lonely planet

Scandinavia

Iceland
p218

Finland
p124

Sweden
p383

Norway
p291

Tallinn
p208

Denmark
p42

Anthony Ham,

Alexis Averbuck, Carolyn Bain, Oliver Berry, Cristian Bonetto, Belinda Dixon, Mark Elliott, Catherine Le Nevez, Virginia Maxwell, Craig McLachlan, Hugh McNaughtan, Becky Ohlsen, Andy Symington, Mara Vorhees, Benedict Walker, Donna Wheeler

PLAN YOUR TRIP

ON THE ROAD

SERGELS TORG,
STOCKHOLM, SWEDEN P389

SKANSEN, SWEDEN P391

Contents

PREIKESTOLEN (PULPIT ROCK), NORWAY P328

Contents

ON THE ROAD

GULLFOSS, ICELAND P23...

Contents

NYHAVN, DENMARK P49

Welcome to Scandinavia

Endless day, perpetual night. Rocking festivals, majestic aurora borealis. With effortlessly chic cities and remote forests, Scandinavia attracts style-gurus and wilderness-hikers alike.

City Style

Stolid Nordic stereotypes dissolve in the region's vibrant capitals. Crest-of-the-wave design can be seen in them all, backed by outstanding modern architecture, excellent museums, imaginative solutions for 21st-century urban living, internationally acclaimed restaurants and a nightlife that fizzes along despite hefty beer prices. Live music is a given: you're bound to come across some inspiring local act, whether your taste is Viking metal or chamber music. Style here manages to be conservative and innovative at the same time, or perhaps it's just that the new and the old blend with less effort than elsewhere.

Green Choices

You'll rarely come across the word 'ecotourism' in Scandinavia, but those values have long been an important part of life here. Generally, green, sustainable solutions are a way of living, rather than a gimmick to attract visitors. Scandinavia will likely be affected by climate change significantly, and big efforts to reduce emissions are being made across the region. Travelling here, you'll be struck by the excellent levels of environmental protection, the sensible 'why don't we do that back home' impact-reducing strategies and the forward thinking. It makes for pleasurably enlightening travel.

Outdoors

The great outdoors is rarely greater than in Europe's big north. Epic expanses of wilderness – forests, lakes, volcanoes – and intoxicatingly pure air mean engaging with nature is a viscerally pleasurable experience. National parks cover the region, offering some of Europe's best hiking as well as anything from kayaking to glacier-walking to bear-watching. Spectacular coasts invite exploration from the sea, with rugged fjords, cliffs teeming with seabirds or archipelagos so speckled with islands it looks like paint flicked at a canvas. Wildlife from whales to wolverines awaits the fortunate observer.

Seasons

They have proper seasons up here. Long winters carpeted with thick snow, the sun making cameo appearances if at all. Despite scary subzero temperatures, there's a wealth of things to do: skiing, sledding behind huskies or reindeer, snowmobile safaris to the Arctic Sea, ice fishing, nights in snow hotels, visiting Santa Claus and gazing at the soul-piercing aurora borealis. Spring sees nature's awakening before the explosive summer's long days, filled with festivals, beer terraces and boating, hiking and cycling. Autumn's glorious array of colours offer marvellous woodland walking before the first snows.

Why I love Scandinavia

By Andy Symington, Writer

I've been visiting regularly for two decades; right from the moment I arrive, those initial gulps of Nordic air seem so pure. I'm entranced by Scandinavia's smart modern cities and cosy cottage culture. My first love, though, is the wilderness. Spotting the first roadside reindeer gives me a far north shiver, anticipating endless Arctic summer days or the eerily sunless polar night. Then, depending on season and place, it's brilliant hikes, the aurora borealis, huskies, smoking volcanoes, indigenous culture or intriguing wildlife. It fascinates me that there's such awe-inspiringly untamed nature in these upright modern nations.

For more about our writers, see p512

Above: Reindeer, Sweden

Scandinavia

Greenland (Denmark)

Svalbard (same scale as main map)

North Pole (1000km)

Kvitøya

Nordaustlandet

Abeløya

Prins Karls Forlandet

Svenskøya

Barentsøya

GREENLAND SEA

Longyearbyen

GREENLAN SEA

Edgeøya

Spitsbergen

Svalbard
You, polar bears, utter north (p364)

Denmark Strait

Jan Mayen (Norway)

Blue Lagoon
Kick back in Iceland's most famous thermal waters (p236)

Akureyri

☆ **Reykjavík**

ICELAND

Arctic Circle

Bergen
Be charmed by venerable wooden buildings (p315)

ATLANTIC OCEAN

Landmannalaugar to Þórsmörk
Fabulous hiking through awesome volcanic scenery (p266)

Faroe Islands (Denmark)

Vestmanna

◎ **Tórshavn**

Oslo
Discover the Vikings' mighty legacy (p294)

Skagen
Be charmed by venerable wooden buildings (p103)

SCOTLAND

Glasgow

☆ **Edinburgh**

Belfast **ENGLAND**

IRELAND

Dublin ☆

Silkeborg
Gaze upon an ancient face (p95)

NORT SEA

0	500 km
0	250 miles

Svalbard (Norway)

See Svalbard inset

Novaya Zemlya (Russia)

BARENTS SEA

Lapland
See the magical
aurora borealis (p183)

Inari
Discover the reindeer-herding
Sámi culture (p196)

Icehotel
Subzero sleeping in
ethereal beauty (p460)

Saariselkä
Husky or reindeer
sled rides (p194)

Nordkapp ○

○ Vardø

Lofoten Islands
Epic rock, timeless fishing
communities (p347)

○ Murmansk

Inarijärvi

Tromsø ○

○
Saariselkä

Gotland
Great cycling around this
church-studded island (p445)

ORWEGIAN SEA

Narvik ○

○ Kiruna

Lofoten
Islands

Bodø ○

○ Rovaniemi

Lakeland
Lakeside cottage,
rowboat and you (p163)

Norway's Fjords
Investigate these awesome
geological serrations (p328)

Oulu
○

Oulujärvi

SWEDEN

FINLAND

Umeå ○

Helsinki
Trendy and edgy design
shopping (p126)

Trondheim ○

○ Vaasa

Kuopio
○

Saimaa

RUSSIA

○ Östersund

○ Jyväskylä

*Lake
Ladoga*

○ Ålesund

*Galdhøpiggen
(2469m)*

*Gulf of
Bothnia*

Tampere ○

Lappeenranta

○ Vyborg

◉ **St Petersburg**

Lillehammer ○

Turku
○

Helsinki
✪

Gulf of Finland

○ **Bergen**

Åland

Tallinn
Evocative medieval
city centre (p208)

Oslo ☆

Uppsala ○

Tallinn
✪

ESTONIA

Västerås ○

☆ **Stockholm**

○ **Stavanger**

Örebro ○

Stockholm
Admire stately,
watery beauty (p385)

Vänern

○ Norrköping

Kristiansand
○

Vättern

○ Linköping

Skagen

○ Jönköping Gotland

*BALTIC
SEA*

Rīga ✪ **LATVIA**

Skagerrak

Göteborg

Aalborg ○

Öland

Copenhagen
Scandinavia's top
foodie scene (p44)

Kattegat

ENMARK

Aarhus Helsingør ○ Helsingborg

RUSSIA

Vilnius ✪

Minsk ✪

Silkeborg ○

Copenhagen

LITHUANIA

BELARUS

Esbjerg ○

○ Billund

○ Odense Malmö

Bornholm

Billund
Discover the world
of Lego (p109)

Funen

Scandinavia's
Top 19

1

Fjords, Norway

1 The drama of Norway's fjords is difficult to overstate. Seen from above, they cut deep gashes into the interior, adding texture and depth to the map of northwestern Scandinavia. Up close, sheer rock walls plunge from high, green meadows into water-filled canyons shadowed by pretty waterside villages. Sognefjorden, over 200km long, and Hardangerfjord are Norway's most extensive fjord networks, but the quiet, precipitous beauty of Nærøyfjorden (part of Sognefjorden), Lysefjord and – the king of Norwegian fjords – Geirangerfjord (p333) are prime candidates for Scandinavia's most beautiful corner. Bottom left: Geirangerfjord (p333)

National Park Hiking

2 Scandinavia's unspoilt wilderness areas are the finest in Europe. If you like dark pine forests populated by foxes and bears, head for northeastern Finland's Karhunkierros trail. Norway's Jotunheimen National Park encompasses hundreds of lofty mountain peaks and crystal-blue lakes. Lying inside the Arctic Circle, Abisko National Park in Sweden is at one end of the epic 440km Kungsleden hiking trail. But walkers will never forget the bleak volcanic slopes, steaming pools and mossy valleys of Iceland's Landmannalaugar to Þórsmörk trek (p266). Botton right: Hiking trail, Finland

5

Lofoten Islands, Norway

3 Few visitors forget their first sighting of the Lofoten Islands (p347), laid out in summer greens and yellows or drowned in the snows of winter, their razor-sharp peaks looming dark against a cobalt clear sky. In the pure, exhilarating air, there's a constant tang of salt and, in the villages, more than a whiff of cod, that staple of the seas whose annual migration brings wealth. A hiker's dream and nowadays linked by bridges, the islands are simple to hop along, whether by bus, car or bicycle. Top left: Sakrisøy (p352), Lofoten Islands

Aurora Borealis, Lapland & Iceland

4 Whether caused by the collision of charged particles in the upper atmosphere, or sparked, as Sámi tradition tells, by a giant snow fox swishing its tail in the Arctic tundra, the haunting, humbling splendour of the aurora borealis, or northern lights, is an experience never to be forgotten. Though theoretically visible year-round, it's much easier to see and more spectacular in the darker winter months. The further north you go, such as the Lapland region of Finland, Norway or Sweden (p462), the better your chances of gazing on nature's light show.

Island Cycling

5 A lazy bike ride around the perimeters of Gotland (p444), the holiday-friendly Baltic Sea island, is one of the most rewarding ways to spend your time in Sweden: the mostly flat, paved Gotlandsleden cycle path circles the island, passing fields of poppies, shady woodlands, historic churches and ancient rune stones at regular intervals. Also just a ferry ride from Stockholm, the autonomous Åland islands have a network of bridges and ferries that makes them a pleasure to pedal around. Or try the 105km-long ride around Bornholm, one of Denmark's National Routes.

Svalbard, Norway

6 Deliciously remote and yet surprisingly accessible, Svalbard (p364) is Europe's most evocative slice of the polar north and one of the continent's last great wilderness areas. Shapely peaks, massive ice fields (60% is covered by glaciers) and heartbreakingly beautiful fjords provide the backdrop for a rich array of Arctic wildlife (including one-fifth of the world's polar bears, which outnumber people up here) and for summer and winter activities that get you out amid the ringing silence of the snows. Top: Longyearbyen, Svalbard (p364)

Icehotel, Sweden

7 Somewhere between a chandelier and an igloo, the famed Icehotel (p460) at Jukkasjärvi is a justifiably popular destination – it may be a gimmick, but it's also really cool (and not just literally). Sleep among reindeer skins in a hotel sculpted anew from ice each winter; hang out in the attached Icebar, sipping chilled vodka out of ice glasses. Beyond its own appeal, the hotel makes a good base for admiring the aurora borealis and learning about Sámi culture in this part of Lapland. Similar hotels exist in Norway and Finland.

Sami Culture

8 The indigenous Sami have a near-mystical closeness to the natural environment: the awesome wildernesses of Lapland. Reindeer-herding is still a primary occupation, but these days it's done with all-terrain vehicles and snowmobiles. The Sámi are a modern people, but still in touch with their roots. Check out the great museums (p196), the parliament buildings and craft workshops in Inari and Karasjok, both in Finland, and try to coincide with a festival or cultural event, whether reindeer-racing or yoiking (traditional singing). Top: Deer with a person in traditional Sami dress

Thermal Springs & Saunas

9 Geothermal pools are Iceland's pride. The most famous of the bathing places is the Blue Lagoon spa (pictured above, p236), whose waters are packed with skin-softening minerals. Visitors can also sink back into warm milky-blue waters at Mývatn Nature Baths, or even inside a volcanic crater at Víti, beside the Askja caldera. The soothing springs plus the mind-bending scenery make for utter relaxation. The sauna is as deeply entrenched in Finnish tradition: participants steam in the nude, whisk themselves with birch twigs and cool off with a cold shower or icy plunge.

Old Town, Tallinn

10 The jewel in Tallinn's crown is its Unesco-protected Old Town (p209), a 14th- and 15th-century twin-tiered jumble of turrets, spires and winding streets. Most travellers' experiences of Estonia's capital begin and end with the cobblestoned, chocolate-box landscape of intertwining alleys and picturesque courtyards. Enjoy the postcard-perfect vistas from up high (climb one of the observation towers) or nestle down below (refuel in one of the vaulted cellars turned into cosy bars and cafes), or simply stroll and soak up the medieval magic.

A Cottage Somewhere

11 Vast numbers of Scandinavians head for summer cottages at the first hint of midyear sunshine. The typical one is simple, by a lake or on an island, with few modern comforts but probably a rowing boat or canoe, a barbecue, a bit of old fishing line and maybe a sauna. The holidays are spent enjoying nature and getting away from city life. Across the region there are numerous rental cottages (p182) – Finland's Lakeland is full of them – that can become venues for you to experience a slice of authentic Nordic peace. Bottom left: Island near Helsinki, Finland

V. BELOV/SHUTTERSTOCK ©

PHOTO: UIO ©

Food Scene

12 Once known for smørrebrød (open sandwiches) and *frikadeller* (meatballs), Denmark's capital Copenhagen (p44) was the leader in developing the New Nordic cuisine that wowed the whole world and further innovations are always on the go. Other countries have followed the lead, and exciting new restaurants now inhabit all the region's capitals, with more popping up like chanterelle mushrooms. The Nordic forage ethos, looking for naturally occurring local ingredients – including many not traditionally considered to be food – has had worldwide culinary influence.

Sledding

13 Once there's healthy snow cover in the north, a classic experience is to hitch up a team of reindeer or husky dogs (p367) to a sled and swish away under the pale winter sun. Short jaunts are good for getting the hang of steering, stopping and working with the animals; once your confidence is high, take off on an overnight trip, sleeping in a hut in the wilderness and thawing those deserving bones with a steaming sauna. Pure magic.

Viking History

14 Mead-swilling pillaging hooligans or civilising craftspeople, poets and merchants? Your Viking preconceptions will likely be challenged during a visit to Scandinavia. A series of memorable burial sites, rune stones, settlements and museums – the one in Oslo (p295) is perhaps the best – across the region brings this fascinating age to life. Gods and beliefs, stupendous feats of navigation, customs, trade, longships, intricate jewellery, carvings and the wonderful sagas – it's all here. Just forget about the horned helmets; they didn't wear them. Bottom right: The Oseberg ship at Viking-skipshuset (p295), Norway

SARAH COGHILL/LONELY PLANET ©

Design Shopping

15 If design is defined as making the practical beautiful, then Scandinavia rules the roost. Elegant, innovative yet functional takes on everyday items have made the region's creativity world famous and mean that you won't have to look far before you experience an 'I need that!' moment. There's great design and handicrafts to be found right across the region, but Copenhagen and Helsinki (p136), closely followed by Stockholm, are where modern flagship stores can be found alongside quirky boutiques that present the best of the edgier new ideas.

Bar Life

16 In Scandinavia's capital cities summer is short and winter is long and bitter. Driving away the darkness is a necessity – so it's no wonder that a near-legendary nightlife has evolved in these cities. After all, what could be better than gathering your friends into a snug, sleek bar to talk, drink, joke, sing, laugh, flirt and dance the night away? Natural Nordic reserve melts away with the application of such local firewaters as *brennivín*, *salmiakkikossu*, *snaps* or aquavit, or plain old beer. Join the party and make fast friends.

Historic Wooden Towns

17 Scandinavian towns and cities were once built exclusively from timber, but 'great fires' were understandably common, and comparatively few of these historic districts remain. They are worth seeking out for their quaint, unusual beauty; among others, Bergen (pictured bottom right; p315) and Stavanger in Norway, Rauma in Finland and Gothenburg in Sweden preserve excellent 'timbertowns', perfect neighbourhoods for strolling around. Across the region, house museums preserve traditional architecture and contents for an enjoyable trip back in time.

Skagen, Denmark

18 Sweeping skies, moving sands and duelling seas: the appeal of Skagen is both ephemeral and constant. The lure of the light has drawn many – packing paintbrushes – from far beyond its coastline, and its blending colour of sky, sea and sand can inspire awe in the most hardened of souls. This is both Jutland's northern tip and Denmark's 'end of the line', where gentle fields give way to ghostly dunes, a buried church and the shape-shifting headland of Grenen (p103), where the Baltic meets its murky North Sea rival.

Stockholm, Sweden

19 Sweden's capital (p385) is the aristocrat among Scandinavian cities with imposing stately buildings arrayed across a complex geography of islands and waterways. Noble museums, palaces and galleries dignify this former seat of empire but there's plenty of contemporary innovation to balance it out. Stockholm's vibrant multiculturalism banishes all the blond stereotypes, while modern trends in design and food are in full flow, adding an exciting energy to the streets and a kick to the city's evening scene. Bottom: Nordiska Museet (p391)

Need to Know

For more information, see Survival Guide (p477)

Currency

Denmark: Danish krone (kr; DKK)
Finland & Tallinn: euro (€; EUR)
Iceland: Icelandic króna (kr; ISK)
Norway: Norwegian krone (kr; NOK)
Sweden: Swedish krona (kr; SEK)

Languages

Danish, Estonian, Finnish, Icelandic, Norwegian and Swedish. English is widely spoken.

Visas

Generally not required for stays of up to 90 days; some nationalities will need a Schengen visa.

Money

ATMs are widespread. Credit/debit cards are generally accepted

Time

Iceland: Western European Time (GMT/UTC)
Denmark, Norway & Sweden: Central European Time (GMT/UTC plus one hour)
Finland & Tallinn: Eastern European Time (GMT/UTC plus two hours)
All but Iceland use summer time from late March to late October.

When to Go

Warm to hot summers, mild winters
Warm to hot summers, cold winters
Mild year round
Mild summers, cold to very cold winters
Polar climate

Svalbard
GO Mar–Aug

Iceland
GO Jun–Aug

Lapland
GO Feb–Apr, Aug–Sep

Fjords
GO Mar–Sep

Helsinki/
Tallinn
GO May–Jul

Copenhagen
GO May–Oct, Dec

High Season
(Jun–Aug)

➡ All attractions and lodgings are open.

➡ Hotels in many parts are often substantially cheaper.

➡ Summer budget accommodation is open.

➡ Boat cruises run.

➡ Numerous festivals held.

Shoulder
(Apr, May, Sep & Oct)

➡ Expect chilly nights and even snow.

➡ Not the cheapest time to travel as summer hostels and camping grounds have closed.

➡ Many rural attractions close or shorten their opening hours.

Low Season
(Nov–Mar)

➡ Outside cities, many attractions are closed.

➡ Hotels charge top rates except at weekends.

➡ January to April is busy for winter sports.

➡ Days are short, and cool or cold.

EXCHANGE RATES

For current exchange rates, see www.xe.com.

CURRENCY	VALUE	DENMARK (DKK)	FINLAND (€)	ICELAND (ISK)	NORWAY (NOK)	SWEDEN (SEK)
Australia	AU$1	4.76	0.64	79.85	6.17	6.30
Canada	C$1	4.83	0.65	81.09	6.26	6.40
Eurozone	€1	7.44	1.00	125.00	9.66	9.86
Japan	¥100	5.53	0.76	92.90	7.18	7.33
New Zealand	NZ$1	4.41	0.59	74.06	5.72	5.84
UK	UK£1	8.41	1.13	141.33	10.92	11.14
US	US$1	6.04	0.81	101.51	7.85	8.01

Useful Websites

Lonely Planet (www.lonelyplanet.com/scandinavia) Destination information, hotel bookings, traveller forum and more.

Go Scandinavia (www.goscandinavia.com) Combined tourist-board website for the four mainland Nordic countries.

IceNews (www.icenews.is) Presents the latest English news snippets from the Nordic nations, principally though Iceland.

Direct Ferries (www.directferries.com) Useful booking site for Baltic and Atlantic ferries.

Important Numbers

General emergency	☑112
International access code	☑00

Daily Costs

Budget: Less than €150

➡ Dorm bed (HI membership gets you good discounts): €15–40

➡ Bike hire per day: €10–25

➡ Lunch specials: €10–18

➡ National parks: free

Midrange: €150–250

➡ Standard hotel double room: €80–160

➡ Weeklong car hire per day: €35–60

➡ Two-course meal for two with wine: €100–150

➡ Museum entry: €5–15

Top end: More than €250

➡ Room in boutique hotel: €150–300

➡ Upmarket degustation menu for two with wine: €200–400

➡ Taxi across town: €20–40

Opening Hours

Opening hours vary significantly across Scandinavia; see individual countries for opening hours.

Arriving in Scandinavia

Copenhagen Kastrup Airport The metro and trains run very regularly into the centre (15 minutes). Around 300kr for the 20-minute taxi ride.

Stockholm Arlanda Airport Express trains run all day to Stockholm; airport buses are cheaper but slower. Think 500kr for the 45-minute taxi drive.

Oslo Gardermoen Airport Regular shuttle buses make the 40-minute journey to the centre. Trains run from the airport into the centre of Oslo in 20 minutes. A taxi costs 700kr to 900kr.

Helsinki Vantaa Airport It's a half-hour train ride from the airport to the centre. Local buses and faster Finnair buses do it in 30 to 45 minutes. Plan on €45 to €55 for the half-hour taxi trip.

Keflavík Airport (Reykjavík) Buses run the 45-minute journey into Reykjavík. Taxis charge around kr16,000.

Getting Around

Getting around populated areas is generally easy, with efficient public transport and connections. Remote areas usually have trustworthy but infrequent services.

Bus Comprehensive network throughout region; only choice in many areas.

Train Efficient services in the continental nations; none in Iceland.

Car Drive on the right. Hire is easy but not cheap. Few motorways, so travel times can be long. Compulsory winter tyres.

Ferry Great-value network around the Baltic; spectacular Norwegian coastal ferry, and service to Iceland via the Faroe Islands.

Bike Very bike-friendly cities and many options for longer cycling routes. Most transport will carry bikes for little or no charge. Hire is widely available.

Planes Decent network of budget flights connecting major centres. Full-fare flights are comparatively expensive.

For much more on **getting around**, see p485

If You Like...

Canoeing & Kayaking

It's hard to beat this region for kayaking and canoeing, whether you're planning a multiday sea-kayaking or afternoon lake-canoeing adventure.

Danish Lake District Glide silent lakes in bucolic Jutland. (p95)

Stockholm Rent a canoe for the day in the Djurgården. (p395)

Geirangerfjorden Kayak some of Norway's prettiest corners, such as this World Heritage–listed fjord, Sognefjorden or Svalbard. (p333)

Ísafjörður Visit this Icelandic destination – perfect for beginners. (p241)

Seyðisfjörður Take guided kayaking tours with affable Hlynur in Iceland. (p259)

Åland Paddle around the low, rocky islands of this quietly picturesque Finnish archipelago. (p149)

Coastal Scenery

Scoured by glaciers, speckled with islands and buffeted by wind and rain, the Nordic coastlines are spectacular. The Atlantic coasts are the most jagged, while the more sedate Baltic archipelagos offer a gentler beauty.

Dueodde Beach Be entranced by Denmark's Bornholm island, where Nordic forest and snow-white dunes back a spectacular beach. (p74)

Møns Klint See gleaming white cliffs against the Baltic blue in far-east Denmark. (p70)

Höga Kusten Take in northern Sweden's dramatic northern coast. (p450)

Lofoten Marvel at nature's sheer improbability in these northern Norwegian islands. (p347)

Svalbard Be spellbound where vast glaciers meet the Arctic Ocean at this remote outpost of Norway. (p364)

Jökulsárlón Watch glaciers float to sea from this glittering Icelandic lagoon. (p263)

Kystriksveien Journey along Norway's lightly travelled but utterly extraordinary route into the Arctic. (p344)

Cycling

Bikes are part of life here: the cities are full of cycle lanes, grab-a-bike stands and marked routes. There are great options for multiday cycling holidays, particularly in the Baltic islands. Bikes are easily transported throughout the region.

Bornholm Pedal your way across this perfect Danish island. (p70)

Gotland Make the easy loop around this Swedish island. (p444)

Hardangervidda Ride across Europe's highest mountain plateau. (p309)

Mývatn Explore the charms of Iceland's Lake Mývatn on a day-long bicycle circuit. (p255)

Åland Visit this archipelago between Finland and Sweden, with numerous flat islands ideal for two-wheeled touring. (p149)

Hiking

Wide open spaces, majestic landscapes and bracing air offer brilliant hiking. Multiday treks are easily accomplished with a great network of national parks, camping grounds and huts. Norway and Iceland offer magnificent scenery, while Finland and Sweden have spectacular autumn forestscapes.

Kungsleden Trek along the King's Trail in Swedish Lappland. (p463)

Jotunheimen Traverse the roof of Norway in the Jotunheimen National Park. (p313)

Hardangervidda Hike in search of wild reindeer atop this Norwegian plateau. (p324)

Hornstrandir Accessible only by boat in high summer, make the ultimate escape to this isolated Icelandic peninsula. (p243)

Laugavegurinn Trek Conquer Iceland's most famous hike, from Landmannalaugar to Þórsmörk, over rainbow-coloured mountains and through pumice deserts. (p266)

Urho Kekkonen National Park Hit Finnish Lapland's national parks for top trekking in one of Europe's last great wildernesses. (p194)

Historic Buildings & Churches

Kronborg Slot Channel Shakespeare at Hamlet's old haunt in Denmark's Helsingør. (p65)

Tallinn Stroll back to the 14th century around the Old Town's narrow, cobbled streets. (p208)

Gotland Pay due reverence to the historic churches that dot this Swedish island.

Gamle Stavanger Visit one of Europe's most spectacular wooden-building districts, which sits at the heart of this Norwegian city. (p326)

Olavinlinna Marvel at this spectacular Finnish island castle, which presides over the centre of the country's prettiest town. (p166)

Roskilde Domkirke Time-travel through eight centuries of Danish architecture under one roof. (p67)

Nidaros Domkirke Gaze in awe at Scandinavia's largest medieval building and tapestry in stone dedicated to St Olav; Trondheim, Norway. (p338)

Top: Reine (p352), Lofoten Islands, Norway

Bottom: Northern Lights Cathedral (p358), Alta, Norway

PLAN YOUR TRIP IF YOU LIKE...

Modern Art & Architecture

Louisiana Channel your inner Picasso at this Copenhagen modern-art must-see, where art meets vistas. (p54)

ARoS Aarhus Kunstmuseum Walk among giants at this Danish cultural showpiece. (p90)

Moderna Museet Visit one of Scandinavia's best modern-art museums, in Stockholm. (p392)

Oslo Enjoy modern architectural icons: the Oslo Opera House or the Astrup Fearnley modern art museum. (p294)

Helsinki Have your head turned by iconic Kiasma's exuberant exterior, and the adjacent concert venue, Musiikkitalo. (p126)

Alvar Aalto Make an architectural pilgrimage to Finland's Jyväskylä, where one of the giants made his name. (p169)

Northern Lights Cathedral Be divinely inspired by this astonishing swirl of rippling titanium, best appreciated with an aurora backdrop, in Alta, Norway. (p358)

Harpa Visit a stunning waterside concert hall that recalls Iceland's volcanic landscape. (p224)

Vikings

Whether you're interested in the structured society, extensive trade networks, dextrous handicrafts and well-honed navigational skills of this advanced civilization, or you glorify in tales of plunder, pillage, dragonships and the twilight of the gods, there's something for you here.

Roskilde Set sail on a faithful Viking replica in Denmark. (p67)

Ribe VikingeCenter Schmooze with modern-day Danish Vikings. (p108)

Gotland Visit this Swedish island's numerous rune stones and ship settings. (p445)

Oslo Admire a Viking longboat at Oslo's marvellous Vikingskipshuset. (p295)

Lofotr Viking Museum Marvel at Norway's largest Viking-era building. (p350)

Settlement Exhibition Take in this fascinating hi-tech exhibition in Reykjavík, based around an original Viking longhouse. (p222)

Saga Museum Visit this Reykjavík museum, a kind of Viking Madame Tussauds, which is heaps of fun. (p224)

Iceland Ferry Follow the Viking colonists' wake by taking the boat from Denmark to Iceland via the Faroes. (p279)

Wildlife-Watching

Seabirds clamour in the Atlantic air while whales roll beneath. Elk are widespread, forests harbour serious carnivores and mighty polar bears still lord it – for now – over Svalbard.

Iceland View the nesting colonies of the comical puffin, which are found all across the island.

Reindeer Look out for these domesticated roamers, which wander at will across the north of Sweden, Norway and Finland.

Central Norway Track down the prehistoric musk ox.

Svalbard Watch out for polar bears in Svalbard, with Arctic foxes and walrus also present. (p364)

Whale watching Head to Norway's Andenes or Húsavík in Iceland. (p355)

Látrabjarg Travel to these dramatic cliffs in Iceland, the world's biggest bird breeding grounds. (p245)

Bear watching Head out to the Finnish forests to observe bears, elk or wolverines. (p178)

Winter Wonders

Saariselkä Explore the frozen Finnish wilderness whilst pulled by huskies or reindeer, or aboard a snowmobile. (p194)

Breaking the ice Crunch through the frozen Gulf of Bothnia aboard an ice breaker at Kemi in Finland. (p188)

Jukkasjärvi Freeze the romantic moment at this Swedish ice hotel, one of several good ones. (p460)

Santa's Grotto Visit the world's most famous beardie at his eerie Finnish grotto. (p185)

Tivoli Gardens Put the magic back into Christmas with wonderful lights and warming mulled wine. (p45)

Abisko Catch the Aurora Borealia at this northern Swedish locale, a prime viewing spot. (p462)

Top: Tivoli Gardens (p45), Copenhagen, Denmark

Bottom: Harpa concert hall (p224), Reykjavík, Iceland

Month by Month

January

It's cold. Very cold and very dark. But this is the beginning of the active winter; there's enough snow for ice hotels, and winter sports are reliable.

❄ Kiruna Snöfestivalen, Sweden

This Lapland snow festival, based around a snow-sculpting competition that draws artists from all over, is held in the last week of January. There's also a husky dog competition and a handicrafts fair. (p461)

❄ Skábmagovat, Finland

In the third week of January, this film festival with an indigenous theme is held in the Finnish Sámi village of Inari. Associated cultural events also happen here throughout the winter. (p197)

February

There's enough light now for it to be prime skiing season in northern Scandinavia. Local holidays mean it gets very busy (and pricey) on the slopes mid-February.

🛍 Jokkmokk Winter Market, Sweden

The biggest Sámi market of the year with all manner of crafts for sale, preceded by celebrations of all things Sámi and featuring reindeer races on the frozen lake. (p458)

❄ Rørosmartnan, Norway

An old-fashioned and traditional winter fair livens the streets of the historic Norwegian town of Røros. (p313)

❄ Þorrablót, Iceland

Held all across the country, nominally in honour of the god Thor, this midwinter festival's centrepiece is a feast for the fearless that includes delicacies such as fermented shark.

March

As the hours of light dramatically increase and temperatures begin to rise again, this is an excellent time to take advantage of the hefty snow cover and indulge in some winter fun.

☆ Reindeer Racing, Finland

Held over the last weekend of March or first of April, the King's Cup is the grand finale of Finnish Lapland's reindeer-racing season and a great spectacle. (p196)

🎿 Sled Safaris & Skiing, Northern Norway, Sweden & Finland

Whizzing across the snow pulled by a team of huskies or reindeer is a pretty spectacular way to see the northern wildernesses. Add snowmobiling or skiing to the mix and it's a top time to be at high latitude.

🎿 Vasaloppet, Sweden

Held on the first Sunday in March, this ski race (www. vasaloppet.se) salutes Gustav Vasa's history-making flight on skis in 1521. It has grown into a week-long ski fest and celebration with different races – short, gruelling or just for fun.

April

Easter is celebrated in a traditional fashion across the region. Spring is underway in Denmark and the southern parts, but there's still solid snow cover in the northern reaches.

☆ Jazzkaar, Tallinn

Late April sees jazz greats from all around the world converge on Estonia's picturesque capital for this series of performances (www.jazzkaar.ee).

☆ Sámi Easter Festival, Norway

Thousands of Sámi participate in reindeer racing, theatre and cultural events in the Finnmark towns of Karasjok and Kautokeino (www.samieasterfestival. com). The highlight is the Sámi Grand Prix, a singing and yoiking (traditional Sámi form of song) contest attended by artists from across Lapland.

Valborgsmässoafton, Sweden

This public holiday (Walpurgis Night) on 30 April is a pagan hold-over that's partly to welcome the arrival of spring. Celebrated across the country, it involves lighting huge bonfires, singing songs and forming parades.

May

A transitional month up north, with snow beginning to disappear and signs of life emerging after the long winter. Down south, spring is in full flow. A rewarding time to visit the southern capitals.

☆ Aalborg Carnival, Denmark

In late May, Aalborg kicks up its heels hosting the biggest Carnival celebrations in northern Europe, with up to 100,000 participants and spectators. (p99)

☆ Bergen International Festival, Norway

One of the biggest events on Norway's cultural calendar, this two-week festival, beginning in late May, showcases dance, music and folklore presentations, some international, some focusing on traditional local culture. (p317)

☆ Reykjavík Arts Festival, Iceland

Running for two weeks from late May to June in even-numbered years, this wide-ranging festival sees Iceland's capital taken over by theatre performances, films, lectures and music. (p229)

June

Midsummer is celebrated with gusto, but it's typically a family event; unless you've local friends it's not necessarily the best time to visit. Lapland's muddy, but the rest of the region is warm and welcoming.

☆ Extreme Sports Festival, Norway

Adventure junkies from across the world converge on Voss in late June for a week of skydiving, paragliding, parasailing and base jumping; music acts keep the energy flowing. (p323)

☆ Frederikssund Vikingespil, Denmark

Held in Frederikssund over a three-week period from late June to early July, this Viking festival (www.vikingespil.dk) includes a costumed open-air drama followed by a banquet with Viking food and entertainment.

☆ Independence Day, Iceland

Held on 17 June, this is the largest nationwide festival in the country. It commemorates the founding of the Republic of Iceland in 1944 with big parades and general celebration.

☆ Midsummer, Denmark, Norway, Sweden & Finland

The year's biggest event in continental Nordic Europe sees fun family feasts, joyous celebrations of the summer, heady bonfires and copious drinking, often at normally peaceful lakeside summer cottages. It takes place on the weekend that falls between 19 and 26 June.

☆ Old Town Days, Tallinn

This week-long Estonian festival (www.vanalinnapaevad.ee) in early June features dancing, concerts, costumed performers and plenty of medieval merrymaking in the heart of Tallinn's stunning historic centre.

☆ Stockholm Jazz Festival, Sweden

Held on the island of Skeppsholmen in the centre of Stockholm, this well-known jazz fest brings artists from all over, including big international names. (p395)

July

Peak season sees long, long days and sunshine. This is when the region really comes to life, with many festivals, boat trips, activities, cheaper hotels and a celebratory feel. Insects in Lapland are a nuisance.

☆ Copenhagen Jazz Festival, Denmark

This is the biggest entertainment event of the year in the capital, with 10 days of music at the beginning of July. The festival features a range of Danish and international jazz, blues and fusion music, with more than 500 indoor and outdoor concerts. (p53)

☆ Moldejazz, Norway

Norway has a fine portfolio of jazz festivals, but Molde's version in mid-July is the most prestigious. With 100,000 spectators, world-class performers and a reputation for consistently high-quality music, it's easily one of Norway's most popular festivals. (p371)

☆ Roskilde Festival, Denmark

Northern Europe's largest music festival rocks Roskilde each summer. It takes place in early July, but advance ticket sales are on offer around October and the festival usually sells out. (p67)

☆ Ruisrock, Finland

Finland's oldest and possibly best rock festival takes place in early July on an island just outside the southwestern city of Turku. Top Finnish and international acts take part. (p145)

☆ Savonlinna Opera Festival, Finland

A month of excellent performances in the romantic location of one of Europe's most picturesquely situated castles makes this Finland's biggest summer drawcard for casual and devoted lovers of opera. (p167)

☆ Skagen Festival, Denmark

Held on the first weekend of July, this festival at Denmark's picturesque northern tip features folk and world music performed by Danish and international artists. (p104)

🏃 Wife-Carrying World Championships, Finland

The world's premier wife-carrying event is held in the village of Sonkajärvi in early July. Winning couples (marriage not required) win the woman's weight in beer as well as significant kudos. (p171)

August

Most Scandinavians are back at work, so it's quieter than in July but there's still decent weather across most of the region. A great time for Lapland hiking, biking the islands or cruising the archipelagos.

☆ Aarhus Festival, Denmark

The 10-day Aarhus Festival starts in late August and features scores of musical performances, theatre, ballet, modern dance, opera, films and sports events at indoor and outdoor venues across Denmark's second-largest city. (p91)

🏃 Air Guitar World Championships, Finland

Tune your imaginary instrument and get involved in this crazy rockstravaganza held in Oulu in late August. This surfeit of cheesy guitar classics and seemingly endless beer is all in the name of world peace. (p180)

🍴 Copenhagen Cooking & Food Festival, Denmark

Scandinavia's largest food festival focuses on the gourmet. It's a busy event that lets you see presentations from top chefs, go on food-oriented tours of the city and taste produce. (p53)

🎊 Copenhagen Pride, Denmark

Six days of revelry in the August sunshine sees Copenhagen turn rainbow-hued. There are lots of events throughout, but the big bash is the parade on the Saturday. (p54)

🛡️ Medieval Week, Sweden

Find yourself an actual knight in shining armour at Medieval Week, an immensely popular annual Swedish fest in Visby, Gotland's medieval jewel. It takes place over a week in early August. (p445)

☆ Menningarnótt, Iceland

On a Saturday in mid-August, this 'cultural night' rocks Reykjavík, when the whole city seems to be out on the streets for quality Icelandic bands on a variety of stages. (p229)

☆ Smukfest, Denmark

This midmonth music marvel in Skanderborg bills itself as Denmark's most beautiful festival, and is second only to Roskilde in terms of scale. It takes place in lush parkland in the scenic Lake District and attracts up to 40,000 music fans. (p97)

🛡️ Þjóðhátíð, Iceland

Held over the first weekend in August, this festival on the Vestmannaeyjar islands is Iceland's biggest piss-up, with three days of music, fireworks and frivolity. It's a big thing for young Icelanders: an enormous bonfire is a focal point. (p269)

September

Winter is fast approaching: pack something warm for those chilly nights. Autumn colours are spectacular in northern forests, making it another great month for hiking. Many attractions and activities close or go onto winter time.

☆ Reykjavík International Film Festival, Iceland

This annual event at the end of September sees blockbusters make way for international art films in cinemas across the city, plus talks from film directors from home and abroad. (p229)

🏃 Ruska Hiking, Finland & Sweden

Ruska is the Finnish word for the autumn colours, and there's a mini high season in Finnish and Swedish Lapland as hikers take to the trails to enjoy nature's brief artistic flourish.

October

Snow is already beginning to carpet the region's north. It's generally a quiet time, as locals face the realities of yet another long winter approaching.

🛡️ Hem & Villa, Sweden

Held across Sweden's two largest cities, this major interior design fair (www.hemochvilla.se) highlights upcoming trends. You'll be years ahead of your Ikea-going friends.

November

Once the clocks change in late October, there's no denying winter. November's bad for winter sports as there's little light and not enough snow. It can be a good month to see the aurora borealis, though.

🏃 Aurora Watching, Iceland, Norway, Sweden & Finland

Whether you are blessed with seeing the aurora borealis is largely a matter of luck, but the further north you are, the better the chances. Dark, cloudless nights, patience and a viewing spot away from city lights are other key factors.

☆ Iceland Airwaves, Iceland

This five-day event in Reykjavík is one of the world's most cutting-edge music festivals: don't expect to sleep. It focuses on new musical trends rather than mainstream acts. (p229)

☆ Stockholm International Film Festival, Sweden

Screenings of new international and independent films, director talks and discussion panels draw cinephiles to this important annual festival. Tickets go fast; book early. (p395)

December

The Christmas period is celebrated enthusiastically, with cinnamon, mulled drinks, romantic lights and festive traditions.

🛡️ Christmas, Region-wide

Whether visiting Santa and his reindeer in Finnish Lapland, admiring the magic of Copenhagen's Tivoli at night or sampling home-baked delicacies, Christmas – especially if you know a friendly local family to spend it with – is a heart-warming time to be here.

Plan Your Trip
Itineraries

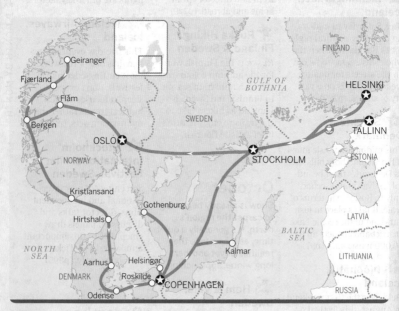

2 WEEKS Scandinavia in a Nutshell

This quick hop jaunts around southern Scandinavia's classic sights. With just a week, it's essentially one city in each of Denmark, Sweden and Norway; extra time allows more detailed exploration.

Start in **Copenhagen**, admiring the waterfront, museums and lights of Tivoli at night. Take a day-trip to the cathedral and Viking Ship Museum at **Roskilde** or Hamlet's castle at **Helsingør**.

Next, train it to **Stockholm** and get into the design scene and the watery town centre. An overnight train takes you to **Oslo** to check out Munch's work and the city's extraordinary museums. From Oslo, a long but scenic day includes the rail trip to **Flåm** and a combination boat and bus journey along the Sognefjord to

Kronborg Slot (p65), Denmark

Bergen, Norway's prettiest city. Out of time? Fly out from Bergen.

Otherwise, head to **Kristiansand**, where there's a ferry to **Hirtshals**. Nose on down to **Aarhus** – don't miss the ARoS art museum. From here, it's an easy train back to Copenhagen.

Extra days? A side trip from Stockholm on a Baltic ferry could take you to **Helsinki** or picturesque **Tallinn**.

Other stops could include **Gothenburg** or **Kalmar**; more fjord-y Norwegian experiences at **Fjærland** and **Geiranger**; or extra Danish time at **Odense**.

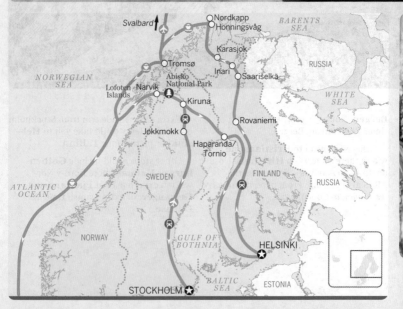

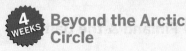

4 WEEKS Beyond the Arctic Circle

This thorough visit to the north takes in Santa, Sámi culture, spectacular coastal scenery and opportunities for excellent activities. It'll be a completely different experience in summer or in winter.

Take the overnight train from **Helsinki** to **Rovaniemi**. Visit the fabulous Arktikum, chat with Santa Claus and stock up on anything you might need for your wilderness adventure; it will be a while before you see another town this big. Head north, crossing the Arctic Circle to **Saariselkä**, a base for great activities, whether hiking in the adjacent Urho Kekkonen National Park in summer or husky-sledding trips in winter. There's a huge range of other things on offer year-round, too.

From here it's a short hop to the Sámi village of **Inari**, where Siida is a wonderful exhibition on Lapland's nature and indigenous cultures. Check out the craft shops too, and the impressive parliament building. To continue the theme, head onward to **Karasjok**, Inari's Norwegian counterpart and an important meeting place for representatives of different Sámi groups.

From Karasjok (and Inari) summer buses run to **Nordkapp**, where you can stand at the top of Europe and gaze out towards the utter north. From nearby **Honningsvåg**, catch the *Hurtigruten* coastal steamer to the stunning **Lofoten Islands**, possibly stopping in lively **Tromsø**. Did we say Nordkapp was the top of Europe? We lied; from Tromsø there are flights way north to **Svalbard**, demesne of polar bears and an epic Arctic experience to really impress the folks back home.

Take some time to enjoy the Lofoten Islands, doing some cycling and visiting the Lofotr Viking Museum. When you're done, the *Hurtigruten* heads right down to Bergen, but jump off in **Narvik** and take the train to **Kiruna**, a remote Swedish mining town, and, in winter, home to the famous Icehotel. On the way, stop off for some hiking or aurora-watching at stunning **Abisko National Park**. Also be sure to check out the Sámi village and typical reindeer-herding region of **Jokkmokk**.

From here, you could fly, train or bus all the way south to **Stockholm**, cut back into Norway to continue your trip down the coast, or head to the Finnish border at **Haparanda/Tornio** to head back to Helsinki from there.

Top: Polar bears (p365), Svalbard, Norway
Bottom: Sami reindeer-fur handicrafts (p467)

3 WEEKS Finland & the Baltic

Starting in Stockholm, this itinerary follows the old trading routes around the Baltic and covers plenty of Finland, including the capital, Helsinki, and beautiful Lakeland, also taking in the sumptuous Baltic city of Tallinn.

Kick things off in **Stockholm**, for centuries a Baltic trading powerhouse. Admire its picturesque Old Town and ponder that famously neutral Sweden once ruled most of the Baltic from here. Take a day trip to ancient **Uppsala** before taking advantage of Stockholm's cheap, luxurious overnight ferries to Helsinki. Don't overdo it on the duty-free booze, because you'll want a good view of the spectacular arrival in **Helsinki**, where you should investigate the cathedrals, market halls, modern architecture and design scene. Catch a classical concert at Musiikkitalo or a rock gig at legendary Tavastia.

From here, a good excursion heads east to the town of **Porvoo**, with its picturesque wooden warehouses and cathedral. Back in Helsinki, it's an easy boat ride across the Baltic to medieval **Tallinn**, a historic treasure trove that's worth a couple of days' exploration. If time's short, take a day trip.

In summer, take the train to the shimmering lakes of **Savonlinna**, with its awesome medieval castle and opera festival, and/or **Kuopio**, to steam up in its large smoke sauna. If you have the time, historic lake boats travel between these and other inland Finnish towns, a fabulously leisurely way to travel on a sunny day. A side trip from either of these towns can take you to **Joensuu**, from where you can visit the Orthodox monastery of **Valamo** or what is deservingly claimed to be Finland's best view at **Koli National Park**.

Turning west, head to the dynamic cultural city of **Tampere**, visiting its quirky museums and re-imagined fabric mills, and patronising its interesting cafes and restaurants. Then it's on to the third member of the trinity of Finnish cities, intriguing **Turku**, with excellent museums of its own, a towering castle and cathedral, and some very quirky drinking dens. From here you can get a ferry back to Sweden via the **Åland islands**. Stop off here for as long as you wish and tour the archipelago by bike.

Top: Koli National Park (p175), Finland
Bottom: Musiikkitalo (p136), Helsinki, Finland

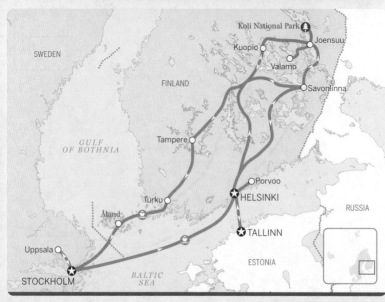

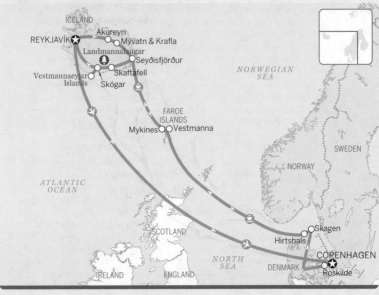

Northern Islands

3½ WEEKS

This trip takes in a little of Denmark then takes to the seas in true Viking style as you head to Iceland, brooding volcanically in the mid-Atlantic, via a stop in the bird-rich archipelago of the Faroes.

Fly into **Copenhagen**, taking some time to absorb its addictive atmosphere. Get in the mood for your sea crossing by visiting the Viking Boat Museum at nearby **Roskilde**. Then hit north Jutland and the beautiful dunes at **Skagen**, where, at the sandy headland of Grenen, two seas meet at Denmark's northernmost tip.

Jump aboard the Smyril Line ferry leaving from nearby **Hirtshals**. In summer there are two ferries running per week, so you can make a three-day stop in the remote **Faroe Islands**, but in the low season it's either nine hours there or a whole week. If you manage some time on the islands, giggle at the comical puffins on the awesome cliffs of **Mykines** and take a boat trip to visit the immense seabird colonies at **Vestmanna**.

The ferry continues to Iceland, arriving at **Seyðisfjörður**. From here journey along the south coast past **Skaftafell**, a national park area that is one of Iceland's most spectacularly scenic regions, offering great hiking and unforgettable glacier walks. If you've got time to explore, head to the interior for the amazing geoscapes of **Landmannalaugar**. Take the three-day hike to Þórsmörk, one of Europe's most spectacular walks. The tough extra day to **Skógar** takes you across some of the country's newest lava fields. Next, you could head out to see the bird life and traditional communities of the **Vestmannaeyjar** islands.

Hit the capital **Reykjavík**, enjoy the nightlife, visit the Saga Museum and take a trip to the Blue Lagoon. Then travel around the Ring Rd to the north of the island, where an R&R stop at peaceful fjord-side **Akureyri** can include a side trip to the **Mývatn** natural thermal baths and the steaming volcanic landscape of **Krafla**.

From here, you can return to the ferry terminal to head back to Copenhagen by sea if you're still game, otherwise you can fly back from Reykjavík.

Top: Landmannalaugar (p266), Iceland
Bottom: Vestmannaeyjar (p269), Iceland

Countries at a Glance

The seductive call of the north is one of wild landscapes, crisp air and cutting-edge city style coloured by the epic changes of the Scandinavian seasons.

Scenically, it's hard to beat. Norway's noble, breathtaking coastline, serrated with fjords, competes with Iceland's harsh, volcanic majesty. Soothing Swedish and Finnish lake- and forest-scapes and Denmark's pastoral landscapes offer a gentler beauty.

Though the towns and cities all have great allure – Copenhagen is the one worth the most time – the big attraction is the outdoors. There are so many ways to get active on land, water and snow. Hiking, kayaking and wildlife-watching are among Europe's best, while the bike-friendly culture makes it great for cyclists, too, particularly Denmark, southern Sweden and various Baltic islands.

Denmark

Cycling
History
Gastronomy

Cycling Pleasures

With a highest point as lofty as your average big-city office building, it's no surprise to find that Denmark is a paradise for cycling. Thousands of kilometres of dedicated cycle routes and islands perfect for two-wheeled exploration make it the best way to get around.

Past Echoes

Denmark's historical sites are great. Hauntingly preserved bog bodies take us back to prehistoric times, while Roskilde's Viking boats and majestic cathedral are important remnants of other periods. Fictional Hamlet's real castle, Kronborg Slot (Elsinore Castle), is a major attraction.

The Foodie Scene

Denmark was at the forefront of the New Nordic cuisine whose forage ethos influenced kitchens across the planet. Now, new trends are emerging in what is Scandinavia's finest eating scene. Copenhagen is the foodie mecca, but excellent regional restaurants hold their own.

p42

Finland

Hiking
Winter Activities
Design

Wild Nature

Finland's vast forested wildernesses are some of Europe's least populated areas. Large national parks with excellent networks of trails, huts and camping grounds make this prime hiking country. Kayaking and canoeing are also great options.

Active Winters

Northern Finland's numerous ski resorts aren't very elevated but are great for beginners and families. Skiing's just the start, though: snowy wildernesses crossed in sleds pulled by reindeer or huskies, snowmobile safaris, ice-breaker cruises, nights in snow hotels and a personal audience with Santa Claus are other wintry delights.

Design & Architecture

Finnish design is world-famous; browsing Helsinki's shops, from flagship emporia to edgy bohemian studios, is one of the city's great pleasures. Some of the world's finest modern architecture can also be found scattered around Finland's towns.

p124

Tallinn

Medieval Streets
Culture
Bars & Cafes

Historic Jewel

A short trip across the water from Helsinki, Estonia's capital, Tallinn, is the jewel of the nation. The medieval Old Town is its highlight, and weaving your way along its narrow, cobbled streets is like strolling back to the 14th century.

Traditional Culture

Despite (or perhaps because of) centuries of occupation, Estonians have tenaciously held onto their national identity and are deeply, emotionally connected to their history, folklore and national song traditions.

Bar Life

Tallinn has numerous cosy cafes decorated in plush style, ideal spots to while away a few hours if the weather's not being kind. Nightlife, with alcohol not such a wallet drain as in other Nordic countries, is pretty vibrant.

p208

Iceland

Scenery
Activities
Wildlife

Volcanic Landscapes

Iceland, forged in fire, has a scenic splendour matched by few nations, a bleak, epic grandeur seemingly designed to remind visitors of their utter insignificance in the greater scheme of things. Get among steaming pools, spouting geysers and majestic glaciers to really appreciate this unique country.

Outdoors

There are so many ways to get active. Truly spectacular hikes give awesome perspectives of Iceland's natural wonder; kayaks let you see it all from the seaward side. Horse riding is a must, and what better way to soothe those aching muscles than luxuriating in a thermal spring?

Whales & Birds

The land may seem inhospitable, but the seas and skies teem with life. Iceland is one of the world's premier whale-watching spots and the quantity of seabirds (10 million puffins!) is quite astounding.

p218

Norway

Fjords
Activities
Wildlife

Coastal Majesty

The famous serrations of the coast are justly renowned; from base to tip, Norway's jagged geography is deeply momentous, inspiring profound awe.

Outdoor Appeal

The rough and rugged contours make this a prime outdoors destination. Mountains and plateaux attract hikers and cyclists, while the coastline invites getting out on the water in anything from a kayak to a cruise ship. Winter switches over to husky-sledding and snowmobile safaris, as well as the region's best skiing.

Unusual Creatures

For a modern European country, Norway has an impressive range of beasts, from whales sporting offshore to roaming elk and reindeer. There's even a reintroduced population of the weird-looking musk ox, as well as plentiful seabird life. Right up north, Svalbard is bossed by polar bears and walruses.

p291

Sweden

Winter Activities
Museums
Boating

Snowy Seduction

Northern Sweden has several top-drawer winter attractions, one of which is the aurora borealis (northern lights). Dark places like Abisko, in the country's top-left corner, make great observatories; other attractions up here include dog-sledding, skiing and Jukkasjärvi's famous Icehotel.

Proud Heritage

Sweden, which once controlled much of northern Europe, has a rich history and proud artistic heritage, which is displayed at great galleries and museums around the country. But it's not all about the rich and famous. Excellent open-air displays dotted across the country document the humbler traditions of everyday life.

Water World

The abundance of water once the snow melts means it's a country that's beautifully set up for boating, whether you're canoeing inland waterways, boating in the many archipelagos, or exploring the coastline in a yacht or kayak.

On the Road

Iceland
p218

Finland
p124

Sweden
p383

Norway
p291

Tallinn
p208

Denmark
p42

Denmark

Best Places to Eat

➡ Kadeau (p70)

➡ Höst (p45)

➡ Langhoff & Juul (p92)

➡ Geranium (p57)

➡ Torvehallerne KBH (p56)

Best Places to Stay

➡ Hotel Nimb (p55)

➡ Broholm Castle (p83)

➡ Nordlandet (p76)

➡ Urban House (p54)

➡ Pension Vestergade 44 (p86)

➡ Hotel Alexandra (p55)

Why Go?

Denmark is the bridge between Scandinavia and northern Europe. To the rest of Scandinavia, the Danes are chilled, frivolous party animals, with relatively liberal, progressive attitudes. Their culture, food, architecture and appetite for conspicuous consumption owe as much, if not more, to their German neighbours to the south than to their former colonies – Sweden, Norway and Iceland – to the north.

Packed with intriguing museums, shops, bars, nightlife and award-winning restaurants, Denmark's capital, Copenhagen, is one of the hippest, most accessible cities in Europe. And while Danish cities such as Odense and Aarhus harbour their own urbane drawcards, Denmark's other chief appeal lies in its photogenic countryside, sweeping coastline and historic sights, from neolithic burial chambers and frozen-in-time peat-bog bodies, to castles.

When to Go
Copenhagen

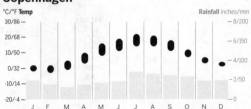

Jun & Jul Long days, buzzing beachside towns, Copenhagen Jazz and A-list rock fest Roskilde.

Sep & Oct Fewer crowds, golden landscapes and snug nights by crackling open fires.

Dec Twinkling Christmas lights, ice-skating rinks and gallons of warming *gløgg* (mulled wine).

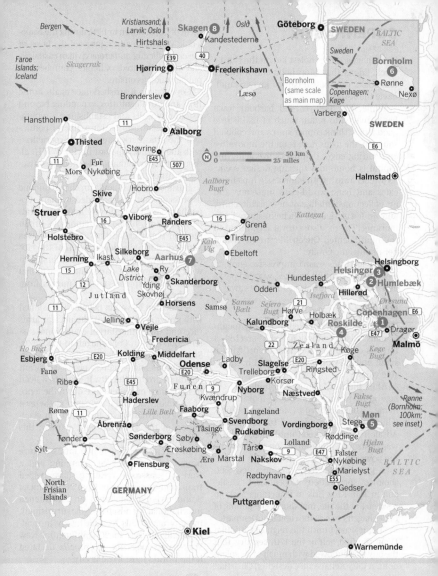

Denmark Highlights

1 **Copenhagen** Shopping, noshing and chilling in Scandinavia's capital of cool. (p44)

2 **Louisiana** (p54) Being inspired by the art and the views in Humlebæk.

3 **Kronborg Slot** (p65) Snooping around Hamlet's epic home in Helsingør.

4 **Roskilde Festival** (p67) Getting your groove on at Denmark's top annual music event.

5 **Møns Klint** (p70) Tackling the toothpaste-white cliffs on picture-perfect Møn.

6 **Bornholm** (p70) Losing yourself in nature and feasting on smoked fish on this beautiful Baltic island.

7 **ARoS** (p90) Seeing through technicolour glass at Aarhus' impressive art museum.

8 **Skagen** (p103) Watching angry seas duel above luminous northern shores.

COPENHAGEN

POP 1.7 MILLION

Copenhagen is the coolest kid on the Nordic block. Edgier than Stockholm and worldlier than Oslo, the Danish capital gives Scandinavia the X-factor.

While this 1000-year-old harbour town has managed to retain much of its historic good looks (think copper spires and cobbled squares), the focus here is on the innovative and cutting edge. Denmark's overachieving capital is home to a thriving design scene, its streets awash with effortlessly hip shops, cafes and bars; world-class museums and art collections; intelligent new architecture; and no fewer than 15 Michelin-starred restaurants. This is also a royal city, home to the multitalented Queen Margrethe II and her photogenic family.

And, as if this wasn't impressive enough, a bounty of beautiful beaches, wooded parks and elegant lakes await just minutes away.

History

Copenhagen was founded in 1167 by tough-as-nails Bishop Absalon, who erected a fortress on Slotsholmen Island, fortifying a small and previously unprotected harbourside village.

After the fortification was built, the village grew in importance and took on the name Kømandshavn (Merchant's Port), which was later condensed to København. Absalon's fortress stood until 1369, when it was destroyed in an attack on the town by the powerful Hanseatic states.

In 1376 construction began on a new Slotsholmen fortification, Copenhagen Castle, and in 1416 King Erik of Pomerania took up residence at the site, marking the beginning of Copenhagen's role as the capital of Denmark.

Still, it wasn't until the reign of Christian IV, in the first half of the 17th century, that the city was endowed with much of its splendour. A lofty Renaissance designer, Christian IV began an ambitious construction scheme, building two new castles and many other grand edifices, including the Rundetårn observatory and the glorious Børsen, Europe's first stock exchange.

In 1711 the bubonic plague reduced Copenhagen's population of 60,000 by one-third. Tragic fires, one in 1728 and the other in 1795, wiped out large tracts of the city, including most of its timber buildings. However, the worst scourge in the city's history is generally regarded as the unprovoked British bombardment of Copenhagen in 1807, during the Napoleonic Wars. The attack targeted the heart of the city, inflicting numerous civilian casualties and setting hundreds of homes, churches and public buildings on fire.

Copenhagen flourished once again in the 19th and 20th centuries, expanding beyond its old city walls and establishing a reputation as a centre for culture, liberal politics and the arts. Dark times were experienced with the Nazi occupation during WWII, although the city managed to emerge relatively unscathed.

During the war and in the economic depression that had preceded it, many Copenhagen neighbourhoods had deteriorated into slums. In 1948 an ambitious urban renewal policy called the 'Finger Plan' was adopted; this redeveloped much of the city, creating new housing projects interspaced with green areas of parks and recreational facilities that spread out like fingers from the city centre.

A rebellion by young people disillusioned with growing materialism, the nuclear arms race and the authoritarian educational system took hold in Copenhagen in the 1960s. Student protests broke out on the university campus and squatters occupied vacant buildings around the city. It came to a head in 1971 when protesters tore down the fence of an abandoned military camp at the east side of Christianshavn and began an occupation of the 41-hectare site, naming this settlement Christiania.

In recent decades, major infrastructure projects, enlightened city planning and a wave of grassroots creativity have helped transform Copenhagen from a provincial Scandinavian capital into an enlightened international trendsetter. Not surprisingly, the city never fails to rank highly in quality-of-life surveys; in 2016 influential New York–based magazine *Metropolis* declared it the world's most liveable city.

Sights

One of the great things about Copenhagen is its size. Virtually all of Copenhagen's major sightseeing attractions – Tivoli Gardens, Nationalmuseet, Statens Museum for Kunst, Ny Carlsberg Glyptotek, Christiansborg, Christiania, Nyhavn, Marmorkirken, Amalienborg and Rosenborg – are in or close to the medieval city centre. Only the perennially disappointing *Little Mermaid* lies outside of the city proper, on the harbourfront.

COPENHAGEN IN...

One Day

Pique your appetite at **Torvehallerne KBH** (p56), Copenhagen's celebrated food market. Warm up with porridge at Grød, browse Danish edibles at Bornholmer Butikken and Omegn, and slurp superlative brew at **Coffee Collective** (p58). From here, it's an easy walk to **Kongens Have** (p51), a former royal backyard turned city park. Snoop around the Hogwarts-worthy rooms of its 17th-century castle, **Rosenborg Slot** (p51), home to the Danish crown jewels, and grab some lunch at **Gasoline Grill** (p56).

Continue east to salty **Nyhavn** (p49), former haunt of Hans Christian Andersen. Capture the perfect snap of the colourful canal, then hop on a canal and harbour tour of the city. Alternatively, walk north along the harbourfront to royal pad **Amalienborg Slot** (p49), the glorious church **Marmorkirken** (p49) and, further north, fortress **Kastellet** (p52). If you must, the **Little Mermaid** (p50) awaits a short walk away from Kastellet. When you're done, catch a Harbour Bus south to **Det Kongelige Bibliotek** (p49). Enjoy the Danish cuisine at **Geist** (p58) for dinner.

Spend the evening swooning and screaming at all-ages **Tivoli Gardens** (p45), Copenhagen's vintage amusement park. If it's Friday night between mid-April and late September, you'll be just in time to catch an open-air concert at Tivoli's Plænen.

Two Days

Start on a high by climbing **Rundetårn** (p50), a 17th-century tower with views fit for its founder, Christian IV. The streets directly to the east – among them Pilestræde and Gammel Mønt – are dotted with Nordic fashion boutiques, as well as Scandi design stores like **Hay House** (p60). Alternatively, explore the streets southwest of Rundetårn, which together form the historic **Latin Quarter** (p50). It's here that you'll find **Vor Frue Kirke** (p50), home to sculptures by the great Bertel Thorvaldsen. For lunch, try celebrated **Schønnemann** (p56) or cosy, hearty **Café Halvvejen** (p56).

You could easily spend the afternoon exploring Viking treasures, bog bodies and Danish interiors at the **Nationalmuseet** (p48), the country's foremost history museum. If impressionist brushstrokes and afternoon coffee in a winter garden appeal more, ditch it for the nearby **Ny Carlsberg Glyptotek** (p49), one of the city's finest art museums and home to the biggest booty of Rodin sculptures outside of France.

Don't forget to reserve a table in advance to enjoy dinner at Michelin-two-starred **Kadeau** (p57) or Michelin-one-starred **Studio** (p58). Continue the night with innovative cocktails at **Ruby** (p59) and maybe a little late-night sax at **La Fontaine** (p60) or **Jazzhus Montmartre** (p60).

⊙ Around Tivoli

★**Tivoli Gardens**   AMUSEMENT PARK
(📞 33 15 10 01; www.tivoli.dk; Vesterbrogade 3; adult/child under 8yr 120kr/free, Fri after 7pm 160kr/free; ⊙ 11am-11pm Sun-Thu, to midnight Fri & Sat early Apr-late Sep, reduced hours rest of year; 🛗; 🚌 2A, 5C, 9A, 12, 14, 26, 250S, 🚆 København H) Dating from 1843, tasteful Tivoli wins fans with its dreamy whirl of amusement rides, twinkling pavilions, carnival games and open-air stage shows. Visitors can ride the renovated, century-old **roller coaster**, enjoy the famous Saturday evening **fireworks display** or just soak up the story-book atmosphere. A good tip is to go on Friday during summer when the open-air Plænen stage hosts free rock concerts by Danish bands

(and the occasional international superstar) from 10pm – go early if it's a big-name act.

Indeed, Tivoli is at its most romantic after dusk, when the fairy lights are switched on, cultural activities unfold and the clock tower of the neighbouring Rådhus soars in the moonlight like the set of a classic Disney film.

Each of Tivoli's numerous entertainment venues has a different character. Perhaps best known is the open-air Pantomime Theatre, built in 1874 by Vilhelm Dahlerup, the Copenhagen architect who also designed the royal theatre. Tivoli's large concert hall features performances by international symphony orchestras and ballet troupes, as well as popular musicians. While the numerous open-air performances are free of charge,

Central Copenhagen

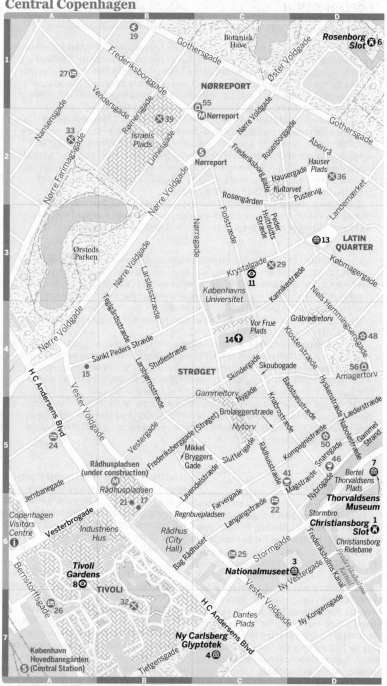

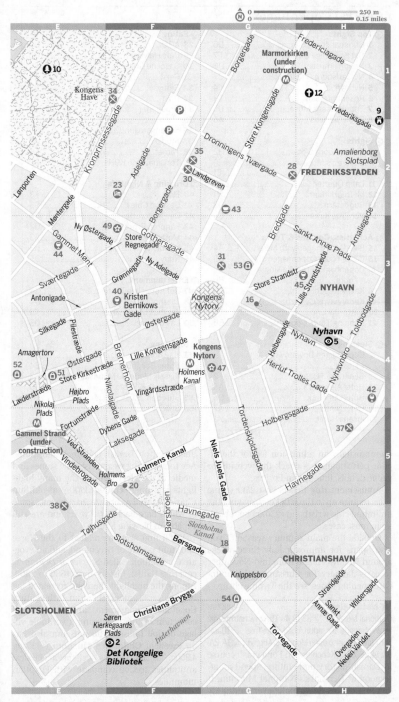

Central Copenhagen

there's usually an admission fee for the indoor performances – check the website for venue details, line-ups and prices.

Amusement ride tickets cost 25kr (some rides require up to three tickets), making the unlimited-ride wristband (230kr) better value in most cases.

Outside the main summer season, Tivoli also opens for approximately three weeks around Halloween and from mid-November to early January for Christmas. For up-to-date opening times, see the Tivoli website.

★**Nationalmuseet**   MUSEUM
(National Museum; ☎ 33 13 44 11; www.natmus.dk; Ny Vestergade 10; adult/child 75kr/free; ⊙10am-5pm Tue-Sun, also open Mon Jul & Aug; ⊞; 🚍 1A, 2A, 9A, 14, 26, 37, Ⓢ København H) For a crash course in Danish history and culture, spend an afternoon at Denmark's National Museum. It has first claims on virtually every antiquity

uncovered on Danish soil, including Stone Age tools, Viking weaponry, rune stones and medieval jewellery. Among the many highlights is a finely crafted 3500-year-old Sun Chariot, as well as bronze *lurs* (horns), some of which date back 3000 years and are still capable of blowing a tune.

You'll find sections related to the Norse and Inuit people of Greenland, and an evocative exhibition called *Stories of Denmark,* covering Danish history from 1660 to 2000. Among the highlights here are recreated living quarters (among them an 18th-century Copenhagen apartment) and a whimsical collection of toys, including a veritable village of doll houses. The museum also has an excellent **Children's Museum** (⊙10am-4.30pm Tue-Sun; ⊞), as well as a classical antiquities section complete with Egyptian mummies.

For a little cerebral relief, find refuge in the well-stocked gift shop.

★ Ny Carlsberg Glyptotek   MUSEUM

(🕽 33 41 81 41; www.glyptoteket.dk; Dantes Plads 7, HC Andersens Blvd; adult/child 95kr/free, Tue free; ☺11am-6pm Tue-Sun, until 10pm Thu; ☐1A, 2A, 9A, 37, ⑤København H) Fin de siècle architecture meets with an eclectic mix of art at Ny Carlsberg Glyptotek. The collection is divided into two parts: Northern Europe's largest booty of antiquities, and an elegant collection of 19th-century Danish and French art. The latter includes the largest collection of Rodin sculptures outside of France and no less than 47 Gauguin paintings. These are displayed along with works by greats like Cézanne, Van Gogh, Pissarro, Monet and Renoir.

⊙ Slotsholmen

★ Christiansborg Slot   PALACE

(Christiansborg Palace; 🕽 33 92 64 92; www.christiansborg.dk; Prins Jørgens Gård 1; adult/child 90kr/free, joint ticket incl royal reception rooms, ruins, kitchen & stables 150kr/free; ☺10am-5pm daily May-Sep, closed Mon Oct-Apr; ♿; ☐1A, 2A, 9A, 26, 37, 66, ⓢ Det Kongelige Bibliotek, Ⓜ Christianshavn) Christiansborg Slot is home to Folketinget (the Danish parliament), the Prime Minister's office and the Supreme Court. Visitor highlights include the glorious royal reception rooms, 11th-century ruins and royal kitchen, all of which can be visited separately or as part of a joint ticket. The palace is free to visit and offers sweeping views of the Danish capital.

★ Thorvaldsens Museum   MUSEUM

(🕽 33 32 15 32; www.thorvaldsensmuseum.dk; Bertel Thorvaldsens Plads 2; adult/child 70kr/free, Wed free; ☺10am-5pm Tue-Sun; ☐1A, 2A, 26, 37, 66) What looks like a colourful Greco-Roman mausoleum is in fact a museum dedicated to the works of illustrious Danish sculptor Bertel Thorvaldsen (1770–1844). Heavily influenced by mythology after four decades in Rome, Thorvaldsen returned to Copenhagen and donated his private collection to the Danish public. In return the royal family provided this site for the construction of what is a remarkable complex housing Thorvaldsen's drawings, plaster moulds and statues. The museum also contains Thorvaldsen's own collection of Mediterranean antiquities.

★ Det Kongelige Bibliotek   LIBRARY

(Royal Library; 🕽 33 47 47 47; www.kb.dk; Søren Kierkegaards Plads; ☺8am-7pm Mon-Fri, from 9am Sat Jul & Aug, 8am-9pm Mon-Fri, 9am-7pm Sat rest of year; ☐66, ⓢ Det Kongelige Bibliotek) **FREE** Scandinavia's largest library is made up of two very distinct parts: the original 19th-century red-brick building and the head-turning 'Black Diamond' extension, the latter a leaning parallelogram of sleek black granite and smoke-coloured glass. From the soaring, harbour-fronting atrium, an escalator leads up to a 210 sq metre ceiling mural by celebrated Danish artist Per Kirkeby. Beyond it, at the end of the corridor, is the 'old library' and its Hogwarts-like northern Reading Room, resplendent with vintage desk lamps and classical columns.

⊙ Around Nyhavn & Habourfront

★ Nyhavn   CANAL

(Nyhavn; ☐1A, 26, 66, 350S, Ⓜ Kongens Nytorv) There are few nicer places to be on a sunny day than sitting at an outdoor table at a cafe on the quayside of the Nyhavn canal. The canal was built to connect Kongens Nytorv to the harbour and was long a haunt for sailors and writers, including Hans Christian Andersen. He wrote *The Tinderbox, Little Claus and Big Claus* and *The Princess and the Pea* while living at number 20, and also spent time living at numbers 18 and 67.

Amalienborg Slot   PALACE

(🕽 33 15 32 86; www.kongernessamling.dk/amalienborg; Amalienborg Plads; adult/child 95kr/free; ☺10am-5pm daily mid-Jun–mid-Sep, reduced hours rest of year; ☐1A, 26) Home of the current queen, Margrethe II, Amalienborg Slot consists of four austere 18th-century palaces around a large cobbled square. The changing of the guard takes place here daily at noon, the new guard having marched through the city centre from the barracks on Gothersgade at 11.30am.

Marmorkirken   CHURCH

(Marble Church; 🕽 33 15 01 44; www.marmorkirken.dk; Frederiksgade 4; dome adult/child 35/20kr, church admission free; ☺church 10am-5pm Mon-Thu & Sat, from noon Fri & Sun, dome 1pm daily mid-Jun–Aug, 1pm Sat & Sun rest of year; ☐1A) Consecrated in 1894, the neo-baroque Marble Church (officially Frederikskirken) is one of Copenhagen's most imposing architectural assets. Its grandiose dome – inspired by St Peter's in Rome

THE LITTLE MERMAID

New York has its Lady Liberty, Sydney its (Danish-designed) Opera House. When the world thinks of Copenhagen, chances are they're thinking of the Little Mermaid (Den Lille Havfrue; Langelinie, Østerport; 🚊1A, 🚢Nordre Toldbod). Love her or loathe her (watch Copenhageners cringe at the very mention of her), this small, underwhelming statue is arguably the most photographed sight in the country, as well as the cause of countless 'is that it?' shrugs from tourists who have trudged the kilometre or so along an often windswept harbourfront to see her.

In 1909 the Danish beer baron Carl Jacobsen was so moved after attending a ballet performance based on the Hans Christian Andersen fairy tale *The Little Mermaid* that he commissioned sculptor Edvard Eriksen to create a statue of the eponymous lady-fish to grace Copenhagen's harbourfront. The face of the famous statue was modelled after the ballerina Ellen Price, while Eline Eriksen, the sculptor's wife, modelled for the body.

The *Little Mermaid* survived the Great Depression and the WWII occupation unscathed, but modern times haven't been so kind to Denmark's leading lady, with several decapitations and lost limbs at the hands of vandals and protesters trying to make various political points.

Partly in response to this, Carlsberg commissioned Danish artist Bjørn Nørgaard to create a new Little Mermaid in 2006. The result is a 'genetically altered' mermaid, sitting only a few hundred metres from the original. While there's no doubt that Eriksen's creation may be the prettier sibling, Nørgaard's misshapen creation is arguably truer in spirit to Andersen's rather bleak, twisted fairy tale, in which the fish-tailed protagonist is physically and emotionally tormented...and never gets her man.

and the largest church dome in Scandinavia – offers an impressive view over the city. The church was ordered by Frederik V and drawn up by Nicolai Eigtved. Construction began in 1749 but spiralling costs saw the project mothballed. Salvation came in the form of Denmark's wealthiest 19th-century financier CF Tietgen, who bankrolled the project's revival.

★ **Designmuseum Danmark**　　MUSEUM
(www.designmuseum.dk; Bredgade 68; adult/child 100kr/free; ⊙11am-5pm Tue & Thu-Sun, to 9pm Wed; 🚊1A, Ⓜ Kongens Nytorv) The 18th-century Frederiks Hospital is now the outstanding Denmark Design Museum. A must for fans of the applied arts and industrial design, its fairly extensive collection includes Danish textiles and fashion, as well as the iconic design pieces of modern innovators like Kaare Klint, Poul Henningsen and Arne Jacobsen.

⊙ Around Strøget

Rundetårn　　HISTORIC BUILDING
(Round Tower; ☑33 73 03 73; www.rundetaarn.dk; Købmagergade 52; adult/child 25/5kr; ⊙10am-8pm May-Sep, reduced hours rest of year, observatory times vary; 🚊14, Ⓜ Nørreport, Ⓢ Nørreport) Haul yourself to the top of the 34.8m-high red-brick 'Round Tower' and you will be following in the footsteps of such luminaries

as King Christian IV, who built it in 1642 as an observatory for the famous astronomer Tycho Brahe. You'll also be following in the hoofsteps of Tsar Peter the Great's horse and, according to legend, the track marks of a car that made its way up the tower's spiral ramp in 1902.

Latin Quarter　　AREA
(🚊5C, 6A, 14, Ⓜ Nørreport, Ⓢ Nørreport) Bordered by Nørre Voldgade to the north, Nørregade to the east, Vestergade to the south and Vester Voldgade to the west, the Latin Quarter gets its nickname from the presence of the old campus of **Københavns Universitet** (Copenhagen University), where Latin was once widely spoken. This is one of Copenhagen's oldest and most atmospheric districts, dotted with historic, pastel-hued buildings and postcard-pretty nooks. Among the latter is **Gråbrødretorv** (Grey Friars' Square), which dates from the mid-17th century.

Vor Frue Kirke　　CATHEDRAL
(☑33 15 10 78; www.koebenhavnsdomkirke.dk; Nørregade 8; ⊙8am-5pm, closed during services & concerts; 🚊14, Ⓜ Nørreport, Ⓢ Nørreport) Founded in 1191 and rebuilt three times after devastating fires, Copenhagen's neoclassical cathedral dates from 1829. Designed by CF Hansen, its lofty, vaulted interior houses

Bertel Thorvaldsen's statues of Christ and the apostles, completed in 1839 and considered his most acclaimed works. In fact, the sculptor's depiction of Christ, with comforting open arms, remains the most popular worldwide model for statues of Jesus. In May 2004, the cathedral hosted the wedding of Crown Prince Frederik to Australian Mary Donaldson.

Around Kongens Have

★Statens Museum for Kunst   MUSEUM
(☎33 74 84 94; www.smk.dk; Sølvgade 48-50; adult/child 110kr/free; ⊙11am-5pm Tue & Thu-Sun, to 8pm Wed; ☐6A, 26, 42, 184, 185) FREE Denmark's National Gallery straddles two contrasting, interconnected buildings: a late-19th-century 'palazzo' and a sharply minimalist extension. The museum houses medieval and Renaissance works and impressive collections of Dutch and Flemish artists, including Rubens, Breughel and Rembrandt. It claims the world's finest collection of 19th-century Danish 'Golden Age' artists, among them Eckersberg and Hammershøi, foreign greats like Matisse and Picasso, and modern Danish heavyweights including Per Kirkeby.

★Rosenborg Slot   CASTLE
(☎33 15 32 86; www.kongernessamling.dk/en/rosenborg; Øster Voldgade 4A; adult/child 110kr/free, incl Amalienborg Slot 145kr/free; ⊙9am-5pm mid-Jun–mid-Sep, reduced hours rest of year; ☐6A, 42, 184, 185, 350S, Ⓜ Nørreport, Ⓢ Nørreport) A 'once-upon-a-time' combo of turrets, gables and moat, the early-17th-century Rosenborg Slot was built in Dutch Renaissance style between 1606 and 1633 by King Christian IV to serve as his summer home. Today the castle's 24 upper rooms are chronologically arranged, housing the furnishings and portraits of each monarch from Christian IV to Frederik VII. The pièce de résistance is the basement Treasury, home to the dazzling crown jewels, among them Christian IV's glorious crown and Christian III's jewel-studded sword.

Kongens Have   PARK
(King's Gardens; http://parkmuseerne.dk/kongens-have; Øster Voldgade; ⊙7am-11pm Jul–mid-Aug, to 10pm May–mid-Jun & mid-late Aug, reduced hours rest of year; ☐; ☐26, Ⓜ Nørreport, Ⓢ Nørreport) FREE The oldest park in Copenhagen was laid out in the early 17th century by Christian IV, who used it as his vegetable patch. These days it has a little more to offer, including wonderfully romantic paths, a fragrant rose garden, some of the longest mixed borders in northern Europe and a marionette theatre with free performances from mid-July to mid-August (2pm and 3pm Tuesday to Sunday).

Botanisk Have   GARDENS
(Botanic Garden; http://botanik.snm.ku.dk; Gothersgade 140, Nørreport; ⊙8.30am-6pm Apr-Sep, to 4pm Tue-Sun Oct-Mar; ☐; ☐6A, 42, 150S, 184, 185, Ⓜ Nørreport, Ⓢ Nørreport) Restorative and romantic, Copenhagen's Botanic Garden lays claim to around 13,000 species of plant life – the largest collection in Denmark. You can amble along tranquil trails, escape to warmer climes in the 19th-century Palmehus (⊙10am-5pm daily Apr-Sep, 10am-3pm Tue-Sun Oct-Apr) glasshouse and even pick up honey made using the garden's own bees at the gorgeous little gift shop.

Christianshavn

★Christiania   AREA
(www.christiania.org; Prinsessegade; ☐9A, Ⓜ Christianshavn) Escape the capitalist crunch and head to Freetown Christiania, a hash-scented commune straddling the eastern side of Christianshavn. Since its establishment by squatters in 1971, the area has drawn nonconformists from across the globe, attracted by the concept of collective business, workshops and communal living. Explore beyond the settlement's infamous 'Pusher St' – lined with shady hash and marijuana dealers who do not appreciate photographs – and you'll

ⓘ COPENHAGEN CARD

The Copenhagen Card (www.copenhagencard.com; adult/child 10-15yr 24hr 389/199kr, 48hr 549/279kr, 72hr 659/329kr, 120hr 889/449kr) gives you access to 79 museums and attractions, as well as free public transport. Each adult card includes up to two children aged under 10. The card can be purchased at the Copenhagen Visitors Centre (p61), as well as at the airport information desk, the tourist information centre inside Central Station, and at various hotels and 7-Eleven stores. A complete list of vendors is available on the website, where you can also purchase the card online.

stumble upon a semi-bucolic wonderland of whimsical DIY homes, cosy garden plots, eateries, beer gardens and music venues.

Vor Frelsers Kirke   CHURCH
(☑41 66 63 57; www.vorfrelserskirke.dk; Sankt Annæ Gade 29; church free, tower adult/child 40/10kr; ⊘11am-3.30pm, closed during services, tower 9.30am-7pm Mon-Sat, 10.30am-7pm Sun May-Sep, reduced hours rest of year; ☐2A, 9A, 37, 350S, Ⓜ Christianshavn) It's hard to miss this 17th-century church and its 95m-high spiral tower. For a soul-stirring city view, make the head-spinning 400-step ascent to the top – the last 150 steps run along the outside rim of the tower, narrowing to the point where they literally disappear at the top. Inspired by Borromini's tower of St Ivo in Rome, the spire was added in 1752 by Lauritz de Thurah. Inside the church, highlights include an ornate baroque altar and elaborately carved pipe organ from 1698.

🏃 Activities

⭐ Mystery Makers   WALKING
(☑30 80 30 50; http://mysterymakers.dk; Mystery Hunt per person 250-400kr; ⊘hours vary) Bring out your inner Detective Sarah Lund with Mystery Makers' interactive mystery hunts. Offered at numerous historical sites around town – including Kastellet (☐1A, Ⓢ Nordre Toldbod) – players are given fictional identities and a mystery to solve, with a series of riddles and clues along the way. Suitable for adults and kids aged 12 and above, it's a stimulating, engaging way to explore Copenhagen's back-story.

⭐ GoBoat   BOATING
(☑40 26 10 25; www.goboat.dk; Islands Brygge 10; boat hire 1/2/3hr 399/749/999kr; ⊘9.30am-sunset; 🅰; ☐5C, 12, Ⓜ Islands Brygge) 🖉 What could be more 'Copenhagen' than sailing around the harbour and canals in your own solar-powered boat? You don't need prior sailing experience, and each boat or vessel comes with a built-in picnic table (you can buy supplies at GoBoat or bring your own). Boats seat up to eight people and rates are per boat, so the more in your group, the cheaper per person.

Københavns Cyklerbørs   CYCLING
(☑33 14 07 17; www.cykelboersen.dk; Gothersgade 157; bicycles per day/week 90/450kr; ⊘10am-5.30pm Mon-Fri, to 2pm Sat, also 10am-2pm Sun May-Aug; ☐5C, 37, 350S, Ⓜ Nørreport, Ⓢ Nørreport) Bicycle rental close to the Botanisk Have (Botanic Garden) on the northwest edge of the city centre.

Amager Strandpark   BEACH
(www.kk.dk/amagerstrandpark; 🅰; Ⓜ Øresund, Amager Strand) A sand-sational artificial lagoon southeast of the city centre, with acres of beach and, during summer, a festive vibe most days, with cafes and bars. Playground facilities and shallow water make it ideal for kids. The beach is also home to Helgoland (⊘24hr daily May-Aug) FREE, a vintage-inspired sea bathing complex with multiple pools open to nonmembers from late June to the end of August.

🧭 Tours

Canal Tours

Kayak Republic   KAYAKING
(☑22 88 49 89; www.kayakrepublic.dk; Børskaj 12; 1/2/3hr rental 175/275/375kr, 2hr guided tour 395kr; ⊘10am-9pm Jun-Aug, reduced hours rest of year; ☐2A, 9A, 37, 350S) 🖉 Kayak Republic runs daily two-hour kayaking tours through the city's canals, as well as less frequent three-hour tours that focus on Nordic food (695kr) or architecture (525kr). While no previous kayaking experience is necessary for the guided tours, only people with an EEP 2 or BCU 2 certificate (and ID) are able to rent sea kayaks for unaccompanied exploration.

Netto-Bådene   BOATING
(☑32 54 41 02; www.havnerundfart.dk; Holmens Bro; adult/child 40/15kr; ⊘tours 2-5 per hour, 10am-7pm Jul & Aug, reduced hours rest of year; ☐1A, 2A, 9A, 26, 37, 66) Netto-Bådene operates good-value one-hour cruises of Copenhagen's canals and harbour. Embarkation points are at Holmens Kirke and Nyhavn. From October to March, tours are conducted in heated, glass-roofed boats. Check the website for timetable updates.

Canal Tours Copenhagen   BOATING
(☑32 96 30 00; www.stromma.dk; Nyhavn; adult/child 80/40kr; ⊘9.30am-9pm late Jun–mid-Aug, reduced hours rest of year; 🅰; ☐1A, 26, 66, 350S, Ⓜ Kongens Nytorv) Canal Tours Copenhagen runs one-hour cruises of the city's canals and harbour, taking in numerous major sights, including Christiansborg Slot, Christianshavn, the Royal Library, Opera House, Amalienborg Palace and the *Little Mermaid*. Embark at Nyhavn or Ved Stranden. Boats depart up to six times per hour from late June to late August, with reduced frequency the rest of the year.

Walking Tours

Copenhagen Free Walking Tours WALKING
(www.copenhagenfreewalkingtours.dk; Rådhuspladsen) This outfit runs free daily walking tours of the city. The three-hour Grand Tour of Copenhagen departs daily at 10am, 11am and 3pm from outside Rådhus (Town Hall), taking in famous landmarks and featuring interesting anecdotes. There's also a 90-minute Classical Copenhagen Tour, departing daily at noon. A 90-minute tour of Christianshavn departs daily at 4pm from Højbro Plads. A tip is expected.

Nordic Noir Tours WALKING
(www.nordicnoirtours.com; per person 150kr, if booked online 100kr; ⊘ The Killing/The Bridge tour 4pm Sat, pre-booked Borgen tour 2pm Sat; Ⓢ Vesterport) Fans of Danish TV dramas *The Bridge* and *The Killing* can visit the shooting locations on these themed 90-minute walks. Tours start at Vesterport S-train station. Bookings are not required, though tickets purchased online at least 48 hours in advance are 50kr cheaper. A 90-minute *Borgen* tour is also offered, though advance booking is necessary. Check website for open tour months.

Other Tours

Bike Copenhagen with Mike CYCLING
(⊡ 26 39 56 88; www.bikecopenhagenwithmike.dk; Sankt Peders Stræde 47; per person 299kr; ⊡ 2A, 5C, 6A, 14, 250S) If you don't fancy walking, Bike Mike runs three-hour cycling tours of the city, departing Sankt Peders Stræde 47 in the city centre, just east of Ørstedsparken (which is southwest of Nørreport Station). The tour cost includes bike, helmet rental and Mike himself, a great character with deep, attention-grabbing knowledge of the city. Cash only.

Running Tours Copenhagen RUNNING
(⊡ 50 59 17 29; www.runningtours.dk; 1-2 people 350kr, each additional person 100kr; ⊡ 2A, 12, 14, 26, 33, 250S, Ⓢ København H) Run (or jog) around town for a cardio-friendly sightseeing session. Choose from various themes, including the Grand Tour, the Night Run, and our favourite, the Pub Run. Tours begin from Rådhuspladsen, though hotel pick-ups can be arranged.

★★ Festivals & Events

Changing of the Guard PARADE
(www.kongehuset.dk/en/changing-of-the-guard-at-amalienborg; Amalienborg Slotsplads; ⊘ noon daily;

⊡ 1A) FREE The Royal Life Guard is charged with protecting the Danish royal family and its city residence, Amalienborg Palace. Every day of the year, these soldiers march from their barracks through the streets of Copenhagen to perform the Changing of the Guard. Clad in 19th-century tunics and bearskin helmets, their performance of intricate manoeuvres is an impressive sight to see.

Vinter Jazz MUSIC
(http://jazz.dk; ⊘ Feb) Toe-tap your blues away at the winter edition of Copenhagen's summertime jazz festival. Featuring top Scandinavian talent and a sprinkling of acts from further afield, the festival usually kicks off on the first Friday of February and runs for around three weeks. Events are held across the city.

★ Copenhagen Jazz Festival MUSIC
(www.jazz.dk; ⊘ Jul) Copenhagen's single largest event, and the biggest jazz festival in northern Europe, hits the city over 10 days in early July. The program covers jazz in all its forms, with an impressive line-up of local and international talent.

Copenhagen Cooking & Food Festival FOOD & DRINK
(www.copenhagencooking.dk; ⊘ Aug) Scandinavia's largest food festival serves up a gut-rumbling program spanning cooking demonstrations from A-list chefs to tastings and foodie tours of the city. Events are held in venues and restaurants across town.

Copenhagen Blues Festival MUSIC
(www.copenhagenbluesfestival.dk; ⊘ Sep/Oct) Taking place in late September or October, Copenhagen celebrates the moody sounds of the blues with this international festival of blues. The line-up includes both Danish and international music acts.

CPH:PIX FILM
(www.cphpix.dk; ⊘ Sep/Oct) Copenhagen's feature film festival runs over two weeks in September and October. Expect a comprehensive program of cinema from Denmark and abroad, as well as numerous film-related events, including director and actor Q&As.

Tivoli Christmas Market CULTURAL
(www.tivoli.dk; ⊘ Nov-Dec) From mid-November to late December, Tivoli gets into the Christmas spirit with a large Yuletide market, costumed staff and theatre shows. Fewer rides are operational but the mulled wine and *æbleskiver* (small doughnuts) are ample compensation.

LOUISIANA

An easy train ride north of Copenhagen, **Louisiana** (www.louisiana.dk; Gammel Strandvej 13, Humlebæk; adult/student/child 125/110kr/free; ⊘ 11am-10pm Tue-Fri, to 6pm Sat & Sun) is more than a powerhouse museum of modern art. It's an extraordinary synergy of culture and natural beauty. Grassy knolls are dotted with sculptures by Miro, Calder and Moore, while its striking modernist buildings house works by heavyweights like Asger Jørn, Warhol, Lichtenstein, Bacon and Rothko. One minute you're pondering Picasso, the next you're gazing out at the Øresund sea and Sweden. Art's answer to Slow Food, this is a place for unhurried pondering, lazy picnics and inspiration both human and green.

It's hard to predict exactly which pieces from the gallery's huge, stellar collection will be on display. Such is the quality and breadth that even works by Pablo Picasso and Francis Bacon stay in storage much of the time. There's a better chance of seeing pieces by Alberto Giacometti and prominent Danish artist Asger Jorn, but rotations every two months or so mean that there's always more to discover. Kids are spoilt with an entire section of their own, where they can create masterpieces inspired by the gallery's exhibitions, using everything from crayons to interactive computers. And an evening program often includes art lectures and live music (typically Fridays). There's a great cafe and shop too.

Louisiana is in the pretty coastal town of **Humlebæk**, 30km north of Copenhagen. From Humlebæk train station, the museum is a 1.5km signposted walk northeast. Trains to Humlebæk run at least twice hourly from Copenhagen (92kr, 35 minutes) but if you're day-tripping, the 24-hour Copenhagen ticket (adult/child 130/65kr) is much better value. Hourly bus 388 from Helsingør stops right outside Louisiana (36kr, 17 minutes) and continues to Rungsted (30 minutes), where it passes the Blixen museum.

Copenhagen Pride   LGBT
(www.copenhagenpride.dk; ⊘ Aug) Rainbow flags fly high during the city's six-day queer fest in August. Expect live music and merry revellers in the city centre, fabulous club parties, and film screenings, as well as cultural and political forums. The Pride parade takes place on the Saturday afternoon, starting in Frederiksberg and ending in Rådhuspladsen in the city centre.

🛏 Sleeping

Copenhagen's accommodation continues to smarten up, with a string of svelte, on-point hotels either recently opened or in the pipeline. These are a refreshing antidote to the city's plethora of soulless, business-geared hotels and 'boutique' digs in need of a refresh. Budget accommodation has also received a boost in recent years with hip, low-frill chains **WakeUp Copenhagen** (www.wakeupcopenhagen.com) and **Generator Hostel** (https://generatorhostels.com). Reserve rooms in advance, especially during the busy summer season.

⭐ **Urban House**   HOSTEL, HOTEL €
(✆ 89 88 32 69; www.urbanhouse.me; Colbjørnsensgade 5-11, Vesterbro; dm/d from 140/530kr; @ 🛜; 🚈 2A, 5C, 9A, 10, 14, 250S, Ⓢ København H) This huge hostel spans a trio of historic buildings close to Central Station and Vesterbro's on-trend venues. Slumber options range from single rooms to dorms with bunks for up to 12 people; all have private bathrooms. Bed linen and towels are included in the price, while in-house facilities include a communal kitchen, laundry, games room, small cinema and even a tattoo parlour!

⭐ **Generator Hostel**   HOSTEL €
(✆ 78 77 54 00; www.generatorhostel.com; Adelgade 5-7; dm/d from 130/595kr; @ 🛜; 🚈 350S, 1A, 26, Ⓜ Kongens Nytorv) A solid choice for 'cheap chic', upbeat, design-literate Generator sits on the edge of the city's medieval core. It's kitted out with designer furniture, slick communal areas (including a bar and outdoor terrace) and friendly, young staff. While the rooms can be a little small, all are bright and modern, with bathrooms in private rooms and dorms.

Danhostel Copenhagen City   HOSTEL €
(✆ 33 11 85 85; www.danhostel.dk; HC Andersens Blvd 50; dm/d from 205/590kr; @ 🛜; 🚈 5C, 250S, Ⓢ København H) Step into the lobby here with its cafe-bar and it looks more like a hotel than a hostel. Set in a tower block overlooking the harbour just south of Tivoli Gardens

(did we mention the views?), the dorms and private rooms are all bright, light and modern, each with bathroom. Laundry facilities available on-site. Book ahead.

Copenhagen Downtown Hostel   HOSTEL €
(⏰70 23 21 10; www.copenhagendowntown.com; Vandkunsten 5; dm from 210kr; 📶; 🚇1A, 2A, 9A, 14, 26, 37, ⑤København H) Centrally located in the city's historic core, this hostel is the perfect jumping-off point for exploring Copenhagen on foot. It's a lively, retro-style place with a community feel, along with a colourful bar and cafe with happy-hour offerings and free dinner nightly (when you book accommodation via the hostel website). Other freebies include live music and social events.

★Hotel Alexandra   BOUTIQUE HOTEL €€
(⏰33 74 44 44; www.hotelalexandra.dk; HC Andersens Blvd 8; d from 1180kr; 🅿@📶; 🚇2A, 10, 250S, ⑤Vesterport) The furniture of Danish design deities such as Arne Jacobsen, Ole Wanscher and Kaare Klint graces the interiors of the crisp, refined yet homey Alexandra. Rooms are effortlessly cool, each decked out in a mix of mid-century Danish pieces. Purists can opt for one of the suites, which are dedicated to single Danish designers. On-site parking costs 180kr per day.

★Ibsens Hotel   BOUTIQUE HOTEL €€
(⏰33 13 19 13; www.ibsenshotel.dk; Vendersgade 23; d from 975kr; @📶; 🚇5C, 37, 350S, Ⓜ Nørreport, ⑤Nørreport) Ibsens is a sound choice for discerning sophisticates. Local creativity underscores everything from the striking textiles to the artwork; the inviting lobby comes complete with industrial French lamps and timber tables from veteran Copenhagen cabinetmakers Jul. Møller & Søns. The rooms themselves are minimalist yet plush, with muted tones, designer fixtures and blissful beds. Book early for the best rates.

★Hotel Danmark   BOUTIQUE HOTEL €€
(⏰33 11 48 06; www.brochner-hotels.com; Vester Voldgade 89; d from 1210kr; 🅿📶; 🚇12, 33, ⑤København H) The revamped Danmark is a svelte boutique hideaway steps away from major sights. Though most of its 88 rooms are rather petite, they're all flawlessly chic and ensconcing, with heavenly beds, tactile fabrics and restrained, elegant Danish furniture. Interestingly, the muted colour accents – which range from sage green to cobalt blue – are inspired by the nearby Thorvaldsen Museum.

★Babette Guldsmeden   BOUTIQUE HOTEL €€
(⏰33 14 15 00; www.guldsmedenhotels.com; Bredgade 78; d from 995kr; @📶✱; 🚇1A) ♠
The 98-room Babette is part of the superb Guldsmeden hotel chain, with the same (unexpectedly) harmonious blend of Nordic and Indonesian design aesthetics. Though on the smaller side, the rooms are inviting and tactile, with four-poster beds, sheepskin throws and vibrant artworks. There's a Balinese-inspired rooftop spa and sauna, tranquil leafy courtyard, buzzing bar popular with locals, as well as a good, mostly organic restaurant.

CPH Living   BOUTIQUE HOTEL €€
(⏰61 60 85 46; www.cphliving.com; Langebrogade 1A; r incl breakfast from 1380kr; 📶; 🚇5C, 12, Ⓜ Christiania) Located on a converted freight boat, Copenhagen's only floating hotel consists of 12 stylish, contemporary rooms with harbour and city views. Perks include modern bathrooms with rain shower head, heated floors and a communal sun deck for summertime lounging. Breakfast is a simple continental affair, while the central location makes it walkable to the city centre, Christianshavn and the harbour pools at Islands Brygge.

★Hotel Nimb   BOUTIQUE HOTEL €€€
(⏰88 70 00 00; www.nimb.dk; Bernstorffsgade 5; r from 2800kr; 🅿@📶; 🚇2A, 5C, 9A, 250S, ⑤København H) Part of historic Tivoli Gardens, this boutique belle offers 17 individually styled rooms and suites that fuse clean lines, beautiful art and antiques, luxury fabrics and tech perks, such as Nespresso coffee machines and Bang & Olufsen TVs and sound systems. All rooms except three also feature a fireplace, while all bar one come with views over the amusement park.

71 Nyhavn Hotel   HOTEL €€€
(⏰33 43 62 00; www.71nyhavnhotel.com; Nyhavn 71; r from 1700kr; ✱@📶✱; 🚇66, Ⓜ Kongens Nytorv) Housed in two striking 200-year-old canal-side warehouses, atmospheric 71 Nyhavn offers great views of both the harbour and Nyhavn canal. Rooms facing Nyhavn are quite small, while those without the magical view compensate with more space. The hotel is popular with business travellers, and therefore can be a bargain on weekends.

✗ Eating

Beneath Copenhagen's galaxy of Michelin stars is a growing number of hot-spots serving innovative contemporary Danish fare at affordable prices. The international food scene is also lifting its game, with a spate of new places serving authentic dishes like pho, ramen and tacos made using top-notch produce. Keeping them company are veritable city institutions serving classic Danish fare, including smørrebrød.

★ Torvehallerne KBH
MARKET €

(www.torvehallernekbh.dk; Israels Plads, Nørreport; ⊙ 10am-7pm Mon-Thu, to 8pm Fri, to 6pm Sat, 11am-5pm Sun; ☐ 15E, 150S, 185, Ⓜ Nørreport, Ⓢ Nørreport) Food market Torvehallerne KBH is an essential stop on the Copenhagen foodie trail. A delicious ode to the fresh, the tasty and the artisanal, the market's beautiful stalls peddle everything from seasonal herbs and berries to smoked meats, seafood and cheeses, smørrebrød, fresh pasta and hand-brewed coffee. You could easily spend an hour or more exploring its twin halls.

★ La Banchina
CAFE €

(☑ 31 26 65 61; www.labanchina.dk; Refshalevej 141A; mains 70-90kr; ⊙ 8am-11pm Mon-Fri, from 9am Sat & Sun May-Sep, reduced hours rest of year; ☐ 9A, ☒ Refshaleøen) There are only two daily mains at this tiny lo-fi shack, cooked beautifully and served on paper plates with little fanfare. The real magic is the setting, in a small harbour cove with picnic tables and a wooden pier where diners dip their feet while sipping decent vino, tucking into grub like tender barbecued salmon, and watching the summer sun sink over Copenhagen.

Copenhagen Street Food
STREET FOOD €

(www.copenhagenstreetfood.dk; Warehouse 7 & 8, Trangravsvej 14; dishes from 50kr; ⊙ noon-9pm Mon-Wed & Sun, to 10pm Thu-Sat; ☒; ☐ 66, ☒ Operaen) 🍴 Take a disused warehouse, pack it with artisan food trucks and stalls, hipster baristas and a chilled-out bar or two, and you have this hot little newcomer. The emphasis is on fresh, affordable grub, from handmade pasta and tacos, to pulled-pork burgers and organic koldskål (cold buttermilk dessert). If the weather's good, grab a sun chair and catch some rays by the harbour.

★ Café Halvvejen
DANISH €

(☑ 33 11 91 12; www.cafehalvvejen.dk; Krystalgade 11; dishes 55-125kr; ⊙ 11am-2am Mon-Thu, to 3am Fri & Sat; ☐ 5A, 6A, 14, 150S, Ⓜ Nørreport, Ⓢ Nørreport) Cosy, creaky, wood-panelled Café Halvvejen channels a fast-fading Copenhagen. The menu is unapologetically hearty, generous and cheap for this part of town,

with faithful open sandwiches, frikadeller (Danish meatballs) and pariserbøf (minced beef steak with egg and onions). The deceptively named miniplatte offers a satisfying overview of classic Nordic flavours. Whatever you choose, wash it down with a (very generous) shot of akvavit.

★ Gasoline Grill
BURGERS €

(www.facebook.com/gasolinegrill; Landgreven 10; burgers 75kr; ⊙ daily 11am until sold out; ☐ 1A, 26, Ⓜ Kongens Nytorv) Some of the city's most famous chefs join the queue at Gasoline, a petrol station-turned-burger takeaway. The menu is refreshingly straightforward: four burgers (one vegetarian), fries with a choice of toppings and homemade dips, and two desserts. The meat is organic and freshly ground daily, the buns brioche, and the flavour rich and decadent without the post-feed grease and guilt.

★ Schønnemann
DANISH €€

(☑ 33 12 07 85; www.restaurantschonnemann.dk; Hauser Plads 16; smørrebrød 75-185kr; ⊙ 11.30am-5pm Mon-Sat; ☎; ☐ 6A, 42, 150S, 184, 185, 350S, Ⓜ Nørreport, Ⓢ Nørreport) A veritable institution, Schønnemann has been lining bellies with smørrebrød and snaps since 1877. Originally a hit with farmers in town selling their produce, the restaurant's current fan base includes revered chefs like René Redzepi; try the smørrebrød named after him: smoked halibut with creamed cucumber, radishes and chives on caraway bread.

★ Pluto
DANISH €€

(☑ 33 16 00 16; http://restaurantpluto.dk/forside; Borgergade 16; mains 135-225kr; ⊙ 5.30pm-midnight Mon-Thu, to 2am Fri & Sat, to 11pm Sun; ☎; ☐ 1A, 26, Ⓜ Kongens Nytorv) Loud, convivial Pluto is not short of friends, and for good reason: superfun soundtrack, attentive staff and beautiful, simple dishes by respected local chef Rasmus Oubæk. Whether it's flawlessly seared cod with seasonal carrots or a side of new potatoes, funky truffles and green beans in a mussel broth, the family-style menu is all about letting the produce sing.

★ Oysters & Grill
SEAFOOD €€

(☑ 70 20 61 71; www.cofoco.dk/da/restauranter/oysters-and-grill; Sjællandsgade 1B, Nørrebro; mains 165-245kr; ⊙ 5.30pm-midnight daily; ☐ 5C) Finger-licking surf and turf is what you get at this rocking, unpretentious neighbourhood favourite, complete with kitsch vinyl tablecloths and a fun, casual vibe. The shellfish is fantastically fresh and, unlike most places, ordered by weight, which means you don't need to pick at measly servings. Meat lovers won't to be disappointed either, with cuts that are lustfully succulent.

★ Aamanns Takeaway
DANISH €€

(☑20 80 52 01; www.aamanns.dk; Øster Farimagsgade 10; smørrebrød 65-115kr; ⊙11am-5.30pm daily, take away 11am-7pm Mon-Fri, to 4pm Sat & Sun; ☐6A, 14, 37, 42, 150S, 184, 185) Get your contemporary smørrebrød fix at Aamanns, where open sandwiches are seasonal, artful and served on Aamanns' organic sourdough bread (arrive before 1pm to avoid waiting). If you can't decide between the braised pork belly with rhubarb and bacon crumble, the avocado with lemon cream, or the smoked cheese with cherry/onion compote, the tasting menu offers four smaller smørrebrød for a scrumptious overview.

★ Tårnet
DANISH €€

(☑33 37 31 00; http://taarnet.dk/restauranten; Christiansborg Slotsplads, Christiansborg Slot; lunch smørrebrød 85-135kr, dinner mains 235kr; ⊙11.30am-11pm Tue-Sun, kitchen closes 10pm; 🖥; ☐1A, 2A, 9A, 26, 37, 66, 🚇Det Kongelige Bibliotek) Book ahead for lunch at Tårnet, owned by prolific restaurateur Rasmus Bo Bojesen and memorably set inside Christiansborg Slot's commanding tower. Lunch here is better value than dinner, with superlative, contemporary smørrebrød that is among the city's best. While the general guideline is two smørrebrød per person, some of the à la carte versions are quite substantial (especially the tartare), so check before ordering.

★ Bæst
ITALIAN €€

(☑35 35 04 63; www.baest.dk; Guldbergsgade 29, Nørrebrø; pizzas 85-150kr; ⊙5-10.30pm daily; 🖥; ☐3A, 5C) Owned by powerhouse Italo-Scandi chef Christian Puglisi, Bæst remains hot years after its 2014 launch. Charcuterie, cheese and competent woodfired pizzas are the drawcards here. Much of the produce is organic, and both the commendable charcuterie and hand-stretched mozzarella are made upstairs (the latter made using jersey milk from Bæst's own farm). To fully appreciate its repertoire, opt for the sharing menu (small/large 375/450kr).

★ Manfreds og Vin
DANISH €€

(☑36 96 65 93; www.manfreds.dk; Jægersborggade 40, Nørrebro; small plates 75-90kr, 7-course tasting menu 285kr; ⊙noon-3.30pm & 5-10pm daily; 🖥🖥; ☐8A) ⚐ Convivial Manfreds is the ideal local bistro, with passionate staffers, boutique natural wines and a regularly changing menu that favours organic produce (most from the restaurant's own farm) cooked simply and sensationally. Swoon over nuanced, gorgeously textured dishes like grilled spring onion served with pistachio purée, crunchy breadcrumbs and salted egg yolk. If you're hungry and curious, opt for the good-value seven-dish menu.

★ Kadeau
NEW NORDIC €€€

(☑33 25 22 23; www.kadeau.dk; Wildersgade 10B; tasting menu 1800kr; ⊙6.30pm-midnight Wed-Fri, noon-4pm & 6.30pm-midnight Sat; ☐2A, 9A, 37, 350S, 🚇Christianshavn) The big-city spin-off of the Bornholm original, this Michelin-two-starred standout has firmly established itself as one of Scandinavia's top New Nordic restaurants. Whether it's salted and burnt scallops drizzled with clam bouillon, or an unexpected combination of toffee, crème fraiche, potatoes, radish and elderflower, each dish evokes Nordic flavours, moods and landscapes with extraordinary creativity and skill.

★ Geranium
NEW NORDIC €€€

(☑69 96 00 20; www.geranium.dk; Per Henrik Lings Allé 4, Østerbro; lunch or dinner tasting menu 2000kr, wine/juice pairings 1400/700kr; ⊙noon-3.30pm & 6.30pm-midnight Wed-Sat; 🖥🖥; ☐14) ⚐ On the 8th floor of Parken Stadium, Geranium is the only restaurant in town sporting three Michelin stars. At the helm is Bocuse d'Or prize-winning chef Rasmus Kofoed, who transforms local ingredients into edible Nordic artworks like lobster paired with milk and the juice of fermented carrots and sea buckthorn, or cabbage sprouts and chicken served with quail egg, cep mushrooms and hay beer.

★ AOC
NEW NORDIC €€€

(☑33 11 11 45; www.restaurantaoc.dk; Dronningens Tværgade 2; tasting menus 1500-1800kr; ⊙6.30pm-12.30am Tue-Sat; 🖥; ☐1A, 26, 🚇Kongens Nytorv) In the vaulted cellar of a 17th-century mansion, this intimate, two-starred Michelin standout thrills with evocative, often surprising Nordic flavour combinations, scents and textures. Here, sea scallops might conspire with fermented asparagus, while grilled cherries share the plate with smoked marrow and pigeon breast. Diners choose from two tasting menus, and reservations should be made around a week in advance, especially for late-week dining.

★**Geist** DANISH €€€

(☑33 13 37 13; http://restaurantgeist.dk; Kongens Nytorv 8; plates 85-225kr; ☺6pm-1am daily; ☐1A, 26, ⓂKongens Nytorv) Chic, monochromatic Geist is owned by celebrity chef Bo Bech, a man driven by experimentation. His long list of small plates pairs Nordic and non-Nordic ingredients in unexpected, often thrilling ways. Create your tasting menu from dishes like grilled avocado with green almonds and curry, turbot and fennel ravioli with gruyère, or out-of-the-box desserts like summer blueberries with black olives and vanilla ice cream.

★**Studio** DANISH €€€

(☑72 14 88 08; www.thestandardcph.dk; Havnegade 44; degustation menus from 1000kr; ☺7pm-midnight Tue-Sat, also noon-3.30pm Sat; ☐66, ⓈNyhavn, ⓂKongens Nytorv) Brainchild of Noma co-founder Claus Meyer and former Noma sous-chef Torsten Vildgaard, Studio bagged its first Michelin star within months of opening. Rooted in Nordic traditions, the open kitchen revels in ingredients and influences from further afield. Whether it's sourdough *æbleskiver* (Danish pancake puffs) filled with truffle and cheese, or grilled pigeon paired with warm cherries cooked in foraged spices, Studio smashes it.

🍷 Drinking & Nightlife

★**Coffee Collective** COFFEE

(www.coffeecollective.dk; Jægersborggade 57, Nørrebro; ☺7am-8pm Mon-Fri, 8am-7pm Sat & Sun; ☐8A) Copenhagen's most prolific microroastery, Coffee Collective has helped revolutionise the city's coffee culture in recent years. Head in for rich, complex cups of caffeinated magic. The baristas are passionate about their single-origin beans and the venue itself sits at one end of creative Jægersborggade in Nørrebro. There are three other outlets, including at gourmet food market Torvehallerne KBH (p56) and in **Frederiksberg** (☑60 15 15 25; Godthåbsvej 34b, Frederiksberg; ☺7.30am-6pm Mon-Fri, from 9am Sat, from 10am Sun).

★**Forloren Espresso** CAFE

(www.forlorenespresso.dk; Store Kongensgade 32; ☺8am-4pm Mon-Wed, to 5pm Thu & Fri, 9am-5pm Sat; ☎; ☐1A, 26, ⓂKongens Nytorv) Coffee snobs weep joyfully into their nuanced espressos and third-wave brews at this snug, light-filled cafe. Bespectacled owner Niels tends to his brewing paraphernalia like an obsessed scientist, turning UK- and Swedish-roasted beans into smooth, lingering cups of Joe. If you're lucky, you'll score the cosy back nook, the perfect spot to browse Niels' collection of photography tomes.

★**Den Vandrette** WINE BAR

(☑72 14 82 28; www.denvandrette.dk; Havnegade 53A; ☺4-11pm Tue-Thu & Sun, to midnight Fri, 2pm-midnight Sat; ☐66, ⓈNyhavn) This is the harbourside wine bar for lauded wine wholesaler **Rosforth & Rosforth** (☑33 32 55 20; www.rosforth.dk; Knippelsbrogade 10; ☺9am-5pm Mon-Fri, from noon Sat; ☐2A, 9A, 37, 350S, ⓂChristianshavn). The focus is on natural and biodynamic drops, its short, sharply curated list of wines by the glass often including lesser-known blends like Terret Bourret–Vermentino. Guests are welcome to browse the cellar and pick their own bottle. Come summer, it has alfresco waterside tables and deckchairs for sun-kissed toasting.

★**Mikkeller & Friends** MICROBREWERY

(☑35 83 10 20; www.mikkeller.dk/location/mikkeller-friends; Stefansgade 35, Nørrebro; ☺2pm-midnight Sun-Wed, to 2am Thu & Fri, noon-2am Sat; ☎; ☐5C, 8A) Looking suitably cool with its turquoise floors and pale ribbed wood, Mikkeller & Friends is a joint venture of the Mikkeller and To Øl breweries. Beer geeks go gaga over the 40 artisan draft beers and circa 200 bottled varieties, which might include a chipotle porter or an imperial stout aged in tequila barrels. Limited snacks include dried gourmet sausage and cheese.

★**Brus** MICROBREWERY

(☑75 22 22 00; http://tapperietbrus.dk; Guldbergsgade 29F, Nørrebro; ☺3pm-midnight Mon-Thu, noon-3am Fri & Sat, noon-midnight Sun; ☎; ☐5C) What was once a locomotive factory is now a huge, sleek, hip brewpub. The world-renowned microbrewery behind it is To Øl, and the bar's 30-plus taps offer a rotating selection of To Øl standards and small-batch specials, as well as eight on-tap cocktails. The barkeeps are affable and happy to let you sample different options before you commit.

★**Nebbiolo** WINE BAR

(☑60 10 11 09; http://nebbiolo-winebar.com; Store Strandstræde 18; ☺3pm-midnight Sun-Thu, to 2am Fri & Sat; ☎; ☐1A, 66, ⓂKongens Nytorv) Just off Nyhavn, this smart, contemporary wine bar and shop showcases wines from smaller, inspiring Italian vineyards. Wines by the glass are priced in one of three categories

(75/100/125kr) and even those in the lowest price range are often wonderful.

Culture Box
CLUB

(📞33 32 50 50; www.culture-box.com; Kronprinsessegade 54A; ⏱Culture Box 6pm-1am Thu-Sat, Red Box 11pm-late Fri & Sat, Black Box midnight-late Fri & Sat; 🚇26) Electronica connoisseurs swarm to Culture Box, known for its impressive local and international DJ line-ups and sharp sessions of electro, techno, house and drum'n'bass. The club is divided into three spaces: preclubbing Culture Box Bar, intimate club space Red Box, and heavyweight Black Box, where big-name DJs play the massive sound system.

⭐1105
COCKTAIL BAR

(📞33 93 11 05; www.1105.dk; Kristen Bernikows Gade 4; ⏱8pm-2am Wed, Thu & Sat, 4pm-2am Fri; 🚇1A, 26, 350S, Ⓜ Kongens Nytorv) Head in before 11pm for a bar seat at this dark, luxe lounge. Named for the local postcode, its cocktail repertoire spans both the classic and the revisited. You'll also find a fine collection of whiskies, not to mention an older 30- and 40-something crowd more interested in thoughtfully crafted drinks than partying hard and getting wasted.

⭐Mother Wine
WINE BAR

(📞33 12 10 00; http://motherwine.dk; Gammel Mønt 33; ⏱10am-7pm Mon-Wed, to 10pm Thu & Sat, to late Fri; 🛜; 🚇350S, Ⓜ Kongens Nytorv) A *hyggelig* (cosy) wine bar/shop with some very prized Finn Juhl chairs, Mother Wine showcases natural, organic and lesser-known Italian drops. From organic Veneto Prosecco to Puglian Negroamaro, guests are encouraged to sample the day's rotating offerings before committing to a glass. Wines start at a very palatable 55kr and come with a small complimentary serve of Italian nibbles.

⭐Ruby
COCKTAIL BAR

(📞33 93 12 03; www.rby.dk; Nybrogade 10; ⏱4pm-2am Mon-Sat, from 6pm Sun; 🛜; 🚇1A, 2A, 14, 26, 37, 66) Cocktail connoisseurs raise their glasses to high-achieving Ruby, hidden away in an unmarked 18th-century townhouse. Inside, suave mixologists whip up near-flawless, seasonal libations created with craft spirits and homemade syrups, while a lively crowd spills into a labyrinth of cosy, decadent rooms. For a gentlemen's club vibe, head downstairs among chesterfields, oil paintings and wooden cabinets lined with spirits.

⭐Bastard Café
CAFE

(📞42 74 66 42; https://bastardcafe.dk; Rådhusstræde 13; ⏱noon-midnight Sun-Thu, to 2am Fri & Sat; 🚇1A, 2A, 9A, 14, 26, 37) A godsend on rainy days, this hugely popular, super-cosy cafe is dedicated to board games, which line its rooms like books in a library. Some are free to use, while others incur a small 'rental fee'. While away the hours playing an old favourite or learn the rules of a more obscure option.

⭐Lidkoeb
COCKTAIL BAR

(📞33 11 20 10; www.lidkoeb.dk; Vesterbrogade 72B, Vesterbro; ⏱4pm-2am Mon-Sat, from 8pm Sun; 🛜; 🚇6A, 26) Lidkoeb loves a game of hide-and-seek: follow the 'Lidkoeb' signs into the second, light-strung courtyard. Once found, this top-tier cocktail lounge rewards with passionate barkeeps and clever, seasonal libations. Slip into a Børge Mogensen chair and toast to Danish ingenuity with Nordic bar bites and seasonal drinks like the Freja's Champagne: a gin-based concoction with muddled fresh ginger, lemon and maraschino liqueur.

⭐Mikkeller Bar
BAR

(📞33 31 04 15; http://mikkeller.dk; Viktoriagade 8B-C, Vesterbro; ⏱1pm-1am Sun-Wed, to 2am Thu & Fri, noon-2am Sat; 🛜; 🚇6A, 9A, 10, 14, 26, 🚆København H) Low-slung lights, milk-green floors and 20 brews on tap: cool, cult-status Mikkeller flies the flag for craft beer, its rotating cast of suds including Mikkeller's own acclaimed creations and guest drops from microbreweries from around the globe. Expect anything from tequila-barrel-aged stouts to yuzu-infused fruit beers. The bottled offerings are equally inspired, with cheese and snacks to soak up the foamy goodness.

☆ Entertainment

Copenhagen's entertainment offerings are wide, varied and sophisticated. On any given night choices will include ballet, opera, theatre, clubbing and live tunes spanning indie and blues to pop. The city has a world-renowned jazz scene, with numerous jazz clubs drawing top talent. Most events can be booked through **Billetnet** (📞70 15 65 65; www.billetnet.dk), which has an outlet at Tivoli. You can also try **Billetlugen** (📞70 26 32 67; www.billetlugen.dk).

Operaen
OPERA

(Copenhagen Opera House; 📞box office 33 69 69 69; www.kglteater.dk; Ekvipagemestervej 10; 🚇9A,

☺Operaen) Designed by the late Henning Larsen, Copenhagen's state-of-the-art opera house has two stages: the Main Stage and the smaller, more experimental Takkeløftet. The repertoire runs the gamut from blockbuster classics to contemporary opera. While the occasional opera is sung in English, all subtitles are in Danish only. Tickets can be booked directly via the website.

Det Kongelige Teater
BALLET, OPERA

(Royal Theatre; ☑33 69 69 69; https://kglteater. dk; Kongens Nytorv; 🚇1A, 26, 350S, ⓂKongens Nytorv) These days, the main focus of the opulent Gamle Scene (Old Stage) is world-class opera and ballet, including productions from the Royal Danish Ballet. The current building, the fourth theatre to occupy the site, was completed in 1872 and designed by Vilhelm Dahlerup and Ove Petersen. Book tickets in advance.

★Jazzhus Montmartre
JAZZ

(☑70 26 32 67; www.jazzhusmontmartre.dk; Store Regnegade 19A; ⊙6pm-midnight Thu-Sat; 🚇1A, 26, 350S, ⓂKongens Nytorv) Saxing things up since the late 1950s, Jazzhus Montmartre is one of Scandinavia's great jazz venues, with past performers including Dexter Gordon, Ben Webster and Kenny Drew. Today, it continues to host local and international talent. On concert nights, you can also tuck into a decent, three-course set menu (375kr) at the cafe-restaurant.

Jazzhouse
JAZZ

(☑33 15 47 00; www.jazzhouse.dk; Niels Hemmingsensgade 10; ⊙from 7pm Mon-Thu, from 8pm Fri-Sat; 🚱; 🚇1A, 2A, 9A, 14, 26, 37) One of Copenhagen's leading jazz joints, Jazzhouse hosts top Danish and visiting talent, with music styles running the gamut from bebop to fusion jazz. On weekdays, concerts usually start at 8pm, on Friday and Saturday, acts normally hit the stage around 9pm. Check the website for upcoming acts, times and prices.

La Fontaine
JAZZ

(☑33 11 60 98; www.lafontaine.dk; Kompagnistræde 11; ⊙7pm-5am daily, live music from 10pm Fri & Sat, from 9pm Sun; 🚇14) Cosy and intimate, Copenhagen's jazz-club veteran is a great spot to catch emerging homegrown musicians and the occasional big name. The club even has an open-mic poetry club every first Monday of the month from 8pm to 10pm. Your lucky break?

Vega Live
LIVE MUSIC

(☑33 25 70 11; www.vega.dk; Enghavevej 40, Vesterbro; 🚱; 🚇3A, 10, 14, ⑤Dybbølsbro) The daddy of Copenhagen's live-music venues, Vega hosts everyone from big-name rock, pop, blues and jazz acts to underground indie, hip-hop and electro up-and-comers. Gigs take place on either the main stage (Store Vega), small stage (Lille Vega) or the ground-floor Ideal Bar. Performance times vary; check the website.

Interestingly, the venue is a 1950s former trade union HQ revamped by leading Danish architect Vilhelm Lauritzen.

🛍 Shopping

What Copenhagen's shopping portfolio lacks in size it more than makes up for with quality and individuality. The city is Scandinavia's capital of cool, with no shortage of locally designed and crafted must-haves. Good buys that are easy enough to carry home include unique streetwear and higher-end fashion, ceramics, glassware, jewellery and textiles.

★Hay House
DESIGN

(☑42 82 08 20; www.hay.dk; Østergade 61; ⊙10am-6pm Mon-Fri, to 5pm Sat; 🚇1A, 2A, 9A, 14, 26, 37, 66, ⓂKongens Nytorv) Rolf Hay's fabulous interior-design store sells its own coveted line of furniture, textiles and design objects, as well as those of other fresh, innovative Danish designers. Easy-to-pack gifts include anything from notebooks and ceramic cups, to building blocks for style-savvy kids. There's a second branch at Pilestræde 29-31.

★Stilleben
DESIGN

(☑33 91 11 31; www.stilleben.dk; Niels Hemmingsensgade 3; ⊙10am-6pm Mon-Fri, to 5pm Sat; 🚇1A, 2A, 9A, 14, 26, 37, 66, ⓂKongens Nytorv) Owned by Danish Design School graduates Ditte Reckweg and Jelena Schou Nordentoft, Stilleben stocks a bewitching range of contemporary ceramic, glassware, jewellery and textiles from mostly emerging Danish and foreign designers. Head up the wooden stairs for posters and prints, including works by celebrated contemporary Danish artist Cathrine Raben Davidsen. There's a second branch opposite gourmet-food market Torvehallerne KBH.

★Illums Bolighus
DESIGN

(☑33 14 19 41; www.illumsbolighus.dk; Amagertorv 8-10; ⊙10am-7pm Mon-Thu & Sat, to 8pm Fri, 11am-6pm Sun; 🚱; 🚇1A, 2A, 9A, 14, 26, 37, 66, ⓂKongens Nytorv) Design fans hyperventilate over this sprawling department store, its four floors packed with all things Nordic and beautiful. You'll find everything from ceramics, glassware, jewellery and fashion to throws, lamps, furniture and more. It's also a handy spot to pick up some X-factor souvenirs, from posters, postcards and notebooks adorned with vintage Danish graphics to design-literate Danish wallets and key rings.

★**Stilleben** DESIGN
(☑22 45 11 31; https://stilleben.dk; Frederiksborggade 22; ⊙10am-6pm Mon-Fri, to 5pm Sat; ☐350S, Ⓜ Nørreport, Ⓢ Nørreport) One of Copenhagen's top design stores, Stilleben is famed for its graphic prints, not to mention its stock of unique objects from mostly smaller-scale Scandi designers. Go gaga over all things beautiful and kooky, from boldly patterned cups, jugs, vases and tea cosies to striking sofa cushions, sculptural candle holders, jewellery, bags, socks and more.

There's another location just off Strøget.

Vanishing Point HANDICRAFTS
(☑25 13 47 55; www.vanishing-point.dk; Jægersborggade 45, Nørrebro; ⊙11am-5.30pm Mon-Fri, to 6pm Sat, to 3pm Sun; ☐8A) On trendy Jægersborggade, Vanishing Point is a contemporary craft shop and studio showcasing quirky ceramics, unique jewellery, handmade knits and quilts, as well as engaging, limited-edition prints. Most items are created on-site, while some are the result of a collaboration with non-profits around the world. The aim: to inspire a sustainable and playful lifestyle through nature, traditional craft techniques and humour.

Klassik Moderne Møbelkunst DESIGN
(☑33 33 90 60; www.klassik.dk; Bredgade 3; ⊙11am-6pm Mon-Fri, 10am-4pm Sat; ☐1A, 26, 350S, Ⓜ Kongens Nytorv) Close to Kongens Nytorv, Klassik Moderne Møbelkunst is Valhalla for lovers of Danish design, with a trove of classics from greats like Poul Henningsen, Hans J Wegner, Arne Jacobsen, Finn Juhl and Nanna Ditzel – in other words, a veritable museum of Scandinavian furniture from the mid-20th century.

ⓘ Information

MEDICAL SERVICES
Private doctor and dentist visits vary but usually cost from around 1400kr. To contact a doctor, call ☑60 75 40 70.

There are numerous pharmacies around the city; look for the sign *apotek*.

Call 1813 before going to a hospital emergency department to save waiting time. The following hospitals have 24-hour emergency wards:

Amager Hospital (☑32 34 32 34; www.amagerhospital.dk; Italiensvej 1, Amager; ☐2A, 4A, 12, Ⓜ Amager Strand) Southeast of the city centre.

Bispebjerg Hospital (☑35 31 23 73; www.bispebjerghospital.dk; Bispebjerg Bakke 23; Ⓢ Bispebjerg, Emdrup) Northwest of the city centre.

Frederiksberg Hospital (☑38 16 38 16; www.frederiksberghospital.dk; Nordre Fasanvej 57, Frederiksberg; ⊙24hr; ☐4A, Ⓜ Fasanvej) West of the city centre.

Steno Apotek (☑33 14 82 66; www.steno apotek.dk; Vesterbrogade 6C; ⊙24hr; ☐6A, 26, Ⓢ København H) A 24-hour pharmacy opposite Central Station.

Tandlægevagten (☑1813; www.tandlæge vagten.dk; Oslo Plads 14; ☐1A, Ⓢ Østerport) Emergency dental service near Østerport station.

TOURIST INFORMATION
Copenhagen Visitors Centre (☑70 22 24 42; www.visitcopenhagen.com; Vesterbrogade 4A, Vesterbro; ⊙9am-8pm Mon-Fri, to 6pm Sat & Sun Jul & Aug, reduced hours rest of year; ☎; ☐2A, 6A, 12, 14, 26, 250S, Ⓢ København H) Copenhagen's excellent and informative information centre has a cafe and lounge with free wi-fi; it also sells the **Copenhagen Card** (p51).

ⓘ Getting There & Away

AIR
Copenhagen Airport (☑32 31 32 31; www.cph.dk; Lufthavnsboulevarden, Kastrup; Ⓜ Lufthavnen, Ⓢ Københavns Lufthavn) is Scandinavia's busiest air hub, with direct flights to cities in Europe, North America and Asia, as well as a handful of Danish cities.

Located in Kastrup, 9km southeast of Copenhagen's city centre, the airport is modern and user-friendly, with quality eating, retail and information facilities.

If you're waiting for a flight, note that this is a 'silent' airport and there are no boarding calls, although there are numerous monitor screens throughout the terminal.

Luggage lockers (24hr locker rental 80-120kr) are available in the airport's P4 car park. Lockers come in three sizes, the largest being big enough to store ski or golf bags. Payment is by Visa or MasterCard only. Lockers can be rented for a maxiumum of seven consecutive days.

BOAT
Copenhagen offers regular direct ferry services to/from Norway. There is also a combined

bus-ferry service to Poland and a train-ferry service to Germany.

DB (www.bahn.com) Runs direct InterCity Express (ICE) trains from København H (Central Station) to Hamburg (one way from 298kr, 4¾ hours, several daily), with a ferry crossing between Puttgarden and Rødby.

DFDS Seaways (☑ 33 42 30 00; www.dfds seaways.com; Dampfærgevej 30; Ⓢ Nordhavn) One daily service to/from Oslo (one way from 675kr, 17¼ hours). Ferries depart from Søndre Frihavn, just north of Kastellet.

Polferries (www.polferries.com) Two daily bus-ferry combos to/from Poland (one way from 400kr). Bus 866 connects Copenhagen to Ystad in Sweden (1¼ hours), from where ferries travel to/from Swinoujscie, Poland. Ferry crossings take between six and 7½ hours.

BUS

Copenhagen is well connected to the rest of Europe by daily (or near-daily) buses.

Flixbus (www.flixbus.com; Ⓢ København H) runs services throughout Europe (limited services into Norway and Sweden, however). Destinations, timetables and prices are all online. Flixbus has dynamic pricing, so it pays to book ahead, and the routes may use stops that are different to the main bus stations, so check your options.

CAR & MOTORCYCLE

The main highways into Copenhagen are the E20 from Jutland and Funen (and continuing towards Malmö in Sweden) and the E47 from Helsingør and Sweden. If you're coming from the north on the E47, exit onto Lyngbyvej (Rte 19) and continue south to reach the heart of the city.

TRAIN

All long-distance trains arrive at and depart from København H (Central Station), an imposing, 19th-century, wooden-beamed hall with numerous facilities, including currency exchange, a police station, lockers, left-luggage facilities and food outlets. **DSB Billetsalg** (DSB Ticket Office; ☑ 70 13 14 15; www.dsb.dk; Central Station, Bernstorffsgade 16-22; ⊙ 7am-8pm Mon-Fri, 8am-6pm Sat & Sun; Ⓢ København H) is best for reservations and for purchasing international train tickets. Alternatively, you can make reservations on its website.

Destinations include the following:

Roskilde (84kr, 20 to 35 minutes, three to nine hourly)

Helsingør (108kr, 45 minutes, around every 20 minutes)

Odense (308kr, 1¼ to two hours, at least twice hourly)

Aarhus (418kr, 2¾ to 3½ hours, one to three hourly)

Aalborg (468kr, 4½ to five hours, one to two hourly)

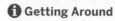 Getting Around

TO/FROM THE AIRPORT
Metro

The 24-hour metro (www.m.dk) runs every four to 20 minutes between the airport arrival terminal (the station is called Lufthavnen) and the eastern side of the city centre. It does not stop at København H (Central Station) but is handy for Christianshavn, the city centre and Nyhavn (get off at Kongens Nytorv for Nyhavn). Journey time to Kongens Nytorv is 14 minutes (36kr).

Taxi

By taxi, it's about 20 minutes between the airport and the city centre, depending on traffic. Expect to pay 250kr to 300kr.

Train

Trains (www.dsb.dk) connect the airport arrival terminal to Copenhagen Central Station (Københavns Hovedbanegården, commonly known as København H) around every 10 to 20 minutes. Journey time is 14 minutes (36kr). Check schedules at www.rejseplanen.dk.

BICYCLE

➡ Copenhagen vies with Amsterdam as the world's most bike-friendly city. Most streets have cycle lanes and, more importantly, motorists tend to respect them.

➡ The city has a superb city-wide rental system: **Bycyklen** (City Bikes; www.bycyklen. dk; per 1hr 30kr) has high-tech 'Smart Bikes' featuring touchscreen tablets with GPS, multispeed electric motors, puncture-resistant tyres and locks. The bikes must by paid for by credit card via the website or the bike's touchscreen. Visit the Bycyklen website for more information.

➡ Bikes can be carried free on S-trains, but are forbidden at Nørreport station on weekdays between 7am and 8.30am and between 3.30pm and 5pm. Enter train carriages with the large white bicycle graphic on the windows. Keep your bike behind the line in the designated bicycle area. Stay with the bike at all times.

➡ Bikes can be carried on the metro (except from 7am to 9am and from 3.30pm to 5.30pm on weekdays). Bike tickets (13kr) are required on metro and city bus services: purchase these at metro and S-train stations (they are not sold on buses).

CAR & MOTORYCLE

Except for the weekday-morning rush hour, when traffic can bottleneck coming into the city (and vice versa around 5pm), traffic in Copenhagen is generally manageable. Getting around by car is not problematic, except for the usual challenge of finding an empty parking space in the most popular places.

That said, Copenhagen's compact size, reliable public transport and bike-friendly roads make driving completely unnecessary.

PUBLIC TRANSPORT

Copenhagen's bus, **metro** (☑70 15 16 15; www.m.dk), **S-train** (www.dsb.dk) and Harbour Bus network has an integrated ticket system based on seven geographical zones. Most of your travel within the city will be within two zones. Travel between the city and airport covers three zones.

➡ The cheapest ticket (*billet*) covers two zones, offers unlimited transfers and is valid for one hour (adult/12 to 15 years 24/12kr). An adult with a valid ticket can take two children under the age of 12 free of charge.

➡ If you plan on exploring sights outside the city, including Helsingør, the north coast of Zealand and Roskilde, you're better off buying a 24-hour ticket (all zones adult/12 to 15 years 130/65kr) or a seven-day FlexCard (all zones 675kr).

➡ Alternatively, you can purchase a Rejsekort (www.rejsekort.dk), a touch-on, touch-off smart card valid for all zones and all public transport across Denmark. Available from the Rejsekort machines at metro stations, Central Station or the airport, the card costs 180kr (80kr for the card and 100kr in credit). To use, tap the Rejsekort against the dedicated sensors at train and metro stations or when boarding buses and commuter ferries, then tap off when exiting. Only tap off at the very end of your journey – if your journey involves a metro ride followed immediately by a bus ride, tap on at the metro station and again on the bus, but only tap off once you exit the bus.

➡ The **Copenhagen Card** (p51) gives you unlimited public transport throughout the greater region of Copenhagen (including the airport). In addition, you get free entrance to 79 attractions and museums as well as discounts on several restaurants, sights, rentals and more.

➡ Another option is the **City Pass** (www.citypass.dk), which covers all bus, train, metro and Harbour Buses in zones 1 to 4 (adult 24/72 hours 80/200kr, children travel half-price). You can purchase the City Pass online and receive it as a text that can be used immediately.

TAXI

➡ Taxis can be flagged on the street and there are ranks at various points around the city centre. If the yellow *taxa* (taxi) sign is lit, the taxi is available for hire.

➡ The fare will start at 24kr for taxis hired on the street and at 37kr for booked taxis (or 40kr and 50kr respectively from 11pm to 7am Friday and Saturday) and costs 15.25kr per kilometre (19.15kr from 11pm to 7am Friday and Saturday and on Danish holidays).

➡ Most taxis accept major credit cards.

➡ Three of the main companies are **DanTaxi** (☑70 25 25 25; www.dantaxi.dk), **Taxa 4x35** (☑35 35 35 35; www.taxa.dk) and **4x27** (Amager-Øbro Taxi; ☑27 27 27 27; https://4x27.dk).

ZEALAND

Denmark's largest island offers much more than the dazzle of Copenhagen. North of the city lie some of the country's finest beaches and most impressive castles. Here you'll find dazzlingly ornate Frederiksborg Slot (p67) in Hillerød and the hulking Kronborg Slot (p65) at Helsingør, Shakespeare's Elsinore. Helsingør also features the excellent Maritime Museum of Denmark (p65). En route don't miss Louisiana (p54), the superb modern/contemporary art gallery, not the US state.

West of Copenhagen awaits history-steeped Roskilde, home to a World Heritage–listed cathedral (p67), Scandinavia's classic rock music festival (p67) and a tremendous Viking Ship Museum (p67). History also comes to life at nearby Sagnlandet Lejre (Land of Legends; www.sagnlandet.dk; Slangealleen 2, Lejre; adult/child 150/95kr; ◷10am-5pm late Jun–mid-Aug, reduced hours rest of year), an engrossing, hands-on archaeology site.

Further west stands the millennia-old Trelleborg ring fortress (www.vikingeborgen-trelleborg.dk; Trelleborg Alle 4; ◷24hr) FREE, while Zealand's southern assets include medieval charm in Køge (☑56 63 42 42; www.koegemuseum.dk; Nørregade 4; adult/child 90/40kr; ◷10am-5pm Jul & Aug, 11am-4pm Tue-Sun Sep-Jun) and the World Heritage–listed cliff geology of Stevns Klint, plus a nearby Cold War fortress-museum (Cold War Museum; ☑56 50 28 06; www.kalklandet.dk; Korsnæbsvej 60, Rødvig; underground fortress guided tour adult/student/child 120/100/70kr, above-ground only 60/50kr/free; ◷site 10am-5pm Apr-Oct).

North Zealand

One of the most popular day trips from Copenhagen is a loop tour taking in Frederiksborg Slot in Hillerød and Kronborg Slot in Helsingør. With an early start you might even have time to reach one of the

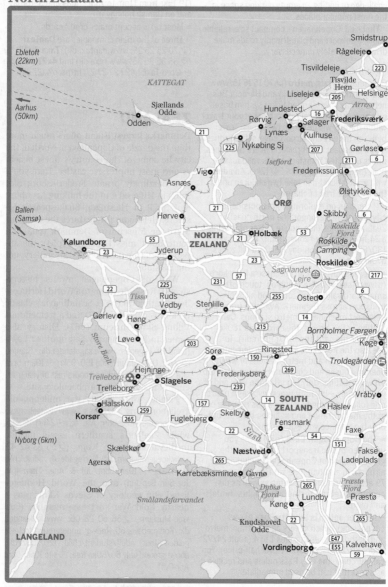

north-shore beaches before making your way back to the city, although it is more rewarding to allow an extra day for wandering between shoreline towns along this gorgeous coastline.

If you're driving between Helsingør and Copenhagen, ditch the motorway for the coastal road, Strandvej (Rte 152), which is far more scenic (though admittedly quite crowded on summer weekends).

the 15th and 16th centuries the city became immensely wealthy by taxing shipping that had to pass this way between the Baltic Sea and the open ocean. For a sizeable town, Helsingør has done a pretty good job of maintaining mementoes of its medieval character, best appreciated by strolling through the grid of narrow cobbled streets between the harbour and the bustling shopping core. Here, half-timbered back-alley houses lean precariously behind towering hollyhocks and creeping ivy. The main sight, however, is the gigantic Kronborg Slot, made famous as Elsinore Castle in Shakespeare's *Hamlet,* although the intimate psychological nature of the play is a far cry from the real-life military colossus.

Very frequent ferries shuttle to Helsingborg (Sweden), generally filled with Swedes on a mission to buy 'cheap' Danish alcohol (it's all relative).

⊙ Sights

★ Kronborg Slot   CASTLE
(www.kronborg.dk; Kronborgvej; interior adult/student 140/130kr; ⊙10am-5.30pm Jun-Sep, 11am-4pm Apr & May, 11am-4pm Tue-Sun Oct-Mar) Best known as the Elsinore Castle of Shakespeare's *Hamlet,* this Unesco World Heritage Site is a vast Renaissance masterpiece topped by baroque green-copper spires. It's ringed by moats, fortifications and powerful Vaubanesque star bastions that you can discover without a ticket. But it's well worth the entry fee to explore the inner palace's rooms, tapestries, ceiling paintings and viewpoints and, best of all, to delve into the spooky maze of casemates – subterranean dungeon passages barely lit by flickering paraffin lamps.

★ M/S Museet for Søfart   MUSEUM
(Maritime Museum of Denmark; www.mfs.dk; Ny Kronborgvej 1; adult/child 110kr/free; ⊙10am-6pm Jul & Aug, 11am-5pm Sep, closed Mon rest of year) Ingeniously built into a dry dock beside Kronborg Slot (p65), this subterranean museum merits a visit as much for its design as for its informative multimedia galleries. These explore Denmark's maritime history and culture in dynamic, contemporary ways. Alongside nautical instruments, sea charts and wartime objects, exhibitions explore themes including the representation of sailors in popular culture, trade and exploitation in Denmark's overseas colonies, and globe-crossing journeys of modern shipping containers.

Helsingør

POP 46,830

Fascinating Helsingør commands the narrowest point of the Øresund, the sound that separates Denmark from today's Sweden. In

Sankt Olai Domkirke
CATHEDRAL

(⊙10am-4pm May-Aug, 10am-2pm Sep-Apr) The handsome, red-brick Sankt Olai Domkirke is a Gothic cathedral built in 1559 on the site of a 13th-century original. Eclectic features include a remarkable 1579 brass baptismal font and an over-the-top gilded altarpiece which, at 12m tall, is one of Denmark's largest.

Sankt Mariæ Kirke & Karmeliterklostret
CHURCH

(www.sctmariae.dk; Sankt Anna Gade 38; ⊙10am-3pm Tue-Sun) Karmeliterklostret is one of Scandinavia's few fully preserved monastic cloisters, its arched brick arcades giving the feel of an Oxford college. The large attached church has a number of rather eclectic 15th-century frescoes, in which frogs, foxes, bulls and rams spring from bizarre-looking faces, and where pipers and lute players burst from giant flowers.

🛏 Sleeping

Danhostel Helsingør
HOSTEL €

(☑49 28 49 49; www.danhostelhelsingor.dk; Nordre Strandvej 24; dm/s/d/tr 225/495/550/650kr; 🅿🛜; 🚌842) Right on its own little sandy beach with fireplace, lawns and kayak hire, this remarkable hostel is based around a count's 1907 summer mansion. Only five of the 40 rooms are within that building, but the restaurant section remains very grand with sea views. Dorm beds are available only in peak summer season. Sheet hire (59kr) obligatory.

★ Kyhns Gæstehus
GUESTHOUSE €€

(☑71 70 84 82; www.kyhnsgaestehus.dk; Stengade 58; r incl breakfast from 995kr; ⊙reception 10am-6pm; 🛜) 🖉 Resurrected over many years of the reconstruction of a derelict 300-year-old house, this super-central luxury guesthouse has immaculate but characterful and spacious rooms above an inviting central courtyard cafe, opposite the historic town hall building. The biggest rooms come with en-suite bathroom and kitchenette. Climbing the brilliantly wobbly old stairway to room 5 can feel rather disorientating.

Madam Sprunck
BOUTIQUE HOTEL €€

(☑49 21 05 91; www.madamsprunck.dk; Bramstræde 5; s/d from 665/895kr; ⊙reception 9am-4.30pm Mon-Fri, 9am-2pm Sat) Combining hotel, restaurant, cafe and DJ-lounge-bar, this characterful family place manages a clever melange of traditional and modern elements, including flame-style torch-lamps on corridors and antique-effect desks. Small kettles are provided. Some rooms are in the roof gables, with sloping ceilings liable to catch your head should you wake suddenly in the night.

🍴 Eating

Rådmand Davids Hus
DANISH €

(☑49 26 10 43; Strandgade 70; dishes 48-108kr; ⊙10am-5pm Mon-Sat; 🛜) What better place to gobble down Danish classics than a snug, lopsided 1694 house, complete with cobbled courtyard? Refuel with honest, solid staples or special 'shopping lunches', typically a generous plate of salad, salmon pâté and slices of pork, cheese and homemade rye bread. Leave room for the Grand Marnier pancakes.

ℹ Information

Kronborg Slot Ticket Office (p65)

Tourist Office (☑49 21 13 33; www.visitnords jaelland.com; Havnepladsen 3; ⊙10am-5pm Mon-Fri, to 2pm Sat & Sun Jul & Aug, reduced hours rest of year) Opposite the train station.

ℹ Getting There & Away

BOAT

Scandlines car ferries (☑33 15 15 15; www. scandlines.dk; adult/child 40/28kr, car with up to 9 passengers single/day return 380/390kr; ⊙24hr) take 20 minutes to sail to/from Helsingborg in Sweden, with several departures an hour for most of the day, at least hourly boats late at night. Cars should use the ticket barriers approached from **Søndre Strandvej** (☑33 15 15 15; www.scandlines.dk; Færgevej 8). Foot passengers should buy tickets from the **waiting hall** (1st fl, Helsingør train station) upstairs, above platform 1. From there a series of boarding gantries leads directly to the boat. For the same price, foot passengers can alternatively use the smaller **Sundbusserne** (☑53 73 70 10; https://sundbusserne.dk; Færgevej 24; adult/child 40/28kr; ⊙10.30am-6.30pm Mon-Thu, to 8.30pm Fri & Sat, to 5.30pm Sun) boats.

TRAIN

Private Lokalbanen trains (www.lokalbanen. dk) operate daily between 5am and midnight, departing once or twice hourly to Hillerød (68kr, 30 minutes) via Fredensborg (60kr, 20 minutes), and to Gilleleje (68kr, 45 minutes).

DSB trains to Copenhagen (108kr, 45 minutes) run about three times hourly from before 5am to around midnight. Daytime Øresundståg trains from Sweden via Copenhagen airport run to Helsingør, but returning they unload at Copenhagen Central Station due to Swedish ID check regulations introduced in 2016.

Roskilde

POP 50,390

Most foreigners who have heard of Roskilde know it either as the home of one of northern Europe's best outdoor music festivals, or the sight of several remarkable Viking ship finds, now housed in an excellent, purpose-built museum. To the Danes, however, it is a city of great royal and religious significance, as it was the capital city long before Copenhagen and is still the burial place of 39 monarchs stretching back several hundred years. Located on the southern tip of Roskilde Fjord, the city was a thriving trading port throughout the Middle Ages. It was also the site of Zealand's first Christian church, built by Viking king Harald Bluetooth in AD 980.

◉ Sights & Activities

★ Ragnarock — MUSEUM

(www.museumragnarock.dk; Rabalderstræde 16; adult/child 90kr/free; ⊙10am-5pm Tue & Fri-Sun, to 10pm Wed & Thu; P; ☐202A) Within a startling architectural statement of a building, this spirit-lifting, highly interactive museum delivers a multisensory, experiential and often humorous journey through the evolution of rock music and youth culture from the 1950s to the present. Walls of headphones let you listen to music time capsules, and spin-to-hear turntables explain about gramophones. Play with interactive musical lights, learn why toilets were integral to Danish music production and practise various dance steps on the hot-spot stage beside the 'world's biggest mirror ball'.

★ Viking Ship Museum — MUSEUM

(Vikingskibsmuseet; ☑46 30 02 00; www.viking eskibsmuseet.dk; Vindeboder 12; adult/child May–mid-Oct 130kr/free, mid-Oct–Apr 85kr/free; ⊙10am-5pm late Jun–mid-Aug, to 4pm rest of year, boat trips daily mid-May–Sep; P⚕) Five original Viking ships, discovered at the bottom of Roskilde Fjord, are displayed in the main hall of this must-see museum. A short walk away, the same ticket gives access to the workshops of Museumsø, where archaeological and reconstruction work takes place, and Nordic longboats depart. There are free 45-minute guided tours in English at noon and 3pm daily from late June to the end of August and at noon on weekends from May to late June and in September.

FREDRIKSBORG SLOT

This gigantic, Dutch Renaissance–styled **fortress-palace** (www.frederiksborgmuseet.dk; adult/child 75/20kr; ⊙10am-5pm Apr-Oct, 11am-3pm Nov-Mar) rises proudly out of photogenic moat-lake Slotsø, and is one of Denmark's most impressive buildings. Access is free to the impressive central courtyards and huge, beautifully tended park with baroque gardens. To visit the interiors (ticket required) you'll need around three hours to do justice to the 80-plus rooms overloaded with beautiful furniture, tapestries, endless portraiture and gilded decor of astonishingly pompous grandiosity. Copious info-cards, along with free audio guides in nine languages, add plentiful context.

★ Roskilde Domkirke — CATHEDRAL

(www.roskildedomkirke.dk; Domkirkestræde 10; adult/pensioner/child 60/40kr/free; ⊙10am-6pm Mon-Sat, 1-6pm Sun Apr-Sep, to 4pm Oct-Mar) The crème de la crème of Danish cathedrals, this twin-spired giant was started by Bishop Absalon in 1170, but has been rebuilt and tweaked so many times that it's now a superb showcase of 850 years' worth of Danish architecture. As the royal mausoleum, it contains the crypts of 37 Danish kings and queens. Now a Unesco World Heritage Site, the entry fee includes a comprehensive, full-colour 48-page guidebook.

Nordic Longboat Trips — BOATING

(☑46 30 02 00; www.vikingeskibsmuseet.dk; Museumsø, Vindeboder 12; per person 100kr; ⊙May-Sep) Want to leap aboard a longboat? The Viking Ship Museum's highly amusing 50-minute trips provide the chance to propel a reconstructed traditional Nordic boat across the water by a mixture of sailing, rowing and ducking overhead ropes. Getting a place is first-come, first-served from the Museumsø ticket office. Departures (one to 10 daily depending on expected demand) are weather-dependent.

✴ Festivals & Events

Roskilde Festival — MUSIC

(www.roskilde-festival.dk; Darupvej; tickets from 1995kr; ⊙early Jul) Denmark's answer to Glastonbury, Roskilde Festival is northern

Europe's largest music festival, a week-long summer binge of bands and booze.

🛏 Sleeping & Eating

B&B Roskilde City
B&B €

(📞25 11 10 55; www.bbroskildecity.dk; Lille Højbrøndsstræde 14; s/d/tr 550/650/900kr) On a quiet, super-central lane, this B&B offers three rooms in a family home, the big selling point of which is the glorious layered garden. Very handy for the cathedral area; there's no sign on the door and you'll need to call ahead to make arrival arrangements.

Zleep Hotel Roskilde
HOTEL €€€

(Hotel Prindsen; 📞70 23 56 35; www.zleep hotels.com; Algade 13; r weekday/weekend from 1795/1095kr; P 🔊) Formerly Hotel Prindsen, this central hotel first opened in 1695, and previous guests have included King Frederik VII and Hans Christian Andersen. Rooms are comfortable if relatively standard business affairs, with a full renovation planned by 2018. The suite maintains a more classic historical look.

CafeKnarr
VIKING €€

(Museumsø, Vindeboder 12; sandwich/sausages/lunch plate 75/95/155kr; ⊙11.30am-3.30pm) The Viking Ship Museum's (p67) outwardly functional cafe makes sandwiches and huge plates of sausage-and-salad partly using Viking recipes, with ingredients like ramson (wild garlic), sea buckthorn and dried rosehips.

Raadhuskælderen
DANISH, INTERNATIONAL €€

(www.raadhuskaelderen.dk; Stændertorvet; smørrebrød 72-138kr; dinner mains 188-358kr; ⊙11am-9pm Mon-Sat; 🔊) Dine in a pretty garden with orchard views of the cathedral (p67), or inside within the modernised ancient cellar of what was once the town hall/hospital. Herring platters, shrimps, salads and open sandwiches feature at lunch. Dinner offerings are predominantly barbecued steaks, but there's also a daily fish option and a tempting rack of lamb with tzatziki and rosemary sauce.

🛈 Information

The helpful **tourist office** (📞46 31 65 65; www.visitroskilde.com; Stændertorvet 1; ⊙10am-4pm or 5pm Mon-Fri, to 1pm Sat) provides information, has a 3D map-model of the city and can help book B&Bs. There's even free coffee and left luggage (same day during opening hours only).

🛈 Getting There & Away

BUS
To Hillerød, bus 600S (76kr, 70 minutes) is marginally faster than taking the train via Copenhagen and runs up to four times hourly. Flixbus (www.flixbus.dk) advertises advance-purchase fares to Odense/Aarhus from 59/89kr (four times daily) but you might find last-minute prices around three times that, and be aware that departures are from Trekoner Station, out near the university.

TRAIN
Trains between Copenhagen and Roskilde run around the clock, up to six times an hour (84kr, 21 to 30 minutes) by day, once or twice an hour at night, 24 hours at weekends but with a two-hour timetable gap midweek from 1.45am to 3.57am. Holders of the Copenhagen Card get free train travel to Roskilde.

Other useful train services include Køge (48kr, 23 minutes), Odense (232kr, 73 minutes) and Vordingborg (100kr, 45-55 minutes), each generally twice an hour. For northeastern Zealand change in Copenhagen.

🛈 Getting Around

Central Roskilde is compact enough to visit the main sights on foot, or by bicycle, which you can rent from **RosCykler** (📞46 32 26 66; Hestetorvet 5; per day 100kr; ⊙9am-6pm Mon-Fri, 9.30am-3pm Sat). A very pleasant downhill walk from the cathedral through Byparken takes around 15 minutes to the **Viking Ship Museum** (p67)/harbour area.

Musicon-bound bus 202A helpfully picks up at **Kornerups Vænge stop** (Bredgade) and on Jernbangade near the train station: for **Ragnarock** (p67), get off at Teknik Skole and walk 350m north. On return using the Margrethehåb-bound service, you could alight at **Schmeltzplads** (Schmeltzplads, Borchsgade; 🚌202A) or the **Absalons Skole stop** (Støden; 🚌202A) for the centre. There's a short-cut route by bicycle.

During the **Roskilde Festival** (p67), a special train station comes into operation near the festival grounds to cope with the crowds.

Køge
POP 36,830

Pretty Køge (*koo*-e) is well worth a look if you're taking the ferry to Bornholm or driving via Stevns Klint towards Denmark's southern islands. The one-time medieval trading centre retains a photogenic core of cobbled streets flanked by a number of well-preserved 17th- and 18th-century buildings. At its heart, Torvet is claimed to be Denmark's largest square.

Around 7km south, Vallø's moat-encircled Renaissance castle (www.valloe-stift.dk; Slotsgade; ⊘ gardens 8am-sunset) makes a great destination for a cycle ride along quiet, tree-lined avenues and country lanes. Either side of Køge bay there are passable beaches, though the semi-industrial backdrop of the modern commercial harbour detracts a little from some of the coastal scenery. Further beaches at Solrød and Greve (8km and 17km north of Køge respectively) are popular S-train escapes for Copenhagen city-dwellers.

Sleeping & Eating

Centralhotellet   HOTEL €€
(☑ 56 65 06 96; www.centralhotellet.dk; Vestergade 3; s/d 860/1135kr, s/d/tr/q without bathroom 705/860/1450/1600kr; P ⊚) A black-and-white colour scheme, picked out with abstract art, brings life to this perfectly central hotel's rooms, whose sizes vary radically from a tiny single (560kr) to family rooms with a shared roof terrace (access via spiral stairs).

Troldegården   B&B €€
(☑ 23 32 57 67; www.troldgaarden.dk; Egøjevej 146, Egøje; apt 850-1050kr; ⊘ check in after 4.30pm; P ⊚) Less a B&B, more a rural retreat, with four luxurious apartments that feel like a home away from home, with kitchen and lots of tastefully chosen elements. One comes in charcoal grey modernist tones, others with old timbers and fireplace.

★ Restaurant Arken   SEAFOOD €€
(☑ 56 66 05 05; www.restaurant-arken.dk; Bådehavnen 21; lunch 70-240kr, dinner mains 158-288kr; ⊘ 11.30am-8.30pm; ⊚) Overlooking the marina, 2.5km north of Torvet, Arken has a sterling reputation for seafood, well cooked with top-quality ingredients. The daily changing 175kr lunch plate includes four flavour-packed mini-dishes and a cheese-and-fruit dessert. Even the chips are superb, triple fried with creamy garlic dip. And there's a scallop shell for a side plate on which to rest delicious home-baked rolls.

ℹ Information

Just off the town's main square, the **tourist office** (☑ 56 67 60 01; www.visitkoege.com; Vestergade 1; ⊘ 9.30am-5pm Mon-Fri, 10am-1pm Sat Sep-Jun, closes 1hr later Jul & Aug; ⊚) offers free wi-fi and a remarkable range of brochures for virtually anywhere in Denmark.

ℹ Getting There & Away

BOAT
Bornholmer Færgen (☑ 70 23 15 15; www.faergen.dk; Østre Kajgade; adult/child 12-15yr/under 12yr 283/141kr/free, low season 232/116kr/free, car incl 5 passengers return 850-1064kr, sleeping berths dm/d/q 225/450/900kr) Daily, year-round ferries to Bornholm depart from Køge at 12.30am, arriving in Rønne at 6am. From Rønne, the return ferry leaves at 5pm, reaching Køge at 10.30pm. Prices vary according to availability and advance purchase. Book online.

TRAIN
Køge is the southernmost station on the E-line of greater Copenhagen's S-train network. Trains to København H (100kr, 37 minutes) run three to six times an hour, continuing all the way to Hillerød (100kr, 80 minutes). Due to start as of 2018, the new high-speed Ringsted line should cut the Copenhagen-Køge journey time to 30 minutes, but will stop at a new Køge Nord station, somewhat more distant from the centre than the present station.

Vordingborg
POP 11,910

Many Møn-bound visitors will need to change transport in Vordingborg. If you're doing that, it's worth stopping at least briefly to visit the site of the town's central, once-formidable castle that played a starring role in early Danish history. Today, all that remains are a few moated bastion ruins plus a single round tower (Goose Tower; www.danmarksborgcenter.dk; Slotsruinen), but the site forms an appealing park with views down across a pretty harbour. Danmarks Borgcenter (Danish Castle Centre; www.danmarksborgcenter.dk; Slotsruinen 1; adult/child 125/75kr; ⊘ 10am-5pm Jul & Aug, Tue-Sun Sep-Jun) brings the site's history vividly to life using an imaginative self-led tour guided by tablet-computer.

ℹ Information

The container box that acts as ticket counter and shop for the **Danmarks Borgcenter** (p69) also doubles as a small **tourist office** (☑ 70 70 12 36; www.sydkystdanmark.dk; Slotsruinen 1; ⊘ 10am-5pm Jul & Aug, Tue-Sun Sep-Jun).

ℹ Getting There & Away

Vordingborg-Copenhagen trains (142kr) take 68 to 80 minutes via Roskilde, with departures once or twice hourly till late evening. Trains arriving before midnight are met by connecting bus 660R (or 664) to Møn.

MØN

POP 9380

One of Denmark's most magical islands, Møn's best-known drawcard is its sweeping stretch of white cliffs, **Møns Klint**. Crowned by deep-green forest, they're a popular inspiration for landscape paintings, possibly explaining the island's healthy artist headcount. But the inspiration doesn't end there. Beautiful beaches span sandy expanses and small secret coves, there are haunting Neolithic graves, and several rural churches are adorned with whimsical medieval frescoes. Every year more stargazers come for what are said to be Denmark's darkest night skies, and now they're joined by hikers flooding in to walk the well-organised network of trails known as Camønoen, named with a punning nod to the classic Camino pilgrim trail.

🏃 Activities

A major new development in Møn, Bogø and **Nyord** is the 175km **Camønoen** (https://camoenoen.dk), a network of walking trails that loops via a series of carefully spaced rest stops equipped with free shelters and facilities like mobile-phone-charging points. The tourist office at Stege, the largest town on Møn, sells an excellent Camønoen map-guide sheet (85kr) with all of the essential information.

🛏 Sleeping & Eating

The Stege tourist office has a guide-map listing the main 25 hotels and B&Bs on the island. There are hostels at Magleby and Elmelunde with a new one planned to open in central Stege during 2017. Hikers wanting to use the network of free shelters on the Camønoen trail network should go to www.friluftsguiden.dk to find the local contact for booking (where necessary).

Stege is the island's gastronomic capital, but there is a handful of rural options, too, including an intriguingly off-the-route ice-cream maker.

ℹ Information

For lots of useful information, browse the tourist website www.visitmoensklint.com or the handy, annually updated booklet *50 Things to Do on Møn.*

Tourist Office (☑ 55 86 04 00; Storegade 75; ⊙10am-4pm Tue-Sun Apr-Oct, to 2pm low season, closed Jan & Feb)

ℹ Getting There & Away

There is no railway on Møn. Trains arriving at the nearest major station in Vordingborg, southern Zealand, are met by connecting bus 660R (and occasionally bus 664) to Stege (48kr, 45 minutes), twice/once hourly on weekdays/weekends.

If driving from Zealand, leave the E47 at exit 41 for Rte 59 or use a series of bridges via the small island of Bogø.

ℹ Getting Around

Hiking the web of **Camønoen** trails is a very popular way to see the island on your own two feet.

BORNHOLM

The sunniest part of Denmark, Bornholm lies way out in the Baltic Sea, 200km east of Copenhagen (and closer to Sweden and Poland than to mainland Denmark). But it's not just (relatively) sunny skies that draw the hordes each year. Mother Nature was in a particularly good mood when creating this Baltic beauty, bestowing on it rocky cliffs, leafy forests, bleach-white beaches and a pure, ethereal light that painters do their best to capture.

Humankind added the beguiling details, from medieval fortress ruins and thatched fishing villages, to the iconic *rundekirke* (round churches) and contemporary Bornholms Kunstmuseum (p74). The island's ceramic and glassware artisans are famed throughout Denmark, as are its historic smokehouses and ever-expanding league of food artisans, doing brilliant things with local harvests. Local produce and foraged ingredients are prepared with Michelin-starred skill at **Kadeau** (☑ 56 97 82 50; www.kadeau.dk; Baunevej 18, Vestre Sømark; lunch 550-700kr, 5-/8-course dinner 800/1100kr; ⊙noon-4pm & 5.30pm-midnight Jul–mid-Aug, shorter hours rest of year, closed Oct–mid-Apr), one of Denmark's most exciting and innovative destination restaurants. It's no wonder that 600,000 people visit this island annually – and expect that number to increase as word continues to spread.

Bornholm

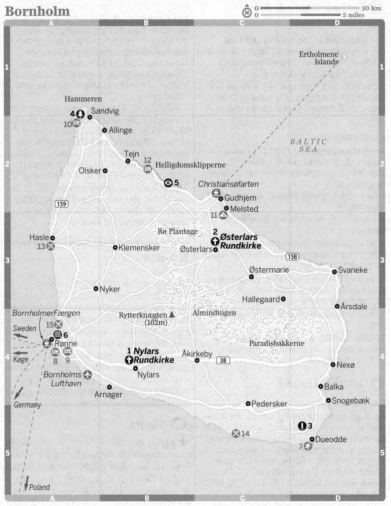

Bornholm

◎ Top Sights
1 Nylars Rundkirke	B4
2 Østerlars Rundkirke	C3

◎ Sights
3 Bornholmertårnet	D5
Bornholms Museum	(see 6)
4 Hammeren	A1
5 Helligdomsklipperne	B2
6 Hjorths Fabrik	A4

◎ Activities, Courses & Tours
7 Dueodde Beach	D5

◎ Sleeping
8 Danhostel Rønne	A4
Fredensborg Badehotel	(see 9)
9 Hotel GSH	A4
10 Nordly	A2
11 Sannes Familiecamping	C3
12 Stammershalle Badehotel	B2

◎ Eating
13 Hasle Røgeri	A3
14 Kadeau	C5
Stammershalle Badehotel	(see 12)
15 Torvehal Bornholm	A4

ℹ️ Getting There & Away

AIR

The island's airport, **Bornholms Lufthavn** (www.bornholms-lufthavn.dk; Søndre Landevej 2, Rønne), is 5km southeast of Rønne. Bus 5 connects the airport with Rønne.

Danish Airport Transport (DAT; www.dat.dk) operates several flights a day between Copenhagen and Bornholm. Book ahead for cheaper fares.

BOAT & TRAIN

BornholmerFærgen (📞 70 23 15 15; www. faergen.dk; Dampskibskajen 3, Rønne) operates ferries connecting Rønne to the following destinations:

➡ Køge (5½ hours) on Zealand, 40km south of Copenhagen

➡ Sassnitz (3½ to four hours) in northern Germany

➡ Ystad (80 minutes) in Sweden, with easy onward train and bus connections to Copenhagen via the Øresund bridge

Fares are determined by season. Children aged 11 and under travel free, while kids aged 12 to 15 pay half the adult fare.

There are online deals available – see the website.

TT-Line (www.ttline.com) has a weekly ferry service in summer connecting Świnoujście (Poland) and Rønne.

ℹ️ Getting Around

BICYCLE

Bornholm is ideal for cycling, with 235km of bike trails crisscrossing the island. Some of the trails go over former train routes, some slice through forests, and others run alongside main roads. You can start right in Rønne, where bike routes fan out to Allinge, Gudhjem, Nexø, Dueodde and the Almindingen forest. Or follow route 10, which circumnavigates the island over 105km.

If you don't feel like pedalling the entire way, you can take your bike on public buses for an additional 24kr.

Ask at tourist offices for the free brochure *Welcome to Our Bike Island* (in Danish, English or German), which maps out routes and describes sights along the way.

You'll find bike rental outlets in most major towns. **Bornholms Cykeludlejning** (📞 56 95 13 59; www.bornholms-cykeludlejning.dk; Nordre Kystvej 5; bike rental per day/week 75/450kr; ⏰ 9am-noon & 2-6pm Mon-Fri, 9.30am-6pm Sat & Sun Jul & Aug, shorter hours rest of year) is the handiest one, close to the Rønne ferry terminal and next door to the island's main tourist office.

BUS

BAT (📞 56 95 21 21; www.bat.dk; Munch Petersensvej 2, Rønne) operates bus services on the island. Fares are based on a zone system, with the maximum fare being for five zones. Tickets cost 13kr per zone, and are valid for unlimited trips within one zone for 30 minutes. Another 15 minutes validity is added for each added zone.

The multiride '*klippekort*' ticket is good for 10 rides and can be used by more than one person. Day/week passes cost 150/500kr and cover all zones. Children travel for half-price. Buses operate all year, but schedules are less frequent from October to April. Most ticket types can be purchased on board (but not the week pass).

Buses 7 and 8 circumnavigate the island, stopping at all major towns and settlements. Other buses make direct runs from Rønne to Nexø, Svaneke, Gudhjem and Sandvig.

Rønne

POP 13,600

Rønne is Bornholm's largest settlement and the main harbour for ferries. The town has been the island's commercial centre since the Middle Ages, and while the place has expanded and taken on a more suburban look over the years, a handful of well-preserved quarters still provides pleasant strolling. Especially appealing is the old neighbourhood west of Store Torv with its handsome period buildings and cobblestone streets, among them Laksegade and Storegade.

⦿ Sights

★ Nylars Rundkirke   CHURCH

(www.nylarskirke.dk; Kirkevej 10K, Nylars; ⏰ 7am-6pm Apr-Sep, 8am-3.30pm Oct-Mar) Built around 1150, Nylars Rundkirke is the most well-preserved and easily accessible round church in the Rønne area. Its central pillar is adorned with wonderful 13th-century frescoes, the oldest in Bornholm. The works depict scenes from the creation myth, including Adam and Eve's expulsion from the Garden of Eden. The cylindrical nave has three storeys, the top one a watchman's gallery that served as a defence lookout in medieval times.

Hjorths Fabrik   MUSEUM

(📞 56 95 07 35; www.bornholmsmuseum.dk; Krystalgade 5; adult/child 70kr/free; ⏰ 10am-5pm Mon-Sat mid-May–late Oct, shorter hours rest of year) This ceramics museum features a working studio, and watching the master artisans turn clay into beautifully moulded works of art is the real highlight. You'll find some fetching locally made wares for sale in the shop in front (which is free to enter).

Bornholms Museum
MUSEUM

(☑56 95 07 35; www.bornholmsmuseum.dk; Sankt Mortensgade 29; adult/child 70kr/free; ☉10am-5pm Jul–mid-Aug, closed Sun mid-May–Jun & mid-Aug–late Oct, shorter hours rest of year) Prehistoric finds including weapons, tools and jewellery are on show at Bornholm's museum of cultural history, which has a surprisingly large and varied collection of local exhibits, including some interesting Viking finds. A good maritime section is decked out like the interior of a ship, and there's a hotchpotch of nature displays, antique toys, Roman coins, pottery and paintings.

🛏 Sleeping

Danhostel Rønne
HOSTEL €

(☑56 95 13 40; www.danhostel-roenne.dk; Arsenalvej 12; dm/s/d/q without bathroom 200/375/475/575kr; ☉Apr-late Oct; P🅿🛜) This immaculately kept 26-room hostel is a secluded building with a neatly tended garden. Expect small, tidy, if somewhat soulless dorms, all with shared bathroom; common areas are cosy. The garden is full of kid-friendly diversions, and there are cycling paths on the doorstep (and on-site bike hire). Breakfast/linen costs 60/80kr.

★Hotel GSH
HOTEL €€

(☑56 95 19 13; www.greensolutionhouse.dk; Strandvejen 79; s/d incl breakfast 1100/1300kr; 🛜) 🌿 The 'Green Solution House' is easily one of Denmark's most innovative places to stay, and gives detailed insight into the possible future of construction. Every aspect of sustainability has been considered, and an exhibit on the ground level explains the decisions made and materials used in the award-winning overhaul and extension of an old hotel on this site.

Fredensborg Badehotel
HOTEL €€

(☑56 90 44 44; www.bornholmhotels.dk; Strandvejen 116; s/d/f incl breakfast 1100/1350/1565kr; P🛜) Perched on a knoll overlooking wave-pounded rocks at the southern end of Rønne, the newly renovated Fredensborg has been transformed into a bathing hotel with on-trend rooms, all with sea views. There's also a fine restaurant renowned for its fish buffets. To cover the 2.5km into Rønne's centre, cycle or walk a delightful forested trail.

🍴 Eating & Drinking

★Torvehal Bornholm
FOOD HALL €

(☑31 43 72 00; www.torvehalbornholm.dk; Gartnervangen 6; mains from grill 145-190kr; ☉10am-5pm Wed & Thu, to 8pm Fri-Sun Jun-Aug, shorter hours rest of year) While food elsewhere on the island went gangbusters, Rønne's food scene lagged – but the summer 2017 opening of this food hall in the town's north changed that. In a former slaughterhouse, peruse the output of some of Bornholm's finest producers, nibble on snacks from a food truck, sample beer brewed on-site and dine on meat fresh off the grill.

★Hasle Røgeri
SEAFOOD €

(☑56 96 20 02; www.hasleroegeri.dk; Søndre Bæk 20, Hasle; dishes 58-115kr; ☉10am-9pm Jul-late Aug, to 5pm May, Jun & late Aug-Oct) The closest traditional smokehouse to Rønne is by the water in Hasle, about 11km north of town. This century-old place has the iconic square chimneys, lots of outdoor seating and a super spread of smoked-fish goodness (herring, salmon, mackerel, eel, prawns) in a 149kr lunch buffet.

ℹ Information

Tourist Office (Bornholms Velkomstcenter; ☑56 95 95 00; www.bornholm.info; Nordre Kystvej 3; ☉9am-5pm Jul–mid-Aug, to 4pm Mon-Fri rest of year, hours vary Sat) A few minutes' walk from the harbour, this large, friendly office has masses of information on all of Bornholm and Christiansø.

Dueodde

Dueodde, the southernmost point of Bornholm, is a vast stretch of breathtaking beach backed by deep-green pine trees and expansive dunes. Its soft sand is so fine-grained that it was once used in hourglasses and ink blotters.

There's no real village at Dueodde – the bus stops at the end of the road where there's a hotel, a steakhouse restaurant, a couple of food kiosks and a boardwalk across the marsh to the beach. The only beachside 'sight' is a lighthouse on the western side of the dunes; you can climb the 197 steps for a view of endless sand and sea. For more views, head 1km back to the main road to visit Bornholmertårnet (☑40 20 52 40; www.bornholmertaarnet.dk; Strandmarksvejen 2; adult/child 75/50kr; ☉10am-5pm May-Oct) tower.

🏃 Activities

⭐ Dueodde Beach   BEACH

(🖼) Dueodde's beach is a fantastic place for children: the water is generally calm and is shallow for about 100m, after which it becomes deep enough for adults to swim. During July and August it can be a crowded trek for a couple of hundred metres to reach the beach. Once there, simply head off to discover your own wide-open spaces.

🛏 Sleeping

⭐ Dueodde Familiecamping & Hostel   HOSTEL, CAMPGROUND €

(📞20 14 68 49; www.dueodde.dk; Skrokkegårdsvejen 17; s/d/q from 375/425/580kr, campsites per adult/child 75/45kr, per site 30-45kr; ⊗May-Sep; P🐾🕸) This upbeat beachside hostel-camping-ground combo is a 10-minute walk east of the bus stop. Hostel rooms come with private bathroom (linen hire is additional). There are pleasant, pine-clad campsites; caravans and apartments are for rent (one-week minimum in summer's peak). Perks include an indoor swimming pool, free wi-fi and a good cafe.

Dueodde Badehotel   APARTMENT €€

(📞56 95 85 66; www.dueodde-badehotel.dk; Sirenevej 2; d per 3 nights incl breakfast 2262-3744kr, self-catering apt per 3 nights 1454-4159kr; P🕸) These smart, Ikea-style apartments 150m from the beach have terraces or balconies overlooking the pleasant garden. Sleeping up to four people, they're an especially good bet for families. The complex also offers double rooms – the cheapest are small and simple, while those with terraces or balconies also feature a sofa and kitchenette.

ℹ Getting There & Away

Two access roads head to Dueodde south from Strandmarksvejen. Bus 7 runs here.

Gudhjem & Melsted

POP 715

Gudhjem is the best-looking of Bornholm's harbour towns. Its rambling high street is crowned by a squat windmill standing over half-timbered houses and sloping streets that roll down to the picture-perfect harbour. The town is a good base for exploring the rest of Bornholm, with cycling and walking trails, convenient bus connections, plenty of places to eat and stay, and a boat service (p75) to Christiansø.

Melsted blends into Gudhjem just a short walk southeast of the town centre.

👁 Sights

⭐ Østerlars Rundkirke   CHURCH

(www.oesterlarskirke.dk; Vietsvej 25, Østerlars; 10kr; ⊗10am-5pm Mon-Sat Apr-Oct, to 2.45pm Tue-Sat Nov-Mar) The largest and most impressive of Bornholm's round churches dates to at least 1150, and its seven buttresses and upper-level shooting positions give away its former role as a fortress. The roof was originally constructed with a flat top to serve as a battle platform, but the excessive weight this exerted on the walls saw it eventually replaced with its present conical one. The interior is largely whitewashed, although a swath of medieval frescoes has been uncovered and restored.

⭐ Bornholms Kunstmuseum   MUSEUM

(📞56 48 43 86; www.bornholms-kunstmuseum.dk; Otto Bruuns Plads 1; adult/child 70kr/free; ⊗10am-5pm Jun-Aug, closed Mon Apr, May, Sep & Oct, shorter hours rest of year) Occupying a svelte, modern building and overlooking sea, fields and (weather permitting) the distant isle of Christiansø, Bornholms Kunstmuseum echoes Copenhagen's Louisiana. Among its exhibits, the museum displays paintings by artists from the Bornholm School, including Olaf Rude, Oluf Høst and Edvard Weie, who painted during the first half of the 20th century.

The grounds are a delight – take a walk past grazing highland cows to reach the photogenic Helligdomsklipperne, high and rugged rock formations by the sea.

⭐ Oluf Høst Museet   MUSEUM

(📞56 48 50 38; www.ohmus.dk; Løkkegade 35; adult/child 75kr/free; ⊗11am-5pm Jun-Aug, Wed-Sun Sep & Oct; 🖼) This wonderful museum contains the workshops and paintings of Oluf Høst (1884–1966), one of Bornholm's best-known artists. The museum occupies the home where Høst lived from 1929 until his death. The beautiful back garden is home to a little hut with paper, paints and pencils for kids with a creative itch.

🛏 Sleeping & Eating

Sannes Familiecamping   CAMPGROUND €

(📞56 48 52 11; www.familiecamping.dk; Melstedvej 39; per adult/child 90/60kr, per site 30-90kr, 4-person cabin per week 3150-11,050kr; ⊗Apr-Oct; P🐾🕸) This lovely four-star camping ground is right beside the beach but also boasts a pool, sauna and wellness area for when the weather doesn't deliver. Camping aside, the place offers cabins accommodating three to eight people in varying degrees of luxury (the top-end options have jacuzzis). There are bikes for rent, too (75/350kr per day/week).

★ Stammershalle Badehotel
BOUTIQUE HOTEL €€

(🖉56 48 42 10; www.stammershalle-badehotel. dk; Søndre Strandvej 128, Stammershalle; s/d incl breakfast from 700/900kr; ☉May-Oct, Wed-Sat Mar, Apr & Nov; 🅿🛜🌊) One of Bornholm's top slumber spots occupies an imposing, early-20th-century bathing hotel overlooking a rocky part of the coast a few kilometres north of Gudhjem. It's a calming blend of whitewashed timber and understated Cape Cod–esque chic, not to mention the home of an excellent **restaurant** (Lassens; small/large tasting menu 450/595kr; ☉6-10pm May-Oct, Wed-Sat Mar & Apr). Book well ahead, especially in the summer high season.

Melsted Badehotel
BOUTIQUE HOTEL €€€

(🖉56 48 51 00; www.melsted-badehotel.dk; Melstedvej 27; d incl breakfast 1510-1975kr; ☉May-Sep) The gorgeous green grounds are a feature of this boutique seaside complex, complete with croquet lawn, putting green and Adirondack chairs that lend a refined air. Rooms are bright, fresh and full of good taste.

Gudhjem Røgeri
SEAFOOD €

(🖉56 48 57 08; www.smokedfish.dk; Ejnar Mikkelsensvej 9; dishes 64-115kr, buffet 130-185kr; ☉from 10am Apr-Oct) Gudhjem's popular smokehouse serves deli-style fish and salads, including the classic smørrebrød topping known as Sol over Gudhjem (Sun over Gudhjem; smoked herring topped with a raw egg yolk, chives and radish on rye bread). There's indoor and outdoor seating, and live music most nights in July and August.

★ Norresan
CAFE €

(🖉20 33 52 85; www.facebook.com/norresand; Nørresand 10; cake/sandwich 35/70kr; ☉11am-9pm Jul, shorter hours Apr-Jun & Aug-Oct) In a beautiful old smokehouse by the water, close to Oluf Høst Museet, this whitewashed cafe wins over visitors with views, home-baked cakes and cookies, tasty ice cream and a sweet ambience. Check its Facebook page for opening hours, and for details of visiting food trucks for sunset-watchers.

ℹ Information

Tourist Office (🖉56 95 95 00; Ejnar Mikkelsensvej 27; ☉10am-3.30pm Mon-Fri Jun-Aug) This small tourist office right by the harbour is staffed during the summer, and open for self-service (brochures, etc) for a few hours in the morning daily from mid-April to mid-October.

ℹ Getting There & Away

Christiansøfarten (🖉56 48 51 76; www. christiansoefarten.dk; Ejnar Mikkelsensvej 25; Christiansø return adult/child 250/125kr; ☉hours vary) operates passenger ferries to Christiansø from Gudhjem. From July to late August, ferries depart Gudhjem daily at 10am, 12.30pm and 3pm; return ferries depart Christiansø at 2pm, 4.15pm and 7.30pm. Sailing time is around an hour. Note that there are fewer sailings outside peak summer.

In a gorgeous gesture, 10am sailings in summer are serenaded from Gudhjem's harbour by the local choir.

From November to mid-April, there is a weekday service with the post-boat – check the website for details.

Sandvig & Allinge
POP 1600

Sandvig is a genteel seaside hamlet with story-book older homes, many fringed by rose bushes and flower gardens. It's fronted by a gorgeous sandy bay and borders a network of walking trails throughout the **Hammeren** area and southwest to Hammershus.

Allinge, the larger and more developed half of the Allinge-Sandvig municipality, is 2km southeast of Sandvig. Although not as quaint as Sandvig, Allinge has the lion's share of commercial facilities, including banks, grocery shops and the area's tourist office (p76).

🛏 Sleeping & Eating

★ Nordly
HOSTEL €

(🖉56 48 03 62; www.nordlybornholm.dk; Hammershusvej 94; d/q without bathroom from 475/610kr; 🅿🛜) A young couple has taken over this old Danhostel in rustic surrounds not far from Hammershus, and transformed it into cosy, stylish budget digs. Double and family rooms surround a courtyard out back, while the main building has some fun retro stylings and inviting common areas. All rooms have shared bathrooms. Linen/breakfast is 70/75kr.

★**Nordlandet**   BOUTIQUE HOTEL €€

(☑56 48 03 44; www.hotelnordlandet.com; Strandvejen 68, Sandvig; r incl breakfast from 1190kr; P﹫) Wowsers, talk about a makeover. The folks behind the first-class Kadeau (p70) restaurant in southern Bornholm have turned their attention to this hotel, with similarly stellar results. The coast-hugging complex offers minimalist, on-trend hotel rooms; most have sea views, some have terraces and/or kitchens. Also on-site: a beautifully appointed restaurant (book ahead) and cool bar serving local beer and snacks.

★**Nordbornholms Røgeri**   SEAFOOD €

(☑56 48 07 30; www.nbr.dk; Kæmpestranden 2, Allinge; dishes 60-115kr, buffet 189kr; ☺11am-10pm; ﹫) Several of Bornholm's top chefs praise this smokehouse as the island's best. Not only does it serve a bumper buffet of locally smoked fish, salads and soup (ice-cream dessert included), but its waterside setting makes it the perfect spot to savour Bornholm's Baltic flavours.

★**Kalas-Kalas**   CAFE €

(☑60 19 13 84; www.kalasbornholm.dk; Strandpromenaden 14, Sandvig; 2/3 ice-cream scoops 34/44kr, coffee 30-40kr; ☺11am-10pm late Jun–mid-Aug, shorter hours rest of year) The perfect island combination: excellent coffee, handmade ice cream the locals queue for, picture-perfect rocky coastline out the windows, and beanbags on the terrace for cocktails at sunset. Ice-cream flavours come courtesy of local gardens and fields: elderflower, rhubarb, redcurrant, various berries. Ask here about boat trips and snorkelling tours run by the owners' sons (www.boatingbornholm.dk). Check the website for hours.

❶ Information

Tourist Office (☑56 95 95 00; Sverigesvej 11, Allinge; ☺11am-5pm Mon-Fri, 10am-4pm Sat & Sun Jul & Aug, shorter hours rest of year) Helpful office by the harbour in Allinge.

❶ Getting There & Away

There are decent bus connections: bus 1 runs frequently from Rønne, bus 4 from Gudhjem.

FUNEN

Funen (Fyn in Danish) is Denmark's proverbial middle child. Lacking Zealand's capital-city pull or Jutland's geographic dominance, it's often overlooked by visitors, who rarely do more than make a whistle-stop visit to Hans Christian Andersen's birthplace, Odense.

Certainly the master of fairy tales makes a worthy favourite son and Odense is a lively cultural and commercial centre. But there is much more to Funen. Thatched farmhouses, picture-book coastal towns and grand Renaissance castles dot the island's patchwork of fields and woodlands. There's a remarkable Viking-era ship grave near Kerteminde. Rolling southern pastures and orchards grow some of the country's best produce. Curiously minimalist shelters are set up for cyclists and kayakers. And handsome harbour towns give access to a yacht-filled archipelago of idyllic seafaring islands. All in all, if you take the trouble to explore, you'll find Funen is a microcosm of the very best of Denmark.

Odense

POP 175,245

Pronounced *o*-thn-se (or *ohn*-se if you're local), Funen's millennium-old hub is Denmark's third-biggest city, a buzzing place undergoing a very major revamp. The birthplace of fairy-tale writer extraordinaire Hans Christian Andersen, there's a profusion of Andersen-related attractions, including museums, a **children's centre** (Tinderbox Children's Culturehouse; www.museum.odense.dk; Hans Jensens Stræde 21; 80-95kr; ☺10am-4pm Fri-Sun Feb–mid-Dec, daily school holidays; ⟡) and sculptures interpreting his most famous stories. Even the lights at pedestrian crossings feature Andersen in silhouette.

Yet there's much more to Odense than top-hatted storytellers, including several great museums, imaginative art galleries, Denmark's best zoo (p78), a superb 'village' museum (p78) of historic houses, and a fizzing bar and cafe scene. With dozens of parks, the city is also a family-friendly destination that lives by its motto: *at leger er at leve* (to play is to live).

Odense is Funen's transport hub and has a small but impressive choice of budget accommodation.

History

Meaning 'Odin's shrine', Odense was named for the Viking god of war, poetry and wisdom who was said to have had his home here. As the era changed, so too did Odense's

Odense

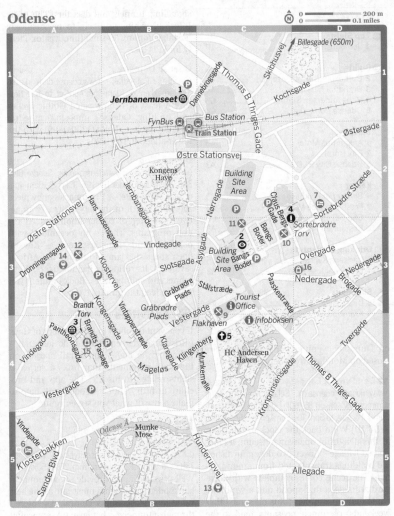

religious associations: after the murder of King Knud II in what would later become the cathedral, the bones of the rapidly canonised monarch quickly became the object of a popular pilgrimage, bringing considerable wealth to the town. Thus, despite having no harbour, Odense was already Denmark's largest provincial town even before it was finally linked to the sea by a large canal (from 1800). With a new harbour and an important textile industry it went from strength to strength until the late 20th century. Facing a changing world, the city has reoriented itself towards education, tourism and high-tech

medical and robotics industries, investing very heavily in new infrastructure to boost its prospects.

◉ Sights

If you are visiting several museums in a day, the tourist office's 24-hour City Pass (169kr) might save you money – it gives free admission to most sights plus 50% off zoo entry and free bus travel. Alternatively, you can save 30% on some museums by showing the entry ticket to another museum (within one week), and a few are free

Odense

on Thursday evenings. Most museums are closed on Mondays from September to May.

★ **Den Fynske Landsby**   MUSEUM
(www.museum.odense.dk; Sejerskovvej 20; adult summer/low season 85/60kr, child free; ⊙10am-6pm Jul & Aug, to 5pm Tue-Sun Apr-Jun, Sep & Oct; ▣110, 111) Wind back the clock to the 1850s at this delightful open-air museum, a landscaped 'village' of over two dozen furnished old buildings transplanted from around Funen. The scene comes complete with farmyard animals, a duck pond and a windmill, while daily in summer (plus on some other weekends) costumed 'peasants' tend to the geese, while children in knickerbockers play with hoops and sticks.

★ **Jernbanemuseet**   MUSEUM
(www.jernbanemuseet.dk; Dannebrogsgade 24; adult/child late Jun-late Aug & holidays 95/50kr, low season 65kr/free; ⊙10am-4pm; ⊛) For train buffs, this fabulous video-rich museum is almost reason enough to come to Denmark. The core collection of over 30 engines and wagons, ranging from 1868 to 1981, includes an 1869 snow plough, a double-decker carriage and Christian IX's plush 1900 royal saloon car. There are also model trains and ships, and, upstairs, extensive exhibitions on

signalling, tunnels and disasters. The 1970s InterRail exhibit is likely to be gushingly nostalgic for any 50-something visitor. Plenty for kids too.

Odense Domkirke   CHURCH
(Canute's Cathedral; www.odense-domkirke.dk; Klosterbakken; ⊙10am-5pm Apr-Oct, to 4pm Nov-Mar) A feast of whitewashed Gothic arches and vaulting, Odense's imposing cathedral took 200 years to build (1300–1499) with the tower added in the 1580s.

Odense Zoo   ZOO
(▢66 11 13 60; www.odensezoo.dk; Søndre Blvd 306; adult/child under 11yr 195/95kr; ⊙10am-4pm or later, see website; ⊛) Denmark's showpiece zoo, 2km south of the city centre, is an active supporter of conservation and education programs. There's an 'oceanium' with penguins and manatees, and a 'Kiwara' open space that aims to mimic the African savannah. Its residents include tigers, lions, zebras and chimpanzees. Book online if you want to feed the giraffes (70kr).

🏃 Activities

If you want to follow in the footsteps of Hans Christian Andersen you can do just that – following the boot-shaped trail marked on the city's pavements that links a series of sights related to his life. The app and brochure at http://andersensodense.dk help to make sense of what you see en route.

🛏 Sleeping

★ **Odense City B&B**   B&B €
(▢71 78 71 77; www.odensecitybb.dk; Vindegade 73B; s/d without bathroom from 250/450kr; ⊛) Well-travelled hosts provide seven immaculate modern rooms that must rate as the best value in Odense. Super central, it's entered through a tunnelway between two appealing little restaurants. Deposit your shoes in the box and head upstairs past a small kitchenette on the landing where there's free coffee, tea and fruit. The two shared bathrooms are on the 1st floor.

Billesgade   B&B €
(▢20 76 42 63; www.billesgade.dk; Billesgade 9; d/apt from 575/900kr; ▣⊛) This spotless B&B has six hotel-standard rooms, each trio sharing a bathroom. There's a communal kitchenette with free coffee and tea, or you can opt for an agreeable breakfast (60kr) made with eggs laid by the hosts' own chickens.

Knutsens Gaard HOTEL €€
(☑ 63 11 43 11; www.knutsensgaard.dk; Hunderup-gade 2; d summer/weekend/high season from 845/945/1245kr; P �) The most photogenic wings of this midrange business hotel occupy part-timbered, red-tiled farm buildings around a pretty cobbled courtyard. Rooms are less special than the exterior, but are still very comfy with botanical prints, minibar, kettle and wine glasses provided.

Ansgarhus Motel HOTEL €€
(☑ 66 12 88 00; www.ansgarhus.dk; Kirkegårds Allé 17; s/d incl breakfast 595/795kr; P �) Though there are several free-parking spaces, the term 'motel' undersells this 15-room family guesthouse in a quiet residential area near the river and parkland. Room sizes vary considerably from very compact singles to some impressively spacious doubles. There's an inviting, plant-filled courtyard-garden behind.

✖ Eating

Bryggeriet Flakhaven BRASSERIE €€
(☑ 66 12 02 99; www.flakhaven.dk; Flakhaven 2; mains 198-298kr, 2-/3-course meal 255/325kr, with beer 313/413kr; ⊙ 11am-11pm Mon-Sat, kitchen noon-2.45pm & 5-9pm) Built into one corner of the historic town hall, Bryggeriet Flakhaven's impressive open kitchen experiments with monthly changing menus designed to produce top-quality gastronomy that complements beers produced in its own microbrewery. If you just want to try the beer, that's fine too, in a tasting room amid the vats downstairs or on the square facing the cathedral.

★ Oluf Bagers Gård DANISH €€€
(☑ 64 44 11 00; http://olufbagersgaard.dk; Nørregade 29; cold/hot lunch dishes from 50/125kr, dinner 325kr; ⊙ noon-5pm & 5.30-9.30pm Mon-Sat) This charming mixture of old beams, yellow-brick floors and big low-wattage ball lights offers lunchtime smørrebrød dishes that are works of art. But it's best known for fixed-menu dinners that give you nine small dishes presented in three trios, all offering seasonal flavours garnished with love.

★ Restaurant No 61 EUROPEAN €€€
(☑ 61 69 10 35; www.no61.dk; Kongensgade 61; 1/2/3 courses 195/275/325kr; ⊙ 5-10pm Mon-Sat; ⊙ ♿) Family-friendly yet gastronomically oriented, this farmhouse-chic bistro has a short, simple, monthly changing menu of seasonal dishes using produce plucked straight from the Funen fields: white asparagus with truffle-infused hollandaise sauce

perhaps, or a confection of strawberry, rhubarb, white chocolate and crème anglaise. Reservations recommended.

🍷 Drinking & Nightlife

★ Carlsens Kvarter PUB
(www.carlsens.dk; Hunderupvej 19; beer from 32kr, craft beers 55-225kr; ⊙ noon-1am Mon-Sat, 1-7pm Sun; ⊙) From outside it looks entirely forgettable, but within, Carlsens offers Odense's best selection of beers (20 on tap, over 130 in bottles), including such hard-to-find delights as Amager's sublimely hopped miracle Batch 1000, and, if you're lucky, Midtfyns Bryghus' fabulous Imperial Stout.

★ Midtfyns Bryghus BREWERY
(☑ 63 90 88 80; http://midtfyns-bryghus.dk; Industrivej 11-13, Årslev) Some of Funen's best and most imaginative beers, including a stupendous 9.5% imperial stout, are brewed 10km south of Odense at Midtfyns Bryghus. It also produces a range of SMaSH (single malt, single hop) pale ales, oddities flavoured with snuff and ginger-wasabi, and a remarkably successful chilli *tripel* (a strong pale ale) with subtly spicy after-burn. Call ahead for opening hours.

★ Den Smagløse Café BAR
(www.facebook.com/densmagloesecafe; Vindegade 57; beer 25-58kr, cocktails 70kr, coffee 25-50kr; ⊙ noon-midnight or later; ⊙) This friendly, utterly offbeat place uses old radios, caged lamps, yellowing newspaper and junk-shop furniture to create an eccentric atmosphere. But it's the collages of dolls' body parts that get your head spinning – until you stumble into the *'pølşeům'*, a museum display of bottled sausages. Yes. Honestly. There's a cosy garden area if all of the above becomes too much.

🔒 Shopping

The main shopping streets are predominantly pedestrianised Vestergade, Kongensgade and Brandts Passage, with quirkier places on Nedergade. There are flea markets at the harbour on summer Sundays and along Overgade on Saturday mornings. On Saturday and Wednesday there's also a *farmers market* (Sortebrødre Torv; ⊙8am-1pm Wed & Sat) in the Hans Christian Andersen quarter.

★ Kramboden   HOMEWARES
(📷 66 11 45 22; www.kramboden.net; Nedergade 24; ⊙10am-5.30pm Mon-Fri, to 2pm Sat) In a late-16th-century merchant's house with neither heating nor running water, this superb place sells everything from brooms to locks to bottles to Danish flags. It is more museum than shop, yet survives entirely on sales along with metal repairs in the dinky workshop behind. Visitors are free to take photos.

Dina Vejling Crafts   DESIGN
(www.dinavejling.dk; Brandts Passage 28; ⊙11am-5.30pm Mon-Fri, 10.30am-2pm Sat) Stylish showroom of contemporary Danish craftwork, including ceramics, glassware and enamelware.

ℹ️ Information

In the town hall, the **tourist office** (📷 63 75 75 20; www.visitodense.com; Vestergade 2; ⊙9.30am-6pm Mon-Fri, 10am-3pm Sat, 11am-2pm Sun Jul & Aug, 10am-4.30pm Mon-Fri, to 1pm Sat Sep-Jun; 📶) and its excellent website are very useful resources. **Infoboksen** (Albani Torv; ⊙noon-5.30pm Mon-Fri, 10am-2pm Sat) has updated exhibitions on Odense's city regeneration projects.

ℹ️ Getting There & Away

BUS

FynBus (📷 63 11 22 00; www.fynbus.dk; Dannebrogsgade 10; ⊙ticket office 9am-5pm Mon, to 3.45pm Tue-Fri) runs most of the bus services within Funen and Odense City. These and other longer-distance buses *(rutebiler)* currently depart from various points north of the rail tracks, an area loosely described as a **bus station** (Dannebrogsgade; ⊙info desk 9.30am-4pm Mon-Fri).

Services run at least hourly to numerous destinations including Faaborg (bus 141; 72kr, one hour) and Kerteminde (bus 150; 42kr, 43 minutes).

CAR & MOTORCYCLE

Odense is 44km northwest of Svendborg and 50km east of the bridge to Jutland. Access from the highway is clearly marked from the Copenhagen–Esbjerg cross-country E20 motorway, which loops south of town.

TRAIN

The train station is within the **Odense Banegård Center** (OBC), a complex containing cafes, shops, the public library and travel facilities including luggage lockers and the train **ticket office** (⊙7am-6pm Mon-Fri, 9am-4pm Sat, 10am-6pm Sun) on the 2nd floor. Note that the concourse closes 1.15am to 5am so for night services use the tunnel between platforms 7 and 8.

Direct trains run at least hourly to:
Aarhus (244kr, 1¾ hours)
Copenhagen (278kr, 75 to 95 minutes)
Esbjerg (222kr, 80 minutes)
Nyborg (53kr, 15 minutes)
Svendborg (78kr, 42 minutes, twice hourly)

ℹ️ Getting Around

At the time of writing, construction of a new light train/tram system (www.odenseletbane.dk) was due for completion by 2020.

BICYCLE

Odense City Bicycle (http://cibi.dk/odense-city-bicycle) is a 24-hour bicycle-hire system operated through automated parking stations, where you release and return bikes using SMS messages on your mobile phone. Assuming you don't have a Danish mobile phone, you'll need to register your credit card details as a deposit. There are handy stations opposite **Brandts 13** (www.brandts.dk; Jernbanegade 13; combined same-day ticket with Brandts adult/child 95kr/free; ⊙10am-5pm Wed & Fri-Sun, noon-9pm Thu), the **zoo** (p78) and **Den Fynske Landsby** (p78), but in our experience, finding empty city-centre stands can put paid to the whole idea.

Alternatively use a more traditional approach by renting bikes at **Odense Cykeludlejning** (📷 29 29 25 89; www.odensecykler.dk; Døckerslundsvej 186; per day 100-300kr; ⊙9am-3pm Mon-Thu, to 2pm Fri). It's rather inconveniently out of the city centre; however, you can book via the website or (late June to early August) pick up/return through **City Hotel** (📷 66 12 14 33; www.city-hotel-odense.dk; Hans Mules Gade 5; incl breakfast s 600-950kr, d 750-1200kr; 🅿️ 📶).

BUS

Painted bright pink, one of the city buses does a free loop of Odense city centre every 10 minutes from 11am to 5pm weekdays and until 4pm Sat-

BIG CHANGES FOR ODENSE

Odense is in the process of reinventing itself. The harbour and a new concert hall have already been (re)developed, a 14km light-railway is under construction, and, since 2014, much of the central arterial road has been permanently closed to traffic. The idea is to enable the city's historic heart to reconnect, replacing traffic with new green spaces, buildings, bike lanes and underground car parks. As a model for town planners it's not been without its critics, but political consensus has helped.

In the short term, until at least 2019, expect the city centre to be divided by a large construction zone; if you're driving, get your hands on an up-to-date map. Or better yet, park on the centre's fringe and walk in. Plans are shown in detail at the red **Infoboksen** hut.

urday. Other routes cost 24kr for a one-way fare (pay the driver, exact change recommended). From June through the summer, **FynBus** offers much better value one-day passes: Odensebillet (40kr) for the city area and Tourist Ticket (50kr) covering travel throughout Funen and Langeland.

The main transit point for city buses is north of the train station behind the **Odense Banegård Center**.

Egeskov Slot

Egeskov Slot is a fairy-tale 16th-century castle (www.egeskov.dk; Egeskov Gade 18, Kværndrup; adult/child castle & grounds 210/130kr, grounds only 180/110kr; ◎10am-7pm Jul–mid-Aug, to 5pm mid-Apr–Jun & mid-Aug–mid-Oct; ⊞), complete with moat and manicured gardens. And that's just the start, as the extensive grounds also include a remarkable series of museums (mostly vehicle based), an array of play-activities and a roster of seasonal events including a **rock festival** (2-day ticket 1290kr; ◎1st weekend Jun), Christmas market and major midsummer-night celebration. You'll need several hours to do the place justice.

❶ Getting There & Away

Hourly bus 920 costs 52kr from Faaborg (25 minutes), 60kr from Nyborg (one hour) or 60kr from Kerteminde (95 minutes). It stops 400m south of the castle entrance gate at Egeskov Gade on Rte 8. That's around 2km west of Kværndrup, which has a station on the Odense–Svendborg railway line.

Faaborg

POP 7100

Faaborg first appears in Danish historical documents in 1229, but its heyday was the 17th century when the town claimed one of the country's largest commercial fishing fleets. While sleepier these days, the port still has island-hopping ferries, and vestiges of Faaborg's former golden years live on in cobblestone streets lined with crooked cottages, as on Adelgade, Tårngade, Feltens Rist and dog-legged Holkegade. You'll also find galleries, statues and museums (including a free one in the bus station), plus one of the oddest public sculptures for miles around.

◉ Sights & Activities

Start any exploration of old Faaborg in the central square, Torvet, with its bizarre milk-sucking **statue**, or from the iconic bell tower, **Klokketårnet** (www.klokketaarnet. dk; Tårnstræde; adult/child 20kr/free; ◎11am-4pm mid-Jun–mid-Aug, 10.30am-1pm mid-Aug–late Aug), outside which a **nightwatchman** (◎from 9pm early Jul-late Aug) FREE starts his costumed perambulations from 9pm on midsummer evenings. The tourist office's free leaflet Kunst-og Kulturguide points you towards a dozen galleries and artists' workshops in and around town.

The countryside north of Faaborg gets its tongue-in-cheek nickname, the 'Funen Alps', from rolling part-wooded hills. They're criss-crossed with cycling and walking trails. Perhaps ride around the bay to Helnæs past the picturesque jetties of Brunhuse, crossing a pretty causeway and spying a unique thatched windmill.

⛏ Sleeping & Eating

Danhostel Faaborg   HOSTEL €
(☎62 61 12 03; www.danhostelfaaborg.dk; Grønnegade 71-72; s/d/tr/q 375/450/550/600kr; ◎Apr-Sep; ⊛) This oh-so-cosy, city-centre hostel has 20 bright-white rooms in its two historic buildings. Most are twins with two further fold-down wall-bunks and rather-too-few in-room electric sockets. Sheets cost 70kr.

Magazin Gaarden Hotel Faaborg   HOTEL €€
(🖉 62 61 02 45; http://hotelfaaborg.dk; Torvet 13-15; s/d/ste incl breakfast 750/950/1200kr; 🛜 🐾) Above a fairy-tale restaurant and a more urban-style cafe, this hotel's 13 rooms are modestly fashion-conscious with wet-room bathrooms, a chocolate on your pillow and the odd Klee print to add colour to the monochrome decor. Room 15 has a particularly good view across the main square.

Det Hvide Pakhus   DANISH €€
(🖉 62 61 09 00; www.dethvidepakhus.dk; Christian IXs Vej 2; lunch 88-155kr; dinner mains 155-265kr; ⏱ 11.30am-10pm Jul & Aug, reduced hours rest of year) Set in a light-infused harbourside warehouse, Det Hvide Pakhus wins on location, obliging service and light-touch fashionable decor. Lunches are Danish standards plus salads and burgers, while dinner menus add steaks and grills.

★ **Falsled Kro**   DANISH €€€
(🖉 62 68 11 11; www.falsledkro.dk; Assensvej 513, Falsled; 6-/8-course dinner menu 1075/1795kr, with wine 2150/3290kr) Book well ahead for a full-on gourmet experience, but with bigger portions and far warmer service than in so many upmarket places. Falsled Kro's cuisine focuses on prime, locally harvested ingredients cooked using French techniques with Nordic twists. Dine on a lawn-front verandah or within the picture-perfect thatched inn (rebuilt 1851). It's 10km west of Faaborg.

🛈 Information

On the 1st floor of the former courthouse, the helpful **tourist office** (🖉 63 75 94 44; www.visit faaborg.com; Torvet 19; ⏱ 9am-5pm Mon-Fri, to 2pm Sat Jun-Aug, 10am-4pm Mon-Fri Sep-May) has cycling and hiking maps, sells a 20kr city walking guide and organises fishing licences. Downstairs, open longer hours (9am to 9pm), is an unstaffed information room full of free leaflets and with a touchscreen computer.

🛈 Getting There & Away

Faaborg is a very scenic 28km drive west of Svendborg (Rte 44). It's 42km south of Odense on Rte 43.

BOAT

The little **M/S Lillebjørn** (🖉 20 29 80 50; www. bjoernoe-faergen.dk; return adult/child/bicycle late Jun–mid-Aug 59/30/18kr, off season 20/10/10kr) passenger ferry to Bjørnø takes 17 minutes each way.

For Ærø, use the **Ærøfærgerne car ferries** (🖉 62 52 40 00; www.aeroe-ferry.dk; Kanalvej) to Søby (one hour), departing at 5.10am (weekdays only), 11.40am and 5pm. For most of the year the return fare is 80/40/166kr per adult/child/car, but between late June and mid-August you'll pay 138/69/296kr. Bicycles cost 29kr at any time. You can use the return section of the ticket on alternative services to Fynshav or Svendborg but with a car, reservations are virtually essential: book a week or more ahead in summer. Pedestrians can generally buy tickets on board without fuss.

Ø-Færgen (🖉 72 53 18 00; http://island ferry.fmk.dk; return adult/child/bicycle 120/85/30kr, off season 45/30/10kr) car ferries operate triangular routes to the small islands of Lyø and Avernakø, five to eight times daily. Tickets are valid for a return trip including stops on one or both islands (overnight stop allowed). In midsummer, foot or cycle passengers can also use the **Sea Hawk** (www.sea-service-express.dk) to island-hop onward from

---

LADBYSKIBET & VIKINGSMUSEET LADBY

Captivating Ladbyskibet (the Ladby Ship) is Denmark's only known Viking Age ship grave. Around the year AD 925, a Viking chieftain was laid to rest in a splendid 21.5m warship, surrounded by weapons, jewellery, clothing and other fine possessions. Archaeologists have ascertained that not long after his burial the grave was plundered and the chieftain's body was removed. But what was left behind is still utterly intriguing. All the wooden planks from the ship decayed long ago, but left a perfect imprint of the hull moulded into the earth, along with 2000 rivets, an anchor, iron curls from the ship's dragon-headed prow, and countless bones of sacrificed dogs and horses.

An explanatory museum, Vikingemuseet Ladby (www.vikingemuseetladby.dk; Vikingevej 123, Ladby; adult/child 70kr/free; ⏱ 10am-5pm Jun-Aug, 10am-4pm Tue-Sun Sep-May), displays finds from the grave and a reconstructed mock-up of the boat (complete with slaughtered animals) as it probably looked just before it was interred. But the site itself is the real attraction, the relics displayed in an eerie, dimly lit, airtight chamber beneath a turfed-over mound. Moored just beyond at a fjordside picnic site, a fully functioning reconstruction of the boat has been built by enthusiasts using Viking-era techniques.

Avernakø via Drejø and Skarø (with a few hours in each) to reach Svendborg the same evening using the same ticket.

BUS

Faaborg's **bus station** (Banegårdspladsen) is near the harbour. To Odense, bus 141 (60kr, one hour) runs once or twice hourly; rarer bus 111 takes 95 minutes. To Svendborg (52kr, one hour), Nyborg-bound bus 931 leaves approximately hourly. Bus 920 via Egeskov Slot (42kr, 26 minutes) eventually heads to Kerteminde (80kr, 2¼ hours) but it's quicker to go via Odense and change.

CAR

If you're driving to Germany, the 50-minute AlsFærgen ferry (www.faergen.dk) from Bøjden to Fynshav saves a long detour via Middelfart. June to August it operates every hour (7am to 7pm; car and passengers 297kr). In low season it departs every second (odd-numbered) hour with prices dropping to 214kr.

Svendborg

POP 27,070

Gateway to Funen's beautiful southern archipelago, Svendborg is the darling of the Danish yachting fraternity, with a harbour packed with yachts and older wooden boats and schooners. Although it has its modern light-industrial sectors, Svendborg has wooded cycling areas, popular beaches, cafe-dotted streets and a summer ferry service that putters south through the island-dotted estuary to Valdemars Slot (p84).

⊙ Sights & Activities

Around Svendborg there are plenty of active pursuits to get the adrenalin flowing, notably the zip lines of Gorilla Park (☑29 16 74 75; http://gorillapark.dk; Rødmevej 45, Stenstrup; adult/child 305/255kr; ⊙daily late Jun–mid-Aug, other dates vary, closed Nov-Mar), scuba diving to the wreck of the M/F Ærøsund (www.dyk-sydfyn.dk/16-home.html; Ballen) and sea kayaking between the shallow inlets around Tåsinge.

★ Sejlskibsbroen   WATERFRONT
This jetty is lined with splendidly preserved wooden sailing ships, including some multi-masted schooners, all seaworthy and making regular sorties, along with a plethora of yachts from the adjoining marina.

★ Danmark's Forsorgsmuseum   MUSEUM
(www.forsorgsmuseet.dk; Grubbemøllevej 13; adult/student/child 50/40kr/free; ⊙10am-4pm Tue-Sun mid-Feb–mid-Dec) Danmark's Forsorgsmuseum is a highly thought-provoking 'welfare museum'. It's housed in Svendborg's old poorhouse, within which paupers lived segregated by sex, as virtual prisoners during its century of operation (from 1872). They became forced labourers making rope-matting or doing mindless chores like packing bundles of ice-lolly sticks.

Egebjerg Mølle   VIEWPOINT
(www.egebjergmollenaturrum.dk; Alpevej 36, Stenstrup; ⊙24hr) FREE North of Otterup, this former windmill has lost its sails and had its crown replaced by faceted-glass viewing windows, creating an observation point to admire the surrounding countryside and distant seascapes.

🛏 Sleeping & Eating

Hotel Ærø   HOTEL €€
(☑62 21 07 60; www.hotel-aeroe.dk; Brogade 1; s/d incl breakfast 850/1025kr; �) This brilliantly located hotel extends through four buildings with over 60 rooms in varying styles, with 1930s- to '40s-style mock antique furniture in many. Harbour views cost 100kr extra. The main section is near the Ærø ferry dock, with an atmospheric pub-reception and a wood-panelled old-world restaurant.

★ Broholm Castle   HERITAGE HOTEL €€€
(http://broholm.dk; Broholmsvej 32, Gudme; d/ste 1795/2195kr, mill house s/d without bathroom 695/895kr; ☐930, 931) Set behind a double moat, Broholm is one of Denmark's most historic castles and much of it remains packed museum-like with antiques, paintings and heirlooms. Indeed it has a 19th-century archaeological museum of its own as well as antique dolls, a well-stoked fireplace and classy restaurant, yet the atmosphere here is less stuffy than at many other upmarket castle hotels.

★ Vester Skerninge Kro   DANISH €€
(☑62 24 10 04; www.vesterskerningekro.dk; Krovej 9, Vester Skerninge; lunch mains 95-168kr, dinner mains 158-225kr, 3-/4-/5-course menu 370/420/470kr; ⊙noon-3pm & 6-9pm Wed-Sun) Beside Vester Skerninge church on the main Svendborg–Faaborg road, this photogenic thatched inn is an absolute classic. The traditional Danish fare is excellent quality, and if you don't fancy accompanying it with wine or one of the fine craft beers try sipping its subtly flavoured homemade rhubarb or elderflower cordials.

ℹ Information

Tourist Office (☑ 63 75 94 80; www.visit svendborg.dk; Maritime Centre, Havnepladsen 2; ☺ 9am-5pm Mon-Fri, 9am-1pm Sat Jul & Aug, 9am-4pm Mon-Fri Sep-Jun) Lots of information on south Funen.

ℹ Getting There & Away

Svendborg, located 44km southeast of Odense, is the main transit point to the South Funen Archipelago.

BOAT

From mid-May to early September, the vintage vessel **M/S Helge** (www.mshelge.dk) sails between Svendborg and **Valdemars Slot** (p84) (60kr, 55 minutes). En route it makes four intermediate stops. First is Vindebyøre (**Svendborg Sund camping ground** (☑ 21 72 09 13; www.svendborgsund-camping.dk; Vindebyørevej 52, Vindeby; per adult/child/dog/site 85/60/20/30kr, Jul–mid-Aug 90/65/20/70kr, small/large hut 450/800kr, Jul–mid-Aug 600/975kr; ☺ Apr-Sep; ☎); 30kr, 10 minutes), then the popular beach area of **Christiansminde** (30kr, 15 minutes), pretty Troense (60kr, 30 minutes) and Grasten on Thurø Island. It departs Svendborg harbour at 10am, 12.30pm and 2.30pm with extra July departures at 4.30pm, 6.30pm and 8.30pm. You can use it as a sightseeing tour (60kr one way) or a short-hop transport option riding two stops for 30kr.

BUS & TRAIN

Trains leave Odense for Svendborg twice an hour (78kr, 42 minutes). Bus 931 stops in Svendborg between Faaborg (52kr, 50 minutes) and Nyborg (72kr, 50 minutes). Both train and main **bus** (Toldbodvej) stations are north of the Ærø ferry terminal, on Toldboldvej, but for Langeland, it's better to pick up bus services at the **Vestergade stop**.

SOUTH FUNEN ARCHIPELAGO

Tåsinge

POP 6110

Administratively part of Svendborg, the island of Tåsinge is connected to Funen and Langeland by road bridges. Its main sights, all located in the northeast, are the pretty sea captain's village of Troense, palatial 17th-century Valdemars Slot (www.valdemars slot.dk; Slotsalleen 100; adult/child 105/55kr; ☺ 10am-5pm Jun-Aug, closed Mon May & Sep), and

the museum (www.taasinge-museum.dk; Kirkebakken 1; adult/child 40kr/free; ☺ 10am-4pm Tue-Sun Jun-Aug, Thu-Sun early–mid-Sep) and (view from the) church (www.bregningekirke.dk; Kirkebakken 2A; tower adult/child 5/2kr; ☺ dawn-dusk) at Bregninge.

ℹ Getting There & Away

Bus 930 between Svendborg and Rudkøbing on Langeland crosses Tåsinge en route passing Bregninge. Bus 250 links Svendborg to Troense but stops 1km short of **Valdemars Slot**. In summer it's more fun to travel on the vintage ferry **M/S Helge**.

Langeland

Great for cycling or bird-watching, Langeland is a long, mainly agricultural island dotted with windmills and farming villages, and fringed by the odd beach. Apart from sometimes frenetic traffic on the main spine road, everything moves at an unhurried pace.

Connected by bridge to Svendborg via Tåsinge, Langeland's major town is gently attractive Rudkøbing. Greater attractions lie north at Tranekær with its castle and sculpture park (Tranekær International Centre for Art & Nature; Botofte Strandvej; adult/child 25kr/free; ☺ sunrise-sunset; 🖳 913), and around Bagenkop on the southern tip, where the former NATO military stronghold of Langelandsfort gives intriguing insights into the paranoia of the 20th-century Cold War era.

◉ Sights

Northern Langeland's main attraction is pretty Tranekær with its castle (☑ stays 62 59 10 12, tours 60 96 80 90; www.tranekaergods. dk; Slotsgade 86; per person 150kr; ☺ tours mid-Jul only, generally 11am & 3pm Tue-Sat mid-Jul only; 🖳 913), windmill and artistic offerings. Heading south there are several megalithic grave sites to seek out plus the Skovsgaard (☑ 62 57 26 66; www.skovsgaard.dn.dk; Kågårdsvej 12, Hennetved; adult/child 60kr/free; ☺ 10am-5pm Apr-Oct) manor house and estate. Around Bagenkop at the island's southern tip is the fascinating Cold War–era relic Langelandsfort (www.langelandsfort.dk; Vognsbjergvej 4B; adult/child 95kr/free; ☺ 10am-4pm May-Sep, to 3pm Apr & Oct) and a chance to spot semi-wild Exmoor ponies. The island's best beaches are at Ristinge and Emmerbølle, both backed by upmarket camping holiday villages.

DENMARK ÆRØ

⚡ Activities

There's a wide range of possible outdoor activities, notably excellent bird-watching sites connected by footpaths around Bagenkop, around the coastal lakes of **Tryggelev Nor** (www.fuglevaernsfonden.dk/fuglereservater/tryggelev-nor; Stenbækvej), and near the island's southern tip. **IBI** (http://bootsverleih.dk/boote) in Spodsbjerg rents a range of motor boats from 440kr per day (plus 1100kr deposit).

🛏 Sleeping & Eating

Accommodation on Langeland tends to be good value by Danish standards. There's a fair scattering of rustic B&B options, holiday homes, several village inns (notably at Bakenkop with its bargain buffet deals), a **hostel** (Rudkøbing Camping; http://rudkobing-camping.dk; Engdraget 11; d/tr/q 450/500/550kr, without bathroom 375/425/475kr; ⊙Feb-Sep; 🅿🛜🐾) in Rudkøbing and two unusually upmarket beach camping grounds.

Ristinge SommerCamp   CAMPGROUND €
(📞62 57 13 29; http://feriepark-langeland.dk; Ristingevej 104, Ristinge; per adult/child 75/50kr, plus site 67-92kr; ⊙May-Sep; @🛜🐾) Within walking distance of Ristinge's long sandy beach, this super camping ground cum holiday village comes with swimming pool, playground, mini-golf, tennis court, bike hire and loads more. En-suite/simple huts sleeping four people cost from 625/420kr per night.

⭐Skovsgaard MadMarked   CAFE, DELI €
(www.skovsgaardmadmarked.dk; Kågårdsvej 12, Hennetved; lunch plate 85kr, Thu dinner 120kr; ⊙10am-5pm Apr-Sep, Thu-Sun Oct-Mar, to 9pm Thu) Located at Skovsgaard's entrance, this deli-cafe brims with fresh, organic local produce, some of it grown on the estate. Lunch plates include your choice of main dish with three salads and bread. Drinks include several local beers and juices. Or go straight for coffee and cake. The best seats are on the rear stilted terrace above the castle's thick pea-green moat.

ℹ Information

Landeland's tourism website (www.langeland.dk) and the Rudkøbing **tourist office** (📞62 51 35 05; www.langeland.dk; Torvet 5; ⊙9.30am-4.30pm Mon-Fri Jan-Dec & 9.30am-2.30pm Sat Jul & Aug) provide an amazingly comprehensive trilingual, 142-page guidebook.

ℹ Getting There & Away

Hourly bus 960 links Svendborg to Rudkøbing (42kr, 30 minutes) where you'll generally change for the rest of the island. However, on weekdays a couple of daily 860U buses from Svendborg continue to Tranekær (55 minutes) and all the way up the island to Lohals (80 minutes), while a few 861 services from Svendborg Vest continue to Bagenkop in southern Langeland.

See www.fynbus.dk for schedules.

The 45-minute Spodsbjerg–Tårs **car ferry** (www.faergen.dk; Spodsbjerg; car/motorbike incl passengers 265/130kr, pedestrians adult/child 80/40kr) runs hourly from 5.15am to 10.15pm in each direction. The Langeland–Marstal (Ærø) ferry has not operated since 2013 but a relaunch is mooted for 2019.

Ærø
POP 6290

Just 30km long and 9km wide, Ærø (pronounced 'with difficulty', or *air*-rue) is the front runner for the title of Denmark's loveliest – and friendliest – island.

Country roads roll through gentle countryside peppered with thatched-roofed, half-timbered houses and old windmills. There's a rich maritime history, beaches with photogenic bathing huts and the little town of Ærøskøbing is a picture-book beauty. The island is famed as Europe's up-and-coming wedding capital, thanks to both its romantic setting and its 'can-do' attitude towards hitching foreigners with awkward paperwork issues.

☉ Sights

Ærøskøbing

⭐Det Gamle Værft   MUSEUM
(www.detgamlevaerft.dk; Havn 2; ⊙11am-4pm Mon-Fri Jun-Sep, to 3pm Mon-Thu Oct-May) In a still-active mini ship-repair yard with century-old boats on the rear slipways, this memorable hands-on activities experience lets you hammer your name in runes into recycled copper, weave rope, catch crabs by hand and learn how to work a blacksmith's forge.

Flaske Peters Samling   MUSEUM
(Smedegade 22; adult/child 40kr/free; ⊙10am-4pm Jul & Aug, 11am-3pm Mon-Sat mid-Apr–Jun & Sep–mid-Oct, by appointment rest of year) In what was once the poorhouse, peruse over 500 ships-in-bottles representing the amazing life's work of Peter Jacobsen, nicknamed 'Bottle Peter'.

Ærø Museum
MUSEUM

(www.arremus.dk; Brogade 3-5; adult/child 30kr/free; ⊙11am-4pm Mon-Fri, to 3pm Sat & Sun Jul & Aug, 11am-3pm Mon-Sat May, Jun & Sep or by appointment) For now, this little museum is a classic clutter of domestic ethnographic items, ship paintings, furniture and glass cases that rattle as you walk by on the creaky floors. But room 10 has a more modern approach with its town model and QR-coded 'tour' of Ærøskøbing in its 1863 heyday. The whole place expects a major revamp by 2018.

⊙ Søby

You might drive or cycle 5km northwest to **Skjoldnæs Fyr** (Skjoldnæsvej 1; adult/child 20/10kr; ⊙sunrise-sunset), a climbable lighthouse on the island's western tip. Or wend your way east via **Søbygaard** (www.arremus.dk; Søbygaardsvej; adult/child 60/25kr; ⊙10am-4pm May-late Oct, by appointment rest of year; ⊞), a small, historic manor house turned exhibition centre. Halfway to Ærøskøbing, the grassy, eroded moraine cliffs of **Voderup Klint** are geologically interesting for their stepped formation and make for lovely sunset viewing spots.

⊙ Marstal

Marstal's charm is still as a seafaring town with a busy if apparently doomed shipyard, marina and excellent **nautical museum** (www.marmus.dk; Prinsensgade 1; adult/child 60kr/free; ⊙9am-5pm daily Jun-Aug, 10am-4pm mid-Apr–May, Sep & Oct, 11am-3pm Mon-Sat Nov–mid-Apr). Across a lagoon-like stretch of water, photographers adore the site of a thatched beach hut on **Erikshale Strand** (Kalkovnsstien). On Sølvgade, a few trees with knitted trunk warmers form one of the island's more offbeat artistic ventures.

⌷ Sleeping

Vitsø
FARMSTAY €

(☑41 48 68 95; www.yoga-aero.info; Søby Landevej 20; apt per week from 2200kr) Between Søby and Søbygaard, this 1868 thatched farmstead sits amid 6 hectares of beautiful lawns, gardens and organic farmland (you can join the harvest). The two apartments, each with two bedrooms, kitchen and lounge, are primarily aimed at longer-stay guests and those joining German owner Dorit's yoga, meditation or shaman-oriented activities. However, two-night B&B stays are possible October to April.

★ Pension Vestergade 44
B&B €€

(☑62 52 22 98; www.vestergade44.com; Vestergade 44; s/d without bathroom incl breakfast 990/1090kr; ☜) Surrey-born Susanna and her laid-back Gordon setter Tillie are perfect hosts at this large, beautifully appointed 1784 house originally built by a sea captain for his daughter. Full of books, framed etchings and period furniture, most rooms are named after their colour scheme, and there's also a self-contained unit in the extensive, tree-shaded garden, itself an oasis of delight.

★ Vesteraas Bed & Nature
COTTAGE €€

(☑61 28 62 52; www.vesteraas.dk; Voderup 41; cottage 750-1250kr; ⊙May-Sep) For a very special middle-of-nowhere experience, stay at this family friendly sustainable farm where cows and chickens roam. Two atmospheric, self-contained units, each sleeping up to six, are well equipped if rambling and very rustic. One is a converted old stable, its facade drowning in wild roses, the rear door opening out to fabulous sweeping views.

✖ Eating & Drinking

Den Gamle Købmandsgaard
DELI €

(The Old Merchant's Court; https://dgkshop.com; Torvet 5; ⊙10am-5.30pm Mon-Fri, 10am-4pm Sat) This picturesque outlet shop for local produce was originally set up by volunteers at a time when the old square seemed set to lose its last surviving shop. Now something of an attraction in itself, DGK sells fine local produce (bread, beer, salami, ice cream, honey and chocolate), and has a charming cafe section and a whisky distillery in the yard.

Restaurant Fru Berg
DANISH, INTERNATIONAL €€

(☑24 63 56 57; www.bergsrestauranter.dk; Havnepladsen 6; lunch mains 119-198kr, dinner mains 198-249kr; ⊙noon-9.30pm Apr-Oct) Ideally placed at the port-side where tall-masted boats dock, this well-pitched restaurant has enviable terrace views and an inviting, clean-lined nautical interior. Particularly popular are variations on freshly-caught plaice or mussels, served on blue plates shaped like fish or sea shells.

Rise Bryggeri
BREWERY

(☑62 52 11 32; www.risebryggeri.dk; Vandværksvej 5, Store Rise; ⊙shop 11am-3pm Jul & Aug, 10am-1pm Sep & Oct, cafe 11.30am-4pm Jul & Aug) You can buy Ærø Øl beers all across the island, cheapest at **Netto** (Vestre Allé 4; ⊙8am-10pm) in Ærøskøbing, where bottles cost 20.95kr plus deposit. But visiting the brewery that produces them makes for a worthy cycling excursion to Store Rise village, 7km south of Ærøskøbing.

ℹ️ Information

Ærøskøbing Tourist Office (📞 62 52 13 00; www.visitaeroe.dk; Havn 4; ⏱ 9am-4pm Mon-Fri) Handily near the ferry terminal, this office is the main info centre for the island.

Marstal Tourist Office (Prinsensgade 21A; ⏱ 1-6pm Mon, Wed & Thu, 10am-1pm Tue & Fri) Inside the library, at the south end of pedestrianised shopping street Kirkestræde.

Tourist Office (Havnevejen 6A) There's an unstaffed tourist office with lots of free brochures beside the harbour office, one block west of the ferry dock.

ℹ️ Getting There & Away

Ærøfærgerne (📞 62 52 40 00; www.aeroe-ferry.dk; Søby Havn; return adult/child/car late Jun–mid-Aug 212/106/463kr, mid-Aug–late Jun 80/40/166kr) runs year-round car ferries on three routes:

➡ **Svendborg–Ærøskøbing** The main service, running up to 12 times daily (75 minutes).

➡ **Faaborg–Søby** Twice/three times daily weekends/weekdays (one hour).

➡ **Fynshav–Søby** From Fynshav on the island of Als (southern Jutland). Three times daily, 70 minutes.

Prices are the same on all three routes. All tickets are return fares that can be combinations of any two routes. For most of the year the return fare is 80/40/166kr per adult/child/car, but it increases steeply between late June and mid-August when you'll pay 212/106/463kr. Bicycles cost 29kr at any time. If you have a car, it's wise to reserve a few days ahead, further ahead for summer weekends.

The ferry link between Marstal and Rudkøbing (on Langeland) has not operated since 2013, but at the time of writing, there were tentative plans to restore it in 2019.

ℹ️ Getting Around

BICYCLE

Cycling is a perfect way to enjoy Ærø, and is in keeping with the island's spirit of promoting sustainable energy sources. Bike rental is available in the three main towns and well-signposted cycle routes create a 60km circuit:

➡ Route 90: Ærøskøbing to Søby (17.5km)

➡ Route 91: Søby to Marstal (31.5km)

➡ Route 92: Marstal to Ærøskøbing (10.5km)

Ærø's tourist offices sell a low-cost English-language cycling map of the island (20kr), listing sights along the way.

Bike Erria (📞 32 14 60 74; www.bike-erria.dk; Pilebækken 5, Ærøskøbing) is a useful company that promotes bicycle tourism on the island and can help you plan a cycle-tour itinerary (one day or longer) – delivering bikes to you, delivering your bags to your accommodation, etc.

BUS

The free local Jesper bus (www.jesperbus. dk) runs the length of the island from Søby to Marstal (50 minutes) via Ærøskøbing (25 minutes) departing essentially hourly on the hour in each direction, but with a few gaps at weekends. After 9am you can take bikes on the bus.

JUTLAND

Denmark doesn't have a north–south divide; culturally, spiritually and to a great extent politically, it is divided into Jutland...and all the rest. You'll find an old-fashioned hospitality here and an engaging frankness – Jutlanders stem from hardy fishing and farming stock, and they're proud of their points of difference from big-city Danes.

Then there are those picture-book Jutland landscapes, an incredible melange of windswept sand dunes, boat-filled harbours, glittering lakes and thatch-roofed villages. These are the scenes that have inspired centuries of great Danish art – visit Skagen for a brilliant introduction.

Add to this top-notch museums, ample outdoor adventures, Denmark's oldest town, endless family attractions and the understated cool of 'second city' Aarhus, and you'll come to understand why Copenhagen isn't the only Danish destination to put on your itinerary.

Aarhus

POP 269,000

Aarhus (*oar*-hus) has long laboured in the shadow of consummate capital Copenhagen, but transformation is afoot. Denmark's second-largest city is busy staking a claim for visitor attention, and building a reputation as an emerging European destination for savvy city-breakers, festival-goers, art and food fans, and those looking beyond the capital-city conga.

This Viking-founded, student-filled hub has accrued some weighty accolades to shore up its appeal, too: in 2017 its titles included European Capital of Culture and European Region of Gastronomy (the latter

Aarhus

Strandbaren (650m);
Aarhus Ø (700m)

Mols-Linien
Ferries to Odden
(300m)

500 m
0.25 miles

Sverigesgade

Bassin 4

Skansegade

Bassin 2

Bassin 1

Nordhavnsgade

Honnørkajen

Skolebakken

Havnegad

Mejlgade

Kystvejen

Knudrisgade

Nørreport

Studsgade

Nørregade

15

LATIN QUARTER

Graven

Rosensgade

Bispegade

Store
Torv

Bispe-
torvet

4

Skolegade

Skolegyde

Kannikegade

Voldgade

Badstuegade

Guldsmedgade

8

14

12

19

17

Lille
Torv

Sankt
Clements
Torv

Aboulevarden

Fiskergade

Telefontorvet Posthussmøgf

Busgaden

Østergade

Sjællandsgade

Klostergade

Møllestien

Christiansgade

Aboulevarden

e

Munkegade

Thunøgade

Nørre Allé

Vestergade

5

Møllegade

Ny Munkegade

Lollandsgade

Grønnegade

Samsøgade

Sejrøgade

Mølle
Parken

Vester Allé

Museumsgade

Thorvaldsensgade

Vestergade

Langelandsgade

Hjortensgade

Vesterbrogade

Botanisk
Have

2 Den
Gamle By

Aarhus Å

Silkeborg
(43km)

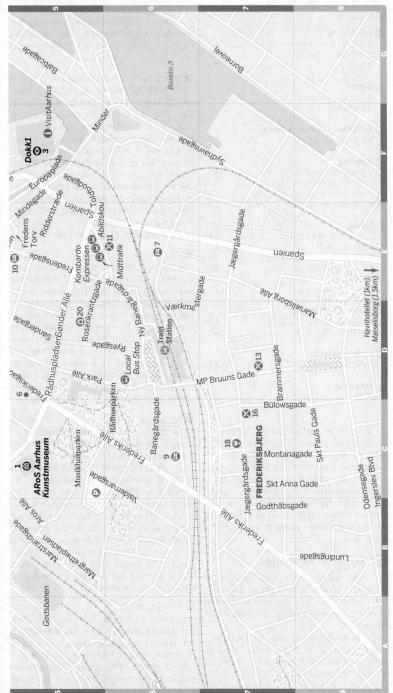

Balticgade

Bornevej

Bassin 3

VisitAarhus **3**

Dokk1 3

Minder

Sydhavnsgade

Europaplads

Toldbodgade

Fredens Mindegade

Torv Ridderstræde

Spanien

Fredensgade

Abildskou

Kombardo **11**

Expressen

Midttrafik

Fredensgade

10

Søndergade

Sønder Allé

Rosenkrantzgade

20

Ryesgade

Banegårdsgade

Park Allé

Rådhuspladsen

Frederiks

Rådhusparken

Jægergårdsgade

Spanien

Jægergårdsgade

Marselisborg Allé

Havnehotellet (1km);
Marselisborg (1.5km)

Værkme Østergade

Train
Station

Local
Bus Stop

Nu Banegårdsgade

MP Bruuns Gade

13

Brammersgade

Skt Pauls Gade

Bülowsgade

16

**ARoS Aarhus
Kunstmuseum 1**

Musikhusparken

Frederiks Allé

Banegårdsgade

9

18

FREDERIKSBJERG

Montanagade

Jægergårdsgade

Skt Anna Gade

Godthåbsgade

Odensegade

Ingerslev Blvd

Marstrandsgade

Aros Allé

Margrethepladsen

Valdemarsgade

Lundingsgade

Godsbanen

Aarhus

was awarded to Aarhus and the larger central Denmark region). The ever-expanding menu of architectural landmarks, lauded restaurants, bars, festivals and boutiques is a mark of a vibrant city on the rise. It's a great place to explore – compact, photogenic and friendly (its local nickname is 'the city of smiles'). Here you'll be left in little doubt why Denmark scores so highly in those liveability lists.

◎ Sights & Activities

The train station marks the south side of the city centre. A pedestrian shopping street extends 850m from here to Aarhus Domkirke, the cathedral, in the heart of the old quarter.

The best neighbourhoods for exploring, shopping and eating are the Latin Quarter, north of the cathedral; and Frederiksbjerg, south of the train station.

The easiest, most enjoyable way to experience the great outdoors surrounding Aarhus is on foot or by bike, and the best hiking and cycling is along the green belt south of the city.

★ ARoS Aarhus Kunstmuseum   MUSEUM
(☑ 87 30 66 00; www.aros.dk; Aros Allé 2; adult/child 130kr/free; ◎ 10am-5pm Tue & Thu-Sun, to 10pm Wed; ◉) Inside the cubist, red-brick walls of Aarhus' showpiece art museum are nine floors of sweeping curves, soaring spaces and white walls showcasing a wonderful selection of Golden Age works, Danish modernism and an abundance of arresting and vivid contemporary art. The museum's cherry-on-top is the spectacular Your Rainbow Panorama, a 360° rooftop walkway offering technicolour views of the city through its glass panes in all shades of the rainbow.

★ Den Gamle By   MUSEUM
(The Old Town; ☑ 86 12 31 88; www.dengamleby.dk; Viborgvej 2; adult/child 135kr/free; ◎ 10am-5pm, hours vary by season; ◉) The Danes' seemingly limitless enthusiasm for dressing up and re-creating history reaches its zenith at Den Gamle By. It's an engaging, picturesque open-air museum of 75 half-timbered houses brought here from all corners of Denmark and reconstructed as a provincial market town from the era of Hans Christian Andersen. Recreated neighbourhoods from 1927 and 1974 are the newest additions.

★ Moesgaard Museum   MUSEUM
(☑ 87 39 40 00; www.moesgaardmuseum.dk; Moesgård Allé; adult/child 140kr/free; ◎ 10am-5pm Tue & Thu-Sun, to 9pm Wed; ◉) Don't miss the reinvented Moesgaard Museum, 10km south of the city, housed in a spectacularly designed, award-winning modern space. The star attraction is the 2000-year-old Grauballe Man, whose astonishingly well-preserved body was found in 1952 in the village of Grauballe, 35km west of Aarhus. Aside from the Grauballe Man, the museum brings various eras (from the Stone Age to the Viking era) to life with cutting-edge archaeological and ethnographic displays.

Aarhus Domkirke   CHURCH
(www.aarhus-domkirke.dk; Store Torv; ◎ 9.30am-4pm Mon-Sat May-Sep, 10am-3pm Mon-Sat Oct-Apr) With a lofty nave spanning nearly 100m in length, Aarhus Domkirke is Denmark's longest church. The original Romanesque chapel at the eastern end dates from the

12th century, while most of the rest of the church is 15th-century Gothic.

Moesgård
AREA

The Moesgård area, 10km south of the city centre, is a must for the Moesgaard Museum, but the area's natural attractions warrant investigation, too. An enjoyable **walking trail**, dubbed the 'Prehistoric Trackway' (Oldtidsstien) leads from behind the museum across fields of wildflowers, past grazing sheep and through beech woods down to **Moesgård Strand**, one of Aarhus' best sandy beaches.

Møllestien
STREET

While you're exploring the old part of town, be sure to wander along idyllic Møllestien, easily Aarhus' prettiest street – all cobblestones, pastel-coloured cottages and climbing roses.

🎆 Festivals & Events

NorthSide Festival
MUSIC

(www.northside.dk; ⊘ Jun) A three-day music festival in mid-June that's building a big reputation – line-ups rival the legendary Roskilde Festival.

Viking Moot
CULTURAL

(www.moesgaardmuseum.dk; ⊘ Jul) The 'moot' is a meet, where the Viking era springs to life at Moesgård Strand over a weekend in late July. Costumed folks? Check. Craftsmanship and authentic food such as spit-roasted meats and mead? Absolutely. Warrior and cavalry displays? Oh yes!

Aarhus Festival
CULTURAL

(www.aarhusfestuge.dk; ⊘ Aug) The city dons its shiniest party gear at the end of August, when this festival transforms the town for 10 days, celebrating music, food, short film, theatre, visual arts and outdoor events (many of which are free) for all ages.

Food Festival
FOOD & DRINK

(www.foodfestival.dk; ⊘ Sep) Wrapping up the 10-day Aarhus Festival (the city's biggest annual party), this tasty weekend in early September celebrates Nordic produce and innovation. There are tastings, workshops and activities, and a showdown to claim the title of the year's best hot dog.

🛏 Sleeping

Aarhus has many smart chain hotels, mainly catering to business and conference crowds – these often have good weekend and summertime rates. If you're after something special, book early at a boutique hotel or B&B.

The 'Where to Sleep' section of the Visit Aarhus website (www.visitaarhus.com) lists rooms in private homes, plus private apartments for rent. Many are central and very well priced.

Note that where parking is offered, it's rarely free.

Havnhotellet
HOTEL €

(BB Hotel; www.bbhotels.dk; Marselisborg Havnevej 20; d/tr incl breakfast 670/920kr; P 🛜) These fresh, good-value rooms at the marina are straight off the Ikea production line. All booking is done online (hence no phone number), and check-in is via a computer. The hotel is 1.5km south of the centre (off Strandvejen; catch bus 19) and walking distance to Marselisborg, a coastal green belt that's great for hiking and cycling; at your doorstep is a handful of restaurants (and free parking).

★ Hotel Guldsmeden
BOUTIQUE HOTEL €€

(📞 86 13 45 50; http://guldsmedenhotels.com/aarhus; Guldsmedgade 40; d with/without bathroom from 1075/895kr; 🛜) 🦎 A top pick for its excellent location, warm staff, French Colonial–style rooms with Persian rugs, pretty garden oasis and relaxed, stylish ambience. Bumper breakfasts (mainly organic) are included, as is Guldsmeden's own organic toiletries range. *Guldsmed* means both goldsmith and dragonfly in Danish – look for sweet use of the dragonfly motif in the decor.

Comwell Aarhus
HOTEL €€

(📞 86 72 80 00; www.comwellaarhus.dk; Værkmestergade 2; d from 1200kr; P 🛜) A new addition to the Comwell chain, this large, modern hotel stylishly showcases Danish design courtesy of furnishings by local company HAY (📞 42 82 08 20; www.hay.dk; Rosenkrantzgade 24; ⊘ 10am-6pm Mon-Fri, to 4pm Sat). Higher rooms have sweeping views, the breakfast spread is top-notch and the location is central.

Hotel Oasia
HOTEL €€

(📞 87 32 37 15; www.hoteloasia.com; Kriegersvej 27; d incl breakfast 895-1695kr; P 🛜) Clearly a subscriber to the minimalist school of design, Oasia offers bright modern rooms full of clean lines and the best of Scandinavian fittings (Hästens beds, Bang & Olufsen TVs, designer chairs). It's well placed for the train station and for Frederiksbjerg dining treats.

★**Villa Provence** BOUTIQUE HOTEL €€€

(☑86 18 24 00; www.villaprovence.dk; Fredens Torv 12; d incl breakfast 1395-1900kr; [P]🐾) Elegant rooms (individually decorated in Provençal country style) for a mature, well-heeled crowd. The superior rooms are large and lovely; standard rooms are smaller but with the same attention to detail – all have TVs, minibar, French linen and original French movie posters. Besides the gourmet breakfast, our favourite feature is the courtyard, with flowering pot plants and fairy-lit trees.

✗ Eating

There's a food revolution sweeping Aarhus, with new restaurants, cafes, microbreweries and provedores springing up regularly and giving diners plenty to hunger over. Options swing from farmers markets to fancy-pants dining; two new food halls feed grazers and hipsters while gourmands can choose from a handful of Michelin-starred restaurants.

★**OliNico** INTERNATIONAL €

(☑86 25 05 70; www.olinico.dk; Mejlgade 35; mains 60-165kr; ☺11.30am-2pm Mon-Sat, 5.30-9pm daily) You may need to fight for one of the sought-after tables at OliNico, a small deli-restaurant with a menu of classic dishes at excellent prices (*moules frites* for 65kr, fish and chips for 60kr). The daily-changing, three-course dinner menu (for a bargain 130kr) may be Aarhus' best-kept food secret. No reservations; takeaway available.

★**Aarhus Street Food** FOOD HALL €

(www.aarhusstreetfood.com; Ny Banegårdsgade 46; mains 50-150kr; ☺11.30am-9pm Sun-Thu, to 10pm Fri & Sat; 🐾☑) ◢ A former garage at the back of the bus station now houses a buzzing street-food venue serving everything from pizza slices to bumper burgers, by way of Thai curries and Vietnamese *banh mi*. The place has fast become one of *the* places to meet, greet and graze in town – on-site bars stay open until midnight Friday and Saturday.

Arla Unika DELI €

(☑91 31 46 66; www.arlaunika.dk; Klostergade 20; toasted sandwich 45kr; ☺10am-5.30pm Mon-Thu, to 7pm Fri, to 4pm Sat) Drop by this sophisticated deli (primarily selling cheese and high-end booze) to see how design permeates all aspects of Danish life. Taste-test local flavours (*gammel knas* and *havgus* are the best-selling cheeses), pick up picnic

supplies, or sit in the back room and enjoy a coffee and top-notch toastie.

★**Langhoff & Juul** DANISH €€

(☑30 30 00 18; www.langhoffogjuul.dk; Guldsmedgade 30; lunch 98-175kr, 1-/2-/3-course dinner 198/258/338kr; ☺9am-10pm Mon-Sat, 10am-4pm Sun) Ticking all the right boxes, Langhoff & Juul is a rustic, informal space in the Latin Quarter, where the casual setting belies the accomplished food coming out of the kitchen, especially of an evening. There's a super brunch spread every day (148kr), and smørrebrød and salads at lunch. Plus: polished service, great aesthetics, and a relaxed and enjoyable atmosphere.

Kähler Spisesalon DANISH €€

(☑86 12 20 53; www.spisesalon.dk; MP Bruuns Gade 33; 1/3 pieces smørrebrød 79/200kr; ☺9am-10pm Mon-Sat, 10am-10pm Sun) This elegant 'salon' charms with plants, lamps, vintage photos and covetable ceramics (made by Kähler, a 175-year-old ceramic company with its flagship store down the road, at No 41). It's a great choice at any time of day: for its weekday breakfast buffet (80kr), weekend brunch (159kr) and excellent coffee, but especially for its artful reinterpretation of classic smørrebrød.

★**Frederikshøj** DANISH €€€

(☑86 14 22 80; www.frederikshoj.com; Oddervej 19-21; 6-course menu 995kr; ☺6pm-midnight Wed-Sat) Bookings are essential to experience this Michelin-starred restaurant's forested setting just south of the centre, and to savour the gastronomic wizardry of Beirut-born owner-chef Wassim Hallal. A variety of menus are offered, from three courses of long-established favourites to a 10-course 'deluxe' extravaganza. Hallal's kitchen has a penchant for high-end headliners like lobster, caviar, oysters and foie gras.

St Pauls Apothek DANISH €€€

(☑86 12 08 33; www.stpaulsapothek.dk; Jægergårdsgade 76; 2-/3-course menu 265/345kr; ☺5.30pm-midnight Tue-Thu, to 2am Fri & Sat) What was once a pharmacy is now one of Aarhus' hottest dining destinations: a Brooklyn-esque combo of hipster mixologists, vintage architectural detailing and slinky mood lighting. The menu is small on choice but big on Nordic produce and confident food pairings – and for 645kr, you can enjoy three courses matched with inspired, delicious cocktails. Book ahead.

🍷 Drinking & Entertainment

Aarhus has a sizeable student population, which enlivens the city's parks and cobblestone streets (and fills its bars). Plenty of eating options are also primed for a drink, like St Pauls Apothek for great cocktails, and Aarhus Street Food for chilled-out grazing and boozing.

★ **Strandbaren** BAR

(www.facebook.com/strandbarenaarhus; Pier 4, Havnebassin 7; ☺May-Sep) Plonk shipping containers and sand on a harbourfront spot and voila: beach bar. This chilled hang-out at Aarhus Ø (docklands) offers food, drink, flirting and weather-dependent activities and events. Check hours and location on the Facebook page (harbour redevelopment may require an annual location change; opening hours are 'when the sun is shining'). Bus 33 comes here, but cycling is best.

Mikkeller Bar BAR

(📞 32 16 01 92; www.mikkeller.dk; Jægergårdsgade 61; ☺2pm-midnight Sun-Wed, to 1am Thu, to 2am Fri, 1pm-2am Sat) Copenhagen's renowned nomad brewer has a popular outpost in Frederiksbjerg, and it's a bright, Scandi-streamlined place in which to sample one (or many) of the uniquely crafted beers. Let knowledgeable staff help you narrow down the 20 options on tap.

★ **Løve's Bog- & VinCafé** BAR

(📞 27 83 16 33; www.loeves.dk; Nørregade 32; ☺9am-midnight Mon-Fri, 10am-midnight Sat, 10am-6pm Sun) This snug 'book and wine cafe' is full of book-lined shelves and old furniture, and reading/laptopping regulars. Occasional poetry readings and live music add to the cultured air, while the short, simple tapas menu nicely fills in any writer's-block moments.

Øst for Paradis CINEMA

(📞 86 19 31 22; www.paradisbio.dk; Paradisgade 7-9) Art-house cinema in the northern reaches of the Latin Quarter. Shows films in their original language, with Danish subtitles.

ℹ️ Information

VisitAarhus (📞 87 31 50 10; www.visitaarhus. com; Hack Kampmanns Plads 2; ☺10am-4pm Mon-Sat, 11am-2pm Sun) has a good website, touchscreens around town and a free app. Its social media pages are useful for up-to-date info. The main staffed information desk is a small one inside **Dokk1** (📞 89 40 92 00; www.dokk1.dk; Hack Kampmanns Plads 2; ☺8am-10pm Mon-Fri, 10am-4pm Sat & Sun; 🚹); there's another info point inside the **bus station**.

ℹ️ Getting There & Away

The best website for planning travel is www. rejseplanen.dk.

AIR
Aarhus Airport

Aarhus Airport (AAR; www.aar.dk; Ny Lufthavnsvej 24, Kolind), also known as Tirstrup Airport, is 45km northeast of the city.

Scandinavian Airlines (SAS) has frequent daily flights to/from Copenhagen; Sun-Air (affiliated with British Airways) operates direct connections to Stockholm, Gothenburg and Oslo. Ryanair has daily connections to/from London (Stansted).

Billund Airport

Billund Airport (www.billundairport.dk; Passagerterminalen 10), 95km southwest of Aarhus, is a larger hub, with more connections than Aarhus Airport.

BOAT

Mols-Linien (📞 70 10 14 18; www.molslinien.dk; Hveensgade 4; 🚹) Operates high-speed ferries between Aarhus and Odden in north Zealand (standard one-way fare adult/car 349/699kr, 1¼ hours), with multiple sailings daily. Rates for car passage include passengers; low-price options available online.

BUS

Regional and long-distance buses stop at Aarhus **bus station** (Rutebilstation; Fredensgade 45), 300m northeast of the train station. From Aarhus you can reach most Jutland towns of note on the blue X-bus network – information is available from operator **Midttrafik** (📞 70 21 02 30; www. midttrafik.dk). There is an info desk at the bus station (staffed from 7am to 7pm).

The following services arrive at and depart from Aarhus bus station. Fare discounts available online.

Abildskou (📞 32 72 93 86; www.abildskou.dk) Express bus line 888 runs up to 10 times daily between Aarhus and Copenhagen (149kr to 249kr, 3½ to 4½ hours), stopping at the capital's train station, bus station or airport.

Kombardo Expressen (www.kombardo expressen.dk) Bus service between Aarhus and Copenhagen (99kr to 299kr, 3½ hours) travelling via the ferry between Aarhus and Odden (rather than driving through Funen).

CAR & MOTORCYCLE

The main highways to Aarhus are the E45 from the north and south and Rte 15 from the west.

The E45 doesn't make it into the city itself – take exits 46 to 50.

TRAIN

Inside the *hovedbanegård* (train station) you'll find the **ticket office** (⊙6am-6pm Mon-Fri, 10am-4.45pm Sat & Sun) with its orderly ticket-queuing system: red for domestic journeys, green for international. For domestic journeys, skip the queues by using one of the ticket machines (instructions available in English; credit cards accepted) or purchasing online (www.rejseplanen.dk). It's best to reserve a seat (35kr) for long journeys.

Trains to Copenhagen (one way 388kr, three to 3½ hours), via Odense (244kr, 1½ hours), leave Aarhus roughly half-hourly.

Other frequent services:

➡ Aalborg (197kr, 1½ hours)

➡ Frederikshavn (256kr, 2½ hours)

➡ Silkeborg (90kr, 45 minutes)

❶ Getting Around

TO/FROM THE AIRPORT
Aarhus Airport

A bus service (route 925X) connects Aarhus with the airport at Tirstrup (115kr, 50 minutes). Buses depart from outside the train station and the changeable schedule is geared to meet all incoming and outgoing flights. See www.midt trafik.dk for more.

A taxi between the airport and Aarhus centre will set you back a hefty 650kr.

Billund Airport

A bus service (route 912X) connects Aarhus with the larger **airport** (p93) at Billund (160kr, 1½ hours). Buses depart from the Aarhus **bus station** (p93), and stop on Banegårdspladsen (outside the train station).

Another option: take a train to Vejle, from where there are plenty of buses to Billund's airport. This usually takes the same time as the direct airport bus.

BICYCLE

Free Aarhusbycykel (www.aarhusbycykel.dk) city bikes are available from locations around the city from April to October (download a map from the website or ask at your accommodation). You need to put a 20kr coin into the slot to obtain the bike (refunded when you return it). Some of the bikes are not in great shape.

If you want a better-quality bike, **Cycling Aarhus** (☑27 29 06 90; www.cycling-aarhus.dk; Frederiksgade 78; 2/3hr tour 199/299kr; ⊙bike rental 9am-1pm May-Oct, other times by arrangement) is your best bet. The company offers tours from a central location, plus bike rental (one day/week 110/595kr). See its website for

details of its free city app with suggestions for cycling destinations.

BUS

Aarhus has an extensive, efficient local bus network. Most in-town (yellow) buses **stop** close to the train station on Park Allé. Buy your ticket from the on-board machine (single ticket 20kr).

Information on tickets, passes, routes and schedules is available from the **bus station** (p93) on Fredensgade or through **Midttrafik** (p93), which has good info in English on its website.

Jelling

POP 3400

A sleepy town with a big history, Jelling is revered as the birthplace of Christianity in Denmark, the monarchy and all that is truly Danish. The town served as the royal seat of King Gorm during the Vikings' most dominant era; Gorm the Old was the first in a millennium-long chain of Danish monarchs that continues unbroken to this day. The site of Gorm's ancient castle remains a mystery, but other vestiges of his reign can still be found at Jelling Kirke.

The town is a kind of spiritual touchstone for the Danes. Virtually all of them will visit at some point, to pay homage at the church, inspect the two rune stones and climb the burial mounds. The area became a Unesco World Heritage Site in 1994.

◉ Sights

★ **Jelling Kirke**   CHURCH
(☑75 87 11 17; www.jellingkirke.dk; Thyrasvej 1; ⊙8am-8pm May-Aug, to 6pm Mar, Apr, Sep & Oct, to 5pm Nov-Feb, opens 12.30pm Sun) Inside this small whitewashed church, erected around 1100, are some vividly restored 12th-century frescoes; the main attractions, however, are the two well-preserved rune stones just outside the church door.

The smaller stone was erected in the early 10th century by King Gorm the Old in honour of his wife. The larger one, raised by Gorm's son, Harald Bluetooth, is adorned with the oldest representation of Christ found in Scandinavia and is commonly dubbed 'Denmark's birth certificate'.

Kongernes Jelling   MUSEUM
(☑41 20 63 31; www.natmus.dk; Gormsgade 23; ⊙10am-5pm May-Oct, closed Mon Nov-Apr) **FREE** Kongernes Jelling is a large interactive museum opposite the church, dedicated to

Jelling at the time of the Viking kings. It provides enthralling insight into the town's monuments and their importance to Danish royal history, and there's a rooftop terrace from which to gain a full perspective over the historic site.

An enlarged coloured version of the larger rune stone from the church helps visitors understand the meaning behind it.

🛏 Sleeping & Eating

Jelling Kro (☑75 87 10 06; www.jellingkro.dk; Gormsgade 16; lunch 79-129kr, dinner mains 95-215kr; ☺11am-9.30pm Wed-Mon) has rooms, and there's a camping ground on the outskirts of town. Sleeping options are best in nearby Givskud or Billund (about 20km west).

★Cafe Sejd CAFE €
(☑29 61 54 16; www.cafesejd.dk; Gormsstorv 7A; lunch 45-79kr; ☺11am-5pm) Bjarne and Ole, the guys behind this stylish, mythologically inspired cafe, are storytellers up for a chat (about Viking times or current affairs). There's good coffee on offer, plus local microbrews and even mead, plus tasty fare such as platters of bread and dips.

Byens Café CAFE €€
(☑76 80 19 90; www.byenshus.com; Møllegade 10; mains 100-160kr; ☺noon-9pm Tue-Sat, to 5pm Sun) Byens Hus (The Town's House) is home to the local library, cinema, gallery and a spacious cafe serving simple all-day dishes (sandwiches, salads, burgers). Inside you'll see the big copper vats of the local microbrewery, Jelling Bryggeri, and can also sample the wares.

ℹ Information

Tourist information is offered at **Kongernes Jelling**, and there are brochures and maps at **Byens Hus**, which is home to the library.

There's information at www.visitvejle.com.

ℹ Getting There & Away

Jelling is 11km northwest of Vejle on Rte 442. From Vejle, trains run at least hourly on weekdays, less frequently on weekends (32kr, 15 minutes). Bus 211 covers the same ground for the same price.

The Lake District

One of Jutland's most prized areas is the Lake District (Søhøjlandet, also called the Lakelands), gently dazzling with hills, forests and lakes not found elsewhere in Denmark. This region is home to Denmark's longest river (the Gudenå, 160km long), Jutland's biggest lake (Mossø) and Denmark's highest point, Møllehøj (a smidge under 171m, bless its cotton socks). It's unlikely to induce nosebleeds, but it's a delightful area for rambling and enjoying the superbly pretty scenery.

Silkeborg
POP 43,200

In a flat country, the modern town of Silkeborg is something of a black sheep, surrounded as it is by hills, sitting on an expansive lake and spaciously laid out. Modern-art lovers and history boffins will find cause to stop here, but nature lovers have the most to celebrate. It's Silkeborg's surrounding landscapes that draw tourists – not thrillseekers but rather families and outdoorsy folk drawn to the lush forests and waterways that are perfect for cycling, rambling and, especially, canoeing.

◎ Sights

★Indelukket PARK
(Åhave Allé; 🚸) Don't miss a stroll through this picturesque riverside park – follow Åhavevej south to reach it. There's a snack bar here, as well as mini-golf, a playground, a marina and an open-air stage. If you're on foot, it's the desired route to get to Museum Jorn, the **camping ground** (☑86 82 22 01; www.gudenaaenscamping.dk; Vejlsøvej 7; per adult/child/site 88/54/72kr; ☺Apr-Oct; @🛜) and points further south.

★Museum Silkeborg MUSEUM
(☑86 82 14 99; www.museumsilkeborg.dk; Hovedgårdsvej 7; adult/child 65kr/free; ☺10am-5pm May-Oct, noon-4pm Tue-Sun Nov-Apr) Here you can check out the amazingly well-preserved body of the 2400-year-old **Tollund Man**, the central (albeit leathery) star in an otherwise smart but predictable collection. The well-preserved face of the Tollund Man is hypnotic in its detail, right down to the stubble on his chin. Like the Grauballe Man at Aarhus' Moesgaard Museum (p90), the life (and death) of the Tollund Man remains a mystery.

Museum Jorn MUSEUM
(☑86 82 53 88; www.museumjorn.dk; Gudenåvej 7-9; adult/child 100kr/free; ☺10am-5pm Tue-Sun) This wonderful art space contains some striking pieces. It displays many of the works

of native son Asger Jorn and other modern artists, including Max Ernst, Le Corbusier and Danish artists from the influential Co-BrA group. It's 1km south of the town centre.

★ Activities

The website www.silkeborg.com has information on canoeing, kayaking, hiking, cycling, swimming and more (including options such as golf, horse riding and fishing).

★ Østre Søbad   SWIMMING
(Horsensvej) For idyllic swimming, head to the lakeshore of Almindsø. Head south of town on Frederiksberggade and take a left at the roundabout in the direction of Horsens. The swimming area is signposted on your right after 1km; there are bathing jetties, change rooms and a kiosk here.

Silkeborg Kanocenter   CANOEING
(☑86 80 30 03; www.silkeborgkanocenter.dk; Østergade 36; canoes per hr/day 100/400kr; ⊙9am-8pm Jun–mid-Aug, to 5pm May & late Aug; ☀) Silkeborg Kanocenter hires out canoes and can help plan a range of tour options (adaptable from two to five days). You can also hire motor boats (per hour/day 200/900kr) if the exertion of canoeing doesn't appeal.

Hjejlen Boat Company   BOATING
(☑86 82 07 66; www.hjejlen.com; Sejsvej 2; one way/return 100/150kr; ⊙May-Sep; ☀) The Hjejlen, the world's oldest operating paddle steamer, has been plying the waters of the Lake District since it was first launched in 1861. These days the boat shuttles tourists from Silkeborg to Himmelbjerget during the summer season, along with a fleet of other boats (departures 10am, 11am, 1.30pm and 2.30pm on operating days; additional sailings in peak summer).

🛏 Sleeping & Eating

★ Danhostel Silkeborg   HOSTEL €
(☑86 82 36 42; www.danhostel-silkeborg.dk; Åhavevej 55; dm 275kr, d with/without bathroom 750/520kr; ⊙Mar-Nov; @☀) The truly lovely riverbank location, good facilities and lack of budget alternatives in town make this hostel popular, so book ahead. Once here, enjoy the outdoor tables and homey communal areas alongside cyclists, families, school groups and Euro-backpackers. Dorm beds are available July to mid-September; breakfast costs 80kr.

★ Villa Zeltner   B&B €
(☑29 82 58 58; www.villa-zeltner.dk; Zeltnersvej 4; s/d/apt from 400/550/700kr; ☀) Super-central and with loads of style, this great-value B&B houses a handful of rooms with shared bathroom and kitchen access, plus a couple of small apartments with private kitchen and bathroom. There's garden access and a grill, too. Breakfast can be arranged at additional cost.

Evald Brasserie & Cafe   INTERNATIONAL €€
(☑86 80 33 66; www.evald.nu; Papirfabrikken 10B; lunch 85-190kr, dinner mains 140-290kr; ⊙11am-11pm Mon-Thu, to midnight Fri, 10am-midnight Sat, 10am-10pm Sun; ☀) Among the family restaurants, cinema and cafe-bars of Papirfabrikken is bustling Evald, wooing patrons with a crowd-pleasing menu. Sit at a riverside table, order a beer from the local Graubal-le Bryghus (brewery), and try the bumper Evald burger or three-course set dinner menu (299kr).

Classique Fiske Restaurant   SEAFOOD €€€
(☑86 20 12 15; www.classiquefiskerestaurant.dk; Åhavevej 2A; lunch 79-235kr, dinner mains 229-259kr; ⊙noon-10pm) From its cheerful yellow exterior to its designer-clad interior, this grand old villa bids a warm welcome. Eat inside, among the owner's great art and furniture collection, or outside in the garden. There's a high-class, fish-focused menu, but guests are equally welcome to stop in for a coffee or glass of wine.

ℹ Information

The website www.silkeborg.com is full of helpful information. Surprisingly, however, the local tourist office has closed, and you're left to your own devices with an assortment of touchscreens and brochure stands around town. A good place to start is the foyer of the **Jysk Musikteater** (www.jmts.dk; Papirfabrikken 80).

ℹ Getting There & Away

Silkeborg is 44km west of Aarhus on Rte 15.

Half-hourly trains connect Silkeborg with Aarhus (90kr, 45 minutes) via Ry (40kr, 15 minutes).

Long-distance buses stop at **Trafikterminalen** (Drewsensvej), next door to the train station.

Ry

Mellow, rural Ry lies in the heart of the Lake District. It has a pretty duck-filled marina, where you'll find canoe hire and tourist boats to Himmelbjerget, which rises 147m above sea level. It's surrounded by lovely landscapes and quaint villages perfect for exploring.

◎ Sights & Activities

Ask at Ry's tourist office for leaflets detailing walking, cycling and boating options.

Cycling allows you to explore the low-key charms of the area. Hire a bike from **Ry Cykler** (☑86 89 14 91; www.rycykler.dk; Parallelvej 9B; regular/mountain-bike rental per day 75/200kr; ⊙9.30am-5.30pm Mon-Fri, to noon Sat), 1.5km east of the train station towards Skanderborg.

Hjejlen Boat Company   BOATING
(☑86 82 07 66; www.hjejlen.com; one way/return 70/100kr) Schedules three boats daily from Ry to Himmelbjerget, operating most days June to August (and weekends in May and September; see the website to confirm sail dates). Boats leave Ry at 10.30am, 12.45pm and 3pm, and sail from Himmelbjerget one hour later. It's good to book a day in advance.

Ry Kanofart   CANOEING
(☑86 89 11 67; www.kanoferie.dk; Kyhnsvej 20; canoes per hr/day 100/400kr; ⊙9am-6pm Jun-Aug, 9am-6pm Sat & Sun May & Sep, or by appointment) Ry Kanofart has canoes for hire. As with the operators in Silkeborg, staff here can help you plan a day or multiday trip paddling on the Gudenå and lakes.

🛏 Sleeping & Eating

Knudhule Badehotel   HOTEL €€
(☑86 89 14 07; www.knudhule.dk; Randersvej 88; s/d from 585/770kr; 🖄) About 2km outside Ry, this sweet hotel is in a pretty locale, across the road from the bathing jetties of Knudsø lake. On offer is a collection of freshly renovated rooms and cabins – the cheapest rooms are petite but well equipped. There are also four family-sized cabins with kitchen. On-site is the excellent **Restaurant Gastronomisk Institut** (lunch 89-199kr, dinner mains 125-299kr; ⊙noon-2pm & from 6pm Mon-Sat).

Hotel Ry   HOTEL €€
(☑86 89 19 11; www.hotelry.dk; Kyhnsvej 2; s/d from 840/1000kr; 🖄) New owners have taken over the town's big main-street hotel. When we visited they were in the process of giving the place a major makeover, and when they're done there will be 55 fresh, colourful and individually styled rooms, plus a raft of new eateries (including a restaurant, gastropub and takeaway). Stop by to check it out.

SMUKFEST
If music festivals are your thing, you need to know about **Smukfest** (www.smukfest.dk; ⊙Aug). This huge annual music fest is held on the second weekend in August and billed as 'Denmark's most beautiful festival'. The title is due to its gorgeous location among beech forest near the Lake District's Skanderborg, which is about 28km southwest of Aarhus, and roughly the same distance from Silkeborg.

Lakeside   INTERNATIONAL €€
(☑70 70 71 13; www.lakesidery.dk; Skimminghøj 2; mains 75-200kr; ⊙5.30-9pm Tue, 11.30am-9pm Wed-Sun Jul & Aug, shorter hours rest of year) The couple behind the popular **Hotel Julsø** (☑86 89 80 40; www.hotel-julso.dk; Julsøvej 14, Ry; lunch 110-245kr, 2-/3-course dinner 325/385kr; ⊙11.30am-10pm Mon & Thu-Sat, to 5pm Tue, Wed & Sun Jun-Aug, shorter hours Apr, May, Sep & Oct) at Himmelbjerget are also responsible for this appealing new option down by the marina. It's an idyllic spot for their relaxed decor and crowd-pleasing menu of pasta, burgers, steak and a couple of French classics like *moules-frites*. Plus, attached is a kiosk selling homemade Italian ice cream, panini and fish and chips.

ℹ Information

Tourist Office (☑86 69 66 00; www.visitskanderborg.com; Klostervej 3; ⊙10am-4pm Mon-Fri, to noon Sat Jul & Aug, 10am-3pm Mon-Fri Apr-Jun & Sep) At the train station. Particularly helpful given that there is no longer a staffed tourist office in Silkeborg. From October to March you can call in on weekdays (11am to 2pm) to help yourself to brochures.

ℹ Getting There & Away

Ry is on Rte 445, 22km southeast of Silkeborg and 34km west of Aarhus. Half-hourly trains connect Ry with Silkeborg (40kr, 15 minutes) and Aarhus (70kr, 30 minutes).

Viborg
POP 39,000

Rich in religious history and bordering two idyllic lakes, Viborg is a sweetly romantic getaway. During its holiest period (just prior to the Reformation), 25 churches lined the streets. Nowadays, only two can be found in the town centre.

◉ Sights & Activities

The town's local history museum (www.viborg museum.dk) owns exhibits that tell the story of Viborg's rich religious past. It has closed in its old location (on Hjultorvet) and there are plans to open a new showcase close to the cathedral. That goal is a few years from fruition (possibly 2021); in the meantime, look for pop-up exhibits in various spots around town, and occasional guided tours.

Viborg Domkirke   CHURCH
(☑87 25 52 55; www.viborgdomkirke.dk; Sankt Mogens Gade 4; adult/child 10kr/free; ☉11am-5pm Mon-Sat, noon-5pm Sun May-Sep, to 3pm Oct-Apr) The striking, twin-towered cathedral is equally impressive inside and out, with frescoes, painted over five years (1908–13) by artist Joakim Skovgaard, evocatively portraying the story of the Protestant Bible. In 1876 the cathedral was almost entirely rebuilt, becoming the largest granite church in Scandinavia (an enduring claim to fame). The crypt is all that survives from its birth date, 1100.

Sankt Mogens Gade   STREET
The old part of town lies just to the north and west of the cathedral. Sankt Mogens Gade has a charming pocket of homes from the mid-16th century, including Den Hauchske Gård at No 7, Villadsens Gård at No 9A and Den Gamle Præstegård at No 11. B&Bs can also be found here.

🛏 Sleeping & Eating

Danhostel Viborg   HOSTEL €
(☑86 67 17 81; www.danhostelviborg.dk; Vinkelvej 36; dm/s/d 210/415/515kr; @ 🛜) This well-run place feels like a country escape, 3km from town in green surrounds and backed by botanic gardens down to the lakeshore. Rooms are top-notch, too (most with bathrooms). Note that the town's camping ground is next door. No bus services.

★**Niels Bugges Hotel**   BOUTIQUE HOTEL €€
(☑86 63 80 11; www.nielsbuggeskro.dk; Egeskovvej 26, Hald Ege; d incl breakfast with/without bathroom 1350/850kr; 🛜) This old inn, set amid forest on the outskirts of town, is a destination hotel where design and gastronomy are taken seriously and the result is something very special. Rooms epitomise farmhouse chic, all florals, patchworks and antiques. Add a library, romantic grounds and wonderful New Nordic–inspired restaurant, Skov

(meaning 'forest'), and you too will be dreading checkout.

ⓘ Information

Tourist Office (☑87 87 88 88; www.visit viborg.dk; Tingvej 2A; ☉10am-4pm Mon-Fri, to 1pm Sat Jul & Aug, 10am-3pm Mon-Fri Sep-Jun) Clued up on the area, with good brochures and maps, plus bike hire (100kr per day). This office is a little out of the centre.

ⓘ Getting There & Away

Viborg is 66km northwest of Aarhus on Rte 26 and 44km west of Randers on Rte 16.

Regular trains run to/from Aarhus (140kr, 65 minutes). The train station is 1km southwest of the cathedral; walk via Jernbanegade and Sankt Mathias Gade.

Aalborg

POP 112.200

Things are on the way up for Aalborg, Denmark's fourth-largest city. It sits at the narrowest point of the Limfjord (the long body of water that slices Jutland in two), and recent developments have seen the waterfront become the focal point of the town. A concerted effort is being made to rejuvenate the central industrial areas and turn neglected spaces into something far more appealing.

Traditionally, Aalborg has flown under the traveller's radar, but that could easily change. There are enough low-key diversions here to occupy a few days for most visitors, from architecture fans to families, and party animals to history boffins.

◉ Sights

★**Kunsten**   MUSEUM
(☑99 82 41 00; www.kunsten.dk; Kong Christians Allé 50; adult/child 95kr/free; ☉10am-5pm Tue & Thu-Sun, to 9pm Wed) Housed in a stunning white-marble building designed by the great Finnish architect Alvar Aalto, Kunsten is Aalborg's high-quality museum of modern art. The building's light-filled interior complements a fine collection of predominantly Danish works and changing exhibitions. Lovely grounds and a smart cafe make it an easy place to spend some time.

★**Lindholm Høje**   ARCHAEOLOGICAL SITE
(Vendilavej, Nørresundby; ☉dawn-dusk) FREE
The Limfjord was a kind of Viking motorway providing easy, speedy access to the

Atlantic for longboat raiding parties. It's not surprising, then, that the most important piece of Aalborg's historical heritage is a predominantly Viking one.

The atmospheric Lindholm Høje is a Viking burial ground where nearly 700 graves from the Iron Age and Viking Age are strewn around a hilltop pasture ringed by a wall of beech trees.

Waterfront   LANDMARK

(Jomfru Ane Parken) The Aalborg waterfront promenade, extending east from Limfjordsbroen, is a great example of urban regeneration, taking what was a scruffy dockside area and opening it up to locals. Here you'll find restaurants, a park, playground, basketball courts and moored boats (including an old ice-breaker, now a restaurant-bar). One of the best features is the Aalborg Havnebad (Jomfru Ane Parken 6; ⊗10am-7pm Jul–mid-Aug, noon-6pm Jun & late Aug) FREE, a summertime outdoor pool that lets you take a dip in the Limfjord.

Utzon Center   ARCHITECTURE, MUSEUM

(☑76 90 50 00; www.utzoncenter.dk; Slotspladsen 4; adult/child 80kr/free; ⊗11am-5pm Tue, Wed & Fri, to 9pm Thu, 10am-5pm Sat & Sun) This impressive 700-sq-metre design and architecture space, with its distinctive silver roofscape, sits pretty on the waterfront. It's the last building designed by celebrated Danish architect, Jørn Utzon (1918–2008), who famously designed the Sydney Opera House. Utzon grew up in Aalborg and died shortly after the eponymous centre was finished.

The centre hosts a changing program of exhibitions on architecture and design – if you're not a huge design buff, you might consider the admission price a little steep.

✪ Festivals & Events

Aalborg Carnival   CULTURAL

(www.aalborgkarneval.dk; ⊗May) Each year in late May, Aalborg kicks up its heels hosting this week-long festival (the biggest Carnival celebrations in northern Europe), when up to 100,000 participants and spectators shake their maracas and paint the town red.

⏏ Sleeping

If only the sleeping options matched the quality of the eating choices. With only a few exceptions, Aalborg's accommodation scene is lacklustre.

The tourist office (p101) has details of budget-priced rooms in private homes.

BBBB i Aalborg   HOSTEL, CAMPGROUND €

(☑98 11 60 44; www.aalborg-vandrerhjem.dk; Skydebanevej 50; s/d/q 470/580/732kr; P⟦@⟧⟦📶⟧) Formerly a Danhostel, this place is handy for boating activities on the fjord but it's hardly central. The surrounds are green and the accommodation is basic (all rooms have bathrooms). It's at the marina area about 3km west of the town centre; take bus 2 (which stops short of the hostel). Linen/breakfast costs 52/62kr; dorm beds are available in summer.

Villa Rosa   GUESTHOUSE €€

(☑98 12 13 38; www.villarosa.dk; Grønnegangen 4; r & apt incl breakfast 500-800kr; P⟦📶⟧) Book early to snare one of only six theatrically decorated rooms over three floors (no lift) at this late-19th-century villa. The three small self-contained apartments are the standout bargain – the English Room is especially lovely. Three rooms share a large bathroom and guest kitchen. It's the town's most interesting option, so the reasonable rates and central location are added bonuses.

First Hotel Aalborg   HOTEL €€

(☑98 10 14 00; www.firsthotels.com; Rendsburggade 5; d incl breakfast from 920kr; P⟦@⟧⟦📶⟧) Some of the newly renovated rooms at this smart fjordside hotel near the Utzon Center have water views. Parking is available (95kr per day), and the central location and on-site gym and bar are a bonus. Best rates are found online.

✗ Eating

It's not in the same league as Aarhus, but the cafe and restaurant scene in Aalborg is of a high quality, and getting better all the time.

Good areas for dining include CW Obels Plads, Ved Stranden and Østerbro.

★Penny Lane   CAFE, DELI €

(☑98 12 58 00; www.pennylanecafe.dk; Boulevarden 1; meals 89-135kr; ⊗8am-6pm Mon-Fri, to 5pm Sat, 10am-5pm Sun) This ace cafe-delicatessen (now with petite attached crêperie) has an in-house bakery, so its freshly baked bread, local cheeses and cured meats are extremely picnic-worthy. There's a buzzing cafe offering a cracker brunch platter (105kr) or lunchtime sandwiches, salads and tapas plates. Leave room for something sweet.

Pingvin   INTERNATIONAL €€

(☑98 11 11 66; www.cafepingvin.dk; Adelgade 12; dinner 4/6/8 tapas 218/258/288kr; ⊗noon-11pm Mon-Sat) This chic restaurant-bar offers a

FAROE ISLANDS

The far-flung Faroes (Føroyar) may be under Danish sovereignty, but this self-governing slice of Scandinavia is a universe unto itself. Midway between Iceland and Scotland, it's an 18-piece jigsaw of majestic rocks jutting out of the frothing North Atlantic swells, a place where multicoloured cottages and grass-roofed wooden churches add focus to grandly stark, treeless moorlands. It's a curiously bewitching place, infused with ancient Norse legends and tight-knit rural communities alive with art and music.

Running the show is capital-city **Tórshavn** (Thor's Harbour), its transport links, solid restaurants and hotels making the place an excellent base from which to explore the rest of the country. Take a day or two to explore the turf-roofed cottages of its historic Tinganes district, as well as the islands' idiosyncratic culture at museums such as **Føroya Fornminnissavn** (☎ 340500; www.savn.fo; adult/child kr30/free; ☺ 10am-5pm Mon-Fri, 2-5pm Sat & Sun mid-May–mid-Sep, indoor museum only also 2-5pm Thu & Sun mid-Sep–mid-May) and **Listasavn Føroya** (☎ 313579; www.art.fo; adult/child/student kr65/free/kr25; ☺ 11am-5pm May-Aug, 1-4pm Tue-Sun Sep-Apr).

The Faroes' ethereal pull, however, lurks beyond the city limits. Sharing the island of **Streymoy** with Tórshavn is tiny **Vestmanna**, from where tour boats reach the inspirational **Vestmanna Bird Cliffs**, bobbing beneath towering cliff faces, passing spiky rock pinnacles and squeezing through tight stone arches. You'll spy the breeding areas of guillemots and razorbills as screeching fulmars and kittiwakes soar above like thousands of white dots.

Another bird-watchers' paradise is the far western island of **Mykines**. Its hiking trail to the 1909 Mykineshólmur Lighthouse leads through densely packed puffin burrows and across a 35m footbridge over a sea gorge brimming with birdlife, including the Faroes' only significant gannet colonies.

Long and thin, the northeast island of **Kalsoy** delivers a surreal succession of abrupt peaks and swales. Nicknamed the 'flute' for its many tunnel holes, the scenery glimpsed all too briefly between them is nothing short of majestic.

Arresting scenery is something the island of **Eysturoy** does especially well. Wedged between Kalsoy and Streymoy, it's here that you'll find the country's grandest fjords and highest peaks. Northern Eysturoy serves up especially spectacular scenery at every turn, and travelling between its criminally cute villages makes for one of the most magical experiences in the country.

Facing Kalsoy's jagged northern tip, the petite village of **Elduvík** is a dreamily cute snaggle of tar-blackened traditional cottages divided into two photogenic clumps by the meandering mouth of the Stórá stream. Then there's **Gøta**. Caught in a fjord end between two jagged mountain arms, this sprawling three-villages-in-one wakes the neighbours in July with the Faroes' foremost rock festival, **G!** (www.gfestival.com), improbably held on a sandy little beach.

While July and August cover the main tourist season, consider visiting in June, when the days are dreamily long, most hotels and museums are open, yet tourist numbers are low. From September to May, rain abounds, and much infrastructure is shut, though the brooding skies, pounding ocean and haunting landscapes will speak to more meditative travellers.

All flights fly into the Faroe Islands' only airport, **Vágar** (www.floghavn.fo). National carrier **Atlantic Airways** (www.atlantic.fo) runs direct flights to/from numerous destinations, including Copenhagen, Billund, Bergen and Reykjavík. Seasonal destinations include Stavanger, Barcelona and Milan. **Air Iceland** (www.airiceland.is) also has flights to Reykjavík.

For details on ferry connections see Hirtshals (Denmark; p105) and Seyðisfjörður (Iceland). For more information on the Faroe Islands themselves, click onto www.faroe-islands.com.

selection of up to 30 'tapas' (not so much shared dishes, but more of an individual tasting-plate approach). Enjoy small portions of Asian-style fish soup, coq au vin or beef carpaccio (with good vegetarian options). There's an excellent global wine list, plus lunchtime offers.

Caféministeriet CAFE €€
(☑ 98 19 40 50; www.cafeministeriet.dk; Møllegade 19; dinner mains 105-189kr; ☺ 9am-midnight Mon-Thu, to 2am Fri & Sat, to 11pm Sun) A fashionable crowd enjoys classic cafe fare here, preferably on the summer terrace in the centre of the traffic-free square, Mølleplads. The menu runs from fruity breakfasts to burgers by way of smørrebrød and tapas selections (the kitchen closes at 9pm); drop by for late-night alfresco drinks.

★ Applaus DANISH €€€
(☑ 71 72 81 81; www.restaurantapplaus.dk; Ved Stranden 9A; 10-course menu 395kr; ☺ 5.30pm-12.30am Tue-Sat) Much effort goes into this kitchen's accomplished output – the results are fab, and the prices incredible value. You can order from the short menu (dishes 50kr to 160kr), but the treat here is to put yourself in the staff's capable hands and enjoy the 10-course 'social menu' that runs from snacks to dessert (375kr for five accompanying wines). Bookings advised.

Drinking & Nightlife

If it's a flirt, drink or loud beats you're after, trawl Jomfru Ane Gade, Aalborg's take-no-prisoners party street, jammed with bars, clubs and kebab joints. The venues themselves are pretty homogenous, so it's best to explore until you find your kind of music/type of crowd. Things are pretty tame early in the week, but get rowdy later from Thursday night.

Wharf PUB
(☑ 98 11 70 10; www.facebook.com/wharf aalborg; Borgergade 16; ☺ 4pm-midnight Mon, 2pm-midnight Tue & Wed, 2pm-1am Thu, noon-2am Fri & Sat) Beer-lovers' heaven, this surprising slice of the UK in deepest Jutland is dedicated to cask ale and serves up to 70 different British, Belgian, Danish, Irish and German beers the length of its capacious bar. Pub food is served weekdays until 7.30pm.

Irish House PUB
(☑ 98 14 18 17; www.theirishhouse.dk; Østerågade 25; ☺ 1pm-1am Mon-Wed, to 2am Thu, noon-4am Fri & Sat, 2pm-midnight Sun) It's almost too

beautiful a setting in which to get sloshed. Inside a 17th-century building loaded with timber carvings and stained glass, this cheerful pub offers live music Thursday to Saturday, big-screen sports, cheap pub grub (Irish stew, beef-and-Guinness pie) and a big range of beers.

Søgaards Bryghus MICROBREWERY
(☑ 98 16 11 14; www.soegaardsbryghus.dk; CW Obels Plads 4; ☺ 11am-11pm Mon-Wed, to midnight Thu, to late Fri & Sat, 10.30am-10pm Sun) Every Danish town worth its salt has a microbrewery, and Aalborg's is a cracker. With loads of outdoor seating and a long meaty menu of beer accompaniments, you could easily lose an afternoon sampling Søgaard's impressive array of brews. The attached Missing Bell Brewpub has 24 beers on tap.

ℹ Information

Det Danske Udvandrerarkiv (The Danish Emigration Archives; ☑ 99 31 42 20; www.udvandrerarkivet.dk; Arkivstræde 1; ☺ 10am-4pm Mon-Wed, to 5pm Thu, to 3pm Fri) Behind Vor Frue Kirke; keeps records of Danish emigration history and (for a fee) helps foreigners of Danish descent trace their roots.
Tourist Office (☑ 99 31 75 00; www.visit aalborg.com; Nordkraft, Kjellerups Torv 5; ☺ 10am-5.30pm Mon-Fri, to 2pm Sat) A small but well-stocked office inside Nordkraft.

ℹ Getting There & Away

AIR
Aalborg Airport (www.aal.dk; Ny Lufthavnsvej 100, Nørresundby) is 6.5km northwest of the city centre. There are plenty of direct connections with Copenhagen, and direct flights to/from Oslo and Amsterdam. Norwegian (www.norwegian.com) and Ryanair (www.ryanair.com) have connections with London.

BUS
Long-distance buses stop at the **bus station** (John F Kennedys Plads 1) south of JF Kennedys Plads (behind the Kennedy Arkaden shopping centre), not far from the train station.

From Aalborg you can reach most Jutland towns of note on the X-bus network – info is online at the site of the regional transport company, **Nordjyllands Trafikselskab** (NT; www.nordjyllandstrafikselskab.dk), or via the helpful **bus station information desk** (☑ 98 11 11 11; ☺ 7am-5pm Mon-Fri, 8.30am-4pm Sat, 10.30am-5.30pm Sun) and its customer-service phone line.

The good-value NT Travel Pass covers 24/72 hours of transport in northern Jutland (train and

bus) for 150/250kr. Buy the pass online (www.
nordjyllandstrafikselskab.dk/travelpass) and
it's delivered to your phone.

Abildskou (📞 70 21 08 88; www.abildskou.
dk) Express bus line 888 operates one to three
times daily between Aalborg and Copenhagen
(from 209kr, 5½ to 6½ hours), stopping at the
capital's train station, bus station or airport.
Good fare discounts available online.

Thinggaard Express (📞 98 11 66 00; www.
expressbus.dk) Bus 980 from Esbjerg to
Frederikshavn runs once or twice daily, calling
at Viborg and Aalborg en route.

TRAIN

Trains run hourly north to Frederikshavn (100kr,
1¼ hours), where there are onward connections
to Skagen (from Aalborg 120kr, two hours).

About two trains hourly run south to Aarhus
(197kr, 1½ hours) and to Copenhagen (438kr, 4½
to five hours).

ⓘ Getting Around

Aalborg spreads along both sides of the Limfjord,
with its two sections linked by bridge and tunnel.
The business, shopping and dining hub, and most
traveller amenities are on the southern side.

BUS

Almost all city buses leave from south of JF
Kennedys Plads and pass the city-centre stops
on Østerågade and Nytorv, near Burger King.
The standard local bus fare is 22kr; buy tickets
from the driver.

Information on tickets, routes and schedules
is available at the helpful bus station information
desk (p101).

CAR

Car-rental companies Hertz, Avis and Europcar
have booths at the airport (p101) and in town.

Apart from a few one-way streets, Aalborg
is easy to travel around by car. There's free
(but time-restricted) parking along many side
streets, and metered parking in the city centre.
There are also several large commercial car
parks, including at Ved Stranden 11 (opposite
the Radisson Hotel), at Kennedy Arkaden (enter
from Østre Allé), and under the **Friis Shopping Centre** (www.friisaalborg.dk; Nytorv 27;
⊙ 10am-7pm Mon-Fri, to 5pm Sat, 11am-4pm 1st
Sun of month) – enter from Nyhavnsgade. These
aren't cheap (up to 18kr per hour, maximum
160kr for a 24-hour period).

Frederikshavn

POP 23,500

A transport hub rather than a compelling
destination, Frederikshavn shuffles more
than three million people through its port

each year, making it Jutland's busiest international ferry terminal. The majority of visitors are Scandinavians raiding Denmark's
supplies of relatively cheap booze and meat.

The town itself lacks the historical glamour of its coastal neighbours but can suc-
cessfully entertain you for a few hours with
its feature attraction, **Bangsbo** (📞 98 42 31
11; www.kystmuseet.dk; Dronning Margrethesvej 6;
adult/child 75kr/free; ⊙ 10am-4pm Mon-Fri, 11am-
4pm Sat & Sun Jun-Aug, Mon-Fri Sep-May), an old
country estate with an interesting mix of
exhibits, including the reconstructed Viking
Ellingå ship. It's also the jumping-off point
for visits to the charming island of Læsø.
Still, Skagen or even Sæby make for more
appealing overnight options.

🛏 Sleeping & Eating

⭐ **Danhostel Frederikshavn City**　HOSTEL €
(📞 98 42 14 75; www.danhostelfrederikshavn.dk;
Læsøgade 18; s/d/q 530/590/715kr; 🅿 @ 🛜) Perfectly positioned behind the tourist office,
this hostel has a supermarket and cafe-bar
as neighbours. It's busy with ferry passengers enjoying the fresh facilities (all rooms
have bathrooms). Communal areas are top-
notch, as is the courtyard garden with barbecue. Breakfast/linen costs 65/60kr.

**Best Western Hotel
Herman Bang**　HOTEL €€
(📞 98422166; www.hermanbang.dk; Tordenskjolds-
gade 3; s/d from 795/995kr; 🛜) The standard
rooms at this business-oriented hotel are
bright and comfortable, and the most expensive ('business') rooms are quite luxurious. The hotel has an upmarket spa and
American-style diner. It also has a better-
value budget annexe, **Herman Bang Bed
& Breakfast** (www.hbbb.dk; Skolegade 2; d
with/without bathroom incl breakfast 650/500kr),
about 350m away.

Karma Sushi　JAPANESE €€
(📞 98 43 22 01; www.karmasushi.dk; Lodsgade
10; 8-piece sushi 135-142kr; ⊙ 4-10pm Sun-Thu,
to 11pm Fri & Sat) When hunger strikes, head
for Lodsgade, which has oodles of eating options. The standout is good-looking Karma,
an oasis of calm and elegance among the
strange hybrid Mexican-Italian buffets – but
its beautifully presented sushi morsels don't
come cheap.

Møllehuset　DANISH €€
(📞 98 43 44 00; www.mollehuset.dk; Skovalléen
45; lunch 115-205kr, 2-/3-course dinner 260/335kr;

⊙ noon-5pm Mon, 11am-10pm Tue-Sat, 11am-5pm Sun) This handsome old mill house from the mid-18th century is in a leafy setting in the Bangsbo area (though its modern extension lacks a little soul). The menu has plenty of appeal in the form of tapas tasters, cheese platters and fresh fish. Bus 3 from central Frederikshavn stops here. The kitchen closes at 9pm.

ℹ Information

Tourist Office (✆ 98 42 32 66; www.visit frederikshavn.dk; Skandiatorv 1; ⊙ 9am-4pm Mon-Sat, 10am-2pm Sun Jul–mid-Aug, 9.30am-4pm Mon-Fri, 10am-1pm Sat mid-Aug–Jul) Over the walkway from the ferry terminal, this office offers the low-down on the town and surrounds.

ℹ Getting There & Away

BOAT

Stena Line (✆ 96 20 02 00; www.stenaline. com; Færgehavnsvej 10) connects Frederikshavn with Gothenburg (Sweden) and Oslo (Norway). Ferries depart from the port on Færgehavnsvej.

There is also a frequent **ferry** (Sydhavnsvej) service to the sweet island of Læsø.

BUS

Bus routes in northern Jutland extend as far as Hirtshals, Hjørring and Løkken (take the train to Skagen). See www.rejseplanen.dk for travel planning that covers all public transport in Denmark.

Thinggaard Express (✆ 98 11 66 00; www. expressbus.dk) operates bus 980 from Frederikshavn to Esbjerg once or twice daily, calling at Viborg and Aalborg en route.

Buses depart from the **bus station** (Skippergade) just north of the train station.

Skagen

POP 8200

Located at Jutland's northern tip where the Baltic meets the North Sea, Skagen (pronounced 'skain') features a rich art heritage, fresh seafood, photogenic neighbourhoods and classic character that combine to create a delicious slice of Denmark.

In the mid-19th century, artists flocked here, charmed by the radiant light's impact on the ruggedly beautiful landscape. Now tourists come in droves, drawn by an intoxicating combination of the busy working harbour, long sandy beaches and buzzing holiday atmosphere. The town gets packed in summer but maintains its charm, espe-

cially in the intimate, older neighbourhoods filled with distinctive yellow houses framed by white-picket fences and red-tiled roofs.

Catering to the tourist influx are numerous museums, art galleries, bike-rental outlets, icecreameries and harbourside restaurants. Come and see why half the Danish population lights up whenever the town's name is mentioned.

◉ Sights

★ **Gammel Skagen**   VILLAGE, BEACH
There's a touch of Cape Cod in refined Gammel Skagen ('Old Skagen', also known as Højen), renowned for its gorgeous sunsets, upmarket hotels and well-heeled summer residents.

It was a fishing hamlet before sandstorms ravaged this windswept area and forced many of its inhabitants to move to Skagen on the more protected east coast. It's a pleasant bike ride 4km west of Skagen: head towards Frederikshavn and turn right at Højensvej, which takes you to the waterfront.

★ **Skagens Museum**   MUSEUM
(✆ 98 44 64 44; www.skagensmuseum.dk; Brøndumsvej 4; adult/child 100kr/free; ⊙ 10am-5pm May-Aug, Tue-Sun Mar, Apr, Sep & Oct, Thu-Sun Nov-Feb; ◈) This wonderful gallery showcases the outstanding art that was produced in Skagen between 1870 and 1930. Artists discovered Skagen's luminous light and its wind-blasted heath-and-dune landscape in the mid-19th century and fixed eagerly on the romantic imagery of the area's fishing life that had earned the people of Skagen a hard living for centuries. Their work established a vivid figurative style of painting that became known internationally as the 'Skagen School'.

Grenen   BEACH
Appropriately enough for such a neat and ordered country, Denmark doesn't end untidily at its most northerly point, but on a neat finger of sand just a few metres wide. You can actually paddle at its tip, where the waters of the Kattegat (an arm of the Baltic Sea) and Skagerrak (part of the North Sea) clash, and you can put one foot in each sea – but not too far. Bathing here is forbidden because of the ferocious tidal currents.

Råbjerg Mile   NATURAL FEATURE
(off Kandestedvej) The country's largest expanse of drifting sand dunes, Råbjerg Mile is an amazing natural phenomenon. These

DENMARK SKAGEN

undulating, 40m-high hills are fun to explore and almost big enough to lose yourself in. The dunes were formed on the west coast during the great sand drift of the 16th century and have purposefully been left in a migratory state (moving towards the forest at a rate of 15m per year). The dunes leave a moist layer of sand behind, stretching westwards to Skagerrak.

☆ Festivals & Events

Skagen Festival
MUSIC

(www.skagenfestival.dk; ☺ Jul) Since 1971 the Skagen Festival has seen the town packed with performers, buskers and appreciative visitors, with acts encompassing rock to folk music. It's held on the first weekend of July; book accommodation well in advance.

🛌 Sleeping

★ Badepension Marienlund
GUESTHOUSE €€

(✆ 28 12 13 20; www.marienlund.dk; Fabriciusvej 8; s/d incl breakfast 680/1190kr; ☺ Apr-Oct; P 🐾 🛜) A cosy atmosphere, idyllic garden and pretty lounge and breakfast areas make Marienlund a top option. There are only 14 rooms, all light, white and simply furnished (all with bathrooms). You'll find the hotel in a peaceful residential neighbourhood west of the centre; bike hire available.

Hotel Plesner
BOUTIQUE HOTEL €€

(✆ 98 44 68 44; www.hotelplesner.dk; Holstvej 8; s/d incl breakfast 1395/1495kr; 🛜) Candy-striped designer touches run throughout this boutique hotel, home to 17 fresh, petite guest rooms. Highlights include an alluring garden lounge (where afternoon tea is served in summer) and a smart breakfast spread.

★ Ruths Hotel
HOTEL €€€

(✆ 98 44 11 24; www.ruths-hotel.dk; Hans Ruths Vej 1, Gammel Skagen; r incl breakfast from 1750kr; P 🛜 ♨) One of Denmark's grand bathing hotels – beautifully positioned in chichi Gammel Skagen (p103), with acclaimed restaurants, a wellness centre and stylish modern-meets-traditional decor. Rooms and apartments are spread over a campus of buildings.

✕ Eating

★ Slagter Munch
DELI €

(✆ 98 44 37 33; www.munch-skagen.dk; Sankt Laurentii Vej 1; ☺ 9am-5.30pm Mon-Fri, 8am-1pm Sat) The queues out the door attest to this butcher's reputation for award-winning *skinke* (ham) and sausages. There's also a selection of fine, picnic-worthy salads and deli produce for sale.

Museumscaféen
CAFE €

(www.skagensmuseum.dk; Skagens Museum, Brøndumsvej; lunch 90-100kr; ☺ 10.30am-4.30pm May-Aug, 11.30am-4.30pm Tue-Sun Sep & Oct) For lunch or a cuppa in a magical setting, head to the Garden House cafe at Skagens Museum (p103), serving lunchtime dishes plus a super spread of home-baked cakes and tarts (35kr). Note: you don't need to pay the museum's admission to visit the cafe. Enter through the garden, opposite Brøndums Hotel (✆ 98 44 15 55; www.broendums-hotel.dk; Anchersvej 3; s/d with shared bathroom incl breakfast from 595/895kr; 🛜).

Ruths Gourmet
DANISH €€€

(✆ 98 44 11 24; www.ruths-hotel.dk; Ruths Hotel, Hans Ruths Vej 1, Gammel Skagen; 4/5/8 courses 795/865/1295kr; ☺ from 6pm Tue-Sat Jul & Aug, Thu-Sat May, Jun & Sep, Fri & Sat Oct-Apr) Modern Danish cuisine shines in the spotlight at this refined and intimate restaurant at Ruths Hotel – the perfect place for a special-occasion dinner. The menu has a regional focus, utilising fine local produce to innovative and creative effect (choose menus from four to eight courses). You'll need to book ahead to score one of only 22 seats.

ℹ️ Information

Tourist Office (✆ 98 44 13 77; www.skagen-tourist.dk; Vestre Strandvej 10; ☺ 9am-4pm Mon-Sat, 10am-2pm Sun late Jun–mid-Aug, shorter hours rest of year) In front of the harbour, with loads of info on regional sights, attractions and activities.

ℹ️ Getting There & Away

Trains run to Frederikshavn roughly hourly (60kr, 35 minutes), where you can change for destinations further south.

ℹ️ Getting Around

The best way to get around is by bike and loads of places offer rental. **Skagen CykelUdlejning** (✆ 98 44 10 70; www.skagencykeludlejning.dk; Banegårdspladsen, Sankt Laurentii Vej; bike hire per day/week 90/375kr; ☺ 9am-5pm Apr–mid-Sep) is adjacent to the train station and has a range of bikes. It has a second, year-round **outlet** (✆ 98 44 10 70; www.skagencykeludlejning.dk; Fiskergangen 10) close to the harbour, inside the bike shop at Fiskergangen 10.

Hirtshals

POP 6000

Frequented by discount-hungry Norwegians and largely inhabited by hardened Hirtshals seafarers, this modern town makes a reasonable base for sightseeing, but its appearance won't take your breath away. It has ferry connections to points further north (way north, such as Iceland, the Faroe Islands and Norway). Beaches, bunkers, lighthouses and an impressive show of sea life may add to the appeal.

Sleeping & Eating

Tornby Strand Camping   CAMPGROUND €
(📞 98 97 78 77; www.tornbystrandcamping.dk; Strandvejen 13; per adult/child/site 85/50/60kr; 🛜🏊) This well-equipped, year-round camping ground is outside town, about 1km inland from **Tornby Strand** (Strandvej). It's loaded with family friendly facilities (indoor and outdoor pools, mini-golf, playroom). It also has budget 'transit rooms' (double 250kr to 350kr) if all you need is a bed before a ferry departure, plus family sized cabins.

Hotel Hirtshals   HOTEL €€
(📞 98 94 20 77; www.hotelhirtshals.dk; Havnegade 2; s/d/f incl breakfast from 845/950/1645kr; 🛜) On the main square above the fishing harbour, Hotel Hirtshals has bright rooms with steepled ceilings – try for one with a sea view (though you'll pay extra). It's well positioned for enjoying the town's restaurants.

Slagter Winther   DELI €
(📞 98 94 16 11; www.slagterwinther.dk; Hjørringgade 5; ⊙9am-9.30pm) Join the Norwegians who come to raid this quality butchers and delicatessen of its discounted meats and booze.

Hirtshals Fiskehus   SEAFOOD €€
(📞 40 55 43 55; www.hirtshalsfiskehus.dk; Sydvestkajen 7; meals 59-159kr; ⊙11am-8pm; 🚗) There's a popular *kro* (inn) on the main square, Grønne Plads, but we recommend you take the steps down to the fishing harbour come mealtime. Here, a fresh-faced fishmonger-cafe enjoys a prime quayside position and offers a menu of good-value fish dishes (*fiskefrikadeller,* fish burger, seafood platter, etc) to eat in or take away.

Information

Tourist Office (📞 98 94 22 20; www.visit hirtshals.dk; Jyllandsgade 10; ⊙9am-4pm Mon-Fri, to 1pm Sat) Small office at the end of Nørregade, about 500m walk from Den Grønne Plads.

Getting There & Away

BOAT

The following international ferries use Hirtshals as their main port. Departure points are well signposted.

Color Line (www.colorline.com; Norgeskajen 2) Service to/from the Norwegian ports of Kristiansand and Larvik.

Fjord Line (www.fjordline.com; Containerkajen 4) Fast catamaran to Kristiansand from mid-May to mid-September, plus year-round ferry to Stavanger and Bergen, and to Langesund (all in Norway).

Smyril Line (www.smyrilline.com; Containerkajen 4) Weekly departures to the Faroe Islands and Iceland.

See the websites for prices, which vary widely according to season, day of the week, whether you're travelling with a car, etc. The highest prices tend to occur on summer weekends and the lowest on winter weekdays. Discounts and packages are often available, including for return tickets, car and passengers. Children's fares are discounted; fares for seniors may also be discounted.

TRAIN

Hirtshals' train station is on Havnegade, west of the ferry terminals. A private railway connects Hirtshals with Hjørring at least hourly (32kr, 22 minutes). At Hjørring you can connect with DSB trains to Aalborg, Frederikshavn or destinations further south.

Esbjerg

POP 72,300

Esbjerg (roughly pronounced *ess*-be-air) has a touch of the 'wild frontier' about it – a new city (by Danish standards) that's grown big and affluent from oil, fishing and trading. Its business focus lies to the west, to the oilfields of the North Sea, but its ferry link with the UK ceased in 2014.

Esbjerg fails to pull heartstrings on first impressions – its silos and smokestacks hardly compete with the crooked, storybook streets of nearby Ribe. In the harbour you may see offshore drilling rigs being repaired. Away from the industrial grit, however, Esbjerg redeems itself with some quirky attractions and its easy access to the beautiful, time-warped island of Fanø, just a 12-minute ferry ride away.

◉ Sights & Activities

★ **Mennesket ved Havet** MONUMENT
(Sædding Strandvej) On the waterfront opposite Fiskeri- og Søfartsmuseet (☑ 76 12 20
00; www.fimus.dk; Tarphagevej 2; adult 115-140kr,
child free; ⊙ from 10am daily; 🚌) is Esbjerg's
most interesting landmark, *Mennesket ved
Havet* ('Man Meets the Sea'): four stark-
white, 9m-high, stylised human figures,
sitting rigid and staring out to sea. They
were created by Danish sculptor Svend Wiig
Hansen to commemorate the city's centen-
nial in 1995 and they make a striking backdrop to holiday snaps.

Musikhuset Esbjerg ARCHITECTURE
(☑ 76 10 90 00; www.mhe.dk; Havnegade 18)
Famed Danish architect Jørn Utzon (he of
the Sydney Opera House) designed Esbjerg's
Music House together with his son, Jan. The
performing arts centre opened in 1997 and
is the city's main venue for cultural events
including concerts, opera and ballet.

🛏 Sleeping

Hotel Britannia HOTEL €€
(☑ 75 13 01 11; www.britannia.dk; Torvegade 24;
s/d incl breakfast 1295/1495kr; 🅿 @ 🛜) This
central, business-oriented hotel has professional service, smart rooms, a well-regarded
restaurant and an English pub, but its rack
rates seem pitched at expense-account business travellers. Weekend and summer rates
(late June to mid-August) are better value at
795/895kr per single/double.

★ **Hjerting Badehotel** HOTEL €€€
(☑ 75 11 70 00; www.hjertingbadehotel.dk; Strandpromenaden 1; s/d incl breakfast from 1195/1395kr;
🛜) If Esbjerg's industry has you yearning
for a little trademark Danish *hygge* (cosiness), make your way 10km northwest of
town to this delightful, century-old 'bathing
hotel' on the beach. As well as housing two
appealing eating options, there are fresh,
pastel-hued rooms and stylish beach houses
sleeping four. There's a wellness centre, too,
plus kayaks and bikes for hire.

✕ Eating & Drinking

★ **Industrien** INTERNATIONAL €€
(☑ 75 13 61 66; www.indubar.dk; Skolegade 27;
meals 100-179kr; ⊙ kitchen 5.30-9pm Mon-Thu,
noon-9pm Fri & Sat) This cool 'rock gastro bar'
is a local darling for its live music, vinyl selection, late hours (till 3am Friday and Saturday) and excellent kitchen. Build a tasty

dinner from the selection of gourmet sliders
(mini-burgers; 50kr a pop, veg options too)
and creative side dishes, then sit back and
enjoy the house gin cocktails and good times.

Sand's Restauration DANISH €€
(☑ 75 12 02 07; www.sands.dk; Skolegade 60; lunch
59-189kr, dinner mains 119-249kr; ⊙ 11.30am-
9.30pm Mon-Sat) One for the traditionalists.
The menu at this classy, century-old restaurant is an ode to old-school Danish favourites: lunchtime smørrebrød and herring
platters (accompanied by snaps), evening
fish (try the *bakskuld,* salted and smoked
flatfish) and plenty of classic *bøf* (beef).

Portlands CAFE, BAR
(☑ 79 30 18 00; www.portlands.dk; Skolegade 48;
⊙ 9am-11pm Mon-Wed, to midnight Thu, to 2am Fri &
Sat, 11am-8pm Sun) A welcoming, all-day cafe-
bar, ideal for daytime smoothies or good
coffee, or evening wine, cocktails or microbrews. There's limited food (cheese or charcuterie platters, plus a few cakes), but there
are plenty of couches, tables and outdoor
seating. Plus: board games. It's the kind of
place you could easily spend hours at.

ℹ Information

Tourist Office (☑ 75 12 55 99; www.visit
esbjerg.dk; Skolegade 33; ⊙ 10am-8pm Sun-
Wed, to 6pm Thu-Sat) Unstaffed central office,
on the corner of Torvet. Offers info screens,
plus self-service racks of brochures and maps.

ℹ Getting There & Away

BUS
The local and long-distance **bus station** (Jernbanegade) is by the train station.
Thinggaard Express (☑ 98 11 66 00; www.
expressbus.dk) operates bus 980 from Esbjerg
to Frederikshavn once daily (340kr, 5¼ hours),
calling at Viborg and Aalborg en route.
   Bus 915X is a handy service, connecting Esbjerg with Ribe (60kr, 30 minutes).

TRAIN
There are regular services running south to Ribe
(60kr, 30 minutes) and Tønder (112kr, 1½ hours);
and east to Kolding (101kr, 45 minutes) and
Aarhus (270kr, 2½ hours).

ℹ Getting Around

Torvet, the city square, can be found where
Skolegade and Torvegade intersect. The train
and bus stations are about 300m east of Torvet;
the **Fanø ferry terminal** (☑ 70 23 15 15; www.
faergen.com; Dockvej) is 1km southwest.

Most city buses can be boarded at the train station; it's 22kr for a local ticket (available from the driver).

City buses 11, 12 and 13 run to the harbour (for the ferry to Fanø).

Parking in the city centre is free but has a time limit (usually two or four hours) and a parking disc (*P-skive*) is required, to show time of arrival.

Rent bikes from **PJ Ferie** (☑ 75 45 62 33; www.pjferie.dk; Hjertingvej 21; bike rental per day/week 50/250kr; ☺ noon-5pm).

Fanø

POP 3200

The island of Fanø holds more charm than the larger, more-popular island of Rømø, further south. It may have something to do with the means of arrival (is it just us, or is a boat more romantic than a 10km-long causeway?). And this island backs it up with two traditional seafaring settlements full of idyllic thatch-roofed houses, blooming gardens, and cobblestone streets lined with boutiques and cafes.

Beach-goers are blessed with wide, welcoming strips of sand on the exposed west coast, and a lively summer-season atmosphere. All this, and it's just 12 minutes from Esbjerg – too easy.

◉ Sights & Activities

The main villages of **Nordby** and **Sønderho** lie at each end of the 16km-long island; ferries from Esbjerg arrive at Nordby. Sønderho in particular is one of Denmark's most charming villages. It dates from the 16th century and has more than a hint of Middle Earth to its jumble of thatched houses.

The tourist office (p107) can provide brochures and maps outlining on-foot exploration. The villages are home to a few low-key **museums** detailing Fanø's rich maritime history. Fanø's golden age peaked in the late 19th century, when it boasted the largest fleet outside Copenhagen; over a period of 150 years it was the site for the construction of more than 1000 vessels.

With time and interest, check out Nordby's maritime or history museum. Sønderho has an art museum and an original 19th-century sea-captain's house known as **Hannes Hus**.

If you're here on a day trip, it can be enjoyable to wander around Nordby to soak up the charm, then jump on the bus to Sønderho, or hire a bike, visit the beach, take a boat trip or see where the mood takes you – maybe to the local links **golf course** (www.fanoe-golf-links.dk), the oldest golf course in Denmark. Other options include horse riding and sea kayaking – ask at the tourist office.

🍽 Sleeping & Eating

Møllesti B&B　　　　　　　　　　GUESTHOUSE €
(☑ 75 16 29 49; www.mollesti.dk; Møllesti 3, Nordby; s/d without bathroom from 300/450kr; ☺ May-Aug; 🛜) This well-priced B&B is hidden away in the atmospheric lanes of Nordby. It's home to four simple, comfy guest rooms sharing two bathrooms and a kitchenette/lounge, in a restored sea-captain's house from 1892. Breakfast costs an additional 50kr; there's a two-night minimum stay.

★ Sønderho Kro　　　　　　　　　　INN €€€
(☑ 75 16 40 09; www.sonderhokro.dk; Kropladsen 11, Sønderho; s/d incl breakfast from 1300/1650kr; ☺ May-Oct, Fri & Sat Nov-Apr) The loveliest place to stay on the island (and renowned around the country) is this thatched-roof slice of *hyggelig* heaven. It dates from 1722, and its 13 individually decorated rooms feature local antiques. The inn has an acclaimed gourmet restaurant, which showcases local and seasonal specialities in a steeped-in-time dining room.

★ Rudbecks Ost & Deli　　　　　　CAFE €€
(☑ 24 93 85 05; www.rudbecks.dk; Hovedgaden 90, Nordby; mains 89-189kr; ☺ 10am-5.30pm Mon-Fri, to 4pm Sat) This fab family-run deli-cafe gives a great snapshot of island flavours: house-made bread, butter and ice cream, salmon smoked on Fanø, burgers made from local marsh-grazing lamb and beef. Grab picnic supplies (there's a great cheese cabinet) or linger over brunch, lunch or delicious cake.

Sønderho Kro　　　　　　　　　　DANISH €€€
(☑ 75 16 40 09; www.sonderhokro.dk; Kropladsen 11, Sønderho; lunch 149kr, 2-/3-/5-course dinner 439/539/650kr; ☺ noon-8.30pm Apr-Oct, by appointment Sat & Sun rest of year) Renowned throughout Denmark, delightful Sønderho Kro has an acclaimed gourmet restaurant, which showcases local and seasonal specialities in a steeped-in-time dining room. Bookings advised.

❶ Information

Tourist Office (☑ 70 26 42 00; www.visitfanoe.dk; Skolevej 5, Nordby; ☺ 10am-4pm Mon-Fri, 11am-3pm Sat & Sun Jul & Aug, 10am-4pm

Mon-Fri Sep-Jun) In Nordby, about 700m south of the ferry harbour (via Hovedgaden).

❶ Getting There & Away

If you're doing a day trip or overnight stay from Esbjerg, you're better off leaving your car on the mainland and hiring a bike or taking the bus once you reach the island.

FanøFærgen (☑ 70 23 15 15; www.fanoe faergen.dk; Langelinie, Nordby) shuttles car ferries between Esbjerg and Nordby one to three times hourly from 5am to 2am. Sailing time is 12 minutes. A return ticket for a foot passenger is 45/25kr per adult/child; bikes travel free. It costs 195/415kr in the low/high season to transport a car (return trip, including passengers).

❶ Getting Around

There's a local bus service (route 431) from the ferry dock that runs about once an hour, connecting Nordby with Fanø Bad (22kr), Rindby Strand (22kr) and Sønderho (32kr).

Bicycles can be hired from a number of places, including **Fri BikeShop** (☑ 75 16 24 60; Mellemgaden 12, Nordby; bike rental per day 100-145kr; ⊙ 10am-5.30pm Mon-Fri, to 2pm Sat & Sun). Taxis can be reached on ☑ 75 16 62 00.

Ribe

POP 8200

The crooked cobblestone streets of Ribe (*ree*-buh) date from the late 9th century, making it Denmark's oldest town. It's easily one of the country's loveliest spots at which to stop and soak up some history.

It's a delightfully compact chocolate-box confection of crooked half-timbered 16th-century houses, a sweetly meandering river and lush water meadows, all overseen by the nation's oldest cathedral. Such is the sense of living history that the entire 'old town' has been designated a preservation zone, with more than 100 buildings registered by the National Trust. Don't miss it.

◎ Sights

Historic Ribe   AREA

For a leisurely stroll that takes in some of Ribe's handsome half-timbered homes and idyllic cobbled lanes, head along any of the streets radiating out from Torvet (note that the **night-watchman walks** (departs Weis Stue, Torvet; ⊙ 8pm May-Oct, also 10pm Jun-Aug; ☉) **FREE** cover much of this ground).

To help you appreciate the surrounds, drop by the tourist office and pick up a copy of the free *Town Walk in Old Ribe* brochure; it's available in Danish, English, German, Dutch, Italian, Spanish and French.

On Puggårdsgade is a 16th-century man-or house, the charmingly skew-whiff **Taarnborg** (Puggårdsgade 3), where no corner is 90°. Next door at No 5 is a half-timbered house from 1550.

From Grønnegade, narrow alleys lead down and across pretty Fiskergade to Skibbroen and the picturesque riverfront.

★ Ribe VikingeCenter   MUSEUM

(☑ 75 41 16 11; www.ribevikingecenter.dk; Lustrupvej 4; adult/child 120/60kr; ⊙ 11am-5pm late Jun-late Aug, 10am-3.30pm Mon-Fri early May-late Jun & late Aug-mid-Oct; ☉) Embrace your inner Viking (ignore any pillaging tendencies, OK?) at this fun, hands-on, open-air museum. It re-creates a slice of life in Viking-era Ribe using various reconstructions, including a 34m longhouse. The staff, dressed in period clothing, bake bread over open fires, demonstrate archery and Viking-era crafts such as pottery and leatherwork, and offer falconry shows and 'warrior training' (for kids, using a sword and shield). You'll undoubtedly learn more about Viking life than you could from a textbook.

Ribe Kunstmuseum   MUSEUM

(☑ 75 42 03 62; www.ribekunstmuseum.dk; Sankt Nicolaj Gade 10; adult/child 75kr/free; ⊙ 11am-5pm Jul & Aug, to 4pm Tue-Sun Sep-Jun) An undeniable benefit of being the oldest town in the land is the opportunity to amass an impressive art collection. Ribe's beautifully restored art museum has been able to acquire some of Denmark's best works, including those by 19th-century 'Golden Age' painters.

Ribe Domkirke   CHURCH

(☑ 24 66 07 37; www.ribe-domkirke.dk; Torvet; tower adult/child 20/10kr; ⊙ 10am-5pm Mon-Sat, noon-5pm Sun May-Sep, shorter hours Oct-Apr) Dominating Ribe's skyline is the impressive Ribe Cathedral, which dates back to at least 948 (the earliest record of the existence of a bishop in Ribe) – making it the oldest in Denmark. The cathedral was largely rebuilt in 1150 when Ribe was at the heart of royal and government money, which paved the way for some fine architectural structures.

🛏 Sleeping

★ Danhostel Ribe   HOSTEL €

(☑ 75 42 06 20; www.danhostel-ribe.dk; Sankt Pedersgade 16; dm 240kr, s/d/q from 455/500/760kr;

LEGOLAND & LEGO HOUSE

Mind-blowing Lego models, fun rides and the happy-family magic associated with great theme parks have transformed **Legoland** ([☎] 75 33 13 33; www.legoland.dk; Nordmarksvej; adult/child 379/359kr; ⊙10am-8pm or 9pm Jul–mid-Aug, shorter hours Apr-Jun & mid-Aug–early Nov, closed early Nov-Mar; [P] [♿]) into Denmark's most visited tourist attraction outside of Copenhagen. It's a great day outing (you'll need a day to do it justice) and it sits smack-bang in the middle of Jutland, 1km north of Billund.

The heart of Legoland is **Miniland** – 20 million plastic Lego blocks snapped together to create miniature cities and replicate global icons (and re-create scenes from *Star Wars* movies).

You can't help but marvel at the brilliant Lilliputian models of the Kennedy Space Center, Amsterdam, Bergen or a Scottish castle and you'll no doubt vow to head home and drag your Lego out of storage to see what masterpiece you can create (surely it's not that hard?). In Miniland you can also do some advance sightseeing of Danish landmarks including Copenhagen's Nyhavn, Ribe, Skagen or various royal palaces. Or take a trip in miniboats past landmarks such as the Statue of Liberty, the Acropolis and an Egyptian temple. The reconstructions are on a scale of 1:20 to 1:40 and the attention to detail is incredible. The park's largest piece, a model of Indian chief Sitting Bull, was built with 1.4 million Lego bricks. (The smallest piece? A Miniland dove, built from four small white bricks.)

Pick up a map to assist with further exploration. The park is divided into themed areas, including **Legoredo Town**, a Wild West area that's home to a haunted house; **Knights' Kingdom**, where a medieval castle awaits; **Pirate Land**, which hosts ships, sword-play and a swimming area; **Adventure Land**, a strange hybrid of Indiana Jones meets Egypt; **Polar Land**, with a roller coaster and a penguin habitat; and **Duplo Land**, with plenty of safe, simple rides and activities for littlies.

For some downtime stop by **Atlantis**, an aquarium built around Lego models of divers and submersibles. For the chilled park-goer there are placid rides, from merry-go-rounds to a tranquil train ride; adrenaline junkies should seek out the roller coasters. Once the entrance fee is paid, all rides are free – the only exception is the **SEAT Driving School** (99kr), for kids aged seven to 13.

Note that the admission price is slightly cheaper if you buy your tickets in advance online. Family passes are also available online (two adults and two kids 1176kr).

Opened in 2017 in the heart of Billund, **Lego House** ([☎] 82 82 04 00; www.legohouse.com; Ole Kirks Plads 1; Experience Zones ticket 199kr; ⊙9.30am-8.30pm most days) is a hands-on 'experience centre' with a thoroughly brilliant design that resembles a stack of 21 gigantic Lego bricks. It is marketed as the 'Home of the Brick' and incorporates top-quality **museum** displays of the company's history, plus exhibition areas and rooftop terraces. The ground level (home to eateries and a Lego store) has free public access; access to the **Experience Zones** requires a prebooked ticket (allocated entry time).

The building is divided into four colour-coded Experience Zones that emphasise Lego's philosophy of learning through play – much planning has gone into these, and the technology is impressive (and super-fun). You can join 20-minute **Creative Labs** (facilitated by teachers) and build a stop-motion movie, for example. As you explore the zones, note the building's standout central feature: the **Tree of Creativity**, 15m high and built of 6.3 million Lego bricks.

The building was seven years in the making and is a design from Danish starchitect Bjarke Ingels. It offers a stellar year-round reason to visit Billund (even in winter, when **Legoland** is closed). Check times and buy tickets online.

[P] [@] [🛜]) [🍴] Knowledgeable staff, sparkling rooms (all with bathroom) and impressive facilities make this a top option for both backpackers and families. It rents bikes and is a stone's throw from Ribe's historic centre; equally impressive is its commitment to the environment, from the Good Origin coffee in its vending machines to its promotion of sustainable travel in the Wadden Sea region.

Ribo B&B GUESTHOUSE €
(www.ribobandb.dk; Giørtz Plads 3; s/d 475/550kr;
🕾) This B&B is one of a new breed of Danish 'self-service' sleeping options, where the guesthouse is unstaffed, you book online and a security code is given so you can access your room. It's impersonal, but the prices are often excellent – as they are at Ribo, a central, modern, three-room guesthouse, with spick-and-span facilities plus access to a kitchen. Breakfast is 75kr.

Hotel Dagmar HOTEL €€
(📞75 42 00 33; www.hoteldagmar.dk; Torvet; s/d incl breakfast from 1125/1325kr; @🕾) Classy, central Hotel Dagmar is Denmark's oldest hotel (1581) and exudes all the charm you'd expect. There's a golden hue to the hallways and rooms, with old-world decor alongside tiling, artworks and antiques. See the website for packages involving meals and accommodation.

✖ Eating & Drinking

★Kolvig DANISH €€
(📞75 41 04 88; www.kolvig.dk; Mellemdammen 13; lunch 88-189kr, dinner mains 230-250kr; ◷11am-midnight Mon-Sat) Kolvig's alfresco terrace overlooks the river, offering prime Ribe-watching. The menu is the most ambitious in town, showcasing local produce; most interesting is the delicious tapas plate of Wadden Sea flavours, including shrimp, ham, smoked lamb and local cheese. It makes for a good drinking spot, too; the kitchen closes at 9.30pm.

★Sælhunden DANISH €€
(📞75 42 09 46; www.saelhunden.dk; Skibbroen 13; lunch 69-169kr, dinner mains 129-289kr; ◷11am-10pm) This handsome old black-and-white inn is by the riverfront, with outdoor seating by the **Johanne Dan** (moored on Skibbroen) boat. *Sælhund* means seal, so it's no surprise there's quality seafood in traditional Danish guises, including lunchtime smørrebrød. Try the delicious house speciality *stjerneskud* (one fried and one steamed fillet of fish served on bread with prawns and dressing).

Ribe Bryghus BREWERY
(📞40 43 17 16; www.ribebryghus.dk; Skolegade 4B; ◷10am-2pm Sat) Look out for this label's locally brewed beers at restaurants and bars around town, or pop into the brewery (in the courtyard) during its limited opening hours. Note it's also 'open' whenever the brewers are inside working their hoppy magic.

Groups of eight or more can arrange a tour (per person 100kr).

ⓘ Information

Tourist Office (📞75 42 15 00; www.visitribe.dk; Torvet 3; ◷9am-6pm Mon-Fri, 10am-4pm Sat Jul & Aug, 9am-4pm Mon-Fri Sep-Jun plus 10am-1pm Sat Sep-Dec & Apr-Jun; 🕾) Has an abundance of information on the town and surrounding areas. There is an unstaffed brochure area open 9am to 10pm every day.

ⓘ Getting There & Away

Ribe is 32km south of Esbjerg via Rte 24 and 48km north of Tønder via Rte 11.

Trains from Ribe run hourly on weekdays and less frequently at weekends north to Esbjerg (60kr, 35 minutes), and south to Skærbæk for Rømø (31kr, 20 minutes) and Tønder (78kr, 50 minutes).

The best website for planning travel is www.rejseplanen.dk.

UNDERSTAND DENMARK

History

Humble Hunters to Mighty Vikings

First settled around 4000 BC, most probably by prehistoric hunter-gatherers from the south, Denmark has been at the centre of Scandinavian civilisation ever since, and there are plenty of reminders of that past in the shape of the ancient burial chambers that pepper the countryside and the traces of fortifications at, for example, Trelleborg.

The Danes themselves are thought to have migrated south from Sweden in around AD 500 but it was their descendants, who were initially a peaceful, farming people, who are better known today. What we think of as modern Denmark was an important trading centre within the Viking empire and the physical evidence of this part of Denmark's history is to be found throughout the country today. In the late 9th century, warriors led by the Viking chieftain, Hardegon, conquered the Jutland peninsula. The Danish monarchy, Europe's oldest, dates back to Hardegon's son, Gorm the Old, who reigned in the early 10th century. Gorm's son, Harald Bluetooth, completed the conquest of Denmark and spearheaded the conversion of the Danes to Christianity; his story and his legacy is well showcased in the tiny hamlet of Jelling. Successive Danish kings sent their subjects to row their longboats to England and conquer most of the Baltic region. They were accomplished fighters, sword-smiths, shipbuilders and sailors, qualities well illustrated at the excellent Viking Ship Museum (p67) in Roskilde.

Reformation & Renaissance

In 1397, Margrethe I of Denmark established a union between Denmark, Norway and Sweden to counter the influence of the powerful Hanseatic League that had come to dominate the region's trade. Sweden withdrew from the union in 1523 and over the next few hundred years Denmark and Sweden fought numerous border skirmishes and a few fully fledged wars, largely over control of the Baltic Sea. Norway remained under Danish rule until 1814.

In the 16th century, the Reformation swept through the country, accompanied by church burnings and civil warfare. The fighting ended in 1536, the Catholic Church was ousted and the Danish Lutheran Church headed by the monarchy was established.

Denmark's Golden Age was under Christian IV (1588–1648), with Renaissance cities, castles and fortresses flourishing throughout his kingdom. A superb example is Egeskov Slot (p81) on Funen. In 1625, Christian IV, hoping to neutralise Swedish expansion, entered an extremely ill-advised and protracted struggle known as the Thirty Years' War. The Swedes triumphed and won large chunks of Danish territory. Centuries' worth of Danish kings and queens are laid to rest in sarcophagi on dramatic display at Roskilde's cathedral.

The Modern Nation

Literature, the arts, philosophy and populist ideas flourished in the 1830s, and Europe's Year of Revolution in 1848 helped inspire a democratic movement in Denmark. Overnight, and in typically orderly Danish fashion, the country adopted male suffrage and a constitution on 5 June 1849, forcing King Frederik VII to relinquish most of his power and become Denmark's first constitutional monarch.

Denmark lost the Schleswig and Holstein regions to Germany in 1864. Denmark remained neutral throughout WWI and also declared its neutrality at the outbreak of WWII. Nevertheless, on 9 April 1940, the Germans invaded, albeit allowing the Danes a degree of autonomy. For three years the Danes managed to walk a thin line, running their own internal affairs under Nazi supervision, until in August 1943 when the Germans took outright control. The Danish Resistance movement mushroomed and 7000 Jewish Danes were smuggled into neutral Sweden.

Although Soviet forces heavily bombarded the island of Bornholm, the rest of Denmark emerged from WWII relatively unscathed. Postwar Social Democrat governments introduced a comprehensive social-welfare state in the postwar period, and still today Denmark provides its citizens with extensive cradle-to-grave social security.

Political Controversies

In 2004 the country's most eligible bachelor, Crown Prince Frederik, married Australian Mary Donaldson in a hugely popular and exhaustively covered story-book wedding. They now have four children.

It has not all been fairy tales, though. The growing political sway of the nationalist, right-wing Danish People's Party (DPP) in the late 1990s and early 2000s led Denmark to impose some of the toughest immigration laws in Europe in 2002. Its influence also contributed to Denmark's joining the USA, UK and other allies in the 2003 Iraq War, as well as to its commitment to maintain its role in Afghanistan.

In 2006, the country became the focus of violent demonstrations around the Middle East following the publication of a cartoon depicting the prophet Mohammed – a deep taboo for many Muslims but an issue of freedom of speech for liberal news editors – in the *Jyllands-Posten* newspaper.

Discontent over the country's stuttering economic performance influenced the election of a new, centre-left coalition in 2011, led by Social Democrat Helle Thorning-Schmidt. During the first year in office her government rolled back anti-immigration legislation enacted by the previous government, and passed a tax reform with support from the liberal-conservative opposition.

Thorning-Schmidt's one-term reign was ended when the pendulum swung again at the next general election in mid-2015. A minority government was formed under Lars Løkke Rasmussen, head of the Venstre party.

The government later formed a coalition with other conservative parties. The next general election is scheduled to be held by June 2019.

People

Denmark's 5.7 million people are a generally relaxed bunch. It takes a lot to shock a Dane, and even if you do, they probably won't show it. This was the first country in the world to legalise same-sex marriages, and it became (in)famous during the 1960s for its relaxed attitudes to pornography.

They are an outwardly serious people, yet with an ironic sense of humour. They have a strong sense of family and an admirable environmental sensitivity. Above all, they are the most egalitarian of people (they officially have the smallest gap between rich and poor in the world), proud of their social equality in which none have too much or too little.

The vast majority of Danes are members of the National Church of Denmark, an Evangelical Lutheran denomination (a proportion of each Dane's income tax goes directly to the church), though less than 5% of the population are regular churchgoers.

Arts

Literature

By far the most famous Danish author is Hans Christian Andersen. Other prominent Danish writers include religious philosopher Søren Kierkegaard, whose writings were a forerunner of existentialism, and Karen Blixen, who wrote under the name Isak Dinesen and penned *Out of Africa* and *Babette's Feast*, both made into acclaimed movies in the 1980s.

Another successful novel turned screenplay is Peter Høeg's 1992 world hit *Miss Smilla's Feeling for Snow*, a suspense mystery about a Danish Greenlandic woman living in Copenhagen. And while the hugely popular genre of Scandinavian crime fiction is dominated by authors from Sweden (Henning Mankell and Stieg Larsson) and Norway (Jo Nesbø), Denmark is not without its noteworthy contributors. Among them is Jussi Adler-Olsen, whose novel *The Message That Arrived in a Bottle* won the 2010 Glass Key award, an annual prize given to a Nordic crime novel. The prize was once again swagged by a Dane in 2012, this time by Erik Valeur for his debut work, *The Seventh Child*.

Architecture & Design

For a small country Denmark has had a massive global impact in the fields of architecture and design. Arne Jacobsen, Verner Panton, the late Jørn Utzon and Hans J Wegner are now considered among the foremost designers of the 20th century, and the tradition of great furniture and interior design remains strong in the country's design schools, museums and independent artisanal workshops.

In recent years, a new league of ecoconscious architectural firms has emerged on the world stage. Among them is Effekt, designers of Tallinn's striking new Estonian Academy of Arts building, and BIG (Bjarke Ingels Group), whose head-turning projects include the cascading VM Bjerget housing complex in Copenhagen's Ørestad district. Indeed, Copenhagen is Denmark's architectural and design powerhouse, with museums such as Desigmuseum Danmark and architectural show-stealers like the Opera House and Royal Library extension maintaining the country's enviable international reputation.

Film & TV

As with its design prowess, Denmark punches well above its weight in the realm of cinema and televison. The country has scored regular Oscar success with films such as *Babette's Feast* (1987), Gabriel Axel's adaptation of a Karen Blixen novel; Bille August's *Pelle the Conqueror* (1988); and Anders Thomas Jensen's short film *Valgaften* (1998). In 2011, Susanne Bier's family drama *In a Better World* (2010) won Best Foreign Film at both the Academy Awards and the Golden Globe Awards. In 2010, Mads Brügger's subversively comic documentary about North Korea, *The Red Chapel* (2009), swooped the World Cinema Documentary Jury Prize at the Sundance Film Festival. In 2017, Denmark's (unsuccessful) Academy nominee was the well-received *Land of Mine*, directed by Martin Zandvliet, exploring the animosity felt by Danes when, following WWII, young German POWs were forced to defuse thousands of landmines along the west coast of Jutland.

The most prolific and controversial of Denmark's 21st-century directors remains

Lars von Trier, whose best-known films to date include the award-winning *Breaking the Waves* (1996) and *Dancer in the Dark* (2000). Dubbed the *enfant terrible* of contemporary cinema, von Trier first scored international attention as a co-founder of the Dogme95, an artistic manifesto pledging a minimalist approach to film-making using only hand-held cameras, shooting in natural light and rejecting special effects and pre-recorded music.

Over the past 15 years, Denmark has also cemented its reputation for superlative TV drama. The most successful series to date include *The Killing* – featuring a Copenhagen police detective known for her astute crime solving abilities and love of Faroese knitwear – and *The Bridge*, which begins with the discovery of severed corpses on the Øresund Bridge. Police tape gives way to spin doctors in the acclaimed political drama *Borgen*, whose idealistic female protagonist is suddenly thrown into the position of Denmark's *statsminister* (prime minister).

Visual Arts

Before the 19th century, Danish art consisted mainly of formal portraiture, exemplified by the works of Jens Juel (1745–1802). A Golden Age ushered in the 19th century with such fine painters as Wilhelm Eckersberg (1783–1853) and major sculptors like Bertel Thorvaldsen (1770–1844), although he chose to spend most of his life in Rome.

Later in the century, the Skagen School evolved from the movement towards alfresco painting of scenes from working life, especially of fishing communities on the northern coasts of Jutland and Zealand. Much of it is exhibited at the Skagens Museum (p103). Leading exponents of the Skagen School were PS Krøyer and Michael and Anna Ancher. In the mid-20th century, a vigorous modernist school of Danish painting emerged, of which Asger Jorn (1914–73) was a leading exponent. Many of his works are on display at the art museum in Silkeborg (p95).

A number of contemporary Danish artists enjoy international acclaim, including conceptual artists Jeppe Hein, duo Elmgreen & Dragset, and Danish-Icelandic Olafur Eliasson. Eliasson's famously large-scale projects have included four temporary 'waterfalls' along New York's East River, as well as a whimsical multicoloured walkway atop the acclaimed ARoS gallery (p90) in Aarhus.

Like Aarhus, many Danish towns and cities contain a vibrant selection of home-grown and international contemporary art; even the smallest towns can surprise. One of the best small art museums and galleries outside the capital is **Faaborg's art museum** (www.faaborgmuseum.dk; Grønnegade 75; adult/student/child 80/50kr/free; ◷10am-4pm Jun-Aug, closed Mon Sep-May). Topping it all off is the magnificent Louisiana (p54), on the coast north of Copenhagen.

Environment

Wildlife

On the nature front, common critters include wild hare, deer and many species of birds, including eagles, magpies, coots, swans, and ducks. Stretching along Jutland's west coast from Ho Bugt to the German border (and including the popular island of Fanø), the Nationalpark Vadehadet (Wadden Sea National Park) provides food and rest for between 10 and 12 million migratory birds each spring and autumn. Among the feathered regulars are eiders, oystercatchers, mallards and widgeons, as well as brent geese and barnacle geese. The park, Denmark's largest and newest, is part of an ambitious plan to restore many of Denmark's wetlands and marshes, and to help endangered species such as the freshwater otter make a comeback.

Environmental Issues

While some Western governments continue to debate the veracity of climate-change science, Denmark gets on with (sustainable) business. Wind power generates around 30% of Denmark's energy supply, and the country is a market leader in wind-power technology, exporting many wind turbines.

The long-term goal for Danish energy policy is clear: the entire energy supply – electricity, heating, industry and transport – is to be covered by renewable energy by 2050. The city of Copenhagen has pledged to go carbon-neutral by 2025.

The cycling culture is another example of Denmark's green outlook. Copenhagen has around 430km of continuous, safe cycle paths, and 52% of all Copenhageners cycle to their place of work or education every day.

Food & Drink

Denmark has rebranded itself from 'dining dowager' to 'cutting-edge gastronome' in less than two decades. At the heart of the revolution is Copenhagen, home to 15 Michelin-starred restaurants. Restaurants like Kadeau (p70), **Kødbyens Fiskebar** (☑32 15 56 56; www.fiskebaren.dk; Flæsketorvet 100; mains 195-275kr; ⊙5.30pm-midnight Mon-Thu, 11.30am-2am Fri & Sat, 11.30am-midnight Sun; ☎; ☐10, 14, ⓈDybbølsbro) and **Pony** (☑33 22 10 00; www.ponykbh.dk; Vesterbrogade 135, Vesterbro; 2/3/4-course menu 325/425/485kr; ⊙5.30-10pm Tue-Sun; ☐6A) have helped redefine New Nordic cuisine by showcasing native produce and herbs, prepared using traditional techniques and contemporary experimentation, and focused on clean, natural flavours.

Staples & Specialties

Proud of it though they are, even the Danes would concede that their traditional cuisine is rather heavy and unhealthy. They eat a great deal of meat, mostly pork and usually accompanied by something starchy and a gravylike sauce. However, one Danish speciality has conquered the world: *smørrebrød*, the Danish open sandwich.

Meaty staples include *frikadeller* (fried minced-pork balls) and fiskefrikadeller (the fish version), *flæskesteg* (roast pork with crackling), *hvid labskovs* (beef-and-potato stew), *hakkebøf* (beefburger with fried onions) and the surprisingly tasty pariserbøf (rare beef patty topped with capers, raw egg yolk, beets, onions and horseradish).

It's not all turf, with coast-sourced classics including *sild* (herring), fresh *rejer* (shrimp)

NEW NORDIC CUISINE

Despite some claims of overexposure, Denmark's New Nordic cuisine continues to garner lots of media attention and praise from food critics, bloggers and general gluttons across the globe. It is evolving, too, which all good trends should do.

The movement stems from 2004, when Nordic chefs attending a food symposium in Copenhagen created a 10-point manifesto defining the cuisine's aims. According to the manifesto, New Nordic is defined by seasonality, sustainability, local ingredients and produce, and the use of Nordic cooking methods to create food that originally and distinctly reflects Scandinavian culture, geography and history.

The movement threw the spotlight on Denmark's fantastic raw ingredients, from excellent pork products, beef, game and seafood, to root vegetables, wild berries and herbs. It also serves as a showcase for rarer ingredients from the wider Nordic region, among them Greenlandic musk ox, horse mussels from the Faroe Islands, obscure berries from Finland, and truffles from the Swedish island of Gotland.

The world's most famous New Nordic restaurant was Noma, four times topping the list of the World's 50 Best Restaurants (2010–12 and again in 2014). In its heyday, owner-chef René Redzepi eschewed all nonindigenous produce in his creations, including olive oil and tomatoes. Redzepi is renowned for playing with modest, often-overlooked ingredients and consulting food historians, digging up long-lost traditions. Famously, he also forages in the wilderness for herbs and plants. At Noma, the ingredients were then skilfully prepared using traditional techniques (curing, smoking, pickling and preserving) alongside contemporary experiments that included, among other things, ants.

From 2014 to 2017, Noma took to the road and set up in new homes (in Tokyo, Sydney and Tulum in Mexico) for a short spell, embracing indigenous ingredients and methods in each location. At the end of 2016, Noma's Copenhagen restaurant closed. There are plans to reopen in a different format, in a different location in the capital – stay tuned.

In the meantime, a newer wave of Danish chefs (many of whom are Noma alumni) seem to be taking a less dogmatic approach, with their own seasonal, Nordic menus splashed with the odd foreign ingredient. Some are creating more casual restaurants, making New Nordic relatively affordable and more accessible.

A newer trend is super high-quality, contemporary 'non-Danish' food made with the same precision and design savvy that defines New Nordic. While some may argue that this compromises the very concept of New Nordic, others see it as the next step in the evolution of contemporary Danish cooking.

and hummer (lobster). The Danes are great fish smokers too; you'll find smokehouses (called *røgeri* in Danish) preserving herring, eel, cod livers, shrimp and other seafood all around the coast. The most renowned are on Bornholm.

Where to Eat

Beyond Copenhagen, Denmark's food scene can be less inspiring. Culinary clichés continue to plague too many menus, from nachos and burgers to inauthentic pasta, pizza and Thai. Yet things are slowly changing. Seasonality and local produce are informing an ever-growing number of kitchens. In Aarhus, New Nordic hot spots such as St Pauls Apothek (p92) have pushed the city onto the foodie radar. Beyond the big cities, destinations like Bornholm's Kadeau (p70) and Skagen's Ruths Gourmet (p104) fly the flag for quality and innovation. And then there are the country's traditional *kroer* (inns), many of which serve authentic Danish home cooking.

SURVIVAL GUIDE

❶ Directory A–Z

ACCOMMODATION

Camping & Cabins

➜ Denmark is very well set up for campers, with nearly 600 camping grounds, Some are open only in the summer months, while others operate from spring to autumn. About 200 stay open year-round (and have low-season rates).

➜ You need a camping card (called Camping Key Europe) for stays at all camping grounds. You can buy a card at the first camping ground you arrive at, at local tourist offices or from the Danish Camping Board (see www.danish-campsites.com). The cost for an annual pass for couples is 110kr; it covers all accompanied children aged under 18.

➜ The per-night charge to pitch a tent or park a caravan is typically around 80kr for an adult, and about half that for each child. In summer, some places also tack on a site charge of 50kr to 80kr per tent/caravan; some also have a small eco tax.

➜ Many camping grounds rent cabins (a few offer on-site caravans) sleeping four to six people. Cabins range from simple huts with bunk beds to full cottages with kitchen and bathroom. You generally BYO linen or pay to hire it. In the summer peak (late June to mid-August), many

cabins can only be hired by the week (around 3500kr, but it very much depends on the cabin's size and facilities).

➜ The Danish Nature Agency (http://eng.naturstyrelsen.dk) oversees some primitive camping areas and shelters in forested areas. See its website for more details and the rules on wild camping.

➜ Backpackers and cyclists, note: even if a camping ground is signposted as fully booked, there may be sites for light-travelling campers.

➜ If you're touring around, look for camping grounds offering 'QuickStop', a cheaper rate whereby you arrive after 8pm and leave again by 10am.

➜ Check www.smaapladser.dk for a list of 34 camping grounds that are smaller and more intimate, with a maximum of 145 camping pitches.

➜ Best online resources: www.danishcampsites.com and www.dk-camp.dk.

Farmstays

➜ A great way to get a feel for rural Denmark is on a farm stay, which can simply mean bed and breakfast accommodation or actually helping out with farm activities.

➜ The website of Landsforeningen for Landboturisme (www.visitfarmen.dk) links to 60 farms throughout Denmark that offer accommodation (from farmhouse rooms to family-sized self-contained flats and small rural houses). You book directly with the farm owner.

➜ Although it's best to plan in advance, if you're cycling or driving around Denmark you may well come across farmhouses displaying *værelse* (room) signs.

Homestay Bed & Breakfast

➜ There's a growing number of B&Bs – some are traditional homestay arrangements, where you stay in the hosts' house, but many more are private rooms in small guesthouses, where you may share a bathroom and kitchen with other guests, or have a studio-style apartment to yourself.

➜ A great example of this is in Ribe (www.visitribe.com), where about 30 locals rent out rooms and apartments in town and around, some of them in beautifully restored old houses.

➜ The number and quality of these places is on the increase. They're often cheaper than a private room at a hostel or budget hotel, at around

---

❶ SLEEPING PRICE RANGES

The following price ranges refer to a double room in high season. Unless otherwise noted, rooms have private bathrooms.

€ less than 700kr
€€ 700kr–1500kr
€€€ more than 1500kr

350/600kr for a single/double. The rate generally includes linen but excludes breakfast, which can often be purchased (around 70kr to 90kr).

➡ Staff at tourist offices maintain lists of B&B options in their area – check the local tourism websites for links.

➡ Many B&Bs that operate more like small guesthouses are bookable on the usual accommodation booking sites.

➡ Best online resource: www.bedandbreakfast guide.dk.

Hostels

➡ Some 68 hostels make up the **Danhostel association** (📞 33 31 36 12; www.danhostel.dk), which is affiliated with Hostelling International (HI). Some are dedicated hostels in holiday areas, while others are attached to sports centres (and hence may be busy with travelling sports teams, etc).

➡ If you hold a valid HI card, you receive a 10% discount on Danhostel rates (these can be purchased from hostels and cost 160kr for non-Danes). We list prices for noncardholders.

➡ Note that there are a growing number of private hostels not affiliated with the Danhostel association.

➡ Danish hostels appeal to all ages and are oriented as much towards families and groups as to budget travellers. Hiring a private room is the norm. Outside Copenhagen, only some hostels offer dorm beds in shared rooms (some may only offer these in the summer, from July to mid-September).

➡ Typical costs are 200kr to 300kr for a dorm bed. For private rooms, expect to pay 400kr to 600kr per single, 450kr to 750kr per double, and up to 100kr for each additional person in larger rooms. All hostels offer family rooms; many rooms come with private bathrooms.

➡ Duvets and pillows are provided, but you'll have to bring or hire your own sheets and towel (typically between 50kr and 80kr per stay).

➡ Almost all hostels provide an all-you-can-eat breakfast costing around 75kr, and some also provide dinner. Most hostels have guest kitchens with pots and pans.

➡ Advance reservations are advised, particularly in summer. In a few places, reception closes as early as 6pm. In most hostels the reception office is closed, and the phone not answered, between noon and 4pm.

➡ Between May and September, hostels can get crowded with children on school excursions, or sports groups travelling for tournaments.

➡ A number of Danish hostels close for part of the low season.

➡ A note on costs: if you need to hire linen, the price of a double room plus sheets and towels may become more expensive than a room at a budget hotel. Consider what you're after (kitchen access, for example, which hostels offer but hotels don't) and book accordingly.

Hotels

➡ A few brands tend to dominate in the hotel business. For budget hotels, look for CabInn (www.cabinn.dk), Zleep (www.zleephotels.com) and self-service BB Hotels (www.bbhotels. dk) across the country, and Wake Up (www. wakeupcopenhagen.com) in Copenhagen and Aarhus.

➡ Business-standard hotel chains include Scandic (www.scandichotels.com), Radisson (www. radisson.com), Comwell (www.comwell.dk) and First Hotels (www.firsthotels.com).

➡ There's a good range of boutique hotels in larger cities and popular upmarket destinations (Bornholm, for example, and Skagen), but true luxury or design hotels are not especially common outside Copenhagen and Aarhus. If you're looking for something more memorable than a chain hotel, consider staying in a castle, historic manor house or rural property. Also look out for a *badehotel* or *strandhotel* (an old seaside 'bathing inn') – many of these are now restored. Great resources for something a little special: www.guldsmedenhotels.com, www. slotte-herregaarde.dk and www.smalldanish hotels.com.

➡ Be careful: the inclusion of *kro* in a name usually implies a country inn, but it is also (less commonly) the Danish version of a motel, found along major motorways near the outskirts of town.

➡ Some hotels have set rates published on their websites; others have dynamic rates that fluctuate according to season and demand. Most hotel websites offer good deals and packages, as do the usual booking engines.

➡ Many business hotels offer cheaper rates on Friday and Saturday nights year-round, and during the summer peak (from late June until the start of the school year in early/mid-August), when business folk aren't travelling.

➡ There is no hard-and-fast rule about the inclusion of breakfast in prices – many hotels include it in their price, but for others it is optional. It is never included in the price of budget hotels (you can purchase it for around 75kr to 100kr). Hotel breakfasts are usually pretty decent all-you-can-eat buffets.

Other Accommodation

➡ Many seaside resort areas are filled with cottages and apartments. These are generally let out by the week and require reservations. Rates vary greatly, depending on the type of accommodation and the season, but generally they're cheaper than hotels.

➡ DanCenter (www.dancenter.com) handles holiday-cottage bookings nationwide. Many tourist offices can also help make reservations. Alternatively, try Novasol (www.novasol.dk), which organises self-catering options in cottages and summer houses.

➡ Hundreds of places (summer cottages, inner-city apartments, family-friendly houses) can be rented direct from the owner via the usual online booking engines.

ACTIVITIES

Denmark offers diverse activities, from island-hopping cycling adventures to Lake District canoeing. The sea, never far away, offers fishing, sailing and wind- and-kitesurfing, while hiking trails are abundant., and cycling opportunities are outstanding.

Cycling

Denmark is a superb country for cyclists, with over 12,000km of signposted cycle routes and relatively quiet country roads that wend through attractive, gently undulating landscapes.

As well as the Danes' use of cycling as a widespread means of commuting, you'll also see locals (and tourists) enjoying cycling holidays. The big draw for touring cyclists are the 11 national routes, which are in excellent condition, but there are oodles of regional and local routes to get you pedalling. The routes are well suited to recreational cyclists, including families with children.

Danish cyclists enjoy rights that, in most other countries, are reserved for motorists. There are bicycle lanes along major city roads and through central areas; road signs are posted for bicycle traffic, and bicycle racks can be found at grocery shops, museums, train stations and many other public places. Overall, cyclists and drivers coexist remarkably well.

When bicycle touring, accommodation is easy to find, be it at a small country inn or camping ground. One advantage of Denmark's small scale is that you're never far from a bed and a hot shower.

For quality rental bikes, Copenhagen and Aarhus are your best starting points, but you can generally rent bikes in every town – enquire locally. Note: you are not legally required to wear a helmet. Bikes are allowed on most trains, some buses and all ferries.

Canoeing & Kayaking

Canoeists and kayakers can paddle the extensive coastline and fjords or the rivers and lakes. White water is about the only thing that's missing in mountain-free Denmark.

The country's best canoeing and kayaking can be experienced along the rivers Gudenå (in Jutland) and Suså (in Zealand). The idyllic forests and gentle waterways of central Jutland's prized Lake District are perfect for cycling, rambling and, especially, canoeing – multiday canoeing-and-camping adventures are possible here. You can hire canoes and equipment in Silkeborg. The lakes are generally undemanding as far as water conditions go, although some previous experience is an advantage.

Canoeing the small coves, bays and peninsulas of several Danish fjords is also an option, including Limfjorden in northern Jutland and the fjords of Zealand: Roskilde Fjord, Holbæk Fjord and Isefjord.

Walking

There's not much wilderness in wee Denmark (especially in comparison to its larger, more mountain-endowed neighbours), and walking or hiking is not as widespread a phenomenon as cycling. But rambling is popular nonetheless, and all local tourist offices will be able to point you in the direction of a local area with walking trails.

In Jutland, there are some picturesque trails through the forested Rold Skov area, the Mols Bjerge and Thy National Parks, and the bucolic Lake District.

The 220km Øhavssti (Archipelago Trail) is a long-distance walking trail spanning Funen and the islands to its south. It snakes its way from west to east Funen along the southern coast, then traverses northern Langeland. It concludes with a delightful 36km stretch across Ærø's countryside.

An increasing number of hikers are heading to Møn to walk the well-organised network of trails known as Camønoen (www.camoenoen.dk), a pun on Spain's Camino de Santiago.

Shorter walks at or around scenic landmarks include the base of the chalk cliffs at Møns Klint; along the coast at Stevns Klint; to Grenen sand spit, Denmark's northernmost point; along Hammeren's heather-lined trails at the northern tip of Bornholm; and in the forests around 147m Himmelbjerget, one of Denmark's highest peaks.

GAY & LESBIAN TRAVELLERS

➡ Given Denmark's high degree of tolerance for alternative lifestyles of all sorts, it's hardly surprising that Denmark is a popular destination for gay and lesbian travellers.

➡ Copenhagen in particular has an active, open gay community with a healthy number of venues, but you'll find gay and lesbian venues in other cities as well (as well as mainstream venues that are welcoming to all).

➡ For general info, contact Landsforeningen for Bøsser, Lesbiske, Biseksuelle og Transpersoner

---

> ### ⓘ EATING PRICE RANGES
>
> The following price ranges refer to a standard main course.
>
> € less than 125kr
> €€ 125kr–250kr
> €€€ more than 250kr

(www.lgbt.dk), the Danish national association for the LGBTQ community.

→ A useful website for travellers with visitor information and listings is www.rainbow businessdenmark.dk. Also see www.oaonline.dk.

→ The main gay and lesbian festival of the year is **Copenhagen Pride** (www.copenhagenpride. dk), a week-long queer fest that takes place in August. There's also the LGBTQ film festival **Mix Copenhagen** (www.mixcopenhagen.dk), held each October.

INTERNET ACCESS

→ With the proliferation of wi-fi, and most locals and travellers carrying tablets and/or smart-phones, the old-fashioned internet cafe is a dying breed in Denmark. There may be a couple catering to gamers and laptop-less travellers in the major cities, but public libraries are your best bet in mid-sized and small towns for free use of computers with internet access.

→ Libraries also have free wi-fi (you will gener-ally need a code), as do many cafes and bars, and trains and buses. Wi-fi is ubiquitous in hotels and hostels and is usually free. Some hostels and hotels will offer a computer for guests to use, free or for a small charge.

MONEY

ATMs Major bank ATMs accept Visa, Master-Card and the Cirrus and Plus bank cards.

Cash If you're exchanging cash, there's a 30kr fee for a transaction. Post offices exchange foreign currency at rates comparable to those at banks.

Credit cards Visa and MasterCard are widely accepted in Denmark. American Express and Diners Club are occasionally accepted. A surcharge of up to 3.75% is imposed on foreign credit-card transactions in some restaurants, shops and hotels.

Tipping Restaurant bills and taxi fares include service charges in the quoted prices. Further tipping is not expected, although rounding up the bill is not uncommon when service has been particularly good.

OPENING HOURS

Opening hours vary throughout the year, espe-cially for sights and activities.

Banks 10am–4pm Monday to Friday

Bars & Clubs 4pm–midnight, to 2am or later Friday and Saturday (on weekends clubs may open until 5am)

Cafes 8am–5pm or midnight

Restaurants noon–10pm (maybe earlier on weekends for brunch)

Shops 10am–6pm Monday to Friday, to 4pm Saturday, some larger stores may open Sunday

Supermarkets 8am–9pm (many with in-store bakeries opening around 7am)

PUBLIC HOLIDAYS

Many Danes take their main work holiday during the first three weeks of July, but there are nu-merous other holidays as well.

Banks and most businesses close on public holidays and transport schedules are usually reduced.

New Year's Day (Nytårsdag) 1 January

Maundy Thursday (Skærtorsdag) Thursday before Easter

Good Friday (Langfredag) Friday before Easter

Easter Day (Påskedag) Sunday in March or April

Easter Monday (2. påskedag) Day after Easter

Great Prayer Day (Store Bededag) Fourth Friday after Easter

Ascension Day (Kristi Himmelfartsdag) Sixth Thursday after Easter

Whitsunday (Pinsedag) Seventh Sunday after Easter

Whitmonday (2. pinsedag) Seventh Monday after Easter

Constitution Day (Grundlovsdag) 5 June

Christmas Eve (Juleaften) 24 December (from noon)

Christmas Day (Juledag) 25 December

Boxing Day (2. juledag) 26 December

New Year's Eve (Nytårsaften) 31 December (from noon)

TELEPHONE

→ As of June 2017, the EU has ended roaming surcharges for people who travel periodically within the EU. EU residents can use mobile devices when travelling in the EU, paying the same prices as at home.

→ For non-EU folk, the cheapest and most practical way to make calls at local rates is to purchase a European SIM card and pop it into your own mobile phone (tip: bring an old phone from home for that purpose). Before leaving home, make sure that your phone isn't blocked from doing this by your home network.

→ If you're coming from outside Europe, also check that your phone will work in Europe's GSM 900/1800 network (US phones work on a different frequency).

→ You can buy a prepaid Danish SIM card at su-permarkets, kiosks and petrol stations through-out the country. Top-up credit is available from the same outlets.

→ The main Danish mobile service providers now work primarily with contract customers. For prepaid SIM-card packages, look for those from Lycamobile (www.lycamobile.dk) and Leb-ara (www.lebara.dk). Lycamobile is best – SIM cards can be obtained for free (see the website) and you can top up online.

Phone Codes

➡ All telephone numbers in Denmark have eight digits; there are no area codes. This means that all eight digits must be dialled, even when making calls in the same city.

➡ For local directory assistance dial ☎118. For overseas enquiries, including for rates and reverse charge (collect) calls, dial ☎113.

➡ The country code for Denmark is ☎45. To call Denmark from another country, dial the international access code for the country you're in followed by ☎45 and the local eight-digit number.

➡ The international access code in Denmark is ☎00. To make direct international calls from Denmark, dial ☎00 followed by the country code for the country you're calling, the area code, then the local number.

TIME

➡ Time in Denmark is one hour ahead of GMT/UTC, the same as in neighbouring European countries.

➡ During the northern hemisphere summer, Denmark is one hour ahead of London, six hours ahead of New York, and eight hours behind Sydney.

➡ Clocks are moved forward one hour for daylight saving time from the last Sunday in March to the last Sunday in October.

➡ Denmark uses the 24-hour clock system and all timetables and business hours are posted accordingly.

➡ *Klokken,* which means o'clock, is abbreviated as kl (kl 19.30 is 7.30pm).

➡ The Danes number their weeks and refer to them as such – eg schools break for winter holidays in week 7 or 8; many businesses are closed for summer holidays in weeks 29 and 30. It might be hard to wrap your head around – www.ugenr.dk can help.

TOURIST INFORMATION

Denmark is generally well served by helpful tourist offices and multilingual staff. Each town and region publishes a glossy annual brochure that covers most of the things travellers need to know, and has a website full of sights, accommodation options and practical info. Many now offer a downloadable app and have installed touchscreens around town (at train and bus stations, for example).

The trend in recent times is for information to be obtained online, with shorter staffed hours at tourist offices (though these offices may be open for self-service pick-up of brochures or use of a touchscreen). A few larger towns have done away with physical tourist offices.

Important websites for visitors to Denmark include www.denmark.dk and www.visitdenmark.

com. Other official websites covering local areas include the following:

Bornholm (www.bornholm.info)
Copenhagen (www.visitcopenhagen.com)
East Jutland (www.visitaarhus.com, www.visitdjursland.com)
Funen (www.visitfyn.com)
North Jutland (www.visitnordjylland.com, www.toppenafdanmark.com)
West Jutland (www.sydvestjylland.com, www.visitnordvestjylland.com)
Zealand (www.visitnorthsealand.com, www.cphcoastandcountryside.com)

TRAVELLERS WITH DISABILITIES

➡ Denmark is improving access to buildings, transport and even forestry areas and beaches all the time, although accessibility is still not ubiquitous.

➡ The official www.visitdenmark.com website has a few links for travellers with disabilities – see www.visitdenmark.com/a-z/6244.

➡ A useful resource is God Adgang (Good Access; www.godadgang.dk), which lists service providers who have had their facilities registered and labelled for accessibility.

VISAS

➡ No entry visa is needed by citizens of EU and Nordic countries.

➡ Citizens of the USA, Canada, Australia and New Zealand need a valid passport to enter Denmark, but they don't need a visa for tourist stays of less than 90 days.

➡ Citizens of many African, South American, Asian and former Soviet bloc countries do require a visa. The Danish Immigration Service publishes a list of countries whose citizens require a visa at its website at www.newtodenmark.dk.

➡ If you're in the country and have questions on visa extensions or visas in general, contact the Danish Immigration Service (see details on www.newtodenmark.dk).

🚹 Getting There & Away

AIR

➡ The majority of overseas flights into Denmark land at Copenhagen Airport (p61) in Kastrup, about 9km southeast of central Copenhagen.

➡ A number of international flights, mostly those coming from other Nordic countries or the UK, land at smaller regional airports, in Aarhus, Aalborg, Billund, Esbjerg and Sønderborg.

➡ Dozens of international airlines fly to/from Danish airports; the airport websites have up-to-date information on all the relevant carriers.

→ **SAS** (☏ 70 10 20 00; www.flysas.com) is the flag carrier of Denmark (and Norway and Sweden).

LAND

→ Technically, Denmark's only land crossing is with Germany, although the bridge over the Øresund from Sweden functions the same way.

→ Comprehensive tips on reaching Denmark from the UK or Europe without flying are online at www.seat61.com/denmark.

Bus

Copenhagen is well connected to the rest of Europe by daily (or near daily) buses. Major Jutland cities also have links south via Aalborg and Aarhus.

Eurolines has closed its operations in Denmark, and the new bus-network operator is **FlixBus** (☏ 32 72 93 86; www.flixbus.dk), which has services throughout Europe (limited services into Norway and Sweden, however). Destinations, timetables and prices are all online. FlixBus has dynamic pricing, so it pays to book ahead, and the routes may use stops that are not the main bus stations, so check your options.

Abildskou (☏ 32 72 93 86; www.abildskou.dk) links Aarhus and Berlin (one way from 219kr, nine hours, daily) with stops in Kolding and Vejle (Denmark), and Flensburg and Neumünster (Germany) en route. There is an option to connect to services to Hamburg. Its bookings are handled by FlixBus.

Car & Motorcycle

If you bring a vehicle that is registered in a non-EEC country to Denmark, you must take out a border insurance policy. These requirements are outlined on the website of the Danish Motor Insurers' Bureau (DFIM; www.dfim.dk).

Germany

→ The **E45 motorway** is the main road link with Germany, although there are several smaller crossings. The E45 runs from the German border north through Jutland to Frederikshavn.

→ Thanks to a bridge linking the Jutland peninsula to the island of Funen, and a toll bridge from Funen to Zealand, it's possible to drive all the way from mainland Europe to Copenhagen (and on to Sweden).

→ There are also car ferries to Danish islands from Germany.

Norway

Unless you fancy a road trip through southern Sweden to cross the Øresund Bridge, car ferries are still the most efficient way to arrive from Norway.

Sweden

The remarkable 16km **Øresundsbroen** (Øresund Bridge) joins Copenhagen with Malmö in Sweden, via the E20 motorway. It's actually a combination of a tunnel beneath the sea, an artificial island (Peberholm) and a suspension bridge catering for cars and trains.

The Øresund Bridge's toll station is situated on the Swedish side. The toll for a regular car/motorcycle is 410/210kr; campervans and cars towing a caravan pay 820kr. You can pay by cash (at the yellow staffed stations, using Danish or Swedish currency or the euro), credit/pay cards (automatic stations) or via a 'BroPas' transponder affixed to your windscreen (for regular commuters). Visit www.oresundsbron.com for more information.

You can also take a car ferry between Sweden and Denmark.

Train

DSB (Danske Statsbaner; ☏ 70 13 14 15; www.dsb.dk), the Danish national railway company, runs virtually all trains in Denmark and has a comprehensive website outlining timetables and fares.

Eurail and InterRail tickets are valid on the DSB.

Rail Passes

→ It may be hard to get your money's worth on a rail pass if you're travelling most of the time in tiny Denmark, although a pass may make sense if you plan on visiting other countries as well.

→ There's a dizzying variety of passes, depending on where you reside and where you're going to travel. Details about rail passes can be found at www.railpass.com or on websites for individual types of passes. And remember, if you buy a rail pass, read the small print.

→ Note: prices depend on age and class of travel. There are cheaper rates for youths (12 to 27 years) and seniors (over 60), and passes for families (adults with kids aged four to 11).

→ Supplements (eg for high-speed services, night trains, seat reservations) are not covered by passes.

SEA

Ferry connections are possible between Denmark and Norway, Sweden, Germany, Poland (via Sweden), Iceland and the Faroe Islands.

Fares on these routes vary wildly, by season and by day of the week. The highest prices tend to occur on summer weekends and the lowest on winter weekdays. Discounts are often available, including for return tickets, car and passengers, holders of rail passes or student cards, and seniors. Child fares are usually half the adult fares.

If travelling in peak times, in particular if you are transporting a car, you should always make reservations well in advance – this is doubly true in summer and on weekends. Taking a bicycle incurs a small fee.

Faroe Islands & Iceland

Smyril Line (www.smyrilline.com) Sails from the Northern Jutland port of Hirtshals to Tórshavn, the capital of the Faroe Islands (38 hours, once weekly year-round, twice weekly in summer peak), and from Hirtshals to Seyðisfjörður (Iceland) via Tórshavn (66 hours, once weekly).

Germany

BornholmerFærgen (www.bornholmerfaergen.dk) Sails from Rønne (on Bornholm) to Sassnitz (3½ to four hours) a handful of times weekly from April to October (daily in July and August).

Scandlines (www.scandlines.dk) Sails from Rødbyhavn (on Lolland) to Puttgarden (45 minutes, every half-hour) and from Gedser (on Falster) to Rostock (1¾ hours, up to 10 daily).

Sylt Ferry (www.syltferry.com) Sails from Havneby (on west-coast Rømø) to the German island of Sylt (40 minutes, up to nine daily).

Norway

Color Line (www.colorline.com) Sails from Hirtshals to Kristiansand (3¼ hours, once or twice daily) and Larvik (3¾ hours, once or twice daily).

DFDS Seaways (www.dfdsseaways.com) Copenhagen to Oslo (17 hours, daily).

Fjordline (www.fjordline.com) Offers a fast catamaran service from Hirtshals to Kristiansand (2¼ hours, two or three services daily mid-May to mid-September). Also sails year-round from Hirtshals to Bergen via Stavanger (Stavanger 10½ hours, Bergen 16½ hours, once daily), and to Langesund (4½ hours, once daily).

Stena Line (www.stenaline.dk) Frederikshavn to Oslo (nine hours, daily).

Poland

Polferries (www.polferries.com) connects Świnoujście with Ystad in southern Sweden (6½ hours, once or twice daily). From Ystad there is a free connecting shuttle-bus service to Copenhagen via the Øresund Bridge for foot passengers; those in cars receive a pass for passage across the bridge. From Ystad there are frequent ferries to Bornholm.

TT-Line (www.ttline.com) has a direct weekly ferry service in summer connecting Rønne (on Bornholm) and Świnoujście.

Sweden

BornholmerFærgen (www.bornholmerfaergen.dk) Rønne (Bornholm) to Ystad (80 minutes, up to nine times daily).

Scandlines (www.scandlines.dk) Helsingør to Helsingborg (20 minutes, up to four sailings an hour).

Stena Line (www.stenaline.com) Sails from Frederikshavn to Gothenburg (3½ hours, up to five times a day) and from Grenaa to Varberg (four to five hours, once or twice daily).

🛈 Getting Around

AIR

Denmark's small size and efficient train network mean that domestic air traffic is limited, usually to business travellers and people connecting from international flights through Copenhagen, from where there are frequent services to a few of the more distant corners of the country.

Internal flights are usually of no more than 30 minutes' duration. SAS (www.flysas.com) is the main domestic carrier and internal flights from Copenhagen include Aarhus, Aalborg and Billund.

Summer flights to Bornholm are popular; these are operated by Danish Airport Transport (DAT; www.dat.dk).

BICYCLE

➡ Denmark is the most cycle-friendly country in the EU and cyclists are well catered for with excellent cycling routes throughout the country.

➡ It's easy to travel with a bike anywhere in Denmark, even when you're not riding it, as bicycles can be taken on ferries and trains for a modest fee.

➡ You need to buy a ticket (cykelbillet) for your bike when travelling on regional and intercity trains (price varies with distance travelled, but is generally quite cheap; you may also need to reserve a place, called the cykelpladsbillet). It's free to take a bike on the S-tog, Copenhagen's suburban train network. You need a bike ticket to ride the metro in the capital, and bikes are not permitted on the metro during weekday peak hours.

BOAT

Boats link virtually all of Denmark's populated islands. These range from large, high-speed car ferries sailing several times daily year-round between Aarhus and Odden in north Zealand, to small summertime boats ferrying day trippers to minor islands in the South Funen Archipelago.

A number of islands can only be reached by ferry; expect there to be a year-round service.

> ### 🛈 THE ESSENTIAL TRANSPORT WEBSITE
>
> For travelling around Denmark, the essential website is www.rejseplanen.dk.
>
> This excellent resource allows you to enter your start and end point, date and preferred time of travel, and will then give you the best travel option, which may involve walking or taking a bus, train or ferry. Bus routes are linked, travel times are given and fares listed. You can't travel without it! Download the app for easy mobile access.

Popular routes include Køge–Bornholm, Svend-borg–Ærø, Frederikshavn–Læsø and Esbjerg–Fanø, but this list is far from exhaustive. It's a good idea to book car passage in advance at any time of year (but especially in summer).

BUS

→ Long-distance buses run a distant second to trains. Still, some cross-country bus routes work out to about 25% cheaper than trains.

→ Check out services from bus lines Abildskou (p120) and **Thinggaard Express** (⟋ 98 11 66 00; www.expressbus.dk), and search online at www.rejseplanen.dk for regional and long-distance bus options (including journey length and price comparisons). Abildskou works with the FlixBus (p120) network and now has dynamic pricing, so you can snare some good deals if you book ahead or travel at quieter times.

→ Daily express buses include Abildskou's route 888 between Copenhagen and Aarhus (from 149kr, 3½ to 4½ hours) and Copenhagen and Aalborg (from 209kr, 5½ to 6½ hours), stopping at a number of Jutland towns en route.

→ Copenhagen to Jutland buses generally drive through Funen, stopping in Odense, but some buses use the ferry service from Odden in northwest Zealand to Aarhus.

CAR & MOTORCYCLE

→ Denmark is an excellent destination for a driving holiday. Roads are high quality and usually well signposted. Except during rush hour, traffic is quite light, even in major cities.

→ One thing to be aware of is the large number of cyclists – they often have the right of way. It is particularly important that you check cycle lanes before turning right.

→ Access to and from Danish motorways is straightforward: roads leading out of town centres are named after the main city that they lead to (eg the road heading out of Odense to Faaborg is called Faaborgvej).

→ Petrol stations, with toilets, baby-changing facilities and minimarkets, are at 50km intervals on motorways. They also generally sell hot dogs and sandwiches.

→ Denmark's extensive ferry network carries vehicles at reasonable rates. Fares for cars average three times the passenger fare. It's wise to make ferry reservations in advance, even if it's only a couple of hours ahead of time. On weekends and holidays, ferries on prime crossings can be completely booked.

Car Hire

→ Rental cars are relatively expensive in Denmark, but a little research can mean big savings. Walk-in rates start at about 600kr per day for a small car, although naturally the per-day rates drop the longer you rent.

→ You may get the best deal on a car rental by booking with an international rental agency before you arrive. Be sure to ask about promotional rates, prepay schemes etc. Ensure you get a deal covering unlimited kilometres.

→ Avis, Budget, Europcar and Hertz are among the largest operators in Denmark, with offices in major cities, airports and other ports of entry. There are very few local budget operators. If you'll be using a rental car for a while, you might consider hiring your car in cheaper Germany and either returning it there afterwards, or negotiating a slightly more expensive one-way deal.

→ Rental companies' weekend rates, when available, offer real savings. For about 1000kr, you can hire a small car from Friday to Monday, including VAT and insurance. These deals may have restrictions on the amount of kilometres included (often around 300km) – request a plan that includes unlimited kilometres if you'll need it.

Road Rules

→ Drive on the right-hand side of the road.

→ Cars and motorcycles must have dipped headlights on at all times.

→ Drivers are required to carry a warning triangle in case of breakdown.

→ Seat belt use is mandatory. Children under 135cm must be secured with approved child restraint appropriate to the child's age, size and weight.

→ Motorcycle riders (but not cyclists) must wear helmets.

→ Speed limits: 50km/h in towns and built-up areas, 80km/h on major roads, up to 130km/h on motorways. Maximum speed for vehicles with trailers: 80km/h. Speeding fines can be severe.

→ Using a hand-held mobile phone while driving is illegal; hands-free use is permitted.

→ It's illegal to drive with a blood-alcohol concentration of 0.05% or more.

→ Motorways have emergency telephones at 2km intervals, indicated by arrows on marker posts. From other telephones, dial 112 for emergencies.

TRAIN

Denmark has a reliable train system with reasonable fares and frequent services. The network extends to most corners of the country, with the exception of the southern islands and a pocket of northwestern Jutland. In these areas, a network of local buses connects towns (and there are frequent services to the nearest train station).

Most long-distance trains on major routes operate at least hourly throughout the day. DSB (p120) runs virtually all trains in Denmark. Types of DSB trains include the following:

InterCity (IC) Modern comforts.

InterCityLyn (ICL) On certain well-travelled routes. Same facilities as InterCity, but with fewer stops.

Regionaltog Regional trains; reservations generally not accepted.

S-tog The combined urban and suburban rail network of Greater Copenhagen.

Fares & Discounts

Standard train fares work out to be a fraction over 1kr per kilometre, with the highest fare possible between any two points in Denmark topping out at around 500kr (Copenhagen to Skagen, a road distance of 525km).

➺ The reservation fee for a seat *(pladsbillet)* is 30kr. It's recommended on IC and ICL services to guarantee your seat.

➺ Note that the '*Stillezone*' on trains is a quiet zone.

➺ Bikes can be taken on many trains, but you need to buy a ticket *(cykelbillet)* for them on intercity and regional trains (price varies with distance travelled, but is generally quite cheap). From May to August bike space must be booked in advance for IC and ICL trains *(cykelpladsbillet)*. It's free to take a bike on the S-tog.

➺ A DSB 1 (1st-class ticket) generally costs about 50% more than the standard fare. DSB 1 tickets give an automatic seat guarantee on IC or ICL services.

Discounts include the following:

Children (under 12) Travel free if they are with an adult travelling on a standard ticket (each adult can take two children free).

Children (aged under 15) Pay half the adult fare.

Group '*Minigruppe*' offers 20% discount for groups of three to seven people travelling on the same ticket (minimum two adults); there are also '*gruppebillet*' rebates for eight or more adults travelling together (contact DSB to access these).

Orange *Orange-billetter* are discounted tickets (as low as 99kr for lengthy IC and ICL journeys – Copenhagen to Aarhus, for example) – although the number of tickets available at that price is limited. To find the cheapest fares, buy your ticket well in advance (up to two months before your travel date), travel outside peak hours and travel Monday to Thursday or on a Saturday.

Youth (aged 16 to 25) Can buy a DSB Ung Kort (youth card) valid for one year for 125kr; it allows discounts that vary from 20% to 50%.

Finland

Best Places to Eat

➡ Grön (p134)

➡ Smakbyn (p153)

➡ Café Fäboda (p163),

➡ Smor (p145)

➡ Ravintola Hugo (p181)

Best Places to Stay

➡ Hotel Katajanokka (p132)

➡ Kylmäpihlajan Majakka (p161)

➡ Kestikievari Herranniemi (p176)

➡ Levi Panorama (p190)

➡ Dream Hostel (p155)

Why Go?

There's something pure in the Finnish air; it's an invitation to get out and active year-round. A post-sauna dip in an ice hole under the majesticaurora borealis (northern lights), after whooshing across the snow behind a team of huskies, isn't a typical winter's day just anywhere. And hiking or canoeing under the midnight sun through pine forests populated by wolves and bears isn't your typical tanning-oil summer either.

Although socially and economically in the vanguard of nations, large parts of Finland remain gloriously remote; trendsetting modern Helsinki is counterbalanced by vast forested wildernesses elsewhere.

Nordic peace in lakeside cottages, summer sunshine on convivial beer terraces, avant-garde design, dark melodic music and cafes warm with aromas of home-baking are other facets of Suomi (Finnish) seduction. As are the independent, loyal, warm and welcoming Finns, who tend to do their own thing and are much the better for it.

When to Go
Helsinki

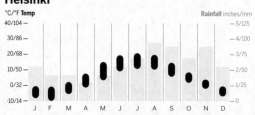

Mar–Apr There's still plenty of snow, but enough daylight to enjoy winter sports.

Jul Everlasting daylight, countless festivals and discounted accommodation.

Sep The stunning colours of the *ruska* (autumn) season make this prime hiking time up north.

Finland Highlights

1 Immersing yourself in **Helsinki's** (p128) harbourside creative melting pot for the latest in Finnish design and nightlife.

2 Marvelling at the shimmering lakescapes of **Savonlinna** (p165) and seeing top-quality opera in its medieval castle.

3 Cruising Lakeland waterways, gorge on tiny fish, and sweat it out in the huge smoke sauna at **Kuopio** (p170).

4 Crossing the Arctic Circle, hit the awesome Arktikum museum, and visit Santa in his official grotto at **Rovaniemi** (p183).

5 Learning about Sami culture and husky-sledding, and meeting reindeer in **Inari** (p196).

6 Cycling the picturesque islands of the **Åland Archipelago** (p148).

7 Checking out the quirky museums in **Tampere** (p154) .

8 Taking an unusual pub crawl around the offbeat watering holes of **Turku** (p142).

9 Crunching out a shipping lane aboard an ice-breaker and spending a night in the ethereal Snow Castle in **Kemi** (p188) .

HELSINKI

🔊 09 / POP 629,512

It's fitting that harbourside Helsinki, capital of a country with such watery geography, melds so graciously into the Baltic. Half the city seems liquid, and the writhings of the complex coastline include any number of bays, inlets and islands.

Though Helsinki can seem a younger sibling to other Scandinavian capitals, it's the one that went to art school, scorns pop music and works in a cutting-edge studio. The design scene here is legendary, whether you're browsing showroom brands or taking the backstreet hipster trail. The city's gourmet side is also flourishing, with new gastro eateries offering locally sourced tasting menus popping up at dizzying speed.

Nevertheless, much of what is lovable in Helsinki is older. Its understated yet glorious art-nouveau buildings, the spacious elegance of its centenarian cafes, dozens of museums carefully preserving Finnish heritage, restaurants that have changed neither menu nor furnishings since the 1930s: all part of the city's quirky charm.

History

Helsinki (Swedish: Helsingfors) was founded in 1550 by the Swedish king Gustav Vasa, who hoped to compete with the Hanseatic trading port of Tallinn across the water. In the 18th century the Swedes built a mammoth fortress on the nearby island of Suomenlinna, but it wasn't enough to keep the Russians out.

Once the Russians were in control of Finland, they needed a capital closer to home than the Swedish-influenced west coast. Helsinki was it, and took Turku's mantle in 1812. Helsinki grew rapidly, with German architect CL Engel responsible for many noble central buildings. In the bitter postwar years, the 1952 Olympic Games symbolised the city's gradual revival.

⊙ Sights

Helsinki has more than 50 museums and galleries, including many special-interest museums that will appeal to enthusiasts. For a full list, check the tourist office website (www.visithelsinki.fi) or pick up its free *Museums* booklet.

★**Ateneum**   GALLERY
(www.ateneum.fi; Kaivokatu 2; adult/child €15/free; ⊙10am-6pm Tue & Fri, to 8pm Wed & Thu, to 5pm Sat & Sun) Occupying a palatial 1887 neo-Rennaissance building, Finland's premier art gallery offers a crash course in the nation's art.

It houses Finnish paintings and sculptures from the 'golden age' of the late 19th century through to the 1950s, including works by Albert Edelfelt, Hugo Simberg, Helene Schjerfbeck, the von Wright brothers and Pekka Halonen. Pride of place goes to the prolific Akseli Gallen-Kallela's triptych from the Finnish national epic, the *Kalevala*, depicting Väinämöinen's pursuit of the maiden Aino.

★**Kiasma**   GALLERY
(www.kiasma.fi; Mannerheiminaukio 2; adult/child €14/free, 1st Sun of month free; ⊙10am-5pm Tue & Sun, to 8.30pm Wed-Fri, to 6pm Sat) Now one in a series of elegant contemporary buildings in this part of town, curvaceous and quirky metallic Kiasma, designed by Steven Holl and finished in 1998, is a symbol of the city's modernisation. It exhibits an eclectic collection of Finnish and international contemporary art, including digital art, and has excellent facilities for kids.

Its outstanding success is that it's been embraced by the people of Helsinki, with a theatre and a hugely popular glass-sided cafe and terrace.

★**Kajsaniemi**   GARDENS
(Botanic Gardens; www.luomus.fi; Kaisaniemenranta 2; gardens free, greenhouses adult/child €9/4.50; ⊙gardens 9am-8pm, greenhouses 10am-5pm Mon-Wed, Fri & Sat, to 6pm Thu, to 4pm Sun) Rambling over 4 hectares in the city centre alongside the north harbour, Töölönlahti, Helsinki's botanic gardens are filled with plants from Finland and other countries on the same latitude, with some 3600 species all up.

The gardens' 10 interconnected greenhouses shelter 800 species from all latitudes, and are a wonderfully warm refuge for visitors in the chillier months.

★**Kansallismuseo**   MUSEUM
(National Museum of Finland; www.kansallismuseo.fi; Mannerheimintie 34; adult/child €10/free, 4-6pm Fri free; ⊙11am-6pm Tue-Sun) Built in National Romantic art-nouveau style and

HELSINKI IN...

One Day

If you're arriving by rail, Helsinki's central **train station** gives you an immediate feel for the city's stunning National Romantic art-nouveau architecture. From here it's just footsteps to **Kiasma** to catch modern and contemporary Finnish and international art in striking contemporary surrounds. More art is on display at the nearby **Ateneum**, Helsinki's – and Finland's – premier showcase for the country's 'golden age' from the late 19th century through to the 1950s.

Grab some lunch at the **Karl Fazer Café** (p133), a Helsinki institution.

After lunch, stroll through the city's central strip of green, **Esplanadin Puisto** (p135), and visit central Finnish design shops such as new emporium **Tre** (p136). Continue your stroll through the city's beautiful botanic gardens, **Kajsaniemi**, and its 10 interlinked greenhouses.

When it's time for some food, experience the swish bistro dining on the upper level of **Strindberg** (☑ 09-6128-6900; www.strindberg.fi; Pohjoisesplanadi 33; mains €21-31.50; ⏰ 11am-10pm Mon-Sat).

Book ahead so at the end of the day you can take in a concert at the **Musiikkitalo** (p136), which hosts everything from classical to jazz, rock and pop. Even if you don't catch a performance, its bar is a great place for a nightcap.

Two Days

Get an early start to beat the crowds at Helsinki's Lutheran cathedral, **Tuomiokirkko** (p129), a masterpiece from architect CL Engel, then head to another resplendent church, the Finnish Orthodox **Uspenskin Katedraali**, built as a Russian Orthodox cathedral and still topped by its distinctive gold onion domes.

Make reservations ahead for the Michelin-starred modern Finnish cuisine at **Olo** (p134).

After lunch, make your way to the **kauppatori** (p131) and board a local ferry bound for **Suomenlinna** (p129), the 'fortress of Finland', set over a series of islands in Helsinki's archipelago. Spend the afternoon exploring its fortifications, bunkers and numerous museums. Highlights here include scrambling through the *Vesikko*, the only WWII-era submarine remaining in Finland.

Enjoy a dinner of game platters and house-brewed beers at **Suomenlinnan Panimo** (p134).

Return by ferry to the kauppatori, and finsih up by taking in a dazzling panorama of Helsinki aboard the **Sky Wheel** (p130).

opened in 1916, Finland's premier historical museum looks a bit like a Gothic church with its heavy stonework and tall square tower.

A major overhaul is under way until 2019, but the museum will remain open throughout. Completed sections include an exceptional prehistory exhibition and the Realm, covering the 13th to the 19th century. Also here is a fantastic hands-on area for kids, Workshop Vintti.

Uspenskin Katedraali CHURCH
(Uspenski Cathedral; www.hos.fi/uspenskin-katedraali; Kanavakatu 1; ⏰ 9.30am-4pm Tue-Fri, 10am-3pm Sat, noon-3pm Sun) **FREE** The eye-catching red-brick Uspenski Cathedral towers above Katajanokka island. Built as a Russian Orthodox church in 1868, it features classic golden onion domes and now serves the Finnish Orthodox congregation. The high, square interior has a lavish iconostasis with the Evangelists flanking panels depicting the Last Supper and the Ascension.

FINLAND HELSINKI

Helsinki

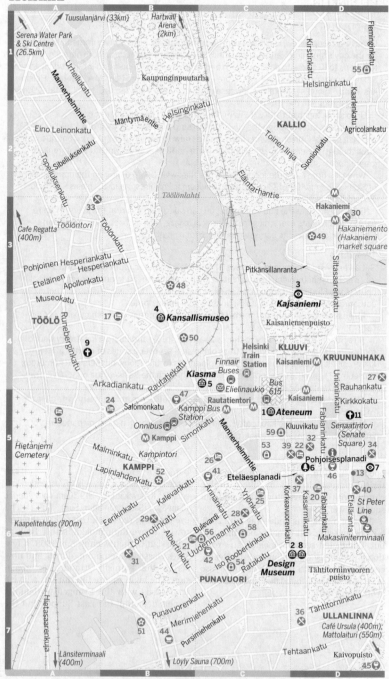

Tuomiokirkko
CHURCH

(Lutheran Cathedral; www.helsinginseurakunnat.fi; Unioninkatu 29; ⊙9am-midnight Jun-Aug, to 6pm Sep-May) FREE One of CL Engel's finest creations, the chalk-white neoclassical Lutheran cathedral presides over Senaatintori. Created to serve as a reminder of God's supremacy, its high flight of stairs is now a popular meeting place. Zinc statues of the 12 Apostles guard the city from the roof of the church. The spartan, almost mausoleum-like interior has little ornamentation under the lofty dome apart from an altar painting and three stern statues of Reformation heroes Luther, Melanchthon and Mikael Agricola.

Temppeliaukion Kirkko
CHURCH

(☎09-2340-6320; www.helsinginseurakunnat.fi; Lutherinkatu 3; adult/child €3/free; ⊙9.30am-5.30pm Mon-Thu & Sat, to 8pm Fri, noon-5pm Sun Jun-Aug, shorter hours Sep-May) Hewn into solid stone, the Temppeliaukio church, designed by Timo and Tuomo Suomalainen in 1969, feels close to a Finnish ideal of spirituality in nature – you could be in a rocky glade were it not for the stunning 24m-diameter roof covered in 22km of copper stripping. Its acoustics are exceptional; regular concerts take place here. Opening times vary depending on events, so phone or search for its Facebook page updates. There are fewer groups midweek.

★Design Museum
MUSEUM

(www.designmuseum.fi; Korkeavuorenkatu 23; adult/child €12/free; ⊙11am-6pm Jun-Aug, 11am-8pm Tue, to 6pm Wed-Sun Sep-May) An unmissable stop for Finnish design aficionados, Helsinki's Design Museum has a permanent collection that looks at the roots of Finnish design in the nation's traditions and nature. Changing exhibitions focus on contemporary design – everything from clothing to household furniture. From June to August, 30-minute tours in English take place at 2pm on Saturday and are included in admission. Combination tickets with the nearby Museum of Finnish Architecture (Arkkitehtuurimuseo; ☎045-7731-0474; www.mfa.fi; Kasarmikatu 24; adult/child €10/free, combination ticket with Design Museum €15/free; ⊙11am-6pm Tue & Thu-Sun, to 8pm Wed) are a great-value way to see the two museums.

★Suomenlinna
FORTRESS

(Sveaborg; www.suomenlinna.fi) Suomenlinna, the 'fortress of Finland', straddles a cluster of car-free islands connected by bridges. The Unesco World Heritage site was originally built by the Swedes as Sveaborg in the mid-18th

Helsinki

century. Several museums, former bunkers and fortress walls, as well as Finland's only remaining WWII submarine, are fascinating to explore; its **tourist office** (☏029-533-8420; ⊙10am-6pm May-Sep, to 4pm Oct-Apr) has info. Cafes and picnic spots are plentiful.

Ferries (www.hsl.fi; one-way/return €3.20/5, 15 minutes, four hourly, fewer in winter) depart from the passenger quay at Helsinki's kauppatori (p131).

🏃 Activities

★**Sky Wheel**　　　　　　　　FERRIS WHEEL
(www.skywheel.fi; Katajanokanlaituri 2; adult/child €12/9; ⊙10am-9pm Mon-Fri, to 10pm Sat, 11am-7pm Sun May-Oct, shorter hours Nov-Apr) Rising above the harbour, this Ferris wheel offers a fantastic panorama over central Helsinki from a height of up to 40m during the 10-minute 'flight'. A truly unique experience is the **SkySauna gondola**, allowing you to sauna and sightsee simultaneously: one hour (up to four people €240 to €320) includes towels, drinks and use of a ground-level Jacuzzi and lounge.

★**Kotiharjun Sauna**　　　　　　SAUNA
(www.kotiharjunsauna.fi; Harjutorinkatu 1; adult/child €13/7; ⊙2-9.30pm Tue-Sun) Helsinki's only original traditional public wood-fired sauna dates back to 1928. It's a classic experience, where you can also get a scrub down and massage (from €30). There are separate saunas for men and women; bring your own towel or rent one (€3). It's a 150m stroll southwest of the Sörnäinen metro station.

★ **Löyly Sauna** SAUNA

(📞 09-6128-6550; www.loylyhelsinki.fi; Hernesaarenranta 4; per 2hr incl towel €19; ⊙ 4-10pm Mon, 1-10pm Tue, Wed & Sun, 7.30-9.30am & 1-10pm Thu, 1-11pm Fri, 7.30-9.30am & 1-11pm Sat) 🍴 Built from striking natural timbers in 2016, with a pine exterior made from 4000 custom-cut planks and a Scandinavian birch interior, Löyly is entirely powered by water and wind. Its two electric saunas and traditional smoke sauna offer direct access to the Hernesaari waterfront (and winter ice hole). All saunas are mixed and swimsuits are required (swimsuit rental €6).

🧭 Tours

Trams (p139) are a great way to tour Helsinki on a budget. Three key routes – trams 2, 4 and 6 – pass through areas of interest. Accompanying guides to the sights can be downloaded from the tourist office website.

If you're short on time, standard hop-on hop-off bus tours are a handy way to see the sights; tickets are sold through Strömma (p138), based at the tourist office. It also sells tickets for cruises, or just head to the quay at the kauppatori to pick one up. Plenty of companies offer 1½-hour sightseeing cruises and there are dinner cruises, bus-boat combinations and sunset cruises. A visit to the zoo (www.korkeasaari.fi; Mustikkamaanpolku 12, Korkeasaari; adult/child €16/8; ⊙ 10am-8pm May-Aug, 10am-4pm Oct-Mar, 10am-6pm Sep & Apr) or Suomenlinna (p129) is a good way to combine a scenic boat ride with other sightseeing. The steamer **JL Runeberg** (📞 019-524-3331; www.msjlruneberg.com; Kauppatori; one way/return €29/39, bicycle €5; ⊙ Tue, Wed, Fri & Sat mid-May–early Sep, plus Sun Jun-Aug & Mon Jul) runs longer trips to the charming Finnish town of Porvoo.

Walking and cycling tours are operated by **Happy Guide Helsinki** (📞 044-502-0066; www.happyguidehelsinki.com; walking/bike tours from €20/55), with themes from berry picking or sunset sauna bike tours, to food or craft-beer walking tours. **Helsinki Cityride** (📞 044-955-8720; www.helsinkicityride.com; tours €45-95) also runs walking, Nordic walking and cycling tours.

For close-up archipelago views, **Natura Viva** (📞 010-292-4030; www.naturaviva.fi; Harbonkatu 13, Vuosaari; 4½-hr tour €69, kayak hire per 2hr/day €22/40; ⊙ May-Sep) runs brilliant summer kayaking tours.

🎊 Festivals & Events

Helsinki Beer Festival FOOD & DRINK

(www.helsinkibeerfestival.fi; ⊙ early Apr) Finnish and guest international beers and ciders, along with DJs and bands, pull in the punters to this rollicking festival held at the Kaapelitehdas (Cable Factory; www.kaapelitehdas.fi; Tallberginkatu 1, Ruoholahti; ⊙ hours vary) over two days. There are also food pairings, barbecues, brewing workshops, pouring workshops and various other events.

Helsinki Coffee Festival FOOD & DRINK

(⊙ late Apr) Helsinki's love of coffee is celebrated during the three-day Helsinki Coffee Festival at the Kaapelitehdas, with roasting demonstrations, tastings, exhibitions, competitions and workshops on themes such as different brewing methods and cooking with coffee.

Helsinki Päivä CULTURAL

(Helsinki Day; www.helsinkipaiva.fi; ⊙ 11-12 Jun) Celebrating the city's anniversary on 12 June, Helsinki Päivä (Helsinki Day) brings many free events to the city, with food stalls, concerts, theatre and dance performances, art exhibitions, workshops, cinema screenings, sports events and wellness activities.

Juhannus CULTURAL

(Midsummer; ⊙ weekend closest to 22 Jun) Juhannus is the most important annual event for Finns, celebrating the longest day of the year. The Seurasaaren Ulkomuseo (Seurasaari Open-Air Museum; www.kansallismuseo.fi/en/seurasaari-openairmuseum; Seurasaari; adult/child €9/3; ⊙ 11am-5pm Jun-Aug, 9am-3pm Mon-Fri, 11am-5pm Sat & Sun mid-late May & early–mid-Sep) on the island of Seurasaari sees the best celebration around Helsinki, with bonfires, midsummer poles and traditional activities.

Helsinki Design Week ART

(www.helsinkidesignweek.com; ⊙ mid-Sep) Spanning 10 days (rather than a week), the Nordic countries' largest design festival has 250-plus events, including workshops, talks, exhibitions, pop-up shops, product launches and parties citywide.

🛏 Sleeping

Helsinki is dominated by chain hotels, particularly Sokos and Scandic, but there are some boutique and designer gems too. Budget accommodation is in short supply.

From mid-May to mid-August bookings are strongly advisable, although July is a quieter time for business and high-end hotels.

Apartment rentals range from one-room studios to multiroom properties that are ideal for families. Often you'll get use of a sauna, parking area and other facilities.

Eurohostel HOSTEL €
(☑09-622-0470; www.eurohostel.eu; Linnankatu 9; dm/s/d/tr from €29/39/46/60; @🖘) Close to the Viking Line ferry on Katajanokka, this busy hostel is easily reached on trams 4 and 5. All rooms share bathrooms. 'Eurohostel' rooms are more modern with TVs and parquet floors. Dorm rates mean sharing a twin – a good deal. Rates include a morning sauna; the cafe-bar serves breakfast (€10) and other meals. HI discount.

Hostel Suomenlinna HOSTEL €
(☑09-684-7471; www.hostelhelsinki.fi; Suomenlinna C9; dm/s/d/tr from €25/56/72/100; ⊘reception 8am-3.30pm Mon-Sat, to noon Sun; @🖘) An excellent alternative to staying in central Helsinki is near the ferry pier on Suomenlinna. Once a Russian primary school then a barracks, the red-brick building's dorms occupy bright, high-ceilinged classrooms, while cosy private rooms upstairs have sloping ceilings. There's a kitchen (and supermarket nearby) and laundry. Outside reception hours, use your booking's keycode to gain access. HI discount.

Hostel Domus Academica HOSTEL €
(☑09-1311-4334; www.hostelacademica.fi; Hietaniemenkatu 14; dm/s/d/tr from €31/58/85/109; ⊘Jun-Aug; P@🖙🖘) Finnish students live well, so take advantage of this summer residence: a clean, busy, environmentally sound spot with a pool and sauna. Its 326 modern en-suite rooms come with kitchenettes (crockery is in the common room) and Finnish textiles. Dorms sleep up to three. Breakfast costs €8.50. HI discount. Rates include a morning sauna.

★Hotel Katajanokka HOTEL €€
(☑09-686-450; www.hotelkatajanokka.fi; Merikasarminkatu 1A; d/f/ste fromm €108/130/185; P🖙@🖘) Set in a spectacularly refurbished 1888-built prison, which was in use until 2002, this fabulous hotel on Katajanokka island offers character in spades. Rooms stretch over two to three former cells, so they're anything but cramped, and have sleek dark-tiled bathrooms. There's a 24-hour gym,

a sauna, a good restaurant and an indoor and outdoor bar. Tram 4 stops right outside.

★Hotelli Helka HOTEL €€
(☑09-613-580; www.hotelhelka.com; Pohjoinen Rautatiekatu 23; s/d/ste from €158/173/248; P🖘) One of Helsinki's best midrange hotels, the Helka has friendly staff and excellent facilities, including parking if you can bag one of the 28 spots. Best are the rooms, with Alvar Aalto–designed furniture, iceblock bedside lights and a backlit print of a rural Suomi scene over the bed. Saunas are situated on the top floor, adjoining the rooftop terrace.

★Hotelli Krapi HOTEL €€
(☑09-274-841; www.krapi.fi; Rantatie 2, Tuusula; s/d from €99/138; P🖘) Belying its name, this historic red wooden estate, 2km north of Tuusula at Tuusulanjärvi, shelters an excellent independent hotel in a former cowshed with countrified rooms, two restaurants, a traditional smoke sauna, summer theatre, golf course, Finnish cookery classes (five hours €145; English available) and resident ghost. Various activity packages are available; rates are cheapest in summer and on weekends.

Hellsten Helsinki Parliament APARTMENT €€
(☑09-5110-5700; www.hellstenhotels.fi; Museokatu 18; apt €132-197; ⊘reception 7am-10pm Mon-Fri; @🖘) A step up in style and comfort from many hotels, the apartments here have sleek modern furnishings and kitchenettes. It's in a peaceful, leafy local neighbourhood setting. There are another two apartment buildings at separate locations: one in Katajanokka (☑09-5110-5243; Kauppiaankatu 5; ⊘s/d/f from €112/122/162; P🖘) and one at Espoo. You will receive a keycode if you arrive outside reception hours. Discounts are available for longer stays.

Hotel Indigo BOUTIQUE HOTEL €€
(☑020-048-105; www.ihg.com; Bulevardi 26; d/ste from €149/207; P🖙@🖘) Helsinki's first branch of branded boutique chain Hotel Indigo opened in the Design District in 2016. Local artists designed and painted unique murals that splash colour across all 120 rooms. Suites have tubs with spa jets. Free bikes are available for guests; there's also a free on-site gym. Bröd, its restaurant, serves Nordic cuisine. Breakfast costs €15.

Sokos Hotel Torni HOTEL €€€
(📞 020-123-4604; www.sokoshotels.fi; Yrjönka-tu 26; d/ste from €199/339; ❄@🛜) In 1931 this building became Finland's tallest, and although it's now been surpassed, it still offers excellent views, especially from its **Ateljee Bar** (www.raflaamo.fi; ☉ 2pm-1am Mon-Thu, to 2am Fri, noon-2am Sat, 2pm-midnight Sun; 🛜). Today some rooms have been stylishly renovated in keeping with the historic feel in art-nouveau and art-deco styles, while other rooms are modern in rich red and black decor. Organic breakfasts include gluten-free options.

⭐ **Klaus K** DESIGN HOTEL €€€
(📞 020-770-4700; www.klauskhotel.com; Bulevardi 2; d/ste from €193/657; ❄@🛜) Independent design hotel Klaus K has a theme of Finnish national epic *Kalevala* quotes throughout, and space-conscious architecture. Contemporary 'Sky Loft' rooms offer access to the roof terrace; some also come with balconies. The highlight is the fabulous all-organic breakfast spread (€25) with superfood juice shots and dishes sourced from small Finnish producers (gluten-free options available). Service is superb.

⭐ **Hotel Kämp** HOTEL €€€
(📞 09-576-111; www.hotelkamp.com; Pohjois-esplanadi 29; d/ste from €272/593; P❄@🛜) A Helsinki emblem, this grand, stylish hotel is where the likes of Sibelius and Gallen-Kallela thrashed out their ideas. Its romantic marble lobby seduces you through to historic rooms furnished with antiques and then surprises in the marble bathrooms with trademark rubber ducks. Facilities include a plush day spa, saunas, an all-day brasserie serving sumptuous afternoon teas and two bars.

⭐ **Hotel F6** BOUTIQUE HOTEL €€€
(📞 09-6899-9666; www.hotelf6.fi; Fabianinkatu 6; s/d from €145/165; ❄🛜) 🥗 Stunningly designed, this 2016 hotel ranges around an internal courtyard (some rooms have direct access and patios); superior rooms come with French balconies. All 66 rooms are spacious (even the smallest are 27 sq metres) and stylishly furnished with cushion-strewn sofas. The courtyard's herb garden supplies the bar (serving great cocktails). Breakfast is organic, and wind and water powers all electricity.

✖ Eating

Helsinki has an extensive range of restaurants, whether for Finnish classics, modern Suomi cuisine or international dishes. Cafes offer some of the cheapest lunchtime options and there are plenty of self-catering opportunities, including large seven-day supermarkets and, better yet, Helsinki's produce-laden outdoor markets in summer and wonderful market halls year-round.

⭐ **Cafe Regatta** CAFE €
(www.caferegatta.fi; Merikannontie 10; dishes €1.50-5; ☉ 8am-10.30pm) In a marvellous waterside location, this historic rust-red wooden cottage is scarcely bigger than a sauna, but has great outdoor seating on the bay. You can hire a canoe or paddleboards alongside, buy sausages and grill them over the open fire, or just kick back with a drink or *korvapuusti* (cinnamon scroll). Expect to queue on sunny weekends. Cash only.

Karl Fazer Café CAFE €
(www.fazer.fi; Kluuvikatu 3; dishes €4-12; ☉ 7.30am-10pm Mon-Fri, 9am-10pm Sat, 10am-6pm Sun; 🛜🥗♿) Founded in 1891 and fronted by a striking art-deco facade, this cavernous cafe is the flagship for Fazer's chocolate empire. The glass cupola reflects sound, so locals say it's a bad place to gossip. It's ideal, however, for buying dazzling confectionery, fresh bread, salmon or shrimp sandwiches, or digging into towering sundaes or spectacular cakes. Gluten-free dishes are available.

⭐ **Vanha Kauppahalli** MARKET €
(www.vanhakauppahalli.fi; Eteläranta 1; ☉ 8am-6pm Mon-Sat, plus 10am-5pm Sun Jun-Aug; 🥗) 🌱 Alongside the harbour, this is Helsinki's iconic market hall. Built in 1888 it's still a traditional Finnish market, with wooden stalls selling local flavours such as liquorice, Finnish cheeses, smoked salmon and herring, berries, forest mushrooms and herbs. Its centrepiece is its superb cafe, **Story** (www.restaurantstory.fi; Vanha Kauppahalli, Eteläranta; snacks €3.20-10; ☉ kitchen 8am-3pm Mon-Fri, to 5pm Sat, bar to 6pm Mon-Sat; 🥗) 🌱. Look out too for soups from Soppakeittiö.

Soppakeittiö SOUP €
(www.sopakeittio.fi; Vanha Kauppahalli; soups €9-10; ☉ 11am-5pm Mon-Sat; 🥗) A great place to warm the cockles in winter, this soup stall inside the Vanha Kauppahalli is renowned for its bouillabaisse, which is almost always on

the menu. Other options might include cauliflower and goat's cheese, smoked reindeer or potato and parsnip. There are also branches at the Hietalahden Kauppahalli (www.hietalahdenkauppahalli.fi; Lönnrotinkatu 34; ⊙8am-6pm Mon-Thu, to 10pm Fri & Sat, 10am-4pm Sun; ♠) ♪ in Kamppi, and Hakaniemen Kauppahalli (www.hakaniemenkauppahalli.fi; Hämeentie 1; ⊙8am-6pm Mon-Fri, to 4pm Sat; ♠) ♪ in Kallio.

★Grön   BISTRO €€
(☑050-328-9181; www.restaurantgron.com; Albertinkatu 36; mains €23-26, 4-course menu €49; ⊙5-10pm Tue-Sat; ♠♠) ♪ Seasonal, often foraged ingredients are used in this exceptional bistro's plant, fish or meat starters and mains, and wild, plant or dairy desserts. Stunning plates might include pike-perch with charred leek parsley emulsion, nasturtium flowers, hazelnuts and burbot roe, followed by beef with sorrel and burnt-butter Béarnaise, and rose-oil-seasoned strawberries with strawberry granita, caramelised strawberry milk and rose petals.

★Suomenlinnan Panimo   FINNISH €€
(☑020-742-5307; www.panimoravintola.fi; Suomenlinna C1; mains €15-30; ⊙noon-10pm Mon-Sat, to 6pm Sun Jun-Aug, shorter hours Sep-May) By the main quay, this microbrewery is the best place to drink or dine on Suomenlinna. It brews three ciders and seven different beers, including a hefty porter, plus several seasonal varieties, and offers good food to accompany it, such as pike-perch with mustard tar sauce, or a game platter with bear salami, smoked reindeer and wild pheasant rillettes.

★Kuu   FINNISH €€
(☑09-2709-0973; www.ravintolakuu.fi; Töölönkatu 27; mains €19-30, 2-/3-course lunch menus €24/28, 4-course dinner menus €47-51; ⊙11.30am-midnight Mon-Fri, 2pm-midnight Sat, 4-11pm Sun) Traditional Finnish fare is given a sharp, contemporary twist at Kuu, which creates dishes from local ingredients such as smoked reindeer heart with pickled forest mushrooms, poached pike-perch with Lappish fingerling potatoes, and liquorice ice cream with cloudberry soup. Wines aren't cheap, but there are some interesting choices. Its casual bistro sibling, KuuKuu, is located 800m south.

Savu   FINNISH €€
(☑09-7425-5574; www.ravintolasavu.fi; Tervasaari; mains €20-26, 3-course menus €41-54; ⊙noon-11pm Mon-Sat, 1-6pm Sun late May-Aug, 6-11pm Tue-Sat Sep) Dating from 1805, a rust-red wooden warehouse that once stored tar on Tervasaari (Tar Island; Tervasaarenkannas) now contains this delightful beam-ceilinged summer restaurant, which reflects its heritage in unique creations such as pine-tar-infused ice cream. Pine tar, birch and alder are all used to smoke meat, fish and vegetables at its smokery. Leafy trees and umbrellas shade the terrace.

Saslik   RUSSIAN €€
(☑09-7425-5500; www.ravintolasaslik.fi; Neitsytpolku 12; mains €24-37, 3-course menus €49-65; ⊙6-11pm Mon-Fri, noon-11pm Sat Sep-Jul, 6-11pm Tue-Sat Aug) Screened by tasselled curtains, Saslik's succession of aristocratic dining rooms have stained-glass windows, gilt-framed paintings of Russian hunting scenes and flowing tablecloths. *Borscht* (sour beetroot soup), lamb *pelmeni* (dumplings made from unleavened dough), blini with aubergine and black caviar, and potted-bear stroganoff are among its specialities, along with desserts such as baked Alaska. Traditional Russian musicians often perform.

★Olo   FINNISH €€€
(☑010-320-6250; www.olo-ravintola.fi; Pohjoisesplanadi 5; 4-course lunch menu €53, dinner tasting menus short/long from €79/109, with paired wines €173/255; ⊙6-11pm Tue-Sat Jun–mid-Aug, 11.30am-3pm & 6-11pm Tue-Fri, 6-11pm Sat mid-Aug–May) At the forefront of new Suomi cuisine, Michelin-starred Olo occupies a handsome 19th-century harbourside mansion. Its memorable degustation menus incorporate both the forage ethos and molecular gastronomy, and feature culinary jewels such as fennel-smoked salmon, herring with fermented cucumber, Åland lamb with blackcurrant leaves, juniper-marinated reindeer carpaccio, and Arctic crab with root celery. Book a few weeks ahead.

★Savoy   FINNISH €€€
(☑09-6128-5300;   www.ravintolasavoy.fi; Eteläesplanadi 14; mains €37-44, 3-course lunch menu €63; ⊙11.30am-3pm & 6pm-midnight Mon-Fri, 6pm-midnight Sat) Designed by Alvar and Aino Aalto in 1937, this is one of Helsinki's grandest dining rooms, with birch walls and ceilings and some of the city's finest views. The food is a modern Nordic tour de force, with the 'forage' ethos strewing flowers and berries across plates that bear the finest Finnish game, fish and meat.

Ask   GASTRONOMY €€€
(☑040-581-8100; www.restaurantask.com; Vironkatu 8; 4-course lunch menu €49, tasting menu €98, with paired wines €178; ☺6pm-midnight Wed & Thu, 11.30am-1pm & 6pm-midnight Fri & Sat) Small organic or biodynamic Finnish farms and foraged game, fish, forest mushrooms, herbs and berries provide the ingredients for Michelin-starred Ask's superb-value lunch menus and 16- to 20-course evening tasting menus. Delicious, exquisitely presented morsels might feature buckwheat and nettle, reindeer and hazelnut, pike-perch and tar butter, beetroot and wild duck or burbot and spruce. Book several weeks ahead.

★**Saaristo**   FINNISH €€€
(☑09-7425-5590; www.ravintolasaaristo.fi; Luoto; mains €21-42, crayfish parties per person €67; ☺by reservation 5-11pm Mon-Fri May-Sep) Most renowned of Helsinki's island restaurants is the Saaristo, set in a spire-crowned art-nouveau villa on Luoto (Swedish: Klippan), and famous for society weddings, refined Finnish cuisine and summer crayfish parties. It's reached by private boat from the pier south of the Olympia Terminaali (p138) ferry terminal; the fare of €6 per person return is automatically added to your bill.

🍷 Drinking & Nightlife

Diverse drinking and nightlife in Helsinki ranges from cosy bars to specialist craft-beer and cocktail venues, and clubs with live music and DJs. In summer early-opening beer terraces sprout all over town. Some club nights have a minimum age of 20 or older; check event details on websites before you arrive.

★**Kaffa Roastery**   COFFEE
(www.kaffaroastery.fi; Pursimiehenkatu 29A; ☺7.45am-6pm Mon-Fri, 10am-5pm Sat; 🐾) Processing up to 4000kg of beans every week, this vast coffee roastery supplies cafes throughout Helsinki, Finland and beyond. You can watch the roasting in progress through the glass viewing windows while sipping Aeropress, syphon or V60 brews in its polished concrete surrounds. It also stocks a range of coffee grinders, espresso machines and gadgets.

★**Birri**   MICROBREWERY
(Il Birrificio; http://ilbirri.fi; Fredrikinkatu 22; ☺11am-11pm Mon-Thu, to 1am Fri & Sat, to 4pm Sun) Birri brews three of its own beers on-site at any one time, stocks a fantastic range of Finnish-only craft beers and also hand-crafts its own seasonally changing sausages. The space is strikingly done out with Arctic-white metro tiles, brown-and-white chequerboard floor tiles, exposed timber beams and gleaming silver kegs.

★**Holiday**   BAR
(http://holiday-bar.fi; Kanavaranta 7; ☺4-11pm Tue-Thu, to 2am Fri, noon-2am Sat; 🐾) Even on the greyest Helsinki day, this colourful waterfront bar transports you to more tropical climes with vibrant rainforest wallpapers and plants such as palms, tropical-themed cocktails such as frozen margaritas and mojitos (plus two dozen different gins) and a seafood menu that includes softshell crab. A small market is often set up out the front in summer, along with ping-pong tables.

★**Steam Hellsinki**   COCKTAIL BAR
(www.steamhellsinki.fi; Olavinkatu 1; ☺4pm-4am Mon-Sat; 🐾) A wonderland of steampunk design – with futuristic-meets-19th-century industrial steam-powered machinery decor, including a giant Zeppelin floating above the gondola-shaped bar, mechanical cogs and pulleys, globes, lanterns, radios, candelabras, Chesterfield sofas and a Zoltar fortune-telling machine – this extraordinary bar has dozens of varieties of gin and DJs spinning electro-swing. Ask about gin-appreciation and cocktail-making courses in English.

★**A21**   COCKTAIL BAR
(www.a21.fi; Annankatu 21; ☺5pm-midnight Tue & Wed, to 1am Thu, to 2am Fri & Sat) At the cutting edge of Helsinki's cocktail scene, this constantly evolving bar revives classic cocktails from past eras, adapts international trends (such as boilermakers, blending craft beers with paired spirits) and crafts new concoctions using Nordic ingredients in cocktails such as Suomen Neito, made with foraged Finnish berries.

Kappeli   BAR
(www.kappeli.fi; Eteläesplanadi 1; ☺10am-midnight; 🐾) Dating from 1867, this grand bar-cafe opens to an outdoor terrace seating 350 people and has regular jazz, blues and folk music in the nearby bandstand in Esplanadin Puisto (Esplanadi Park) from May to August. Locals and visitors alike flock here on a sunny day.

Mattolaituri
BAR

(☑ 045-119-6631; Ehrenströmintie 3A, Kaivopuisto; ⊙ 9am-midnight May-Sep) In **Kaivopuisto** (Puistokatu) park, this summer beach bar overlooking the sand and glittering sea is an idyllic spot to lounge in a deck chair or umbrella-shaded sofa with a coffee, glass of wine or a cocktail. Live music plays most nights from 6pm from June to August. Michelin-starred restaurant **Demo** (☑ 09-2289-0840; www.restaurantdemo.fi; Uudenmaankatu 9; 4-/5-/6-/7-course menus €62/75/92/102, with paired wines €110/138/170/185; ⊙ 4-11pm Tue-Sat) sets up an outdoor kitchen here from June to mid-August.

Kaivohuone
BAR, CLUB

(☑ 020-775-9825; www.kaivohuone.fi; Iso Puistotie 1, Kaivopuisto; ⊙ bar noon-midnight May-Aug, club 10pm-4am Wed, Fri & Sat May-Aug; 🛜) Built in 1838 as a spa in the Kaivopuisto park, this pavilion was later remodelled in art deco style and has been fabulously restored with dazzling multicoloured chandeliers, and opens on to a vast terrace. Food is served until 4pm. DJs pack the club three nights weekly in summer. Minimum age is 20 on Wednesday and Friday, and 24 on Saturday.

☆ Entertainment

Catching live music – from metal to opera – is a highlight of visiting Helsinki. The latest events are publicised in the free *Helsinki This Week* (http://helsinkithisweek.com). Tickets for big events can be purchased from Ticketmaster (www.ticketmaster.fi), Lippupiste (www.lippu.fi), LiveNation (www.livenation.fi) and Tiketti (www.tiketti.fi), which also has a booking office in Kamppi.

★ Musiikkitalo
CONCERT VENUE

(Helsinki Music Centre; ☑ 020-707-0400; www.musiikkitalo.fi; Mannerheimintie 13; tickets free-€30) Home to the Helsinki Philharmonic Orchestra, Finnish Radio Symphony Orchestra and Sibelius Academy, the glass- and copper-fronted Helsinki Music Centre, opened in 2011, hosts a diverse program of classical, jazz, folk, pop and rock. The 1704-capacity main auditorium, visible from the foyer, has stunning acoustics. Five smaller halls seat 140 to 400. Buy tickets at the door or from www.ticketmaster.fi.

Finlandia Talo
CONCERT VENUE

(☑ 09-40241; www.finlandiatalo.fi; Mannerheimintie 13) Designed by Alvar Aalto, this 1971 concert hall in angular white marble is one of Helsinki's landmark buildings. It received its congress wing in 1975 and was expanded in 2011. Alongside a varying program of music, it also mounts art exhibitions. Book tickets through www.lippu.fi. Hour-long guided tours (€15/10 per adult/child) take place in English; check the calendar online.

Orion Theatre
CINEMA

(☑ 029-533-8000; www.kavi.fi; Eerikinkatu 15; adult/child €6.50/3; ⊙ screenings Tue-Sun) Opened in 1927, this gorgeous art-deco cinema with chequerboard tiles has 216 plush red seats. It shows classics from the Finnish Film Archive through to new art-house releases, either in English or with English subtitles.

Juttutupa
LIVE MUSIC

(☑ 020-742-4240; www.juttutupa.fi; Säästöpankinranta 6; ⊙ bar 10.30am-midnight Mon & Tue, to 1am Wed & Thu, to 3am Fri, 11am-3am Sat, noon-11pm Sun) A block from Hakaniemi metro station, in an enormous granite building, Juttutupa is one of Helsinki's better bars for live music, focusing on contemporary jazz and rock fusion. All gigs are free. There's a great beer terrace and an on-site sauna.

Nosturi
LIVE MUSIC

(www.elmu.fi; Telakkakatu 8) This atmospheric harbourside warehouse, with a capacity of 900, hosts regular concerts with known Finnish and international performers. Acts range from folk to hip-hop to metal. Book tickets on its website or at www.lippu.fi.

🔒 Shopping

Helsinki is a design epicentre, from fashion to furniture and homewares. Its hub is the Design District Helsinki (https://designdistrict.fi), spread out between chic Esplanadi to the east, retro-hipster Punavuori to the south and Kamppi to the west. Hundreds of shops, studios and galleries are mapped on its website; you can also pick up a map at the tourist office.

★ Tre
DESIGN

(www.worldoftre.com; Mikonkatu 6; ⊙ 11am-7pm Mon-Fri, to 6pm Sat) If you only have time to visit one design store in Helsinki, this 2016 emporium is a brilliant bet. Showcasing the works of Finnish designers in fashion, jewellery and accessories, including umbrellas, furniture, ceramics, textiles, stationery and art, it also stocks a superb range of architecture and design books to fuel inspiration.

★ **Artek** DESIGN

(www.artek.fi; Keskuskatu 1B; ⊙ 10am-7pm Mon-Fri, to 6pm Sat) Originally founded by architects and designers Alvar Aalto and his wife Aino Aalto in 1935, this iconic Finnish company maintains the simple design principle of its founders. Textiles, lighting and furniture are among its homewares. Many items are only available at this 700-sq-metre, two-storey space.

★ **Lasikammari** ANTIQUES

(www.lasikammari.fi; Liisankatu 9; ⊙ noon-5pm Tue, Wed & Thu, to 2pm Mon, Fri & Sat) Vintage Finnish glassware from renowned brands such as Iittala, Nuutajärvi and Riihimäki, and individual designers such as Alvar Aalto and Tapio Wirkkala, make this tiny shop a diamond find for collectors. Along with glass, you'll find vases, jugs, plates, bowls, light fittings and artistic sculptures. Prices are exceptionally reasonable; international shipping can be arranged.

Awake DESIGN

(www.awake-collective.com; Fredrikinkatu 25; ⊙ 12.30-6.30pm Tue-Fri, 11am-4pm Sat) ✏ At this super-minimalist art gallery–concept store, changing displays of handmade, Finnish-only designs range from men's and women's fashion and accessories, including watches, jewellery, bags and shoes, to birch plywood furniture and homewares such as rugs, carpets, sheets and blankets. Everything is ecologically and sustainably produced. Regular evening art and fashion shows are accompanied by Champagne – check the website for announcements.

Jukka Rintala FASHION & ACCESSORIES

(www.jukkarintala.fi; Fredrikinkatu 26; ⊙ 11am-6pm Mon-Fri, to 3pm Sat) Leading Finnish fashion designer Jukka Rintala is renowned for his women's evening wear, which is often worn at presidential functions and other high-profile events. His talents also extend to jewellery, art and interior design. In addition to his fashion creations, you'll also find prints of his artwork, jewellery pieces and wallpaper designs at this flagship boutique.

Lokal DESIGN

(www.lokalhelsinki.com; Annankatu 9; ⊙ 11am-6pm Tue-Fri, 11am-4pm Sat, noon-4pm Sun) ✏ A Design District standout, this hybrid design shop-gallery has rotating exhibitions from Finnish-based artists and designers, including traditional woodcarver Aimo Katajamäki, ceramicist Kristina Riska, birch-bark painter and jeweller Janna Syvänoja, contemporary painter Visa Norros and industrial furniture designer Jouko Kärkkäinen. All pieces exhibited are for sale.

Fargo VINTAGE, MUSIC

(www.fargoshop.fi; Fleminginkatu 20; ⊙ 3-7pm Tue-Thu, noon-4pm Fri & Sat) Vintage homewares from the 1950s, '60s and '70s, such as Finnish-designed lamps, chandeliers, crockery, vases, furniture and clocks, are scattered haphazardly throughout Fargo's large space. Music fans will love the racks of vinyl from the same era, as well as retro music and movie posters.

ⓘ Information

EMERGENCY

Drop the initial zero from area/mobile codes if dialling from abroad.

Finland's country code	☑ 358
International access code	☑ 00
General emergency	☑ 112

INTERNET ACCESS

Internet access at public libraries is free. Large parts of the city centre have free wi-fi, as do many restaurants, cafes and bars, and nearly all hotels.

Data is very cheap. If you have an unlocked smartphone, you can pick up a local SIM card for a few euros and charge it with a month's worth of data at a decent speed for under €20. Ask at R-kioski shops for the latest deals.

MEDICAL SERVICES

Pharmacy Yliopiston Apteekki has a late-opening branch in the **city centre** (www.yliopistonapteekki.fi; Mannerheimintie 5; ⊙ 10am-9pm) and a 24-hour branch in **Töölö** (www.yliopistonapteekki.fi; Mannerheimintie 96; ⊙ 24hr) .

Haartman Hospital (☑ 09-3106-3231; www.hel.fi; Haartmaninkatu 4; ⊙ 24hr) For emergency medical assistance.

Töölön Terveysasema (Töölö Health Station; ☑ 09-3104-5588; www.hel.fi; Sibeliuksenkatu 14; ⊙ 8am-4pm Mon, Tue, Thu & Fri, to 6pm Wed) A medical centre for non-emergencies.

MONEY

Credit cards are widely accepted. ATMs (bearing the name 'Otto') are prevalent. There are currency-exchange counters at all transport terminals; visit www.forex.fi to locate others.

POST

Main Post Office (www.posti.fi; Elielinaukio 2F; ⊙8am-8pm Mon-Fri, 10am-2pm Sat, noon-4pm Sun) Across from the train station.

TOURIST INFORMATION

Between June and August, multilingual 'Helsinki Helpers' – easily spotted by their lime-green jackets – are a mine of tourist information.

Helsinki City Tourist Office (☑09-3101-3300; www.visithelsinki.fi; Pohjoisesplanadi 19; ⊙9am-6pm Mon-Sat, to 4pm Sun mid-May–mid-Sep, 9am-6pm Mon-Fri, 10am-4pm Sat & Sun mid-Sep–mid-May) Busy multilingual office with a great quantity of information on the city. Also has an office at the **airport** (www.visithelsinki.fi; Terminal 2, Helsinki-Vantaa Airport; ⊙10am-8pm May-Sep, 10am-6pm Mon-Sat, noon-6pm Oct-Apr).

Strömma (www.stromma.fi; Pohjoisesplanadi 19; ⊙9am-6pm Mon-Sat, to 4pm Sun mid-May–mid-Sep, 9am-6pm Mon-Fri, 10am-4pm Sat & Sun mid-Sep–mid-May) In the city tourist office; sells various tours and local cruises, as well as package tours to Stockholm, Tallinn and St Petersburg. Also sells the Helsinki Card and Helsinki & Region Card.

WEBSITES

City of Helsinki (www.hel.fi) Helsinki City website, with links to copious information.

HSL/HRT (www.hsl.fi) Public-transport information and journey planner.

Lonely Planet (www.lonelyplanet.com/finland) Destination information, hotel bookings, traveller forum and more.

Visit Helsinki (www.visithelsinki.fi) Excellent tourist-board website full of information.

❶ Getting There & Away

AIR

Helsinki-Vantaa Airport (www.helsinki-vantaa.fi), 19km north of the city, is Finland's main air terminus. Direct flights serve many major European cities and several intercontinental destinations.

Finnair (☑09-818-0800; www.finnair.fi) covers 18 Finnish cities, usually at least once per day.

BOAT

International ferries sail to Stockholm, Tallinn, St Petersburg and German destinations.

Ferry companies have detailed timetables and fares on their websites. Fares vary widely according to season. Purchase tickets online, at the terminal, or at ferry company offices. Book well in advance during high season (late June to mid-August) and on weekends.

There are five main terminals: **Katajanokan Terminaali** (Katajanokan), **Makasiiniterminaali** (Eteläranta 7), **Olympia Terminaali** (Olympi-aranta 1), **Länsiterminaali** (West Terminal; Tyynenmerenkatu 8) and **Hansaterminaali** (Proviantikatu 5, Vuosaari). The first three are closest to central Helsinki.

BUS

Kamppi bus station (www.matkahuolto.fi; Salomonkatu) has a terminal for local buses to Espoo in one wing, while longer-distance buses also depart from here to destinations throughout Finland. **Onnibus** (www.onnibus.com; Kamppi bus station, Salomonkatu) runs budget routes to several Finnish cities.

Destinations with several daily departures include the following:

Jyväskylä €30, 4½ hours, up to three hourly

Kuopio €34, six hours, hourly

---

❶ TICKETS & PASSES

The city's public-transport system, HSL (www.hsl.fi), operates buses, metro and local trains, trams and local ferries. Hours of operation vary depending on the route.

➡ A one-hour flat-fare ticket for any HSL transport costs €3.20 when purchased on-board, or €2.90 when purchased in advance. The ticket allows unlimited transfers, but must be validated at the machine on-board on first use.

➡ A night ticket, for use between 2am and 4.30am, costs €5.

➡ For destinations further afield, including the airport, you'll need a more expensive regional ticket (€5 advance purchase; €5.50 on-board a bus or tram; €8 for night tickets).

➡ Day or multiday tickets (€9/13.50/18 per 24/48/72 hours) are worthwhile; tickets up to seven days (€36) are available.

➡ Sales points at Kamppi bus station (p138) and the Rautatientori and Hakaniemi metro stations sell tickets and passes, as do many R-kioskis and tourist offices.

➡ The *Helsinki Route Map*, available at tourist offices, maps bus, metro and tram routes. Online, www.reittiopas.fi is a useful route planner.

ⓘ TO/FROM ST PETERSBURG

One of Russia's most beautiful cities feels tantalisingly close to Helsinki, but for most visits, including on the fast trains, you'll need a Russian visa. The exception to this is the overnight Helsinki–St Petersburg ferry run by **St Peter Line** (☑ 09-6187-2000; www.stpeterline.com; Makasiiniterminaali), which allows you a 72-hour, visa-free stay in the city. A mandatory shuttle bus (for visa-free requirements) takes you from the harbour to the centre in St Petersburg.

Applying in your home country for a Russian visa is the easiest option. If you want to apply in Finland, it's simpler to do it via a travel agent such as **Russian Expert** (☑ 045-870-3450; www.russianexpert.fi; Töölönkatu 7; ☺ 9.30am-5pm Mon-Fri), **Rustravel** (☑ 050-585-0955; www.rustravel.fi; Tehtaankatu 12; ☺ 9am-5pm Mon-Fri), which is also helpful with visas for other former Soviet states, or **Venäjän Viisumikeskus** (☑ 010-235-0530; www.venajanviisumikeskus.fi; Urho Kekkosenkatu 2C; ☺ 9am-5pm Mon-Fri). Visas start from €78 for the normal seven- to eight-working-day processing time, and from €218 for express processing (three to four working days). Prices depend on nationality.

In all cases, you'll need a passport with more than six months' validity, two free pages, a couple of photos and 'visa support', namely an invitation document, typically issued either by accommodation you've booked in Russia (even hostels) or by an authorised tour agent. Travel agencies can also organise this for you, and there are reliable set-ups that arrange visa support documents online, such as Way to Russia (http://waytorussia.net). These cost US$30. Once you've got the paperwork sorted, it's easy to jump on a train, bus or boat and head east.

Lappeenranta €30, 3½ hours, up to three hourly
Oulu €55, 9½ hours, up to 13 per day
Savonlinna €30, 5½ hours, nine daily
Tampere €25, 2½ hours, up to four hourly
Turku €28, 2½ hours, up to four hourly

TRAIN

Helsinki's central **train station** (Rautatieasema; www.vr.fi; Kaivokatu 1) is linked to the metro (Rautatientori stop) and situated 500m east of Kamppi bus station.

The train is the fastest and cheapest way to get from Helsinki to major centres.

Destinations include the following:
Joensuu €44, 4½ hours, three daily
Kuopio €45, 4¼ hours, four daily
Lappeenranta €28, two hours, six daily
Oulu €56, six hours, four daily
Rovaniemi €80, eight hours, four daily
Tampere €21, 1½ hours, two hourly
Turku €20, two hours, hourly
There are also daily trains (buy tickets from the international counter) to the Russian cities of Vyborg, St Petersburg and Moscow; you'll need a Russian visa.

ⓘ Getting Around

Bicycle Helsinki's shared-bike scheme City Bikes (www.hsl.fi/citybikes) has some 1500 bikes at 150 stations citywide.
Bus Buses serve the northern suburbs, Espoo and Vantaa; most visitors won't need to use them.

Ferry Local ferries serve island destinations, including Suomenlinna.
Metro Helsinki's single, forked metro line has 17 stations. Most are beyond the centre; the most useful for visitors are in the centre and Kallio.
Tram Ten main routes cover the city. Three of these, trams 2, 4 and 6, can double as budget sightseeing tours.
Walking Central Helsinki is compact and easily covered on foot.

TO/FROM THE AIRPORT

Bus 615 (€3.20, 50 minutes, every 30 minutes, 24 hours) shuttles between Helsinki-Vantaa airport and the Rautatientori (Railway Sq), next to Helsinki's train station.

Faster **Finnair buses** (www.finnair.com; Eliel-inaukio) head to and from Elielinaukio, outside Helsinki's train station (€6.30, 30 minutes, every 20 minutes, 5am to midnight). The last service leaves the airport at 1.10am.

The airport–city rail link (www.hsl.fi, €5, 30 minutes, 5.05am to 12.05am) serves Helsinki's train station.

Door-to-door **Yellow Line Airport Taxis** (☑ 0600-555-555; www.airporttaxi.fi; per two/four passengers €29.50/39.50) need to be booked the previous day before 6pm if you're leaving Helsinki.

A regular **Taksi Helsinki** (☑ 010-00700; www.taksihelsinki.fi) cab should cost €45 to €50.

TURKU & THE SOUTH COAST

Anchoring the country's southwest is Finland's former capital, Turku. This striking seafaring city stretches along the broad Aurajoki from its Gothic cathedral to its medieval castle and vibrant harbour. Turku challenges Helsinki's cultural pre-eminence with cutting-edge galleries, museums and restaurants, and music festivals that electrify the summer air.

Throughout the south, the coastline is strung with characterful little towns. The Swedish and Russian empires fought for centuries over the area's ports, and today they're commandeered by castles and fortresses that seem at odds with the sunshine and sailing boats. Inland, charming *bruk* (ironworks) villages offer an insight into the area's industrial past.

Scattered offshore, islands provide yachting opportunities, sea-salt retreats and stepping stones across to Åland and Sweden. Most of the charming, history-steeped coastal towns offer summer cruises, guestharbour facilities, and charter boats to discover your own island.

Porvoo

☑ 019 / POP 50,000

Finland's second-oldest town is a popular day or weekend trip from Helsinki. Porvoo (Swedish: Borgå) officially became a town in 1380, but even before that it was an important trading post. Its historic centre includes oft-photographed riverside warehouses that once stored goods bound for destinations across Europe. Away from the river, the cobblestone streets are lined with charming wooden houses of every colour. Birthplace of national poet Johan Runeberg, the town is peppered with signs commemorating his whereabouts on various occasions.

Porvoo is home to a fantastic dining scene and a burgeoning arts movement. During the day these ancient streets are bustling with visitors, but spending a weeknight will mean you'll have the place more or less to yourself.

◎ Sights & Activities

Summer cruises leave from the passenger harbour for the Porvoo archipelago and elsewhere. It's also possible (and pleasant) to arrive in Porvoo on a cruise from Helsinki.

★ Vanha Porvoo   HISTORIC SITE
(Old Town) One of Finland's most enticing old quarters, this tangle of cobbled alleys and wooden warehouses is entrancing. Once a vibrant port and market, Porvoo now has craft boutiques, galleries, souvenir stores and antique shops jostling for attention on the main roads, Välikatu and Kirkkokatu. The rows of rust-red storehouses along the Porvoonjoki are a local icon: cross the old bridge for the best photos. The relatively less-touristed area is east of the cathedral; Itäinen Pitkäkatu is one of the nicest streets.

★ Tuomiokirkko   CATHEDRAL
(www.porvoonseurakunnat.fi; ⊙ 10am-2pm Tue-Sat, 2-4pm Sun Oct-Apr, 10am-6pm Mon-Fri, to 2pm Sat, 2-5pm Sun May-Sep) Porvoo's historic stone-and-timber cathedral sits atop a hill overlooking the quaint Old Town. This is where Tsar Alexander I convened the first Diet of Finland in 1809, giving Finland religious freedom. Vandalised by fire in 2006, the church has been completely restored, so you can admire the ornate pulpit and tiered galleries. The magnificent exterior, with free-standing bell tower, remains the highlight.

Saaristolinja Ky   CRUISE
(☑ 019-523-1350; www.saaristolinja.com; Rantakatu; adult/child €10/5; ⊙ noon Tue-Sun mid-Jun–mid-Aug) ☑ Runs 45-minute river jaunts past the Old Town hourly in summer from the passenger harbour.

🛏 Sleeping

Porvoon Retkeilymaja   HOSTEL €
(☑ 019-523-0012; www.porvoohostel.fi; Linnankoskenkatu 1-3; s/d/tr/q €37/52/85/105; ⊙ reception 7-10am & 4-11pm; ℗ ⩙) Four blocks from the kauppatori, and set in a grassy garden, this historic wooden house holds a well-kept hostel. All rooms (for one to six people) have lockers, television and fridge, while bathrooms, showers and a common kitchen are in the corridor. There's also a great indoor pool and sauna complex over the road.

Ida-Maria   B&B €€
(☑ 045-851-2345; www.idamaria.fi; Jokikatu 10A; s/d/f without bathroom €65/85/125, apt €165; ⩙) The hospitable owner of this charming B&B does her utmost to make guests feel welcome. Housed in a wooden building on the main square, the rooms are imbued with historic character. All share a bathroom, but the ambience, sauna and appetising breakfast make this place a winner.

★ **Hotelli Onni**   BOUTIQUE HOTEL €€€
(🖉 044-534-8110; www.hotelonni.fi; Kirkkotori 3; r/ ste €199/295; P❄☎) Opposite the cathedral, this gold-coloured wooden building is perfectly placed. The rooms are all unique, from the four-poster bed and slick design of the Funkishuone to the rustic single Talonpoikaishuone. Top of the line is the honeymoon suite, a small self-contained apartment with bath-tub and complimentary Champagne. *Onni* means 'happiness' in Finnish; this place delivers.

✗ Eating & Drinking

Porvoo's most atmospheric cafes and restaurants are in the Old Town and along the riverfront. For cheaper eats, hit the area around the kauppatori market square. Porvoo is famous for its sweets, which you'll discover in the cafes and confectioners in the Old Town.

★ **Cafe Postres**   DESSERTS €
(www.cafepostres.fi; Gabriel Hagertinkuja; ◷ 10am-6pm Mon-Fri, to 4pm Sat) Tantalise your sweet tooth at this delightful dessert cafe, brainchild of Michelin-starred chef Samuli Wirgentius. Take your pick from rich, creamy gelato and to-die-for desserts, or sample the savoury open-face *smørrebrød* sandwiches on house-made sourdough bread.

Meat District   STEAK €€
(🖉 020-770-5390; www.meatdistrict.fi; Jokikatu 43; mains €18-25, set menu €59-79; ◷ 5pm-midnight Mon-Fri, 2pm-midnight Sat, terrace noon-8pm Fri & Sat, to 4pm Sun) 🍴 When you go to a place called 'Meat District', you probably expect high-quality, organic, grass-fed beef – and that's what you'll get here (the house speciality is the dry-aged beef for two; €84). What you might not expect is the fresh local produce and everything made from scratch, which is what makes this place so special.

Fryysarinranta   SEAFOOD, STEAK €€
(🖉 040-073-2038; www.fryysarinranta.fi; Jokikatu 20; mains €23-28, lunch buffet €25; ◷ 11am-11pm Jun-Aug) A delightful setting, delicious food and laid-back service (ahem) characterise this Old Town newcomer. Set in one of the iconic red wooden warehouses along the river, the restaurant has a tempting lunchtime fish buffet and an irresistible terrace.

ℹ Information

Tourist Office (🖉 040-489-9801; www. visitporvoo.fi; Läntinen Aleksanterinkatu 1; ◷ 9am-6pm Mon-Fri, 11am-4pm Sat; ☎) Offers maps and local information in the Taidetehdas (Art Factory) building across the river.

ℹ Getting There & Away

BOAT

The noble old steamship **JL Runeberg** (🖉 019-524-3331; www.msjlruneberg.fi; ◷ Tue, Wed, Fri & Sat mid-May–early Sep, plus Sun Jun-Aug & Mon Jul) cruises from Helsinki's kauppatori to Porvoo's passenger harbour in summer (one way/return €27/39) and makes an excellent day trip, with various lunch options available. The trip takes 3½ hours each way, so you may prefer to return by bus.

BUS

Buses travel between Porvoo **bus station** (Kauppatori) and Helsinki's Kamppi every 30 minutes or so (€9 to €15, one hour). There are also frequent buses to/from towns further east.

Hanko

🖉 019 / POP 8800

On a long, sandy peninsula, Hanko (Swedish: Hangö) grew up as a well-to-do Russian spa town in the late 19th century. During this period entrepreneurs and industrialists built opulent seaside villas, with fabulous Victorian and art-nouveau architectural detailing. These beauties are still a star attraction here, especially as many of them now house guesthouses and restaurants.

Summertime visitors flock to Hanko for sun and sand, and there are several attractive beaches. There's a party atmosphere throughout summer, especially around the huge Hanko Regatta in July. For island hoppers, Hanko's a good jumping-off point for the southern archipelago. Or you can stay on dry land and relish the fruits of the sea at the town's many excellent restaurants.

RUNEBERG TORTE

A local speciality is Runeberg torte: an almond-rum cake topped with sugar icing and raspberry jam that was supposedly the favourite breakfast of national poet Johan Runeberg. Traditionally it's a treat eaten on the poet's birthday, but in Porvoo you can sample it on any day at the **Helmi Tea & Coffee House** (www. porvoonhelmet.net; Välikatu 7; cakes €3-7; ◷ 11am-6pm Mon-Sat, to 4pm Sun).

◉ Sights

Hanko is a treasure trove of interesting architecture, with notable buildings by Lars Sonck, Selim Lindqvist and other renowned architects. Appelgrenintie, east of East Harbour, is an impressive stretch, featuring many fine 20th-century villas. Pick up the brochure *An Architecture Walk in the Centre of Hanko* from the tourist office.

Hauensuoli   HARBOUR
(Pike's Gut) This narrow strait between Tullisaari and Kobben is a protected natural harbour where ships from countries around the Baltic Sea once waited out storms. The sailors killed time by carving their initials or tales of bravery into the rocks, earning the area the nickname 'Guest Book of the Archipelago'. Some 600 carvings dating back to the 17th century remain. Hauensuoli can be reached by charter taxi boat or on a **cruise** (🖉cruises 040-044-0802, rentals 040-414-5681; www.sunfun.fi; East Harbour; boat trips €25-35, bike rental per 2hr/day €10/16) from Hanko.

⊨ Sleeping & Eating

★**Villa Maija**   VILLA €€€
(🖉050-505-2013; www.villamaija.fi; Appelgrenintie 7; s/d €135/175, without bathroom €100/130, f €200; P🖥) Built in 1888, this is Hanko's best villa accommodation. Spread over three lovely buildings, the rooms are flawlessly restored and packed with character, featuring wooden floors and ceilings, decorative wainscotting, tile stoves and period chandeliers. Rooms vary widely in size and layout – some lack bathrooms and others sport balconies with wonderful sea views. There's a delightful garden.

Hangon Portti   SEAFOOD €€
(🖉010-05516; www.hangonportti.fi; Smultrongrundet; mains €15-32; ⊗noon-10pm Mon-Sat, 5-10pm Sun mid-Jun–Aug) You'll need to take a two-minute ferry journey from the **East Harbour pier** to this little whitewashed, wicker-furnished cottage, perched on a rugged granite island. Sailor's meatballs (with mashed potatoes and lingonberry jam), a smoked-and-glazed-pork 'captain's burger' with potato salad, and archipelago tapas are among the dishes on the menu.

Origo   SCANDINAVIAN €€
(🖉019-248-5023; www.restaurant-origo.com; Satamakatu 7; lunch buffet €30.50, mains €18-32; ⊗11am-10pm) 🖉 At the eatery-clad East Harbour, Origo distinguishes itself with geothermal heating, local, organic ingredients and a seasonal gourmet menu. Braised pork cheek cooked overnight is a treat, as is the salmon soup with dark bread. Vegetarians can choose from unusual dishes such as black-salsify pie.

❶ Information

Tourist Office (🖉019-220-3411; www.hanko.fi; Raatihuoneentori 5; ⊗9am-6pm Mon-Fri, 10am-4pm Sat & Sun Jun-Aug, 9am-4pm Mon-Fri Sep-May) Helpful office with a large list of private accommodation.

❶ Getting There & Away

Buses run to/from Helsinki (€25.20, 2½ hours, three daily) via Ekenäs (Raseborg; €8.40, 35 minutes, six daily). Services depart from the bus station.

Trains go to Karis (Finnish: Karjaa) and connect to Helsinki (€23.80, 1¾ hours, hourly) or Turku (€26.80, two hours, eight daily).

Turku

🖉02 / POP 187,600

Turku (Swedish: Åbo) is Finland's second city – or first, by some accounts, as it was the capital until 1812. The majestic Turun Linna (Turku Castle) and ancient Tuomiokirkko (cathedral) – both dating from the 13th century – are testament to the city's long and storied past.

Contemporary Turku is even more enticing, a hotbed of experimental art and vibrant music festivals, designer boutiques and innovative restaurants. University students populate the cafes and clubs, keeping the place buzzing.

Through the age-old network of bustling streets and squares, the Aurajoki river meanders picturesquely, heading out to sea. For nature-lovers, Turku is the gateway to the glorious Turku Archipelago. As one of the country's main ports of entry (as many visitors arrive by ferry from Sweden and Åland), it's a fabulous introduction to mainland Finland.

◉ Sights & Activities

Archipelago cruises are popular in summer; most departures are from the **quay at Martinsilta bridge**.

★**Luostarinmäen Käsityöläismuseo**   MUSEUM
(Luostarinmäki Handicrafts Museum; 🖉02-262-0350; www.turku.fi/handicraftsmuseum; Vartiovuorenkatu 2; adult/child €6/4; ⊗10am-6pm daily

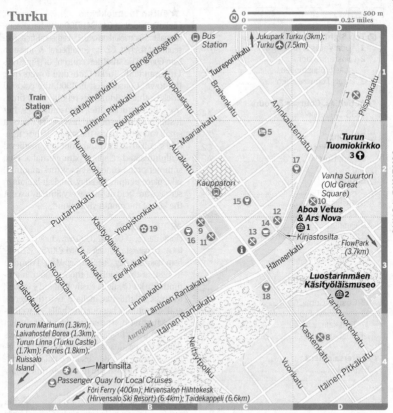

Jun-Aug, Tue-Sun May & Sep, 10am-4pm Tue-Sun late Nov–early Jan) When the savage Great Fire of 1827 swept through Turku, the lower-class quarter Luostarinmäki escaped the flames. Set along tiny lanes and around grassy yards, the 19th-century wooden workshops and houses now form the outdoor handicrafts museum, a national treasure since 1940. All the buildings are in their original locations, including 30 workshops (among them a silversmith, a watchmaker, a bakery, a pottery, a shoemaker, a printer and a cigar shop), where artisans in period costume ply their trades.

★Taidekappeli   CHAPEL
(Art Chapel; www.taidekappeli.fi; Seiskarinkatu 35; suggested donation €5; ◎11am-4pm Mon-Fri, noon-3pm Sat & Sun May-Aug, 11am-3pm Tue-Fri, noon-3pm Sat & Sun Sep-Apr) Like the bow of a ship tipped on its end, this unusual structure is perched on a rock and surrounded by forest on Hirvensalo island, 7km south of Turku centre. Looking at its oddly shaped, copper-clad exterior, you wouldn't know it's a chapel – St Henry's Ecumenical Art Chapel, to be precise. But the timber interior feels holy indeed, with its high walls curving up to form a Reuleaux triangle, framing an altar of light. It's spectacular. Take bus 54 from Turku.

★Aboa Vetus & Ars Nova   MUSEUM, GALLERY
(www.aboavetusarsnova.fi; Itäinen Rantakatu 4-6; adult/child €10/5.50; ◎11am-7pm) Art and archaeology unite here under one roof. Aboa Vetus (Old Turku) draws you underground to Turku's medieval streets, showcasing some of the 37,000 artefacts unearthed from the site (digs still continue). Back in the present, Ars Nova presents contemporary art exhibitions upstairs. English-language tours lasting 45 minutes (included in admission) take place daily from 11.30am in July and August.

Turku

ⓘ DISCOUNT CARDS

The **Tourist Office** (p146) offers several discount programs:

Food Walk (€44) Ten participating restaurants – including **Pinella** (☑ 02-445-6500; www.pinella.fi; Vanha Suurtori 2; mains lunch €9-22, dinner €16-27; ⊙ 11am-11pm Mon-Fri, noon-11pm Sat, noon-9pm Sun) and **Smör** – offer specific menu items, such as a free appetiser or a free dessert. Choose the five restaurants you like and visit them within three days. You'll get an additional 15% off your total bill.

Museum Walk (€38) Includes one-time access to each of 12 participating museums, including **Aboa Vetus & Ars Nova** and **Turun Linna** The card expires three days after your first visit.

★ **Turun Tuomiokirkko**   CATHEDRAL
(Turku Cathedral; ☑ 040-341-7100; www.turunseurakunnat.fi; Tuomiokirkonkatu 1; cathedral free, museum adult/child €2/1; ⊙ cathedral & museum 9am-6pm) The 'mother church' of Finland's Lutheran faith, Turku Cathedral towers over the town. Consecrated in 1300, the colossal brick Gothic building was rebuilt many times over the centuries after damaging fires, but it still looks majestic and historic. Upstairs, a small **museum** traces the stages of the cathedral's construction, and contains medieval sculptures and religious paraphernalia. Free summer organ concerts (www.turkuorgan.fi) take place at 8pm Tuesday. English-language services are held at 4pm every Sunday except the last of the month year-round.

★ **Turun Linna**   CASTLE
(Turku Castle; ☑ 02-262-0300; www.turku.fi/turunlinna; Linnankatu 80; adult/child €10/5; ⊙ 10am-6pm daily Jun-Aug, Tue-Sun Sep-May) Founded in 1280 at the mouth of the Aurajoki, mammoth Turku Castle is easily Finland's largest fortress. Highlights include two dungeons and sumptuous banqueting halls, as well as a fascinating **historical museum** of medieval Turku in the castle's Old Bailey. Models depict the castle's growth from a simple island fortress to a Renaissance palace. Guided tours in English run four to six times daily from June to August.

Forum Marinum   MUSEUM
(www.forum-marinum.fi; Linnankatu 72; adult/child €9/5, incl ships €16/10; ⊙ 11am-7pm May-Sep, to 6pm Tue-Sun Oct-Apr) Partly housed in an old granary, this excellent maritime museum offers a comprehensive look at ships and shipping, from scale models to full-size vessels. Highlights include the museum's hydrocopter, WWII torpedoes and multimedia displays, plus a cabin from a luxury cruise liner (many of which were built in Turku). At the museum's cafe-restaurant, you'll find its namesake *Daphne*, a cute little boat that was home to author Göran Schild. Anchored outside is a small fleet of **museum ships** (adult/child €6/4; ⊙ 11am-7pm Jun-Aug).

✶ Festivals & Events

Keskiaikaiset Markkinat   CULTURAL
(Medieval Market; www.keskiaikaisetmarkkinat.fi) Held over a variable long weekend in summer (usually late June), this lively four-day event brings a Middle Ages market back to the Vanha Suurtori (Old Great Sq) near Tuomiokirkko (Turku Cathedral).

★Ruisrock MUSIC
(www.ruisrock.fi; 1-/2-/3-day ticket €90/135/155; ⏲Jul) Finland's oldest and largest annual rock festival – held since 1969 and attracting 100,000-strong crowds – takes over Ruissalo island for three days.

Turku Jazz MUSIC
(☎040-582-9366; www.turkujazz.fi; tickets €16-32, 1-/2-day pass €35/58.50; ⏲early–mid-Aug) Hot bebop and smoking sax hits the city at three venues, including the main stage in the **Panimoravintola Koulu** (School Brewery-Restaurant; www.panimoravintolakoulu.fi; Eerikinkatu 18; ⏲11am-2am) courtyard.

Sleeping

★Ruissalo Camping CAMPGROUND €
(☎02-262-5100; www.visitturku.fi/en/ruissalo-camping_-0; Saaronniemi, Ruissalo; tent sites €18 plus per person €5, 2-/4-/6-person cabins €68/125/165; ⏲May-Sep; P) On idyllic Ruissalo island, 10km west of the city centre, this sprawling campground has gently sloping grassy sites and a great choice of cabins, along with saunas, a cafe and Turku's closest beaches (including a naturist beach). Minigolf, ball courts, playgrounds and hiking trails will keep the troops entertained. Bus 8 runs from the kauppatori.

Laivahostel Borea HOSTEL €
(☎040-843-6611; www.msborea.fi; Linnankatu 72; dm/s/tw/d/tr/q from €30/51/82/92/112/135; P 📶) Built in Sweden in 1960, the enormous passenger ship SS *Bore* is docked outside the Forum Marinum museum, just 500m north-east of the ferry terminal. It now contains an award-winning HI-affiliated hostel with 120 vintage en-suite cabins. Most are squishy, but if you want room to spread out, higher-priced doubles have a lounge area. Rates include a morning sauna.

Centro Hotel HOTEL €€
(☎02-211-8100; www.centrohotel.com; Yliopistonkatu 12; s/d from €96/119; P @ 📶) The 62-room Centro Hotel is central (as you would guess), but its courtyard location cuts out street noise. Service is friendly and the blond-wood rooms are a good compromise between size and price. The breakfast buffet is worth getting out of bed for. Arrive early to nab one of the 14 parking spaces.

★Park Hotel BOUTIQUE HOTEL €€€
(☎02-273-2555; www.parkhotelturku.fi; Rauhankatu 1; s/d/f €135/177/205; P 📶) Overlooking a hilly park, this art-nouveau building was the home of a shipyard magnate. Nowadays it's a truly atmospheric place to stay, with classical music playing in the lift and a resident parrot in the lobby. Its 20 rooms are decorated in a lovably chintzy style. This is the antithesis of a chain hotel, thanks to the owners' wonderful hospitality.

Eating

Turku is the home town of the ubiquitous Hesburger chain, Finland's answer to McDonald's. But the city also has a sophisticated dining scene. Stroll along the north bank of the Aurajoki to scope out some of the most enticing options, especially at the east end, opposite the Vanha Suurtori.

Kauppahalli MARKET €
(www.kauppahalli.fi; Eerikinkatu 16; ⏲8am-6pm Mon-Fri, to 4pm Sat; ✎) 🌿 Filled with speciality products, this historic covered market also contains the **ininen Juna Aschan Café** (http://aschan.fi; pastries & sandwiches €2.50-6; ⏲8am-6pm Mon-Fri, to 4pm Sat), in a converted-train carriage, run by top-quality Turku bakery chain Aschan.

Hus Lindman FINNISH €€
(☎0400-446-100; www.huli.fi; Piispankatu 15; lunch buffet €16.80; ⏲11am-9pm Mon-Sat, noon-7pm Sun Jun-Aug, 11am-3pm Mon-Fri Sep-May) Hidden at the bottom of a garden and opening to the Aurajoki, this cream-coloured wooden building is an elegant affair, featuring local seafood, steaks and a daily vegetarian option. There's live music from 6pm to 9pm Thursday in July and August.

Tintå BISTRO €€
(☎02-230-7023; www.tinta.fi; Läntinen Rantakatu 9; mains lunch €7.50-14.50, dinner €17-32, pizza €13-16; ⏲11am-midnight Mon-Thu, to 2am Fri, noon-2am Sat, to 10pm Sun) With a cosy exposed-brick interior, this riverside wine bar is also a great bet for weekday lunches, gourmet pizzas and classy mains (such as raspberry and rhubarb salmon or Moroccan-style lamb skewers). Grab a glass of wine and a seat on the summer terrace, and watch the world go by.

★Smor GASTRONOMY €€€
(☎02-536-9444; www.smor.fi; Läntinen Rantakatu 3; mains lunch €12-21, dinner €21-30, 4-course dinner menu €57; ⏲11am-11pm Mon-Fri, 4.30-10pm Sat) A vaulted cellar lit by flickering candles makes a romantic backdrop for appetising, organic, locally sourced food, such as roast lamb with organic currant sauce or the

catch of the day with roasted hay sauce. Desserts are truly inspired: try quark mousse with wild blueberries and oat ice cream or caramelised yoghurt with thyme cookies and honey.

Kaskis
SCANDINAVIAN €€€

(📱044-723-0200; www.kaskis.fi; Kaskenkatu 6A; 4-/6-course menu €55/66; ⊙ 4pm & 7pm Tue-Sat, plus 10.30pm Fri & Sat) Foodies are buzzing about Kaskis, where there's no written menu – not only because it changes daily but also because there are no real decisions to make. You choose four courses or six, but the rest is up to the chefs. Rest assured: ingredients are fresh, seasonal and local, with a result that shows off the versatility of the Finnish forests and sea.

🍷 Drinking & Nightlife

★ Tiirikkala
COCKTAIL BAR

(www.tiirikkala.fi; Linnankatu 3; ⊙ 11am-10pm Tue-Thu, to 2am Fri & Sat, noon-10pm Sun) Fresh from a cool, contemporary Nordic–style makeover, this gorgeous old wooden house opens to a street-level terrace and fabulous roof terrace. Unique cocktails and tasty tapas soothe the soul, as does the jazz and blues heading up the weekend live-music program. Weekend brunch is also a highlight.

Uusi Apteekki
PUB

(www.uusiapteekki.fi; Kaskenkatu 1; ⊙ 10am-2am) Lovely old fittings in this historic pharmacy include wooden dispensing drawers fashioned into tables where you can rest your pint.

CaféArt
CAFE

(www.cafeart.fi; Läntinen Rantakatu 5; ⊙ 10am-7pm Mon-Fri, to 5pm Sat, 11am-5pm Sun) With freshly ground coffee, prize-winning baristas, a beautifully elegant interior and an artistic sensibility, CaféArt is an ideal place to get your caffeine fix, but be sure not to miss its cakes, which include sea buckthorn and carrot, apple and coffee, blueberry and white chocolate, and tangy lemon-meringue cheesecake. In summer, the terrace spills onto the riverbank, shaded by linden trees.

Cosmic Comic Café
BAR

(www.cosmic.fi; Kauppiaskatu 4; ⊙ 3pm-2am Mon-Thu, to 3am Fri & Sat) This fab late-night haunt is a fanboy's dream – comics paper the walls and you can browse its huge (mostly English-language) collection. More than 70 kinds of beer and 25 ciders rotate on the eclectic menu. Located inside the shopping mall.

Monk
JAZZ

(📱02-251-2444; www.monk.fi; Humalistonkatu 3; ⊙ 10pm-4am Fri & Sat year-round, plus 9pm-1am Mon spring & autumn) Intimate venue for live jazz, funk and Latin.

ℹ️ Information

Tourist Office (📱02-262-7444; www.visit-turku.fi; Aurakatu 4; ⊙ 8.30am-6pm Mon-Fri year-round, plus 9am-4pm Sat & Sun May-Sep, 10am-3pm Sat & Sun Oct-Mar; 🛜) Busy but helpful office with information on the entire region.

ℹ️ Getting There & Away

AIR

Turku Airport (TKU; www.finavia.fi; Lentoasemantie 150) is 8.5km north of the city. Facilities are minimal and there are no ATMs – bring euros for the bus.

Airlines include the following:

AirBaltic (www.airbaltic.com) Serves Riga (Latvia).

Finnair (www.finnair.com) Regular flights to/from Helsinki and Mariehamn; seasonal flights to Kittilä.

Nextjet (www.nextjet.se) Flies to Mariehamn.

SAS (www.flysas.com) Flights to/from Stockholm Arlanda (Sweden).

Wizz Air (http://wizzair.com) Seasonal flights to/from Gdańsk (Poland).

BOAT

Turku is a main gateway to Sweden and Åland. The harbour, about 3km southwest of the city centre, has terminals for **Tallink/Silja Line** (📱060-017-4552; www.tallinksilja.com; Linnankatu 91; ⊙ 6.45am-8.15pm) and **Viking Line** (www.vikingline.fi; Ensimmäinen linja 6). Both companies sail to Stockholm, Sweden (10½ hours) via Åland (5½ hours). Book ahead during high season if you plan to take a car. Prices vary according to season and class:

Mariehamn Deck-class one-way tickets from €23/45 per passenger/car

Stockholm Cabin required; from €69/45 per passenger/car

Finnlink (www.finnlines.com) sails to Sweden from nearby Naantali, though this service doesn't take foot passengers. It's also possible to travel to Åland via the Turku Archipelago.

BUS

Long-distance buses use the **bus station** (www.matkahuolto.fi; Aninkaistenkatu 20), while regional buses (including for Naantali) depart from the **kauppatori** (www.foli.fi; single ride before/after 11pm €3/4, day pass €7.50).

Major intercity services:

Helsinki €25, 2½ hours, up to four hourly

Korpo €15.50, two hours, six daily (via Nagu; €11.80, 1¼ hours)

Pori €15, 2¼ hours, hourly (via Rauma; €10, 1½ hours)

Tampere €25, 2½ hours, hourly

TRAIN

Turku's train station is 400m northwest of the city centre; trains also stop at the ferry harbour.

Direct trains include the following:

Helsinki €20, two hours, hourly

Oulu €60 to €67, eight to 10 hours, two daily

Tampere €23, 1¾ hours, six daily

ⓘ Getting Around

BICYCLE

Bike Rent (☏ 044-022-4161; www.polkupy-oravuokraamo.fi; per day/week from €14/63, delivery €5; ⊙ 9am-7pm) Offers good city-riding bikes, as well as tandems and kickbikes.

Tourist Office Rents seven-gear bikes and publishes an excellent free *pyörätiekartta* (bike-route map) of the city and surrounding towns.

BUS

Regional buses depart from the kauppatori (market square). Timetables are available from the tourist office, long-distance bus station and train station.

Naantali

☏ 02 / POP 19,000

Most visitors to charming Naantali (Swedish: Nådendal) are summer day-trippers from Turku, 18km east. They come to meet their friends at Muumimaailma (Moominworld) or to browse the shops and galleries in the quaint Old Town. Even the Finnish president spends his summer holidays here – at the stately mansion overlooking the harbour at Kulturanta.

Out of season, Muumimaailma closes its gates and the Old Town acquires the melancholic air of an abandoned film set. But Naantali continues to work hard behind the scenes, with Finland's third-busiest port, an oil refinery and an electricity plant.

◉ Sights & Activities

Surrounding the harbour, Naantali's photogenic Old Town is made up of narrow cobbled streets and wooden houses, many of which now house handicraft shops, art galleries, antiques shops and cafes.

Naantalin Kirkko CHURCH
(Naantali Convent Church; www.naantalinseura-kunta.fi; organ concerts €5-10; ⊙ 10am-6pm Wed-Sun mid-May–end May, 10am-4pm Tue-Sun Jun–mid-Aug, noon-2pm Wed, 9am-noon Sun mid-Aug–mid-May) Medieval Naantali grew up around the Catholic Convent of the Order of St Birgitta, which was dissolved after the 1527 Reformation. Towering above the harbour, the massive 1462 Convent Church is all that remains. Archaeological digs have unearthed some 2000 pieces of jewellery, coins and relics now in the **Naantali Museum** (www.naantali.fi/museo; Katinhäntä 1; adult/child €5/3; ⊙ 11am-6pm Tue-Sun mid-May–Aug). At 8pm on summer evenings a trumpeter plays vespers (evensong) from the belfry; there are also regular organ concerts.

Muumimaailma AMUSEMENT PARK
(Moominworld; ☏ 02-511-1111; www.muumimaailma.fi; 1/2 days €28/38; ⊙ 10am-6pm early Jun–mid-Aug, noon-6pm late Aug; ⊕) Crossing the bridge from the Old Town to Kailo island takes you into the delightful world of the Moomins. The focus is on hands-on activities and exploration, not rides. Kids love the costumed characters wandering through the Moominhouse, the Groke's Cave and Snork's Workshop (where they can help with inventions). Other Muumimaailma highlights include a swimming beach and Emma's Theatre.

Väski Adventure Island ADVENTURE SPORTS
(☏ 02-511-1111; www.vaski.fi; 1/2 days €24/43; ⊙ 11am-6pm early Jun–mid-Aug) Older adventure-seekers will get their thrills at Väski, an island that features rock climbing, gold panning, zip lining and rope obstacle courses. Free shuttle boats depart every 30 minutes from Naantali, near the bridge to Muumimaailma, where you can also use your two-day ticket.

🛏 Sleeping & Eating

★**Hotel Bridget Inn** GUESTHOUSE €€
(☏ 02-533-4026; www.bridgetinn.fi; Kaivokatu 18; d €140-199; 🛜) Steeped in history, this dove-white 1880-built wooden inn (a one-time cafe frequented by former Finnish president PE 'Ukko-Pekka' Svinhufvud) has gorgeous period-furnished rooms in champagne and chocolate hues, some with patios or balconies. Two luxury suites feature private terraces and private saunas – worth a splurge!

Naantalin Kylpylä   SPA HOTEL €€€
(☑ 02-445-5100; www.naantalispa.fi; Matkailijantie 2; tw €168-188, d €188-218, ste from €244; @ 🎧 🏊) There's a large variety of rooms at this up-market spa complex, from spacious, contemporary hotel rooms to Moomin-themed family suites and luxurious apartments with private balconies. All guests have access to facilities at the spa (Naantali Spa; pool adult/child from €20/8, manicure/pedicure/massage from €34/41/46; ⊙ 8am-8pm Mon-Sat, to 7pm Sun), as well as two recommended restaurants.

★ **Uusi Kilta**   SCANDINAVIAN €€
(☑ 02-435-1066; www.uusikilta.fi; Mannerheiminkatu 1; mains €18-33; ⊙ kitchen 10am-10pm May-Sep) Naantali's best restaurant has a sun-drenched terrace overlooking the pier and a superb, seafood-oriented menu. The selection changes seasonally, but you're likely to find Kilta's creamy fish soup (with pike-perch and salmon) any time of the year. Other favourites include smoked-reindeer pie with chanterelle cream and roasted Arctic char with crayfish and potato stew.

ℹ Information

Naantalin Matkailu (☑ 02-435-9800; www.visitnaantali.com; Kaivotori 2; ⊙ 9am-6pm Mon-Fri, 10am-4pm Sat & Sun Jun-Aug, 9am-4.30pm Mon-Fri Sep-May) Helpful harbour-front tourist office.

ℹ Getting There & Away

Naantali's bus station is 1km east of the harbour. Local buses 6 and 7 run to/from Turku's kauppatori (market square; €3.20, 30 minutes, four per hour).

SS Ukkopekka (www.ukkopekka.fi; Naantali return adult/child €24/12, Loistokari €48-55; ⊙ Naantali 10am & 2pm Tue-Sat Jun-Aug, Loistokari 7pm Tue-Sat May-Sat) sails between Turku and Naantali in summer, arriving at the passenger quay on the south side of the harbour.

Finnlink (p146) car ferry runs between Naantali, Finland, and Kapellskär, Sweden, with a stop in Långnäs in Lumparland (either leg from €45 including passenger and vehicle). Långnäs is five hours from Naantali and 3½ hours from Kapellskär.

ÅLAND ARCHIPELAGO

Glorious Åland Archipelago is a geopolitical anomaly: it is Finnish owned and Swedish speaking, but it has its own parliament, flies its own blue, gold and red flag, issues its own stamps and uses its own web suffix: 'dot ax'. Its 'special relationship' with the EU means it can sell duty-free and make its own gambling laws.

Åland is the sunniest spot in northern Europe and its sweeping white-sand beaches and flat, scenic cycling routes attract crowds of holidaymakers during summer. Yet outside the lively capital, Mariehamn, a sleepy haze hangs over the islands' tiny villages: finding your own remote beach among the 6500 skerries (rocky islets) is surprisingly easy. A lattice of bridges and free cable ferries connects the central islands, while larger car ferries run to the archipelago's outer reaches.

ℹ Information

Aland.ax (www.aland.ax) Official website of the government of Åland.

Aland.com (www.aland.com) Reams of information about local events, culture and more.

Ålandsresor (☑ 018-28040; www.alandsresor.fi) Online booking for accommodation and tours.

Visit Åland (Ålands Turistinformation; ☑ 018-24000; www.visitaland.com; Storagatan 8; ⊙ 9am-6pm early Jun-Aug, to 4pm Apr, May & Sep, to 4pm Mon-Fri Oct-Mar; 🎧) Helpful tourist office in Mariehamn.

ℹ Getting There & Away

AIR

Åland's **airport** (www.finavia.fi; Flygfältsvägen 67) is 4km northwest of Mariehamn. NextJet (www.nextjet.se) flies twice daily to/from Stockholm-Arlanda Airport and once daily to/from Turku (both 30 minutes, from €95 return). Finnair (www.finnair.com) operates a flight between Mariehamn and Helsinki.

There are no regular buses from the airport. In the terminal there's a free hotline to order a taxi.

BOAT

Several car ferries run between Finland and Sweden, stopping at Fasta Åland (Mainland Åland) en route.

In Finland, ferries originate in Helsinki, Turku or Naantali. In Sweden, the ferries come from Stockholm, Kapellskär or Grisslehamn. In Åland, ferries call at Mariehamn, Eckerö or Långnäs, depending on company and point of origin. Prices vary with season and web specials are common; cars and cabins cost extra.

The smaller archipelago ferries travel from mainland Finland to the outer islands. Namely, ferries travel from Kustavi to Åva on Brändö, from where you can connect to the northern route to Vårdö. Ferries also travel from Galtby,

ÅLAND SPECIALITIES

With its abundance of seafood, produce and dairy products, not to mention the ingenuity of local chefs, Åland boasts special cuisine indeed. Don't miss the chance to sample a few specialities that you may not see anywhere else in Finland.

Ålandspannkaka They call it an Åland pancake, but it's not really a pancake at all. It's a spongy dessert made of semolina and subtly flavored with cardamom. Traditionally, it's topped with stewed prunes, though it's also good with jam.

Ålands svartbröd The ubiquitous local dark bread is a malt fruit loaf that takes four days to make. It's the perfect complement to *sill* (pickled herring) and light local cheeses.

Korpo, to Kökar and then follow the southern route to Lumparland.

ⓘ Getting Around

BICYCLE

Ro-No Rent (☑ 018-12820; www.rono.ax; Österhamn; ⊙ 9am-6pm Jun–mid-Aug, by arrangement Sep–May) has bicycles available near Mariehamn harbour. Many campgrounds and guest harbours also have bike hire.

Green-and-white signs trace cycling routes through the islands. Routes generally follow smaller, less busy roads; dedicated bicycle paths run parallel to some main roads.

BOAT

Three kinds of inter-island ferry serve the islands. For short trips, free vehicle ferries sail nonstop. There's also one private summer bicycle ferry running between Hammarland and Geta.

For longer routes – namely to the outer islands – ferries run to a schedule, which is available **online** (Transportation Office; ☑ 018-25600; www.alandstrafiken.ax; Styrmansgatan 1; ⊙ 10am-5pm Mon-Fri). These ferries are generally free for foot passengers, but you must buy tickets for bicycles or cars.

Mariehamn

☑ 018 / POP 11,470

The capital of Åland, Mariehamn was named by Alexander II after the Empress Maria, and its broad streets lined with linden trees recall its Russian heritage. Nowadays it's a bustling, touristy place – home to parks, museums, minigolf, hotels, restaurants, bars, clubs, shops, galleries and more. During summer, visitors flood the bike paths, tour boats and pavement cafes. The calendar is packed with music festivals and cultural fairs, and folks stay out all night soaking up the midnight sun.

Of course, it's not all fun and games in the archipelago's only city. Two out of every five Ålanders live and work in Mariehamn, and Åland's parliament and government are also here. In summer, however, this workaday world fades into the background as holiday-makers take over the town.

◉ Sights & Activities

★ Sjöfartsmuseum   MUSEUM
(Maritime Museum; www.sjofartsmuseum.ax; Hamngatan 2; adult/child incl Museumship Pommern €10/6; ⊙ 10am-5pm Jun-Aug, 11am-4pm Sep-May) Preserved boats make up most of the exhibitions at this state-of-the-art museum exploring Åland's marine heritage. In fact, the centrepiece is a reproduction of a ship, complete with mast, saloon, galley and cabins. The museum is a great place to discover your inner pirate, with plenty of ships in bottles, sea chests and accoutrements. Anchored outside is the Museumship Pommern. Also here is Mariehamn's top restaurant, Nautical (p151).

Sjökvarteret   WATERFRONT, MUSEUM
(Maritime quarter; ☑ 018-16033; www.sjokvarteret.com; Österleden 110; museum adult/child €4/free; ⊙ museum 10am-4pm Mon-Fri, 11am-3pm Sat & Sun mid-Jun–mid-Aug, 9.30am-4pm Tue-Thu May–mid-Jun) At the northern end of Österhamn, Sjökvarteret has long been devoted to boat building. You can stroll along the atmospheric quay, lined with traditional schooners, and perhaps see boats under construction. The **museum**, with exhibitions on shipbuilding (no English information), is located in a small timber boat shed. Don't miss the tiny reconstructed **seafarers' chapel** at the end of the pier.

Museumship Pommern   MUSEUM
(Sjopromenaden; adult/child incl Sjöfartsmuseum €10/6; ⊙ 10am-5pm Jun-Aug, 11am-4pm Sep & May) Just behind the Sjöfartsmuseum

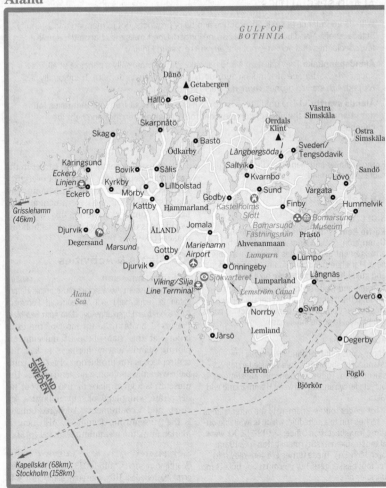

(p149), this beautifully preserved, four-masted, merchant barque was built in 1903 in Glasgow, Scotland. The ship once carried tonnes of cargo and a 26-man crew on the trade route between Australia and England. Its record run was a speedy 110 days.

🛏 Sleeping

Mariehamn contains the bulk of Åland's lodgings. Business and tourist hotels, as well as campgrounds and guesthouses, cover a wide range of prices and styles. As throughout the islands, rates are highest between mid-June and the end of August, and especially in July. Booking ahead is recommended, especially for weekends.

Gröna Udden Camping   CAMPGROUND €
(☎ 018-528-700; www.gronaudden.com; Östernäsvägen; tent sites €10 plus per adult €10, 2-/4-/6-person cabins €105/140/180; ☉ early May-early Sep; 🐊) By the seaside, 15 minutes' stroll south of the city centre, this campground is a family favourite, so you'll need to book its fully equipped spruce cabins ahead. Outdoor fun includes a safe swimming beach, a minigolf course (admission €5) and bike hire (€15). Linen costs €8.50 per person.

0 — 20 km
0 — 10 miles

Enklinge

Lappo

Krokarno

Kumlinge

Seglinge   Snäckö

Skaget   Galtby (130km);
Sottunga   Houtskar (142km);
              Turku (158km);
              Helsinki (326km)

Finholma

Husö

Southern
Archipelago
              Kökar
Hamnö   Hellsö

Karlby

Källskär

with business visitors, though water views from the balconies are tempting for anyone. Rooms are large, with wooden floors, modern furnishings and minimalist decor. Super facilities include indoor and outdoor pools, a freshly refurbished sauna, a nightclub, a casino, three restaurants and several bars.

✖ Eating & Drinking

Mariehamn has an exciting dining scene that shows off the island's freshest ingredients and the talent of its most creative chefs. No other place in the archipelago rivals the capital in terms of variety and quality of eating options. Mariehamn also has the islands' biggest and best food store, so you may want to stock up here before heading to the outer islands.

Nightlife in Mariehamn is hopping in summer, and many bars and clubs stay open until sunrise (which is about 3am at that time of year). Restaurant bars also keep later hours in summer, and there's often live music to keep the party going.

★ Pub Niska   PIZZA €
(☑ 018-19151; www.pubniska.com; Sjökvarteret; pizza €11.50-12.50; ⊙ 11am-7pm Mon-Sat, 3-9pm Sun May & Sep, 11am-9pm Jun-Aug) ◢ Star chef Michael 'Micke' Björklund of Smakbyn (p153) is the brains behind this *plåtbröd* (Åland-style pizza) restaurant in the maritime quarter. Toppings are diverse and delicious, including favourites such as cold-smoked salmon and horseradish cream. In true locavore spirit, the cheese is from Åland's dairy. The atmospheric interior feels like the inside of a ship, but the place to be is the glorious sunny terrace.

Bagarstugan Cafe & Vin   CAFE €
(www.bagarstugan.ax; Ekonomiegatan 2; mains €6-15; ⊙ 10am-6pm Mon-Fri, to 4pm Sat Jun-Aug, 10am-5pm Mon-Fri, 11am-4pm Sat Sep-May) ◢ This sweet cafe is set in a cosy house crowded with bookshelves, chandeliers and tile stoves. It's a charming backdrop for homemade soups, salads, quiches, pies and cakes (scattered with flower petals and far too pretty to eat!) made from local, often organic produce. The courtyard is a delight in summer.

★ Indigo   FINNISH €€
(☑ 018-16550; www.indigo.ax; Nygatan 1; lunch €12-13, dinner mains €23-33, courtyard summer mains €18-22; ⊙ 11am-10pm Mon-Sat year-round,

Park Alandia Hotel   HOTEL €€
(☑ 018-14130; www.parkalandiahotel.com; Norra Esplanadgatan 3; s/d €120/150; @🛜🏊) Recently revamped, all rooms at this sophisticated spot on the main boulevard now feature big windows, sandy hues and hardwood floors. There's a swimming pool and sauna, and a recommended restaurant with an irresistible terrace. Bonus: guests can borrow bikes for free.

Hotell Arkipelag   HOTEL €€€
(☑ 018-24020; www.hotellarkipelag.com; Strandgatan 35; s/d €150/180, with sea view €180/210; ✳@🛜🏊) High-class Arkipelag is popular

plus 2-10pm Sun May-Aug) The building might be historic brick and timber, but the menu is contemporary, with expertly cooked dishes like grilled Åland beef with Béarnaise sauce and homemade fries. There's a buzzing summer courtyard and a beautiful loft space. It's a stylish spot for a drink, with late-night hours for the bar.

Nautical
FINNISH €€€

(☑ 018-19931; www.nautical.ax; Hamngätan 2; mains lunch €12-16, dinner €34-41, 6-course tasting menu €79; ⊙ 11am-11pm Mon-Fri, 5pm-midnight Sat; 🛜) Taking its cue from its maritime-museum (p149) location, this spiffy marine-blue restaurant overlooking the western harbour and *Pommern* is decked out with a ship's wheel and has a splendid umbrella-shaded summer terrace. Sea-inspired dishes range from salmon tartare with horseradish and fennel to pan-fried Åland perch with caraway foam; land-based options include red-wine-braised oxtail with forest mushrooms.

Kvarter 5
FINNISH €€€

(☑ 018-1555; www.kvarter5.ax; Norragatan 10; lunch buffet €12, dinner mains €17-33, 3-course tasting menu €38; ⊙ 7am-10.30pm Mon-Sat, 7.30am-9pm Sun) This newish spot has received rave reviews for its sophisticated Nordic cuisine, featuring local ingredients and everything made from scratch. The location – inside the Hotell Pommern (☑ 018-15555; www.alandhotels.fi; Norragatan 8-10; s/d/q €165/175/205, Moomin r €225; 🛜⛱🐾) – detracts a bit from the atmosphere, but service and cuisine are spot on.

ⓘ Information

Ålandsresor (p148) Handles hotel, guesthouse and cottage bookings for the entire archipelago. Also books tours.

Ålandstrafiken (p149) Information on buses and ferries around Åland, and Archipelago Ticket bookings.

Tourist Office (p148) Helpful office with region-wide info.

ⓘ Getting There & Away

The airport (p148) is 4km northwest of the city centre.

Viking (☑ 018-26211; www.vikingline.fi; Storagatan 3; ⊙ 9am-6pm Mon-Fri) and **Tallink/Silja** (☑ 018-16179; www.tallinksilja.com; Västrahamnen; ⊙ 9.30am-5pm Mon-Fri) ferries dock at the ferry terminal at Västerhamn (West Harbour). The guest harbour for small boats is at Österhamn (East Harbour).

Eckerö Linjen (☑ 018-28000; www.eckerolinjen.ax; Torggatan 2; ⊙ 8.30am-5pm Mon-Fri) ferries sail from Eckerö to Grisslehamn, Sweden (adult/car €4.50/15, two hours); buy tickets at this office in Mariehamn.

Island buses depart from the **bus station** (Styrmansgatan) opposite the post office; enquire at Visit Åland (p148) for timetables.

Around the Archipelago

Sund
POP 1030

Sund is situated 30km from Mariehamn, just east of the main island group. It's connected to Saltvik by bridge, but it's still a long haul from the capital. It's worth the trip, however, as Sund is home to Åland's highlight attractions: the muscular medieval castle Kastelholm and the battle-scarred ruins of the Russian stronghold at Bomarsund. In the midst of these historic sights is the island's most talked-about eatery, Smakbyn, which spearheaded the locavore movement on Åland.

Midway between Kastelholm and Bomarsund is Sund's largest town, Finby, with all services.

⊙ Sights

⭐ **Kastelholms Slott**
CASTLE

(☑ 018-432-150; www.kastelholm.ax; adult/child €6/4.50; ⊙ 10am-5pm mid-May–Jun & Aug–mid-Sep, to 6pm Jul) One of Åland's premier sights is this striking 14th-century castle on a picturesque inlet (signposted off Rd 2). The keep towers are 15m high in parts, with walls of 3m-thick red granite; it's easy to see how it would once have ruled over Åland. Exhibits showcase the castle's evolution and archaeological finds, including a medieval silver-coin hoard. English-language tours (included in admission) depart at 2pm Saturday and Sunday from June to early August and last around 45 minutes.

⭐ **Bomarsund Fästningsruin**
RUINS

(Bomarsund Fortress Ruin; www.bomarsund.ax) Following the war of 1808–09, Russia began building this major military structure as its westernmost defence against the Swedes. The fortress was still incomplete when the Crimean War began in 1854, and a French-British naval force bombarded it heavily from the sea. Within four days the Russians were forced to surrender it.

The evocative ruins stretch for a couple of kilometres, straddling the road and overlooking the sea. Across the water on Prästö, the small **Bomarsund Museum** (☑018-44032; Prästö; admission by donation; ☺10am-5pm Mon-Fri Jun-Aug, plus 10am-5pm Sat & Sun Jul) displays excavated artefacts.

🍴 Sleeping & Eating

Puttes Camping   CAMPGROUND €
(☑018-44040, 0457-313-4177; www.visitaland.com/puttescamping; Bryggvägen 2, Bomarsund; tent sites €12 plus per person €4, cabins without bathroom €35-55, cottages €75; ☺May-Aug) Right on Bomarsund's doorstep, Puttes has plenty of grassy sites and simple four-bed cabins, plus a beach sauna, bike hire, rowing boats and a canoe jetty. Its cafe does a brisk trade in pancakes and other treats.

Kastelholms Gästhem   B&B €€
(☑018-43841; Tosarbyvägen 47, Kastelholm; s/d €91/98, without bathroom €64/86; ☺May–mid-Oct; 🛜) The closest accommodation to Kastelholms Slott (p152) is this pleasant little guesthouse. Most of its spotless floral rooms have private bathrooms, and there's access to a self-catering kitchen and laundry. The patios are perfect for evening lazing.

★**Smakbyn**   FINNISH €€€
(☑018-43666; www.smakbyn.ax; Slottsvägen 134, Kastelholm; lunch €10, light bites €15-19, evening menu €36-44; ☺11am-7pm Mon-Fri, 1-8pm Sat; 🍴) 🍷 The brainchild of award-winning chef Michael 'Micke' Björklund, this 'taste village' incorporates a farm shop, cookery courses and a distillery (tours and tastings available). The centrepiece is the airy open-kitchen restaurant, where the cooks work magic, using seasonal organic produce in creative ways. The menu is always different but usually features delicious local perch fillets and the beloved Hunter's sandwich.

❶ Getting There & Away

Bus 4 from Mariehamn to Vårdö serves Sund. The bus goes via Kastelholm (€3.20, 30 minutes), Bomarsund (€4.40, 40 minutes) and Prästö (€4.50, 45 minutes).

Eckerö

POP 930

On the far-western edge of mainland Åland, delightful Eckerö is the archipelago's closest point to mainland Sweden – just a two-hour ferry ride from Grisslehamn. While the island maintains an off-the-beaten-track atmosphere, it does contain a handful of excellent accommodation options and some offbeat but interesting sights. Eckerö is also home to Åland's loveliest stretch of sand at Degersand beach.

◉ Sights & Activities

Käringsund Harbour   HARBOUR
About 2km north of Storby, Käringsund harbour is delightfully picturesque, with rustic red wooden boathouses reflected in the calm waters. A nature trail leads to a small beach; **Käringsund Resort** (☑018-38000; www.karingsund.ax; Käringsundsvägen 194; 🛜) rents out canoes and rowing boats.

JaRo Guiding   FISHING, OUTDOORS
(☑0457-342-7467; www.jaroguiding.com) Jakob Rosenqvist offers a variety of nature tours and fishing excursions, including birding, boat tours of the archipelago and snake walks.

🍴 Sleeping & Eating

★**Degersands Resort** CAMPGROUND, COTTAGE €€
(☑018-38004; www.degersand.ax; Degersandsvägen 311; tent sites €9 plus per person €6, 1-2 person/3-4 person cabins €145/170; 🛜) 🍷 Bang on Åland's most beautiful beach, this haven has stunning cottages in sleek Scandinavian blond wood with full kitchens, indoor and outdoor showers, and wraparound timber decks with barbecues. Awesome facilities include a traditional smoke sauna on the beach, and rowing-boat, kayak, fishing-gear and bike hire. Weekly discounts available.

Hotel Elvira   HOTEL €€
(☑0457-343-1530; www.elvira.ax; Sandmovägen 85, Storby; d from €115; 🛜) Fronting a small beach, this guesthouse is a charmer, with 20 individually decorated rooms, some with sea views. Sewing machines, typewriters and other antique items enhance the retro atmosphere, as do the animal hides and other recycled items. Excellent restaurant and sauna also on-site. It's just up the road from the **Post och Tullhuset** (Post & Customs House; www.postochtullhuset.ax; Storby; museum €3; ☺main bldg 10am-5pm May-Aug, museum 10am-3pm May-Aug).

★**Bodegan**   SEAFOOD €€
(☑018-38530; www.karingsundsgasthamn.ax; Käringsund Harbour; mains lunch €15-16, dinner €18-25; ☺11am-7pm mid-late Jun, 8am-10pm late Jun–mid-Aug; 🛜) Right on the pier, this delightful spot is perfect for a drink or a meal

while watching the seagulls soar above the creaking red boathouses. The classic Nordic dishes are delectable: marinated salmon with dill potatoes; grilled tenderloin; or a plate of 'sea tapas', including smoked salmon, shrimp or whitefish, served with archipelago black bread.

ℹ Information

Tourist Information Desk (☑ 018-39462; www.eckero.ax; ☉10am-6pm Jun-Aug, to 5pm Sep-May) At Eckerö's ferry terminal.

ℹ Getting There & Away

Eckerö Linjen (☑ 018-28300; www.eckerolinjen. ax; Berghamn) ferries sail from Eckerö to Grisslehamn, Sweden (adult/car €4.50/15, two hours).

Williams Buss (bus 1) runs from Mariehamn to Eckerö about six times a day (€4.50, 50 minutes).

SOUTHWESTERN FINLAND

Tampere

☑ 03 / POP 228,907

Set between two vast lakes, scenic Tampere has a down-to-earth vitality and pronounced cultural focus that make it a favourite for many visitors. The Tammerkoski rapids churn through the centre, flanked by grassy banks that stand in contrast with the red brick of the imposing fabric mills that once drove the city's economy. Regenerated industrial buildings now house quirky museums, enticing shops, pubs, cinemas and cafes.

◎ Sights

★**Amurin Työläismuseokortteli** MUSEUM
(Amuri Museum of Workers' Housing; ☑03-5656-6690; www.museokortteli.fi; Satakunnankatu 49; adult/child €7/3, 3-6pm Fri free; ☉10am-6pm Tue-Sun early May-early Sep) An entire block of wooden houses – including 32 apartments in five residential buildings, a bakery, a shoemaker, a public sauna, two general shops and a cafe – is preserved at the Amuri Museum of Workers' Housing, evoking life from 1882 to 1973. Interpretative panels (English translation available) outlining the fictional lives of residents give plenty of historical information and make for a visit that is as entertaining as it is educational. There's a good on-site cafe (soup lunch €7).

★**Vapriikki** MUSEUM
(www.vapriikki.fi; Alaverstaanraitti 5; adult/child €12/6, free 3-6pm Fri; ☉10am-6pm Tue-Sun) This bright, modern glass-and-steel exhibition space in the renovated Tampella textile mill hosts regularly changing exhibitions on anything from bicycles to Buddhism. It also has a permanent display on Tampere's history, a beautiful **mineral museum**, a **natural history museum** and a small but cluttered **ice-hockey museum**, with memorabilia of star players and teams from Finland's sporting passion. There's also a **museum of shoes** – Tampere was known for its footwear industry – and a pleasant cafe (open 11am to 2pm Tuesday to Friday, noon to 3pm Saturday and Sunday).

★**Tuomiokirkko** CHURCH
(☑ 040-804-8765; www.tampereenseurakunnat.fi; Tuomiokirkonkatu 3; ☉10am-5pm May-Aug, 11am-3pm Sep-Apr) FREE An iconic example of National Romantic art-nouveau architecture, Tampere's cathedral dates from 1907. Hugo Simberg created the frescoes and stained glass; you'll appreciate that they were controversial. A procession of naked childlike apostles holds the 'garland of life', graves and plants are tended by skeletal figures, and in the upstairs gallery a wounded angel is stretchered off by two children. Magnus Enckell's dreamlike Resurrection altarpiece is designed in a similar style. The serpent on the dome adds to the strange ambience.

★**Särkänniemi** AMUSEMENT PARK
(www.sarkanniemi.fi; Laiturikatu 1; 1-day pass over/under 120cm €45/39; ☉rides mid-May–Aug, hours vary) This promontory-set amusement park complex offers dozens of rides, an observation tower, art gallery, aquarium, farm zoo and planetarium. A one-day pass gives you access to them all. Among the best rides are the Tornado roller coaster, super-fast High Voltage, speedboat rides on the lake and an Angry Birds area for younger kids. Opening times are complex; check the website. Indoor attractions stay open year-round. Take bus 20 (€3) from the train station or central square.

The **aquarium** (€12.90; ☉11am-9pm) is mediocre, with Finnish fish more interesting than the hobby-tank favourites. The planetarium is in the same complex, above which soars the 168m **Näsinneula Observation Tower** (€5.90; ☉11am-11.30pm), the tallest in these northern lands. It commands spectacular city and lake views and has a revolving restaurant.

Sara Hildénin Taidemuseo (Sara Hildén Art Museum; ☑ 03-5654-3500; www.tampere.fi/sarahilden; Laiturkatu 13; adult/child €8/4; ☉ 10am-6pm Tue-Sun Sep–mid-May, noon-7pm daily mid-May–Aug) has a collection of international and Finnish modern art and sculpture, and also hosts travelling exhibitions.

🏃 Activities

The www.visittampere.fi website has plenty more ideas for getting active in and around Tampere, including fishing information.

Rajaportin Sauna   SAUNA
(☑ 050-310-2611; www.rajaportinsauna.fi; Pispalan Valtatie 9; adult/child €10/3, midweek €6/3; ☉ 6-10pm Mon & Wed, 3-9pm Fri, 2-10pm Sat) This traditional place is Finland's oldest operating public sauna. It's a great chance to experience the softer steam from a traditionally heated sauna rather than the harsher electric ones. It's a couple of kilometres west of the city centre; buses 8, 11 and 13 among others head out there. There's a cafe on-site, and massages can be arranged. Take a towel or rent one there.

Suomen Hopealinja   CRUISE
(☑ 010-422-5600; www.hopealinja.fi) Departing from **Laukontori Quay**, the Finnish Silver Line operates short cruises on Pyhäjärvi between June and August and there's also a shuttle service (adult/child return €13/8) to nearby **Viikinsaari**, a pleasant picnic island. There are various lunch- and dinner-cruise options, and pirate cruises for kids.

🎉 Festivals & Events

Tampere Biennale   MUSIC
(www.tamperemusicfestivals.fi/biennale; ☉ Apr) A festival of contemporary Finnish music, held in even-numbered years.

Tampere International Theatre Festival   THEATRE
(www.teatterikesa.fi; ☉ early Aug) Week-long showcase of international and Finnish theatre. **Off-Tampere** is a fringe festival held at the same time.

Tampere Jazz Happening   MUSIC
(www.tamperemusicfestivals.fi/jazz/en; ☉ Nov) International artists join musicians from across Scandinavia at this high-profile event. Gigs are held at the Old Customs House Hall, **Klubi** (www.klubi.net; Tullikamarinaukio 2; ☉ 11am-6pm Mon-Tue, to 4am Wed-Sat) and Telakka (p158).

🛏 Sleeping

As well as better-known nationwide operators, there are several options in the countryside around Tampere for seeking out that perfect cottage haven or warm and welcoming stay on an organic farm. Check www.visittampere.fi for ideas.

★ Dream Hostel   HOSTEL €
(☑ 045-236-0517; www.dreamhostel.fi; Åkerlundinkatu 2; dm €27-41, tw with shared bathroom from €53, s/d & tw from €65/72; ✴@🛜) 🅿 With its contemporary Nordic design, switched-on staff and good facilities, this hostel is consistently ranked Finland's best. Narrow dorms (mixed and female-only) have small under-bed lockers; bathrooms are barracks-like but clean. Facilities include a laundry and fully kitted-out self-catering kitchen (free tea and coffee). It's a 200m walk southeast of the train station in a quiet area. Breakfast costs €6.50.

Scandic Tampere Station   HOTEL €€
(☑ 03-339-8000; www.scandichotels.com; Ratapihankatu 37; standard s/d €139/159, superior s €160-220, superior d €180-240; 🅿✴@🛜🛁) As the name suggests, this sleek, modern chain hotel is located right by the train station. Rooms are spacious and well equipped; those in the superior category have a kettle and some even have a dark-wood sauna and balcony, and don't cost much more. Service is excellent, as befits a business hotel. Parking costs €18.

Radisson Blu Grand Hotel Tammer   HISTORIC HOTEL €€
(☑ 020-123-4632; www.radissonblu.com/hotel-tampere; Satakunnankatu 13; standard s/d €140/160, superior d €180, ste €200-250; 🅿✴@🛜🛁) Constructed in 1929, this is one of Finland's oldest hotels and enjoys a fine location beside the rapids. After the gloriously old-fashioned elegance of the public areas, the rooms are a little disappointing, though they have the expected facilities and Nordic comfort levels. Parking costs €18; a good breakfast buffet and sauna are included.

★ Lapland Hotel Tampere   DESIGN HOTEL €€€
(☑ 03-383-000; www.laplandhotels.com; Yliopistonkatu 44; s €180-210, d €200-230; 🅿✴@🛜) Part of the excellent portfolio of contemporary hotels operated by the Lapland hotel group, this place has a chic ground-floor lounge bar, a sauna, well-equipped and extremely comfortable rooms and a restaurant

Tampere

Särkänniemi ⊚ 2

Näsijärvi

Verstaank

Tampellan

6

7 ⊚❶ 5

Laiturikatu

Näsinpuisto Park

Alaverstaanraitti

4 Vapriikki

ⓟ

Paasikiventie

Näsijärvenkatu

Tammerkoski

Niemikatu

Mariankatu

Amurinkatu

Kortelahdenkatu

Puuvillatehtaankatu

Finlaysoninkatu

Mustalahdenkatu

Satakunnankatu

Amurin
Työläismuseokortteli
1

Frenckellinaukio

ⓟ
19

Puutarhakatu

Aleksis Kivenkatu

Pirkankatu

Kauppakatu

Hämeenpuisto

Hämeenkatu

16 ⊗

Local
Buses

← Rajaportin
Sauna (1.5km)

17 ⊗

Hallituskatu

Laukontori
Market
Square

Näsilinnankatu

Kuninkaankatu

Laukontori
Quay

⊗ 8

Pyynikintie

Satamakatu

✗ Eating

There's a vibrant restaurant and cafe scene in Tampere, with eateries catering to almost every taste and budget. Most are open year-round.

The city's speciality, *mustamakkara*, is a mild, tasty sausage made with cow's blood, normally eaten with lingonberry jam. Try it at the kauppahalli (covered market).

★ **Bistro 14**　　　　　　　　　INTERNATIONAL €
(📞 050-462-8204; http://bistro14.fi; Rautatienkatu 14; lunch buffet €7.50-9.70, 3-course dinner menu €33, mains €18; ⊗ 11am-9pm Wed & Thu,

---

where a generous and delicious buffet breakfast is served. Staff members are young and very helpful; on-site parking costs €18.

Sokos Hotel Ilves　　　　　　HOTEL €€€
(📞 020-123-4631; www.sokoshotels.fi; Hatanpään valtatie 1; r from €169; ⓟ ❋ @ 🛜 🏊) This tower hotel was big news when it opened in the 1980s, and still keeps standards high. Very high: the view from upper-floor rooms is memorable, so ask for as lofty a chamber as you can get. Rooms are attractively furnished with Finnish design classics; superiors are the same size but with even better views.

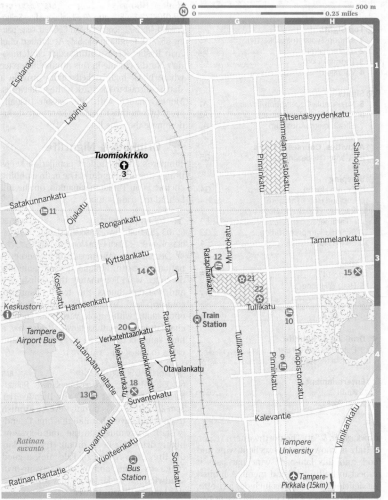

Tampere-Pirkkala (15km)

to 10pm Fri & Sat, to 3pm Sun Jun-Sep, 11am-3pm Mon & Tue, to 9pm Wed & Thu, to 10pm Fri & Sat, to 3pm Sun Oct-May; 🔊🖋) With its sleek modern interior and talented French chef, this small place near the train station is garnering lots of local attention. The food is fresh and light, with expertly balanced flavours and pretty presentation; diners who are gluten-free, lactose intolerant or vegetarian are catered for. The weekday lunch buffet is simply amazing value, as is the Sunday brunch (€12.50).

Kauppahalli MARKET €

(Hämeenkatu 19; ⊘8am-6pm Mon-Fri, to 3pm Sat; 🖋) 🖋 This intriguing indoor market is one of Finland's best, with picturesque wooden stalls serving a dazzling array of wonderful meats, fruit, baked goodies and fish. If hungry, you can snack on cheap *mustamakkara* (sausage made with cow's blood) with berry jam or sit down for a French feast at Neljä Vuodenaikaa.

★ Piemonte ITALIAN €€

(📞03-225-5505; www.piemonte.fi; Suvantokatu 9; mains €19-29; ⊘11am-9pm Mon, to 11pm Tue-Thu,

Tampere

to midnight Fri & Sat) The northwestern region of Italy is known for its excellent wine and food, and this laid-back wine bar pays it respect in both name and menu. A limited but delicious list of dishes includes a risotto, one or two pastas, a fish dish and one or two meat mains – the steak is particularly good. Excellent service and Italian wine list.

★**Neljä Vuodenaikaa**   BISTRO €€
(4 Saisons; www.4vuodenaikaa.fi; Kauppahalli; soup €9.50, mains €18-22; ⊙8am-3.45pm Mon-Fri, to 3.30pm Sat) Tucked into the rear right-hand corner of the kauppahalli, the Four Seasons brings Gallic flair to the Finnish lunch hour with delicious plates such as bouillabaisse, escargots and *steak fritte* augmented by excellent daily specials and wines by the glass.

Hella & Huone   GASTRONOMY €€€
(🖉010-322-3898; http://hellajahuone.fi; Salhojankatu 48; 6-/12-course menu €65/90, wine pairing €52/70; ⊙6-10pm Thu-Sat) Acclaimed chef Arto Rastas serves cutting-edge contemporary Nordic cuisine in this minimalist space where black high-backed chairs provide a sharp contrast to the stark white tablecloths. Menus change with the season (usually every two months). Organic European drops dominate the wine list.

🍷 Drinking & Nightlife

Tampere's strong student population keeps things vibrant after dark. The main clubbing enclave is on Tullikamarinaukio, on the hill behind the train station.

★**Mokka Mestarit**   COFFEE
(🖉03-253-0145; www.mokkamestarit.fi; Verkatehtaankatu 9; ⊙10am-6pm Mon-Fri, to 4pm Sat; 🛜) 🍴 Despite being the most caffeine-addicted nation on earth, Finland doesn't generally do coffee well. Fortunately this stylish cafe and roastery bucks the trend. Espresso, cold-drip and Aeropress variations are on offer, along with hippie variations such as chai lattes and matcha bowls. It also has a huge range of tea and an array of panini and cakes to snack on – we love it.

★**Deli 1909 & Wine Bar**   BAR
(🖉050-441-1722; www.gastropub.net; Puutarhakatu 11; sandwiches €8.50; ⊙4-11pm Tue-Thu, 3pm-2am Fri & Sat) If only every Finnish town could have a bar like this one. Friendly staff, great music on the sound system, highly drinkable beers on tap (try the Nordic Brewery's American Pale Ale), a good range of wine and a choose-your-own sandwich bar make for a great mix. Closes one hour earlier in winter.

☆ Entertainment

★**Telakka**   LIVE PERFORMANCE
(🖉03-225-0700; www.telakka.eu; cnr Tullikamarinaukio & Tullikatu; cover €5-12; ⊙11am-midnight Mon-Thu, noon-3am Fri & Sat Jun-Aug, noon-3am Fri & Sat Sep-May) Comics and musicians regularly take to the stage at this much-loved venue, which attracts arty, hip and fun-loving locals of every age. Drinkers and diners claim the tables in the front garden; the stage is inside. It's always fun, but is absolutely irresistible during the Tampere Jazz Happening (p155).

ℹ Information

Visit Tampere (☑ 03-5656-6800; www.
visittampere.fi; Hämeenkatu 14B; ⊗ 10am-6pm
Mon-Fri, to 3pm Sat & Sun Jun-Aug, 10am-5pm
Mon-Fri, to 3pm Sat Sep-May; 🛜) On the main
street in the centre of town. Can book activities
and events.

ℹ Getting There & Away

AIR

Tampere-Pirkkala Airport (TMP; ☑ 020-708-
5521; www.finavia.fi; Tornikaari 50) is situated
17km southwest of the city. Airlines flying to/
from Tampere:

AirBaltic Flies to Riga, Latvia.

Finnair Flies to Helsinki (though the train is
more convenient, with connections to other
Finnish cities.

Primera Air Nordic Flies to various destinations in Spain, Greece and Portugal.

Ryanair Flies to Bremen, Germany, and Buda-
pest, Hungary.

SAS Flies to Stockholm, Sweden.

BUS

From the **bus station** (Hatanpään valtatie 7),
express buses serve Helsinki (€25 to €27, 2¾
hours, up to four hourly) and Turku (€15 to €25,
two hours, hourly). There are services to most
other major towns in Finland.

TRAIN

Trains link Tampere's central **train station**
(www.vr.fi; Rautatienkatu 25) with Helsinki
(€21, 1½ to 1¾ hours, up to three hourly), Turku
(€19 to €23, 1¾ hours, up to six daily) and other
cities.

ℹ Getting Around

The local bus system is extensive. A one-day
ticket costs an adult/child €8/4 for inner-city
zones and €16/8 to cover the complete network;
single-trip tickets for short trips cost €3/1.50.
Check route maps online at http://joukko-
liikenne.tampere.fi.

TO/FROM THE AIRPORT

Tampere-Pirkkala airport is 15km southwest;
arriving flights are met by **bus** (☑ 0100-29400;
www.paunu.fi; €5) 1A, which heads to the city
centre (€5, 30 minutes). **Tokee** (☑ 0200-
39000; www.airpro.fi) serves Ryanair flights,
leaving from the train station forecourt about
2½ hours before take-off (€6).

Shared **airport taxis** (☑ 0100-4131; www.
taksitampere.fi) must be booked in advance
from the city to the airport (€19 per person). A
regular cab will cost around €35.

Hämeenlinna

☑ 03 / POP 67,706

Dominated by its namesake castle, Hämeenlinna (Swedish: Tavastehus) is Finland's oldest inland town, founded in 1649, though a
trading post had existed here since the 9th
century. The Swedes built the castle in the
13th century, and Hämeenlinna developed
into an administrative, educational and garrison town around it. The town is quiet but
picturesque, and its wealth of museums will
keep you busy for a day or two. It makes a
good stop between Helsinki and Tampere.

◉ Sights

★ **Hämeenlinna** CASTLE
(Häme Castle; ☑ 029-533-6932; www.kansallis-
museo.fi/en/hame-castle; adult/child €9/4.50;
⊗ 10am-3.30pm Tue-Fri, 11am-4pm Sat & Sun mid-
Aug–mid-Dec & mid-Jan–Apr, 10am-4pm Mon-Fri,
11am-4pm Sat & Sun May, daily 10am-5pm Jun–mid-
Aug) Hämeenlinna means Häme Castle, so
it's no surprise that this bulky, twin-towered,
red-brick fortress is the town's pride and
most significant attraction. Construction was
begun in the 1260s by the Swedes, who wanted to establish a military redoubt against the
power of Novgorod. It was originally built on
an island, but the lake receded and necessi-
tated the building of new walls. It never saw
serious military action and, after the Russian
takeover of 1809, was converted into a jail.

★ **Palanderin Talo** MUSEUM
(☑ 03-621-2967; www.hmlmuseo.fi; Linnankatu 16;
adult/child €5/2; ⊗ noon-4pm Tue-Sun May-Aug, Sat
& Sun Sep-Apr) Finland loves its house-muse-
ums and this is among the best, offering a wonderful insight into well-off 19th-century Finnish life, thanks to excellent English-speaking
guided tours. There's splendid imperial and
art-nouveau furniture as well as delicate little
touches including a double-sided mirror to
spy on street fashion, and a set of authentic
children's drawings from the period.

🛏 Sleeping & Eating

Sokos Hotel Vaakuna HOTEL €€
(☑ 020-1234-636; www.sokoshotels.fi; Possentie 7;
s/d from €116/131; 🅿 @ 🛜 🐾) Across the river
from the town centre and very near the train
station, this attractive hotel echoes Häme
Castle with its design. Many of the rooms
have great water views, as does the in-house
French restaurant. The sunny bar terrace is
particularly pleasant on a summer evening.

FINLAND RAUMA

Café Kukko
CAFE €

(☑ 03-616-5670; www.cafekukko.fi; Palokunnankatu 11; sandwiches €4-6, buns & pastries €2.60; ⊙ 8am-8pm Mon-Fri, 10am-5pm Sat & Sun; ☎) Every town needs a good cafe, and Kukko certainly fits the bill. Its bright, diner-style interior has a long counter with an espresso machine and displays of buns, brownies and pastries. A refrigerated cabinet is filled with healthy sandwiches (choose from salad, falafel or smoked salmon), making it as popular at lunch as it is at breakfast. Good coffee too.

★ Piparkakkutalo
FINNISH €€

(☑ 03-648-040; www.ravintolapiparkakkutalo.fi; Kirkkorinne 2; mains €20-34; ⊙ 11am-10pm Tue-Thu, to 11pm Fri, noon-11pm Sat) This fairytale-style 'gingerbread house' was built in 1907 for merchant August Skogster, whose department store was next door, and it is now home to the town's best restaurant. The interior still has a warm, domestic feel. Food includes Finnish classics, a few vegetarian choices and burgers, all made using fresh local produce. The cosy pub downstairs is open between Wednesday and Saturday.

❶ Information

Tourist Office (☑ 03-621-3373; www.visithameenlinna.fi; Raatihuoneenkatu 11; ⊙ 9am-4pm Mon-Fri; ☎) In the Kastelli information centre. Supplies maps and brochures.

❶ Getting There & Away

Hourly buses between Helsinki (€17 to €20, 1½ to 1¾ hours) and Tampere (€12.60, 65 minutes) stop at the **bus station** (Eteläkatu 1), as do regular buses to/from Lahti (€10 to €13.20, 75 minutes). From Turku, there are several buses daily (€15 to €21, 2¼ hours).

The train station is 1km from the town centre, across the bridge. Frequent trains between Helsinki (€15, one hour) and Tampere (€7 to €11, 40 to 60 minutes) stop here. From Turku, change in Toijala.

Rauma

☑ 02 / POP 39,700

Centred on its lively kauppatori (market square), Rauma's Old Town district, Vanha Rauma, is the largest preserved wooden town in the Nordic countries. The main pleasure here is simply meandering the quaint streets of this Unesco World Heritage site.

In the Middle Ages Rauma's lacemakers ignored King Gustav Wasa's order to move to Helsinki to boost the capital's industry. By the 18th century Rauma (Swedish: Raumo) was a thriving trade centre, thanks to the European fashion for lace-trimmed bonnets. Locals still turn out the delicate material, and celebrate their lacemaking heritage with an annual festival.

You might hear snatches of Rauman giäl, the local dialect that mixes English, Estonian, German and other languages that worked their way into the lingo from Rauma's intrepid sailors. Rauma remains an important shipping centre, transporting Finnish paper around the world.

◉ Sights

In the heart of modern Rauma, Vanha Rauma (the Old Town) remains a living centre, with cosy cafes, shops and a few artisans working in small studios; try to visit between Tuesday and Saturday, when everything is open and the town hums with life.

There are more than 600 18th- and 19th-century wooden buildings here, each with its own name – look for small oval nameplates near the door. For a detailed history, pick up a free copy of *A Walking Tour in the Old Town* from the tourist office.

★ Sammallahdenmäki
ARCHAEOLOGICAL SITE

(Lappi; ⊙ dawn-dusk) FREE The Unesco World Heritage–listed Bronze Age burial complex Sammallahdenmäki dates back more than 3500 years. Thirty-six stone burial cairns of different shapes and sizes are spread over a kilometre of forest. The two biggest are kirkonlattia (church floor), a monumental quadrangle measuring 16m by 19m, and the huilun pitkä raunio (long cairn of Huilu). The moss-covered rocks and light-filtering forest create an evocative setting for the mysterious site.

Pyhän Ristin Kirkko
CHURCH

(Church of the Holy Cross; www.rauma.seurakunta.net; Luostarinkatu 1; ⊙ 10am-5pm Mon-Fri, 11am-3pm Sat, 10am-4pm Sun May-Sep) Picturesquely sited next to the little Rauma river, this stone beauty was built around 1520 as part of a Franciscan monastery on the site. The interior frescoes date from this era. The church was abandoned after the Reformation; it was re-established as a Lutheran church in 1640, after a fire destroyed the other church in town. The bell tower was constructed with the stones of the destroyed church.

Sleeping & Eating

Hotelli Vanha Rauma BOUTIQUE HOTEL €€
(☑02-8376-2200; www.hotelvanharauma.fi; Van-
hankirkonkatu 26; s/d €130/160; ☎) Once a
warehouse in the old fish market, this is
now the only hotel in the Old Town proper.
Its 20 rooms embrace modern Scandinavian
design, with lino flooring, leatherette chairs,
flat-screen TV and views of the park or
courtyard. Service is attentive, and the restaurant, SJ Nyyper, is well respected.

★**Kylmäpihlajan Majakka** BOUTIQUE HOTEL €€
(☑045-175-0619; www.kylmapihlaja.com; s €99-
119, d €135-155, ste €265; ☺early Jun-Aug) Fall
asleep to the sound of crashing waves in
this authentic lighthouse, which rises 36m
above the sea on the island of Kylmäpihla-
ja. Nautical-styled rooms are atmospherically furnished with wrought-iron beds. All
bathrooms are shared, even the suite with
fantastic four-way views. There's a restaurant. Catch a boat from **Poroholma campground** (☑02-533-5522; www.poroholma.fi;
Poroholmantie 8; tent sites €15 plus per person €6,
d €85, cottages €80-110; ☺May-Aug; adult/child
return €20/10, 30 minutes).

Kontion Kahvilat CAFE €
(Kontion Cafe; www.kontion.fi; Kuninkaankatu 9;
dishes €4-8, mains €8-14; ☺7.30am-5pm Mon-Fri,
8am-3pm Sat, 11am-4pm Sun) This 50-year-old
bakery is a local institution – it even has its
own cookbook. Breads, cakes and pastries
are the main attraction, but light lunches
such as soups and stews are also available.
And this is your chance to sample a local
speciality: gingerbread cookies.

★**Wanhan Rauman Kellari** FINNISH €€
(☑02-866-6700; www.wrk.fi; Anundilankatu 8;
mains €14.50-34; ☺11am-10pm Mon, to 11pm Tue-
Thu, to midnight Fri & Sat, noon-10pm Sun) A Rauma institution, this restaurant has served as
a potato cellar and an air-raid shelter. Nowadays the atmospheric dining room and
sun-drenched rooftop summer terrace are
delightful settings for a sophisticated menu
of Finnish faves. Desserts are a highlight.

Information

Main Tourist Office (www.visitrauma.fi;
Valtakatu 2; ☺9am-4pm Mon-Fri) Open year-
round.
Summer Tourist Office (☑02-834-3512; www.
visitrauma.fi; Kauppakatu 13; ☺9am-6pm Jun-
Aug) In Vanha Raatihuone (the Old Town Hall)
on the kauppatori.

Getting There & Away

Note that fewer buses run on Saturday and es-
pecially on Sunday. Direct services from the **bus
station** (Tehtaankatu 5):
Helsinki €25, four hours, eight daily
Pori €10, one hour, two hourly
Tampere €15, 2¾ hours, hourly
Turku €10, 1½ hours, hourly
Uusikaupunki €10.10, one hour, six daily

Vaasa
☑06 / POP 67,500
Vaasa (Swedish: Vasa) sits above the 63rd
parallel – southern Finns consider it 'The
North'. Just 45 nautical miles from Sweden,
the city has a significant Swedophone population, with a quarter of residents speaking
Swedish as a first language.

The 17th-century town was named after
Swedish royalty: the noble Wasa family. But
200 years later it was in Russian hands. The
Old Town burned down in Vaasa's Great Fire
of 1852 – caused by a careless visitor who fell
asleep and dropped his pipe – and the new
city was built from scratch, 7km away from
the cinders.

Vaasa has long been a family-holiday
playground, with plenty of outdoor recreation and easy access to the Kvarken Archipelago. It's a cultural centre too, with three
universities and a thriving arts scene, exemplified by its excellent museums.

Sights

★**Pohjanmaan Museo** MUSEUM
(Ostrobothnian Museum; www.pohjanmaanmuseo.
fi; Museokatu 3; adult/child €7/free; ☺10am-5pm
Tue-Sun) This dynamic, modern regional museum is divided into three sections. Downstairs, Terranova has a brilliant evocation of
the region's natural history – complete with
dioramas and storm-and-lightning effects.
This is a great place to start if you're heading
to the Kvarken Archipelago.

Stundars Handicraft Village MUSEUM
(☑06-344-2200; www.stundars.fi; Solf; adult/child
€7/3; ☺11am-4pm Jul–mid-Aug) In the attractive village of Solf (Finnish: Sulva), about
15km south of Vaasa, is this fine open-air
museum and crafts centre. Its 60 traditional wooden buildings were moved here from
surrounding villages and include crofts,
cottages and cowsheds, a pottery, windmills
and a schoolhouse. Admission includes a
guided tour.

🛏 Sleeping

Top Camping Vaasa CAMPGROUND €
(☑ 020-796-1255; www.topcamping.fi; Niemeläntie 1; tent sites €12.50 plus per person €8, 4-person cabins €70; ☺ mid-May–mid-Aug) This popular family getaway is 2km from town on the island of Vaskiluoto. There's loads of fun to be had at this place, including minigolf, pedal cars, a bouncy house, beach volleyball and various other diversions. Ask about discount packages with nearby Tropiclandia water park (☑ 020-796-1300; www.tropiclandia. fi; Sommarstigen 1, Vaskiluoto; adult/child €17/12; ☺ 10am-8pm Sun-Tue, to 9pm Wed-Sat; ☝).

Hotel Astor HOTEL €€
(☑ 06-326-9111; www.astorvaasa.fi; Asemakatu 4; s/d €130/152; ☺ reception noon-midnight; @ 🛜) Handy for the bus and train station, this great little hotel has a historic interior and a personal feel, down to the freshly baked cakes at breakfast. Rooms in the older wing feature polished floors and dark-wood furnishings. Higher-priced doubles have their own sauna.

🍴 Eating

Kauppahalli MARKET €
(Market Hall; www.vaasankauppahalli.fi; Vaasaesplanaden 18; ☺ 8am-6pm Mon-Fri, 9am-3pm Sat) Vaasa's covered market has stalls selling fresh pastries and market goodies.

Seglis FINNISH €€
(☑ 010-320-3779; www.seglis.fi; Niemeläntie 14; lunch buffet €12, mains €16-32; ☺ 11am-2pm Mon-Fri May, 11am-10pm Mon-Fri Jun-Aug) On the island of Vaskiluoto, you can dine on Finnish classics (smoked herring, hare, reindeer) on this wooden pavilion's waterside terrace overlooking the city.

★ Gustav Wasa FINNISH €€€
(☑ 050-466-3208; www.gustavwasa.com; Raastuvankatu 24; mains €19-33, 7-course tasting menu €69, wine pairing €50; ☺ gastropub 5-10pm Mon-Fri, 3-10pm Sat, restaurant 6-10pm Mon-Fri, 4-10pm Sat) A former coal cellar is home to one of Finland's finest restaurants, with sublime seven-course tasting menus served in the intimate candlelit dining room. There's also a casual gastropub with wines by the glass and Finnish beers on tap.

ℹ Information

Tourist Office (☑ 06-325-1145; www.visit-vaasa.fi; 2nd fl, Rewell Shopping Center, Ylätori; ☺ 9am-5pm Mon-Fri year-round, plus 10am-2pm Sat Sep-Apr)

ℹ Getting There & Away

AIR

Accessible by local bus, the **airport** (www. finavia.fi) is 12km southeast of the town centre. Finnair (p138) flies several times daily to Helsinki (from €125, 45 minutes).

BOAT

From late June to early August **Wasaline** (☑ 020-771-6810; www.wasaline.com; Laivanvarustajankatu 4, Helsinki) runs daily ferries (adult/car/bicycle €38/53/5, 4½ hours) between Vaasa and the Swedish town of Umeå (Finnish: Uumaja). The ferry terminal is on the western side of the island of Vaskiluoto.

BUS

Up to five direct buses serve Helsinki (7½ hours) via Tampere (four hours). Frequent buses run up and down the west coast. Services depart from the bus station.

TRAIN

Vaasa trains connect via Seinäjoki (€10, one hour, up to 10 daily) to main-line destinations such as Tampere (€31, two hours, five daily) and Helsinki (€45, 3½ hours, five daily).

Jakobstad

☑ 06 / POP 19,500

In 1652, war widow Ebba Braha founded the town of Jakobstad in honour of her husband, Swedish war hero Jacob de la Gardie. The site was previously the harbour of the parish of the Pedersöre Kyrka. The church still stands today, lending its name to the town's Finnish name, Pietarsaari. But the Swedish identity runs deep, as more than half the population are Swedophone. Jakobstad is also the birthplace of Finland's (Swedish-speaking) national poet, JL Runeberg (1804–77).

Jakobstad's main attraction is its Skata (Old Town), which contains some 300 of the best-preserved wooden houses in Finland, with the picturesque Gamla Hamn (Old Port) beyond.

◉ Sights

Skata OLD TOWN
(Old Town) Originally the stamping ground of sailors and factory workers, Skata occupies several blocks north of the centre (beyond Skolparken). The oldest street is Hamngatan, lined with 18th-century houses. But the prettiest street is Norrmalmsgatan, with a stunning clock tower bridging the street.

Pedersöre Kyrka · CHURCH

(☑040-310-0447; Vasavägen 118; ⊙9am-4pm mid-May–mid-Aug) Dating from the 1400s, this is one of the region's oldest churches. King Gustav III of Sweden personally signed off on the plans to expand the church into the cruciform, though builders ignored his instruction to demolish the towering spire. The church is located about 2km south of the town centre.

Sleeping & Eating

Hotel Epoque · HOTEL €€

(☑06-788-7100; www.hotelepoque.fi; Jakobsgatan 10; s/d €125/143; ⊙reception 7am-10pm Mon-Fri, 8am-10pm Sat, 8am-4pm Sun; P❋◉) Housed in the elegantly restored customs house, the Epoque is the town's best place to stay, with 16 modern rooms and a refined, intimate atmosphere. Most rooms overlook the nearby Skolparken botanic garden.

Stadshotellet Kaupunginhotelli · HOTEL €€

(☑06-788-8111; www.cfhotel.fi; Kanalesplanaden 13; s/d from €105/125) Prominently placed on the main pedestrian thoroughfare, this stately hotel offers super-easy access to the town centre. The 100 rooms – all spruced up after a recent renovation – feature contemporary furnishings, hardwood floors and splashes of colour. There are also three restaurants, two nightclubs and two saunas.

After Eight · CAFE €

(☑06-781-6500; www.aftereight.fi; Storgatan 6; lunch €10; ⊙10am-4pm Mon-Fri) This smashing cafe–cultural centre is the best hang-out in town, with a relaxed atmosphere, well-spaced tables, chilled-out music and a grassy courtyard garden. Lunch (served from 10am to 1pm) offers simple but tasty dishes such as salmon soup and Swedish meatballs, while homemade cakes are available throughout the day. The place sometimes opens in the evenings for special events.

★ Café Fäboda · FINNISH €€

(☑06-723-4533; www.faboda.fi; Lillsandvägen 263; sandwiches €13.50, mains €22-32; ⊙noon-9pm May-Aug; ⊞) On a picturesque rocky perch overlooking the beach, this breezy spot is the best place to dine for miles around. Specialities include gourmet cheeseburgers on brioche buns, freshly caught whitefish with white wine–butter sauce, and steaks such as Chateaubriand in thyme-Madeira sauce. Coffee and dessert are also divine, as is the glorious view of sea and forest.

❶ Information

Tourist Office (☑044-785-1425; www.jakobstad.fi; Salutorget 1; ⊙8am-6pm Mon-Fri, 9am-3pm Sat Jun-Aug, 8am-4pm Mon-Fri Sep-May) Next to the town square.

❶ Getting There & Away

Kokkola-Pietarsaari Airport (www.finavia.fi; Kronoby) is 30km northeast of Jakobstad, with flights from Helsinki, Tampere and Stockholm (Sweden). **City Taxi Jeppis** (☑50-550-9866; www.citytaxijeppis.fi) provides a taxi service into town (€20 per person).

There are regular buses to Jakobstad's **bus** station from Vaasa (€18, 1¾ hours), Kokkola (€8.20, 45 minutes) and other west-coast towns.

The closest train station is at Bennäs (Finnish: Pännäinen), 11km away. A shuttle bus (€4, 15 minutes) meets arriving trains.

LAKELAND & KARELIA

Most of Finland could be dubbed lakeland, but around here it seems there's more aqua than terra firma. Reflecting the sky and forests as clearly as a mirror, the sparkling, clean water leaves an indelible impression. When exploring the region, it's almost obligatory to get waterborne, whether it be while practising your paddling skills in a canoe or by hopping aboard a historic steamboat for leisurely progress down canals and across lakes.

On land, there's just as much to do. Architecture buffs from around the globe make the pilgrimage here to visit Alvar Aalto's buildings, opera aficionados arrive en masse to attend the world-famous Savonlinna Opera Festival and outdoor enthusiasts shoulder their packs and set out to hike through tranquil forests of spruce, birch and pine. And at the end of active days, there are always saunas to relax in.

Lappeenranta

☑05 / POP 73,101

On the banks of Lake Saimaa – Finland's largest lake – Lappeenranta has encountered dramatic swings of fortune. Once famous for its scarlet-clad garrison, the 17th-century 'Cavalry City' was a humming trade port at the edge of the Swedish empire. In 1743 it came under Russian control, where it remained for the next 68 years, becoming an exclusive spa town. Much of the town was destroyed during the Winter and

Continuation Wars, but its massive fortress and spa endure.

Russia still owns half of the 43km Saimaa Canal, which links Lappeenranta to the Gulf of Finland. It's currently 'leased' to Finland until 2063 – popular day trips run through its eight locks and across the Russian border.

◉ Sights

★ Linnoitus
FORTRESS

(www.lappeenranta.fi; Kristiinankatu; fortress free, combined museum ticket adult/child €8/free; ⊙10am-6pm Mon-Fri, 11am-5pm Sat & Sun Jun-late Aug, 11am-5pm Tue-Sun late Aug-May) Standing guard above the harbour, this hulking hilltop fortification was begun by the Swedes and finished by the Russians in the late 18th century. Today it contains galleries, craft workshops and fascinating museums, including the history-focused South Karelian Museum (Etelä-Karjalan Museo; ⊙10am-6pm Mon-Fri, 11am-5pm Sat & Sun Jun-late Aug, 11am-5pm Tue-Sun late Aug-May) and Cavalry Museum (Ratsuväkimuseo; ⊙10am-6pm Mon-Fri, 11am-5pm Sat & Sun), and the Lappeenranta Art Museum (Etelä-Karjalan Taidemuseo; ⊙10am-6pm Mon-Fri, 11am-5pm Sat & Sun Jun-late Aug, 11am-5pm Tue-Sun late Aug-May). Its Orthodox Church (www.2ort.fi; ⊙10am-5pm Tue-Sun Jun–mid-Aug), Finland's oldest church, was completed in 1785 by Russian soldiers. Pick up the tourist office's free walking guide *The Fortress of Lappeenranta,* or download its free app.

★ Hiekkalinna
PUBLIC ART

(http://hiekkalinna.lappeenranta.fi; Satamatie 11; ⊙10am-9pm early Jun-Aug) FREE Every summer, around 30 sand artists from Finland and abroad gather to build the Hiekkalinna, a giant themed 'sandcastle' made from some 3 million kg of sand. Previous themes have included dinosaurs, a Wild West scene incorporating a gigantic steam train, and 'outer space' featuring ET and Darth Vader. Kids' entertainment here includes small carousel-style rides.

⌲ Tours

★ Saimaan Matkaverkko
CRUISE

(☎05-541-0100; www.saimaatravel.fi; Kipparinkatu 1; Vyborg day cruise/St Petersburg 3-day trip from €63/310, Vyborg port fee €8.80; ⊙late May–mid-Sep) Saimaan Matkaverkko runs 'visa-free' trips for all nationalities to Russia: there are day cruises along the canal to Vyborg (with an overnight option; prices vary seasonally). In July and August, longer trips continue to St Petersburg by bus, with two nights in the city before returning to Lappeenranta.

⊨ Sleeping

★ Huhtiniemi
Tourist Resort
CAMPGROUND, COTTAGE €

(☎05-451-5555; www.huhtiniemi.com; Kuusimäenkatu 18; tent sites €14 plus per person €5, 2-/4-person cottages €40/50, apt €80-98; P⊙) Situated 2km west of the centre, this 10-hectare lakeside campground has waterside sites, cottages and wi-fi–equipped apartments that fill to the gills in summer – reservations are a must except for camping, which is first come, first served (although the site is so large there's almost always space). Bus 5 from the city stops here, as do most intercity buses.

★ Asko & Maija's
Farmhouse
HOMESTAY, COTTAGE €

(☎040-507-5842; www.rantatupa.net; Suolahdentie 461, Taipalsaari; homestay per person €30, cottages per 2 days from €230; ⊙homestay Jun-Aug, cottages year-round; P) Homestay accommodation at this lakeside property 27km northwest of Lappeenranta off Rd 408 is in a traditional log cabin built in 1843. Guests have access to the lakeside smoke sauna. There are also four charming timber cottages (linen and cleaning cost extra depending on the length of stay) sleeping up to eight people, with private saunas, kitchenettes and rowboats.

★ Salpalinjan Hovi
BOUTIQUE HOTEL €€

(☎050-336-0986; www.salpalinjanhovi.com; Vanha Mikkelinte 125, Rutola; s/d/f from €89/99/144; P✳@⊙) Topped by a tin roof, this yellow-painted wooden schoolhouse dating from 1901 now has six rooms themed for different subjects once taught here: Languages and Literature, History, Science, Art, Music and Geography. All come with kitchens; there's a sauna, spa, ski storage and a courtyard barbecue area. It's a 400m stroll from a lakeside beach, 9km west of Lappeenranta.

✕ Eating & Drinking

Kahvila Majurska
CAFE €

(www.majurska.com; Kristiinankatu 1; cakes & pastries €3-6; ⊙10am-8pm Mon-Sat, 11am-8pm Sun Jun-Aug, to 5pm Sep-May) If you can't border-hop to a genuine Russian teahouse, this is as close as you'll get in Finland. A former officers' club (check out the vintage furniture and august portrait of Mannerheim), it still serves tea from the samovar and does a range of home-made pastries and cakes.

Kasino FINNISH €€
(☑040-716-8097; www.fazer.fi; Ainonkatu 10; lunch buffet €12.60, mains €14.50-23.50; ☺11am-3pm & 5-9pm Mon-Wed, 11am-3pm Thu & Fri, 11am-3pm & 5-11pm Sat Jun-Aug) Pork tenderloin with dill and sour-cream sauce, crumbed white lake fish with salmon roe, and perch with cider sauce are among the options served at this venerable century-old wooden building. On sunny days, the best seats are on the floating terrace moored on the lake. Kid-pleasers include fish fingers. Enter via the lakeside promenade.

★ **Lehmus Roastery** COFFEE
(www.lehmusroastery.com; Satamatie 6; ☺10am-6pm Mon-Thu & Sat, 10am-8pm Fri, noon-6pm Sun; ☏) Crowned Finland's best coffee roastery at 2017's Suomen Paras Paahtimo awards, Lehmus occupies a red-brick former warehouse overlooking the lake. Behind the gleaming espresso machine, passionate staff roast four types of organic coffee, which they serve in the open-plan, whitewashed interior along with fresh pastries. You can also buy bags of beans, along with Finnish design products (ceramics etc).

★ **Prinsessa Armaada** BAR
(☑044-754-5504; www.prinsessaarmaada.fi; Satamatori 10; ☺10am-2am mid-Apr–mid-Sep) Built in 1902, this tar steamship, which once transported timber to St Petersburg (and briefly served in the Russian Imperial Navy in 1914) has operated as a bar since 1959 and has great ciders and craft beers. Its cargo hold has a restaurant (reservations essential); up on deck is a 12-person sauna with its own minibar. There's regular live music.

ⓘ Information

Main Tourist Office (☑05-667-788; www.visitlappeenranta.fi; Brahenkatu 1; ☺10am-5pm Mon-Fri, to 4pm Sat; ☏) In the **IsoKristiina** (www.isokristiina.fi; Brahenkatu 5; ☺7am-9pm Mon-Fri, 9am-9pm Sat, 9am-6pm Sun) shopping centre.
Summer Tourist Office (☑040-352-2178; www.visitlappeenranta.fi; Satamatie 11; ☺10am-8pm Jun-early Aug, to 6pm early Aug-late Aug) Located at the sandcastle Hiekkalinna.

ⓘ Getting There & Away

AIR
Lappeenranta airport (LPP; www.lppairport.fi; Lentokentäntie 21) is 2.5km west of the city centre. Finnair has year-round domestic flights; there are also seasonal flights to a handful of European destinations. Bus 4 (€3.20) links it with the bus station via the city centre. A **taxi** (☑020-060-400; www.taksisaimaa.fi) to the city centre costs around €9.

BUS
Lappeenranta's **bus station** (Ratakatu 23) is 1.2km south of the city centre; most intercity buses also stop on Valtakatu in the middle of town. Bus 9 (€3.20) runs between the bus station and the city centre.

Major **Matkahuolto** (www.matkahuolto.fi) services include the following:
Helsinki (€30, 3½ hours, eight daily)
Imatra (€9.30, 35 minutes, two daily)
Joensuu (€30, 4½ hours, two daily)
Mikkeli (€20, 1¾ hours, three daily)
Savonlinna (€25, four hours, three daily)

Onnibus (www.onnibus.com) has cheaper but less frequent services to destinations including Helsinki (€7, three hours, four daily), Imatra (€5, 30 minutes, one daily) and Joensuu (€10, three hours, one daily).

TRAIN
Intercity trains use **Lappeenranta train station** (Ratakatu 23), next to the bus station, 1.2km south of town. Services include Helsinki (€28, two hours, six daily), Imatra (€5, 25 minutes, eight daily) and Joensuu (€30, 2¼ hours, four daily).

International trains to/from Russia use **Vainikkala train station** (Rajamiehentie 147, Vainikkala), 29.5km south of Lappeenranta, linked by bus (€6.50, 40 minutes, up to 10 daily) from the bus station and Valtakatu in town. Trains run to Vyborg (€47, 25 minutes, two daily) and on to St Petersburg (€75, 1½ hours).

Book through VR (Finnish Railways; www.vr.fi).

Savonlinna
☑015 / POP 34,905
The historic frontier settlement of Savonlinna is one of Finland's prettiest towns and most compelling tourist destinations. Scattered across a garland of small islands strung between Haukivesi and Pihlajavesi lakes, its major attraction is the visually dramatic Olavinlinna Castle, constructed in the 15th century and now the spectacular venue of July's world-famous Savonlinna Opera Festival. In summer, when the

FINLAND SAVONLINNA

Savonlinna

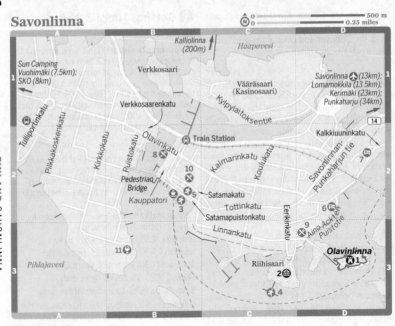

Savonlinna

lakes shimmer in the sun and operatic arias waft through the forest-scented air, the place is quite magical. In winter it's blanketed in fairy-tale-like snow, and its friendly locals can be relied upon to offer visitors a warm welcome.

◉ Sights & Activities

The countryside around Savonlinna has quiet country lanes and gently sloping hills, and is terrific for **bicycle touring**. Bikes can be carried on-board lakeboats for a small fee.

See http://visitsavonlinna.fi/en for information about canoe and kayak hire in and around the city.

★ Olavinlinna   CASTLE
(St Olaf's Castle; ☏029-533-6941; www.kansallismuseo.fi; adult/child €9/4.50; ⊙11am-5.15pm Jun–mid-Aug, 10am-3.15pm mid-Aug–mid-Dec & Feb-May) Built directly on rock in the middle of the lake (now accessed via bridges), this heavily restored 15th-century fortification was constructed as a military base on the Swedes' restless eastern border. The currents in the surrounding water ensure that it remains unfrozen in winter, which prevented enemy attacks over ice. To visit the castle's upper levels, including the towers and chapel, you must join an hour-long guided tour. Guides bring the castle to life with vivid accounts of its history.

Riihisaari   MUSEUM
(Lake Saimaa Nature & Culture Centre; ☏044-417-4466; www.savonlinna.fi/museo; adult/child €7/3, incl Olavinlinna €10/4.50; ⊙10am-5pm

Tue-Sun Sep-Apr, 9am-5pm Mon-Fri & 10am-5pm Sat & Sun May, 10am-5pm daily Jun-Aug) On an island that was once a naval port, this museum housed in a handsome 16th-century granary recounts local history and the importance of water transport. It also has a number of exhibits about the history, flora and fauna of Lake Saimaa, including a 12-minute video about the underwater world of Torsti, an endangered ringed seal pup living in the lake. Exhibits on the ground floor are more interesting than those upstairs.

Outside, there's a group of historic watercraft to board (open mid-May to mid-September). These include the **SS Mikko** (☑044-417-4466; adult/child €15/10; ☺Jul). Information about the town and region, including the Linnansaari National Park, is available from the ground-floor ticket office/information desk.

VIP Cruise CRUISE
(☑050-025-0075; www.vipcruise.info/en; Satamapuistonkatu; ☺Jun-Aug) Operates three historic steamships – S/S *Paul Wahl,* S/S *Punkaharju* and S/S *Savonlinna* – offering 90-minute sightseeing cruises on Lake Saimmaa (adult/child €20/10).

★☆ Festivals & Events

For a list of festivals and events staged in Savonlinna, go to http://visitsavonlinna.fi/en/events-in-savonlinna-region.

Savonlinna Opera Festival MUSIC
(Savonlinnan Oopperajuhlat; ☑015-476-750; www.operafestival.fi; Olavinkatu 27; ☺early Jul-early Aug) This internationally renowned event is Finland's most famous festival, with an enviably dramatic setting: the covered courtyard of Olavinlinna Castle.

🛏 Sleeping

★Lomamokkila FARMSTAY €€
(☑015-523-117; www.lomamokkila.fi; Mikonkiventie 209; farmhouse s/d €105/110, guesthouse s €75-85, guesthouse d €80-90, cottages €55-180; P☎) 🍃 This farmstay 12km northwest of Savonlinna is run by a genial Finnish family and incorporates a handsome century-old farmhouse, two nearby guesthouses and lakeside cottages with sauna and their own jetty and rowboat (but no wi-fi). There are three pretty rooms in the main farmhouse and eight rooms in each guesthouse; the latter share a kitchen and lounge.

★Lossiranta Lodge BOUTIQUE HOTEL €€
(☑044-511-2323; www.lossiranta.net; Aino Acktén Puistotie; s €85-160, d €110-290, extra person €60; P☎) The dress-circle views of Olavinlinna Castle are one of many good reasons to stay at this boutique hotel on the lakeshore. There are five rooms sleeping between two and four on offer year-round, the best of which has its own wood sauna and outdoor spa. All are attractively decorated and most have kitchenettes. Staff are both friendly and helpful.

Tavis Inn GUESTHOUSE €€
(☑044-511-2323; www.lossiranta.net; Kalkkiuuninkatu; s €85-160, d €100-220, ste & apt €110-260, extra person €60; P☎) In a tranquil end-of-the-road spot that's a short lakeside stroll from Olavinlinna Castle, this annexe of Lossiranta Lodge (where you check in) offers two rooms, four suites and one apartment in a 1915 timber house; all are stylishly decorated. Some have kitchenettes; others a kettle, microwave and small fridge. Bathrooms are small.

🍴 Eating & Drinking

Kalastajan Koju SEAFOOD €
(www.kalastajankoju.com; Kauppatori; fried muikku €9.50, with dip, mayonnaise or remoulade €10.50, with potato & salad €16.90; ☺11am-10pm Mon-Thu, to midnight Fri & Sat, to 9pm Sun) Owned by a fisherman who heads out on the lake each morning to catch the *muikku* (vendace, or whitefish, a common lake fish) that this place specialises in, Kalastajan Koju is conveniently located on the water by the kauppatori and is particularly busy in summer. The menu also includes fish and chips, bratwurst and fried salmon.

Linnakrouvi FINNISH €€
(☑015-576-9124; www.linnakrouvi.fi; Linnankatu 7; mains €18-33; ☺noon-10pm or later Mon-Sat, 3-10pm or later Sun late Jun–mid-Aug) Overlooking Olavinlinna Castle, this summer restaurant employs chefs from Helsinki and serves Savonlinna's most sophisticated food. Unsurprisingly it's hugely popular during the opera season. There's tiered outdoor seating, an attractive interior and a range of fare running from burgers to freshly caught and beautifully prepared fish from Lake Saimaa. There's a limited but impressive wine list.

Majakka FINNISH €€
(☑015-206-2825; www.kattaasavon.fi; Satamakatu 11; mains €17-32, kids' menu €8; ☺11am-10pm Mon-Thu, to 11pm Fri, noon-11pm Sat, noon-10pm

FINLAND SAVONLINNA

Sun; ❄ 🛜 🍴) The name of this popular family bistro means 'lighthouse', reflecting its location overlooking the harbour. Steaks, burgers and locally caught fish are well cooked, generously sized and fairly priced; the select-your-own appetiser plate is a nice touch. Service is brisk but friendly.

★Huvila MICROBREWERY
(📄 015-555-0555; www.panimoravintolahuvila.fi; Puistokatu 4; mains €24-35, 3-course menu €45-50; ⊙ noon-10pm Jun-Aug; 🛜) Sitting across the harbour, Huvila is operated by the Waahto brewery and is a delightful destination in warm weather, when its lakeside deck is full of patrons relaxing over a pint or two of the house brew (try the Golden Ale). There's also an attractive dining area in the old timber house. Sadly the menu promises more than it delivers.

In high summer, live bands play in the evening and the opening hours are extended to midnight.

ℹ️ Information

Savonlinna has no official tourist office, but the ticket desk in the Riihisaari (p166) stocks maps and brochures about the city and region. Other information can be accessed via www.savonlinna.fi.

ℹ️ Getting There & Away

AIR

Savonlinna Airport (SVL; 📄 020-708-8101; www.finavia.fi; Lentoasemantie 50) is 14km north of town, and is predominantly used by charter flights. Finnair flies here during the opera season.

BOAT

Boats connect Savonlinna's **passenger harbour** (Satamapuistonkatu) with many lakeside towns; check www.oravivillage.com for seasonal schedules. The **M/S Puijo** (📄 015-250-250; www.mspuijo.fi; Satamapuistonkatu; one way €95, return by same-day car €130, return with/without overnight cabin €180/150; ⊙ mid-Jun–mid-Aug) cruises between Savonlinna and both Kuopio and Lappeenranta in summer.

BUS

Savonlinna is not on major bus routes, but buses link the **bus station** (Tulliportinkatu 1) with Helsinki (€30, 5½ hours, up to nine daily), Mikkeli (€20, 1½ hours, up to 14 daily) and Jyväskylä (€30, 3½ hours, up to eight daily).

TRAIN

Punkaharju (€3, 30 minutes, at least four daily) is one of the few destinations that can be accessed via a direct service from Savonlinna. To get to Helsinki (€48, 4¼ hours, up to four daily) and Joensuu (€25, 2¼ hours, up to four daily), you'll need to change in Parikkala. The train station is in the town centre near the kauppatori. Buy your ticket at the machines – there's no ticket office.

Around Savonlinna

Punkaharju
📄 015 / POP 3645

Punkaharju, the famous pine-covered esker (sand or gravel ridge) on the shore of Lake Saimaa, is touted in tourist brochures as 'Finland's national landscape'. The region was first declared a protected area by Tsar Alexander in 1803 and became a favoured summering spot for St Petersburg gentry. The unspoiled landscape is extremely picturesque and great for walking, cycling and cross-country skiing. It can be reached on an easy day trip from Savonlinna, but is also an appealing place to stay. For more information, go to www.visitpunkaharju.fi and www.nationalparks.fi/en/punkaharju.

⊙ Sights

★Lusto Suomen Metsämuseo MUSEUM
(The Finnish Museum of Forestry; 📄 015-345-100; www.lusto.fi; Lustontie 1; adult/child €10/5; ⊙ 10am-5pm Tue-Sun Jan-Apr & Oct-Dec, to 5pm daily May & Sep, to 7pm daily Jun-Aug) 'Lusto' is the Finnish word for a tree's annual growth ring, and this well-curated and cleverly presented museum is all about forests and the growth of the local timber industry. Displays (with English labels) cover everything from forest biodiversity, forest healers and forest myths, to the history of forest settlements and forestry technology. The huge hall filled with machinery features a tower of chainsaws and various interactive displays – everyone will enjoy testing their motor skills with a timber loader.

Punkaharju NATURAL FEATURE
(www.nationalparks.fi) During the ice age, formations similar to this 7km-long sand ridge were created all over Finland. Because it crosses a large lake, it's always been an important travel route. Short sections of the original unsealed road along

the ridgetop remain – once part of a route to Russia connecting the Olavinlinna and Vyborg (Viipuri) castles. The national parks website carries information about hiking on the ridge.

ℹ Getting There & Away

Trains between Savonlinna and Parikkala (€3.80, 55 minutes, five daily) stop at Retretti (€3, 20 minutes), Lusto (€3, 25 minutes) and Punkaharju (€3, 30 minutes).

Jyväskylä

⬛ 014 / POP 138,459

Vivacious and modern, western Lakeland's main town has a wonderful waterside location, an optimistic feel and an impeccable architectural pedigree. Thanks to the work of Alvar Aalto, who started his career here, Jyväskylä (yoo-vah-skoo-lah) is of global architectural interest. At the other end of the cultural spectrum, petrolheads around the world know it as a legendary World Rally Championships venue. The large student population and lively arts scenes give the town plenty of energy and nightlife.

◎ Sights & Activities

For architecture buffs the best visiting days are Tuesday to Friday, as many buildings are closed on weekends and the Alvar Aalto Museum is closed on Monday.

Jyväskylä's museums are all free on Fridays between September and May.

An enjoyable 12km circuit can be walked or cycled around the lake, and can be cut in half using the road bridge. There are numerous boating options – check http://visitjyvaskyla.fi for information, or wander along the pleasant harbour area, where you'll also find boat bars, jet-ski hire, houseboats (www.houseboat.fi) and floating saunas for rent.

Water craft can be hired from www.tavinsulka.com.

★ **Säynätsalon**
Kunnantalo　　　　　　　　NOTABLE BUILDING
(Säynätsalo Town Hall; ⬛ 040-197-1091; www.aaltoinfo.com; Parviaisentie 9, Säynätsalo; tours €8; ◎ tours noon-6pm Mon-Fri, 2-6pm Sat & Sun Jun-Sep) FREE One of Aalto's most admired works, this town hall was conceived as a 'fortress of democracy' and constructed between 1949 and 1952. Its sturdy brick tower references the medieval *palazzi communale* (town halls) Aalto had admired in Italy,

but the grassy inner courtyard bathes the interior with light and reflects a relationship with nature that is distinctively Nordic. Guided tours (no booking necessary) visit the council chamber, Artek-furnished library and meeting rooms. The complex is remarkably intact and utterly magnificent.

Alvar Aalto Museo　　　　　　　MUSEUM
(⬛ 040-135-6210; www.alvaraalto.fi; Alvar Aallonkatu 7; adult/child €6/free; ◎ 11am-6pm Tue-Sun Sep-Jun, 10am-6pm Tue-Fri Jul & Aug) The town's most famous son and the subject of this museum was a giant of 20th-century architecture. Schooled in Jyväskylä, Aalto opened his first offices here, designed many buildings in the town and later spent his summers in nearby Muuratsalo. Aalto devotees should start their pilgrimage at this informative museum in the university precinct, one of the last buildings he designed. Displays chronicle his life and work, focusing on his major buildings, as well as his furniture design and glassware.

🛏 Sleeping

Hotelli Milton　　　　　　　　　HOTEL €€
(⬛ 014-337-7900; www.hotellimilton.com; Hannikaisenkatu 29; s €70-85, d €90-120; ℗ 🛜) Designed by Erkki Kantonen and Sakari Nironen and constructed in 1963, this architecturally notable building is one of the city's major landmarks. Family-run, it is extremely popular with visiting businesspeople – book ahead. Spacious rooms offer plenty of natural light; most have a balcony. It's very handy for the bus and train stations.

★ **Hotel Yöpuu**　　　　　　BOUTIQUE HOTEL €€€
(⬛ 014-333-900; www.hotelliyopuu.fi; Yliopistonkatu 23; standard s/d €145/168, superior €159/189, ste €237; ℗ ❄ 🛜 🐾) Among Finland's most alluring boutique hotels, the Yöpuu has 26 rooms varying in size, decoration and facilities; those in the superior category are larger, with air-conditioning and tea and coffee facilities. Service is extremely professional, with personal touches including a welcome drink. There's a classy bar next to the highly recommended Pöllöwaari (p170) restaurant; an excellent buffet breakfast is served in the latter.

🍴 Eating & Drinking

★ **Beans & More**　　　　　　　　　VEGAN €
(⬛ 050-351-7731; www.beansandmore.fi; Asemakatu 11; dishes €10-15; ◎ 10am-6pm Mon-Fri, 9am-5pm Sat; 🅿 🐾) Artek furniture, a vaulted ceiling and artfully dangling light fittings provide a

stylish setting at this on-trend vegan cafe. The friendly staff serve up burgers, salads piled with kale and other goodies, sandwiches on gluten-free bread and vegetarian snack plates featuring seasonal produce. Coffee is made with oat, almond or soy milk, and there's a range of teas to choose from.

★Figaro Winebistro   TAPAS €€
(☑020-766-9811; www.figaro.fi; Asemakatu 2; lunch mains €15-18, tapas €3-9, dinner mains €16-28; ☺11am-11pm Mon-Fri, 1-11pm Sat, 2-10pm Sun; ☎) The three-course lunch menu (€25) at this this welcoming wine bar is an excellent deal, but most regulars head here after work or on weekends to graze on tapas and order drinks from the large and top-quality wine and beer list. It's so pleasant that many choose to stay on for a steak or burger dinner.

★Pöllöwaari   FINNISH €€€
(☑014-333-900; www.ravintolapollowaari.fi; Yliopistonkatu 23; mains €22-29; ☺11am-10.30pm Mon-Fri, 1-10.30pm Sat; ☎) We're of the view that Hotel Yöpuu's fine-dining restaurant is the best in the region. Its menu places a laudable emphasis on seasonality, and the kitchen's execution is exemplary. Choose one of the set menus (€56 to €79, or €84 to €127 with wine pairing) or order à la carte – the main courses are exceptionally well priced considering their quality. Excellent wine list, too.

★Papu   CAFE
(☑050-368-0340; www.paahtimopapu.fi; Yliopistonkatu 26D; ☺10am-6pm Mon & Tue, to 9pm Wed-Fri, noon-6pm Sat) It would be easy to describe Papu as a hipster haunt, but this laid-back cafe doesn't lend itself to easy categorisation. Yes, its baristas have sleeve tattoos and a preference for pour-over coffee, but the loyal customer base is multi-aged and eclectic. The coffee is made with house-roasted organic beans, and there's also espresso tonic and iced chocolate on offer.

❶ Information

Tourist Office (☑014-266-0113; www.visitjyvaskyla.fi; Asemakatu 7; ☺10am-5pm Mon-Fri, to 3pm Sat Jun-Aug, 10am-4pm Mon-Fri Sep-May) Helpful office where you can source plenty of information. Staff can arrange visits to the **Muuratsalon Koetalo** (Muuratsalo Experimental House; ☑014-266-7113; www.alvaraalto.fi; Melalammentie, Muuratsalo; adult/student €18/9; ☺1.30pm Mon, Wed & Fri Jun, Jul & 1st half Sep, 1.30pm Mon-Fri Aug).

❶ Getting There & Away

AIR
The airport is at Tikkakoski, 23km northwest of the city centre. Finnair flies to/from Helsinki.

BUS & TRAIN
The bus and train stations share the **Matkakeskus** (Jyväskylä Travel Centre; ☺6am-10pm Mon-Sat, from 8am Sun). Daily express buses connect Jyväskylä to southern Finnish towns, including frequent departures to Tampere (€20, 2¼ hours) and Helsinki (€25 to €30, 3½ to 4½ hours).

There are regular trains to/from Helsinki (from €32, 3½ hours), many of which travel via Tampere and Hämeenlinna.

Kuopio

☑017 / POP 117,383

Kuopio is the quintessential summery lakeside town, offering pleasure cruises on the azure water, hikes in spruce forests, tasty local fish specialities and plenty of terraces and beer gardens where you can enjoy a drink. Those visitors who are more interested in cultural diversions than the great outdoors will enjoy visiting the town's portfolio of museums; note that all of these are closed on Mondays.

◉ Sights

Puijon Torni   TOWER
(Puijo Tower; ☑044-552-4887; www.puijo.com; Puijontie 135; adult/child €6/3; ☺10am-9pm Mon-Sat, to 7pm Sun Jun-Aug, 11am-7pm Mon-Thu, to 9pm Fri & Sat, to 4pm Sun Sep-May) The views from the top of the 75m Puijon Torni are very impressive; the vast perspectives of lakes and forests represent a sort of idealised Finnish vista. Atop the structure is a revolving restaurant (lunch menu €26.50, dinner mains €25 to €37), a daytime cafeteria and an open-air viewing deck.

Kuopion Korttelimuseo   MUSEUM
(Old Kuopio Museum; ☑017-182-625; www.korttelimuseo.kuopio.fi; Kirkkokatu 22; adult/child €6/free; ☺10am-5pm Tue-Sat mid-May–Aug, 10am to 3pm Sep–mid-May) This block of 11 wooden townhouses dating from the 18th and 19th centuries includes several period-furnished homes representing family life between 1800 and 1930. **Apteekkimuseo** in building 11 contains old pharmacy paraphernalia, while in another building it's fascinating to compare photos of Kuopio from different decades. Interpretative information is

in English and Finnish. The museum's cafe serves delicious sweet and savoury dishes including a traditional *rahkapiirakka* (a local cheesecake-style pastry).

Kuopion Museo MUSEUM
(☑017-182-603; www.kuopionmuseo.fi; Kauppakatu 23; adult/child €8/free; ⏰10am-5pm Tue-Sat) In a castle-like art-nouveau mansion, this museum has a wide scope. The top two floors are devoted to cultural history, but the real highlight is the natural history display, which includes a wide variety of beautifully presented Finnish wildlife, including a mammoth and an ostrich wearing snowboots. The ground floor has temporary exhibitions. Pick up English explanations at the ticket desk.

🎯 Activities

★ Jätkänkämppä SAUNA
(☑030-60830; www.rauhalahti.fi/en/restaurants/jatkankamppa/public-traditional-finnish-evenings; Katiskaniementie 8; adult/child €14/7; ⏰4-10pm Tue & Thu Jun-Aug, 4-10pm Tue Sep-May) This giant *savusauna* (smoke sauna) is a memorable, sociable experience. It seats 60 and is mixed: you're given towels to wear. Bring a swimsuit for lake dipping – devoted locals and brave tourists do so even when it's covered with ice. Repeat the process several times. Then buy a beer and relax, looking out over the lake in Nordic peace.

Rauhalahti OUTDOORS
(☑030-60830; www.rauhalahti.com; Katiskaniementie 8) This estate is full of activities for families, including boating, cycling, tennis and minigolf in summer, and skating, ice-fishing and snowmobiling in winter. You can hire bikes, rowboats, canoes and in-line skates. To get here, take bus 7 or 20 from the town centre (€3.30) or take a **Koski-Laiva Oy cruise** (☑0400-207-245; www.koskilaiva.com; adult/child €16/8; ⏰mid-May–late Aug) in summer. There's also a variety of **accommodation** (Spa Hotel Rauhalahti; ☑030-60830; www.rauhalahti.fi; Katiskaniementie 8; s/d from €105/120; P🐕🛜⛱🐾) here.

🧭 Tours

Several different cruises depart from the town's passenger harbour daily during summer. Tickets for all cruises are available at the Matkustajasatama (harbour) or directly on the boats.

Saimann Laivamatkat Oy CRUISE
(☑015-250-250; www.mspuijo.fi) Operates the M/S *Puijo*, which sails along the Heinävesi Canal Route to/from Savonlinna (one way €95, 10½ hours) on Tuesdays, Thursdays and Saturdays, returning on Monday, Wednesday and Friday. Return same-day transport by car (€130, minimum four passengers) is offered.

Roll Risteilyt CRUISE
(Roll Cruises; ☑017-266-2466; www.roll.fi; adult/child €18/9; ⏰Tue-Sat Jun & Aug, daily Jul) Runs regular 90-minute scenic cruises on M/S *Ukko and* M/S *Queen* leaving from Kuopio's harbour, as well as a four-hour lunch cruise to the Alahovi Berry Wine Farm (adult/child €36/17).

🎉 Festivals & Events

Kupio Dance Festival DANCE
(Kuopion Tanssii ja Soi; www.kuopiodancefestival.fi; ⏰mid-Jun) Open-air classical and modern dance performances are staged at this week-long festival, and there are also comedy and theatre gigs. There's a real buzz in town at this time.

Wife-Carrying World Championships SPORTS
(Eukonkanto; www.eukonkanto.fi; ⏰Jul) What began as a heathenish medieval habit of pillaging neighbouring villages in search of nubile women has now become one of Finland's oddest – and most publicised – events. It's held in Sonkajärvi, 18km northeast of Iisalmi.

🛏 Sleeping

Matkailukeskus Rauhalahti CAMPGROUND €
(☑017-473-000; www.visitrauhalahti.fi; Rauhankatu 3; tent/caravan sites €15/23 plus per person €6, d/q camping cottages €35/65, q cottages €120-197; ⏰mid-May–late Aug; P🐕🛜⛱) On a lake near the Rauhalahti hotel complex, this campground has top-notch facilities including a cafe, minigolf and croquet courses, volleyball and basketball courts, a children's playground, sauna (€18 for 50 minutes), excellent camp kitchen and good ablution blocks. Camping cabins are extremely basic; most standard cottages have a kitchen and sauna. Bus 16 (€3.30) will get you here.

Apartment Hotel Rauhalahti APARTMENT €€
(☑030-60830; www.rauhalahti.fi; Katiskaniementie 8; 1-/2-/4-person apt from €115/120/159; P🛜⛱) Part of the Spa Hotel Rauhalahti

complex, this has modern apartments with all the trimmings, including (for not much extra cash) a sauna. Guests have full use of the hotel's facilities.

★ **Scandic Hotel Kuopio** HOTEL €€€
(☑ 017-195-111; www.scandichotels.fi; Satamakatu 1; s €220, standard/superior d €240/260, ste €300; P@🛜📶🐾) ✔ Kuopio's best hotel has a tranquil lakeside location and a wealth of facilities, including a gym, sauna, spa, indoor swimming pool and kids' play room, plus free bike hire. The rooms have an attractive decor, but are on the small side. Superior rooms are worth the extra €20, as they have king-sized beds, kettles and balconies with lake views.

✗ Eating

Budget eats can be sourced at stalls on the kauppatori (market square) or in the **Kauppahalli** (http://kuopionkauppahalli.fi; Kauppatori; ⊘8am-5pm Mon-Fri, to 3pm Sat; ✍) ✔. There are plenty of midrange options in the city, but no fine-dining options of note.

Lounas-Salonki FINNISH €
(☑ 017-281-1210; www.lounassalonki.fi; Kasarmikatu 12; mains €9-27; ⊘9am-9pm Mon-Sat, noon-9pm Sun; ✍🔷) This charming wooden building west of the town centre features little rooms sporting elegant imperial furniture. It serves soup (€8 to €14), has a lunchtime salad buffet (€9.90) and offers simple Finnish fare such as meatloaf, bratwurst and stews. The food is unexceptional, but offers excellent value. Between meals, a slice of cheesecake and tea or coffee will set you back €5.

Kummisetä FINNISH €€
(☑ 017-369-9880; www.kummiseta.com; Minna Canthin Katu 44; mains €17-29; ⊘4-9pm Mon, to 10pm Tue-Thu, 3-10.30pm Fri & Sat) The menu at this old-fashioned eatery places an emphasis on comfort food, offering excellent burgers, steaks and ribs; the more-adventurous items on offer aren't as successful. In summer, dining on the spacious two-level back terrace is a pleasure, and there's live music on weekends.

Jätkänkämppä Restaurant FINNISH €€
(☑ 030-60830; www.rauhalahti.fi; Katiskaniementie 8; buffet adult/child €23/11.50, incl sauna €35/17.50; ⊘4-8pm Tue & Fri Jun-Aug, 4-8pm Tue Sep-May; 🔷) Head to the loggers' cabin adjacent to the Jätkänkämppä (p171) smoke sauna at Spa Hotel Rauhalahti to enjoy a traditional Finnish buffet when the sauna

is operating. You'll be serenaded with accordion entertainment and a lumberjack show – it's great fun.

🍷 Drinking & Nightlife

Kuopio's nightlife is conveniently strung along Kauppakatu, running east from the market square to the harbour. Look out for traditional liqueurs, such as cloudberry, from 1852-founded local company Lignell & Piispanen.

Wanha Satama PUB
(☑ 050-342-9276; www.wanhasatama.net; Matkustajasatama; mains €15-26; ⊘11am-9pm Mon-Thu, to 11pm Fri-Sun) In a blue-and-white timber building right on the harbour, this popular place has a rear deck and front terrace where patrons can sit and watch the boats come and go. It offers decent Finnish food and international favourites, including burgers, as well as a semi-regular program of live music.

Helmi PUB
(www.satamanhelmi.fi; Kauppakatu 2; ⊘11am-11pm Mon-Thu, to midnight Fri, noon-midnight Sat, noon-8pm Sun) This historic 19th-century sailors' hang-out by the harbour is a cosy, comfortable spot with a range of local characters. It has a decent pool table and a sociable beer garden. If hungry, you'll need to rely on the house-made pizzas (from €9), which would be publicly vilified if served up in Italy.

❶ Information

Kuopio Info (☑ 017-182-584; www.kuopio.fi; Apaja Shopping Centre, Kauppakatu 45; ⊘9am-4pm Mon-Fri) Underneath the kauppatori. Information on local and regional attractions.

❶ Getting There & Away

AIR

Kuopio Airport (KUO; ☑ 020-708-7202; www.finavia.fi; Lentokentäntie 275) is 14km northeast of Kuopio. Finnair (www.finnair.fi) operates daily flights to/from Helsinki.

BOAT

In summer, Saimann Laivamatkat Oy (p171) operates regular cruises between Kuopio and Savonlinna.

BUS

Services depart from the **bus station** (Puijonkatu 45). Express services include the following:
Helsinki (from €10, 5½ hours, frequent) Some require a change in Jyväskylä.

Jyväskylä (€20, two hours, frequent)
Savonlinna (€27.30, 2¾ hours, four daily)
Change in Varkaus.

TRAIN
Daily train services include the following:
Helsinki (€41 to €45, 4½ hours, six daily)
Kajaani (€19 to €23, 1¾ hours, five daily)
Mikkeli (€18 to €21, 1¾ hours, four daily)
Oulu (€38 to €45, 4¾ hours, four daily)

Change at Pieksämäki or Kouvola for other destinations.

Joensuu

📞 013 / POP 75,557

At the egress of the Pielisjoki (Joensuu means 'river mouth' in Finnish), North Karelia's capital is a spirited university town, with students making up almost a third of the population. Joensuu was founded by Tsar Nikolai I and became an important trading port following the 1850s completion of the Saimaa Canal. During the Winter and Continuation Wars, 23 bombing raids flattened many of its older buildings, and today most of its architecture is modern. It's a lively place to spend some time before heading into the Karelian wilderness.

◉ Sights

★**Carelicum** MUSEUM
(www.joensuu.fi; Koskikatu 5; adult/child €5/3; ⊙10am-4.30pm Mon-Fri, 10am-3pm Sat & Sun) Themed displays – on the region's prehistory, its war-torn past, the Karelian evacuation, the importance of the sauna etc – cover both sides of Karelia's present-day border at this excellent museum. Highlights include a Junkers bomber engine, and local hunting and fishing equipment including a 200-year-old crossbow.

Taitokortteli ARTS CENTRE
(📞013-220-140; www.taitokortteli.fi; Koskikatu 1; ⊙10am-5pm Mon-Fri, 10am-3pm Sat year-round, plus noon-4pm Sun Jul) Dating back over a century, these charming wooden buildings are some of the few remaining in Joensuu; some have been relocated here from other parts of town. They now comprise an arts and crafts centre where you can see weavers at work, browse contemporary art and purchase clothing, toys and homewares by local designers. There's a gallery space as well as cafes and bars.

Orthodox Church of St Nicholas CHURCH
(Pyhän Nikolaoksen Kirkko; 📞020-610-0590; www.joensuunortodoksit.fi; Kirkkokatu 32; ⊙10am-4pm Mon-Fri mid-Jun–mid-Aug or by appointment) Joensuu's most intriguing church is the wooden Orthodox church, built in 1887 with icons painted in St Petersburg during the late 1880s. Services are held at 6pm Saturday and 10am Sunday; visitors are welcome.

★⚲ Festivals & Events

Ilosaari Rock Festival MUSIC
(www.ilosaarirock.fi; Linnunlahdentie; ⊙mid-Jul) Founded in 1971, this massive three-day rock festival has a waterside location with its own beach, and attracts more than 60 Finnish and international acts on its five stages. It has received awards for its environmental record.

🛏 Sleeping

Finnhostel Joensuu HOSTEL €
(📞050-408-4587; www.islo.fi; Kalevankatu 5B; s/d/q from €50/76/152; ⊙reception 3-8pm; 🅿🛜) Great-value, sizeable rooms here come with bathroom and kitchen facilities as well as small balconies. Prices include breakfast, and access to a sauna and gym. Kids have indoor and outdoor play areas. HI discount.

Cumulus Joensuu HOTEL €€
(📞020-048-118; www.cumulus.fi; Kirkkokatu 20; d from €130; 🅿❄🛜) The pick of Joensuu's central chain hotels has squeaky-clean rooms with ultrapowerful showers, a small gym, free parking, friendly staff and fast wi-fi. Breakfast is served in the cellar dining room.

🍴 Eating

Kahvila & Konditoria Houkutus CAFE, BAKERY €
(www.houkutus.fi; Torikatu 24; small dishes €1.50-5.50, mains €8-17; ⊙7.30am-7pm Mon-Fri, 8.30am-5pm Sat) Houkutus does great coffee and even better cakes (the mint blackcurrant cake is a treat), along with savoury pastries such as quiches, meal-sized salads and filled bread rolls.

★**Teatteri** KARELIAN €€
(📞010-231-4250; www.teatteriravintola.fi; Rantakatu 20; lunch buffet €8.60-10.50, mains €18-32, menus €46-65; ⊙11am-10pm Mon & Tue, 11am-11pm Wed & Thu, 11am-midnight Fri, 11.30am-midnight Sat) 🍃 Locally sourced ingredients prepared in innovative ways are served in the town hall's art-deco surrounds and on its beautiful summer terrace. Dishes span

nettle ricotta with wild herb salad to liquorice-glazed goose with kale pesto; desserts such as fennel and apple sorbet with blackberry panna cotta are the icing on the cake. Menus can be accompanied by wine or craft-beer pairings.

❶ Information

Karelia Expert (☑040-023-9549; www.visitkarelia.fi; Koskikatu 5; ☺10am-5pm Mon-Fri; ☞) In the Carelicum, enthusiastic staff handle tourism information and bookings for the region.

❶ Getting There & Away

Joensuu is the transport hub for North Karelia.

AIR

The **airport** (JOE; www.finavia.fi; Lentoasemantie 30) is 11km northwest of central Joensuu. An airport bus service (one way €5) meets all incoming flights, and departs from the bus station (65 minutes before flight departures) and from the corner of Koskikatu and Kauppakatu (one hour before departures). A **taxi** (☑060-110-100; www.taksiitasuomi.fi) costs €25.

Finnair operates several flights a day between Helsinki and Joensuu.

BUS

The bus station is on the eastern side of the river.

Major **Matkahuolto** (www.matkahuolto.fi) services include the following:

Helsinki (€30, 6½ hours, five express services daily)

Jyväskylä (€30, four hours, five daily)

Kuopio (€29.90, 2¼ hours, three express services daily)

Lappeenranta (€30, 4½ hours, two daily)

Nurmes (€20, two hours, three daily)

Oulu (€40, 6½ hours, two daily)

Onnibus (www.onnibus.com) has cheaper but less frequent services to destinations including Helsinki (€15, 6¼ hours, two daily), Imatra (€5, 2½ hours, one daily) and Lappeenranta (€7, 3¼ hours, one daily).

TRAIN

The **train station** (Itäranta) is east of the river, next to the bus station. Services include the following:

Helsinki (€44, 4½ hours, four daily)

Lieksa (€14, 1¼ hours, two daily)

Nurmes (€21, two hours, one daily)

Savonlinna (€25, 2¼ hours, four daily) Change at Parikkala.

Ilomantsi

☑013 / POP 5316

The closest North Karelian town to the Russian border, Ilomantsi has an Orthodox religion and its own dialect. There is a handful of interesting sights here, but with little tourist infrastructure you're better off visiting during the day and then heading for the national parks and scenic areas beyond.

✕ Eating & Drinking

★Parppeinpirtti   KARELIAN €€

(☑010-239-9950; www.parppeinpirtti.fi; Parppeintie 4, Parppeinvaara; buffet adult/child €23.50/11.50; ☺11am-6pm Jul, to 4pm Jun & Aug) Ilomantsi's one foodie highlight is this traditional house in the Parppeinvaara village, which does a real-deal *pitopöytä* (Karelian buffet) complete with a *kantele* soundtrack. Heap your plate with *vatruskoita* (salmon-stuffed pastry), swill down nonalcoholic *kotikalja* (a fermented drink that tastes like home-brewed beer) and finish with sticky berry soup.

★Hermanni Wine Tower   WINE BAR

(Viintorni; ☑020-778-9233; www.hermannin.fi; Kappalaisentie; ☺10am-11pm Jun–mid-Aug) Blackcurrants, crowberries and white currants from the fields and bogs around Ilomantsi are blended by Hermanni Winery (Käymiskuja 1; ☺9am-4pm Mon-Fri, 10am-5pm Sat, noon-5pm Sun Jul, closed Sun Jun & Aug, closed Sat-Sun Sep-May). At the top of the local 33m-high water tower, you can sample its local berry wines and liqueurs by the glass or tasting tray (€12 for five wines and one liqueur). The balcony's panoramas are fabulous.

❶ Getting There & Away

There's no public transport in the area; if you don't have your own wheels, you'll have to rely on **taxis** (☑013-88111).

Lake Pielinen Region

At the heart of northern Karelia is Pielinen, Finland's fourth-largest lake. On its shores, precipitous Koli National Park has epic views and winter skiing.

Bring your hiking boots because this is a place to be active; towns here are really just bases for getting into the great outdoors.

Koli National Park

The magnificent 347m-high Koli inspired Finland's artistic National Romantic era with artists including Pekka Halonen and Eero Järnefelt setting up their easels here. Koli was declared a national park in 1991 after intense debate between environmentalists and landowners. The area remains relatively pristine with more than 90km of marked walking tracks and superb cross-county and downhill skiing.

◉ Sights & Activities

Summer walking and winter skiing are the twin highlights here. Myriad other activities range from boating to horse riding and dog-sledding.

Summer Chair Lift CHAIR LIFT
(one way/return €4/6; ⊙ 11am-5.45pm mid–late Jun & early Aug, 10am-5.45pm Jul) Across from the Sokos Hotel Koli's upper car park, a summer chair lift sweeps you down the east side of Koli Hill to the shore of Lake Pielinen and back. The dizzying 212m descent/ascent, over a distance of 770m each way, is definitely not for the vertigo-prone, but the vistas are sublime.

Koli Activ OUTDOORS
(☑ 040-085-7557; www.koliactiv.fi; ⊙ Jun-Aug & Nov-Feb) During summer, Koli Activ rents out mountain bikes (€20/35 per three hours/day), canoes (€25/40 per two hours/day), kayaks and stand-up paddleboards (€25 or €50 per two hours) and rowboats (€15/30 per four hours/day) from its restaurant, Alamaja. In winter it offers ski or snowshoe rental (€20/30 per three hours/day) from the Luontokeskus Ukko nature centre.

Koli Husky DOG SLEDDING
(☑ 040-876-6587; www.kolihusky.com; adult/child 10-minute ride €25/10, 2hr €135/70; ⊙ Nov-Feb) Winter husky trips take place on Lake Pielinen. Seasonal operating hours and departure points can vary depending on weather conditions.

🛏 Sleeping & Eating

Koli National Park has eight basic cabins that can be booked through the Luontokeskus Ukko nature centre. To rent other holiday cottages in the area, use Karelia Expert's **Koli accommodation service**

(☑ 045-138-7429; www.visitkarelia.fi; Ylä-Kolintie 2; ⊙ Jun-Sep).

The ski-in **Break Sokos Hotel Koli** (☑ 020-123-4600; www.sokoshotels.fi; Ylä-Kolintie 39; d from €135; P🐾) sits atop the hill; other accommodation, including hostel accommodation and guesthouses, is scattered throughout the area.

★**Alamaja** CAFE €
(www.koliactiv.fi; Ranatatie 12; lunch buffet €13, mains €16-19; ⊙ 11am-8pm Jun–mid-Aug, 11am-5pm mid-Aug–Sep & Dec-Easter) Right on the lake's shore at Koli harbour, this rust-red, double-storey timber building has two terraces overlooking the water (or, in winter, ice) and some of the best food for miles around: reindeer steaks with lingonberry jam, butter-fried vendace (whitefish) with sour cream and dill potatoes, delicious halloumi burgers and a different soup each day (plus, this being Finland, two saunas).

ℹ Information

Koli's **summer tourist office** (☑ 045-138-7429; www.koli.fi; Ylä-Kolintie 2; ⊙ Jun-Sep) has a comprehensive range of information and maps. It opens daily in July but shuts most weekends in June, August and September. If it's closed, the **Luontokeskus Ukko** (☑ 020-639-5654; www.luontoon.fi/kolinluontokeskus; Ylä-kolintie 39; exhibition adult/child €5/2; ⊙ 10am-5pm mid-Aug–mid-Apr, shorter hours mid-Apr–mid-Aug) nature centre has tourist information.

ℹ Getting There & Away

On weekends during the ski season, buses run to Koli *kylä* (village) from Joensuu (€10, 1½ hours, one daily Saturday and Sunday from early December to Easter).

Lieksa

☑ 013 / POP 11,739
On the banks of Lake Pielinen, Lieksa is unlovely in itself, but from here you can easily explore Koli or go whitewater rafting, horse riding, canoeing and bear-watching.

◉ Sights & Activities

Karelia Expert (p176) can book most trips and activities, and provides detailed driving instructions for out-of-the-way operators. Pick-ups from Lieksa for whitewater rafting trips in the Ruunaa Recreation Area can also be arranged.

Pielisen Museo MUSEUM
(☑040-104-4151; www.lieksa.fi; Pappilantie 2; adult/child €7/1.50; ☺10am-6pm mid-May–mid-Sep) More than 70 Karelian buildings and open-air exhibits at this outdoor museum are organised by century or trade (such as farming, milling and fire-fighting). A fascinating insight into the forestry industry includes a look at a logging camp and floating rafts and machinery used for harvest and transport.

In winter the only section open is the **indoor museum** (winter admission adult/child €3/1; ☺10am-3pm Tue-Fri mid-Sep–mid-May) featuring photographs and displays on Karelian history.

★ **Erä Eero** WILDLIFE WATCHING
(☑040-015-9452; www.eraeero.com; €175; ☺4pm-6am) Erä Eero runs awesome overnight trips to its 18-person observation cabin (six places are accessible for wheelchairs), where you may see bears and beavers between April and October, as well as wolves, lynx, wolverines and birds of prey year-round. Coffee and snacks are included, along with sleeping bags (bunks are available). Breakfast costs €8. It's 27km southeast of Lieksa.

⌙ Sleeping & Eating

Timitraniemi Camping CAMPGROUND €
(☑045-123-7166; www.timitra.com; Timitrantie 25; tent sites €15 plus per person €4.50, cabins €45-165; ☺mid-May–mid-Sep; P) At the mouth of the river, well-equipped Timitraniemi has 45 log cabins of varying sizes and plushness and plenty of grassy pitches. Facilities include a lakeside cafe, saunas, and bikes and boats for hire; rafting and fishing trips can be arranged.

★ **Kestikievari Herranniemi** GUESTHOUSE €€
(☑013-542-110; www.herranniemi.com; Vuonislahdentie 185, Vuonislahti; s/d/tr from €59/84/102, cabins €30-78, cottage €145; P) In an idyllic lakeside setting 2km south of Vuonislahti's train station, this quaint 200-year-old farm has a range of comfortable accommodation, home-cooked local dishes (€14 to €18), two lakeside saunas, canoes and rowboats for hire (€6/15 per hour/day) and bike hire (€3/15 per hour/day). Treatment therapies span herbal baths (€17) to *turvesauna* (a sauna and mud bath; €30 per hour). Cots are available by request.

In winter, staff can also arrange ice-fishing equipment, cross-country skis and snowshoes.

Lieksan Leipomo BAKERY, CAFE €
(☑013-521-777; www.liekasnleipomo.fi; Pielisentie 31; dishes €3.50-8.50, lunch buffet €8.30; ☺7am-5pm Mon-Fri, 9am-2pm Sat) In a beautiful wooden building, this endearing bakery is a local favourite for filling lunch buffets featuring a daily soup (such as smoked reindeer) and fantastic cakes.

❶ Information

Karelia Expert (☑040-017-5323; www.visitkarelia.fi; Pielisentie 20; ☺9am-5pm Mon-Fri Jun & Aug, to 5pm Mon-Fri, to 2pm Sat Jul, to 4pm Mon-Fri Sep-May) Books tours and accommodation.

❶ Getting There & Away

BOAT
The car ferry **M/F Pielinen** (☑040-088-9845; pielislaivat@gmail.com; one way adult/child/car/bicycle €20/12/12/6; ☺late Jun-late Aug) makes the 1¾-hour trip from Lieksa to Koli twice daily, departing from Lieksa at 10am and 3pm, and departing from Koli at noon and 5pm. Book ahead by phone as space is limited.

BUS
Buses (€18, 1¾ hours, one daily Monday to Friday) link Lieksa with Joensuu, but the train is faster and more frequent.

TRAIN
Trains run from Helsinki to Lieksa (€56, six hours, two daily) via Joensuu (€14, 1¼ hours).

Nurmes
☑013 / POP 7983
On the northern shores of Lake Pielinen, Nurmes is a great base for activities such as snowmobiling, ice-fishing, dog-sledding and cross-country skiing tours in winter, and wildlife-watching, canoeing, hiking and more come summer.

Founded in 1876 by Tsar Alexander II, the town is pleasant in its own right, with an Old Town area (Puu-Nurmes) of historical wooden buildings along Kirkkokatu.

◉ Sights & Activities

Karelia Expert takes bookings (at least 24 hours in advance) for most services; **Bomba Action** (☑040-087-9890; www.bomba-action.fi; Suojärventie 1, Bomba Village; ☺10am-2pm Mon-

Fri, by appointment Sat & Sun) and Hyvärilä also offer a huge range of high-energy activities.

Bomba Village   VILLAGE

(☑010-783-0450; Tuulentie 10) The centrepiece of this recreated Karelian 'village' encompassing the Sokos Hotel Bomba is the imposing Bomba Talo, with its high roof and ornate wooden trim. It's a replica of a typical 19th-century Karelian family house and was completed in 1978. It now houses the Bomban Talo restaurant and eating here is the only way to see inside. Outside are craft studios and a summertime market. Activities company Bomba Action is also located on the grounds.

🛏 Sleeping & Eating

Hyvärilä   HOTEL, CAMPGROUND €

(☑040-104-5960; www.hyvarila.com; Lomatie 12; tent sites €10 plus per person €6, cabins €54-65, hostel dm €22, hotel s/d/f €85/103/170; ⊙camping Jun–mid-Sep; P🌐) Next door to a nine-hole golf course, and home to a golf simulator, this lakeside resort incorporates a campground, hostel accommodation, a 14-room hotel and a restaurant, all managed by cheerful staff. Golf aside, activities include a small swimming beach, tennis courts, and canoe and boat hire. Two saunas are by the lake. Wi-fi is available in the main hotel building.

Sokos Hotel Bomba   SPA HOTEL €€

(☑010-783-0450; www.sokoshotels.fi; Tuulentie 10; s/d/cabin from €119/131/168, spa for nonguests from €12.50; ⊙spa 10am-10pm May-Aug, to 9pm Sep-Apr; P🌐@🌐🌐) This sprawling complex has an enormous indoor pool and spa area overlooking the lake and stylish modern rooms. There are also atmospheric Karelian-style log cabins (all with private bathrooms and several with their own saunas) amid the replica Karelian buildings of Bomba Village. On-site adventure company Bomba Action can arrange no end of outdoor activities.

Bomban Talo   KARELIAN €€

(☑010-783-045; www.sokoshotels.fi; Suojärvenkatu 1; Karelian buffet €21, mains €19-29; ⊙noon-9.30pm, buffet until 7pm) The mammoth wood cabin at Bomba Village contains the Sokos Bomba Hotel's restaurant serving a Karelian buffet to the masses, with *karjalanpiirakka* (rice-filled savoury pastry) designed to mop up *karjalanpaisti* (stew), and *sultsina*

(semolina porridge pie) with *puolukkahillo* (lingonberry jam). À la carte options include rainbow trout with rosehips.

🛈 Information

Karelia Expert (☑050-336-0707; www.visitkarelia.fi; Kauppatori 3; ⊙9am-5pm Mon-Fri; 🌐) Local information and bookings.

🛈 Getting There & Away

Buses and trains depart from just by the main square.

Up to three daily buses run to/from Joensuu (€20, two hours), Kajaani (€20, two hours) and Lieksa (€12, one hour).

Trains run to Joensuu (€21, two hours, three daily) via Lieksa (€8, 45 minutes). The train station is unstaffed; buy tickets online before you travel or on the train.

NORTH-CENTRAL FINLAND

Kuhmo

☑08 / POP 8755

Surrounded by wilderness, Kuhmo makes a natural base for hiking and wildlife-watching. Vast taiga forests run from here right across Siberia and harbour wolves, bears and lynx. Kuhmo is also the unofficial capital of Vienan Karjala, the Karelian heartland now in Russia, explored by artists in the movement that was crucial to the development of Finnish national identity. Most of their expeditions set off from Kuhmo, as did one of Elias Lönnrot's, when he headed into 'Songland' to record the verses of bards that he later wove into the *Kalevala* epic. There's a fine *Kalevala* resource centre in town.

This likeable little town also has a great chamber music festival (p178) in July.

◉ Sights & Activities

Hiking is the big drawcard in Kuhmo – the eastern 'branch line' of the UKK route passes through here – but there are plenty of other ways to get active.

The website www.wildtaiga.fi has details of activities offered in the region, including operators with hides for viewing bears, elk, flying squirrels, beavers, wolverines and wild reindeer.

★ Juminkeko
CULTURAL CENTRE

(www.juminkeko.fi; Kontionkatu 25; adult/child €5/2; ⊙noon-6pm Mon-Fri, daily in Jul) If you're interested in the *Kalevala* or Karelian culture, pay a visit to this excellent resource centre inside a beautiful hand-hewn timber building made using traditional methods and modern styling – its 24 wooden pillars support a roof covered with lingonberries and heather. Passionate staff are very knowledgeable; there are also themed art and photography exhibitions here each year.

Wild Brown Bear
WILDLIFE WATCHING

(✆040-546-9008; www.wildbrownbear.fi; Kostamustie 5644, Vartius; bear-watching from €140; ⊙Apr-Sep) With 26 hides, this operator's wildlife and photography excursions offer a high chance of spotting bears (and possibly cubs in September), wolverines, wolves and other creatures. Accommodation is available in its wooden lodge, with rooms sharing bathrooms (from €60 per person including breakfast, dinner and sauna). It's in a conservation area 63km north of Kuhmo by the Russian border.

★★ Festivals & Events

Kuhmon Kamarimusiikki
MUSIC

(Kuhmo Chamber Music Festival; www.kuhmofestival.fi; concert tickets from €18.50; ⊙mid-Jul) This two-week festival in mid-July has a full program performed by a variety of Finnish and international musicians, many youthful. Most concerts, usually five or six short pieces bound by a tenuous theme, are held in the Kuhmo-Talo (✆08-6155-5451; www.kuhmotalo. fi; Koulukatu 1) arts and cultural centre.

🛏 Sleeping & Eating

Book well ahead during July's Kuhmon Kamarimusiikki (p178) festival, when prices rise. Wildlife-watching operators such as Taiga Spirit (✆040-746-8243; www.taigaspirit. com; Lentiirantie 4282, Lentiira; wildlife-watching/safaris from €80/130) and Wild Brown Bear (p178) have their own lodges out in the surrounding wilderness.

Matkakoti Parkki
GUESTHOUSE €

(✆08-655-0271; www.matkakotiparkki.fi; Vienantie 3; s/d €40/60; P 🖥) Run by kind-hearted hosts, this quiet little family guesthouse offers excellent value near the centre of town. Its 19 rooms share bathrooms, which are spotless. There's a kitchen you can use and a home-cooked breakfast is included.

★ Hotelli Kalevala
HOTEL €€

(✆08-655-4100; www.hotellikalevala.fi; Väinämöinen 9; s/d/ste from €98/132/209; P @ 🖥) Built in the shape of the *Kalevala kokko* (eagle), this striking wood-and-concrete building 4.5km southeast of central Kuhmo is the area's best place to stay. Most of its 47 warm-hued rooms have lake views, and the hotel takes full advantage of its gorgeous setting with a relaxing Jacuzzi and sauna area with vistas and plenty of activity options year-round.

Neljä Kaesaa
CAFE €

(✆08-652-1573; www.neljakaesaa.fi; Koulukatu 3; lunch buffet €10.50, Saturday brunch €19.50; ⊙9am-4.30pm Mon-Fri, 11am-4pm Sat; 🖥) In a charming white-painted wooden building, Neljä Kaesaa is the best central option for lunch, when it serves a buffet of warming and traditional Finnish comfort food like stews (sometimes with elk) or fried *muikku* (vendace, or whitefish, a small lake fish) from Monday to Friday; Saturday's brunch features the same dishes.

ℹ Information

There's no tourist office but hotels can provide information.

ℹ Getting There & Away

Buses serve Kajaani (€20.40, 1¾ hours, one daily) and Sotkamo (€13.70, one hour, one daily).

Oulu

✆08 / POP 200,526

Prosperous Oulu (Swedish: Uleåborg) is one of Finland's most enjoyable cities to visit. In summer angled sunshine bathes the kauppatori (market square) in light and all seems well with the world. Locals, who appreciate daylight when they get it, crowd the terraces, and market stalls groan under the weight of Arctic berries.

The city centre is spread across several islands, connected by pedestrian bridges and cycleways. Oulu is also a significant technology city; the university turns out top-notch IT graduates and the corporate parks on the city's outskirts employ people from all over the globe.

◎ Sights & Activities

Free maps from the tourist office (p181) detail Oulu's extensive network of bicycle paths.

Oulu

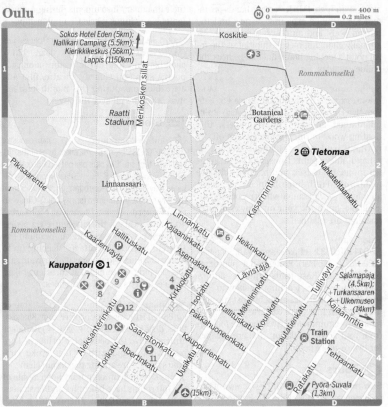

A good 3km walk or ride is from the kauppatori, across the bridge to Pikisaari and across another bridge to Nallikari, where there's a lovely beach facing the Gulf of Bothnia and activities including kitesurfing.

★ **Kauppatori** SQUARE
Oulu has one of Finland's liveliest market squares, and its position at the waterfront makes it all the more appealing. The square is bordered by several old wooden storehouses now serving as restaurants, bars and craft shops. The squat *Toripolliisi* statue, a humorous representation of the local police, is a local landmark. Made from bronze, the lovable figure is the work of sculptor Kaarlo Mikkonen, and was installed here in 1987.

★ **Tietomaa** MUSEUM
(www.tietomaa.fi; Nahkatehtaankatu 6; adult/child €15/11, IMAX cinema €5.50/4; ⊙10am-6pm, hours vary) This huge, excellent science museum can occupy kids for the best part of a day with a

Oulu

giant, 35m-high IMAX screen, hands-on interactive exhibits exploring planets and the human body, and an observation tower. An annually changing mega-exhibition is the focal point. Opening hours fluctuate; check the online calendar.

Kesän Sauna SAUNA
(www.kesansauna.fi; Koskitie 58; sauna €5; ⊙5-9pm Mon-Fri, from 3pm Sat & Sun Jun-Aug) Built, maintained and run by volunteers, this floating wood-burning sauna sits 5m off the northern bank of the Oulujoki, reached by a hand-pulled punt. Unusually for a Finnish sauna, it's unisex, and bathing suits are mandatory. Fresh birch branches are available for a *vihta* (sauna whisk). Lockers are available, but bring your own towel. Winter openings are planned.

Salamapaja OUTDOORS
(☑044-210-0033; http://salamapaja.fi; 4hr tour €120-175; ⊙Sep-Mar) Professional photographer Thomas Kast leads fantastic aurora photography tours, teaching you how to capture the glowing skies at their most spectacular. He also has spare cameras if you need to borrow equipment. Prices include pick-up from your accommodation, and are cheaper for two or more people.

🧭 Tours

Summer tours (☑08-4152-7770; www.oulun-seudunoppaat.fi; Kirkkokatu 2A; ⊙late Jun-late Aug) by bus, bicycle and foot in English (many free) leave from the town hall, usually Wednesdays and Saturdays: check the website for times. Reservations can be made online.

Between September and March, when dark skies permit, Salamapaja (p180) offers aurora photography tours.

✨ Festivals & Events

QStock MUSIC
(www.qstock.fi; Raatintie 4, Kuusisaari; ⊙late Jul) Hip-hop, rock and – this being Finland – metal acts, play over six stages during this two-day festival in late July, which attracts more than 60 different artists and 30,000 visitors. Most bands are Finnish, but past international performers have included Marilyn Manson, Megadeath, Twisted Sister and Alice Cooper.

Air Guitar World Championships MUSIC
(www.airguitarworldchampionships.com; ⊙late Aug) Contestants from all over the world take the stage to show what they can do with their imaginary instruments during August's famous Air Guitar World Championships.

Oulun Juhlaviikot PERFORMING ARTS
(www.oulunjuhlaviikot.fi; ⊙Aug) Jazz, blues, chamber and folk music feature alongside poetry, stand-up comedy, theatre, film and art exhibitions during this month-long festival at venues all over the city.

🛏 Sleeping

⭐**Nallikari Camping** CAMPGROUND €
(☑044-703-1353; https://nallikari.fi; Leiritie 10, Nallikari; tent site €15 plus per person €5, cottages €105-157, villas from €366; ⊙campground & cottages May-Sep, villas year-round; 🅿🛜; 🚃15 from the city centre, 🚂summer tourist train) Close to the lifeguard-patrolled beach at Nallikari, a 40-minute walk to the city centre via pedestrian bridges, this excellent campground has 150 tent pitches, 28 cottages sleeping up to five, and 24 luxurious villas with private saunas sleeping up to eight. It hires out bikes, cross-country skis and snowshoes.

⭐**Lapland Hotel Oulu** DESIGN HOTEL €€
(☑08-881-1110; www.laplandhotels.com; Kirkkokatu 3B; d/ste from €122/347; 🅿@🛜🌊) Reindeer antlers above the beds, large prints of Lappish wildlife and carpets that evoke Lapland's forests are among the design elements of this striking contemporary hotel. Some of the 160 rooms have balconies and/or saunas, and cots are available. There's also a large lake-inspired, free-form swimming pool and rental bikes. Kitchen & Bar Oula (p180), its on-site restaurant, is superb.

⭐**Hotel Lasaretti** HOTEL €€
(☑020-757-4700; www.lasaretti.com; Kasarmintie 13; s/d/f from €108/125/155; 🅿🛜🌊) In a tranquil parkside location, this inviting hotel sits in a group of renovated red-brick buildings that once housed a hospital. Stylish rooms have gleaming hardwood floors: ask for one with a water view. Excellent facilities include an indoor swimming pool with big windows overlooking the surrounding greenery and a busy bar-restaurant with a sunny terrace.

⭐**Kitchen & Bar Oula** FINNISH €€
(☑040-671-0539; www.laplandhotels.com; Kirkkokatu 3; mains €17-32, 3-/5-course menu €56/65; ⊙5-10pm Mon-Sat Jun–mid-Sep, shorter hours mid-Sep–May) Beneath an igloo-inspired glass atrium, this restaurant inside the Lapland Hotel Oulu (p180) features outsized prints of Lapland scenes, such as spawning salmon.

Gourmet Lappish dishes include cold-smoked Arctic perch soup with birch and fennel, chargrilled reindeer with redcurrant and moss jus, and smoked whitefish carpaccio with parsnip mayo and pickled dandelion, accompanied by an extensive wine list and Lapland-influenced cocktails.

Eating

Rooster
CAFE €

(📱 020-711-8280; https://rooster.fi; Torikatu 26; mains €11-18, lunch buffet Mon-Fri/weekend €10.20/21; ⊙10.30am-2pm Mon-Fri, noon-4pm Sat & Sun, bar to midnight; 🖋) Inside a beautiful wooden building, Rooster has a minimalist Finnish-design interior. Burgers, such as its *Lohiburgeri* (salmon, marinated fennel and horseradish mayo), *Vuohenjuustoburgeri* (beef, grilled goat's cheese, watermelon and fig balsamic) and *Vegaanburgeri* (gado gado, mango, rocket and red-onion compote), are a speciality. Light lunch dishes include spicy sweet potato lasagne or nettle and pepper soup. Hours vary seasonally.

Oulun Kauppahalli
MARKET €

(www.oulunkauppahalli.fi; Kauppatori; ⊙8am-5pm Mon-Thu, to 6pm Fri, to 3pm Sat) On the square, the 1901-built kauppahalli has freshly filleted salmon glistening in the market stalls and plenty of spots to snack on anything from cloudberries to sushi.

1881 Uleåborg
FINNISH €€€

(📱 08-881-1188; www.uleaborg.fi; Aittatori 4; mains €31.50-36.50, 3-course menu €54.50; ⊙5-10pm Mon-Sat) In an old timber warehouse near the kauppatori, this classy spot combines a traditional setting with chic Finnish style and creative cooking (smoked reindeer and morel terrine, Åland lamb with spruce-smoked potatoes, lingonberry crème brûlée with cloudberry meringue). The awning-shaded, glassed-in terrace by the water is one of Oulu's loveliest summer spots.

Ravintola Hugo
FINNISH €€€

(📱 020-143-2200; www.ravintolahugo.fi; Rantakatu 4; 3-/5-course menus €45/65, with paired wines €71/109; ⊙5-9pm Tue-Thu, to 10pm Fri & Sat) Innovative cuisine using locally sourced products makes this elegant restaurant with white tablecloths and richly coloured walls a real Oulu highlight. Some outstanding flavour combinations feature in its menus (no à la carte), such as pike-perch with liquorice leaves and parsnip; lichen-smoked reindeer with wild mushrooms and powdered roast beetroot; and spruce and strawberry sorbet with clotted reindeer cream.

Drinking & Nightlife

Oulu has plenty going on at night. The kauppatori is the spot to start in summer: bars set in traditional wooden warehouses have terraces that soak up every last drop of the evening sun. Year-round, you'll find regular live music and clubs.

Viinibaari Vox
WINE BAR

(www.viinibaarivox.fi; Pakkahuoneenkatu 8; ⊙3pm-midnight Mon-Thu, to 2am Fri & Sat) Hefty timber beams and low lighting give this wine bar a cosy, atmospheric ambience. A rotating menu of 30 to 40 wines are available by the glass each month, served with Finnish cheese and charcuterie plates. In summer, bentwood chairs are set up on the pavement terrace; the mulled wine is an instant winter warmer when it's snowing outside.

Graali
PUB

(www.graali.fi; Saaristonkatu 5; ⊙2pm-2am) When it's cold and snowy outside, there's nowhere cosier than this pub, decorated with suits of armour and sporting trophies. Sink into a leather armchair by the open fire and feel the warmth return to your bones. A good whisky selection will help you along.

45 Special
CLUB

(www.45special.com; Saaristonkatu 12; ⊙8pm-4am) This grungy three-level club pulls a good mix of people for its downstairs rock and more mainstream top floor. There's a small cover charge on weekends and regular live gigs. It serves food until 3am.

Information

Free wi-fi is available throughout the city centre on the PanOulu network.

Tourist Office (📱 08-5584-1330; www.visitoulu.fi; Torikatu 18; ⊙9am-5.30pm Mon-Fri Jun, 9am-5.30pm Mon-Fri, 10am-4pm Sat Jul & Aug) Oulu's summer-opening tourist office has a good range of information on Oulu and other Finnish destinations.

Getting There & Away

AIR

Oulu's **airport** (OUL; www.finavia.fi; Lentokentäntie 720; 🖥) is 14km southwest of the centre. Finnair and Norwegian have daily direct services to Helsinki; Arctic Airlink has several flights a week to Luleå, Sweden, and Tromsø, Norway. Buses 8, 9 and 56 link it to the city centre (€5.80, 25 minutes, half-hourly at least). A taxi costs around €45. There are car-hire desks and an ATM.

BUS

The **bus station** (Ratakatu) is on the eastern side of the city centre, adjacent to the train station.

Matkahuolto (www.matkahuolto.fi) services include the following:

Helsinki (€55, 9½ hours, up to 14 daily)
Kajaani (€20, 2¾ hours, four daily)
Rovaniemi (€24, 3½ hours, eight daily)
Tornio (€25.20, 2½ hours, six daily)

Budget operator Onnibus (www.onnibus.com) has services to destinations including Helsinki (€23, eight hours, four daily) and Vaasa (€9, 4½ hours, two daily).

TRAIN

Direct **trains** (Rautatienkatu) run daily to Helsinki (€56, six hours, four daily) via Kajaani (€12.40, 2¾ hours). From Oulu, trains continue north to Rovaniemi (€14, 2¼ hours).

Kuusamo & Ruka

📞 08 / POP 15,673

Kuusamo is a remote frontier town 217km northeast of Oulu and close to the Russian border, while Ruka is its buzzy ski resort 30km north. Both make great activity bases.

⊙ Sights & Activities

The Kuusamo/Ruka area is probably Finland's best equipped for outdoor activities. In summer, there's great walking and bird-watching as well as good mountain-biking trails. In winter it's a centre for skiing (p182), husky-sledding, snowmobiling and more. The Ruka webpage, www.ruka.fi, is a useful place to look for activity ideas.

Kuusamon
Suurpetokeskus   WILDLIFE RESERVE

(www.kuusamon-suurpetokeskus.fi; Keronrannan-tie 31; adult/child €10/5; ⊙ 10am-5pm Apr-Sep) There's a great backstory to this bear sanctuary 35km south of Kuusamo on the Kajaani road. Rescued as orphans, the bears were nursed by their 'father' Sulo Karjalainen, who then refused to have them put down (they can't return to the wild) when government funding dried up. He casually takes them fishing and walking in the forest, but you'll meet them in their enclosures here. It's thrilling to see these impressive, intelligent animals up close and appreciate their different personalities.

★ Karhu-Kuusamo   WILDLIFE

(📞 040-021-0681; www.karhujenkatselu.fi; Kit-ulantie 1, Mustaniemi; evening/overnight trips €120/140) Thrilling bear-watching trips spend the evening at a comfortable hide overlooking a meadow where bears regularly stop by: most of the summer you have a high chance of seeing a honeypaw. Evening trips return to town around midnight; overnight trips return the next morning. Tuomo, the knowledgeable guide, can also arrange birdwatching. It's 13km southeast of Kuusamo off Rd 866.

★ Kota-Husky   DOG SLEDDING

(📞 040-718-7287; http://kota-husky.fi; Jaksamon-tie 60, Karjalaisenniemi; 1hr husky visit €45, 2/6hr sleigh ride €95/210, 3½hr aurora tour €150) Kota-Husky has picturesque kennels in an old barn and runs excellent, great-value husky excursions for a maximum of 12 people. Most memorable are the aurora-watching tours in husky-pulled sleighs. It's 48km west of Ruka via Rd 9471.

★ Rukatunturi   SNOW SPORTS

(www.ruka.fi; Rukatunturintie 9, Ruka; lift pass per day/week €41.50/202; ⊙ Nov–mid-Apr) Busy Ruka fell has 34 ski slopes, of which 30 are illuminated, 26 lifts, a vertical drop of 201m and a longest run of 1300m. Dedicated snowboard areas include a half-pipe. Cross-country trails total an impressive 500km, with 40km illuminated. Lift passes allow you to ski at Pyhä (www.pyha.fi; Kultakeronkatu, Pyhä; lift tickets per day/week €44/213; ⊙ Dec–mid-Apr) in Lapland too.

🍴 Sleeping & Eating

Ruka has the lion's share of accommodation. Book well ahead for winter; in summer it's great value. There are numerous apartments in Ruka itself, and hundreds of cabins and cottages dotted throughout the surrounding area. For rentals, contact the tourist offices or booking services such as Lomarengas (📞 030-650-2502; www.lomarengas.fi), ProLoma (📞 020-792-9700; www.proloma.fi), Ski-Inn (📞 08-860-0300; www.ski-inn.fi) or Ruka-ko (📞 020-734-4790; www.rukako.fi).

If you stay in Ruka in summer, accommodation providers offer a 'Summer Wristband', with discounts on dining and activities.

Royal Hotel Ruka   BOUTIQUE HOTEL €€

(📞 040-081-9840; https://royalruka.fi; Mestantie 1, Ruka; d/ste from €90/179; ⊙ Jul-Apr; 🅿 🐾 🛜) At the foot of the fell at the turn-off to Rukajärvi, this intimate 16-room hotel looks like a children's fort waiting to be populated with toy soldiers. Rooms are plainer than the exterior suggests, but service is excellent. The classy restaurant offers such wild delicacies as hare, elk and bear; from July to November it only opens by reservation.

Cumulus Rantasipi Rukahovi　　HOTEL €€
(☑ 020-048-126; www.cumulus.fi; Rukankyläntie 15, Ruka; s/d/ste/apt from €86/96/160/186; P @ 🛜) Right by the major slopes in Ruka's centre, this huge 219-room complex draws everyone from conferencing execs to snowball-lobbing families. Standard rooms are a long hike from reception; spacious superiors have balconies. Both have drying cupboards. Duplex apartments are down the road. Its restaurant, bars and nightclub are the heart of Ruka nightlife in the ski and autumn *ruska* seasons.

Riipisen Riistaravintola　　FINNISH €€
(☑ 08-868-1219; www.riipisen.fi; Rukaturintie 6, Ruka; mains €16-45; ⏱ 1-9pm Mon-Sat Sep-May) At the Kelo ski-lift area, 500m south of Ruka's main square, this log cabin has a rustic interior and attracts a convivial crowd. It specialises in game dishes, and you'll find Rudolf, Bullwinkle and, yes, poor Yogi on the menu here in various guises, depending on availability and season. Arctic hare, willow grouse and boar also feature.

❶ Information

Kuusamo Info (☑ 040-860-8365; www.ruka. fi; Torangintaival 2, Kuusamo; ⏱ 9am-5pm Mon-Fri, 10am-2pm Sat, plus noon-4pm Sun Jun-Aug; 🛜) This large visitor centre is at the highway junction, 2km from central Kuusamo. It offers comprehensive tourist information, rental cottage booking and a cafe-shop. There's also a wildlife photography exhibition and national park information desk.

Ruka Info (☑ 08-860-0250; www.ruka.fi; Rukatunturintie 9, Ruka; ⏱ 9am-5pm early Jun & late Aug, 9.30am-7pm Sep & late Jun–mid-Aug, 10am-8pm daily Oct-May) Tourist information and accommodation booking in Ruka's village centre.

❶ Getting There & Away

Kuusamo airport (KAO; www.finavia.fi; Lentokentäntie, Kuusamo) is 4km northeast of town. Finnair has year-round services to/from Helsinki; winter services are much more frequent. Major car-hire companies have desks here. Buses serve incoming and outbound flights (€7, 10 minutes to Kuusamo; €10, 30 minutes to Ruka). Call 0100-84200 for a taxi.

Buses run to/from Kajaani (€25, 3½ hours, two daily), Oulu (€25, three hours, up to eight daily) and Rovaniemi (€34.50, three hours, three daily).

LAPLAND

Lapland casts a powerful spell: there's something lonely and intangible here that makes it magical. The midnight sun, the Sami peoples, the aurora borealis (Northern Lights) and roaming reindeer are all components of this – as is Santa Claus himself, who 'officially' resides here – along with the awesome latitudes: at Nuorgam, the northernmost point, you have passed Iceland and nearly all of Canada and Alaska.

Spanning 30% of Finland's land area, Lapland is home to just 3% of its population. Its vast wilderness is ripe for exploring on foot, skis or sled. The sense of space, pure air and big skies are what's most memorable here, more so than the towns.

Lapland's far north is known as Sápmi, home of the Sami, whose main communities are around Inari, Utsjoki and Hetta. Rovaniemi, on the Arctic Circle, is the most popular gateway to the north.

Rovaniemi

☑ 016 / POP 62,231

Situated right by the Arctic Circle, the 'official' terrestrial residence of Santa Claus is the capital of Finnish Lapland and a tourism boom town. Its wonderful Arktikum museum is the perfect introduction to these latitudes, and Rovaniemi is a fantastic base from which to organise activities.

Thoroughly destroyed by the retreating Wehrmacht in 1944, the town was rebuilt to a plan by Alvar Aalto, with the major streets in the shape of a reindeer's head and antlers (the stadium near the bus station is the eye). Its utilitarian buildings are compensated for by its marvellous riverside location.

◉ Sights & Activities

A Culture Pass combination ticket (adult/child €20/10) offering unlimited access to the three major sights – the Arktikum (p185), Pilke Tiedekeskus (p185) and Rovaniemen Taidemuseo (p185) – is valid for a week. Pick it up from the museums or the tourist office (p187).

Rovaniemi's concert hall, **Lappia-talo** (☑ 040-028-2484;　　www.rovaniementeatteri.fi;

Rovaniemi

Rovaniemi

Hallituskatu 11; ⊙ box office 1-5pm Tue-Fri, 11am-1pm Sat & 1hr prior to performances), is one of several buildings in Rovaniemi designed by Alvar Aalto; others include the adjacent library and town hall.

Rovaniemi is a great launching pad for winter and summer activities, offering frequent departures with multilingual guides. You need a driving licence to operate a snowmobile; there's a 50% supplement if you want one to yourself.

Rovaniemi's ski area, **Ounasvaara** (☑ 044-764-2830; https://ounasvaara.fi; Taunontie 14; winter lift ticket per day €38, ski hire per day €38; ☻ winter activities early Nov-late Mar, summer activities late Jun–mid-Aug), is just east of the river.

★ Arktikum   MUSEUM
(www.arktikum.fi; Pohjoisranta 4; adult/child €12/5; ☻ 9am-6pm Jun-Aug, 10am-6pm Tue-Sun mid-Jan–May & Sep-Nov, 10am-6pm Dec–mid-Jan) With its beautifully designed glass tunnel stretching out to the Ounasjoki, this is one of Finland's finest museums. One half deals with Lapland, with information on Sami culture and the history of Rovaniemi; the other offers a wide-ranging display on the Arctic, with superb static and interactive displays focusing on flora and fauna, as well as on the peoples of Arctic Europe, Asia and North America. Downstairs an audiovisual – basically a pretty slide show – plays on a constant loop.

★ Pilke Tiedekeskus   MUSEUM
(www.tiedekeskus-pilke.fi; Ounasjoentie 6; adult/child €7/5; ☻ 9am-6pm Mon-Fri, 10am-4pm Sat & Sun mid-Jun–Aug, shorter hours rest of year) Downstairs in the Metsähallitus (Finnish Forest and Park Service) building next to the Arktikum (p185), this is a highly entertaining exhibition on Finnish forestry with a sustainable focus. It has dozens of interactive displays that are great for kids of all ages, who can clamber up into a bird house, build a timber-framed dwelling, get behind the wheel of a forest harvester or play games about forest management. Multilingual touch screens provide interesting background information.

Rovaniemen Taidemuseo   GALLERY
(Korundi; www.korundi.fi; Lapinkävijäntie 4; adult/child €8/4; ☻ 11am-6pm Tue-Sun) A wide collection of contemporary Finnish art rotates in the clean white exhibition space of this gallery in an old brick truck depot. Performances by the Lapland Chamber Orchestra regularly take place in its concert hall.

Santa Claus Village   AMUSEMENT PARK
(www.santaclausvillage.info; Tarvantie 2, Napapiiri; ☻ 9am-6pm Jun-Aug, 10am-5pm mid-Jan–May, Sep & Nov, 9am-7pm Dec–mid-Jan) **FREE** The 'official' Santa Claus Village is built atop the **Arctic Circle marker**, denoted by a line painted on the pavement (Arctic Circle certificates cost €4.20). There's a mixture

of humdrum souvenir stands and classier shops, some selling Sami handicrafts. Other attractions here include reindeer-pulled sleigh rides (on wheels in summer, traditional runners in snow; per adult/child from €17/13 for 400m) and **Santa's Grotto** (www.santaclausvillage.info; Sodankyläntie, Napapiiri; visit free, photographs from €20; ☻ 9am-6pm Jun-Aug, 10am-5pm mid-Jan–May, Sep & Nov, 9am-7pm Dec–mid-Jan) **FREE**.

You can also visit a **husky park** (☑ 040-824-7503; www.huskypark.fi; Joulumaantie 3, Napapiiri; adult/child €10/5; ☻ 11am-4pm Jun-Aug, 10am-4pm Sep-May), and view ice sculpting and varying Christmassy exhibitions. There are Christmas-themed dining options; on-site accommodation includes cabins at **Santa Claus Holiday Village** (☑ 040-159-3811; www.santaclausholidayvillage.fi; Tähtikuja 2, Napapiiri; d from €109; P �), and the new **Snowman World** (http://snowmanworld.fi), with glass-sided apartments and a winter-only ice hotel complete with restaurant and bar.

Bus 8 heads here from the train station, via the city (p188) and airport (€3.90, 25 minutes, up to three hourly 6.30am to 6.30pm).

Bear Hill Husky   DOG SLEDDING
(☑ 040-760-0020; www.bearhillhusky.com; Sinettäjärventie 22; kennel tours incl sled ride adult/child €59/29, expeditions from €119/59; ☻ Jul-Mar) Wintertime husky-pulled sled expeditions start at two hours' duration (prices include transport to/from Rovaniemi). Overnight tours run on Saturdays from late January to March, with accommodation in a traditional wilderness cabin with smoke sauna. If you just want a taster, kennel tours, where you meet the Alaskan huskies, include a 1km ride with their mushers (sled drivers).

☞ Tours

Safartica   OUTDOORS
(☑ 016-311-485; www.safartica.com; Koskikatu 9; ☻ 3hr reindeer sled tour €148, 4hr mountain-bike tour €121) In addition to reindeer-pulled sled tours and mountain-bike tours, this superb outfit runs river activities such as summer berry-picking trips (€75,three hours), midnight-sun lake floating in special flotation suits (€92, three hours), ice fishing (€89, 2½ hours), snowshoe hiking (€69, two hours) and a snowmobile adventure (€192, six hours).

Rovaniemi Food Walk   FOOD

(☑040-488-7173; www.aittadeli.com; €50, with drinks €75; ☺ by reservation) Offering a taster of Lapland cuisine, these three-hour tours are a moveable feast, starting at street-food restaurant **Roka** (☑050-311-6411; www.ravintolaroka.fi; Ainonkatu 3; lunch buffet €9.90, street-food dishes €8.50-12, mains €15.50-23; ☺10.30am-9pm Mon-Thu, to 11pm Fri, noon-11pm Sat, noon-9pm Sun), followed by a contemporary Finnish main course (such as slow-cooked reindeer or whitefish with pickled cucumber) at Aitta Deli & Dine, and finishing with dessert and a cocktail at Cafe & Bar 21.

🎊 Festivals & Events

Jutajaiset   CULTURAL

(www.jutajaiset.fi; ☺ late Jun/early Jul) Held over three days, Jutajaiset is a celebration of Lapland folklore, with music, dance and theatre at venues around town.

🛏 Sleeping

Guesthouse Borealis   GUESTHOUSE €

(☑044-313-1771; www.guesthouseborealis.com; Asemieskatu 1; s/d/tr/apt from €58/68/99/175; P🞡) Friendly owners and proximity to trains make this family-run spot a winner. Rooms are simple, bright and clean, and guests can use a kitchen. Breakfast, served in an airy dining room, features Finnish porridge. The two apartments each have their own entrance and full kitchen; one has a private balcony and private sauna.

City Hotel   HOTEL €€

(☑016-330-0111; www.cityhotel.fi; Pekankatu 9; s/d/ste from €96/126/236; P🞡) Epicentral City Hotel has 90 compact, stylish rooms with large windows and plush maroon and brown fabrics, but it retains an intimate feel. Luxe rooms offer proper double beds (rather than two singles joined together), while smart suites have a sauna. There are also two free saunas on the top floor and free summertime bike hire.

Its restaurant, **Monte Rosa** (☑016-330-0111; www.monterosa.fi; Pekankatu 9; mains restaurant €23-37, bar €10-28; ☺11am-11pm Mon-Fri, 5-11pm Sat & Sun; 🞡), specialises in steak.

★ Arctic Light Hotel   BOUTIQUE HOTEL €€€

(☑020-171-0100; www.arcticlighthotel.fi; Valtakatu 18; d/apt from €150/349; P✳🞡) In Rovaniemi's former 1950s town hall, with original fixtures including wood panelling,

a vintage lift and wrought-iron balustrades, Lapland's top hotel has handcrafted artworks adorning individually designed rooms (some with private saunas). Loft rooms have skylights for aurora-borealis views; the two apartments sleep four, with separate living rooms. Buffet breakfasts are designed by Finnish-American TV chef Sara La Fountain.

Arctic Snow Hotel   ICE HOTEL €€€

(☑040-769-0395; www.arcticsnowhotel.fi; Lehtoahontie 27, Sinettä; s/d/ste €180/260/350, glass-igloo tw €499; ☺Nov-Mar; P) On Lehtojärvi's lakeshore, this place offers the complete snow-hotel experience and also has a snow restaurant as well as warmer eating choices. Alongside the snow hotel is an array of glass igloos (available from the beginning of December), ideal for aurora-watching. It's 26km northwest of Rovaniemi; pick-ups can be arranged.

The temperature of the ice-hotel rooms never gets above 5°C, but reindeer furs and sleeping bags keep you warm.

You can visit the complex (adult/child €15/8) even if you're not a guest.

🍴 Eating

Cafe & Bar 21   CAFE €

(www.cafebar21.fi; Rovakatu 21; dishes €10-14; ☺11am-8.30pm Mon & Tue, to 9.30pm Wed & Thu, to 11pm Fri, noon-11pm Sat, noon-8.30pm Sun; 🞡) A reindeer-pelt collage on the grey-concrete wall is the only concession to place at this artfully modern designer cafe-bar. Black-and-white decor makes it a stylish haunt for salads, superb soups, tapas and its house-speciality waffles (both savoury and sweet), along with creative cocktails. The bar stays open late.

★ Aitta Deli & Dine   FINNISH, DELI €€

(☑040-488-7173; www.aittadeli.com; Rovakatu 26; lunch buffet €10, platters €10-30, 4-course dinner menu €44, with paired wine or beer €69; ☺restaurant 11am-4pm Mon & Tue, to 10pm Wed-Sat, to 3pm Sun, deli 11am-6pm Mon-Fri, to 3pm Sat) 🍃 Locally sourced, organic food at Aitta includes sharing platters piled high with reindeer heart and tongue, lingonberry and elk stew, bear and nettle sausages, and rye and barley breads. Two- and three-course menus are available at lunch and dinner, but the pick of the dinner offerings is the four-course Taste of Lapland menu paired with natural wines or craft beers.

★Restaurant Sky Ounasvaara

FINNISH €€€

(☑ 016-323-400; www.laplandhotels.com; Juhannuskalliontie; mains €24-36, 5-course menu €69, with wine €127; ☺ 6-9.30pm Mon-Sat, to 9pm Sun Jun-Apr) For a truly memorable meal, head to the 1st floor of the **Sky Ounasvaara** d/tr/f/ apt from €101/126/135/143; ☺ Jun-Apr; ⓟ🐾) hotel, where wraparound floor-to-ceiling glass windows looking onto the forest outside create the impression of dining in a tree house. Specialities include Lappish potato dumplings with local mushrooms, reindeer tartare with spruce-smoked mayo, arctic char with sour-milk sauce, and sea-buckthorn meringue with reindeer yoghurt.

🍷 Drinking & Nightlife

Excluding ski resorts, Rovaniemi is the only place north of Oulu with half-decent nightlife. Bars and clubs concentrate in the city centre.

Paha Kurki

BAR

(www.pahakurki.com; Koskikatu 5; ☺ 4pm-3am; 🐾) Dark yet clean and modern, this rock bar has a fine variety of bottled beers, memorabilia on the walls and a good sound system. A Finnish rock bar is what other places might call a metal bar: expect more Pantera than Pixies.

Kauppayhtiö

BAR

(www.kauppayhtio.fi; Valtakatu 24; ☺ 11am-9pm Tue-Thu & Sun, to 3.30am Fri, 1pm-3.30am Sat; 🐾) Almost everything at this oddball gasoline-themed bar-cafe is for sale, including colourful plastic tables and chairs, and retro and vintage toys, as well as new streetwear and Nordic clothing at the attached boutique. DJs play most evenings and there are often bands at weekends – when it's rocking, crowds spill onto the pavement terrace. Its burgers are renowned. Bonus: pinball machines.

🛍 Shopping

Rovaniemi has Lapland's largest array of shops, including malls in the city centre and some wonderful traditional arts and craft shops. Souvenir shops selling Christmas paraphernalia abound at Napapiiri.

★Lauri Tuotteet

ARTS & CRAFTS

(www.lauri-tuotteet.fi; Pohjolankatu 25; ☺ 10am-5pm Mon-Fri) Established in 1924, this former knife factory in a charming log cabin at the northwestern edge of town still makes knives today, along with jewellery, buttons, felt boots and traditional Sami items including engraved spoons and sewing-needle cases. Everything is handmade from local materials, including reindeer antlers, curly birch and goats willow timbers, and Finnish steel.

ℹ Information

Metsähallitus (☑ 020-564-7820; www.metsa. fi; Pilke Tiedekeskus, Ounasjoentie 6; ☺ 9am-6pm Mon-Fri, 10am-4pm Sat & Sun mid-Jun–Aug, shorter hours rest of year) Information centre for the national parks; sells maps and fishing permits.

Tourist Information (☑ 016-346-270; www. visitrovaniemi.fi; Maakuntakatu 29; ☺ 9am-5pm Mon-Fri mid-Aug–mid-Jun, plus 10am-3pm Sat mid-Jun–mid-Aug; 🐾) On the square in the middle of town.

ℹ Getting There & Away

AIR

Rovaniemi's **airport** (RVN; ☑ 020-708-6506; www.finavia.fi; Lentokentäntie), 8km northeast of the city, is the 'official airport of Santa Claus' (he must hangar his sleigh here) and a major winter destination for charter flights. Finnair and Norwegian have several flights daily to/from Helsinki. There are car-hire desks, cafes, ATMs, moneychangers, a children's playground and a **Santa Claus Post Office** (www.santaclausvillage.info; Sodankyläntie, Napapiiri; ☺ 9am-6pm Jun-Aug, 10am-5pm mid-Jan–May, Sep & Nov, 9am-7pm Dec–mid-Jan) outpost.

Airport minibuses (☑ 016-362-222; http:// airportbus.fi) meet arriving flights, dropping off at hotels in the town centre (€7, 15 minutes). They pick up along the same route about an hour before departures.

A taxi to the city centre costs €20 to €30 depending on the time of day and number of passengers.

BUS

Express buses go south from the **bus station** (Matkahuolto Rovaniemi; ☑ 020-710-5435; www. matkahuolto.fi; Lapinkävijäntie 2) to Kemi (€22, 1½ hours, up to six daily) and Oulu (€24, 3½ hours, up to eight daily). Night buses serve Helsinki (€83.90, 12¾ hours, up to four daily). Daily connections serve just about everywhere else in Lapland. Some buses continue north into Norway.

TRAIN

One direct train per day runs from Rovaniemi to Helsinki (€80, eight hours), with two more requiring a change in Oulu (€14, 2¼ hours).

There's one train daily northeast to Kemijärvi (€11, one hour).

FINLAND ROVANIEMI

❶ Getting Around

Major car-hire agencies have offices at the airport and in town; book vehicles well ahead at peak times.

Bus 8 (Rovakatu P; Poromiehentie) to the attractions at Napapiiri runs from the train station via the city and airport (€3.90, 25 minutes, up to three hourly 6.30am to 6.30pm).

Many hotels offer bike rental in summer for around €20 per day; sports complex **Santasport** (☑ 020-798-4202; http://santasport. fi; Hiihtomajantie 2; P 🛜 ♿) also rents bikes to nonguests.

For a taxi, call **Taksi Rovaniemi** (☑ 020-088-000; www.rovaniemenaluetaksi.fi).

Western Lapland

Kemi

☑ 016 / POP 21,766

Kemi is an important deep-water harbour and heavy-industry town. It's home to two of Finland's blockbuster winter attractions – a snow castle and an ice-breaker cruise – while summer diversions include a gem museum and a wide waterfront where you'll find a handful of kid-friendly activities at Santa's Seaside Office.

◉ Sights & Activities

★ Lumilinna   CASTLE

(Snow Castle; ☑ 016-258-878; www.visitkemi.fi; Lumilinnankatu 15; adult/child €20/12; ⊙ 10am-6pm late Jan-early Apr) Few things conjure fairy-tale romance like a snow castle. First built in 1996 as a Unicef project, this is a Lapland winter highlight and a favoured destination for weddings, honeymoons, and general marvelling at the ethereal light and sumptuously decorated interior. The design changes every year but always includes a chapel, a snow hotel, an ice bar and a restaurant (lunch menus €26, dinner menus €51 to €58; by reservation 11am to 2pm and 7pm to 9.30pm).

Santa's Seaside Office   VISITOR CENTRE

(☑ 040-637-0653; www.visitkemi.fi; Luulajantie 6; ⊙ 10am-6pm early Jun-late Aug & mid-Dec–mid-Apr) Kemi's newest attraction, opened in 2017, is Santa's Seaside Office – a collection of cute red-painted timber buildings overlooking the waterfront, which house a gift shop, a cafe and, from Thursday to Saturday afternoons, Santa himself. Activities include writing a letter to Santa and sealing it in a bottle,

elf sailor workshops and gingerbread decorating. Prices for individual activities vary.

Sampo   CRUISE

(☑ 016-258-878; www.visitkemi.fi; Sampotie 137, Ajos Harbour; 4hr cruise €270, summer visit €10; ⊙ cruises late Dec–mid-Apr, summer visits by reservation 10am-2pm Tue-Sat late Jun-late Aug) This retired ice-breaker runs memorable, though overpriced, excursions. The four-hour cruise includes a warming soup (a three-course meal is €32) and ice swimming in special drysuits. The best experience is when the ice is thickest, usually in March. Book well in advance. Kids under 12 aren't allowed to take part in ice swimming. Online bookings are cheapest.

🛏 Sleeping & Eating

Hotelli Palomestari   HOTEL €€

(☑ 016-257-117; www.hotellipalomestari.com; Valtakatu 12; s/d/tr from €75/95/130; P 🛜) Near the train and bus stations on a pedestrian street, the 'fire chief' has 32 timber-floored rooms with trademark Finnish furniture, including a desk and sofa, and blackout curtains, friendly service and a downstairs bar with outside seating. Rates are cheapest at weekends and in summer.

★ Lumihotelli   HOTEL €€€

(☑ 016-258-878; www.visitkemi.fi; Lumilinnankatu 15; s/d/ste with shared bathroom from €220/350/400, apt from €230; ⊙ late Jan-early Apr; P) The snow hotel's interior temperature is -5°C (23°F) – somewhat temperate when the outside temperate is closer to -30°C (-22°F) – but a woolly sheepskin and a sturdy sleeping bag keep you warm(ish) atop the ice bed. From late June to April, seaside glass villas with transparent walls and ceilings offer private bathrooms, kitchenettes and, conditions permitting, aurora-watching.

Panorama Cafe   CAFE €

(☑ 050-410-3605; www.panoramacafekemi.fi; Valtakatu 26; lunch buffet €9, dishes €4.50-9.50; ⊙ 8am-3.30pm Mon-Fri) Panorama's great-value lunch buffet includes home-brewed beer. Dishes like arctic char and potato bake, wild-mushroom soup, reindeer meatballs with turnip mash, and elk sausages with cranberry sauce are delicious, but the ultimate reason to head up to the 13th floor of Kemi's town hall is for its sweeping views over the Bay of Bothnia from the dining room and terrace.

ℹ️ Information

Tourist Office (📞 016-258-878; www.visitkemi.fi; Valtakatu 26; ⊙ 8am-4pm Mon-Fri) In the town hall.

ℹ️ Getting There & Away

Kemi-Tornio Airport (KEM; www.finavia.fi; Lentokentäntie 75) is 6.5km north. Finnair has regular Helsinki flights. Airport **taxis** (📞 020-068-000; www.merilapintaksit.fi) cost €20 and must be prebooked.

Buses departing from the **train station** (Rautatiekatu) serve Tornio (€6.80, 35 minutes, frequent), Rovaniemi (€22, 1½ hours, up to six daily) and Oulu (€20.40, 1¾ hours, up to 10 daily).

There's one direct train daily to Helsinki (€70, seven hours), and four daily services to Oulu (€14, one hour) and Rovaniemi (€15, 1½ hours).

Tornio

📞 016 / POP 22.187

Situated on the impressive Tornionjoki, northern Europe's longest free-flowing river, Tornio is joined to its Swedish counterpart Haparanda by short bridges. After Russia claimed the Finnish trading centre in 1809, Haparanda was founded in 1821 across the river. Upon joining the EU, the twin towns reunited as a 'Eurocity'. Cross-border shopping has boomed here in recent years, with a vast Ikea on the Swedish side and new malls on the Finnish side. Finland is an hour ahead of Sweden (meaning double celebrations on New Year's Eve).

👁️ Sights

Aineen Taidemuseo   GALLERY
(www.tornio.fi/aine; Torikatu 2; adult/child €5/free, combination ticket with Tornionlaakson Maakuntamuseo €8/free; ⊙ 11am-6pm Tue-Thu, to 3pm Fri-Sun) Finnish art from the 19th and 20th centuries from the private collection of Veli Aine, a local business tycoon, is displayed at the attractive modern Tornio gallery. There are regular temporary exhibitions and a good cafe.

Tornion Kirkko   CHURCH
(www.tornio.seurakunta.net; Seminaarinkatu 2; ⊙ 10am-6pm Mon-Fri, 1.30-6pm Sat & Sun Jun & Jul, 10am-5pm Mon-Fri Aug) **FREE** Completed in 1686, this charming wooden church, visited by King Charles XI of Sweden in 1694, is topped by a shingle roof.

🏃 Activities

The tourist office (p190) can book trips and handles fishing permits; there are several excellent spots along the Tornionjoki.

River rafting is popular in summer on the Kukkolankoski rapids north of town.

Pohjolan Safarit   OUTDOORS
(Nordic Safaris; 📞 040-069-2301; www.pohjolansafarit.fi; Koskitie 130) Rafting on the Tornionjoki takes place on inflatable rubber rafts or traditional wooden boats from June to October. The 90-minute rafting trips cost €40 per person, with a minimum of six people. From December to March the outfit runs four-hour snowmobile tours to a reindeer farm (€225 per person including lunch and a reindeer sleigh ride; single supplement €68).

It's 15km north of Tornio.

🎉 Festivals & Events

Kalott Jazz & Blues Festival   MUSIC
(www.kalottjazzblues.net; ⊙ late Jun/early Jul) Established in 1983, this three-day festival takes place in churches, parks, museums, shops, bars and restaurants on both sides of the Finland–Sweden border. A free bus service travels between venues. Many concerts are also free.

🛏️ Sleeping & Eating

⭐ **Hotel Mustaparta**   BOUTIQUE HOTEL €€
(📞 040-010-5800; http://mustaparta.fi; Hallituskatu 6; d/ste from €107/227; 🅿️ 🛜) Tornio's best hotel by far tells the story of Iisakki Mustaparta (Isaac Blackbeard), an 18th-century leader of local farmers who defied the ruling merchant class, in its bar-restaurant Mustaparran Päämaja, and themed rooms stunningly decorated with wooden floors reflecting his ship's decking, woven willow baskets, fur rugs, cushions and throws. Some rooms open to French balconies.

⭐ **Mustaparran Päämaja**   FINNISH €€
(📞 040-126-0222; http://mustaparta.fi; Hallituskatu 6; lunch buffet €10.50, mains €15.50-32.50; ⊙ 11am-9.30pm Mon-Fri, noon-9.30pm Sat, noon-7.30pm Sun; 🛜🚸) At the fabulous Hotel Mustaparta, this atmospheric restaurant styled after local hero Iisakki Mustaparta has hefty timber beams, ships' wheels, wooden barrels and a buffet served on a skiff, and inspired modern Finnish cuisine: smoked arctic char with fennel sauce, beetroot-marinated local lamb with blueberry jus,

and a reindeer burger with smoked cheese, lingonberry pickle and tar-mustard mayo.

Finish with desserts such as lingonberry and apple pie with lingonberry-rum ice cream. Kids can order special pared-down versions of adults' dishes.

ℹ Information

Tourist Office (☑ Finland 050-590-0562; www.haparandatornio.com; Krannigatan 5, Haparanda, Sweden; ⊙ 8am-4pm Mon-Fri Swedish time; ☎) The tourist office for both towns in located in the shared Tornio-Haparanda bus station.

ℹ Getting There & Away

Kemi-Tornio airport (p189), 22km east of town, has regular flights to/from Helsinki. Bus 76 (€6.80, 20 minutes) drops off on Rd 926, 800m west of the terminal, or it's a €40 **taxi** (☑ 020-068-000; www.merilapintaksit.fi).

From the shared Tornio-Haparanda **bus station** (Krannigatan 5, Haparanda, Sweden), there are two direct daily services to Rovaniemi (€23.50, 1¾ hours), and several others that require a change (to a bus or train) in Kemi (€6.80, 35 minutes, frequent). Swedish buses run to Luleå, from where buses and trains run to other destinations in Sweden.

Levi

☑ 016 / POP

One of Finland's most popular ski resorts, Levi has a compact centre, top-shelf modern facilities and a large accommodation capacity. It hosts many high-profile winter events and is also a very popular destination for hiking during the *ruska* (autumn leaves) season. There's enough going on here in summer that it's not moribund, and great deals on smart modern apartments make it an excellent base for exploring western Lapland, particularly for families.

Levi is actually the name of the fell, while Sirkka is the village, but most people refer to the whole place as Levi. The ski season runs from around late October to early May, depending on conditions; in December overseas charter flights descend at nearby Kittilä, bringing families in search of reindeer and a white Christmas.

◉ Sights & Activities

Winter brings a full complement of snowy activities, from husky, reindeer and snowmobile trips to snowshoeing and ice-fishing. In summer, canoeing on the Ounasjoki is popular, as is the **mountain-biking park** (www.levi.fi; Hissitie; lift €4, bike hire per day €47; ⊙ 10am-6pm Jun-Sep) on the ski slopes. The tourist office can book most activities.

Samiland   MUSEUM
(www.samiland.fi; Tunturitie 205; adult/child €12/9; ⊙ 10am-8pm May-Nov, to 6pm Dec-Apr) Attached to the Levi Panorama (p190) hotel at the top of the main ski lift, this museum is a Unesco project. The illuminating exhibition gives plenty of good multilingual information on the Sami, including details about their traditional beliefs and reindeer herding, accompanied by past and present photographs. Outdoors on the hillside is a collection of traditional *kota* huts and storage platforms.

★**Levitunturi**   SNOW SPORTS
(www.levi.fi; Hissitie; lift pass per day/week €43.50/202.50; ⊙ late Oct-early May) Levi's ski resort has 43 downhill slopes, many lit, and 28 lifts. The vertical drop is 325m and the longest run is 2.5km. There are two snow parks with half-pipes and a superpipe for snowboarders, and several runs and free lifts for children. Equipment hire and lessons are available. Cross-country skiing is also superb here, with 230km of trails, some illuminated.

Lapland Safaris   OUTDOORS
(☑ 016-654-222; www.laplandsafaris.com; Keskuskuja 2; 2hr snowmobile safari from €99; ⊙ Dec-early Apr) Winter excursions include snowmobile safaris, full-day husky safaris (€417) and snowshoe hikes (€66 for two hours).

🛏 Sleeping & Eating

★**Levi Panorama**   HOTEL €€
(☑ 016-336-3000; www.golevi.fi; Tunturitie 205; d/ste/chalets from €72/129/126; 🅿 @ ☎) High up on the fell, with a great ski-in, ski-out area, this stylish hotel has brilliant rooms with lots of space, streamlined Nordic furniture, big photos of Lapland wildlife and views over the pistes. Superiors add a balcony, although most face the forest. There are several in-house restaurants and bars; you can nip up and down to town on the gondola.

Golden Crown   IGLOO €€€
(☑ 045-162-5609; http://leviniglut.net; Harjatie 4; igloos standard/premium €429/529; ⊙ Dec-mid-Apr; 🅿 ☎) On the side of the fell, these perspex igloos sleeping up to four people have kitchenettes, en-suite bathrooms and motorised

beds so that you can move around while sky-watching. Once you're paying these sorts of prices, you might as well upgrade to the premium igloos in the front row.

Jängällä FINNISH €€
(☑044-086-0090; www.jangalla.fi; Tähtitie 4; mains €19-34; ☺4-10pm Sep-Apr) Amazing flavour combinations at this rustic-contemporary restaurant with rough-hewn timber tables span roast wild boar with blackcurrant sauce, reindeer shank with lingonberry hollandaise and an elk burger with tar mayo on a rye bun to blueberry pudding with salted-caramel cloudberries. Local produce is also used in its craft cocktails, like Kettu (birch-infused vodka, bilberry, soda, egg white and bitters).

Panimo & Pub FINNISH €€€
(www.levinpanimo.fi; Levinraitti 1; mains €19.50-36.50, tapas plate €14; ☺kitchen noon-10pm; ☎) The atmospherically candlelit downstairs Kellari restaurant cooks inventive dishes such as gooseberry-stuffed reindeer, wild boar and elk sausages or roast whitefish with cranberry sauce. For a taster, order the Lapland tapas platter. Upstairs, the bar serves house-brewed beers and homemade tar-wood liqueur, and opens to a terrace that catches the evening sun.

❶ Information

Tourist Office (☑016-639-3378; www.levi.fi; Myllyjoentie 2; ☺9am-6pm Mon-Fri, 10am-4pm Sat Jun-Apr, 9am-6pm Mon-Fri May; ☎) Behind the tepee-like building on the roundabout in the centre of the resort.

❶ Getting There & Away

Levi is on Rd 79, 170km north of Rovaniemi. Buses from Rovaniemi (€32.80, 2½ hours, four daily) continue to Muonio (€13.70, 50 minutes). A bus (www.tunturilinjat.fi; €8, reservations essential) meets all incoming flights at **Kittilä airport** (KTT; www.finavia.fi; Levintie 259, Kittilä), 15km to the south.

Major car-hire franchises are at Kittilä airport; they will deliver to Levi free of charge.

Muonio

☑016 / POP 2362

The last significant stop on Rd 21 before Kilpisjärvi and Norway, Muonio sits on the scenic Muonionjoki that forms the border between Finland and Sweden. It's a fine base for summer and winter activities,

including low-key skiing at nearby Olos. Most of the town was razed during WWII, but the 1817 wooden church escaped that fate.

🏃 Activities

Arktinen Rekikoirakeskus DOG SLEDDING
(Arctic Sled-dog Centre; ☑040-015-5100; www.harriniva.fi; Harrinivantie 35; ☺guided tour adult/child €8/5, dog-sledding safaris 1½hr/2 days €90/580) At Harriniva (p191), the Arktinen Rekikoirakeskus has more than 400 lovable dogs, all with names and their own personalities. A great guided tour of their town departs up to two times daily. In winter wonderful dog-sledding safaris range from 1½-hour trips to excursions of two days, a week or more. Multiday trips include meals and hut accommodation.

★Harriniva OUTDOORS
(☑040-015-5100; www.harriniva.fi; Harrinivantie 35) Attached to the Arktinen Rekikoirakeskus, this excellent set-up has a vast program of activities. In summer these include canoe and boat trips (€50, three hours), midnight-sun rafting trips (€45, 1½ hours), foraging tours (€50, four hours), and fishing (€80, five hours) on the salmon-packed Muonionjoki. In winter, try reindeer sledding (€140, five hours) and snowmobiling (€110, two hours).

🛌 Sleeping

★Harriniva HOTEL, CAMPGROUND €€
(☑040-015-5100; www.harriniva.fi; Harrinivantie 35; s/d from €88/98, cabins d/q from €41/56, tent sites €12 plus per person €5, glamping dome €150; ℗@☎) Activities operator Harriniva offers a wide range of accommodation. Hotel rooms are simple but attractively done out in wood and have plenty of space; some have their own sauna. There are also cabins and tent sites by the river and, best of all, state-of-the-art perspex glamping domes for aurora-watching; these have their own open fireplaces.

❶ Getting There & Away

Muonio is at the junction of western Lapland's main two roads: Rd 21, which runs from Tornio to Kilpisjärvi, and Rd 79, which runs northwest from Rovaniemi via Kittilä.

Buses connect Muonio with Rovaniemi (€43.90, 3½ hours, three daily) and Kittilä (€15.50, 1½ hours, up to five daily).

Hetta

🎵 016 / POP 202

The spread-out village of Hetta, usually sign-posted as Enontekiö (the name of the municipal district), is an important Sami town and a good place to start trekking and exploring the area. It's also the northern end of the popular Hetta–Pallastunturi Trek.

👁 Sights & Activities

There's a small ski resort (www.hettahii-htomaa.fi; Peuratie 23; 1-day lift pass €25; ⊙1-7pm Tue-Fri, noon-5pm Sat & Sun Feb–mid-Apr) here in winter, and various guides offering husky, snowmobile and ski-trekking excursions.

ℹ Information

Head to the **Fell Lapland Visitor Centre** (☑020-564-7950; www.nationalparks.fi; Peuratie 15; ⊙9am-5pm Mar, Apr & Jun-late Sep, to 4pm Mon-Fri late Sep-Feb & May) for information on the national park and trekking routes.

Tourist information (www.tosilappi.fi; Ounastie 165; ⊙9am-4.30pm Mon-Fri) is available in the municipal building on the main road.

ℹ Getting There & Away

Enontekiö airport (ENF; www.finavia.fi; Hetantie 775) is 7km west of Hetta. It's mainly used for winter charters; scheduled services to Helsinki are infrequent.

Buses travel to Rovaniemi (€56.90, 4¾ hours, up to two daily) and Kilpisjärvi (€29.20, 3½ hours) via a swap-over at Palojoensuu. There are also buses to Hetta from Muonio (€15.50, 1¼ hours, one daily).

Pallas-Yllästunturi National Park

🎵 016

Covering 102,000 hectares, Finland's third-largest national park forms a long, thin area running from Hetta in the north to the Ylläs ski area in the south.

There are 350km of hiking trails, 80km of mountain-bike trails and 500km of cross-country-skiing trails. The main attraction is the excellent 55km trekking route from the village of Hetta to Pallastunturi in the middle of the park, where there's a hotel, the Pallastunturi Luontokeskus nature centre and transport connections. You can continue from here to Ylläs, although there are few facilities on that section. In winter Pallastunturi Fell is a small but popular place for both cross-country and downhill skiing.

🏃 Activities

The 55km trek/ski from Hetta to Pallastunturi (or vice versa) is a Lapland classic and offers some of the best views in the country from the top of the fells. While there's plenty of up and down, it's not a difficult route, though long stretches of it are quite exposed to wind and rain – pack weatherproof gear. The route is well marked, and there are several wilderness huts along the way. The popularity of the trek means huts get pretty crowded at peak times. See www.national-parks.fi for the route and wilderness huts.

The Hetta trailheads are separated from town by the lake. Various operators in town will run you across (around €10 to €15). Some can also drive your car to Pallastunturi while you are doing the trek (around €100). Contact the Fell Lapland Visitor Centre for operators.

From Pallastunturi you can extend your trek a further 72km to the park's southernmost border, by the ski resorts at Ylläs.

🛏 Sleeping

The park has wilderness huts; Pallastunturi Luontokeskus and the Fell Lapland Visitor Centre in Hetta make reservations and provide keys for the lockable huts (€12 per person). At Pallastunturi the seasonally opening Hotelli Pallas has a wonderful natural setting.

Hotelli Pallas HOTEL €€
(☑016-323-355; www.laplandhotels.com; Pallastunturintie 560, Pallastunturi; d/q from €67/150, d with shared bathroom from €55; ⊙mid-Feb–Apr & mid-Jun–late Sep; 🅿🛜) Built in 1938, this old wooden place up in the fells is just what a weary trekker wants to see. The upstairs rooms are the most modern. Connecting rooms are good for families; cheaper rooms have a toilet but share a shower. There's a good Finnish restaurant, a lakeside sauna (with winter ice-hole), and walks and skiing on the doorstep.

ℹ Information

Pallastunturi Luontokeskus (☑020-564-7930; www.nationalparks.fi; Pallastunturintie 557, Pallastunturi; ⊙9am-5pm Jun-Sep & mid-Feb–Apr, to 4pm rest of year; 🛜) This nature centre at Pallastunturi Fell sells trekking maps, makes hut reservations and offers advice about the region. The Hetta route (p192) leaves from here; good shorter walks include a 9km loop across the tops of Taivaskero and Laukukero.

ℹ️ Getting There & Away

From Monday to Friday, one bus runs from Muonio (€7.40, 30 minutes) via Pallastunturi to Kittilä (€18.70, 1¾ hours). In summer a return service runs in the other direction. Otherwise, you'll have to call a local taxi on 016-538-582.

Kilpisjärvi

📍 016 / POP 114

The remote village of Kilpisjärvi, the northernmost settlement in the 'arm' of Finland, sits on the doorstep of both Norway and Sweden. At 480m above sea level, this small border post, wedged between the lake of Kilpisjärvi and the magnificent surrounding fells, is also the highest village in Finland. The main reason to venture out here is for brilliant summer and *ruska* (autumn colour) trekking or spring cross-country skiing.

Kilpisjärvi consists of two small settlements 5km apart – the main (southern) centre has most services; the northern knot has the hiking centre and trailheads.

🔘 Sights & Activities

Hiking is the big draw here. For aerial access to remote hiking and fishing locations, take a float plane (📍040-039-6087; www.harriniva.fi; Lentosatama; 10min scenic flight from €180) or helicopter flight (📍040-015-5111; www.heliflite.fi; Lentosatama; ⊘30min scenic flights from €310). Summer lake cruises (📍040-848-5494; www.mallalaiva.com; Lentosatama; one way/return €20/30; ⊘10am, 2pm & 6pm Jun-Sep) take you to within 3km of the point where Finland, Norway and Sweden converge, with a couple of hours to walk to the tri-border marker.

The Kilpisjärvi area offers fantastic long and short hikes. All trekking routes and wilderness huts around the area are clearly displayed on the 1:100,000 *Halti Kilpisjärvi* map. See also www.nationalparks.fi.

🛌 Sleeping

⭐ Tundrea   CHALET, APARTMENT €€
(Kilpisjärven Lomakeskus; 📍040-039-6684; www.tundrea.com; Käsivarrentie 14188; chalet/apt from €93/149; 🅿🛜) Alongside the tumbling Tsahkaljoki, this riverside spot is the best of the clutch of cabin complexes in the centre of Kilpisjärvi. In addition to beautifully furnished wooden chalets and apartments with their own sauna, loft bedroom and fully equipped kitchen, there's a wood-and-stone restaurant (mains €13.50 to €32; open June to September) with an open fire.

Kilpisjärven
Retkeilykeskus   GUESTHOUSE, CABIN €€
(Kilpisjärvi Hiking Centre; 📍016-537-771; www.kilpisjarvi.info; Käsivarrentie 14663; tent sites €12 plus per person €4, s/d €65/75, 2-/4-person cottages €82/92; ⊘mid-Mar–late Sep; 🅿🛜) Situated 4.5km northwest of the main village, this hiking centre is conveniently close to the trekking routes and M/S Malla. You'll find a range of en-suite rooms and cottages here, as well as camping. From June to August only, the no-frills restaurant dishes up a good all-you-can-eat buffet lunch (€14; open noon to 9pm) as well as breakfast (€10).

ℹ️ Information

Kilpisjärven luontokeskus Visitor Centre
(📍020-564-7990; www.nationalparks.fi; Käsivarrentie 14145; ⊘9am-5pm late Mar-Sep, to 4pm Mon-Fri early-late Mar; 🛜) At the southern end of the village, this national-park centre is effectively the tourist information office. It has maps, advice on trekking and a nature display, and it sells fishing permits.

ℹ️ Getting There & Away

Buses connect Kilpisjärvi with Rovaniemi (€72.90, six hours, two daily) via Muonio (€34.50, three hours), Levi (€43.60, 5¼ hours) and Kittilä (€46.60, 5½ hours). In summer one heads on to Tromsø, Norway (€33.20, 3¾ hours).

It's a spectacular 196km drive between Muonio and Kilpisjärvi. There are petrol stations in Kaaresuvanto (where there's a border crossing into Sweden) and Kilpisjärvi itself.

Northern Lapland

Sparsely populated and extraordinarily beautiful, with fells, lakes and forests, Lapland's north is a magical place for hiking, snow sports and learning about Sami culture. At these latitudes, your chances of seeing the aurora borealis (Northern Lights) are high when skies are clear and dark.

Sodankylä

📍 016 / POP 8739

Sodankylä is the main service centre for one of Europe's least populated areas, with a density of just 0.75 people per square kilometre. It's at the junction of Lapland's two main highways and makes a decent staging post between Rovaniemi and the north; even if you're just passing through, stop to see the humble but exquisite wooden church

Vanha Kirkko. A contrast is provided by the high-tech observatory Aurora House just outside town, an important collection point for data on the atmosphere and the aurora borealis.

Sights

Aurora House VISITOR CENTRE
(Revontulikota Pohjan Kruunu; ☎040-514-2858; www.arcticacademy.fi; Välisuvannontie 13; up to 4 people €88; ⏲by reservation) If you miss witnessing the aurora borealis, this 45-minute simulation in a purpose-built riverside tepee is the next best thing. Lean back on a reclining chair to watch images gathered over three decades projected on the ceiling while a local guide explains the science and folklore. You'll also hear radio signals as they hit the ionosphere. The centre is 11km south of Sodankylä.

Vanha Kirkko CHURCH
(☎040-019-0406; www.sodevl.fi; Kirkkotie 1; ⏲9am-6pm Jun-Aug) FREE One of the few buildings in Lapland to survive the Nazis' scorched-earth retreat in WWII is this, the region's oldest church, dating from 1689. It stands in a graveyard encircled by a low wooden fence and is noteworthy for its decorative shingles and prominent prong-like standards. The interior is simple and charming, with gnarled wooden benches and pulpit, and a simple altar made from leftover beams. The stone church nearby was built in 1859.

Festivals & Events

Midnight Sun Film Festival FILM
(https://msfilmfestival.fi; ⏲mid-Jun) Dubbed the 'anti-Cannes', this four-day festival sees the village's population double, with round-the-clock screenings in three venues, often with high-profile directors in attendance.

Sleeping & Eating

Majatalo Kolme Veljestä GUESTHOUSE €
(☎040-053-9075; www.majatalokolmeveljesta.fi; Ivalontie 1; s/d with shared bathroom from €55/69; P @ ≈) Situated 500m north of the town centre, this family-run guesthouse has small but spotless rooms with Ikea-style furniture such as wire storage units. Guests share decent bathrooms and have the use of a lounge and kitchen facilities (there's a big supermarket across the road). Prices include breakfast, sauna, tea and coffee.

Hotelli Karhu HOTEL €€
(Hotel Bear Inn; ☎040-122-8250; http://hotel-bearinn.com; Lapintie 7; s/d/tr from €105/115/125; P ≈) This central hotel offers old-fashioned but decent rooms with grey-wood floors and modern bathrooms. Some single rooms come with a cute mini-sauna. There's an on-site restaurant, but there are better options elsewhere.

Päivin Kammari FINNISH €€
(www.paivinkammari.fi; Jäämerentie 11; lunch buffet €10.80, mains €15-28; ⏲10am-9pm Mon-Sat, noon-6pm Sun; ≈) Cosy and homelike, this is the best eating spot in town, with a good-value lunch buffet, soups, quiches and cakes, along with hearty mains incorporating local *muikku* (vendace, or whitefish, a small lake fish) and reindeer. Tables set up on the streetside terrace in warm weather.

Information

Tourist Office (☎040-746-9776; www.visitsodankyla.fi; Jäämerentie 3; ⏲9am-4pm Mon-Fri) At the intersection of the Kemijärvi and Rovaniemi roads.

Getting There & Away

Sodankylä is on the main Rovaniemi–Ivalo road (E75), and the E63 from Kemijärvi and Karelia ends here.

Buses serve Rovaniemi (€27.10, two hours, four daily), Ivalo (€31.40, two hours, four daily) and Kemijärvi (€20.40, two hours, three daily Monday to Friday, one Saturday and Sunday).

Saariselkä

☎016 / POP 354

The bustling, touristy village of Saariselkä (Sami: Suolocielgi), 250km north of the Arctic Circle, is more resort than community, as it's basically a collection of enormous hotels and holiday cottages, but it's a great spot to get active. It's a major winter destination for Christmassy experiences, sled safaris and skiing, and in summer it serves as the main base for trekkers heading into the awesome Saariselkä Wilderness.

Sights & Activities

Saariselkä bristles with things to do year-round. Things are most active in winter, with numerous snowy excursions, such as husky- and reindeer-sledding, snowmobiling and ice-fishing trips, organised by the many companies in town.

Summer options include visiting the gold-panning settlement of Tankavaara (www.kultamuseo.fi; Tankavaarantie 11C, Tankavaara; adult/child €12/6, gold panning per hr/day €12/45; ☺9am-5pm Jun-Sep, 10am-4pm Mon-Fri Oct-May), reindeer farms, canoeing, fishing, white-water rafting and various guided walks.

Tankavaara Nature Centre NATURE CENTRE
(Tankavaaran Luontokeskus; ☑020-564-7251; www.nationalparks.fi; Tankavaarantie 11B, Tankavaara; ☺10am-5pm Mon-Fri Jun-Aug, 9am-4pm Mon-Fri Sep) FREE Next door to Tankavaara's gold-panning museum, Kultamuseo, this nature centre has advice on activities and trekking in Urho Kekkonen National Park. Good exhibitions cover the local environment, including a display on raptors; you can also watch a half-hour audiovisual presentation. It sells maps and fishing permits, and has keys to the huts in the national park. Circular nature trails (1km to 6km) arc out from the centre.

Lapland Safaris OUTDOORS
(☑016-668-901; www.laplandsafaris.com; Saariseläntie 13) Based at the Lapland Hotel Riekonlinna (p195), this is one of Saariselkä's major activity operators, with a full summer and winter program. Summer options include a 2½-hour mountain-bike ride (€71) and a five-hour hiking and fishing trip (€125); winter highlights include a two-hour reindeer safari (€118) and a four-hour aurora-spotting snowmobile tour (€144). Children under 12 pay half-price.

Ski Saariselkä SNOW SPORTS
(http://skisaariselka.fi; Kullanhuuhtojantie; ski pass per day/week €37/132; ☺late Nov-May) Ski Saariselkä's 15 downhill slopes are served by six lifts; the longest run is 1300m and the vertical drop is 180m. There's also a freestyle park and some 240km of cross-country trails, some lit. Saariselkä is known for snow-kiting; lessons are available.

Husky & Co DOG SLEDDING
(☑044-729-0006; www.huskyco.fi; Hirvaspirtti 1; 1hr summer farm tour adult/child €40/20, 2½hr summer husky hike €80/40, 3/5hr winter safari €135/170) Husky & Co has more than 250 dogs and offers great-value sledding safaris in winter, and farm tours and hikes with huskies (one dog per person) in summer. Other activities include reindeer sleigh rides, quad-bike tours and aurora tours.

🛌 Sleeping & Eating

Saariselkä Inn INN €
(☑044-729-0006; www.saariselkainn.com; Saariseläntie 10; d/tr/apt from €66/128/138; 🅿🤙) In the heart of Saariselkä, this friendly village pub brews its own beer and offers good accommodation in a variety of neighbouring buildings. Rooms are spacious and warm, with en-suite bathrooms and comfortable mattresses; they're an absolute steal in summer. Apartments are equipped with saunas. A simple breakfast is served in winter only.

Lapland Hotel Riekonlinna HOTEL €€
(☑016-559-4455; www.laplandhotels.com; Saariseläntie 13; d/ste/apt from €114/128/150; 🅿@🤙) Some of the spacious rooms at this central 232-room hotel come with saunas and all have balconies. Apartments sleeping up to six people are in a separate building 100m away and are great for families, with fully equipped kitchens, drying cupboards, saunas and private parking with heating. Top-notch amenities include two restaurants and activities operator Lapland Safaris (p195).

Restaurant Kaunispään Huippu CAFE €€
(☑016-668-803; www.kaunispaanhuippu.fi; Kaunispää; mains incl salad buffet €21-32.50; ☺10am-5pm, closed May & Oct) Attached to the Kaunispään Huippu (www.kaunispaanhuippu.fi; Kaunispää; ☺10am-5pm, closed May & Oct) arts-and-crafts shop, this panoramic restaurant on top of Kaunispää fell has views across to Russia. Smoked-reindeer mousse with blackcurrant sauce, willow-grouse breast with Inarijärvi vendace roe, roast elk with morel sauce, and oatmeal pie with salmon and arctic char are among the savoury dishes; afterwards, don't miss the crowberry jam–filled doughnuts.

Laanilan Kievari FINNISH €€
(☑040-023-9868; www.laanilankievari.fi; Sateenkaarenpääntie 9; lunch buffet €7.90, dinner mains €27-39.50; ☺11am-3pm, dinner by reservation early Jun–mid-May) Off the main road 2.5km south of Saariselkä, this cute wooden hut with a roaring open fire has good-value lunch buffets. It's well worth booking in for dinner, though, when the game-oriented mains might include wood pigeon or elk fillet. In winter a small pond is cut into the ice for you to brave after you use the on-site sauna.

FINLAND NORTHERN LAPLAND

ℹ️ Information

Kiehinen (📞 020-564-7200; www.national-parks.fi; Siula Centre, Kelotie 1; ⏱9am-9pm Mon-Fri, to 4pm Sat & Sun mid-Jun–Aug, shorter hours rest of year) In the Siula building, just off the main road near the petrol station, this nature centre offers hiking information, cabin reservations, fishing permits, maps and a small nature display. It also contains Saariselkä's **tourist information desk** (📞 040-168-7838; www.inarisaariselka.fi; Siula Centre, Kelotie 1; ⏱9am-9pm Mon-Fri, to 4pm Sat & Sun mid-Jun–Aug, shorter hours rest of year).

ℹ️ Getting There & Away

Buses run from Rovaniemi to Saariselkä (€50.20, 4¼ hours, four daily), continuing to Ivalo (€7.40, 30 minutes).

Inari

📞 016 / POP 565

The tiny village of Inari (Sami: Anár) is Finland's most significant Sami centre and the ideal starting point to learn something of Sami culture. Home to the wonderful Siida museum and Sajos (cultural centre and seat of the Finnish Sami parliament), it also has a string of superb handicrafts shops. It's a great base for forays into Lemmenjoki National Park and the Kevo Strict Nature Reserve.

The village sits on Lapland's largest lake, Inarijärvi, a spectacular body of water with more than 3000 islands in its 1084-sq-km area.

👁 Sights & Activities

Hiking opportunities in the area include the walk to the wilderness church **Pielpajärven Kirkko** (⏱24hr) **FREE**, and a 9km trail from the Siida museum to the top of Otsamo fell. Other summer activities include lake cruises, scenic flights and horse riding; in winter there are snowmobiling safaris as well as aurora-watching trips.

⭐ **Siida**　　　　　　　　　　　MUSEUM

(www.siida.fi; Inarintie 46; adult/child €10/5; ⏱9am-7pm Jun-Aug, to 6pm Sep, 10am-5pm Wed-Mon Oct-May) One of Finland's most absorbing museums, state-of-the-art Siida offers a comprehensive overview of the Sami and their environment. The main exhibition hall consists of a fabulous nature exhibition around the edge, detailing northern Lapland's ecology by season, with wonderful photos and information panels.

In the centre of the room is detailed information on the Sami, from their former semi-nomadic existence to modern times.

Bears' Nest　　　　　　　NATURAL FEATURE

(Karhunpesäkivi; www.inarisaariselka.fi; Karhunpesäkivi rest stop, Myössäjärvi; ⏱sunrise-sunset) **FREE** At the edge of Myössäjärvi, 16km south of Inari, look out for the Karhunpesäkivi rest stop. From here, a 300m timber boardwalk (mainly comprising steps) leads through the forest to Finland's largest tafone (cave-like formation found in granular rock), the only one in the world known to have shifted from its original base during the last ice age. You can enter the hollow boulder; although you have to crawl to enter, the honeycomb-like structure is high enough to stand upright.

Sajos　　　　　　　　　　CULTURAL CENTRE

(www.samediggi.fi; Siljotie 4; ⏱9am-5pm Mon-Fri) **FREE** The spectacular wood-and-glass Sami cultural centre stands proud in the middle of town. It holds the Sami parliament as well as a library and music archive, a restaurant, exhibitions and a craft shop.

Visit Inari　　　　　　　　　　　CRUISE

(📞 040-179-6069; www.visitinari.fi; Inarintie 38; 3hr cruise adult/child €35/15; ⏱cruises Jun-Sep) From June (as soon as the ice melts) to late September, cruises on Inarijärvi sail to Ukko Island (Sami: Äjjih), which is sacred to the Sami. During the brief (20-minute) stop, most people climb to the top of the island, but there are also cave formations at the island's northern end. There are one or two daily departures from Siida car park.

🎿 Festivals & Events

Skábmagovat　　　　　　　　　　FILM

(http://skabmagovat.fi; ⏱late Jan) This indigenous-themed film festival (with many films in English) sees collaborations with groups from other nations.

King's Cup　　　　　　　　　　SPORTS

(www.siida.fi; ⏱late Mar/early Apr) Held over the last weekend in March or the first weekend in April, this is the grand finale of Lapland's reindeer-racing season. It's a great spectacle as the beasts race around the frozen lake, jockeys sliding like waterskiers behind them. The semifinals are on Saturday and the finals on Sunday; plenty of betting livens things up.

Ijahis Idja
MUSIC

(Nightless Night; www.ijahisidja.fi; ⊘ Aug) Over a weekend, usually in August, this excellent music festival features groups from all spectra of Sami music.

🛏 Sleeping & Eating

Uruniemi Camping
CAMPGROUND €

(☑ 050-371-8826; www.uruniemi.fi; Uruniementie 7; tent sites €16, d with shared bathroom from €25, cabins €28-120; ⊘ Jun–mid-Sep; P 🛜) The most pleasant place to pitch a tent hereabouts is this well-equipped lakeside campground 2km south of town. Along with campsites, there are basic rooms and cottages; facilities include a cafe and a sauna, and kayaks, boats and bikes for hire. Heated cottages are available year-round.

Hotelli Inari
HOTEL €€

(☑ 040-179-6069; http://visitinari.fi; Inarintie 40; s/d/apt from €119/130/180; P 🛜) On the lakeshore in Inari's village centre, this well-run hotel has spacious rooms with powerful showers. Those in the annexe have stylish grey-and-black decor and private saunas or glassed-in balconies for viewing the aurora. From December to April there's a two-night minimum stay. The restaurant (mains €15 to €28) serves local fish and reindeer alongside pizza and burgers.

★ Aanaar
FINNISH €€

(☑ 016-511-7100; www.hotelkultahovi.fi; Saarikoskentie 2; mains €13.50-31.50, 3-/5-course menu €43.50/62, with paired wines €62/85; ⊘ 11am-2.30pm & 5-10.30pm) 🍽 A panoramic glassed-in dining room overlooks the Juutuanjoki's Jäniskoski rapids at Inari's best restaurant, situated in the Tradition Hotel Kultahovi (☑ 016-511-7100; www.hotelkultahovi.fi; Saarikoskentie 2; d with/without sauna from €140/110; P 🛜). Seasonal local produce is used in dishes such as morel and angelica-root soup, smoked reindeer heart with pine-needle vinaigrette, grilled Inarijärvi lake trout with bilberry sauce and smoked beetroot, and Arctic king crab with nettle butter.

🛍 Shopping

Inari is the main centre for Sami handicrafts, including silversmithing, antler carving and clothing, and there are several studios and boutiques in the village.

Sami Duodji Ry
ARTS & CRAFTS

(www.duodjishop.fi; Siljotie; ⊘ 10am-5pm Mon-Fri) 🍽 In the Sajos (p196) building, this is the main shop of the Finnish association of Sami craftspeople. It has a good range of Sami books and CDs, as well as beautifully crafted silverware and handmade clothing.

Samekki
JEWELLERY

(☑ 016-671-086; www.saariselka.fi/samekki; Lehtolantie 5; ⊘ 10am-4pm mid-Jun–Aug, Mon-Fri only Sep–mid-Jun) 🍽 Down a small lane behind the library is the studio of Petteri Laiti, a famous Sami artisan. The silverwork and handicrafts are very highly regarded; you'll often see the artist at work here.

ℹ Information

Inari's **tourist office** (☑ 040-168-9668; www.inarisaariselka.fi; Inarintie 46; ⊘ 9am-7pm Jun-Aug, to 6pm Sep, 10am-5pm Wed-Mon Oct-May; 🛜) is in the Siida museum and is open the same hours. There's also a nature information point here.

ℹ Getting There & Away

Inari is 38km northwest of Ivalo on the E75. Up to four daily buses run here from Ivalo (€8.20, 30 minutes). Shuttle buses (€30, 45 minutes) serving **Ivalo Airport** (IVL; ☑ 020-708-8610; www.finavia.fi; Lentokentäntie 290) can be booked through Inari's tourist office website (www.inarisaariselka.fi).

Two direct daily buses serve Inari from Rovaniemi (€60.10, five hours). Both continue to Norway: one to Karasjok (€23.70, three hours) and, in summer, on to Nordkapp (€77.90, 5½ hours); and another to Tana bru (€37.60, three hours, up to four per week).

Lemmenjoki National Park

At 285,550 hectares, Lemmenjoki (Sami: Leammi) is Finland's largest national park, covering a remote wilderness area between Inari and Norway. This is prime hiking territory, with desolate wilderness rivers, rough landscapes and the mystique of gold, as solitary prospectors slosh away with their pans in the middle of nowhere. Boat trips on the river allow more leisurely exploration of the park.

The launch pad is Njurgulahti, an Inari Sami community by the river; it's often simply referred to as Lemmenjoki. It's 11km down a turn-off signposted 34km southwest of Inari on the Kittilä road.

◉ Sights & Activities

Most trails start from Njurgulahti, including a family-friendly 4.5km marked nature trail. Marked trekking routes are in the relatively small 'basic area' between the rivers Lemmenjoki and Vaskojoki; a 20km loop between Kultahamina and Ravadasjärvi huts takes you to some of the most interesting gold-panning areas. Another route heads over Látnjoaivi Fell to Vaskojoki hut and back, taking you into the 'wilderness area', which has fewer restrictions on where to camp but no trail markings. For any serious trekking, you will need the 1:100,000 *Lemmenjoki* map.

From Kultahamina, it's a 21.5km walk back to Njurgulahti along the river, via Ravadas, 6.5km closer. You can get the boat one way and walk the other.

🛏 Sleeping

Paltto CABIN €

(📞 040-028-7544; www.lemmenjoki.org; Lemmenjoen Kylätie 100; cabins from €65; ☻ Jun–mid-Oct; 🅿) This home of an active Sami family has a felt **studio** (☻10am-5pm early Jun-late Sep & by appointment) 🎨 selling some extraordinary works of art, as well as comfortable accommodation in log cabins, with access to a sauna and a boat. Excellent boat trips (from €70; minimum two people) range from half-day to full-day trips that can include Sami yoiks (chants), meeting reindeer, gold panning and a traditional lunch.

Hotel Korpikartano LODGE €€

(📞 040-777-4339; www.korpikartano.fi; Meneskartanontie 71, Menesjärvi; s/d/apt from €85/96/157; 🅿🛜) On the shores of one of the region's most beautiful lakes, 3.5km northeast of the Lemmenjoki turn-off from Rd 955, this remote wilderness lodge has colourful rooms (some with kitchenettes), rental equipment including skis, canoes and kayaks, and a flexible attitude that makes staying here a delight. Lunch is available for €18; a three-course evening meal is €29.

ℹ Getting There & Away

No public transport serves the area – some accommodation options can arrange transport for guests. Otherwise your own vehicle is essential (make sure you've fuelled up beforehand, as there are no petrol stations).

UNDERSTAND FINLAND

History

Finnish history is the story of a people who for centuries were a wrestling mat between two heavyweights, Sweden and Russia, and the nation's eventful emergence from their grip to become one of the world's most progressive and prosperous nations.

Prehistory

Though evidence of pre–ice age habitation exists, it wasn't until around 9000 years ago that settlement was re-established after the big chill. Things are hazy, but the likeliest scenario seems to be that the Finns' ancestors moved in to the south and drove the nomadic ancestors of the Sami north towards Lapland.

Sweden & Russia

The 12th and 13th centuries saw the Swedes begin to move in, Christianising the Finns in the south, and establishing settlements and fortifications. The Russians were never far away, though. There were constant skirmishes with the power of Novgorod, and in the early 18th century Peter the Great attacked and occupied much of Finland. By 1809 Sweden was in no state to resist, and Finland became a duchy of the Russian Empire. The capital was moved to Helsinki, but the communist revolution of October 1917 brought the downfall of the Russian tsar and enabled Finland to declare independence.

Winter & Continuation Wars

Stalin's aggressive territorial demands in 1939 led to the Winter War between Finland and the Soviet Union, conducted in horribly low temperatures. Finland resisted heroically, but was eventually forced to cede a 10th of its territory. When pressured for more, Finland accepted assistance from Germany. This 'Continuation War' against the Russians cost Finland almost 100,000 lives. Eventually Mannerheim negotiated an armistice with the Russians, ceding more land, and then waged a bitter war in Lapland to oust the Germans. Against the odds, Finland remained independent, but at a heavy price.

Recent Times

Finland managed to take a neutral stance during the Cold War, and once the USSR collapsed, it joined the EU in 1995, and adopted the euro in 2002.

In the new century, Finland has boomed on the back of the technology sector – which, despite the plunge of Nokia, continues to be strong – the traditionally important forestry industry, design and manufacturing, and, increasingly, tourism. Despite suffering economically along with most of the rest of the world in recent years, it's nevertheless a major success story of the new Europe with a strong economy, robust social values, and super-low crime and corruption.

Parliamentary politics have twisted and turned, with immigration issues at the forefront of the national agenda. In 2017 one of three parties in Prime Minister Juha Sipilä's ruling coalition, the nationalist Finns Party, elected anti-immigration hardliner Jussi Halla-aho as its leader, and the other two coalition partners announced that they would no longer govern with the Finns Party. The government averted collapse when 20 members of parliament defected from the Finns Party, forming the breakaway New Alternative party. Sipilä's government retained a parliamentary majority with New Alternative, and the Finns Party was relegated to the opposition. The next parliamentary elections are due in 2019.

People

Finland is one of Europe's most sparsely populated countries, with 17 people per sq km, falling to fewer than one in parts of Lapland. Both Finnish and Swedish are official languages, with some 5% of Finns having Swedish as their mother tongue, especially on the west coast and the Åland Archipelago. Around 5% of all Finnish residents are immigrants, a low percentage but one that has increased substantially in recent years.

Finland's minorities include some 6000 Roma in the south and, in the north, the Sami, from several distinct groups. Some 78% of Finns describe themselves as Lutherans, 1.5% are Orthodox and most of the remainder unaffiliated. Finns have one of the lowest rates of church attendance in the Christian world.

A capacity for silence and reflection are the traits that best sum up the Finnish character, though this seems odd when weighed against their global gold medal in coffee consumption, their production line of successful heavy bands and their propensity for a tipple. The image of a log cabin with a sauna by a lake tells much about Finnish culture: independence, endurance (*sisu* or 'guts') and a deep love of nature.

FINLAND PEOPLE

THE SAUNA

Nothing is more traditionally or culturally Finnish than the sauna. For centuries it has been a place to bathe, meditate, warm up during cold winters and even give birth, and most Finns still use the sauna at least once a week. An invitation to bathe in a family's sauna is an honour.

There are three principal types of sauna around these days. The most common is the electric sauna stove, which produces a fairly dry, harsh heat compared with the much-loved chimney sauna, which is driven by a log fire and is the staple of life at Finnish summer cottages. Even rarer is the true *savusauna* (smoke sauna), which is without a chimney.

Bathing is done in the nude (there are some exceptions in public saunas, which are almost always sex-segregated anyway) and Finns are quite strict about the nonsexual – even sacred – nature of the sauna.

Proper sauna etiquette dictates that you use a *kauha* (ladle) to throw water on the *kiuas* (sauna stove), which then gives off the *löyly* (sauna steam). At this point, at least in summer in the countryside, you might take the *vihta* (a bunch of fresh, leafy birch twigs) and lightly strike yourself. This improves circulation and has cleansing properties. When you are sufficiently warmed, you'll jump in the lake, river or pool, then return to the sauna to warm up and repeat the cycle several times. If you're indoors, a cold shower will do.

Arts

Architecture

Finland's modern architecture – sleek, functionalist and industrial – has been admired throughout the world ever since Alvar Aalto started making a name for himself during the 1930s. His works can be seen all over Finland today, from the angular Finlandia-talo in Helsinki to the public buildings and street plan of Rovaniemi. Jyväskylä is another obligatory stop for Aalto fans.

Earlier architecture in Finland can be seen in churches made from stone or wood – Kerimäki's oversized church is a highlight, as are the cathedrals at Turku and Tampere. Low-rise Helsinki boasts a patchwork of architectural styles, including the neoclassical buildings of Senate Square, the rich ornamentation of art nouveau (Jugendstil), the modern functionalism of Aalto's buildings and the postmodern Kiasma museum.

Design

Finland, like Scandinavia as a whole, is also famous for its design. Aalto again laid a foundation with innovative interior design, furniture and the famous Savoy vase. Finns have created and refined their own design style through craft traditions and using natural materials such as wood, glass and ceramics. Glassware and porcelain such as Iittala and Arabia are world-famous, while Marimekko's upbeat, colourful fabric is a Finnish icon. A new wave of young designers is keeping things from stagnating. Stereotypes are cheerfully broken without losing sight of the roots: an innate practicality and the Finns' almost mystical closeness to nature.

Literature

The *Kalevala*, a collection of folk stories, songs and poems compiled in the 1830s by Elias Lönnrot, is Finland's national epic and a very entertaining read. As part of the same nationalistic renaissance, poet JL Runeberg wrote *Tales of the Ensign Ståhl*, capturing Finland at war with Russia, while Aleksis Kivi wrote *Seven Brothers* (1870), the nation's first novel, about brothers escaping conventional life in the forest, allegorising the birth of Finnish national consciousness.

This theme continued in the 1970s with *The Year of the Hare*, looking at a journalist's escape into the wilds by the prolific, popular and bizarre Arto Paasilinna. Other 20th-century novelists include Mika Waltari who gained international fame with *The Egyptian*, and FE Sillanpää who received the Nobel Prize for Literature in 1939.

The national bestseller during the postwar period was *The Unknown Soldier* by Väinö Linna. The seemingly endless series of autobiographical novels by Kalle Päätalo and the witty short stories by Veikko Huovinen are also very popular in Finland. Finland's most internationally famous author is Tove Jansson, whose books about the fantastic Moomin family have long captured the imagination. Notable living writers (apart from Paasilinna) include the versatile Leena Krohn and Mikko Rimminen, who has attracted attention for both novels and poetry.

Music

Music is huge in Finland, and in summer numerous festivals all over the country revel in everything from mournful Finnish tango to soul-lifting symphony orchestras to crunchingly potent metal.

Revered composer Jean Sibelius (1865–1957) was at the forefront of the nationalist movement. His stirring tone-poem *Finlandia* has been raised to the status of a national hymn. Classical music is thriving in Finland, which is an assembly line of orchestral and operatic talent: see a performance if you can.

The Karelian region has its own folk-music traditions, typified by the stringed *kantele*, while the Sami passed down their traditions and beliefs not through the written word but through the songlike chant called the *yoik*.

Finnish bands have made a big impact on the heavier, darker side of the music scale in recent years. The Rasmus, Nightwish, Apocalyptica, HIM and the 69 Eyes are huge worldwide. But there is lighter music, such as surf-rockers French Films, pop-rockers Sunrise Avenue, the Von Hertzen Brothers, indie band Disco Ensemble, emo-punks Poets of the Fall and melodic Husky Rescue.

Increasingly though, what young people in Finland are listening to is local hip-hop, or Suomirap. Artists such as Elastinen and Pyhimys have taken the airwaves by storm in recent years, and there's always some new underground project.

Environment

People often describe Finland offhand as a country of 'forests and lakes', and the truth is that they are spot on. Some 10% of Suomi is taken up by bodies of water, and nearly 70% is forested with birch, spruce and pine. It's a fairly flat expanse of territory: though the fells of Lapland add a little height to the picture, they are small change compared to the muscular mountainscapes of Norway.

Measuring 338,000 sq km and weighing in as Europe's seventh-largest nation, Finland hits remarkable latitudes: even its southernmost point is comparable with Anchorage in Alaska, or the lower reaches of Greenland. Its watery vital statistics are also impressive, with 187,888 large lakes and many further wetlands and smaller bodies of water. Geographers estimate that its total coastline, including riverbanks and lakeshores, measures 315,000km, not far off the distance to the moon.

Finland has one of the world's highest tree coverages; much of this forest is managed, and timber-harvesting and the associated pulp-milling is an important industry.

Wildlife

Brown bears, lynx, wolverines and wolves are native to Finland, although sightings are rare unless you go on an organised excursion. You're more likely to see an elk, though hopefully not crashing through your windscreen; drive cautiously. In Lapland, the Sami keep commercial herds of some 230,000 reindeer. Finland is a bird-watcher's paradise, with species such as the capercaillie and golden eagle augmented by hundreds of migratory arrivals in spring and summer.

National Parks

Finland's excellent network of national parks and other protected areas is maintained by Metsähallitus (p187). In total, more than 30,000 sq km, some 9% of the total area, is in some way protected land. The largest and most pristine national parks are in northern Finland, particularly Lapland, where vast swathes of wilderness invite trekking, cross-country skiing, fishing and canoeing.

WILDLIFE-WATCHING

The deep forests in eastern and northeastern Finland offer excellent wildlife-spotting opportunities. While you're unlikely to spot bears, wolves, lynx or wolverines on a casual hike, there are plenty of reliable operators, especially in eastern Finland, that specialise in trips to watch these creatures in their domain. The excellent bird life, both migratory and local, offers further opportunities. Ask at tourist offices for local services.

Sustainable Finland

As a general model for environmentally sustainable nationhood, Finland does very well. Though it has a high per-capita carbon-emission rate, this is largely due to its abnormal heating requirements and is offset in many ways. As in much of northern Europe, cycling and recycling were big here decades ago, littering and waste-dumping don't exist, and sensible solutions for keeping the houses warm and minimising heat loss have long been a question of survival, not virtue. Finns in general have a deep respect for and understanding of nature and have always trodden lightly on it.

But the forest is also an important part of Finland's economy. Most of the forests are periodically logged, and privately owned plots are long-term investments for many Finns. Hunting is big here, and animals are kept at an 'optimum' population level by the keen shooting contingent.

Finland's own commitment to combating climate change is strong, having set a legally binding target in 2014 of 80% emissions reduction by 2050. A large nuclear-power sector is backed by an increasing percentage of renewable energy.

Climate Change

Southern Finland has already noticed dramatically changed weather patterns, with much milder winters. The once-unthinkable prospect of a non-white Christmas in Helsinki is now a reality. Scientists in the Arctic are producing increasingly worrying data and it seems that northern nations like Finland may be some of the earliest to be seriously affected.

Food & Drink

Finland's eating scene has perked up dramatically in the last few years as a wave of gourmet restaurants in the major cities has added gastronomic innovation to the always-excellent fresh local produce.

Staples & Specialities

Finnish cuisine has been influenced by both Sweden and Russia and draws on what was traditionally available: fish, game, meat, milk and potatoes, with dark rye used to make bread and porridge, and few spices employed.

Soups are a Finnish favourite and one common in homes and restaurants. Heavy pea, meat or cabbage soups are traditional workers' fare, while creamier fish soups have a more delicate flavour.

One light snack that you'll see everywhere is the rice-filled savoury pastry from Karelia, the *karjalanpiirakka*. These are tasty cold, heated, toasted or with egg butter, and have several variations.

Fish is a mainstay of the Finnish diet. Fresh or smoked *lohi* (salmon), *silli* (marinated herring), *siika* (lavaret, a lake whitefish), *kuha* (pike-perch or zander) and delicious Arctic *nieriä* or *rautu* (char) are common, and the tiny lake fish *muikku* (vendace, or whitefish) is another treat.

Two much-loved favourites that you'll see in many places are grilled liver, served with mashed potatoes and bacon, and meatballs. Finns have been known to fight over whose granny cooks the best ones.

Reindeer has always been a staple food for the Sami. The traditional way to eat it is sautéed with lingonberries. Many restaurants also offer it on pizza or as sausages. It also comes in fillet steaks, which, though expensive, is the tastiest way to try this meat.

Elk is also eaten, mostly in hunting season, and you can even get a bear steak – or more commonly, a potted or preserved meat – in some places, although the latter is very expensive, as only a small number are hunted every year.

Drinking

The Finns lead the world in coffee (*kahvi*) consumption, downing over 20 million cups per day – that's around four each for every man, woman and child.

Finns drink plenty of beer (*olut*) and among the big local brews are Karhu, Koff, Olvi and Lapin Kulta. The big brands are all lagers, but there's quite a number of microbreweries in Finland (look for the word *panimo* or *panimo-ravintola*), and these make excellent light and dark beers. Cider is also popular, as is *lonkero*, a ready-made mix of gin and fruity soft drink. A half-litre in a bar costs around €5 to €7. Finns don't tend to drink in rounds; everybody pays their own. Beer, wine and spirits are sold by the state network, Alko (www.alko.fi). There are stores in every town. The legal age for drinking is 18 for beer and wine, and 20 for spirits.

Beer and cider with less than 4.8% alcohol can be bought at supermarkets, service stations and convenience stores. If you buy cans or bottles, you pay a small deposit (about €0.20). This can be reclaimed by returning them to the recycling section at a supermarket.

Wine is widely drunk, but very pricey in restaurants, where you might pay €45 for a bottle that would cost €10 in an Alko store.

Other uniquely Finnish drinks include *salmiakkikossu*, which combines dissolved liquorice sweets with the iconic Koskenkorva vodka (an acquired taste); *fisu*, which does the same but with Fisherman's Friend pastilles; and cloudberry or cranberry liqueurs.

Vegetarians & Vegans

Most medium-sized towns in Finland will have a vegetarian restaurant (*kasvisravintola*), usually open weekday lunchtimes only. It's easy to self-cater at markets, or take the salad/vegetable option at lunch buffets (which is usually cheaper). Many restaurants also have a salad buffet. The website www.vegaaniliitto.fi has a useful listing of vegetarian and vegan restaurants; follow 'ruoka' and 'kasvisravintoloita' (the Finnish list is more up-to-date than the English one).

SURVIVAL GUIDE

ⓘ Directory A–Z

ACCOMMODATION
Camping

Finland's campgrounds are a delight, and have much to offer to all types of travellers.

Most campgrounds are open only from June to August, and popular spots are crowded during July and the midsummer weekend.

Almost all campgrounds have cabins or cottages for rent, which are usually excellent value – from €40 for a basic double cabin to €120 for a cottage with kitchen, bathroom and sauna.

The Camping Key Europe (http://campingkeyeurope.com) offers useful discounts. You can buy it at most campgrounds for €16 per year, or online at www.camping.fi, where you'll also find an extensive listing of campgrounds across the country.

Finland's *jokamiehenoikeus* (everyman's right) allows access to most land, and means you can pitch a tent almost anywhere on public land or at designated free campsites in national parks.

Farmstays

A growing, and often ecologically sound, accommodation sector in Finland is that of farmstays. Many rural farms, particularly in the south, offer B&B accommodation, a unique opportunity to meet local people and experience their way of life. Plenty of activities are also usually on offer. Home-cooked breakfasts are typically included; evening meals are also usually available. Your hosts may not speak much English; if you have difficulties, the local tourist office will be happy to help arrange the booking.

ECEAT (www.eceat.fi) lists a number of organic, sustainable farms in Finland that offer accommodation. Local tourist offices keep lists of farmstay options in the surrounding area; the website www.visitfinland.com links to a few, and Lomarengas (p182) also has many listed on its website.

Guesthouses

A Finnish *matkakoti* (guesthouse) is a no-frills spot offering simple but usually comfy accommodation with shared bathroom, typically for travelling salespeople. It can be pretty good value, usually includes breakfast and sometimes rises well above the norm: check out places such as Naantali and Hanko for some exceptional options in this class.

Hostels & Summer Hotels

For solo travellers, hostels generally offer the cheapest bed and can be good value for twin rooms. Finnish hostels are invariably clean, comfortable and very well equipped, though most are in somewhat institutional buildings.

Some Finnish hostels are run by the Finnish Youth Hostel Association (SRM), and many more are affiliated. It's worth being a member of HI (Hostelling International; www.hihostels.com), as members save 10% per night at affiliated places. You'll save money with a sleep sheet or your own linen, as hostels tend to charge extra for this.

From June to August, many student residences are made over as summer hostels and hotels. These are often great value, as you usually get your own room, with kitchen (bring your own utensils, though) and bathroom either to yourself or shared between two people.

Hotels

The majority of hotels in Finland belong to one of a few major chains, including the following:

Cumulus (www.cumulus.fi)

Scandic (www.scandichotels.com)

Sokos (www.sokoshotels.fi)

Omenahotelli (www.omena.com) Offers good-value unstaffed hotels booked online.

Hotels in Finland are designed with the business traveller in mind and tend to charge robustly. But on weekends and during the July summer holidays, prices in three- and four-star hotels tend to drop by 40% or so.

Superior rooms vary in value. In many places they are identical to the standard and your extra cash gets you only a bathrobe and a fancier shampoo. In others an extra €20 can get you 50% more space, views over the town and a private sauna. It's worth asking. The discount for singles is marginal at all times, so you may prefer to pay the little extra for a twin room, which is usually much larger.

Most hotel rooms have tiny Nordic bathrooms. If you want a bath-tub, this can usually be arranged. Many hotels have 'allergy rooms', which have no carpet and minimal fabric.

Nearly all Finnish hotels have a plentiful buffet breakfast included in the rate and many include a sauna session.

Self-Catering Accommodation

One of Finland's joys is its plethora of cottages for rent, ranging from simple camping cabins to fully equipped bungalows with electric sauna and gleaming modern kitchen. These can be remarkably good value and are perfect for families. There are tens of thousands of cabins and cottages for rent in Finland, many in typical, romantic forest lakeside locations. Local booking agents are mentioned under individual destinations. Local tourist offices and town websites also have lists.

Lomarengas (p182) is by far the biggest national agent for cottage rentals.

ACTIVITIES

Finland's beauty and appeal lie in its fantastic natural environment, with vast forests, long waterways, myriad lakes and Arctic northern wilderness. Getting outdoors is the ultimate way to experience the country and Finland is remarkably well set up for all types of activities, from safari-style packages to map-and-compass DIY adventures.

Boating, Canoeing & Kayaking

Every waterside town has a place (most frequently the camping ground) where you can rent a canoe, kayak or rowing boat by the hour or day. Rental cottages often have rowing boats that you can use free of charge to investigate the local lake and its islands. Canoe and kayak rentals range in price from €25 to €45 per day, and €90 to €200 per week, more if you need overland transport to the start or end point of your trip.

Fishing

Several permits are required for foreigners (between the ages of 18 and 64) who wish to go fishing in Finland, but they are very easy to arrange. The website www.mmm.fi has all the details. Ice-fishing is popular and requires no licence.

Hiking

Hiking is best from June to September, although in July mosquitoes and other biting insects can be a big problem in Lapland. Wilderness huts line the northern trails (both free and bookable ones, on a shared basis). According to the law, a principle of common access to nature applies, so you are generally allowed to hike in any forested or wilderness area. The website www.outdoors.fi provides comprehensive information on trekking routes and huts in national parks.

Saunas

Many hotels, hostels and camping grounds have saunas that are free with a night's stay. Large towns have public saunas.

Skiing

The ski season in Finland runs from late November to early May and slightly longer in the north, where it's possible to ski from October to May. You can rent all skiing or snowboarding equipment at major ski resorts for about €30/110 per day/week. A lift pass costs around €35/170 per day/week. Cross-country skiing is popular: it's best during January and February in southern Finland, and from December to April in the north.

Snowmobiles

You'll need a valid driver's licence to use one.

CHILDREN

Finland is an excellent country to travel in with children, with many kid-friendly attractions and outdoor activities, whether you visit in winter or in summer.

All hotels will put extra beds in rooms, restaurants have family-friendly features and there are substantial transport discounts.

GAY & LESBIAN TRAVELLERS

Finland's cities are open, tolerant places. Helsinki has a small but welcoming gay scene and the country's largest pride festival. Tampere and Turku also host pride festivals. Same-sex marriage became legal in Finland on 1 March 2017.

The tourist-board website, www.visitfinland.com, is a good starting point for information.

INTERNET ACCESS

Wireless internet access is widespread. Several cities have extensive free networks and nearly all hotels, as well as many restaurants, cafes and bars, offer free access to customers and guests.

Data is very cheap. If you have an unlocked smartphone, you can pick up a local SIM card for a few euros and charge it with a month's worth of data at a decent speed for under €20. Ask at R-kioski shops for the latest deals.

MONEY

ATMs Using ATMs with a credit or debit card is by far the easiest way of getting cash in Finland. ATMs have a name, Otto, and can be found even in small villages.

Credit cards Widely accepted; Finns are dedicated users of plastic even to buy a beer or cup of coffee.

Currency Finland adopted the euro (€) in 2002. Euro notes come in five, 10, 20, 50, 100 and 500 denominations and coins in five, 10, 20, 50 cents and €1 and €2. Note that one- and two-cent coins are not used in Finland.

Moneychangers Travellers cheques and cash can be exchanged at banks; in the big cities, independent exchange facilities such as Forex (www.forex.fi) usually offer better rates.

Tipping Service is considered to be included in bills, so there's no need to tip at all unless you want to reward exceptional service.

OPENING HOURS

Many attractions in Finland only open for a short summer season, typically mid-June to late August. Opening hours tend to shorten in winter in general.

Alko (state alcohol store) 9am–8pm Monday to Friday, to 6pm Saturday

Banks 9am–4.15pm Monday to Friday

Businesses and Shops 9am–6pm Monday to Friday, to 3pm Saturday

Nightclubs 10pm–4am Wednesday to Saturday

 EATING PRICE RANGES

The following price ranges refer to a standard main course.

€ less than €17

€€ €17–27

€€€ more than €27

Pubs 11am–1am (often later on Friday and Saturday)

Restaurants 11am–10pm, lunch 11am–3pm. Last orders are generally an hour before closing.

Finland grinds to a halt twice a year: around Christmas and New Year, and during the midsummer weekend.

National public holidays:

New Year's Day 1 January

Epiphany 6 January

Good Friday March/April

Easter Sunday & Monday March/April

May Day 1 May

Ascension Day May

Whitsunday Late May or early June

Midsummer's Eve & Day Weekend in June closest to 24 June

All Saints Day First Saturday in November

Independence Day 6 December

Christmas Eve 24 December

Christmas Day 25 December

Boxing Day 26 December

Public telephones basically no longer exist in Finland.

The country code for Finland is ☑ 358. To dial abroad first dial ☑ 00.

Mobile Phones

Purchasing a Finnish SIM card at any R-kioski shop for your own phone (provided it's unlocked) is cheapest. Top the credit up at the same outlets, online or at ATMs. Roaming charges within the EU have been abolished.

Finland is on Eastern European Time (EET), an hour ahead of Sweden and Norway. In winter it's two hours ahead of UTC/GMT; from 3am on the last Sunday in March to 3am on the last Sunday in October, the clocks go forward an hour to three hours ahead of UTC/GMT.

Public toilets are widespread in Finland, but expensive – often €1 a time. On doors, 'M' is for men, while 'N' is for women.

The main website of the Finnish Tourist Board is www.visitfinland.com. Cities, large towns and major tourist destinations have tourist offices.

A valid passport or EU identity card is required to enter Finland. Most Western nationals don't need a tourist visa for stays of less than three months. South Africans, Indians and Chinese, however, are among those who need a Schengen visa. For more information, contact the nearest Finnish embassy or consulate, or check the website www.formin.finland.fi.

❶ Getting There & Away

Finland is easily reached by air, with direct flights to Helsinki from many European, North American and Asian destinations. It's also served by budget carriers from several European countries. Most other flights are with Finnair, Norwegian or Scandinavian Airlines (SAS).

Most flights land at Helsinki-Vantaa airport (p138), 19km north of the capital. Winter charters serve Rovaniemi (p187), Lapland's main airport, and other smaller regional airports. Other international airports include Tampere (p159), Turku (p146) and Oulu (p181). The website www.finavia.fi includes information for Finnish airports.

There are several border crossings from northern Sweden and Norway to northern Finland, with no passport or customs formalities.

There are nine main border crossings between Finland and Russia, including several in the southeast and two in Lapland. They are more serious frontiers; you must already have a Russian visa.

Sweden

The linked towns of Tornio (Finland) and Haparanda (Sweden) share a bus station (p190) from where you can get onward transport into their respective countries. A possible, if remote, crossing point is the Lapland villages of Kaaresuvanto (Finland) and Karesuando (Sweden), separated by a bridge and both served sporadically by domestic buses.

Norway

Three routes link Finnish Lapland with northern Norway, some running only in summer. These are operated by Eskelisen Lapin Linjat (www.eskelisen.fi), whose website has detailed maps and timetables, as does the Finnish bus website Matkahuolto (www.matkahuolto.fi).

All routes originate or pass through Rovaniemi. The two northeastern routes continue via Inari to Tana Bru/Vadsø or Karasjok. The Karasjok bus continues in summer to Nordkapp (North Cape). On the western route, a Rovaniemi–Kilpisjärvi bus continues to Tromsø in summer.

Russia

Daily express buses run to Vyborg and St Petersburg from Helsinki and Lappeenranta. These services appear on the website of Matkahuolto (www.matkahuolto.fi).

Finland's only international trains are to/from Moscow and St Petersburg in Russia.

High-speed Allegro train services (known as Sapsan trains in Russia) run daily from Helsinki to the Finland Station in St Petersburg (3½ hours, four daily). The evening train is usually cheaper. The Tolstoi sleeper runs from Helsinki via St Petersburg (Ladozhki station) to Moscow (14½ hours, one daily). Fares include a sleeper berth, with upmarket sleeper options available.

All trains go via Lahti, Kouvola, Vainikkala (26km south of Lappeenranta) and the Russian city of Vyborg. At Helsinki station tickets are sold at the international ticket counter.

You must have a valid Russian visa; immigration procedures are carried out on-board.

There are significant discounts for families and small groups. See www.vr.fi.

SEA

For ferry companies and route information, see Transport (p484).

Getting Around

AIR

Finnair (www.finnair.com) runs a fairly comprehensive domestic service out of Helsinki. Standard prices are expensive, but check the website for offers. Multitrip journeys can be significantly cheaper than one-way flights. Some Lapland destinations are winter only.

BICYCLE

Finland is as bicycle-friendly as any country you'll find, with plenty of paths and few hills. Bikes can be taken on most trains, buses and ferries. Åland is particularly good for cycling. Helmets are recommended but no longer required by law.

Hire

You can hire a bike in nearly every Finnish town. Most campgrounds and many urban hotels offer bikes for a small fee or for free, but these are made for cycling around town, not for ambitious road trips. Better bikes are available at dedicated outlets. Expect to pay around €15 per day or €90 per week for a good-quality road bike and €45/120 for a mountain bike.

BOAT

Lake boats were once important summer transport. These services are now largely kept on as cruises, and make a great, leisurely way to journey between towns. The most popular routes are Tampere–Hämeenlinna, Tampere–Virrat, Savonlinna–Kuopio and Lahti–Jyväskylä.

Coastal routes include Turku–Naantali, Helsinki–Porvoo and ferries to the Åland Archipelago.

The website http://lautta.net is handy for domestic lake-boat and ferry services.

BUS

Bus is the main form of long-distance transport in Finland, with a far more comprehensive network than the train system. Buses run on time and are rarely full.

Intercity buses fall into two main categories: *vakiovuoro* (regular), stopping frequently at towns and villages; and slightly pricier *pikavuoro* (express). Because there are few motorways, even express buses aren't that fast, averaging about 60km/h.

Ticketing is handled by Matkahuolto (www.matkahuolto.fi), which has an excellent website with all the timetables. Matkahuolto offices work normal business hours, but you can always just buy the ticket from the driver.

Towns have a *linja-autoasema* (bus terminal), with local timetables displayed (*lähtevät* is departures, *saapuvat* arrivals).

Separate from the normal system (though its timetables appear on the Matkahuolto website), Onnibus (www.onnibus.com) runs a variety of budget inter-city routes in comfortable double-decker buses. Most of these radiate from Helsinki and can be much cheaper than normal fares if booked in advance.

Departures between major towns are frequent, but reduce substantially at weekends. In more remote areas there may be no weekend buses at all. Schedules change during the summer holidays, when it can be much harder to move around isolated regions.

CAR & MOTORCYCLE

Finland's road network is excellent, although there are few motorways. When approaching a town or city, *keskusta* on signs indicates the town centre. There are no road tolls but *lots* of speed cameras.

Petrol is expensive in Finland; check current prices at www.fuel-prices-europe.info. Many petrol stations are unstaffed, but machines take cash and most (but not all) chip- and PIN-enabled credit and debit cards. Change for cash is not given.

Hire

Car rental is expensive, but rates can work out reasonably with advance booking or with a group. A small car costs from €65/205 per day/week with 300km free per day, not including insurance. One-way rentals attract a surcharge and are not always possible. Book ahead at peak times to ensure a car is available. Most cars have manual transmission; automatic cars may be available but at a premium and should be reserved well in advance of travel. As ever, the cheapest deals are online.

In larger towns, look out for weekend rates. These can cost little more than the rate for a single day, and you can pick up the car early afternoon on Friday and return it late Sunday or early Monday.

Car-hire franchises with offices in many Finnish cities include the following:

➡ Avis (www.avis.com)

➡ Budget (www.budget.com)

➡ Europcar (www.europcar.com)

➡ Hertz (www.hertz.com)

➡ Sixt (www.sixt.com)

Road Conditions & Hazards

Conditions Snow and ice on the roads, potentially from September to April, and as late as June in Lapland, make driving a serious undertaking. Snow chains are illegal: people use either snow tyres, which have studs, or special all-weather tyres. The website http://liikennetilanne.liikennevirasto.fi has road webcams around Finland that are good for checking conditions. Select kelikamerat on the map.

Wildlife Beware of elk and reindeer, which don't respect vehicles and can dash onto the road unexpectedly. This sounds comical, but elk especially constitute a deadly danger. Notify the police if there is an accident involving these animals. Reindeer are very common in Lapland; slow right down if you see one, as there will be more nearby.

Road Rules

➡ Finns drive on the right.

➡ The speed limit is 50km/h in built-up areas, from 80km/h to 100km/h on highways, and 120km/h on motorways.

➡ Use headlights at all times.

➡ Seat belts are compulsory for all.

➡ Blood alcohol limit is 0.05%.

An important feature of Finland is that there are fewer give-way signs than most countries. Traffic entering an intersection from the right has right of way. While this doesn't apply to highways or main roads, in towns cars will often nip out from the right without looking: you must give way, so be careful at smaller intersections in towns.

TRAIN

State-owned Valtion Rautatiet (VR; www.vr.fi) runs Finnish trains. It's a fast, efficient service, with prices roughly equivalent to buses on the same route.

VR's website has comprehensive timetable information. Major stations have a VR office and ticket machines. Tickets can also be purchased online, where you'll also find discounted advance fares. You can also board and pay the conductor, but if the station where you boarded had ticket-purchasing facilities, you'll be charged a small penalty fee (€2 to €5).

Classes

The main types of trains are the high-speed Pendolino (the fastest and most expensive class), fast Intercity (IC), Express and 2nd-class-only Regional trains (H on the timetable).

On longer routes there are two types of sleeping carriage. Traditional blue ones offer berths in one-, two- or three-bed cabins, while newer sleeping cars offer single and double compartments in a double-decker carriage. There are cabins with bathroom, and one equipped for wheelchair use. Sleeper trains transport cars.

Costs

Fares vary slightly according to the type of train, with Pendolino the priciest. A one-way ticket for a 100km express train journey costs approximately €25 in 2nd ('eco') class. First-class ('extra') tickets cost around 35% more than a 2nd-class ticket. A return fare gives a 10% discount.

Children under 17 pay half-fare; those under six years travel free (but without a seat). A child travels free with every adult on long-distance trips, and there are also discounts for seniors, local students and any group of three or more adults travelling together.

Train Passes

Various passes are available for rail travel within Finland, or in European countries including Finland. There are cheaper passes for students, people aged under 26 and seniors. Supplements (eg for high-speed services) and reservation costs are not covered, and terms and conditions change – check carefully before buying. Always carry your passport when using the pass.

Tallinn

POP 426,538

Best Places to Eat

➡ Leib (p216)
➡ Moon (p216)
➡ NOA (p216)
➡ Sfäär (p215)
➡ Von Krahli Aed (p215)

Best Places to Stay

➡ Villa Hortensia (p214)
➡ Three Sisters (p215)
➡ Hotel Cru (p215)
➡ Hotel Telegraaf (p215)
➡ Old House Apartments (p215)
➡ Tabinoya (p214)

Why Go?

No longer the plaything of greater powers – Danish, Swedish, Polish, German and Soviet – Tallinn is now a proud European capital with an allure all its own. It's lively yet peaceful, absurdly photogenic and bursting with wonderful sights – ancient churches, medieval streetscapes and noble merchants' houses. Throw in delightful food and vibrant modern culture and it's no wonder Tallinn seems in danger of being loved to death, especially after a few cruise ships dock. But it's one of those blessed places that seems to cope with all the attention.

Despite the boom of 21st-century development, Tallinn safeguards the fairy-tale charms of its Unesco-listed Old Town – one of Europe's most complete walled cities. Some examples of exuberant post-Soviet development aside, the city clearly realises it's better to be classy than brassy. Hence the blossoming of first-rate restaurants, atmospheric hotels and a well-oiled tourist machine that makes visiting a breeze.

When to Go
Tallinn

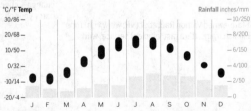

Dec–Jan Christmas markets, New Year's parties and the certainty of snow.

Jun–Jul Long, gentle, sunny days, festivals, a city open for business (and peak tourism season).

Sep The nights close in, the crowds fade, prices drop and you'll have more elbow room.

◉ Sights

◉ Old Town

The medieval jewel of Estonia, Tallinn's *vana-linn* (Old Town) is without a doubt the country's most fascinating locality. Picking your way along the narrow, cobbled streets is like strolling into the 15th century. You'll pass the ornate stone facades of Hanseatic merchants' houses, wander into hidden medieval courtyards, and find footworn stone stairways leading to sweeping views of the red-roofed city. It's staggeringly popular with tourists, but manages to remain largely unspoilt.

St Mary's Lutheran Cathedral   CHURCH
(Tallinna Püha Neitsi Maarja Piiskoplik toomkirik; ☑644 4140; www.toomkirik.ee; Toom-Kooli 6; church/tower €2/5; ⊙9am-5pm May & Sep, to 6pm Jun-Aug, shorter hours/days rest of year) Tallinn's cathedral (now Lutheran, originally Catholic) had been initially built by the Danes by at least 1233, although the exterior dates mainly from the 15th century, with the tower completed in 1779. This impressive building was a burial ground for the rich and titled, and the whitewashed walls are decorated with the elaborate coats-of-arms of Estonia's noble families. Fit view-seekers can climb the tower.

Alexander Nevsky Orthodox Cathedral   CATHEDRAL
(☑644 3484; http://tallinnanevskikatedraal.eu; Lossi plats 10; ⊙8am-7pm, to 4pm winter) The positioning of this magnificent, onion-domed Russian Orthodox cathedral (completed in 1900) at the heart of the country's main administrative hub was no accident: the church was one of many built in the last part of the 19th century as part of a general wave of Russification in the empire's Baltic provinces. Orthodox believers come here in droves, alongside tourists ogling the interior's striking icons and frescoes. Quiet, respectful, demurely dressed visitors are welcome but cameras aren't.

Museum of Occupations   MUSEUM
(Okupatsioonide muuseum; ☑668 0250; www.okupatsioon.ee; Toompea 8; adult/child €6/3; ⊙10am-6pm) The displays here illustrate the hardships and horrors of five decades of occupation, under both the Nazis (briefly) and the Soviets. The photos and artefacts are interesting but it's the videos (lengthy but enthralling) that leave the greatest impression – and the joy of a happy ending. The museum

has also opened the former **KGB prison cells** (www.okupatsioon.ee; Pagari 1, enter from Pikk 59; adult/child €5/4) as a separate historical site.

St Catherine's Cloister   CHURCH
(www.claustrum.eu; Müürivahe 33; adult/child €2/1; ⊙11am-5pm mid-May–Sep) Perhaps Tallinn's oldest building, St Catherine's Monastery was founded by Dominican monks in 1246. In its glory days it had its own brewery and hospital. A mob of angry Lutherans torched the place in 1524 and the monastery languished for the next 400 years until its partial restoration in 1954. Today the ruined complex includes the gloomy shell of the barren church (which makes an atmospheric venue for occasional recitals) and a peaceful cloister lined with carved tombstones.

◉ Lower Town

★ Town Hall Square   SQUARE
(Raekoja plats) In Tallinn all roads lead to Raekoja plats, the city's pulsing heart since markets began setting up here in the 11th century. One side is dominated by the Gothic town hall (p209), while the rest is ringed by pretty pastel-coloured buildings dating from the 15th to 17th centuries. Whether bathed in sunlight or sprinkled with snow, it's always a photogenic spot.

Tallinn Town Hall   HISTORIC BUILDING
(Tallinna raekoda; ☑645 7900; www.raekoda.tallinn.ee; Raekoja plats; adult/student €5/2; ⊙10am-4pm Mon-Sat Jul & Aug, shorter hours rest of year; 🖭) Completed in 1404, this is the only surviving Gothic town hall in northern Europe.

ℹ TALLINN CARD

If you're in Tallinn for more than a fleeting visit, and are keen to see the sights, the **Tallinn Card** (www.tallinncard.ee) is a godsend. You'll pay €25/37/45 for a 1-/2-/3-day adult card (children pay €14/19/23) and get free entry to over 40 sights and attractions (including most of the big-ticket ones), unlimited use of public transport and plenty of other discounts on shopping, dining and entertainment. Single tickets to Tallinn's myriad museums, bastions and other diversions are increasingly dear, so you won't need to visit many to start racking up the savings. You can buy the Tallinn Card online, from the **Tourist Information Centre** (p217), or from many hotels.

Tallinn

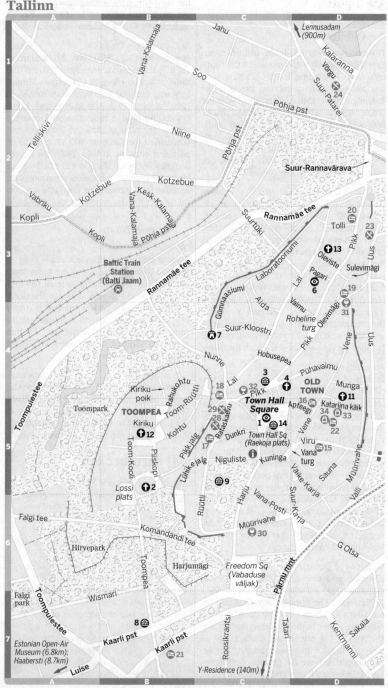

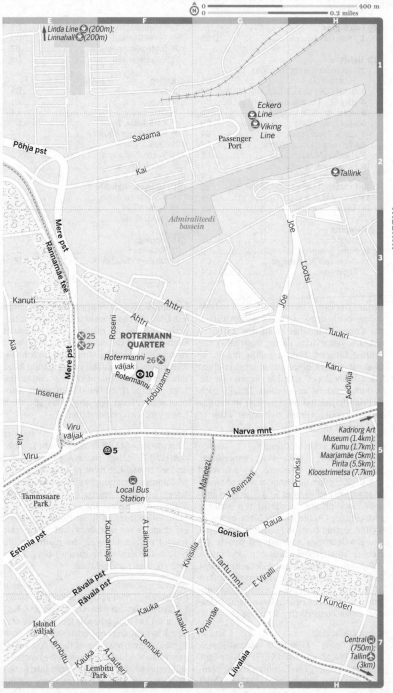

Linda Line (200m);
Linnahall (200m)

Põhja pst

Sadama

Kal

Passenger Port

Eckerö Line

Viking Line

Tallink

Mere pst

Rannamäe tee

Kanuti

Admiraliteedi bassein

Jõe

Lootsi

Ahtri

Ahtri

Roseni

Jõe

Tuukri

25
27

ROTERMANN QUARTER

Rotermanni väljak

26

Karu

Aedvilja

Mere pst

Aia

Inseneri

10

Rotermanni

Hobujaama

Viru väljak

Narva mnt

Kadriorg Art Museum (1.4km); Kumu (1.7km); Maarjamäe (5km); Pirita (5.5km); Kloostrimetsa (7.7km)

Aia

Viru

5

Maneezi

Pronksi

Tammsaare Park

Local Bus Station

V Reimani

Estonia pst

Kaubamaja

A Laikmaa

Kivisilla

Gonsiori

Raua

Rävala pst

Rävala pst

Tartu mnt

E Viralli

J Kunderi

Islandi väljak

Kauka

Maakri

Tornimäe

Lennuki

Central (750m); Tallin (3km)

Lembitu

Kauka

A Lauteri

Lembitu Park

Liivalaia

Tallinn

Inside, you can visit the Trade Hall (whose visitor book drips with royal signatures), the Council Chamber (featuring Estonia's oldest woodcarvings, dating from 1374), the vaulted Citizens' Hall, a yellow-and-black-tiled councillor's office and a small kitchen. The steeply sloped attic has displays on the building and its restoration. Details such as brightly painted columns and intricately carved wooden friezes give some sense of the original splendour.

Holy Spirit Lutheran Church   CHURCH
(Pühavaimu kirik; ☑646 4430; www.eelk.ee/tallinna.puhavaimu; Pühavaimu 2; adult/child €1.50/0.50; ◷9am-6pm Mon-Sat when no service underway, between services Sun) The blue-and-gold clock on the facade of this striking 13th-century Gothic church is the oldest in Tallinn, dating from 1684. Inside are exquisite woodcarvings and painted panels, including an altarpiece dating to 1483 and a 17th-century baroque pulpit. Johann Koell, a former pastor here, is considered the author of the first Estonian book, a catechism published in 1535. The church hosts regular classical music concerts (try Mondays at 6pm).

Great Guild Hall   MUSEUM
(Suurgildi hoone; ☑696 8693; www.ajaloomuuseum.ee; Pikk 17; adult/child €6/3; ◷10am-6pm, closed Wed Oct-Apr) The Estonian History Museum has filled the striking 1410 Great Guild

building with a series of ruminations on the Estonian psyche, presented through interactive and unusual displays. Coin collectors shouldn't miss the old excise chamber, with its numismatic relics stretching back to Viking times, while military nuts should head downstairs. The basement also covers the history of the Great Guild itself, while Estonian music, language, geography and deep history all win consideration.

Lower Town Wall   FORTRESS
(Linnamüür; ☑644 9867; Väike-Kloostri 1; adult/child €2/0.75; ◷11am-7pm Jun-Aug, shorter hours/days rest of year) The most photogenic stretch of Tallinn's remaining walls connects nine towers lining the western edge of Old Town. Visitors can explore the barren nooks and crannies of three of them (there are modest displays on weaponry and castle-craft inside) with cameras at the ready for the red-rooftop views. The gardens outside the wall are pretty and relaxing.

St Olaf's Church   CHURCH
(Oleviste kirik; ☑641 2241; www.oleviste.ee; Lai 50; ◷10am-6pm Apr-Jun & Sep-Oct, to 8pm Jul & Aug) From 1549 to 1625, when its 159m steeple was struck by lightning and burnt down, this (now Baptist) church was one of the tallest buildings in the world. The current spire reaches a still-respectable 124m and you can take a confined, 258-step staircase up the tower (adult/

child €3/1) for wonderful views of Toompea over the lower town's rooftops.

Niguliste Museum
MUSEUM

(☑ 631 4330; www.nigulistemuuseum.ekm.ee; Niguliste 3; adult/student €6/5; ☺10am-5pm Tue-Sun May-Sep, Wed-Sun Oct-Apr) Dating from the 13th century, the imposing St Nicholas' Church (Niguliste kirik) was badly damaged by Soviet bombers in 1944 and a fire in the 1980s, but today stands restored to its Gothic glory. Now deconsecrated, it's a strikingly apt site for a branch of the Estonian Art Museum devoted to religious art. The acoustics are first-rate, and organ recitals are held here most weekends.

⊙ City Centre

Hotel Viru KGB Museum
MUSEUM

(☑ 680 9300; www.viru.ee; Viru väljak 4; tour €12; ☺daily May-Oct, Tue-Sun Nov-Apr) When the Hotel Viru was built in 1972, it was not only Estonia's first skyscraper, it was the only place for tourists to stay in Tallinn – and we mean that literally. Having all the foreigners in one place made it much easier to keep tabs on them and the locals they had contact with, which is exactly what the KGB did from its 23rd-floor spy base. The hotel offers fascinating tours of the facility in various languages; bookings essential.

Rotermann Quarter
ARCHITECTURE

(Rotermanni kvartal; ☑ 626 4200; www.rotermann. eu; Rotermanni 8) With impressive contemporary architecture wedged between 19th-century brick warehouses, this development has transformed an outmoded (if historically very valuable) factory complex into the city's swankiest shopping and dining precinct. An artisan baker and butcher, together with a well-stocked cheese shop, also make it a good place to stock up on some supplies.

⊙ Kadriorg

★Kadriorg Art Museum
MUSEUM

(Kadrioru kunstimuuseum; ☑ 606 6400; www. kadriorumuuseum.ekm.ee; A Weizenbergi 37, Kadriorg Palace; adult/child €6.50/4.50; ☺10am-6pm Tue & Thu-Sun May-Sep, to 5pm Thu-Sun Oct-Apr, to 8pm Wed year-round) Kadriorg Palace, a baroque beauty built by Peter the Great between 1718 and 1736, houses a branch of the Estonian Art Museum devoted to Dutch, German and Italian paintings from the 16th to the 18th centuries, and Russian works from the 18th to early 20th centuries (check

out the decorative porcelain with Communist imagery upstairs). The pink building is exactly as frilly and fabulous as a palace ought to be and there's a handsome French-style formal garden at the rear.

★Kumu
GALLERY

(☑ 602 6000; www.kumu.ekm.ee; A Weizenbergi 34, near Kadriorg Park; adult/student €8/6; ☺10am-8pm Thu, to 6pm Wed & Fri-Sun year-round, plus 10am-6pm Tue Apr-Sep) This futuristic, Finnish-designed, seven-storey building is a spectacular structure of limestone, glass and copper, nicely integrated into the landscape. Kumu (the name is short for *kunstimuuseum*, or art museum) contains the country's largest repository of Estonian art as well as constantly changing contemporary exhibits. There's everything from venerable painted altarpieces to the work of contemporary Estonian artists such as Adamson-Eric.

⊙ Other Neighbourhoods

★Lennusadam
MUSEUM

(Seaplane Harbour; ☑ 620 0550; www.meremuuseum.ee; Vesilennuki 6; adult/child €14/7; ☺10am-7pm daily May-Sep, to 6pm Tue-Sun Oct-Apr; ℗) Surrounded on two sides by island-dotted waters, Estonia has a rich maritime history, explored in this fascinating museum filled with interactive displays. When the building, with its triple-domed hangar, was completed in 1917, its reinforced-concrete shell frame construction was unique in the world. Resembling a classic Bond-villain lair, the vast space was completely restored and opened to the public in 2012. Highlights include exploring the cramped corridors of a 1930s naval submarine, and the ice-breaker and minehunter ships moored outside.

★Estonian Open-Air Museum
MUSEUM

(Eesti vabaõhumuuseum; ☑ 654 9101; www.evm.ee; Vabaõhumuuseumi tee 12, Rocca Al Mare; adult/child high season €9/6, low season €7/5; ☺10am-8pm 23 Apr-28 Sep, to 5pm 29 Sep-22 Apr) If tourists won't go to the countryside, let's bring the countryside to them. That's the modus operandi of this excellent, sprawling complex, where historic Estonian buildings have been plucked and transplanted among the tall trees. In summer the time-warping effect is highlighted by staff in period costume performing traditional activities among the wooden farmhouses and windmills. There's a chapel dating from 1699 and an old wooden tavern, Kolu Kõrts, serving traditional Estonian cuisine.

Tallinn TV Tower VIEWPOINT
(Tallinna teletorn; ☎686 3005; www.teletorn.ee; Kloostrimetsa tee 58a; adult/child €12/7; ⏰10am-7pm) Opened in time for the 1980 Olympics, this futuristic 314m tower offers brilliant views from its 22nd floor (175m). Press a button and frosted glass disks set in the floor suddenly clear, giving a view straight down. Once you're done gawping, check out the interactive displays in the space-age pods. Daredevils can try the exterior, 175m-high 'edge walk' (€20, 10am-6pm).

Tours

The tourist office (p217) and most travel agencies can arrange tours in English or other languages with a private guide; advance booking is required. The free tours leaving from the tourist office are excellent, and should be acknowledged with tips.

Euroaudioguide WALKING
(www.euroaudioguide.com; iPod rental €15) Preloaded iPods are available from the tourist office (p217) offering excellent commentary on most Old Town sights, with plenty of history thrown in. If you've got your own iPod, iPhone or iPad you can download the tour as an e-book (€10).

Reimann Retked KAYAKING
(☎5114099; www.retked.ee) Offers sea-kayaking excursions, including a four-hour paddle out to Aegna Island (from €35 per person). Other interesting possibilities include diving, rafting, bog shoeing, snowshoeing and beaver watching.

Tallinn Traveller Tours TOURS
(☎58374800; www.traveller.ee) This outfit runs entertaining tours – including a two-hour Old Town walk departing from outside the tourist office (p217) (private groups of one to 15 people from €80, or there's a larger free tour, for which you should tip the engaging guides). There are also ghost tours (€15), bike tours (from €19), pub crawls (€20) and day trips as far afield as Rīga (€55).

Sleeping

Tallinn has a good range of accommodation to suit every budget. Most of it is congregated in Old Town and its immediate surrounds, where even backpackers might find themselves waking up in a converted merchant's house. Of course, Tallinn is no secret any more, and it can be extremely difficult to find a bed on the weekend in summer.

★ **Tabinoya** HOSTEL €
(☎632 0062; www.tabinoya.com; Nunne 1; dm/d from €17/50; @📶) The Baltic's first Japanese-run hostel occupies the two top floors of a charming old building, with dorms (the four-person one is for females only) and a communal lounge at the top, and spacious private rooms, a kitchen and a sauna below. Bathroom facilities are shared. The vibe's a bit more comfortable and quiet than most of Tallinn's hostels. Book ahead.

Tallinn Backpackers HOSTEL €
(☎644 0298; www.tallinnbackpackers.com; Olevimägi 11; dm/r from €12/50; @📶) In an ideal Old Town location, this place has a global feel and a roll-call of traveller-happy features: a convivial common room, free wifi and lockers, cheap dinners, a games room with tabletop football and a kitchen and laundry. There's also a regular roster of pub crawls and day trips to nearby attractions.

United Backpackers HOSTEL €
(☎56850415; www.unitedbackpackers.ee; Kaarli pst 11; dm/tw from €14/45; @📶) Spread over three floors in a nondescript building off a busy road just south of Old Town, this well-kept, friendly wee hostel offers six-, eight- and 12-bed dorms or twin/quad rooms. There's a pleasant and well-patronised common area, pool table, bar, board games, and shared laundry, kitchen and bathrooms. A simple breakfast can be had for €5 extra.

★ **Y-residence** APARTMENT €€
(☎5021477; www.yogaresidence.eu; Pärnu mnt 32; apt from €65; 📶) The 'Y' stands for 'yoga', which seems a strange name for a collection of clean-lined new apartments in several locations around Tallinn, until you realize the operators also run yoga, tai chi and meditation sessions. You can expect friendly staff, a basic kitchenette and, joy of joys, a washing machine!

Villa Hortensia APARTMENT €€
(☎641 8083; www.hoov.ee; Vene 6, Masters' Courtyard; s/d from €45/65; 📶) Situated in the sweet, cobbled Masters' Courtyard (p217), Hortensia has four split-level studio apartments with kitchenettes and access to a shared communal lounge, but the two larger apartments are the real treats, with balconies and loads of character. In summer they can get hot and the downstairs cafe is open until midnight, so pack earplugs if you're an early sleeper.

Romeo Family Apartments APARTMENT €€
(☎56904786; www.romeofamily.ee; apt €55-110; 📶) With 14 spic-and-span apartments scat-

tered around Old Town, this family-run operation is an extremely good option. Most units are spacious and nicely furnished, with kitchens and clothes-washing facilities, and you can also book an airport pick-up service (€10).

★**Hotel Cru** HOTEL €€€
(📋611 7600; www.cruhotel.eu; Viru 8; s/d/ste €170/285/585; 📶) Behind the pretty powder-blue facade of this boutique hotel you'll find 15 richly furnished rooms scattered along a rabbit warren of corridors. All make sensitive use of original 14th-century features such as timber beams and limestone walls, but the cheapest are a little snug. The attached restaurant prides itself as one of Tallinn's best.

Hotel Telegraaf HOTEL €€€
(📋600 0600; www.telegraafhotel.com; Vene 9; r €225-255; 🅿 ❄ 📶 ⊠) This upmarket hotel in a converted 19th-century former telegraph station delivers style in spades. It boasts a spa, a pretty courtyard, an acclaimed restaurant, swanky modern-art decor and smart, efficient service. 'Superior' rooms, in the older part of the building, have more historical detail but we prefer the marginally cheaper 'executive' rooms for their bigger proportions and sharp decor.

Old House Apartments APARTMENT €€€
(📋641 1464; www.oldhouseapartments.ee; Rataskaevu 16; apt from €109; 🅿 📶) The name 'Old House' does poor justice to this wonderfully refurbished 14th-century merchant's house. It's been split into beautifully furnished apartments (including a spacious two-bedroom unit with traces of a medieval painted ceiling), and there are a further 20-odd units scattered around Old Town. All are in similar buildings, but the quality and facilities varies.

Three Sisters HOTEL €€€
(📋630 6300; www.threesistershotel.com; Pikk 71; r/ste from €200/315; 📶) Offering sumptuous luxury in three conjoined merchant houses dating from the 14th century, Three Sisters has 23 spacious rooms, each unique but with uniformly gorgeous details, including old-fashioned freestanding bathtubs, wooden beams, tiny balconies, blackout blinds and canopy beds. If you've got regal aspirations, the piano suite is the usual choice of visiting royalty.

✗ **Eating**

Tallinn is a dining gem. Its abundance of casual yet clued-up and innovative restaurants (not to mention its slew of fine diners

and taverns aimed at 'medieval' trencherman) shouldn't be unexpected: it's at a cultural crossroads surrounded by wonderful seafood, fecund farms, forest produce and New Nordic exemplars, so the food really *should* be good.

★**Vegan Restoran V** VEGAN €
(📋626 9087; www.vonkrahl.ee; Rataskaevu 12; mains €9-11; ⊙noon-11pm Sun-Thu, to midnight Fri & Sat; 🍴) Visiting vegans are spoiled for choice in this wonderful restaurant. In summer everyone wants one of the four tables on the street, but the atmospheric interior is just as appealing. The food is excellent – expect the likes of tempeh and veggies on brown rice with tomato-coconut sauce, and kale and lentil pie with creamy hemp-seed sauce.

RØST Pagar & Kohvik BAKERY €
(📋55604732; http://rost.ee; Rotermanni 14; snacks €3; ⊙9am-6pm Tue-Fri, 10am-5pm Sat) This fabulous little artisan bakery makes dense, almost fruity Estonian bread, sourdoughs, spiced pastries and other delightful things to accompany its carefully selected and expertly prepared coffee.

★**Von Krahli Aed** MODERN EUROPEAN €€
(📋58593839; www.vonkrahl.ee; Rataskaevu 8; mains €13-16; ⊙noon-midnight Mon-Sat, to 11pm Sun; 📶🍴) You'll find plenty of greenery on your plate at this rustic, plant-filled restaurant (*aed* means 'garden'), beneath the rough beams of a medieval merchant's house. Veggies star here (although all dishes can be ordered with some kind of fleshy embellishment) and there's care taken to offer vegan dishes and gluten-, lactose- and egg-free options.

Sfäär MODERN EUROPEAN €€
(📋56992200; www.sfaar.ee; Mere pst 6e; mains €13-14; ⊙8am-10pm Mon-Fri, from 10am Sat, 10am-5pm Sun; 📶) Chic Sfäär delivers an inventive menu highlighting great Estonian produce in dishes that gesture east (tempura) and west (beef tartare). The warehouse-style setting is like something out of a Nordic design catalogue, the cocktail and wine list won't disappoint and if the lubrication loosens the purse strings sufficiently, there's a pricey fashion store attached.

Rataskaevu 16 ESTONIAN €€
(📋642 4025; www.rataskaevu16.ee; Rataskaevu 16; mains €14-16; ⊙noon-11pm Sun-Thu, to midnight Fri & Sat; 🍴) If you've ever had a hankering for braised elk roast, this warm, stone-walled place, named simply for its Old Town address, can sate it. Although it's hardly traditional, plenty of Estonian faves fill the

menu – fried Baltic herrings, grilled pork tenderloin and Estonian cheeses among them. Finish, if you can, with a serve of the legendary warm chocolate cake.

★ **Moon**   RUSSIAN €€€
(☑ 631 4575; www.restoranmoon.ee; Võrgu 3; mains €15-17; ⊙ noon-11pm Mon-Sat, 1-9pm Sun, closed briefly in Jul) Quietly but consistently the best restaurant in ever-increasingly hip Kalamaja, Moon ('poppy') is a Tallinn gem, combining Russian and broader European influences to delicious effect. The staff are delightfully friendly and switched-on, the decor is cheerily whimsical, and dishes such as *piroshki* (little stuffed pies) and reputation-transforming chicken Kiev showcase a kitchen as dedicated to pleasure as to technical excellence.

★ **NOA**   INTERNATIONAL €€€
(☑ 5080589; www.noaresto.ee; Ranna tee 3; mains €19-26; ⊙ noon-11pm Mon-Thu, to midnight Fri & Sat, to 10pm Sun; ☑) It's worth the trek out to the far side of Pirita to reach this top-notch waterside restaurant, which consistently backs up its elevated reputation. Housed in a stylish low-slung pavilion with superb views over Tallinn Bay to Old Town, it plays knowledgeably with Asian influences while keeping a focus on the best Estonian and European ingredients and techniques.

NOA's adjoining 'Chef's Hall' offers wonderful set dining for larger parties, Wednesday to Saturday evenings. If you have the time, cash and inclination, the €79 degustation menu is a perfect demonstration of how good Estonian food can be.

★ **Leib**   ESTONIAN €€€
(☑ 611 9026; www.leibresto.ee; Uus 31; mains €17-19; ⊙ noon-11pm) *Leib* (Estonian black bread) is a thing of great beauty and quiet national pride, and you'll find a peerless rendition here: dense, moist, almost fruity in its Christmas-cake complexity. Thick-sliced and served with salt-flaked butter, it's the ideal accompaniment to the delightful new-Nordic ('new Estonian'?) food at this garden restaurant in the Old Town headquarters of Tallinn's Scottish club (really!).

★ **Ö**   NEW NORDIC €€€
(☑ 661 6150; www.restoran-o.ee; Mere pst 6e; degustation menus €59-76; ⊙ 6-11pm Mon-Sat, closed Jul) Award-winning Ö (pronounced 'er' and named for Estonia's biggest island, Saaremaa) has carved a unique space in Tallinn's culinary world, delivering inventive degustation menus showcasing seasonal Estonian produce. There's a distinct 'New Nordic' influence at play, deploying unusual ingredients such as fermented birch sap and spruce shoots. The understated dining room nicely complements the theatrical but always delicious cuisine.

🍷 Drinking & Nightlife

Don't worry about Tallinn's reputation as a stag-party paradise: it's easy to avoid the 'British' and 'Irish' pubs in the southeast corner of Old Town where lager-louts congregate (roughly the triangle formed by Viru, Suur-Karja and the city walls). Elsewhere you'll find a diverse selection of bars where it's quite possible to have a quiet, unmolested drink.

★ **No Ku Klubi**   BAR
(☑ 631 3929; Pikk 5; ⊙ noon-1am Mon-Thu, to 3am Fri, 2pm-3am Sat, 6pm-1am Sun) A nondescript red-and-blue door, a key-code to enter, a clubbable atmosphere of regulars lounging in mismatched armchairs – could this be Tallinn's ultimate 'secret' bar? Once the surreptitious haunt of artists in Soviet times, it's now free for all to enter – just ask one of the smokers outside for the code. Occasional evenings of low-key music and film are arranged.

★ **Levist Väljas**   BAR
(☑ 5077372; Olevimägi 12; ⊙ 3pm-3am Mon-Thu, to 6am Fri & Sat, to midnight Sun) Inside this much-loved Tallinn cellar bar (usually the last pit stop of the night) you'll find broken furniture, cheap booze and a refreshingly motley crew of friendly punks, grunge kids and anyone else who strays from the well-trodden tourist path. The discreet entrance is down a flight of stairs.

Gloria Wine Cellar   WINE BAR
(☑ 640 6804; www.gloria.ee; Müürivahe 2; ⊙ noon-11pm Mon-Sat) Set in a cellar beneath the inner face of the town wall, this atmospheric wine bar and shop stocks thousands of bottles across a series of vaulted stone chambers. Credenzas, heavy carpets, antique furniture and walls hung with paintings greet you inside, and the passing life of Tallinn outside, should the weather encourage an alfresco glass.

🛍 Shopping

★ **Katariina Käik**   ARTS & CRAFTS
(St Catherine's Passage; www.katariinagild.eu; off Vene 12; ⊙ noon-6pm Mon-Sat) This lovely medieval lane is home to the Katariina Guild,

comprising eight artisans' studios where you can happily browse the work of 14 female creators. Look for ceramics, textiles, patchwork quilts, hats, jewellery, stained glass and beautiful leather-bound books. Opening hours can vary amongst the different studios.

★ **Masters' Courtyard**   ARTS & CRAFTS
(Meistrite Hoov; www.hoov.ee; Vene 6; ☺10am-6pm) Archetypal of Tallinn's amber-suspended medieval beauty, this cobbled 13th-century courtyard offers rich pickings – a cosy chocolaterie/cafe, a guesthouse and artisans' stores and workshops selling quality ceramics, glass, jewellery, knitwear, woodwork and candles.

ⓘ Information

Tallinn Tourist Information Centre (☎ 645 7777; www.visittallinn.ee; Niguliste 2; ☺9am-7pm Mon-Sat, to 6pm Sun Jun-Aug, shorter hours rest of year) A very well-stocked and helpful office. Many Old Town walking tours leave from here.

ⓘ Getting There & Away

AIR

Tallinn Airport (Tallinna Lennujaam; ☎ 605 8888; www.tallinn-airport.ee; Tartu mnt 101) is conveniently located just 4km southeast of the city centre and offers air connections with 34 other Baltic and European destinations. A few domestic flights are scheduled to the islands of Saaremaa and Hiiumaa, routes currently handled by Transbaltika (www.transaviabaltika.lt).

LAND

There are no direct bus connections from Tallinn to Scandinavian destinations, although there are services to Russia, Latvia and Lithuania.

SEA

Eckerö Line (☎ 6000 4300; www.eckeroline.fi; Passenger Terminal A, Vanasadam; adult/child/ car from €19/12/19; ☺ ticket office 8.30am-7pm Mon-Fri, to 3pm Sat & Sun) Twice-daily car ferry from Helsinki to Tallinn (2½ hours).

Linda Line (☎ 699 9331; www.lindaliini.ee; Patarei Sadam, Linnahall Terminal) Operates smaller, faster (and more expensive) hydrofoil connections between Tallinn and Helsinki, from late March to late December.

Tallink (☎ 631 8320; www.tallink.com; Terminal D, Lootsi 13) Runs multiple daily services between Tallinn and Helsinki, and an overnight ferry to Stockholm and Tallinn, via the Åland islands.

Viking Line (☎ 666 3966; www.vikingline.com; Terminal A, Varasadam; passenger & vehicle from €42) At least four daily car ferries between Helsinki and Tallinn (2½ hours).

ⓘ Getting Around

TO/FROM THE AIRPORT

➠ From the airport, bus 2 will take you into central Tallinn and then on to the passenger ferry port. Running an average of three times an hour between 6.30am and 11.30pm, it should get you from the airport to the A Laikmaa stop by Viru Keskus in about 20 minutes, traffic depending. Unless you've had a chance to buy a Tallinn Card (p209) or Ühiskaart (smartcard) you'll buy a single-journey ticket from the driver (€2, exact change required). Simply reverse the process to get back to the airport.

➠ A taxi between the airport and the city centre should cost less than €10.

TO/FROM THE FERRY TERMINALS

There are three main passenger docks, all less than 1km from Old Town. Most ferries and cruise ships dock at Old City Harbour (Vanasadama). Eckerö Line, Viking Line and St Peter Line use **Terminals A & B** (Sadama 25/2 & 3) while Tallink uses **Terminal D** (Lootsi 13), across the marina. Linda Line ferries dock a little further west, beside the **Linnahall** (Kalasadama).

Bus 2 runs one to four times every hour between 6.30am and 11.30pm (slightly less frequently on weekends) from the stop by Terminal A, calling at Terminal D, the city centre, **Central Bus Station** (Tallinna bussijaam; ☎ 12550; www.bussijaam.ee; Lastekodu 46; ☺ ticket office 7am-9pm Mon-Sat, 8am-8pm Sun) and **airport** (p217). If you're heading to the port from the centre, catch the bus from the A Laikmaa stop, out front of the Tallink Hotel. Also from the heart of town, buses 3 and 73 go to the Linnahall stop (on Põhja pst, near the start of Sadama), five minutes' walk from all of the terminals.

A taxi between the city centre and any of the terminals should cost about €5.

PUBLIC TRANSPORT

Tallinn has an excellent network of buses, trams and trolleybuses running from around 6am to 11pm or midnight. The major **bus station** is beneath the Viru Keskus shopping centre. Public transport timetables are online at www.tallinn.ee.

Public transport is free for Tallinn residents, children under seven and adults with children under three. Others need to pay, either buying a paper ticket from the driver (€2 for a single journey, exact change required) or by buying a Ühiskaart (a smartcard, requiring a €2 deposit which can't be recouped within six months of validation) at an R-Kiosk, post office or the Tallinn City Government customer service desk; you can add credit and then validate the card at the start of each journey using the orange card-readers. E-ticket fares are €1.10/3/6 for an hour/day/five days.

The Tallinn Card (p209) includes free public transport on all services throughout its validity.

TALLINN INFORMATION

Iceland

POP 340,000

Best Places to Eat

➡ Dill (p231)

➡ Slippurinn (p269)

➡ Pakkhús (p265)

➡ Eldhúsið (p258)

➡ Norð Austur Sushi & Bar (p260)

Best Places to Stay

➡ Hótel Egilsen (p239)

➡ Kvosin Downtown Hotel (p230)

➡ River Hotel (p237)

➡ Halllandsnes (p249)

Why Go?

Iceland is literally a country in the making, a vast volcanic laboratory where mighty forces shape the earth: geysers gush, mudpots gloop, sulphurous clouds puff from fissures and glaciers grind great pathways through the mountains. Experience the full weirdness of Icelandic nature by bathing in milky blue pools, kayaking under the midnight sun or crunching across a dazzling-white ice cap.

Iceland's creatures are larger than life too: minke, humpback and even blue whales are common visitors to the deeper fjords. Record-breaking numbers of birds nest in the sea cliffs: cutest are the puffins who flutter here in their millions. Clean, green Reykjavík must contain the world's highest concentration of dreamers, authors, poets and musicians. Little wonder, as the magnificent scenery of this Atlantic island forged in fire and ice make it one of the world's most awe-inspiring sights.

When to Go
Reykjavík

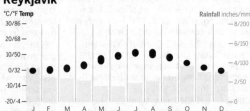

Jun–Aug In endless daylight, crowds and prices peak. Festivals and hiking are plentiful.

May & Sep Breezy weather with occasional snows; best time to avoid the crowds.

Oct–Apr Long nights with Northern Lights; winter activities on offer; some roads closed.

REYKJAVÍK

POP 122,460

The world's most northerly capital combines colourful buildings, quirky people, eye-popping design, wild nightlife and a capricious soul to devastating effect.

In many ways Reykjavík is strikingly cosmopolitan for its size. After all, it's merely a town by international standards, and yet it's loaded with excellent museums, captivating art, rich culinary choices, and hip cafes and bars.

ICELAND REYKJAVÍK

Iceland Highlights

1 Reykjavík Exploring the all-star assortment of boutiques, museums and galleries, restaurants and lively bars.

2 Skaftafell (p261) Donning crampons for an easy but exhilarating glacier walk.

3 Mývatn (p255) Wandering around the otherworldly geological wonderland.

4 Blue Lagoon (p236) Soaking in steaming lagoons at the world-famous site.

5 Vestmannaeyjar (p269) Setting sail with puffins galore and a small town tucked between lava flows.

6 Húsavík (p253) Admiring the giants of the ocean on a whale-watching trip.

7 Hornstrandir (p243) Roving around sawtoothed cliffs and lonely coves on an inspiring hike.

8 Jökulsárlón (p263) Cruising among the everchanging ice sculptures at the bewitching lagoon.

9 Snæfellsnes Peninsula (p238) Touring 'Iceland in miniature' – wild beaches, lava fields, a glacier-topped mountain.

Reykjavík

See Central Reykjavík Map (p226)

ICELAND

A

7 Fiskislóð

Grandagarður

14

19

5

Ananaust

Mýrargata

Framnesvegur

Bræðraborgarstígur

Öldugata

Sólvallagata

Ásvallagata

Hofsvallagata

Hringbraut

Birkimelur

1

National Museum

Dunhagi

Suðurgata

Aragata

Oddagata

Sæmundargata

Njarðargata

Sturlugata

Þorragata

VATNSMÝRI

17 Einarsnes

Bauganes

Skeljanes

NORTH ATLANTIC OCEAN

Fossvogur

B

Old Harbour

Geirsgata

Tryggvagata

Austurvöllur

Tjörnin

Hljómskálagarður Park

Miðbæjarsund

Laufásvegur

Smáragata

BSÍ Bus Terminal

Reykjavík Domestic Airport

C

Summer-only ferry to Viðey Island

Kalkofnsvegur

Lindargata

Skúlagata

Hverfisgata

Laugavegur

Njálsgata

Óðinsgata

Freyjugata

Barónsstígur

Eiríksgata

Gamla

Hringbraut

Flugvallarvegur

Öskjuhlíð

D

Borgartún

Laugavegur

20

18

Snorrabraut

Rauðarárstígur

Einholt

Háteigsvegur

Reykjavík Art Museum – Kjarvalsstaðir 2

4

Flókagata

Langahlíð

Miklabraut

Mjóah

Reykjahlíð

Eskihlíð

Barmahlíð

Mávahlíð

Dráupuhlíð

Blönduhlíð

Bústaðavegur

Hörgshlíð

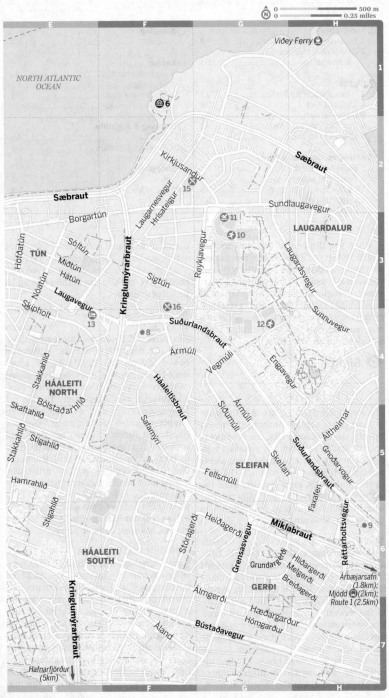

Reykjavík

When you slip behind the shiny tourist-centric veneer you'll find a place and its people that are both creative and utterly quaint, embracing their know-your-neighbours sense of community. Add a backdrop of snow-topped mountains, churning seas and crystal-clear air, and you, like many visitors, may fall helplessly in love, returning home already saving to come back.

◎ Sights

◎ Old Reykjavík

The area dubbed Old Reykjavík is the jaunty heart of the capital. Anchored by placid Tjörnin, the city-centre lake, the neighbourhood is loaded with brightly coloured residential houses and a series of great sights and interesting historic buildings. Old Reykjavík is also tops for a wander: from the seafront to Austurvöllur park, Alþingi (Parliament) and Ráðhús (city hall) and on to the National Museum.

★ **National Museum**   MUSEUM
(Þjóðminjasafn Íslands; Map p220; ☎530 2200; www.nationalmuseum.is; Suðurgata 41; adult/child kr2000/free; ☉10am-5pm May–mid-Sep, closed Mon mid-Sep–Apr; ☐1, 3, 6, 12, 14) This superb museum displays artefacts from settlement to the modern age. Exhibits give an excellent overview of Iceland's history and culture, and the free smartphone audio guide adds loads of detail. The strongest section describes the Settlement Era – including the rule of the chieftans and the introduction of Christianity – and features swords, drinking horns, silver hoards and a powerful bronze figure of Thor. The priceless 13th-century Valþjófsstaðir church door is carved with the story of a knight, his faithful lion and a passel of dragons.

★ **Reykjavík Art Museum – Hafnarhús**   GALLERY
(Map p226; ☎411 6400; www.artmuseum.is; Tryggvagata 17; adult/child kr1600/free; ☉10am-5pm Fri-Wed, to 10pm Thu) Reykjavík Art Museum's Hafnarhús is a marvellously restored warehouse converted into a soaring steel-and-concrete exhibition space. Though the well-curated exhibitions of cutting-edge contemporary Icelandic art change frequently (think installations, videos, paintings and sculpture), you can always count on the comic book-style paintings of Erró (Guðmundur Guðmundsson), a political artist who has donated several thousand works to the museum. The cafe, run by Frú Lauga (Map p220; ☎534 7165; www.frulauga.is; Laugalækur 6; ☉11am-6pm Mon-Fri, to 4pm Sat; 🅿) 🌱 farmers market, has great harbour views.

★ **Settlement Exhibition**   MUSEUM
(Landnámssýningin; Map p226; ☎411 6370; www.reykjavikmuseum.is; Aðalstræti 16; adult/child kr1600/free; ☉9am-6pm) This fascinating archaeological ruin/museum is based around a 10th-century Viking longhouse unearthed here from 2001 to 2002, and other settlement-era finds from central Reykjavík. It imaginatively combines technological wizardry and archaeology to give a glimpse into early Icelandic life. Don't miss the fragment of boundary wall at the back of the mu-

seum that is older still (and the oldest human-made structure in Reykjavík). Among the captivating high-tech displays, a wraparound panorama shows how things would have looked at the time of the longhouse.

Tjörnin   LAKE
(Map p226) This placid lake at the centre of the city is sometimes locally called the Pond. It echoes with the honks and squawks of more than 40 species of visiting birds, including swans, geese and Arctic terns; feeding the ducks is a popular pastime for the under-fives. Pretty sculpture-dotted parks like **Hljómskálagarður** (Map p220) `FREE` line the southern shores, and their paths are

much used by cyclists and joggers. In winter hardy souls strap on ice skates and the lake transforms into an **outdoor rink**.

⊙ Old Harbour

Largely a service harbour until recently, the Old Harbour and the adjacent Grandi (Örfirisey) neigbourhood have blossomed into a hot spot for tourists, with several museums, volcano and Northern Lights films, and interesting eateries and shops. Whale-watching and puffin-viewing trips depart from the pier, and, as boat bells ding, photo ops abound with views of the Harpa concert hall and snowcapped mountains beyond. On

---

REYKJAVÍK IN...

One Day

Explore the historic Old Reykjavík quarter, taking in the **Ráðhús** (Vonarstræti; ⊙8am-4pm Mon-Fri) `FREE` (town hall) and **Alþingi** (Parliament; ☑563 0500; www.althingi.is; Kirkjustraeti) `FREE` (Parliament), then peruse the city's best museums, such as the impressive **National Museum** (p222), **Reykjavík Art Museum** (Listasafn Reykjavíkur; www.artmuseum.is; adult/child kr1600/free) or the **Settlement Exhibition** (p222), built around a Viking longhouse. Lunch at hip **Nora Magasin** (Map p226; ☑578 2010; Pósthússtræti 9; mains kr1800-2600; ⊙11.30am-1am Sun-Thu, to 3am Fri & Sat) or **Bergsson Mathús** (Map p226; ☑571 1822; www.bergsson.is; Templarasund 3; mains kr2100-2500; ⊙7am-10pm; ☑).

Wander up arty Skólavörðustígur, shop for the latest Icelandic music at **12 Tónar** (p234), then photograph the immense church, **Hallgrímskirkja** (p224). For a perfect view, zip up the tower. Then stroll Laugavegur, the main shopping drag, with boutiques such as **Kiosk** (p234) and **KronKron** (p234). Grab some dinner at cheerful **Hverfisgata 12** (☑437 0203; www.hverfisgata12.is; Hverfisgata 12; pizza kr2450-3450; ⊙5pm-1am Mon-Thu, 11.30am-1am Fri-Sun; ♠) or **Public House** (Map p226; ☑555 7333; www.publichouse.is; Laugavegur 24; small plates kr1100-2000; ⊙11.30am-1am).

Enjoy people-watching and drinks at **Kaldi** (p232). Many cafes and restaurants turn into night-time party hang-outs, perfect for joining Reykjavík's notorious *djammið* (pubcrawl). Don't miss perennial favourite **Kaffibarinn** (p232), and tag along with locals to the latest drinking holes, wrapping up for a late-night dance session.

Two Days

After a late night out, brunch on your way over to the Old Harbour, or head straight for **Coocoo's Nest** (p231) then take in the area's museums, such as **Saga Museum** (p224) or **Whales of Iceland** (p224), or head out on a **whale-watching tour** (p228). Lunch on skewered fish at **Sægreifinn** (p231) or juicy burgers at **Hamborgara Búllan** (Hamborgarabúlla Tómasar; Map p226; ☑511 1888; www.bullan.is; Geirsgata 1; mains kr1500-2000; ⊙11.30am-9pm; ☎♠).

In the afternoon, visit Laugardalur, east of the city centre, for a soak at the geothermal pools, gardens and cool art at the **Reykjavík Art Museum – Ásmundarsafn** (Ásmundur Sveinsson Museum; ☑411 6430; www.artmuseum.is; Sigtún; adult/child kr1600/free; ⊙10am-5pm May-Sep, 1-5pm Oct-Apr; ☐2, 4, 14, 15, 17, 19) or at **Sigurjón Ólafsson Museum** (p224).

Book ahead for dinner to land a spot at one of the top Icelandic restaurants, such as **Dill** (p231) or **Matur og Drykkur** (p231), or try Reykjavík's most revered hot dogs at **Bæjarins Beztu** (Map p226; www.bbp.is; Tryggvagata; hot dogs kr420; ⊙10am-1am Sun-Thu, to 4.30am Fri & Sat; ♠).

After dark, hit one of the new breed of cocktail bars on Old Reykjavík, or go on a beer crawl, sampling the brews at **Micro Bar** (p232) or **Mikkeller & Friends** (p232).

WORTH A TRIP

VIÐEY

On fine-weather days, the tiny uninhabited island of Viðey (www.reykjavikmuseum.is) makes a wonderful day trip. Just 1km north of Reykjavík's Sundahöfn Harbour, it feels a world away. Well-preserved historic buildings, surprising modern art, an abandoned village and great bird-watching add to its remote spell. The only sounds are the wind, the waves and the golden bumblebees buzzing among the tufted vetch and hawkweed.

Little Viðey was settled around 900 and was farmed until the 1950s. It was home to a powerful monastery from 1225, but in 1539 it was wiped out by Danish soldiers during the Reformation. In the 18th and 19th centuries several significant Icelandic leaders lived here.

the western edge of the harbour the Grandi area, named after the fish factory there, has burgeoned with eateries and shops.

Saga Museum
MUSEUM

(Map p220; ☏ 511 1517; www.sagamuseum.is; Grandagarður 2; adult/child kr2100/800; ◷ 10am-6pm; 🖫 14) The endearingly bloodthirsty Saga Museum is where Icelandic history is brought to life by eerie silicon models and a multi-language soundtrack featuring the thud of axes and hair-raising screams. Don't be surprised if you see some of the characters wandering around town, as moulds were taken from Reykjavík residents (the owner's daughters are the Irish princess and the little slave gnawing a fish).

Whales of Iceland
MUSEUM

(Map p220; ☏ 571 0077; www.whalesoficeland.is; Fiskislóð 23-25; adult/child kr2900/1500; ◷ 10am-5pm; 🖫 14) Ever strolled beneath a blue whale? This museum houses full-sized models of the 23 species of whale found off Iceland's coast. The largest museum of this type in Europe, it also displays models of whale skeletons, and has good audio guides and multimedia screens to explain what you're seeing, plus has a cafe and gift shop. Online ticket discounts and family tickets (kr5800) are available.

◉ Laugavegur & Skólavörðustígur

Reykjavík's main street for shopping and people-watching is bustling, pedestrianised

Laugavegur. The narrow, one-way lane and its side streets blossom with the capital's most interesting shops, cafes and bars. At its western end, its name changes to Bankastræti, then Austurstræti. Running uphill off Bankastræti, artists street Skólavörðustígur ends at the spectacular modernist church, Hallgrímskirkja.

★ Hallgrímskirkja
CHURCH

(Map p226; ☏ 510 1000; www.hallgrimskirkja.is; Skólavörðustígur; tower adult/child kr900/100; ◷ 9am-9pm Jun-Sep, to 5pm Oct-May) Reykjavík's immense white-concrete church, star of a thousand postcards, Hallgrímskirkja (1945–86) dominates the skyline and is visible from up to 20km away. Get an unmissable view of the city by taking an elevator trip up the 74.5m-high tower. In contrast to the high drama outside, the Lutheran church's interior is quite plain. The most eye-catching feature is the vast 5275-pipe organ installed in 1992. The church's size and radical design caused controversy, and its architect, Guðjón Samúelsson (1887–1950), never saw its completion.

National Gallery of Iceland
MUSEUM

(Listasafn Íslands; Map p226; ☏ 515 9600; www.listasafn.is; Fríkirkjuvegur 7; adult/child kr1500/free; ◷ 10am-5pm daily mid-May–mid-Sep, 11am-5pm Tue-Sun mid-Sep–mid-May) This pretty stack of marble atriums and spacious galleries overlooking Tjörnin offers ever-changing exhibits drawn from a 10,000-piece collection. The museum can only exhibit a small sample at any one time; shows range from 19th- and 20th-century paintings by Iceland's favourite artists (including Jóhannes Kjarval and Nína Sæmundsson) to sculptures by Sigurjón Ólafsson and others. The museum ticket also covers entry to the Ásgrímur Jónsson Collection (Map p226; ☏ 515 9625; www.listasafn.is; Bergstaðastræti 74; adult/child kr1000/free; ◷ 2-5pm Tue, Thu, Sat & Sun mid-May–mid-Sep, 2-5pm Sat & Sun mid-Sep–Nov & Feb–mid-May) and Sigurjón Ólafsson Museum (Listasafn Sigurjóns Ólafssonar; Map p220; ☏ 553 2906; www.lso.is; Laugarnestanga 70; adult/child kr1000/free; ◷ 2-5pm Tue-Sun Jun-Aug, 2-5pm Sat & Sun Sep-Nov & Feb-May; 🖫 12, 16).

★ Harpa
ARTS CENTRE

(Map p226; ☏ box office 528 5050; www.harpa.is; Austurbakki 2; ◷ 8am-midnight, box office 10am-6pm) With its ever-changing facets glistening on the water's edge, Reykjavík's sparkling Harpa concert hall and cultural centre is a beauty to behold. In addition to a season of top-notch shows (some free), the shimmering interior with harbour vistas is worth stopping in for, or take a 30-minute guided **tour** (kr1500; 1pm, 3.30pm and 4.30pm Monday to Friday, and 3.30pm, 11am, 1pm and 3.30pm Saturday and Sunday).

Reykjavík Art Museum – Kjarvalsstaðir   GALLERY

(Map p220; ☑411 6420; www.artmuseum.is; Flókagata 24, Miklatún Park; adult/child kr1600/free; ⊙10am-5pm) The angular glass-and-wood Kjarvalsstaðir, which looks out onto **Miklatún Park** (Map p220), is named for Jóhannes Kjarval (1885–1972), one of Iceland's most popular classical artists. He was a fisherman until his crew paid for him to study at the Academy of Fine Arts in Copenhagen, and his wonderfully evocative landscapes share space alongside changing installations of mostly Icelandic 20th-century paintings.

🏃 Activities

Locally you can tour the city, rent bikes to zoom along lake or seaside trails, or pop into hot-pots all over town. Reykjavík is also the main hub for every kind of activity tour to all manner of destinations beyond the city limits.

Pools

Reykjavík's naturally hot water is the heart of the city's social life (as in many Icelandic towns); children play, teenagers flirt, business deals are made and everyone catches up on the latest gossip at the baths. Volcanic heat keeps the temperature at a mellow 29°C, and most baths have *heitir pottar* (hot-pots): jacuzzi-like pools kept at a toasty 37°C to 42°C. Bring towels and bathing suits or rent them on-site. For further information and more locations, see www.spacity.is.

Reykjavikers get very upset by dirty tourists in their clean, chemical-free pools. To avoid causing huge offence, you must wash thoroughly with soap and without a swimsuit before hopping in.

★Laugardalslaug   GEOTHERMAL POOL, HOT-POT

(Map p220; ☑411 5100; www.reykjavik.is/stadir/laugardalslaug; Sundlaugavegur 30a, Laugardalur; adult/child kr950/150, suit/towel rental kr850/570; ⊙6.30am-10pm Mon-Fri, 8am-10pm Sat & Sun; ⊕) One of the largest pools in Iceland, with the best facilities: an Olympic-sized indoor pool, and outdoor pools, seven hot-pots, a salt-water tub, a steam bath and a curling 86m water slide.

★Laugar Spa   SPA, GYM

(Map p220; ☑553 0000; www.laugarspa.com; Sundlaugavegur 30a, Laugardalur; day pass kr5500; ⊙6am-11pm Mon-Fri, 8am-9.30pm Sat & Sun) Super-duper Laugar Spa, next door to the Laugardalslaug geothermal pool, offers myriad ways to pamper yourself. There are six themed saunas and steam rooms, a seawater tub, a vast and well-equipped gym, fitness classes, and beauty and massage clinics with detox wraps, facials and hot-stone therapies. The spa is open to visitors over 18 years of age, and entry includes access to Laugardalslaug.

🧭 Tours

Walking, bike and bus tours are the main way to take in the city. Whale-watching, puffin-spotting and sea-angling trips allow a jaunt offshore.

As lovely as the capital's sights are, though, Reykjavík is also the main hub for tours to amazing landscapes and activities around Iceland. Those without wheels, time or the desire to travel the countryside independently can use Reykjavík as a cosmopolitan base for all forms of tours from super-Jeeps and buses to horse riding, snowmobiling and helitours. Regional operators like **Midgard Adventure** (☑578 3370; www.midgardadventure.is; Dufpaksbraut 14) and **Southcoast Adventure** (☑867 3535; www.southadventure.is) will also pick up in Reykjavík. If you have time, you can also head out on your own.

There are also smartphone apps (p235) for the city and Iceland as a whole, featuring everything from art and design to film locations.

Atlantsflug   FLIGHT TOUR

(☑854 4105; www.flightseeing.is; Reykjavík Domestic Airport; from adult/child kr20,000/10,000) Offers flightseeing tours from Reykjavík, Bakki Airport and Skaftafell. From Reykjavík Domestic Airport you can fly over Eyjafjallajökull crater or Reykjanes Peninsula, or take a day trip with tours around Skaftafell and Jökulsárlón glacial lagoon. There are also scheduled flights to Vestmannaeyjar.

Free Walking Tour Reykjavik   WALKING

(Map p226; www.freewalkingtour.is; ⊙noon & 2pm Jun-Aug, 1pm Sep-May) A one-hour, 1.5km walking tour of the city centre, starting at the little clock tower on Lækjartorg Sq.

Central Reykjavík

ICELAND

12

Summer-only ferry to Viðey Island

10
Boardwalk
Ægisgarður

Mýrargata
Nýlendugata

3 Old Harbour
Old Harbour

29
34

Small cruise ship dock

Geirsgata

Vesturgata
Ránargata
Ægisgata
Bárugata
Öldugata
Túngata

20

Tryggvagata

47

8

35
38
41

Naustin

48

Geirsgata

Fisch
Mjóstræti
Aðalstræti
Veltus
Hafnarstræti
Grjótagata

26
Ingólfstorg

Austurstræti

22

Tryggvagata

Lækjargata

Settlement Exhibition 5

Torvaldsensstræti

Pósthússtræti

11
13
28
31

Bankastræti

17

Kirkjustræti

Old Reykjavík 4

Vonarstræti
Templarasund

30
Kirkjutorg
16
24

Lækjargata

Amtmannsst
Skólastræti
Þingholtsstræti
Ingólfsstræti

46

Hólavallagata
Garðastræti
Hávallagata
Sólvallagata

Suðurgata
Tjarnargata

Bókhlöðust
Laufásvegur
Miðst
Skálholtsst

Spítalast

+ Hólavellir + Cemetery +

Suðurgata

9

7

Þingholtsstræti
Grundarst
Bjargarst
Bergstaðastræti

Tjarnargata
Bjarkargata

Skothúsvegur

Frikirkjuvegur
Hallargarðurinn

Hellus

Öðinsgata

Hringbraut

Tjörnin

Sóleyjargata
Fjölugata

Baldursgata
Nönnugata
Urðarst

6

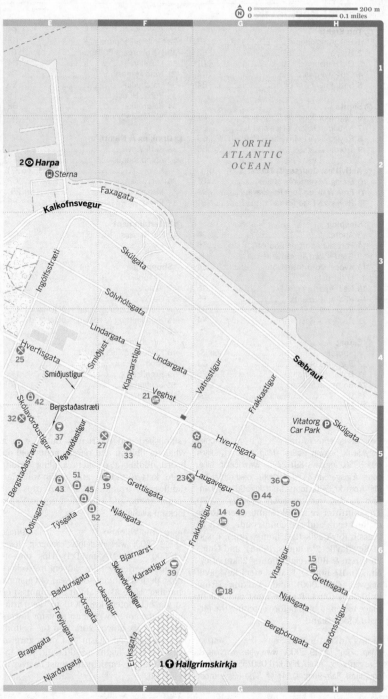

ICELAND

Central Reykjavík

Reykjavík Bike Tours CYCLING
(Reykjavík Segway Tours; Map p226; ☑ bikes 694 8956, segways 897 2790; www.icelandbike. com; Ægisgarður 7, Old Harbour; bike rental per 4hr from kr3500, tours from kr7500; ◷ 9am-5pm Jun-Aug, reduced hours Sep-May; ☐ 14) This outfitter rents bikes and offers tours of Reykjavík and the countryside, such as Classic Reykjavík (2½ hours, 7km); Coast of Reykjavík (2½ hours, 18km); and Golden Circle & Bike (eight hours, 25km of cycling in 1½ hours). It also offers Reykjavík Segway (kr15,000) and walking (from kr20,000) tours. It's the most convenient place to rent a bike before catching the ferry to Viðey island.

Elding Adventures at Sea WILDLIFE
(Map p226; ☑ 519 5000; www.whalewatching.is; Ægisgarður 5; adult/child kr11,000/5500; ◷ harbour kiosk 8am-9pm; ☐ 14) ⚲ The city's most established and ecofriendly outfit, with a whale exhibition and refreshments sold on board. Elding also offers angling (adult/child kr14,200/7100) and puffin-watching (adult/child from kr6500/3250) trips and combo tours, and runs the ferry to Viðey. Pick-up available.

Inside the Volcano ADVENTURE
(☑ 519 5609; www.insidethevolcano.com; tours kr42,000; ◷ mid-May–mid-Oct) This one-of-a-kind experience takes adventure-seekers into a perfectly intact 4000-year-old magma chamber. Hike 3km (about 50 minutes) or go via helicopter (kr87,000) to the Thrihnukagigur crater where an elevator lowers groups of six down 120m into the bottom of a vase-shaped chasm that once gurgled with hot lava. Lights are dim and time inside is limited. Participants must be over 12 years old.

★☆ Festivals & Events

Reykjavík Arts Festival CULTURAL
(www.listahatid.is; ☉May & Jun) Culture vultures flock to Iceland's premier cultural festival, which showcases two weeks of local and international theatre performances, film, dance, music and visual art.

★ Secret Solstice MUSIC
(www.secretsolstice.is; ☉Jun) This excellent music festival with local and international acts coincides with the summer solstice, so there is 24 hours of daylight for partying. It's held at Reykjavík's Laugardalur.

★ Reykjavík Culture Night CULTURAL
(www.menningarnott.is; ☉Aug) On Menningarnótt, held mid-month, Reykjavíkers turn out in force for a day and night of art, music, dance and fireworks. Many galleries, ateliers, shops, cafes and churches stay open until late. It's held on the same date as the city's marathon.

Reykjavík Pride CULTURAL
(www.hinsegindagar.is; ☉Aug) This festival brings carnival-like colour to the capital in early August. About 90,000 people (more than 25% of the country's population) have been known to attend the Pride march and celebrations.

**Reykjavík International
Film Festival** FILM
(www.riff.is; ☉Sep-Oct) This intimate 11-day event from late September features quirky programming highlighting independent filmmaking, both homegrown and international.

★ Iceland Airwaves MUSIC
(www.icelandairwaves.is; ☉Nov) You'd be forgiven for thinking Iceland is just one giant music-producing machine. Since the first edition of Iceland Airwaves was held in 1999, this fab festival has become one of the world's premier annual showcases for new music (Icelandic and otherwise).

⌂ Sleeping

★ Reykjavík Downtown Hostel HOSTEL€
(Map p226; ☏ 553 8120; www.hostel.is; Vesturgata 17; 4-/10-bed dm kr10,100/7400, d with/without bathroom kr28,000/24,500; @🛜) Squeaky clean and well run, this effortlessly charming hostel gets such good reviews that it regularly lures large groups and the nonbackpacker set. Enjoy friendly service, a guest

kitchen and excellent rooms. There's a kr700 discount for HI members.

★ Loft Hostel HOSTEL €€
(Map p226; ☏ 553 8140; www.lofthostel.is; Bankastræti 7; dm kr8300-9800, d/q kr25,500/35,800; @🛜) Perched high above the action on bustling Bankastræti, this modern hostel attracts a decidedly young crowd, including locals who come for its trendy bar and cafe terrace. This sociable spot comes with prim dorms (linen included) and en suite bathrooms. HI members get a kr800/3000 discount for a dorm/double.

Nest Apartments APARTMENT €€
(Map p226; ☏ 893 0280; http://nestapartments. is; Bergthorugata 15; apt from kr20,000; 🛜) Four thoroughly modern apartments with neat antique touches make a superb home away from home on this peaceful residential street just north of Hallgrímskirkja. In a tall town house, each apartment has a different layout, and the largest sleeps four people. Two-night minimum.

REY Apartments APARTMENT €€
(Map p226; ☏ 771 4600; www.rey.is; Grettisgata 2a; apt kr27,250-52,500; 🛜) For those leaning towards private digs rather than hotel stays, REY is a very handy choice with a huge cache of modern apartments scattered across several Escher-like stairwells. They're well maintained and stylishly decorated.

Forsæla

Apartmenthouse
GUESTHOUSE, APARTMENT €€

(Map p226; ☑551 6046; www.apartmenthouse.is; Grettisgata 33b; d/tr without bathroom incl breakfast kr24,700/33,500, apt/house from kr44,200/88,300; 🛜) This lovely option in Reykjavík's centre stars a 100-year-old wood-and-tin house for four to eight people, which comes with all the old beams and tasteful mod cons you could want. Three apartments have small, cosy bedrooms and sitting rooms, kitchens and washing machines. Plus there's B&B lodging with shared bathrooms. Minimum three-night stay in apartments and the house.

Grettisborg Apartments
APARTMENT €€

(Map p226; ☑666 0655; www.grettisborg.is; Grettisgata 51; apt kr22,000-55,200; 🛜) It's like sleeping in a magazine for Scandinavian home design; these thoroughly modern studios and apartments sport fine furnishings and sleek built-ins. The largest sleeps six or seven.

Reykjavík Residence
APARTMENT €€€

(Map p226; ☑561 1200; www.rrhotel.is; Hverfisgata 45; apt from kr41,000-82,500; @🛜) Plush city-centre living feels just right in these two converted historic mansions. Linen is crisp, service attentive and the light a glowing gold. The residences come in loads of configurations, from suites and studios with kitchenettes to two- and three-bedroom apartments.

Apotek
BOUTIQUE HOTEL €€€

(Map p226; ☑512 9000; www.keahotels.is; Austurstræti 16; d incl breakfast from kr49,000; 🛜) This hotel in a well-renovated 1917 Guðjón Samúelsson building, a former pharmacy, smack in the centre of Old Reykjavík, offers slick contemporary rooms in muted tones and a popular ground-floor tapas-style restaurant-bar (p232) as well.

Kvosin Downtown Hotel
APARTMENT €€€

(Map p226; ☑571 4460; www.kvosinhotel.is; Kirkjutorg 4; apt incl breakfast kr43,000-110,500; 🛜) Firmly a part of the luxury-apartment wave, these superbly located mod pads range from 'Junior Suite' and 'Executive' to the 'Valkyrie Suite'. Nespresso machines adorn the kitchenettes and all the mod cons are standard, including Sóley Organics toiletries. The Valkyrie Suite has amazing balconies.

Eating

★ Stofan Kaffihús
CAFE €

(Map p226; ☑546 1842; www.facebook.com/stofan.cafe; Vesturgata 3; dishes kr1500-1700; ⊙9am-11pm Mon-Wed, to midnight Thu-Sat, 10am-10pm Sun; 🛜) This laid-back cafe in a historic

---

EATING THE LOCALS: WHALE, SHARK & PUFFIN

Many restaurants and tour operators in Iceland tout more unusual delicacies: whale (*hvál/hvalur*), shark (fermented and called *hákarl*) and puffin (*lundi*). Before you dig in, consider that what may have been sustainable with 332,000 Icelanders becomes taxing on species and delicate ecosystems when around 1,800,000 tourists annually try them. Be aware:

➡ as much as an estimated 40% to 60% of Icelandic whale meat consumption is by tourists

➡ as many as two-thirds of Icelanders say they never eat whale meat

➡ an estimated 3% of Icelanders eat whale regularly

➡ between 75% and 85% of minke whale is thrown away after killing

➡ fin whales are classified as endangered globally; their status in the North Atlantic is hotly debated

➡ Iceland's Ministry of Industries and Innovation maintains the whale catch is sustainable, at less than 1% of local stock, despite international protest

➡ the Greenland shark, which is used for *hákarl*, has a conservation status of 'near threatened' globally

➡ in 2002 there were an estimated 7 million puffins in Iceland, in 2015 there were about 4 million – a 43% drop, with much more among juveniles (65% drop) due to consistently poor chick production

➡ while we do not exclude restaurants that serve these meats from our listings, you can opt not to order the meat, or easily find whale-free spots at www.icewhale.is/whale-friendly-restaurants.

brick building has a warm feel, with worn wooden floors, plump couches and a spacious main room. Settle in for coffee, cake or soup, and watch the world go by.

★ Bakarí Sandholt   BAKERY €
(Map p226; 📞 551 3524; www.sandholt.is; Laugavegur 36; snacks kr600-1200; ⊙ 7am-9pm; 📶) Reykjavík's favourite bakery is usually crammed with folks hoovering up the generous assortment of fresh baguettes, croissants, pastries and sandwiches. The soup of the day (kr1600) comes with delicious sourdough bread.

Sægreifinn   SEAFOOD €
(Seabaron; Map p226; 📞 553 1500; www.saegreifinn.is; Geirsgata 8; mains kr1350-1900; ⊙ 11.30am-11pm mid-May–Aug, to 10pm Sep–mid-May) Sidle into this green harbourside shack for the most famous lobster soup (kr1400) in the capital, or choose from a fridge full of fresh fish skewers to be grilled on the spot. Though the original sea baron sold the restaurant some years ago, the place retains a cosy, laid-back feel.

Gló   ORGANIC, VEGETARIAN €
(Map p226; 📞 553 1111; www.glo.is; Laugavegur 20b; mains kr1400-2000; ⊙ 11am-9pm Mon-Fri, 11.30am-9pm Sat & Sun; 📶🖊) Join the cool cats in this airy upstairs restaurant serving fresh, large daily specials loaded with Asian herbs and spices. Though not exclusively vegetarian, it's a wonderland of raw and organic foods, with a broad bar of elaborate salads, from root veggies to Greek, to choose from. It also has branches in **Laugardalur** (Map p220; 📞 553 1111; Engjateigur 19; mains kr1250-2000; ⊙ 11am-9pm Mon-Fri; 📶🖊) and **Kópavogur** (Hæðasmári 6; mains kr1300-2300; ⊙ 11am-9pm Mon-Fri, 11.30am-9pm Sat & Sun; 📶🖊).

Matur og Drykkur   ICELANDIC €€
(Map p220; 📞 571 8877; www.maturogdrykkur.is; Grandagarður 2; lunch mains kr1900-2700, dinner mains/tasting menus kr3700/10,000; ⊙ 11.30am-3pm & 6-10pm Mon-Sat, 6-10pm Sun; 🖥14) One of Reykjavík's top high-concept restaurants, Matur Og Drykkur means 'food and drink', and you surely will be plied with the best of both. The brainchild of brilliant chef Gísli Matthías Auðunsson, who also owns excellent Slippurinn (p269) in the Vestmannaeyjar, creates inventive versions of traditional Icelandic fare. Book ahead in high season and for dinner.

Messinn   SEAFOOD €€
(Map p226; 📞 546 0095; www.messinn.com; Lækjargata 6b; lunch mains kr1850-2100, dinner mains kr2700-4100; ⊙ 11.30am-3pm & 5-10pm; 📶) Make a beeline to Messinn for the best seafood that Reykjavík has to offer. The speciality here is amazing pan-fry dishes: your pick of fish is served up in a sizzling cast-iron skillet, accompanied by buttery potatoes and salad. The mood is upbeat and comfortable, and the staff is friendly.

Coocoo's Nest   CAFE €€
(Map p220; 📞 552 5454; www.coocoosnest.is; Grandagarður 23; mains kr1700-4500; ⊙ 11am-10pm Tue-Sat, to 4pm Sun; 📶) Pop into this cool eatery tucked behind the Old Harbour for popular weekend brunches (dishes kr1700 to kr2500; 11am to 4pm Friday to Sunday) paired with decadent cocktails (kr1800). It's casual, small and groovy, with mosaic plywood tables. The menu changes and there are nightly themes, but it's always scrumptious.

Ostabúðin   DELI €€
(Cheese Shop; Map p226; 📞 562 2772; www.ostabudin.is; Skólavörðustígur 8; mains kr3750-5000; ⊙ restaurant noon-10pm, deli 10am-6pm Mon-Thu, to 7pm Fri, 11am-4pm Sat) Head to the large dining room at this gourmet cheese shop and deli and order the friendly owner's cheese and meat platters (from kr1900 to kr4000), or the catch of the day accompanied by homemade bread. You can pick up other local goods, such as terrines and duck confit, on the way out.

Dill   ICELANDIC €€€
(Map p226; 📞 552 1522; www.dillrestaurant.is; Hverfisgata 12; 5-course meals from kr12,000; ⊙ 6-10pm Wed-Sat) Top 'New Nordic' cuisine is the major drawcard at this elegant yet simple bistro. The focus is very much on the food – locally sourced produce served as a parade of courses. The owners are friends with Copenhagen's famous Noma clan and take Icelandic cuisine to similarly heady heights. It's popular with locals and visitors alike; a reservation is a must.

Grillmarkaðurinn   FUSION €€€
(Grill Market; Map p226; 📞 571 7777; www.grillmarkadurinn.is; Lækargata 2a; mains kr4600-9900; ⊙ 11.30am-2pm Mon-Fri, 6-10.30pm Sun-Thu, to 11.30pm Fri & Sat) Top-notch dining is the order of the day here, from the moment you enter the glass atrium with its golden-globe lights to your first snazzy cocktail, and on throughout the meal. Service is impeccable, and locals and visitors alike rave about the food, which uses locally sourced Icelandic ingredients prepared with imagination by master chefs.

Fiskmarkaðurinn
SEAFOOD €€€

(Fishmarket; Map p226; ☑578 8877; www.fisk-markadurinn.is; Aðalstræti 12; mains kr5100-8900; ⊙5-11.30pm) This restaurant excels in infusing Icelandic seafood and local produce with unique flavours like lotus root. The tasting menu (kr11,900) is tops, and the place is renowned for its excellent sushi bar (kr3300 to kr4700).

Apotek
FUSION €€€

(Map p226; ☑551 0011; www.apotekrestaurant.is; Austurstræti 16; mains kr2500-6000; ⊙11.30am-11pm, Sun-Thu, to midnight Fri & Sat) This beautiful restaurant and bar with shining glass fixtures and a cool ambience is equally known for its delicious menu of small plates that are perfect for sharing and its top-flight cocktails. It's on the ground floor of the hotel of the same name.

🍷 Drinking & Nightlife

Sometimes it's hard to distinguish between cafes, restaurants and bars in Reykjavík, because when night rolls around (whether light or dark out) many coffee shops and bistros turn lights down and volume up, swapping cappuccinos for cocktails. Craftbeer bars, high-end cocktail bars and music and dance venues flesh out the scene. Some hotels and hostels also have trendy bars.

★ Mikkeller & Friends
CRAFT BEER

(Map p226; ☑437 0203; www.mikkeller.dk; Hverfisgata 12; ⊙5pm-1am Sun-Thu, 2pm-1am Fri & Sat; 🖥) Climb to the top floor of the building shared with excellent pizzeria Hverfisgata 12 and you'll find this Danish craft-beer pub; its 20 taps rotate through Mikkeller's own offerings and local Icelandic craft beers. The vibe is laid-back and colourful.

★ Kaffi Vínyl
CAFE

(Map p226; ☑537 1332; www.facebook.com/vinil-rvk; Hverfisgata 76; ⊙8am-11pm; 🖥) This bright light shining in the Reykjavík coffee, restaurant and music scene is popular for its chilled vibe, great music and delicious vegan and vegetarian food.

Kaffibarinn
BAR

(Map p226; ☑551 1588; www.kaffibarinn.is; Bergstaðastræti 1; ⊙3pm-1am Sun-Thu, to 4.30am Fri & Sat; 🖥) This old house with the London Underground symbol over the door contains one of Reykjavík's coolest bars; it even had a starring role in the cult movie *101 Reykjavík* (2000). At weekends you'll feel like you need either a famous face or a battering ram to get in. At other times it's a place for artistic types to chill with their Macs.

Kaldi
BAR

(Map p226; ☑581 2200; www.kaldibar.is; Laugavegur 20b; ⊙noon-1am Sun-Thu, to 3am Fri & Sat) Effortlessly cool with mismatched seats and teal banquettes, plus a popular smoking courtyard, Kaldi is awesome for its full range of Kaldi microbrews, not available elsewhere. Happy hour (4pm to 7pm) gets you a brew for kr700. Anyone can play the in-house piano.

Reykjavík Roasters
CAFE

(Map p226; ☑517 5535; www.reykjavikroasters.is; Kárastígur 1; ⊙8am-6pm Mon-Fri, 9am-5pm Sat & Sun) These folks take their coffee seriously. The tiny hipster joint is easily spotted on warm days by its smattering of wooden tables on a small square. Swig a perfect latte and savour a flaky croissant. Also has a **branch** (Map p220; ☑552 3200; www.reykjavikroasters.is; Brautarholt 2; ⊙8am-6pm Mon-Fri, 9am-5pm Sat & Sun; 🖥) in the Hlemmur area.

Micro Bar
BAR

(Map p226; ☑865 8389; www.facebook.com/MicroBarIceland; Vesturgata 2; ⊙4pm-12.30am Sun-Thu, to 1.30am Fri & Sat) Boutique brews are the name of the game at this low-key spot in the heart of the action. Bottled beers represent a slew of brands and countries, but on tap you'll discover 10 local draughts from the island's top microbreweries; it's one of the best selections in Reykjavík. Happy hour (4pm to 7pm) offers kr870 beers.

☆ Entertainment

The ever-changing vibrant Reykjavík performing-arts scene features shows at bars and cafes, local theatres and the Harpa concert hall.

For the latest in Icelandic music and performing arts, and to see who's playing, consult the free English-language newspaper *Grapevine* (www.grapevine.is; with events listing app Appening); websites Visit Reykjavík (www.visitreykjavik.is), and Musik.is (www.musik.is); or city music shops.

★ Bíó Paradís
CINEMA

(Map p226; ☑412 7711; www.bioparadis.is; Hverfisgata 54; adult kr1800; 🖥) This totally cool cinema, decked out in movie posters and vintage officeware, screens specially curated Icelandic films with English subtitles. It's a chance to see movies that you may not find elsewhere.

★ **Húrra**   LIVE MUSIC
(Map p226; www.facebook.com/pg/hurra.is; Tryggvagata 22; ⊙6pm-1am Mon-Thu, to 4.30am Fri & Sat, to 11.30pm Sun; 🛜) Dark and raw, this large bar opens up its back room to create a concert venue, with live music or DJs most nights, and is one of the best places in town to close out the evening. There's a range of beers on tap and happy hour runs till 9pm (beer or wine kr750).

🔒 **Shopping**

Reykjavík's vibrant design culture makes for great shopping: from sleek fish-skin purses and knitted *lopapeysur* (Icelandic woollen sweaters) to unique music or Icelandic schnapps (*brennivín*). Laugavegur is the most dense shopping street. You'll find interesting shops all over town, but fashion concentrates near the Frakkastígur and Vitastígur end of Laugavegur. Skólavörðustígur is strong for arts and jewellery, while Bankastræti and Austurstræti have touristy shops.

★ **Kolaportið Flea Market**   MARKET
(Map p226; www.kolaportid.is; Tryggvagata 19; ⊙11am-5pm Sat & Sun) Held in a huge industrial building by the harbour, this weekend market is a Reykjavík institution. There's a huge tumble of secondhand clothes and old toys, plus cheap imports. A food section sells traditional eats like *rúgbrauð* (geothermally baked rye bread), *brauðterta* ('sandwich cake'; a layering of bread with mayonnaise-based fillings) and *hákarl* (fermented shark).

★ **Kirsuberjatréð**   ARTS & CRAFTS
(Cherry Tree; Map p226; ☑562 8990; www.kirs.is; Vesturgata 4; ⊙10am-6pm Mon-Fri, to 5pm Sat & Sun) This women's art-and-design collective in an interesting 1882 former bookshop sells weird and wonderful fish-skin handbags, music boxes made from string, and, our favourite, beautiful coloured bowls made from radish slices. It's been around for 25 years and now has 11 designers.

Geysir   CLOTHING
(Map p226; ☑519 6000; www.geysir.com; Skólavörðustígur 16; ⊙10am-7pm Mon-Sat, 11am-6pm Sun) If you're looking for traditional Icelandic clothing and unique modern designs, Geysir boasts an elegant selection of sweaters and blankets, and men's and women's clothes, shoes and bags. There's also a branch down the street at Skólavörðustígur 7 with the same opening hours.

Kron   SHOES
(Map p226; ☑551 8388; www.kron.is; Laugavegur 48; ⊙10am-6pm Mon-Fri, to 5pm Sat) Kron sells its own outlandishly wonderful handmade shoes with all the flair you'd expect of an Icelandic label. Colours are bright, textures are cool; and they're even wearable (those practical Icelanders!).

Skúmaskot   ARTS & CRAFTS
(Map p226; ☑663 1013; www.facebook.com/skumaskot.art.design; Skólavörðustígur 21a; ⊙10am-6pm Mon-Fri, to 5pm Sat) Ten local designers create unique handmade porcelain items, women's and kids' clothing, paintings and cards.

WOOLLY JUMPERS: LOPAPEYSUR

Lopapeysur are the ubiquitous Icelandic woolly jumpers you will see worn by locals and visitors alike. Made from naturally water-repellant Icelandic wool, they are thick and cosy, with simple geometric patterns or regional motifs. They are no longer the bargain they were in the 1960s, so when shopping, be sure to make the distinction: do you want hand-knit or machine made? You'll notice the price difference (some cost well over €200), but either way these beautiful but practical items (and their associated hats, gloves and scarves) are exceptionally wearable souvenirs.

Traditional handmade hats, socks and sweaters are sold at the **Handknitting Association of Iceland** (Handprjónasamband Íslands; Map p226; ☑552 1890; www.handknit. is; Skólavörðustígur 19; ⊙9am-10pm Mon-Fri, to 6pm Sat, 10am-6pm Sun) knitting collective. Or you can buy yarn, needles and knitting patterns and do it yourself. The association's smaller **branch** (Laugavegur 53b; ⊙9am-7pm Mon-Fri, 10am-5pm Sat) sells made-up items only.

Álafoss (Map p226; ☑562 6303; www.alafoss.is; Laugavegur 8; ⊙10am-6pm) sells loads of hand- or machine-made *lopapeysur* and other wool products. Its **outlet store** (Álafossvegur 23, Mosfellsbær; ⊙8am-8pm Mon-Fri, 9am-8pm Sat & Sun; 🚌15) in Mosfellsbær also sells yarn, patterns and needles.

It's in a large, renovated gallery that beautifully showcases the creative Icelandic crafts.

Orrifinn JEWELLERY
(Map p226; ☑789 7616; www.orrifinn.com; Skólavörðustígur 17a; ⊙10am-6pm Mon-Fri, 11am-4pm Sat) Orrifinn's subtle, beautiful jewellery captures the natural wonder of Iceland and its Viking history. Delicate anchors, axes and pen nibs dangle from understated matte chains.

KronKron CLOTHING
(Map p226; ☑561 9388; www.kronkron.com; Laugavegur 63b; ⊙10am-6pm Mon-Thu, to 6.30pm Fri, to 5pm Sat) This is where Reykjavík goes high fashion, with labels such as Marc Jacobs and Vivienne Westwood. But we really enjoy its Scandinavian designers (including Kron by KronKron) and their offering of silk dresses, knit capes, scarves and even woollen underwear. The handmade shoes are off the charts, and are also sold down the street at Kron (p233).

Kiosk CLOTHING
(Map p226; ☑571 3636.; www.kioskreykjavik.com; Ingólfsstræti 6; ⊙11am-7pm Mon-Fri, to 5pm Sat) This wonderful designers' cooperative is lined with creative women's fashion in a glass-fronted boutique. Designers take turns staffing the store.

Icelandic Music

The den of musical goodness that is **Lucky Records** (Map p220; ☑551 1195; www.luckyrecords.is; Rauðarárstígur 10; ⊙10am-6pm Mon-Fri, 11am-5pm Sat & Sun) holds loads of modern Icelandic music, but plenty of vintage vinyl too. The huge collection spans from hip-hop to jazz and electronica, and it has occasional live music.

12 Tónar (Map p226; ☑511 5656; www.12tonar.is; Skolavörðustígur 15; ⊙10am-6pm Mon-Sat, from noon Sun) has launched some of Iceland's favourite bands. The two-storey shop is a very cool place to hang out, and you can listen to CDs, drink coffee and sometimes catch a live performance.

ℹ Information

DISCOUNT CARDS

Reykjavík City Card (www.citycard.is; 24/48/72hr kr3700/4900/5900) offers admission to Reykjavík's municipal swimming/thermal pools and to most of the main galleries and museums, plus discounts on some tours, shops and entertainment. It also gives free travel on the city's Strætó buses and on the ferry to Viðey. The Children's City Card (24/48/72

hours kr1300/2400/3100) is less useful, since kids enter free at many museums anyway. The cards are available at the Main Tourist Office, some travel agencies, 10-11 supermarkets, HI hostels and some hotels.

TOURIST INFORMATION

Main Tourist Office (Upplýsingamiðstöð Ferðamanna; Map p226; ☑411 6040; www.visitreykjavik.is; Ráðhús City Hall, Tjarnargata 11; ⊙8am-8pm) Friendly staff and mountains of free brochures, plus maps, Reykjavík City Card and Strætó city bus tickets. Books accommodation, tours and activities.

Besides the Main Tourist Office, Reykjavík has loads of travel agencies. **Visit Iceland** (☑511 4000; www.inspiredbyiceland.com; Borgartún 35) offers Iceland-wide information.

ℹ Getting There & Away

AIR

Iceland's primary international airport, **Keflavík International Airport** (p279) is 48km west of Reykjavík, on the Reykjanes Peninsula. The airport has ATMs, money exchange, car hire, an **information desk** (☑425 0330, booking service 570 7799; www.visitreykjanes.is; ⊙6am-8pm Mon-Fri, noon-5pm Sat & Sun) and cafes. The duty-free shops in the arrival area sell liquor at far better prices than you'll find in town. There's also a desk for collecting duty-free cash back from eligible purchases in Iceland. The 10-11 convenience store sells SIM cards, and major tour companies like Reykjavík Excursions and Gray Line have desks.

Reykjavík Domestic Airport (p279) is in central Reykjavík, just south of Tjörnin. Sightseeing services, domestic flights and those to/from Greenland and the Faroe Islands fly here.

Air Iceland Connect (☑570 3030; www.airicelandconnect.is; Reykjavík Domestic Airport) has a desk at the airport and serves Akureyri, Egilsstaðir, Ísafjörður and Greenland; but you can usually save money by booking online.

Atlantic Airways (☑in Faroe Islands 298 34 10 00; www.atlantic.fo) flies to the Faroe Islands.

Eagle Air Iceland (Map p220; ☑562 4200; www.eagleair.is; Reykjavík Domestic Airport) operates sightseeing services and five set routes from Reykjavík: Vestmannaeyjar Islands; Höfn; Húsavík; and in the Westfjords, Bíldudalur and Gjögur.

BUS

You can travel from Reykjavík by day tour (many of which offer hotel pick-up), or use Strætó and several of the tour companies for transport, getting on and off their scheduled buses. They also offer a multitude of bus transport passes. Things are changing rapidly in Iceland; the official tourism website (www.inspiredbyiceland.com)

has links to bus providers under the Plan Your Trip – Getting Around section.

The bus network operates frequently from around mid-May to mid-September. Outside these months services are less frequent (or nonexistent).

For destinations on the northern and eastern sides of Iceland (eg Egilsstaðir, Mývatn and Húsavík), you usually change in Höfn or Akureyri; for the West and Westfjords change in Borgarnes.

Strætó (p280) Operates Reykjavík long-distance buses from **Mjódd bus terminal** (☑540 2700; www.bus.is; ⊙ticket office 7am-6pm Mon-Fri, 10am-6pm Sat, 12.30-6pm Sun), 8km southeast of the city centre, which is served by local buses 3, 4, 11, 12, 17, 21, 24 and 28. Strætó also operates city buses and has a smartphone app. For long-distance buses only you can use cash, credit/debit card with PIN or (wads of) bus tickets.

BSÍ bus terminal (Map p220; ☑580 5400; www.bsi.is; Vatnsmýrarvegur 10; 🛜) Reykjavík Excursions (and its Flybus) uses the BSÍ bus terminal (pronounced 'bee-ess-ee'), south of the city centre. There's a ticketing desk, tourist brochures, lockers, luggage storage (www.luggagelockers.is), Budget car hire and a cafeteria with wi-fi. The terminal is served by Reykjavík buses 1, 3, 5, 6, 14 and 15. Reykjavík Excursions offers prebooked hotel pick-up to bring you to the terminal. Some Gray Line buses also stop here.

Sterna (Map p226; ☑551 1166; www.sternatravel.com; 🛜) Sales and departures from the Harpa concert hall. Buses around the Ring Road and to tourist highlights.

Trex (☑587 6000; www.trex.is) Departs from the Main Tourist Office, Kringlan's Shell petrol station or Reykjavík Campsite. Buses go to Þórsmörk and Landmannalaugar in the South.

❶ Getting Around

The best way to see compact central Reykjavík is on foot.

BICYCLE

Reykjavík has a steadily improving network of cycle lanes; ask the Main Tourist Office for a map. You are allowed to cycle on pavements as long as you don't cause pedestrians problems.

At the Old Harbour, rent bikes at **Reykjavík Bike Tours** (p228) and get service at **Kría** (Map p220; ☑534 9164; www.kriacycles.com; Grandagarður 5; ⊙10am-6pm Mon-Fri, 11am-3pm Sat) bicycle shop, or do your own repairs at **Bike Cave** (Map p220; ☑770 3113; www.facebook.com/pg/bikecavereykjavik; Einarsnes 36; ⊙9am-11pm, shorter hours in winter; 🖵12) cafe.

SMARTPHONE APPS

Useful, practical apps include the vital 112 Iceland app for safe travel and Veður for weather. Bus companies such as Strætó also offer apps.

There are plenty more apps that cover all sorts of interests, from history and language to aurora-spotting, or walking tours of the capital. Smartguide offers many of those. Reykjavík *Grapevine*'s apps (Appy Hour, Craving and Appening) deserve a special mention for getting you to good bars, food and events in Reykjavík.

BOAT

Whale-watching tours leave from the Old Harbour.

Viðey Ferry (Map p220; ☑533 5055; www.videy.com; return adult/child kr1500/750; ⊙from Skarfabakki hourly 10.15am-5.15pm mid-May–Sep, weekends only Oct–mid-May) The ferry to Viðey island takes five minutes from Skarfabakki, 4.5km east of the city centre. During summer two boats a day start from Elding at the Old Harbour and the Harpa concert hall. Bus 5 stops closest to Skarfabakki, and it's a point on the Reykjavík hop-on-hop-off tour bus.

BUS

Strætó (www.bus.is) operates regular, easy buses around Reykjavík and its suburbs (Seltjarnarnes, Kópavogur, Garðabær, Hafnarfjörður and Mosfellsbær); it also operates long-distance buses. It has online schedules, a smartphone app and a printed map. Many free maps like *Welcome to Reykjavík City Map* also include bus-route maps.

Buses run from 7am until 11pm or midnight (from 11am on Sunday). Services depart at 20-minute or 30-minute intervals. A limited night-bus service runs until 2am on Friday and Saturday. Buses only stop at designated bus stops, marked with a yellow letter 'S'.

TAXI

Taxi prices are high. Flagfall starts at around kr700. Tipping is not required. From BSÍ bus terminal to the Harpa concert hall costs about kr2200. From Mjódd bus termimal it's about kr4300.

There are usually taxis outside bus stations, airports and bars on weekend nights (huge queues for the latter), plus on Bankastræti near Lækjargata.

BSR (☑561 0000; www.taxireykjavik.is)
Hreyfill (☑588 5522; www.hreyfill.is)

AROUND REYKJAVÍK

Blue Lagoon

As the Eiffel Tower is to Paris, so the Blue Lagoon (Bláa Lónið; ☑ 420 8800; www.bluelagoon.com; adult/child from kr6990/free; ☉ 7am-midnight Jul–mid-Aug, 7am-11pm mid-May–Jun, 8am-10pm Jan–mid-May & mid-Aug–Sep, 8am-9pm Oct-Dec) is to Iceland...with all the positive and negative connotations implied. Those who say it's too commercial and too crowded aren't wrong, but you'll be missing something special if you don't go. Pre-booking is essential or you will be turned away.

In a magnificent black-lava field, the milky-teal spa is fed water from the futuristic Svartsengi geothermal plant; with its silver towers, roiling clouds of steam and people daubed in white silica mud, it's an other-worldly place.

The superheated water (70% sea water, 30% fresh water, at a perfect 38°C) is rich in blue-green algae, mineral salts and fine sil-ica mud, which condition and exfoliate the skin – sounds like advertising speak, but you really do come out as soft as a baby's bum. The water is hottest near the vents where it emerges, and the surface is several degrees warmer than the bottom.

ℹ Getting There & Away

The lagoon is 47km southwest of Reykjavík and 23km southeast of Keflavík International Airport. The complex is just off the road between Keflavík and Grindavík. Bus services run year-round, as do tours (which sometimes offer better deals than a bus ticket plus lagoon admission). You must book in advance. If your bus or tour does not include lagoon entry, you must pre-book at www.bluelagoon.com.

Blue Lagoon partners with **Reykjavík Excursions** (p257), which runs buses to the lagoon from/to Reykjavík and from/to the airport. With frequent buses (10 to 16 daily, June to August; see www.bluelagoon.com for details), you can do a round trip from either Reykjavík or the airport, or stop off at the lagoon on your way between

---

DIY GOLDEN CIRCLE

It's very easy to tour the Golden Circle on your own (by bike or car) – plus, it's fun to tack on additional elements that suit your interests. In the Golden Circle area, signs are well marked, roads well paved and the distances relatively short (it takes about four hours to drive the loop without any add-on stops). You can also cobble some of it together by bus (and buses do go into highlands not accessible by 2WD). The excellent, free *Uppsveitir Árnessýslu* map details the region; find it at tourist offices.

The primary points of the Golden Circle are Þingvellir, Geysir and Gullfoss. DIYers can add the following elements to their tour:

Laugarvatn Located between Þingvellir and Geysir, this small lakeside town has two must-tries: Lindin, an excellent restaurant, and Fontana, an upmarket geothermal spa.

Þjórsárdalur Largely untouristed, the quiet valley along the Þjórsá river is dotted with ancient Viking ruins and mysterious natural wonders such as the Gjáin canyon. Ultimately it leads up into the highlands (a main route to Landmannalaugar, the starting point of the famous Laugavegurinn hike).

Reykholt & Flúðir On your way south from Gullfoss, you can go river-rafting on the Hvítá river from Reykholt or swing through the geothermal area of Flúðir, for its beautiful natural spa and to pick up fresh veggies for your evening meal.

Eyrarbakki & Stokkseyri South of Selfoss, these two seaside townships are strikingly different from others nearby. Feast on seafood, peruse seasonal local galleries and bird-watch in nearby marshes.

Kaldidalur Corridor Not all rentals are allowed to drive this bumpy dirt track (Rte 550), but if you have a sanctioned vehicle, you can explore this isolated road that curves around hulking glaciers. It starts near Þingvellir and ends near Húsafell, so if you have time, do the traditional Golden Circle in reverse, then head westward, where many more adventures await.

Kerlingarfjöll You'll need a 4WD (or to go by bus) to travel beyond Gullfoss, but if you have one, it's worth continuing on to this highland reserve, a hiker haven, about two hours beyond the falls.

the two. These bus tickets can be booked when you book lagoon entry.

Bustravel (☑ 511 2600; www.bustravel.is) also runs return transfers from the airport or Reykjavík (both kr4400).

The Golden Circle

The Golden Circle takes in three popular attractions all within 100km of the capital: Þingvellir, Geysir and Gullfoss. It is an artificial tourist circuit (ie no natural topography marks its extent) loved (and marketed) by thousands, and not to be confused with the Ring Road, which wraps around the entire country (and takes a week or more to properly complete). The Golden Circle offers the opportunity to see a meeting-point of the continental plates and site of the ancient Icelandic parliament (Þingvellir), a spouting hot spring (Geysir) and a roaring waterfall (Gullfoss), all in one doable-in-a-day loop. Visiting under your own steam allows you to visit at off-peak hours and explore exciting attractions further afield. Almost every tour company in the Reykjavík area offers a Golden Circle excursion (from bus to bike to super-Jeep), often combinable with other sights as well.

◎ Sights

Þingvellir National Park   NATIONAL PARK
(www.thingvellir.is) Þingvellir National Park, 40km northeast of central Reykjavík, is Iceland's most important historical site. The Vikings established the world's first democratic parliament, the **Alþingi** (pronounced *ál-thingk-ee*, also called Alþing) here in AD 930. The meetings were conducted outdoors, and as with many saga sites, there are only the stone foundations of ancient encampments. The site has a superb natural setting, in an immense, fissured rift valley, caused by the meeting of the North American and Eurasian tectonic plates, with rivers and waterfalls.

Gullfoss   WATERFALL
(Golden Falls; www.gullfoss.is) FREE Iceland's most famous waterfall, Gullfoss is a spectacular double cascade dropping a dramatic 32m. As it descends, it kicks up magnificent walls of spray before thundering down a rocky ravine. On sunny days the mist creates shimmering rainbows, while in winter the falls glitter with ice. Although it's a popular sight, the remote location still makes you feel the ineffable forces of nature that have worked this landscape

for millennia. Above the falls there's a small tourist information centre, shop and cafe.

Geysir   GEYSER
FREE One of Iceland's most famous tourist attractions, Geysir (gay-zeer; literally 'gusher') is the original hot-water spout after which all other geysers are named. Earthquakes can stimulate activity, though eruptions are rare. Luckily for visitors, the very reliable geyser, **Strokkur**, sits alongside. You rarely have to wait more than five to 10 minutes for the hot spring to shoot an impressive 15m to 30m plume.

⌑ Sleeping & Eating

If you're planning to spend the night in the relatively small Golden Circle region, the Laugarvatn area is a good base, or choose from accommodation scattered along Rte 35.

River Hotel   HOTEL €€
(☑ 487 5004; www.riverhotel.is; Þykkvabæjarvegur, Rte 25; d/f kr24,000/33,000; P 🛜) Relax and watch the river glide by through giant plate-glass windows in the lounge areas of this immaculate hotel on the banks of the Ytri-Rangá river. Contemporary rooms and a separate cottage are super-comfortable and there's an on-site restaurant for dinner. It's ideal for Northern Lights watching as well, and the owners are avid anglers.

❶ Getting There & Away

A huge array of tours take in the Golden Circle, or Reykjavík Excursions (www.re.is) offers hop-on-hop-off bus service (kr13,400). It's also very easy to drive on your own, which allows flexibility in routes and timing.

Reykjanesfólkvangur Reserve

For a taste of Iceland's raw countryside, visit this 300-sq-km wilderness reserve, a mere 40km from Reykjavík. Established in 1975, the reserve protects the elaborate lava formations created by the dramatic Reykjanes ridge volcanoes. Its three show pieces are Kleifarvatn, a deep mineral lake with submerged hot springs and black-sand beaches; the spitting, bubbling Krýsuvík geothermal zone at Seltún; and the Southwest's largest bird cliffs, the epic Krýsuvíkurberg. The whole area is criss-crossed by walking trails. Get good maps at Keflavík, Grindavík or Hafnarfjörður tourist offices. You'll see parking turnouts at the head of the most popular walks, including the loop around Kleifarvatn, and the tracks along the craggy Sveifluháls and Núpshlíðarháls ridges.

⊙ Sights & Activities

Seltún
HOT SPRINGS

The volatile geothermal field Austurengjar, about 2km south of Kleifarvatn, is often called Krýsuvík after the nearby abandoned farm. At the main sight, Seltún, boardwalks meander round a cluster of seething hot springs. The mud pots and steaming sulphuric solfataras (volcanic vents) shimmer with rainbow colours from the minerals in the earth.

Grænavatn
LAKE

Just to the south of the Seltún hot springs, this lake is an old explosion crater filled with gorgeous teal water, caused by a combination of minerals and warmth-loving algae.

Kleifarvatn
LAKE

This deep, brooding lake sits in a volcanic fissure, surrounded by wind-warped lava cliffs and black-sand shores. A walking trail runs around the edge, offering dramatic views and the crunch of volcanic cinders underfoot. Legend has it that a wormlike monster the size of a whale lurks below the surface – but the poor creature is running out of room, as the lake has been shrinking ever since two major earthquakes shook the area in 2000.

Krýsuvíkurberg Cliffs
BIRDWATCHING

About 3km south of Seltún across the Krýsuvíkurhraun lava fields, a dirt track leads down to the coast at Krýsuvíkurberg (marked on the main road as Krýsuvíkurbjarg). These sweeping black cliffs stretch for 4km and are packed with some 57,000 seabird breeding pairs in summer, from guillemots to occasional puffins. A walking path runs the length of the cliffs.

ⓘ Getting There & Away

There is no public transport within the wilds of the park, so either come with your own wheels, or on one of the many guided tours on offer.

THE WEST

Geographically close to Reykjavík, yet far, far away in sentiment, West Iceland (known as Vesturland) is a splendid microcosm of what Iceland has to offer. Yet many tourists have missed the memo, and you're likely to have remote parts of this wonderful region to yourself.

The long arm of Snæfellsnes Peninsula is a favourite for its glacier, Snæfellsjökull, and the area around its national park is tops for birding, whale watching, lava-field hikes and horse riding. Inland beyond Reykholt you'll encounter lava tubes and remote highland glaciers, including enormous Langjökull with its unusual ice cave. Icelanders honour West Iceland for its local sagas: two of the best known, *Laxdæla Saga* and *Egil's Saga*, took place along the region's brooding waters, marked today by haunting cairns and an exceptional museum in lively Borgarnes. West Iceland offers everything from windswept beaches to historic villages and awe-inspiring terrain in one neat little package.

Snæfellsnes Peninsula

Sparkling fjords, dramatic volcanic peaks, sheer sea cliffs, sweeping golden beaches and crunchy lava flows make up the diverse and fascinating landscape of the 100km-long Snæfellsnes Peninsula. The area is crowned by the glistening ice cap Snæfellsjökull, immortalised in Jules Verne's *Journey to the Centre of the Earth*. Good roads and regular buses mean that it's an easy trip from Reykjavík, offering a cross section of the best Iceland has to offer in a very compact region.

Stykkishólmur, on the populated northern coast, is the region's largest town and a logical base. Moving west along the northern coast, you'll pass smaller townships. On the western part of the peninsula, Snæfellsjökull National Park encompasses not only its glacier but bird sanctuaries and lava fields. The quiet southern coast has several good horse farms beneath towering crags.

Stykkishólmur
POP 1110

The charming town of Stykkishólmur (www. visitstykkisholmur.is), the largest on the Snæfellsnes Peninsula, is built up around a natural harbour tipped by a basalt islet. It's a picturesque place with a laid-back attitude and a sprinkling of brightly coloured buildings from the late 19th century. With a comparatively good choice of accommodation and restaurants, and handy transport links, Stykkishólmur makes an excellent base for exploring the region. There's free wi-fi throughout the whole town. Stykkishólmur featured in Ben Stiller's *The Secret Life of Walter Mitty* (2013).

◉ Sights

★ Súgandisey
ISLAND

The basalt island Súgandisey features a scenic lighthouse and grand views across Breiðafjörður. Reach it via the stone causeway from Stykkishólmur harbour.

★ Norska Húsið
MUSEUM

(Norwegian House; ☑ 433 8114; www.norskahusid.is; Hafnargata 5; adult/child kr1000/free; ⊙ 11am-6pm daily May-Aug, 2-5pm Tue-Thu Sep-Apr) Stykkishólmur's quaint maritime charm comes from the cluster of wooden warehouses, shops and homes orbiting the town's harbour. Most date back about 150 years. One of the most interesting (and oldest) is the Norska Húsið, now the regional museum. Built by trader and amateur astronomer Árni Thorlacius in 1832, the house has been skilfully restored and displays a wonderfully eclectic selection of local antiquities. On the 2nd floor you visit Árni's home, an upper-class 19th-century residence, decked out with his original wares.

Helgafell
MOUNTAIN

About 5km south of Stykkishólmur, the holy mountain Helgafell (73m) was once venerated by worshippers of the god Þór. Although quite small, the mountain was so sacred in Saga times that elderly Icelanders would seek it out near the time of their death. Today, locals believe that wishes are granted to those who climb the mount.

✦ Activities

Stykkishólmur Swimming Pool
GEOTHERMAL POOL, HOT-POT

(Sundlaug Stykkishóms; ☑ 433 8150; Borgarbraut 4; adult/child kr800/220; ⊙ 7am-10pm Mon-Thu, to 7pm Fri, 10am-6pm Sat & Sun Jun-Aug, reduced hours Sep-May) Water slides and hot-pots are the highlights at the town's geothermal swimming pool, in the municipal sports complex.

Seatours
BOATING

(Sæferðir; ☑ 433 2254; www.seatours.is; Smiðjustígur 3; ⊙ 8am-8pm mid-May–mid-Sep, 9am-5pm mid-Sep–mid-May) Various boat tours, including the much-touted 'Viking Sushi', a one- or two-hour boat ride (kr6220/7700) taking in islands, bird colonies (puffins until August) and basalt formations. A net brings up shellfish to devour raw. Also offers dinner cruises and runs the Baldur Ferry to Flatey.

WISHING AT HELGAFELL

It is commonly believed that those who ascend humble Helgafell will be granted three wishes, provided that the requests are made with a pure heart. However, you must follow three important steps to make your wishes come true:

Step 1 Start at the grave of Guðrún Ósvífursdóttir, heroine of an ancient local saga.

Step 2 Walk up to the Tótt (the chapel ruins), not uttering a single word, and (like Orpheus leaving Hades) never looking back.

Step 3 Once at the chapel ruins, you must face east while wishing. And never tell your wishes to anyone, or they won't come true.

Partners with Reykjavík Excursions for Reykjavík pick-up. On-site shop and cafe. Children under 15 travel free.

⌇ Sleeping

Harbour Hostel
HOSTEL €

(☑ 517 5353; www.harbourhostel.is; Hafnargata 4; dm/d/q without bathroom from kr4400/9400/14,300; ☑) This simple harbourside hostel offers some of the town's best cheap lodging, with dorm rooms (four-, eight- and 12-bed dorms), doubles and family rooms.

★ Hótel Egilsen
BOUTIQUE HOTEL €€€

(☑ 554 7700; www.egilsen.is; Aðalgata 2; s/d kr25,600/31,500; @☑) One of our favourite little inns in Iceland, this boutique hotel fills a lovingly restored timber house that creaks in the most charming way when winds howl off the fjord. The friendly owner has outfitted cosy (tiny!) rooms with traditional woollen blankets, original artwork and organic Coco-Mat mattresses. Complimentary iPads and a homemade breakfast (kr2500) sweeten the deal.

Fransiskus Hotel
HOTEL €€€

(☑ 422 1101; www.fransiskus.is; Austurgata 7; s with/without bathroom incl breakfast from kr18,900/13,900, d/f incl breakfast from kr30,100/35,400; ℗☑) This hotel in a renovated wing of a Catholic monastery and hospital complex offers well-maintained modern rooms with private bathrooms and flat-screen TVs.

✖ Eating

Meistarinn   FAST FOOD €
(📞848 0153; www.facebook.com/meistarinnsth;
Aðalgata; hot dogs kr540-600, sub sandwiches
kr1400-1600; ⊙noon-8pm Jun-Aug) This friendly *pylsuvagninn* (hot-dog wagon) has the
best hot dogs in town. Each menu item is
named after someone from Stykkishólmur.

★Narfeyrarstofa   ICELANDIC €€
(📞533 1119; www.narfeyrarstofa.is; Aðalgata 3;
mains kr2000-5000; ⊙11.30am-midnight Mon-Thu,
to 1am Fri-Sun May-Sep, reduced hours Oct-Apr; 🖋)
This charming restaurant is the Snæfellsnes'
darling fine-dining destination. Book a table
on the 2nd floor for the romantic lighting of
antique lamps and harbour views. Ask your
waiter about the portraits on the wall – the
building has an interesting history.

Sjávarpakkhúsið   ICELANDIC €€
(📞438 1800; www.sjavarpakkhusid.is; Hafnargata 2; mains kr2790-3500; ⊙noon-11pm Sun-Thu,
to 3am Fri & Sat Jun-Aug, reduced hours Sep-May;
🖥) This old fish-packing house has been
transformed into a wood-lined cafe-bar with
harbour-front outdoor seating. The speciality is blue-shell mussels straight from the
bay. It's a great daytime hang-out too, and
on weekend evenings it turns into a popular
bar where locals come to jam.

❶ Getting There & Away

You can get to Reykjavík (2½ hours) by changing
in Borgarnes. All services are greatly reduced
in winter.

Strætó (p280) services from the **bus stop**
(Aðalgata) at the Olís petrol station:
➡ Bus 58 to Borgarnes (kr2640, 1½ hours, two
daily).
➡ Bus 82 to Arnarstapi via Grundarfjörður–
Ólafsvík–Rif–Hellissandur (kr2200, 1¼ hours,
two daily June to mid-September). The rest
of the year it only goes from Stykkishólmur to
Hellissandur, four days per week.

Snæfellsjökull National Park

Snæfellsjökull National Park (📞436 6860;
www.snaefellsjokull.is) encompasses much of
the western tip of Snæfellsnes Peninsula
and wraps around the rugged slopes of the
glacier Snæfellsjökull, the icy fist at the end
of the long Snæfellsnes arm. Around its
flanks lie lava tubes, protected lava fields,
which are home to native Icelandic fauna,
and prime hiking and coastal bird- and
whale-watching spots.

When the fog swirling around the glacier
lifts, you'll see the mammoth ice cap, which
was made famous when Jules Verne used it
as the setting for *Journey to the Centre of
the Earth*. In his book, a German geologist
and his nephew embark on an epic journey into the crater of Snæfells, guided by a
16th-century Icelandic text with the following advice:

*Descend into the crater of Yocul of Sneffels,
which the shade of Scartaris caresses, before
the kalends of July, audacious traveller, and
you will reach the centre of the earth.*

◉ Sights

★Snæfellsjökull   GLACIER
It's easy to see why Jules Verne selected
Snæfell for his adventure *Journey to the
Centre of the Earth*: the peak was torn apart
when the volcano beneath it exploded and
then collapsed back into its own magma
chamber, forming a huge caldera. Among
certain New Age groups, Snæfellsjökull is
considered one of the world's great 'power
centres'. Today the crater is filled with the ice
cap (highest point 1446m) and is a popular
summer destination.

The best way to reach the glacial summit is to take a tour with **Summit Adventure Guides** (📞787 0001; www.summitguides.
is), **Snæfellsjökull Glacier Tours** (📞663
3371; www.theglacier.is; snowcat/snowmobile
tours kr12,500/28,000; ⊙Mar-Jul) or **Go West!**
(📞695 9995; www.gowest.is) 🖋. These companies approach the peak from the south,
on Rte F570; Rte F570's northern approach
(near Ólafsvík) is frustratingly rutty (4WD
needed) and frequently closed due to weath-
er-inflicted damage. Even the well trained
and outfitted are not allowed to ascend the
glacier without a local guide; contact the National Park Visitor Centre (p241) in Malarrif
for more information.

★Djúpalón Beach   BEACH
(Djúpalónssandur) On the southwest coast,
Rte 572 leads off Rte 574 to wild black-sand
beach Djúpalónssandur. It's a dramatic place
to walk, with rock formations (an elf church,
and a *kerling* – a troll woman), two brackish
pools (for which the beach was named), and
the rock-arch **Gatklettur**. Some of the black
sands are covered in pieces of rusted metal
from the English trawler *Eding*, which was
shipwrecked here in 1948. An asphalt car
park and public toilets allow tour-bus access,
and crowds.

☆ Activities

Today, the park is criss-crossed with hiking trails, and during proper weather it is possible to visit the glacier with a tour or guide. Malarrif is home to the National Park Visitor Centre (p241), and in the area tourist offices sell maps and give advice, too. The park's online map is also excellent. Rangers have an active summer program of free park guided tours; check online or email.

ℹ Information

National Park Visitor Centre – Gestastofa (Snæfellsjökull National Park Visitor Centre; ☑ 591 2000, 436 6888; www.snaefellsjokull. is; Malarrif; ⊙10am-5pm daily Jun-Sep, 11am-4pm Mon-Fri Oct-May; ☜) This office in Malarrif is the go-to spot for information on Snæfellsjökull National Park, with maps and brochures, as well as displays on local geology, history, flora, fauna and customs. NB: the park office in Hellissandur is administrative only and not open to the public.

ℹ Getting There & Away

Strætó bus 82 Stykkishólmur–Anarstapi runs twice daily from June to mid-September (four days per week in the rest of the year, when it only goes as far as Hellissandur).

Having your own wheels is the best way to see the park.

THE WESTFJORDS

To the east of Snæfellsjökull National Park, coastal Rte 574 passes the hamlets of Hellnar and Arnarstapi, with their glacier tour companies and interesting sea-sculpted rock formations. It continues east along the broad southern coastal plain, hugging huge sandy bays such as Breiðavík on one side, and towering peaks with waterfalls on the other. This stretch has some super horse riding.

Ísafjörður

POP 2559

The hub of Westfjords adventure tours, and by far the region's largest town, Ísafjörður (www.isafjordur.is) is a pleasant and prosperous place and an excellent base for travellers. The town is set on an arcing spit that extends out into Skutulsfjörður, and is hemmed in on all sides by towering peaks and the dark waters of the fjord.

The centre of Ísafjörður is a charming grid of old timber and tin-clad buildings, many unchanged since the 18th century, when the harbour was full of tall ships and Norwegian whaling crews. Today it is a surprisingly cosmopolitan place, and after some time spent travelling in the Westfjords, it'll feel like a bustling metropolis with its tempting cafes and fine choice of restaurants.

There's hiking in the hills around the town, skiing in winter, and regular summer boats ferry hikers across to the remote Hornstrandir Peninsula.

◉ Sights

★**Westfjords Heritage Museum** MUSEUM (Byggðasafn Vestfjarða; ☑ 456 3293; www.ned-sti.is; Neðstíkaupstaður; adult/child kr1000/free; ⊙9am-6pm mid-May–mid-Sep) Part of a cluster of historic wooden buildings by the harbour, the Westfjords Heritage Museum is in the Turnhús (1784), which was originally a warehouse. It is crammed with fishing and nautical exhibits, tools from the whaling days, accordions and fascinating old photos depicting town life over the centuries. To the right is the Tjöruhús (1781), now an excellent seafood restaurant. The Faktorhús (1765), which housed the manager of the village shop, and the Krambúd (1757), originally a storehouse, are now private residences.

☞ Tours

West Tours (Vesturferðir; ☑ 456 5111; www.westtours.is; Aðalstræti 7; ⊙8am-6pm Mon-Fri, 8.30am-4.30pm Sat, 10am-3pm Sun Jun-Aug, 8am-4pm Mon-Fri Sep-May) and **Wild Westfjords** (☑456 3300; www.wildwestfjords.com; Hafnarstræti 9; ⊙9am-6pm Jun-Aug, reduced hours Sep-May) offer cultural walking tours around Ísafjörður; you can also book online at http://isafjordur-guide.is. Both West Tours and **Borea** (☑456 3322; www.borea.is; Aðalstræti 22b; ⊙9am-7pm Mon-Fri, to 6pm Sat & Sun Jun-Aug, reduced hours Sep-May) run summer ferry services to Hornstrandir Nature Reserve (p243).

⊨ Sleeping

Tungudalur Campground CAMPGROUND € (☑864 8592; www.gih.is; sites per adult/child kr1700/free; ⊙mid-Jun–mid-Sep; ☜) This campground is almost 5km out of town and very scenic, set by pretty waterfall Bunarfoss, in Tungudalur. The last stop on the town bus will take you to within 1km of the site. Kitchen and coin laundry available.

★ Gentle Space
Guesthouse & Apartments   APARTMENT €€

(☑ 892 9282; www.gentlespace.is; Hlíðarvegur 14; r/apt from kr13,500/20,800; 🛜) This family-run outfit offers three rooms with kitchenettes and flat-screen TVs in a small, well-run guesthouse, and rents immaculate, fully equipped apartments in the centre.

Gamla Gistihúsið   GUESTHOUSE €€

(☑ 456 4146; www.gistihus.is; Mánagata 5; d/tr without bathroom incl breakfast kr23,500/30,000; @🛜) Bright, cheerful and well kept, this excellent guesthouse owned by Hótel Ísafjörður (p242) has simple but comfortable rooms with plenty of cosy touches. The bathrooms are shared, but each double room has a telephone, washbasin and bathrobes. An annexe just down the road has a guest kitchen and more modern rooms.

✖ Eating

★ Gamla Bakaríð   BAKERY €

(☑ 456 3226; Aðalstræti 24; ⊙ 7am-6pm Mon-Fri, to 4pm Sat, 8am-4pm Sun) For breakfast, lunch or a mid-morning sugar fix, there's a clutch of tempting bakeries in town. Gamla Bakaríð is usually packed for its full range of sweet treats (cookies, doughnuts and cakes) as well as fresh bread.

★ Tjöruhúsið   SEAFOOD €€

(☑ 456 4419; www.facebook.com/tjoruhusid; Neðstakaupstaður 1; mains kr2500-5500; ⊙ noon-2pm & 7-9pm Jun-Sep, reduced hours Oct-May) The warm and rustic restaurant next to the heritage museum (p241) offers some of the best seafood around. Go for the *plokkfiskur* – flaked fish, potatoes and onions – or try the various catches of the day, fresh off the boat from the harbour down the street, all served up in hot skillets. There's outdoor seating on benches when it's sunny. Occasional live music.

Húsið   INTERNATIONAL €€

(☑ 456 5555; Hrannargata 2; mains kr1700-3200; ⊙ 11am-10pm Sun-Thu, to 2am Fri & Sat; 🛜) Sidle up to the varnished, rough-hewn wood tables inside this tin-clad house, or kick back on the sunny terrace for scrumptious, relaxed meals and local beer on tap. Groovy tunes play as hip staff serve soup, sandwiches, burgers, pizza and Icelandic staples such as lamb. It's a fun hang-out regardless of what you're up to, and there are occasional DJs and live music.

❶ Information

Westfjords Regional Information Centre
(☑ 450 8060; www.isafjordur.is; Aðalstræti 7, Edinborgarhús; ⊙ 8am-6pm Mon-Fri, 8.30am-2pm Sat, 10am-2pm Sun Jun-Aug, reduced hours Sep-May) The friendly tourist information centre is down by the harbour in the Edinborgarhús, built in 1907. Luggage storage is available for kr200 a day.

❶ Getting There & Away

AIR

Air Iceland Connect (☑ 570 3030; www.airicelandconnect.is) flies between **Ísafjörður Airport** (IFJ; ☑ 570 3000), 5km south on the fjord, and Reykjavík's domestic airport twice daily. It also offers day tours.

A **Flybus** (p243), timed to meet flights, runs between the airport and Bolungarvík (kr1500), and stops near the **Hótel Ísafjörður** (☑ 456 4111; www.hotelisafjordur.is; Silfurtorg 2;) (kr1000).

BOAT

In summer **West Tours** (p245) and **Borea** (p245) ferries to Hornstrandir depart from the **Sundahöfn docks** (p245) on the eastern side of the town promontory.

BUS

Ísafjörður is the major bus hub in the Westfjords. The **long-distance bus stop** (www.westfjords.is; Aðalstræti) is at the tourist information centre.

Westfjords Adventures (www.wa.is) services:
➡ From June to August there's a bus to Patreksfjörður (kr9900) and Brjánslækur (the terminal for the Stykkishólmur ferry; kr8400) via Þingeyri, Dynjandi and Flókalundur (one daily each direction Monday, Wednesday and Friday).
➡ You must prebook in late May and early September.
➡ There are no buses in the off season.

Hópferðamiðstöð Vestfjarða (vidfjordinn@ vidfjordinn.is) operates buses mid-May to mid-September between Ísafjörður and Hólmavík, four times a week.

To get to Reykjavík, take a bus to Hólmavík or Brjánslækur then transfer. In Hólmavík, catch Strætó (www.bus.is) bus 59 to Borgarnes, where you transfer again. In Brjánslækur, take the ferry to Stykkishólmur then catch Strætó bus 58 to Borgarnes. To get to Akureyri, you also need to transfer in Borgarnes; alternatively you can transfer in Bifröst to the middle-of-the-night Sterna (www.sternatravel.com) bus 60, or stay overnight (no campground there, though) and catch the Strætó bus 57 to Akureyri in the morning.

Municipal buses (☑ 456 5518; www.isafjordur. is) stop at marked **stops** (Skutulsfjarðarbraut) along the waterfront:

➡ Flateyri and Þingeyri (kr350, three daily Monday to Friday)

➡ Suðureyri (kr350, 20 minutes, three daily Monday to Friday)

➡ A bus for Bolungarvík (kr1000, 15 minutes, four daily Monday to Friday) leaves from the kiosk at Hamraborg, near the **Samkaup** (Hafnarstræti 9, Neisti Centre; ⊙10am-8pm Mon-Sat, noon-8pm Sun) supermarket.

Flybus (www.isafjordur.is; Hafnarstræti) services:

➡ Buses are timed to meet Icelandair flights (but anyone can use them); they run the route Bolungarvík–Ísafjörður–Airport–Ísafjörður–Bolungarvík.

➡ In Ísafjörður they stop near the **Hótel Ísafjörður**, about 45 minutes before departure.

Check with the **information centre** (p242) or www.westfjords.is for current schedules.

Hornstrandir

Craggy mountains, precarious sea cliffs and plunging waterfalls ring the wonderful, barely inhabited Hornstrandir Peninsula, at the northern end of the Westfjords. This is one of Europe's last true wilderness areas, covering some of the most extreme and inhospitable parts of the country. It's a fantastic destination for hiking, with challenging terrain and excellent opportunities for spotting Arctic foxes, seals, whales and teeming bird life.

A handful of hardy farmers lived in Hornstrandir until the 1950s, but since 1975 the 580 sq km of tundra, fjord, glacier and alpine upland have been protected as **Hornstrandir Nature Reserve** (📷591 2000; www.ust.is/hornstrandir) and are a national monument. The area has some of the strictest preservation rules in Iceland, thanks to its incredibly rich, but fragile, vegetation. Descendants of some of the old farmers have recently returned and rebuilt their old houses; much of the land is privately owned (so be respectful towards the privacy of landowners). Always stick to marked trails, and don't disturb or take things along the way.

🧭 Tours

The main operators running tours (boating, hiking, kayaking, skiing etc) into Hornstrandir are West Tours (p241), Borea (p241) and Wild Westfjords (p241), based in Ísafjörður.

🛏 Sleeping

Camping is the main way to stay in Hornstrandir. There are also three options for sleeping-bag accommodation in the main part of Hornstrandir: Hesteyri, Hornbjargsviti and Bolungarvík á Ströndum. Two additional options are in the far-eastern part of the reserve at Reykjarfjörður and Bolungarvík.

Hornbjargsviti   HOSTEL €
(📷852 0333, Ferðafélag Íslands 568 2533; www.fi.is; sites per person kr2000, dm kr8000; ⊙ Jul–early-Aug) Run by Ferðafélag Íslands (FI), and attached to the lighthouse of the same name on

ICELAND HORNSTRANDIR

ⓘ WEATHER, SAFETY & GEAR

There are no services available in Hornstrandir and hikers must be fully prepared to tackle all eventualities. The passes are steep, heavy rains will make rivers impassable, fog can be dense and you'll need to carry all your gear, so hiking can be slower than you might expect. In addition, most trails are unmarked, primitive and uneven, so it's essential to carry a good map (try *Vestfirðir & Dalir: 1*), a compass and a GPS. Rangers stress the need for high-quality, completely weatherproof gear as you will often be hiking in rain, without any way to get dry. Don't force a rescue operation due to ill preparation.

The best time to visit is in July. Outside the summer season (which runs from late June to mid-August; ferry boats run June to August) there are few people around and the weather is even more unpredictable. It is essential to plan ahead and get local advice, as vast snow drifts with near-vertical faces can develop on the mountain passes, rivers can be unfordable etc. Before 15 June it is mandatory to register with a **ranger** (p245). It's also always smart to register your plans with www.safetravel.is. At various points in the park there are emergency huts with VHF radios preset to the Icelandic Coast Guard in case of emergency. Emergency huts are often located near campsites.

You always need to book your return boat in advance; this serves as a safety measure, in case you don't turn up for it. Ask local operators about current conditions before setting off. Guided trips can also be easily arranged with Ísafjörður operators.

the east coast, this hostel sleeps 40 and has a kitchen and coin-operated showers. Campers have access to toilets but not the hut kitchen.

Reykjarfjörður
HUT €

(☎ 456 7545; www.reykjarfjordur.is; sites per person kr1000; dm kr4000, cottage from kr15,000; ☺ Jun & Jul) Choose from camping, a sleeping-bag bed (no electricity) or a small cottage that sleeps five. There's also a geothermal pool and hot-pot. The hut is located in the Hornstrandir Nature Reserve (p243), not to be confused with Reykjarfjörður further south on the Strandir coast.

Bolungarvík á Ströndum
HUT €

(☎ 893 6926, 861 1425; hut per person kr4000; ☺ Jul, rest of year by appointment) Bolungarvík's basic hut sits on the southeast coast of Hornstrandir and is usually used by hikers walking in or out.

Old Doctor's House
HOSTEL €€

(☎ 845 5075, Hesteyri 899 7661; www.hesteyri.net; Hesteyri; d incl breakfast & dinner kr16,000; ☺ Jun–Aug) By far the most developed lodging in Hornstrandir. A stay at this cafe-guesthouse involves dinner, bed and a buffet breakfast. Book well ahead for June and July.

HIKING HORNSTRANDIR

How is one supposed to choose from the array of trails that zigzag across Hornstrandir's peninsula? Locals and tourists agree: the Royal Horn (or 'Hornsleið') is, hands down, your best option for getting a taste of all that the reserve has to offer. This four- to five-day hike from Veiðileysufjörður to Hesteyri can also be easily modified if you run into bad weather. The trail is marked with cairns, but there are very few tourists, so keep track of the route. It's a great way to experience this remote land.

The Royal Horn

Day 1 Sail from Ísafjörður to Veiðileysufjörður, one of the local jökulfirðir (glacier fjords). The hike begins on a street near the bottom of the fjord and follows a cairn-marked trail up the slope and through the mountain pass. From the pass you can descend the mountain on either side until you reach the campground at Höfn in Hornvík. The hike from Veiðileysufjörður to Hornvík can take anywhere between four and eight hours. There's a ranger station at the campground at Höfn in Hornvík, so feel free to get the latest weather forecast and information about trail conditions.

Day 2 Stay in Hornvík for a second night and use your second day to visit **Hornbjarg**, one of Iceland's most beautiful bird cliffs with diverse flora and fauna. Alternatively, you could spend the second day exploring the area around the lighthouse, **Hornbjargsviti**.

Day 3 Hike from Hornvík to Hlöðuvík. The partly marked trail goes through a mountain pass and is relatively easy to find. At Hlöðuvík, the campsite is situated next to **Hlöðuvíkurós** (the mouth of the Hlöðuvík river). Like Hornvík, Hlöðuvík faces north – it's the perfect place to watch the spectacular midnight sun. Figure around six hours to reach Hlöðuvík.

Day 4 Hike through **Kjarnsvíkurskarð** (a mountain pass) and **Hesteyrarbrúnir** pass to Hesteyri (figure around eight hours). **Hesteyri** is an old village that was abandoned around the middle of the 20th century. There are still several well-kept houses amid the fields of angelica. Ruins of a turn-of-the-century whaling station are found near the village. The **coffee shop** in Hesteyri is a good place to stop at the end of your hike – you can wait here for the ferry back to Bolungarvík or Ísafjörður.

Day 5 If the ferry isn't running the day you arrive, enjoy a night in Hesteyri and spend one more day exploring the area before catching the boat. Pitch your tent at the campground or, if you prebooked, stay at the **Old Doctor's House** (p244).

Abridged Hike

You can take the ferry to Veiðileysufjörður, hike up to Hornvík, spend a night (or two) there, and walk down to Lónafjörður to link back up with a boat, but only if you have prebooked it. The walk from Hornvík to Lónafjörður takes around six to seven hours. Or you could backtrack to Veiðileysufjörður.

Alternatively, just sail in and use Hesteyri as a day-hike base (prebook if you want sleeping-bag accommodation).

✕ Eating

Besides the basic meals available at the Old Doctor's House (p244) in Hesteyri, you'll need to bring in all food and supplies.

Campfires are prohibited in the reserve, and cooking equipment should be used with caution.

ℹ Information

Hornstrandir Park Rangers (Environmental Agency of Iceland; ☑ 591 2000; www.ust.is/hornstrandir)

ℹ Getting There & Away

Take a ferry from Ísafjörður (at the **Sundahöfn** docks on the eastern side of the town promontory) or Norðurfjörður (on the Strandir Coast) to Hornstrandir from June to August. One-way rides cost kr10,200–16,700, depending on your destination; children are half-price.

It is strongly advised to book your return boat ticket, for safety reasons. You can book all boats direct, or through **West Tours** (p241).

From Ísafjörður, West Tours runs **Sjóferðir** (☑ bookings 456 5111; www.sjoferdir.is) boats to the following, among other destinations:

➡ Aðalvík (kr10,600, two weekly)
➡ Grunnavík (kr10,200, one weekly)
➡ Hesteyri (kr10,200, six weekly)
➡ Hornvík (kr16,700, one weekly)
➡ Hrafnfjörður (kr14,800, one weekly)
➡ Veiðileysufjörður (kr12,600, two weekly)

Also from Ísafjörður, **Borea** (p241) runs **Bjarnarnes** (☑ 456 3322; www.boreaadventures.com) boats to:

➡ Aðalvík (kr10,600, two weekly)
➡ Grunnavík (kr10,200, three weekly)
➡ Hesteyri (kr10,200, four weekly)
➡ Hornvík (kr16,700, two weekly)
➡ Veiðileysufjörður (kr12,600, five weekly)

Hornbjargsviti, Hlöðuvík, Fljótavík, Slétta (Sléttunes) and Lónafjörður are by request only. In early June and late August there is an eight-person minimum.

From Norðurfjörður on the Strandir coast, **Strandferðir** (☑ 849 4079, 859 9570, West Tours bookings 456 5111; www.strandferdir.is; Norðurfjörður, Hornstrandir) boats run on a schedule from June to mid-August or can be chartered to Drangar (kr8500), Reykjarfjörður (kr9500), Þaralátursfjörður/Furufjörður (kr12,500), Bolungarvík (in Hornstrandir, not the town of the same name west of Ísafjörður), Látravík/Hornbjargsviti (kr14,500) and Hornvík (kr15,500).

Látrabjarg Peninsula

Best known for its dramatic cliffs and abundant bird life, the remote Látrabjarg Peninsula also has wonderful, deserted, multihued beaches, like exquisite Rauðasandur (p245), and plenty of long, leisurely walks. Roads are sandy, pitted and bumpy.

◉ Sights & Activities

Rauðasandur   BEACH
Stunning Rauðasandur beach stretches out in shades of pink and red sands on the southern edge of the peninsula. Pounded by surf and backed by a huge azure lagoon, it's an exceptionally beautiful, serene place. You can walk out to the lagoon edge at low tide; always keep a lookout for seals. A coastal path (about 20km one way) runs between Rauðasandur and the Látrabjarg bird cliffs (p245). Approach Rauðasandur by car from Rte 612 by taking bumpy Rte 614 for about 10km.

Breiðavík   BEACH
An enormous and stunning golden-sand beach is framed by rocky cliffs and the turquoise waters of the bay. Certainly one of Iceland's best beaches, this idyllic spot is usually deserted. The large **Hotel Breiðavík** (☑ 456 1575; www.breidavik.is; Breiðavík Bay; sites per adult/child kr2000/free, d with/without bathroom incl breakfast kr31,500/21,500; ☉ mid-May–mid-Sep; 🛜) is here.

Látrabjarg Bird Cliffs   BIRDWATCHING
These renowned and dramatic bird cliffs, just up from **Bjargtangar Lighthouse**, extend for 12km along the coast. They range from 40m to 400m and are mobbed by nesting seabirds in early summer; it's a fascinating place even for the most reluctant of twitchers. Unbelievable numbers of puffins, razorbills, guillemots, cormorants, fulmars, gulls and kittiwakes nest here from June to mid-August.

ℹ Getting There & Away

From June to August there's one Westfjords Adventures (www.wa.is) bus (kr14,500, Monday, Wednesday and Friday) from Brjánslækur to Patreksfjörður, Látrabjarg and **Rauðasandur** (p245), then back to Patreksfjörður and Brjánslækur, returning to Brjánslækur in time for the ferry back to Stykkishólmur. If you get on at **Breiðavík** (p245) it costs kr8000 to the bird cliffs and back.

Two-wheel-drive cars can traverse the rutted tracks slowly, but there is no petrol on the peninsula. Fuel up in Patreksfjörður.

THE NORTH

Iceland's mammoth and magnificent north is a geologist's heaven. A wonderland of moonlike lava fields, belching mudpots, epic waterfalls, snowcapped peaks and whale-filled bays – this is Iceland at its best. The region's top sights are variations on one theme: a grumbling, volcanically active earth.

There are endless treats to uncover: little Akureyri, with its surprising moments of big-city living; windy fjordside pastures full of stout Viking horses; fishing villages clinging tenaciously to life at the end of unsealed roads.

Prepare to be enticed. Offshore islands are populated by colonies of seabirds and a few hardy locals while lonely peninsulas stretch out towards the Arctic Circle. White-water rapids are ready to deliver an adrenalin kick and national-park walking trails reach unparalleled views. Unhyped and underpopulated ski fields await and underwater marvels woo divers into frigid depths.

Siglufjörður

POP 1200

Sigló (as the locals call it) sits precariously at the foot of a steep slope overlooking a beautiful fjord. In its heyday it was home to 10,000 workers; fishing boats crammed into the small harbour to unload their catch for the waiting women to gut and salt.

After the herring abruptly disappeared from Iceland's north coast in the late 1960s, Siglufjörður declined and never fully recovered.

New tunnels now link the town with Ólafsfjörður and points further south, and these days Sigló is receiving warranted attention from travellers smitten by its fishing, marina and excellent diversions (and its role as the sordid small town in the 2015 Icelandic TV series *Trapped,* which was filmed here). Just reaching the town (from either direction) involves a journey that will take your breath away.

⊙ Sights

★ Herring Era Museum   MUSEUM
(Síldarminjasafnið; ☑467 1604; www.sild.is; Snorragata 10; adult/child kr1800/free; ☉10am-6pm Jun-Aug, 1-5pm May & Sep, by appointment Oct-Apr) Lovingly created over 16 years, this award-winning museum does a stunning job of recreating Siglufjörður's boom days between 1903 and 1968, when it was the herring-fishing capital of Iceland. Set in three buildings that were part of an old Norwegian herring station, the museum brings the work and lives of the town's inhabitants vividly to life. Start at the red building on the left, and move right.

🏃 Activities

Siglufjörður is a great base for hikers, with a series of interesting hikes in the area. Some 19km of paths are marked along the avalanche-repelling fence above town, with numerous access points. There's a worthwhile information panel on the northern outskirts of town, beside a parking area, detailing these avalanche defences.

Another popular option is over the passes of Hólsskarð and Hestsskarð into the beautiful, uninhabited Héðinsfjörður, the next fjord to the east. This is where the tunnels connecting Siglufjörður and Ólafsfjörður see the light.

There's a lot of hiking-trail info at www.fjallabyggd.is – go to About, then Hiking.

In winter ski lifts operate in the expanded, improved ski fields at Skarðsdalur (☑878 3399; www.skardsdalur.is) above the head of the fjord. A growing number of heliskiing operators work in Tröllaskagi over the winter; contact Viking Heliskiing (☑846 1674; www.vikingheliskiing.com) based out of Ólafsfjörður for info.

🛏 Sleeping & Eating

The street opposite the supermarket is Aðalgata; it's home to a busy bakery (Aðalgata 28; soup buffet kr1600; ☉7am-5pm Mon-Fri, 8am-5pm Sat, 9am-4pm Sun) and pizzeria, but come mealtime many appetites are focused on the primary-coloured marina.

It's well worth investigating whether Siglunes Guesthouse (p247) has anything interesting cooking – it recently had a Moroccan chef preparing authentic Moroccan cuisine.

★ Herring Guesthouse   GUESTHOUSE €€
(☑868 4200; www.theherringhouse.com; Hávegur 5; s/d without bathroom kr15,500/19,900, 4-person apt kr47,800; 🛜) Þórir and Erla are charming, knowledgable hosts (he's a former town mayor) offering personalised service at their stylish, view-blessed guesthouse, now with two locations (the second is at Hlíðarvegur 1, behind the church). There is a guest kitchen at the main house, and a lovely (optional) breakfast spread (kr2500). Families will appreciate the two-bedroom apartment.

★ **Siglunes Guesthouse**   GUESTHOUSE €€
(📞 467 1222; www.hotelsiglunes.is; Lækjarga-ta 10; s from kr16,500, d with/without bathroom from kr20,900/17,4000; 🛜) Personality shines through in this cool guesthouse, where vintage furniture is paired with contemporary art and ultra-modern bathrooms in the hotel-standard wing. There are equally appealing guesthouse rooms (shared bathrooms, no kitchen), a big dining hall for breakfast (kr2200), and a cosy bar area celebrating happy hour from 5pm to 7pm. Free bikes for guests to use are a nice touch.

Sigló Hótel   HOTEL €€€
(📞 461 7730; www.siglohotel.is; Snorragata 3; d incl breakfast kr41,500) The town's 'patron', a local man made good in the US, is behind the vibrant marina redevelopment; his most recent project is this upmarket, 68-room harbourside hotel. Rooms are smart and well fitted out, but it's the public areas that shine brightest: the elegant restaurant and bar, stylish lounge and waterside hot-pot.

ℹ Information

The town has services such as a bank, pharmacy, post office etc. The **Herring Era Museum** (p246) offers some tourist info.

There's also information on the website www.fjallabyggd.is (Fjallabyggð is the municipality covering Siglufjörður and Ólafsfjörður), and more at www.visittrollaskagi.is.

Tourist Information Centre (📞 467 1555; Gránugata 24; ⊙ 9am-5pm Mon-Fri, 11am-3pm Sat & Sun Jun-Aug, reduced hours Sep-May) A helpful desk inside the Ráðhús (town hall) on Gránugata.

ℹ Getting There & Away

BUS

Strætó (p280) services:

➡ Bus 78 to Ólafsfjörður (kr880, 15 minutes, three daily Monday to Friday, one daily Sunday)

➡ Bus 78 to Akureyri (kr2640, 70 minutes, three daily Monday to Friday, one daily Sunday) runs via Dalvík.

Akureyri

POP 18,200

Akureyri (pronounced *ah*-koo-rare-ee) stands strong as Iceland's second city, but a Melbourne, Manchester or Montréal it is not. And how could it be with only 18,000 residents? It's a wonder the city (which would be a 'town' anywhere else) generates this much

buzz. Expect cool cafes, quality restaurants, a handful of art galleries and even some late-night bustle – a far cry from other rural Icelandic towns.

Akureyri nestles at the head of Eyjafjörður, Iceland's longest (60km) fjord, at the base of snowcapped peaks. In summer flowering gardens belie the location, just a stone's throw from the Arctic Circle. Lively winter festivals and some of Iceland's best skiing provide plenty of off-peak (and off-piste) appeal. With its relaxed attitude and extensive food and accommodation choices, it's the natural base for exploring Eyjafjörður and around, and it's seeing a growing number of cruise ships calling by (passenger numbers can sometimes overwhelm the town).

◉ Sights & Activities

In winter the snowfields draw skiers from all over the country, while independent summertime activities include hiking, golf and hot-pot-hopping. A helpful resource is the collection of *Útivist & afþreying* hiking maps (there are seven in the series; #1 and #2 focus on the Eyjafjörður area); these are available at **Ferðafélag Akureyrar** (Touring Club of Akureyri; 📞 462 2720; www.ffa.is; Strandgata 23; ⊙ 3-6pm Mon-Fri May-Aug, 11am-1pm Mon-Fri Sep-Apr) and the tourist office (p251).

At the time of writing there were no businesses offering bike rental, but it's worth enquiring at the tourist office to see if this has changed.

Akureyri is also the base for a multitude of tours and guided activities all over Iceland's north.

Akureyrarkirkja   CHURCH
(📞 462 7700; www.akureyrarkirkja.is; Eyrarlandsvegur; ⊙ generally 10am-4pm Mon-Fri) Dominating the town from high on a hill, Akureyri's landmark church was designed by Guðjón Samúelsson, the architect responsible for Reykjavík's Hallgrímskirkja. Although the basalt theme connects them, Akureyrarkirkja looks more like a stylised 1920s US skyscraper than its big-city sibling.

Skjaldarvík   HORSE RIDING, ADVENTURE TOUR
(📞 552 5200; www.skjaldarvik.is; horse rides kr10,900, buggy tours kr19,900) As well as operating a superb guesthouse (p249) and restaurant, Skjaldarvík offers a couple of top-notch activities from its scenic fjordside locale 6km north of town: horse-riding tours, plus a fun new adrenaline-inducing option of buggy

Akureyri

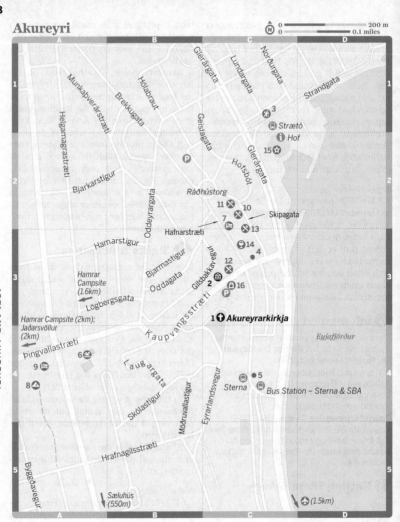

rides. These buggies are golf carts on steroids and can seat two; you'll drive along trails on the surrounding farm (driver's licence required; helmet and overalls supplied).

Sundlaug Akureyrar SWIMMING
(☎461 4455; www.facebook.com/Sundlaug-Akureyrar; Þingvallastræti 21; adult/child kr750/200; ☉6.45am-9pm Mon-Fri, 8am-7.30pm Sat & Sun; 🏊) The hub of local life, Akureyri's outdoor swimming pool is one of Iceland's finest. It has three heated pools, plus hotpots, water slides, saunas and steam rooms.

Saga Travel ADVENTURE TOUR
(☎558 8888; www.sagatravel.is; Kaupvangsstræti 4; ☉booking office 7.30am-5pm Jun-Aug, reduced hours rest of year) Offers a rich and diverse year-round program of excursions and activities throughout the north. Includes obvious destinations such as Mývatn, Húsavík (for whale watching) and Askja in the highlands, but also offers innovative tours along themes such as food or art and design. Check out Saga's full program online, or drop by its central booking office.

Akureyri

★ Festivals & Events

The Calendar page of the www.visitakureyri.is website lists events big and small. Winter events are growing in stature.

Iceland Winter Games   SPORTS
(www.icelandwintergames.com; ☉Mar) Snowy activities take centre stage in Iceland's winter-sports capital, including international freeski and snowboard competitions. Tour operators offer ways to get out into gloriously wintry landscapes (such as dog sledding, snowmobiling, and super-Jeep or helicopter tours). Rug up!

Arctic Open   SPORTS
(www.arcticopen.is; ☉late Jun) Akureyri's golf course (☑462 2974; www.golficeland.org; per round kr8500; ☉mid-May–Oct) is home to the annual 36-hole Arctic Open, a golf tournament played under the midnight sun over two nights in late June.

⌂ Sleeping

Akureyri Backpackers   HOSTEL €
(☑571 9050; www.akureyribackpackers.com; Hafnarstræti 98; dm kr4900-5800, d without bathroom kr20,300; ☎) Supremely placed in the town's heart, this backpackers has a chilled travellers' vibe and includes a tour-booking service and a popular bar. Rooms spread over three floors: four- to eight-bed dorms, plus private rooms with made-up beds are on the top floor. Minor gripe: there are toilets and sinks on all levels but showers are in the basement, as is the free sauna.

Hamrar Campsite   CAMPGROUND €
(☑461 2264; www.hamrar.is; sites per person kr1400; ☉mid-May–late Sep) This huge site, 1.5km south of town in the leafy setting of Kjarnaskógur woods, has newer facilities than the city campsite (☑462 3379; www.hamrar.is; Þórunnarstræti; sites per person kr1500; ☉Jun–mid-Sep), and mountain views. There's a hostel-style building here that has the cheapest beds in town: mattresses on the floor in a sleeping loft for kr2000.

★**Skjaldarvík**   GUESTHOUSE €€
(☑552 5200; www.skjaldarvik.is; s/d without bathroom incl breakfast kr22,700/24,500; @☎) A slice of guesthouse nirvana, Skjaldarvík lies in a bucolic farm setting 6km north of town. It's owned by a young family and features quirky design details (plants sprouting from shoes, vintage typewriters as artwork on the walls). Plus: bumper breakfast buffet, horse-riding and buggy tours (p247), mountain-bike rental, a hot-pot, and an honesty bar in the comfy lounge.

★**Icelandair Hotel Akureyri**   HOTEL €€
(☑518 1000; www.icelandairhotels.com; Þingvallastræti 23; d from kr23,000-29,000; @☎) This high-class hotel showcases Icelandic designers and artists within its fresh, white-and-caramel-toned decor; rooms are compact but well designed. Added extras: outdoor terrace, good on-site restaurant, and a lounge (www.icelandairhotels.com; Þingvallastræti 23; high tea kr2750; ☉high tea 2-5pm) serving high tea of an afternoon and happy-hour cocktails in the early evening.

Halllandsnes
APARTMENT €€€

(📲 895 6029; www.halllandsnes.is; Rte 1; apt from kr40,000; 🛜) There's an unexpected touch of the Mediterranean at this outstanding property 6km east of Akureyri along Rte 1. Its whitewashed buildings and delightful outdoor area enjoy sweeping fjord views, while inside are impeccable, well-furnished apartments with quality appliances, full kitchens including dishwasher, and washer-dryers – you may not want to leave. Each apartment sleeps four or six in comfort.

Sæluhús
APARTMENT €€€

(📲 412 0800; www.saeluhus.is; Sunnutröð; studios/houses kr31,000/47,700; 🛜) This awesome mini-village of modern studios and houses is perfect for a few days' R & R. The houses may be better equipped than your own back home: three bedrooms (sleeping seven), kitchen, washing machine and verandah with hot tub and barbecue. Smaller studios are ideal for couples, with kitchen and access to a laundry (some have a hot tub, but these cost extra).

✖ Eating

★ Berlin
CAFE €

(📲 772 5061; www.facebook.com/berlinakureyri; Skipagata 4; breakfast kr800-1700; ⏰ 8am-6pm; 🛜🧒) Breakfast served all day? Hello Berlin! If you need a fix of bacon and eggs or avocado on toast, this cosy timber-lined cafe is your spot. Good coffee is a bonus, and you can linger over waffles with caramel sauce too. From 11.30am the menu adds lunch-y offerings such as vegetable dhal and chicken wings.

★ Strikið
INTERNATIONAL €€

(📲 462 7100; www.strikid.is; Skipagata 14; lunch mains kr2300-3200, dinner mains kr3700-5100; ⏰ 11.30am-9.30pm Mon-Thu, to 11pm Fri & Sat) Huge windows with fjord views lend a magical glitz to this 5th-floor restaurant, and the cool cocktails help things along. The menu showcases prime Icelandic produce (reindeer burgers, super-fresh sushi, lamb shoulder, shellfish soup). Passionfruit crème brûlée makes for a sweet ending. The three-course signature menu is decent value at kr7500.

Akureyri Fish Restaurant
FISH & CHIPS €€

(📲 414 6050; www.facebook.com/pg/Akureyrifish-and-chips; Skipagata 12; mains kr1500-4000; ⏰ 11.30am-10pm) The short blackboard at this bustling, casual place highlights piscatorial pleasures: fish and chips is the bestseller, or there's oven-baked salmon, crumbed cod, fish soup, fish burger, mussels and *plokkfiskur* (a tasty, traditional, creamy mashed-fish stew served with rye bread). Fish and chips taste good washed down with local beers.

Rub23
INTERNATIONAL €€€

(📲 462 2223; www.rub23.is; Kaupvangsstræti 6; lunch mains kr1990-3990, dinner mains kr4300-6700; ⏰ 11.30am-2pm Mon-Fri, 5.30-10pm daily) This sleek, seafood-showcasing restaurant has a decidedly Japanese flavour, but also promotes its use of 'rubs' or marinades (along the lines of sweet mango chilli or citrus rosemary). At dinner, there's a confusing array of menus (including a 'summer menu', sushi menu and tasting menus) – it's a good thing that the food is first-rate. Bookings advised.

🍷 Drinking & Nightlife

Akureyri Backpackers
BAR

(www.akureyribackpackers.com; Hafnarstræti 98; ⏰ 7.30am-11pm Sun-Thu, to 1am Fri & Sat) Always a hub of convivial main-street activity, the fun timber-clad bar at Akureyri Backpackers (p249) is beloved of both travellers and locals for its occasional live music, good-value burgers and weekend brunches. There's a wide beer selection – this is a fine spot to sample local microbrews Kaldi and Einstök.

Götubarinn
BAR

(📲 462 4747; www.facebook.com/gotubarinn; Hafnarstræti 96; ⏰ 8pm-1am Thu, to 3am Fri & Sat) The locals' favourite drinking spot, fun and central Götubarinn (Street Bar) has a surprising amount of cosiness and charm for a place that closes at 3am. It's all timber, mirrors and couches, and there's even a downstairs piano for late-night singalongs.

🛍 Shopping

Several shops on Hafnarstræti sell traditional *lopapeysur* Icelandic woollen sweaters, books, knick-knacks and souvenirs. Remember to look for Icelandic-made knitwear (some is now mass-produced in China) and ask about the tax-free scheme.

The Glerártorg shopping mall, on Rte 1 about 1km north of the town centre, is home to a large Nettó supermarket and other shops and services.

★ Geysir
CLOTHING

(www.geysir.com; Hafnarstræti 98; ⏰ 9am-10pm, shorter hours in winter) We covet everything in this unique store, from the woollen blankets to the hipster-chic *lopapeysur* and the old

Iceland maps. Looks like it dresses all the stylish lumbersexuals in town.

Sjoppan DESIGN

(📞 864 0710; www.facebook.com/sjoppanvoruhus; Kaupvangsstræti 21; ⊙ hours vary) Cute as a button, this tiny store dispenses cool design items and gifts from a hutch out the front (ring the bell for service). It's across from the **art museum** (Listasafnið á Akureyri; 📞 461 2610; www.listak.is; Kaupvangsstræti 8; kr500; ⊙ 10am-5pm daily Jun-Aug, noon-5pm Tue-Sun Sep-May). Check out its Facebook page for hours and other details.

ℹ️ Information

MEDICAL SERVICES

Akureyri Hospital (📞 463 0100; www.sak.is; Eyrarlandsvegur) Just south of the botanical gardens.

Apótekarinn (Hafnarstræti 95; ⊙ 9am-5.30pm Mon-Fri) Central pharmacy.

On-Call Doctor Service (📞 1700; ⊙ 24hr) Only for urgent issues.

Primary Health Care Clinic (Heilsugæslustöðin; 📞 460 4600; 3rd fl, Hafnarstræti 99; ⊙ 8am-4pm Mon-Fri)

TOURIST INFORMATION

Tourist Office (📞 450 1050; www.visitakureyri. is; Hof, Strandgata 12; ⊙ 8am-6.30pm mid-Jun–mid-Sep, shorter hours rest of year; 📶) This friendly, efficient office is inside **Hof** (📞 450 1000; www.mak.is; Strandgata 12). There are loads of brochures and maps, as well as internet access and a great design store. Knowledgeable staff can advise on tours and transport; they may also be able to help if you arrive without an accommodation booking (kr500 reservation fee), but only if they have time – which is not common, so don't rely on this service! (We don't recommend arriving in town without a booking.) There's a complex range of opening hours outside of summer, with the office generally closing at 4pm in winter, 5pm in spring and autumn.

ℹ️ Getting There & Away

AIR

Akureyri Airport (www.isavia.is) is 3km south of the city centre.

Air Iceland Connect (📞 460 7000; www. airicelandconnect.is) runs flights up to eight times daily between Akureyri and Reykjavík (45 minutes), and daily in summer (three times a week in winter) from Akureyri to Grímsey (30 minutes). There's also a weekday link with Vopnafjörður and Þórshöfn in northeast Iceland. All other domestic (and international) flights are routed via Reykjavík.

Icelandair (www.icelandair.com) has one weekly flight from June to September from Keflavík, meaning international travellers arriving into Iceland don't need to travel to Reykjavík's domestic airport to connect to Akureyri. These flights are only bookable as part of an international flight to and from Iceland with Icelandair.

BUS

Bus services are ever-changing in Iceland, so it pays to get up-to-date information on schedules and fares, from the companies themselves (websites are handy) or from tourist information centres.

Akureyri's **bus station** (Hafnarstræti 82) is currently the hub for bus travel in the north provided by SBA-Norðurleið and Sterna; at time of writing Strætó operates from a stop in front of **Hof** (p251). (Note: double check departure points as they might change.)

If you need to return to Reykjavík, consider taking an all-terrain bus route through the interior highlands, rather than travelling along Rte 1.

SBA-Norðurleið (📞 550 0700; www.sba.is; Hafnarstræti 82) services (departing from Hafnarstræti bus terminal):

➡ Bus 62 to Mývatn (kr4200, two hours, one daily June to mid-September)

➡ Bus 62 to Egilsstaðir (kr10,100, four hours, one daily June to mid-September)

➡ Bus 62 to Höfn (kr20,000, 9½ hours, one daily June to mid-September)

➡ Bus 610a to Reykjavík via the Kjölur route (kr17,900, 10½ hours, one daily mid-June to mid-September).

Reykjavik Excursions (p257) services:

➡ Bus 641 to Húsavík (kr4050, 1¾ hours, one daily mid-June to August)

➡ Bus 641 to Ásbyrgi (kr7150, three hours, one daily mid-June to August)

➡ Bus 641 to Dettifoss (kr10,150, 4½ hours, one daily mid-June to August).

Sterna (📞 551 1166; www.icelandbybus.is; Hafnarstræti 77) services beginning at **City Campsite** (p249):

➡ Bus 60a to Reykjavík via Rte 1 (kr9500, 5½ hours, one daily mid-June to early September).

Strætó (📞 540 2700; www.straeto.is) services generally run year-round (departing from Hof building):

➡ Bus 56 to Mývatn (kr2520, 1½ hours, two daily) drops to two services a week in winter

➡ Bus 56 to Egilsstaðir (kr7920, 3½ hours, one daily) drops to two services a week in winter

➡ Bus 57 to Reykjavík via Rte 1 (kr10,140, 6½ hours, two daily)

➡ Bus 78 to Siglufjörður (kr2640, 70 minutes, three daily Monday to Friday, one daily Sunday) runs via Dalvík and Ólafsfjörður

➡ Bus 79 to Húsavík (kr2640, 1¼ hours, three daily) winter services are reduced on weekends (no services Saturday, two on Sunday)

➡ Bus 79 to Þórshöfn (kr7480, four hours, one daily Sunday to Friday summer, three weekly winter) this service only operates beyond Húsavík to Þórshöfn (via Ásbyrgi, Kópasker and Raufarhöfn) if prebooked. Call Strætó at least four hours before departure.

Check to see whether **Airport Express North** (www.airportexpress.is) is running its usual, through-the-night, direct bus service linking Akureyri with Keflavík airport (kr11,000, six hours, one a day between June and September). Also contact the bus line for less-frequent services in other months.

Around Akureyri

If you have time and wheels, it's well worth getting off the Ring Road to explore the region around Akureyri's fjord, Eyjafjörður.

Eyjafjarðarsveit is the valley south of Akureyri, accessed by Rtes 821 and 829. The Eyjafjarðará river runs through fertile farmland with idyllic pastoral views and mountain backdrops.

Eyjafjörður's **eastern shore** is much quieter than its western counterpart, and offers a few good places to pause among the sweeping vistas, including the eclectic **Icelandic Folk & Outsider Art Museum** (Safnasafnið; ☑ 461 4066; www.safnasafnid.is; adult/child kr1000/free; ⊙ 10am-5pm mid-May–Aug), 12km from Akureyri on Rte 1.

Further north, Rte 83 branches off the Ring Road to lead you 20km north to the tiny, tidy fishing village of **Grenivík**, which has a spectacular outlook and good facilities: campground and pool, a small maritime museum, and a small supermarket with attached restaurant. En route are the photogenic turf roofs at **Laufás** (☑ 462 4162; www.minjasafnid.is; Rte 83; adult/child kr1400/free; ⊙ 9am-5pm Jun-Aug) and the acclaimed stables of **Pólar Hestar** (☑ 463 3179; www.polarhestar.is; Rte 83; 2hr horse rides kr10,000).

❶ Getting There & Away

You'll need your own wheels to explore here.

Grímsey

Best known as Iceland's only true piece of the **Arctic Circle**, the remote island of Grímsey, 40km from the mainland, is a lonely little place where birds outnumber people by about 10,000 to one. The island is small (5 sq km, with a year-round population of 60) but the welcome is big.

Grímsey's appeal probably lies less in the destination itself, and more in what it represents. Tourists flock here to snap up their 'I visited the Arctic Circle' certificate, pose for a photo with the 'You're standing on the Arctic Circle' monument and appreciate the windswept setting. Scenic coastal cliffs and dramatic basalt formations make a popular home for dozens of species of **seabirds**, including loads of puffins, plus the kamikaze Arctic tern. We're particularly fond of the anecdote that the airport runway has to be cleared of the terns a few minutes before aircraft are scheduled to arrive.

🏃 Activities

A new local company **Arctic Trip** (☑ 848 1696; www.arctictrip.is) offers the unique opportunity to **dive or snorkel** with the bird life – puffins and especially guillemots swoop down deep as they search for food. A couple of notes to birders: puffins are not guaranteed beyond about 10 August (they usually arrive in April; viewing is best from May to July). Terns arrive in May and are pretty aggressive in July, when their chicks begin to be active; they commonly leave in early September. And remember to *take care* walking around cliff edges.

🛌 Sleeping & Eating

If sleeping in the Arctic Circle sounds too good to pass up, two places offer accommodation. The island's campground is due to move to a new location by the swimming pool – check with www.akureyri.is/grimsey for the latest.

Básar   GUESTHOUSE €€
(☑ 467 3103; www.gistiheimilidbasar.is; s/d without bathroom incl breakfast kr13,000/18,000) Homey Básar is right next to the airport. Sleeping-bag accommodation costs kr6000, and there is a guest kitchen and lounge area. Meals can be arranged, as can sailing and sea-angling trips (with notice).

Gullsól   GUESTHOUSE €€
(☑ 467 3190; gullsol@visir.is; r without bathroom per person kr8000) Follow the stairs up through the trapdoor at cosy Gullsól to find teeny-tiny rooms perched above the island's gift shop (which opens in conjunction with ferry arrivals and serves snacks). The full kitchen is handy for self-caterers.

Krían
ICELANDIC €€

(☎467 3112; ⊘noon-9pm mid-May–early Sep)
The island's only restaurant (named after the Arctic tern, *kría* in Icelandic) is open daily in summer, but has varied winter hours. It's an agreeable place with an outdoor deck that enjoys views over the harbour. Soups and fish dishes are generally available.

ⓘ Information

The Akureyri **tourist office** (p251) can help with information for a visit, or see www.akureyri.is/grimsey.

ⓘ Getting There & Away

There are a number of options for reaching Grímsey. Norlandair (www.norlandair.is) offers summer flights to/from Akureyri, while Sæfari (www.saefari.is) offers a year-round ferry service between Dalvík and Grímsey. Tours and excursions to the island are normally only an option in summer months: try Myflug Air (www.myflug.is), Air Iceland Connect (www.airicelandconnect.is) or Circle Air (www.circleair.is), or arrive over the water with Arctic Sea Tours (www.arcticseatours.is), Ambassador (www.ambassador.is) or Gentle Giants (www.gentlegiants.is).

Húsavík

POP 2240

Húsavík, Iceland's whale-watching capital, has become a firm favourite on travellers' itineraries – and with its colourful houses, unique museums and stunning snowcapped peaks across the bay, it's easily the northeast's prettiest fishing town.

◉ Sights

Skrúðgarður
GARDENS

A walk along the duck-filled stream of the endearing front park, which is as scenic as the waterfront area, offers a serene break. Access is via a footbridge on Ásgarðsvegur, or beside Árból (p255) guesthouse.

Húsavíkurkirkja
CHURCH

(☎464 1317; www.husavikurkirkja.is; Garðarsbraut; ⊘9am-5pm) Húsavík's beloved church is quite different from anything else seen in Iceland. Constructed in 1907 from Norwegian timber, the delicately proportioned red-and-white church would look more at home in the Alps. Its cruciform shape becomes apparent inside and is dominated by a depiction of the resurrection of Lazarus (from lava!) on the altarpiece. It's open most days in summer.

Húsavík Whale Museum
MUSEUM

(Hvalasafnið; ☎414 2800; www.whalemuseum.is; Hafnarstétt; adult/child kr1900/500; ⊘8.30am-6.30pm daily May-Sep, 10am-4pm Mon-Fri Oct-Apr) This excellent museum provides all you ever need to know about the impressive creatures that visit Skjálfandi bay. Housed in an old harbourside slaughterhouse, the museum interprets the ecology and habits of whales, conservation and the history of whaling in Iceland through beautifully curated displays, including several huge skeletons soaring high above (they're real!).

ⓒ Tours

Whale Watching

This is why you came to Húsavík. Although there are other Iceland locales where you can do whale-watching tours (Reykjavík and Eyjafjörður, north of Akureyri), this area has become Iceland's premier whale-watching destination, with up to 11 species coming here to feed in summer. The best time to see whales is between June and August when you'll have a near-100% chance of a sighting. This is also, of course, the height of tourist season.

Four whale-watching companies now operate from Húsavík harbour. Don't stress *too* much over picking an operator; prices are similar and services are comparable for the standard three-hour tour (guiding and warm overalls supplied, plus hot drinks and a pastry).

Where the differences are clear, however, is in the excursions that go beyond the standard. When puffins are nesting (from roughly mid-April to mid-August), all companies offer tours that incorporate whale watching with a sail by the puffin-festooned island of Lundey: **North Sailing** (☎464 7272; www.northsailing.is; Garðarsbraut; 3hr tours adult/child kr10,500/4500) does this on board an atmospheric old schooner over four hours (hoisting sails when conditions are right); **Gentle Giants** (☎464 1500; www.gentlegiants.is; Garðarsbraut; 3hr tours adult/child kr10,300/4200) does it over 2½ hours in a high-speed rigid inflatable boat (RIB).

Trips depart throughout the day (June to August) from around 8am to 8pm, and large signs at the ticket booths advertise the next departure time. Boats also run in April, May, and September to November with less frequency (North Sailing has daily tours from early March). You can't miss the offices on the waterfront: North Sailing with its yellow flags, Gentle Giants dressed in blue, and smaller Salka (☑464 3999; www.salkawhalewatching.is; Garðarsbraut 7; 3hr tours adult/child kr9950/4200; ⊗May-Sep) operating from its cafe across the road. A fourth player, Húsavík Adventures (☑853 4205; www.husavikadventures.is; Garðarsbraut 5; 2hr RIB tours adult/child kr16,000/12,000), has recently entered the market, offering RIB tours.

When booking a last-minute standard tour, it's worth enquiring about how big the boat is and how many passengers are booked on the tour. Consider taking an early-morning or evening cruise (bus groups visit in the middle of the day). Note that RIB tours are not suitable for kids under about eight years.

Other Tours

Both major whale-watching operators offer combo tours that involve cruises plus a horse ride at Saltvík (☑847 9515; www.saltvik.is; Rte 85; 2hr tours kr9500). Gentle Giants (p253) also offers sea angling expeditions or a two-day hiking trip; North Sailing (p253) offers a unique 'Ski to the Sea' multiday package in April and May, working with ski guides. North Sailing also has week-long sailing trips to Greenland each summer. See websites for full details.

🛏 Sleeping

Árbót
HOSTEL €

(☑464 3677; www.hostel.is; dm/d without bathroom kr5000/13,600; ⊗Apr-Sep; @🖀) One of two HI hostels on tranquil, remote rural properties in the area (owned by the same family) – both are about 20km south of Húsavík off Rte 85. You'll need your own transport and will have to BYO all food. There are decent facilities and comfy common areas. HI members get a discount; linen can be hired.

★ Kaldbaks-Kot
COTTAGES €€

(☑892 1744; www.cottages.is; 2-/4-person cottages excl linen kr22,000/30,7000; ⊗May-Sep; @🖀) Located 3km south of Húsavík is this spectacular, spread-out settlement of cosy timber cottages that all feel like grandpa's log cabin in the woods (but with considerably more comfort). Choose your level of service: BYO linen or hire it; bring supplies or buy breakfast here (kr1500), served in the magnificent converted cowshed.

★ Árból
GUESTHOUSE €€

(☑464 2220; www.arbol.is; Ásgarðsvegur 2; s/d without bathroom incl breakfast kr12,200/29,900) This 1903 heritage house has a pretty stream

---

THE WHALES OF HÚSAVÍK

With the help of Edda Elísabet Magnúsdóttir, marine biologist, we investigated the whales of Húsavík and what's gone into making this town the whale-watching capital of Iceland.

Húsavík sits on a super-scenic bay known as Skjálfandi, which is often translated into English as 'Shaky Bay'. The name is apt, since little earthquakes occur very frequently in the bay, usually without being noticed. These tremors occur because the bay sits atop a wrench fault in the earth's crust.

Skjálfandi's bowl-shaped topography and fresh water flowing in from two river estuaries means that there is a great deal of nutrients collecting in the bay. The nutrient deposits accumulate during the winter months, and when early summer arrives – with its long sunlit days – the cool waters of Skjálfandi bay come alive with plankton blooms. These rich deposits act like a beacon, kick-starting each year's feeding season. This is when the whales start appearing in greater numbers.

The first creatures to arrive are the humpback whales (Megaptera novaeangliae) and the minke whales (Balaenoptera acutorostrata). The humpback whale is known for its curious nature, equanimity and spectacular surface displays, whereas the minke whale is famous for its elegant features: a streamlined and slender black body and white-striped pectoral fin.

Several minke and humpback whales stay in the bay throughout the year, but most migrate south during the winter. The enormous blue whale (Balaenoptera musculus), undoubtedly the most exciting sight in Skjálfandi, usually starts coming in mid-June and stays until the middle of July.

Other summer sightings in Skjálfandi include the orca, also known as the killer whale (Orcinus orca; some come to the bay to feed on fish, others come to hunt mammals), northern bottlenose whales (Hyperoodon ampullatus; a mysterious, deep-diving beaked whale), fin whales (Balaenoptera physalus), sei whales (Balaenoptera borealis), pilot whales (Globicephala melas) and sperm whales (Physeter macrocephalus).

and the town park as neighbours. Spacious, spotless rooms are spread over three levels – those on the ground and top floors are loveliest (the pine-lined attic rooms are particularly sweet). Note: no kitchen.

Fosshótel Húsavík   HOTEL €€€
(☑ 464 1220; www.fosshotel.is; Ketilsbraut 22; d incl breakfast from kr32,000; ☜) Fast-growing hotel chain Fosshótel has expanded this hotel (from 67 to 110 rooms) and put its stylish, contemporary stamp on much-needed renovations: charcoal tones, bright colour accents etc. Deluxe rooms are a good step up from standard rooms. The airy lobby creates a great first impression, and the bar and bistro have a subtle whale theme.

✖ Eating

Café Hvalbakur   CAFE €
(☑ 464 7278; www.gamlibaukur.is; Garðarsbraut; snacks & meals kr350-1300; ☉ 8am-8pm Jun-Aug, 11.30am-8pm Sep-May) With a sun-trap terrace overlooking the waterfront, this friendly cafe – owned by North Sailing (p253) – serves a big cabinet full of baguettes, wraps, muffins and cakes. Good coffee too. It's just down the stairs from the North Sailing ticket office.

Fish & Chips   FAST FOOD €
(Hafnarstétt 19; fish & chips kr1800; ☉ 11.30am-8pm May-Oct) Doing exactly what it says on the label, this small window-front on the harbour doles out good-value fish (usually cod) and chips, with a few picnic tables out front and a simple seating area upstairs. To find it, walk down the stairs opposite the church and turn left.

★ Naustið   SEAFOOD €€
(☑ 464 1520; www.facebook.com/naustid; Ásgarðsvegur 1; mains kr2000-4900; ☉ noon-10pm) In a new location away from the harbour, buttercup-yellow Naustið wins praise for its super-fresh fish and a simple concept that's well executed: skewers of fish and vegetables, grilled to order. There's also fish soup (natch), fish tacos and langoustine, plus home-baked rhubarb cake for dessert.

❶ Information

Tourist Information Centre (☑ 464 6165; www.visithusavik.is; Hafnarstétt; ☉ 8.30am-6.30pm daily May-Sep, 10am-4pm Mon-Fri Oct-Apr) At the Whale Museum, with plentiful maps and brochures.

❶ Getting There & Away

AIR

Húsavík's airport is 12km south of town. **Eagle Air** (p280) flies year-round between Reykjavík and Húsavík.

BUS

Reykjavik Excursions (p257) operates the following services:
➠ Bus 641a to Akureyri (kr3950, 1½ hours, one daily mid-June to August)
➠ Bus 641 to Ásbyrgi (kr2750, 1¼ hours, one daily mid-June to August)
➠ Bus 641 to Dettifoss (kr6750, 2¾ hours, one daily mid-June to August) From Dettifoss you can connect to bus 661a to Mývatn.
➠ Bus 650a to Mývatn (kr3750, 55 minutes, one daily mid-June to August)

Strætó (☑ 540 2700; www.straeto.is) services (departing from the N1 service station):
➠ Bus 79 to Akureyri (kr2640, 1¼ hours, three daily)
➠ Bus 79 to Ásbyrgi (kr2240, one hour, one daily Sunday to Friday summer, three weekly winter) This service only operates from Húsavík to Þórshöfn (via Ásbyrgi, Kópasker and Raufarhöfn) if prebooked. Call Strætó at least four hours before departure.
➠ Bus 79 to Þórshöfn (kr5260, 2¾ hours, one daily Sunday to Friday summer, three weekly winter) See booking advice as per Bus 79 to Ásbyrgi.

Mývatn Region

Undisputed gem of the northeast, Mývatn (pronounced *mee*-vaht) lake (and the surrounding area) is starkly beautiful. It's an other-worldly terrain of spluttering mudpots, weird lava formations, steaming fumaroles and volcanic craters, set around a bird-filled lake.

The Mývatn basin sits squarely on the Mid-Atlantic Ridge and the violent geological character of the area has produced an astonishing landscape unlike anywhere else in the country; this is the Iceland you've always imagined.

🏃 Activities

Mýflug Air   SCENIC FLIGHT
(☑ 464 4400; www.myflug.is; Reykjahlíð Airport) Mýflug Air operates daily flightseeing excursions (weather permitting). A 20-minute trip over Mývatn and Krafla costs kr19,000; a two-hour 'super tour' (kr57,000) also includes Dettifoss, Ásbyrgi, Kverkfjöll,

Mývatn & Krafla

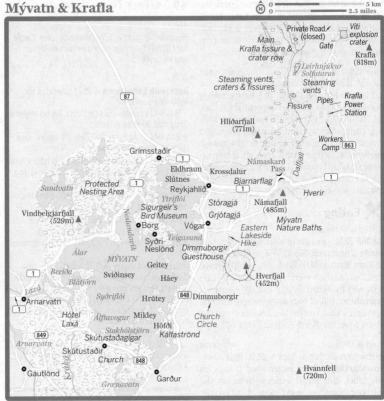

Herðubreið and Askja. You can fly north for a one-hour stop in Grímsey (kr48,000).

Snowdogs DOG SLEDDING
(☑ 847 7199; www.snowdogs.is; tours adult/child kr30,000/5000; ⊘ Nov-Apr or May) On the remote farm Heiði, about 8km off the main road in southern Mývatn (take Rte 849 west of Skútustaðir), Sæmi and his family run dog-sledding tours across the snow-white wilderness. Tours vary depending on the dogs, people, weather and trail conditions involved, but guests are generally on the snow for about 45 to 60 minutes and cover around 8km.

Saga Travel ADVENTURE TOUR
(☑ 558 8888; www.sagatravel.is) Saga Travel operates a variety of fabulous year-round tours in the Mývatn area, including sightseeing, caving, birdwatching and lava walks (see website for the full selection). Northern Lights tours include photography tips.

There is often the option of joining tours from Akureyri or Reykjahlíð.

Geo Travel ADVENTURE TOUR
(☑ 464 4442; www.geotravel.is) Geo Travel is a small company owned by two well-connected local guys. They work with the local operators to offer year-round tours, from summer super-Jeep excursions to Askja and Holuhraun (kr35,000), to Northern Lights tours (kr17,500), to half-hour snowmobile trips (kr15,000).

🛏 Sleeping

Mývatn's popularity means that room rates have soared; demand is far greater than supply, so be sure to book ahead. Most prices are very inflated, with kr35,500 being the norm for a run-of-the-mill hotel double in summer's peak. Off-season rates are considerably cheaper. To save money at guesthouses, ask about sleeping-bag options.

Most places are located either in Reykjahlíð or at Vógar, on the lake's eastern shore, with additional options at Dimmuborgir and Skútustaðir.

🍴 Eating

Most dining choices are found either in Reykjahlíð or at Vógar, a small cluster of buildings along the lake's eastern shore. Additional options are at Dimmuborgir and along the southern shore at Skútustaðir. The large hotels all have restaurants.

The local food speciality is a moist, cake-like rye bread known as *hverabrauð* (often translated as 'geysir bread'). It's slow-baked underground using geothermal heat and is served in every restaurant in the area.

ℹ️ Information

Mývatnsstofa Visitor Centre (☎ 464 4390; www.visitmyvatn.is; Hraunvegur 8, Reykjahlíð; ⏱ 7.30am-6pm Jun-Aug, shorter hours Sep-May) This well-informed centre in Reykjahlíð (by the supermarket) has good displays on the local geology, and can book accommodation, tours and transport. Pick up a copy of the hugely useful *Mývatn* brochure, which gives a good overview of hiking trails in the area.

Because the Mývatn region is a protected nature reserve, there are rangers here too (from Umhverfisstofnun, the Environment Agency of Iceland), with a staffed desk from 9am to 6pm in summer.

All tours and buses leave from the car park here.

ℹ️ Getting There & Away

All buses pick up/drop off passengers at the **visitor centre** (p257) in Reykjahlíð; bus routes 62/62a, 56, 14/14a and 17/17a also stop in Skútustaðir, by the **Sel-Hótel** (☎ 464 4164; www.myvatn.is; Skútustaðir; s/d incl breakfast kr31,900/39,900; @ 🛜).

SBA-Norðurleið (p280) services:
➡ Bus 62a to Akureyri (kr4200, 1¾ hours, one daily June to mid-September).
➡ Bus 62 to Egilsstaðir (kr6900, two hours, one daily June to mid-September).
➡ Bus 62 to Höfn (kr16,100, 7½ hours, one daily June to mid-September).

Reykjavik Excursions (☎ 580 5400; www.re.is) services:
➡ Bus 650 to Húsavík (kr3750, 40 minutes, one daily mid-June to August).
➡ Bus 661 to Krafla (kr2150, 15 minutes, two daily mid-June to early September).
➡ Bus 661 to Dettifoss (kr4350, one hour, one daily mid-June to early September) From Dettifoss you have the option of linking with bus 641a to Ásbyrgi, Húsavík or on to Akureyri.

LAKE OF MIDGES

Mývatn's name translates as 'Lake of Midges', and plague-like swarms of these small flies are a lasting memory for many summer visitors. As infuriating as they can be, these midges are a vital food source for wildlife.

If they bother you, consider wearing a head net (which you can buy at the supermarket in Reykjahlíð, and elsewhere) – then splash on the repellent and pray for a good wind to send the little blighters diving.

Strætó (p280) services:
➡ Bus 56 to Akureryi (kr2520, 1½ hours, two daily) Drops to two weekly services in winter.
➡ Bus 56 to Egilsstaðir (kr5720, two hours, one daily) Drops to two weekly services in winter.

Reykjavík Excursions (☎ 580 5400; www.re.is) services:
➡ Bus 14a to Landmannalaugar along the highland Sprengisandur route (kr17,000, 10 hours, three per week July to August)
➡ Bus 17a to Reykjavík along the highland Sprengisandur route (kr21,700, 11½ hours, three per week July to August)

ℹ️ Getting Around

There are wonderful hiking trails around Mývatn, but they're not all connected. Without wheels you may find yourself on long walks along the lakeshore road.

You might consider renting a car in Akureyri. During calmer weather, a good option is to hire a mountain bike from **Hike&Bike** (☎ 899 4845; www.hikeandbike.is). The 36km ride around the lake can be done in a day.

If you need a taxi (June to August), call 893 4389.

THE EAST

As far as you can get (some 650km) from Reykjavík, Iceland's impressively varied and sparsely populated east doesn't announce itself as loudly as other parts of the country, preferring subtle charms over big-ticket attractions. The Eastfjords is the area's most wondrous destination – the scenery is particularly spectacular around the northern fjord villages, backed by sheer-sided mountains etched with waterfalls. If the weather's fine, several days spent hiking here may be some of your most memorable in Iceland.

Away from the convoluted coast, the country's longest lake stretches southwest from Egilsstaðir, its shores lined with perfect diversions. Further inland are the forgotten farms, fells and reindeer-roamed heathlands of the empty east, and Snæfell, one of Iceland's prime peaks.

Ring Road motorists often simply overnight in Egilsstaðir then speed out of the east. Lunacy! The east's spectacular fjords, scenic hiking trails, fascinating geology and friendly villages are some of Iceland's unsung treasures.

Egilsstaðir

POP 2330

However much you strain to discover some underlying charm, Egilsstaðir isn't a ravishing beauty. It's the main regional transport hub, and a centre for local commerce, so its services are quite good (including quality accommodation and dining options). It's growing fast, but in a hotchpotch fashion and without a proper town centre.

Egilsstaðir's saving grace is its proximity to lovely Lagarfljót, Iceland's third-largest lake. Since Saga times, tales have been told of a monster living in its depths. If you want to do some beastie-hunting, or explore the forest on the lake's eastern bank, Egilsstaðir makes a good base.

🛏 Sleeping

Rooms and campsites in the area are in hot demand on Wednesday nights in summer, as the ferry to Europe sails from Seyðisfjorður (27km away) on Thursday mornings. If you are taking the ferry, book your accommodation well ahead. Refer to accommodation websites for up-to-date rates.

Olga Guesthouse
GUESTHOUSE €€

(📞 860 2999; www.gistihusolgu.com; Tjarnabraut 3; d with/without bathroom incl breakfast kr25,990/21,200; 🛜) In a good central location, dressed-in-red Olga offers five rooms that share three bathrooms and a small kitchen – all rooms come with tea- and coffee-making facilities, TV and fridge. Two doors down is Olga's sister, yellow Birta Guesthouse, under the same friendly ownership and with similar high-quality facilities. Both guesthouses have an additional annexe containing en-suite rooms.

Gistihúsið – Lake Hotel Egilsstaðir
HOTEL €€€

(📞 471 1114; www.lakehotel.is; r incl breakfast kr36,300; @🛜) The town was named after this farm and splendid heritage guesthouse (now big enough to warrant the 'hotel' label) on the banks of Lagarfljót, 300m west of the crossroads. In its old wing, en suite rooms retain a sense of character. In contrast, a new extension houses 30 modern, slightly anonymous hotel rooms. There's a great restaurant (p258) on-site, and a spa (📞 471 1114; www.lakehotel.is; hotel guest/nonguest kr2000/3500; ⏰10am-10pm).

Icelandair Hótel Hérað
HOTEL €€€

(📞 471 1500; www.icelandairhotels.is; Miðvangur 1-7; r from kr31,500; @🛜) This stylish, friendly, business-standard hotel is kitted out with the expected bells and whistles, and appealing splashes of colour. The restaurant (mains kr2200 to kr7600) here is a good place to indulge. The house speciality is reindeer. Breakfast buffet is kr2600.

🍴 Eating

Refuelling motorists don't have to look far – quick eats can be found at the busy service stations in town. Supermarkets should be utilised by self-caterers. Good restaurants showcase local produce – hotel restaurants are a high-quality option, especially at Gistihúsið (p258), Hótel Valaskjálf (📞471 1600; www.valaskjalf.is; Skógarlönd 3; s/d incl breakfast kr23,000/31,200) and Icelandair Hótel Hérað (p258).

⭐ Eldhúsið
ICELANDIC €€

(📞 471 1114; www.lakehotel.is; lunch kr1400-4000, dinner mains kr3400-6400; ⏰11.30am-10pm; 🛜) Some of the east's most creative cooking happens at the restaurant inside Gistihúsið – Lake Hotel Egilsstaðir (p258). The menu is an ode to locally sourced produce (lamb, fish and game), and the speciality is the beef, raised right here on the farm. Try a rib-eye with Béarnaise foam, or fish from the fjords with grape salad and dill mayonnaise. Desserts are pretty, polished affairs. Bookings advised.

ℹ Information

East Iceland Regional Information Centre
(📞 471 2320; www.east.is; Miðvangur 1-3; ⏰8.30am-6pm Mon-Fri, 10am-4pm Sat, 1-6pm Sun Jun-Aug, noon-6pm Mon-Fri, 11am-2pm Sat Sep-May; 🛜) Maps and brochures are plentiful here – you'll find everything you need to explore the entire eastern region.

Egilsstaðastofa Visitor Center (☑ 470 0750; www.visitegilsstadir.is; Kaupvangur 17; ☺7am-11pm Jun-Aug, 8.30am-3pm Mon-Fri May & Sep, 8.30am-12.30pm Mon-Fri Oct-Apr; ☎) From its info desk at the campground reception, this place focuses on Egilsstaðir and surrounds and can hook you up with bus tickets and various activity tours: hiking, super-Jeep tours, sea-angling etc. Bike hire is available (kr2900 for up to four hours, kr3900 for 24 hours).

❶ Getting There & Away

Egilsstaðir is the transport hub of East Iceland. There's an airport, and all bus services pass through. The main **bus stop** is at the campground.

Seyðisfjörður

POP 665

If you visit only one town in the Eastfjords, this should be it. Made up of multicoloured wooden houses and surrounded by snow-capped mountains and cascading waterfalls, obscenely picturesque Seyðisfjörður is the most historically and architecturally interesting town in East Iceland. It's also a friendly place with an international community of artists, musicians, craftspeople and students.

If the weather's good, the scenic Rte 93 drive from Egilsstaðir is a delight, climbing to a high pass then descending along the waterfall-filled river Fjarðará.

Summer is the liveliest time to visit, particularly when Smyril Line's ferry sails majestically up the 17km-long fjord to town – a perfect way to arrive in Iceland. Note: you may wish to avoid Seyðisfjörður on Wednesday nights in summer, as the ferry to Europe sails on Thursday mornings and accommodation and meals in town are in hot demand. If you are taking the ferry, book accommodation well ahead.

◉ Sights

Seyðisfjörður is stuffed with 19th-century timber buildings, brought in kit form from Norway; several of these have been transformed into cosy ateliers where local artisans work on various projects. A quick loop around town will reveal half a dozen places to drop some krónur, on art, handicrafts, knitwear and designer homewares.

⚡ Activities

Short walking trails lead from the museum area uphill to waterfalls, and to the 'sound sculpture' Tvísöngur – five interconnected concrete domes. Another short walk leads from the road on the north shore of the fjord (about 6km beyond the Bláa Kirkjan (www.blaakirkjan.is; Ránargata)) to the signposted Dvergasteinn (Dwarf Rock) – according to folklore, this is a dwarf church that followed the people's church across the fjord.

The hills above Seyðisfjörður are the perfect spot for longer hiking. Vestdalur is a grassy valley north of town – just before the Langahlíð (p260) cottages – renowned for its glorious waterfalls. Following the Vestdalsá river, after two to three scenic hours you'll arrive at a small lake, Vestdalsvatn, which remains frozen most of the year (it's generally covered by snow until July).

Trails are marked on the widely available *Víknaslóðir – Trails of the Deserted Inlets* map (kr1000). The www.visitseydisfjordur.com website outlines some options, including the Seven Peaks Hike (trails climbing seven of the 1000m-plus peaks surrounding the town).

For a sublime outdoor experience, contact Hlynur Oddsson (☑ 865 3741; hlynur@hotmail.de; Austurvegur 15b; ☺ Jun-Aug), a charming Robert Redford–esque character who spends his summers around town and offers tailor-made kayaking tours. Options on the fjord range from one to six hours, visiting a shipwreck or waterfalls (one/three hours kr4000/8000). Experienced kayakers can choose longer trips, including to Skálanes (full day kr25,000, minimum two people).

🛏 Sleeping

⭐ **Hafaldan Old Hospital Hostel**   HOSTEL €
(☑ 611 4410; www.hihostels.com; Suðurgata 8; dm kr5500, d with/without bathroom kr17,400/14,000; @☎) Seyðisfjörður's first-class HI budget digs are housed in two locations: the Harbour Hostel (☑ 611 4410; www.hihostels.com; Ránargata 9; dm/d/quad without bathroom kr5000/12,100/19,400; ☎) is a little out of town past the Blue Church (p259); and the Old Hospital Hostel is the more central summertime annexe. The Old Hospital houses the main reception for both buildings from May to August, plus dorms, a handful of en-suite rooms and a beautiful kitchen-dining facility.

⭐ **Hótel Aldan**   HOTEL €€
(☑ 472 1277; www.hotelaldan.com; Norðurgata 2; s/d incl breakfast from kr19,400/28,900; ☎) This wonderful hotel is shared across three old

wooden buildings: reception and a bar-restaurant (where breakfast is served) are at the Norðurgata location. Guest rooms are in two other buildings: Snæfell (p260) and the **Old Bank** (☑472 1277; www.hotelaldan.com; Oddagata 6; s/d incl breakfast kr28,900/36,900; 🛜). Ask about the hotel's central apartments (from kr50,400), with full kitchens, lots of space (two and three bedrooms) and some fun retro styling.

Hótel Aldan (Snæfell)   HOTEL €€
(☑472 1277; www.hotelaldan.com; Austurvegur 3; s/d incl breakfast kr19,400/28,900; 🛜) Snæfell is a creaky, characterful three-storey place with the cheapest rooms, fresh white paintwork and Indian bedspreads. The ground-floor has family suites.

★ Langahlið   COTTAGES €€€
(☑897 1524; www.langahlid.com; cottages from kr36,500-41,500; 🛜) Book *very* early for these three-bedroom cottages, sleeping up to six in a whole lot of comfort, including a kitchen, lounge, and a hot-pot on the deck with astounding views. They're about 2km north of Hótel Aldan (p259). The friendly Italian owners plan to build smaller, one-bedroom cottages on the property, too.

✖ Eating

Norð Austur Sushi & Bar   SUSHI €€
(☑787 4000; www.nordaustur.is; 2nd fl, Norðurgata 2; mains kr2000-4500; ⊙6-10pm Sun-Thu, to 11pm Fri & Sat mid-May–mid-Sep) Locals rave about this place – and with good reason: the salmon, trout and char come straight off the fishers' boats and into the hands of accomplished sushi chefs with international pedigree. Set tasting menus offer excellent value (five/seven courses for kr6300/7500); the decor is cool, as are the cocktails. Bookings recommended.

Skaftfell Bistro   INTERNATIONAL €€
(☑472 1633; http://skaftfell.is/en/bistro; Austurvegur 42; mains kr1300-4000; ⊙noon-9pm Jun-Aug, 3-9.30pm Sep-May; 🛜☑🐕) This fabulous bistro-bar and cultural centre is perfect for chilling, snacking and/or meeting locals. There's a short menu that changes weekly, plus popular pizza options (including 'reindeer bliss' and 'langoustine feast'). Be sure to check out the exhibitions in the **gallery** (☑472 1632; www.skaftfell.is; ⊙noon-6pm Jun-Aug, 3-9.30pm Sep-May) upstairs. Bookings recommended for larger groups.

ℹ Information

Tourist office (☑472 1551; www.visitseydisfjordur.com; Ferjuleira 1; ⊙8am-4pm Mon-Fri May-Sep, 1-5pm Mon-Fri Oct-Apr) In the ferry terminal building, stocking local brochures, plus info on the entire country. The website is invaluable. In March, April and October the office is open Tuesdays and Wednesdays during the stops of the Smyril Line ferry. The office is also open during cruise-ship visits.

ℹ Getting There & Away

FAS (☑472 1515, 893 2669) runs a bus service between Egilsstaðir and Seyðisfjörður (kr1050, around 45 minutes). Services operate year-round, one to three times daily Monday to Saturday (Sunday services operate from mid-June to August). Services run to coincide with the ferry arrival and departure. An up-to-date schedule can be found on www.visitseydisfjordur.com. The bus stops by the **ferry terminal**, and also outside the library on **Austurvegur**.

ℹ Getting Around

As well as offering walking and cycling tours, **Seyðisfjörður Tours** (☑785 4737; www.seydisfjordurtours.com; Norðurgata 6; ⊙Jun-Aug, plus Sep by request) rents mountain bikes (one/four hours kr2000/4500).

THE SOUTH

Containing glittering glaciers, toppling waterfalls, the iceberg-filled Jökulsárlón lagoon and Iceland's favourite walking area, Skaftafell, it's no wonder that the south is the country's most visited region. Various places along the coast offer hiking, snowmobiling, dog sledding and glacier explorations; or head offshore to the charming, puffin-friendly Vestmannaeyjar (Westman Islands).

Vatnajökull National Park

Vast, varied and spectacular, Vatnajökull National Park was founded in 2008, when authorities created a giant megapark by joining the Vatnajökull ice cap with two previously established national parks: Skaftafell (p261) in southeast Iceland and Jökulsárgljúfur in the northeast. With recent additions, the park measures 13,900 sq km – nearly 14% of entire Iceland (it's one of the largest national parks in Europe).

The park boundaries encircle a staggering richness of landscapes and some of Iceland's greatest natural treasures, created by the combined forces of rivers, glacial ice, and volcanic and geothermal activity. The entirety of the Vatnajökull ice cap is protected, including countless glistening outlet glaciers and glacial rivers. There are incredible rock formations around Ásbyrgi canyon, brilliant waterfalls such as Dettifoss and Svartifoss, the storied Lakagígar crater row, Askja and other volcanoes of the highlands. The park is home to an unending variety of areas where geology, ecology and history lessons spring to life.

Skaftafell (Vatnajökull National Park – South)

Skaftafell, the jewel in the crown of Vatnajökull National Park, encompasses a breathtaking collection of peaks and glaciers. It's the country's favourite wilderness: 500,000 visitors per year come to marvel at thundering waterfalls, twisted birch woods, the tangled web of rivers threading across the sandar, and brilliant blue-white Vatnajökull with its lurching tongues of ice, dripping down mountainsides like icing on a cake.

Skaftafell deserves its reputation, and few visitors – even those who usually shun the great outdoors – can resist it. In the height of summer it may feel that every traveller in the country is here. However, if you're prepared to get out on the more remote trails and take advantage of the fabulous hiking on the heath and beyond, you'll leave the crowds behind. Avoid the crowds by visiting Svartifoss under the midnight sun.

🏃 Activities

Skaftafell is ideal for **day hikes** and also offers **longer hikes** through its wilderness regions. The park produces good maps outlining shorter hiking trails (kr350), and stocks larger topo maps from various publishers.

Most of Skaftafell's visitors keep to the popular routes on Skaftafellsheiði. Hiking in other accessible areas, such as the upper Morsárdalur and Kjós valleys, requires more time, motivation and planning. Before embarking on more remote routes, speak to the staff at the visitor centre, who are keen to impart knowledge and help you prepare, as well as make you aware of potential risks. You should enquire about river crossings along your intended route; you should also leave a travel plan at www.safetravel.is.

Other possibilities for hikes include the long day trip beyond Bæjarstaðarskógur into the rugged Skaftafellsfjöll. A recommended

Skaftafell

destination is the 862m-high summit of the **Jökulfell ridge**, which affords a commanding view of the vast expanses of Skeiðarárjökull. Even better is an excursion into the **Kjós** dell.

Note that from mid-June to mid-August, rangers guide **free daily interpretive walks** that depart from the visitors centre – a great way to learn about the area. Check the website, or ask staff.

Glacier Hikes & Ice Climbing

The highlight of a visit to the southern reaches of Vatnajökull is a glacier hike. It's utterly liberating to strap on crampons and crunch your way around a glacier, and there's much to see on the ice: waterfalls, ice caves, glacial mice (moss balls, not actual mice!) and different-coloured ash from ancient explosions. But – take note: as magnetic as the glaciers are, they are also riven with fissures and are potentially dangerous, so don't be tempted to stride out onto one without the right equipment and guiding.

A number of authorised guides operate year-round in the area (and at lesser-visited glacier tongues further east, toward Höfn). One of the largest companies, Glacier Guides (☑ 562 7000; www.glacierguides.is; ⊙ 8.30am-6pm Apr-Oct, reduced hours Nov-Mar), has info and booking huts in the car park at Skaftafellsstofa Visitor Centre (p263), where you can talk to experts and get kitted out for glacier walks (warm clothes essential, waterproof gear and hiking boots available for hire).

Glacier Guides goes further than just easy glacier hikes, offering more challenging options and ice climbs, right up to summiting Iceland's highest peak (Hvannadalshnúkur). Both operators offer combos, such as a glacier hike plus a lagoon boat trip. See the websites for suggestions and for the most up-to-date rates.

Ice Caves

In hot demand: winter visits to ice caves, glorious dimpled caverns of exquisite blue light, which are accessible (usually at glacier edges) only from around November to March – they can be viewed in cold conditions, and become unstable and unsafe in warmer weather. Temporary ice caves are created anew each season by the forces of nature, and are scouted by local experts. They *must* be visited with guides, who will ensure safety and correct equipment. As

with glacier hikes, tours generally involve getting kitted out (crampons, helmets etc), then driving to the glacier edge and taking a walk to reach the destination. Reasonable fitness and mobility are required.

With their rapid growth in popularity, the largest and most accessible ice caves can become busy and crowded when tour groups arrive (from as far afield as Reykjavík). It is often the case that guided groups all visit the same cave – some tourists are disappointed to find queues of visitors waiting to enter. Catering to this, a few tour companies offer private tours to more remote caves: these tours are longer, more expensive, and generally require a higher level of fitness to reach.

Local Guide (☑ 894 1317; www.localguide.is; Fagurhólsmýri) is the regional expert on ice caves in the south, and can get you to some more remote, private caves if you have more time, stamina and cash. Other good, locally owned companies offering ice-cave exploration include Glacier Adventure (☑ 571 4577; www.glacieradventures.is; Hali), IceGuide (☑ 661 0900; www.iceguide.is; ⊙ Jun-Sep) and Glacier Trips (☑ 779 2919; www.glaciertrips.is; from kr15,500).

🛏 Sleeping

Inside the park, the only option is to camp. There's very little accommodation close to the park, and hotels in the southeast are in huge demand in summer – you'll need either a tent or a firm hotel booking if you're heading this way.

The nearest hotel is at Freysnes, 5km east of the national-park entrance, and there's a handful of options at Hof, a further 15km east.

VATNAJÖKULL & OUTLET GLACIERS

Vatnajökull is the world's largest ice cap outside the poles. At 8100 sq km, it's more than three times the size of Luxembourg, with an average thickness of 400m to 600m (and a maximum of 950m). Under this enormous blanket of ice lie countless peaks and valleys, including a number of live volcanoes and subglacial lakes, plus Iceland's highest point – the 2110m mountain Hvannadalshnúkur.

Huge outlet glaciers, pleated with crevasses, flow down from the centre of Vatnajökull to the lowlands. There are around 30 of them, with many visible (and accessible, to varying degrees) from the Ring Road (Rte 1) in the southeast.

The best known is possibly Skaftafellsjökull, a relatively small glacier that ends within 1.5km of the campsite at Skaftafell. Another famous beauty is Breiðamerkurjökull, which crumbles into icebergs at the breathtaking Jökulsárlón lagoon.

Close to Skaftafell, companies guide glacier walks on tongues such as Svínafellsjökull and Falljökull. Between Jökulsárlón and Höfn, there are now walks on lesser-visited Breiðamerkurjökull and Fláajökull.

ℹ️ Information

Skaftafellsstofa Visitor Centre (☎ 470 8300; www.vjp.is; ⊙ 8am-9pm Jun-Aug, 9am-7pm May & Sep, 9am-6pm Oct & Nov, 9am-5pm Dec-Apr; 🛜) The helpful year-round visitor centre has an information desk plus maps for sale, informative exhibitions, a summertime cafe and internet access. The staff here know their stuff.

ℹ️ Getting There & Away

Skaftafell is a stop on Reykjavík–Höfn bus routes and also a departure point for wilderness areas such as Landmannalaugar and Lakagígar. There are frequent services to Jökulsárlón.

Buses stop in front of the visitor centre.

Reykjavík Excursions (p257) services:
➡ Bus 10/10a to Landmannalaugar (kr9400, five hours, one daily mid-June to mid-September) Runs via Eldgjá. Can be used as a day tour, or as regular transport.
➡ Bus 15 to Jökulsárlón (kr2750, 45 minutes, three daily June to August).
➡ Bus 16/16a to Lakagígar (one daily late June to August) Use as a day tour, with 3½ hours at Laki (day tour kr18,100).
➡ Bus 19 to Höfn (kr5750, two hours, one daily June to August).
➡ Bus 20a to Reykjavík (kr11,250, seven hours, one daily June to August) Stops for one hour at Vík.

Sterna (p280) services:
➡ Bus 12 to Höfn (kr3000, 2¾ hours, one daily June to mid-September) Stops for one hour at Jökulsárlón.
➡ Bus 12a to Reykjavík (kr9600, 6¾ hours, one daily June to mid-September).

Strætó (p280) services:
➡ Bus 51 to Höfn (kr4400, 1¾ hours, two daily June to mid-September, one daily Sunday to Friday mid-September to May) Stops at Freysnes and Jökulsárlón en route.
➡ Bus 51 to Reykjavík (kr9680, 5¼ hours, two daily June to mid-September, one daily Sunday to Friday mid-September to May).

Jökulsárlón

A host of spectacular, luminous-blue icebergs drift through Jökulsárlón glacier lagoon, right beside the Ring Road between Höfn and Skaftafell. It's worth spending a couple of hours here, admiring the wondrous ice sculptures (some of them striped with ash layers from volcanic eruptions), scouting for seals or taking a boat trip.

The icebergs calve from Breiðamerkurjökull, an offshoot of Vatnajökull, crashing down into the water and drifting towards the Atlantic Ocean. They can spend up to five years floating in the 25-sq-km-plus, 260m-deep lagoon, melting, refreezing and occasionally toppling over with a mighty splash, startling the birds. They then move on via Jökulsá, Iceland's shortest river, out to sea.

Although it looks as though it's been here since the last ice age, the lagoon is only about 80 years old. Until the mid-1930s Breiðamerkurjökull reached the Ring Road; it's now retreating rapidly (up to a staggering 500m per year), and the lagoon is consequently growing.

🏃 Activities

Breiðármörk Trail WALKING
A new walking trail has been marked from the western car park at Jökulsárlón, leading to Breiðárlón (10km one way) and Fjallsárlón (15.3km) lagoons. It is classified as challenging. In time, there is a plan to build out this walking route from Skaftafell in the west to Lónsöræfi in the east. The visitor centre at Höfn sells a trail map (kr250).

Glacier Lagoon Amphibious Boat Tours BOAT TOUR
(☎ 478 2222; www.icelagoon.is; adult/child kr5500/2000; ⊙ 9am-7pm Jun-Sep, 10am-5pm May & Oct) Take a memorable 40-minute trip in an amphibious boat, which trundles along the shore like a bus before driving into the water. On-board guides regale you with factoids about the lagoon, and you can taste 1000-year-old ice. There is no set schedule; trips run from the eastern car park (by the cafe) regularly – up to 40 a day in summer.

Ice Lagoon Zodiac Boat Tours BOAT TOUR
(☎ 860 9996; www.icelagoon.com; adult/child kr9500/6000; ⊙ 9am-5.30pm mid-May–mid-Sep) This operator deals exclusively with Zodiac tours of the lagoon. It's a one-hour experience, with a maximum of 20 passengers per boat, and it travels at speed up to the glacier edge (not done by the amphibious boats) before cruising back at a leisurely pace. It pays to book these tours in advance, online; minimum age six years.

ℹ️ Getting There & Away

Countless tours take in Jökulsárlón. We *don't* recommend trying to do a trip from Reykjavík to the lagoon and back to the capital in one day (it's 375km, or about a 4½-hour drive each way).

Reykjavík Excursions (p257) has two summer services of note:

➧ Bus 15 runs a loop between Skaftafellsstofa Visitor Centre and Jökulsárlón (kr2750, 45 minutes, three daily June to August).

➧ Bus 19 runs from Höfn to Skaftafell and back again each day, stopping for a lengthy spell at the lagoon in either direction (to Höfn kr3750, one hour, one daily mid-June to August).

Sterna (p280) Bus 12/12a between Reykjavík and Höfn runs once daily from June to mid-September. Travelling in either direction, it stops for one hour at Jökulsárlón (enough time for a boat ride).

Strætó (p280) Bus 51 between Reykjavík and Höfn runs twice daily from June to mid-September (once daily the rest of the year) and stops here. It simply drops off or picks up passengers, it doesn't linger.

Höfn

POP 1700

Although it's no bigger than many European villages, the Southeast's main town feels like a sprawling metropolis after driving through the emptiness on either side. Its setting is stunning; on a clear day, wander down to the waterside, find a quiet bench and just gaze at Vatnajökull and its guild of glaciers.

Höfn simply means 'harbour', and is pronounced like an unexpected hiccup (just say 'hup' while inhaling). It's an apt name – this modern town still relies heavily on fishing and fish processing, and is famous for its *humar* (often translated as lobster, but technically it's langoustine).

Bus travellers use Höfn as a transit point, and most travellers stop to use the town's services, so prebook accommodation in summer. On bus timetables and the like, you may see the town referred to as Höfn í Hornafirði (meaning Höfn in Hornafjörður) to differentiate it from all the other *höfn* (harbours) around the country.

🏃 Activities

Activities that explore Vatnajökull's icy vastness – such as glacier walks, super-Jeep tours, lagoon kayaking and snowmobile safaris – are accessed along the Ring Road west of Höfn.

In town there are a couple of short **waterside paths** where you can amble and gape at the views; one by Hótel Höfn and another on Ósland.

Ósland   WALKING

This promontory – about 1km beyond the harbour (head for the **seamen's monument**

(Óslandsvegur) on the rise) – boasts a walking path round its marshes and lagoons. The path is great for watching seabirds, but watch out for dive-bombing Arctic terns.

From the seamen's monument, you can follow a **nature trail** that has been set up to model the solar system – it's been 'scaled down 2.1-billion-fold', and has its sizes and distances in correct proportion.

🛏 Sleeping

HI Hostel   HOSTEL €

(☑ 478 1736; www.hostel.is; Hvannabraut 3; dm/d without bathroom kr5700/19,000; 🛜) Follow the signs from the N1 to find Höfn's sole budget option, hidden away in a residential area. It's a sprawling, dated space (a former aged-care home) that's usually bustling with travellers in summer. It has the requisite facilities (kitchen, laundry) but no lounge areas. There's a kr700 discount for members; linen is kr1850.

★ Guesthouse Dyngja   GUESTHOUSE €€

(☑ 866 0702; www.dyngja.com; Hafnarbraut 1; d without bathroom incl breakfast kr19,100; @🛜) A lovely young couple owns this petite five-room guesthouse in a prime harbourfront locale. They have filled it with charm and good cheer: rich colours, a record player and vinyl selection, self-service breakfast, an outdoor deck and good local knowledge. There's also a good new addition: a downstairs suite with private bathroom (kr23,400).

Old Airline Guesthouse   GUESTHOUSE €€

(☑ 478 1300; www.oldairline.com; Hafnarbraut 24; d without bathroom incl breakfast kr19,200; 🛜) This central guesthouse sparkles under the care of friendly host Sigga. On offer are five fresh rooms with shared bathrooms, plus a large lounge and guest kitchen (with self-service breakfast). Big brownie points for free laundry access. It's attached to a small electronics/IT store.

★ Milk Factory   GUESTHOUSE €€€

(☑ 478 8900; www.milkfactory.is; Dalbraut 2; d/q incl breakfast kr30,000/39,500; 🛜) Full credit to the family – and the designers – behind the masterful restoration of an old dairy factory north of town. There are 17 modern, hotel-standard rooms here, including two with disabled access. The prize allotments are the six spacious mezzanine suites that sleep four – good for families or friends, although they don't have kitchens. There are also free bikes for guest use.

Eating

Look out for the Heimahumar food truck, parked out front of Nettó in the summer, for the cheapest lobster wraps and panini in town (priced around kr2000).

Hafnarbúðin
FAST FOOD

(☎478 1095; Ránarslóð 2; snacks & meals kr400-2800; ⊙9am-10pm Mon-Fri, 10am-10pm Sat & Sun, shorter hours in winter) A fabulous relic, this tiny old-school diner has a cheap-and-cheerful vibe, a menu of fast-food favourites (hot dogs, burgers, toasted sandwiches) and a fine *humarloka* – langoustine baguette – for kr2200. There's even a drive-up window!

Nýhöfn
ICELANDIC €€

(☎865 2489; www.nyhofn.is; Hafnarbraut 2; mains kr2900-5900; ⊙noon-10pm mid-May–mid-Sep) This sweet 'Nordic bistro' is in the home that Höfn's first settler built in 1897, and it retains its refined, old-world atmosphere. The menu spotlights local produce, but is an interesting nod to influences near and far, from langoustine bruschetta to Peruvian ceviche to organic vegetarian barley burgers. There's a small bar in the cellar, too.

★ Humarhöfnin
ICELANDIC €€

(☎478 1200; www.humarhofnin.is; Hafnarbraut 4; mains kr2900-8400; ⊙noon-10pm May-Sep, to 9pm Oct-Nov) Humarhöfnin offers 'Gastronomy Langoustine' in a cute, cheerfully Frenchified space with superb attention to detail: herb pots on the windowsills, roses on every table. Mains that centre on pincer-waving critters cost upwards of kr7000, but there are also more budget-friendly dishes including a fine langoustine baguette (kr3900) or pizza (kr2900).

★ Pakkhús
ICELANDIC €€€

(☎478 2280; www.pakkhus.is; Krosseyjarvegur 3; mains kr3200-6850; ⊙noon-10pm mid-May–mid-Sep, 5-9pm mid-Sep–mid-May) Hats off to a menu that tells you the name of the boat that delivers its star produce. In a stylish harbour-side warehouse, Pakkhús offers a level of kitchen creativity you don't often find in rural Iceland. First-class local langoustine, lamb and duck tempt taste buds, while clever desserts end the meal in style; who can resist a dish called '*skyr* volcano'?

ℹ Information

Gamlabúð Visitor Centre (☎470 8330; www.visitvatnajokull.is; Heppuvegur 1; ⊙9am-7pm Jun-Aug, to 6pm May & Sep, to 5pm Oct-Apr) Harbourfront Gamlabúð houses a national park visitor centre with excellent exhibits, plus local tourist information. Ask about activities and hiking trails in the area.

ℹ Getting There & Away

Höfn is about 6km south of the Ring Road on Rte 99. The nearest towns in either direction are Kirkjubæjarklaustur, 200km west, and Djúpivogur, 105km east.

AIR

Höfn's airport is 6.5km northwest of town. Eagle Air (www.eagleair.is) flies year-round between Reykjavík and Höfn (one way from kr16,000).

BUS

Bus companies travelling through Höfn have different stops, so make sure you know what operator you're travelling with and confirm where they pick up from.

Buses heading from Höfn to Reykjavik stop at all major towns and landmarks, including Jökulsárlón, Skaftafell, Kirkjubæjarklaustur, Vík, Skógar, Hvolsvöllur, Hella and Selfoss. See websites for up-to-date rates and schedules.

Note that there is no winter bus connection between Egilsstaðir and Höfn (ie bus 62a doesn't run).

Reykjavík Excursions (p257) services (stop at N1 petrol station):

➡ Bus 19 to Skaftafell (kr5750, 4¼ hours, one daily June to August). Stops at Jökulsárlón for 2½ hours. Can be used as a day tour returning to Höfn (with 5¼ hours at Skaftafell).

SBA-Norðurleið (☎550 0700; www.sba.is) services (stop at N1 petrol station):

➡ Bus 62a to Egilsstaðir (kr10,000, five hours, one daily June to August; stops at Djúpivogur, Breiðdalsvík and fjords along Rtes 92 and 96).

➡ Bus 62a to Mývatn (kr16,100, 7½ hours, one daily June to August).

➡ Bus 62a to Akureyri (kr20,000, 9¼ hours, one daily June to August).

Sterna (☎551 1166; www.icelandbybus.is) services (pick-up/drop-off at campground):

➡ Bus 12a to Reykjavik (kr12,600, 10¼ hours, one daily June to August).

Strætó (☎540 2700; www.straeto.is) services (pick-up/drop-off out front of the swimming pool):

➡ Bus 51 to Reykjavik (kr12,760, 7¼ hours, two daily June to mid-September, one daily Sunday to Friday mid-September to May).

Landmannalaugar

Mind-blowing multicoloured mountains, soothing hot springs, rambling lava flows and clear blue lakes make Landmannalaugar one of Iceland's most unique destinations, and a must for explorers of the interior. It's a favourite with Icelanders and visitors alike... as long as the weather cooperates.

Part of the Fjallabak Nature Reserve, Landmannalaugar (600m above sea level) includes the largest geothermal field in Iceland outside the Grímsvötn caldera in Vatnajökull. Its multihued peaks are made of rhyolite – a mineral-filled lava that cooled unusually slowly, causing those amazing colours.

The area is the official starting point for the famous **Laugavegurinn hike**, and there's some excellent day hiking as well. The day-use fee for the facilities at Landmannalaugar is kr600.

🏃 Activities

★ Ljótipollur   HIKING

Day-hike to the ill-named Ljótipollur (Ugly Puddle), an incredible magenta crater filled with bright-blue water. The intense, fiery red colour comes from iron-ore deposits. Oddly enough, although it was formed by a volcanic explosion, the lake is rich in brown trout. The walk to the Puddle offers plenty of eye candy, from tephra desert and lava flow to marsh and braided glacial valleys.

Frostastaðavatn   HIKING

This blue lake lies behind the rhyolite ridge immediately north of the Landmannalaugar hut. Walk over the ridge and you'll be rewarded with far-ranging views as well as close-ups of the interesting rock formations and moss-covered lava flows flanking the lake. If you walk at least one way on the road and spend some time exploring around the lake, the return trip takes two to three hours.

Brennisteinsalda   HIKING

When the weather is clear, opt for a walk that takes in the region's spectacular views. From Landmannalaugar climb to the summit of rainbow-streaked Brennisteinsalda – covered in steaming vents and sulphur deposits – for a good view across the rugged and variegated landscape. It's a 6.5km return trip from Landmannalaugar. From Brennisteinsalda it's another 90 minutes along the Þórsmörk route to the impressive Stórihver geothermal field.

ℹ Getting There & Away

Landmannalaugar can be reached by rugged, semi-amphibious buses from three different directions. They run when the roads are open to Landmannalaugar (check www.road.is).

From Reykjavík Buses travel along the western part of the Fjallabak Rte, which first follows Rte 26 east of the Þjorsá to F225.

From Skaftafell Buses follow the Fjallabak Rte (F208).

LAUGAVEGURINN HIKE: LANDMANNALAUGAR TO ÞÓRSMÖRK

The hike from Landmannalaugar to Þórsmörk – commonly known as Laugavegurinn – is where backpackers earn their stripes in Iceland. It means 'Hot Spring Road', and it's easy to understand why. The harsh, other-worldly beauty of the landscape morphs in myriad ways as you traipse straight through the island's interior, with much of the earth steaming and bubbling from the intense activity below its surface. Expect wildly coloured mountainsides, glacial rivers and the glaciers themselves, and then you'll finally emerge at a verdant nature reserve in Þórsmörk. It is the most popular hike in Iceland and infrastructure is sound, with carefully positioned huts along the zigzagging 55km route. But it is essential that you book months in advance if you intend to use them. Campers do not need to reserve.

Ferðafélag Íslands (www.fi.is) runs facilities in the area and its website is loaded with information. They break Laugavegurinn into four sections (see the website for a detailed description), and many hikers opt to tackle one section each day for four days. Some hikers add an extra day to their trek, continuing along the Fimmvörðuháls trail from Þórsmörk to Skógar.

Check www.safetravel.is before setting out (and log your plan with them), and be sure to register at the information hut in Landmannalaugar. It is imperative not to attempt the hike out of season (opening dates vary according to weather, but tend to be early July to early September), as the conditions can be lethal and there will be no services on the route. Even in summer there will be snow and fog along the way, and rivers to cross; prepare accordingly.

Laugavegurinn Hike

From Mývatn Buses cut across the highlands via Nýidalur on the Sprengisandur Rte (F26).

It's possible to travel from Reykjavík and be in Landmannalaugar for two to 10 hours before returning to Reykjavík, or three to five hours before going on to Skaftafell. That's about enough time to take a dip in the springs and/or a short walk. Schedules change, but morning buses usually reach Landmannalaugar by midday. Alternatively, stay overnight and catch a bus out when you're done exploring.

Reykjavík Excursions (p257) services:
➡ Bus 10/10a Skaftafell–Landmannalaugar (kr9400, five hours, one daily late June to early September).

➡ Bus 11/11a Reykjavík–Landmannalaugar (kr8250, 4¼ hours, three to four daily mid-June to mid-September).

➡ Bus 14/14a Mývatn–Landmannalaugar (kr18,750, 10 hours, one daily late June to early September).

Sterna (p280) services:
➡ Bus 13/13a Reykjavík–Landmannalaugar (kr8000, four hours, one daily late June to early September).

Trex (p235) services:
➡ Bus T21 Reykjavík–Landmannalaugar (kr8200, 4¼ hours, two daily mid-June to early September).

Vestmannaeyjar

Jagged and black, the Vestmannaeyjar (sometimes called the Westman Islands) form 15 eye-catching silhouettes off the southern shore. The islands were formed by submarine volcanoes around 11,000 years ago, except for Surtsey, the archipelago's newest addition, which rose from the waves in 1963. Surtsey was made a Unesco World Heritage Site in 2008, but its unique scientific status means that it is not possible to land there, except for scientific study.

Heimaey is the only inhabited island. Its little town and sheltered harbour lie between dramatic *klettur* (escarpments) and two ominous volcanoes – blood-red Eldfell and conical Helgafell. These days Heimaey is famous for its puffins (around 10 million birds come here to breed); Þjóðhátíð (National Festival Þjóðhátíð Vestmannaeyjar; www.dalurinn.is; kr23,900; ☉ Jul or Aug), Iceland's biggest outdoor festival, held in August; and its state-of-the-art volcano museum. It's also home to one of Iceland's most lively and creative restaurants, **Slippurinn** (☑ 481 1515; www.slippurinn.com; Strandvegur 76; lunch

kr2200-3000, dinner mains kr3490-6990, set menu kr7990-11,990; ☉ noon-2.30pm & 5-10pm early May–mid-Sep; ☎).

All ferries and flights go to Heimaey, from where you can catch tour boats that sail among the other islands.

Vík & Around

POP 320

The welcoming little community of Vík (aka Vík í Mýrdal) has become a booming hub for a very beautiful portion of the south coast. Iceland's southernmost town, it's also the rainiest, but that doesn't stop the madhouse atmosphere in summer, when every room within 100km is booked solid. With loads of services, Vík is a convenient base for the beautiful basalt beach Reynisfjara and its puffin cliffs, and the rocky plateau Dyrhólaey (both just to the west), and for the volcanoes running from Skógar to Jökulsárlón glacier lagoon and beyond. Along the coast, white-capped waves wash up on black sands and the cliffs glow green from all that rain. Put simply, it's gorgeous.

◉ Sights

★ **Reynisfjara**   BEACH

On the west side of Reynisfjall, the high ridge above Vík, Rte 215 leads 5km down to the black-sand beach of Reynisfjara. It's backed by an incredible stack of **basalt columns** that look like a magical church organ, and there are outstanding views west to Dyrhólaey.

Surrounding cliffs are pocked with caves formed from twisted basalt, and puffins belly-flop into the crashing sea during summer. Immediately offshore are the towering Reynisdrangur (p268) sea stacks. At all times watch for rogue waves: people are regularly swept away.

Reynisdrangur   LANDMARK

Vík's most iconic cluster of sea stacks is known as Reynisdrangur, which rise from the ocean like ebony towers at the western end of Vík's black-sand beach. Tradition says they're masts of a ship that trolls were stealing when they got caught in the sun. The nearby cliffs are good for puffin watching. A bracing walk up from Vík's western end takes you to the top of **Reynisfjall** ridge (340m), which offers superb views.

Vestmannaeyjar

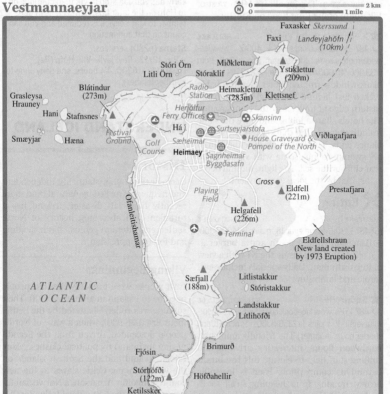

★ **Dyrhólaey**   WILDLIFE RESERVE

One of the South Coast's most recognisable natural formations is the rocky plateau and huge stone sea arch at Dyrhólaey (*deer-lay*), which rises dramatically from the surrounding plain 10km west of Vík, at the end of Rte 218. Visit its crashing black beaches and get awesome views from atop the promontory. The islet is a nature reserve that's rich in bird life, including puffins; some or all of it can be closed during nesting season (15 May to 25 June).

🛏 Sleeping

★ **Garðar**   GUESTHOUSE €€

(📞 487 1260; www.reynisfjara-guesthouses.com; Reynisfjara; cottages kr16,000-29,000) At the end of Rte 215, to the west of Vík, Garðar is a magical, view-blessed place. Friendly farmer Ragnar rents out self-contained beachside huts: one stone cottage sleeps four; other timber cottages sleep two to four.

★ **Guesthouse Carina**   B&B €€

(📞 699 0961; www.guesthousecarina.is; Mýrarbraut 13; s/d/q without bathroom incl breakfast from kr21,900/25,900/31,500; 🅿 🕾) Friendly Carina and her husband Ingvar run one of the best lodging options in Vík. Neat-as-a-pin, spacious rooms with good light and clean shared bathrooms fill a large converted house near the centre of town.

Grand Guesthouse Garðakot   B&B €€

(📞 487 1441; www.ggg.is; Garðakot farm; d kr27,500; 🕾) Set on a pastoral sheep farm, this small, tidy house holds four beautiful rooms, two with private bathrooms and two that share. Heated hardwood floors downstairs, sweeping views of volcanoes and sea upstairs, and friendly proprietors, pretty decor, serenity and flat-screen TVs for all. It's 14km west of Vík, south of the Ring Road on Rte 218.

★ **Icelandair Hótel Vík**   HOTEL €€€
(☑ 487 1480, bookings 444 4000; www.ice-landairhotels.com; Klettsvegur 1-5; d/tr/f from kr33,800/40,000/50,500; ℙ 🛜) This sleek black-window-fronted hotel is improbably tucked just behind the Hótel Edda, on the eastern edge of town, near the campground. The hotels share a lobby (and have the same friendly owners), but that's where the resemblance ends. The Icelandair hotel has suitably swanky rooms, some with views to the rear cliffs or the sea. The light, natural decor is inspired by the local environment.

✗ Eating

Víkurskáli   INTERNATIONAL €
(☑ 487 1230; Austurvegur 18; mains kr1400-3000; ⊙ 11am-9pm) Grab a booth and a burger at the old-school grill inside the N1 with a view of Reynisdrangur. Daily specials include casserole and lamb stew.

★ **Suður-Vík**   ICELANDIC, ASIAN €€
(☑ 487 1515; www.facebook.com/Sudurvik; Suður-víkurvegur 1; mains kr2250-5350; ⊙ noon-10pm, shorter hours in winter) The friendly ambience, hardwood floors, interesting artwork and smiling staff help to elevate this restaurant beyond its competition. Food is Icelandic hearty, ranging from heaping steak sandwiches with bacon and Béarnaise sauce to Asian (think Thai satay with rice). In a warmly lit silver building atop town. Book ahead in summer.

❶ Information

Tourist Information Centre (☑ 487 1395; www.visitvik.is; Víkurbraut 28; ⊙ 10am-7pm Mon-Fri, 11am-5pm Sat & Sun Jun-Aug; 🛜) Inside the iron-clad house Brydebúð.

❶ Getting There & Away

Vík is a major stop for all Reykjavík–Höfn bus routes; buses stop at the N1 petrol station.

Reykjavík Excursions (p257) services:
➡ Bus 20/20a Reykjavík–Skaftafell (Reykjavík–Vík kr7750, four hours, one daily June to early September).

➡ Bus 21/21a Reykjavík–Skógar (Reykjavík–Vík kr7750, 3¾ hours, one daily June to August) One of the two services to Skógar goes as far as Vík each day.

Strætó (p280) services:
➡ Bus 51 Reykjavík–Vík–Höfn (Reykjavík–Vík kr6160, 2¾ hours, two daily) If you take the

early bus you can stop in Vík then continue on to Höfn on the later bus; however, from September to May service is reduced and you can't count on that connection.

Sterna (p280) services:
➡ Bus 12/12a Reykjavík–Vík–Höfn (Reykjavík–Vík kr6200, 4¼ hours, one daily June to mid-September).

UNDERSTAND ICELAND

History

Geologically young, staunchly independent and frequently rocked by natural (and more recently financial) disaster, Iceland has a turbulent and absorbing history of Norse settlement, literary genius, bitter feuding and foreign oppression.

Viking Beginnings

Irish monks were probably the first people to come to Iceland in around AD 700. Their solitude was rudely shattered by the Settlement Era (871–930), when a wave of Nordic people descended, driven from the Scandinavian mainland by political clashes. Many raided Ireland and the Scottish islands on the way, bringing Celtic slaves to the new country. Ingólfur Arnarson, a Norwegian fugitive, became the first official Icelander (AD 871). He settled at Reykjavík (Smoky Bay), which he named after steam he saw rising from geothermal vents.

According to 12th-century sources, Ingólfur built his farm on Aðalstræti. Recent archaeological excavations have unearthed a Viking longhouse on that very spot; the dwelling is now the focus of the Reykjavík 871+/-2 museum. The settlers rejected monarchy and established the world's first democratic parliament at Þingvellir (Parliament Plains), outside Reykjavík. The country converted to Christianity in the year 1000.

Six-Hundred Years of Misery

Two hundred years of peace ended during the Sturlung Age (1230–62), when Iceland's chieftains descended into bloody territorial fighting. Under pressure from the Norwegian king and with few alternatives, Iceland ceded control of the country to Norway in 1262. In 1397 the Kalmar Union of Norway, Sweden and Denmark brought Iceland under Danish rule. For the next six centuries, the forgotten country endured a dark age of famine, disease and disastrous volcanic eruptions.

In the early 17th century the Danish king imposed a trade monopoly that was exploited by foreign merchants. In an attempt to bypass the crippling embargo, weaving, tanning and wool-dyeing factories were built, which led to the foundation of the city of Reykjavík.

Iceland's next calamity was volcanic. In 1783 the vast crater row Lakagígar (Laki) erupted for 10 months, devastating southeastern Iceland and creating a lingering poisonous haze. Nearly 75% of Iceland's livestock and 20% of the human population perished in the resulting famine; an evacuation of the country was discussed.

Birth of a New Nation

In spite (or perhaps because) of such neglectful foreign rule and miserable living conditions, a sense of Icelandic nationalism slowly began to grow.

Perversely, while the rest of Europe endured the horrors of WWII, Iceland went from strength to strength: at the outbreak of war it was an independent state within the Kingdom of Denmark, asserting its neutrality; by war's end, it was a republic (triggered by the German occupation of Denmark). The Republic of Iceland was established on 17 June 1944, symbolically at Þingvellir.

British and then US troops were stationed at Keflavík (right up until 2006), bringing with them undreamt-of wealth. Subsistence farming gave way to prosperity and a frenzy of new building, funded mainly by American dollars. The Ring Road, Iceland's main highway that circles the whole country, was finally completed in 1974.

Boom...& Bust

A corresponding boom in the fishing industry saw Iceland extend its fishing limit in the 1970s to 200 miles (322km). This precipitated the worst of the 'cod wars', when the UK initially refused to recognise the new zone and continued fishing inside what were now deemed to be Icelandic waters. During the seven-month conflict, Icelandic ships cut the nets of British trawlers, shots were fired and ships on both sides were rammed.

Iceland's booming economy suffered when the world financial crisis dealt the country a sledgehammer blow in 2008, thanks to massive foreign debt and a severely overvalued currency. All three national banks went into receivership, and the country teetered on the brink of bankruptcy.

Help came in the form of International Monetary Fund (IMF) loans, and bailouts from Scandinavian neighbours. Protestors rioted in Reykjavík, suffering the effects of spiralling inflation and furious with a government they felt had betrayed them in not downsizing the bloated banking system.

The government fell, and in May 2009 a new left-wing government was elected, headed by Jóhanna Sigurðardóttir, Iceland's first female prime minister. Her first major act was to apply for EU membership, with the eventual aim of adopting the euro as the country's new currency in an effort to stabilise the economy. EU membership was then (and continues to be) a contentious issue.

The banking collapse was a terrible blow to Icelanders – its legacy included high household debt, high inflation, record unemployment and emigration for work.

But, incredibly, the economic situation has begun to right itself. Where other countries chose to bail out their financial institutions, the Icelandic government refused to use taxpayers' money to prop up the failing banks, and let the private banks' creditors take the hit.

Ash, Cash & the Road to Recovery

Icelanders went to the polls in April 2013 with the national economy on the path to recovery, but with the population smarting from the government's tough austerity measures (higher taxes, spending cuts). The results showed a clear backlash against the ruling Social Democrats; two centre-right parties formed a coalition government. In early 2014 the government halted all membership negotiations with the EU.

In volcano news, the ash cloud from the April 2010 eruption under Eyjafjallajökull glacier shut down European air traffic for six days, causing travel chaos across much of the continent. The Grímsvötn volcano, which erupted the following year, was a mere trifle by comparison: its ash cloud only managed three days of air-traffic disruption. In mid- to late 2014, all eyes were on the Bárðarbunga eruption.

However, erupting volcanoes tickled people's interest and this, combined with the devalued króna, gave the nation's tourism industry an unforeseen jolt. Recently, Iceland has been registering record-breaking tourist numbers; the country hosted one million annual visitors in 2014, doubling numbers from 2010. The trend seems to be continuing, with that figure rising to 1.8 million in 2016, a 40% increase on the year before.

Religion

Iceland officially converted to Christianity around 1000, although followers of the old pagan gods were allowed to worship in private. The Danes imposed Lutheranism in the 1550 Reformation: today, as in mainland Scandinavia, most Icelanders (around 80%) belong to the Protestant Lutheran Church – but many are nonpractising.

Arts

Literature

Iceland produces the most writers and literary translations per capita of any country in the world.

Bloody, black, humorous and powerful, the late-12th- and 13th-century sagas are some of Iceland's greatest cultural achievements. Written in Old Norse, these epics look back on the disputes, families, doomed romances and larger-than-life characters (from warrior and poet to outlaw) who lived during the Settlement Era. They continue to entertain Icelanders and provide them with a rich sense of heritage.

Iceland's most celebrated 20th-century author is Nobel Prize-winner Halldór Laxness (1902–98). His darkly comic work gives a superb insight into Icelandic life. His most famous book, *Independent People* (1934), concerning the bloody-minded farmer Bjartur and the birth of the Icelandic nation, is an unmissable read.

Modern Icelandic writers include Einar Kárason, who wrote the outstanding *Devil's Island* (1983; about Reykjavík life in the 1950s). Hallgrímur Helgason's *101 Reykjavík* (1996) is the book on which the cult film was based. Currently surfing the Nordic Noir tidal wave is Arnaldur Indriðason, whose Reykjavík-based crime fiction permanently tops the bestsellers list.

Music

Iceland punches above its weight in the pop-music world. Internationally famous Icelandic musicians include (of course) Björk, and her former band, The Sugarcubes. Sigur Rós have followed Björk to stardom; their biggest-selling album *Takk* (2005) garnered rave reviews around the world.

Indie-folk band Of Monsters and Men stormed the US charts in 2011 with their debut album *My Head is an Animal*. More recently Ásgeir Trausti, who records simply as Ásgeir, had a breakout hit with *In the Silence* (2014), an English-language album, and he has been selling out concerts internationally.

Back home, Reykjavík has a flourishing music scene with a constantly changing line-up of new bands and sounds; see www.icelandmusic.is for an idea of the variety. If your trip coincides with one of the country's many music festivals, go! The fabulous Iceland Airwaves music festival (held in Reykjavík in November) showcases Iceland's talent along with international acts, as does Secret Solstice (June).

Environment

The Land

Contrary to popular opinion, Iceland isn't completely covered in ice, nor is it a treeless, lunar landscape of congealed lava flows and windswept tundra. Both of these habitats exist, but so too do steep-sided fjords, rolling emerald-green hills, glacier-carved valleys and bubbling mudpots.

A mere baby in geological terms, Iceland is the youngest country in Europe, formed by underwater volcanic eruptions along the joint of the North American and Eurasian plates 17 to 20 million years ago. At 103,000 sq km, it is roughly the size of Portugal, or the US state of Kentucky. Within its borders are some 30 active volcanoes. Its landscape is 3% lakes, 11% ice caps and glaciers, 23% vegetation and 63% wasteland. Its highest point, Hvannadalshnúkur, rises 2110m.

Iceland's active volcanic zone runs through the middle of the country, from southwest to northeast. Active-zone geological features include lava flows, tubes, geysers, hot springs and volcanoes, and rocks such as basalt, pumice and rhyolite. Geysir, Krýsuvík and Krafla are very accessible active areas.

There are few trees, although more are being planted to combat erosion. Most of the native flora consists of grasses, mosses, lichens and wildflowers.

Wildlife

Apart from birds, sheep and horses, you'll be lucky to have any casual sightings of land animals in Iceland. The only indigenous land mammal is the elusive Arctic fox. Reindeer were introduced from Norway in the 18th century and now roam the mountains in the east. Polar bears very occasionally drift across from Greenland on ice floes, but armed farmers make sure they don't last long.

In contrast, Iceland has a rich marine life. On whale-watching tours from Húsavík in northern Iceland (among other places), you'll have an excellent chance of seeing cetaceans, particularly dolphins, porpoises, minke whales and humpback whales. Sperm, fin, sei, pilot, killer and blue whales also swim in Icelandic waters. Seals can be seen in a handful of regions.

Birdlife is prolific, at least from May to August. On coastal cliffs and islands around the country you can see a mind-boggling array of seabirds, often in massive colonies. Most impressive for their sheer numbers are gannets, guillemots, gulls, razorbills, kittiwakes, fulmars and puffins.

National Parks & Reserves

Iceland has three national parks and more than 100 nature reserves, natural monuments and country parks, with a protected area of 18,806 sq km (about 18% of the entire country).

Iceland's three national parks:

Snæfellsjökull In west Iceland. Protects the Snæfellsjökull glacier (made famous by Jules Verne), the surrounding lava fields and coast.

Þingvellir Part of the Golden Circle, southeast of the capital, and a Unesco World Heritage Site.

Vatnajökull Founded in 2008, joining the Vatnajökull ice cap and the former Skaftafell and Jökulsárgljúfur national parks to form one giant, 13,900-sq-km megapark.

Environmental Issues

Historically, sheep farming and timber extraction caused immense environmental damage. At the time of settlement (9th century) an estimated quarter of the country was covered by birch woodlands, whereas today forests only cover a little over 1%. Large-scale aerial seeding and intensive tree-planting programs are combating erosion.

To ensure prosperity continues even if the tourism boom comes to a crashing halt, Iceland is shoring up its position as a green-energy superpower, looking at exporting its geothermal and hydroenergy knowhow (and quite possibly its actual energy, transmitting via undersea cables) to foreign shores. It's also wooing more big-business energy-users to consider setting up shop (it already has large aluminium smelters here for the cheap, abundant power).

The most controversial project in Icelandic history was the Kárahnjúkar hydroelectric station in east Iceland. Completed in 2009, it created a network of dams and tunnels, a vast reservoir, a power station and kilometres of power lines to supply electricity to a fjordside smelter 80km away. In the process, it altered the courses of two glacial rivers and flooded a vast area of untouched wilderness. Environmentalists fear that other tracts of Iceland's wilderness may be threatened by industrial megaprojects.

An important debate is also taking place, questioning whether Iceland's fragile environment can withstand the pressure it is now under due to the rapid increase in visitor numbers. There is a nascent government proposal to introduce a one-off fee (perhaps an arrival tax payable at the airport, or a nature pass you purchase depending on the length of your stay), ensuring travellers contribute to the protection and maintenance of natural sites.

Food & Drink

If people know anything about Icelandic food, it's usually the punchline of a plucky population tucking into boundary-pushing dishes like fermented shark. It's a pity the spotlight doesn't shine as brightly on Iceland's delicious, fresh-from-the-farm ingredients, the seafood bounty hauled from the surrounding icy waters, the innovative dairy products (hello, *skyr!*) or the clever historic food-preserving techniques that are finding new favour with today's much-feted New Nordic chefs.

Where to Eat & Drink

Iceland's best restaurants are in Reykjavík, but some magnificent finds are mushrooming up beyond the capital. In rural Iceland you may not have a huge choice – the town's only eating place may be the restaurant in the local hotel, supplemented by the grill in the petrol station. And in peak summer you may struggle to get a table without a reservation, and/or face long waits.

À la carte menus usually offer at least one fish dish, one vegie choice (invariably pasta) and a handful of meat mains (lamb stars, of course). Many restaurants also have a menu of cheaper meals such as hamburgers and pizzas. Soup will invariably appear as a lunchtime option (perhaps in the form of a soup-and-salad buffet), or as a dinnertime starter. Large petrol stations often have good, cheap, well-patronised grills and cafeterias attached.

Downtown Reykjavík has a great range of bohemian cafe-bars. The cafe scene is spreading too, with some cool new spots scattered around the country. Many of Reykjavík's cafes morph into wild drinking dens in the evenings (Fridays and Saturdays mostly).

Every town and village has at least one small supermarket. Bónus is the country's budget supermarket chain. Alcohol is available to people aged over 20 from licensed hotels, bars, restaurants and Vínbúð (state monopoly) stores.

SURVIVAL GUIDE

❶ Directory A–Z

ACCOMMODATION

Iceland has a broad range of accommodation, but demand often outstrips supply. If you're visiting in the shoulder and high seasons (from May to September), book early.

Campgrounds There's no requirement to book, so camping allows some degree of spontaneity – but also exposure to the elements. Campervans are growing in popularity.

Hostels Popular budget options are spread across the country.

Guesthouses Run the gamut from homestyle B&Bs to large hotel-like properties.

Hotels From small, bland and business-like hotels to designer dens with all the trimmings (and prices to match).

Mountain huts These are a basic option for hikers and explorers, but book ahead.

Camping

Tjaldsvæði (organised campsites) are found in almost every town, at some rural farmhouses and along major hiking trails. The best sites have washing machines, cooking facilities and hot showers, but others just have a cold-water tap and a toilet block. Some are attached to the local *sundlaug* (swimming pool), with shower facilities provided by the pool for a small fee.

Icelandic weather is notoriously fickle, and if you intend to camp it's wise to invest in a good-quality tent. There are a few outfits in Reykjavík that offer rental of camping equipment, and some car-hire companies can also supply you with gear such as tents, sleeping mats and cooking equipment.

With the increase in visitors to Iceland, campgrounds are getting busier, and service blocks typically housing two toilets and one shower are totally insufficient for coping with the demand of dozens of campers. If the wait is long, consider heading to the local swimming pool and pay to use the amenities there.

It is rarely necessary (or possible) to book a camping spot in advance. Many small-town campsites are unstaffed – look for a contact number for the caretaker posted on the service block, or an instruction to head to the tourist information centre or swimming pool to pay. Alternatively, a caretaker may visit the campsite in the evening to collect fees.

A few things to keep in mind:
➥ When camping in parks and reserves the usual rules apply: leave sites as you find them; use biodegradable soaps; carry out your rubbish.

➥ Campfires are not allowed, so bring a stove. Butane cartridges and petroleum fuels are available in petrol stations. Blue Campingaz cartridges are not always readily available; the grey Coleman cartridges are more common.

➥ Camping with a tent or campervan/caravan usually costs kr1200 to kr1800 per person. Electricity is often an additional kr800. Many campsites charge for showers.

➥ A 'lodging tax' of kr111 per site exists; some places absorb this cost in the per-person rate, others make you pay it in addition to the per-person rate.

➥ Consider purchasing the good-value Camping Card (www.campingcard.is), which costs kr18,200 and covers 28 nights of camping at 41 campsites throughout the country for two adults and up to four children. Note that the card doesn't include the lodging tax, or any charges for electricity or showers. Get full details online.

➥ Most campsites open from mid-May to mid-September. Large campsites that also offer huts or cottages may be open year-round. This is a fluid situation, as an increasing number of visitors are hiring campervans in the cooler months and looking to camp with facilities – ask at local tourist offices for info and advice.

→ If camping in summer, be aware that if the weather turns bad and you'd like to sleep with a roof over your head, you'd be extremely lucky to find last-minute availability in guesthouses or hostels.

→ Free accommodation directory *Áning* (available from tourist information centres) lists many of Iceland's campsites, but is not exhaustive.

Farmhouse Accommodation

Many rural farmhouses offer campsites, sleeping-bag spaces, made-up guestrooms, and cabins and cottages. Over time, some 'farmhouses' have evolved into large country hotels.

Facilities vary: some farms provide meals or have a guest kitchen, some have outdoor hot-pots (hot tubs), and many provide horse riding or can organise activities such as fishing. Roadside signs flag which farmhouses provide accommodation and what facilities they offer.

Rates are similar to guesthouses in towns, with sleeping-bag accommodation around kr6900 and made-up beds from kr10,300 to kr17,000 per person. Breakfast is usually included in the made-up room price, while an evening meal (generally served at a set time) costs around kr7500.

Some 170 farm properties are members of **Icelandic Farm Holidays** (www.farmholidays.is), which publishes an annual map called *Discover Iceland,* available free from most tourist information centres. Its website helpfully allows you to search by area, type (hotel, B&B, self-catering, hostel etc) and to further narrow down the search with categories such as farmstay, or local food on-site. The company can arrange package self-drive holidays.

Guesthouses

The Icelandic term *gistiheimilið* (guesthouse) covers a broad range of properties, from family homes renting out a few rooms, to a cluster of self-contained cottages, to custom-built blocks of guestrooms.

Guesthouses vary enormously in character, from stylish, contemporary options to those with plain, chintzy or dated decor. A surprisingly high number offer rooms only with a shared bathroom.

Most are comfortable and cosy, with guest kitchens, TV lounges and buffet-style breakfasts (either included in the price or for around kr2000 extra). If access to a self-catering kitchen is important to you, it pays to ask beforehand to ensure availability.

Some guesthouses offer sleeping-bag accommodation at a price significantly reduced from that of a made-up bed. Some places don't advertise a sleeping-bag option, so it's worth asking.

As a general guide, sleeping-bag accommodation costs kr7000 per night, double rooms in summer are kr18,000 to kr27,000, and self-contained units excluding linen from kr19,500. Guesthouse rooms with their own bathroom are often similarly priced to hotel rooms.

Hostels

Iceland has 32 well-maintained hostels administered by **Hostelling International Iceland** (www.hostel.is). In Reykjavík, Akureyri and a handful of other places, there are also independent backpacker hostels. Bookings are recommended at all of them, especially from June to August.

About half the HI hostels open year-round. Check online for opening-date info.

All hostels offer hot showers, cooking facilities and sleeping-bag accommodation, and most offer private rooms (some with a private bathroom). If you don't have a sleeping bag, you can hire linen (prices vary, but reckon on around kr2000 per person, per stay).

Breakfast (where available) costs kr1750 to kr2500.

Join **Hostelling International** (www.hihostels.com) in your home country to benefit from HI member discounts of kr700 per person. Non-members pay around kr6100 for a dorm bed; single/double rooms cost kr8500/13,500 (more with private bathrooms). Children aged five to 12 get a discount of kr1500.

Hotels

Every major town has at least one business-style hotel, usually featuring comfortable but innocuous rooms with a private bathroom, phone, TV and sometimes minibar. Invariably, hotels also have decent restaurants.

Summer prices for singles/doubles start at around kr22,000/29,000 and usually include a buffet breakfast. Rates for a double room at a nice but nonluxurious hotel in a popular tourist area in peak summer can easily top kr36,000.

Prices drop substantially outside high season (June to August), and cheaper rates may be found online.

The largest local chains are Icelandair Hotels (www.icelandairhotels.is), Fosshótel (www.fosshotel.is), Keahotels (www.keahotels.is) and CenterHotels (www.centerhotels.is). New chain

Stracta Hótels (www.stractahotels.is) has plans to expand beyond its first base in Hella.

Many international hotel chains are eyeing the growing Reykjavík market – Hilton has recently added to its portfolio in the capital, and a new five-star Marriott Edition is set to open in 2018.

Mountain Huts

Private walking clubs and touring organisations maintain *skálar* (mountain huts; singular *skáli*) on many of the popular hiking tracks. The huts are open to anyone and offer sleeping-bag space in basic dormitories. Some huts also offer cooking facilities, campsites and have a summertime warden.

The huts at Landmannalaugar, Þórsmörk and around Askja are accessible by 4WD; huts in Hornstrandir are accessed by boat; many other mountain huts are on hiking trails and accessible only by foot.

GPS coordinates for huts are included in our reviews.

The main organisation providing mountain huts is **Ferðafélag Íslands** (Iceland Touring Association; Map p220; ☑ 568 2533; www.fi.is; Mörkin 6), which maintains 15 huts around Iceland (some in conjunction with local walking clubs). The best huts have showers (for an additional fee, around kr600), kitchens, wardens and potable water; simpler huts usually just have bed space, toilet and a basic cooking area. Beds cost kr5000 to kr8000 for nonmembers. Camping is available at some huts for kr2000 per person.

Other organisations include **Ferðafélag Akureyrar** (p247), which operates huts in the northeast (including along the Askja Trail), and **Útivist** (Map p220; ☑ 562 1000; www.utivist.is; Laugavegur 178; ⊙ noon-5pm Mon-Fri), which has huts at Básar and Fimmvörðuháls Pass in Þórsmörk.

It's essential to book with the relevant organisation, as places fill up quickly.

ACTIVITIES

Iceland's spectacular natural beauty encompasses Western Europe's largest national park and the mightiest ice cap outside the poles, plus a whale-filled ocean and the world's largest puffin colonies. Prepare to greet soaring mountains, hidden valleys, dark canyons, roaring waterfalls, twisting rivers and fjord-riven coastlines. Getting among it is easy, and utterly exhilarating.

Glacier Walking & Snowmobiling

Trekking across an icy white expanse can be one of the most ethereal experiences of your Iceland visit. The island has several options that offer a taste of winter even on the warmest of days – strap on the crampons!

Common-sense safety rules apply: don't get too close to glaciers or walk on them without the proper equipment and guiding.

Hiking & Mountaineering

Opportunities for hiking are endless, from leisurely hour-long strolls to multiday wilderness treks. Setting off on foot will open up vast reaches of unspoilt nature; however, the unpredictable weather is always a consideration, and rain, fog and mist can turn an uplifting hike into a miserable trudge. Always be prepared.

Horse Riding

Horses are an integral part of Icelandic life; you'll see them all over the country. Many farms around the country offer short rides, including a handful of stables within a stone's throw of Reykjavík. Reckon on around 7500kr or 11,000kr for a one- or two-hour ride.

Kayaking & Rafting

Sea-kayaking opportunities abound in the Westfjords (organise these from Ísafjörður), while Seyðisfjörður in the east also has scenic paddling opportunities.

White-water rafting bases are Varmahlíð in northern Iceland (tour pick-ups can be arranged from Akureyri; www.vikingrafting.com) and Reykholt, in the southwest (www.arcticrafting.com). Reykholt also has adrenalin-pumping jetboat rides.

Scuba Diving & Snorkelling

Little-known but incredibly rewarding, diving in Iceland is becoming increasingly popular. The clear water (100m visibility!), great wildlife, spectacular lava ravines, wrecks and thermal chimneys make it a dive destination like no other. The best dive sites are Silfra at Þingvellir and the geothermal chimneys in Eyjafjörður.

A PADI Dry Suit Diver certificate is recommended – you can obtain this in Iceland through a handful of diving companies. The unique PADI Tectonic Plate Awareness course (designed by Dive.is – www.dive.is) gives you an understanding of plate tectonics and what it means to dive between them.

Swimming

Thanks to Iceland's abundance of geothermal heat, swimming is a national institution, and nearly every town has at least one *sundlaug* (heated swimming pool – generally outdoors). Most pools also offer *heitir pottar* (hot-pots; small heated pools for soaking, with the water around 40°C), saunas and Jacuzzis. Admission is usually around 850kr (half-price for children).

The clean, chemical-free swimming pools and natural hot springs require a strict hygiene regimen, which involves a thorough shower without swimsuit before you enter the swimming area. Instructions are posted in a number of languages. Not following these rules is a sure-fire way to offend the locals.

Whale Watching

The most common sightings are of minke and humpback whales, but you can also spot fin, sei and blue whales, among others. Húsavík, Reykjavík and Akureyri all have tour operators.

Prices hover around kr9500 for a two- or three-hour tour. Sailings do in fact run all year, with the best chances of success from June to August.

EMERGENCY & IMPORTANT NUMBERS

To call from outside Iceland, dial your international access code, Iceland's country code (354) then the seven-digit number. There are no area codes in Iceland.

Emergency services (police, ambulance, fire, Search & Rescue)	☑ 112
Directory enquiries	☑ 118
Iceland country code	☑ 354
International access code	☑ 00
Weather	☑ 902 0600 (press 1 after the introduction)
Road condition information	☑ 1777

GAY & LESBIAN TRAVELLERS

Icelanders have a very open, accepting attitude towards homosexuality, though the gay scene is quite low-key, even in Reykjavík.

INTERNET ACCESS

Wi-fi is common in Iceland.

➼ Most accommodation and eating venues across the country offer online access, and often buses do, too. Access is usually free for guests/customers, but there may be a small charge. You may need to ask staff for an access code.

➼ Most of the N1 service stations have free wi-fi.

➼ The easiest way to get online is to buy an Icelandic SIM card with a data package and pop it in your unlocked smartphone. Other devices can then access the internet via the phone.

➼ To travel with your own wi-fi hot spot, check out Trawire (http://iceland.trawire.com) for portable 4G modem rental with unlimited usage, from US$10/day (kr1050; up to 10 laptops or mobile devices can be connected).

➼ Some campervan-hire companies offer portable modem devices as an optional extra.

➼ Most Icelandic libraries have computer terminals for public internet access, even in small towns; there's often a small fee.

➼ Tourist information centres often have public internet terminals, often free for brief usage.

MONEY

Iceland is an almost cashless society where credit cards reign supreme, even in the most rural reaches. PINs are required for purchases. ATMs are available in all towns.

ATMs

➼ As long as you're carrying a valid card, you'll need to withdraw only a limited amount of cash from ATMs.

➼ Almost every town in Iceland has a bank with an ATM *(hraðbanki),* where you can withdraw cash using MasterCard, Visa, Maestro or Cirrus cards.

➼ Diners Club and JCB cards connected to the Cirrus network have access to all ATMs.

➼ You'll also find ATMs at larger petrol stations and in shopping centres.

Credit & Debit Cards

➼ Locals use plastic for even small purchases.

➼ Contact your financial institution to make sure that your card is approved for overseas use – you will need a PIN for purchases.

➼ Visa and MasterCard (and to a lesser extent Amex, Diners Club and JCB) are accepted in most shops, restaurants and hotels.

➼ You can pay for the Flybus from Keflavík International Airport to Reykjavík using plastic – handy if you've just arrived in the country.

➼ If you intend to stay in rural farmhouse accommodation or visit isolated villages, it's a good idea to carry enough cash to tide you over.

Exchange Rates

Australia	A$1	kr78
Canada	C$1	kr80
Europe	€1	kr122
Japan	¥100	kr92
NZ	NZ$1	kr71
UK	UK£1	kr138
US	US$1	kr103

For current exchange rates, see www.xe.com.

OPENING HOURS

Opening hours vary throughout the year (some places are closed outside the high season). In general hours tend to be longer from June to August, and shorter from September to May.

Standard opening hours:

Banks 9am–4pm Monday to Friday

Cafe-bars 10am–1am Sunday to Thursday, 10am to between 3am and 6am Friday and Saturday

Cafes 10am–6pm

Offices 9am–5pm Monday to Friday

Petrol stations 8am–10pm or 11pm

Post offices 9am–4pm or 4.30pm Monday to Friday (to 6pm in larger towns)

Restaurants 11.30am–2.30pm and 6pm–9pm or 10pm

Shops 10am–6pm Monday to Friday, 10am–4pm Saturday; some Sunday openings in Reykjavík malls and major shopping strips.

Supermarkets 9am–8pm (11pm in Reykjavík)

Vínbúðin (government-run alcohol stores) Variable; many outside Reykjavík only open for a couple of hours per day.

PUBLIC HOLIDAYS

Icelandic public holidays are usually an excuse for a family gathering or, when they occur on weekends, a reason to rush to the countryside and go camping. If you're planning to travel during holiday periods, particularly the Commerce Day long weekend, you should book mountain huts and transport well in advance.

National public holidays in Iceland:

New Year's Day 1 January

Easter March or April; Maundy Thursday and Good Friday to Easter Monday (changes annually)

First Day of Summer First Thursday after 18 April

Labour Day 1 May

Ascension Day May or June (changes annually)

Whit Sunday and Whit Monday May or June (changes annually)

National Day 17 June

Commerce Day First Monday in August

Christmas 24 to 26 December

New Year's Eve 31 December

TAXES & REFUNDS

Anyone who has a permanent address outside Iceland can claim a tax refund on purchases when they spend more than kr6000 at a single point of sale. Look for stores with a 'tax-free shopping' sign in the window, and ask for a form at the register.

Before you check in for your departing flight at Keflavík, go to the refund office at Arion Banki and present your completed tax-free form, passport, receipts/invoices and purchases. Make sure the goods are unused. Opening hours of the office match flight schedules.

If you're departing Iceland from Reykjavík airport or a harbour, go to the customs office before check-in.

Full details outlined at www.globalblue.com.

TELEPHONE

➡ Public payphones are elusive in Iceland. You may find them outside post offices, bus stations and petrol stations. Many accept credit cards as well as coins. Local calls are charged at around kr20 per minute.

➡ To make international calls from Iceland, first dial the international access code 00, then the country code, the area or city code, and the telephone number.

➡ To phone Iceland from abroad, dial your country's international access code, Iceland's country code (354) and then the seven-digit phone number.

➡ Iceland has no area codes.

➡ Toll-free numbers begin with 800; mobile (cell) numbers start with 6, 7 or 8.

➡ An online version of the phone book with good maps is at http://en.ja.is.

➡ Useful numbers: directory enquiries 118 (local), 1811 (international).

Also see Emergency & Important Numbers (p285).

Mobile Phones

➡ The cheapest and most practical way to make calls at local rates is to purchase an Icelandic SIM card and pop it into your own mobile phone (tip: bring an old phone from home for that purpose).

➡ Before leaving home, make sure that your phone isn't locked to your home network.

➡ Check your phone will work on Europe's GSM 900/1800 network (US phones work on a different frequency).

➡ Buy prepaid SIM cards at bookstores, grocery stores and petrol stations throughout the country, and also on Icelandair flights. Top-up credit is available from the same outlets.

➡ Iceland telecom Síminn (www.siminn.is/prepaid) provides the greatest network coverage; Vodafone (www.vodafone.is/english/prepaid) isn't far behind. Both have voice-and-data starter packs including local SIM cards; Síminn's costs kr2000 (including kr2900 voice and data credit).

TIME

➡ Iceland's time zone is the same as GMT/UTC (London).

➡ There is no daylight saving time.

➡ From late October to late March Iceland is on the same time as London, five hours ahead of New York and 11 hours behind Sydney.

→ In the northern-hemisphere summer, Iceland is one hour behind London, four hours ahead of New York and 10 hours behind Sydney.

→ Iceland uses the 24-hour clock system, and all transport timetables and business hours are posted accordingly.

TOURIST INFORMATION

Inspired by Iceland (www.inspiredbyiceland. com) is the official tourism site for the country.

Each region also has its own useful site/s:

East Iceland (www.east.is)

North Iceland (www.northiceland.is; www. visitakureyri.is)

Reykjavík (www.visitreykjavik.is)

Southeast Iceland (www.south.is; www. visitvatnajokull.is)

Southwest Iceland (www.visitreykjanes.is; www.south.is)

The Westfjords (www.westfjords.is)

West Iceland (www.west.is)

VISAS

Iceland is one of 26 member countries of the Schengen Convention, under which the EU countries (all but Bulgaria, Croatia, Romania, Cyprus, Ireland and the UK) plus Iceland, Norway, Liechtenstein and Switzerland have abolished checks at common borders.

The visa situation for Iceland is as follows:

→ Citizens of EU and Schengen countries – no visa is required for stays of up to three months.

→ Citizens or residents of Australia, Canada, Japan, New Zealand and the USA – no visa is required for tourist visits of up to three months. Note that the total stay within the Schengen area must not exceed three months in any six-month period.

→ Other countries – check online at www.utl.is.

To work or study in Iceland a permit is usually required – check with an Icelandic embassy or consulate in person or online.

For questions on visa extensions or visas and permits in general, contact the Icelandic Directorate of Immigration, Útlendingastofnun (www.utl.is).

❶ Getting There & Away

Iceland has become far more accessible in recent years, with more flights arriving from more destinations. Ferry transport (from northern Denmark) makes a good alternative for Europeans wishing to take their own car.

Flights, cars and tours can be booked online at lonelyplanet.com/bookings.

AIR

Keflavík International Airport (KEF; ☑ 425 6000; www.kefairport.is) Iceland's main

international airport is 48km southwest of Reykjavík.

Reykjavík Domestic Airport (Reykjavíkur-flugvöllur; Map p220; www.reykjavikairport. is; Innanlandsflug) Internal flights and those to Greenland and the Faroes use this small airport in central Reykjavík.

A growing number of airlines fly to Iceland (including budget carriers) from destinations in Europe and North America. Some airlines have services only from June to August. Find a list of airlines serving the country at www.inspired-byiceland.com (under Plan Your Trip/Travel to Iceland).

Icelandair (www.icelandair.com) The national carrier has an excellent safety record.

Air Iceland Connect (www.airicelandconnect. is) The main domestic airline (not to be confused with Icelandair) also flies to destinations in Greenland and the Faroe Islands.

WOW Air (www.wowair.com) Icelandic low-cost carrier, serving a growing number of European and North American destinations.

SEA

Smyril Line (www.smyrilline.com) operates a pricey but well-patronised weekly car ferry, the *Norröna*, from Hirtshals (Denmark) through Tórshavn (Faroe Islands) to Seyðisfjörður in East Iceland. It operates year-round, although winter passage is weather-dependent – see the website for more.

Fares vary greatly, depending on dates of travel, what sort of vehicle (if any) you are travelling with, and cabin selection. The journey time from Hirtshals to Seyðisfjörður is 47 hours.

It's possible to make a stopover in the Faroes. Contact Smyril Line or see the website for trip packages.

❶ Getting Around

Air If you're short on time, domestic flights can help you get around efficiently.

Bus A decent bus network operates from around mid-May to late-August or mid-September, shuttling you between major destinations and into the highlands. Outside these months, services are less frequent (even nonexistent). Find an invaluable online map at www.public-transport.is.

Car The most common way for visitors to get around is by car. Vehicles can be expensive to hire but provide great freedom. A 2WD vehicle will get you almost everywhere in summer. Driving into the highlands and on F roads requires 4WDs.

AIR

Iceland has an extensive network of domestic flights, which locals use almost like buses. In winter a flight can be the only way to get between destinations, but weather at this time of year can play havoc with schedules.

Domestic flights depart from the small **Reykjavík Domestic Airport** (p279), not from the major international airport at Keflavík.

A handful of airstrips offer regular sightseeing flights – eg Mývatn, Skaftafell, and Reykjavík and Akureyri domestic airports – and helicopter sightseeing is increasingly popular.

Airlines in Iceland

Air Iceland Connect (⌨570 3030; www.airicelandconnect.is) Not to be confused with the international airline Icelandair. Destinations covered: Reykjavík, Akureyri, Grimsey, Ísafjörður, Vopnafjörður, Egilsstaðir and Þórshöfn. Offers some fly-in day tours.

Eagle Air (⌨Reykjavík 562 4200; www.eagleair.is) Operates scheduled flights to five small airstrips from Reykjavík: Vestmannaeyjar, Húsavík, Höfn, Bíldudalur and Gjögur. It also runs a number of day tours.

BICYCLE

Cycling is an increasingly popular way to see the country's landscapes, but be prepared for harsh conditions.

Gale-force winds, driving rain, sandstorms, sleet and sudden flurries of snow are possible year-round. We recommend keeping your plans relatively flexible so you can wait out bad weather if the need arises.

You'll be forced to ride closely alongside traffic on the Ring Road (there are no hard shoulders to the roads).

The large bus companies carry bikes, so if the weather turns bad or that highlands bike trip isn't working out as planned, consider the bus. Note that space can't be reserved. It's free to take a bike on **Strætó** (p280) services; other companies, such as **Sterna** (p280), **SBA-Norðurleið** (p280) and **Reykjavík Excursions** (p257), charge around kr3500.

Puncture-repair kits and spares are hard to come by outside Reykjavík; bring your own or stock up in the capital. On the road, it's essential to know how to do your own basic repairs.

If you want to tackle the interior, the Kjölur route has bridges over all major rivers, making it fairly accessible to cyclists. A less-challenging route is the F249 to Þórsmörk. The Westfjords also offers some wonderful, challenging cycling terrain.

BOAT

Several year-round ferries operate in Iceland. Major routes all carry vehicles, but it's worthwhile booking ahead for car passage.

Baldur (www.seatours.is) Connecting Stykkishólmur in West Iceland to Brjánslækur in the Westfjords.

Herjólfur (www.herjolfur.is) Connecting Landeyjahöfn in South Iceland to Vestmannaeyjar islands.

Sæfari (www.saefari.is) Connecting Dalvík in North Iceland to Grímsey island on the Arctic Circle.

Sævar (www.hrisey.net) Frequent and easy connections from Árskógssandur in North Iceland, north of Akureyri, to the island of Hrísey.

From June to August, regular boat services run from Bolungarvík and Ísafjörður to points in Hornstrandir (Westfjords).

BUS

Iceland has an extensive network of long-distance bus routes, with services provided by a handful of main companies. The free *Public Transport in Iceland* map has an overview of routes; pick it up at tourist offices or view it online at www.public transport.is.

From roughly June through to early to mid-September regular scheduled buses run to most places on the Ring Road, into the popular hiking areas of the southwest, and to larger towns in the Westfjords and Eastfjords, and on the Reykjanes and Snæfellsnes Peninsulas. For the rest of the year, services range from daily, to a few weekly, to nonexistent.

In summer, 4WD buses run along some F roads (mountain roads), including the highland Kjölur, Sprengisandur and Askja routes (inaccessible to 2WD cars).

Many bus services can be used as day tours: buses spend a few hours at the final destination before returning to the departure point, and may stop for a half-hour at various tourist destinations en route.

Bus companies may operate from different terminals or pick-up points. Reykjavík has several bus terminals; in small towns, buses usually stop at the main petrol station, but it pays to double-check.

Many buses are equipped with free wi-fi.

Many buses have GPS tracking, so you can see when your bus is approaching your stop.

Bus Companies

Main bus companies:

Reykjavík Excursions (p257)
SBA-Norðurleið (⌨550 0700; www.sba.is)
Sterna (⌨551 1166; www.icelandbybus.is)
Strætó (⌨540 2700; www.bus.is)

CAR & MOTORCYCLE

Driving in Iceland gives you unparalleled freedom to discover the country and, thanks to (relatively) good roads and (relatively) light traffic, it's all fairly straightforward.

➡ The Ring Road (Rte 1) circles the country and, except for a couple of small stretches in East Iceland, is paved.

➤ Beyond the Ring Road, fingers of sealed road or gravel stretch out to most communities.

➤ Driving coastal areas can be spectacularly scenic, and incredibly slow, as you weave up and down over mountain passes and in and out of long fjords.

➤ A 2WD vehicle will get you almost everywhere in summer (note: *not* into the highlands, or on F roads).

➤ In winter heavy snow can cause many roads to close; mountain roads generally only open in June and may start closing as early as September. For up-to-date information on road conditions, visit www.road.is.

➤ Don't be pressured into renting a GPS unit – if you purchase a good, up-to-date touring map, and can read it, you should be fine without a GPS. If you are planning to take remote trails, it will be worthwhile.

Driving Licences

You can drive in Iceland with a driving licence from the US, Canada, Australia, New Zealand and most European countries. If your licence is not in Roman script, you need an International Driving Permit (normally issued by your home country's automobile association).

Fuel & Spare Parts

➤ Petrol stations are regularly spaced around the country, but in the highlands you should check fuel levels and the distance to the next station before setting off.

➤ At the time of research, unleaded petrol and diesel cost about kr200 per litre.

➤ Some Icelandic roads can be pretty lonely, so carry a jack, a spare tyre and jump leads just in case (check your spare when you pick up your rental car).

➤ In the event of a breakdown or accident, your first port of call should be your car-hire agency.

➤ Although the Icelandic motoring association **Félag Íslenska Bifreiðaeigenda** (FÍB; www.fib. is) is only open to locals, if you have breakdown cover with an automobile association affiliated with ARC Europe you may be covered by the FÍB – check with your home association.

➤ FÍB's 24-hour breakdown number is 511 2112. Even if you're not a member, it can provide information and phone numbers for towing and breakdown services.

Hire

Travelling by car is the only way to get to some parts of Iceland. Although car-hire rates are expensive by international standards (actually the most expensive in Europe, according to one recent study), they compare favourably to bus or internal air travel, especially if there are a few of you to split the costs. Shop around and book online for the best deals.

To rent a car you must be 20 years old (23 to 25 years for a 4WD) and hold a valid licence.

The cheapest cars, usually a small hatchback or similar, cost from around kr12,000 to kr14,000 per day in high season (June to August). Figure on paying from around kr16,500 for the smallest 4WD that offers higher clearance than a regular car but isn't advised for large river crossings, and from kr23,000 for a larger 4WD model.

Rates include unlimited mileage and VAT (a hefty 24%), and usually collision damage waiver (CDW).

Weekly rates offer some discount. From September to May you should be able to find considerably better daily rates and deals.

Check the small print, as additional costs such as extra insurance, airport pick-up charges and one-way rental fees can add up.

In winter you should opt for a larger, sturdier car for safety reasons, preferably with 4WD (ie absolutely not a compact 2WD).

In the height of summer many companies run out of rentals. Book ahead.

Many travel organisations (eg Hostelling International Iceland, Icelandic Farm Holidays) offer package deals that include car hire.

Most companies are based in the Reykjavík and Keflavík areas, with city and airport offices. Larger companies have extra locations around the country (usually in Akureyri and Egilsstaðir). Ferry passengers arriving via Seyðisfjörður should contact car-hire agencies in nearby Egilsstaðir.

Car-hire companies:

Átak (www.atak.is)

Avis (www.avis.is)

Budget (www.budget.is)

Cars Iceland (www.carsiceland.com)

Cheap Jeep (www.cheapjeep.is)

Europcar (www.europcar.is) The biggest hire company in Iceland.

Geysir (www.geysir.is)

Go Iceland (www.goiceland.com)

Hertz (www.hertz.is)

SADcars (www.sadcars.com) Older fleet, therefore (theoretically) cheaper prices.

Saga (www.sagacarrental.is)

Road Conditions & Hazards

Good main-road surfaces and light traffic (especially outside the capital and Southwest region) make driving in Iceland relatively easy, but there are some specific hazards. Watch the 'Drive Safely on Icelandic Roads' video on www.drive. is for more.

Ash- & sandstorms Volcanic ash and severe sandstorms can strip paint off cars; strong winds can even topple your vehicle. At-risk areas are marked with orange warning signs.

Blind rises In most cases roads have two lanes with steeply cambered sides and no hard shoulder; be prepared for oncoming traffic in the centre of the road, and slow down and stay to the right when approaching a blind rise, marked as 'Blindhæð' on road signs.

F roads Roads suitable for 4WD vehicles only are F-numbered.

Livestock Sheep graze in the countryside over the summer, and often wander onto roads. Slow down when you see livestock on or near roadsides.

River crossings Few highland roads have bridges over rivers. Fords are marked on maps with a 'V'.

Single-lane bridges Slow down and be prepared to give way when approaching single-lane bridges (marked as 'Einbreið Brú'). Right of way is with the car closest to the bridge.

Sun glare With the sun often sitting low to the horizon, sunglasses are recommended.

Tunnels There are a number of tunnels in Iceland – a couple are single lane, and a little anxiety-inducing! Before you enter such tunnels, a sign will indicate which direction has right of way. There will be a couple of pull-over bays inside the tunnel (signed 'M'). If the passing bay is on your side in the tunnel, you are obligated to pull in and let oncoming traffic pass you.

Unsurfaced roads The transition from sealed to gravel roads is marked with the warning sign 'Malbik Endar' – slow right down to avoid skidding when you hit the gravel. Most accidents involving foreign drivers in Iceland are caused by the use of excessive speed on unsurfaced roads. If your car does begin to skid, take your foot off the accelerator and gently turn the car in the direction you want the front wheels to go. Do not brake.

Winter conditions In winter make sure your car is fitted with snow tyres or chains; carry a shovel, blankets, food and water.

Road Rules

→ Drive on the right.

→ Front and rear seatbelts are compulsory.

→ Dipped headlights must be on at all times.

→ Blood alcohol limit is 0.05%.

→ Mobile phone use is prohibited when driving except with a hands-free kit.

→ Children under six years must use a car seat.

→ Do not drive off-road (ie off marked roads and 4WD trails).

Natural Wonders

Scandinavia's wide, wild expanses encompass forests, lakes, Arctic and volcanic landscapes, all governed by the seasons' spectacular swing. Life is abuzz in summer under the endless daylight, while winter's snowfall is a rapid scene change for the second act of this northern drama.

➡ **Great Outdoors**
➡ **Winter Wonderland**
➡ **Summer Adventures**
➡ **Wildlife**

Above Blue Lagoon (p236), Iceland

284

1. Puffins, Faroe Islands (p100), Denmark 2. Skaftafell (p261),
Iceland 3. Reine (p352), Lofoten Islands, Norway 4. Forest, Finland

PETER ADAMS/GETTY IMAGES ©

Great Outdoors

The scenery in Scandinavia is one of its great attractions. Wild, rugged coasts and mountains, hundreds of kilometres of forest broken only by lakes and the odd cottage, and unspoilt Baltic archipelagos make up a varied menu of uplifting visual treats.

Forests

Mainland Scandinavia has some of the world's top tree cover, and the forests stretch much further than the eye can see. Mainly composed of spruce, pine and birch, these forests are responsible for the crisp, clean, aromatic northern air.

Iceland

Thrown up in the middle of the Atlantic by violent geothermal activity, Iceland offers bleak and epic scenery that is at once both harsh and gloriously uplifting. The juxtaposition of frozen glaciers and boiling geysers make it a wild scenic ride.

Norway

Fjords are famous for a reason; coastal views here take the breath away. There are spectacular views the length of this long country. Near the top, the Lofoten Islands present picturesque fishing villages against the awesome backdrop of glacier-scoured mountains.

Lakes

Once the ice melts, Scandinavia is a watery land. A Finnish or Swedish lake under a midnight sun, pines reflected in the calm, chilly water, and a stillness broken only by the landing of waterbirds: these are enduring images.

Archipelagos

Thousands of islands lie offshore and the Baltic is the place to grab a boat and find an islet to call your own. Out in the Atlantic, the Faroes offer stern cliffs housing vast seabird colonies.

GORAN ASSNER/GETTY IMAGES ©

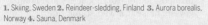

1. Skiing, Sweden 2. Reindeer-sledding, Finland 3. Aurora borealis, Norway 4. Sauna, Denmark

ALTRENDO IMAGES/GETTY IMAGES ©

Winter Wonderland

Once the snows come, bears look for a place to sleep through the winter, but for the rest of us, there's no excuse. The ethereal beauty of the whitened land combines with numerous exciting activities to make this a great time to visit.

Skiing

There's not much you can teach Scandinavians about skiing; they invented it. There are numerous places to hit the powder, with excellent facilities for all levels. Cross-country is big, with lit trails compensating for the long nights.

Winter Activities

Snowmobiles are a part of life up north, and it's lots of fun to whiz about on one. More sedate is ice fishing, but you'd better pack a warm drink. Ice climbing, nights in snow hotels, the aurora borealis (northern lights), snowshoe treks and kick sledding are other popular possibilities.

Sledding

The whoosh of the runners as a team of huskies or reindeer whisks you through the icy northern landscapes – it's tough to beat the feeling. Don't expect a pampered ride though – learn on the job or eat snow!

Landscapes

It's cold, but low winter light and the eerie blue colours the sky takes on make it spectacularly scenic. Trees glistening with ice crystals and snow carpeting the ground add to this magical landscape.

Saunas

If the cold has seeped into your bones, there's nothing like a log fire or, even better, a sauna, to warm the extremities again. Too hot? Get somebody to drill a hole in the lake and jump in. Good for the pores!

1. Snaefellsnes (p238), Iceland 2. Nærøyfjord (p328), Norway
3.Vaxholm (p403), Sweden 4. Summer celebrations, Sweden

Summer Adventures

When the snows melt and the sun returns, it's like a blessing bestowed upon the land. Nature accelerates into top gear, and locals pack a year's worth of fun and festivals into the short but memorably vibrant summer season.

Nordic Peace

For many Scandinavians, summer is spent at a lakeside cottage or campsite where simple pleasures – swimming, fishing, chopping wood, picking berries – replace the stresses of urban life for a few blissful weeks.

Kayaking & Canoeing

It's a perfect time to get the paddles out and explore the rivers and lakes of the interior, or the coastal serrations and islands. Throughout the region, kayaking and canoeing are extremely popular and easy to organise.

Hiking

There's fabulous walking across the whole region, from the jaw-droppingly majestic Icelandic routes to the remote Finnish wilderness. Excellent facilities mean it's easy to plan short walks or multiday hiking adventures.

Midsummer

The summer solstice is celebrated throughout the region, whether with traditional midsummer poles and dancing, or beer, sausages and a lakeside barbecue and bonfire with friends.

Terraces

Once the first proper rays bathe the pavement, coat racks in bars and cafes disappear, and outdoor terraces sprout onto every square and street, packed with people determined to suck up every last drop of the precious summer sun.

Brown bear, Fir

Wildlife

Vast tracts of barely populated land away from the bustle of central Europe make Scandinavia an important refuge for numerous species, including several high-profile carnivores, myriad seabirds and lovable marine mammals.

Elk & Reindeer

If antlers are your thing, you won't be disappointed. The sizeable but ungainly elk (moose) is widespread in the mainland forests, often blundering onto roads or into towns. In Lapland, the domesticated reindeer is the herd animal of the indigenous Sámi.

Brown Bears

The ruler of the forest is deeply rooted in Finnish culture, and there's still a fairly healthy population of them in the east of the country, near the Russian border. Bear-watching trips offer a great opportunity to see these impressively large, shaggy beasts.

Polar Bears & Walrus

Svalbard is as close to the North Pole as most are going to get, and the wildlife is appropriately impressive. The mighty polar bear means you'll need a just-in-case weapon if you want to leave town, while the weighty walrus is also an impressive sight.

Whales & Seabirds

Iceland has important seabird colonies; they breed there in huge numbers. Off Iceland's and Norway's coastlines, several varieties of whale are in regular attendance, best seen on a dedicated boat trip.

Nordic Creatures

The region is stocked with a range of animals: lynx and wolves pace the forests, while golden eagles, ospreys, ptarmigans and capercaillie add feathered glory to the mix. There are seals and dolphins aplenty, and the lonely wolverine prowls the northern wastes in search of prey or carrion.

Norway

Best Places to Eat

➡ Lysverket (p321)

➡ Pjoltergeist (p303)

➡ Bass (p303)

➡ Fiskekrogen (p352)

➡ Børsen (p349)

Best Places to Stay

➡ Engholm Husky Design Lodge (p363)

➡ Basecamp Spitsbergen (p367)

➡ The Thief (p299)

➡ Svinøya Rorbuer (p348)

Why Go?

Norway is a once-in-a-lifetime destination and the essence of its appeal is remarkably simple: this is one of the most beautiful countries on earth.

The drama of Norway's natural world is difficult to over-state. Impossibly steep-sided fjords cut deep gashes into the interior. But this is also a land of glaciers, grand and glori-ous, snaking down from Europe's largest ice fields, and of the primeval appeal of the Arctic.

The counterpoint to so much natural beauty is found in the country's vibrant cultural life. Norwegian cities are cos-mopolitan and brimful of architecture that showcases the famous Scandinavian flair for design. At the same time, a busy calendar of festivals, many of international renown, are worth planning your trip around.

Yes, Norway is one of the most expensive countries on Earth. But Norway will pay you back with never-to-be-forgotten experiences many times over.

When to Go
Oslo

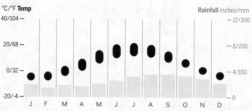

Mid-Jun–mid-Aug	May–mid-Jun & mid-Aug–Sep	Oct–Apr Short
No guarantees of nice weather; book ahead for accommodation	Mild, clear weather and fewer crowds: a good time to travel.	days bitterly cold and many attrac-tions are closed.

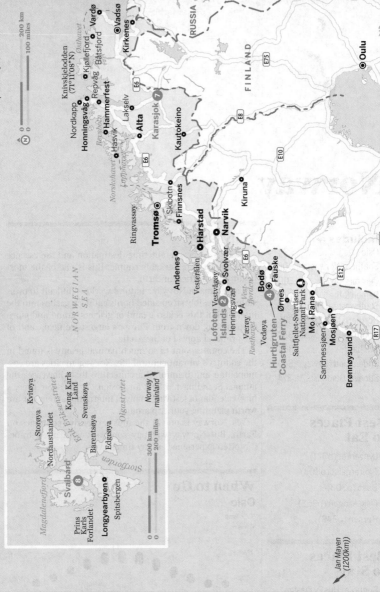

Norway Highlights

1 Aurlandsfjorden
(p328) Taking the ferry Flåm to Gudvangen through some of Norway's most spectacular fjord scenery.

2 Lofoten Islands
(p347) Sleeping in a fisherman's *robu* (shanty) on the craggy and beautiful archipelago.

3 Bergen (p315)
Journeying by train from Oslo to Bergen, arguably Norway's most attractive coastal city.

4 Hurtigruten coastal ferry (p378)
Riding Norway's jagged, beautiful coast.

5 Jotunheimen National Park
(p313) Hiking amid the soaring peaks and countless glaciers.

Svalbard (550km)
(see inset)

200 km
100 miles

N

NORWEGIAN SEA

RUSSIA

FINLAND

Oulu

Vardø
Vadsø
Kirkenes
Båtsfjord
Kjøllefjord
Knivskjelodden (71°11'08"N)
Nordkapp
Honningsvåg
Repvåg
Hammerfest
Lakselv
Hasvik
Alta
Karasjok 7
Kautokeino

E6
E6
E8
E10

Ringvassøy
Tromsø
Skibotn
Finnsnes
Harstad
Kiruna

Andenes
Vesterålen
Lofoten Islands 2
Svolvær
Henningsvær
Narvik
A
Vest-fjorden
Røst
Værøy
Bodø 4
Fauske
Ørnes
Vedøya
Hurtigruten Coastal Ferry
Saltfjellet-Svartisen National Park 4
Mo i Rana

E6
E12
E75
45
R17

Mosjøen
Sandnessjøen
Brønnøysund
Namsos

Jan Mayen (1200km)

Svalbard inset

300 km
200 miles

Kvitøya
Storøya
Nordaustlandet
Kong Karls Land
Kvilip Eriksenstretet
Svenskøya
Barentsøya
Edgeøya
Magdalenefjord
Prins Karls Forlandet
Svalbard 8
Longyearbyen
Spitsbergen
Olgastretet
Storfjorden

Norway mainland

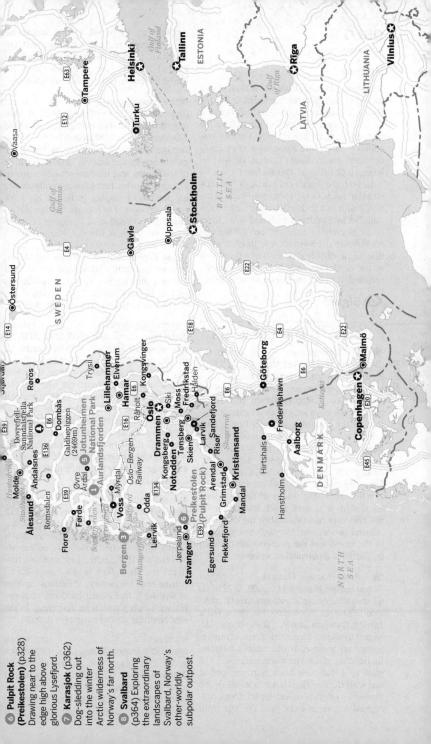

6 Pulpit Rock (Preikestolen) (p328)
Drawing near to the edge high above glorious Lysefjord.

7 Karasjok (p362)
Dog-sledding out into the winter Arctic wilderness of Norway's far north.

8 Svalbard (p364)
Exploring the extraordinary landscapes of Svalbard, Norway's other-worldly subpolar outpost.

OSLO

POP 5.2 MILLION

History

Founded by Harald Hardråda in 1049, Oslo is the oldest Scandinavian capital. In 1299, King Håkon V constructed the Akershus Festning here, to counter the Swedish threat from the east. Levelled by fire in 1624, the city was rebuilt in brick and stone on a more easily defended site by King Christian IV, who renamed it Christiania, after his humble self.

In 1814, the framers of Norway's first constitution made Oslo the official capital of the new realm but their efforts were effectively nullified by Sweden, which had other ideas about Norway's future and unified the two countries under Swedish rule. In 1905, when that union dissolved, Christiania flourished as the capital of modern Norway. The city reverted to its original name, Oslo, in 1925.

◉ Sights

◎ Central Oslo & Aker Brygge

★ **Oslo Opera House** ARCHITECTURE

(Den Norske Opera & Ballett; Map p300; ☎ 21 42 21 21; www.operaen.no; Kirsten Flagstads plass 1; foyer free; ⊙ foyer 10am-9pm Mon-Fri, 11am-9pm Sat, noon-9pm Sun; Ⓣ Sentralstasjonen) The centrepiece of the city's rapidly developing waterfront is the magnificent Opera House, considered one of the most iconic modern buildings of Scandinavia. Designed by Oslo-based architectural firm Snøhetta and costing around €500 million to build, the Opera House opened in 2008, and resembles a glacier floating in the waters of the Oslofjord. Its design is a thoughtful meditation on the notion of monumentality, the dignity of cultural production, Norway's unique place in the world and the conversation between public life and personal experience.

★ **Astrup Fearnley Museet** GALLERY

(Astrup Fearnley Museum; Map p300; ☎ 22 93 60 60; www.afmuseet.no; Strandpromenaden 2; adult/child 120kr/free; ⊙ noon-5pm Tue, Wed & Fri, to 7pm Thu, 11am-5pm Sat & Sun; ⎙ Aker brygge) Designed by Renzo Piano, this private contemporary art museum is housed in a wonderful building of silvered wood, with a sail-like glass roof that feels both maritime and at one with the Oslofjord landscape. While the museum's original collecting brief was conceptual American work from the '80s (with artists of the ilk of Jeff Koons, Tom Sachs, Cindy Sherman and Richard Prince well represented), it has in recent times broadened beyond that, with, for example, a room dedicated to Sigmar Polke and Anselm Kiefer.

★ **Nasjonalgalleriet** GALLERY

(National Gallery; Map p300; ☎ 21 98 20 00; www.nasjonalmuseet.no; Universitetsgata 13; adult/child 100kr/free, Thu free; ⊙ 10am-6pm Tue, Wed & Fri, to 7pm Thu, 11am-5pm Sat & Sun; ⎙ Tullinløkka) The gallery houses the nation's largest collection of traditional and modern art and many of Edvard Munch's best-known creations are on permanent display, including his most renowned work, *The Scream*. There's also an impressive collection of European art, with works by Gauguin, Claudel, Picasso and El Greco, plus Impressionists such as Manet, Degas, Renoir, Matisse, Cézanne and Monet. Nineteenth-century Norwegian artists have a strong showing too, including key figures such as JC Dahl and Christian Krohg.

The gallery is set to relocate in 2020.

Nobels Fredssenter MUSEUM

(Nobel Peace Center; Map p300; ☎ 48 30 10 00; www.nobelpeacecenter.org; Rådhusplassen 1; adult/student 100/65kr; ⊙ 10am-6pm; ⎙ Aker brygge) Norwegians take pride in their role as international peacemakers, and the Nobel Peace Prize is their gift to the men and women judged to have done the most to promote world peace over the course of the previous year. This state-of-the-art museum celebrates the lives and achievements of the winners with an array of digital displays that offer as much or as little information as you feel like taking in.

Museet for Samtidskunst GALLERY

(National Museum of Contemporary Art; Map p300; www.nasjonalmuseet.no) The highly regarded National Museum of Contemporary Art is keeper of the National Gallery's collections of post-WWII Scandinavian and international art. The gallery is also known for its cutting-edge temporary exhibitions. At time of writing it had closed its doors at Bankplassen in preparation for reopening in the new National Museum complex in 2020.

Rådhus ARCHITECTURE

(Map p300; Fridtjof Nansens plass; ⊙ 9am-6pm, guided tours 10am, noon & 2pm Jun–mid-Jul; ⎙ Kontraskjæret) **FREE** This twin-towered town hall, completed in 1950 to commemorate Oslo's 900th anniversary, houses the city's political administration and is filled with mid-century tributes to Norwegian cultural and working life. Something of an Oslo landmark, the bombast of its red-brick functionalist exterior is polarising, if unmissable. It's here that the Nobel Peace Prize is awarded on 10 December each year.

★ **Akershus Festning** FORTRESS
(Akershus Fortress; Map p300; ⊙6am-9pm; 🚇Christiania Square) **FREE** When Oslo was named capital of Norway in 1299, King Håkon V ordered the construction of Akershus, strategically located on the eastern side of the harbour, to protect the city from external threats. It has, over the centuries, been extended, modified and had its defences beefed up a number of times. Still dominating the Oslo harbourfront, the sprawling complex consists of a medieval castle, **Akershus Slott** (Akershus Castle; Map p300; ☑ 22 41 25 21; www. nasjonalefestningsverk.no; Kongens gate; adult/child 60/30kr, with Oslo Pass free; ⊙11am-4pm Mon-Sat, noon-5pm Sun; 🚇Christiania Square), a fortress and assorted other buildings, including still-active military installations.

★ **Ibsen Museet** MUSEUM
(Ibsen Museum; Map p300; ☑ 40 02 36 30; www. ibsenmuseet.no; Henrik Ibsens Gate 26; adult/child 115/30kr; ⊙11am-6pm May-Sep, to 4pm Oct-Apr, guided tours hourly; 🚇Slottsparken) While downstairs houses a small and rather idiosyncratic museum, it's Ibsen's former apartment, which you'll need to join a tour to see, that is unmissable. This was the playwright's last residence and his study remains exactly as he left it, as does the bedroom where he uttered his famously enigmatic last words, *'Tvert imot!'* ('To the contrary!'), before dying on 23 May 1906.

◉ Bygdøy Peninsula

Vikingskipshuset MUSEUM
(Viking Ship Museum; Map p296; ☑ 22 13 52 80; www.khm.uio.no; Huk Aveny 35; adult/child 80kr/free; ⊙9am-6pm May-Sep, 10am-4pm Oct-Apr; 🚌91) Around 1100 years ago, Vikings dragged up two longships from the shoreline and used them as the centrepiece for grand ceremonial burials, most likely for important chieftains or nobles. Along with the ships, they buried many items for the afterlife: food, drink, jewellery, furniture, carriages, weapons, and even a few dogs and servants for companionship. Discovered in Oslofjord in the late 19th century, the ships are beautifully restored and offer an evoc-

ative, emotive insight into the world of the Vikings.

Kon-Tiki Museum MUSEUM
(Map p296; ☑ 23 08 67 67; www.kon-tiki.no; Bygdøynesveien 36; adult/child 100/40kr, with Oslo Pass free; ⊙9.30am-6pm Jun-Aug, 10am-5pm Mar-May, Sep & Oct, 10am-4pm Nov-Feb; 🚌91) A favourite among children, this worthwhile museum is dedicated to the balsa raft *Kon-Tiki*, which Norwegian explorer Thor Heyerdahl sailed from Peru to Polynesia in 1947. The museum also displays the totora-reed boat *Ra II*, built by Aymara people on the Bolivian island of Suriqui in Lake Titicaca. Heyerdahl used it to cross the Atlantic in 1970.

Polarship Fram Museum MUSEUM
(Frammuseet; Map p296; ☑ 23 28 29 50; www. frammuseum.no; Bygdøynesveien 36; adult/child 100/40kr, with Oslo Pass free; ⊙9am-6pm Jun-Aug, 10am-5pm May & Sep, to 4pm Oct-May; 🚌91) This museum is dedicated to one of the most enduring symbols of early polar exploration, the 39m schooner *Fram* (meaning 'Forward'). You can wander the decks, peek inside the cramped bunk rooms and imagine life at sea and among the polar ice. There are detailed exhibits complete with maps, pictures and artefacts of various expeditions, from Nansen's attempt to ski across the North Pole to Amundsen's discovery of the Northwest Passage.

Norsk Folkemuseum MUSEUM
(Norwegian Folk Museum; Map p296; ☑ 22 12 37 00; www.norskfolkemuseum.no; Museumsveien 10; adult/child 130/40kr, with Oslo Pass free; ⊙10am-6pm mid-May–mid-Sep, 11am-3pm Mon-Fri, 11am-4pm Sat & Sun mid-Sep–mid-May; 🚌91) This folk museum is Norway's largest open-air museum and one of Oslo's most popular attractions. The museum includes more than 140 buildings, mostly from the 17th and 18th centuries, gathered from around the country, rebuilt and organised according to region of origin. Paths wind past old barns, elevated *stabbur* (raised storehouses) and rough-timbered farmhouses with sod roofs sprouting wildflowers. Little people will be entertained by the numerous farm animals, horse and cart rides, and other activities.

◉ Greater Oslo

Munchmuseet GALLERY
(Munch Museum; Map p296; ☑ 23 49 35 00; www. munchmuseet.no; Tøyengata 53; adult/child 100kr/free; ⊙10am-4pm, to 5pm mid-Jun–late Sep;

Oslo

T Tøyen) A monographic museum dedicated to Norway's greatest artist Edvard Munch (1863–1944), and housing the largest collection of his work in the world: 28,000 items including 1100 paintings and 4500 watercolours, many of which were gifted to the city by Munch himself (although his best-known pieces, including *The Scream,* are held in the Nasjonalgalleriet, p294).

To get here, take a bus or the T-bane to Tøyen, followed by a 300m signposted walk.

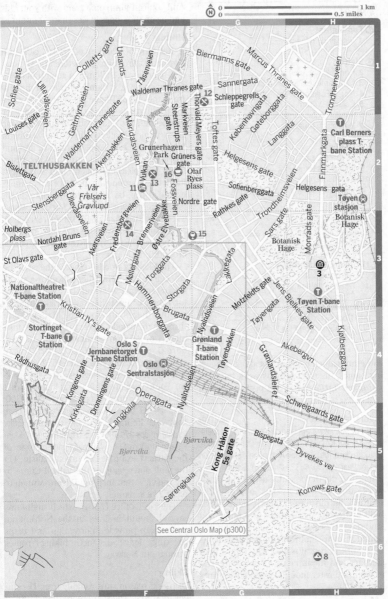

★ **Vigelandsanlegget** PARK
(Vigeland Sculpture Park; Map p296; www.vigeland.
museum.no/no/vigelandsparken; Nobels gate 32;
⊙ Tue-Sun noon-4pm; ⊤ Borgen) The centrepiece of Frognerparken is an extraordinary
open-air showcase of work by Norway's best-

loved sculptor, Gustav Vigeland. Statistically
one of the top tourist attractions in Norway,
Vigeland Park is brimming with 212 granite and bronze Vigeland works. His highly
charged oeuvre includes entwined lovers,
tranquil elderly couples, bawling babies and

Oslo

contempt-ridden beggars. Speaking of bawling babies, his most famous work here, *Sinataggen (Little Hot-Head)*, portrays a child in a mood of particular ill humour.

Vigeland Museum   GALLERY
(Map p296; www.vigeland.museum.no; Nobelsgata 32; adult/child 60/30kr, with Oslo Pass free; ⊙10am-5pm Tue-Sun May-Aug, noon-4pm Tue-Sun rest of year; 🚌20, 🚌12, 🚌N12, 🚇Borgen) For a more in-depth look at Gustav Vigeland's work, this museum is just opposite the southern entrance to Frognerparken. It was built by the city in the 1920s as a home and studio for the sculptor in exchange for the donation of a significant proportion of his life's work. It contains his early collection of statuary and monuments to public figures, as well as plaster moulds, woodblock prints and sketches.

🏃 Activities

Avid skiers, hikers and sailors, Oslo residents will do just about anything to get outside. That's not too hard given that there are more than 240 sq km of woodland, 40 islands and 343 lakes within the city limits.

And you can jump on a train with your skis and be on the slopes in less than 30 minutes.

Hiking

A network of 1200km of trails leads into Nordmarka from Frognerseteren (at the end of T-bane line 1), including a good trail down to Sognsvann lake, 6km northwest of the centre at the end of T-bane line 5. If you're walking in August, be sure to take a container for blueberries, and a swimsuit to cool off in the lake (bathing is allowed in all the woodland lakes around Oslo except Maridalsvannet and Skjersjøen lakes, which are drinking reservoirs). The pleasant walk around Sognsvann itself takes around an hour, or for a more extended trip, try hiking to the cabin at **Ullevålseter** (www.ullevalseter.no; Maridalen; waffles 35-59kr; ⊙10am-4pm Tue-Fri, 9am-7pm Sat & Sun), a pleasant old farmhouse that serves waffles and coffee. The return trip (about 11km) takes around three hours.

The Ekeberg woods to the southeast of the city centre is another nice place for a stroll. During summer weekends it's a popular spot for riding competitions and cricket matches, and there's an Iron Age heritage path through the woods. To get to the woods, take bus 34 or 46 from Jernbanetorget to **Ekeberg Camping** (Map p296; ☎22 19 85 68; www.ekebergcamping.no; Ekebergveien 65; 2-/4-person tent 220/330kr; ⊙Jun-Aug; 🅿; 🚌Ekebergparken). For a piece of architectural history, don't miss the **Ekeberg Restaurant** (Map p300; ☎23 24 23 00; www.ekebergrestauranten.com; Kongsveien 15; mains 295-310kr, set menu 650kr, terrace mains 170-190kr; ⊙11am-midnight Mon-Sat, noon-10pm Sun; 🚌Ekebergparken), one of the earliest examples of functionalism. On the way down, stop at the Valhall Curve to see the view that inspired Edvard Munch to paint *The Scream*.

The DNT office (p304), which maintains several mountain huts in the Nordmarka region, can provide information and maps covering longer-distance hiking routes throughout Norway.

Skiing

Oslo's ski season runs roughly from December to March. There are more than 2400km of prepared nordic tracks (1000km in Nordmarka alone), many of them floodlit, as well as a ski resort within the city limits. Easy-access tracks begin at the end of T-bane lines 1 and 5. The **Skiservice Centre** (☎22 13 95 00; www.skiservice.no; Tryvannsveien 2; ⊙10am-8pm; 🚇Holmen), at Voksenkollen station, one

T-bane stop before Frognerseteren, hires out snowboards and nordic skis. The downhill slopes at **Oslo Vinterpark** (☏404 62 700; www.oslovinterpark.no; ⊙10am-10pm Mon-Fri, to 5pm Sat & Sun Dec–mid-Apr; Ⓣ Holmen) are open in the ski season. Check out www.holmen-kollen.com for more ski-related info.

✦ Festivals & Events

Holmenkollen Ski Festival   SPORTS
(☏22 92 32 00; http://skifest.no/; Kongeveien 5; ⊙early Mar) One of the world's most revered ski festivals. Its penultimate day is so loved by locals it's dubbed 'second National Day'.

OverOslo   MUSIC
(www.overoslo.no; Grefsenkollveien 100; ⊙Jun) A three-day event with a broad range of acts set in a stunning natural amphitheatre with views all the way down to the Oslofjord.

Oslo International Jazz Festival   MUSIC
(www.oslojazz.no; ⊙mid-Aug) Jazz and Oslo's long summer evenings go well together, and the festival brings big names to venues across the city.

⨳ Sleeping

Central Oslo & Aker Brygge

★ Saga Poshtel Oslo   HOSTEL €€
(Map p300; ☏23 10 08 00; www.sagahoteloslo-central.no; Kongens gate 7; dm/d 520/1100; 🛜; ⛐Øvre Slottsgate) A crossover hostel-hotel (posh-tel, if you didn't already get it), smart-ly designed and very central, with a big social lounge with decent wi-fi. Rooms are basic but spotless; there are lots of doubles, plus four- and six-bunk-bed dorms, all with en suites.

Hotel Folketeateret   HOTEL €€
(Map p300; ☏22 00 57 00; www.choiceno; Storga-ta 21-23; s/d half-board 2200/2400kr; 🛜; ⛐Kirk-eristen) The rooms here are smart, large and decorated in a fabulously idiosyncratic style with more character than most Oslo ho-tels. It's located within the always buzzing theatre complex with Youngstorget at the other side. Comfortable public spaces, from a lounge to a dining room where a compli-mentary dinner is served each night, give it a friendly vibe.

★ The Thief   BOUTIQUE HOTEL €€€
(Map p300; ☏24 00 40 00; www.thethief.com; Landgangen 1; d 2900-4000kr; 🛜⛱; ⛐Aker bry-

gge) Overlooking the Astrup Fearnley Mu-seum, Oslo's best design hotel is more dark glamour than Scandinavian sparse, though is packed with playful touches from beauti-ful artisan objects to video art. Views from many of the rooms, and the rooftop bar, are stunning.

Grims Grenka   BOUTIQUE HOTEL €€€
(Map p300; ☏23 10 72 00; www.firsthotels. no; Kongens gate 5; s/d 1350/1500kr; P⚹🛜; Ⓣ Kongens gate) Grims Grenka has simple, contemporary rooms – the loft suites are particularly stylish and generous – that are well equipped and totally tech-savvy. If you're here in summer, don't miss the roof terrace bar.

Greater Oslo

★ Ellingsens Pensjonat   PENSION €€
(Map p296; ☏22 60 03 59; www.ellingsenspens-jonat.no; Holtegata 25; s/d 700/1050kr, without bathroom 590/800kr, apt s/d 850/1300kr; 🛜; ⛐Rosenborg) Located in a quiet, pleasant neighbourhood, this warm B&B offers one of the best deals in the capital. The building dates from 1890 and many of the original features (high ceilings, rose designs) re-main. Rooms are bright, airy and smartly decorated, with fridges and kettles, and there's a small garden to lounge about in on sunny days.

Saga Hotel Oslo   BOUTIQUE HOTEL €€
(Map p296; ☏22 55 44 90; www.sagahoteloslo. no; Eilert Sundts gate 39; s/d from 995/1395kr; 🛜; ⛐Rosenborg) In a quiet, leafy street right be-hind the Royal Palace, this smart 46-room hotel occupies a grand corner building from the 1890s. Rooms and public spaces make the most of the elegant 19th-century bones with a restrained modern fit-out and lots of smart monochromes. There's a highly regarded sushi restaurant, Fangst, in the basement too.

Scandic Vulkan   HOTEL €€€
(Map p296; ☏21 05 71 00; www.scandichotels. com; Maridalsveien 13; d 1395-1700kr; ⛐54) Floorboards and rough-hewn bedheads give this contemporary chain hotel a warmth and tactility that you might not expect from the exterior architecture; some rooms even come with quirks such as a vintage vinyl col-lection tacked to the wall. The lobby is lots of fun and you're right by Mathallen for all-day drinking and eating too.

Central Oslo

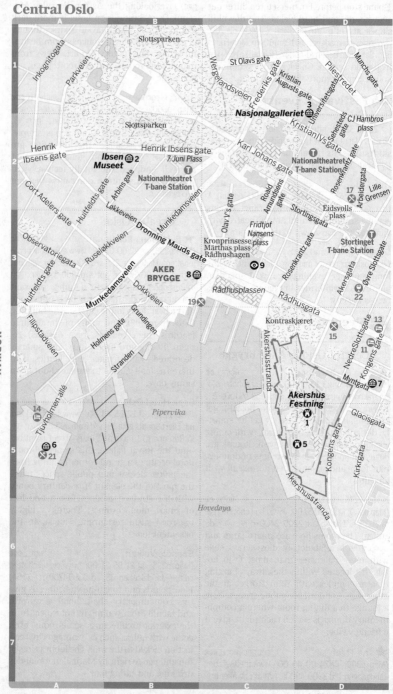

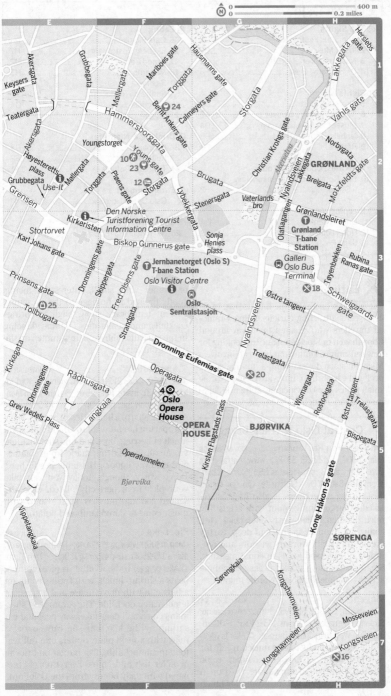

400 m
0.2 miles

E • F • G • H

NORWAY

Hestebs gate

Lakkegata gate

Heslebs gate

Akersgata

Keysers gate

Grubbegata

Mollergata

Mariboes gate

Hausmanns gate

Torggata

Storgata

Vahls gate

Teatergata

Hammersborggata

Bernt Ankers gate

Calmeyers gate

Christian Krohgs gate

GRØNLAND

Norbygata

Motzfeldts gate

Breigata

24

Youngstorget

Youngs gate

Akersgata

Høyesteretts plass

Mollergata

Ploens gate

Brugata

Nylandsveien

Lakkegata

Grubbegata

Use-It

10

23

12

Storgata

Lybekkergata

Stenersgata

Vaterlands bro

Olafiagangen

Grønlandsleiret

Grensen

Torggata

Stortorvet

Kirkeristen

Den Norske Turistforening Tourist Information Centre

Sonja Henies plass

Grønland T-bane Station

Rubina Ranas gate

Karl Johans gate

Biskop Gunnerus gate

Galleri Oslo Bus Terminal

Tøyenbekken

Schweigaards gate

Prinsens gate

Dronningens gate

Skippergata

Fred Olsens gate

Jernbanetorget (Oslo S) T-bane Station

Oslo Visitor Centre

18

Østre tangent

Tollbugata

25

Oslo Sentralstasjon

Nylandsveien

Trelastgata

Kirkegata

Dronningens gate

Rådhusgata

Strandgata

Dronning Eufemias gate

20

Wismargata

Rostockgata

Østre tangent

Trelastgata

Grev Wedels Plass

Langkaia

Operagata

4 ◉ Oslo Opera House

Kirsten Flagstads Plass

OPERA HOUSE

BJØRVIKA

Bispegata

Vippetangkaia

Operatunnelen

Bjørvika

Kong Håkon 5s gate

SØRENGA

Sørengkaia

Kongshavnveien

Mosseveien

Kongsveien

Kongshavnveien

16

Central Oslo

✗ Eating

Oslo's food scene has come into its own in recent years, attracting curious culinary-minded travellers who've eaten their way around Copenhagen or Stockholm and are looking for new sensations. Dining out here can involve a Michelin-starred restaurant, a hot-dog stand, peel-and-eat shrimp, innovative New Nordic small plates or a convincingly authentic Japanese, Italian, French, Indian or Mexican dish.

✗ Central Oslo & Aker Brygge

★ Sentralen Restaurant NEW NORDIC €€
(Map p300; ☑22 33 33 22; www.sentralen.no; Øvre Slottsgate 3; small plates 85-195kr; ⊙11am-10pm Mon-Sat; 🚇 Øvre Slottsgate) One of Oslo's best dining experiences is also its most relaxed. A large dining room with a bustling open kitchen, filled with old social club chairs and painted in tones of deep, earthy green, draws city workers, visitors and natural-wine-obsessed locals in equal measure. Small-plate dining makes it easy to sample across the appealing New Nordic menu.

Vingen NEW NORDIC €€
(Map p300; ☑901 51 595; http://vingenbar.no; Strandpromenaden 2; mains 145-240kr; ⊙10am-9pm Sun-Wed, to midnight Thu-Sat; 🚇 Aker brygge) While honouring its role as museum cafe for Astrup Fearnley (p294) and a super-scenic pit stop, Vingen is so much more. Do drop in for excellent coffee, but also come for lunch

or dinner with small, interesting menus subtly themed in homage to the museum's current temporary show. Nightfall brings cocktails, and sometimes DJs and dancing in the museum lobby and, in summer, on the waterfront terrace.

Grand Café NORWEGIAN €€
(Map p300; ☑23 21 20 18; www.grand.no; Karl Johans gate 31; mains 145-295kr; ⊙11am-11pm Mon-Fri, from noon Sat, noon-9pm Sun; 🚇 Stortinget) At 11am sharp, Henrik Ibsen would leave his apartment and walk to Grand Café for a lunch of herring, beer and one shot of aquavit (an alcoholic drink made from potatoes and caraway liquor). His table is still here. Don't worry, though, today you can take your pick from perfectly plated, elegantly sauced cod and mussels, spelt risotto with mushrooms or cured lamb and potato.

Pipervika SEAFOOD €€
(Map p300; www.pipervika.no; Rådhusbrygge 4; mains 175-250kr, shrimp per kg 130kr; ⊙7am-11pm; 🚇 Aker brygge) If the weather is nice, nothing beats a shrimp lunch, with fresh shrimp on a baguette with mayonnaise and a spritz of lemon eaten dockside. The revamped fisherman's co-op still does takeaway peel-and-eat shrimp by the kilo, but you can now also relax with a sushi plate, oysters or a full seafood menu including fish burger on brioche or killer fish and chips. Everything is prepared with daily bounty from the Oslofjord.

Maaemo NEW NORDIC €€€
(Map p300; ☑22 17 99 69; https://maaemo.no;
Schweigaards gate 15; menu 2600kr; ☺6pm-mid-
night Wed & Thu, from noon Sat & Sun; ☑Busster-
minalen Grønland) This is not a meal to be tak-
en lightly: firstly, you'll need to book many
months in advance, and secondly, there will,
for most of us, be the indenting of funds. But
go if you can, not for the three Michelin stars
and other accolades but for Esben Holmboe
Bang's 20 or so courses that are one of the
world's most potent culinary experiences
and a sensual articulation of what it means
to be Norwegian.

Café Skansen MEDITERRANEAN €€€
(Map p300; ☑24 20 13 11; www.cafeskansen.no;
Rådhusgata 32; mains 205-248kr; ☺11am-mid-
night Mon-Fri, noon-midnight Sat, noon-11pm Sun;
☑Kontraskjæret) A dark wood and tiled dining room makes for an atmospheric change
from Aker Brygge's stringent contemporary architecture and the menu here is in
keeping with its surrounds, with lots of
traditional seafood dishes, lamb and steaks.
The Danish sausages with red-wine gravy
are a great 4pm dinner if you've been out
exploring the Oslofjord and need warming
sustenance.

⭐**Vaaghals** NORWEGIAN €€€
(Map p300; ☑920 70 999; www.vaaghals.com;
Dronning Eufemias gate 8; lunch mains 179-199kr,
7-course dinner menu 695kr; ☺11am-10pm Mon-
Fri, from 4.30pm Sat; ☑Bjørvika) There's a lot of
sharing going on at Vaaghals, but don't mention the 'sh' world. Here it's definitely *skifte*,
a uniquely Norwegian way of communal
dining. This intriguing restaurant combines
a resolutely contemporary address and
surroundings with rustic, quintessentially
Norwegian ingredients, including dry-aged
meats, lots of offal, wild fish and foraged
herbs and vegetables.

Greater Oslo

⭐**Mathallen Oslo** FOOD HALL €€
(Map p296; www.mathallenoslo.no; Maridalsveien
17, Vulkan; ☺8am-1am Tue-Fri, from 9.30am Sat &
Sun; ☑54) Down by the river, this former industrial space is now a food court dedicated
to showcasing the very best of Norwegian
regional cuisine, as well as some excellent
internationals. There are dozens of delis, cafes and miniature restaurants, and the place
buzzes throughout the day and well into the
evening.

Bass NEW NORDIC €€
(Map p296; ☑482 41 489; http://bassoslo.
no; Thorvald Meyers gate 26; dishes 70-175kr;
☺5pm-1am Tue-Sat, 3-8pm Sun; ☑Birkelunden)
In what could be yet another Grünerløkka corner cafe, you'll find one of the
city's best small-plate dining options,
served beneath vintage seascapes by classic Norwegian ceramics by jovial Løkka locals. Most dishes are what might
be called contemporary Norwegian-
meets-international – from fried chicken
and potato pancakes to deep-sea cod in
sorrel butter and death-by-chocolate cake.

Pjoltergeist NEW NORDIC, KOREAN €€
(Map p296; ☑402 37 788; http://pjoltergeist.no;
Rosteds gate 15; ☺6pm-12.30am Tue-Sat; ☑54)
One peek into this dim basement space and
the intrigue begins, only to grow when you
discover the menu. Icelandic chef Atly Mar
Yngvason combines ingredients from his
home country and his adopted Norwegian
home, with the techniques and seasonings
of Korea and Japan. Flavours are always
bold, ingredients occasionally confronting
(moose heart!), and the presentation insou-
ciantly playful.

🍷 Drinking & Nightlife

⭐**Tim Wendelboe** CAFE
(Map p296; ☑400 04 062; www.timwendelboe.
no; Grüners gate 1; ☺8.30am-6pm Mon-Fri, 11am-
5pm Sat & Sun; ☑Schous plass) Tim Wendelboe is often credited with kick-starting
the Scandinavian coffee revolution, and
his eponymous cafe and roastery is both
a local freelancers' hang-out and an international coffee-fiend pilgrimage site. All
the beans are, of course, self-sourced and
hand-roasted (the roaster is part of the
furniture), and all coffees – from an iced
pour-over to a regular cappuccino – are
world class.

⭐**Torggata Botaniske** COCKTAIL BAR
(Map p300; ☑980 17 830; Torggata 17b; ☺5pm-
1am Sun-Wed, to 2am Thu, 2pm-3am Fri & Sat;
☑Brugata) The greenhouse effect done right,
with a lush assortment of indoor plants (including a warm herb-growing area) as well
as beautiful mid-century light fittings and
chairs, chandeliers, and lots of marble and
mirrors. If you're not already seduced by the
decor, the drinks will do it, with a list that
features the bar's own produce, fresh fruit
and good-quality spirits.

★ Territoriet WINE BAR

(Map p296; http://territoriet.no/; Markveien 58; ◷4pm-1am Mon-Fri, from noon Sat & Sun; 🚌Schous plass) A true neighbourhood wine bar that's also the city's most exciting. The grape-loving owners offer up more than 300 wines by the glass and do so without a list. Talk to the staff about your preferences and – yes, this is Norway – your budget, and they'll find something you'll adore. Ordering beer or gin and tonic won't raise an eyebrow, we promise.

Gullbaren BAR

(Map p300; www.sentralen.no/arrangement/gullbaren; 3rd fl, Øvre Slottsgate 3; ◷check website for details; 🚌Øvre Slottsgate) Hidden at the top of the grand marble staircase in the original bank section of Sentralen, and decorated with found objects from the pre-renovation bank headquarters, this tiny bar might just be Oslo's most atmospheric.

Kulturhuset BAR, PUB

(Map p300; http://kulturhusetioslo.no; Youngs gate 6; ◷8am-3.30am Mon-Fri, from 11am Sat & Sun; 🚌Brugata) The Norwegian notion of culture being an interactive, collective enterprise combines here with their exceptional ability to have a good time. The city's 'culture house' moved into this beautiful, rambling old four-storey building in 2017, but it feels as if it's been part of the Oslo fabric for years.

☆ Entertainment

Oslo has a thriving live-music scene – it's said that the city hosts more than 5000 gigs a year. Its venues are spread across the city but concentrate on Møllegata and in Vulkan, Grünerløkka and Grønland. World-class opera or ballet performances are held at the **Oslo Opera House** (Den Norske Opera & Ballett; Map p300; www.operaen.no; Kirsten Flagstads plass 1; tickets 100-795kr; Ⓣ Sentralstasjonen). Book ahead or try for the last-minute 100kr standing tickets.

🛍 Shopping

Oslo's centre and its inner neighbourhoods have a great selection of small shops if you're not into the malls. The city centre's Kirkegaten, Nedre Slottsgate and Prinsens gate are home to a well-considered collection of Scandinavian and international fashion and homewares shops, with Frogner and St Hanshaugen also having some good upmarket choices. Grünerløkka is great for vintage and Scandinavian fashion too.

★ Norwegian Rain FASHION & ACCESSORIES

(Map p300; ☑996 03 411; http://norwegianrain.com; Kirkegata 20; ◷10am-6pm Mon-Fri, to 5pm Sat; 🚌Nationaltheatret) Bergen comes to Oslo! The west-coast design superstar creates what might be the world's most coveted raincoats. This Oslo outpost stocks the complete range as well as creative director T-Michael's woollen suits, detachable-collar shirts, leather shoes and bags, not to mention limited editions of Kings of Convenience LPs.

★ Utopia Retro Modern VINTAGE, HOMEWARES

(Map p296; ☑408 60 460; www.utopiaretromodern.com; Bygdøy allé 7; ◷12.30-6pm Thu & Fri, 1-4pm Sat; 🚌Solli) Take note of this lovely 1929 functionalist shopfront before browsing the great mid-century design within; designed by Arne Korsmo and Sverre Aasland, it remains super-characteristic of the era. While you'll also find plenty of fantastic international pieces here, look out for the beautiful Norwegian design pieces, both original and reissued, from names such as Torbjørn Afdal, Gunnar Sørlie and Sven Ivar Dysthe.

Vestkanttorget Flea Market MARKET

(Map p296; Amaldus Nilsens plass; ◷10am-4pm Sat; Ⓣ Majorstuen) If you're happy sifting through heaps of, well, junk in search of an elusive vintage band T-shirt or mid-century ceramic coffee pot, take a chance here. It's at the plaza that intersects Professor Dahls gate, a block east of Vigeland Park, and it's a more than pleasant way to pass a Saturday morning.

ℹ Information

Den Norske Turistforening Tourist Information Centre (DNT, Norwegian Mountain Touring Club; Map p300; www.turistforeningen.no; Storget 3, Oslo; ◷10am-5pm Mon-Wed & Fri, to 6pm Thu, to 3pm Sat; 🚌Jernbanetorget) DNT provides information, maps and brochures on hiking in Norway and sells memberships that include discounted rates on mountain huts along the main hiking routes. You can also book some specific huts and pick up keys, as well as buy hiking gear.

Oslo Visitor Centre (Map p300; ☑81 81 05 55; www.visitoslo.com; Jernbanetorget 1; ◷9am-6pm; 🚌Sentralstasjon) Right beside the main train station. Sells transport tickets as well as the useful Oslo Pass; publishes free guides to the city.

Use-It (Map p300; ☑24 14 98 20; http://use-it.unginfo.oslo.no/; Møllergata 3; ◷10am-5pm Mon-Fri, noon-5pm Sat; 🚌Brugata) The exceptionally helpful and savvy Ungdomsinformasjonen (Youth Information Office, better known as Use-It) is aimed at, but not restricted to, backpackers under the age of 26. It makes (free) bookings for inexpensive or private accommodation and provides information on anything from current events to possibilities for hitching (note: hitching is never entirely safe, so we don't recommend it).

ℹ Getting There & Away

AIR

Oslo Gardermoen International Airport

Oslo Gardermoen International Airport (https://avinor.no/flyplass/oslo), the city's main airport, is 50km north of the city. It's used by international carriers, including Norwegian, SAS, Air France and British Airways. It's one of the world's most beautiful airports and has an amazing selection of places to eat and drink as well as Norwegian design shops alongside standard airport shopping.

Torp International Airport

Some budget flights, including those run by SAS Braathens, Widerøe and Ryanair, operate from Torp International Airport (www.trop.no) in Sandefjord, some 123km southwest of Oslo. Check carefully which airport your flight is going to. It has limited but good restaurants and bars and extensive parking facilities.

BUS

Long-distance buses arrive and depart from the **Galleri Oslo Bus Terminal** (Map p300; ☑ 23 00 24 00; Schweigaards gate 8; Ⓣ Sentralstasjon). The train and bus stations are linked via a convenient overhead walkway for easy connections.

Nor-Way Bussekspress (☑ 81 54 44 44; www. nor-way.no) provides timetables and bookings. International services also depart from the bus terminal. Destinations include the following:

Bergen (522kr, 11 hours, three daily)

Stavanger (802kr, seven hours, usually one daily) Via Kristiansand.

CAR & MOTORCYCLE

The main highways into the city are the E6 from the north and south, and the E18 from the southeast and west. Each time you enter Oslo, you must pass through (at least) one of 19 toll stations and pay the 33kr toll.

TRAIN

All trains arrive and depart from Oslo S in the city centre. It has **reservation desks** (Jernbanetorget 1; ⊘ 6.30am-11pm; 🚇 Sentralstasjon) and an **information desk** (☑ 81 50 08 88; Jernbanetorget 1; 🚇 Sentralstasjon) that provides details on routes and timetables throughout Norway.

There are frequent train services around Oslofjord (eg Drammen, Skien, Moss, Fredrikstad and Halden). Other major destinations:

Destination	Cost (kr)	Time (hr)	Frequency (daily)
Bergen via Voss	950	6½-7½	four
Røros via Hamar	810	5	every 2hr
Stavanger via Kristiansand	997	7¾	six
Trondheim via Hamar & Lillehammer	965	6½-7½	six

ℹ Getting Around

All public transport is covered off by the Ruter (https://ruter.no/en/) ticketing system; schedules and route maps are available online or at **Trafikanten** (☑ 177; www.ruter.no; Jernbanetorget; ⊘ 7am-8pm Mon-Fri, 8am-6pm Sat & Sun).

Train Suburban trains and services to the Oslofjord where the T-bane doesn't reach.

Tram Oslo's tram network is extensive and runs 24 hours.

T-bane The six-line Tunnelbanen underground system, better known as the T-bane, is faster and extends further from the city centre than most city buses or tram lines.

SOUTHERN NORWAY

Arendal

POP 41,665

Arendal, one of the larger south-coast towns, has an undeniable buzz throughout summer, with the outdoor restaurants and bars around the harbour (known as Pollen) filling up with holidaymakers, and a full calendar of festivals and open-air concerts by the water most weekends. Even in winter, some of the larger bars stay open and have live music on weekends. It's a nice place to spend a few days, with enough going on to keep you amused while retaining an intimate village-like vibe.

The matchbox-sized old district of Tyholmen, with its tightly wound core of timbered houses, adds considerable charm, while those seeking greater communion with the sea than a harbourside cafe can set off to the offshore islands of Merdø, Tromøy and Hisøy.

◉ Sights

★ **Bomuldsfabriken Kunsthall** GALLERY
(www.bomuldsfabriken.no; Oddenveien 5; ⊘noon-4pm Tue-Sun) FREE This highly regarded contemporary art gallery is a 15-minute walk from the town centre on the northern reaches of Arendal. One of the largest contemporary galleries in southern Norway, its exhibitions are housed in a stunning example of Norwegian industrial architecture, a former cotton factory from the late 19th century.

Tyholmen AREA
Rising up behind the Gjestehavn (Guest Harbour) is the old harbourside Tyholmen district, home to beautiful 17th- to 19th-century timber buildings featuring neoclassical, rococo and baroque influences. Tyholmen was once separated from the mainland by a canal, which was filled in after the great sailing era. Look out for the **rådhus** (town hall), a striking wooden building dating from 1815.

🎉 Festivals & Events

Canal Street Jazz & Blues Festival MUSIC
(www.canalstreet.no) World-class jazz and blues, with surprise acts such as Patti Smith.

🛏 Sleeping

★ **Clarion Tyholmen
Hotel** HISTORIC HOTEL €€€
(☑37 07 68 00; www.nordicchoicehotels.no; Teaterplassen 2; s/d 1470/1710kr; ❄️🐾) Undoubtedly Arendal's best hotel, the Clarion combines a prime waterfront position in a restored old dockside building that emulates Tyholmen's old-world ambience. Rooms in the original wing are the most atmospheric, and have ridiculously lovely views, as do the corner suites in the new wing. The hotel restaurant is a relaxed and stylish option too.

Thon Hotel Arendal HOTEL €€€
(☑37 05 21 50; www.thonhotels.no; Friergangen 1; s/d 1095/1395kr; ❄️🐾) It might not have waterfront views, but this typical Thon is just 50m from the water's edge. Bland on the exterior, the rooms are modern, large and comfortable. There's a public pay car park nearby.

🍴 Eating

Pigene på Torvet BAKERY €
(☑465 49 136; www.facebook.com/pigenepaatorvet; Tollbodgaten 5; snacks 79-169kr; ⊘10am-4pm Sat-Wed, to 5pm Thu & Fri) What you miss out on views here, you'll make up for in flavour. A brimming display of cakes and pastries – the town's best – can be taken away or wolfed at a table with coffee. Or come for a thin-crust pizza, chilli con carne or salad lunch. It also has gourmet grocery supplies to take away.

★ **Blom Restaurant** SEAFOOD €€€
(☑37 00 14 14; www.blomrestaurant.no; Lang-brygge 5; mains 310kr; ⊘5-10pm) The most upmarket of the Pollen harbour crowd, Blom provides a respite from the overfilled plates and boozy vibe that sometimes wins out at the other waterside places. Mains are elegantly traditional (instead of fish soup, it's creamy seafood with a lobster stock), but the sharing menu does aquavit-cured reindeer as well as sashimi and satays.

ℹ Information

Tourist Office (☑37 00 55 44; www.arendal.com; Sam Eydes Plass 1; ⊘10am-4pm Mon-Fri) Outside the high season, hours can be erratic. Even if the office is shut, someone will be on hand to answer phone calls.

ℹ Getting There & Away

MS *Merdøy*, or one of the other ferries run by **Skilsoferga** (www.skilsoferga.no; one way adult/child 35/25kr), sails from Arendal (Pollen) to Merdø up to hourly from early July to mid-August. It also leaves hourly between 11am and 4pm on weekends year-round from Merdø and returns on the half-hour. Timetables are available from the tourist office and displayed on the dock; it costs 30kr return.

There are also ferries to Hisøy (adult/child 50/30kr).

Nor-Way Bussekspress (p378) buses to and from Kristiansand (232kr, 1½ hours, up to nine daily) and **Nettbuss** (p380) services to and from Oslo (364kr, four hours) call in at the Arendal Rutebilstasjon, a block west of Pollen harbour. Nettbuss' local TIMEkspressen buses connect Arendal with Grimstad (79kr, 30 minutes, half-hourly) and Risør (139kr, 1¼ hours, hourly).

Grimstad

POP 12,172

Grimstad is at its most lovely in the pedestrianised streets that lie inland from the waterfront; these are some of the most atmospheric on the Skagerrak coast. The town has a number of interesting calling cards. It was home to young playwright Henrik Ibsen and has a good museum in the pharmacy in which he once worked. And it is the sunniest spot in Norway, with an average of 266

NORWAY GRIMSTAD

hours of sunshine per month in June and July. The town also has an unmistakably, and welcome, young vibe, thanks to its large student population.

◉ Sights

★ Ibsenhuset Museum   MUSEUM
(www.gbm.no; Henrik Ibsens gate 14; adult/child 90/65kr; ⊙11am-4pm Mon-Sat, noon-4pm Sun Jun–mid-Sep, closed mid-Sep–May) Norway's favourite playwright, Henrik Ibsen, washed up in Grimstad in January 1844. The house where he worked as a pharmacist's apprentice, and where he lived and first cultivated his interest in writing, has been converted into the Ibsenhuset Museum. It contains a re-created pharmacy and many of the writer's belongings, and is one of southern Norway's most interesting museums. The young staff here are wonderful, their tours full of fascinating detail and the odd spot of salacious gossip.

⌶ Sleeping

Café Ibsen B&B   B&B €€
(☑909 12 931; www.cafeibsen.no; Løkkestredet 7; s/d 600/900kr) This is a great central B&B option, run by the friendly owners of Café Ibsen (☑37 27 57 63; Henrik Ibsens gate 12; sandwiches 79-99kr; ⊙10am-4pm Mon-Sat, noon-4pm Sun). There are six simple but character-filled rooms in a historic house, all with private bathrooms.

Scandic Grimstad   HISTORIC HOTEL €€
(☑37 25 25 25; www.scandichotels.no; Kirkegata 3; s/d 1145/1345kr; P ✳ ☎) At the town's heart, this historic hotel spans a number of converted and conjoined timber houses, with an atmospheric breakfast room and basement restaurant. Rooms here can be absolutely delightful, if a little staid, but make sure you're not allocated one of the dark, stuffy and very noisy internal rooms overlooking the lobby.

✕ Eating

★ Apotekergården   SEAFOOD €€
(☑37 04 50 25; www.apotekergaarden.no; Skolegata 3; mains 160-260kr, pizzas 125kr; ⊙noon-midnight) The Apotekergården is a fun, busy restaurant with a cast of regulars who wouldn't eat anywhere else. It can be difficult to get a table out on the terrace in summer, especially as the night wears on. If so, head up the old wooden stairs for a beer and a game of shuffleboard.

Smag & Behag   CAFE, DELI €€
(www.smag-behag.no; Storgaten 14; mains 115-165kr; ⊙10am-10pm Mon-Sat) We concur with this upmarket deli-cafe's name: 'taste and enjoy'. Come for lunch or a casual dinner and sample the region's best produce (which is also available from the deli counter) and a carefully selected wine list. A summer salad of beets and 40°C cured salmon is a riot of colour; an open sandwich of pulled beef and coleslaw is a revelation.

Information

Tourist Office (☑37 25 01 68; www.visitgrimstad.com; Storgaten 1a; ⊙9am-6pm Mon-Fri, 10am-4pm Sat mid-Jun–mid-Aug, 8.30am-4pm Mon-Fri mid-Aug–mid-Jun) On the waterfront inside the big white timber building. Staff run guided tours of the town every Wednesday and Friday in July at 1pm (adult/child 100kr/free).

❶ Getting There & Away

The Grimstad Rutebilstasjon is on Storgata at the harbour, though some buses only stop up at the highway, rather than coming into town. **Nor-Way Bussekspress** (p378) buses between Oslo (400kr, 4½ hours) and Kristiansand (240kr, one hour) call at Grimstad three to five times daily. **Nettbuss** (p380) TIMEkspressen buses run to/from Arendal once or twice hourly (80kr, 30 minutes).

Kristiansand

POP 87,400

Kristiansand is Norway's fifth-largest city and styles itself as 'Norway's No 1 Holiday Resort'. That can be a bit misleading: sun-starved Norwegians do flock to this charming big town in the summer, and there's a petite town beach and flash marina, but it tends to serve as a gateway to the villages of Norway's southern coast and the inland region of Setesdalen.

What Kristiansand offers in spades, though, is a lively cultural and shopping scene, some excellent restaurants and very healthy nightlife. In addition, anyone travelling with children will more than likely find themselves cajoled into visiting the town's outstanding children's park and zoo.

◉ Sights

★ Sørlandets Kunstmuseum   GALLERY
(SKMU; ☑38 07 49 00; www.skmu.no; Skippergata 24b; adult/child 60kr/free; ⊙11am-5pm Tue-Sat, noon-4pm Sun) This exceptional regional art museum focuses on both fine and craft-based practices, and the collection includes

some particularly strong contemporary work from local, Norwegian and Nordic artists. There is a bright, beautifully designed, pleasingly sophisticated children's wing. For anyone interested in Norwegian ceramics, the 44 works by local Kari Christensen will prove a treat.

Posebyen AREA

The Kristiansand Posebyen takes in most of the 14 blocks at the northern end of the town's characteristic *kvadraturen* (square grid pattern of streets). It's worth taking a slow stroll around this pretty quarter; its name was given by French soldiers who came to *reposer* here (it's French for 'relax').

Kristiansand Dyrepark ZOO

(www.dyreparken.no; high season adult/child 319/299kr; ⊙10am-7pm mid-Jun–mid-Aug, to 3pm mid-Aug–mid-Jun; 🖼) Off the E18, 10km east of Kristiansand, Dyrepark is probably *the* favourite holiday destination for Norwegian kids. The former zoo is several parks rolled into one. There's a **fun fair** that includes rides such as the pirate-ship cruise, Captain Sabretooth's Treasure Trove and enchanted houses. **Cardamom Town** (Kardamomme By) is a fantasy village based on the children's stories of Thorbjørn Egner. There's a **water park** with heated pools and water slides. The biggest attraction, though, is still the **zoo** itself.

🛌 Sleeping

⭐**Sjøglott Hotell** HOTEL €€

(📞38 70 15 66; www.sjoglott.no; Østre Strandgate 25; s/d 895/975kr; 🖥) This low-key 15-room hotel in a historic building is run by a lovely young couple. The rooms are small, but have big windows and are well designed, and include extras unusual at this price, such as Nespresso machines. Breakfast, afternoon tea-time waffles and evening pizza and wine are served in an atmospheric basement, or you can relax in the sun in the cute courtyard.

⭐**Scandic Kristiansand Bystranda** HOTEL €€

(📞21 61 50 00; www.scandichotels.no; Østre Strandgate 76; s/d 1290/1390kr; 🅿🔊) This beachside place is big and brash, but very beautifully designed. It has a warm, textured and relaxed kind of style, and has all the facilities and extras you can expect in a hotel of this size. It's a wonderful spot for families with its beach, park and poolside position.

Hotel Q42 HOTEL €€

(📞38 04 40 00; http://q42.no/; Elvegata 11a; s/d 1000/1300kr) This hotel is part of a church conference centre, so doesn't possess as much of a holiday vibe as some of the others in town. The 11 junior suites and suites here are beautifully furnished, calm, spacious and stylish.

✖ Eating

Drømmeplassen BAKERY, CAFE €

(📞38 04 71 00; www.drommeplassen.no; Skippergata 26; sandwiches, salads & soups 99-119kr; ⊙7am-6pm Mon-Sat, 10am-5pm Sun) This big, bustling bakery has lots of tables inside and on the pretty footpath. Locals flock here every morning for a great range of freshly baked *boller* (buns) and loaves of bread, or pop in later for chicken salads, tuna melts and big soups.

Pieder Ro SEAFOOD €€

(📞38 10 07 88; www.pieder-ro.no; Gravane 10; mains 285-345kr, smørrebrød & burgers 145-215kr; ⊙11am-10pm Mon-Sat, 1-9pm Sun) Kristiansand might be very good at smart-casual coastal, but it also keeps the traditionalists happy with places such as Pieder Ro, with its chandlery-chic nautical decor (How nautical? The bar *is* a boat...), chequered blinds and upholstered chairs. There's an all-day casual menu and an elegant evening one, with a focus on fresh fish but also decent steaks (including kangaroo).

⭐**Bønder i Byen** NEO NORDIC, INTERNATIONAL €€€

(📞911 47 247; www.bønderibyen.com; Rådhusgata 16; mains 295kr, 4-course menu 485kr; ⊙11am-10pm Mon-Sat, noon-8pm Sun) A beautiful extended riff on Norway's spectacular produce and on the country's rural life, Bønder i Byen's menu is both gorgeous to read, with its redolent roll call of local farmers, and to eat. This is one place on the coast where you won't get seafood; instead it's best-quality organic beef, pig and chicken (long-tailed, of course), along with vibrant tumbles of vegetables.

ⓘ Information

DNT Sør (📞38 12 07 50; www.dntsor.no; Gyldenløvesgate 2b; ⊙10am-4pm Mon-Fri) Maps and information on hiking, huts and organised mountain tours in southern Norway.

Tourist Office (📞38 12 13 14; www.visitkrs. no; Rådhusgata 6; ⊙8am-6.15pm Mon-Fri, 10am-6pm Sat, noon-6pm Sun Jul & Aug, 8am-3.30pm Mon-Fri rest of year)

🛈 Getting There & Away

BOAT

Ferries to Denmark and Sweden leave from the Colour Line Terminal.

BUS

There's a bus information office and left-luggage facilities inside the bus station. Note, most local buses, including those to Lillesand, Grimstad and Arendal, leave from central Henrik Wergelands gate, rather than the bus station.

TRAIN

There are up to four trains daily to Oslo (259kr to 687kr, 4½ hours) and up to five to Stavanger (249kr to 489kr, 3¼ hours).

Rjukan

POP 3385

Sitting in the shadow of what is arguably Norway's most beautiful peak, Gausta (1883m), Rjukan is a picturesque introduction to the Norwegian high country as well as southern Norway's activities centre par excellence.

The town stretches like elastic for 6km along the floor of the steep-sided Vestfjorddalen and while the centre, which consists of a couple of blocks of pastel-painted wooden buildings, is attractive, the remainder stands in utter contrast to its majestic setting.

If you're here from late September to March, you'll notice the expected winter gloom is absent, with the town's valley floor illuminated by 'concentrated solar power' – three giant remote-controlled mirrors track and reflect the much needed sunshine from the mountain above.

🅞 Sights

★ **Gaustabanen Cable Railway**   RAILWAY
(www.gaustabanen.no; one way/return adult 250/350kr, child 125/175kr; ⊙10am-5pm late Jun–mid-Oct) Gaustabanen runs 860m deep into the core of Gausta before a different train climbs an incredible 1040m, alongside 3500 steps at a 40-degree angle, to 1800m, just below the Gaustahytte, not far from the summit. It was built by NATO in 1958 at a cost of US$1 million to ensure it could access its radio tower in any weather. Taking the railway is an incredible experience, although it's not for the claustrophobic. The base station is 10km southeast of Rjukan.

★ **Norwegian Industrial Workers Museum**   MUSEUM
(Norsk Industriarbeidermuseet Vemork; www.visitvemork.com; Vemork; adult/child 90/60kr; ⊙10am-6pm mid-Jun–mid-Aug, to 4pm May–mid-Jun & mid-Aug–Sep, noon-3pm rest of year) This museum, 7km west of Rjukan, is in the Vemork power station, which was the world's largest when completed in 1911. These days it honours the Socialist Workers' Party, which reached the height of its Norwegian activities here in the 1950s. There's an interesting exhibition about the race in the 1930s and '40s to make an atom bomb, plus a fabulous miniature power station in the main hall.

Krossobanen   CABLE CAR
(www.krossobanen.no; one way/return adult 65/130kr, child 30/60kr, bike 51/110kr; ⊙9am-8pm mid-Jun–Aug, 10am-4pm Sun-Thu, to 8pm Fri & Sat rest of year) The Krossobanen cable car was constructed in 1928 by Norsk Hydro to provide its employees with access to the sun. It now whisks tourists up to Gvepseborg (886m) for a view over the deep, dark recesses. The best panoramas are from the viewing platform atop the cable-car station. It also operates as the trailhead for a host of hiking and cycling trails.

🏃 Activities

The whole area around Rjukan is pockmarked with excellent ski runs. You can also rug up against the winter cold and take a **horse-drawn sleigh ride** through a forested, magical winter wonderland or strike out across the bleak Hardangervidda plateau on the back of a sleigh pulled by a team of **husky dogs**. The tourist office (p310) can put you in touch with local tour operators running either of these winter-only activities.

Rjukan also makes a superb base from which to strike out into the surrounding wilderness on foot or by mountain bike. To get an idea of what's possible, visit the tourist office to pick up the free *Rjukan – og Tinn,* which has a number of route suggestions.

Ice Climbing   ADVENTURE SPORTS
(Kvitåvatnvegen 372) If the idea of hauling yourself up a giant vertical icicle that looks suspiciously as if it's going to crack and send you tumbling to an early grave sounds like fun, then Rjukan, fast becoming known as *the* place for ice climbing, is the place for you. There are more than 150 routes in the immediate area of the town.

NORWAY RJUKAN

Bungee Jumping　　ADVENTURE SPORTS
(☑995 13 140; www.telemark-opplevelser.no; per jump 790kr; ☺mid-May–Sep, exact times vary) Described as Norway's highest land-based bungee jump, this 84m plunge into the canyon from the bridge leading to the Norwegian Industrial Workers' Museum is Rjukan's biggest adrenalin rush. Book through the tourist office.

🛏 Sleeping & Eating

★**Rjukan Hytteby & Kro**　　CABIN €€
(☑35 09 01 22; www.rjukan-hytteby.no; Brogata 9; large cabins 950-1500kr, small cabins s/d 990/1195kr; 🛜) Easily the best choice in town, Rjukan Hytteby & Kro sits in a pretty spot on the river bank and has carefully decorated, very well-equipped huts that sweetly emulate the early-20th-century hydroelectric workers' cabins. The owner is exceptionally helpful. It's a pleasant 20-minute walk along the river bank to the town centre.

Gaustablikk Høyfjellshotell　　LODGE €€€
(☑35 09 14 22; www.gaustablikk.no; Kvitåvatnvegen 372; d 1700kr; 🅿🛜) With a prime location overlooking the lake and mountain, this lodge is one of Norway's better mountain hotels. Rooms have a calm modern Alpine style, with lots of raw wood, felt sofas and antlers all about, and many have lovely views of Gausta.

Geared towards a winter skiing crowd (with high prices and advance reservations necessary), it's nonetheless a great place in summer. The **restaurant** (mains 129-179kr, dinner buffet 405kr; ☺noon-5pm & 6.30-9pm) is a destination in itself.

Kinokafeen　　INTERNATIONAL €€
(☑408 56 048; Storstulgate 1; mains 139-189kr; ☺10am-9pm Mon-Sat) Kinokafeen, at the cinema, has a pleasing airy art-deco style and its outdoor tables (summer only!) and fading interior make it the most memorable place to eat in the town centre.

ℹ Information

Tourist Office (☑35 08 05 50; www.visitrjukan.com; Torget 2; ☺9am-6pm Mon-Fri, 10am-4pm Sat & Sun) Possibly the best tourist office in Telemark, with loads of information and knowledgeable staff.

ℹ Getting There & Away

Buses connect Rjukan with Oslo (390kr, 3½ hours) via Notodden (146kr, 1¼ hours; where you need to change buses) roughly every two hours

between 5.30am and 3.30pm. These buses also stop in Kongsberg (295kr, two hours).

Rjukan's linear distances will seem intimidating, but the local Bybuss runs from Vemork, 6.5km west of Rjukan, to the eastern end of the valley.

CENTRAL NORWAY

Lillehammer
POP 27,476

◎ Sights

★**Olympic Park**　　AREA
(☑61 05 42 00; www.olympiaparken.no; Nordsetervegen 45) After Lillehammer won its bid for the 1994 Winter Olympics, the Norwegian government ploughed more than two billion kroner into the town's infrastructure. In an example to other Olympic host cities, most amenities remain in use and visitors can tour the main Olympic sites over a large area called the Olympiaparken.

Norwegian Olympic Museum　　MUSEUM
(www.ol.museum.no; Olympiaparken; adult/child 130/65kr; ☺10am-5pm Jun-Aug, 11am-4pm Tue-Sun Sep-May) The excellent Olympic museum is at the Håkons Hall ice-hockey venue. On the ground floor there is a well-presented display covering the ancient Olympic Games, as well as all of the Olympic Games of the modern era, with a focus on the exploits of Norwegian athletes and the Lillehammer games.

Maihaugen Folk Museum　　MUSEUM
(www.maihaugen.no; Maihaugveien 1; adult/child/family Jun-Aug 170/85/425kr, Sep-May 130/65/325kr; ☺10am-5pm Jun-Aug, 11am-4pm Tue-Sun Sep-May) Step back into the past at this surprisingly fascinating folk museum, which has collected around 180 buildings from other parts of Norway, mostly from the early 1900s. They've been rebuilt to resemble a small inland village: among the buildings on show are a stave church from Garmo, traditional turf-topped houses and shops, a post office, a schoolroom, fishing cabins and farmers' barns. Costumed actors help bring the experience to life.

🏃 Activities

★**Lygårdsbakkene Ski Jump**　　SKIING
(tower adult/child 25/15kr; ☺9am-7pm Jun–mid-Aug, 9am-5pm May & late Aug, 11-4pm Sat & Sun

Sep) The main ski jump (K120) here drops 136m with a landing-slope angle of 37.5 degrees. The opening ceremony of the Lillehammer Games was held here; the **Olympic flame tower** stands near the foot of the jump. The ski-jump chairlift ascends to a stunning panoramic view over the town and includes entry to the viewing tower; alternatively, you can walk up the 952 steps.

Hafjell Alpine Centre SKIING
(☑61 27 47 00; www.hafjell.no) Fifteen kilometres north of town, not far from Hunderfossen, this was the venue for downhill events in the '94 Winter Olympics.

🛏 Sleeping

★**HI Lillehammer Vandrerhjem** HOSTEL €
(☑61 26 00 24; www.stasjonen.no; 1st fl, Railway Station; dm/s/d/f from 395/795/895/1395kr; P ☐ ☎) If you've never stayed in a youth hostel, this one above the train station is the place to break the habit of a lifetime. The rooms are simple but come with a bathroom, bed linen and free wi-fi. There's a spick-and-span communal kitchen, but approach the downstairs cafe with caution (hot-dog soup anyone?!). Free parking is a bonus.

Øvergaard B&B €€
(☑61 25 99 99; www.oevergaard.net; Jernbanegata 24; s/d with shared bathroom 445/790kr; P ☎) Just above the centre of town, this friendly B&B has simple rooms with plenty of family character in quiet surrounds. It's a well-run place and about as cheap as you'll get in Norway. It's an equally short walk to both the town centre and the Olympic sites.

★**Clarion Collection Hotel Hammer** HOTEL €€€
(☑61 26 73 73; www.nordicchoicehotels.com; Stortorget 108b; tw/d incl half-board from 1345/1545kr; ☎) In an architecturally pleasing, mustard-yellow building that echoes traditional Norwegian architecture, this hotel is a solid choice. Monochrome rooms are a bit short on character, but comfortable enough – and the inclusion of both breakfast and a dinner buffet make it great value (at least for Norway).

🍴 Eating

★**Lykellige Dager** CAFE €€
(☑921 32 682; www.lykkeligedager.no; Storgata 49; lunch mains 129-199kr; ☉7.30am-5pm Mon-Fri, 10am-4pm Sat) In a hard-to-miss glass-and-steel box on the main street of Storgata, this excellent cafe serves a range of tempting, on-trend lunch dishes – açai bowls, Asian-style chicken salads, Thai soups and detox smoothies. The cakes are really good too – and on a nice day, you can sit outside on the pavement tables.

Heim GASTROPUB €€
(☑61 10 00 82; www.heim.no; Storgata 84; dinner mains 179-269kr; ☉3pm-midnight Mon-Thu, 3pm-3am Fri, noon-3pm Sat) This warm and welcoming gastropub has fast become one of the town's most frequented hang-outs since opening its doors in 2014. It attracts all kinds of diners, from hipsters to ale enthusiasts, and the hearty menu of fish and chips, bangers and mash and meat-and-cheese platters is just the ticket for easy, all-hours dining.

🍷 Drinking & Nightlife

★**Lillehammer Bryggeri** BREWERY
(☑950 19 108; www.lillehammerbryggeri.no; Elvegata 19; ☉5-11pm Wed & Thu, 5pm-1am Fri & Sat) This is a cracking spot to down beers with the locals – an enthusiast-run brewery with an ale-making history dating back to 1847, bar a few closures here and there. Beer bottles line the walls, and vaulted ceilings provide an atmospheric place to down some brews. There's also a no-frills, beer-friendly menu of sausages, stews and the like.

ℹ Information

Lillehammer Tourist Office (☑61 28 98 00; www.lillehammer.com; Jernbanetorget 2, Lillehammer Skysstasjon; ☉8am-6pm Mon-Fri, 10am-4pm Sat & Sun mid-Jun–mid-Aug, 8am-4pm Mon-Fri, 10am-2pm Sat rest of year) Inside the train station.

ℹ Getting There & Away

Lillehammer Skysstasjon is the main transport terminal for buses, trains and taxis.

BUS

Lavprisekspressen (www.lavprisekspressen. no) bus services run to/from Oslo (300kr, three hours, three to four daily) via Gardermoen Airport.

Nor-Way (www.nor-way.no) runs to Bergen (646kr, nine hours, one or two daily).

TRAIN

Trains run to/from Oslo (414kr, 2¼ hours, around hourly) and Trondheim (from 754kr, 4¼ to seven hours, four to six daily). Some trains also stop at Hamar.

Røros

POP 5576

Røros, a charming Unesco World Heritage-listed site set in a small hollow of stunted forests and bleak fells, is one of Norway's most beautiful villages. The Norwegian writer Johan Falkberget described Røros as 'a place of whispering history'. This historic copper-mining town (once called Bergstad, or mountain city) has wonderfully preserved, colourful wooden houses that climb the hillside, as well as fascinating relics of the town's mining past. It feels a little bit like a Norwegian version of the Wild West.

Røros has become something of a retreat for artists, who lend even more character to this enchanted place. It is also one of the coldest places in Norway – the temperature once dropped to a mighty bracing -50.4°C.

☉ Sights

Røros' **historic district**, characterised by the striking log architecture of its 80 protected buildings, takes in the entire central area. The two main streets, **Bergmannsgata** and **Kjerkgata**, are lined with historical homes and buildings, all under preservation orders. The entire area is like an architectural museum of old Norway. For one of the loveliest turf-roofed homes you'll see, head up to the top of Kjerkgata to the house signposted as **Harald Sohlsbergs Plass 59**.

If Røros looks familiar, that's because several films have been made here, including Røros author Johan Falkberget's classic *An-Magrit*, starring Jane Fonda. Flanderborg gate starred in some of Astrid Lindgren's *Pippi Longstocking* classics and Røros even stood in for Siberia in *A Day in the Life of Ivan Denisovich*.

In addition to the main museum website, www.worldheritageroros.no is an excellent resource about Røros' historical sites.

★ **Smelthytta**   MUSEUM
(www.rorosmuseet.no; Malmplassen; adult/student/child incl guided tour 100/80kr/free; ☉ 10am-6pm mid-Jun–mid-Aug, 10am-4pm early Jun & mid-Aug–mid-Sep, 10am-3pm mid-Sep–May) Built on the site of a former copper-smelting works that burnt down in 1975, this museum brings the town's mining heritage to life. Intricate working models demonstrate the water- and horse-powered smelting processes, and if you want to watch the real thing, live copper smelting demonstrations are held daily at 3pm in July and August.

Outside the museum entrance spreads the large open area known as the **Malmplassen** (Ore Place), where loads of ore were dumped and weighed on the large wooden scale. Just across the stream from the museum are the protected **Slegghaugen** (slag heaps), from which there are lovely views over town. Off the southwestern corner of the slag heaps, the historic smelting district with its tiny turf-roofed **miners' cottages**, particularly along **Sleggveien**, is one of Røros' prettiest corners.

Røros Kirke   CHURCH
(Kjerkgata; adult/child 50kr/free; ☉ 10am-4pm Mon-Sat, 12.30-2.30pm Sun mid-Jun–mid-Aug, 11am-1pm Mon-Sat early Jun & mid-Aug–mid-Sep, 11am-1pm Sat rest of year) Røros' copper industry was booming when local notables decided to finance the construction of this lovely – and large – Lutheran church in 1784, at a cost of 23,000 riksdaler (at the time, miners earned about 50 riksdaler per year). It's vast, with space for 1600 worshippers, and a fittingly grand monument to the town's mining fortunes.

☆ Activities

Guided Walking Tours   WALKING
(adult/child 100kr/free; ☉ tours 11am, 1pm & 3pm mid-Jun–mid-Aug, 11am early Jun & mid-Aug–mid-Sep, 11am Thu & Sat mid-Sep–May) These interesting walking tours are run by the tourist office and illustrate the town's past, as well as some of the important characters who shaped its history. They last just over an hour and start at Smelthytta/Malmplassen and end at Røros church. Sign up at the tourist office (p313).

Husky Point   DOG SLEDDING
(✆977 38 903; www.huskypoint.no; Kopparleden 9001, Os; dog-sledding winter/summer adult from 1200/1100kr, child year-round 600kr) ⚑ Based near the town of Os, about 20km south of Røros, this dog-sledding company can take you on a 90-minute husky-driven ride whatever the time of year: in winter, the sleds are on skis, and in summer they're on wheels. If you feel up to it, you can even opt to take the reins.

Røros Rein   WILDLIFE
(✆97974966; www.rorosrein.no; Hagaveien 17; ☉ Nov-Apr) ⚑ If you've always wanted to learn how to steer a reindeer sleigh, then this winter-only company can help. It's run by a local Sami family, the Nordfjells, who will teach you all about the reindeer and even let you join in with herding if you wish. Afterwards, a traditional meal is served in a Sami *lavvo* (hut).

✨ Festivals & Events

Rørosmartnan CULTURAL
(Røros Market; ⊘ Feb) The biggest winter event is Rørosmartnan (Røros Market), which began in 1644 as a rendezvous for hunters who ventured into town to sell their products to miners and buy supplies.

Fermund Race SPORTS
(www.femundlopet.no; ⊘ Feb) One of Europe's longest dog-sled races starts and ends in Røros in the first week of February.

🛌 Sleeping

★ Erzscheidergården GUESTHOUSE €€
(☑ 72 41 11 94; www.erzscheidergaarden.no; Spell Olaveien 6; s 900-1150kr, d 1250-1350kr; P ₷) For our money, this cosy guesthouse is the top place to stay in Røros. It has the vibe of a traditional mountain hostelry, so expect wood, rugs, rustic furniture and old-fashioned beds – but it's all tastefully done and exceedingly comfortable. The home-cooked buffet breakfast is an absolute feast and almost worth coming for on its own.

Frøyas Hus B&B €€
(☑ 72 41 10 10; www.froyashus.no; Mørkstugata 4; s/d 950/1050kr; ₷) With only two rooms, this gorgeous guesthouse has an intimacy you won't find elsewhere. Rooms are small and have scarcely changed in over 300 years – it's rustic in the best sense of the word. Throw in friendly service, a lovely courtyard cafe and public areas strewn with local antiques and curiosities, and it's all perfectly integrated into the Røros experience.

Vertshuset Røros HISTORIC HOTEL €€
(☑ 72 41 93 50; www.vertshusetroros.no; Kjerkgata 34; r 1100-1700kr; ₷) Located in a historic 17th-century inn on the main pedestrian thoroughfare, the Vertshuset Røros is a wonderful choice. The wood-clad rooms are generously sized and have numerous period touches, such as original timber beams. Pricier rooms have small kitchenettes, while the two-bed apartments are perfect for families. As with all old buildings, noise can be an issue.

🍴 Eating

Trygstad Bakeri BAKERY €
(☑ 72 41 10 29; www.trygstadbakeri.no; Kjerkgata 12; snacks 30-80kr; ⊘ 8.30am-7pm Mon-Fri, 9am-4pm Sat, noon-5pm Sun) This standout cafe and bakery will treat you to the town's most popular coffee and baked goodies.

Kaffestugu Cafeteria NORWEGIAN €€
(www.kaffestuggu.no; Bergmannsgata 18; mains 129-250kr; ⊘ 10am-11pm) Set in one of Røros' classic timber buildings, with a small outdoor courtyard, this perennially popular cafe has the air of an old Norwegian tearoom, and it's a good spot, indeed, for coffee, cake and pastries. Main meals tend towards the hearty and filling: *smørbrød* (open sandwich), reindeer steak, sausages and stews, often served with heaps of potato and cabbage.

★ Vertshuset Røros NORWEGIAN €€€
(☑ 72 41 93 50; Kjerkgata 34; mains lunch 110-190kr, dinner 295-340kr, 3-/6-course menu 450/798kr; ⊘ 10am-10pm) The town's best food is served at the Vertshuset Inn, with a strong focus on local flavours: mountain trout, Arctic char, local beef, pork and a great selection of cheeses. The highlight is the six-course evening menu, a feast of mountain flavours, served in the inn's cosy beamed dining room. Lunch mains are tasty, but less ambitious.

ℹ Information

Tourist Office (☑ 72 41 00 00; www.roros.no; Peder Hiortsgata 2; ⊘ 9am-3.30pm Mon-Fri, 10am-4pm Sat) The first port of call for town info.

World Heritage Roros (www.worldheritage roros.no) Details Røros' historical sites.

ℹ Getting There & Away

AIR
Widerøe (www.wideroe.no) flies from Oslo a couple of times a day except Saturday. There's no airport bus; a taxi into town costs about 100kr.

BUS
There are daily buses from Røros to Trondheim (319kr, four hours, two to four daily) leaving from the **bus station** (Johan Falkbergets vei). You can see timetables at the ATB (www.atb.no) website.

TRAIN
Røros lies on the eastern railway line between Oslo (249kr to 810kr, five hours, four or five daily) and Trondheim (from 249kr to 304kr, 2½ hours).

Jotunheimen National Park

This is it. This is the big one. The high peaks and glaciers of the 1151-sq-km **Jotunheimen National Park** (www.jotunheimen.com; 17km SW of Lom) whose name means the 'Home of the Giants', make for Norway's best-loved, busiest and, arguably, most spectacular wilderness destination. Seemingly hundreds of hiking routes lead through ravine-like valleys past deep lakes, plunging waterfalls and 60 glaciers to the tops of all the peaks in Norway over 2300m; these include Galdhøpiggen (the highest peak in northern Europe at 2469m), Glittertind (2452m) and Store Skagastølstind (2403m). By one count, there are more than 275 summits above 2000m inside the park.

◉ Sights

★ Mímisbrunnr Klimapark 2469 TUNNEL
(⟳61 21 16 00; www.mimisbrunnr.no; adult/child 345/175kr; ⊙guided tours 10.30am & 2pm late Jun–late Aug, Sat & Sun late Aug–mid-Sep) If you want to learn all about the wonders of ice, this impressive experience takes you closer than you ever thought possible. Guided tours take you 60m under the ice through a specially created ice tunnel that reveals the ice's structure and colours, and documents more than six millennia of time. It's a surprisingly moving experience, with the obvious topic of climate change looming constantly in the background.

🏃 Activities

Jotunheimen's hiking possibilities are practically endless and all are spectacular. The best maps are Statens Kartverk's *Jotunheimen Aust* and *Jotunheimen Vest* (1:50,000).

The tourist office and the Norsk Fjellmuseum in Lom can offer advice, route descriptions and guided hikes through the park.

★ Sognefjellet SCENIC DRIVE
Town councillors of the world: You may have built a lot of roads in your time, and many of them are probably very useful, but chances are none of them are as spectacular as this one. Snaking through Jotunheimen National Park (and providing access to most of the trailheads), the stunningly scenic Sognefjellet Rd (Rv55) connects Lustrafjorden with Lom, and is billed as 'the road over the roof of Norway'. With little doubt, it's one of Norway's most beautiful drives.

Tindevegen SCENIC DRIVE
(www.tindevegen.no; per car 80kr; ⊙May-Nov) Sometimes known as the shortcut through Jotunheimen, this is yet another of Norway's most epic roads. Running from Turtagrø to Øvre Årdal and beyond all the way to Sognefjorden, it's a 32km route that offers a cinematic view of several of Norway's highest mountains, most of which stay snow capped year-round – among them

Fanaråken (2069m), Skagastølstindane (2405m) and Austabotntindane (2203m). Though it's not one of Norway's official Tourist Routes, it's an absolute stunner nonetheless. Don't miss it.

★ Besseggen HIKING
No discussion of hiking in Jotunheimen would be complete without mention of Besseggen, the most popular hike in Norway. Indeed, some travellers find it too popular, with at least 30,000 hikers walking it in the three months a year that it's passable. The day hike between Memurubu Lodge (⟳460 16 100, 61 23 89 99; www.ut.no/hytte/3.2002; dm DNT nonmembers 970-1130kr) and Gjendesheim (⟳61 23 89 10; www.gjendesheim.no; Gjendesheim; dm adult/child 210/105kr; r 1-3 beds 350/175kr, 4-6 beds 300/150kr; 🛜) takes about six hours and climbs to a high point of 1743m. Park at Gjendesheim, hop on the M/S *Gjende* ferry and cross the lake to begin the hike.

Galdhøpiggen Summer Ski Centre SKIING
(⟳61 21 17 50; www.gpss.no; day lift pass adult/child 405/325kr) This ski centre, at 1850m on the icy heights of Norway's highest mountain, is a stunning spot for summer skiing. From Galdesand on the Rv55, follow the Galdhøpiggen road (100kr toll) to its end at 1841m. The main season runs from June to mid-November. Apart from skiing opportunities, this road takes you to the highest point reachable by road in Norway.

🛏 Sleeping & Eating

DNT maintains staffed huts along most of the routes and there's also a choice of private lodges along the main roads. The majority of accommodation is to be found along the Sognefjellet Rd. On the Rv51, options are more limited to campsites, although there are some lodges in the vicinity of Gjendesheim, which are handy for an early start on the Besseggen ridge. Most open from May to September.

Apart from the hotel and hostel restaurants, there's hardly anywhere to eat – so either bring supplies or reserve dinner wherever you're staying.

Juvasshytta LODGE €
(⟳61 21 15 50; www.juvasshytta.no; dm per adult/child 250/200kr) With a name that sounds like it came from *Star Wars,* and a location above 1800m, Juvasshytta is a fine base. It sits in the shadow of Galdhøpiggen, Norway's highest peak, and staff can arrange guided walks, glacier hikes and climbs to

the summit. The lodge-style accommodation ranges from barn-basic to quite comfortable.

Leirvassbu Lodge LODGE €€
(☑61211210; www.ton.no/en/leirvassbu-mountain-lodge; s/d/tr 755/1190/1725kr; P🐾) Run by the same family as the Elvesæter Hotel, this typically Norwegian mountain lodge sits at an altitude of 1400m, hunkered down beside Lake Leirvatnet. It's predominantly a walking and skiing base, and its 100-odd rooms get full up in the height of the season. You can save some krone by opting for a shared bathroom.

⭐ **Elvesæter Hotell** HOTEL €€€
(☑61 21 99 00; www.ton.no/en/elveseter-culture-and-art-hotel; Bøverdalen; s/d from 1100/1550kr; P🐾) 🐾 This extraordinary old hostelry looks for all the world like something out of Tolkien's notebook. Accessed through wooden gates, the hotel's timber buildings are home to a higgledy-piggledy collection of storybook-style rooms, complete with painted murals, sleigh beds, antiques and artworks. The plumbing is creaky, the soundproofing is non-existent and it gets busy – but it sure scores high on heritage.

⭐ **Turtagrø Hotel** LODGE €€€
(☑57 68 08 00; www.turtagro.no; Fortun; s/d/f 1610/2200/3200kr, campsite per person 135kr; P🐾) An intriguing meeting of mountain heritage old and new. This alpine hotel has two buildings: the original Swiss chalet dating from 1888 and the strikingly modern main lodge, a zig-zag structure built in 2002. Rooms reflect their era: modern ones are clean and sleek in pine and glass, older ones have a more trad feel. Excellent meals are served nightly.

ℹ Information

For general information on the park, contact the **Norsk Fjellmuseum** (Norwegian Mountain Museum; ☑61 21 16 00; www.norskfjellsenter.no; Brubakken 2; adult/child 12-16yr 80/50kr; ⊙9am-7pm Mon-Fri, 9am-5pm Sat & Sun mid-Jun–mid-Aug, 9am-4pm Mon-Fri, 10am-3pm Sat & Sun mid-Aug–mid-Jun) or the small **tourist office** (☑61 21 29 90; www.visitjotunheimen.com; ⊙9am-5pm Mon-Sat, 9am-4pm Sun Jul–mid-Aug, 9am-4pm Mon-Sat mid-Aug–early Sep; 🐾), both in Lom.

ℹ Getting There & Away

Between June and September, the Valdreseks-pressen bus connects Lom with various areas in the park, including Gjendesheim (126kr, one hour 20 minutes).

BERGEN & THE SOUTHWESTERN FJORDS

Bergen
POP 278,121

Surrounded by seven hills and seven fjords, Bergen is a beguiling city. During the early Middle Ages, it was an important seaport and a member of the Hanseatic League, as well as Norway's capital – a heritage that can still be glimpsed in the beautifully preserved wooden houses of Bryggen, now protected as a Unesco World Heritage site. Colourful houses creep up the hillsides, ferries flit around the fjords, and a cluster of excellent art museums provide a welcome detour in case Bergen's notoriously fickle weather sets in. Meanwhile, a large student population ensures the city has a buzzy bar scene and nightlife.

◉ Sights

Making time just to wander Bergen's historic neighbourhoods is a must. Beyond Bryggen, the most picturesque are the steep streets climbing the hill behind the Fløibanen funicular station, Nordnes (the peninsula that runs northwest of the centre, including along the southern shore of the main harbour) and Sandviken (the area north of Håkonshallen). It's a maze of winding lanes and clapboard houses, perfect for a quiet wander.

⭐ **Bryggen** HISTORIC SITE
FREE Bergen's oldest quarter runs along the eastern shore of Vågen Harbour (*bryggen* translates as 'wharf') in long, parallel and often leaning rows of gabled buildings. Each has stacked-stone or wooden foundations and reconstructed rough-plank construction. It's enchanting, no doubt about it, but can be exhausting if you hit a cruise-ship and bus-tour crush.

⭐ **KODE** GALLERY
(☑53 00 97 04; www.kodebergen.no; Rasmus Meyers allé; adult/child 100kr/free, includes all 4 museums, valid 2 days)) A catch-all umbrella for Bergen's art museums, KODE showcases one of the largest art-and-design collections in Scandinavia. Each of the four buildings has its own focus: **KODE 1** (Nordahl Bruns gate 9; ⊙11am-5pm) houses a national silver collection and the renowned

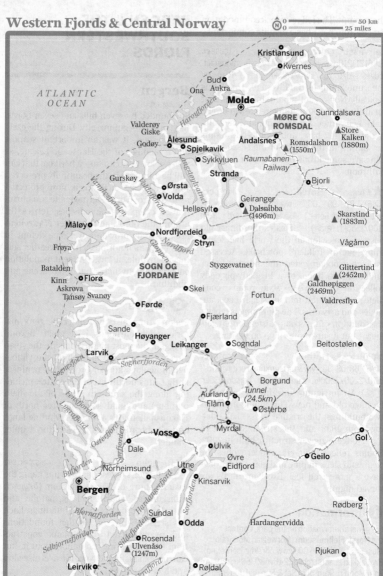

Singer art collection; **KODE 2** (Rasmus Meyers allé 3) is for contemporary exhibitions; **KODE 3** (Rasmus Meyers allé 7; ☺10am-6pm) majors in Edvard Munch; and **KODE 4** (Rasmus Meyers allé 9; ☺11am-5pm; ♿) focuses on modern art.

★**Edvard Grieg Museum** MUSEUM
(Troldhaugen; ☎55 92 29 92; http://griegmuseum.no; Troldhaugvegen 65, Paradis-Bergen; adult/child 100kr/free; ☺9am-6pm May-Sep, 10am-4pm Oct-Apr) Composer Edvard Grieg and his wife Nina Hagerup spent summers at this

charming Swiss-style wooden villa from 1885 until Grieg's death in 1907. Surrounded by fragrant, tumbling gardens and occupying a semi-rural setting – on a peninsula by coastal Nordåsvatnet lake, south of Bergen – it's a truly lovely place to visit.

★**Ole Bull Museum** MUSEUM

(Museet Lysøen; ☑ 56 30 90 77; www.lysoen.no; adult/child incl guided tour 60/30kr; ☉ 11am-4pm mid-May–Aug, Sun only Sep) This beautiful estate was built in 1873 as the summer residence of Norway's first musical superstar, violinist Ole Bull. Languishing on its own private island, it's a fairy-tale concoction of turrets, onion domes, columns and marble inspired by Moorish architecture. Of particular note is the soaring pine music hall: it's hard not to imagine Bull practising his concertos in here.

Damsgård HISTORIC BUILDING

(www.bymuseet.no; Alleen 29, Laksevåg; adult/child 80kr/free; ☉ noon-4pm Jun-Aug, tours at noon & 2pm) The 1770 Damsgård manor, 3km west of town, may well be Norway's (if not Europe's) finest example of 18th-century rococo timber architecture. The building's superbly over-the-top garden includes sculptures, ponds and plant specimens that were common 200 years ago. To get here, take bus 19 from Bergen's centre.

🏃 **Activities**

★**Bergen Food Tours** FOOD

(☑ 960 44 892; www.bergenfoodtours.com; adult/child 800/700kr) These three-hour food tours are a great way to ease yourself into Nordic cuisine. The classic walk includes stops at about eight different spots around the city, where you get to sample the goods: seafood, reindeer, pastries, craft beer and *trekroneren* (hot dogs), as well as fish soup made by none other than Bergen's top chef, Christopher Håtuft of Lysverket (p321).

Fløibanen Funicular CABLE CAR

(☑ 55 33 68 00; www.floibanen.no; Vetrlidsalmenning 21; adult/child return 90/45kr; ☉ 7.30am-11pm Mon-Fri, 8am-11pm Sat & Sun) For an unbeatable view of the city, ride the 26-degree Fløibanen funicular to the top of Mt Fløyen (320m), with departures every 15 minutes. From the top, well-marked hiking tracks lead into the forest; the possibilities are mapped out on the free *Walking Map of Mount Fløyen*, available from the Bergen tourist office (p322).

Ulriken643 CABLE CAR

(☑ 53 64 36 43; www.ulriken643.no; adult/child/family return 170/100/460kr; ☉ 9am-9pm May-Sep, 9am-5pm Tue-Sun Oct-Apr) Look up to the mountains from the harbour, and you'll spy a radio mast clad in satellite dishes. That's the top of Mt Ulriken (643m) you're spying, and on a clear day it offers a stunning panorama over city, fjords and mountains. Thankfully you don't have to climb it; a cable car speeds from bottom to top in just seven minutes.

★**Fjord Tours** TOURS

(☑ 81 56 82 22; www.fjordtours.com) Bergen is a great place for a quick one-day jaunt into the fjords – especially if you have limited time. Hardangerfjord and Sognefjord can both easily be visited in a day from Bergen, or even from Oslo thanks to the popular **Norway in a Nutshell** tour, which packs in more in a single day than you thought possible.

🎭 **Festivals & Events**

For a full list of events, see the website www.visitbergen.com.

Bergen International Festival CULTURAL

(www.fib.no; ☉ late May) Held over 14 days, this is the big cultural festival of the year, with dance, music, theatre and visual-arts shows throughout the city.

Night Jazz Festival MUSIC

(www.nattjazz.no; ☉ May) May jazz festival that is popular with Bergen's large student population.

Bergen Beer Festival BEER

(Bergen Ølfestival; www.bergenolfestival.no; ☉ Sep) Bergen's beer-drinkers get to taste brews from across the globe in this lively two-day celebration of all things ale. Well, this is a Viking nation after all.

🛏 **Sleeping**

★**Hotel Park** HISTORIC HOTEL €€

(☑ 55 54 44 00; www.hotelpark.no; Harald Hårfagresgate 35; s/d 1290/1790kr; 🛜) Two 19th-century houses combined comprise this family-run beauty, still managed by the daughters of the long-time owner. Packed with curios and antiques, it's a lovely, welcoming place to stay – all 33 rooms are slightly different, with quirky layouts and surprising design touches; corner rooms have the best views over Bergen's rooftops and Mt Fløyen.

Bergen

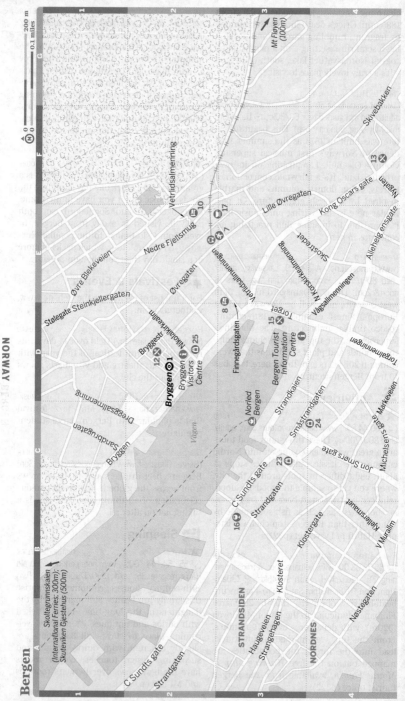

NORWAY

200 m
0.1 miles

Mt Fløyen (100m)

Vetrlidsalmenning

Nedre Fjellsmug

Øvre Blekeveien

Stølegate Steinkjellergaten

Øvregaten

Nikolaikirkeallm

Bryggestr

Bryggen

Dreggsallmenning

Sandbrugaten

Bryggen
Visitors
Centre

Vågen

Norled
Bergen

Finnegårdsgaten

Vetrlidsalmenningen

N Korskirkeallmenning

Torget

Bergen Tourist
Information
Centre

Strandkaien

Strandsgaten

Småstrandgaten

C Sundts gate

Strandgaten

Klostergate

Klosteret

Haugeveien

Strangehagen

STRANDSIDEN

NORDNES

Nøstegaten

V Muralln

Kjøttbasaren

Jon Smørs gate

Michelsens gate

Markeveien

Torgallmenningen

Vågsallmenningen

Skostredet

Lille Øvregaten

Kong Oscars gate

Skivebakken

Nigjen

Allehelgensgate

C Sundts gate

Strandgaten

Skoltegrunnskaien
(International Ferries; 300m);
Skuteviken Gjestehus (500m)

1
8
10
12
13
15
16
17
23
24
25

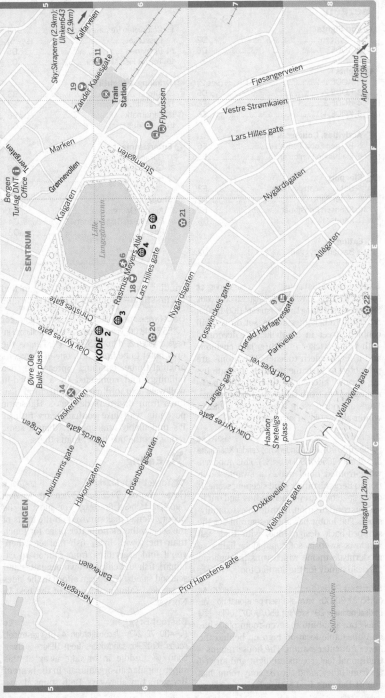

NORWAY

Bergen

Skuteviken Gjestehus   GUESTHOUSE €€
(☑934 67 163; www.skutevikenguesthouse.com; Skutevikens smalgang 11; 2-person apt 1100-1200kr; ☎) This timber guesthouse, set on a small cobbled street in Sandviken, is decorated with white wicker furniture, lace cushions and a few modern touches. The rooms are promoted as apartments, with separate living rooms, kitchenette and en-suite bathrooms, but in truth they're just large rooms. Rates are per person; they start at 450kr in winter and 550kr in summer.

Zander K   HOTEL €€
(☑55 36 20 40; www.zanderk.no; Zander Kaaesgate 8; s/d from 1050/1690kr; ✱☎) This modern, white-fronted hotel makes a swanky addition to Bergen's rather staid sleeping scene. It offers spacious, grey-toned rooms, laid out in various configuration, from doubles to family-sized. The lobby, bar and restaurant set the stripped-back design tone, with their tall windows, swooshy sofas and globe lights – a modernistic theme which runs throughout. It's dead handy for the station, too.

Skansen Pensjonat   GUESTHOUSE €€
(☑55 31 90 80; www.skansen-pensjonat.no; Vetrlidsalmenning 29; s/d/apt 550/900/1100kr; ☎) This cute-as-a-button, seven-room place has an unbeatable location high up behind the lower funicular station. The house retains a traditional feel, rooms are light and airy (if far from fancy), and the 'balcony room' has one of Bergen's best views. It's on a steep,

winding lane, and extremely tricky to find the first time – phone ahead if you're unsure.

Det Hanseatiske Hotel   HISTORIC HOTEL €€€
(☑55 30 48 00; www.dethanseatiskehotell.no; Finnegårdsgaten 2; d from 1890kr; ☎) This is the only hotel to be housed in one of Bryggen's original timber buildings. Spread over two buildings and connected by a glassed-in walkway, extraordinary architectural features from Bryggen's days as a Hanseatic port mix with luxe contemporary fittings. It's undeniably atmospheric, though some rooms get the mix better than others.

✗ Eating

★**Torget Fish Market**   SEAFOOD €
(Torget; lunches 99-169kr; ⊙7am-7pm Jun-Aug, 7am-4pm Mon-Sat Sep-May) For most of its history, Bergen has survived on the fruits of the sea, so there's no better place for lunch than the town's lively fish market, where you'll find everything from salmon to calamari, fish and chips, prawn baguettes and seafood salads. If you can afford it, the sides of smoked salmon are some of the best in Norway.

Bastant Bryggen   CAFE €
(☑400 72 247; Jacobsfjorden 4, Bryggestredet; soups 99-129kr; sandwiches from 119kr; ⊙11am-5pm) ✐ Cuddle in or take away at this super-popular, all-organic cafe in the heart of Bryggen's tiny alleyways. Daily soups always

include a vegan, vegetarian and meat option, and sandwiches are hearty. There are home-made lemonade and strawberry frappés in summer, killer hot chocolates when it's cold and excellent coffee year-round.

Pingvinen
NORWEGIAN €€

(☑ 55 60 46 46; www.pingvinen.no; Vaskerelven 14; daily specials 119kr, mains 159-269kr; ☺ noon-3am) Devoted to Norwegian home cooking, Pingvinen is the old favourite of *everyone* in Bergen. They come for meals their mothers and grandparents used to cook, and the menu always features at least one of the following: fish-cake sandwiches, reindeer, fish pie, salmon, lamb shank and *raspeballer* (sometimes called *komle*) – west-coast potato dumplings. Note that whale is served here.

★Lysverket
NORWEGIAN €€€

(☑ 55 60 31 00; www.lysverket.no; KODE 4, Rasmus Meyers allé 9; lunch mains 165-195kr, lunch sharing menu with/without dessert 295/395kr, 4-/7-course menu 745/995kr; ☺ 11am-1am Tue-Sat) If you're going to blow the budget on one meal in Norway, make it here. Chef Christopher Haatuft is pioneering his own brand of Nordic cuisine, which he dubs 'neo-fjordic' – in other words, combining modern techniques with the best fjord-sourced produce. His food is highly seasonal, incredibly creative and full of surprising textures, combinations and flavours. Savour every mouthful.

Colonialen Restaurant
NORWEGIAN €€€

(☑ 55 90 16 00; www.colonialen.no/restaurant/; Kong Oscars gate 44; 6-/8-course tasting menu 895/1195kr; ☺ 6-11pm Mon-Sat) Part of an ever-expanding culinary empire, this flagship fine-diner showcases the cream of New Nordic cuisine. It's playful and pushes boundaries, sure, but the underlying flavours are classic, and employ the very best Norwegian ingredients, especially from the west coast. Presentation is impeccable – expect edible flowers and unexpected ingredients aplenty. Strange it's on the dingy side of town.

🍷 Drinking & Nightlife

★Terminus Bar
BAR

(Zander Kaaesgate 6, Grand Terminus Hotel; ☺ 5pm-midnight) Consistently voted one of the world's best whisky bars, this grand old bar in the Grand Hotel Terminus is the perfect place for a quiet dram. It promises more than 500 different tastes, and the oldest whisky dates back to 1960. The 1928 room looks gorgeous both before and after you've sampled a few.

★Landmark
BAR, CAFE

(☑ 940 15 050; Bergen Kunsthalle, Rasmus Meyers allé 5; ☺ cafe 11am-5pm Tue-Sun, bar 7pm-1am Tue-Thu, to 3.30am Fri & Sat) This large, airy room is a beautiful example of 1930s Norwegian design and is named for architect Ole Landmark. It multitasks: daytime cafe, lecture and screening hall; live-performance space, bar and venue for Bergen's best club nights. It's a favourite with the city's large creative scene. The cafe serves yummy lunches, with a choice of open-faced sandwiches and a weekly melt (995kr to 1295kr).

Det Lille Kaffekompaniet
CAFE

(Nedre Fjellsmug 2; ☺ 10am-8pm Mon-Fri, 10am-6pm Sat & Sun) This was one of Bergen's first third-wave coffee places and retains a super-local feel. Everyone overflows onto the neighbouring stairs when the sun's out and you're not sure which table belongs to whom.

Altona Vinbar
WINE BAR

(☑ 55 30 40 00; www.augustin.no/en/altona; C Sundts gate 22; ☺ 6pm-12.30am Mon-Thu, to 1.30am Fri & Sat) Set in a warren of vaulted underground rooms that date from the 16th century, Altona's huge, carefully selected wine list, soft lighting and murmured conversation make it Bergen's most romantic bar (particularly appealing when the weather's cold and wet). The bar menu tends towards tasty comfort food, such as Norwegian lamb burgers (190kr).

☆ Entertainment

Garage
LIVE MUSIC

(☑ 55 32 19 80; www.garage.no; Christies gate 14; ☺ 3pm-3am Mon-Sat, 5pm-3am Sun) Garage has taken on an almost mythical quality for music lovers across Norway. They do have the odd jazz and acoustic act, but this is a rock-and-metal venue at heart, with well-known Norwegian and international acts drawn to the cavernous basement. Stop by for their Sunday jam sessions in summer.

Hulen
LIVE MUSIC

(☑ 55 32 31 31; www.hulen.no; Olaf Ryes vei 48; ☺ 9pm-3am Thu-Sat) Another minor legend of the Norwegian music scene, this basement club has hosted top rock and indie bands since opening its doors in 1968. *Hulen* means 'cave' and the venue is indeed underground, in a converted bomb shelter.

Grieghallen
CLASSICAL MUSIC

(☑ 55 21 61 50; www.grieghallen.no; Edvard Griegs plass; ☺ Aug-Jun) Performances by the

NORWAY BERGEN

respected Bergen Philharmonic Orchestra take place inside this striking glass hall.

🛍 Shopping

⭐ Aksdal i Muren
CLOTHING

(☎55 24 24 55; www.aksdalimuren.no; Østre Muralmenning 23; ⊙10am-5pm Mon-Fri, 10am-6pm Sat) This enticing shop in a historic landmark building has been ensuring the good people of Bergen are warm and dry since 1883. The city's best selection of rainwear includes cult Swedish labels such as Didriksons, big names including Helly Hansen and Barbour, but also local gems such as Blæst by Lillebøe. We can't think of a better Bergen souvenir than a stripey sou'wester.

⭐ Colonialen Strandgaten 18
DELI

(☎55 90 16 00; www.colonialen.no; Strandgaten 18; ⊙8am-6pm Mon-Fri, 10am-6pm Sat) The latest addition to the Colonialen arsenal, this impeccably cool cafe-deli serves up lavish lunchtime sandwiches, plus an irresistible selection of cold cuts, cheeses, oils, smoked fish and so much more. It's also the best place in town to try baked goodies and breads from Colonialen's own bakery – including their to-die-for cinnamon buns.

Røst
GIFTS & SOUVENIRS

(☎488 94 499; www.butikkenrost.no; Bryggen 15; ⊙10am-8pm Mon-Fri, 10am-7pm Sat & Sun) Short on souvenir-buying time and want something a bit more upmarket than a troll doll? This bright boutique right in the centre of Bryggen has a large range of well-designed Norwegian and Scandinavian objects and homewares, as well as local fashion for women, children and babies.

ℹ Information

Bergen Turlag DNT Office (☎55 33 58 10; www.bergen-turlag.no; Tverrgaten 4; ⊙10am-4pm Mon-Wed & Fri, to 6pm Thu, to 3pm Sat) Maps and information on hiking and hut accommodation throughout western Norway.

Bryggen Visitors Centre (Jacobsfjorden, Bryggen; ⊙9am-5pm mid-May–mid-Sep) Maps and activities in the Bryggen neighbourhood.

Tourist Office (☎55 55 20 00; www.visitbergen. com; Strandkaien 3; ⊙8.30am-10pm Jun-Aug, 9am-8pm May & Sep, 9am-4pm Mon-Sat Oct-Apr) One of the best and busiest in the country, Bergen's tourist office distributes the free and worthwhile *Bergen Guide* booklet, as well as a huge stock of information on the entire region. They also sell rail tickets. If booking or making an enquiry, come early or be prepared to queue.

ℹ Getting There & Away

Bergen is 463km from Oslo via Rv7, and 210km from Stavanger via E39.

AIR

Bergen Airport (www.avinor.no/en/airport/bergen-airport) is at Flesland, about 18km southwest of the centre. It's served by the following airlines:

Norwegian (www.norwegian.com) Flights to Oslo and Tromsø.

SAS (www.sas.no) Connects with Oslo and Stavanger.

Widerøe (www.wideroe.no) Flies to Oslo, Haugesund, Stavanger and many coastal destinations as far north as Tromsø.

BUS

Flybussen (www.flybussen.no; one way/return adult 90/160kr, child 50/80kr) runs up to four times hourly between the airport, the Radisson Blu Royal Hotel, the main bus terminal and opposite the tourist office on Vågsallmenningen.

Various companies run long-distance routes across Norway from Bergen's **bus terminal** (Vestre Strømkaien), located on Vestre Strømkaien. **Nor-Way** (www.nor-way.no) provides a useful travel planner.

TRAIN

The spectacular train journey between Bergen and Oslo (349 to 905kr, 6½ to eight hours, five daily) runs through the heart of Norway. Other destinations include Voss (204kr, one hour, hourly) and Myrdal (299 to 322kr, 2¼ hours, up to nine daily) for connections to the Flåmsbana railway.

Early bookings can secure you some great discounts.

ℹ Getting Around

BICYCLE

Bergen Bike (☎400 04 059; www.norway-active.no; Bontelabo 2; adult per 2hr/day 200/500kr) Rental bikes near the quay.

Sykkelbutikken (www.sykkelbutikken.no; Kong Oscars gate 81; touring bikes per day/week 250/850kr; ⊙10am-8pm Mon-Fri, 10am-4pm Sat) Bicycle hire near the train station.

CAR & MOTORCYCLE

Parking is a bit of an expensive headache in Bergen. Few hotels have their own car parks, which means you'll have to resort to one of the public car parks in the city centre. The largest and cheapest is the 24-hour **Bygarasjen** (per 24 hours 150kr) next to the bus terminal, which also has a covered walkway leading straight to the train station. Elsewhere you'll pay upwards of 200kr per day. The **tourist office** (p322) has two brochures covering where to park in Bergen.

Voss

POP 14,168

Voss (also known as Vossevangen) sits on a sparkling lake not far from the fjords and this position has earned it a world-renowned reputation as Norway's adventure capital. The town itself is far from pretty, but everyone is here for white-water rafting, bungee jumping and just about anything you can do from a parasail, most of it out in the fjords.

◎ Sights

Vangskyrkja   CHURCH

(Uttrågata; adult/child 20kr/free; ⊙10am-4pm Tue-Sat) Voss' stone church occupies the site of an ancient pagan temple. A Gothic-style stone church was built here in the mid-13th century and although the original stone altar and unique wooden spire remain, the Lutheran Reformation of 1536 saw the removal of many original features. The 1923 stained-glass window commemorates the 900th anniversary of Christianity in Voss. Miraculously, the building escaped destruction during the intense German bombing of Voss in 1940.

Nearby is the important monument of St Olav's Cross.

🏃 Activities

Voss lives for its outdoor activities, and there are loads to choose from. Bookings can be made directly or through the tourist office (p324).

Although normally done from Oslo or Bergen, the Norway in a Nutshell tour run by Fjord Tours (p317) can also be done from Voss.

Voss Vind   SKYDIVING

(☑401 05 999; www.vossvind.no; Oberst Bulls veg 28; adult/child 765/565kr; ⊙10am-8pm mid-June–mid-Aug, noon-8pm Wed-Sun rest of year) If you've always wanted to feel what it's like to skydive, but the thought of actually hurling yourself out of a plane fills you with mortal terror, then this amazing place can help. It has a wind tunnel that simulates the experience of free fall only without any danger of turning yourself into a cowpat. There's a minimum age of five years.

Nordic Ventures   ADVENTURE SPORTS

(☑56 51 00 17; www.nordicventures.com; on the water, near Park Hotel; adult/child 1095/750kr; ⊙Apr–mid-Oct) Take a guided kayak along the fjords from Voss, or book in for a multinight adventure. They have a floating office on the

water near the Park Hotel, as they also run tours out of Gudvangen.

Voss Active   ADVENTURE SPORTS

(☑56 51 05 25; www.vossactive.no; Nedkvitnesvegen 25; ⊙9am-9pm mid-May–Sep) This outdoors company specialises in organising rafting trips on local rivers including the Stranda, Raundalen and Vosso, but more recently it's branched out into lots of other activities, too, from canyoning and rappelling to fishing, guided hikes and – the kids' favourites – a high-wire rope course.

🎊 Festivals & Events

Extreme Sports Festival   SPORTS

(Veko; www.ekstremsportveko.com; ⊙Jun) A week long festival at the end of June that combines all manner of extreme sports (skydiving, paragliding and base jumping) with local and international music acts.

Vossajazz   MUSIC

(www.vossajazz.no; ⊙late Mar-early Apr) An annual innovative jazz, folk and world-music festival.

🛏 Sleeping

Fleischer's Hotel   HISTORIC HOTEL €€

(☑56 52 05 00; www.fleischers.no; Evangervegen; d 1495-2095kr; P 🕸 🛰) This venerable old hotel was built in 1889, and looks antique, with its striking facade and turrets, supplemented by a modern extension. Unfortunately rooms seem to have got stuck in the olden days, too – expect flock carpets, heavy drapes and old furniture here. Still, it has a quaint charm, and the dining room is majestic.

★Store Ringheim   B&B €€€

(☑954 06 135; www.storeringheim.no; Mølstervegen 44; d/f 1590/3390kr; P 🛰) This old farmhouse has been impeccably renovated with style, grace and supremely good taste to provide six lovely rooms. Choices include a cosy attic room, an elegant bedroom that was once the kitchen and a romantic bolt-hole in the old house that has its own stone fireplace and a hand-painted box bed straight out of *Sleeping Beauty*.

🍴 Eating

★Tre Brør   CAFE €

(☑951 03 832; www.trebror.no; Vangsgata 28; sandwiches & light meals 85-185kr; ⊙cafe 11am-8pm Mon-Wed, 11am-2.30am Thu-Sat, 11am-8pm Sun; 🛰) The Three Brothers is the heart of Voss's social scene, and rightly so – it's everything you want from a small-town cafe. There's super coffee from Oslo's Tim Wendleboe and Ålesund's Jacu Roastery, a great range of microbrewed beers from Voss Brewery down the road, and an on-trend menu of salads, soups, wraps, burgers and Asian-tinged dishes. What's not to like?

Ringheim Kafé NORWEGIAN **€€**
(☑56 51 13 65; www.ringheimkafe.no; Vangsgata 32; mains 160-220kr; ☉10am-6pm Mon-Fri, 10am-5pm Sat, noon-6pm Sun) If you're just after a quick lunchtime elk burger or a bowl of *hjortekoru* (smoked sausage with potato-and-cabbage stew), this traditional cafe on the main Vangsgata thoroughfare is a reasonable option, but don't go expecting any culinary fireworks. The cakes and desserts are homemade, and generally good.

🍷 Drinking & Nightlife

Voss Bryggeri MICROBREWERY
(☑975 40 517; www.vossbryggeri.com; Kytesvegen 396; ☉by appointment) This much-respected brewery has made a real splash on the beer scene in recent years, with standout brews such as their Oregonian pale ale, Natabjødn ('Nut Beer'), an English-style brown beer, and traditional Vossaøl, brewed with juniper tea. It's about 6km north of Voss; guided tours are available by arrangement, otherwise you can taste their beers at Tre Brør (p323).

❶ Information

Voss Tourist Office (☑406 17 700; www.visitvoss.no; Skulegata 14; ☉9am-6pm Mon-Sat, 10am-5pm Sun mid-June–Aug, 9am-4pm Mon-Fri Sep–mid-June)

❶ Getting There & Away

Voss is about 100km east of Bergen on the E16, and 45km southwest of Gudvangen.

BUS
Buses stop at the train station, west of the centre. There are frequent services to the following:
Bergen (186kr, two hours)
Flåm (121kr, 1¼ hours)
Sogndal (149kr to 229kr, three hours) via Gudvangen and Aurland.

TRAIN
Voss has fast and efficient train links. At Myrdal, you can connect with the **Flåmsbåna Railway** (p328). Booking ahead can get you some fantastic deals.
Bergen (204kr, one hour, hourly)
Oslo (249kr to 860kr, 5½ to six hours, five daily)

Hardangerfjord

Running from the Atlantic to the steep wall of central Norway's Hardangervidda plateau, Hardangerfjord is classic Norwegian fjord country. There are many beautiful corners, although our picks would take in Eidfjord, Ulvik and Utne, while Folgefonna National Park offers glacier walks and top-level hiking. It's also well known for its many fruit farms, especially apples – Hardanger is sometimes known as the orchard of Norway.

You can easily explore Hardangerfjord from Bergen; www.hardangerfjord.com is a good resource.

Eidfjord
POP 950
Eidfjord is one of the most beautifully sited towns in this part of Norway, dwarfed by sheer mountains and cascading waterfalls. Eidfjord's beauty does, however, come at a price. Although it's only accessible by ferry or spiral tunnels, in summer cruise ships arrive on an almost daily basis, and the town can get overwhelmed.

◉ Sights

Hardangervidda Natursenter MUSEUM
(☑53 67 40 00; www.hardangerviddanatursenter.no; Øvre Eidfjord; adult/child 130/65kr; ☉9am-7pm mid-Jun–mid-Aug, 10am-6pm Apr–mid-Jun & mid-Aug–Oct) For an all-encompassing overview of the Hardangervidda National Park, this excellent visitor centre should be your first port of call. Interactive exhibits explore the park's flora and fauna, while staff provide copious information on the many activities you can get up to, from hiking to skiing.

Kjeåsen Farm FARM
Perched 600m above Eidfjord are two farms that were, until 1974, completely inaccessible by road. Until then, residents had no choice but to lug all their goods and supplies up the mountainside – a back-breaking task. (It's said that one of the buildings took 30 years to build.) Nowadays it's mainly visited by tourists for the absolutely breathtaking view.

Vøringsfossen WATERFALL
At the summit after a steep 20km drive, and where Hardangervidda begins, is the stunning, 182m-high Vøringfoss Waterfall. There are actually numerous waterfalls here, which together are called Vøringsfossen. They plunge over the plateau's rim and

down into the canyon, some with a vertiginous drop of 145m, and can be viewed via a series of lookouts along the road.

Viking Burial Mounds   ARCHAEOLOGICAL SITE
(Hæreid; Troll Train 90/40kr; ⊘ Troll Train hourly 10am-5.30pm Jun-Aug) The 350 Viking burial mounds found here make this the largest Iron Age site in western Norway, dating from AD 400 to 1000. The tourist office can point you in their direction and supply a basic map with a marked 90-minute walking trail.

🏃 Activities

🌟 Flat Earth   ADVENTURE SPORTS
(☑ 476 06 847; www.flatearth.no) This excellent outdoors company offers pretty much every way of exploring the fjord country that you can think of. The highlight, of course, is the chance to steer a sea kayak down the epic fjord: there's a choice of three-hour trips (adult/child 590/450kr) or full-day expeditions (1150/1000kr) that include a BBQ lunch. Climbing, rafting and mountain biking are also offered.

🛏 Sleeping & Eating

All the hotels in Hardangerfjord have their own restaurants.

🌟 Eidfjord Gjestegiveri   GUESTHOUSE €
(☑ 53 66 53 46; www.ovre-eidfjord.com; Øvre Eidfjord; huts 400kr, s/d 600/890; ⊘ May-Aug; P 🛜) Pass through the tunnel to Øvre Eidfjord and you can't miss this handsome guesthouse, an old-fashioned, whitewashed, gabled beauty with a covered porch out front. Inside, the eight double rooms are simple but proper, stocked with vintage furniture; all share a corridor bathroom. There are also a few basic camping-style huts in the front garden, and a super pancake cafe.

Vik Pensjonat   GUESTHOUSE €€
(☑ 53 66 51 62; www.vikpensjonat.com; Eidfjord; s/d with shared bathroom 650/1200kr, with private bathroom 1200/1600kr, cabins 800-1450kr; P) An attractive option if being by the fjord is what matters. With its slate-topped gables and clapboard exterior, it looks every inch the traditional Norwegian guesthouse, but inside it's spruce and modern: uncluttered rooms, wooden floors and the essential fjord views. Rooms with balconies are unsurprisingly the best, or you can go for the riverside cabins in the garden.

ℹ Information

Eidfjord Tourist Office (☑ 53 67 34 00; www.visiteidfjord.no; Simadalsvegen 3; ⊘ 9am-7pm Mon-Fri, 10am-6pm Sat & Sun mid-Jun–mid-Aug, 10am-5pm Mon-Fri mid-Aug–mid-Jun)

ℹ Getting There & Away

Skyss (☑ 177; www.skyss.no) Bus 991/990 (seven to nine daily Monday to Friday, five to seven on weekends) travels from Øvre Eidfjord to Eidfjord (19kr, 10 minutes), Kinsarvik (93kr, 50 minutes), Lofthus (115kr, one hour) and Odda (195kr, 1½ hours).

In the opposite direction, some buses run to Geilo (242kr, 80 minutes, one or two daily), where you can catch the train on to Bergen.

Stavanger

POP 123.369

There's a reason this coastal town has been twinned with Houston and Aberdeen: it's sometimes known as Norway's 'Oil City' for its importance in oil exploration in the North Sea since the 1970s (Norway's largest oil company, Statoil, is based here). But while much of the outskirts are modern, you won't find too many skyscrapers – Stavanger's old centre has some of the most beautiful and best-preserved wooden buildings anywhere in Norway, many dating back to the 18th century. It's all very pretty, and in summer the waterfront comes alive in the best port-town style.

What Stavanger's oil boom has brought, however, is suburban sprawl and sky-high prices, even for Norway. It's notorious as one of the country's priciest locations, and finding a bed and a bite comes with a hefty price tag.

Nevertheless, it's a perfect launch pad for exploring nearby Lysefjorden, and for tackling the classic hike to Preikestolen (Pulpit Rock).

◉ Sights

🌟 Norsk Oljemuseum   MUSEUM
(Oil Museum; www.norskolje.museum.no; Kjeringholmen; adult/child 120/60kr; ⊘ 10am-7pm daily Jun-Aug, 10am-4pm Mon-Sat, to 6pm Sun Sep-May; ♿) Admittedly, the prospect of an 'oil museum' doesn't sound like the most promising option for an afternoon out. But this state-of-the-art place is well worth visiting – both for its striking, steel-clad architecture and its high-tech displays exploring the history of North Sea oil exploration. Highlights include the world's largest drill bit, simulated rigs, documentary films, archive testimony

and a vast hall of oil-platform models. There are also exhibitions on natural history, energy use and climate change.

Gamle Stavanger
AREA

Gamle (Old) Stavanger, above the western shore of the harbour, is a delight. The Old Town's cobblestone walkways pass between rows of late-18th-century whitewashed wooden houses, all immaculately kept and adorned with cheerful, well-tended flowerboxes. It well rewards an hour or two of ambling.

Canning Museum
MUSEUM

(☑51 84 27 00; www.museumstavanger.no; Øvre Strandgate 88a; adult/child incl other Stavanger museums 90/50kr; ☉11am-5pm Tue-Fri, 11am-4pm Sat & Sun) Don't miss this museum housed in an old cannery: it's one of Stavanger's most entertaining. Before oil, there were sardines, and Stavanger was once home to more than half of Norway's canning factories. By 1922 the city's canneries provided 50% of the town's employment. The exhibits take you through the whole 12-stage process from salting through to threading, smoking, decapitating and packing. Guides are on hand to answer your questions or crank up some of the old machines.

✹✹ Festivals & Events

Stavanger Vinfest
WINE

(www.stavangervinfest.no; ☉mid-Apr) A week long wine celebration at the city's best restaurants.

Gladmat
FOOD & DRINK

(www.gladmat.no; ☉mid-Jul) Reportedly Scandinavia's largest food festival.

🛏 Sleeping

★Thompsons B&B
B&B €

(☑51 52 13 29; www.thompsons-bed-and-breakfast.com; Muségata 79; s/d with shared bathroom 400/500kr; ℗) You won't find a bigger bargain in Stavanger than this homely B&B. Housed in a 1910 villa in a peaceful residential area, this four-bed B&B has a home-away-from-home vibe engendered by the warm and welcoming owner, Sissel Thompson. Rooms are cosy and comfortable, and the traditional Norwegian breakfast, taken around the downstairs dining table, is generous.

★Darby's Inn
B&B €€

(☑476 25 248; www.darbysbb.com; Oscars gate 18; r 1180-1280kr; ℗❅🖼) The two front rooms at this understated, opulent B&B might be Stavanger's nicest, even without a sea view. Traditional interiors in this historic house

combine dark wood with antique furniture, paintings, Persian rugs and a baby grand in the lounge and dining room. The large guest rooms are simpler but still have luxury linen, plump cushions and suitably heavy curtains.

Clarion Collection
Hotel Skagen Brygge
HOTEL €€€

(☑51 85 00 00; www.nordicchoicehotels.com; Skagenkaien 30; r Mon-Fri 2010-2990kr, Sat & Sun 1290-1910kr; ❅🖼) Built to resemble a modern take on a row of harbour townhouses, this swish number is the preferred choice of overnighting oil execs. It's quietly luxurious, with large, water-view rooms, plush turquoise-velour chairs and tasteful tones of cappuccino and chocolate. There's a gym, free afternoon cakes and waffles, and a nice lounge. Rates almost halve at weekends.

🍴 Eating

Stavanger has a large choice of restaurants, including some tasty Thai and Indian, but also what we suspect is the most expensive dining scene in Norway.

★Renaa Matbaren
INTERNATIONAL €€

(☑51 55 11 11; www.restaurantrenaa.no; Breitorget 6, enter from Bakkegata; small dishes 59-125kr; mains 165-395kr; ☉4pm-1am Mon-Fri, 11am-1am Sat, 2pm-midnight Sun) Run by top chef Sven Erik Renaa, this smart bistro offers a taste of his food at (reasonably) affordable prices. The menu is classic – mussels in beer, rib-eye with rosemary fries, squid with fennel and shallots, all with a Nordic twist. The glass and wood feels uber-Scandi, and the art collection is stellar (yes, that's an Antony Gormley statue).

Renaa Xpress Sølvberget
NORWEGIAN €€

(Stavanger Kulturhus; ☑51 55 11 11; www.restaurantrenaa.no; Sølvberggata 2; panini 89-98kr; salads 170kr; pizzas 180-199kr; ☉10am-10pm Mon-Thu, to midnight Fri & Sat, noon-10pm Sun) One of three Renaa restaurants in Stavanger, this upmarket cafe pretty much corners the lunchtime market. Go for the daily soup deal, tuck into a huge salad, enjoy a panino topped with *Parmaskinke* (Parma ham) or *røkelaks* (smoked salmon), or order a wood-fired, wild-yeasted pizza (available from 3pm). Needless to say, the cake, pastries and coffee are delicious, too.

★Eggett
BISTRO €€€

(☑984 07 700; Steinkargata 23; dishes from 800kr; ☉6-11pm Tue-Sat) In a clapboard building off Steinkargata, this ramshackle, rough-and-ready eatery is small in size but strong on ambition: the food is modern, creative and bang on trend, with an emphasis on freshness, seasonality and Asian-inspired flavours. There's no set menu; dishes are chalked above the bar, from wild trout to kimchi, braised ribs or Asian slaws. The only drawback? It's pricey.

Torget Fish Market SEAFOOD €€€
(Rosenkildetorget; ☉ market 9am-4.30pm Mon-Sat, restaurant 11am-9pm Mon-Wed, 11am-midnight Thu-Sat) Stavanger's small fish market isn't a patch on the Bergen version. Still, you can pick up fresh fish here, and try locally harvested oysters, mussels, clams, lobsters and crabs, and the market restaurant does good fish dishes including a majestic, if eye-wateringly-priced, shellfish platter (1550kr for two people). Even if you're not eating, it's fun to look around.

🍷 Drinking & Nightlife

★ **Bøker & Børst** BAR
(☎51 86 04 76; www.bokerogborst.webs.com; Øvre Holmegate 32; ☉10am-2am) With all the decorative chic of a well-worn living room – complete with book-lined shelves, retro floor -lamps and old wallpaper – this lovely coffee bar is a fine spot to while away a few hours. There are plenty of beers on tap, plus pub-type snacks and pastries, and a covered courtyard at the back.

B.broremann B.bar BAR
(☎406 36 783; www.broremann.no; Skansegata 7; ☉6pm-2am Tue-Thu & Sun, 4pm-2am Fri & Sat, closed Mon) One of Stavanger's best-loved bars, this low-key shopfront place draws a discerning over-30s crowd and, later, local hospitality staff for post-shift beers and cocktails.

ℹ️ Information

Stavanger Turistforening DNT (☎51 84 02 00; www.stf.no; off Muségata; ☉10am-4pm Mon, Wed, Fri & Sat, 10am-6pm Tue & Thu) Information on hiking and mountain huts.

Tourist Office (☎51 85 92 00; www.regionstavanger.com; Strandkaien 61; ☉9am-8pm Jun-Aug, 9am-4pm Mon-Fri, 9am-2pm Sat Sep-May) Local information and advice on Lysefjord and Preikestolen.

ℹ️ Getting There & Away

AIR

Stavanger Airport (☎51 65 80 00; https://avinor.no/en/airport/stavanger-airport) is at Sola, 14km south of the city centre. As well as international airlines, there are a number of domestic-airline services. Seasonal flights are also available to destinations in the UK and Europe.

Norwegian (www.norwegian.com) Flights to Oslo, Bergen and Trondheim.

SAS (www.sas.no) Services to Oslo and Bergen, plus international destinations including London and Aberdeen.

Widerøe (www.wideroe.no) Flies to Bergen, Kristiansand, Sandefjord, Florø and Aberdeen.

BUS

Destination	Cost (kr)	Time (hr)	Frequency (daily)
Bergen	475	5½	hourly
Haugesund	241	2	hourly
Kristiansand	406	4½	4
Oslo	742-811	9½	3

CAR & MOTORCYCLE

Stavanger is about 210km south of Bergen, and 138km south of Haugesund, both via the E39. It's an expensive route when you factor in ferries, road tolls and city tolls.

TRAIN

Destination	Cost (kr)	Time (hr)	Frequency (daily)
Egersund	177	1¼	hourly
Kristiansand	512	3	5
Oslo	997	8	up to 5

Lysefjord

All along the 42km-long Lysefjord (Light Fjord), the granite rock glows with an ethereal light and even on dull days it's offset by almost-luminous mist. This is the favourite fjord of many visitors, and there's no doubt that it has a captivating beauty.

There are two compelling reasons to explore this wonderful place: a cruise along the fjord, or the four-hour hike to the top of Preikestolen, the plunging cliff face that's graced a million postcards from Norway, not to mention as many Instagram posts. Daredevils might also want to brave standing on the Kjeragbolten, a boulder wedged between two sheer cliff faces.

The ferry ride from Stavanger takes you to the fjord head at Lysebotn, where a narrow and much-photographed road corkscrews spectacularly 1000m up towards Sirdal in 27 hairpin bends. From Lysebotn, the road twists up the mountain and on into the Setesdalen region and Oslo.

VISITING LYSEFJORD

Lysefjord & Pulpit Rock

If you want to hike Preikestolen (Pulpit Rock) but don't have your own car, the cheapest option is to book a ticket through **Norled** (p328) or Tide (www.tide.no). The trip costs 320/150kr per adult/child, including the return fare on the Stavanger–Tau ferry, and the return bus fare between Tau and the trailhead at Preikestolhytta.

Rødne Fjord Cruises (p328) runs its own cruise-and-hike excursions (adult 780/500kr); the cruise boat fare to Tau and the bus fare between Tau and Preikestolhytta are included, but you'll need to add on the ferry fare back to Stavanger (adult/child 56/28kr).

Having your own car makes things easier. Catch the **Stavanger–Tau ferry** (www.tide.no; adult/child 56/28kr, car incl driver 167kr; ⊘ every 40-45min) from Fiskespiren Quay and follow the Rv13 for 13km to the turn-off for Preikestolhytta Vandrerhjem, another 6km further on. It's a drive of about 1½ hours.

Cruises to Lysefjord

Two companies offer three-hour cruises from Stavanger to Lysefjord. Along the way, sights visited include the **Vagabonds' Cave** and the **Hengjane waterfall** – and look out for mountain goats on the hillsides as you go.

Rødne Fjord Cruises (☑ 51 89 52 70; www.rodne.no; Skagenkaien 35-37, Stavanger; adult/child/family 490/300/1300kr, Preikestolen boat-and-hike ticket 720kr)

Norled (www.norled.no; Lysefjord cruise adult/child/family 450/280/1100kr, Preikestolen boat-and-bus-ticket 320kr)

Sognefjorden

Sognefjorden, the world's second-longest (203km) and Norway's deepest (1308m) fjord, cuts a deep slash across the map of western Norway. In places, sheer walls rise more than 1000m above the water, while elsewhere a gentler shoreline supports farms, orchards and villages.The broad, main waterway is impressive but it's worth detouring into its narrower arms, such as the deep and lovely Nærøyfjord, for idyllic views of abrupt cliff faces and cascading waterfalls.

There's a comprehensive guide to the area at www.sognefjord.no.

Flåm

POP 450

At the head of Aurlandsfjorden, Flåm sits in a truly spectacular setting beside Sognefjord. The main attraction here is the stunning mountain railway that creeps up into the surrounding peaks and offers truly eye-popping panoramas. Unfortunately it's far from a well-kept secret, and on the busiest summer days the tiny village can find itself swamped by several thousand visitors – it's probably best left for the quieter seasons of spring and au-

tumn, or early summer at a push. The popular Norway in a Nutshell tour also stops here.

🏃 Activities

The tourist office (p329) has free sheets describing local walks, varying from 45 minutes to five hours. Various places around town rent bikes, including for the Rallarvegen (p329) trail.

★ **Flåmsbana Railway**   RAIL
(www.visitflam.com/en/flamsbana; adult/child one way 360/180kr, return 480/240kr) This 20km-long engineering wonder hauls itself up 864m of altitude gain through 20 tunnels. At a gradient of 1:18, it's the world's steepest railway that runs without cable or rack wheels. It takes a full 45 minutes to climb to Myrdal on the bleak, treeless Hardangervidda plateau, past thundering waterfalls (there's a photo stop at awesome Kjosfossen). The railway runs year-round, with up to 10 departures daily in summer, dropping to four in winter.

Njord Sea Kayak   KAYAKING
(☑ 913 16 628; www.seakayaknorway.com; adult/child from 660/480kr) Operating from Flåm's postage stamp of a beach, this kayak company offers two daily guided trips: a three-hour paddle around the fjord (adult/child

660/480kr) or a four-hour kayak-and-hike trip along the old King's Path (800/580kr). Multiday wild-camping expeditions for budding Bear Grylls are also possible.

★ Rallarvegen
CYCLING

(Navvies' Road; www.rallarvegen.com) The Rallarvegen is the service route that was once used by workers who built the Flåmsbana railway. It's now been converted into a super cycle track, running for 83km from Haugastøl (1000m) or an easier 56km from Finse. It can also be done as a very manageable day trip from Myrdal, 18km south of Flåm.

🛌 Sleeping

★ Flåm Camping & Hostel
HOSTEL, CAMPGROUND €

(☑ 940 32 681; www.flaam-camping.no; Nedre Brekkevegen 12; 1-/2-person tent 120/205kr; dm/s/tw/q with bathroom 335/550/920/1315kr, with shared bathroom 260/450/720/995kr; ☺ Mar–Nov; P 🛜) Everyone's favourite when looking for a budget place in Flåm, this conveniently positioned hostel and campsite has accommodation options to suit all wallets: bunk-bed dorms, singles, twins, triples and quads, in simple lodge buildings with pine walls and colourful fabrics. There's also tonnes of green grassy space for caravans and campers and it's just a short walk to the marina.

Flåm Marina & Apartments
APARTMENT €€

(☑ 57 63 35 55; www.flammarina.no; s/tw 1095/1295kr, apt 1150-2450kr) This waterside establishment offers something different in Flåm: a selection of self-catering apartments sleeping one to five people, simply furnished but with the great advantage of a small lounge and proper kitchen. It's ideal for family travellers (some apartments have rooms with bunk beds). Most have a fjord view from the living room. There are also standard hotel-style rooms.

Flåmsbrygga
HOTEL €€€

(☑ 57 63 20 50; www.flamsbrygga.no; r 1295-2590kr; 🌬 🛜) Right beside the dock, this modern hotel has been made to look reassuringly rustic, with wood cladding, rugs, beams and the like. All but two of the rooms have a balcony, making for some superb fjord vistas. It's a busy location, but super-handy to everything, including the attached pub and restaurant, Ægir Bryggeri (☑ 57 63 20 50; www.flamsbrygga.no/aegir-bryggeripub; ☺ noon-10pm May–mid-Sep, 6-10pm mid-Sep–Apr).

✖ Eating

Flåm Bakery
BAKERY €

(cakes & pastries 25-40kr; ☺ 8am-5pm) This little bakery turns out muffins, Danish pastries, croissants and cakes, along with some lovely traditional Norwegian breads.

★ Restaurant Arven
NORWEGIAN €€€

(☑ 57 63 63 00; www.fretheimhotel.no; Fretheim Hotel; mains 165-315kr, buffet 495kr; ☺ 6.30-9.30pm) On the 2nd floor of the Fretheim Hotel, this reliably good restaurant offers a grandstand view over the harbour and fjord. It's not quite New Nordic, but there's a strong emphasis on seasonality and local sourcing, and an interest in reinterpreting classic Norwegian dishes with a more modern twist: smoked reindeer, halibut ceviche or brown cheese ice cream, for example.

ⓘ Information

The seasonal **tourist office** (☑ 57 63 33 13; www.visitflam.com; Stasjonsvegen; ☺ 8.30am-8pm Jun-Aug, to 4pm May & Sep) is located within the train station.

ⓘ Getting There & Away

BOAT

From Flåm, boats head out to towns around Sognefjorden.

The most scenic trip from Flåm is the **passenger ferry** (www.thefjords.no; one way/return 400/870kr) up Nærøyfjord to Gudvangen (five daily), with a connecting bus to Voss for trains to Bergen or Oslo. The **tourist office** (p329) sells tickets.

From May to September, **Norled** (☑ 51 86 87 00; www.norled.no; Kong Christian Frederiks plass 3) runs a direct ferry to Bergen (adult/child 825/415kr, 5½ hours). There's at least one daily express boat to Balestrand (280/143kr, two hours) year-round. There are good discounts if you buy in advance online.

BUS

The following destinations are serviced by bus from Flåm.

Destination	Cost (kr)	Time	Frequency (daily)
Aurland	38	15min	4-8
Bergen	285-350	3hr	2-6
Gudvangen	45-56	20min	4-8
Lærdalsøyri	101	45min	2-6
Sogndal	165	1¾hr	2-6

NORWAY IN A NUTSHELL

Although most visitors do the classic Norway in a Nutshell tour from either Oslo or Bergen, you also can do a mini version (adult/child 775/400kr). This circular route from Flåm – boat to Gudvangen, bus to Voss, train to Myrdal, then train again down the spectacular Flåmsbana railway back to Flåm – is truly the kernel within the nutshell and takes in all the most dramatic elements. The Gudvangen boat leaves Flåm at 9am and the Flåmsbana train brings you home at 4.55pm.

TRAIN

Flåm is the only Sognefjorden village with a rail link, via the magnificent **Flåmsbana railway** (p328). There are train connections via Myrdal to Oslo (1141kr, 5½ hours) and Bergen (669kr, 2¾ hours).

Aurland

POP 1715

Peaceful Aurland is much less hectic than its neighbour, Flåm, a mere 10km south along the fjord. These days it's renowned as one end of Lærdalstunnel (24.5km), the world's longest road tunnel. This is an essential link in the E16 highway that connects Oslo and Bergen; before its completion, traffic had to ferry-hop between Lærdal and Gudvangen. It's a fast alternative to the sinuous, 45km-long Aurlandsfjellet, sometimes known as the Snow Road, which crests over the mountains via one of Norway's loftiest road passes. As such, it's generally only passable from June to October.

It's your choice: speed and convenience via the Lærdalstunnel, or driving fun and massive views via the mountain road. We know which we'd choose.

◉ Sights

★**Aurlandsfjellet**   SCENIC ROAD
(SnøVegen; www.nasjonaleturistveger.no/en/routes/aurlandsfjellet; ⊙Jun–mid-Oct) This 45km road is one of Norway's most fabulous, climbing from sea level to the desolate, boulder-strewn high plateau that separates Aurland and Lærdalsøyri (Lærdal). Even if you don't opt for the whole route, drive the first 8km from Aurland to the magnificent Stegastein observation point.

It's a strictly summer-only drive: the road is impassable in winter, and even in midsummer you'll probably still see snowbanks lining the roadsides (hence it's local nickname, Snøvegen – the Snow Road).

★**Stegastein**   VIEWPOINT
Projecting out high above the fjord at an altitude of 630m, this marvel of modern engineering is one of Norway's great viewing points. Clad in pine and balancing on worryingly slender steel legs, it seems to roll down into the fjord, with nothing but a glass rail between you and a long, long drop. It's popular, so it's worth getting up early or staying late to have it to yourself.

It's about 8km up the narrow, winding road (p330) from Aurland.

🏃 Activities

The Aurland and Lærdal tourist offices have produced six walker-friendly sheets of local walks, where the route is mapped upon an aerial photo.

Flåm to Aurland Path   HIKING
For consistently outstanding views and virtual solitude, hike the 12km trail that mainly follows the old road between Aurland and Flåm, passing by **Otternes** (☑57 63 11 32; www.visitflam.com/en/se-og-gjore1/se/otternes; ⊙10am-6pm May–mid-Sep). Until 1919 and the construction of the coast road, it was the only means of land communication between the two villages. Allow around three hours.

🛌 Sleeping

Lunde Gard & Camping   CAMPGROUND €
(☑997 04 701; www.lunde-camping.no; campsite for tent, car & 2 adults 210kr, cabin 650-850kr; ⊙May-Sep; 🛜) Reasonably quiet and popular with families, this campsite has a green riverside location, and all the facilities you need: decent shower block, TV room and plug-in power for campers and caravans.

Vangsgaarden Gjestegiveri   HOTEL €€
(☑57 63 35 80; www.vangsgaarden.no; s 1350kr, d 1395-1590kr, f 1890kr, 4-bed cabin from 1350kr; 🅿🛜) This whitewashed hotel is a peaceful alternative to the hectic places in nearby Flåm, and looks pretty as a picture, with its clapboard facade and 18th-century architecture. Rooms are simple but sweet, and at least most have fjord views. There are also six cabins down at water level.

The on-site Duehuset restaurant and pub is a good spot for dinner.

Aurland Fjordhotell
HOTEL €€€

(☑ 57 63 35 05; www.aurland-fjordhotel.com; s/d/f from 1190/1590/1890kr; ℗ ☎) With its white-wood exterior and gabled roof, this place certainly looks the ticket – unfortunately its rooms are considerably less starry, and feel more roadside motel than historic ho-tel. Still, it's a good fallback if everywhere in Flåm is booked out.

✖ Eating

Aurlandskafeen
CAFE €

(☑ 57 63 36 66; mains 110-180kr; ⏱ 10am-5pm Mon-Sat) This cute cafe is good for ear-ly-morning coffee, homemade pastries and cakes, and lunchtime sandwiches. It has a small terrace overlooking the river.

Duehuset
PUB, CAFE €€

(☑ 57 63 35 80; www.vangsgaarden.no; mains 140-330kr; ⏱ 3-11pm Jun-Aug) Part of the Vangs-gaarden Gjestegiveri (p330), the Dovecot is a great spot for an early dinner or a pint while the sun sets. The menu is nothing fancy – mainly burgers, salads and fish dishes – but it's not expensive, especially by Norwegian standards, and the cracking terrace with fjord views and old-fashioned pub interior are big sells.

ℹ Getting There & Away

Buses run between Aurland and Flåm (38kr, 15 minutes, up to eight times daily). The express bus to/from Bergen (350kr, three hours) stops in Aurland on the way to Flåm.

Watch out for the speed cameras in Lærdal-stunnelen – along the entire stretch.

Stalheim

POP 200

High above the valley, Stalheim is a place of extraordinary natural beauty with an interesting, lively past. Between 1647 and 1909, Stalheim was a stopping-off point for travellers on the Royal Mail route be-tween Copenhagen, Christiania (Oslo) and Bergen. A road was built for horses and carriages in 1780. The mailmen and their weary steeds rested in Stalheim and changed to fresh horses after climbing up the valley and through the Stalheimskleiva gorge, flanked by the thundering Stalheim and Sivle waterfalls.

Although a modern road winds up through two tunnels from the valley floor, the old mail road (Stalheimskleiva) climbs up at an astonishing 18% gradient. As tour buses, improbably, use this road, it's one way only: you can drive down it, but not up.

🏃 Activities

Brekkedalen
HIKING

🌿 This three-hour return hike leads up into the valley above Stalheim. Locals in the know claim it's the region's prettiest walk, and the views are magnificent. It's a rela-tively easy way to leave behind the crowds and have this stunning high country all to yourself. The tourist office in Voss (p324) has route guides, or ask at Stalheim Hotel (p331) for directions.

Husmannsplassen Nåli
HIKING

🌿 This cotter's farm, along the ledge from Stalheim high above Nærøydalen, was occu-pied until 1930. The route there (two hours return) is not for the faint-hearted. The path beneath the cliff wall is extremely narrow in parts and there is nothing between you and the valley floor far below; don't even think of walking here after rain.

🛏 Sleeping

★ Stalheim Hotel
HISTORIC HOTEL €€€

(☑ 56 52 01 22; www.stalheim.com; s/d/superior from 1160/1880/2350kr; ⏱ mid-May–mid-Sep; ℗ @ ☎) There's one reason to stay at this sprawling sky-high hotel, and it's not the dat-ed decor. It's all about the view: vast, snowy mountain panoramas unfurl through the win-dows here, so compelling that you probably won't even notice the rather twee furnishings. The public areas are grand, filled with Nor-wegian design pieces and historical paintings.

ℹ Getting There & Away

Stalheim is about 34km north of Voss. It's reached via a steep turn-off on the E16, heading northeast towards Gudvangen.

To reach Stalheim from Voss, take any bus (110kr, one hour, hourly) towards the towns of Gudvangen and Aurland, but you may have to hike 1.3km up from the main road unless you can persuade the bus driver to make the short detour.

Jostedalsbreen & Nigardsbreen

For years mighty Jostedalsbreen, mainland Europe's largest ice cap, crept countercur-rent, slowly advancing while most glaciers elsewhere in the world were retreating. Now Jostedalsbreen itself has succumbed and is also withdrawing.

It's still a powerful player, though, eroding an estimated 400,000 tonnes of rock each year. With an area of 487 sq km and in places 600m thick, Jostedalsbreen rules over the highlands of Sogn og Fjordane county. The main ice cap and several outliers are protected as the Jostedalsbreen National Park.

The northern and southern sides of the national park are some distance apart, so they need to be visited separately – and you'll have a tough time without your own car. For accessing the southern side of the park, the towns of Solvorn, Sogndal and Fjærland are the most useful gateways, while on the northern side, Stryn, Loen and Olden are within easy driving distance and have plenty of accommodation.

Fjærland

POP 310

If you're still looking for that perfect fjord-side village, then here's another strong contender. Beautifully sited at the end of Fjærlandsfjorden, it's a sleepy one-street town lined with clapboard buildings and surrounded on all sides by huge cliffs. Most people come to experience its pair of particularly accessible glacial tongues, Supphellebreen and Bøyabreen, but Fjærland is also known as the Book Town of Norway (www.bokbyen.no) – 10 shops in town sell second-hand books, mostly in Norwegian, but some in English and other languages too.

The village virtually hibernates from October onwards, then leaps to life in early May, when the ferry runs again.

◉ Sights

★ **Norwegian Glacier Museum**   MUSEUM
(Norsk Bremuseum; ☑ 57 69 32 88; www.bre.museum.no; adult/child 125/65kr; ◉ 9am-7pm Jun-Aug, 10am-4pm Apr-May, Sep & Oct) You can't miss this striking museum: it's a concrete wedge marooned among a sea of grass on the way into Fjærland, and even has a couple of model woolly mammoths outside. It provides a great overview of general glacier geology, as well as process of fjord formation, and the ecology and wildlife of Jostedalsbreen itself. Highlights are the simulated ice tunnel and the tusk of a Siberian woolly mammoth who met an icy demise 30,000 years ago.

Bøyabreen   GLACIER
The more spectacular of the two glacial tongues accessible from Fjærland, Bøyabreen looms majestically at the end of the

wooded valley. There's a car park next to the visitors centre and cafe, from where it's a short walk down to the glacial lake and an uninterrupted panorama over the glacier itself. It's a mighty hunk of ice indeed.

Supphellebreen   GLACIER
Reached via a turn-off from the main road north from Fjærland, this small glacier creeps down the mountainside into an isolated valley. Trails lead from the small car park right up to a rushing stream fed by the glacier's meltwater. Depending on the time of year and how the ground underfoot is, it might even be possible to get close to the ice itself – but take care.

🏃 Activities

Fjærland Guiding (☑ tourist office 57 69 32 33; www.fjaerland.org/fjaerland-guiding; Sandaneset; guided hikes from 500kr, glacier hikes from 800kr) offers guided hikes and glacier walks on request.

The tourist office (p333) provides a free *Escape the Asphalt* guide listing 12 marked walking routes, varying from 30 minutes to three hours. For greater detail, supplement this with *Turkart Fjærland* (80kr) at 1:50,000, which comes complete with route descriptions and trails indicated. Pull on your boots and you're away. Most walks follow routes the local shepherds would have used until quite recently to lead their flocks to higher summer pastures.

🛏 Sleeping & Eating

Bøyum Camping   CAMPGROUND €
(☑ 57 69 32 52; www.boyumcamping.no; dm 225kr, campsites 230kr, r 390-590kr, cabins 810-1490kr; ◉ May-Sep; 🅿 🛜) Three kilometres from the Fjærland ferry landing, Bøyum Camping has something for all pockets and sleeping preferences, not to mention a great view of the Bøyabreen glacier at the head of the valley. Pitches are grassy and spacious, and there's a small shop and cafe.

★ **Hotel Mundal**   HOTEL €€€
(☑ 57 69 31 01; www.hotelmundal.no; s/d from 1045/1650kr; ◉ May-Sep; 🅿 🛜) What a sight this historic hotel is. Gabled and slate-topped, it's been in the same family since 1891, and is a classic slice of late-19th-century grandeur, with a wonderful period interior filled with oil paintings, rugs, leather armchairs and burnished furniture. Rooms feel endearingly old-fashioned, with wooden

floors, metal bedsteads and antiques aplenty. Fjord views are essential.

Brævasshytta
CAFE €

(📱57 69 32 96; www.facebook.com/brevasshytta; mains 1400-2100kr; ⊙8am-8pm May-Sep) Do visit the Brævasshytta, built into the moraine of Bøyabreen glacier's latest major advance, even if it's only for a cup of coffee. With the glacier right there and in your face, it's like you're in an IMAX cinema – only it's real. Simple meals such as meatballs, grilled chicken, sandwiches and burgers are on offer throughout the day and evening.

🛍 Shopping

Various spots around town sell books, ranging from just a few shelves to the large selection at Bøk & Bilde, where the town's tourist office is located. Most titles tend to be in Norwegian, although you can occasionally find an English title or two.

ℹ Information

Tourist Office (📱57 69 32 33; www.fjaerland. org; ⊙10am-6pm Jun-Aug, to 4pm Sep-May) Inside the Bøk & Bilde bookshop, this small tourist office handles accommodation bookings and rents out bikes.

ℹ Getting There & Away

BOAT

In the summer only, from June to August, a ferry (one-way/return 480/950kr, 1¾ hours, twice daily) runs from Balestrand to Fjærland via Hella.

BUS

Buses bypass the village and stop on the Rv5 near the Norwegian Glacier Museum. Four to six services run daily to/from Sogndal (90kr, 30 minutes) and Stryn (230kr, two hours). Timetables are available from Kringom (www. kringom.no).

Geirangerfjorden

Well, this is the big one: the world-famous, Unesco-listed, oft-photographed fjord that every visitor to Norway simply has to tick off their bucket list. And in purely scenic terms, it's impossible to argue against the case for its inclusion: it is, quite simply, one of the world's great natural features, a majestic combination of huge cliffs, tumbling waterfalls and deep blue water that's guaranteed to make a lasting imprint on your memory.

Unfortunately with prestige comes popularity. Some 600,000 visitors come here to see the sights every year and scores of cruise ships dock at the port every day in summer. You're unlikely to enjoy much peace and quiet, especially around the main port of Geiranger.

Thankfully, out on the fjord itself, peace and tranquillity remain and a ride on the Geiranger–Hellesylt ferry is an essential part of your Norwegian adventure.

⦿ Sights

Flydalsjuvet
VIEWPOINT

Somewhere you've seen that classic photo, beloved of brochures, of the overhanging rock Flydalsjuvet, usually with a figure gazing down at a cruise ship in Geirangerfjord. The car park, signposted Flydalsjuvet, about 5km uphill from Geiranger on the Stryn road, offers a great view of the fjord and the green river valley, but doesn't provide the postcard view down to the last detail.

Dalsnibba
VIEWPOINT

(www.dalsnibba.no) For the highest and perhaps most stunning of the many stunning views of the Geiranger valley and fjord, take the 5km toll road (130kr per car) that climbs from the Rv63 to the Dalsnibba lookout (1500m). Since August 2016, the view has been enhanced by a new viewing platform, the Geiranger Skywalk, with a see-through floor and glass rail making it seem as though you're walking on air.

🏃 Activities

Get away from the seething ferry terminal and life is altogether quieter. All around Geiranger there are great signed hiking routes to abandoned farmsteads, waterfalls and vista points. The tourist office's aerial-photographed *Hiking Routes* map (10kr) gives ideas for 18 signed walks of between 1.5km and 5km.

A popular longer trek begins with a ride on the Geiranger Fjordservice sightseeing boat. A steep 45-minute ascent from the landing at Skagehola brings you to Skageflå, a precariously perched hillside farm. You can retrace your steps to the landing, where the boat stops (on request; tell the crew on the way out or just wave). To stretch your legs more, continue over the mountain and return to Geiranger via Preikestolen and Homlung.

⭐ Geiranger Fjordservice
BOATING

(📱70 26 30 07; www.geirangerfjord.no; Homlong; 1½hr tours adult/child 250/135kr) This long-running company runs sightseeing boat trips up and down the fjord from Geiranger. The standard 1½-hour trip runs up to five times daily in midsummer, just once daily in April and October, and not at all from November to March.

From mid-June to August, they also operate a smaller, 15-seater RIB boat (adult/child 695/395kr) and run kayaking tours (525/469kr), all from their base at Homlong, 2km from Geiranger.

🛏 Sleeping

Geirangerfjorden Feriesenter   CAMPGROUND €
(📞951 07 527; www.geirangerfjorden.net; Grande; lakefront campsite for car, tent & 2 adults 255kr, cabin from 990kr; ☺ late Apr–mid-Sep; 🅿🛜) A more tranquil option than camping in town is to head along the northern shore to this lovely spot, with spacious pitches, well-maintained facilities and particularly pretty, well-decorated cabins. If you don't mind not being right beside the water, you can save 300kr.

★ Westerås Farm   CABIN €€
(📞932 64 497; 2-bed cabin 870-1040kr, apt 1250kr; ☺May-Sep) This beautiful old working farm, 4km along the Rv63 towards Grotli, sits at the end of a narrow road dizzyingly high above the bustle. Stay in one of the two farmhouse apartments or five pine-clad cabins. The barn, dating from 1603, is home to a restaurant, where Arnfinn and Iris serve dishes made with their own produce.

Hotel Utsikten   HOTEL €€€
(📞70 26 96 60; www.classicnorway.no/hotell/hotell-utsikten-geiranger; s/d 1290/1590kr; ☺May-Sep; 🅿🛜) 'A temple to lift your spirits' – so observed King Rama V of Siam when he stayed during his grand tour. High on the hill above Geiranger (take Rv63, direction Grotli), the family-owned Utsikten, constructed in 1893, still has stunning views over town and fjord over a century later. Rooms, however, are small and a little more prosaic.

🍴 Eating

Olebuda & Cafe Olé   INTERNATIONAL €
(📞70 26 32 30; www.olebuda.no; Maråkvegen 19, Geiranger; restaurant mains lunch 155-255kr, dinner 310-355kr; ☺cafe 9am-7pm, restaurant 6-10pm) Occupying Geiranger's old general store, the pretty upstairs restaurant does a range of international-style dishes and good local standards including poached salmon rou-

lade and house-smoked goat; all fish and meat are local. Downstairs is a colourful, casual cafe with cakes, all-day snacks and good coffee.

Brasserie Posten   BRASSERIE €€
(📞70 26 13 06; www.brasserieposten.no; lunch mains 140-250kr, dinner mains 195-290kr; ☺noon-11pm Apr-Sep, shorter hours rest of year) 🍴 A simple menu of salads, burgers, steaks, fish and pizza is elevated above the norm by a passionate local chef who sources organic dairy from Røros and makes the most of fresh herbs and vegetables. The modern Scando interior is bright and atmospheric, but the fjord-side terrace wins.

ℹ Information

Tourist Office (📞70 26 30 99; www.geiranger. no; ☺9am-6pm mid-May–mid-Sep, shorter hours rest of year) This efficient, if occasionally overwhelmed, tourist office books boat and cruise tickets, hands out hiking leaflets, and generally aims to make your stay as pleasurable as possible. It's located right beside the pier.

ℹ Getting There & Away

BOAT
The car ferry between Geiranger and Hellysylt is a stunner. There are four to eight sailings a day between May and early October (adult/child one way 260/130kr, return 360/180kr, 1½ hours). With a car, the one-way fare is 530kr for one passenger or 1040kr with up to five people. Tickets can be booked online through the Visit Flåm (www.visitflam.com) website.

From mid-April to mid-October, the Hurtigruten coastal ferry makes a detour from Ålesund (departs 9.30am) to Geiranger (departs 1.30pm) on its northbound run.

BUS
From mid-June to mid-August, sightseeing buses make the spectacular run from Geiranger to Åndalsnes (adult/child 478/239kr, three hours, twice daily), known as the 'Golden Route'.

Åndalsnes
POP 2244

There are two equally dramatic ways to approach Åndalsnes: by road through the Trollstigen Pass or along Romsdalen as you ride the spectacularly scenic Rauma Railway. The rail route down from Dombås ploughs through a deeply cut glacial valley flanked by sheer walls and plummeting waterfalls. Badly bombed during WWII, the modern town, nestled beside Romsdalfjord, might be nondescript, but the locals are delightful and the surrounding landscapes are absolutely magnificent.

⊙ Sights

★ Trollstigen   MOUNTAIN ROAD
(www.trollstigen.net; ⊙ May-Oct) This twisting, sky-topping corkscrew of a road is the most famous stretch of tarmac in Norway. Completed in 1936 after eight years of labour, the Troll's Ladder is a stunning feat of road building, spiralling up the mountainside through 11 hairpin bends and a 1:12 gradient, and after heavy rain, waterfalls cascade down the mountainside, drenching cars as they pass. To add to the thrill, much of it is effectively single-lane, meaning traffic jams and passing vehicles are part of the hair-raising experience.

★ Rauma Railway   SCENIC RAILWAY
(adult 297kr, 1 child per adult free; ⊙ 4 daily) A classic Norwegian train ride that railway buffs definitely won't want to miss, the 114km-long Rauma Railway clatters from Åndalsnes and Dombås, high in the mountains of central Norway. It's a super trip, taking in fjords, forests, valleys, lakes and mountains en route, and passing through six tunnels and 32 bridges. There's also a shorter summer-only tourist train with onboard commentary that runs twice daily from June to August from Åndalsnes' lakeside station up to Bjorli, at 600m.

Trollveggen   NATURAL FEATURE
(Troll Wall) From Dombås, the E136 and rail line drop in parallel northwest down to Romsdalen (you might have a sense of déjà vu if you've seen *Harry Potter and the Half-Blood Prince*, in which the valley features). Near Åndalsnes, the dramatic Trollveggen, first conquered in 1958 by a joint Norwegian and English team, rears skywards. The highest vertical mountain wall in Europe, its ragged and often cloud-shrouded summit, 1800m from the valley floor, is considered the ultimate challenge among mountaineers.

🏃 Activities

Hiking
The *Geiranger Trollstigen* (30kr) pamphlet describes seven signed hiking trails in the Trollstigen area. You'll need to supplement this with the *Romsdals-Fjella* map at 1:80,000. The tourist office (p336) carries both and can also arrange mountain walks of four to six hours with a qualified guide.

★ Aksla/Nesaksla   HIKING
(www.romsdal.com) An excellent half-day day hike begins in town, along Romsdalsvegen, 50m north of the roundabout before the Esso petrol station. It takes around one to 1½ hours to reach the summit of Nesaksla (715m), the peak that rises above Åndalsnes. The ascent rewards with the most astonishing views of the Romsdal Alps, the River Rauma and the Romsdal fjord.

Climbing
The best local climbs are the less extreme sections of the 1500m-high rock route on Trollveggen and the 1550m-high Romsdalshorn, but there are a wealth of others. Serious climbers should buy *Klatring i Romsdal* (300kr), which includes rock- and ice-climbing information in both Norwegian and English.

✦ Festivals & Events

Norsk Fjellfestival   SPORTS
(Norway Mountain Festival; www.norsk-fjellfestival.no; ⊙ Jul) A weeklong get together in early July for lovers of the great outdoors, with plenty of folk events thrown in.

Rauma Rock   MUSIC
(www.raumarock.com; ⊙ Aug) Central Norway's largest outdoor rock gathering held over two days in early August.

🛏 Sleeping & Eating

Åndalsnes Vandrerhjem   HOSTEL €
(🗐 71 22 13 82; www.hihostels.no/hostels/andalsnes; dm/s/d/f 365/760/860/1160kr; ⊙ Mar-Nov; 🅿🛜) This is a great hostel, spread across several buildings and surrounded by lawns, greenery and nature, 1.5km from Åndalsnes. As you'd expect, the rooms are nothing to write home about, but they're fine for a couple of nights. There's a nice lounge area if you want to mingle with other guests and the breakfast spread is particularly generous.

★ Hotel Aak   HOTEL €€€
(🗐 71 22 17 00; www.hotelaak.no; s/d 1300/1600kr; ⊙ mid-May–Sep; 🅿🛜) 🍴 What a beauty: a historic mountain hotel that's been given a thoughtful, charming overhaul by the young Rønning family. The decor in the rooms is sparse but tasteful, and the best rooms have lots of space and knockout mountain

NORWAY ÅNDALSNES

views. The building's rustic past still shines through, though. Breakfast is a real mountain feast, and you can arrange dinners too.

★ **Sødahl-Huset** CAFE €€
(📞📧400 66 401; Romsdalsvegen 8; mains 120-200kr; ⊙11am-7pm Sun-Fri, to 2am Sat, shorter hours in winter) 🍴 This place is the model of what every small-town cafe should be like. Mix-and-match furniture, regular beer tastings and gigs, and a blackboard menu chock-a-block with delicious, homemade, local-produce food, from sinful chocolate cake and *kraftkar* (blue cheese) burgers to more healthy options like Asian salmon salad. As the sign says, it's run by three lovely ladies, and the welcome is warm.

❶ Information

Tourist Office (📞71 22 16 22; www.visitandalsnes.com; ⊙9am-8pm Jun-Aug, to 3pm Mon-Fri Sep-May) Located next to the train station, this tourist office has tonnes of info on ways to explore the area, and can hook you up for guided hikes, climbing lessons, stand-up paddleboarding and more. Bikes (per hour/day 100/400kr), both standard and electric, can be rented here.

❶ Getting There & Away

BUS

Åndalsnes is on the Golden Route to the stunning Trollstigen Pass. Buses run across the route to Geiranger (one way/return 239/478kr, three hours, twice daily) from mid-June to August.

There are also buses to Molde (169kr, 1½ hours, up to eight daily) and Ålesund (345kr, 2¼ hours, four daily).

TRAIN

Trains to/from Dombås (249kr to 297kr, 1½ hours, up to four daily) link up with the Oslo–Trondheim route.

Ålesund

POP 42,317

The far northern port of Ålesund might be far from the bright lights of metropolitan Norway, but it's rich with some of the country's finest examples of Jugendstil (art nouveau) architecture – a legacy of a huge rebuilding project that took place after a devastating fire in 1904. Set out over a hook-shaped peninsula, the town is now the home base for Norway's largest cod-fishing fleet, and it's an attractive, lively town and unsurprisingly has some superb seafood to try.

◉ Sights

★ **Jugendstil Senteret** MUSEUM
(Art Nouveau Centre; 📞70 10 49 70; www.jugendstilsenteret.no; Apotekergata 16; adult/child incl KUBE 80kr/free; ⊙10am-5pm Jun-Aug, 11am-4pm Tue-Sun Sep-May, to 8pm Thu year-round) The city's unique architectural heritage is documented in a former pharmacy, the first listed Jugendstil monument in Ålesund. Apart from the building's own exquisite and almost entirely original interior, including a sinuous staircase and florid dining room, displays include textiles, ceramics, furniture, posters and other ephemera. Even if you're not a keen aesthete, a 'Time Machine' capsule is great fun, presenting 'From Ashes to Art Nouveau', a 14-minute multimedia story of the rebuilding of Ålesund after the great fire.

Kniven Viewpoint VIEWPOINT
For the best view over Ålesund and its fishhook-shaped peninsula, as well as the mountains and islands beyond, head up the 418 steps to the summit of Aksla Hill and this panoramic viewing point. On a sunny day it's a cracking scene indeed, and it looks pretty special when the town lights start to twinkle at twilight, too.

🏃 Activities

Kayak More Tomorrow KAYAKING, HIKING
(📞911 18 062; www.kayakmoretomorrow.com/en; Notenesgata 3) 🍴 However you want to get out on the water, this company will cater for you. There's a range of daily sea kayaking and stand-up paddleboarding expeditions (from around 515kr per person) and kayak and SUP rentals (from 185kr per hour) are available. Away from the water, they also run guided bike tours, rent out bikes and offer city walks.

Guided Town Walk WALKING
(adult/child 100kr/free; ⊙noon-1.30pm mid-Jun–mid-Aug) To get to know Ålesund's architecture with a knowledgeable local, sign on for the tourist office's excellent 1½- to two-hour guided town walk, which runs daily during the summer.

🎊 Festivals & Events

Norwegian Food Festival FOOD & DRINK
(www.matfestivalen.no; ⊙Aug) A celebration of local food with stalls and cooking demos held in the last week of August.

Ålesund Boat Festival SAILING
(www.batfestivalen.no; ⊙Jul) A week of watery pleasures in the first half of July.

🛏 Sleeping

Ålesund Vandrerhjem
HOSTEL €

(☑ 70 11 58 30; www.hihostels.no; Parkgata 14; dm 295-345kr, s/d/tr/q 690/890/990/1290kr; ☺ year-round; @ 🛜) In a pretty residential area a few minutes' walk from the port, this attractive Jugendstil building has big, pristine rooms. There's a large self-catering kitchen and breakfast is included. Most doubles come with a bathroom and there are apartments with their own kitchens and sea views.

Scandic Scandinavie Hotel
HOTEL €€

(☑ 70 15 78 00; www.scandichotels.com; Løvenvoldgata 8; r 1190-1490kr; P ❋ 🛜) Ålesund's oldest hotel, the first constructed after the 1904 fire, has beautiful Jugendstil bones indeed, and since being taken over by the Scandic chain, it's been given a much-needed refresh. Through the lovely art-nouveau doorway, there's a bright lobby filled with modern art and, upstairs, lots of clean-lined rooms in whites, beiges and greys. There's private parking underground.

★ Hotel Brosundet
HOTEL €€€

(☑ 70 11 45 00; www.brosundet.no; Apotekergata 5; s/d 1330/1530kr, d with view 1730kr; P ❋ 🛜) Right on the waterfront and designed by superstar architects Snøhetta, this former warehouse is one of Norway's most charming hotels. Wonderful old beams and exposed brick walls are combined with contemporary comfort and style. Bedroom furnishings are of white oak, bathrooms are set behind smoky glass walls and beds are draped with brown velvet and sheepskins.

✗ Eating

Invit
CAFE €€

(☑ 70 15 66 44; www.invit.no; Apotekergata 9; sandwiches 35-55kr, mains 85-165kr, seafood buffet 300-450kr; ☺ 8.15am-4.30pm Mon-Fri, 6pm-midnight Thu, 10am-4.30pm Sat) Invit does central Ålesund's best coffee and is its most stylish lunch spot. Daily changing sandwiches and salads are super-fresh and inventive, healthy soups are warming and the nutty, fragrant cakes are homemade. If the streetside bar is full, spread out downstairs at one of the beautiful big wooden tables.

Lyspunktet
CAFE €€

(☑ 70 12 53 00; www.lyspunktet.as; Kipervikgata 1; mains 130-170kr; ☺ noon-5pm Sat-Mon, 10am-1pm Tue-Fri, to late summer weekends) Premium coffee, local craft beers and a comforting menu of foccacias, pulled-pork rolls, home-style fish soup, pies, burgers and tacos make this shabby-chic hang-out a favourite for the town's groovesters. There are deep sofas to lounge in, art on the walls and a bare-brick hearth that provides warmth in winter. All in all, the Spotlight is spot on.

★ Maki
SEAFOOD €€€

(☑ 70 11 45 00; Apotekergata 5; mains 150-360kr, 4-/6-course menu 600/780kr; ☺ 6-10pm) In a nautical cellar space of the hip Hotel Brosundet, this first-rate seafooderie is Ålesund's most creative and interesting place for a fine-dining dinner. Fish, crustaceans and seafood from along the Sunnmore and Runde coastline form the core of the menu, from delicate cured pollack fillets to crispy halibut and a sublimely creamy fish soup. Expensive, but justified.

🍷 Drinking & Nightlife

★ Jacu Coffee Roastery
COFFEE

(☑ 997 28 802; www.jacu.no; Parkgata 18; ☺ 9am-3pm Mon-Fri, 10am-2pm Sat) The west coast's most highly respected coffee roastery is headquartered in this sensitively remodelled industrial space. Drop in for an espresso or a made-to-order filter, breakfast pastries and lunch sandwiches. If you're keen to discover more about the Norwegian coffee scene, they offer tastings and classes, too. Apart from roasting the best beans, they also host art exhibitions.

Apoteker'n
CAFE

(☑ 70 10 49 70; Apotekergata 16; sandwiches around 50kr; ☺ 10am-5pm Jun-Aug, 11am-4pm Tue-Sun Sep-May) Within Jugendstil Senteret (p336), this stylish, friendly little place offers excellent coffee and cake. There's also a good lunch menu of sandwiches and salads, made from top-quality local produce sourced from Matbuda, a Stranda providore.

🛍 Shopping

★ Ingrids Glassverksted
GLASS

(www.ingridsglassversted.no; Molovegen 15; ☺ 10am-5pm Mon-Fri, to 3pm Sat) In the old harbour district near the fishing museum, this quirky glassworks turns out all manner of curious creations – from technicolour chicken jugs to delicate bowls, glasses and miniature houses. You can watch the process in action at the studio here. They also have a shop in the town centre on Løvenvoldgata.

★ **Trankokeriet Antikk** ANTIQUES
(☑70 12 01 00; www.trankokeriet.no; Molovegen 6b; ⊙10am-5pm Mon-Sat) A delver's dream, this place: a chaotic antiques shop stacked floor to ceiling with curiosities and collectibles, from nautical pieces such as old diver's helmets and barometers to traditional Norwegian craft pieces, ceramics, vintage dolls and design pieces. It's not cheap, but it's huge fun just to wander round and see what's for sale. There's a quirky cafe (☑971 58 985; Apotekergata 10; sandwiches 79kr; ⊙11am-5pm Wed-Sun) here, too.

❶ Information

Tourist Office (☑70 15 76 00; www.visi-talesund.com; Skaregata 1; ⊙8.30am-6pm Jun-Aug, 9am-4pm Mon-Fri Sep-May) This efficient, modern office is full of fun ideas on things to do in the Sunnmore region. Its booklet *Along the Streets of Ålesund* (30kr) details the town's architectural highlights in a walking tour.

❶ Getting There & Away

AIR

Ålesund has great air links to the rest of Norway, with frequent flights to Bergen, Oslo, Trondheim and Stavanger. European destinations include Amsterdam, Copenhagen and London.

BUS

To get to Oslo and Trondheim, it works out cheaper (and obviously quicker) to fly than to take the bus, but the bus to Bergen (700kr, 9¼ hours, one to two daily) is competitive, if excruciatingly slow.

There are also buses to Molde (69kr, 1½ hours, up to eight daily) and Åndalsnes (345kr, 2¼ hours, four daily).

❶ Getting Around

Ålesund's airport is on Vigra island, which is connected to the town by an undersea tunnel.

The **airport bus** (www.frammr.no; 113/57kr), which takes about 25 minutes, stops at the Skateflukaia ferry terminal and the **bus station**.

NORTHERN NORWAY

Trondheim

POP 190,464

With its colourful warehouses, waterways and wooded hills, Trondheim is without doubt one of Norway's most photogenic towns. Norway's third-largest city and its historic capital is a pleasure to explore, with wide streets and a partly pedestrianised heart, some great cafes, restaurants and museums to visit – plus Europe's northernmost Gothic cathedral. Fishing boats putter around the harbour, gulls wheel and screech overhead, and beyond the city's outskirts there's a wealth of wilderness to explore.

◉ Sights

★ **Nidaros Domkirke** CATHEDRAL
(☑73 89 08 00; www.nidarosdomen.no; Kongsgårdsgata; adult/child/family 90/40/220kr, tower 40kr, with Archbishop's Palace & crown jewels 180/90/440kr; ⊙9am-6pm Mon-Fri, to 2pm Sat, to 5pm Sun mid-Jun–mid-Aug, shorter hours rest of year) Nidaros Cathedral is Scandinavia's largest medieval building, and the northernmost Gothic structure in Europe. Outside, the ornately embellished, altar-like west wall has top-to-bottom statues of biblical characters and Norwegian bishops and kings, sculpted in the early 20th century. Several are copies of medieval originals, nowadays housed in the museum. Note the glowing, vibrant colours of the modern stained-glass in the rose window at the west end, a striking contrast to the interior gloom.

★ **Archbishop's Palace** MUSEUM, HISTORIC BUILDING
(Kongsgårdsgata; adult/child/family 90/40/220kr, crown jewels 90/40/220kr, with cathedral & crown jewels 180/80/440kr; ⊙10am-5pm Mon-Fri, 10am-3pm Sat, noon-4pm Sun mid-Jun–mid-Aug, shorter hours rest of year) The 12th-century archbishop's residence (Erkebispegården), commissioned around 1160 and Scandinavia's oldest secular building, is beside the cathedral. In its west wing, you'll find Norway's shimmering crown jewels and its museum. After visiting the well-displayed statues, gargoyles and carvings from the cathedral, drop to the lower level with a selection of the myriad artefacts revealed during the museum's late-1990s construction.

★ **Stiftsgården** PALACE
(www.nkim.no/stiftsgarden; Munkegata 23; adult/child 90/50kr; ⊙10am-4pm Mon-Sat, noon-4pm Sun Jun-late Aug) Scandinavia's largest wooden palace, the 140-room late-baroque Stiftsgården, was constructed as a private residence in the late 18th century, at the height of Trondheim's golden age. It is now the official royal residence in Trondheim. Admission is by tour only, every hour on the hour. The publicly accessible garden around the east side (enter via Dronningens gate) is one of Trondheim's loveliest corners.

Trondheim Kunstmuseum
GALLERY

(📞 73 53 81 80; www.trondheimkunstmuseum.no; Bispegata 7b; adult/child 100/50kr; ⏱ 10am-4pm Jun-Aug, noon-4pm Tue-Sun Sep-May) Trondheim's Art Museum, a stone's throw from the cathedral, houses a permanent collection of modern Norwegian and Danish art from 1800 onwards, including a hallway of Munch lithographs. It also runs temporary exhibitions.

Rockheim
MUSEUM

(www.rockheim.no; Brattørkaia 14; adult/concession/child 130/100/free; ⏱ 11am-6pm Tue-Sun) This terrific museum is devoted to pop and rock music, mainly Norwegian, from the 1950s until yesterday. It's a dockside temple to R&B, where a huge projecting roof featuring Norwegian record covers extends above an equally vast converted warehouse. Within, there's plenty of action and interaction (mix your own hip-hop tape, for example). Home of Rock is on the quayside, very near Pirbadet and the fast-ferry landing stage.

Sverresborg Trøndelag Folkemuseum
MUSEUM, ARCHITECTURE

(📞 73 89 01 00; www.sverresborg.no; Sverresborg Allé 13; adult/5-15yr/under 5 incl guided tour mid-Jun–Aug 155/115kr/free, Sep–mid-Jun 115/95kr/free; ⏱ 10am-5pm Jun-Aug, 10am-3pm Tue-Fri, noon-4pm Sat & Sun Sep-May; 🚌 18, 🚌 8) Three kilometres west of the centre, this folk museum is one of the best of its kind in Norway. The indoor exhibition, Livsbilder (Images of Life), displays artefacts in use over the last 150 years – from clothing to school supplies to bicycles. The rest of the museum is open-air, comprising more than 60 period buildings, adjoining the ruins of King Sverre's castle and giving fine views of the city.

🏃 Activities

Hiking is the main attraction, even in Trondheim itself, and there also some outstanding trails begin just beyond city limits. Skiing is possible in winter.

The free map, *Friluftsliv i Trondheimsregionen* (*Outdoor Life in the Trondheim Region*; text in Norwegian), available at the tourist office (p344), shows nearby outdoor recreation areas and walking trails.

Two easy strolls within town are the steep, but short, ascent through the traffic-free lanes of Bakklandet to Kristiansten Fort and the riverbank footpaths beside the Nidelva between Bakke Bru and Gangbrua bridges.

🛈 COMBINATION TICKET

If you're planning to visit all three sights within the Nidaros Cathedral (p338) complex, it's worthwhile purchasing a combined ticket (adult/child/family 180/90/440kr) that gives access to the cathedral, Archbishop's Palace museum and the crown jewels.

West of town spreads the Bymarka, a gorgeous green woodland area laced with wilderness footpaths and ski trails. Take the Gråkallbanen tram, in itself a lovely scenic ride through the leafy suburbs, from the St Olavsgata stop to Lian. There you can enjoy excellent views over the city and a good swimming lake, Lianvannet.

To the east of Trondheim, Ladestien (the Lade Trail) follows the shoreline of the Lade peninsula, beginning only 1km from the town centre.

Harbour Sightseeing
BOATING

(Tripps; 📞 950 82 144; www.trippsbatservice.no; adult/child 170/60kr; ⏱ cruises 11am, 12.30pm & 3pm Tue-Sun mid-Jun–mid-Aug, noon Thu-Sun mid-May–Jun & mid-Aug–Sep) Tripps runs a one-hour cruise (at 11am) along the estuary of the River Nidelva, with two longer 90-minute versions (at 12.30pm and 3pm) out into the fjord. Departures are from beside the Ravnkloa Fish Market (p342) and you buy your ticket at the small kiosk next to the wharf.

Walking Tours
WALKING

(📞 73 80 76 60; www.visittrondheim.no; tours 130-2540kr; ⏱ 2pm daily late Jun–mid-Aug, 2pm Sat rest of year) In addition to their standard two-hour guided city walk (185kr per person), the tourist office organises a fascinating portfolio of walks, some guided, some self-guided, with themes that range from coffee or music to gourmet-food experiences.

Trondheim Kajakk
KAYAKING

(📞 483 38 318; www.trondheimkajakk.no; 2hr tour incl rental per person 400kr, rental per day 400kr; ⏱ 8am-11pm; 🚌 3, 4, 9, 46) A fine way to get an alternative perspective on Trondheim, these kayak tours paddle from down through the old town along the Nidelven River to where it meets the fjord. Prices vary with the number of people.

Trondheim

3
Rockheim

Brattørkaia

Havnegata

Trondheimfjord

Trondheim
Sentralstasjon

Intercity Bus
Terminal
(Rutebilstasjon)

Østre
Kanalhavn

Fjordgata

7

Brattørgata
25 **23**

15

Olav Tryggvasonsgate

Søndre gate

*Vestre
Kanalhavn*

Thomas Angells gate
22
8

9

Dronningens gate

Nordre gate

Sandgata

20

4
Stiftsgården

10

Tordenskjolds gate

St Olavsgata

Prinsens gate

Torvet

Kongens gate

Kongens gate

21

Kjøpmannsgata

*Ila Brannstasjon (350m);
Sverresborg Trøndelag
Folkemuseum (1.6km);
Vertshuset Tavern (1.7km)*

Erling Skakkes gate

Munkegata

16

5

14

KALVSKINNET

Prinsens gate

Bispegata

Gangbrua

6

Kongsgårdsgata

2
*Nidaros
Domkirke*

Nidelva

Klostergata

Arkitekt
Christies gate

1
*Archbishop's
Palace*

Øvre Bakklandet

*Elgeseter
Bru*

Mauritz Hansens gate

Klostergata

Elgesetergate

Christian Frederiks gate

19

*Trondheim
Kajakk (2km)*

Trondheim

◎ Top Sights
1	Archbishop's Palace	D6
2	Nidaros Domkirke	D6
3	Rockheim	D2
4	Stiftsgården	C4

◎ Sights
5	Gamle Bybro	D5
6	Trondheim Kunstmuseum	C5

✦ Activities, Courses & Tours
7	Harbour Sightseeing	C3
8	Walking Tours	D4

🛏 Sleeping
9	City Living Hotel & Apartments	C4
10	Pensjonat Jarlen	B4
11	Radisson Blu Royal Garden Hotel	E3
12	Scandic Nidelven Hotel	E2

✖ Eating
13	Baklandet Skydsstasjon	E5
14	Folk & Fe	D5
15	Ravnkloa Fish Market	C3

🍷 Drinking & Nightlife
16	Antikvariatet	D5
17	Cafe Løkka	E3
18	Jacobsen og Svart	E4
19	Studentersamfundet	C7
20	Trondheim Microbryggeri	C4

🛍 Shopping
21	Bryggerekka Bruktmarked	D4
22	Moods of Norway	D4
23	Småting	D3
24	Sukker	E5
25	Ting	D3

🎎 Festivals & Events

★ **Nidaros Blues Festival**   MUSIC
(www.nidarosbluesfestival.com; ☉ Apr) A who's who of the international blues scene with local acts as well.

★ **Olavsfestdagene**   CULTURAL
(www.olavsfestdagene.no; ☉ Jul & Aug) In honour of St Olav and held during the week around his saint's day, 29 July. There's a medieval market and a rich program of classical music, folk, pop and jazz.

★ **UKA**   CULTURAL
(www.uka.no; ☉ Oct/Nov) Trondheim's 25,000 university students stage this three-week celebration, Norway's largest cultural festival. Every other year (in odd-numbered years) in October and November, it's a

HISTORIC BUILDINGS & NEIGHBOURHOODS

From **Gamle Bybro** (Old Town Bridge) there's a superb view of the Bryggen, the colourful 18th- and 19th-century riverfront warehouses similar to their better-known counterparts in Bergen. To the east, the one-time working-class neighbourhoods of **Møllenberg** and **Bakklandet** are now gentrified latte-land, all cobbles, car-free alleys, trim houses in pastel shades and gardens scarcely bigger than a towel that burst with flowers. Here, within old warehouses and renovated workers' housing, are some of the city's most colourful places to eat and drink.

The cobblestone streets immediately west of the centre are also lined with mid-19th-century wooden buildings, notably the octagonal 1705 timber church, **Hospitalkirken**, in the hospital grounds.

continuous party with concerts, plays and festivities based at the round, red **Studentersamfundet** (Student Centre; www.samfundet. no; Elgesetergate 1).

🛏 Sleeping

⭐ **Pensjonat Jarlen** GUESTHOUSE €
(☎73 51 32 18; www.jarlen.no; Kongens gate 40; s/d/tr 540/690/960kr; cat or dog 100kr; 🛜) Price, convenience and value for money are a winning combination here. After a 2010 overhaul, the rooms at this central spot have a contemporary look and are outstanding, although some bathrooms could do with a spruce-up. Some rooms have polished floorboards, others carpet, and most have a hot plate and fridge thrown in.

⭐ **Radisson Blu Royal Garden Hotel** HOTEL €€
(☎73 80 30 00; www.radissonblu.com; Kjøpmannsgata 73; s/d from 895/1245kr; 🅿🌐@🛜🏊) This first-class, contemporary riverside hotel (you can fish from your window in some rooms, although most overlook a leafy internal patio) is open and airy from the moment you step into the atrium, where the light streams in through the all-glass walls. Rooms are supremely comfortable.

City Living Hotel & Apartments HOTEL, APARTMENTS €€
(Schøllers Hotel; ☎73 87 08 00; www.cityliving.no; Dronningens gate 26; r/apt from 637/922kr) Slick modern rooms in the heart of the city, just across from the town's loveliest little garden, and with just the right mix of style and comfort.

Most rooms have parquetry floors and modern furnishings, but some have carpets. The prices, too, are brilliant value for what you get and where you get it.

Scandic Nidelven Hotel HOTEL €€€
(☎73 56 80 00; www.scandichotels.com; Havnegata 1-3; r 1449-2149kr, ste from 3995kr; 🅿@🛜) A big business hotel with more than 340 rooms and the full suite of facilities (conference rooms, gym, meeting spaces etc). It's split into several box-shaped wings projecting over the water, so many rooms have river views. Rooms are smallish but attractive, and the breakfast is a corker – Twinings awarded it 'Norway's best hotel breakfast' for 10 years running from 2006 to 2015.

In 2016 it came third, but it still wins our vote. Why? A fresh juice bar, a real-life barista and astonishing choice of every possible breakfast food imaginable...

🍴 Eating

⭐ **Ravnkloa Fish Market** SEAFOOD €
(☎73 52 55 21; www.ravnkloa.no; Munkegata; snacks from 50kr, mains 140-215kr; ⏰10am-5pm Mon-Fri, to 4pm Sat) Everything looks good at this fish market that doubles as a cafe with quayside tables out the front. The fish cakes are fabulous and it also does shrimp sandwiches, mussels and a fine fish soup. In addition to seafood, it sells an impressive range of cheeses and other gourmet goods.

⭐ **Baklandet Skydsstasjon** NORWEGIAN €€
(☎73 92 10 44; www.skydsstation.no; Øvre Bakklandet 33; mains 158-275kr; ⏰11am-1am Mon-Fri, noon-1am Sat & Sun) If you're still searching for that quintessentially Norwegian meal, then you won't get much more traditional than this. Originally an 18th-century coaching inn, it's now everyone's favourite homely hang-out in Trondheim, with rambling rooms crammed with old furniture and clad in flock wallpaper, and a menu stuffed with comforting classics such as fish or reindeer soup, baked salmon and liver paste.

★ **Vertshuset Tavern** NORWEGIAN €€€
(☑73 87 80 70; www.tavern.no; Sverresborg Allé
11; mains 175-315kr; ⊙4-9pm Mon, to 10pm Tue-Fri,
2-10pm Sat, to 9pm Sun) Once in the heart of
Trondheim, this historic (1739) tavern was
lifted and transported, every last plank, to
the Sverresborg Trøndelag Folkemuseum
(p339) on the outskirts of town. Tuck into
rotating specials of traditional Norwegian
fare or just graze on waffles with coffee in
one of its 16 tiny rooms, each low-beamed,
with sloping floors, candlesticks, cast-iron
stoves and lacy tablecloths.

★ **Folk & Fe** NORWEGIAN €€€
(☑975 18 180; www.folkogfe-bistro.no; Øvre Bakklandet 66; 3-/5-course menu 525/815kr; ⊙noon-4pm &
5-11pm Tue-Sun) Rustic-chic is the modus operandi at the Folk & Fe. Lauded by the *White
Guide* (Scandinavia's equivalent of the *Michelin Guide*), it's vintage New Nordic, with a
taste for minimalist presentation and seasonal dishes maxing out on local ingredients. The
menu changes constantly, but expect smoked
fish, reindeer carpaccio, farm cheeses and foraged berries, served on wooden platters.

🍷 Drinking & Nightlife

Trondheim buzzes after dark. The free papers, *Natt & Dag* and *Plan B,* have listings,
mostly in Norwegian. Solsiden (Sunnyside) is
Trondheim's trendiest leisure zone. A whole
wharfside of bars and restaurants nestles beneath smart new apartment blocks, converted warehouses and long-idle cranes.

★ **Antikvariatet** CAFE, BAR
(☑942 20 557; Nedre Bakklandet 4; drinks from
79kr; ⊙2pm-1.30am Tue-Fri, noon-1.30am Sat &
Sun) Now this is our kind of place – craft
beers on tap, shelves lined with books, lovely views over the water and regular live gigs
to boot. Unsurprisingly it's popular with students and trendy types, and it's in a delightful location among the wooden houses of the
Bakklandet. You'll have to be lucky to snaffle
a balcony table.

★ **Ila Brainnstasjon** BAR, LIVE MUSIC
(☑489 55 036; www.ilabrainnstasjon.no; Ilevollen
32b; ⊙4-11pm Tue-Thu, to 1am Fri, noon-1am Sat,
to 9pm Sun) This Trondheim institution is
the best place in the city to see live music
(most nights around 9pm; on Thursdays
at 6pm), but it's a fine little bar-cafe even
when nothing's on the bill. We especially
love its 2pm Sunday jazz jam session when
local musicians turn up to play – when it

works, it's one of our favourite places to be
in Trondheim.
Check the website (select 'Hvar Skjer') to
see what's coming up.

Cafe Løkka BAR
(☑400 00 974; www.cafelokka.no; Dokkgata 8;
⊙11am-midnight Sun-Tue, to 2am Wed-Sat) Long
before its latest makeover, mustard-yellow
Cafe Løkka was a boat-repair workshop.
It now carries a good range of beers, on
draught and in bottle, and also does milkshakes. It's more an early-evening venue
than a serious late-night drinking den. It
also does a good range of meals.

Jacobsen og Svart CAFE
(☑902 44 226; www.jacobsenswart.no; Ferjemannsveien 8; ⊙7am-6pm Mon-Fri, 9am-6pm
Sat, 11am-6pm Sun) One of Trondheim's
trendiest coffee cafes, Jacobsen og Svart
does what many claim to be the city's best
coffee. Throw in a very cool soundtrack and
near-perfect, freshly baked cinnamon rolls
and you're somewhere close to cafe heaven.

Trondheim Microbryggeri MICROBREWERY
(☑73 51 75 15; www.tmb.no; Prinsens gate 39;
⊙3pm-midnight Mon, 3pm-2am Tue-Fri, noon-2am
Sat) This splendid home-brew pub deserves
a pilgrimage as reverential as anything accorded to St Olav from all committed øl
(beer) quaffers. After a 2014 renovation and
with up to eight of its own brews on tap and
good light meals available, it's a place to linger, nibble and tipple. It's down a short lane,
just off Prinsens gate.

🛍 Shopping

★ **Bryggerekka Bruktmarked** MARKET
(www.midtbeyn.no/bruktmarked; Kjøpmannsgata;
⊙10am-4pm Sun mid-May–early Sep) Along the
waterfront close to where Kongens gate hits
the water, the colourful wharfside warehouses
provide a lovely backdrop for this summer-only Sunday flea market. It's mostly antiques,
secondhand and the occasional vintage, with
coffee and waffles at regular intervals.

★ **Ting** HOMEWARES
(☑452 00 700; www.ting.no; Olav Tryggvasonsgate
10; ⊙10am-6pm Mon-Sat) Modern designer
homewares dominate this funky shop – it's
all about Scandinavian cool without an
outrageous price tag. A couple of doors up,
Småting (☑47 48 92 88; www.ting.no; Olav Tryggvasonsgate 6; ⊙10am-6pm Mon-Sat), run by
the same people, brings the same creative
eye to children's toys.

Sukker DESIGN
(📋 476 53 637; www.sukkerdesign.no; Nedre Bakklandet 9; ⊙ 2-5pm Fri, 11-4pm Sat & Sun) Designer just about anything is what this gorgeous little boutique is all about – jewellery and other accessories, clothing, artworks, ceramics, homewares…the designers actually run the shop and you'll want to spend both serious time and money here. It's just a pity (or perhaps just as well) it doesn't open longer hours.

Moods of Norway FASHION & ACCESSORIES
(📋 924 25 722; www.moodsofnorway.com; Olav Trygvassonsgate 29; ⊙ 10am-6pm Mon-Sat) The quirky fashions of this stunning Norwegian success story make a virtue out of eccentricity. Bright colours and harmless fun are recurring themes.

❶ Information

Tourist Office (📋 73 80 76 60; www.visittrondheim.no; 1st fl, Nordre gate 11; ⊙ 9am-6pm mid-Jun–mid-Aug, to 6pm Mon-Sat rest of year) In the heart of the city, with an accommodation booking service.

❶ Getting There & Away

AIR

Værnes airport is 32km east of Trondheim, with flights operated by SAS (www.sas.no), Norwegian (www.norwegian.no) and Widerøe (www.wideroe.no). There are flights to all major Norwegian cities, as well as Copenhagen and Stockholm. Norwegian flies to/from London (Gatwick) and Berlin, and KLM covers Amsterdam.

BUS

The **intercity bus terminal** (Rutebilstasjon; Fosenkaia) adjoins Trondheim Sentralstasjon (train station, also known as Trondheim S).

As the main link between southern and northern Norway, Trondheim is a bus-transport crossroads. **Nor-Way Bussekspress** (p305) services run to/from destinations including the following:
Bergen (808kr, 14 hours) One overnight bus.
Namsos (413kr, 3¾ hours) Four daily via Steinkjer (273kr, 2¼ hours).

If you're travelling by public transport to Narvik and points north, it's quicker – all is relative – to take the train to Fauske or Bodø (the end of the line), then continue by bus.

TRAIN

There are two to four trains daily to/from Oslo (937kr, 6½ hours). Two head north to Bodø (1088kr, 9¾ hours) via the following:
Fauske (1052kr, nine hours)

Mo i Rana (908kr, 6½ hours)
Mosjøen (817kr, 5½ hours)
As always, a *minipris* ticket will considerably undercut these standard prices.

You can also train it to Steinkjer (241kr, two hours, hourly).

❶ Getting Around

As befits such a cycle-friendly city, Trondheim has a bike-hire scheme (50kr per day). Pick up a card at the tourist office in return for a refundable deposit of 200kr or €25, then borrow a bike from any of the 12 cycle stations around town. You then return the bike to one of the stations, and return the card to the tourist office to claim back your deposit.

Other cycle-friendly measures include clear signing of cycle routes, often traffic-free and shared with pedestrians, a lane of smooth flagstones along cobbled streets that would otherwise uncomfortably judder your and the bike's moving parts – and Trampe, the world's only **bike lift**, a low-tech piece of engineering to which cyclists heading from the Gamle Bybro up the Brubakken hill to Kristiansten Fort can hitch themselves.

Bodø

POP 50,000

Bodø, the northernmost point of the staggeringly beautiful Kystriksveien Coastal Route and 63km west of Fauske on the Arctic Highway, is the gateway to Norway's true north. It's also the northern terminus of Norway's railway system and a jumping-off point for the Lofoten Islands.

The town centre, rebuilt after being almost completely levelled by WWII bombing, is unexciting architecturally. The city's main charm lies in its backdrop of distant rugged peaks and vast skies. Dramatic islands that support the world's densest concentration of white-tailed sea eagles – not for nothing is Bodø known as the Sea Eagle Capital – dot the seas to the north.

◉ Sights

Kjerringøy Trading Post MUSEUM
(Kjerringøy Handelssted; 📋 75 50 35 05; www.nordlandsmuseet.no/kjerringoy_handelssted; Rv 834; adult/child 100/50kr; ⊙ 11am-5pm late May-late Aug) At Kjerringøy, some 40km north of Bodø, the entrepreneurial Zahl family established an important trading station in the 19th century. The trading post provided local fishing families with supplies in

exchange for their catch. Most of the timber-built structures of this self-contained community have been preserved. The spartan quarters and kitchens of the fishing families contrast with the sumptuous decor of the merchants' housing.

There's a 20-minute audiovisual presentation included with admission. Entry to the main building is by guided tour.

Norsk Luftfartsmuseum MUSEUM
(Norwegian Aviation Museum; www.luftfartsmuseum.no; Olav V gate; adult/child/family 160/80/450kr; ⊙10am-7pm) Norway's 10,000-sq-metre aviation museum is huge fun to ramble around if you have a passing interest in flight and aviation history – allow at least half a day. If you're flying into Bodø for real, you'll see that from above, the striking modern grey and smoked-glass main museum building has the shape of an aeroplane propeller.

Exhibits include a complete control tower and hands-on demonstrations. In 2016, it opened the excellent, interactive Civil Gallery on the dream of flying.

🛏 Sleeping

★ Skagen Hotel HOTEL €€
(📞75 51 91 00; www.skagen-hotel.no; Nyholmsgata 11; s/d from 915/1135kr; @🛜) Skagen occupies two buildings (one originally a butcher's, though you'd never guess it). Facing each other, they're connected by a passage that burrows beneath the street. Rooms are attractively decorated and a continent away from chain-hotel clones. There's a bar and free afternoon waffles and coffee, and excellent breakfasts. Staff can give advice on a raft of vigorous outdoor activities.

Thon Hotel Nordlys HOTEL €€
(📞75 53 19 00; www.thonhotels.no; Moloveien 14; s/d from 995/1205kr; 🛜) Arguably Bodø's most stylish hotel, with touches of subtle Scandinavian design throughout, it overlooks the marina and runs a reasonable restaurant. We love the wall-sized photos of the Northern Lights in some rooms.

🍴 Eating

Bryggeri Kaia NORWEGIAN €€
(📞75 52 58 08; www.bryggerikaia.no; Sjøgata 1; snacks from 150kr; mains 215-335kr; ⊙11am-3.30am Mon-Sat, noon-3.30am Sun) Bryggeri Kaia is a firm favourite. You can dine well, snack, enjoy its weekday lunch buffet (195kr), its Saturday herring buffet (195kr) or quaff one of its several beers. Enjoy your choice in its large pub-decor interior, on the streetside terrace or, best of all should you find a seat spare, on the verandah overlooking the harbour.

★ Roast INTERNATIONAL €€
(📞75 50 38 35; www.roastfood.no/bodo; Tollbugata 5, 17th fl; mains 189-350kr; ⊙11am-1am Mon-Thu, to 2.30am Fri & Sat, to 5pm Sun) High above the city on a 17th-floor perch in the Scandic Havet (📞75 50 38 00; www.scandichotels.no/hotell/norge/bodo/scandic-havet; Tollbugata 5; s/d 1449/1649kr; 🛜) hotel, Roast is true to its name – you could play around with different tastes but you really must order the roast board, with its different meats (ribs, steak...) all beautifully presented. And the views from up here are simply wonderful.

ℹ️ Information

Tourist Office (📞75 54 80 00; www.visitbodo.com; Sjøgata 15-17; ⊙9am-8pm Mon-Fri, 10am-6pm Sat & Sun mid-Jun–Aug, 9am-3.30pm Mon-Fri Sep–mid-Jun) Publishes the excellent free *Bodø* brochure and offers free wi-fi.

ℹ️ Getting There & Away

AIR
From Bodø's airport (www.avinor.no), southwest of the city centre, there are at least 10 daily flights to Oslo, Trondheim and Tromsø. Other destinations in northern Norway include Leknes, Narvik, Harstad and Mo i Rana.

BOAT
Bodø is a stop on the **Hurtigruten coastal ferry** (📞97 05 70 30).

Car ferries (www.torghatten-nord.no) sail five to six times daily in summer (less frequently during the rest of the year) between Bodø and Moskenes on Lofoten (car including driver/adult/child 702/196/98kr, three to 3½ hours). If you're taking a car in summer avoid a potential long wait in line by booking in advance (an additional 100kr; online reservation at www.torghatten-nord.no).

Most days, at least one ferry calls in at the southern Lofoten Islands of Røst and Værøy.

There's also a daily **express passenger ferry** (www.torghatten-nord.no) between Bodø and Svolvær (adult/child 385/198kr, 3¾ hours) once daily.

BUS
From the **bus station** (📞177), buses run to/from Narvik (325kr, 6½ hours) via Fauske (105kr, 1½ hours) twice daily, with extra services to/from Fauske.

TRAIN

Destination	Cost (kr)	Time	Frequency (daily)
Fauske	138	45min	5
Mo i Rana	507	3hr	3
Mosjøen	675	4¼hr	3
Trondheim	1088	9¾hr	2

Narvik

POP 18,787

Narvik has a double personality. On the one hand, its location is spectacular, pincered by islands to the west and mountains in every other direction, while spectacular fjords stretch north and south. At the same time, heavy industry casts a pall of ugliness over the rather scruffy downtown area – the town was founded in 1902 as the port for the coal-mining town of Kiruna in Swedish Lapland and the trans-shipment facility bisecting the city still loads several million tonnes of ore annually from train wagons on to ships.

But Narvik's appeal lies elsewhere, with unique sporting and sightseeing activities offered by its majestic surroundings and the spectacular Ofotbanen Railway to Sweden.

Activities

Narvik og Omegns Turistforening (NOT; Narvik Trekking Association; ☑915 52 908, 402 40 987; www.turistforeningen.no/narvik) is an excellent source of information about hiking. It maintains more than 15 cabins, mostly between Narvik and the Swedish border. Collect keys from the tourist office against a deposit of 150kr.

★**Narvikfjellet**   CABLE CAR
(☑905 40 888; www.narvikfjellet.no; Mårveien; adult one way/return 120/180kr, child under 7yr free; ☺1pm-1am Jun–mid-Jul, 1-8pm mid-Jul–mid-Aug, shorter hours rest of year) Climbing 656m above town, this cable car offers breathtaking views over surrounding peaks and fjords – even as far as Lofoten on a clear day. Several marked walking trails radiate from its top station or you can bounce down a signed mountain-bike route. From February to April, it will whisk you up high for trail, off-piste and cross-country skiing with outstanding views.

Ofotbanen Railway   RAIL
(☑76 92 31 21; www.nsb.no/en/our-destinations/our-regional-railway-lines/ofotenrailway; one way adult/ child 160kr/free) The spectacular mountain-hugging Ofotbanen Railway trundles beside fjordside cliffs, birch forests and rocky plateaus as it climbs to the Swedish border. The route from Narvik to Riksgränsen, the ski resort just inside Sweden, features some 50 tunnels and snow sheds. Towards the Narvik end, you might make out the wreck of the German ship *Georg Thiele* at the edge of the fjord.

🛏 Sleeping

★**Breidablikk Gjestehus**   GUESTHOUSE €€
(☑76 94 14 18; www.breidablikk.no; Tore Hunds gate 41; dm 350kr, s 600-1150kr, d 1195-1750kr; P@🛜) It's a steep but worthwhile walk from the centre to this pleasant hillside guesthouse with rooms for all budgets and sweeping views over the town and fjord. There's a cosy communal lounge and dorms have six beds.

Scandic Hotel Narvik   HOTEL €€
(☑76 96 14 00; www.scandichotels.no/hotell/norge/ narvik; Kongens gate 33; d 895-1495kr; 🛜) Towering over the downtown area, this striking glass edifice houses Narvik's most stylish hotel. Rooms are slick and contemporary and those on the upper floors have fabulous views. There's also a fine restaurant and 16th-floor **bar** (16th fl, ☺11am-1am Mon-Fri, 11am-2am Sat, 6pm-1am Sun).

🍴 Eating

Fiskekroken   CAFE €
(☑76 94 36 60; Kongens gate 42; mains 80-190kr; ☺noon-6pm Tue-Thu, 1-9pm Fri & Sat) This tiny cafe, offshoot of the adjacent fish shop, offers tasty ready-to-eat dishes, such as fish cakes and fish and chips to eat in or take away. The fish couldn't be fresher.

Kafferiet   INTERNATIONAL €€
(☑76 96 00 55; Dronningensgate 47; light meals 109-179kr, mains 159-309kr; ☺10.30am-1.30am Tue-Thu, to 3am Fri & Sat) Narvik's slickest venue is a stylish, modern place with outdoor tables that tumble down the steps. Pasta, fish and grilled meats dominate an extensive if largely unimaginative menu, while it turns into a bar and nightclub once the kitchen closes.

ℹ Information

In the centre of town, the **tourist office** (☑76 96 56 00; www.destinationnarvik.com; Kongens gate 41-43; ☺10am-7pm Mon-Fri, to 6pm Sat & Sun mid-Jun–mid-Aug, 10am-4pm Mon-Sat & noon-4pm Sun rest of year) holds Narvik og Omegns Turistforening cabin keys (150kr deposit), has free wi-fi and rents out bikes (250kr per day).

ⓘ Getting There & Away

AIR
Nearly all flights leave from Harstad-Narvik Evenes airport, 1¼ hours away by road. Narvik's tiny Framneslia airport, about 3km west of the centre, serves only Bodø, Tromsø and Andenes.

BUS
Express buses run from the **bus station** northwards to Tromsø (280kr, 4¼ hours, three daily) and south to Bodø (325kr, 6½ hours, two daily) via Fauske (315kr, 5½ hours, two daily). For Lofoten, two Lofotekspressen buses run daily between Narvik and Svolvær (from 280kr, 4¼ hours) and continue to Å.

Between late June and early September, bus 91 runs twice a day up the E10 to Riksgränsen (45 minutes) in Sweden and on to Abisko and Kiruna (three hours).

TRAIN
Heading for Sweden, there are two daily services between Narvik and Riksgränsen (one hour) on the border, and Kiruna (three hours). Trains continue to Lulea (7¼ hours) via Boden, from where you can pick up connections to Stockholm. The route takes you up the spectacular Ofotbanen Railway and, in Sweden, past Abisko National Park, which offers excellent hiking and lovely Arctic scenery.

ⓘ Getting Around
Narvik's Framneslia airport is 3km from the centre.

Flybuss runs four to eight times daily between Narvik's **Scandic Hotel Narvik** (p346) and the bus station, and Harstad-Narvik Evenes airport (adult/child one way 260/130kr, adult return 400kr, 1¼ hours), 79km away.

For a taxi phone **Narvik Taxi** (☑ 07550; www.narviktaxi.no).

Lofoten
You'll never forget your first approach to the Lofoten Islands. The islands spread their tall, craggy physique against the sky like some spiky sea dragon. The beauty of this place is simply staggering.

The main islands, Austvågøy, Vestvågøy, Flakstadøy and Moskenesøy, are separated from the mainland by Vestfjorden, but all are connected by road bridges and tunnels. On each are sheltered bays, sheep pastures and picturesque villages. The vistas and the special quality of the Arctic light have long attracted artists, represented in galleries throughout the islands. One of the best ways to appreciate

the view is to follow the E10 road, which runs along the islands from tip to toe, taking just about every detour you have time for en route.

Svolvær
POP 4598

The port town of Svolvær is as busy as it gets in Lofoten. The town once sprawled across a series of skerries, but the in-between spaces are being filled in to create a reclaimed peninsula. Although the setting is beautiful with a backdrop of high mountains, the hotchpotch of modern buildings clutters things somewhat. It's a good place to eat and refuel, but the magic of Lofoten lies elsewhere.

⊙ Sights

★**Foto Galleri** GALLERY
(☑ 954 98 150; www.lofotfotografen.no; cnr Vestfjordgata & Kirkegata; ⊙ 10am-4pm & 6.30-8pm Mon-Fri, 10am-3pm & 6.30-8pm Sat mid-Jun–mid-Aug, closed evenings rest of year) FREE Stunning photos of the Lofoten Islands in all their brooding glory, most of them for sale, are the work of photographer Anders Finsland. It's worth stopping by even if you don't plan to buy.

★**Magic Ice** SCULPTURE
(☑ 76 07 40 11; www.magicice.no; Fiskergata 36; adult/child 175/95kr; ⊙ 11am-11pm Sun-Thu, to midnight Fri & Sat mid-May–mid-Sep, 4-11pm Sun-Thu, to midnight Fri & Sat rest of year) Housed appropriately in what was once a fish-freezing plant, this is the ultimate place to chill out (perhaps with something to warm the spirit).

TROLLFJORD BOAT TRIPS

From the port, several competing companies offer sailings into the constricted confines of nearby Trollfjord, spectacularly steep and narrowing to only 100m. Take the two-hour sea-eagle trip, the three-hour cruise or sign on for a four-hour trip that includes the chance to dangle a line and bring home supper. Buy your ticket at the quayside (Vestfjordgata) or at operators such as Lofoten Explorer (☑ 971 52 248; www.lofoten-explorer.no; adult/child 795/600kr; ⊙ 9am, 11.30am & 2pm Jul, 11.30am & 2pm Jun & Aug, 11.30am rest of year), RiB Lofoten (☑ 904 16 440; www.rib-lofoten.com; adult/child 750/600kr; ⊙ 11am & 1pm May-Aug) or Trollfjord Cruise (☑ 451 57 587; www.trollfjordcruise.com; adult/child 700/350kr).

Lofoten

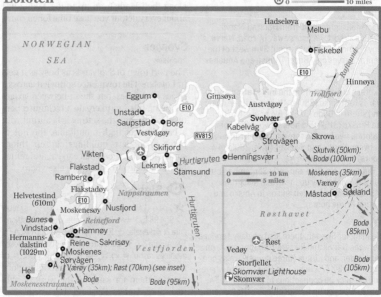

The 500-sq-metre space is filled with huge ice sculptures, illustrating Lofoten life. If you can't return to northern Norway in winter, this is a great, if brief, approximation. Admission includes warm clothing and a drink in an ice glass.

🏃 Activities

★Svolværgeita
HIKING, CLIMBING

You'll see it on postcards all over Lofoten – some daring soul leaping between two fingers of rock high above Svolvær. To hike up to a point just behind the two pinnacles (355m), walk northeast along the E10 towards Narvik, past the marina, then turn left on Nyveien and right on Blatind veg. The steep climb begins just behind the children's playground.

The climb takes around half an hour, or an hour if you continue up to the summit of Floya. To actually climb Svolværgeita and take the leap, you'll need to go with a climbing guide – ask the tourist office for recommendations or try Northern Alpine Guides (p350).

🛏 Sleeping

Scandic Hotel Svolvær
HOTEL €€

(📞 76 07 22 22; www.scandichotels.no; Lamholmen; r from 995kr; P🛜) The Rica here is built on a tiny island, above the water and support-ed by piles. Room 121 has a hole in the floor so guests can drop a fishing line directly into the water below. Such novelties aside, the rooms are functional rather than memorable – make sure you get one with a balcony.

★Lofoten Suite Hotel
BOUTIQUE HOTEL €€€

(📞 476 70 100; www.lofoten-suitehotel.com; Havnepromenaden; ste 1450-3300kr; 🛜) This striking wood-and-glass structure seems to hover above the harbour-front of Svolvær, so it's perhaps unsurprising that practically all its swanky suites have an ocean view with floor-to-ceiling windows. Stripped wood and colourful fabrics conjure a contemporary feel, and some rooms have little kitchenettes for preparing snacks.

★Svinøya Rorbuer
CABIN €€€

(📞 76 06 99 30; www.svinoya.no; Gunnar Bergs vei 2; cabins & ste 1600-3500kr) Across a bridge on the islet of Svinøya, site of Svolvær's first settlement, are several cabins, some historic, most contemporary, and all cosy and comfortable. Reception is a veritable museum – a restored and restocked *krambua* (general store), constructed in 1828, which was Svolvær's first shop. It has properties all over the area and some of the best *rorbuer* (fisher's cabins) in Lofoten.

Eating

Hjerterommet Kafe
CAFE €

(Vestfjordgata; snacks from 80kr; ⊙10am-4pm Mon-Fri, 11am-4pm Sat) More a coffee and cake kind of place, this eclectic little cafe is a fine little pit stop. The decor ranges from a bed mattress to cutesy and colourful wood, and the whole place is brimful of personality and warmth.

Bacalao
CAFE €€

(☑76 07 94 00; www.bacalaobar.no; Havnepromenaden 2; mains 175-225kr; ⊙10.30am-1am Mon-Thu, 10.30am-2.30am Fri & Sat, noon-1am Sun) With its upbeat interior, Bacalao offers leafy, innovative salads, sandwiches and some equally creative pasta dishes; the hot *rekepasta* (shrimp pasta) will set your taste buds tingling. Bacalao also expresses some of Lofoten's best coffee. It transforms into a popular bar once the kitchen closes.

★ Børsen
NORWEGIAN €€€

(☑76 06 99 30; www.svinoya.no; Gunnar Bergs vei 2; mains lunch 195-235kr, dinner 295-345kr; ⊙11.30am-3.30pm & 6-10pm mid-Jun–mid-Aug, 6-10pm rest of year) Located at the Svinøya complex, this is one of the town's top tables. A former fish house, it was called the 'stock exchange' after the bench outside, where the town's old geezers would gather to debate. In its dining room, with its beams and wooden floors, stockfish and Lofoten lamb are the specialities.

ℹ Information

Tourist Office (☑76 07 05 75; www.lofoten.info; Torget; ⊙9am-9pm Mon-Fri, to 7pm Sat & Sun mid-Jun–mid-Aug, shorter hours rest of year) Provides information on the entire archipelago.

ℹ Getting There & Away

AIR

From Svolvær's small airport there are up to six flights daily to Bodø, and at least one daily Wideroe flight direct to Oslo.

There's no airport shuttle, so you'll have to catch a taxi.

BOAT

Svolvær is a stop on the **Hurtigruten coastal ferry** (Torget). Two other sea routes connect Svolvær to the mainland. For timetables and reservations, visit www.torghatten-nord.no.

Skutvik (car/passenger 383/112kr, 1¾ to 2¼ hours, up to 10 daily) The most regular and popular crossing.

Bodø (adult/child 385/198kr, 3¾ hours) Daily **express** (p347) passenger-only boat.

BUS

Destinations:

Leknes (143kr, 1½ hours, four to six times daily) With connections to Å (230kr, 3½ hours).

Narvik (from 280kr, 4¼ hours, two direct daily).

Sortland (202kr, 2¼ hours, three to five times daily) On Vesterålen via Stokmarknes (1¾ hours).

Kabelvåg

POP 1733

Kabelvåg, 5km southwest of Svolvær, is an intimate and cosy place. At its heart is a small square and tiny harbour, while its Storvågen district, 2km off the E10 to the south, has an enticing trio of museums and galleries.

⊙ Sights

A combination ticket (adult/child 220/110kr) gives entry to Lofotmuseet (p349), Lofoten Aquarium (p349) and Galleri Espolin (p349), all in Storvågan. They're an easy walk from each other.

Galleri Espolin
GALLERY

(☑76 07 84 05; www.museumnord.no/galleri-espolin; adult/child 90/40kr; ⊙10am-6pm Jun–mid-Aug, shorter hours rest of year) This gallery features the haunting etchings and lithographs of one of Norway's great artists, Kaare Espolin-Johnson (1907–94). Espolin – his work all the more astounding as he was nearly blind for much of his life – loved Lofoten and often featured its fisherfolk, together with other Arctic themes.

Lofotmuseet
MUSEUM

(☑76 15 40 00; www.museumnord.no/lofotmuseet; Storvåganveien; adult/child 90/40kr; ⊙10am-6pm Jun-Aug, shorter hours rest of year) The islands' major folk museum is on the site of what can be considered the first town in the polar region, where traces of the original *rorbuer* (fisher's cabins) have been excavated. The museum's main gallery was once the merchant's mansion. An easy, undulating, scenic 2km heritage path leads from the museum to the centre of Kabelvåg.

Lofoten Aquarium
AQUARIUM

(Lofotakvariet; www.museumnord.no/lofotakvariet; Storvåganveien 28; adult/child 130/70kr; ⊙10am-6pm Jun-Aug, shorter hours Feb-May & Sep-Nov) If you want to learn all about the deep, cold waters that surround Lofoten, then this aquarium is a good place to start. There are various exhibits relating to the *skrei* – the species of east Atlantic cod that migrates

NORWAY LOFOTEN

DON'T MISS

LOFOTR VIKING MUSEUM

In 1981 at Borg, near the centre of Vestvågøy, a farmer's plough hit the ruins of the 83m-long dwelling of a powerful Viking chieftain, the largest building of its era ever discovered in Scandinavia. The resulting **Lofotr Viking Museum** (☑ 76 15 40 00; www. lofotr.no; adult/child incl guided tour mid-Jun–mid-Aug 200/150kr, rest of year 140/100kr; ⊙10am-7pm Jun–mid-Aug, shorter hours rest of year;), 14km north of Leknes, offers a glimpse of life in Viking times. You can walk 1.5km of trails over open hilltops from the replica of the chieftain's longhouse (the main building, shaped like an upside-down boat) to the Viking-ship replica on the water.

from the Barents Sea to Lofoten every winter to spawn – as well as tanks filled with king crab, salmon and other species, plus playful troupes of seals and sea otters (feeding times are noon, 3pm and 6pm).

🏃 Activities

Lofoten Kajakk   ADVENTURE
(☑76 07 30 00; www.lofoten-aktiv.no; Kabelvåg) A reliably good adventure company that offers a range of seasonal activities. In summer you can kayak or sail in the fjords, or take a guided mountain-bike tour, while in winter you can go aurora-hunting, experience cross-country skiing or try out your snowshoeing skills. It also rents out kayaks, mountain bikes and other outdoor gear.

Northern Alpine Guides   ADVENTURE SPORTS
(☑942 49 110; www.alpineguides.no; Kalleveien 21) Offers climbing and sailing expeditions in the Lofoten Islands in summer; ski adventures in winter. A very professional group that comes highly recommended.

🛌 Sleeping

**Sandvika Fjord
og Sjøhuscamp**   CAMPGROUND €
(☑90 66 02 07; www.lofotferie.no/nb; car/caravan site 200/225kr, cabins 500-1850kr, sea-house apt 1100kr) This shoreside campground has its own small beach. It rents motorboats (from 220kr per hour) and is a base for sea-kayak trips. The camping area is significantly larger than its neighbour's.

Nyvågar Rorbuhotell   CABIN €€€
(☑76 06 97 00; www.classicnorway.no/hotell/ nyvagar-rorbuhotell; Storvåganveien 22; 4-bed sea-facing/land-facing rorbu incl breakfast 2450/2050kr) At Storvågan, this snazzy complex of seafront cottages is almost entirely modern, but its contemporary *rorbuer* are extremely attractive and fully equipped. They're available in various configurations and sizes, and the hotel can organise nearby activities from cycling to sea-fishing. Rates drop sharply outside the high summer season.

🍴 Eating

Præstengbrygga   PUB, CAFE €€
(☑76 07 80 60; www.prestengbrygga.no; Torget 9; mains 130-175kr; ⊙10.30am-1am Mon-Thu, 10.30am-2.30am Fri & Sat, noon-1am Sun) This is a general-purpose hang-out, as popular for laid-back pub lunches as for late-night drinking. It's a cosy space, with lashings of wood and a lovely dockside terrace. The food is hearty and filling, with dishes such as reindeer stew, seafood platters (sometimes including whale) and big, generous pizzas. Occasional live music in summer make this a great place to chill.

⭐ **Lorchstua Restaurant**   NORWEGIAN €€€
(☑76 06 97 00; www.classicnorway.com/hotels/ nyvagar-rorbuhotell/restaurant; Storvåganveien 26; mains lunch 105-205kr, dinner 219-325kr; ⊙6-10.30pm Jun–mid-Aug) 🌿 The acclaimed Lorchstua restaurant, run by Nyvågar Rorbuhotell, serves primarily local specialities with a subtle twist, such as baked fillet of halibut in a cod brandade. The atmosphere is formal and the food excellent.

ℹ️ Getting There & Away

The regular bus between Henningsvær and Svolvær stops in Kabelvåg (50kr, at least six daily).

Henningsvær

POP 444

A delightful (and rather narrow) 8km shoreside drive southwards from the E10 brings you to the still-active fishing village of Henningsvær, perched at the end of a thin promontory. Its nickname, 'the Venice of Lofoten', may be a tad overblown, but it's certainly the lightest, brightest and trendiest place in the archipelago.

It's also been an important fishing centre for many centuries. There's even a local saying dedicated to the town's piscatorial heritage: 'A real Lofoten cod am I, for I was born in Henningsvær.'

◉ Sights

Engelskmannsbrygga GALLERY
(☑ 481 29 870; www.engelskmannsbrygga.no; Dreyersgate 1; ⊙ 10am-9pm mid-Jun–mid-Aug, shorter hours rest of year) FREE Here at 'Englishman's Wharf' is the open studio and gallery of three talented local artists: potter Cecilie Haaland, wildlife photographer and guide John Stenersen and glass-blower Mette Paalgard, with whom you can sometimes try your hand at blowing your own glass.

Kaviar Factory GALLERY
(☑ 907 34 743; www.kaviarfactory.com; Henningsværveien; adult/child 100/80kr; ⊙ 10am-7pm Sun-Thu, 2.30-7pm Fri & Sat) This fabulous art gallery inhabits an arresting, restored 1950s factory with a changing cast of cutting-edge temporary art exhibitions. The design shop at the entrance is also very cool.

🏃 Activities

Lofoten Oppleveiser OUTDOORS
(Lofoten Adventure; ☑ 905 81 475; www.lofoten-opplevelser.no; Misværveien) Based in Henningsvær, this adventure company offers a wealth of maritime activities. In summer, try sea-eagle safaris (adult/child 650/500kr, 1½ hours), midnight-sun safaris (900/750kr, 2½ hours) and snorkelling sorties (850/700kr, two hours). In winter, chase the Northern Lights (700kr, two hours) or take an orca safari (including snorkelling with them!) in Andenes, a four-hour drive north of Henningsvær.

North Norwegian Climbing School CLIMBING
(Nord Norsk Klatreskole; ☑ 905 74 208; www.nordnorskklatreskole.no; Misværveien 10; ⊙ Mar-Oct) This outfit offers a wide range of technical climbing and skiing courses all around northern Norway. Climbing the peaks with an experienced guide costs around 2200kr per day, including equipment, for one to four people.

Kayak Lofoten KAYAKING
(☑ 468 05 648; www.kayaklofoten.com; Gammelveien 6; kayak rental per day 450kr, 3hr guided tour 650kr) Take a three-hour tour out on the water or go it alone – whichever you choose, the waters around Henningsvær are magnificent for a paddle.

🛌 Sleeping

Johs H Giæver
Sjøhus og Rorbuer GUESTHOUSE €
(☑ 76 07 47 19; www.giaever-rorbuer.no; Hellandsgata 79; rorbu 650-1200kr, sea house 500-750kr)

From mid-June to mid-August workers' accommodation in a modern sea house belonging to the local fish plant is hired out to visitors. Spruce rooms (some with space for four) have shared facilities, including a large kitchen and dining area, and are good value. The company also has 10 *rorbuer* with bathrooms in the heart of town.

Lofoten Arctic Hotel HOTEL €€
(☑ 76 07 07 77; www.lofotenarctichotel.no; Sauøya 2; r 1353kr) Simple motel-style rooms at the entrance to the village make this a decent if uninspiring choice – some rooms are better than others so ask to see a few. Views are stunning from many parts of the property.

⭐**Henningsvær Bryggehotel** HOTEL €€€
(☑ 76 07 47 19; www.henningsvaer.no; Hjellskjæret; d from 1395-1895kr; 🛜) In a beautiful wood-clad building by the harbour, this heritage hotel is hands down the best place to stay in Henningsvær. The rooms are styled in cool greys and creams; most have watery views, and some have fun loft-space beds for kids. Its restaurant, the Bluefish, is excellent – the menu prides itself on serving fish species 'you've probably never heard of'.

🍴 Eating

⭐**Kafé Lysstoperiet** CAFE €
(☑ 905 51 877; www.henningsvarlys.no; Gammelveien 2; mains 98-149kr; ⊙ 10am-8pm) This casual place in the heart of town is wildly (and deservedly) popular. The organic food ranges from Lofoten's best cakes and sweet treats to light meals such as soup, open sandwiches, pies, pasta salad and homemade pizzas. There are a couple of small outside tables, but the interior is warmly eclectic and filled with personality. Great coffee, too.

Klatre Kafeen CAFE €€
(☑ 909 54 619; www.nordnorskklatreskole.no/klatrekafeen; Misværveien; mains 140-210kr; ⊙ 11am-1am Sun-Thu, 11am-2.30am Fri & Sat mid-Jun–mid-Aug, 6pm-1am Wed, 6pm-2am Fri & Sat mid-Aug–mid-Jun) With a few tables out over the water and an inviting interior dining area, this relaxed place is run by the neighbouring North Norwegian Climbing School (p351). The food ranges from open shrimp sandwiches and couscous salad to codfish soup. Watch for live music on Friday and Saturday nights in summer. It also has some simple rooms (dorm/single/double 300/500/600kr).

★ **Fiskekrogen** SEAFOOD €€€
([📞] 76 07 46 52; www.fiskekrogen.no; Dreyersgate 29; mains lunch 185-265kr, dinner 245-325kr; ⊘12.30-10pm Jun-Aug, shorter hours rest of year) This dockside restaurant – a favourite of the Norwegian royal family – is Henningsvær's culinary claim to fame. Try, in particular, the outstanding fish soup (198kr), but there's everything else on the menu from fish and chips to fried cod tongues. Between 4pm and 5pm in summer it serves fish soup and seafood stew only. Quite right, too.

❶ Getting There & Away

There's a regular bus to Henningsvær from Svolvær (50kr, 40 minutes, at least six daily) via Kabelvåg (35 minutes).

Nusfjord
POP 50

If you take one detour off the E10 between Svolvær and Å, make it Nusfjord, one of the loveliest villages in Norway's north. The road in here, just 6km long, is a stunning byway, hemmed in by towering bare crags. The ox-blood-red wooden buildings of Nusfjord, which feels like a hidden treasure, hug its tiny, tucked-away harbour. Many artists consider it to be the essence of Lofoten but be warned: so do tour operators and in summer it gets so crowded that parking attendants manoeuvre vehicles this way and that. But don't let this put you off – even with all this, it's worth every second you spend here.

It costs 50kr for adults (children under 12 free) just to walk around plus a further 50kr to see *The People & The Fish,* a 12-minute video about Nusfjord, past and present.

◎ Sights

In the country store that recently celebrated its centenary, upper shelves are crammed with vintage cans, bottles and boxes while the lower ones are stocked with contemporary fare. There's the old cod-liver-oil factory, boathouse, sawmill and a cluster of more than 40 *rorbuer* (fisher's huts).

To snap the postcard-perfect shot of Nusfjord that you'll see everywhere around the island, you'll need to climb the rocky slope above the closed end of the little harbour. The path can be slippery after rain.

🛏 Sleeping & Eating

Nusfjord Rorbuer CABIN €€
([📞]76 09 30 20; www.classicnorway.no/hotell/nusfjord/rorbuene; rorbuer 1395-2795kr) Many of the *rorbuer* here are quite simple on the inside (most have photos on the website), but they're faithful representations of the traditional fishing cabin and they're all extremely comfortable. Apart from anything else, it's the wonderful silence that descends on the village in the evening that's the real draw. Reception is at the village entrance.

Karoline Restaurant CAFE €€
([📞]76 09 30 20; mains from 149kr; ⊘11am-4pm & 5-10pm mid-Jun–mid-Aug, shorter hours rest of year) Wonderful views from the terrace, local dishes with fish in abundance and a casual atmosphere add up to a fine place for a meal – if you can snaffle a table, which can be a challenge.

❶ Getting There & Away

There's no public transport in Nusfjord. Parking is on a hill at the entrance to the village.

Reine
POP 309

Reine is a characterless place but gosh, it looks splendid from above, beside its placid lagoon and backed by the sheer rock face of Reinebringen. You get a great view from the head of the road that turns to the village from the E10 at the southern end of town. This is one of the signature Lofoten views you'll have seen on postcards across the archipelago – pray for some sun.

❶ Getting There & Away

Buses between Svolvær or Leknes and Å pass through Reine.

Sakrisøy

In the heart of some stunning country on an arm of Reinefjord, Sakrisøy is a small, pretty island with services far out of proportion to its size – two places to eat, a place to stay and plenty to do.

🏃 Activities

Aqua Lofoten Coast Adventure AS BOATING
([📞] 990 19 042; www.aqualofoten.no; E10) From June to mid-August, three-hour boat trips are run by Aqua Lofoten to the bird- and fish-rich Moskenesstraumen maelstrom, as

well as other nearby attractions, with snorkelling and fishing also possible.

Sleeping & Eating

Sakrisøy Rorbuer CABIN €€

(76 09 21 43; www.sakrisoyrorbuer.no; cabin 1100-2150kr; P 🛜) Sakrisøy Rorbuer is a relatively authentic complex of ochre-coloured cottages hovering above the water. They're postcard-perfect from the outside and the supremely comfortable interiors have an authentic wood-panelled aesthetic. Views are splendid in this area – you don't have to walk far to see what we mean.

★ Anitas Sjømat CAFE €

(900 61 566; www.sakrisoy.no/sjomat; E10; 10am-8pm mid-Jun–mid-Aug, shorter hours rest of year) Part delicatessen and part waterside cafe, this fab place sells all sorts of stockfish snacks, Kong Oskar sardines and dishes such as uncommonly good fish soup, fish cakes, fresh shrimp and fish burgers – our favourite is the pulled-salmon burger. Go on, be adventurous, try the seagulls' eggs...and don't be put off by the fearsome dried cod heads outside.

Underhuset Restaurant NORWEGIAN, SEAFOOD €€

(900 35 419; www.sakrisoyrorbuer.no/restaurant; mains lunch from 149kr, dinner 242-315kr; noon-11pm mid-Jun–mid-Aug, 4-11pm rest of year) The Sakrisøy Rorbuer's more formal (though only just...) restaurant doesn't mess around with a wide variety of dishes – it's cod/bacalao, sirloin of ox or a bucket of shrimp. And they're all exceptionally good. A terrific range of local beers and a wickedly good homemade chocolate mousse round things out nicely.

ⓘ Getting There & Away

Sakrisøy lies along the E10 – buses between Leknes and Å pass through here.

Å

POP 1162

At the southern tip of Moskenesøy and the Lofoten Islands, the bijou village of Å (appropriately, the last letter of the Norwegian alphabet), sometimes referred to (and signposted across Lofoten) as Å i Lofoten, is something of a living museum – a preserved fishing village with a shoreline of red *rorbuer* (fisher's huts), cod-drying racks and picture-postcard scenes at almost every turn. It's an almost feudal place, carved up between two families, now living very much from tourism but in its time

a significant fishing port (more than 700,000 cod would be hung out to dry here every season until as recently as WWII).

Do the village a favour and leave your vehicle at the car park and walk in through the short tunnel.

◉ Sights

★ Norsk Fiskeværsmuseum MUSEUM

(Norwegian Fishing Village Museum; 76 09 14 88; www.museumnord.no/fiskevarsmuseum; adult/child 80/40kr; 9am-7pm mid-Jun–Aug, 10am-5pm Sep-May) This museum takes in 14 of Å's 19th-century boathouses, storehouses, fishing cottages, farmhouses and commercial buildings. Highlights (pick up a pamphlet in English at reception) include Europe's oldest cod-liver-oil factory, where you'll be treated to a taste of the wares and can pick up a bottle to stave off those winter sniffles; the smithy, who still makes cod-liver-oil lamps; the still-functioning bakery, established in 1844; the old *rorbu* with period furnishings; and a couple of Lofoten fishing boats.

Sleeping

Å-Hamna Rorbuer & Vandrerhjem HOSTEL €

(76 09 12 11; www.lofotenferie.com; dm 280kr, 2-4 bed cabins 1200-1700kr, 6-bed cabin 2150kr) Most of the *rorbuer* (fisher's huts) in Å have been turned into holiday cabins, offering the chance for an atmospheric night's sleep. Wood-clad inside and out, the cabins are simple but cosy, and some are furnished with antiques and fishing ephemera.

Å Feskarbrygga Rorbuer RORBUER €€

(911 61 999; www.lofoten-info.no/aa-fb; cabins 1000-1400kr, 4-bed apt 900kr) Open year-round this collection of self-catering *rorbuers* and apartments lies scattered around the harbour area; furnishings are simple rather than luxurious. They're at their best after day trippers have headed home.

✖ Eating

★ Bakeri BAKERY €

(76 09 14 88; 9am-3pm daily mid-May–Aug, shorter hours rest of year) In a building that dates from 1844 and whose stone oven dates from the same year, this atmospheric bakery is the essence of Å. It turns out fresh bread every day, plus a small number of other pastries, among which is the utterly divine *kanelsnurr* (cinnamon roll; 35kr) that tastes every bit as good as its rather lovely name sounds.

Brygga Restaurant SEAFOOD €€€
(☑ 76 09 11 21; mains 195-329kr, lunch specials 185-205kr; ☺ 11am-10pm Jun-Sep) Hovering above the water, this is Å's one decent sit-down dining choice. The menu, as is right and proper in a village with such a strong fishing tradition, includes mainly things with fins.

❶ Getting There & Away

Å is pretty much as far south as you can go in Lofoten.

There are between three and six buses a day to Moskenes (52kr, 10 minutes), where you can catch the car ferry back to Bodø on the mainland.

Most buses continue onwards to Reine, Marka, Hamnøy and Leknes.

Vesterålen

Although the landscapes here aren't as dramatic as those in Lofoten, they tend to be much wilder and the forested mountainous regions of the island of Hinnøya are a unique corner of Norway's largely treeless northern coast. There are many reasons to visit, but our top three would be whale-watching from Andenes or Stø, a drive along Andøya's lovely west coast and a visit to the reborn hamlet of Nyksund.

Tromsø

POP 72,681

Located 400km north of the Arctic Circle at 69°N, the small town of Tromsø bills itself as Norway's gateway to the Arctic, and there's definitely more than a hint of polar atmosphere around town. Surrounded by chilly fjords and craggy peaks that remain snowcapped for much of the year, Tromsø sits on the eastern edge of Tromsøya, and is linked to the mainland by a gracefully arched bridge.

In previous centuries, the town was a centre for seal hunting, trapping and fishing, and was later a launch pad for several important Arctic expeditions, including some led by Roald Amundsen. These days it's best known as one of the better places in the north of the country to spot the Northern Lights.

It's also a notoriously lively city, with a large university, a happening cultural calendar and an animated nightlife. (Tromsø prides itself on having more pubs per capita than any other Norwegian town.)

◉ Sights

★ **Arctic Cathedral** CHURCH
(Ishavskatedralen; ☑ 476 80 668; Hans Nilsens veg 41; adult/child 50kr/free, organ recitals 70-170kr; ☺ 9am-7pm Mon-Sat, 1-7pm Sun Jun–mid-Aug, 3-6pm mid-Aug–mid-May, from 2pm Feb) The 11 triangles of the Arctic Cathedral (1965), aka Tromsdalen Church, suggest glacial crevasses and auroral curtains. The glowing stained-glass window that occupies the east end depicts Christ descending to earth. The west end is filled by a futuristic organ and icicle-like lamps of Czech crystal. Unfortunately, its position beside one of Tromsø's main thoroughfares somewhat spoils the serenity outside. It's on the southern side of the Bruvegen bridge, about 1km from town. Take bus 20 or 24.

★ **Fjellheisen** CABLE CAR
(☑ 77 63 87 37; www.fjellheisen.no; Solliv.eien 12; adult/child 170/60kr; ☺ 10am-1am late May–mid-Aug, shorter hours rest of the year) For a fine view of the city and the midnight sun, take the cable car to the top of Mt Storsteinen (421m). There's a restaurant at the top, from where a network of hiking routes radiates. Take bus 26 to get here.

★ **Polar Museum** MUSEUM
(Polarmuseet; ☑ 77 62 33 60; www.uit.no/tmu/polarmuseet; Søndre Tollbodgate 11; adult/child 60/30kr; ☺ 9am-6pm mid-Jun–mid-Aug, 11am-5pm rest of the year) Fittingly for a town that was the launch pad for many pioneering expeditions to the Pole, Tromsø's fascinating Polar Museum is a rollicking romp through life in the Arctic, taking in everything from the history of trapping to the ground-breaking expeditions of Nansen and Amundsen. There are some fascinating artefacts and black-and-white archive photos; the stuffed remains of various formerly fuzzy, once-blubbery polar creatures are rather less fun. It's in a harbourside building that served as Tromsø's customs house from 1833 to 1970.

★ **Polaria** MUSEUM, AQUARIUM
(☑ 77 75 01 11; www.polaria.no; Hjalmar Johansens gate 12; adult/child 130/65kr; ☺ 10am-7pm mid-May–Aug, 10am-5pm Sep–mid-May) This Arctic-themed attraction provides a multimedia introduction to northern Norway and Svalbard. Kick things off by watching the two films *In the Land of the Northern Lights* and *Spitsbergen – Arctic Wilderness*, then follow the Arctic walkway past exhibits on shrinking sea ice, the aurora borealis, aquariums of cold-water fish and – the big draw

– some yapping, playful bearded seals (feeding time is at 12.30pm year-round, plus 3pm in summer or 3.30pm in winter).

🏃 Activities

For many people, the main reason to visit Tromsø is the chance to hunt for the Northern Lights. There are lots of companies around town offering aurora-spotting safaris. Go with a small, independent operator, otherwise you might end up with a coach party from one of the city's big hotels.

Summer activities in the Tromsø hinterland include hiking, fishing, visits to Sami camps, food-centric excursions, boat sightseeing and sea kayaking. Trips to scenic locations to see the midnight sun and general sightseeing trips are widely available. Wildlife enthusiasts can also go looking for seabirds and seals.

In and around Tromsø (operators will normally collect you from your hotel), winter activities outnumber those in summer, and include chasing the Northern Lights, cross-country skiing, Sami cultural visits, reindeer herding, reindeer- and dog-sledding, snowshoe safaris, ice fishing and snowmobiling. Whale-watching in a variety of boats (including kayaks!) is also an exciting possibility, with the season running from late October to mid-January or into February.

The tourist office's *Summer Activities in Tromsø* and its winter equivalent provide comprehensive checklists of tours and activities.

Tromsø Villmarkssenter   OUTDOORS
(📞 77 69 60 02; www.villmarkssenter.no; Stortorget 1, Kystens Hus) Tromsø Villmarkssenter offers dog-sled excursions ranging from a one-day spin to a four-day trek with overnight camping. This booking office is in town; the centre, 24km south of Tromsø on Kvaløya, also offers a range of summer activities such as trekking, glacier hiking and sea kayaking, as well as seal and seabird safaris.

Tromsø Friluftsenter   ADVENTURE SPORTS
(📞 907 51 583; www.tromso-friluftsenter.no; Kvaløyvågvegen 669) Tromsø Friluftsenter runs summer sightseeing, boat trips and a full range of winter activities (including trips to Sami camps). One intriguing possibility is their five-hour humpback-whale and orca safari from late November to mid-January. Book online or at Tromsø's tourist office (p357).

Wandering Owl Tours   ADVENTURE
(📞 48460081;www.wanderingowl.com;Sommerlyst vegen 7a) One of the more creative operators

---

WHALE-WATCHING IN VESTERÅLEN

Far and away Andøya's biggest outfit, **Whale Safari** (📞 76 11 56 00; www.whalesafari. no; Hamnegata; adult/concession/child 975/850/690kr; ⊘ late May–early Sep) runs popular whale-watching cruises between late May and mid-September. It also operates the **Whale Centre** (Havnegate 1; adult/child 110/55kr; ⊘ 8.30am-7pm mid-Jun–mid-Aug). Tours begin with a guided visit to the centre, followed by a two- to four- or five-hour boat trip. There's a good chance of spotting (and getting really close to) sperm whales in summer.

The smaller of Andenes' whale-watching outfits, with its base on the docks just off the road to the lighthouse, **Sea Safari Andenes** (📞 916 74 960; www.seasafariandenes.no; Hamnegata; whale-watching adult/child 995/850kr, birdwatching 495/400kr; ⊘ May-Sep) runs 1½- to three-hour whale-watching trips in smaller boats with up to two daily departures in season. It also offers shorter seal- and birdwatching trips (1½ hours, adult/child 450/400kr), plus winter outings to look for orcas, humpbacks and fin whales.

Whale-watching (including from November to March) is only a part of what **Wild Ocean** (📞 469 32 899; www.wildocean.no) does here – it also runs coastal sightseeing, fishing and birdwatching trips. It doesn't have an office – make your booking through the **tourist office** (📞 76 14 12 03; www.visitandoy.info; Kong Hans gate 8; ⊘ 9am-5.30pm Mon-Fri, 10am-5.30pm Sat, noon-4.30pm Sun mid-Jun–mid-Aug, 9am-4pm early Jun & late Aug, shorter hours rest of year).

Summer whale safaris have returned to Stø with the excellent **Arctic Whale Tours** (📞 76 13 43 00; www.arcticwhaletours.com; adult/child 1100/600kr; ⊘ 10am late May–Aug) . Its all-day safaris offer a whale guarantee – if you don't see at least one whale or dolphin, you get a free second trip. Sperm whales are most commonly sighted. The boat trip also visits seabird and seal colonies, making for a wonderful day's outing.

around town, Wandering Owl Tours has excellent summer guided hikes, a trip to a wilderness sauna and scenic driving tours from mid-May to mid-August, with a host of winter activities that include northern-lights photography workshops.

Active Tromsø ADVENTURE
(☑481 37 133; www.activetromso.no) An excellent company offering the full range of summer and winter activities, with dog-sledding expeditions a particular speciality – including overnight husky trips with the chance to spot the aurora en route. Bookings can be made online or at the tourist office (p357).

Arctic Adventure Tours ADVENTURE
(☑456 35 288; www.arcticadventuretours.no; Straumsvegen 993) A range of activities from dog-sledding and skiing in winter, to fishing and hiking expeditions in summer. You can book ahead via their website or at Tromsø's tourist office (p357).

🎉 Festivals & Events

Tromsø International Film Festival FILM
(☑77 75 30 90; www.tiff.no; ⊙mid-Jan) One of the world's most northerly film festivals kicks off for a week in mid-January, with film screenings and talks at various locations around town (there are even a few outdoor screenings for hard-core film-goers). As you'd expect, there's a strong Arctic theme to many of the films.

Sami Week CULTURAL
(www.msm.no/sami-week-in-tromsoe.242995. en.html; ⊙early Feb) Includes the national reindeer-sledge championship, where skilled Sami whoop and crack the whip along the main street in Tromsø. It centres on the week surrounding Sami National Day (6 February).

Northern Lights Festival MUSIC
(☑77 68 90 70; www.nordlysfestivalen.no; ⊙Jan) Six days of music of all genres. If it coincides with a Northern-Lights spectacular, you've hit the jackpot.

Midnight Sun Marathon SPORTS
(www.msm.no; ⊙Jun) The world's most northerly marathon is held one Saturday in June. In January there's also the Polar Night Half Marathon.

🛏 Sleeping

Smart Hotel Tromsø HOTEL €
(☑415 36 500; www.smarthotel.no/en/tromso; Vestregata 12; d from 695kr; 🛜) The northern-

most outpost of this budget mini-chain offers some of the best rates in town, and it's a fine base – as long as you don't mind the boxy rooms, basic facilities and institutional decor (battleship-grey is the colour of choice, combined with graffiti-style slogans like 'You Are Smart'). It's deservedly popular, so book ahead. The buffet breakfast costs 110kr.

★ Tromsø Bed & Books GUESTHOUSE €€
(☑77 02 98 00; www.bedandbooks.no; Strandvegen 45; s/d 850/950kr; 🛜) Run by a pair of seasoned globetrotters, this lovely guesthouse has two 'homes' – a Fisherman's and a Writer's – all stuffed with books, retro furniture, old maps and curios, and thoughtfully designed for budget travellers. The rooms can feel cramped when full, and are noisy, but that's part of the budget trade-off. There's no breakfast, but both houses have shared kitchens.

Radisson Blu Hotel Tromsø HOTEL €€
(☑77 60 00 00; www.radissonblu.com/hotel-tromso; Sjøgata 7; s/d from 995/1295kr; 🅿@🛜) Bedrooms have been comprehensively renovated and an attractive new wing has been grafted onto the solid, rectangular block of the original building. Of its 269 rooms (it's worth the 200kr extra for one in the new wing), around half have harbour views. It runs a decent pub, the Rorbua, and a fine Arctic Menu restaurant.

★ Scandic Ishavshotel HOTEL €€€
(☑77 66 64 00; www.scandichotels.no; Fredrik Langes gate 2; d/ste from 1699/2499kr; 🅿🛜) This is the prime spot in Tromsø if you want a waterside view – the Scandic Ishavshotel's architecture evokes an ocean-going vessel, complete with a flag-topped mast and crow's nest. The rooms are sleek, smart and business-like, in cappuccino-browns and slate-greys. Breakfast is included; rooms are 20% cheaper on weekends.

🍴 Eating

★ Risø CAFE €
(☑416 64 516; www.risoe-mk.no; Strandgata 32; mains 95-179kr; ⊙7.30am-5pm Mon-Fri, 9am-5pm Sat) You'll find this popular coffee and lunch bar packed throughout most of the day: young trendies come in for their hand-brewed Chemex coffee, while local workers pop in for the daily specials, open-faced sandwiches and delicious cakes. It's small, and the tables are packed in tight, so you might have to queue.

★ Emma's Under NORWEGIAN €€

(☑ 77 63 77 30; www.emmasdrommekjokken.no; Kirkegata; lunch mains 165-335kr; ☉ 11am-10pm Mon-Fri, noon-10pm Sat) Homely and down-to-earth Norwegian cuisine is the dish of the day here. You'll find hearty dishes such as fish gratin, king crab and baked *klippfisk* on the lunch menu, served in a cosy space designed to echo a traditional kitchen à la grandma. Upstairs is the more formal Emma's Drømmekjøkken (p357), which shares its menu with Emma's Under after 5.30pm.

★ Kitchen
& Table NORWEGIAN, INTERNATIONAL €€€

(☑ 77 66 84 84; www.kitchenandtable.no/tromso; Kaigata 6; mains 235-375kr; ☉ 5-10pm Mon-Sat, to 9pm Sun) Combining a touch of Manhattan style with Arctic ingredients, chef Marcus Samuelsson serves up some of the freshest and most original tastes in Tromsø – there's reindeer fillet with mango chutney, reindeer ratatouille, burgers with quinoa or kimchi, and even slow-cooked Moroccan lamb.

★ Emma's Drømmekjøkken NORWEGIAN €€€

(☑ 77 63 77 30; www.emmasdrommekjokken.no; Kirkegata; mains 285-365kr, 3-/5-course menu 390/630kr; ☉ 6pm-midnight Mon-Sat) Upstairs from Emma's Under (p357), this stylish and highly regarded place pulls in discriminating diners with its imaginative cuisine, providing traditional Norwegian dishes married with top-quality local ingredients such as *lutefisk* (stockfish), blueberry-marinated halibut, ox tenderloin and gratinated king crab. Advance booking is essential.

🍷 Drinking & Nightlife

Ølhallen Pub PUB

(☑ 77 62 45 80; www.olhallen.no; Storgata 4; ☉ 10am-7.30pm Mon-Wed, 10am-12.30am Thu-Sat) Reputedly the oldest pub in town, and once the hang-out for salty fishermen and Arctic sailors, this is now the brewpub for the excellent Mack Brewery (Mack Ølbryggeri; ☑ 77 62 45 80; www.mack.no; Storgata 5). There are 67 ales to try, including eight on tap – so it might take you a while (and a few livers) to work your way through them all.

Kaffebønna CAFE

(☑ 77 63 94 00; www.kaffebonna.no; Stortorget 3; ☉ 8am-6pm Mon-Fri, 9am-6pm Sat, 10am-6pm Sun) One of our favourite Tromsø cafes, this cool little spot right in the town centre does the city's best coffee, accompanied by tasty pastries.

Blå Rock Café BAR

(☑ 77 61 00 20; www.facebook.com/Blaarock; Strandgata 14/16; ☉ 11.30am-2am Mon-Thu, 11.30am-3am Fri & Sat, 1pm-2am Sun) The loudest, most raving place in town has theme evenings, almost 50 brands of beer, occasional live bands and weekend DJs. The music is rock, naturally. Every Monday hour is a happy hour.

ℹ Information

Tourist Office (☑ 77 61 00 00; www.visit tromso.no; Kirkegata 2; ☉ 9am-5pm Mon-Fri, 10am-5pm Sat & Sun Jan-Mar & mid-May–Aug, shorter hours rest of year; ☎) In a wooden building by the harbour, Tromsø's busy tourist office books accommodation and activities, and has free wi-fi. It also publishes the comprehensive *Tromsø Guide*.

ℹ Getting There & Away

AIR

Tromsø Airport (☑ 77 64 84 00; www.avinor. no/flyplass/tromso) is about 5km from the town centre, on the western side of Tromsøya and is the main airport for the far north. Destinations with direct Scandinavian Airlines flights to/from the airport include Oslo, Narvik/Harstad, Bodø, Trondheim, Alta, Hammerfest, Kirkenes and Longyearbyen.

Norwegian (www.norwegian.no) flies to and from most major cities in Norway, plus UK destinations including London (Gatwick), Edinburgh and Dublin.

Widerøe (www.wideroe.no) has several flights a day to Svolvær and Leknes in the Lofoten Islands. All flights are via Bodø.

BOAT

Tromsø is a major stop on the Hurtigruten coastal-ferry route. All ferries on the route will stop at the **Hurtigruten ferry quay** (Samuel Arnesens quay), until the opening of the new terminal (at the time of research scheduled for autumn 2018).

Express boats connect Tromsø and Harstad (2½ hours), via Finnsnes (1¼ hours), two to four times daily and leave from the **Express Ferry Terminal** (Strandskillet).

BUS

The **main bus terminal** (Prostneset; Samuel Arnesens gate) is on Kaigata, beside the Hurtigruten ferry quay. There are up to three daily express buses to/from Narvik (280kr, 4¼ hours) and one to/from Bodø (410kr, 6½ hours). To get further south, you need to catch the daily bus to Fauske, then the night train to Trondheim and Oslo – but it's a long and pricey journey, so it's much more practical to fly.

Heading north, there's a daily bus to Alta (620kr, 6½ hours). The fare includes the two Lyngen ferries.

Tromskortet (www.tromskortet.no) has a daily bus on weekdays to Narvik, where there's a connecting bus to Svolvær (eight hours) in the Lofoten Islands.

CAR & MOTORCYCLE

Having your own vehicle is easily the best way to negotiate Norway's far northern reaches. All major car-hire companies have offices at the airport. Contrasting with steep rates in summer (when it's essential to reserve in advance), car rental can be very reasonable in winter.

FINNMARK

Alta

POP 14,472

⊙ Sights

★ **Alta Museum** MUSEUM
(📞 417 56 330; www.alta.museum.no; Altaveien 19; adult/child May-Sep 110/35kr, Oct-Apr 75/20kr; ⊙ 8am-8pm mid-Jun–Aug, shorter hours rest of year) This superb museum is in Hjemmeluft, at the western end of town. It features exhibits and displays on Sami culture, Finnmark military history, the Alta hydroelectric project and the aurora borealis (northern lights). The cliffs around it, a Unesco World Heritage site, are incised with around 6000 late–Stone Age carvings, dating from 6000 to 2000 years ago, and it's these petroglyphs that will live longest in the memory.

★ **Northern Lights Cathedral** CHURCH
(Løkkeveien; adult/child 50/25kr, incl Borealis Alta show 150/75kr; ⊙ 11am-9pm Mon-Sat & 4-9pm Sun mid-Jun–mid-Aug, 11am-3pm Mon-Sat rest of year) Opened in 2013, the daringly designed Northern Lights Cathedral, next to the Scandic Hotel Alta, is one of the architectural icons of the north, with its swirling pyramid structure clad in rippling titanium sheets. The interior is similarly eye-catching, with an utterly modern 4.3m-high bronze *Christ* by Danish artist Peter Brandes – note how the figure gets lighter as your eyes move up the body.

Sautso-Alta Canyon CANYON
The Altaelva hydroelectric project has had very little effect on the most scenic stretch of river, which slides through 400m-deep Sautso, northern Europe's grandest canyon.

🏃 Activities

★ **Trasti i Trine** DOG SLEDDING, COOKING
(Northern Lights Husky; 📞 458 53 144; www.trasti-ogtrine.no; Gargiaveien 29; 2hr dog-sledding adult/child 1450/750kr) Dog-sledding trips from 2½ hours to multiday expeditions. They also run cooking courses, have special meals with commentary and offer accommodation (p359). Located about 10km outside Alta.

Alta Adventure ADVENTURE SPORTS
(📞 78 43 40 50; www.alta-adventure.no) Trekking, canoeing and salmon fishing. Also, on request and not something you'll do around home: ptarmigan hunting.

Sorrisniva BOATING
(📞 78 43 33 78; www.sorrisniva.no; Sorrisniva 20; 1/2hr riverboat tours per person 895/1495kr) Sorrisniva, at the **Sorrisniva Igloo Hotel** (B&B s/d 3000/5000kr; ⊙ mid-Dec–mid-Apr; 🅿), runs several riverboat rides along the Altaelva. Boats set out at noon daily from June to mid-September. They also offer winter snowmobiling. To reach Sorrisniva, head 16km south of Alta along the Rv93, then a further 6.5km along a marked road.

Winter Activities

Sorrisniva (p358) also has 80 snowmobiles, the largest such fleet in northern Norway. It offers guided outings (one-/two-person snowmobile 1450/1700kr), and, after your exertions, you can relax in its steaming hot tub. **Gargia Fjellstue** (📞 78 43 33 51; www.gargia-fjellstue.no; Gargiaveien 96; r from 1100kr) also offers a range of summer and winter outdoor activities.

Holmen Husky DOG SLEDDING
(📞 78 43 66 45; www.holmenhusky.no; Holmen 48; 3hr dog-sledding per adult/child 1450/625kr) Holmen Husky specialises in dog-sledding (mid-December to April; dog-carting in summer), with outings ranging from three hours to five days.

🛏 Sleeping

★ **Wisløff Camping** CAMPGROUND €
(📞 78 43 43 03; www.wisloeff.no; per person/site 50/220kr, cabins 500-1450kr) One of three excellent riverside campsites in Ovre Alta, 3.5km south of the E6 along the Rv93 to Kautokeino, Wisløff Camping was declared Campground of the Year in 2000, and it still deserves the accolade. Travellers also sing its praises.

★ **Trasti i Trine** LODGE €€
(☑ 78 40 30 40; www.trastiogtrine.no/accommodation; s/d from 750/1300kr) Some 10km outside Alta and in a forest down by the river, this wonderful wooden lodge is classy, sophisticated and warmly inviting all at once. The on-site husky farm adds loads of personality, the rooms are impeccably turned out and the food is outstanding. The communal living area has a fireplace and overall it's the kind of place you'll never want to leave.

Scandic Hotel Alta HOTEL €€€
(☑ 78 48 27 00; www.scandichotels.no; Løkkeveien 61; s/d from 1450/1690kr; @ 🕏) Alta's classiest hotel has attractive rooms (some have large photos of the Northern Lights) and excellent service, although some rooms are on the small side. Try for one of the west-facing rooms with views over the Northern Lights Cathedral. The **Alta restaurant** (mains from 265kr, dinner buffet per person 295kr; ⊘ 5-11pm) is also also excellent and there's a bar (closed Sundays).

✗ Eating

Du Verden Matbar NORWEGIAN, INTERNATIONAL €€
(☑ 459 08 213; www.duverden.no/alta; Markedsgata 21; mains 185-365kr; ⊘ 10am-midnight Mon-Sat, 1-10.20pm Sun) A cool brasserie-style place, Du Verden does fish soup, king crab, stockfish, shellfish platters, reindeer fillet and tapas, as well as salads and a wide range of drinks.

★ **Restaurant Haldde** NORWEGIAN €€€
(☑ 78 48 22 22; Fogdebakken 6; mains 249-349kr; ⊘ 4-11pm Mon-Sat, 2-10pm Sun) ✈ This quality restaurant within **Thon Hotel Vica** (☑ 78 48 22 22; www.thonhotels.no; Fogdebakken 6; s/d from 950/1200kr; P @ 🕏) relies almost entirely upon local ingredients in the preparation of choice dishes such as reindeer steak, grilled stockfish and its *Flavour of Finnmark* dessert of cloudberries and cowberry-blueberry sorbet.

ℹ Information

Tourist Office (☑ 991 00 022; www.visitalta. no; Bjørn Wirkolasvei 11; ⊘ 9am-8pm daily mid-Jun–mid-Aug, shorter hours rest of year) This should be your first stop for organising summer and winter activities.

ℹ Getting There & Away

Alta's **airport** (☑ 78 44 95 55; www.avinor.no) is 4km northeast of Sentrum at Elvebakken. SAS has direct flights to/from Oslo, Tromsø, Hammerfest, Lakselv and Vadsø. Norwegian connects Alta with Oslo.

Buses leave from the terminal in Sentrum:
Hammerfest (335kr, 2¼ hours, two daily)
Honningsvåg (496kr, four hours, one daily)
Karasjok (525kr, 4¾ hours, two daily except Saturday)
Kautokeino (298kr, 2¼ hours, one daily except Saturday)
Tromsø (620kr, 6½ hours, one daily)

Hammerfest

POP 7938

Welcome to Norway's, and perhaps even the world's, northernmost town – other Norwegian communities, while further north, are, Hammerfest vigorously argues, too small to qualify as towns!

If you're arriving on the Hurtigruten coastal ferry, you'll have only 1½ hours to pace around, pick up an Arctic souvenir or two and visit the Royal & Ancient Polar Bear Society. For most visitors that will be ample, Hurtigruten or not.

⊙ Sights

★ **Royal & Ancient Polar Bear Society** MUSEUM
(Isbjørklubben; ☑ 78 41 21 85; www.isbjornklubben.no; Hamnegata 3; ⊘ 8am-6pm Jun & Jul, 9am-4pm Mon-Fri, 10am-2pm Sat & Sun Aug-May) **FREE** Dedicated to preserving Hammerfest culture, the Royal & Ancient Polar Bear Society (founded in 1963) features exhibits on Arctic hunting and local history and shares premises with the tourist office. For 200kr you can become a life member and get a certificate, ID card, sticker and pin. At times, the link to polar bears here can feel a little tenuous. But if you think of the place in terms of the Norwegian name (Isbjørklubben, simply Polar Bear Club), you're less likely to be disappointed.

★ **Hammerfest Kirke** CHURCH
(Kirkegata 33; ⊘ 9am-2pm mid-Jun–mid-Aug) The design of Hammerfest's contemporary church, consecrated in 1961, was inspired by the racks used for drying fish in the salty sea air all across northern Norway. Behind the altar, the glorious stained-glass window positively glows in the summer sun, while the wooden frieze along the organ gallery depicts highlights of the town's history. The chapel in the cemetery across the street is the only building in town to have survived WWII.

🛏 Sleeping

⭐ Smarthotel Hammerfest — HOTEL €€
(📱415 36 500; www.smarthotel.no/hammerfest; Strandgata 32; s/d 950/1050kr; 📶) From the outside, Smarthotel Hammerfest looks like a stylish designer hotel, so it comes as a pleasant surprise to find simple but stylish contemporary rooms at excellent prices within; prices also drop considerably when things are quiet. The rooms with harbour views are best, and there's a decent buffet breakfast included in the price.

Scandic Hotel Hammerfest — HOTEL €€
(📱78 42 57 00; www.scandichotels.no; Sørøygata 15; d 950-1799kr; 🅿@📶) Constructed in agreeable mellow brick, this hotel has an attractive if somewhat dated bar and lounge, and well-furnished rooms – they're worth it if you get a harbour view, but overpriced if not. Some of the bathrooms are so small that they require a contortionist's flexibility. Its Arctic Menu restaurant, Skansen Mat og Vinstue (p360), serves excellent local fare.

🍴 Eating

Skansen Mat og Vinstue — NORWEGIAN €€€
(📱78 42 57 00; www.scandichotels.no; Sørøygata 15; mains 185-355kr; ⊗6-11pm) A cut above most of the other restaurants in town, the Scandic Hotel Hammerfest's restaurant serves up fine local specialities such as king-crab soup and reindeer stew, although the menu changes with the seasons. Sea views are thrown in for good measure.

⭐ Havørna — SEAFOOD €€
(📱480 29 661; www.havorna.com; Strandgata 16; mains lunch 88-156kr, dinner 185-318kr; ⊗1-10pm) The hugely popular Havørna couldn't be closer to where the fishing fleet comes in, and it serves up suitably fresh fish, from fish cakes or fish and chips for lunch to fish soup or oven-baked salmon in the evening. It also does takeaway.

ℹ Information

Tourist Office (📱78 41 21 85; www.visit hammerfest.no; Hamnegata 3; ⊗8am-6pm Jun & Jul, 9am-4pm Mon-Fri & 10am-2pm Sat & Sun Aug-May; 📶) Has free wi-fi and rents out electric bikes for 159/399kr per hour/day.

ℹ Getting There & Away

Buses (Hamnegata) run to/from Alta (335kr, 2¼ hours, two daily), Honningsvåg (468kr, 3½ hours, one to two daily) and Karasjok (450kr, 4¼ hours, twice daily except Saturday), with one service extending to Kirkenes (1155kr, 10¼ hours) via Tana Bru (810kr, eight hours) four times weekly.

The **Hurtigruten coastal ferry** (Hurtigrutenkai, Hamnegata) stops in Hammerfest for 1½ hours in each direction. A Hurigruten hop to Tromsø (11 hours) or Honningsvåg (five hours) makes a comfortable alternative to a long bus journey.

There's a **taxi office** (📱78 41 12 34; www. hammerfesttaxi.no) opposite the tourist office.

Nordkapp

Nordkapp is the one attraction in northern Norway that everybody seems to visit. It is a tourist trap, however – billing itself as the northernmost point in continental Europe, it sucks in visitors by the busload – some 200,000 every year.

Nearer to the North Pole than to Oslo, Nordkapp sits at latitude 71°10'21" N, where the sun never drops below the horizon from mid-May to the end of July. Long before other Europeans took an interest, it was a sacrificial site for the Sami, who believed it had special powers.

Yes, it's a rip-off, but Nordkapp is a stunning, hauntingly beautiful place. Even after the novelty wears off, it's the view that thrills the most. In reasonable weather you can gaze down at the wild surf more than 300m below, watch the mists roll in and simply enjoy the moment.

◉ Sights

Nordkapp Visitor Centre — VISITOR CENTRE
(📱78 47 68 60; www.visitnordkapp.net; ⊗11am-1am mid-May–mid-Aug, 11am-10pm mid-end Aug, 11am-3pm Sep–mid-May) Presiding over a scene of considerable natural beauty is this visitor centre, a vast bunker of a place, topped by a giant, intrusive golf ball. Within you'll find a detailed account of WWII naval actions off the cape; a cafeteria and restaurant; the Grotten bar, with views of Europe's end through its vast glass wall; a one-room Thai museum; the St Johannes chapel ('the world's northernmost ecumenical chapel'); a post office (for that all-important Nordkapp postmark); and an appropriately vast souvenir shop.

ℹ Getting There & Away

A good road, the 36km-long E69, connects Honningsvåg with Nordkapp. In winter you may need to travel in a convoy behind a snowplough.

Buses, both tour and the public variety, connect the two – ask **Honningsvåg's tourist office**

(📞 78 47 70 30; www.nordkapp.no; Fiskeriveien 4; ⏱ 10am-10pm Mon-Fri, noon-8pm Sat & Sun mid-Jun–mid-Aug, 11am-2pm Mon-Fri rest of the yr; 📶) for advice on what's leaving next.

Kirkenes

POP 3498

This is it: you're as far east as Cairo, further east than most of Finland, a mere 15km from the border with Russia – and at the end of the line for the Hurtigruten coastal ferry. It's also road's end for the E6, the highway that runs all the way down to Oslo.

This tiny, nondescript place, anticlimactic for many, has a distinct frontier feel. You'll see street signs in Norwegian and Cyrillic script and hear Russian spoken by trans-border visitors and fishermen, who enjoy better prices for their catch here than in their home ports further to the east.

The town reels with around 100,000 visitors every year, most stepping off the Hurtigruten to spend a couple of hours in the town before travelling onward. But you should linger a while here, not primarily for the town's sake but to take one of the many excursions and activities on offer.

🏃 Activities

Kirkenes offers a wealth of tours and activities. For an overview according to season, get one of the comprehensive brochures, *Summer Activities* or *Winter Activities*, from your hotel.

There's a summertime reservation point in the Scandic Arctic Hotel lobby, or book directly with tour operators. Do your research – operations are professional and well-run, but prices and timings sometimes vary so find out what best suits your needs.

Summer

The following activities are popular from late June to mid-August, sometimes into September:

➡ King-crab safari (adult/child 1650/825kr)

➡ Quad-bike safari (per person from 1490kr)

➡ Half-day tours of the Pasvik River Valley (adult/child 1000/500kr)

➡ Visiting the Russian border and iron-ore mines (adult/child 700/350kr)

➡ Boat trips along the Pasvik River (adult/child 990/500kr)

Winter

Activities to try between December and mid-April:

➡ Snowmobile safaris (per person from 1890kr)

➡ Ice fishing (from 1800kr)

➡ Snowshoe rental (half-/full day from 250/400kr)

➡ Dog-sledding (adult/child from 2100/1050kr)

➡ King-crab safari (adult/child 1500/750kr)

👉 Tours

Tour agencies can arrange in-town or hotel pick-ups. In addition to the following, it's also worth checking what **BIRK Husky** (📞 909 78 248; www.birkhusky.no), based in the Pasvik River Valley, and Sollia Gjestegård (p361) have on offer.

Barents Safari (📞 901 90 594; www.barents-safari.no; Fjellveien 28)

Pasvikturist (📞 78 99 50 80; www.pasvikturist.no; Dr Wessels gate 9)

Kirkenes Snow Hotel (📞 78 97 05 40; www.kirkenessnowhotel; Sandnesdalen 14)

🛏 Sleeping

⭐ **Sollia Gjestegård** HOTEL €€
(📞 78 99 08 20; www.storskog.no; apt 1420kr, 2- to 4-bed cabins 1215-1825kr, s/d 665/815kr) The Sollia, 13km southeast of Kirkenes, was originally constructed as a tuberculosis sanatorium and you can see why. The air could scarcely be more pure or the atmosphere more relaxed at this wonderful getaway. The whole family can sweat it out in the sauna and outdoor tub, while children will enjoy communing with the resident huskies. Rooms are simple.

Scandic Arctic Hotel HOTEL €€
(📞 78 99 11 59; www.scandichotels.no; Kongensgate 1-3; d from 1050kr; 🅿 @ 🏊) The Scandic Arctic, a pleasing modern block in the town centre, boasts Norway's most easterly swimming pool, heated and open year-round. The other special attribute, its **Arctic Menu** restaurant (summer buffet 395kr), is the best of the town's limited hotel dining options.

⭐ **Kirkenes Snow Hotel** HOTEL €€€
(📞 78 97 05 40; www.kirkenessnowhotel.com; Sandnesdalen 14; adult/child including half-board from 3100/1550kr; ⏱ 20 Dec–mid-Apr) Yes, the prices are steep but you'll remember the

occasion for life. And bear in mind that 25 tonnes of ice and 15,000 cu metres of snow are shifted each winter to build this ephemeral structure. For dinner, guests cook reindeer sausages over an open fire, then enjoy a warming main course of baked salmon.

✖ Eating

Surf & Turf INTERNATIONAL, NORWEGIAN **€€**
(☑464 45 245; Dr Wessels gate 2; mains from 189kr; ☺11am-10pm Mon-Sat) One of the better in-town options in a place of few, Surf & Turf does a decent fish soup and serves up everything from steaks to pasta and even whale. The setting, too, is much nicer than others in town and the thoughtful presentation of dishes is rare in Kirkenes.

★ Gapahuken NORWEGIAN **€€€**
(☑78 99 08 20; www.storskog.no/en/restaurant-gapahuken; Storskog; mains 290-395kr, buffet 450kr; ☺4-10pm Mon-Sat, 3-7pm Sun mid-Jun–Aug, on demand rest of year) The restaurant of the Sollia Gjestegård hotel (p361) is clad in wood and glass, and from its broad picture windows there's a grand panorama of the lake at its feet and the Russian frontier post just beyond. Discriminating diners drive out from Kirkenes to enjoy gourmet Norwegian cuisine made with fresh local ingredients such as reindeer, king crab, salmon and halibut. Sunday is buffet only.

❶ Information

Kirkenes has no functioning tourist office. Your best bet for information and brochures are hotels or tour operators. A collection of local tour operators and hotels have set up the generally excellent website www.visitkirkenes.no.

❶ Getting There & Away

From **Kirkenes Airport** (☑67 03 53 00; www.avinor.no), 13km southwest of town, there are direct flights to Oslo (SAS and Norwegian) and Tromsø (Widerøe).

Kirkenes is the terminus of the Hurtigruten coastal ferry, which heads southwards at 12.45pm daily. A bus (120kr) meets the boat and runs into town and on to the airport.

From the bus stop, buses run four times weekly to Karasjok (five hours), Hammerfest (10¼ hours), Alta (10½ hours) and many points in between.

Independent travellers armed with a Russian visa (which you'll need to get in your home country) can hop aboard one of the two daily buses to Murmansk (one way/return 510/780kr, five hours).

❶ Getting Around

The airport is served by the Flybuss (85kr, 20 minutes), which connects the bus terminal and the Scandic Arctic Hotel with all arriving and departing flights.

Kirkenes Taxi (☑78 99 13 97; www.kirkenestaxi.no; Presteveien 1) charges 350/425kr for a day/evening run between town and the airport.

There are car-rental agencies at the airport, or ask at your hotel.

Karasjok
POP 2668

Kautokeino may have more Sami residents, but Karasjok (Kárásjohka in Sami) is Sami Norway's indisputable capital. It's home to the Sami Parliament and library, NRK Sami Radio, a wonderful Sami museum and a Sami theme park. This is also one of the best places in Norway to go dog-sledding in winter.

It's a lovely forested drive between Karasjok and Kautokeino, following, for the most spectacular stretch, the River Jiešjokka.

◎ Sights

Sami National Museum MUSEUM
(Sámiid Vuorká Dávvirat, De Samiske Samlinger; ☑78 46 99 50; www.rdm.no; Museumsgata 17; adult/concession/child 90/60kr/free; ☺9am-6pm mid-Jun–mid-Aug, shorter hours rest of year) Exhibits at the Sami National Museum, also called the Sami Collection, include displays of colourful, traditional Sami clothing, tools and artefacts, and works by contemporary Sami artists. Outdoors, you can roam among a cluster of traditional Sami constructions and follow a short trail, signed in English, that leads past and explains ancient Sami reindeer trapping pits and hunting techniques. In summer a guided walk is included in the ticket price.

Sami Parliament NOTABLE BUILDING
(Sámediggi; ☑78 47 40 00; www.samediggi.no; Kautokeinoveien 50; ☺hourly tours 8.30am-10.30 & 12.30- 2.30pm Mon-Fri late Jun–mid-Aug, 1pm Mon-Fri rest of year) FREE The Sami Parliament was established in 1989 and meets four times annually. In 2000 it moved into a glorious new building, encased in mellow Siberian wood, with a birch, pine and oak interior. The main assembly hall is shaped like a Sami tent, and the Sami library, lit with tiny lights like stars, houses more than 35,000 volumes, plus other media. Tours last 30 minutes. There are similar Sami parliaments in Finland and Sweden.

Sápmi Park AMUSEMENT PARK, MUSEUM
(78 46 88 00; www.visitsapmi.no; Leavnn-jageaidnu 1, off Porsangerveien; adult/child/family 160/80/400kr; 9am-7pm mid-Jun–mid-Aug, 9am-4pm late Aug, 9am-4pm Mon-Fri, 11am-3pm Sat Sep–mid-Dec, 10am-2pm Mon-Fri Jan-May) Sami culture is big business here, and this impressive theme park includes a wistful, hi-tech multimedia introduction to the Sami in the 'Magic Theatre', plus Sami winter and summer camps and other dwellings to explore on the grounds. There's also, of course, a gift shop and cafe – and **Boble Glasshytte**, Finnmark's only glass-blowing workshop and gallery. Reindeer are also often around.

🏃 Activities

⭐ **Engholm's Husky** ADVENTURE SPORTS
(www.engholm.no; 1hr dog-sledding 1000kr, 1-/4-/5-/8-day winter husky safari 2000/8700/11,600/19,900kr) Engholm's Husky, in the lodge (p363) bearing the same name, offers winter dog-sled tours. These are sometimes run by Sven Engholm, one of dog-sledding's most celebrated names. They can also arrange summer walking tours with a dog to carry at least some of your gear. Consult the website for the full range of activities.

🛏️ Sleeping

⭐ **Engholm Husky Design Lodge** CABIN €€
(915 86 625; www.engholm.no; s/d incl full board from 1500/2500kr, s/d hut only from 750/1100kr; 🅿 🛜) 🌿 About 6km from Karasjok along the Rv92, Sven Engholm has built this wonderful haven in the forest with his own hands. Each rustic cabin is individually furnished with great flair, with every item (from reindeer-horn toilet brushes to creative lampshades) hand-carved by Sven. All have kitchen facilities; two have bathrooms. You sink into sleep to the odd bark and yelp from the sled dogs.

Scandic Hotel Karasjok HOTEL €€
(78 46 88 60; www.scandichotels.no; Porsangerveien; d 850-1600kr; 🅿 @ 🛜) Adjacent to Sápmi Park, this is Karasjok's premier hotel lodging, with handsome rooms and Sami motifs throughout, plus, outside in summertime, **Gammen**, an impressive Arctic Menu restaurant. They also have a range of budget rooms.

MIDNIGHT SUN & POLAR NIGHT

Because the Earth is tilted on its axis, polar regions are constantly facing the sun at their respective summer solstices and are tilted away from it in the winter. The Arctic and Antarctic Circles, at 66° 33' north and south latitude respectively, are the northern and southern limits of constant daylight on their longest day of the year.

The northern half of mainland Norway, as well as Svalbard and Jan Mayen Island, lie north of the Arctic Circle but during summer, between late May and mid-August, nowhere in the country experiences true darkness. In Trondheim, for example, the first stars aren't visible until mid-August.

Conversely, winters here are dark, dreary and long, with only a few hours of twilight to break the long polar nights. In Svalbard, not even a twilight glow can be seen for over a month. During this period of darkness, many people suffer from SAD syndrome, or 'seasonal affective disorder'. Its effects may be minimised by using special solar-spectrum light bulbs for up to 45 minutes after waking up. Not surprisingly, most northern communities make a ritual of welcoming the sun the first time it peeks above the southern horizon.

Town/Area	Latitude	Midnight Sun	Polar Night
Bodø	67° 18'	4 Jun – 8 Jul	15 Dec – 28 Dec
Svolvær	68° 15'	28 May – 14 Jul	5 Dec – 7 Jan
Narvik	68° 26'	27 May – 15 Jul	4 Dec – 8 Jan
Tromsø	69° 42'	20 May – 22 Jul	25 Nov – 17 Jan
Alta	70° 00'	16 May – 26 Jul	24 Nov – 18 Jan
Hammerfest	70° 40'	16 May – 27 Jul	21 Nov – 21 Jan
Nordkapp	71° 11'	13 May – 29 Jul	18 Nov – 24 Jan
Longyearbyen	78° 12'	20 Apr – 21 Aug	26 Oct – 16 Feb

✗ Eating

Biepmu Kafeà CAFE €€
(Biepmu Cafe; ☑ 78 46 61 51; Finlandsveien; mains 140-240kr; ⊙1-8pm) This simple cafeteria in the centre of town serves up hearty local dishes and snacks, with daily specials (starting at 175kr) including a fish buffet on Wednesday. Other dishes include shredded reindeer meat. The heavy wooden benches resemble church pews and it's very much only locals in attendance.

★ Gammen NORWEGIAN €€€
(☑ 78 46 88 60; off Porsangerveien; mains 265-395kr; ⊙11am-10pm mid-Jun–mid-Aug) It's reindeer or reindeer plus a couple of fish options at this summer-only rustic complex of four large interconnected Sami huts, run by the Scandic Hotel. Although it may be busy with bus-tour groups, it's an atmospheric place to sample traditional Sami dishes, from reindeer stew to reindeer fillet, or simply to drop in for coffee or beer around the fire.

🔒 Shopping

★ Knivsmed Strømeng ARTS & CRAFTS
(☑ 78 46 71 05; www.samekniv.no; Markangeaidnu 10; ⊙8.30am-6pm Mon-Fri, 10am-4pm Sat mid-Jun–mid-Aug, shorter hours rest of year) This shop calls on five generations of local experience to create original handmade Sami knives for everything from outdoor to kitchen use. They're real works of art, but stay true to the Sami need for durability, made with birch-and-brass handles and varying steel quality. Prices start at around 1000kr for a Sami kid's knife up to 2000kr for the real deal.

❶ Information

The **tourist office** (☑ 78 46 89 81; Leavnnjageaidnu 1, off Porsangerveien; ⊙9am-7pm mid-Jun–mid-Aug) is in Sápmi Park, near the junction of the E6 and the Rv92. It will change money if you're stuck with euros after crossing the border from Finland.

❶ Getting There & Away

Twice-daily buses (except Saturday) connect Karasjok with Alta (525kr, 4¾ hours) and Hammerfest (450kr, 4¼ hours). There's a service to Kirkenes (580kr, five hours) three times weekly.

A daily Finnish Lapin Linjat bus runs to Rovaniemi (785kr, eight hours) via Ivalo (315kr, 3½ hours), in Finland.

SVALBARD

Svalbard is the Arctic North as you always dreamed it existed. This wondrous archipelago is a land of dramatic snow-drowned peaks and glaciers, of vast ice fields and forbidding icebergs, an elemental place where the seemingly endless Arctic night and the perpetual sunlight of summer carry a deeper kind of magic. One of Europe's last great wildernesses, this is also the domain of more polar bears than people, a terrain rich in epic legends of polar exploration.

Svalbard's main settlement and entry point, scruffy Longyearbyen, is merely a taste of what lies beyond and the possibilities for exploring further are many: boat trips, glacier hikes, and expeditions by snowmobile or led by a team of huskies. Whichever you choose, coming here is like crossing some remote frontier of the mind: Svalbard is as close as most mortals can get to the North Pole and still capture its spirit.

Longyearbyen

POP 2100

Longyearbyen is like a portal to a magical sub-polar world. Just about every Svalbard experience begins here, but if you came to Svalbard and spent the whole time in Longyearbyen (Svalbard's only town of any size), you'd leave disappointed. That's because although Longyearbyen enjoys a superb backdrop including two glacier tongues, Longyearbreen and Lars Hjertabreen, the town itself is fringed by abandoned mining detritus and the waterfront is anything but beautiful, with shipping containers and industrial buildings. The further you head up the valley towards the glaciers, the more you'll appreciate being here. Even so, Longyearbyen is a place to base yourself for trips out into the wilderness rather than somewhere to linger for its own sake.

◎ Sights

★ Wild Photo Gallery GALLERY
(☑ 405 17 775; www.wildphoto.com; ⊙10am-4pm Jun-Aug, shorter hours Mar-May, Sep & Oct) FREE This gallery of stunning Svalbard photos by Ole Jørgen Liodden and Roy Mangersnes is small but filled with utterly unforgettable images. A book that contains most of the displayed images, *Svalbard Exposed*, is sold here, and the two photographers run photo expeditions in Svalbard and elsewhere.

Svalbard Museum   MUSEUM
(☑79 02 64 92; www.svalbardmuseum.no; adult/student/child 90/50/15kr; ☺10am-5pm Mar-Sep, noon-5pm Oct-Feb) Museum is the wrong word for this impressive exhibition space. Themes on display include life on the edge formerly led by whalers, trappers, seal and walrus hunters and, more recently, miners. It's an attractive mix of text, artefacts, and birds and mammals, stuffed and staring. There's a cosy book-browsing area for lounging, too, with sealskin cushions and rugs.

Svalbard Bryggeri   BREWERY
(☑902 86 205; www.svalbardbryggeri.no; guided tour 350kr; ☺guided tours 6pm Mon, Wed & Sat) Having opened for business in 2015, Svalbard's very own brewery makes the very quaffable Spitsbergen IPA, Spitsbergen Pilsener and Spitsbergen Pale Ale – 16% of the water used in making their beers comes from the Bogerbreen glacier. They also of-

fer 90-minute guided tours of their operations with free tastings thrown in. Advance reservations are essential and can be made through the tourist office (p368).

North Pole Expedition Museum   MUSEUM
(Spitsbergen Airship Museum; ☑957 35 742; www.spitsbergenairshipmuseum.com; adult/child 90/40kr; ☺10am-5pm) This fascinating private museum houses a stunning collection of artefacts, original newspapers and other documents relating to the history of polar exploration. There's intriguing archive footage and labels are in English – you could easily spend a couple of hours here reliving some of the Arctic's most stirring tales. It's across the road from the back side of the Svalbard Museum (p364), down near the waterfront.

Galleri Svalbard   GALLERY
(☑79 02 23 40; www.gallerisvalbard.no; adult/concession/child 70/40/20kr; ☺11am-5pm Mar-Sep,

POLAR BEARS UNDER THREAT

Polar bears are one of the most enduring symbols of the Arctic wilderness – loners, immensely strong and survivors in one of the world's most extreme environments. But for all the bears' raw power, some scientists predict that they could be extinct by the end of this century if the world continues to heat up.

Polar bear numbers had been in decline since the late 19th century, when intensive hunting began. But ever since the 1973 treaty for the Conservation of Polar Bears and their Habitat, signed by all the countries whose lands impinge upon the Arctic, polar bear numbers have been gradually increasing again and latest estimates by the World Wildlife Fund (WWF) suggest that there are between 22,000 and 31,000 left in the wild; Svalbard has a population of around 3500.

But as is the case throughout the Arctic, Svalbard's glaciers are retreating and the ice sheet, their natural habitat and prime hunting ground for seals, the mainstay of their diet (an adult bear needs to eat between 50 and 75 seals every year), is shrinking. In 2017, a particularly bad year, even most of Svalbard's north coast remained ice-free throughout the winter – one polar bear that was being tracked by the WWF remained stranded on the island of Storøya, off the archipelago's far northeastern coast, after sea ice that usually connects the island to the rest of Svalbard failed to form.

Shrinking sea ice matters because although polar bears are classified as marine mammals and are powerful swimmers, many risk drowning as they attempt to reach ice floes that are ever more separated by open water. Less sea ice also means that some populations will become isolated and inbred, weakening their genes. The birth rate may also fall since females need plenty of deep snow to dig the dens in which they whelp. And hungry bears, on the prowl and desperate for food, could lead to increasing confrontations with humans.

Your chances of seeing one, unless you're on a cruise and observing from the safety of a ship, are minimal, especially in summer. In any event, contact is actively discouraged, both for your and the bear's sake (if a snowmobiler gives chase, for example, he or she will be in for a stiff fine). Bears under pressure quickly become stressed and overheat under their shaggy coats and may even die of heat exhaustion if pursued.

Should you come within sight of one on land, don't even think about approaching it. An altogether safer way to track polar bears is to log onto www.panda.org/polarbears, managed by the WWF. Here, you can track the movements of bears that scientists have equipped with a collar and satellite transmitter.

SVALBARD GLOBAL SEED VAULT

Deep inside a mountain, down beneath the permafrost, a vast artificial cavern, **Svalbard Global Seed Vault** (www.seedvault.no), already dubbed the Doomsday Vault or a vegetarian Noah's Ark, was opened in 2008. It's a repository with a capacity for up to four million different seed types (and up to 2.25 billion seeds in all), representing the botanical diversity of the planet. Note that casual visitors are not welcome.

1-5pm Tue-Sat & 11am-3pm Sun Oct-Feb) Galleri Svalbard features the Svalbard-themed works of renowned Norwegian artist Kåre Tveter (1922–2012), so pure and cold they make you shiver, as well as works by other artists, such as Olav Storø (www.storoe.no). It also has fascinating reproductions of antique maps of Svalbard, historical drawings with a Svalbard focus and temporary exhibitions. The gallery has a small cafe and an excellent shop.

Summer Activities

Restrict yourself to Longyearbyen and you'll leave with little sense of the sheer majesty of Svalbard's wilderness. Fortunately, there's a dizzying array of short trips and day tours. The tourist office (p368) has an extensive weekly activities list. All outings can be booked through individual operators (directly or via their websites; see also www.svalbard.net).

Boat Trips

The range of boat day trips you can undertake to get out into the further reaches of Svalbard is growing with each passing year. Barentsburg and Pyramiden are the most popular with daily departures, but Ny Ålesund is also now within reach.

Food & Drink Sightseeing

There are tours and tastings at Longyearbyen's brewery, Svalbard Bryggeri (p365), three times a week, while **Karlsberger Pub** (☑79 02 20 00; www.karlsbergerpub.no; Lompensenteret; ☺5pm-2am Sun-Fri, 3pm-2am Sat) also offers whisky tastings thrice weekly.

Arctic Tapas (☑46 27 60 00; www.arcticta-pas.com; per person 895kr; ☺6.30-9pm Tue, Thu, Fri & Sun) This tour bus with a difference offers a sightseeing tour of Longyearbyen accompanied by an on-board four-course meal with a focus on northern Norwegian produce and specialities – think cheese, trout, salmon, reindeer, herring... There's one free drink included in the cost of the tour.

Spitsbergen Travel (Hurtigruten Svalbard; ☑79 02 61 00; www.spitsbergentravel.com) Offers an Arctic Wilderness Evening at 7pm four nights a week, which includes dinner out in the wilds of Adventdalen, with an informative lecture on polar bears and Spitsbergen history thrown in (1045/500kr per adult/child).

Hiking

Summer hiking possibilities are endless and any Svalbard tour company worth its salt can organise half-, full- and multi-day hikes. The easiest options are three-hour fossil-hunting hikes (from 400kr), some of which take you up onto the moraine at the base of the Longyearbreen glacier.

Some popular destinations for other hikes, many of which include glacier hikes, are Platåberget (500kr, three hours); up onto the Longyearbreen glacier itself (750kr, five hours); Sarkofagen (525m above sea level; 690kr, six hours); Trollsteinen via Lars glacier (795kr, six hours); Fuglefjella (990kr, seven hours); and Nordensköldtoppen (990kr, eight hours).

Spitsbergen Outdoor Activities (☑917 76 595; www.spitsbergenoutdooractivities.com) and **Poli Arctici** (☑913 83 467, 79 02 17 05; www.poliartici.com) are among the better smaller operators, with numerous options, but all companies can get you out and walking.

Walrus Safaris

One of the most exciting new types of tours to hit Svalbard in years, walrus safaris now run to Prins Karls Forlandet (with a glacier stop en route) from mid- or late May to August or mid-September. You can get to within 30m (either on land or at sea) of the great blubbery things lounging on the beach. A warming soup is included in tours prices and both of these companies are excellent:

Better Moments (☑400 95 965; www.bettermoments.no) Four departures weekly (2190kr, seven hours)

Svalbard Booking (☑79 02 50 00; www.svalbardbooking.com) Four trips weekly (1990kr to 2390kr, seven hours)

🏃 Winter Activities

Basecamp Spitsbergen (☎79 02 46 00; www.basecampexplorer.com/spitsbergen) and Spitsbergen Travel (p366) in particular offer some truly epic, multiday cross-country ski expeditions, but it's worth spending time looking at what all of the tour companies have to offer.

Dog-Sledding

The environmentally friendly rival to snowmobiling, dog-sledding is in many ways the iconic Svalbard winter activity – the soundtrack of huskies barking and the scrape of the sled across the ice are a far more agreeable accompaniment in the wilderness than the drone of a snowmobile engine. Expect to pay around 1590kr for a four-hour excursion, although longer expeditions are possible.

Dedicated dog-sledding operators include the following:

Green Dog Svalbard (☎79 02 61 00; www.greendog.no)

Polardogs Svalbard (☎966 59 126; www.polardogssvalbard.com)

Svalbard Husky (☎78 40 30 78; www.svalbardhusky.no)

Svalbard Villmarkssenter (☎79 02 17 00; www.svalbardvillmarkssenter.no)

Snowmobiling

Riding or driving a snowmobile is the main way of getting around Svalbard in winter and it certainly enables you to cover a greater distance and see more than is otherwise possible.

Before setting out, pick up a copy of *Driving a Snowmobile in Svalbard* from the tourist office (p368). To drive a snowmobile scoot, you'll need to flash your home driving licence. Check with the tourist office; many areas are off-limits for snowmobiles. Daily rates start from 1200kr to 1500kr for the basic model.

Most companies will offer snowmobile safaris. Spitsbergen Travel (p366) has a particularly wide range of excursions, while Svalbard Booking (p366) offers snowmobile rental.

Sample expeditions (prices may vary between companies) include the following:

➡ Barentsburg (2400kr, eight hours)

➡ Coles Bay (1900kr, four hours)

➡ East coast Spitsbergen (2500kr, 10 hours)

➡ Elveneset (1900kr, four hours)

➡ Northern-lights safari (1750kr, three hours)

➡ Pyramiden (2500kr, 11 hours)

➡ Von Post glacier (2400kr, eight hours)

🛏 Sleeping

Coal Miners' Cabins   GUESTHOUSE €
(Spitsbergen Guesthouse; ☎79 02 63 00; www.spitsbergentravel.no; dm 400kr, s 590-1050kr, d 875-1400kr; ☉mid-Mar–mid-Sep; ☎) This guesthouse is a subsidiary of Spitsbergen Travel (p366) and can accommodate up to 136 people. Spread over four buildings (the terrific Coal Miners' Bar & Grill (p368) is housed in one), the renovated rooms are simple and generally great value for money, albeit at Norway prices.

★**Basecamp Spitsbergen**   LODGE €€€
(☎79 02 46 00; www.basecampexplorer.com; s 1150-2600kr, d 1600-3000kr; ☎) Imagine a recreated sealing hut, built in part from recycled driftwood and local slate. Add artefacts and decorations culled from the local refuse dump and mining cast-offs. Graft on 21st-century plumbing and design flair and you've got this fabulous place, also known as Trapper's Lodge. The 16 cabin-like rooms are the definition of cosiness and comfort, and the breakfasts are splendid.

★**Svalbard Hotell & Lodge**   HOTEL €€€
(☎79 02 50 00; www.svalbardbooking.com/Accommodation/Svalbard-Hotell; s/d/apt from 1790/1990/2250kr; ☎) Svalbard Hotell & Lodge offers stylish rooms with dark Scandinavian wood tones offset by stunning large photos above the beds and splashes of colour in the linens. There are flat-screen TVs, and you couldn't be more centrally located for the main shops and restaurants of Longyearbyen. The two- and three-bedroom apartments, known as Svalbard Lodge, are similarly outstanding.

🍴 Eating

★**Fruene Kaffe og Vinbar**   CAFE €
(The Missus; ☎79 02 76 40; Lompensenteret; lunch mains 45-89kr; ☉10am-6pm Mon-Fri, 10am-5pm Sat, 11am-5pm Sun; ☎) 'The Missus' is a welcoming and popular cafe, serving decent coffee, baguettes, pizza, snacks and other light meals. There's free wi-fi, the walls are adorned with stunning photography and the food's good – lunch specials usually include a soup or a salad. The soups are particularly outstanding.

★ **Huset**   NORWEGIAN €€
(☑ 79 02 50 02; www.huset.com; bistro mains 150-220kr, restaurant mains 295-369kr, Nordic Tasting Menu 900-1100kr; ☺ bistro 4-10pm Sun-Fri, 2-10pm Sat, restaurant 7-10pm Tue-Sun) It's something of a walk up here but it's worth it. Dining in the bistro is casual, with well-priced dishes such as reindeer burgers or reindeer stew with lingonberries on the menu. Its signature dish is the coal-grilled hamburger (160kr) – a meaty burger with all the trimmings, so juicy, we're told, that lonely scientists in their tents dream of it.

Coal Miners' Bar & Grill   NORWEGIAN, INTERNATIONAL €€
(☑ 79 02 63 00; www.spitsbergentravel.com/start/food/coal-miners-bar-grill; mains from 199kr; ☺ kitchen 3-10pm) A renovation of this former mining mess hall has transformed it into one of Longyearbyen's coolest venues. There's warming decor, fabulous charcoal-grilled meals (the spare ribs and burgers are excellent) and the humming backdrop of a happy crowd that often hangs around to drink long after the kitchen closes; they throw people out at midnight (1am on Friday and Saturday).

★ **Gruvelageret**   NEW NORDIC, INTERNATIONAL €€€
(☑ 79 02 20 00; www.gruvelageret.no/en; 4-course set menu 895kr; ☺ 6-10pm) Opened in the winter of 2015, Gruvelageret occupies a stunningly converted wooden mining warehouse and serves up an exceptional set menu that begins with Atlantic salmon, moves on to borscht soup and reindeer fillet before climaxing with the gorgeous 'crushed cheesecake'. The location, high on a hill deep in the valley, is as splendid as the food.

Advance reservations are essential and payment is by credit card only.

🍷 **Drinking & Nightlife**

Svalbar   BAR
(☑ 79 02 50 03; www.svalbar.no; ☺ 11am-2am Mon-Thu, noon-2am Fri-Sun) Svalbar is your fairly standard Norwegian bar with a dartboard, billiard table, and small menu of food until 11pm. It's popular with a younger crowd.

> ℹ **AIRPORT BUS**
> The airport bus **Svalbard Busservice** (☑ 79 02 10 52; www.svalbardbuss.no/flybussen; adult/student/child 75/50/25kr) meets arriving and departing planes and takes passengers to hotels around town.

Huset   BAR, CLUB
(The House; ☑ 79 02 50 02; www.huset.com; ☺ bar 4-11pm Mon-Sat, 2-11pm Sun, nightclub 10pm-4am Fri & Sat) Huset is your all-purpose night spot, with a bar and nightclub (cover charge 100kr) where live acts take to the stage on weekends. The wine cellar here has a staggering 20,000 bottles and is one of Scandinavia's best – tastings can be arranged with advance reservations.

Kroa   BAR
(The Pub; ☑ 79 02 13 00; www.kroa-svalbard.no; ☺ 11.30am-2am) Bustling Kroa, with metal bar stools fashioned from old mine stanchions and sealskin rugs, is enduringly popular and blurs the line between restaurant and bar in a most agreeable way.

🛍 **Shopping**

Skinnboden   CLOTHING, ARTS & CRAFTS
(☑ 79 02 10 88; www.skinnboden.no; ☺ 10am-6pm Mon-Fri, 10am-3pm Sat, noon-3pm Sun) This place stocks all manner of rather unusual 'Arctic Products' – reindeer-skin boots, sealskin gloves, hats and vests, and even rugs made from the pelts of musk ox and other Arctic creatures. It also has a small range of jewellery. It won't be everyone's cup of tea, but at least it's different.

Svalbardbutikken   DEPARTMENT STORE
(☑ 79 02 25 20; www.svalbardbutikken.no; ☺ 10am-8pm Mon-Fri, 10am-6pm Sat, 3-6pm Sun) Part supermarket, part department store and with a small but decent selection of local souvenirs, Svalbardbutikken is Longyearbyen's catch-all shopping experience.

ℹ **Information**

Sysselmannen På Svalbard (☑ 79 02 43 00; www.sysselmannen.no; ☺ 8.30am-3.30pm Mon-Fri) For independent hiking and gun permits.

Tourist Office (☑ 79 02 55 50; www.visitsvalbard.com; ☺ 10am-5pm May-Sep, noon-5pm Oct-Apr) Produces a helpful weekly activities list and has other information about the Svalbard archipelago.

ℹ **Getting There & Away**

SAS (www.flysas.com) flies from Longyearbyen to/from Oslo directly in summer (three flights weekly) or via Tromsø (three to five times weekly) year-round.

Norwegian (www.norwegian.com) also flies three times a week between Oslo Gardermoen and Longyearbyen.

ℹ Getting Around

BICYCLE

Bicycles can be rented for between 150kr and 350kr from **Poli Arctici** (p366) or **Basecamp Spitsbergen** (p367) and various other, well-signposted outlets around town. Street bikes (no off-roading) are available for those staying at **Longyearbyen Camping** (☏ 79 02 10 68; www. longyearbyen-camping.com; ☺ Apr & Jun-Aug).

CAR & MOTORCYCLE

You can't go that far by car, but **Arctic Autorent** (☏ 917 02 258; www.autorent.no; per day 890-1050kr), with an office in the airport arrivals hall, can get you your own set of wheels.

TAXI

Svalbard Maxi Taxi (☏ 79 02 13 05) and **Longyearbyen Taxi** (☏ 79 02 13 75) charge 120kr to 150kr for the journey between town and airport.

UNDERSTAND NORWAY

History

Norway's first settlers arrived around 11,000 years ago with the end of the ice age. As the glaciers melted, the earliest hunter-gatherers moved in from Siberia, pursuing migrating reindeer herds. You can see the prehistoric rock drawings of these hunters in the far north on Alta. Shortly afterwards, nomadic European hunters arrived in the south of the country.

The Vikings

Norway greatly affected Western civilisation during the Viking Age, a period usually dated from the plundering of England's Lindisfarne monastery by Nordic pirates (AD 793).

Through the next century, the Vikings conducted raids throughout Europe and established settlements in the Shetland, Orkney and Hebridean islands, the Dublin area (Ireland) and in Normandy (named after the 'North men'). The Viking leader Harald Hårfagre (Fairhair) unified Norway after the decisive naval battle at Hafrsfjord near Stavanger in 872.

King Olav Haraldsson, adopting the religion of the lands he had conquered, converted the Norwegians to Christianity and founded the Church of Norway in 1024. You can see Viking artefacts firsthand in Oslo's Vikingskipshuset (p295) and the Lofotr Viking Museum (p350) in Lofoten. The Viking Age declined after 1066, with the defeat of the Norwegian king, Harald Hardråda, at the Battle of Stamford Bridge in England. Norwegian naval power was finished off for good when Alexander III, King of Scots, defeated a Viking naval force at the Battle of Largs (Scotland) in 1263.

Under Occupation

In the early 14th century, Oslo emerged as a centre of power. A period of growth followed until 1349 when the bubonic plague swept the country, wiping out two-thirds of the population. In 1380, Norway was absorbed into a union with Denmark that lasted more than 400 years.

Denmark ceded Norway to Sweden in 1814. In 1884 a parliamentary government was introduced in Norway and a growing nationalist movement eventually led to a constitutional referendum in 1905. As expected, virtually no one in Norway favoured continued union with Sweden. The Swedish king, Oskar II, was forced to recognise Norwegian sovereignty, abdicate and reinstate a Norwegian constitutional monarchy, with Håkon VII on the throne. His descendants rule Norway to this day, with decisions on succession remaining under the authority of the *storting* (parliament). Oslo was declared the national capital of the Kingdom of Norway.

Independent Norway

Norway stayed neutral during WWI. Despite restating its neutrality at the start of WWII, it was attacked by the Nazis on 9 April 1940, falling to the Germans after a two-month struggle. King Håkon set up a government in exile in England, and placed most of Norway's merchant fleet under the command of the Allies. Although Norway remained occupied until the end of the war, it had an active Resistance movement.

The royal family returned to Norway in June 1945. King Håkon died in 1957 and was succeeded by his son, Olav V, a popular king who reigned until his death in January 1991. The current monarch is Harald V, Olav's son, who was crowned in June 1991.

In the late 1960s, oil was discovered in Norway's offshore waters, thereafter transforming Norway from one of Europe's poorest to arguably its richest. Although Norway joined the European Free Trade Association (EFTA) in 1960, it has been reluctant to forge closer bonds with other European nations, in part due to concerns about the effect on its fishing and small-scale farming industries. During 1994 a national referendum on joining the EU was held and rejected.

On 22 July 2011, a lone assailant killed 77 people in a bomb attack on government buildings in Oslo and a youth camp on the island of Utøya, close to Oslo. The killings, reportedly in protest against growing multiculturalism in the country, shocked and deeply traumatised the country. The perpetrator, a right-wing extremist, was later sentenced to 21 years for the attacks (the maximum possible sentence), with an option to renew the sentence thereafter.

People

Norway has one of Europe's lowest population densities. Most Norwegians are of Nordic origin (86.2% according to one recent study), and are thought to have descended from central and northern European tribes who migrated northwards around 8000 years ago. In addition, there are about 40,000 Sami, the indigenous people of Norway's far north who now make up the country's second-largest ethnic minority (after the Polish community). Some Sami still live a traditional nomadic life, herding reindeer in Finnmark.

Norway has become an increasingly multicultural society in recent years and was, at last count, home to around 635,000 immigrants (around 15% of the population) from 216 countries (compared with just 1.5% of population in 1970).

Around 82% of Norwegians nominally belong to the Church of Norway, a Protestant Evangelical Lutheran denomination, although actual church attendance is low. The Muslim population (around 2.5% of the total) is growing due to recent immigration.

The Arts

In the late 19th century and into the early 20th century, three figures – playwright Henrik Ibsen, composer Edvard Grieg and painter Edvard Munch – towered over Norway's cultural life like no others. Their emergence came at a time when Norway was forging its path to independence and pushing the creative limits of a newly confident national identity.

Ibsen (1828–1906) became known as 'the father of modern drama', but to Norwegians he was the conscience of a nation. The enormously popular *Peer Gynt* (1867) was Ibsen's international breakthrough, while other well-known works include *The Doll's House* (1879), *Ghosts* (1881), *An Enemy of the People* (1882) and *Hedda Gabler* (1890).

Edvard Grieg (1843–1907) was greatly influenced by Norway's folk music and melodies and his first great, signature work, *Piano Concerto in A Minor*, has come to represent Norway as no other work before or since. Thanks to his formidable repertoire, he became Norway's best-known composer. According to his biographer, it was impossible to listen to Grieg without sensing a light, fresh breeze from the blue waters, a glimpse of grand glaciers and a recollection of the mountains of Western Norway's fjords.

Edvard Munch (1863–1944), Norway's most renowned painter, was a tortured soul: his first great work, *The Sick Child*, was a portrait of his sister Sophie shortly before her death. In 1890 he produced the haunting *Night*, depicting a lonely figure in a dark window. The following year he finished *Melancholy* and began sketches of what would become his best known work, *The Scream*, which graphically represents Munch's own inner torment.

Literature

In the 20th century, three Norwegian writers – Bjørnstjerne Bjørnson (1832–1910), the hugely controversial Knut Hamsun (1859–1952) and Sigrid Undset (1882–1949) – won the Nobel Prize in Literature.

One of the best-known modern Norwegian writers is Jan Kjærstad (b 1953), whose *The Seducer* (2003) combines the necessary recipes for a bestseller – a thriller with a love affair and a whiff of celebrity – with seriously good writing. Among other recent Norwegian winners of the prestigious Nordic Council Literature Prize is the prolific Per Petterson (b 1952), who won the prize in 2009. If you're lucky enough to get hold of a copy, Angar Mykle's *Lasso Round the Moon* (1954) might be the best book you've never read.

In the crime fiction genre, it's Jo Nesbø (http://jonesbo.com/en) who is considered the king of Norwegian crime fiction. His stories are darker than many in the genre and are almost all set in Norway from WWII to the present.

KARL OVE KNAUSGAARD

Karl Ove Knausgaard (b 1968) is the most extraordinary Norwegian literary phenomenon of recent times. Although he wrote two critically acclaimed novels, in 1998 *(Out of this World)* and 2004 *(A Time for Everything)*, it was his six-part *Min Kamp* (My Struggle) series of intensely autobiographical novels, written between 2009 and 2011, that truly took the literary world by storm. The first five books sold more than half a million copies in Norway, with millions more sold around the world.

Knausgaard's work has been compared to that of Marcel Proust, and while the critical acclaim has been near universal, the series has attracted great controversy. Partly that derives from the title – *Min Kamp* is the Norwegian translation for Hitler's *Mein Kampf*. More enduringly, Knausgaard has been criticised for the unsparing portrayal of the private lives of his family members (including his father, ex-wife and grandmother), and he is now estranged from many of them.

The first five books in the series have been translated into English as *A Death in the Family*, *A Man in Love*, *Boyhood Island*, *Dancing in the Dark* and *Some Rain Must Fall*.

Music

There's more to Norwegian music than a-ha and Kings of Convenience.

JAZZ

Norway has a thriving jazz scene, with world-class festivals throughout the year. Jazz saxophonist Jan Garbarek is one of the most enduring Norwegian jazz personalities. His work draws on classical, folk and world music influences and he has recorded 30 albums. His daughter, Anja Garbarek, is seen as one of the most exciting and innovative performers on the Norwegian jazz scene, bringing pop and electronica into the mix.

Norway has some fine jazz festivals:

Moldejazz (www.moldejazz.no; ⊙ Jul)

Oslo International Jazz Festival (p299)

Canal Street Jazz & Blues Festival, Arendal (p306)

Night Jazz Festival, Bergen (p317)

Vossajazz, Voss (p323)

Polar Jazz, Longyearbyen (www.polarjazz.no; ⊙ Feb)

ELECTRONICA

Norway is at once one of Europe's most prolific producers and most devoted fans of electronica. Röyksopp (www.royksopp.com) took the international electronica scene by storm with its debut album Melody A.M. in 2001 and it's never really left the dance charts since.

METAL

Metal is another genre that Norway has taken to heart. Although traditional heavy metal is popular, Norway is particularly known for its black-metal scene. For a time in the early 1990s, black metal became famous for its anti-Christian, Satanist philosophy with a handful of members of black-metal bands burning down churches. Among the better-known Norwegian black-metal bands are Darkthrone, Mayhem, Emperor, Enslaved, Gorgoroth, Satyricon and Arcturus.

Environment

The Land

Norway's geographical facts tell quite a story. The Norwegian mainland stretches 2518km from Lindesnes in the south to Nordkapp in the Arctic North with a narrowest point of 6.3km wide. Norway also has the highest mountains in northern Europe and the fourth largest landmass in Western Europe (behind France, Spain and Sweden).

Norway is also home to continental Europe's largest ice-cap (Jostedalsbreen), the world's second- and third-longest fjords (Sognefjorden and Hardangerfjord), Europe's largest and highest plateau (Hardangervidda) and several of the 10 highest waterfalls in the world. Norway's glaciers cover some 2600 sq km (close to 1% of mainland Norwegian territory and 60% of the Svalbard archipelago).

Wildlife

Norway has wild and semi-domesticated reindeer herds, thriving elk populations and a scattering of Arctic foxes, lynxes, musk oxen, bears and wolverines. Polar bears (population around 3000, or around one-eighth of the world's surviving population, and declining) and walrus are found in Svalbard. Several species of seal, dolphin and whale may be seen around most western and northern coasts. Bird life is prolific in coastal areas.

National Parks

At last count, Norway had 44 national parks (including seven in Svalbard, where approximately 65% of the land falls within park boundaries). Thirteen new national parks have been created since 2003, with further new parks and extensions to existing parks planned. National parks cover 15% of the country. In many cases, the parks don't protect any specific features, nor do they necessarily coincide with the incidence of spectacular natural landscapes or ecosystem boundaries. Instead, they attempt to prevent development of remaining wilderness areas and many park boundaries simply follow contour lines around uninhabited areas.

Norwegian national parks are low profile and lack the traffic and overdeveloped facilities that have overwhelmed parks in other countries. Some parks, notably Jotunheimen and Rondane, are increasingly suffering from overuse, but in most places pollution and traffic are kept to a minimum.

Environmental Issues

Norway has led many contemporary environmental initiatives, such as the creation of the Svalbard Global Seed Vault (2008), where seeds are stored to protect biodiversity. In 2007 the government declared a goal of making Norway carbon-neutral and cutting net greenhouse gas emissions to zero by 2050, largely by purchasing offsets from developing countries. Around 98% of Norway's electricity supplies come from renewable (primarily hydropower) sources, with fossil fuels accounting for just 2%.

Loss of habitat has placed around 1000 species of plants and animals on the endangered or threatened species lists, and sport hunting and fishing are more popular here than in most of Europe. Hydroelectric schemes have devastated some mountain landscapes and waterfalls, and over-fishing perpetually haunts the economy.

Whaling in Norway is regulated by the International Whaling Commission. Norway resumed commercial whaling of minke whales in 1993, defying an international ban. The government, which supports the protection of threatened species, contends that minke whales, with an estimated population of 100,000, can sustain a limited harvest.

THE MUSK OX

The musk ox (Ovibos moschatus) is one of nature's great survivors; it has changed little in two million years. Although a member of the family Bovidae, the musk ox bears little resemblance to any other animal and its only known relative is the takin of northern Tibet.

Musk oxen weigh between 225kg and 445kg, and have incredibly high shoulders and an enormous low-slung head with two broad, flat horns that cross the forehead, curving outwards and downwards before twisting upwards and forwards. Its thick and shaggy coat, with a matted fleece of soft hair underneath, covers the whole body. Only the bottom part of the legs protrude, giving the animal the appearance of a medieval horse dressed for a joust. During the rutting season, when the males gather their harems, they repeatedly charge each other, butting their heads together with a crash heard for miles around. This heated battle continues until one animal admits defeat and lumbers off. In winter, they stand perfectly still for hours to conserve energy, a position some scientists have described as 'standing hibernation'.

Traditionally, the musk oxen's main predator has been the wolf; their primary defence is to form a circle with the males on the outside and females and calves inside, trusting in their collective horns to rip open attackers. This defence has proven useless against human hunters, especially the Greenlandic Inuit, and numbers have been seriously depleted.

The musk ox died out in Norway almost 2000 years ago, but in 1931, 10 animals were reintroduced to Dovrefjell-Sunndalsfjella from Greenland. Musk oxen all but vanished during WWII, but 23 were transplanted from Greenland between 1947 and 1953. The herd has now grown to around 300 animals and some have shifted eastwards into Femundsmarka National Park to form a new herd. Wild herds can also be found in parts of Greenland, Canada and Alaska.

Food & Drink

Norwegian food can be excellent. Abundant seafood and local specialities such as reindeer are undoubtedly the highlights, and most medium-sized towns have fine restaurants in which to eat. The only problem (and it's a significant one) is that prices are prohibitive, meaning that a full meal in a restaurant may become something of a luxury item for all but those on expense accounts.

Striking a balance between eating well and staying solvent requires a clever strategy. For a start, most Norwegian hotels and some hostels offer generous buffet breakfasts, ensuring that you'll rarely start the day on an empty stomach. Many restaurants, especially in larger towns, serve cheaper lunch specials. These are often filling and well sized for those wanting more than a sandwich. Some hotels also lay on lavish dinner buffets in the evening – they're generally expensive, but excellent if it's your main meal of the day.

Staples & Specialities

Norwegian specialities include grilled or smoked *laks* (salmon), *gravat laks* (marinated salmon), *reker* (boiled shrimp), *torsk* (cod), *fiskesuppe* (fish soup) and other seafood. *Reinsdyrstek* (roast reindeer) is something every nonvegetarian visitor to Norway should try at least once; it's one of the tastier red meats.

Expect to see sweet brown goat's-milk cheese called *geitost*, and *sild* (pickled herring) with the breads and cereals in breakfast buffets. A fine Norwegian dessert is warm *moltebær syltetøy* (cloudberry jam) with ice cream. *Lutefisk* (dried cod made almost gelatinous by soaking in lye) is popular at Christmas but it's an acquired taste.

If Norway has a national drink, it's strong black coffee. Most of the beer you'll drink is pilsner. At the other end of the taste spectrum is Norway's bitter aquavit, which does the job at 40% proof.

Where to Eat & Drink

Norway has a fairly standard range of eating options, and advance reservations are rarely required anywhere except for dinner in top-end restaurants.

Restaurants From simple diner-style eateries to Indian or Thai outposts to high-end gourmet experiences.

Cafes Open usually for breakfast and lunch only, most serve light meals and pastries to go with the coffee that's the main event.

Hotels Almost all of Norway's hotels have restaurants; many serve evening buffets and most are open to nonguests.

Kiosks Cheap alternatives to sit-down restaurants, serving fast food (hamburgers, hot dogs etc).

Fish Markets In larger towns, with fresh fish on offer.

Vegetarians & Vegans

Being vegetarian in Norway is a challenge and vegan almost impossible. In rural parts of the country, vegetarians will live out of a grocery store, though some cafes serve token dishes such as vegetables with pasta. Another easily found option is pizza, however, Norwegian pizza is often bland and soggy. You'll find more options in bigger cities, although most menus are entirely based on fish and meat. About half of the kebab stands serve falafel.

Habits & Customs

The Norwegian day starts with coffee (always!), a boiled egg and some sort of bread or dry crispbread (normally Ryvita) topped with cheese, cucumber, tomato and a type of pickled herring.

For lunch, most people opt for an open sandwich, a slice of bread topped with sardines, shrimp, ham, olives, cucumber or egg. In the mid-afternoon Norwegians often break for coffee and one of the highlights of the day, waffles with cream and jam. Unlike the firm Belgian waffles, which are better known abroad, Norwegian waffles are flower-shaped, soft and often strongly flavoured with cardamom.

The main meal is eaten between 4pm and 6pm, considerably later in summer. Usually the only hot meal of the day, it normally includes a meat, seafood or pasta dish, with boiled potatoes, a scoop of vegetables and perhaps even a small salad or green garnish.

SURVIVAL GUIDE

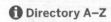 Directory A–Z

ACCOMMODATION

During summer, it's wise to book accommodation in advance. The main tourist season runs from mid-June to mid-August.

During the high season, accommodation prices are at their lowest and many hotels offer their best deals. During the rest of the year, prices are much higher, except on weekends.

B&Bs

Some places operate as B&Bs, where prices (usually with shared bathrooms) start from single/double 500/700kr and can go up to 700/950kr.

Camping

Norway has more than 1000 campsites. Tent space costs from 100kr at basic campsites up to 250kr for those with better facilities or in more popular areas, such as Oslo and Bergen. Quoted prices usually include your car, motorcycle or caravan. A per-person charge is also added in some places, electricity often costs a few kroner extra and almost all places charge at least 10kr for showers.

Most campsites also rent simple cabins with cooking facilities, starting at around 450kr for a very basic two- or four-bed bunkhouse. Bring a sleeping bag, as linen and blankets are only provided at an extra charge (anywhere from 50kr to 150kr).

Unless you opt for a more expensive deluxe cabin with shower and toilet facilities (750kr to 1500kr), you'll also have to pay for showers and washing water (there are a few exceptions). Normally, cabin occupants must clean their cabin before leaving or pay an additional cleaning charge (around 150kr).

Note that although a few complexes remain open year-round, tent and caravan sites are closed in the off-season (normally early September to mid-May).

NAF Camp (www.nafcamp.no) is an excellent online resource listing more than 250 campsites around Norway.

Norsk Camping (www.camping.no) is a useful resource for general camping info, as well as the comprehensive *Camping* guide, available in book (there's a charge of 98kr for it to be sent) or pdf format (free); you can also pick it up for free from some tourist offices and campsites. It has hundreds of listings, although most entries are in Norwegian.

Mountain Huts

Den Norske Turistforening (DNT, Norwegian Mountain Touring Club; Map p300; ☑ 40 00 18 68, 22 82 28 22; www.turistforeningen.no; Youngstorget 1, Oslo) maintains a network of 460 mountain huts or cabins located a day's hike apart along the country's 20,000km of well-marked and -maintained wilderness hiking routes. Of these, more than 400 have beds for sleeping, with the remainder reserved for eating, rest stops or emergency shelter.

DNT huts range from unstaffed huts with two beds to large staffed lodges with more than 100 beds and renowned standards of service. At both types of huts, DNT members receive significant discounts.

Annual membership for adult/senior/19 to 26 years/13 to 18 years/child 12 and under costs 660/510/340/205/125kr.

Most DNT huts are open from 16 February to 14 October. Staffed DNT lodges also open from the Saturday before Palm Sunday until Easter Monday, but staffed huts along the Oslo–Bergen railway and a few others open for the cross-country ski season from late February. DNT can provide lists of opening dates for each hut.

Members/nonmembers who prefer to camp outside the huts and use the facilities will pay 70/90kr.

There are also numerous private hikers' huts and lodges peppered around most mountain areas, but not all are open to the public. Some offer DNT members a discount.

Guesthouses & Pensions

Many towns have *pensjonat* (pensions) and *gjestehus* (guesthouses), and some, especially the latter, are family run and offer a far more intimate option than the hostel or hotel experience. Prices for a single/double with shared bathroom usually start at 550/800kr but can cost significantly more; linen and/or breakfast will only be included at the higher-priced places.

Hostels

In Norway, reasonably priced hostels *(vandrerhjem)* offer a dorm bed for the night, plus use of communal facilities that usually include a self-catering kitchen (you're advised to take your own cooking and eating utensils), internet access and bathrooms. Some also have single or double rooms with either shared or private bathroom facilities, but these often represent poor value.

While some hostels have quite comfortable lodge-style facilities and are open year-round,

---

ℹ PRICE RANGES

The following price ranges relate to a double room with private bathroom in high season and, unless stated otherwise, include breakfast:

€ less than 750kr

€€ 750kr–1400kr

€€€ more than 1400kr

a few are used for school accommodation and others are the cheaper wing of a hotel; occasionally prices work out to be more expensive than a cabin or budget hotel. In most hostels, guests must still bring their own sleeping sheet and pillowcase, although most hire out sleeping sheets for a one-off fee (starting from 50kr) regardless of the number of nights.

Most hostels have two- to six-bed rooms, and beds cost from 220kr to 450kr. The higher-priced hostels usually include a buffet breakfast, while other places may charge from 70kr to 150kr for breakfast. Some also provide a good-value evening meal for around 150kr.

A welcome addition to the budget end of the market are chains such as Citybox, Smarthotels and Basic Hotels. These hostel-hotel hybrids are slick and excellent value, but you'll only find them in larger cities.

Several hostel guides are available, including Hostelling International's annually updated Europe guide.

Hotels

Norway's hotels are generally modern and excellent, although those with any character are pretty thin on the ground. Comfortable, nationwide chain hotels are the norm and the rooms can all start to look the same after a while, whether you're sleeping in Oslo or Kirkenes. The advantage of these chains or hotel networks, however, is that some offer hotel passes, which can entitle you to a free night if you use the chain enough times; some passes only operate in summer.

ACTIVITIES

Norway's portfolio of activities is simply extraordinary, from Europe's best summer hiking to fabulous winter sports. Better still, it caters equally for first-timers leaving the car behind and hard-core adventurers who think nothing of leaping off a cliff. And whichever you choose, it'll be against an utterly magnificent backdrop.

Summer

Norway is a popular thrill-seeker destination thanks to professional operators and spectacular settings. Extreme sports include paragliding, parasailing, bungee jumping and skydiving. Voss is the centre of most of the action. Norway has some of Europe's best hiking, including around 20,000km of marked trails that range from easy strolls through the green zones around cities, to long treks through national parks and wilderness areas. Many trails are maintained by **DNT** (p374) and marked with cairns or red Ts at 100m or 200m intervals.

The hiking season runs from late May to early October, with a much shorter season in the higher mountain areas and the far north. In the highlands, the snow often remains until June

and returns in September, meaning many routes are only possible in July and August.

Norway's premier kayaking sites are clustered around the western fjords and there are numerous operators offering guided excursions. Kayaking is also possible in Svalbard.

The cascading, icy-black waters and white-hot rapids of central Norway are a rafting paradise from mid-June to mid-August. These range from Class II through to Class V.

Winter

Downhill and cross-country skiing are possible throughout the country in winter.

Dog-sledding is popular as it enables you to experience Arctic and sub-Arctic wilderness areas at a slow pace and free from engine noise. Expeditions can range from half-day to multiday trips with overnight stays in remote forest huts. Depending on the number of travellers in your group, most operators will allow you to 'mush' your own sled (after a brief primer course) or sit atop the sled as someone else urges the dogs onwards.

Snowmobile operators usually allow you to ride as a passenger behind an experienced driver. For an additional charge you may be able to drive the snowmobile, but you will need a valid driving licence.

CHILDREN

Norway is a terrific destination in which to travel as a family. This is a country that is world-famous for creating family-friendly living conditions and most hotels, restaurants and many sights are accordingly child-friendly. It's worth remembering, however, that the old parental adage of not trying to be too ambitious in how far you travel is especially relevant in Norway – distances are vast and, due to the terrain, journey times can be significantly longer than for equivalent distances elsewhere.

GAY & LESBIAN TRAVELLERS

Norwegians are generally tolerant of alternative lifestyles, although this is less the case in rural areas. Homosexuality has been legal in Norway since 1973, and the country was the first in the world to pass a law prohibiting discrimination against homosexuals. Then, in 2009, Norway became the sixth country in the world to legalise same-sex marriage when its parliament passed a gender-neutral marriage law. The new law granted full rights to church weddings, adoption and artificial insemination to married couples regardless of their sexual orientation.

All of that said, public displays of affection are not common practice, except perhaps in some areas of Oslo. Oslo is generally the easiest place to be gay in Norway, although even here there have been occasional recent attacks on gay couples holding hands, especially in the central-eastern areas of the capital. You're most likely to encounter difficulties wherever conservative religious views predominate, whether among newly arrived Muslim immigrant communities or devoutly Lutheran communities in rural areas.

Oslo has the liveliest gay scene, and it's worth stopping by **Use-It** (p304), where you can pick up the excellent annual *Streetwise* booklet with its 'Gay Guide' section.

INTERNET ACCESS

With wi-fi widely available, good cybercafes that last the distance are increasingly hard to find; ask at the local tourist office.

Free internet access is available in most municipal libraries (*biblioteket*). As it's a popular service, you may have to reserve a timeslot earlier in the day; in busier places, you may be restricted to a half-hour slot.

Wi-fi is widely available at most hotels, cafes and tourist offices, as well as some restaurants; it's generally (but not always) free and you may need to ask for a password.

MONEY

ATMs accept most international cards and are available in most towns.

The Norwegian kroner is most often written NOK in international money markets, Nkr in northern Europe and kr within Norway.

Not all banks will change money and in some places you may need to shop around to find one that does. Rates at post offices and tourist offices are generally poorer than at banks, but can be convenient.

OPENING HOURS

These standard opening hours are for high season (mid-June to mid-August) and tend to decrease outside that time.

Banks 8.15am to 3pm Monday to Wednesday and Friday, to 5pm Thursday

Central Post Offices 8am to 8pm Monday to Friday, 9am to 6pm Saturday; otherwise 9am to 5pm Monday to Friday, 10am to 2pm Saturday

Restaurants noon to 3pm and 6pm to 11pm; some don't close between lunch and dinner

Shops 10am to 5pm Monday to Wednesday and Friday, to 7pm Thursday, to 2pm Saturday

Supermarkets 9am to 9pm Monday to Friday, to 6pm Saturday

PUBLIC HOLIDAYS

New Year's Day (Nyttårsdag) 1 January

Maundy Thursday (Skjærtorsdag) March/April

Good Friday (Langfredag) March/April

Easter Monday (Annen Påskedag) March/April

Labour Day (Første Mai, Arbeidetsdag) 1 May

Constitution Day (Nasjonaldag) 17 May

Ascension Day (Kristi Himmelfartsdag) May/June, 40th day after Easter

Whit Monday (Annen Pinsedag) May/June, 8th Monday after Easter

Christmas Day (Første Juledag) 25 December

Boxing Day (Annen Juledag) 26 December

TAXES & REFUNDS

Norway has a well-organised system of tax refunds on items purchased at participating shops.

TELEPHONES

Telephone kiosks are still fairly widespread in Norway, but many won't accept cash. Instead you have to use either a credit card or a phonecard, which you can buy at 7-Elevens and convenience stores.

Mobile Phones

There aren't too many places where you can't get mobile (cell) access; there's coverage in close to 90% of the country. This doesn't, of course, apply to wilderness areas and the hiking trails of most national parks.

If you want to use your home-country mobile phone in Norway, always check with your carrier about the cost of roaming charges to avoid a nasty surprise when your next bill arrives. In theory EU phones should have no roaming charges, but do check first. An increasing number of providers now offer packages that allow you to take your minutes, texts and data allowances overseas for a small charge.

If you wish to use your mobile, but with a Norwegian SIM card, check that your phone is unlocked. If your phone accepts a foreign SIM card, these can be purchased from any 7-Eleven store and some Narvesen kiosks. However, as the connection instructions are entirely in Norwegian, you're better off purchasing the card from any Telehuset outlet, where they'll help you connect on the spot. SIM cards start from 200kr, which includes 100kr worth of calls.

There are three mobile-service providers:

Chess (www.chess.no) A relatively new mobile operator.

Telenor Mobil (www.telenor.no) The largest mobile-service provider.

Telia (www.telia.no) Norway's second-largest operator.

Phone Codes

All Norwegian phone numbers have eight digits. Numbers starting with '800' usually indicate a toll-free number, while those beginning with '9' are mobile (cell) phone numbers. There are no extra local area codes (these are incorporated into listed numbers).

International access code	✆ 00
Norway's country code	✆ 47

TIME

Note that when telling the time, Norwegians use 'half' as signifying 'half *before*' rather than 'half past'. Always double-check unless you want to be an hour late! Although the 24-hour clock is used in some official situations, you'll find people generally use the 12-hour clock in everyday conversation.

Norway shares the same time zone as most of Western Europe (GMT/UTC plus one hour during winter, and GMT/UTC plus two hours during the daylight-saving period). Daylight saving starts on the last Sunday in March and finishes on the last Sunday in October.

Note the following time differences:

Australia During the Australian winter, subtract eight hours from Australian Eastern Standard Time to get Norwegian time; during the Australian summer, subtract 10 hours.

Finland One hour ahead of Norway.

Russia One hour ahead of Norway.

Sweden and Denmark Same time as Norway.

UK and Ireland One hour behind Norway.

USA USA Eastern Time six hours behind Norway, USA Pacific Time nine hours behind Norway.

TOURIST INFORMATION

It's impossible to speak highly enough of tourist offices in Norway. Most serve as one-stop clearing houses for general information and bookings for accommodation and activities. Nearly every city and town has its own tourist office, and most tourist offices in reasonably sized towns or major tourist areas publish comprehensive booklets giving the complete, up-to-date low-down on their town and the surrounding area.

Offices in smaller towns may be open only during peak summer months, while in cities they're open year-round, but with shorter hours in the low season.

Tourist offices operate under a variety of names – *turistkontor* and *reiseliv* are among the most common – but all have the information symbol (i) prominently displayed outside and are easy to identify and find.

Norwegian Tourist Board (Norges Turistråd; ☏ 22 00 25 00; www.visitnorway.com) has general info on travelling in Norway.

VISAS

Norway is one of 26 member countries of the Schengen Convention, under which 22 EU countries (all but Bulgaria, Cyprus, Ireland, Romania and the UK) plus Iceland, Norway, Liechtenstein and Switzerland have abolished checks at common borders. The process towards integrating Bulgaria, Cyprus and Romania has slowed but they may join sometime in the future.

Visa for entering Norway are as follows:

Citizens of Denmark, Finland, Iceland and Sweden No visa or passport required.

Citizens or residents of other EU and Schengen countries No visa required.

Citizens or residents of Australia, Canada, Israel, Japan, New Zealand and the USA No visa required for tourist visits of up to 90 days.

Other countries Check with a Norwegian embassy or consulate.

To work or study in Norway A special visa may be required – contact a Norwegian embassy or consulate before travel.

ⓘ Getting There & Away

Norway is well linked to other European countries by air. There are also regular bus and rail services to Norway from neighbouring Sweden and Finland (from where there are connections further afield to Europe), with less regular (and more complicated) services to/from Russia. Regular car and passenger ferries also connect southern Norwegian ports with Denmark, Sweden and Germany.

Flights, cars and tours can be booked online at lonelyplanet.com/bookings.

AIR

For a full list of Norwegian airports, visit www.avinor.no; the page for each airport has comprehensive information.

The main international Norwegian airports are Gardermoen (Oslo), Flesland (Bergen), Sola (Stavanger), Tromsø, Værnes (Trondheim), Vigra (Ålesund), Karmøy (Haugesund), Kjevik (Kristiansand) and Torp (Sandefjord).

Dozens of international airlines fly to/from Norwegian airports. There are direct flights to Norway from East Coast USA and the UK. If coming from Australia or New Zealand, you'll need to connect via an airport in Asia, the Middle East or Europe.

Norwegian (www.norwegian.com) Low-cost airline with an extensive and growing domestic and international network.

SAS (www.sas.no) The longest established of Norway's carriers with a large domestic and international route network.

Widerøe (www.wideroe.no) Local carrier that predominantly operates between smaller towns and cities, and also provides flights to the Lofoten Islands and the far north.

LAND

Norway shares land borders with Sweden, Finland and Russia. Crossing most borders into Norway is usually hassle-free. That's particularly the case if you're arriving by road where, in some cases, you may not even realise that you've crossed the border.

If you're arriving in Norway from a non-EU or non-Schengen country, expect your papers to be checked carefully. If you're from a non-Western country, expect that you and your baggage will come under greater scrutiny than other travellers at airports and some of the staffed border crossings; this also applies for all travellers crossing by land into Norway from Russia.

Train travel is possible between Oslo and Stockholm, Gothenburg, Malmö and Hamburg, with less frequent services to northern and central Swedish cities from Narvik and Trondheim.

Eurolines (www.eurolines.com) The main operator for many international bus services to/from Norway is Eurolines, which acts as a feeder for national companies.

Nor-Way Bussekspress (www.nor-way.no) Has a reasonable range of international routes.

Swebus Express (☑ 0200 218 218; www. swebusexpress.se) Numerous cross-border services between Norway and Sweden.

Finland

Options for bus travel between Finland and Norway include the following (some in summer only):

From	To	Fare (€)	Duration (hr)
Rovaniemi	Alta	101	10
Rovaniemi	Karasjok	77.90	6
Rovaniemi	Tromsø (Jun-Sep only)	102.20	8-10
Rovaniemi	Nordkapp	132.10	10½
Saariselkä	Karasjok	33.10	2¾

The E8 highway extends from Tornio, in Finland, to Tromsø; secondary highways connect Finland with the northern Sami towns of Karasjok and Kautokeino – if you're travelling by car or motorcycle between Kautokeino and Tromsø, it generally works out quicker to take the southern route via Finland. Regular buses serve all three routes.

Russia

Buses run twice daily between Kirkenes in Norway and Murmansk in Russia (one way/return 460/750kr, five hours). From Murmansk, trains connect to the Russian rail network. Russian visas are required and must usually be applied for and issued in your country of residence.

Sweden

Swebus Express (p475) has the largest (and cheapest) buses between Oslo and Sweden.

Among the numerous cross-border bus services between Sweden and Norway, there are twice-daily services between Narvik and Riksgränsen (one hour), on the border, and Kiruna (three hours).

There are also less-frequent bus services between Bodø and Skellefteå, and along the Blå Vägen, or 'Blue Highway', between Mo i Rana and Umeå. Swedish companies **Länstrafiken i Norrbotten** (☑ 0771-10 01 10; www.ltnbd.se) and **Länstrafiken i Västerbotten** (☑ 0771-10 01 10; www.tabussen.nu) offer some cross-border services.

Rail services between Sweden and Norway are operated by **Norwegian State Railways** (p382) and **Sveriges Järnväg** (p473). It's worth noting that some of the Stockholm–Oslo services require a change of train in the Swedish city of Karlstad. It's also possible to travel from Trondheim to Sweden via Storlien and Östersund, although you'll need to change trains at the border.

SEA

Ferry connections are possible between Norway and Denmark, Germany and Sweden. Most ferry operators offer package deals that include taking a car and passengers, and most lines offer substantial discounts for seniors, students and children. Taking a bicycle incurs a small extra fee.

If you're travelling by international ferry and plan on drinking at all while in Norway, consider picking up your maximum duty-free alcohol allowance while on-board.

NORWAY GETTING THERE & AWAY

HURTIGRUTEN COASTAL FERRY

There are few better ways to drink in the scenery of the fjords than to hop aboard the iconic **Hurtigruten coastal ferry** (☑ 81 00 30 30; www.hurtigruten.com), which has been ploughing Norway's waters since 1894. Every day of every year, there's at least one Hurtigruten boat shuttling along Norway's coastline, stopping at 35 ports between Bergen and Kirkenes.

Though it was conceived to provide a vital link between Norway's most far-flung communities, these days the Hurtigruten is a full-blown cruise-ship service, complete with cabins, cafeteria, shops and restaurant – although the 11-strong fleet includes vessels of varying ages (the oldest dates from 1956, but all were substantially remodelled in the 1990s). There are also three 'expedition' ships that voyage all the way to Svalbard and the high Arctic.

Famously, Hurtigruten also provides a 'Northern Lights' promise – if you take the full 12-day cruise in winter and don't manage to spot the aurora, they'll give you another six- or seven-day cruise free of charge.

Denmark

The following companies operate ferries between Norway and Denmark.

Color Line (☑ in Denmark 99 56 19 00, in Germany 0431-7300 300, in Norway 81 00 08 11, in Sweden 0526-62000; www.colorline.com) Operates two express ferries from Denmark: Hirtshals to Larvik (3¾ hours) and Hirtshals to Kristiansand (3¼ hours).

DFDS Seaways (☑ in Denmark 33 42 30 00, in Norway 21 62 13 40, in UK 0871 522 9955; www.dfdsseaways.com) Copenhagen to Oslo (17 hours, once daily).

Fjord Line (☑ in Denmark 97 96 30 00, in Norway 51 46 40 99; www.fjordline.com) Hirtshals to Kristiansand, Bergen, Stavanger and Langesund (Oslo).

Stena Line (☑ in Denmark 96 20 02 00, in Norway 02010; www.stenaline.no) Fredrikshavn to/from Oslo.

Germany & Sweden

Color Line (p379) connects Norway with Germany and Sweden. Check the website for different fare and accommodation types. From Oslo to Kiel, Germany, there are seven weekly departures (from €327, 20 hours), while ferries (operated by both Color Line and Fjord Line) from Sandefjord to Strömstad in Sweden depart up to 20 times weekly (from €15, 2½ hours).

ⓘ Getting Around

Norway has an extremely efficient public transport system and its trains, buses and ferries are often timed to link with each other. The handy *NSB Togruter*, available free at most train stations, details rail timetables and includes information on connecting buses. Boat and bus departures vary with the season and the day (services on Saturday are particularly sparse, although less so in the summer high season), so pick up the latest *ruteplan* (timetables) from regional tourist offices.

Rail lines reach as far north as Bodø (you can also reach Narvik by rail from Sweden); further north you're limited to buses and ferries. A fine alternative to land travel is the Hurtigruten coastal ferry, which calls in at every sizable port between Bergen and Kirkenes.

AIR

Due to the time and distances involved in overland travel, even budget travellers may want to consider a segment or two by air. The major Norwegian domestic routes are quite competitive, meaning that it is possible (if you're flexible about departure dates and book early) to travel for little more than the equivalent train fare.

Keep an eye out for *minipris* return tickets, which can cost just 10% more than full-fare one-way tickets. In addition, spouses (including gay partners), children aged two to 15, travellers aged under 26, students and senior citizens over 67 years of age may be eligible for significant discounts on some routes – always ask.

Airlines in Norway

Aside from tiny charter airlines and helicopter services, three airlines fly domestic routes.

Norwegian (www.norwegian.com) Low-cost airline with an extensive and growing domestic network that now includes Longyearbyen (Svalbard).

SAS (www.sas.no) Large domestic network on mainland Norway, plus flights to Longyearbyen (Svalbard).

Widerøe (www.wideroe.no) A subsidiary of SAS with smaller planes and flights to smaller regional airports.

BICYCLE

Given Norway's great distances, hilly terrain and narrow roads, only serious cyclists engage in extensive cycle touring, but those who do rave about the experience.

Assuming that you've steeled yourself for the challenge of ascending mountain after mountain, the long-distance cyclist's biggest headache will be tunnels, and there are thousands of them. Most of these, especially in the western fjords, are closed to nonmotorised traffic; in many (although not all) cases there are outdoor bike paths running parallel to the tunnels. If no such path exists, alternative routes may involve a few days' pedalling around a long fjord or over a high mountain pass.

Rural buses, express ferries and nonexpress trains carry bikes for various additional fees (around 150kr), but express trains don't allow them at all and international trains treat them as excess baggage (350kr). Nor-Way Bussekspress charges a child's fare to transport a bicycle!

The Norwegian government takes cycling seriously enough to have developed an official Cycling Strategy (www.sykkelbynettverket.no), among the primary goals of which is to increase cycling in larger Norwegian cities.

BOAT

Norway's excellent system of ferries connects otherwise inaccessible, isolated communities, with an extensive network of car ferries criss-crossing the fjords; express boats link offshore islands to the mainland. Most ferries accommodate motor vehicles, but some express coastal services normally take only foot passengers and cyclists, as do the lake steamers.

Long queues and delays are possible at popular crossings in summer. Ferries do, however, run late at night, especially in summer, albeit less frequently. Details on schedules and prices for vehicle ferries and lake steamers are provided in the timetables published by the Norwegian Tourist Board, or *Rutebok for Norge*. Tourist offices can also provide timetables for local ferries.

Norway Fjord Cruise (☏ 57 65 69 99; www.fjordcruise.no) and **Fjord1** (☏ 55 90 70 70; www.fjord1.no) both offer boat-based tours and/or ferries in the fjord region; the former also covers Lofoten and Svalbard.

BUS

Buses on Norway's extensive long-distance bus network are comfortable and make a habit of running on time. You can book tickets and consult timetables for most routes online.

In addition to the larger networks, there are a number of independent long-distance companies that provide similar prices and levels of service. In northern Norway there are several Togbuss (train–bus) routes, while elsewhere there's a host of local buses, most of which are confined to a single *fylke* (county). Most local and some long-distance bus schedules everywhere in Norway are drastically reduced on Saturday, Sunday and in the low season (usually mid-August to mid-June).

To get a complete listing of bus timetables (and some prices) throughout the country, pick up a copy of the free *Rutehefte* from any reasonably sized bus station and some tourist offices. All bus stations and tourist offices have smaller timetables for the relevant routes passing through town.

Lavprisekspressen (www.lavprisekspressen.no) The cheapest buses are operated by Lavprisekspressen, which sells tickets online. Its buses run along the coast between Oslo and Stavanger (via Kristiansand) and along two north–south corridors linking Oslo with Trondheim. If you're online at the right moment, Oslo–Trondheim fares can cost as little as 99kr; even its most expensive tickets are cheaper than those of its competitors.

Nettbuss (www.nettbuss.no) Nettbuss has a big network that includes the subsidiaries TIMEkspressen, Nettbuss Express and Bus4You (Bergen to Stavanger).

Nor-Way Bussekspress (p378) Nor-Way Bussekspress operates the largest network of express buses in Norway, with routes connecting most towns and cities.

Costs & Reservations

Advance reservations are rarely required in Norway. That said, you're more likely to find cheaper fares the earlier you book. Buying tickets over the internet is usually the best way to get the cheapest fare (special *minipris* tickets are frequently offered in summer), and online bookings are often the only option for Lavprisekspressen buses. Tickets are also sold on most buses or in advance at the bus station, and fares are based on the distance travelled. Some bus companies quote bus fares excluding any ferry costs, so always check.

Many bus companies offer student, child, senior and family discounts of 25% to 50%, so it pays to ask when purchasing. Groups (including two people travelling together) and holders of InterRail and Eurail passes may also be eligible for discounts.

CAR & MOTORCYCLE

There are no special requirements for bringing your car to Norway. Main highways, such as the E16 from Oslo to Bergen and the entire E6 from Oslo to Kirkenes, are open year-round; the same cannot be said for smaller, often more scenic mountain roads that generally only open from June to September, snow conditions permitting.

Statens Vegvesen's Road User Information Centre **Vegmeldingssentralen** (☏ 175, press 9 for English 22 07 30 00; www.vegvesen.no) provides 24-hour, up-to-date advice on road closures and conditions throughout the country.

Automobile Associations

By reciprocal agreement, members affiliated with AIT (Alliance Internationale de Tourisme) national automobile associations are eligible for 24-hour breakdown recovery assistance from the **Norges Automobil-Forbund** (NAF; ☏ 92 60 85 05; www.naf.no). NAF patrols ply the main roads from mid-June to mid-August. Emergency phones can be found along motorways, in tunnels and at certain mountain passes.

Driving Licences

Short-term visitors may hire a car with only their home country's driving licence.

Fuel

Norway's petrol prices are some of the most expensive in the world: at the time of research prices ranged from around 15kr to 16kr per litre. Diesel usually costs around 1kr per litre less. Most petrol stations sell unleaded petrol and diesel and take payment by major credit cards.

In towns, petrol stations may be open until 10pm or midnight, but there are some 24-hour services. In rural areas, many stations close in the early evening and don't open at all on weekends. Some have unstaffed 24-hour automatic pumps operated with credit cards.

A word of warning for those driving a diesel vehicle: don't fill up at the pump labelled '*augiftsfri diesel*', which is strictly for boats, tractors etc.

Hire

Norwegian car hire is costly and geared mainly to the business traveller. Walk-in rates for a compact car (with 200km per day included) typically approach 1200kr per day (including VAT, but insurance starts at 100kr per day extra). Per-day rates drop the longer you rent, and booking through online brokers can bring the price down as low as 600kr per day.

ROAD TOLLS

Around one-quarter of Norway's road construction budget comes from road tolls – you'll soon become accustomed to the signs warning of toll points.

Most of Norway's toll stations are automated. If you're driving a Norwegian rental car, they'll be fitted with an automatic sensor – after you return your car, the hire company adds up the accumulated tolls and then charges it to your credit card.

If you're driving a foreign-registered car (including some rental cars from other countries), you're expected to register your credit card in advance online at www.autopass.no (whereupon you pay a 200kr deposit) and the tolls are later deducted. The alternative is to pay at one of the pay stations (sometimes the first petrol station after the toll station). If you don't pay, the authorities will, in theory, attempt to track you down (often as much as six months later) and you'll be expected to pay both the toll and a penalty fee of 300kr.

Check the terms carefully before booking – look out for extra charges like collision damage waiver and high excesses. Also avoid contracts with limited mileage, as this can rapidly make a cheap deal very expensive. Check the condition of the tyres and the spare wheel (especially if you're travelling in winter); make sure to note any damage to the vehicle before departure, and have it noted on your copy of the contract.

Car-hire companies:

Avis (☑ 81 56 30 44; www.avis.no)

Bislet Bilutleie (☑ 22 60 00 00; www.bislet.no)

Budget (☑ 81 56 06 00; www.budget.no)

Europcar (☑ 67 16 58 20; www.europcar.no)

Hertz (☑ 67 16 80 00; www.hertz.no)

Rent-a-Wreck (☑ 81 52 20 50; www.rent-a-wreck.no)

Sixt (☑ 81 52 24 66; www.sixt.no)

Insurance

Third-party car insurance (unlimited cover for personal injury and 1,000,000kr for property damage) is compulsory and, if you're bringing a vehicle from abroad, you'll have fewer headaches with an insurance company Green Card. Ensure that your vehicle is insured for ferry crossings.

If you're renting, it's worth paying extra for comprehensive insurance – in the case of even a small accident, the difference between having to pay 1000kr and 10,000kr is considerable.

Road Conditions

If Norway were Nepal they'd have built a road to the top of (or underneath) Mt Everest. There are roads that can inspire nothing but profound admiration for the engineering expertise involved. The longest tunnels link adjacent valleys, while shorter tunnels drill through rocky impediments to straighten routes. To get an idea of just how hard-won were Norway's roads and tunnels through the mountains, visit the **Norwegian Museum of Road History** (Norsk Vegmuseum; ☑ 61 28 52 50; www. vegmuseum.no; Hunderfossvegen 757; ⊙ 10am-5pm mid-Jun–mid-Aug, 10am-3pm Tue-Sun rest of year), outside Lillehammer.

Most tunnels are lit and many longer ones have exhaust fans to remove fumes. Motorcyclists must be wary of fumes in longer tunnels and may want to avoid them where possible.

Although the roads are generally excellent, plan on taking longer than you expect, especially in summer high season. Speed limits rarely reach 90km/h and you'll share narrow roads with trucks, campervans and buses.

Road Hazards

Older roads and mountain routes are likely to be narrow, with multiple hairpin bends and very steep gradients. Although most areas are accessible by car (and very often tour bus), some of the less-used routes have poor or untarred surfaces only suitable for 4WD vehicles, and some seemingly normal roads can narrow sharply with very little warning. On some mountain roads, caravans and campervans are forbidden or advisable only for experienced drivers, as it may be necessary to reverse in order to allow approaching traffic to pass.

If you're expecting snowy or icy conditions, use studded tyres or carry snow chains.

Vegdirektoratet (☑ press 9 for English 22 07 30 00; www.vegvesen.no) outlines on a map the restricted roads for caravans; its website also has a handy route planner.

Road Rules

For more detail than you probably need, there's a downloadable PDF of Norway's road rules on the website for **Vegdirektoratet** (p381); follow the links to 'Traffic', then 'Traffic Rules'.

Blood-alcohol limit The limit is 0.02%. Mobile breath-testing stations are reasonably common, and violators are subject to severe fines and/or imprisonment. Because establishments serving alcohol may legally share liability in the case of an accident, you may not be served even a small glass of beer if the server or bartender knows you're driving.

Foreign vehicles Should bear an oval-shaped nationality sticker on the back. UK-registered vehicles must carry a vehicle registration document (Form V5) or a Certificate of Registration (Form V379, available from the Driver and Vehicle Licensing Agency in the UK). For vehicles not registered in the driver's name, you'll require written permission from the registered owner.

Headlights The use of dipped headlights (including on motorcycles) is required at all times and right-hand-drive vehicles must (in theory) have beam deflectors affixed to their headlight in order to avoid blinding oncoming traffic.

Motorcycle parking Motorcycles may not be parked on the pavement (sidewalk) and are subject to the same parking regulations as cars.

Red warning triangles Compulsory in all vehicles for use in the event of a breakdown.

Roundabouts (traffic circles) Give way to cars coming from the left.

Side of the road Drive on the right side.

Speed limits The national speed limit is 80km/h on the open road, but in villages limits range from 50km/h to 60km/h and in residential areas the limit is 30km/h. A few roads have segments allowing 90km/h, and you can drive at 100km/h on a small part of the E6 – bliss! The speed limit for caravans (and cars pulling trailers) is usually 10km/h less than for cars.

Vehicle Ferries

While travelling along the west coast may be spectacular, it also requires numerous ferry crossings that can prove time-consuming and costly. For a complete list of ferry schedules and fares, get hold of the *Rutebok for Norge*, a phone-book-sized transport guide sold in bookshops and larger Narvesen kiosks.

TRAIN

Norwegian State Railways (Norges Statsbaner, NSB; ☑ press 9 for English 81 50 08 88; www.nsb.no) operates an excellent, though limited, system of lines connecting Oslo with Stavanger, Bergen, Åndalsnes, Trondheim, Fauske and Bodø; lines also connect Sweden with Oslo, Trondheim and Narvik. Most train stations offer luggage lockers for 50kr to 90kr and many also have baggage storage rooms.

Most long-distance day trains have 1st- and 2nd-class seats and a buffet car or refreshment trolley service. Public phones can be found in all express trains and most intercity trains. Doors are wide and there's space for bulky luggage. Free wi-fi is available on most routes, although the service can be unreliable in the countryside.

Buying Tickets

The easiest – and usually cheapest – way to book tickets is online at the NSB website (www.nsb.no/en/frontpage). Look out for cheap *minipris* fares. Reservations sometimes cost an additional 50kr and are mandatory on some long-distance routes. Usually you'll be sent an online ticket with a barcode, to be scanned on-board by the conductor.

Alternatively, you can buy tickets from automated machines at most main stations, as well as at customer-service counters. It is possible to buy tickets on-board from the conductor, using either cash or credit card. For shorter journeys this is usually at the standard fare, but for longer journeys you might be missing out on cheap and discounted tickets such as the *minipris* fares, so always try booking online as far in advance as you can.

Classes & Costs

On long-distance trains, 2nd-class carriages provide comfortable reclining seats with footrests. First-class carriages, which cost 50% more, offer marginally more space and often a food trolley, but they're generally not worth the extra expense.

Travelling by train in Norway is expensive: it often costs less to fly. However, if you learn how to work the *minipris* system, or the train passes, train travel suddenly becomes affordable. And think of the scenery...

There's a 50% discount on rail travel for people aged 67 and older, for travellers with disabilities, and for children aged between four and 15; children under four travel free. Students get discounts of between 25% and 40%.

On long-distance overnight routes, sleeper compartments (you pay for the whole two-bed compartment) are additional to the standard fares.

MINIPRIS

If you plan to travel on longer routes by train through Norway and you know your itinerary in advance, this tip will save you hundreds of kroner. On every route, for every departure, Norwegian State Railways sets aside a limited number of tickets known as *minipris*. Those who book the earliest can get just about any route for just 299kr. Once those are exhausted, the next batch of *minipris* tickets goes for 399kr and so on. These tickets cannot be purchased at ticket counters and must instead be bought over the internet (www.nsb.no) or in ticket-vending machines at train stations. Remember that *minipris* tickets may only be purchased in advance (minimum one day), reservations are nonrefundable and cannot be changed once purchased. In peak seasons (especially from mid-June to mid-August) on popular routes, you may need to book up to three weeks in advance to get the cheapest fares. That said, the savings are considerable, often as much as 75% off the full fare.

Sweden

Best Places to Eat

➡ Woodstockholm (p398)

➡ Rutabaga (p398)

➡ SPiS (p461)

Best Places to Stay

➡ Icehotel (p460)

➡ Treehotel (p456)

➡ U&Me Hotel (p454)

➡ Green Hotel (p411)

Why Go?

As progressive and civilised as it may be, Sweden is a wild place. Its scenery ranges from barren moonscapes and impenetrable forests in the far north to sunny beaches and lush farmland further south. Its short summers and long winters mean that people cling to every last speck of sunshine on a late August evening – crayfish parties on seaside decks can stretch into the wee hours. In winter locals rely on candlelight and *glögg* to warm their spirits. But lovers of the outdoors will thrive here in any season: winter sees skiing and dogsledding while the warmer months invite long hikes, swimming and sunbathing, canoeing, cycling – you name it – if it's fun and can be done outdoors, you'll find it here. For less rugged types, there's always restaurant and nightclub hopping and museum perusing

When to Go
Stockholm

Jun–Aug Summers are short but intense, and the 'white nights' beyond the Arctic Circle magical.

Sep–Oct Nothing's open, but the countryside is stunning in autumn.

Mar–Apr Winter sports and the aurora borealis (northern lights) keep Norrland towns buzzing.

Sweden Highlights

❶ Stockholm
(p385) Touring the urban waterways, exploring top-notch museums and wandering the labyrinthine Old Town.

❷ Jukkasjärvi
(p460) Hiking through wild landscapes, spotting herds of reindeer, absorbing Sami culture and sleeping in the world-famous Icehotel.

❸ Gothenburg
(p424) Digging into the art, fashion and originality that make Sweden's 'second city' first-rate.

❹ Visby (p445)
Joining the feasting, archery and other medieval fun and frolics in this historic town.

❺ Kiruna (p460)
Racing a dog-sled under the northern lights.

❻ Lake Siljan
(p410) Celebrating Midsummer in the heartland villages surrounding this lovely lake.

❼ Arvidsjaur
(p456) Taking a car for a spin on a frozen lake.

STOCKHOLM

♪ 08 / POP 932,000

Beautiful capital cities are no rarity in Europe, but Stockholm must surely be near the top of the list for sheer loveliness. The saffron-and-cinnamon buildings that cover its 14 islands rise starkly out of the surrounding ice-blue water, honeyed in sunlight and frostily elegant in cold weather. The city's charms are irresistible. From its movie-set Old Town (Gamla Stan) to its ever-modern fashion sense and impeccable taste in food and design, the city acts like an immersion school in aesthetics.

History

Its creation shaped by waterways, Stockholm originally came into existence when Vikings moved their trade centre here from northern Mälaren lake for easier sea–lake trade. Around 1250, Stockholm's leaders wrote a town charter and signed a trade treaty with the Hanseatic port of Lübeck. Stockholm's official founder, Birger Jarl, commissioned the Tre Kronor castle in 1252.

A century later, Stockholm was hurting. The Black Death of 1350 wiped out a third of the population, and in 1391 the Danish queen Margareta Valdemarsdotter besieged the city for four years. This led to the Union of Kalmar, which linked the crowns of Sweden, Norway and Denmark in 1397. But Sweden soon began to chafe under the union. Discontent peaked with the Stockholm Bloodbath of 1520, when Danish king Christian II tricked, trapped and beheaded 82 Swedish burghers, bishops and nobles on Stortorget in Gamla Stan.

One of the 82 victims was the father of Gustav Eriksson Vasa; Gustav Vasa's quest to retaliate eventually led to widespread rebellion against Danish rule, and he became King of Sweden on 6 June 1523. These days, Swedes view Gustav Vasa as equal parts 'father of the country' and ruthless tyrant.

By the end of the 16th century, Stockholm's population was 9000 and had expanded beyond Gamla Stan to the neighbouring islands of Norrmalm and Södermalm. The city was officially proclaimed Sweden's capital in 1634, and by 1650 the city had a thriving artistic and intellectual culture and a grand new look, courtesy of father-andson architects the Tessins. The next growth spurt came in 1871, when Sweden's northern and southern train lines met at Centralstationen (Central Station) and started an industrial boom. The city's population reached 245,000 in 1890.

Sweden's famed neutrality left it and its capital city in good shape through both world wars. These days, the capital is part of a major European biotechnology region, not to mention star on the world stages of fashion and culinary arts.

⊙ Sights

Stockholm can seem a baffling city to navigate at first, strewn over 14 islands. Although the city centre and other neighbourhoods are easily walkable, the excellent transport system, comprising trams, buses and metro, is the best way to cover the city's more far-flung sights. Most people start their visit at Gamla Stan, a medieval tangle of narrow alleyways and colourful buildings which,

SWEDEN STOCKHOLM

STOCKHOLM IN...

Two Days

Beat the crowds to the labyrinthine streets of Gamla Stan, the city's historic old town. Watch St George wrestle the dragon inside **Storkyrkan** (p389), the old-town cathedral, and join a tour of the royal palace, **Kungliga Slottet** (p388). Then trek to **Södermalm** (p393) for dizzying views from the Söder heights. See what's on at the photography gallery **Fotografiska** (p393) – you can grab a bite here, too. If the weather's nice, party at the bars in Medborgarplatsen. Spend the next day exploring the outdoor museum **Skansen** (p391).

Four Days

On day three take a guided boat tour of Stockholm's waterways. Visit the impressive **Vasamuseet** (p391), then stroll up to **Hötorgshallen** (p397) for a big bowl of fish soup and speciality-food browsing. Next day, head to **Drottningholm Slott** (p394) in the morning, then spend the afternoon doing what Stockholmers do best: shopping. Start with pedestrianised **Biblioteksgatan** (p400) off Stureplan, then transition to Drottninggatan for souvenirs.

SWEDEN STOCKHOLM

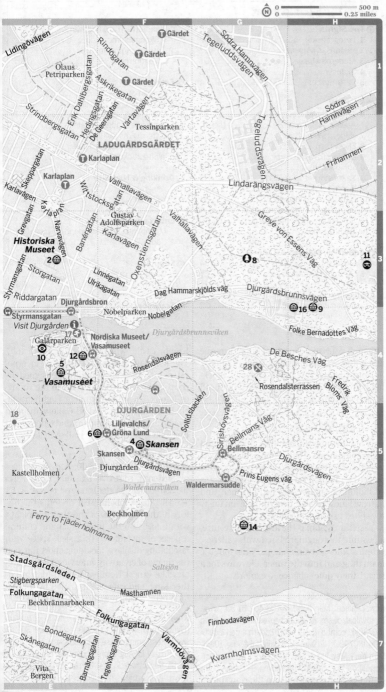

Greater Stockholm

although touristy, is extremely picturesque and home to several truly splendid sights.

Note that very few museums in Stockholm are open before 10am – often not until 11am. Plan to *ta det lugnt* ('take it easy').

◎ Gamla Stan

The old town is Stockholm's historic and geographic heart. Here, cobblestone streets wriggle past Renaissance churches, baroque palaces and medieval squares. Spice-coloured buildings sag like wizened old men, and narrow lanes harbour everything from dusty toy shops to candlelit cafes.

Västerlånggatan is the area's nerve centre, a bustling thoroughfare lined with galleries, eateries and souvenir shops. Step off the main drag and into the tinier alleyways for a surprisingly quiet chance to explore.

★**Kungliga Slottet**   PALACE
(Royal Palace; Map p390; ☎ 08-402 61 30; www. theroyalpalace.se; Slottsbacken; adult/child 160/80kr, combo ticket incl Riddarholmen adult/ child 180/90kr; ☺ 9am-5pm daily Jul & Aug, 10am-5pm daily May-Jun & Sep, 10am-4pm Tue-Sun Oct-Apr; ☒ 43, 46, 55, 59 Slottsbacken, ☒ Gamla Stan) Kungliga Slottet was built on the ruins of Tre

Kronor castle, which burned down in 1697. The north wing survived and was incorporated into the new building. Designed by court architect Nicodemus Tessin the Younger, it took 57 years to complete. Highlights include the decadent Karl XI Gallery, inspired by Versailles' Hall of Mirrors and Queen Kristina's silver throne in the Hall of State.

Nobelmuseet   MUSEUM
(Map p390; ☒ 08-54 43 18 00; http://nobelcenter. se; Stortorget; adult/child 120kr/free; ☺ 9am-8pm Tue-Sun Jun-Aug, shorter hours rest of year; ☒ 53, ☒ Gamla Stan) Nobelmuseet presents the history of the Nobel Prizes and their recipients, with a focus on the intellectual and cultural aspects of invention. It's a slick space with fascinating displays, including short films on the theme of creativity, interviews with laureates like Ernest Hemingway and Martin Luther King, and cafe chairs signed by the visiting prize recipients (flip them over to see!).

Royal Armoury   MUSEUM
(Livrustkammaren; Map p390; ☎ 08-402 30 30; www.livrustkammaren.se; Slottsbacken 3; ☺ 10am to 6pm daily Jul-Aug, shorter hours rest of year; ☒ 43, 46, 55, 59 Slottsbacken, ☒ Gamla Stan) **FREE** The Royal Armoury is housed in the cellar vaults

of the palace but has separate hours. It's a family attic of sorts, crammed with engrossing memorabilia spanning more than 500 years of royal childhoods, coronations, weddings and murders. Meet Gustav II Adolf's stuffed battle steed, Streiff; see the costume Gustav III wore to the masquerade ball on the night he was shot in 1792; or let the kids try on a suit of armour in the playroom.

Riddarholmskyrkan CHURCH
(Riddarholmen Church; Map p390; ☑ 08-402 61 30; www.kungahuset.se; Riddarholmen; adult/child 50/25kr; ⊘ 10am-5pm daily mid-May–mid-Sep, 10am-4pm Sat & Sun Oct-Nov; ☑ 3, 53 Riddarhustorget, ☒ Gamla Stan) The strikingly beautiful Riddarholmskyrkan, on the equally pretty and under-visited islet of Riddarholmen, was built by Franciscan monks in the late 13th century. It has been the royal necropolis since the burial of Magnus Ladulås in 1290, and is home to the armorial glory of the Seraphim knightly order. There's a guided tour in English at noon (included with admission) and occasional concerts. Holiday closures are frequent; check the website for updates. Admission fee is by credit card only.

Storkyrkan CHURCH
(Great Church; Map p390; www.stockholmsdomkyrkoforsamling.se; Trångsund 1; adult/child 60kr/free; ⊘ 9am-4pm, to 6pm Jun-Aug; ☒ Gamla Stan) The one-time venue for royal weddings and coronations, Storkyrkan is both Stockholm's oldest building (consecrated in 1306) and its cathedral. Behind a baroque facade, the Gothic-baroque interior includes extravagant royal-box pews designed by Nicodemus Tessin the Younger, as well as German Berndt Notke's dramatic sculpture *St George and the Dragon*, commissioned by Sten Sture the Elder to commemorate his victory over the Danes in 1471. Keep an eye out for posters and handbills advertising music performances here.

Medeltidsmuseet MUSEUM
(Medieval Museum; www.medeltidsmuseet.stockholm.se; Strömparterren; ⊘ noon-5pm Tue-Sun, to 8pm Wed; ☑ 62, 65, Gustav Adolfs torg) **FREE** Tucked beneath the bridge that links Gamla Stan and Norrmalm, this child-friendly museum was established when construction workers preparing to build a car park here in the late 1970s unearthed foundations from the 1530s. The ancient walls were preserved as found, and a museum was built around them. The circular plan leads visitors through faithful reconstructions of typical

homes, markets and workshops from medieval Stockholm. Tickets are valid for one year.

Riksdagshuset NOTABLE BUILDING
(Swedish Parliament; ☑ 020-34 80 00; www.riksdagen.se; Riksgatan 3; ⊘ 1hr tours in English noon, 1, 2 & 3pm Mon-Fri mid-Jun–mid-Aug, 1.30pm Sat & Sun Oct–mid-Jun; ☑ 3, 59, Riddarhustorget, ☒ Gamla Stan, T-Centralen) **FREE** Technically situated on Helgeandsholmen, the little island in the middle of Norrström, rather than on Gamla Stan, the Swedish Parliament building is an unexpected pleasure to visit. The building consists of two parts: the older front section (facing downstream) dates from the early 20th century, but the other more-modern part contains the current debating chamber. Tours of the building offer a compelling glimpse into the Swedish system of consensus-building government.

⊙ Central Stockholm

The fashionable, high-heeled heart of modern-day Stockholm beats in bustling Norrmalm. Near T-Centralen station is Sergels Torg, a severely modern public square (actually round) bordered on one side by the imposing Kulturhuset, Stockholm's cultural centre and theatre space. Norrmalm is also home to the beloved public park Kungsträdgården – home to an outdoor stage, winter ice-skating rink and restaurants, cafes and kiosks. Vasastan is the somewhat quieter, more residential area that extends to the north of Norrmalm.

★ Historiska Museet MUSEUM
(Map p386; ☑ 08-51 95 56 20; www.historiska.se; Narvavägen 13-17; ⊘ 10am-5pm Jun-Aug, 11am-5pm Tue-Sun, to 8pm Wed Sep-May; ☑ 44,56, ☒ Djurgårdsbron, ☒ Karlaplan, Östermalmstorg) **FREE** The national historical collection awaits at this enthralling museum. From Iron Age skates and a Viking boat to medieval textiles and Renaissance triptychs, it spans 10,000 years of Swedish culture and history. There's an exhibit about the medieval Battle of Gotland (1361), an excellent multimedia display on the Vikings, a room of breathtaking altarpieces from the Middle Ages, a vast textile collection and a section on prehistoric culture.

Bonniers Konsthall GALLERY
(Map p386; ☑ 08-736 42 48; www.bonnierskonsthall.se; Torsgatan 19; ⊘ noon-5pm Thu-Sun, to 8pm Wed; ☒ St Eriksplan) **FREE** This ambitious gallery keeps culture fiends busy with a fresh dose of international contemporary art, as well as a reading room, a fab cafe and a busy

Gamla Stan

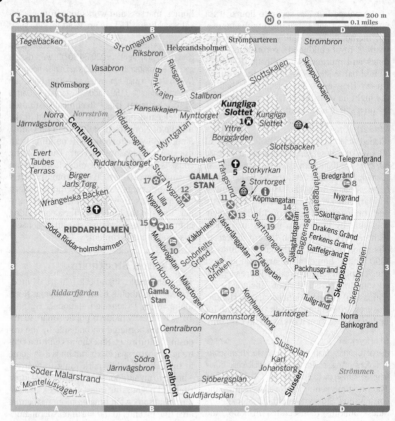

Gamla Stan

schedule of art seminars and artists-in-conversation sessions. The massive, transparent flatiron building was designed by Johan Celsing. There are discussions about the exhibitions in English at 1pm, 3pm, 5pm and 7pm on Wednesday, and 1pm and 4pm Thursday to Sunday. Curators lead free guided tours on Sunday at 2pm.

Wetterling Gallery
GALLERY

(☑08-10 10 09; www.wetterlinggallery.com; Kungsträdgården 3; ☺11am-5pm Wed-Fri, 1-4pm Sat; 🚇Kungsträdgården) This cool gallery space at the edge of Kungsträdgården always has something interesting going on – usually a boundary-pushing contemporary painter, but there's also often photography or multimedia work, from big names (eg Frank Stella) to soon-to-be-big names.

Konstakademien
MUSEUM

(Royal Academy of Fine Arts; ☑08-23 29 25; www.konstakademien.se; Fredsgatan 12; ☺11am-5pm Tue-Fri, noon-4pm Sat & Sun; 🚇Centralen) **FREE** The Royal Academy of Fine Arts has a beautiful gallery space and puts on several exhibitions a year, well worth investigating if you're interested in Swedish art.

⊙ Djurgården

★Vasamuseet
MUSEUM

(Map p386; www.vasamuseet.se; Galärvarvsvägen 14; adult/child 130kr/free; ☺8.30am-6pm Jun-Aug, 10am-5pm Thur-Tue, to 8pm Wed Sep-May; 🅿; 🚌44, 🚢Djurgårdsfärjan, 🚋7) A good-humoured glorification of some dodgy calculations, Vasamuseet is the custom-built home of the massive warship *Vasa;* 69m long and 48.8m tall, it was the pride of the Swedish crown when it set off on its maiden voyage on 10 August 1628. Within minutes, the top-heavy vessel tipped and sank to the bottom of Saltsjön, along with many of the people on board.

★Skansen
MUSEUM

(Map p386; www.skansen.se; Djurgårdsvägen; adult/child 180/60kr; ☺10am-6pm, extended hours in summer; 🅿; 🚌69, 🚢Djurgårdsfärjan, 🚋7) The world's first open-air museum, Skansen was founded in 1891 by Artur Hazelius to provide an insight into how Swedes once lived. You could easily spend a day here and not see it all. Around 150 traditional houses and other exhibits dot the hilltop – it's meant to be 'Sweden in miniature', complete with villages, nature, commerce and industry. Note that prices and opening hours and days vary seasonally; check the website before you go.

Nordiska Museet
MUSEUM

(Map p386; ☑08-51 95 47 70; www.nordiskamuseet.se; Djurgårdsvägen 6-16; adult/child 120kr/free; ☺10am-5pm Sep-May, 9am-5pm rest of year, to 8pm Wed; 🚌44, 69, 🚢Djurgårdsfärjan, 🚋7) The epic Nordiska Museet is Sweden's largest cultural-history museum and one of its largest indoor spaces. The building itself (from 1907) is an eclectic, Renaissance-style castle designed by Isak Gustav Clason, who also drew up Östermalms Saluhall (p397); you'll notice a resemblance. Inside is a sprawling collection of all things Swedish, from sacred Sami objects to clothing and table settings. The museum boasts the world's largest collection of paintings by August Strindberg, as well as a number of his personal possessions.

ABBA: The Museum
MUSEUM

(Map p386; ☑08-12 13 28 60; www.abbathemuseum.com; Djurgårdsvägen 68; adult/child 250/95kr; ☺9am-7pm Mon-Fri Jun-Aug, shorter hours rest of year; 🚌67, 🚢Djurgårdsfärjan, Emelie, 🚋7) A sensory-overload experience that might appeal only to devoted ABBA fans, this long-awaited and wildly hyped cathedral to the demigods of Swedish pop is almost aggressively entertaining. It's packed to the gills with memorabilia and interactivity – every square inch has something new to look at, be it a glittering guitar, a vintage photo of Benny, Björn, Frida or Agnetha, a classic music video, an outlandish costume or a tour van from the band members' early days.

Prins Eugens Waldemarsudde
MUSEUM

(Map p386; ☑08-54 58 37 07; www.waldemarsudde.com; Prins Eugens väg 6; adult/child 150kr/free; ☺11am-5pm Tue-Sun, to 8pm Thu, gardens 8am-9pm; 🚋7) Prins Eugens Waldemarsudde, at the southern tip of Djurgården, is a soul-perking combo of water views and art. The palace once belonged to the painter prince (1865–1947), who favoured art over typical royal pleasures. In addition to Eugen's own work, it holds his impressive collection of Nordic paintings and sculptures, including works by Anders Zorn and Carl Larsson. The museum stages top-notch temporary exhibitions several times a year, usually highlighting the careers of important Scandinavian artists.

Junibacken
AMUSEMENT PARK

(Map p386; www.junibacken.se; Djurgården; adult/child 159/139kr; ☺10am-6pm Jul-Aug, to 5pm rest of year; 🚼; 🚌44, 69, 🚢Djurgårdsfärjan, 🚋7) Junibacken whimsically recreates the fantasy scenes of Astrid Lindgren's books for children. Catch the flying Story Train over Stockholm, shrink to the size of a sugar cube and end up at Villekulla cottage, where kids can shout, squeal and dress up like Pippi Longstocking. The bookshop is a treasure trove of children's books, as well as a great place to pick up anything from cheeky Karlsson dolls to cute little art cards with storybook themes.

Central Stockholm

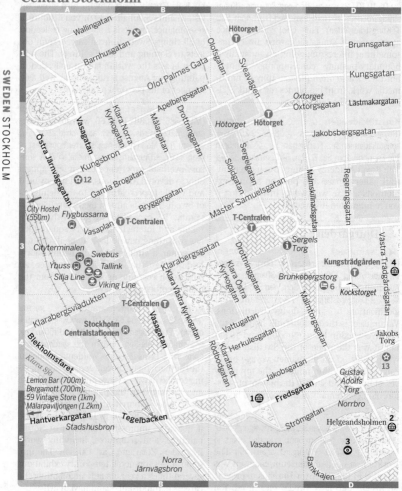

Skeppsholmen

★ Moderna Museet
MUSEUM

(Map p386; ☎08-52 02 35 00; www.modernamuseet.se; Exercisplan 4; ⏲10am-8pm Tue & Fri, to 6pm Wed-Thu, 11am-6pm Sat & Sun; 🅿; 🚌65, 🚢Djurgårdsfärjan) **FREE** Moderna Museet is Stockholm's modern-art maverick, its permanent collection ranging from paintings and sculptures to photography, video art and installations. Highlights include works by Pablo Picasso, Salvador Dalí, Andy Warhol, Damien Hirst and Robert Rauschenberg, plus several key figures in the Scandinavian and Russian art worlds and beyond. There are important pieces by Francis Bacon, Marcel Duchamp and Matisse, as well as their contemporaries, both household names and otherwise.

At the time of research, the museum was closed for renovations, with plans to reopen in November 2018.

ArkDes
MUSEUM

(Map p386; ☎08-58 72 70 00; www.arkdes.se; Exercisplan 4; special exhibits adult/child 120kr/free; ⏲10am-8pm Tue & Fri, to 6pm Wed & Thu, 11am-6pm Sat & Sun; 🚌65, 🚢Djurgårdsfärjan) **FREE** Adjoining Moderna Museet (p392) and housed in a converted navy drill hall, this architecture

narrow building displays Asian decorative arts, including one of the world's finest collections of Chinese stoneware and porcelain from the Song, Ming and Qing dynasties. The museum also houses the largest and oldest Asian library in Scandinavia, from which several notable specimens are displayed. The often refreshing temporary exhibitions cover a wide range of themes, with past shows including a look at Japanese anime characters and Chinese video art.

◎ Södermalm

Once-working-class 'Söder' – the southern island – is Stockholm's coolest neighbourhood, jammed with up-and-coming boutiques and galleries, hip cafes and bars and a museum of city history. 'SoFo' (the area south of Folkungagatan) is the trendiest district.

★ **Fotografiska**   GALLERY
(Map p386; www.fotografiska.eu; Stadsgårdshamnen 22; adult/child 135kr/free; ⊘9am-11pm Sun-Wed, to 1am Thu-Sat; ⊠Slussen) A stylish photography museum, Fotografiska is a must for shutterbugs. Its constantly changing exhibitions are huge, interestingly chosen and well presented; examples have included a Robert Mapplethorpe retrospective, portraits by

and design centre has a permanent exhibition spanning 1000 years of Swedish architecture and an archive of 2.5 million documents, photographs, plans, drawings and models. Temporary exhibitions also cover international names and work. The museum organises occasional themed architectural tours of Stockholm; check the website or ask at the information desk.

Östasiatiska Museet   MUSEUM
(Museum of Far Eastern Antiquities; Map p386; www.ostasiatiska.se; Tyghusplan; ⊘11am-5pm Wed-Sun, to 8pm Tue; ⊠65) FREE This long,

WORTH A TRIP

DROTTNINGHOLM SLOTT

Home to the royal family for part of the year, **Drottningholm Slott** (🌐 08-402 62 80; www.kungahuset.se; Ekerö; adult/child 130/65kr, combined ticket incl Kina Slott 190/90kr; ⊙10am-4.30pm May-Sep, 11am-3.30pm Oct & Apr, noon-3.30pm Sat & Sun rest of year (closed mid-Dec–Jan); 🅿; 🚢 Stadshuskajen (summer only), 🚇 Brommaplan, then bus 301-323), Drottningholm's Renaissance-inspired main palace, was designed by architectural great Nicodemus Tessin the Elder and begun in 1662, about the same time as Versailles. You can roam on your own, but it's worth taking a one-hour guided tour (30kr; in English at 10am, noon, 2pm and 4pm June to August, noon and 2pm other months). Guides are entertaining, and provide insight into the cultural milieu that influenced some of the decorations.

indie filmmaker Gus Van Sant and an enormous collection of black-and-white photos by Sebastião Salgado. The attached cafe-bar draws a crowd on summer evenings, with DJs, good cocktails and outdoor seating. Follow signs from the Slussen tunnelbana stop to reach the museum.

Stockholms Stadsmuseum MUSEUM
(City Museum; Map p386; www.stadsmuseum.stockholm.se; Ryssgården, Slussen; 🚇 Slussen) The evocative exhibits here cover Stockholm's development from fortified port to modern metropolis via plague, fire and good old-fashioned scandal. The museum is housed in a late-17th-century palace designed by Nicodemus Tessin the Elder. Temporary exhibitions are fresh and eclectic, focused on the city's ever-changing shape and spirit. Admission gets you a card good for one year here and at Medeltidsmuseet (p389).

◉ Ladugårdsgärdet

The vast parkland of Ladugårdsgärdet is part of the 27-sq-km **Ekoparken** (Royal National City Park; Map p386; www.ekoparken.org; ⊙24hr; 🚇; 🚌 69) 🌿 **FREE**, the world's first national park within a city. An impressive 14km long, its combo of forest and open fields stretches far into the capital's northern suburbs. Reached by bus 69 from Centralstationen or Sergels Torg, it boasts several fine museums and one of Stockholm's loftiest views.

Etnografiska Museet MUSEUM
(Museum of Ethnography; Map p386; 🌐 010-456 12 99; www.etnografiska.se; Djurgårdsbrunnsvägen 34; ⊙11am-5pm Tue-Sun, to 8pm Wed; 🚌 69 Museiparken) **FREE** The Museum of Ethnography stages evocative displays on various aspects of non-European cultures, including dynamic temporary exhibitions and frequent live performances. Recent examples include displays about the cultural treasures of Afghanistan, a gender norms in different cultures, and 'reallife' voodoo. If there's a dance or musical performance scheduled, don't miss it. The cafe is a treat, with great music, imported sweets and beverages, and authentic global dishes.

Kaknästornet VIEWPOINT
(Map p386; www.kaknastornet.se; Mörka Kroken 28-30; adult/child 70/25kr; ⊙10am-6pm Sun-Thu, to 9pm Fri & Sat; 🚌 69 Kaknästornet) A handy landmark for navigating this part of town, the 155m-tall Kaknästornet is the automatic operations centre for radio and TV broadcasting in Sweden. Opened in 1967, it's among the tallest buildings in Scandinavia. There's a small visitor centre (mainly a gift shop) on the ground floor and an elevator up to the observation deck, restaurant and cafe near the top, from where there are stellar views of the city and archipelago.

Tekniska Museet MUSEUM
(Museum of Science & Technology; Map p386; 🌐 08-450 56 00; www.tekniskamuseet.se; Museivägen 7; adult/child 150/100kr, free 5-8pm Wed; ⊙10am-5pm Thu-Tue, to 8pm Wed; 👶; 🚌 69 Museiparken) Tekniska is a sprawling wonderland of interactive science and technology exhibits. The Teknorama is a vast room of kinetic experiments and stations designed to do things like test your balance, flexibility and strength. In one corner is a dark and genuinely scary mining exhibit. There's also a model railroad, a survey of inventions by women, and a climate-change game.

🏃 Activities

Fjäderholmarna BOATING
(Feather Islands; 🌐 08-2155000; www.fjaderholmslinjen.se; Nybroplan, Berth 13; adult/child roundtrip 145/70kr; ⊙hourly 10.30am-10.30pm May–early Sep) A trip to the Feather Islands takes about 25 minutes from Stockholm, and is a fantastic way to get a taste of the archipelago in a very short time. You can swim and sunbathe, visit traditional workshops including smiths and glassblowers, admire old boats, visit a brewery and stuff yourself on smoked fish. Recommended!

Strömma Kanalbolaget   BOATING

(Map p386; ☑08-12 00 40 00; www.stromma.se; Svensksundsvägen 17; 200-400kr) This ubiquitous company offers tours large and small, from a 50-minute 'royal canal tour' around Djurgården (200kr) to a 50-minute ABBA tour, which visits places where the *ABBA* movie was shot and drops you off at the ABBA museum (p391) (315kr). There are also hop-on, hop-off tours by bus (from 300kr), boat (180kr) or both (400kr).

Sjöcaféet   CYCLING

(Map p386; ☑08-660 57 57; www.sjocafeet.se; Djurgårdsvägen 2; per hour/day bicycles 80/275kr, canoes 150/400kr, kayaks 125/400kr; ⊙9am-9pm Apr-Sep; 🚲7) Rent bicycles from the small wooden hut below this restaurant, cafe and tourist-info centre beside Djurgårdsbron, Stockholm's centrally located bridge; it also offers canoes and kayaks for hire.

👉 Tours

Millennium Tour   WALKING

(www.stadsmuseum.stockholm.se; per person 130kr; ⊙11.30am Sat year-round, 6pm Thu Jul-Sep) Fans of Stieg Larsson's madly popular crime novels (*The Girl with the Dragon Tattoo*) will enjoy this walking tour (in English) pointing out key locations from the books and films. While the Stadsmuseum is closed for renovations, buy tickets online or at the Medeltidsmuseet (p389). Tour meeting points are printed on the tickets.

Stockholm Ghost Walk   WALKING

(Map p390; ☑07-61 46 66 00; www.stock-holmghostwalk.com; Tyska Brinken 13; adult/child 200/100kr, cash only; ⊙7pm; 🚇Gamla Stan) This 90-minute walking tour features tales of murder, mayhem, hauntings and executions, narrated with gusto by multilingual costumed guides. The walk starts at Järntorget in Gamla Stan. Dinner packages available (from 575kr per person). Check online for tour availability on particular days.

Far & Flyg   BALLOONING

(☑070-340 41 07; www.farochflyg.se; 10-person group 25,000kr; ⊙late May–mid-Sep) Float over Stockholm in a hot-air balloon for up to an hour and see the city from a rare vantage point. Note that only groups can book trips, so bring your friends, and reserve well ahead.

Svenska Turistföreningen   TOURS

(STF | Swedish Touring Association; ☑08-463 21 00; www.svenskaturistforeningen.se) Events and tours are generally affordable, ecologically minded and fun, and mostly based on outdoor activities (eg kayaking and hiking). Equipment rental is often available. Prices are usually lower for STF members.

🎊 Festivals & Events

Smaka På Stockholm   FOOD & DRINK

(A Taste of Stockholm; www.smakapastockholm. se; ⊙early Jun) FREE A five-day celebration of the Stockholm area's food scene. The program includes gourmet food stalls (including representatives from several archipelago restaurants), cooking demos and entertainment on Kungsträdgården. It's free to get in, and food offerings tend to be good value.

Stockholm Pride   LGBT

(www.stockholmpride.org/en; ⊙late Jul or early Aug) Stockholm goes pink with a week of parties and cultural events, plus a pride parade.

Stockholms Kulturfestival   CULTURAL

(www.kulturfestivalen.stockholm.se; ⊙mid-Aug) FREE This festival is one big party week, with everything from sidewalk opera to street theatre and dancing in and around Sergels Torg. Free admission.

**Stockholm International
Film Festival**   FILM

(www.stockholmfilmfestival.se; tickets 170kr; ⊙Nov) A major celebration of local and international cinema whose guest speakers include top actors and directors. The ticket office is in **Kulturhuset** (☑tickets noon-5pm 08-50 62 02 00; www.kulturhusetstadsteatern.se; Sergels Torg; ⊙11am-5pm, some sections closed Mon; 🚹; 🚌52, 56, 59, 69, 91 Sergels Torg, 🚲7 Sergels Torg, 🚇T-Centralen).

Stockholm Jazz Festival   MUSIC

(www.stockholmjazz.com; ticket price varies by venue; ⊙Oct) One of Europe's premier jazz festivals, headquartered at Fasching (p399).

🛏 Sleeping

⭐**Långholmen Hotell &
Vandrarhem**   HOSTEL, HOTEL €

(☑08-720 85 00; www.langholmen.com; Långholmsmuren 20, Långholmen; dm from 290kr, cell with bath s/d from 650/810kr, hotel r from 1095kr; 🅿🚭@🛜; 🚌4, 40, 77, 94 Högalidsgatan, 🚇Hornstull, 🚌54 Bergsunds strand) Guests at this hotel-hostel, in a former prison on Långholmen island, sleep on bunks in a cell, with either shared or private baths (it's much nicer than that sounds; there's a playful vibe throughout). There's laundry service, a good guest kitchen, excellent breakfast, a restaurant serving meals all day June to August, and a popular Långholmen bathing spot a towel flick away.

Zinkensdamm Hotell & Vandrarhem
HOTEL, HOSTEL €

(Map p386; ☑08-616 81 00; www.zinkensdamm. com; Zinkens Väg 20; dm from 270kr, s/d from 490/850kr; P➡☀@🖰; 🚇Zinkensdamm) 🍴 In a cheery yellow building next to the adorable Tantolunden park, the Zinkensdamm STF is fun, attractive and well equipped – complete with a sleek guest kitchen and personal lockers in each room – and caters for families with kids as well as pub-going backpackers. It can be crowded and noisy, but that's the tradeoff for an upbeat vibe.

2kronor Hostel Old Town
HOSTEL €

(Map p390; ☑08-22 92 30; www.2kronor. se; Skeppsbron 40; dm from 195kr, s/d from 495/590kr; ⊗reception 3-6pm; ➡@🖰; 🚇Gamla Stan, Slussen) This small, quiet, family-run hostel has a fantastic location and a friendly vibe. Rooms are on the basement level, slightly cavelike but pretty and well kept (and there are windows). Shared bathrooms are down the hall. Breakfast isn't available, but there's a guest kitchen and dining area by the reception upstairs. Dorms (six- and eight-bed rooms with bunks) are mixed.

⭐Hobo Hotel
BOUTIQUE HOTEL €€

(☑08-57 88 27 00; https://hobo.se; Brunkebergstorg 4; r without/with windows from 1000/1250kr, breakfast 120kr; ➡; 🚇T-Centralen) This new 200-room boutique hotel has a great location in the city centre, plus a mega-hip style that feels both cool and comfortable. The cheapest rooms are small and windowless, but well designed, with full bath and comfy beds. Details like comic books on the bedside table and borrowable umbrellas add to the fun vibe.

⭐Vandrarhem af Chapman & Skeppsholmen
HOSTEL €€

(Map p386; ☑08-463 22 66; www.stfchapman.com; Flaggmansvägen 8; dm/s/d from 325/595/940kr; ➡@🖰; 🚇65 Skeppsholmen) The *af Chapman* is a storied vessel that has done plenty of travelling of its own. It's anchored in a superb location, swaying gently off Skeppsholmen. Bunks are in dorms below deck. Apart from showers and toilets, all facilities are on dry land in the Skeppsholmen hostel, including a good kitchen, a laid-back common room and a TV lounge.

Victory Hotel
HOTEL €€

(Map p390; ☑08-50 64 00 00; www.thecollectorshotels.se/en/victory-hotel/; Lilla Nygatan 5; r from 1120kr; ➡☀@🖰; 🚇Gamla Stan) Nautical antiques, art and model ships define the wonderfully quirky Victory. Most rooms are fairly small (though perfectly comfy), while the museum-like suites (from 2300kr) are larger. There are also four apartments available for long-term rentals (three nights or more).

Birger Jarl Hotel
HOTEL €€

(Map p386; ☑08-674 18 00; www.birgerjarl.se; Tulegatan 8; cabin r from 1190kr, s/d from 1200/1400kr; P➡☀@🖰; 🚌43 Tegnérgatan, 🚇Rådmansgatan) One of Stockholm's original design hotels, the Birger Jarl has a wide variety of room choices. Cabin rooms are tiny and windowless; local fashion designers customised one wall in each. Standard rooms are all done up in modern Swedish style, and the superior rooms are interior-design showpieces, some of them by big-name Swedish designers – they're well worth the price upgrade.

⭐Rival Hotel
HOTEL €€€

(Map p386; ☑08-54 57 89 00; www.rival.se; Mariatorget 3; s/d from 2395/2695kr; ➡☀@🖰; 🚇Mariatorget) Owned by ABBA's Benny Andersson and overlooking leafy Mariatorget, this ravishing design hotel is a chic retro gem, complete with vintage 1940s movie theatre and art-deco cocktail bar. The super-comfy rooms feature posters from great Swedish films and a teddy bear to make you feel at home. All rooms have luxurious, well-equipped bathrooms.

⭐Grand Hôtel Stockholm
HOTEL €€€

(☑08-679 35 00; www.grandhotel.se; Södra Blasieholmshamnen 8; s/d from 2340/3300kr; P➡☀@🖰; 🚌2, 43, 55, 62, 65, 76 Karl XII's Torg, 🚢Strömkajen, 🚇Kungsträdgården, T-Centralen) This is where the literati, glitterati and nobility call it a night. A waterfront landmark, with several exclusive restaurants and a see-and-beseen piano bar, it remains Stockholm's most sumptuous lodgings. Room styles span royal Gustavian to contemporary chic.

Hotel Scandic Gamla Stan
HOTEL €€€

(Map p390; ☑08-723 72 50; www.scandichotels. com; Lilla Nygatan 25; r from 1750kr; ➡☀@🖰; 🚇Gamla Stan) The former Rica chain has been absorbed by Scandic, and this is one of the most atmospheric hotels in its vast collection. Each of the smallish 52 rooms is individually decorated in classic Swedish style – think powder-blue wallpaper and vintage chandeliers. The 17th-century building has up-to-the-minute modern amenities, and the location is perfect for soaking up Gamla Stan's history.

First Hotel Reisen HOTEL €€€

(Map p390; 08-22 32 60; www.firsthotels.com; Skeppsbron 12; r from 1668kr; 🐾 📶; 🚇 Gamla Stan) Stockholm's oldest hotel once hummed with sailors. These days the impressive waterfront building draws in passers-by with a slinky restaurant-bar. Some rooms have exposed brick walls, others are light and open in classic Scandi style; several have French doors with sea views. There's also a gym in the 16th-century vault-ceilinged basement, as well as a candlelit plunge pool and spa.

✕ Eating

La Neta MEXICAN €

(www.laneta.se; Barnhusgatan 2; tacos & quesadillas 22-52kr; ⏰11am-9pm Mon-Fri, noon-9pm Sat, noon-4pm Sun; 🚇Hötorget) Competition for the title of 'Stockholm's Best Taqueria' is not fierce, but La Neta wins hands down. Fastfood pseudo-Mexican eateries are all over town, but this is the real deal, with homemade corn tortillas, nuanced flavours and zero frills in the dining area (unless you count the bowls of delicious salsa). It's great value for money.

Chokladkoppen CAFE €

(Map p390; www.chokladkoppen.se; Stortorget 18; cakes & coffees from 35kr, mains 85-125kr; ⏰9am-11pm Jun-Aug, shorter hours rest of year; 📶; 🚇Gamla Stan) Arguably Stockholm's best-loved cafe, hole-in-the-wall Chokladkoppen sits slap bang on the old town's enchanting main square. It's an atmospheric spot with a sprawling terrace and pocket-sized interior with low-beamed ceilings, custard-coloured walls and edgy artwork. The menu includes savoury treats like broccoli-and-blue-cheese pie and scrumptious cakes.

Hötorgshallen FOOD HALL €

(Hötorget; prices vary; ⏰10am-6pm Mon-Thu, to 6.30pm Fri, to 6pm Sat; 🚇Hötorget) Located below Filmstaden cinema, Hötorgshallen is Stockholm at its multicultural best, with stalls selling everything from fresh Nordic seafood to fluffy hummus and fragrant teas. Ready-to-eat options include Lebanese spinach parcels, kebabs and vegetarian burgers. For the ultimate feed, squeeze into galley-themed dining nook Kajsas Fiskrestaurang for a huge bowl of soulful *fisksoppa* (fish stew) with aioli (110kr).

★ Rosendals Trädgårdskafe CAFE €€

(Map p386; 08-54 58 12 70; www.rosendalstradgard.se; Rosendalsterrassen 12; mains 99-145kr; ⏰11am-5pm Mon-Fri, to 6pm Sat & Sun May-Sep, closed Mon Feb-Apr & Oct-Dec; 🅿️ 🍴; 🚌44, 69, 76 Djurgårdsbron, 🚋7) 🌿 Set among the greenhouses of a pretty botanical garden, Rosendals is an idyllic spot for heavenly pastries and coffee or a meal and a glass of organic wine. Lunch includes a brief menu of soups, sandwiches (such as ground-lamb burger with chanterelles) and gorgeous salads. Much of the produce is biodynamic and grown on site.

★ Hermitage VEGETARIAN €€

(Map p390; www.hermitage.gastrogate.com; Stora Nygatan 11; buffet weekday/weekend 130/140kr; ⏰11am-8pm Mon-Fri, noon-8pm Sat & Sun, to 9pm Jun-Aug; 🍴; 🚇Gamla Stan) Herbivores love Hermitage for its simple, tasty vegetarian buffet, easily one of the best bargains in Gamla Stan. Salad, homemade bread, tea and coffee are included in the price. Pro tip: don't miss the drawers of hot food hiding under the main buffet tabletop. Vegan fare is also available, including cakes.

★ Hermans Trädgårdscafé VEGETARIAN €€

(Map p386; 08-643 94 80; www.hermans.se; Fjällgatan 23B; buffet 195kr, desserts from 35kr; ⏰11am-9pm; 🍴; 🚌2, 3, 53, 71, 76 Tjärhovsplan, 🚇Slussen) 🌿 This justifiably popular vegetarian buffet is one of the nicest places to dine in Stockholm, with a glassed-in porch and outdoor seating on a terrace overlooking the city's glittering skyline. Fill up on inventive, flavourful vegie and vegan creations served from a cosy, vaulted room – you might need to muscle your way in, but it's worth the effort.

Blå Dörren SWEDISH €€

(Map p386; 08-743 07 43; www.bla-dorren.se; Södermalmstorg 6; mains 148-258kr; ⏰10.30am-11pm Mon, to midnight Tue-Thu, to 1am Fri, 1pm-1am Sat, 1-11pm Sun; 🚇Slussen) A stone's throw from Gamla Stan and facing Stockholm City Museum, Blå Dörren (The Blue Door) honours its historic surroundings with a variety of traditional Swedish dishes. You can't go wrong with the pan-fried herring or elk meatballs, both accompanied with fresh lingonberries.

Östermalms Saluhall MARKET €

(Map p386; www.saluhallen.com; Östermalmstorg; ⏰9.30am-7pm Mon-Fri, to 5pm Sat; 🚇Östermalmstorg) Östermalms Saluhall is a gourmet food hall that inhabits a delightful many-spired brick building. It's a sophisticated take on the traditional market, with fresh produce, fish counters, baked goods, butcher shops and tea vendors and some top places to grab a meal. For best results, arrive hungry and curious.

Under Kastanjen
SWEDISH €€

(Map p390; ☑ 08-21 50 04; www.underkastanjen.se; Kindstugatan 1, Gamla Stan; mains 182-289kr, dagens (daily special) lunch 105kr; ☺ 8am-11pm Mon-Fri, 9am-11pm Sat, 9am-9pm Sun; ☞; ⓡ Gamla Stan) This has to be just about the most picturesque corner of Gamla Stan, with tables set on a cobbled square under a beautiful chestnut tree surrounded by ochre and yellow storybook houses. Enjoy classic Swedish dishes like homemade meatballs with mashed potato. The downstairs wine bar has a veritable Spanish-bodega feel with its whitewashed brick arches and moody lighting.

Caffé Nero
CAFE €€

(Map p386; www.nerostockholm.se; Roslagsgatan 4; lunch mains 110-145kr, dinner mains 145-175kr; ☺ 7am-4pm Mon-Fri, 9am-5pm Sat & Sun; ⓡ Odenplan, Rådmansgatan) Packed with local hipsters during the busy lunch hour, this stylish but casual neighbourhood cafe serves substantial Italian meals (fish, pasta, salads) at good prices, plus sublime coffee and pastries. Next door is a more formal bar-restaurant, Buco Nero, with DJs most nights.

★ Woodstockholm
SWEDISH €€€

(Map p386; ☑ 08-36 93 99; www.woodstockholm. com; Mosebacketorg 9, Södermalm; mains 265-285kr; ☺ 11.30am-2pm Mon, 11.30am-2pm & 5-11pm Tue-Sat; ☞☑; ⓡ Slussen) ✿ This hip dining spot incorporates a wine bar and furniture store showcasing chairs and tables by local designers. The menu changes weekly and is themed, somewhat wackily: think Salvador Dalí or Aphrodisiac, the latter including scallops with oyster mushrooms and sweetbreads with yellow beets and horseradish cream. This is fast becoming one of the city's classic foodie destinations. Reservations essential.

★ Rutabaga
VEGETARIAN €€€

(☑ 08-679 35 84; www.mdghs.se; Södra Blasieholmshamnen 6, Grand Hôtel Stockholm; dishes 125-295kr; ☺ 5pm-midnight Mon-Sat Aug-Jun; ☑; ⓡ Kungsträdgården) At Rutabaga, celebrity chef Mathias Dahlgren pushes vegetarian cuisine into the realm of art: the menu features vividly colourful salads and other unusual combinations (an egg-truffle-white-bean dish, a mango and mozzarella salad) which, as always, Dahlgren presents impeccably on the plate. Most dishes are meant for sharing (if you can bear to give any up). Closes in July.

★ Grands Verandan
SWEDISH €€€

(☑ 08-679 35 86; www.grandhotel.se; Södra Blasieholmshamnen 6, Grand Hôtel Stockholm; smörgåsbord 545kr, mains 205-365kr; ☺ 7-10.30am & 11.30am-11pm; ⓡ Kungsträdgården) Head here, inside the Grand Hôtel, for the famous smörgåsbord – especially during the Christmas holidays, when it becomes even more elaborate (reservations recommended). Arrive early for a window seat and tuck into both hot and cold Swedish staples, including gravadlax with almond potatoes, herring, meatballs and lingonberry jam. It's like a belt-busting crash course in classic Nordic flavours.

Bergamott
FUSION €€€

(Map p386; ☑ 08-650 30 34; www.restaurangbergamott.se; Hantverkargatan 35; mains 195-325kr; ☺ 5.30pm-midnight Tue-Sat; ⓡ Rådhuset) The very cool French chefs in this kitchen don't simply whip up to-die-for French-Italian dishes, they'll probably deliver them to your table, talk you through the produce and guide you through the wine list. It's never short of a convivial crowd, so it's best to book, especially when jazz musicians drop in for a soulful evening jam. Menu changes daily.

Kryp In
SWEDISH €€€

(Map p390; ☑ 08-20 88 41; www.restaurangkrypin. nu; Prästgatan 17; lunch mains 135-168kr, dinner mains 198-290kr; ☺ 5-11pm Mon-Fri, noon-4pm & 5-11pm Sat & Sun; ☞; ⓡ Gamla Stan) Small but perfectly formed, this spot wows diners with creative takes on traditional Swedish dishes. Expect the likes of salmon carpaccio, Kalix roe, reindeer roast or gorgeous, spirit-warming saffron aioli shellfish stew. The service is seamless and the atmosphere classy without being stuffy. The three-course set menu (455kr) is superb. Book ahead.

🍷 Drinking & Nightlife

★ Berns Salonger
BAR

(☑ 08-56 63 22 00; www.berns.se; Berzelii Park; ☺ club 11pm-4am Thu-Sat, occasionally Wed & Sun, bar from 5pm daily; ⓡ Kungsträdgården) A Stockholm institution since 1862, this glitzy entertainment palace remains one of the city's hottest party spots. While the gorgeous ballroom hosts some brilliant live-music gigs, the best of Berns' bars is in the intimate basement, packed with cool creative types, top-notch DJs and projected art-house images. Check the website for a schedule of events; some require advance ticket purchase.

★**Café Opera**   CLUB
(☑08-676 58 07; www.cafeopera.se; Karl XII's Torg; cover from 160kr; ⏱10pm-3am Wed-Sun; ⓇKungsträdgården) Rock stars need a suitably excessive place to schmooze, booze and groove, one with glittering chandeliers, ceiling frescoes and a jet-set vibe. This bar-club combo fits the bill, but it's also welcoming enough to make regular folk *feel* like rock stars. If you only have time to hit one primo club during your visit, this is a good choice.

Monks Wine Room   WINE BAR
(Map p390; ☑08-23 12 14; www.monkscafe.se; Lilla Nygatan 2; ⏱5pm-midnight Tue-Thu, 4pm-midnight Fri & Sat; ⓇGamla Stan) Set in atmospheric 17th-century surroundings in the heart of the old town, Monks Wine Room has a well-stocked cellar with hundreds of bottles to choose from. Stop by for a quick glass of wine to recharge the batteries or take some time to sample a cheese and wine pairing.

Monks Porter House   PUB
(Map p390; ☑08-23 12 12; www.monkscafe.se; Munkbron 11; ⏱6pm-1am Tue-Sat; ⓇGamla Stan) This cavernous brewpub has an epic beer list, including 56 taps, many of which are made here or at the Monks microbrewery in Vasastan. Everything we tried was delicious, especially the Monks Orange Ale – your best bet is to ask the bartender for a recommendation (or a taste). Check online for beer-tasting events.

East   BAR
(☑08-611 49 59; http://east.se; Stureplan 13; dinner mains 247-385kr; ⏱11.30am-3am Mon-Sat, 5pm-3am Sun; ⓇÖstermalmstorg) East is a bar, restaurant and club rolled into one. Great cocktails make it a bartender hang-out. Dishes have a predominantly modern Asian twist (locals recommend the sushi), carrying influences from Vietnam, Korea and Japan. Set right in the heart of Östermalm on Stureplan, it's a good place for fuelling up before or during a club night.

Kvarnen   BAR
(Map p386; ☑08-643 03 80; www.kvarnen.com; Tjärhovsgatan 4; ⏱11am-1am Mon & Tue, to 3am Wed-Fri, noon-3am Sat, noon-1am Sun; ⓇMedborgarplatsen) An old-school Hammarby football fan hang-out, Kvarnen is one of the best bars in Söder. The gorgeous beer hall dates from 1907 and keeps tradition; if you're not the clubbing type, get here early for a nice pint and a meal (mains from 210kr). As the night progresses, the nightclub vibe takes over. Queues are fairly constant but justifiable.

Akkurat   BAR
(Map p386; ☑08-644 00 15; www.akkurat.se; Hornsgatan 18; ⏱3pm-midnight Mon, to 1am Tue-Sat, 6pm-1am Sun; ⓇSlussen) Valhalla for beer fiends, Akkurat boasts a huge selection of Belgian ales as well as a good range of Swedish-made microbrews and hard ciders. It's one of only two places in Sweden to be recognised by a Cask Marque for its real ale. Extras include a vast wall of whisky and live music several nights a week.

☆ **Entertainment**

Stockholm has a good variety of entertainment, from spectator sports to live music, theatre and opera. The city also hosts a number of festivals that are worth planning a trip around.

For an up-to-date events calendar, see www.visitstockholm.com. Another good source, if you can navigate a little Swedish, is the Friday 'På Stan' section of *Dagens Nyheter* newspaper (www.dn.se/pa-stan).

Operan   OPERA
(☑08-791 44 00; www.operan.se; Gustav Adolfs Torg, Operahuset; tickets 240-1070kr; ⓇKungsträdgården) The Royal Opera is the place to go for thunderous tenors, sparkling sopranos and classical ballet. It has some bargain tickets in seats with poor views, and occasional lunchtime concerts for 275kr (including light lunch).

Fasching   JAZZ
(☑08-53 48 29 60; www.fasching.se; Kungsgatan 63; ⏱6pm-1am Mon-Thu, to 4am Fri & Sat, 5pm-1am Sun; ⓇT-Centralen) Music club Fasching is the pick of Stockholm's jazz clubs, with live music most nights. DJs often take over with Afrobeat, Latin, neo-soul or R&B on Friday night and retro-soul, disco and rare grooves on Saturday.

Stampen   JAZZ
(Map p390; ☑08-20 57 93; www.stampen.se; Stora Nygatan 5; cover free-200kr; ⏱5pm-1am Tue-Fri & Sun, 2pm-1am Sat; ⓇGamla Stan) Stampen is one of Stockholm's music-club stalwarts, swinging to live jazz and blues six nights a week. The free blues jam (currently on Sundays) pulls everyone from local noodlers to the odd music legend.

Mosebacke Etablissement   LIVE MUSIC
(Map p386; http://sodrateatern.com; Mosebacketorg 3; ⏱6pm-late; ⓇSlussen) Eclectic theatre and club nights aside, this historic culture palace hosts a mixed line-up of live music. Tunes span anything from home-grown pop to Antipodean rock. The outdoor terrace

(featured in the opening scene of August Strindberg's novel *The Red Room*) combines dazzling city views with a thumping summertime bar. It adjoins Södra Teatern and a couple of other bars.

Södra Teatern
THEATRE, LIVE MUSIC

(Map p386; ☑08-53 19 94 90; www.sodrateatern. com; Mosebacketorg 1; ⊙8am-4pm Mon & Tue, to 11pm Wed & Thu, to 2am Fri, 11.30am-2am Sat, noon-4pm Sun; ⊠Slussen) Accessible from Mosebacketorg and adjoining Mosebacke Etablissement (p399), up the winding streets of old Södermalm, Södra Teatern is the original multifunctional event space, with its assortment of bars, stages and a restaurant. Whether you're relaxing in the beer garden or simply soaking up the ornate decor, this is a great place to dine and dance, or mingle with locals. Check the website for upcoming events.

🛍 Shopping

Stockholm is a seasoned shopper's paradise. For big-name Swedish and international retail outlets, hit the pedestrianised Biblioteksgatan from Östermalm to Norrmalmstorg, as well as the smaller streets that branch off it.

For slightly funkier and artier stores and galleries, head to Södermalm. And for souvenirs and postcards, check out picturesque Gamla Stan.

★ Svenskt Tenn
ARTS, HOMEWARES

(☑08-670 16 00; www.svenskttenn.se; Nybrogatan 15; ⊙10am-6pm Mon-Fri, 10am-4pm Sat; ⊠Kungsträdgården) As much a museum of design as an actual shop, this iconic store is home to the signature fabrics and furniture of Josef Frank and his contemporaries. Browsing here is a great way to get a quick handle on what people mean by 'classic Swedish design' – and it's owned by a foundation that contributes heavily to arts funding.

E Torndahl
DESIGN

(Map p390; www.etorndahl.se; Västerlånggatan 63; ⊙10am-8pm; ⊠Gamla Stan) This spacious design shop, run by the women of the Torndahl family since 1864, is a calm and civilised oasis on busy Västerlånggatan, offering jewellery, textiles and clever Scandinavian household objects.

Studio Lena M
GIFTS & SOUVENIRS

(Map p390; www.studiolenam.wordpress.com; Kindstugan 14; ⊙10am-6pm, to 5pm Sat; ⊠Gamla Stan) This tiny, dimly lit shop is chock full of adorable prints and products featuring the distinctive graphic design work of Lena M. It's a great place to find a unique – and uniquely Swedish – gift to bring home, or even just a cute postcard.

DesignTorget
DESIGN

(Map p386; www.designtorget.se; Götgatan 31; ⊙10am-7pm Mon-Fri, 10am-6pm Sat, 11am-5.30pm Sun; ⊠Slussen) If you love good design but don't own a Gold Amex, head to this chain, which sells the work of emerging designers alongside established denizens. There are several other locations, including one right next to the main tourist information office in Sergels Torg.

Papercut
BOOKS

(Map p386; ☑08-13 35 74; www.papercutshop. se; Krukmakargatan 24; ⊙11am-6.30pm Mon-Fri, 11am-5pm Sat, noon-4pm Sun, closed Sun Jul; ⊠Zinkensdamm) This artfully curated shop sells books, magazines and DVDs with a high-end pop-culture focus. Pick up a new Field Notes journal and a decadent film journal or a gorgeous volume devoted to one of the many elements of style.

Nordiska Galleriet
ARTS & CRAFTS

(☑08-442 83 60; www.nordiskagalleriet.se; Nybrogatan 11; ⊙10am-6pm Mon-Fri, to 5pm Sat; ⊠Östermalmstorg) This sprawling showroom is a design freak's El Dorado – think Hannes Wettstein chairs, Hella Jongerius sofas, Alvar Aalto vases and mini Verner Panton chairs for style-sensitive kids. Luggage-friendly options include designer coathangers, glossy architecture books and bright Marimekko paper napkins.

ℹ Information

MEDICAL SERVICES

Apoteket CW Scheele (www.apoteket.se; Klarabergsgatan 64; ⊠T-Centralen) A 24-hour pharmacy located close to T-Centralen.

CityAkuten (☑010-601 00 00; www.cityakuten.se; Apelbergsgatan 48; ⊙8am-5pm) Emergency health and dental care.

Södersjukhuset (☑08-616 10 00; www. sodersjukhuset.se; Ringvägen 52; ⊠Skanstull) The most central hospital.

MONEY

ATMs are plentiful, but many businesses in Stockholm are now cash-free and accept payment by credit or debit card only.

TOURIST INFORMATION

Stockholm Visitors Center (☑08-50 82 85 08; www.visitstockholm.com; Kulturhuset, Sergels Torg 3; ⊙9am-7pm Mon-Fri, 9am-4pm

Sat, 10am-4pm Sun May–mid-Sep, shorter hours rest of year; 🕿; 🚇T-Centralen) The main visitors centre occupies a space inside Kulturhuset on Sergels Torg.

Tourist Center (Map p390; 🖉 08-550 882 20; www.guidestockholm.info; Köpmangatan 22; ⊘10am-4pm Mon-Fri year-round, 11am-2pm Sat & Sun Jun-Sep; 🚇 Gamla Stan) Tiny office in Gamla Stan, with brochures and information.

Visit Djurgården (Map p386; 🖉 08-667 77 01; www.visitdjurgarden.se; Djurgårdsvägen 2; ⊘9am-dusk) With tourist information specific to Djurgården, this office at the edge of the Djurgården bridge is attached to Sjöcaféet, so you can grab a bite or a beverage as you plot your day.

ℹ Getting There & Away

AIR
Stockholm Arlanda Airport
Stockholm Arlanda Airport (ARN; 🖉10-109 10 00; www.swedavia.se/arlanda) Stockholm's main airport, 45km north of the city centre, is reached from central Stockholm by bus, local train and express train. Terminals two and five are for international flights; three and four are domestic; there is no terminal one.

Left Luggage Stockholm Arlanda Airport has self-service lockers for luggage storage (small/large locker for 24 hours 70/90kr), payable with a credit card. There's also a baggage counter.

Bromma Airport
Bromma Airport (BMA; 🖉 010-109 40 00; www.swedavia.se/bromma; Ulvsundavägen; 🚇 Brommaplan) Located 8km west of the city centre, Bromma is handy for domestic flights but services only a handful of airlines, primarily British Airways, Brussels Airlines and Finnair.

Stockholm Skavsta Airport
Stockholm Skavsta Airport (Nyköping Airport (NYO); 🖉 0155-28 04 00; www.skavsta.se/en; General Schybergs Plan 22, Nyköping; 🚇 Flygbussarna) Small airport 100km southwest of Stockholm, near Nyköping, served by low-cost carriers Ryanair and WizzAir.

BOAT
The main ferry lines with routes from Stockholm are **Silja Line** (🖉 08-22 21 40; www.tallinksilja.com; Silja & Tallink Customer Service Office, Cityterminalen; ⊘9am-6pm Mon-Fri, to 3pm Sat) and **Viking Line** (p474), which operate a regular ferry line to both Turku and Helsinki in Finland. **Tallink** (p474) ferries head to Tallinn (Estonia) and Riga (Latvia).

BUS
Most long-distance buses arrive at and depart from **Cityterminalen** (www.cityterminalen.com; ⊘7am-6pm), which is connected to Centralstationen. The main counter sells tickets for several bus companies, including **Flygbuss** (p401) (airport coaches), **Swebus** (www.swebus.se; Cityterminalen) and **Ybuss** (www.ybuss.se; Cityterminalen). You can also buy tickets from Pressbyrå shops and ticket machines. Destinations include:

Gothenburg from 419kr, six hours, eight daily

Halmstad from 569kr, 12 hours, two daily

Jönköping from 269kr, five hours, six daily

Malmö from 549kr, 8½ hours, two to four times daily

Nyköping from 89kr, two hours, eight daily

Uppsala 79kr, one hour, six daily

CAR & MOTORCYCLE
The E4 motorway passes through the city, just west of the centre, on its way from Helsingborg to Haparanda. The E20 motorway from Stockholm to Gothenburg via Örebro follows the E4 as far as Södertälje. The E18 from Kapellskär to Oslo runs from east to west and passes just north of central Stockholm.

Car hire companies have offices at Arlanda Airport, near Centralstationen and elsewhere across town.

TRAIN
Stockholm is the hub for national train services run by **Sveriges Järnväg** (SJ; 🖉 0771-75 75 75; www.sj.se), with a network of services that covers all the major towns and cities, as well as services to the rest of Scandinavia. Destinations include:

Gällivare from 795kr, 15 hours, one daily

Gothenburg from 422kr, three to five hours, hourly

Jönköping from 696kr, 3½ hours, one daily

Kiruna from 795kr, 17 hours, one daily

Lund from 632kr, 4½ hours, four daily

Malmö from 632kr, five hours, frequent

Oslo from 1000kr, five hours, four daily

Uppsala from 95kr, 35 to 55 minutes, frequent

Centralstationen has left luggage lockers on the lower level (small/large locker for 24 hours 70/90kr).

ℹ Getting Around

TO/FROM THE AIRPORTS
Stockholm Arlanda Airport
Arlanda Express (www.arlandaexpress.com; Centralstationen; one-way adult/child 280/150kr, 2 adults one-way in summer 350kr; 🚇 Centralen) Trains between the airport and Centralstationen run every 10 to 15 minutes from 5am to 12.30am (less frequently after 9pm), taking 20 minutes.

Flygbussarna (www.flygbussarna.se; Cityterminalen; 🚇 Centralen) Buses to/from Cityterminalen leave from stop 11 in Terminal 5 every

10 to 15 minutes (adult/child one-way 119/99kr, 40 minutes). Tickets can be purchased online, at Cityterminalen or at the Flygbuss self-service machine in Terminal 5.

Airport Cab (📞 08-25 25 25; www.airportcab.se), **Sverige Taxi** (p402), **Taxi Stockholm** (p402) Reliable taxi services.

Bromma Airport

Flygbussarna (p401) Runs to/from Cityterminalen every 20 to 30 minutes (adult/child 85/69kr, 20 minutes).

Stockholm Skavsta Airport

Flygbussarna (p401) Runs to/from Cityterminalen every 30 minutes (adult/child 159/135kr, 80 minutes).

BICYCLE

Bicycles can be carried free on SL local trains as foldable 'hand luggage' only. They're not allowed in Centralstationen or on the tunnelbana (metro), although you'll occasionally see some daring souls.

Stockholm City Bikes (www.citybikes.se; 3-day/season card 165/300kr) Has self-service bicycle-hire stands across the city. Bikes can be borrowed for three-hour stretches and returned at any City Bikes stand. Purchase a bike card online or from the tourist office. Rechargeable season cards are valid April to October.

BOAT

Djurgårdsfärjan city ferry services connect Gröna Lund Tivoli on Djurgården with Nybroplan (summer only) and Slussen (year-round) as frequently as every 10 minutes in summer; SL transport passes and tickets are valid on these services.

CAR & MOTORCYCLE

Driving in central Stockholm is not recommended. Skinny one-way streets, congested bridges and limited parking all present problems; note that Djurgårdsvägen is closed near Skansen at night, on summer weekends and some holidays. Don't attempt driving through the narrow streets of Gamla Stan.

Parking is a hassle, but there are *P-hus* (parking stations) throughout the city; they charge up to 100kr per hour, though the fixed evening rate is usually lower.

PUBLIC TRANSPORT
Bus

Inner-city buses radiate from Sergels Torg, Odenplan, Fridhemsplan (on Kungsholmen) and Slussen. Bus 47 runs from Sergels Torg to Djurgården, and bus 69 from Centralstationen and Sergels Torg to the Ladugårdsgärdet museums and Kaknästornet. Useful buses for hostellers include bus 65 (Centralstationen to Skeppsholmen) and bus 43 (Regeringsgatan to Södermalm). Most buses run until midnight, but check schedules.

Tickets cannot be bought on buses.

Metro (Tunnelbana)

Stockholm's underground train system, tunnelbana, connects its various neighbourhoods; it's fast and efficient, although some stops are so close together that you might be better off walking, so check maps first. There are three main lines: green, red and blue. Route maps are easy to navigate and posted at all stations. Trains generally run from 5am to 2.30am, but check schedules online.

Train

Local trains (pendeltåg) are most useful for connections to Nynäshamn (for ferries to Gotland), Märsta (for buses to Sigtuna) and Uppsala (requires supplementary fee). They now depart from inside Centralstationen near the T-Centralen tunnelbana station.

Tram

The historic No 7 tram (and its sleek modern siblings) runs between Norrmalmstorg and Skansen, passing most attractions on Djurgården. SL passes are valid.

Taxi

Taxis are readily available but fees are unregulated – be sure to check for a meter or arrange the fare first. Use one of the established, reputable firms, such as **Taxi Stockholm** (📞 15 00 00; www.taxistockholm.se) or **Sverige Taxi** (📞 020-20 20 20; www.sverigetaxi.se). The ride-sharing company **Uber** (www.uber.com) also covers Stockholm.

AROUND STOCKHOLM

Stockholm Archipelago

Mention the archipelago to Stockholmers and prepare for gushing adulation – well-deserved, too. Buffering the city from the open Baltic Sea, it's a mesmerising wonderland of rocky isles carpeted with deep forests and fields of wildflowers, dotted with yachts and picturesque red wooden cottages.

Exactly how many islands there are is debatable, with the count ranging from 14,000 to 100,000 (the general consensus is 24,000). Whatever the number, it's an unmissable area, unique in the world and much closer to the city than many visitors imagine (Vaxholm is less than an hour away), with regular ferry services and various tours. You can see most of the islands on day trips, but it's worth staying overnight if you have the time.

Most have good boat connections, provided you check timings in advance – although there are worse places in the world to get stranded!

Vaxholm

There are plenty of reasons to come to Vaxholm, the most obvious being that this is the closest archipelago island to Stockholm and thus provides a charming taster to this extraordinarily diverse array of pine-clad islands and islets. Vaxholm is more than just a gateway, however. With cobbled sloping streets flanked by well-preserved wooden houses painted in candy-coloured pastels, plus a slew of excellent restaurants and idiosyncratic family-owned shops, it holds its own as a charming place to visit.

Vaxholm dates from 1647; to glean a sense of its history head to Norrhamn, just north of the town hall and home to the **oldest buildings** (☑ 08-54 13 19 80; Trädgårdsgatan 19; ☺ 11am-5pm May–mid-Sep; FREE, including a 19th-century typical fisher's house (now also one of the island's top cafes). And don't miss the island's most prominent sight: the imposing fortress that once guarded the waterways into the city and now holds a museum and a charming B&B.

ℹ Information

Tourist Office (☑ 08-54 13 14 80; www.vaxholmdestination.se; Rådhuset; ☺ 10am-6pm Mon-Fri, to 4pm Sat & Sun May-Aug, shorter hours rest of year) The tourist office is located inside the *rådhus* (town hall), off Hamngatan; look for the onion dome.

ℹ Getting There & Away

Bus 670 from the Tekniska Högskolan tunnelbana station in Stockholm runs regularly to Vaxholm's town centre and harbour; SL passes valid.

Waxholmsbolaget (☑ 08-600 10 00; www.waxholmsbolaget.com/visitor; Strömkajen; ☺ 7am-2pm Mon, 8am-2pm Tue-Thu, 7.30am-4.30pm Fri, 8am-noon Sat, 8.30am-noon Sun; ☒ Kungsträdgården) Boats sail at least hourly between Vaxholm and Strömkajen in Stockholm from 8am to 7.15pm (50 to 70 minutes, one-way 79kr).

Strömma Kanalbolaget (p395) Sails between Strandvägen (Stockholm; berth 16) and Vaxholm at noon and 3pm daily from April to December (three hours, round trip from 280kr).

Sigtuna

☑ 08 / POP 8444

Just 40km northwest of Stockholm, Sigtuna is one of the cutest, most historically relevant villages in the area. Founded around AD 980, it's the oldest surviving town in Sweden, and the main drag, Storagatan, is very likely Sweden's oldest main street.

Around the year 1000, Olof Skötkonung ordered the minting of Sweden's first coins in the town, and ancient church ruins and rune stones are scattered everywhere.

◎ Sights

Mariakyrkan   CHURCH
(Uppsalavägen; ☺ 9am-5pm) During medieval times, Sigtuna boasted seven stone-built churches, though most have since crumbled. Mariakyrkan is the oldest brick building in the area – it was a Dominican monastery church from around 1250 but became the parish church in 1529 after the monastery was demolished by Gustav Vasa. Pop in for restored medieval paintings and free weekly concerts in summer.

Rosersbergs Slott   CASTLE
(☑ 08-59 03 50 39; www.kungahuset.se; adult/child 100/50kr; ☺ tours hourly 11am-4pm Jun-Aug, Sat & Sun only May & Sep; ☒ J-Slottsvägen, Rosersberg) Rosersbergs Slott is on lake Mälaren about 9km southeast of Sigtuna. Built in the 1630s, it was used as a royal residence from 1762 to 1860; the interior boasts exquisite furnishings from the Empire period (1790–1820) and is noted for its textiles. Highlights include the lavishly draped State Bedchamber and Queen Hedvig Elisabeth Charlotta's conversation room. The palace cafe serves delicious light meals and cakes in regal surrounds.

ℹ Information

Tourist Office (☑ 08-59 48 06 50; www.destinationsigtuna.se/turistbyra; Storagatan 33; ☺ 10am-5pm Mon-Fri, 11am-4pm Sat, noon-4pm Sun Jun-Aug, shorter hours rest of year) The tourist office inhabits an 18th-century wooden house in Drakegården, on the main street.

ℹ Getting There & Away

Travel connections from Stockholm are easy. Take a local train to Märsta, from where there are frequent buses (570 or 575, SL pass is valid) to Sigtuna.

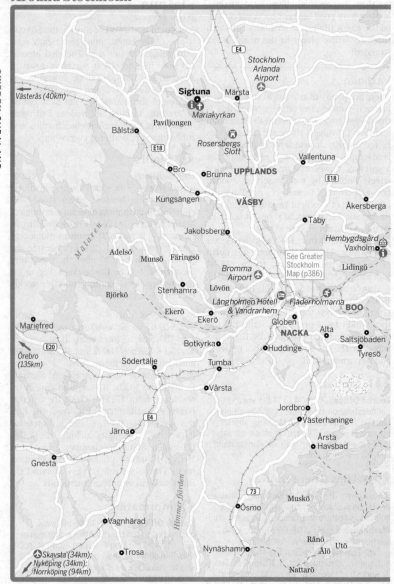

SVEALAND

This area, the birthplace of Sweden, offers evidence of the region's long history, including rune stones so plentiful you might stumble over them. Pre-Viking bur-

ial mounds in Gamla Uppsala light the imaginations of myth-builders and history buffs. There's also the trip into the bowels of the earth at the old mine in Falun, which accidentally provided the red paint for all

those little cottages dotting the landscape. And in Mora, the definitive Swedish king's path towards the crown is still retraced today, by thousands of skiers each year in the Vasaloppet.

Uppsala

📞 018 / POP 214,559

The historical and spiritual heart of the country, Uppsala is one of Sweden's oldest yet most dynamic cities; the latter thanks in part to a student population nudging 40,000. Peaceful by day and lively by night, the resulting youthful buzz manifests most strikingly in the sheer number of laid-back boho-vibe cafes and bars – as well as all those bicycles on the streets. The city's charm also lies in its sheer picturesque value, with the meandering river Fyris flowing through the centre, flanked by pathways and still more cafes. History buffs have plenty to soak up here, with Gamla (Old) Uppsala just up the road. This fascinating archaeological site was once a flourishing 6th-century religious centre where human sacrifices were made, as well as an ancient burial ground.

The city makes an easy day trip from Stockholm, though it's worth lingering overnight to wander the deserted streets and soak up the atmosphere.

⊙ Sights

Aside from Gamla Uppsala, which is a short distance outside of town, Uppsala's sights are located centrally and many focus on the university, which is Sweden's oldest, and one of the oldest and most esteemed in the world.

The city is eminently walkable and rarely is anything more than a 15-minute walk away. Uppsala dates back to the 3rd century; among its more ancient sights are the fascinating rune stones to be seen around town. Other noteworthy sights include both the castle and the Domkyrka (cathedral).

★**Domkyrka**   CHURCH
(Cathedral; 📞018-430 35 00; www.uppsaladomkyrka.se; Domkyrkoplan; ⊙8am-6pm, tours in English 11am & 2pm Mon-Sat, 4pm Sun Jul & Aug) **FREE** The Gothic Domkyrka dominates the city and is Scandinavia's largest church, with towers soaring an inspiring 119 m. The interior is imposing, with the French Gothic ambulatory flanked by small chapels. Tombs here include those of St Erik, Gustav Vasa and the scientist Carl von Linné. Regular tours in English are conducted in July and August and at other times by appointment.

★**Gamla Uppsala**   ARCHAEOLOGICAL SITE
(www.arkeologigamlauppsala.se; ⊙24hr; 🅿; 🚌2) **FREE** One of Sweden's largest and most important burial sites, Gamla Uppsala (4km

north of Uppsala) contains 300 mounds from the 6th to 12th centuries. The earliest are also the three most impressive. Legend has it they contain the pre-Viking kings Aun, Egil and Adils, who appear in *Beowulf* and Icelandic historian Snorre Sturlason's *Ynglingsaga*. More recent evidence suggests the occupant of Östhögen (East Mound) was a woman, probably a female regent in her 20s or 30s.

★ **Museum Gustavianum**   MUSEUM

(☑018-471 75 71; www.gustavianum.uu.se; Akademigatan 3; adult/child 50/40kr; ⊙10am-4pm Tue-Sun Jun-Aug, from 11am rest of year) A wonder cabinet of wonder cabinets, the Museum Gustavianum rewards appreciation of the weird and well organised. The shelves in the pleasantly musty building hold case after case of obsolete tools and preserved oddities: stuffed birds, astrolabes, alligator mummies, exotic stones and dried sea creatures. A highlight is the fascinating 17th-century **Augsburg Art Cabinet** and its 1000 ingenious trinkets. Don't miss Olof Rudbeck's vertiginous **anatomical theatre**, where executed criminals were dissected. Admission includes a tour in English at 1pm Saturday and Sunday.

Uppsala Slott   CASTLE

(☑018-727 24 82; www.uppsalaslott.com; Slottet; admission by guided tour only, adult/child 90/15kr; ⊙tours in English 1 & 3pm Tue-Sun late Jun-Sep) Uppsala Slott was built by Gustav Vasa in the 1550s. It contains the state hall where kings were enthroned and Queen Kristina abdicated. It was also the scene of a brutal murder in 1567, when King Erik XIV and his guards killed Nils Sture and his two sons, Erik and Svante, after accusing them of high treason. The castle burned down in 1702 but was rebuilt and took on its present form in 1757. Contact Destination Uppsala Tourist Centre (p407) for tour bookings.

Linnémuseet   MUSEUM

(☑018-13 65 40; www.linnaeus.se; Svartbäcksgatan 27; adult/child 80kr/free; ⊙11am-5pm Tue-Sun May-Sep) No matter how many times the brochures refer to the 'sexual system' of classification, the excitement to be had at Linnémuseet is primarily intellectual; still, botanists and vegetarians will enjoy a visit to the pioneering scientist's home and workshop, where he lived with his wife and five kids (1743–78). Visits to the adjoining Linneträdgården (☑018-471 25 76; adult/child 60kr/free, admission with Linnémuseet ticket free; ⊙shop & exhibit 11am-5pm Tue-Sun May-Sep, park

11am-8pm Tue-Sun May-Sep), a reconstruction of Sweden's oldest botanical garden, is included in the admission fee.

🛏 Sleeping

Uppsala City Hostel   HOSTEL €

(☑018-10 00 08; www.uppsalacityhostel.se; Sankt Persgatan 16; dm/s/d from 220/440/560kr; ⊙reception 8am-11pm; ❋@🛜) The no-nonsense Uppsala City Hostel is recommended for its sheer convenience – you really can't stay anywhere more central for these prices. Rooms, all named after famous Uppsala landmarks, are small but decent (although dorms suffer from traffic and level-crossing noise). There's wi-fi access in parts of the hostel. Breakfast costs 50kr, and a kitchen is available.

★ **Sunnersta Herrgård**   HOSTEL €€

(☑018-32 42 20; www.sunnerstaherrgard.se; Sunnerstavägen 24; dm 280kr, s/d from 715/850kr; P@🛜; 🛜20) In a historic manor house about 6km south of the city centre, this hostel has a park-like setting at the water's edge and a good restaurant on site. You can rent bikes (per day/week 50/200kr) or borrow a boat. Hotel-standard rooms include breakfast and share a bathroom with one other room; hostel guests can add breakfast for 95kr.

★ **Grand Hotell Hörnan**   HOTEL €€

(☑018-13 93 80; www.grandhotellhornan.com/en/; Bangårdsgatan 1; d from 1495kr; P🛜) This 1907 grand riverfront dame, re-invented in 2013, succeeds in blending that golden age of architecture with the amenities of today. You feel like you're staying in an old hotel, without that fusty furniture feeling, false airs and graces or failing to balance old and new. The Hörnan is smart, affordable and honours the tradition of which it is part.

Elite Hotel Academia   HOTEL €€

(☑018-780 99 00; www.elite.se/en/hotels/uppsala/hotel-academia/; Suttungs gränd 6; d from 1490kr; P❋🛜) New in 2017, the Elite Academia has gotten off to a grand start, mostly by getting the service side of running a big, central hotel right. Rooms are as fresh and high-tech as you'd expect for a present-day build, while the design theme is understated, if not a little bland, and pricing is on the high side. Still, it's a great choice.

🍴 Eating

Ofvandahls   CAFE €

(☑018-13 42 04; www.ofvandahls.se; Sysslomansgatan 3-5; cakes & light meals 35-90kr; ⊙8am-

6pm Mon-Fri, 9am-5pm Sat, 11am-5pm Sun) Something of an Uppsala institution, this classy but sweet *konditori* (bakery-cafe) dates back to the 19th century and is a cut above your average coffee-and-bun shop. It's been endorsed by no less a personage than the king, and radiates old-world charm with antique furniture and fittings. Try the star turn – homemade blueberry cake.

★ **Jay Fu's**   FUSION €€
(☎018-15 01 51; www.jayfu.se; Sankt Eriks Torg 8; mains 145-295kr; ☺5pm-late Mon-Sat; 🛜) Fusion doesn't always work, but while some of the combinations here sound mildly indigestible – like mac and cheese with grilled lobster, truffles and bok choy – they are actually well planned and beautifully presented. While steaks and the mixed grill take centre stage, lighter bites like corn-fried crab cakes and salmon sashimi also receive rave reviews from diners.

★ **Güntherska**   SWEDISH €€
(☎018-13 07 57; www.guntherska.se; Östra Agatan 31; mains 145-220kr; ☺9am-7pm Mon, Tue & Sat, to 9pm Wed-Fri, 10am-7pm Sun; 🛜) An 1870 grande dame of a cafe that enjoys an exemplary position with terraced seating across from the river, and an elegant interior with regency-style wallpaper and chandeliers. The menu includes treats like hummus salad, and the sweet treats are in a league of their own, particularly the sticky buns. They also produce their own muesli, which is available for purchase.

Hamnpaviljongen   SWEDISH €€
(☎018-69 66 53; www.hamnpaviljongen.com; Hamnplan 5; mains 189-299kr, lunch menu 100kr; ☺11am-2pm & 3-9pm Mon-Fri, from noon Sat & Sun; 🅿🛜) This restaurant may look pricey, but the reality is that it serves one of the best value lunchtime menus in town. However, when the sun goes down the prices go up for the evening's á la carte menu, which is of exactly the same quality. Head for the spacious glassed-in terrace for views across the water to the leafy park beyond.

❶ Information

Destination Uppsala Tourist Centre (☎018-727 48 00; www.destinationuppsala.se; Kungsgatan 59; ☺10am-6pm Mon-Fri, to 3pm Sat, plus 11am-3pm Sun Jul & Aug) Can offer helpful advice, maps and brochures covering the region and beyond.

❶ Getting There & Away

Uppsala is 71km north of Stockholm on the E4 motorway.

Upplands Lokaltrafik (☎0771-14 14 14; www.ul.se) bus 801 shuttles between Uppsala and Arlanda Airport (91kr, 40 minutes).

SJ Rail (Statens Järnvägar; ☎0771-75 75 75; www.sj.se/en) operates regular services to/from Stockholm (from 105kr, 40 minutes) and less frequent services to/from Gävle (from 116kr, 1¼ hours), Östersund (from 566kr, five hours) and Mora (from 407kr, 3¼ hours).

Örebro

☑ 019 / POP 146.631

A substantial, culturally rich city, Örebro buzzes around its central feature: the huge and romantic castle surrounded by a moat filled with water lilies. The city originally sprang up as a product of the textile industry, but it continues to gain steam as a university town, since Uppsala University started offering some courses here in 1960. In 1999, the then Örebro University College became Sweden's 12th university, and though, by national standards, Örebro's pedagogical status hardly rates a mention, the presence of students on bikes, in cafes and in parks is more evident with each passing year.

Örebro's proximity to Stockholm, which is fast outgrowing its borders, makes it an appealing city for young families, while the equally short distance to Vänern lake lends the city a relaxed, on-holidays kind of vibe: nursing a beer in a terrace cafe and shopping unhurriedly along cobbled streets are favoured local pastimes.

◎ Sights

★ **Tiveden National Park**   PARK
(☎0584-47 40 83; www.nationalparksofsweden.se; ☺visitor centre 10am-4pm May-Sep, 11am-4pm Sat & Sun Apr & Oct) **FREE** Carved by glaciers, this trolls' home and former highwayrobber's haunt 84km southwest of Örebro makes for wonderful wild walking. The park, reopened in 2017 after extensive works, is noted for its rare, ancient virgin forests, and has lots of dramatic bare bedrock, extensive boulder fields and a scattering of lakes. Several self-guided walks, including the 6km Trollkyrka ('troll church') trail, start from the visitor centre in the southeastern part of the park, 5km north of Rd 49 (turn-off at Bocksjö).

Örebro Slottet
CASTLE

(☑019-21 21 21; www.orebroslott.se; Kansligatan 1; tours adult/child 60/30kr; ☺tours noon & 2pm daily May-Sep, 1pm Sat & Sun rest of year, history exhibition 10am-5pm daily May-Aug) Örebro's hulking and magnificent castle is unmissable in town and now serves as the county governor's headquarters. It was originally built in the late 13th century, but most of what you see today is from 300 years later. The outside is far more dramatic than the interior. To explore you'll need to take a tour.

Örebro Konsthall (OBKHL)
GALLERY

(Örebro Art Gallery; ☑019-21 49 00; Olaigatan 17b; ☺11am-5pm) Örebro's excellent art gallery is responsible for the fact that there are over 200 public art pieces scattered about the city and is integral in the organisation of the Örebro Open Art festival (www.openart. se; ☺Jun-Sep). With a diverse permanent collection of primarily contemporary art and frequent visiting exhibitions, there's always something going on.

Stadsparken
PARK

(☑019-21 10 00; Stadsparken; 🅿🚻) Stadsparken is an idyllic and kid-friendly park once voted Sweden's most beautiful. It stretches alongside Svartån (the Black river) and merges into the Wadköping museum village (☑019-21 10 00; www.orebro.se/wadkoping; Bertil Waldéns-gata 1; ☺11am-5pm daily May-Aug, 11am-4pm Tue-Sun Sep-Apr; 🚻) FREE. The village, named after what author Hjalmar Bergman called his hometown in his novels, is a cobblestone maze of workshops, cafes, a bakery and period buildings – including Kungsstugan (the King's Lodgings; a medieval house with 16th-century ceiling paintings) and Cajsa Warg's house (home of an 18th-century celebrity chef).

🛏 Sleeping & Eating

★STF Tivedstorp Vandrarhem
HOSTEL €

(☑0584-47 20 90; www.tivedstorp.se/english/; Tivedstorp; dm/s/d from 200/370/500kr, sites 100kr; ☺Apr-Oct; 🅿) This STF complex has hostel accommodation in cute red grass-roofed cabins, plus an activity centre and a tiny cafe (open noon to 7pm June to August, and noon to 4pm Sunday March to May and September to October). It's about 3km north of the Tiveden National Park visitor centre; you'll need your own transport to get here.

★Clarion Collection Hotel Borgen
HERITAGE HOTEL €€€

(☑019-20 50 00; www.nordicchoicehotels.com/hotels/sweden/orebro/clarion-collection-hotel-borgen/; Klostergatan 1; d from 1680kr) You can't miss this fabulous, central hotel by the Svartån river which looks like an extension of Örebro Slottet (p408). Occupying a building completed in 1891 that was once a bank, then a newspaper office, this otherwise thoroughly modern establishment boasts spacious, light-flooded rooms with high ceilings, furnished in a contemporary style. The included afternoon tea, dinner and breakfast make for excellent value.

Hälls Konditori
CAFE €

(☑019-611 07 66; www.hallsconditori.se; Engelbrektsgatan 12; pastries 20-45kr, lunch specials 84-98kr, brunch 85kr; ☺7.30am-6pm Mon-Fri, 10am-4pm Sat; 🚻) This bakery-cafe is a classic old-style *konditori* and a favourite hang-out for locals. Go for *fika* (coffee and cake) or more substantial salads, quiche and sandwiches. If the weather's nice, sit out back in the hidden courtyard area – part of Stallbacken, the tiny Old Town square. Brunch is served on Fridays from 8am to 11am and on weekends from 9am to noon.

★A-mano
ITALIAN €€€

(☑019-32 33 70; www.a-mano.se; Kungsgatan 1; mains 178-298kr, set menus 365-735kr; ☺6pm-midnight Mon-Sat) Escalated Italian fare, the likes of pistachio-crusted fillet of pesto-roasted lamb, from Gotland, served with fragrant gorgonzola gnocchi and baby red onions, and excellent value menus are the order of the day in this classy downtown restaurant off Stallbacken. It's best to dress to impress and is much more enjoyable if you're not dining alone.

ℹ Information

The office of Visit Örebro (☑019-21 21 21; www.orebrotown.se; ☺10am-5pm summer, noon-4pm Sat & Sun rest of year) is in the southwest tower of Örebro Slottet (p408), on the 1st floor.

ℹ Getting There & Away

Örebro is 202km west of Stockholm on the E18 motorway.

It is a popular hub for long-distance buses, which leave from the Örebro Resecentrum (Östra Bangatan) adjoining the train station.

Swebus Express (☑0200-21 82 18; www.swebusexpress.se) has direct connections to Norrköping (from 149kr, two hours), Karlstad (from 99kr, 1¾ hours) and Oslo (Norway; from

289kr, five hours), Västerås (from 69kr, 1¼ hours) and Stockholm (from 169kr, 2¾ hours).

SJ Rail (p407) operates direct trains to/from Stockholm (195kr, two hours) every hour with some via Västerås (95kr, one hour); and frequently to and from Gothenburg (145kr, three hours) and Borlänge (235kr, two hours), where you can change for Falun and Mora.

Falun

☑ 023 / POP 57,685

An unlikely combination of industrial and adorable, Falun is home to one of Sweden's oldest and most important copper mines, now retired from service and a protected World Heritage Site. As a consequence, the town was for hundreds of years the primary source of the ruddy red tint that renders Swedish country houses so uniformly cute.

Falun is the main city of Dalarnas *län* (Dalarna county), a region known for its year-round outdoor activities from lowlands hiking to biking, swimming and sailing, and in the colder months, cross-country and downhill skiing and even ski-jumping. It is positioned between lakes Runn (25km south) and Siljan (50km north), and there's a selection of worthwhile sights within striking distance of the city, including one of Sweden's best-loved historic home museums in the village of Sundborn.

⊙ Sights

★**Carl Larsson-gården** HISTORIC BUILDING

(☑ 023-600 53; www.clg.se; Carl Larssonsvägen 12, Sundborn; adult/child/family 180/60/550kr; ⊙ tours 10am-5pm daily May-Sep, 11am Mon-Fri & 1pm Sat & Sun Jan-Apr; 🚼; 🚌 64) Don't miss Sweden's 'most famous home', located 13km northeast of Falun in the picturesque village of Sundborn. After their deaths, the early-20th-century residence of artist Carl Larsson and his wife Karin was preserved in its entirety by their children, but it's no gloomy memorial: 'Lilla Hyttnäs' is itself a work of art, full of brightness, humour and love. Admission is by hour-long guided tour: call in advance to book English-language tours or grab an English handbook and follow the Swedes.

★**Falu Gruva** MINE

(☑ 023-78 20 30; www.falugruva.se; Gruvplatsen 1; tours adult/child 220/90kr, above-ground only 90/50kr; ⊙ tours hourly 10am-5pm Jun-Aug, less frequent rest of year; 🅿; 🚌 53, 708 Timmervägen) Falun's *kopparbergs gruva* was the world's most important copper mine by the 17th cen-

tury. Called 'Sweden's treasure chest', it drove the small country's international aspirations, funded wars and helped paint all those summer cottages that distinctive red. You can opt to take a one-hour underground tour of the mines or simply explore above ground where you'll find the interesting and informative **Mine Museum** (☑ 023-78 20 30; www.falugruva.se; Gruvplatsen 7; adult/child 80/40kr; ⊙ 10am-5:30pm daily Jul & Aug, 10am-5:30pm Mon-Fri & noon-4pm Sat & Sun May, Jun & Sep) and some heritage outbuildings, cafes and boutiques.

🛏 Sleeping & Eating

★**Clarion Collection**
Hotel Bergmastaren HOTEL €€

(☑ 023-70 17 00; www.nordicchoicehotels.se; Bergskolegränd 7; d from 1280kr; 🅿🐾🛜) This thoroughly renovated modern hotel keeps the classics in mind. Antique-styled furnishings, compact chandeliers, old-world wallpapers and wood-panelled walls shift your focus from the HDTV and high-speed wi-fi to the snuggly bed where it just feels right to read a book. A complimentary light dinner served between 6pm and 9pm and a decent breakfast spread round out this noteworthy downtown offering.

STF Falun Hotell HOTEL €€

(☑ 023-291 80; www.hotelfalun.se; Trotzgatan 16; s/d from 910/1040kr; 🅿🐾@🛜) This hotel adjacent to Falu Turistbyrå (p410) is a member of the Swedish Tourist Association and has been thoroughly renovated in recent years in a variety of bright and quirky themes. All rooms have private bathrooms, free wi-fi, modern TVs and rates include a light breakfast of predominantly locally sourced items.

Restaurang Geschwornergården CAFE €

(☑ 023-702 20 75; www.smakochmera.se/geschwornergarden; Gruvplatsen 1, Falu Gruva; lunch sets Mon-Fri 105kr, Sat-Sun 125kr; ⊙ 11am-3pm; 🅿🍴) Opposite the main reception at Falu Gruva (p409) you'll find this funky smart-casual eatery that does excellent two-course hot lunch specials (frequently including knockout paella). It can get quite crowded (and noisy) in the busy summer months.

★**Kopparhattan** CAFE €€

(☑ 023-191 69; www.kopparhatten.se; Stigaregatan 2; lunch buffet 95kr, mains 149-259kr; ⊙ 11am-3pm Mon-Tue, to 10pm Wed-Sat, noon-5pm Sun; 🍴) An excellent choice is this funky, arty cafe-restaurant in the **Dalarnas Museum** (☑ 023-666 55 00; www.dalarnasmuseum.se; Stigaregatan

2-4; ⊙10am-5pm Tue-Fri, noon-5pm Sat-Mon, to 9pm Wed summer; P 🖐) FREE complex. Choose from sandwiches, soup or a good buffet including vegetarian-friendly choices for lunc,; and light vegie, fish and meat evening mains. There's an outside terrace overlooking the river, and live music on Friday nights in summer. Oh, and burgers...really good burgers (from 85kr)... day and night.

❶ Information

Falu Turistbyrå (Falu Tourist Office; ☑ 023-830 50; www.visitsodradalarna.se; Trotzgatan 10-12; ⊙10am-6pm Mon-Fri, to 4pm Sat) The friendly staff have maps and brochures which place Falun in its historical context and pinpoint the neighbourhoods, smelteries, slag heaps and mine estates protected under the World Heritage designation.

❶ Getting There & Away

By road, Falun is 223km northwest of Stockholm via the E18 motorway and Rte 70, and 91km west of Gävle on the E16.

Swebus Express (p408) operates daily buses on the Gothenburg–Karlstad–Falun route.

Regional transport is run by **Dalatrafik** (☑ 0771-95 95 95; www.dalatrafik.se), which covers all corners of Dalarnas *län*. Tickets cost 30kr for trips within a zone, and 15kr extra for each new zone. A 30-day *länskort* (county pass) costs 1390kr and allows you to travel throughout the county; cards in smaller increments are also available.

Regional bus 132 goes hourly to Rättvik (70kr, one hour) and Mora (96kr, 1½ hours).

SJ Rail (p407) operates at least hourly services between Falun and Gävle (164kr, 1¼ hours), but if you're coming from Stockholm or Mora, you'll need to change at Borlänge.

Lake Siljan Region

It's difficult to imagine that 377 million years ago the area around picturesque Lake Siljan bore the brunt of Europe's greatest meteor impact, when a giant lump of space rock hit with the force of 500 million atomic bombs, obliterating all life and creating a 75km ring-shaped crater.

Today, the area is a picture of tranquillity just a few hours' drive from Stockholm and is close to the hearts of many Swedes for whom it's a favoured summer destination.

The 354-sq-km lake and its surrounding countryside combine sparkling waters with lush green landscapes, outdoor activities galore, a rich tradition of folk arts and some of Sweden's prettiest villages. If outdoor pursuits

aren't your thing, you'll be able to see Swedish folk-art Dala horses being hand painted in Nusnäs, learn about the life of one of the nation's best-loved artists, Anders Zorn, in Mora, or just relax and enjoy life in lovely Tällberg.

Leksand

☑0247 / POP 15.507

For most of the year, the town of Leksand, the southernmost settlement on the shores of Lake Siljan, is quiet. But for one weekend in summer (always from the Friday between 19 and 25 June) around 20,000 spectators flood the town for one of Sweden's most popular Midsummer Festivals where you can join in the festivities amid much singing and costumed dancing around maypoles.

Leksand is the southern gateway to Lake Siljan and a logical first port of call as you begin your explorations of the area. The town has strong trade ties with Japan and, in honour of its sister city, Tobetsu, there's a pleasant Japanese garden that's free to enjoy all year.

◉ Sights

★**Munthe's Hildasholm** HISTORIC BUILDING
(☑0247-100 62; www.hildasholm.org; Klockaregatan 5; adult/child 140/60kr, garden only 40kr; ⊙10am-5pm Jun-early Sep, 11am-5pm Sat & Sun early Sep-Oct; P) Built by Axel Munthe (1857–1949), who served as the Swedish royal physician and wrote the best-selling memoir *The Story of San Michele*, this sumptuously decorated National Romantic–style mansion is set in beautiful gardens with views over Lake Siljan. Built for Munthe's second wife, an English aristocrat, in 1910–11, the mansion was rarely visited by Munthe as he spent most of his time attending to Queen Viktoria on the island of Capri. Admission is by guided tour only.

❶ Information

Siljan Turism Leksand Tourist Center
(☑0248-79 72 00; info@siljan.se; Norsgatan 28; ⊙9am-6pm Mon-Fri, 10am-4pm Sat & Sun) Has information on Dalarna county and Lake Siljan, and can assist with planning your explorations of the lake.

❶ Getting There & Away

Leksand is 260km northwest of Stockholm along Rte 70.

Dalatrafik (p410) buses and **SJ Rail** (p407) local trains run frequently between Leksand and the rest of the Lake Siljan region, including Mora (one hour, 105kr), Rättvik (from 65kr, 20 minutes) and Tällberg (from 55kr, 20 minutes).

Rättvik

📞 0248 / POP 10,856

Rättvik is a totally unpretentious town on the shores of Lake Siljan in an area that sometimes borders on the precious. It's a very pretty place, stretching up a hillside and gently hugging the shoreline. There are things to do year-round, for kids and adults alike, whether you like skiing, cycling, hiking or just lolling around in the town's numerous parks and beaches.

A full program of special events in summer includes a folklore festival in late July, Classic Car Week in late July or early August, and a season of world-class opera from a unique and unforgettable outdoor venue.

🛏 Sleeping & Eating

★ **Green Hotel** BOUTIQUE HOTEL €€
(📞 0247-500 00; www.greenhotel.se/en/; Ovabacksgattu 17; d/ste from 1100/3200kr; P 🖕 🔊) 🍴 Originally built as a private residence in 1917 and converted into a hotel 30 years later, nearby Tällberg's quintessentially 'country Swedish' Green Hotel is something special. Privately owned and operated, the hotel feels like part of a more exclusive brand, from its exceptionally decorated guestrooms (many with gorgeous views) and decadent suites, to its attentive, personalised service. One to remember.

Opt for at least a 'Classic' room if you can – you won't regret paying extra for the balcony and wonderful views over Lake Siljan.

Jöns-Andersgården B&B B&B €€
(📞 0248-130 15; http://bokasiljan.visitdalarna.se; Bygatan 4; r 495-995kr; 🕐 mid-Apr–mid-Oct; P 🖕 🔊) Beds here are in traditional wooden houses dating from the 15th century, high on a hill with superb views. Rooms are all in tip-top shape with modern interiors, and one suite has its own sauna. If you don't have transport, the owners will pick you up from the train station by arrangement. Breakfast is included in the price.

Dala Wärdshus HOTEL €€
(📞 0248-302 50; www.dalawardshus.se/hotell-rattvik-vid-siljan-dalarna/hantverksbyn-hotell/; Hantverksbyn 4; s/d from 675/1195kr; breakfast 90kr; P 🔊) You might just fall in love with this rustic joint offering budget accommodation in basic, grass-roofed (real grass, not thatched) huts, some with lake views. The attached restaurant (open May to August; *dagens* lunch 89kr, coffee and cakes from 35kr) has a great view from its outdoor

tables, and occasional live music. Wi-fi is patchy outside common areas.

☆ Entertainment

★ **Dalhalla Opera** OPERA
(📞 070-610 03 39; www.dalhallaopera.se; Sätra Dalhallavägen 201; tickets from 250kr; 🕐 Aug) Held at the magnificent **Dalhalla amphitheatre** (📞 0455-61 97 00; www.dalhalla.se; Sätra Dalhallavägen 201; ticket prices vary), the Dalhalla Opera's summer season always plays to packed crowds.

ℹ Information

Siljan Turism Rättvik Tourist Center (📞 0248-79 72 00; Riksvägen 40; 🕐 9am-6pm Mon-Fri, 10am-4pm Sat & Sun) Located at the train station; has info for the entire Siljan region.

ℹ Getting There & Away

Rättvik is 20km north of Leksand and 39km southeast of Mora along Rte 70.

Dalatrafik (p410) bus 132 runs regularly between Falun, Rättvik and Mora. Buses depart from outside the train station.

SJ Rail (p407) operates up to three services per day from Stockholm that stop at Rättvik (492kr, 3¼ hours). Otherwise you have to change at Borlänge. Local trains from Leksand stop at Rättvik then continue on to Mora (85kr, 25 minutes).

Mora

📞 0250 / POP 10,896

Mora is spliced with Sweden's historic soul. Legend has it that in 1520 Gustav Vasa arrived here in a last-ditch attempt to start a rebellion against the Danish regime. The people of Mora weren't interested and Gustav was forced to put on his skis and flee for the border. After he left, the town reconsidered and two yeomen, Engelbrekt and Lars, volunteered to follow Gustav's tracks, finally overtaking him in Sälen and changing Swedish history.

Today the world's biggest cross-country ski race commemorates that epic chase and its finish-line is in Mora. Participants number more than one and a half times the town's year-round population. Summer sees holidaymakers from Stockholm and beyond come for sunny antics on Lake Siljan, while year-round, lovers of Swedish folk art and lore visit the nearby village of Nusnäs for the chance to observe local artisans carving and painting the nation's beloved Dalahästar (Dala horses).

⊙ Sights

★ **Zorngården**   HISTORIC BUILDING

(☑ 0250-59 23 10; www.zorn.se/en/visit-us/zorn-house/; Vasagatan 36; adult/child 100/40kr; ⊙ 10am-4pm Jun-Aug, noon-4pm Tue-Fri Sep-May; P) The Zorn family house, Zorngården, is an excellent example of a wealthy artist's residence and reflects Anders Zorn's National Romantic aspirations (check out the Viking-influenced hall and entryway). Access to the house is by guided tour (in Swedish) on the hour and half-hour. Guided tours in English are conducted over the summer season at 11.15am and 2.15pm and must be booked in advance. Combination tickets including the adjacent Zornmuseet (☑ 0250-59 23 10; www.zorn.se/en/visit-us/zorn-museum/; Vasagatan 36; adult/child 70kr/free; ⊙ 9am-5pm Jun-Aug, noon-4pm Sep-May; P) are 160kr (no child discount).

🍴 Sleeping & Eating

Mora Hotell & Spa   HOTEL €€

(☑ 0250-59 26 50; www.morahotell.se; Strandgatan 12; r from 1295kr; P ❄ ✳ 🛜) There's been a hotel here since 1830, although its current incarnation is far from antique. Full of personality, modern rooms combine clean lines, wooden floors and earthy tones with bright folk-art accents. Head to the spa for steam rooms, jacuzzis, massage and body treatments.

★ **Korsnasgarden**   EUROPEAN €€

(☑ 046-250 102 84; www.korsnasgarden.se; Moragatan 9; mains 195-385kr; ⊙ 11am-8pm Mon-Sat, shorter hours in winter) This delightful restaurant cafe serves a small selection of hot and cold meals and a plethora of freshly made sandwiches within Mora's most delightful dining environs – a smartly renovated historic house and garden. It's kid friendly, too (but there's enough space that the place doesn't feel flooded with children).

ⓘ Information

Siljan Turism Mora Tourist Center (☑ 0248-79 72 00; Köpmannagatan 3a; ⊙ 9am-6pm Mon-Fri, 10am-4pm Sat & Sun) The friendly folk can deck you out with maps of Siljansleden, an excellent network of walking and cycling paths extending for more than 300km around Lake Siljan, from among their wealth of local information.

ⓘ Getting There & Away

Mora is 39km northwest of Rättvik on Rte 70 and 17km southwest of Orsa on the E45.

All **Dalatrafik** (p410) buses depart from the main bus stop at Moragatan 23. Bus 132 runs to Rättvik and Falun and bus 141 runs to Orsa.

Mora is the Lake Siljan terminus for **SJ Rail** (p407) trains and the southern terminus of the Inlandsbanan (Inland Railway), which runs north to Gällivare (mid-June through mid-August). Mora train station is about 1km east of town. There's also a more central station called Morastrand but not all trains stop there: be sure to check timetables before setting out.

Mora has direct rail links year-round to Stockholm (545kr, 3¾ hours) and seasonally to Östersund (from 595kr, 6¼ hours) via the Inlandsbanan. Outside its operating season, you'll need to catch bus 45 (278kr, 5¼ hours).

SKÅNE

Skåne (Scania) is Sweden at its most continental. Connected to Denmark by bridge, its trademark mix of manors, gingerbread-style abodes and delicate, deciduous forests are a constant reminder that central Europe is just beyond the horizon.

Dominating the scene is metropolitan Malmö, defined by its cosmopolitan culture and striking, twisting tower. Further out, velvety fields, sandy coastlines and stoic castles create one of Sweden's most bucolic landscapes. Add to this the fact that Skåne is often dubbed Sweden's larder and you have yourself one scrumptious Scandi treat.

Malmö

☑ 040 / POP 328,494

Sweden's third-largest city is a place where old meets new: from its proud castle and showpiece squares Stortorget and Lilla Torget, in the heart of Gamla Staden (the 'Old Town'), to the cosmopolitan promenades of Västra Hamnen's vibrant redeveloped waterfront. Here, Scandinavia's tallest building twists its way skyward, gazing down over the vast Öresund bridge – both are modern engineering marvels reflecting multicultural Malmö's progressive outlook.

'The bridge', connecting the city to cool-cat Copenhagen's downtown and busy international airport, has helped forge a dynamic urban conglomeration. This, and the fact that Germany is just a short hop across the Baltic, helps explain why more than 150 nationalities call Malmö home.

It's no wonder then that Malmö is so fabulously worldly – Middle Eastern markets, Italian coffee culture, edgy international eateries and cruisy, chic bars counter its intrinsic Nordic reserve, while its classical and contemporary fine-arts and theatre scenes are thriving.

◎ Sights

★ Västra Hamnen   AREA
(Western Harbour) Located about 2.5km northwest of the Old Town, buzzing, bayside Västra Hamnen represents the modern face of Malmö. It's a popular spot to stroll, sip coffee and browse boutiques, but mostly people come to marvel at the Öresund bridge and ogle the Turning Torso (www.turningtorso.se; Lilla Varvsgatan 14) twisting its way skyward: it's beautiful and an engineering marvel, but one can't help feel it's out of place here.

★ Gamla Staden   AREA
(Old Town) Focusing on the area around Stortorget (the town square) and lively Lilla Torget (the little square) Malmö's Old Town is a gorgeous warren of cobblestone streets, half-timbered houses and bold facades that feel like they'd be more at home in Hamburg.

★ Malmö Museer   MUSEUM
(✆040-34 44 23; www.malmo.se/museer; Malmöhusvägen 6; adult/child 40kr/free; ⊘10am-5pm; 🚸) Located within the vast Malmöhus Slott, operating under the broad banner (and one low admission fee) of the Malmö Museer, are three main museums within a museum: the Malmö Konstmuseum (✆040-34 44 37; Malmöhusvägen 6; adult/child 40kr/free; ⊘10am-5pm), Stadsmuseum (City Museum; ✆040-34 44 37; Malmöhusvägen 6; adult/child 40kr/free; ⊘10am-5pm) and a large and unexpected Aquarium complete with an impressive nocturnal hall, wriggling with everything from bats to electric eels. There are gift shops and cafes inside all the museums, and plenty for kids, but be prepared for lots of walking, narrow staircases and cobblestones.

Moderna Museet Malmö   MUSEUM
(✆040-685 79 37; www.modernamuseet.se/malmo; Gasverksgatan 22; ⊘11am-6pm Tue-Sun) **FREE** Architects Tham & Videgård chose to make the most of the distinct 1901 Rooseum, once a power-generating turbine hall, by adding a contemporary annexe, complete with a bright, perforated orange-red facade. Venue aside, the museum's galleries are well worth visiting, with the permanent exhibition including works by Matisse, Dalí and Picasso.

Kungsparken   PARK
(King's Park) Since 1872, the 34,000-sq-metre King's Park in the shadow of Malmöhus Slott (p413) has been delighting Malmö's residents and visitors with its magnificent collection of more than 130 mature trees from around the world, as well as ponds, an organic vegetable garden and a fountain. It's a great spot for a picnic when the weather is fine. For those partial to a flutter, Malmö's only casino, the Cosmopol (✆020-21 92 19; www.casinocosmopol.se; Slottsgatan 33, Kungsparken; ⊘1pm-4am), is within the park bounds.

Teknikens och sjöfartens hus   MUSEUM
(Technology & Maritime Museum; ✆040-34 44 38; Malmöhusvägen 7A; adult/child 40kr/free; ⊘10am-5pm) A short distance to the west of Malmöhus Slott, the Technology and Maritime museum is home to aircraft, vehicles, a horse-drawn tram, steam engines, and the amazing 'U3' walk-in submarine, outside the main building. The submarine was launched in Karlskrona in 1943 and decommissioned in 1967. Upstairs, a superb hands-on experiment room will keep kids (of all ages) suitably engrossed. Admission includes access to all the museums of the Malmö Museer conglomeration.

Öresund Bridge   BRIDGE
(www.oresundsbron.com; motorcycle/car/minibus 265/520/1040kr) This bridge is the longest cable-tied road and rail bridge in Europe, measuring 7.8km from Lernacken (on the Swedish side, near Malmö) to the artificial island of Peberholm (Pepper Island), south of Saltholm (Salt Island).

Local commuters pay via an electronic transmitter, while tolls for everyone else are payable by credit card, debit card or in euros, Danish or Swedish currency at the Lernacken toll booths or online.

Malmöhus Slott   CASTLE
(✆040 34 44 37; Malmöhusvägen 6; adult/child 40kr/free; ⊘10am-5pm, tours 3pm Wed-Sun Jul-Sep) Erik of Pomerania built the first fortress here in 1436 but it was destroyed between 1534 and 1536 during a popular uprising in Skåne. After this rebellion, Denmark's King Christian III had the castle rebuilt in a Danish Gothic/Renaissance style, but his castle was devastated by fire in 1870. It lay in ruins until the 1930s when the functionalist, factory-like red-brick buildings were added to what remained of the main building and the intact gun towers, and Malmo Museer was born.

Malmö

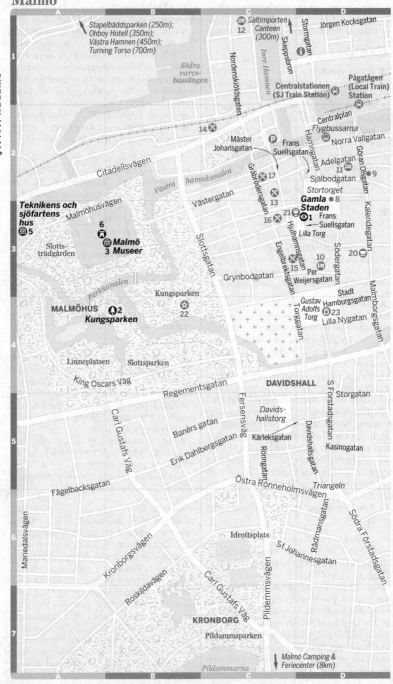

Stapelbäddsparken (250m);
Ohboy Hotell (350m);
Västra Hamnen (450m);
Turning Torso (700m)

12 Saltimporten Canteen (300m)

Jörgen Kocksgatan

Stormgatan

Södra varvsbassängen

Nordenskiöldsgatan

Inre Hamnen

Skeppsbron

Centralstationen (SJ Train Station)

Pågatågen (Local Train) Station

Citadellsvägen

14

Västra hamnkanalen

Centralplan

Flygbussarna

Harmogatan

Norra Vallgatan

Mäster Johansgatan

Frans Suellsgatan

Adelgatan

11

Göran Olsgatan

9

Grävlögersgatan

17

Själbodgatan

Stortorget

Gamla Staden

8

Kalendegatan

Teknikens och sjöfartens hus
5

Malmöhusvägen

6

Västergatan

13

Vastergatan

16

21

1

Frans Suellsgatan

Lilla Torg

Slottsträdgården

Malmö Museer
3

Hjulhammsgatan

Engelbrektsgatan

Per Weijersgatan

15

10

Södergatan

20

Slottsgatan

Grynbodgatan

Stadt Hamburgsgatan

Malmborgsgatan

MALMÖHUS

Kungsparken
2

Parkkanalen

Kungsparken

22

Gustav Adolfs Torg

23

Lilla Nygatan

Gustav Adolfs Torggatan

Linneplatsen

Slottsparken

DAVIDSHALL

S Förstadsgatan

Storgatan

King Oscars Väg

Regementsgatan

Fersensväg

Davids-hallstorg

Davidshallsgatan

Carl Gustafs Väg

Banérs gatan

Kärleksgatan

Kasinogatan

Erik Dahlbergsgatan

Römgatan

Triangeln

Fågelbacksgatan

Östra Rönneholmsvägen

Rådmansgatan

Södra Förstadsgatan

Mariedalsvägen

Idrottsplats

St Johannesgatan

Kronborgsvägen

Pildemmsvägen

Roskildavägen

Carl Gustafs Väg

KRONBORG

Pildammsparken

Malmö Camping & Feriecenter (8km)

Pildammarna

N

0 — 200 m
0 — 0.1 miles

🏃 Activities

⭐ Ribersborgs kallbadhus
SWIMMING

(📞040-26 03 66; www.ribersborgskallbadhus.se; Limhamnsvägen; adult/child 65kr/free; ⏱9am-8pm Mon, Tue & Thu, to 9pm Wed, to 6pm Fri-Sun May-Sep, shorter hours rest of year) Ribersborg is a fetching sandy beach backed by parkland, about 2km west of the town centre. Off the beach, at the end of a 200m-long pier, is an open-air naturist saltwater pool, with separate sections for men and women, and a wood-fired sauna dating from 1898. There is also a pleasant cafe.

Stapelbäddsparken
SKATING

(📞020-34 45 00; www.stpln.se; Stapelbäddsgatan 3; ⏱10am-5pm Mon-Fri; ♿) FREE Swing by this intense urban jungle near the Turning Torso, at the northwestern harbour redevelopment, to gasp at skaters – local and international – sliding, flying and occasionally tumbling from dizzying heights. Check out www.bryggeriet.org for more details on the city's vibrant skateboarding scene.

☞ Tours

Malmö By Foot
WALKING

(📞0708-43 50 20; www.malmobyfoot.com; 1¼hr tour 80kr; ⏱11am & 12.45pm Jul & Aug) A guided walk covering the history of Malmö from the Middle Ages to today. Tours in Swedish leave twice a day from Sankt Petri Kyrka. Book online, by phone or through the tourist office. Customised tours in English are available for groups of 10 or more.

Malmö Bike Tours
CYCLING

(📞0708-46 25 40; www.malmobiketours.se; 2hr tour adult/child 350/250kr, rental day/week 150/650kr) Starting from Stortorget, Malmö Bike Tours runs two-hour and 3½-hour cycling trips around the city, covering major landmarks and lesser-known neighbourhoods. It also rents bicycles if you'd rather tour on your own. Book online, by phone or through the tourist office.

🎊 Festivals

⭐ Malmö Festival
MUSIC

(www.malmofestivalen.se; ⏱mid-Aug) Malmö's premier annual event – with an average of some 1.5 million visitors – is the weeklong Malmö Festival. The mostly free events include theatre, dance, live music, fireworks and sizzling food stalls.

Malmo Pride
LGBT

(www.malmopride.com; ⏱late Sep) Called the Regnbågsfestivalen (Rainbow Festival) until

Malmö

2016, Malmö Pride celebrates LGBT diversity with exhibitions, films, workshops and parties, culminating in a pride parade.

🛏 Sleeping

Malmö Camping & Feriecenter CAMPGROUND €
(☑040-15 51 65; www.firstcamp.se/malmo/; Strandgatan 101; sites from 320kr, 2-bed cabins from 795kr; P🖥🐕) By a little beach, this camping ground is in the shadow of the Öresund (p413) bridge, about 5km southwest of the centre of town: take bus 4 from Gustav Adolfs Torg (16kr).

★**Hotel Noble House** HOTEL €€
(☑040-664 30 00; www.hotelnoblehouse.se; Per Weijersgatan 6; s/d from 995/1195kr; 🖥@🛜) The rooms of this low-cost Best Western have been recently refurbished and feature parquet floors and a variety of tasteful design themes, with smart wallpaper and colourful accents. For comfort, price and location the hotel is an excellent choice.

★**Story Hotel Studio Malmö** BOUTIQUE HOTEL €€
(☑040-616 52 00; www.storyhotels.com/studiomalmo/; Tyfongatan 1; d/ste from 990kr; 🖥🛜) If you love Swedish design, make a beeline for the fresh and funky Story Hotel, one of Malmö's newest offerings. Exposed concrete walls, heavy red curtains, plush sofas, ocean views and sumptuous suites all tempt you to stay indoors...at least for a sleep-in. All rooms have queen or king beds, muted tones and raindrop showers. Most have wonderful views.

Quality Hotel View HOTEL €€
(☑040-37 41 00; www.nordicchoicehotels.com/hotels/sweden/malmo/quality-hotel-view/; Hyllie Stationstorg 29; d from 975kr; P🖥🛜) For the location and price, you really can't go past the soaring heights of Malmö's most typically international hotel, with large rooms (many with bath-tubs), a superb breakfast buffet, great views and an excellent location directly atop Hyllie subway station putting you midway between Copenhagen airport and central Malmö. Access is everything.

Ohboy Hotell BOUTIQUE HOTEL €€
(☑046-40 856 06; www.ohboy.se; Lilla Varvsgatan 24; ⏲d from 1050kr; 🛜) 🚲 Malmö's newest and quirkiest hotel is this concrete whopper designed by cyclists, for cyclists. There's a foldable bike in every room, pump and wash stations on-site, a rooftop terrace and garden and a variety of compact living solutions including lofts with additional hammock bedding and apartments. While it won't be to everyone's tastes, those who love it will love it a lot.

Mayfair Hotel Tunneln BOUTIQUE HOTEL €€€
(☑040-10 16 20; www.mayfairtunneln.com/en/; Adelgatan 4; s/d from 1325/1825kr; P🛜) Central, classic and stylish, this boutique hotel in a heritage-listed building in the heart of Gamla Staden is great for history lovers. Rooms are bright and comfortable and a hearty breakfast spread is served in the hotel's vaulted cellar. With lots of staircases, nooks and narrow corridors it's not a great choice for mobility-impaired guests.

✖ Eating

Surf Shack
BURGERS €

(📞0761-76 40 18; www.surfshacksmashburgers.com; Västergatan 9a; burgers from 70kr; ⏰10.30am-8pm Mon-Thu, to 11pm Fri-Sun; 🚗) Enjoy a surfing-dude theme and a menu of top-range burgers, including a vegie option of tofu and black beans, 'no roll' (wrapped in lettuce) and healthy extra toppings like avocado, feta and grilled mushrooms. There are also sodas and shakes, including double chocolate and peanut butter if you are determined to sink that board.

★ Bastard
EUROPEAN €€

(📞040-12 13 18; www.bastardrestaurant.se; Mäster Johansgatan 11; mains 95-185kr; ⏰5pm-midnight Tue-Thu, to 2am Fri & Sat) 🚗 This hipster restaurant with possibly the best and hipster-est name anyone has ever thought to call a restaurant is about as close as you'll get to a gastropub in Sweden. It serves predominantly small and share plates, ranging from gourmet meat platters to blackened grilled chicken for two or pizza with snails. The bar is a popular choice with well-heeled locals.

★ Namu
FUSION €€

(📞040-12 14 90; www.namu.nu; Landbygatan 5; mains 109-225kr; ⏰11.30am-2pm & 5-11pm Tue-Thu, to 1am Fri & Sat) Brainchild of *Masterchef Sweden* winner Jennie Walldén, Namu (meaning 'tree') serves up artfully prepared Korean dishes adapted according to the availability of seasonal local ingredients and presented in surroundings that merge Scandinavian design elements and traditional Korean styling beautifully. The result: a cultural and culinary synergy that fans of either genre won't want to miss.

Eatery Social Taqueria
MEXICAN €€

(📞040-20 75 00; www.eaterysocial.se/en/; Dag Hammarskjölds Torg 2; small plates 70-165kr; ⏰5pm-midnight Mon-Sat, noon-4pm Sun; 🚗) This fun, boutique *taqueria* belonging to Swedish celebrity chef Marcus Samuelsson's stable serves the best Tex-Mex small plates you'll get this side of Tijuana. All the favourites are there: tacos, quesadillas, tostadas, tequila!

Saltimporten Canteen
SWEDISH €€

(📞070-651 84 26; www.saltimporten.com; Grimsbygatan 24; dagens lunch 95kr; ⏰noon-2pm Mon-Fri) This wonderfully minimalist open canteen housed in the old Salt Importing Warehouse,

---

SWEDEN MALMÖ

WORTH A TRIP

IKEA MUSEUM

When in 1958, a 17-year-old businessman by the name of Ingvar Kamprad opened a hulking furniture store in the little town of Älmult (population: 8,955), people thought he was stark raving bonkers. And when you visit Älmhult and imagine what it was like in 1958, you'll understand why. Sweden didn't even have supermarkets. If you look around you now, you'll probably see a 'something' in your room that got there because Ingvar the entrepreneur had a vision.

Kamprad's store grew into the global base of a Swedish brand that is known the world over: that's right, IKEA! The store (which closed in 2012) was spared from demolition and re-imagined as the world's first IKEA Museum (📞0476-44 16 00; www.ikeamuseum.com; Ikeagatan 5, Älmhult; adult/child 60/40kr; ⏰10am-7pm; 🅿), opened in June 2016. It's well worth a visit so you can learn straight from the horse's mouth how IKEA shaped the future. There's an obligatory resturant selling real-deal IKEA *köttbullar* (Swedish meatballs) and a shop with museum-only products, but if you need a hard-core IKEA fix, there's a megastore up the road.

Trains run almost hourly from Malmö to Älmhult (143kr, 1¼ hours) so it's an easy day trip if you don't fancy spending the night. But because Älmhult really is a little town in the middle of nowhere, the purpose-built IKEA Hotell (📞0476-64 11 00; www.ikeahotell.se; Ikeagatan 1, Älmhult; s/d from 495/995kr; 🅿🛜), opposite the museum, is another world first – allowing visitors even more time to shop. Clever IKEA.

Having retired at 87, Ingvar passed away in early 2018, aged 91. His empire has passed into the hands of his three sons, notably the youngest, who until 2016 held the hotseat as Chairman. At the end of his life Kamprad's estimated net worth was roughly US$58 billion.

The moral of the story is: the next time someone says you're nuts for following your dreams, don't pay them too much attention – you just might change the world.

now a haven of creative and design offices, has polished concrete floors and a design palette that emphasizes its harbour views. Each day there's a different set lunch menu, and that's it – and it's almost always executed perfectly.

★ **Johan P** SEAFOOD €€€
(📞040-97 18 18; www.johanp.nu; Hjulhamnsgatan 5; mains 225-375kr, 4-course set menu 695kr; ⏰11.30am-11pm Mon-Fri, noon-11pm Sat, 1-10pm Sun) Old-timer Johan P continues to enthral diners with its fresh-off-the-boat seafood. Choose your fishy favourite from the market-style counter out back or go for the set menu. There are lovely bisques, *moules meunière* (mussels cooked in wine) and chilled shellfish platters. For snacks, Basque-style *pintxos* (tapas) are available.

🍷 Drinking & Nightlife

★ **Far i hatten** BAR
(📞040-615 36 51; www.farihatten.se; Folkets Park; ⏰5pm-1am Mon-Fri, from 11.30am Sat & Sun, shorter hours in winter) Smack bang in the middle of Folkets Park (www.malmofolketspark.se; Norra Parkgatan 2A; ⏰park 7am-9pm Mon-Fri, 8am-9pm Sat & Sun, to 11pm Jun-Aug, attractions noon-7pm May–mid-Aug, shorter hours rest of year; 🚻) **FREE**, Far i hatten is a popular summer hang-out that transforms from smart casual cafe by day into an illuminated alfresco wonderland of an evening. There's a massive beery patio and even a ping-pong table!

Lilla Kafferosteriet CAFE
(📞040-48 20 00; www.lillakafferosteriet.se; Baltzarsgatan 24; sandwiches from 55kr; ⏰8am-7pm Mon-Fri, 10am-5pm Sat, 11am-5pm Sun) 🍵 Have a mosey around the warren of atmospheric rooms here before you bag your table, or head out to the pretty patio. This is a serious-about-coffee cafe with freshly ground (Fairtrade) beans, plus plenty of sweet and savoury goodies. You may just stay for a while; it's that kind of place.

Victors COCKTAIL BAR
(📞040-12 76 70; www.victors.se; Lilla Torg 1; ⏰11.30am-1am Mon-Thu, til 2am Fri & Sat, til midnight Sun) Appealing to a 30-something and older crowd, Victors does glam cocktails on Lilla Torg with light late-night snacks available to accompany your tipple.

Grand Öl & Mat BAR
(📞040-12 63 13; www.grandolomat.se; Monbijougatan 17; ⏰10pm-3am Fri & Sat May-Sep) Billed as a meeting place for food, drinks, culture and events, the Grand is a popular late-night weekend venue in summer, with regular cross-genre live performances and DJs, then reverts to more of a cafe-restaurant vibe in the winter months.

🛍 Shopping

The hot spots for up-and-coming designers and vintage threads are the streets around Davidshallstorg, south of Gamla Staden. Close to here is Triangeln, one of the city's better shopping malls, which has an excellent range of national and international stores and boutiques.

You'll also find a diverse range of shops in the vibrant Västra Hamnen area.

★ **Julmarknad i city** MARKET
(Gustav Adolfs torg) For 30 days leading up to 23 December, Malmö's Christmas markets warm the hearts of all who visit. Sip on some mulled wine and they'll warm your insides too!

ℹ Information

MEDICAL SERVICES

You can call the dentist and doctor on duty on 📞1177.

Akutklinik (📞1813; Eentrance 36, Södra Förstadsgatan 101) Emergency ward at the general hospital.

Apotek Gripen (📞0771-45 04 50; Bergsgatan 48; ⏰8am-10pm) After-hours pharmacy.

TOURIST INFORMATION

In 2017 Malmö closed its tourist-information offices due to increasing numbers of visitors sourcing their own information on the web or using the number of touch-screen tourist-information kiosks located around town. The official homepage (www.malmotown.com) is still operational but is mainly a placeholder with links to other sites.

Travel Shop (📞040-33 05 70; www.travelshop.se; Carlsgatan 4A; ⏰9am-5pm Mon-Fri, 10am-3pm Sat & Sun) North of Malmö Centralstationen, sells tickets for bus and train companies, as well as offering a wide range of tours, bike rental (per 24 hours 150kr) and help with accommodation. There's also an official touch-screen Tourist InfoPoint located here.

Visit Skåne (www.visitskane.com) Provincial tourist board for the Skåne region.

ℹ Getting There & Away

AIR

Malmö Sturup Airport (📞010-109 45 00; www.swedavia.com/malmo; Malmö-Sturup) is a relatively small international and domestic ter-

ⓘ PUBLIC TRANSPORT PASSES

If you'll be travelling around Malmö by public transport, consider buying a 24-/72-hour *Tim-marsbijett* (65/165kr) offering unlimited public transport (buses and trains) within the service area for the duration of the ticket. And yes, Skånetrafiken inspectors check tickets vigilantly.

If you're sticking around for more than a few days, you can purchase a reusable Jojo card (20kr) at **Skånetrafiken** (☑0771-77 77 77; www.skanetrafiken.se) counters (Central-station and Triangeln station) and load it with an amount to cover your estimated travel. This will get you a discount of 10% on each trip, but if you don't end up using what you loaded, your money stays wastefully locked on the card.

To use the card, tap it on the Jojo readers onboard the bus. For trains, you still have to buy a ticket at ticket machines and use the Jojo card as your method of payment. If the printed ticket doesn't come out, your card hasn't been debited, meaning you don't have a valid rail ticket.

minal with limited facilities. Located some 33km southeast of Malmö, it's serviced primarily by **SAS** (☑0770-727 727; www.sas.se), with up to eight daily flights to/from Stockholm Arlanda, and low-cost domestic carrier **BRA** (☑0771-44 00 10; www.flygbra.se), with daily flights to Stockholm Bromma and a number of domestic destinations, including Visby on Gotland.

BUS

Malmö is easy to reach via bus from other major towns and cities in Sweden. The excellent Res-robot website (www.kopbiljett.resrobot.se) has the nation covered for fares and timetables.

TRAIN

Pågatågen (local trains) operated by **Skåne-trafiken** (p420) run regularly to Helsingborg (118kr, from 40 minutes), Landskrona (99kr, 30 minutes), Lund (63kr, 10 minutes), Simrishamn (118kr, 1½ hours), Ystad (99kr, 50 minutes) and other towns in Skåne. Bicycles are half-fare but are not allowed during peak times except from mid-June to mid-August.

SJ Rail (p407) operates several trains per day to/from Gothenburg (from 206kr, 2½ hours) and Stockholm (417kr, 4½ hours, hourly) also servicing many intermediary stations in central Sweden.

Baggage lockers at Malmö Centralstation start at 30kr per 24 hours.

Local operator **Snälltåget** (☑0771-26 00 00; www.snalltaget.se/en; Norra vallgatan 34) stepped in to start up a new and alternative night train to Berlin, when Deutsche Bahn pulled its service in 2015. A bed in a six-berth sleeper car (three departures a week in each direction) costs 399kr and the carriages are delightfully old-worldy. If you don't want to share, you can rent the whole compartment for 1999kr – a great deal if you're travelling with a few friends. At the time of writing the service was only oper-ational from May to September, but check the website for detailed timetables and updates.

ⓘ Getting Around

TO/FROM THE AIRPORT

Flygbussarna (☑0771-51 52 52; www.flygbus-sarna.se; ☺customer service line 8am-11pm) runs regular scheduled shuttles to/from **Malmö Sturup Airport** (p418) and Centralstation (adult/child one way 115/95kr) roughly every 40 minutes on weekdays, with six services on Saturday and seven on Sunday. Tickets can be purchased at a ticket machine at the bus stop, online, or on the bus, but it's cheaper to pur-chase online and tickets can only be purchased on-board with a credit card, no cash.

A taxi to/from the airport will set you back around 500kr.

Lund

☑046 / POP 118,542

Founded by the Danes around 1000 AD, Lund is the second-oldest city in Sweden. Sur-rounded by copses of beech trees and with an impressive architectural legacy, it just might be Sweden's loveliest city. Lund's magnifi-cent, medieval old town – centred upon its strikingly beautiful cathedral, around which Sweden's oldest, most prestigious university (c1666) radiates – is up there with the best.

Once the seat of the largest archbishopric in Europe, the city today has a much more low-key, out-of-the-limelight vibe, which helps make it feel so special. The beauty of its old bones and a throng of engaged youth drive a lively arts and culinary scene.

Just a few hundred metres from the sta-tion, the old town's endlessly photogenic lanes reveal a clutch of impressive muse-ums, cafes and bars spilling over the cob-bles, and soft, leafy parks.

Lund is an essential day trip from Malmö and an excellent base for stays in Skåne.

◉ Sights

★ Lunds domkyrka CATHEDRAL

(☑ 046-35 87 42; www.lundsdomkyrka.se; Kyrkogatan; ⊙ 8am-6pm Mon-Fri, 9.30am-5pm Sat, 9.30am-6pm Sun) Lund's twin-towered Romanesque cathedral is magnificent. Try to pop in at noon or 3pm (plus 1pm on Sunday and holidays) when the marvellous astronomical clock strikes up *In Dulci Jubilo* (a traditional Christmas carol) and the wooden figures at the top whirr into action. Within the crypt, you'll find Finn, the mythological giant who helped construct the cathedral, and a 16th-century well, carved with comical scenes.

Kulturen MUSEUM

(☑ 046-35 04 00; www.kulturen.com; Tegnerplatsen; adult May-Aug 120kr, Sep-Apr 90kr, child free; ⊙ 10am-5pm May-Aug, noon-4pm Tue-Sun Sep-Apr; ⊕) Kulturen, opened in 1892, is a huge open-air museum filling two whole blocks. Its 30-odd buildings include everything from the meanest birch-bark hovel to grand 17th-century houses. Permanent displays encompass Lund in the Middle Ages, vintage toys, ceramics, silver and glass (among many others); ask about guided tours in English. The popular outdoor cafe flanks several rune stones.

Skissernas Museum ARTS CENTRE

(Sketch Museum; ☑ 046-222 72 83; www.skissernasmuseum.se; Finngatan 2; adult/child 80/60kr; ⊙ noon-5pm Tue & Thu-Sun, to 9pm Wed) The exhibition rooms here, with their visual feast of paintings and sculpture, are designed for maximum impact and art immersion. Several sculptures and installations are huge, including the 6m-high *Women by the Sea* by Ivar Johnsson. Formerly a private collection, it includes works by some of the world's greats, including Joan Miró, Henri Matisse, Raoul Dufy, Sonia Delaunay and Fernand Léger. A sculpture park includes pieces by Henry Moore.

⏢ Sleeping

Hotel Finn HOTEL €

(☑ 046-280 63 00; www.hotelfinn.se; Dalbyvägen 20; d from 795kr) This modern, self-service hotel has crisp, clean lines and stylish though minimal facilities. Room rates are kept low by not having full-time front-end staff.

★ Hotell Oskar BOUTIQUE HOTEL €€

(☑ 046-18 80 85; www.hotelloskar.se; Bytaregatan 3; s/d from 995/1195kr; @ 🛜) Tucked away in a petite 19th-century townhouse, this central hotel has superb rooms reflecting sleek Scandi design. It's also well equipped, with DVD players, kettles and stereos, plus it has a pretty back garden. The adjacent cafe is handy for coffee and cake.

✖ Eating

★ St Jakobs Stenugnsbageri BAKERY €

(☑ 046-13 70 60; www.stjakobs.se; Klostergatan 9; baked goods 20-55kr; ⊙ 8am-6pm Mon-Fri, to 4pm Sat, to 3pm Sun) Mouth-watering is the only way to describe the selection of stone-baked breads, knotted cardamom rolls, melt-in-your-mouth coconut-lemon towers and crisp sugar cookies overflowing from the countertops and baking trays at St Jakobs. During the summer you're likely to see an enormous bowl of strawberries at the centre of it all, served with fresh cream, of course.

Malmstens Fisk & Köj SEAFOOD €€

(☑ 046-12 63 54; www.malmstensfisk.se; Saluhallen, Mårtenstorget; mains 145-205kr; ⊙ 11.30am-6pm Mon-Wed, to 7pm Thu, to 10pm Fri & Sat) Locals swear the seafood here is the best in town. Tucked into a classy corner in the gourmet market, the menu is reassuringly brief, depending on what is fresh that day. If you're just a tad peckish, go for a simple starter such as mussels in white wine with parsley or the signature Malmstens fish soup with bread and aioli.

★ Mat & Destillat SWEDISH €€€

(☑ 046-12 80 00; www.matochdestillat.se; Kyrkogatan 17; mains 129-279kr; ⊙ noon-midnight Mon-Sat; ☑) This high-end experimental kitchen and cocktail bar is turning heads on the Scanian culinary circuit for its artful, inventive locavore dishes offering modern twists on Swedish classics. It's also a popular spot for classy cocktails with superb bar snacks.

ⓘ Information

Lund Tourist Centre (☑ 046-35 50 40; www.lund.se; Botulfsgatan 1A; ⊙ 10am-6pm Mon-Fri, to 2pm Sat) Located at the southern end of Stortorget, with an excellent range of information about Lund. It can help with sourcing accommodation if you're stuck for a bed for the night and can provide you with a handy map of town, as well as a map that shows bicycle routes.

ⓘ Getting There & Away

Lund is just 21km northeast of Malmö by road or rail. Frequent trains and buses make the journey between the two cities.

It takes just 15 minutes from Lund to Malmö by train (63kr) and some trains run to Copenhagen airport in less than 35 minutes (147kr). Other direct services include Kristianstad (118kr, 50 minutes) and Karlskrona (241kr, 2½ hours).

All long-distance trains operated by **SJ Rail** (☑ 0771–75 75 75; www.sj.se) from Stockholm or Gothenburg enroute to Malmö stop in Lund.

FlixBus (☑ 0850-51 37 50; www.flixbus.se) operates daily services to Gothenburg (49kr, 3¾ hours) and Stockholm (from 299kr, eight hours).

Flygbuss (☑ 0771-77 77 77; www.flygbussarna. se) operates services to Malmö's Sturup Airport.

Trelleborg

☑ 0410 / POP 43,913

Trelleborg is home to a truly extraordinary (although reconstructed) sight: a 9th-century, wooden, Viking ring fortress. The city is also known for its beautiful gardens, palm-flanked main avenue and excellent shopping Trelleborg is the main gateway between Sweden and Germany, with frequent ferry services.

◉ Sights

★ **Trelleborgen** HISTORIC SITE
(☑ 0410-73 30 21; www.trelleborgen.se; Västra Vallgatan 6; visitors centre adult/child 30kr/free; ⊗ 10am-4pm Jun-Aug, 1-5pm Mon-Thu rest of year; **P ♿**) **FREE** Trelleborgen is a 9th-century Viking ring fortress, discovered in 1988 off Bryggaregatan (just west of the town centre). A quarter of the palisaded fort and a wooden gateway have been recreated, as has a Viking farmhouse and a medieval house built within the walls. A small museum showcases finds from the archaeological digs, including Viking jewellery, grooming implements and a 10th-century skull illustrating the ancient trend of teeth filing.

ℹ Information

Trelleborg Tourist Center (☑ 0410-73 33 20; www.trelleborg.se/turism; Kontinentgatan 2; ⊗ 9am-6pm Mon-Fri, 10am-4pm Sat, 10am-2pm Sun) is located directly opposite the ferry terminal.

ℹ Getting There & Away

Trelleborg is 32km south of Malmö on the E6 motorway and 48km west of Ystad.

Skånetrafiken (p420) bus 190 runs from Ystad to Trelleborg (87kr, one hour) and bus 146 runs to Malmö (64kr, 50 minutes). You can also catch trains to Malmö (75kr, 35 minutes) and Helsingborg (110kr, 1½ hours).

Stena Line (☑ 031-85 80 00; www.stenaline. com) ferries connect Sweden to Germany with

sailings to Sassnitz (from 190kr, twice daily each way) and Rostock (from 315kr, two or three daily) from the **Stena Line Ferry Terminal**.

TT-Line (☑ 0450-28 01 81; www.ttline.com) ferries also make the link, shuttling to Travemünde (from 310kr) and Rostock (from 450kr) three to four times daily.

Fares vary by sailing and capacity: check online for the best rates and to make bookings.

Ystad

☑ 0411 / POP 29,338

Medieval market town Ystad has an intoxicating allure thanks to its half-timbered houses, rambling cobbled streets and the frequently haunting sound of its nightwatchman's horn. Fans of crime novels may recognise Ystad as the setting for the best-selling Inspector Wallander crime thrillers.

Ystad was Sweden's window to Europe from the 17th to the mid-19th century, with new ideas and inventions – including cars, banks and hotels – arriving here first. Now a terminal for ferries to Poland and the Danish island of Bornholm, the port area's transitory feel thankfully doesn't spread to the rest of the city. Once you start to explore you might find the place will work its magic and you'll want to linger longer.

◉ Sights

Half-timbered houses are scattered liberally round town, especially on Stora Östergatan. Most date from the latter half of the 18th century, although **Pilgrändshuset** (☑ 0411-147 31; Stora Östergatan) on the corner of Pilgrand and Stora Östergatan is Scandinavia's oldest half-timbered house and dates from 1480. Take a peek, too, at the facade of beautiful **Änglahuset**, on Stora Norregatan, which originates from around 1630.

★ **Sankta Maria Kyrka** CHURCH
(☑ 0411-692 00; Stortorget 2A; ⊗ 10am-6pm Jun-Aug, to 4pm Sep-May) **FREE** Among the church's highlights are a fabulously ornate 17th-century baroque pulpit, an elaborate pipe organ, chandeliers and excellent acoustics. It's from the church's clock tower that the town's nightwatchman famously sounds his horn – a tradition that's been upheld since 1250.

★ **Cineteket** MUSEUM
(☑ 0411-57 70 57; www.ystad.se/cineteket; Elis Nilssons väg 8; adult/child 60kr/free; ⊗ 10am-4pm Mon-Thu, Sat & Sun mid-Jun–Aug, hours vary rest of year) Fans of crime thrillers most likely

know the name Henning Mankell (1948-2015), author of the best-selling Inspector Wallander series. The books are set in the small, seemingly peaceful town of Ystad. The gloomy inspector paces its medieval streets, solving gruesome murders through his meticulous police work...but at a cost to his personal life, which is slowly and painfully disintegrating. Cineteket film museum runs guided tours (by appointment; adult/child 120/70kr) of the adjoining Ystad Studios, from May to September.

★ Klostret i Ystad   MUSEUM
(☑ 0411-57 72 86; www.klostret.ystad.se; St Petri Kyrkoplan; adult/child 40kr/free; ☺ noon-5pm Tue-Fri, noon-4pm Sat & Sun) Klostret i Ystad, in the Middle Ages Franciscan monastery of Gråbrödraklostret, features local textiles and silverware. The monastery includes the 13th-century deconsecrated Sankt Petri Kyrkan (now used for art exhibitions), which has around 80 gravestones from the 14th to 18th centuries. Admission also includes entry to Ystads Konstmuseum (☑ 0411-57 72 85; www.konstmuseet.ystad.se; St Knuts Torg; adult/child 40kr/free; ☺ 10am-5pm Mon-Fri, noon-4pm Sat & Sun Jul & Aug, shorter hours rest of year) FREE.

🍽 Sleeping & Eating

★ Sekelgården Hotel   HOTEL €€
(☑ 0411-739 00; www.sekelgarden.se; Långgatan 18; s/d from 995/1395kr; P @ 🛜) A romantic family-run hotel in a superb half-timbered house (1793); staying here is a bit like staying with your (affluent) country cousins. Rooms are set around a delightful garden and are all different, although typically decorated with a combination of William Morris–style wallpaper and pastel paintwork combined with colourful quilts, rugs and fabrics.

★ Saltsjobad   SPA HOTEL €€€
(☑ 0411 136 30; www.ysb.se; Saltsjöbadsvägen 15; d/ste from 1400/2250kr; P ❄ 🛜 ⛉) One of the finest hotels and day spas in Skåne can be found here in Ystad, right on the beach. Generous rooms and suites furnished in a variery of chic styles all feature downy bedding, natural light and big bathrooms. The on-site amenities, from the swimming pool to the restaurant and treatment rooms, are all first class.

Maltes Mackor   SANDWICHES €
(☑ 0411-101 30; Stora Östergatan 12; baguettes from 60kr; ☺ 10am-6pm, to 3pm Sat) Short on space but long on choice, the baguettes and wraps here are made with only the freshest locally sourced produce. If you're not peckish, grab a coffee – it's reputed to be the best in town.

★ Sandskogens Värdshus   EUROPEAN €€€
(☑ 0411-23 73 00; www.villastrandvagen.se/en/; Strandvägen 1; 5-course set menu 595kr (with wine 795kr); ☺ 5-11pm Mon-Sat) Under the tutelage of one of Sweden's most highly regarded chefs, Daniel Müllern, this restaurant serves up exquisite five-course dinners served in an historic mansion (where you can also stay if you choose). The regularly changing menu is posted online. Dress to impress and bring someone special.

ℹ Information

Ystads Turistbyrå (☑ 0411-57 76 81; www.ystad.se; St Knuts Torg; ☺ 9am-7pm Mon-Fri, 10am-6pm Sat & Sun mid-Jun–mid-Aug; 🛜) is located just outside the train station and has free internet access.

ℹ Getting There & Away

Ystad is 60km southeast of Malmö on the E65 motorway, and 45km southwest of Simrishamn via Rte 9.

Ystad is a popular ferry port. **Unity Line** (☑ 0411-55 69 00; www.unityline.se; adult one way from 418kr) and **Polferries** (☑ 040-12 17 00; www.polferries.se; adult one way 353kr) operate daily crossings between Ystad and Swinoujscie (Poland). Fares start at around 353kr and the journey takes approximately 6½ hours. **Faergen** (☑ +45-702 315 15; www.faergen.dk; adult one way from 200kr) runs frequent ferries and catamarans between Ystad and Rønne, on the Danish island of Bornholm. Fares start at 200kr and it takes under 90 minutes to get across.

Skånetrafiken (p420) bus 190 runs from Ystad to Trelleborg (87kr, one hour) via Smygehuk. Bus 570 to Simrishamn (69kr, 40 minutes) via Löderup runs hourly in the summer. Buses depart from outside Ystad train station.

SJ Rail (p407) and **Skånetrafiken** (p420) operate regular trains between Ystad and Malmö (99kr, 50 minutes), Lund (111kr, 1¼ hours) and Simrishamn (69kr, 40 minutes).

Helsingborg

☑ 042 / POP 106,388

At its heart, Helsingborg boasts a showcase of rejuvenated waterfront restaurants, lofty castle ruins and lively cobblestone streets, which in summer, thrive to the beat of a banging cultural drum: Helsingborg is a proud patron of theatre and the arts, and lovers of either discipline will find like-minded people here.

Perhaps this longing for creative expression stems from the fact that its strategic position on the Öresund, a mere 4km from Denmark, saw Helsingborg battled over with ferocious regularity during the many Swedish–Danish wars, until in 1710 Danish invaders were finally defeated just outside the city.

In this historical context it's easier to get a sense of the brazen statement the architects of Helsingborg's wealth of flouncy, turreted, buildings might have been making. A happy denouement is that today, almost 15 million passengers traverse the waterway shared by the city and its Danish counterpart Helsingør, with friendly, seasoned nonchalance.

◎ Sights & Activities

★ **Dunkers Kulturhus**   MUSEUM
(☑ 42 10 74 00; www.dunkerskulturhus.se; Kungsgatan 11; exhibition prices vary; ⏲ 8am-6pm Mon-Fri, from 10am Sat & Sun) Just north of the transport terminal, the crisp white Dunkers Kulturhus encompasses an interesting town museum (free) and temporary exhibitions (admission varies), plus a concert hall, an urbane cafe and a design-savvy gift shop and school of the arts. The building's creator, Danish architect Kim Utzon, is the son of Sydney Opera House architect Jørn Utzon.

★ **Fredriksdal museer
och trädgårdar**   MUSEUM
(Fredriksdal Museum and Gardens; ☑ 042-10 45 00; www.fredriksdal.se; off Hävertgatan; adult/child May-Sep 70kr/free, Oct-Mar free; ⏲ 10am-6pm May-Sep, shorter hours rest of year; P 🚼) One of Sweden's best open-air museums, based around an 18th-century manor house (not open to the public), the houses and shops you see here once graced the streets of central Helsingborg; they were moved here, brick by brick, in the 1960s. Thankfully, this is no contrived theme park; the whole place is charming and there's plenty of scope for souvenir shopping at the art and craft workshops. There are also herb, rose and vegetable gardens and blissfully leafy grounds.

Kärnan   RUINS
(☑ 042-10 50 00; www.helsingborg.se/karnan; Slottshagsgatan; adult/child 50kr/free; ⏲ 10am-6pm Jun-Aug, closed Mon rest of year) Dramatic steps and archways lead up from Stortorget to the square tower Kärnan (34m), all that remains of the medieval castle. The castle became Swedish property during the 17th-century Danish–Swedish War, and was mostly demolished once the fighting stopped. The tower

---

> ### ⓘ KULTURKORT
>
> If you are planning on visiting Helsingborg's main sights, consider investing 120kr in a **Kulturkort** (www.mittkulturkort.se), which can save you close to 200kr in admission costs over two days. Purchase at **Dunkers kulturhus** (p423) or by the entrance to **Fredriksdal museer och trädgårdar** (p423).

was restored from its derelict state in 1894, and the view is regal indeed.

Toy World   MUSEUM
(☑ 042-453 97 00; www.toyworld.se; Kullagatan 12; 60kr; ⏲ noon-5pm Wed-Fri, to 4pm Sat & Sun; P 🚼) We think you'll be hard pressed to find an adult who won't also enjoy this dinky collection of toys and games from around the world – there's something to whisk almost everyone back to the carefree days of youth. The admission price includes a small toy – kids love it!

🛏 Sleeping

★ **V Hotel**   HOTEL €€
(☑ 042-14 44 20; www.vhotel.se; Fågelsångsgatan 1; s/d from 995/1395kr; P @ 🛜) Trendy and urbane, this hipster hotel sets the tone with velvet cushions, modern bookshelves and brass candlesticks decorating the lobby. Rooms are similarly chic and stylish, although they do vary considerably: some are swing-a-cat size, while the most luxurious has a spa.

★ **Elite Hotel Mollberg**   HOTEL €€
(☑ 042-37 37 00; www.elite.se/helsingborg/mollberg⫝; 18 Stortorget; d/ste from 846/1272kr; 🛜) This grand old dame has been lovingly maintained and updated although it has changed management many times over the years. The current team runs a tight ship, which means great-value rooms and the chance to experience a wonderful historic hotel without suffering through painfully out-of-date decor or ridiculously overpriced rates. The Mollberg is a happy medium.

Hotel Maria   HOTEL €€
(☑ 042-24 99 40; www.hotelmaria.se; Mariagatan 8A; s/d from 900/1150kr; P @ 🛜) Tucked away behind Olsons Skafferi restaurant, Hotel Maria is utterly inspired, with each room flaunting a different historical style. Themes include national romantic, art deco and '70s disco. Beds are divinely comfy, the staff are friendly and there's a tapas bar downstairs.

✗ Eating

Globetrotter FUSION €

(☑ 042-37 18 00; www.theglobetrotter.se; Stortorget 20; small plates 35-85kr; ⊙ 5-10pm Sun-Thu, to 1am Fri & Sat; 🖗) These beautifully presented gastro-Asian tapas and mains hit the spot and, combined with the mood music and superb Stortorget people-watching potential from the terrace, make it hard to get a table at weekends.

★ Ebbas Fik CAFE €€

(☑ 042-28 14 40; www.ebbasfik.se; Bruksgatan 20; mains 85-169kr; ⊙ 9am-6pm Mon-Fri, to 4pm Sat; 🖗) It's still 1955 at this kitsch-tastic cafe, complete with jukebox (1kr), retro petrol pump and hamburgers made to Elvis' recipe. You can also buy '50s memorabilia here, ranging from vinyl records to Enid Blyton books (in Swedish!). The extensive cafe menu also includes sandwiches, baked potatoes, Coca-Cola floats and American-style pie.

Merry Widow HUNGARIAN €€€

(☑ 042-21 45 22; www.hungarian-restaurant.com; 29 Bruksgatan; mains 185-305kr; ⊙ 6-10pm Mon-Sat) For something a little out of the ordinary, this fabulously authentic restaurant serves hearty Hungarian fare – and when we say hearty we mean portion sizes are on the food-coma-inducing end of the scale. We're talking pork medallions, goulash and of course, schnitzel. Vegetarians will want to keep walking.

ℹ Information

At time of writing the local tourist office had closed its doors and was not planning to reopen.

Friendly staff now roam the area's key attractions and there's an automated information point at Helsingborg Centralstation. Otherwise, you can use the city-wide free wi-fi to log on to www.visithelsingborg.com and chat with a live representative or find the location of the nearest roaming tourist information officer. Neat idea!

ℹ Getting There & Away

BOAT

Knutpunkten (Drottninggatan) is the terminal for the **Scandlines** (☑ 042-18 61 00; www. scandlines.se) car ferry to Helsingør. There are five different boats: three have the Scandlines mark, while the other two are branded HH ferries. The one-way journey for a car under 6m, including driver, is 480kr. As a foot passenger, the fare is adult/child 36/22kr.

Sundbusserne (☑ +45 53 73 70 10; www. sundbusserne.se; adult/child 38/24kr), a Danish line, also operates from the terminal,

using smaller, passenger-only ferries (adult/child 45/30kr).

BUS

Helsingborg Bus Terminal is located on the ground level of **Knutpunkten** (p424).

Skånetrafiken (p420) operates local and regional bus services throughout the Skåne region.

Swebus (☑ 0771-21 82 18; www.swebus.se) runs north to Gothenburg, continuing on to Oslo, and south to Malmö. It also operates services northeast to Stockholm via Jönköping and Norrköping. Fares to Stockholm start at 469kr (7½ hours), to Gothenburg 139kr (three hours) and to Oslo as low as 249kr (seven hours) if you book in advance.

TRAIN

Underground platforms in **Knutpunkten** (p424) serve regular **SJ Rail** (p407) services to destinations including Stockholm (from 523kr, five hours), Gothenburg (343kr, 2¼ hours), Lund (99kr, 30 minutes), Malmö (118kr, 40 minutes) and Kristianstad (118kr, 1½ hours).

GÖTALAND

Gothenburg (Göteborg)

☑ 031 / POP 580,000

Gregarious, chilled-out Gothenburg (Göteborg) has considerable appeal for tourists and locals alike. Neoclassical architecture lines its tram-rattled streets, locals sun themselves beside canals, and there's always an interesting cultural or social event going on. Gothenburg is a very walkable city. From Centralstationen in the north, shop-lined Östra Hamngatan leads southeast across one of Gothenburg's 17th-century canals, through verdant Kungsparken (King's Park) to the city's boutique and upscale bar-lined 'Avenyn' (Kungsportsavenyn) boulevard.

The waterfront abounds with all things nautical, from ships, aquariums and sea-related museums to the freshest fish. To the west, the Vasastan, Haga and Linné districts buzz with creativity and an appreciation for well-preserved history.

◉ Sights

★ Universeum MUSEUM

(www.universeum.se; Södra Vägen 50; adult/child 250/195kr; ⊙ 10am-6pm, to 8pm Jul & Aug; 🅿 🖗; 🚊 2 Korsvägen) In what is arguably the best museum for kids in Sweden, you find yourself in the midst of a humid rainforest, complete with trickling water, tropical birds and butterflies flitting through the greenery and tiny marmosets. On a level above, roaring dinosaurs maul each other, while next door, denizens of the deep float through the shark tunnel and venomous beauties lie coiled in the serpent tanks. In the 'technology inspired by nature' section, stick your children to the Velcro wall.

★ **Konstmuseum**   GALLERY

(www.konstmuseum.goteborg.se; Götaplatsen; adult/child 40kr/free; ⊙11am-6pm Tue & Thu, to 8pm Wed, to 5pm Fri-Sun; ⊛; ☒4 Berzeliigatan) Home to Gothenburg's premier art collection, Konstmuseet displays works by the French Impressionists, Rubens, Van Gogh, Rembrandt and Picasso; Scandinavian masters such as Bruno Liljefors, Edvard Munch, Anders Zorn and Carl Larsson have pride of place in the **Fürstenburg Galleries**. Other highlights include a superb sculpture hall, the **Hasselblad Center** with its annual *New Nordic Photography* exhibition, and temporary displays of next-gen Nordic art.

Liseberg   AMUSEMENT PARK

(www.liseberg.se; Södra Vägen; 1-day pass 455kr; ⊙11am-11pm Jun–mid-Aug, hours vary rest of year; P ⊛; ☒2 Korsvägen) The attractions of Liseberg, Scandinavia's largest amusement park, are many and varied. Adrenalin blasts include the venerable wooden roller coaster Balder; its 'explosive' colleague Kanonen, where you're blasted from 0km/h to 75km/h in under two seconds; AtmosFear, Europe's tallest (116m) free-fall tower; and the park's biggest new attraction, Loke, a fast-paced spinning 'wheel' that soars 42m into the air. Softer options include carousels, fairy-tale castles, an outdoor dance floor, adventure playgrounds, and shows and concerts.

★ **Röda Sten Konsthall**   GALLERY

(www.rodastenkonsthall.se; Röda Sten 1; adult/child 40kr/free; ⊙noon-5pm Tue, Thu & Fri, to 8pm Wed, to 6pm Sat & Sun; ☒3 Vagnhallen Majorna) Occupying a defunct power station beside Älvsborgsbron (the city's huge western bridge), Röda Sten's four floors are home to such temporary exhibitions as edgy Swedish photography and cross-dressing rap videos by Danish-Filipino artist Lillibeth Cuenca Rasmussen that challenge sexuality stereotypes in Afghan society. The indie-style cafe hosts weekly live music and club nights, and offbeat one-offs like punk bike races, boxing matches and stand-up comedy. To get here, walk towards the Klippan precinct, continue under Älvsborgsbron and look for the brown-brick building.

Haga District   AREA

(www.hagashopping.se; ☒25 Hagakyrkan, ☒2 Handelshögskolan) The Haga district is Gothenburg's oldest suburb, dating back to 1648. A hardcore hippie hang-out in the 1960s and '70s, its cobbled streets and vintage buildings now host a cool blend of cafes, trendy shops and boutiques. During some summer weekends and at Christmas, store owners set up stalls along Haga Nygata, turning the neighbourhood into one big market. Check out the charming three-storey timber houses, built as housing for workers in the 19th century.

Trädgårdsföreningen   PARK

(www.tradgardsforeningen.se; Nya Allén; ⊙7am-8pm; ☒3, 4, 5, 7, 10 Kungsportsplatsen) Laid out in 1842, the lush Trädgårdsföreningen is a large protected area off Nya Allén. Full of flowers and tiny cafes, it's popular for lunchtime escapes and is home to Europe's largest **rosarium**, with around 2500 varieties. The gracious 19th-century **Palmhuset** (open 10am to 8pm) is a bite-size version of the Crystal Palace in London, with five differently heated halls: look out for the impressive camellia collection and the 2m-wide tropical lily pads.

Mölndals Stadsmuseum   MUSEUM

(☎031-431 34; www.museum.molndal.se; Kvarnbygatan 12; ⊙noon-4pm Tue-Sun; P ⊛; ☒752, 756, ☒Mölndal) **FREE** Located in an old police station, this museum is like a vast warehouse, with a 10,000-strong collection of local nostalgia ranging from a 17th-century clog to kitchen kitsch and a re-created 1930s worker's cottage. With a focus on memories and feelings, it's an evocative place where you can plunge into racks of vintage clothes, pull out hidden treasures and learn the individual items' secrets on the digital catalogue.

From Gothenburg, catch a Kungsbacka-bound train to Mölndal station, then bus 752 or 756.

☞ Tours

Paddan City Boat Tour   BOATING

(www.stromma.se; tours from 175kr; ⊙Apr-Oct) Strömma runs 50-minute city tours on its Paddan boats from Kungsportsplatsen, right across from the tourist office. They're an information-packed way to get your bearings and are free with the Göteborg City Card (p429). Longer tours (p428) into the archipelago and various canals are also available.

Gothenburg (Göteborg)

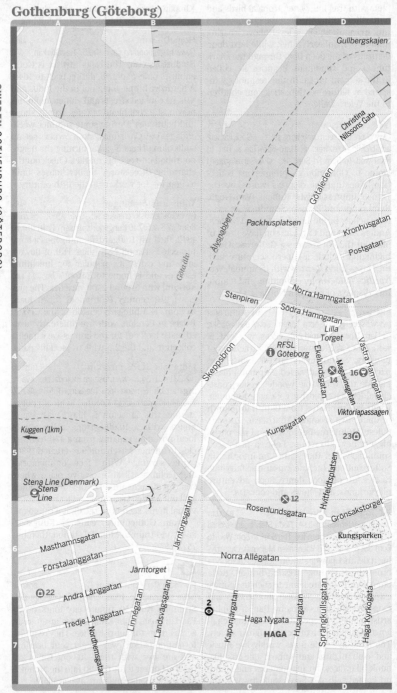

Gullbergskajen

Christina Nilssons Gata

Göталeden

Packhusplatsen

Kronhusgatan

Postgatan

Älvsnabben

Göta älv

Norra Hamngatan

Stenpiren

Södra Hamngatan

Lilla Torget

Skeppsbron

RFSL Göteborg

Ekelundsgatan

Magasinsgatan

Västra Hamngatan

14

16

Viktoriapassagen

Kuggen (1km)

Kungsgatan

23

Hvitfeldtsplatsen

Stena Line (Denmark)
Stena Line

Järntorgsgatan

12
Rosenlundsgatan

Grönsakstorget

Kungsparken

Masthamnsgatan

Norra Allégatan

Förstalanggatan

Järntorget

22

Andra Långgatan

Linnégatan

Landsvägsgatan

2

Haga Nygata

HAGA

Husargatan

Sprängkullsgatan

Haga Kyrkogata

Tredje Långgatan

Nordhemsgatan

Kaponjärgatan

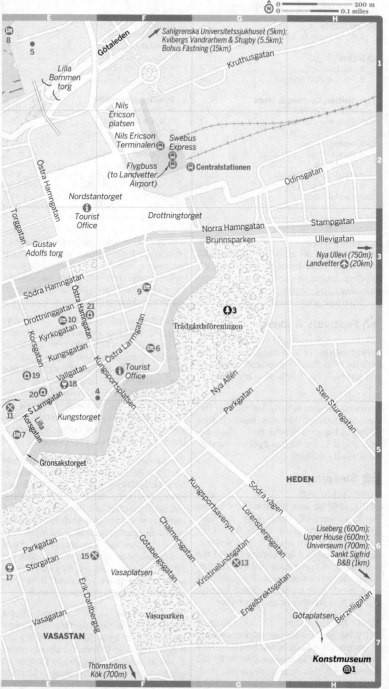

Gothenburg (Göteborg)

Strömma Cruises   BOATING
(www.stromma.se; per person from 280kr) Along with several other tours, Strömma runs archipelago cruises of varying duration. Most leave from just southeast of Götaälvbron, but departure points vary.

✦ Festivals & Events

Göteborg International Film Festival   FILM
(www.giff.se) One of Scandinavia's major film festivals, with flicks spanning all continents and genres. It's usually held in late January.

Way Out West   MUSIC
(www.wayoutwest.se) In early August, Way Out West is a mighty three-day music festival pulling in big guns like the Pixies, Ryan Adams, Major Lazer, Regina Spektor, Band of Horses and the Shins.

🛏 Sleeping

Sankt Sigfrid B&B   B&B €
(📞0735-51 52 80; www.sanktas.se; Sankt Sigfrids Plan 7; s/d from 480/730kr; 🅿🛜; 🚌5 Sankt Sigfrids Plan) Particularly handy for hitting Liseberg or Avenyn nightlife, this welcoming guesthouse in a quiet area offers all the perks of staying practically in the city centre, minus the city-centre prices. The rooms are snug, guests have access to a small kitchen, and the host couldn't be more attentive.

★ STF Göteborg City   HOSTEL €€
(📞031-756 98 00; www.svenskaturistforeningen.se; Drottninggatan 63-65; hostel r from 995kr, hotel s/d from 1400/1500kr, breakfast 85kr; @🛜; 🚌1 Brunnsparken) This large super-central hostel is all industrial chic in the cafe/dining area and lounge and plush comfort on each of its individually themed floors. All rooms are private, with en-suite bathroom, plush carpeting and comfortable bed-bunks, and – rarity of rarities! – your bed linen and towels are provided for you.

Hotell Barken Viking   HOTEL €€
(📞031-63 58 00; www.barkenviking.com; Lilla Bommens torg 10; r from 1395/1495kr; 🛜; 🚌5, 10 Lilla Bommen) If staying aboard a schooner floats your boat, try the *Barken Viking,* an elegant four-masted sailing ship converted into a stylish hotel. The wood-panelled rooms are cosy (read: small), with Hamptons-style linen, and designed for those who travel light. You won't run into any sailors, however, as there's no access to the upper deck.

Vanilla Hotel   BOUTIQUE HOTEL €€
(📞031-711 62 20; www.vaniljhotel.se; Kyrkogatan 38; s/d 1295/1445kr; 🅿✳@🛜; 🚌1, 3, 5, 6, 9 Domkyrkan) This petite slumber spot has the cosy, welcoming feeling of a Swedish home. The compact rooms are pleasantly light and decorated in sparing Scandinavian style, with wooden floors and furniture, crisp sheets and immaculate bathrooms, but they get rather hot in summer. Ask for a garden-view room, as the street gets noisy from early morning. Weekend rates drop sharply.

★ Dorsia Hotel   BOUTIQUE HOTEL €€€
(📞031-790 10 00; www.dorsia.se; Trädgårdsgatan 6; s/d from 1950/2950kr; 🅿✳@🛜; 🚌3 Kungsportsplatsen) If heaven had a bordello, it would resemble this lavish, flamboyant establishment that combines old-world

decadence with cutting-edge design. Rooms delight with their heavy velvet curtains, purple-and-crimson colour scheme and opulent beds; thick carpet in the corridors muffles your footsteps; and the fine art adorning the walls comes from the owner's own collection.

★ **Upper House** BOUTIQUE HOTEL €€€
(📞 031-708 82 00; www.upperhouse.se; Mässans Gata 24; r from 2290kr; 🅿 ❄ 🛜 🏊; 🚊 2, 4, 5, 6, 7 Korsvägen) One of the highest hotels in Sweden, sumptuous Upper House takes up the top four floors of one of the Gothia Towers. The decor is cool Scandinavian chic, the beds are the ultimate in slumbering comfort, and the superlative spa comes with a hammam and a 19th-floor outdoor pool encased in glass, with killer views of the city.

Hotel Flora BOUTIQUE HOTEL €€€
(📞 031-13 86 16; www.hotelflora.se; Grönsakstorget 2; s/d from 1675/1760kr; @ 🛜; 🚊 1 Grönsakstorget) Fabulous Flora's slick, individually themed rooms flaunt black, white and spot colour interiors, designer chairs, flat-screen TVs and sparkling bathrooms, though lack of storage facilities may dismay those with extensive sartorial needs. The top-floor rooms have air-con, several rooms offer river views, and rooms overlooking the chic split-level courtyard are for night owls rather than early birds.

🍴 Eating

Da Matteo CAFE €
(www.damatteo.se; Vallgatan 5; sandwiches & salads 65-95kr; ⏲ 7.30am-6pm Mon-Fri, 8am-6pm Sat, 10am-5pm Sun; 🚊 1, 3, 5, 6, 9 Domkyrkan) The perfect downtown lunch pit stop and a magnet for coffee lovers, this cafe serves wickedly fine espresso, mini *sfogliatelle* (Neapolitan pastries), sandwiches, pizza and great salads. There's a sun-soaked courtyard and a second branch on Viktoriapassagen.

Feskekörka MARKET €
(www.feskekorka.se; Rosenlundsgatan; salads from 75kr; ⏲ 9am-5pm Tue-Thu, to 6pm Fri, 10am-3pm Sat; 🚊 3, 5, 9, 11 Hagakyrkan) A market devoted to all things that come from the sea, the 'Fish Church' is heaven for those who appreciate slabs of gravadlax, heaped shrimp sandwiches and seafood-heavy salads. The outdoor picnic tables are the ideal place to munch on them.

★ **Moon Thai Kitchen** THAI €€
(www.moonthai.se; Kristinelundsgatan 9; mains 139-189kr; ⏲ 11am-11pm Mon-Fri, noon-11pm Sat & Sun; 🚊 4, 5, 7, 10 Göteborg Valand) The owners have opted for a 'Thailand' theme and decided to run with it a few miles, hence the kaleidoscopic whirl of tuktuks, flowers and bamboo everything. Luckily, the dishes are authentic, the whimsical menu features such favourites as *som tum* (spicy papaya salad) and the fiery prawn red curry will make you weep with pleasure and gratitude.

Restaurant 2112 BURGERS €€
(📞 031-787 58 12; Magasinsgatan; burgers 189kr; ⏲ 4pm-1am, from 2pm Sat; 🚊 1, 3, 5, 6, 9 Domkyrkan) Appealing to refined rockers and metalheads, this upmarket joint serves only burgers and beer. But what burgers! These masterpieces range from the superlative Smoke on the Water with its signature Jack Daniels glaze to the fiery Hell Awaits Burger, featuring habanero dressing. The hungriest of diners will meet their match in the 666g monster Number of the Beast (399kr).

★ **Thörnströms Kök** SCANDINAVIAN €€€
(📞 031-16 20 66; www.thornstromskok.com; Teknologgatan 3; mains 325-355kr, 4-course menu 675kr; ⏲ 6pm-1am Mon-Sat; 🛜; 🚊 7 Kapellplatsen) Specialising in modern Scandinavian cuisine, chef Håkan shows you how he earned that Michelin star through creative use of local, seasonal ingredients and flawless presentation. Feast on the likes of rabbit with pistachios, pickled carrots and seaweed; don't

---

ℹ️ GÖTEBORG CITY CARD

The brilliant Göteborg City Card (www. goteborg.com/citycard; 24-/48-/72hr card adult 395/545/695kr, child 265/365/455kr) is particularly worthwhile if you're into intensive sightseeing: it gives you free access to most museums and Liseberg amusement park, discounted and free city tours, unlimited travel on public transport and free parking in the city with the most dedicated traffic wardens. The card is available at tourist offices, hotels, Pressbyrån newsstands and online.

The Göteborgspaketet (http:// butik.goteborg.com/en/package; adult from 635kr) is an accommodation-and-entertainment package offered at various hotels, with prices starting at 635kr per person per night in a double room. It includes the Göteborg City Card for the number of nights you stay; book online in advance.

miss the remarkable milk-chocolate pudding with goat's-cheese ice cream. À la carte dishes are available if a multicourse menu overwhelms you.

★ Smaka
SWEDISH €€€

(☑031-13 22 47; www.smaka.se; Vasaplatsen 3; mains 175-285kr; ☺5-11pm; 🛜; 🚊1 Vasaplatsen) For top-notch Swedish *husmanskost*, like the speciality meatballs with mashed potato and lingonberries, it's hard to do better than this smart yet down-to-earth restaurant-bar. Mod-Swedish options might include hake with suckling pig cheek or salmon tartar with pickled pear.

🍷 Drinking & Nightlife

While Kungsportsavenyn brims with beer-downing tourists and after-work locals, there are some savvier options – in summer, seek out a perch on a sun-soaked terrace and watch the street life go by.

Clubs have minimum-age limits ranging from 18 to 25, and many have a cover charge on popular nights.

★ Champagne Baren
WINE BAR

(www.forssenoberg.com; Kyrkogatan; ☺5-11pm Tue-Thu, 4pm-midnight Fri & Sat; 🛜; 🚊1 Domkyrkan) What's not to like? This champagne bar has an idyllic setting on an inner courtyard with uneven cobbles, picturesque buildings and plenty of greenery. Along with glasses of bubbly, there are platters of cheese, oysters and cold cuts. Very popular with the boho-chic set. You can expect some cool background beats, as well as occasional live jazz.

NOBA Nordic Bar
BAR

(www.noba.nu; Viktoriagatan 1A; ☺4pm-1am Mon-Thu, to 3am Fri & Sat, 5pm-1am Sun; 🚊1, 2, 3, 7, 10 Viktoriagatan) With ye olde maps of Scandinavia on the walls and a glassed-over beer patio with birch tree stumps for stools, this bar takes its Nordic beers very seriously. From Iceland's Freja to Denmark's Kärlek, you name it, they've got it. The free-flowing whiskies liven up the scene on weekends.

Ölhallen 7:an
BEER HALL

(Kungstorget 7; ☺11am-midnight Sun-Tue, to 1am Wed-Sat; 🚊3, 4, 5, 7, 10 Kungsportsplatsen) This well-worn Swedish beer hall – the last remaining from its era – hasn't changed much in over 100 years. It attracts an interesting mix of bikers and regular folk with its homey atmosphere and friendly service. The illustrations lining the walls are Liss Sidén's portraits of regulars in the old days.

Shopping

Gothenburg is right up with Stockholm when it comes to shopping. For idiosyncratic small shops selling everything from handmade jewellery to organic honey, head to the Haga district. At the other end of the scale are designer boutiques and national chains on 'Avenyn' boulevard. For one-stop shopping head to central Nordiska Kompaniet, a hub of Swedish and international brands.

DesignTorget
HOMEWARES

(www.designtorget.se; Vallgatan 14; ☺10am-7pm Mon-Fri, to 5pm Sat, noon-4pm Sun; 🚊1, 2, 5, 6, 9 Domkyrkan) Cool, brightly coloured, affordable designer kitchenware, jewellery and more from both established and up-and-coming Scandi talent.

Nordiska Kompaniet
DEPARTMENT STORE

(www.nk.se; Östra Hamngatan 42; ☺10am-8pm, to 6pm Sat, 11am-5pm Sun; 🚊3, 4, 5, 7, 10 Kungsportsplatsen) A local institution since 1971, the four floors of this venerable department store host the likes of Tiger, RedGreen, NK Boutique and Mayla amid its mix of Swedish and international designers.

Shelta
SHOES

(☑031-24 28 56; www.shelta.eu; Andra Långgatan 21; ☺noon-6.30pm Mon-Fri, to 5pm Sat; 🚊3, 9, 11 Masthuggstorget) Pimp your style with limited-edition sneakers and streetwear from big players and lesser-known labels.

J. Lindeberg
CLOTHING

(www.jlindeberg.com; Korsgatan 17; ☺11am-6pm Mon-Fri, to 5pm Sat; 🚊1, 6, 9, 11 Domkyrkan) This established Stockholm designer offers slick knitwear, casual shirts and those perfect autumn/winter coats for the discerning gent.

Velour by Nostalgi
CLOTHING

(www.velour.se; Magasinsgatan 19; ☺11am-6.30pm Mon-Fri, to 5pm Sat, noon-4pm Sun; 🚊1, 6, 9, 11 Domkyrkan) Revamped flagship store of local label. Stocks slick, stylish streetwear for guys and girls.

❶ Information

MEDICAL SERVICES

For 24-hour medical information, phone ☑1177.

Apotek Hjärtat (☑0771-45 04 50; Nils Eriksongatan; ☺8am-10pm) Late-night pharmacy inside the Nordstan shopping complex.

Sahlgrenska Universitetssjukhuset (☑031-342 00 00; www.sahlgrenska.se; 🚊1) Major hospital about 5km northeast of central Gothenburg, near the terminus of tram line 1.

MONEY

Banks with ATMs are readily available, including inside the Nordstan shopping complex and along Kungsportsavenyn.

Forex (www.forex.se) Foreign-exchange office with branches at Centralstationen, Kungsportsavenyn 22, Kungsportsplatsen, Landvetter Airport and Nordstan shopping complex.

TOURIST INFORMATION

Cityguide Gothenburg (www.goteborg.com/apps) Info on the city's attractions, events and more, available as an Android and iPhone app. City map available offline.

Tourist Office (www.goteborg.com; Nils Eriksongatan; ⏰10am-8pm Mon-Fri, to 6pm Sat, noon-5pm Sun) Branch office inside the Nordstan shopping complex.

Tourist Office (☑031-368 42 00; www.goteborg.com; Kungsportsplatsen 2; ⏰9.30am-8pm late Jun–mid-Aug, shorter hours rest of year) Central and busy; has a good selection of free brochures and maps.

RFSL Göteborg (☑031-788 25 10; www.rfsl.se/goteborg; Stora Badhusgatan 6; ⏰6-9pm Wed) Comprehensive information on the city's gay scene, events and more.

🛈 Getting There & Away

AIR

Göteborg Landvetter Airport (www.swedavia.se/landvetter; 🚌 Flygbuss) is located 25km east of the city. It has daily flights to/from Stockholm Arlanda and Stockholm Bromma airports, as well as weekday services to Umeå and several weekly services to Borlänge, Falun, Visby and Sundsvall.

Direct European routes include Amsterdam (KLM), Brussels (SAS), Copenhagen (SAS and Norwegian), Frankfurt (Lufthansa), Berlin (Air Berlin), Helsinki (Norwegian and SAS), London (British Airways and Ryanair), Munich (Lufthansa), Oslo (Norwegian) and Paris (Air France and SAS).

BOAT

Gothenburg is a major ferry terminal, with several services to Denmark and Germany.

Stena Line (Denmark) (www.stenaline.se; Danmarksterminalen, Masthuggskajen; foot-passenger one-way from 200kr; 🚃3 Masthuggstorget)

Stena Line (Germany) (www.stenaline.se; Elof Lindälusgata 11; foot passenger one-way/return from 500kr; 🚃3 Jaegerdorffsplatsen)

For a special view of the region, jump on a boat for an unforgettable journey along the **Göta Canal** (www.gotakanal.se/en). Starting in Gothenburg, you'll pass through Sweden's oldest lock at Lilla Edet, opened in 1607. From there the trip crosses the great lakes Vänern and Vättern through the rolling country of Östergötland and on to Stockholm.

BUS

Västtrafik (☑0771-41 43 00; www.vasttrafik.se) and **Hallandstrafiken** (☑0771-33 10 30; www.hlt.se) provide regional transport links. If you're planning to spend some time exploring the southwest counties, a monthly pass or a *sommarkort* (summer card) offers cheaper travel in the peak summer period (from late June to mid-August).

The bus station, **Nils Ericson Terminalen**, is next to the train station and has excellent facilities including luggage lockers (medium/large up to 24 hours 70/90kr). There's a Västtrafik information booth here, providing information and selling tickets for all city and regional public transport within the Gothenburg, Bohuslän and Västergötland area.

Swebus (☑0771-21 82 18; www.swebus-express.com) operates frequent buses to most major towns and cities; non-refundable advance tickets work out considerably cheaper than on-the-spot purchases. Services include:

➡ Copenhagen (from 239kr, 4¾ hours, four daily)

➡ Halmstad (from 109kr, 1¾ hours, five to seven daily)

➡ Helsingborg (from 139kr, 2¾ hours, five to eight daily)

➡ Malmö (from 119kr, 3½ to four hours, seven to nine daily)

➡ Oslo (from 229kr, 3½ hours, five to 10 daily)

➡ Stockholm (from 159kr, 6½ to seven hours, four to five daily)

CAR & MOTORCYCLE

The E6 motorway runs north–south from Oslo to Malmö just east of the city centre. There's also a complex junction where the E20 motorway diverges east for Stockholm.

International car-hire companies have desks at Göteborg Landvetter Airport and near the central train/bus stations.

TRAIN

All trains arrive at and depart from Centralstationen, Sweden's oldest railway station and a heritage-listed building. The main railway lines in the west connect Gothenburg to Karlstad, Stockholm, Malmö and Oslo. In the east, the main line runs from Stockholm via Norrköping and Linköping to Malmö. Book tickets online via **Sveriges Järnväg** (SJ; www.sj.se) or purchase from ticket booths at the station.

Left Luggage Luggage lockers (medium/large up to 24 hours 70/90kr) are available at Centralstationen.

🛈 Getting Around

TO/FROM THE AIRPORT

Flygbuss (☑0771-51 52 52; www.flygbussarna.se; one-way/return adult 95/185kr, child

79/155kr) runs to Landvetter Airport from **Nils Ericson Terminalen** (p431) every 15 to 20 minutes from 4.20am to 9pm and from the airport to the city between 5am and 11.30pm. Discounts are available for online bookings.

The fixed taxi rate with **Taxi Göteborg** (☑ 031-65 00 00; www.taxigoteborg.se) from the city to the airport is 453kr.

BICYCLE

Cyclists should ask at the tourist office for the free route map *Cykelkarta Göteborg*.

Styr & Ställ (www.goteborgbikes.se; per season 75kr) is Gothenburg's handy city-bike system. It involves buying a 'season pass' that then gives you unlimited access to bicycles stationed across the city. With the pass, all journeys under half an hour are free, making this ideal for quick trips. (There's a small fee for longer journeys.) You can also download directly onto your smart phone the app allbikesnow.com, which has a city map showing all the bike locales, plus how many bikes are free at any given time.

Cykelkungen (☑ 031-18 43 00; www.cykelkungen.se; Chalmersgatan 19; per day/weel 200/700kr; ☺ 10am-6pm Mon-Fri) is a reliable spot for longer-term bike hire.

PUBLIC TRANSPORT

Buses, trams and ferries run by **Västtrafik** (p431) make up the city's public-transport system; there are Västtrafik information booths selling tickets and giving out timetables inside **Nils Ericson Terminalen** (p431), in front of the train station on **Drottningtorget** and at **Brunnsparken**, a block from the train station.

The most convenient way to travel around Gothenburg is by tram. Colour-coded lines, numbered 1 to 13, converge near Brunnsparken. Trams run every few minutes between 5am and midnight; some lines run a reduced service after midnight on Friday and Saturday.

A city **transport ticket** costs 29/22kr per adult/child. One- and three-day **travel cards** (90/180kr, from Västtrafik information booths, 7-Eleven minimarkets or Pressbyrån newsagencies) can work out much cheaper. Holders of the **Göteborg City Card** (p429) travel free.

Västtrafik also has a handy app, Västtrafik To Go, which allows you to buy tickets on your phone.

Strömstad

☑ 0526 / POP 6288

A resort, fishing harbour and spa town, Strömstad is laced with ornate wooden buildings echoing those of Norway. There are several fantastic Iron Age remains in the area, and some **sandy beaches** at Capri and Seläter. Boat trips run to the most westerly islands in Sweden, popular for cycling and swimming.

☉ Sights

Koster Islands   ISLAND
(www.kosteroarna.com; adult/child round trip 130/100kr) Boat trips run from Strömstad's north harbour to the beautiful cluster of forested Koster Islands every 30 minutes from July to mid-August, less frequently at other times. Tiny North Koster is hilly and has good beaches. Larger South Koster is flatter and better for cycling, with bike-rental facilities, numerous restaurants scattered about and two large beaches at Rörvik and Kilesand. Trips are booked through the tourist office.

Stone-Ship Settings   ARCHAEOLOGICAL SITE
(Blomsholm; ☺ 24hr) **FREE** One of Sweden's largest, most magnificent stone-ship settings (an oval of stones, shaped like a boat) lies 6km northeast of Strömstad. There are 49 stones in total, with the stem and stern stones reaching over 3m in height; the site has been dated to AD 400 to 600. Across the road is a huge site containing approximately 40 **Iron Age graves**. The tourist office can help with transport. Alternatively, there's a gorgeous walking path from the north of town.

🛏 Sleeping & Eating

⭐ **Emma's Bed and Breakfast**   B&B €€
(☑ 0916-65 046; www.emmasbedandbreakfast.se; Kebal 2; r from 1195kr; **P 🤖**) A 10-minute walk from central Strömstad, this stately house, dating back to 1734, sits at the edge of a golf course amid quiet wooded grounds. The rooms are bright and airy and the friendly hostess whips up a full Scandinavian spread at breakfast time.

Lexö på Resö   SWEDISH €€
(☑ 0525-250 00; Hamnholmen, Resö; pizzas 115-159kr, mains 155-220kr, herring buffet 145kr; ☺ noon-midnight mid-Jun–mid-Aug) Ever wished you could get still-in-the-shell mussels on your pizza? Here you can – along with more ordinary varieties. There's also fish stew, baked tuna, a salmon burger, and on the weekends a herring buffet (noon-3pm) with an impressive selection. The outdoor tables look over the water, so you can watch boats come and go. Live music some nights.

ℹ Information

The **tourist office** (☑ 0526-623 30; www.vastsverige.com/stromstad; Ångbåtskajen 2; ☺ 9am-8pm Mon-Sat, 10am-7pm Sun Jun-Aug, shorter hours rest of year) sits just opposite the boat landing for the Koster Islands.

ℹ Getting There & Away

Buses and trains both use the train station near the southern harbour. **Västtrafik** (p431) runs bus 871 to Gothenburg (180kr, 2¼ hours, three to four daily). Direct trains connect Strömstad to Gothenburg (190kr, 2¼ to three hours, one to two hourly). Color Line ferries run from Strömstad to Sandefjord in Norway (2½ hours).

Norrköping

☑ 011 / POP 139,363

It's hard to imagine Norrköping (norr-sher-ping) as it would've been 20 years ago – a grotty has-been past its use-by date.

Norrköping's industrial identity began in the 17th century but took off in the late 19th century when textile mills and factories sprang up alongside the swift-flowing Motala *ström*. Seventy per cent of Sweden's textiles were once made here, the last mill shutting shop in the 1970s.

Forward planning and Swedish design smarts stepped in at the right time to cleverly redevelop the city's defunct historical mills and canals into a hip posse of cultural hang-outs and Manhattan-style lofts against a backdrop of fringing waterfalls and locks. As Stockholm grapples with a high cost of living and little room for growth, nearby cities like Norrköping are on the radar.

While parts of town have already reverted to their working-class roots, the proliferation of construction sites indicates Norrköping's transformation is far from over.

◉ Sights

★**Arbetets Museum** MUSEUM
(Museum of Work; ☑ 011-18 98 00; www.arbetetsmuseum.se; Laxholmen; ⊙ 11am-5pm Wed-Mon, to 8pm Tue May-Sep) **FREE** The innovative Arbetets Museum documents working life. There's one permanent display about Alva Carlsson, a typical worker in the former cotton mill, and temporary exhibitions focusing mainly on gender issues, human rights or multiculturalism. The seven-sided building, completed in 1917 and dubbed the 'flatiron', is a work of art in itself.

★**Norrköpings konstmuseum** MUSEUM
(Norrköping Art Gallery; ☑ 011-15 26 00; www.norrkoping.se/konstmuseet; Kristinaplatsen 6; ⊙ noon-4pm Tue-Sun, to 8pm Wed Jun-Aug) **FREE** Overlooking leafy Vasaparken, the city's impressive art gallery boasts a collection of important early-20th-century works, including modernist and cubist gems as well as one of Sweden's largest collections of graphic art.

Norrköpings stadsmuseum MUSEUM
(Norrköping City Museum; ☑ 011-15 26 20; www.norrkoping.se/stadsmuseet; Holmbrogränden 2; ⊙ 11am-4pm Tue-Sun) **FREE** Stadsmuseum delves into the town's industrial past, complete with still-functioning machinery, a great cafe and dynamic temporary exhibitions.

🛏 Sleeping

Abborrebergs Veranda HOSTEL €
(☑ 073-385 44 00; www.abborreberg.se; Abborreberg Friluftsgård 2; dm/s/d from 275/325/525kr; ⊙ Apr–mid-Oct; 🅿; ☐ 116) Stunningly situated in a coastal pine wood 7km east of town, this sterling hostel offers accommodation in huts scattered through the surrounding park. The associated ice-cream parlour is always a hit. Take bus 116 to Lindö (42).

★**Strand Hotell** BOUTIQUE HOTEL €€
(☑ 011-16 99 00; www.hotellstrand.se; Drottninggatan 2; s/d from 995/1295kr, apt 2100kr; @ 🛜) A real gem in the heart of town, the Strand takes up the 2nd floor of a gorgeous 1890 building overlooking the Motala river and Drottninggattan. It has operated as a hotel since the 1930s, and the furniture and fabrics make the most of the building's existing features, such as cut-glass chandeliers and big bay windows.

🍴 Eating

Fiskmagasinet SEAFOOD €€
(☑ 011-13 45 60; www.fiskmagasinet.se; Skolgatan 1; lunch 90kr, mains 135-285kr; ⊙ 11.30am-2pm & 5-10pm Mon-Fri, noon-10pm Sat) Housed in a converted 19th-century *snus* (snuff) factory, urbane Fiskmagasinet combines an intimate bar with a casually chic dining room serving savvy seafood dishes like grilled scampi with mashed potato, truffle and port-wine reduction, as well as cheaper Swedish classics.

Lagerqvist EUROPEAN €€
(☑ 011-10 07 40; www.restauranglagerqvist.se; Gamla Torget 4; mains 125-285kr; ⊙ 5-11pm Tue-Sun) This perennially popular restaurant-pub has a great summer garden courtyard and snug vaulted cellar. Meat dishes are the speciality, with innovative sides such as green beans with truffle butter. There are also platters for sharing.

Bryggeriet SWEDISH €€€
(☑ 011-10 30 20; www.gamlabrygg.se; Sandgatan 1; mains 195-298kr; ⊙ 4-10pm Mon-Fri, to 11pm Sat &

Sun) Enjoy a dreamy position overlooking the water. The menu here includes finely crafted game dishes with fillet of deer and wild boar, while lunch is more along the lines of posh burgers and pasta. The atmosphere is elegant – don't turn up in thongs (flip-flops).

ⓘ Information

Experience Norrköping (☏ 011-15 50 00; www.upplev.norrkoping.se/en/; Källvindsgatan 1; ☺10am-6pm daily Jul–mid-Aug, shorter hours rest of year) Runs free one-hour walking tours of the industrial area in summer.

Norrköping

Norrköping

◉ **Top Sights**
1 Arbetets Museum B3
2 Norrköpings konstmuseum D5

◉ **Sights**
3 Norrköpings stadsmuseum B3

🛏 **Sleeping**
4 Strand Hotell C2

🍴 **Eating**
5 Bryggeriet B2
6 Fiskmagasinet C3
7 Lagerqvist C4

ℹ Getting There & Away

Norrköping is 43km northeast of Linköping on the E4 and 61km southwest of Nyköping.

Regional buses depart from the bays next to the train station, while the long-distance buses leave from the bays opposite.

Swebus Express (☑ 0771-21 82 18; www. swebus.se) has frequent services to Stockholm (from 149kr, 2¼ hours), Jönköping (from 219kr, 2½ hours), Gothenburg (from 299kr, five hours) and Kalmar (from 269kr, four hours).

Norrköping is on the main **SJ Rail** (p421) railway line with regular services to Stockholm (206kr, 1½ hours), Malmö (206kr, 3¼ hours), Nyköping (75kr, one hour) and Linköping (65kr, 25 minutes).

Sweden's third-largest airport, **Stockholm Skavsta** (p401), is 60km away.

Local **Norrköping Airport** (☑ 011-15 37 22; www.norrkopingairport.com) has direct flights from Copenhagen, Munich and Helsinki.

ℹ Getting Around

If you're flying into **Skavsta** airport, **Flygbussarna** (☑ 0771-51 52 52; www.flygbussarna.se/en/; ⊙ customer service 8am-11pm) operates shuttle services into Norrköping (and Linköping).

Getting around the main downtown sights in Norrköping is easy on foot, but if you need a taxi, try **Taxi Norrköping** (☑ 16 00 00; www.taxi160000.se).

Linköping

☑ 013 / POP 112,013

Most famous for its mighty medieval cathedral, Linköping fancies itself as Norrköping's more upmarket rival. Its most infamous claim to fame is the 'bloodbath of Linköping'. Following the Battle of Stångebro (1598), many of King Sigismund's defeated Catholic army were executed here, leaving Duke Karl and his Protestant forces in full control of Sweden.

While quite the modern, industrial city today (manufacturer Saab is the major employer), pockets of its past survive in its churches, castle and museums and in the picture-perfect streets around Hunnebergsgatan and Storgatan.

⦿ Sights & Activities

★ Gamla Linköping   AREA
(☑ 013-12 11 10; www.gamlalinkoping.info; Tunnbindaregatan 1; P 🚻) **FREE** Located 2km west of the city, this is one of the biggest living-museum villages in Sweden. It's a gorgeous combo of cobbled streets, picket-fenced gardens

and around 90 19th-century houses. Just 300m through the forest is **Valla Fritidsområde**, a recreation area with domestic animals, a children's playground, minigolf, small museums and vintage abodes.

★ Ekenäs Slott   CASTLE
(☑ 073-650 24 20; www.ekenasslott.se; Ekenäs Slott 1; tours adult/child 80/40kr; ⊙ guided tours on the hour 1-3pm Tue-Sun Jul, Sat & Sun Jun & Aug; P) Built between 1630 and 1644, this is one of the best-preserved Renaissance castles in Sweden. Features include three spectacular towers, a moat, and furnishings from the 17th to 19th centuries. It's located 20km east of Linköping; you'll need your own transport to get here.

★ Kinda Canal Cruises   CRUISE
(☑ 070-637 17 00; www.rederiabkind.se; half-day cruises from 515kr; ⊙ May-Oct) While it's upstaged by the Göta Canal, Linköping boasts its own canal system, the 90km Kinda Canal. Opened in 1871, it has 15 locks, including Sweden's deepest. Cruises include evening sailings, musical outings and wine-tasting trips. For a simple day excursion, from late June to early August, the M/S *Kind* leaves Tullbron dock at 10am on Tuesday, Thursday and Saturday, and travels to Rimforsa (return by bus or train).

🛏 Sleeping & Eating

Hotell du Nord   HISTORIC HOTEL €€
(☑ 013-12 98 95; www.hotelldunord.se; Repslagaregatan 5; s/d from 695/895kr; P 🛜) Located across from the beautiful Järnvägsparken, Hotell du Nord is appropriately leafy and tranquil. The main dusky-rose 19th-century building looks like a doll's house, staff are friendly and the rooms are light filled and welcoming (those in the aesthetically challenged rear building are freshly renovated and larger). There's a patio for outdoor summer breakfasts.

Park Hotel   HOTEL €€
(☑ 013-12 90 05; www.fawltytowers.se; Järnvägsgatan 6; s/d from 1145/1345kr; P @ 🛜) Close to the train station and somewhat disturbingly billed as Sweden's 'Fawlty Towers', this smart family-run establishment resembles that madhouse in appearance only (yes, there's an elk head at reception). The public spaces sport chandeliers and oil paintings, and clean, parquet-floored rooms are crisply modern. You have to love the Swedish sense of humour.

★ **Stångs Magasin** SWEDISH €€€

(☑ 013-31 21 00; www.stangsmagasin.se; Södra Stånggatan 1; lunch 115kr, mains 145-505kr; ⏱ 11.30am-2pm Mon-Fri, 6pm-midnight Tue-Fri, 5pm-midnight Sat Jul & Aug; 🛜) In a 200-year-old warehouse down near the Kinda Canal docks, this elegant award-winner fuses classic Swedish cuisine with continental influences – think stuffed trout with beet aioli. There is an extensive wine list and a sommelier on hand to help you choose.

ℹ Information

Bergs Slussar Tourist Office (☑ 013-190 00 70; Oscars Slussar 2; ⏱ 9.30am-5pm May-Aug) This small tourist office is located near the locks.

Visit Linköping (☑ 013-190 00 70; www.visitlinkoping.se; Storgatan 15; ⏱ 10am-6pm Mon-Fri, to 4pm Sat, to 6pm Sun) For brochures, maps and good advice.

ℹ Getting There & Away

Linköping is 43km southwest of Norrköping and 50km east of Vadstena.

Östgöta Trafiken (☑ 0771-21 10 10; www.ostgotatrafiken.se) operates scheduled regional buses to Vadstena (150kr, 1¼ hours), which leave from outside the train station.

Swebus Express (p435) runs frequently to Jönköping (from 169kr, 1½ hours), Gothenburg (from 149kr, four hours) and north to Norrköping (from 59kr, 45 minutes). These long-distance buses depart from **Linköping Fjärrbussterminal** (Linköping Long-distance Bus Terminal; ☑ 070-318 41 09; Järnvägsgatan; 🛜), 500m northwest of the train station.

Linköping is on the main north–south **SJ Rail** (p421) line between Malmö (206kr, three hours) and Stockholm (also 206kr, 1¾ hours). Frequent regional trains run north to Norrköping (from 85kr, 25 minutes).

Linköping City Airport (☑ 013-18 10 30; www.linkopingcityairport.se; Åkerbogatan) is only 2km east of town. There's no airport bus, but taxi company **Taxibil** (☑ 013-14 60 00; www.taxibil.se) charges around 180kr for the ride into town.

Vadstena

☑ 0143 / POP 5646

Sublimely situated beside Lake Vättern, Vadstena is a legacy of both church and state power, and today St Birgitta's abbey and Gustav Vasa's castle compete with each other for admiration.

The atmosphere in the old town, with its wonderful cobbled lanes, intriguing small shops and wooden buildings, makes it an especially satisfying place to end a day of touring along the Göta Canal.

Vadstena really is a wonderfully quiet and pretty lakeside town with a hell of a lot of charm. There's something about the place that, if you've come for a day trip, you will wish you were spending the night. To prevent disappointment, book a night in advance.

◎ Sights & Activities

★ **Vadstena Slott** CASTLE

(☑ 0143-62 16 00; www.vadstenaslott.com; Slottsvägen; tours adult/child 90/70kr; ⏱ 11am-6pm daily Jun-early Aug, hours & days vary rest of year) Overlooking the lake, and considered one of the finest early Renaissance buildings in the Nordic region, construction commenced on Vadstena Slott, the family project of the early Vasa kings, in 1545. View their gloomy portraits inside, along with a modest historical display. The furnished upper floors are the most interesting, and be sure to visit the chapel, with its incredible 17-second echo! There are guided tours (in English, adult/child 130/90kr) from mid-July to mid-September; call ahead for times.

Väversunda kyrka CHURCH

(Väversunda) Located 15km southwest of Vadstena, just beyond the tiny hamlet of Skedet, this bizarre-looking church contains some interesting 13th-century wall paintings. Opening hours vary.

Sancta Birgitta Klostermuseet MUSEUM

(☑ 0143-100 31; www.klostermuseum.se; Lasarettsgatan; adult/child 80/40kr; ⏱ 10.30am-5pm Jul–mid-Aug, 11am-4pm Jun & rest of Aug) The Sancta Birgitta Klostermuseet is in Bjälboättens Palats (a royal residence that became a convent in 1384). It tells the story of St Birgitta's roller-coaster life and those of all her saint-and-sinner children. Artefacts include the coffin that carried her back from Rome.

Motala Motor Museum MUSEUM

(☑ 0141-564 00; www.motormuseum.se; Platensgatan 2, Motala; adult/child 100/45kr; ⏱ 10am-8pm) If you're a rev-head or just a lover of beautiful machines, this vehicle museum in a lovely lakeside spot is a must for its staggering collection of more than 300 vehicles of all makes, shapes, sizes and eras, from the humble to the extravagant.

🛏 Sleeping & Eating

Pensionat Solgården
B&B €

(📞 0143-143 50; www.pensionatsolgarden.se; Strågatan 3; s/d from 540/790kr; ☀May-Sep; 🅿🛜) Set in a classic 1905 wooden house, this family-run hotel boasts lovingly decorated rooms; some have private bathrooms and all have an art/artist connection. They're each *very* different – check the photos on the website to choose your favourite (number 25 is particularly grand).Vadstena

Vadstena Klosterhotel
HISTORIC HOTEL €€

(📞 0143-315 30; www.klosterhotel.se; Lasarettsgatan 5; r from 1475kr; 🅿 @ 🛜) History and luxury merge at this wonderfully atmospheric hotel in St Birgitta's old convent. The bathrooms are a wee bit dated, but the medieval-style rooms are great, with chandeliers and high wooden beds. Most boast lake views. The hotel also has simpler rooms with shared bathrooms and showers in a nearby cottage (single/double 790/990kr).

Rådhuskällaren
INTERNATIONAL €€

(📞 0143-121 70; www.radhuskallaren.com; Rådhustorget; mains 145-270kr; ☀noon-10pm Wed-Sat, to 6pm Sun) Under the old courthouse, this affable 15th-century cellar restaurant dishes out simple but satisfying burger, pasta and fish meals. Its outdoor area is a favourite afternoon drinking spot in summer.

⭐Restaurant Munkklostret
EUROPEAN €€€

(📞 0143-130 00; www.klosterhotel.se; Lasarettsgatan 5; mains 198-295kr; ☀noon-11pm daily Jun-Aug, from 6pm rest of year; 🅿🛜) The Vadstena Klosterhotel's (p437) ravishing restaurant is the best dining spot in town. Seasonal, succulent steak, lamb, game and fish dishes are flavoured with herbs from the monastery garden, and served in the monks' old dorms.

ℹ Information

Vadstena Turistbyrå (📞 0143-315 70; www.vadstena.se; Storgatan 31; ☀10am-2pm Mon-Sat, longer hours in summer) Has plenty of local info on Lake Vättern.

ℹ Getting There & Away

Vadstena is 58km north of Gränna on the E4 and 51km west of Linköping.

Only buses run to Vadstena – take bus 610 to Motala (for trains to Örebro), or bus 661 to Mjölby (for trains to Linköping and Stockholm). **Blåklints Buss** (📞 0142-121 50; www.blaklintsbuss.se) runs one to three services daily from the Viking Line Terminal in Stockholm to Vadstena (250kr).

Cykelaventyr (📞 076-831 48 25; www.cykelaventyr.se; Kanalvägen 17, Borensberg) in Motala (15km north of Vadstena) has bikes for rent (165kr per day).

SMÅLAND

The province of Småland isn't small at all, but occupies some 29,400-sq-km of dense forests, glinting lakes and bare marshlands from the Baltic Sea coast, deep into the Swedish interior. In fact, it's so big that its broken up into five smaller counties or *län*: Kalmar, Östergötland, Jönköpings, Kronobergs and Halland, of which Kalmar is the largest and Östergötland the most populous.

Historically, Småland served as a buffer between the Swedes and Danes who were forever having territorial tussles. Today, it's known for its Glasriket 'Kingdom of Glass' (think Orrefors and Kosta Boda glassware), the scenic Lake Vänern towns of Jönköping-Huskvarna, Gränna and Vadstena, and as the jump-off point for island explorations to Öland (from Kalmar, with its magnificent castle) and Gotland (from Oskarshamn, with its hulking ferries).

From nature to history and culture, Småland has a lot to offer – plan for a few days here if you can.

Växjö

📞 0470 / POP 89,500

A venerable old market town, pretty Växjö (vek-hwa), in Kronobergs *län*, is today a growing city and an important stop for Americans seeking their Swedish roots. An annual festival commemorates the mass 19th-century emigration from the area, which is well documented in the insightful emigration museum.

Vaxjö's glass museum, packed with gorgeous works of art and plenty of history, is another highlight, as are its waterfront parklands, historic church and laid-back vibe.

⊙ Sights & Activities

Enquire at the tourist office (p438) about guided summer **walking tours** (50kr, 5.30pm Tuesday and Thursday) around town.

⭐Utvandrarnas Hus
MUSEUM

(House of Emigrants; 📞 0470-70 42 00; www.utvandrarnashus.se; Vilhelm Mobergs gata 4; adult/child 90kr/free; ☀10am-5pm Tue-Fri, to 4pm Sat & Sun) Boasts engrossing displays on the emigration of more than one million Swedes to America (1850–1930) and includes a replica of Vilhelm Moberg's office and original manuscripts of his famous emigration novels. Entry price also covers admission to the neighbouring Smålands Museum (p438).

Smålands Museum
MUSEUM

(☑0470-70 42 00; www.kulturparkensmaland. se; Södra Järnvägsgatan 2; adult/child 90kr/free; ☉10am-5pm Tue-Fri, to 4pm Sat & Sun) Among the varied exhibits at Sweden's oldest provincial museum is a truly stunning exhibition about the country's 500-year-old glass industry, with objects spanning medieval goblets to cutting-edge contemporary sculptures. It even houses a Guinness World Record collection of Swedish cheese-dish covers – 71 in total. There's a great cafe and the ticket price covers the adjacent Utvandrarnas Hus (p437).

🛏 Sleeping & Eating

★B&B Södra Lycke
B&B €€

(☑0706-76 65 06; www.sodralycke.se; Hagagatan 10; s/d from 500/800kr; P 🛜) This charming B&B in an atmospheric mid-19th-century family house is in a residential area 10 minutes' walk southwest from the centre via Södra Järnvägsgatan (check online for a map). There are three rooms and an appealingly overgrown garden complete with vegetable plot, wildflowers, greenhouse and black hens.

Clarion Collection Cardinal
HOTEL €€

(☑0470-72 28 00; www.nordicchoicehotels.com/ hotels/sweden/vaxjo/clarion-collection-hotel-cardinal/; Bäckgatan 10; s/d from 895/1095kr; P @ 🛜) A jump up in quality, the central Cardinal offers simple, stylish rooms with Persian rugs and the odd antique touch. There's also a small fitness centre, a bar and a restaurant serving modern Nordic cuisine. Note that, as with all Clarion Collection hotels, a buffet dinner (as well as breakfast) is generously included in the room price.

★Kafe de Luxe
INTERNATIONAL €€

(☑0470-74 04 09; www.kafedeluxe.se; Sandgärdsgatan 19; mains from 140-245kr; ☉11am-midnight Mon-Thu, to 2am Fri & Sat, 10am-1am Sun; ☑) An urban-boho vibe, great music (live at weekends) and '50s- to '60s-style decor, including an adjacent candy-coloured ice-cream parlour, contribute to the special feel of this place. The burgers are renowned, as is the eclectic dinner menu with its French-inspired dishes such as entrecôte with a classic *Béarnaise* sauce and its innovative vegie choices: nettle gnocchi, anyone? Occasional DJs.

❶ Information

Vaxjo turistbyrå (☑0470-73 32 80; www. vaxjoco.se; Stortorget, Residencet; ☉9.30am-6pm Mon-Fri & 10am-2pm Sat Jun-Aug) Located on the main square.

❶ Getting There & Away

Växjö is 80km west of Nybro on Rte 25 and 120km south of Jönköping on Rte 30.

Småland Airport (☑0470-75 85 00; www. smalandairport.se) is 9km northwest of Växjö and is serviced by low-cost carriers **Ryanair** (☑0900-20 20 240; www.ryanair.com) and **BRA** (www.flygbra.se). **Växjö Taxi** (☑0470-135 00; www.vaxjotaxi.se) will get you to the airport from the centre of town for around 250kr.

Jönköpings Länstrafiken (JLT; ☑0771-444 333; www.jlt.se; ☉7.30am-6pm Mon-Fri) runs daily buses to Jönköping (198kr, 1¾ hours) while **Kronoberg Länstrafiken** (p439) shuttles back and forth to Kosta, in the Glasriket (94kr, one hour). Buses depart from the train station.

SJ Rail (p421) trains connect Växjö to Kalmar (164kr, 1¼ hours), Malmö (216kr, two hours) and Jönköping (198kr, 1¾ hours).

Glasriket

With its hypnotic glass-blowing workshops, the so-called 'Kingdom of Crystal' is an attempt to revive the fading Swedish art of glass-blowing, which began in Kosta in 1742. With the closure of major factories in Boda (2008) and Orrefors (2013), the 'Glasriket' banner seeks to unify the remaining glass-blowing and crystal workshops that are spread out over a broad area around the villages of Kosta, Boda, Orrefors and Nybro. It's a niche market and a difficult task.

Kosta, with its full-scale factory, is the epicentre of the revival, but it's become a bit of an outlet shopping paradise, frequented by the busload. Glass-lovers will want to augment their shopping trip with a visit to at least one of the smaller *glasbruks* – each has something to offer.

The region is also popular with Americans tracing their ancestors: many emigrated from the area at the end of the 19th century.

Kosta

☑0478 / POP 884

The little town of Kosta is where Glasriket first fired up, way back in 1742. It's a crucial stop for those exploring the area, which will either be something you're very interested in, or not at all. In fact, if you just have a passing interest in glass and glass-blowing and you're not sure which of the Glasriket villages to visit – Kosta is the one-stop shop.

Most visitors to the village – which today feels a bit like a glass-blowing theme park – will either take a tour of the **Kosta Glassworks factory** (☎ 0478-345 00; www. kostaboda.se/en/about-kosta-boda/glassworks; Stora vägen 96; ☺ shops 10am-6pm Mon-Fri, to 5pm Sat & Sun, glass-blowing demonstrations 9am-3.30pm Mon-Fri, 10am-4pm Sat & Sun) or head to the **Kosta Glascenter** (☎ 070-684 61 91; www. kostaglascenter.se; Stora vägen 96; ☺ 10am-6pm Mon-Fri, to 5pm Sat & Sun; P) FREE, where you can witness glass-blowing firsthand, or try it yourself.

Otherwise, there's a fancy hotel, a variety of discount and high-end shopping outlets and not much else.

🛏 Sleeping & Eating

⭐ **Kosta Boda Art Hotel**   HOTEL €€€
(☎ 0478-348 30; www.kostabodaarthotel.com; Stora vägen 75; s/d from 1295/2590kr; P🅿❄🛜🏊) One of the only truly luxury hotel offerings in Småland, the Art Hotel showcases the famed glass and crystal brand's creations in unusual ways – like its designer glass bar. Each of the 102 decadent hotel rooms also features Kosta glasswork and textiles designed by local artists. Outdoors, you'll find the finest private swimming pool for miles.

Linnéa Art Restaurant   SWEDISH €€€
(☎ 0478-348 40; www. kostabodaarthotel.com; Stora vägen 75; buffet 245kr, mains 189-325kr; ☺ noon-3.30pm) This swish restaurant within the Kosta Boda Art Hotel (p439) serves up a delicious lunchtime buffet prepared from local seafood and produce. Of an evening, things get decidedly classier when the lights go down – dress to be seen. Reservations are recommended.

ⓘ Information

Located inside the **Kosta Glascenter** (p439), the staff of **Kosta turistbyrå** (☎ 0478-507 05; www. destinationkosta.se; Stora Vägen 98; ☺ 9am-5pm Mon-Fri, 10am-4pm Sat & Sun) can help you make sense of the somewhat sprawly Glasriket region – you don't want to drive reasonable distances to get to a glass-blowing workshop only to find it closed or not what you had in mind.

ⓘ Getting There & Away

Kosta is almost midway between Växjö (49km to the west) and Nybrö (39km east).

Kronoberg Länstrafiken (☎ 0470-72 75 50; www.lanstrafikenkron.se) bus 218 runs a few times daily between Kosta and Växjö (94kr, 1¼ hours).

Oskarshamn

☎ 0491 / POP 27,006

Oskarshamn is a busy but otherwise unremarkable port city. The main reason people come here is to leave here – taking the regular car ferries to Gotland and Öland or seasonal cruises to the mythical, mystical, off-the-beaten-track island of Blå Jungfrun.

That's not to say Oskarshamn isn't a pleasant, attractive little town – it is; but while you're waiting for the boat, there's really not much to do here but daydream about the next phase of your adventurous voyage.

ⓘ Information

Attraktiva Oskarshamn (☎ 0491-770 72; www. oskarshamn.se; Hantverksgatan 3; ☺ 9am-5pm Mon-Fri, 10am-3pm Sat & Sun) This tourist office is located in the big shopping plaza on the main square. Follow the signs.

ⓘ Getting There & Away

Oskarshamn is 75km north of Kalmar on the E22 motorway and 69km south of Västervik.

Destination Gotland (p444) operates a fleet of huge car ferries from its terminal near the train station, daily in winter and twice daily in summer. Passenger-only fares start as low as 495kr, but prices vary wildly due to demand and other factors: get a real-time quote online.

M/S Solsund (☎ 0499-449 20; www. olandsfarjan.se; Skeppsbron) operates two ferries each day to Byxelkrok, on Northern Öland (adult/child 150/100kr), from June to August. Boats depart from the ferry terminal off Skeppsbron – follow the signs. A limited number of spots for vehicles are available, starting at 450kr. The usually smooth journey takes 2¼ hours.

Trains no longer run to Oskarshamn Central-station, but most buses stop there.

Kalmar Länstrafik (p441) operates regular bus services from Oskarshamn to Kalmar (102kr, 1¼ hours).

Swebus Express (p435) has daily buses from Kalmar that stop in Oskarshamn en route to Stockholm (5¼ hours, from 339kr).

The closest **SJ Rail** (p421) station is in Berga, 25km southwest of town, with connections to Linköping and Nässjö. Local buses connect Oskarshamn with Berga (68kr, 30 minutes).

Kalmar

📞 0480 / POP 66,571

Sheltered from the wild Baltic Sea by the island of Öland, Kalmar's maturity and medieval charm are immediately evident. The classy, compact city claims one of Sweden's most spectacular castles, within which the Kalmar Union of 1397, which united the crowns of Sweden, Denmark and Norway, was signed.

Dominating the landscape from its ever so slightly elevated position overlooking the Kalmar Strait, the fortress possesses all the elements a storybook castle should have, including opulent interiors even more spectacular than its robust turreted armour. The castle is reason alone to visit the city.

Other local assets include Sweden's largest gold hoard, from the 17th-century ship *Kronan*, and the cobbled streets of its immaculately preserved Old Town. But the main reason people come by Kalmar – many of them totally unaware of the treasures that lie beyond the motorway – is to cross the whopping 6km-long Öland bridge, to the mystical island of Öland, beyond.

👁 Sights & Activities

★ Kalmar Slott   CASTLE
(📞 0480-45 14 90; www.kalmarslott.se; Kungsgatan 1; adult/child 120/100kr; ☺ 10am-6pm daily Jul–mid-Aug, shorter hours rest of year; 🚻) Fairy-tale turrets, a drawbridge, a foul dungeon and secret passages...Kalmar Slott has everything that a proper castle should. This dominant Renaissance stronghold was once the most important building in the land and is appropriately fortified outside and sumptuously furnished inside. You're free to wander around the castle as you please, but the engaging and fun hour-long guided tours (at least one a day, at 11.30am) included in your admission fee really help you appreciate the significance of this magnificent relic.

★ Kalmar läns museum   MUSEUM
(Kalmar County Museum; 📞 0480-45 13 00; www.kalmarlansmuseum.se; Skeppsbrogatan; adult/up to 19yr 100kr/free; ☺ 10am-4pm Mon-Fri, 11am-4pm Sat & Sun; 🅿) The highlight of this fine museum, in an old steam mill by the harbour, are finds from the 17th-century flagship *Kronan*. The ship exploded and sank just before a battle in 1676, with the loss of almost 800 men. It was rediscovered in 1980, and more than 30,000 wonderfully preserved items have been excavated so far, including a spectacular gold hoard, clothing and musical instruments.

Krusenstiernska Gården   GARDENS
(📞 0480-41 15 52; www.krusenstiernskagarden.se; Stora Dammgatan 11; tours adult/child 40/15kr; ☺ 11am-5pm) Krusenstiernska Gården is a 19th-century middle-class home around 500m from the entrance to Kalmar Slott that seems to be delightfully stuck in a time-warp. From May to September, tours of the house are held at noon, 1pm and 2pm, but entry to the beautiful gardens and cafe is free, anytime.

World of Dinosaurs   MUSEUM
(📞 0480-49 57 00; www.aworldofdinosaurs.com; Tingby gård; adult/child 175/125kr; ☺ 11am-5pm Sat & Sun; 🅿 🚻) Kids go gaga for the massive monsters of the past in this gargantuan indoor Dino Museum about 10km west of Kalmar. While it's not quite Jurassic Park and some of the Sauropod's feel distinctly plasticky, the museum's redeeming feature is its collection of more than 100 authentic skeletons and an impressive bunch of convincing full-scale dino models to cower beneath.

🛏 Sleeping

★ Hotell Svanen   HOTEL €
(📞 0480-255 60; www.hotellsvanen.se/en/; Rappegatan 1; dm/d from 195/575kr; 🅿) This smart budget hotel, surrounded by water, is excellent value considering the overall quality of its rooms, range of options (like bike and canoe rentals), bright, clean, common areas, and overall good vibes. Room types range from dorms to private, freshly renovated, 'extra comfort rooms' with smart styling and downy beds. There's free parking and all guests can use the communal kitchen.

★ Slottshotellet   HOTEL €€
(📞 0480-882 60; www.slottshotellet.se; Slottsvägen 7; r/ste from 1395/1795kr, annexe s/d 795/995kr; 🅿 🐾 🛜) This wonderfully cosy, romantic hotel is housed in four buildings in a gorgeous green setting near Kalmar Slott. Most rooms have antique furniture with textured wallpaper, crystal chandeliers and oriental rugs. Across the road, a budget wing, sporting a white minimalist look in stark contrast to the fluffy main wing, has crisp, clean rooms from 995kr.

Calmar Stadshotell   HOTEL €€
(📞 0480-49 69 00; www.ligula.se/en/profilhotels/calmar-stadshotell/; Stortorget 14; d from 895kr;

P 🔁) There's been a hotel on this site since 1741 but the current building dates from 1906. It's a classic hotel that has big old bones and brand new clothes – there's nothing old-fashioned about the relatively plain Jane styling. Service, however, is from another era, when the guest was treated like royalty – and why shouldn't you be? You're a long way from home.

🍴 Eating & Drinking

⭐ **Ming Palace**   CHINESE €€
(📞0480-166 86; www.mingpalacekalmar.se/en/; Fiskaregatan 7; buffet lunch/dinner from 108/145kr; ⏱11am-10pm Mon-Sat, to 8pm Sun) The daily lunch buffet at this friendly, central Cantonese restaurant (with retro booths) is always heaving with patrons. There's a wide range of dishes (including tofu and vegies, and salt and pepper squid) that are constantly topped up while the counter is kept clean by hawk-eyed staff who swoop in to tidy any spills. It's delicious and great value all-you-can-eat.

Gröna Stugan   EUROPEAN €€€
(📞0480-158 58; www.gronastuganikalmar.se; Larmgatan 1; mains 185-295kr; ⏱5-11pm Mon-Sat, to 9pm Sun; 🍴) Located in an unassuming sage-green building complete with round windows reminiscent of a ship, this gem of a restaurant serves up beef tartar, whole witch flounder and New Zealand lamb – gorgeous on the plate and even better to eat. Leave space for the blueberry pancakes with raspberry panna cotta. Vegetarians are catered for.

Lilla Puben   PUB
(📞0480-42 24 22; www.lillapuben.se; Larmgatan 24; ⏱5pm-1am Tue-Sat) Thirsty? This bar is almost obscenely decorated with shelf after shelf of every imaginable brand of beer, some 700 varieties, plus a choice of 120 whiskies.

ℹ️ Information

Kalmar Turism (📞0480-41 77 00; www.kalmar.com; Ölandskajen 9; ⏱9am-9pm Mon-Fri, 10am-5pm Sat & Sun Jun-Aug, shorter hours rest of year) Does an excellent job of promoting the city. You'll find colourful chests of drawers full of brochures and maps popping up in unexpected locations around town.

ℹ️ Getting There & Away

Kalmar is 109km east of Växjö via Rte 25 and 75km south of Oskarshamn via the E22 motorway. It's 40km to Borgholm via the 6km-long Öland bridge.

Swebus Express (p435) operates daily services to Norrköping (from 309kr, four hours) and Stockholm (from 359kr, 6½ hours). All buses depart from the terminal at Centralstation.

SJ Rail (p421) trains run every hour or two between Kalmar and Alvesta (195kr, 1¼ hours), where you can connect with services to Stockholm, Malmö and Gothenburg. Direct trains also run to Linköping (224kr, three hours), with connections to Stockholm.

Kalmar Airport (📞480-45 90 00; www.kalmarairport.se) is located 6km west of town. **SAS** (📞08-797 4000; www.flysas.com) flies several times daily to Stockholm Arlanda, but if you've been staying in town and are feeling adventurous, check the airport website for last-minute deals on charter flights to destinations in Europe.

ℹ️ Getting Around

Kalmar Länstrafik (KLT; 📞010-21 21 000; www.klt.se) operates regular bus services around town and on regional routes like Kalmar to Oskarshamn (102kr, 1¼ hours). Services originate and terminate at Centralstation.

Taxi Kalmar (📞0480-44 44 44; www.kalmar.com/en/taxi) can help you get around town. A taxi to/from the airport costs about 200kr.

Öland

Like a deranged vision of Don Quixote, Öland is *covered* in old wooden windmills. Symbols of power and wealth in the mid-18th century, they were a must-have for every social climber and the death knell for many of Öland's oak forests. Today 400 or so remain, many lovingly restored by local windmill associations.

At 137km long and 16km wide, the island is Sweden's smallest province. Once a regal hunting ground, it's now a hugely popular summer destination for Swedes – the royal family still has a summer pad here. The island gets around two million visitors annually, mostly in July. Around 90% of them flock to the golden shores fringing the northern half of the island to bask and bathe. Behind the beaches, fairy-tale forests make for soulful wanders.

Borgholm

📞0485 / POP 3071
Öland's 'capital' and busiest town, Borgholm has a pleasant centre 'grid' of pedestrian streets lined with shops and restaurants that can get packed out in midsummer. The most dramatic (and satisfying) sight is the enormous ruined castle on its outskirts.

◉ Sights

★ **Solliden Palace** PALACE
(Sollidens Slott; ☑ 048-51 53 56; www.sollidens-slott.se; adult/child 105/80kr; ⊙ 11am-6pm May-Sep) Sweden's most famous 'summer house', Solliden Palace, 2.5km south of Borgholm town centre, is still used by the Swedish royals. Its exceptional gardens are open to the public and are well worth a wander. The idyllic cafe is ideal for a post-garden break.

★ **Borgholms Slott** CASTLE
(☑ 0485-885 00; www.borgholmsslott.se; adult/child 95/60kr; ⊙ 10am-6pm Jun-Aug) Northern Europe's largest ruined castle, Borgholms Slott looms just south of town. This epic limestone structure was burnt and abandoned early in the 18th century, after life as a dyeworks. There's a great museum inside and a nature reserve nearby, as well as summer concerts, children's activities and a cafe.

Gärdslösa Kyrka CHURCH
(⊙ 11am-5pm daily mid-May–mid-Sep) **FREE**
On the east coast, about 13km southeast of Borgholm, is Gärdslösa *kyrka*, the best-preserved medieval church (1138) on Öland.

VIDA Museum & Konsthall MUSEUM
(☑ 0485-774 40; www.vidamuseum.com; Landsvägen; adult/child 80kr/free; ⊙ 10am-6pm daily Jul-early Aug, shorter hours rest of year; P) VIDA Museum & Konsthall is a strikingly modern museum and art gallery in Halltorp, about 9km south of Borgholm. Its finest halls are devoted to two of Sweden's top glass designers.

🍽 Sleeping & Eating

**Ebbas Vandrarhem
& Trädgårdscafé** HOSTEL €
(☑ 0485-103 73; www.ebbas.se; Storgatan 12; dm/s/d from 300/375/580kr; ⊙ May-Sep; 🛜) Look for the classic 1950s Morris Minor 1000 out front here. Five of the lemon-yellow rooms overlook the gorgeous rose-laced garden, and four the bustling Borgholm main street. There's a kitchen for self-caterers...or just pop downstairs to the cafe for decent hot and cold grub (lunch 100kr), served until 9pm in summer.

★ **Hotell Borgholm** HOTEL €€€
(☑ 0485-770 60; www.hotellborgholm.com; Trädgårdsgatan 15-19; s/d from 1295/1535kr; ❄ @ 🛜) Cool grey hues, bold feature walls, pine-wood floors and smart functionalist furniture make for stylish slumber at this urbane hotel. Rooms are spacious, with those on the top floor being especially chic.

Owner Karin Fransson is one of Sweden's top chefs, so a table at the restaurant here is best booked ahead (tasting menu with/without wine 2260/1295kr).

Robinson Crusoe EUROPEAN €€
(☑ 0485-44 477; www.robinsoncrusoe.se; Hamnvägen 1; lunch buffet 160kr, mains 135-260kr; ⊙ noon-10pm Apr-Sep) Slouch back on the plush, purple terrace sofas for a cocktail or an excellent coffee, or make a date for the daily buffet. The setting is sublime, overlooking the bobbing boats in Borgholm harbour.

ⓘ Information

Ölands Turistbyrå (☑ 0485-890 00; www.oland.se/en; Storgatan 1; ⊙ 9am-6pm Mon-Fri, to 5pm Sat, 10am-4pm Sun) Down by the marina end of Storgatan.

ⓘ Getting There & Away

Borgholm is 40km northeast of Kalmar, across the 6km-long Ölandsbron.

Karlskrona

☑ 0455 / POP 66,262
This handsome military-base town is included on the Unesco World Heritage list for its impressive collection of 17th- and 18th-century naval architecture, which could best be described as being in the Danish baroque style.

It was the failed Danish invasion of Skåne in 1679 that sparked Karlskrona's conception, when King Karl XI decided that a southern naval base was needed for better control over the Baltic Sea. Almost immediately, it became Sweden's third-biggest city – hard to imagine today, given it's now so delightfully compact and quiet.

Much of the town still has military ties, so for many sights you'll only be granted admission if you join a tour.

◉ Sights & Activities

★ **Drottningskärs kastell** FORT
(☑ 0455-33 93 00; Drottningskär, Aspö; ⊙ noon-9pm Jun-Aug, noon-5.30pm Fri-Sun Sep-May; 🚢) Bristling with cannons, this fortified tower on the island of Aspö was described by Admiral Nelson of the British Royal Navy as 'impregnable'. You can visit it on an Äspoleden (p444), a free car ferry that runs up to twice hourly in July and August from Handelshamnen, north of the Marinmuseum.

★**Kungsholms Fort** FORT
(Tjurkö; adult/child 230/100kr; ⊙May-Sep) Karl-skrona's star is the extraordinary offshore Kungsholms Fort, with its curious circular harbour, established in 1680 to defend the town. The fort can only be visited on two-hour guided boat tours that must be booked through Karlskrona Turistbyrå (p443) or at the Marinmuseum. Highly recommended.

★**Marinmuseum** MUSEUM
(www.marinmuseum.se; Stumholmen; adult/child 100kr/free; ⊙10am-6pm daily Jun-Aug, shorter hours rest of year; P) The striking Marinmuse-um is the national naval museum. Dive in for reconstructions of a battle deck in wartime, a hall full of fantastic figureheads, piles of model boats, and even some of the real thing – such as a minesweeper, the HMS *Väster-vik* and Sweden's royal sloop. There is also a pleasant restaurant (mains from 100kr).

Stortorget SQUARE
Karlskrona's monumental square, Stortor-get, was planned to rival Europe's best. Alas, the funds ran out, resulting in a somewhat odd mix of grand architectural gestures and humble stand-ins. Dominating the square are the courthouse, along with the baroque churches **Fredrikskyrkan** (☑0455-33 47 00; Stortorget 3; ⊙11am-4pm Mon-Fri, 9.30am-2pm Sat) FREE and **Trefaldighetskyrkan** (Trinity Church; ☑0455-33 47 00; Stortorget; ⊙11am-4pm Mon-Fri, 9.30am-2pm Sat) FREE, the latter inspired by Rome's Pantheon.

🛏 Sleeping & Eating

Karlskrona's architectural heritage and at-tractive waterfront position make it a popular tourist destination year-round and you'll find the hotel industry is doing its bit to main-tain the status quo: there's some great-value, good-quality accommodation in the city.

Dragsö Camping CAMPGROUND €
(☑0455-153 54; www.dragso.se; Dragsövägen; sites/d/2-bed cabins from 250/500/575kr; ⊙Apr–mid Sep; P) This large, good-looking campground, 2.5km northwest of town, is situated on a scenic bay. Facilities include boat and bicycle hire, plus a Karlskro-na-themed minigolf course. Bus 7 stops about 1km short of the campground.

First Hotel Ja HOTEL €€
(☑0455-555 60; www.firsthotels.se; Borg-mästaregatan 13; s/d from 895/1075kr; P@ 🛜) Karlskrona's top slumber spot boasts fash-ionable rooms with stripey wallpaper and

decorative fabrics. Hotel perks include a sauna, a bar-restaurant and a full-blown breakfast buffet served in a pleasant atri-um. There are also several more decorative 'Ladies Rooms', exclusively for women.

Clarion Collection Hotel Carlscrona HOTEL €€
(☑0455-36 15 00; www.hotelcarlscrona.se; Skepps-brokajen; s/d from 1095/1345kr; P 🛜) Handy for the train station, this chain hotel combines original rustic beams and slinky furniture in the bar, and navy blues, greys and handsome wooden furnishings in its stately rooms. An added bonus is an included mid-afternoon snack and nightly evening meal.

★**Nya Skafferiet** DELI €€
(☑0455-171 78; www.nyaskafferiet.se; Rådhusgatan 9; buffet 100kr, light meals 125-180kr; ⊙9am-6pm Mon-Fri, to 3pm Sat) Worldly Mediterranean cafe right behind the main square. There is a superb lunch buffet, as well as a well-stocked deli offering a bounty of cheeses, charcuterie, breads and excellent coffee. If you've not yet tried *köttbullar* (Swedish meatballs), here's a good place to start: order them off the à la carte menu.

2 Rum & Kök EUROPEAN €€€
(Två Rum & Kök; ☑0455-104 22; www.2rok.se; Södra Smedjegatan 3; fondue for 2 from 318kr, mains 225-295kr; ⊙5-10.30pm Mon-Sat) This gourmet dinner spot is best known for its magnificent fondue, with flavours ranging from French to barbecue.

❶ Information

Karlskrona Turistbyrå (☑0455-30 34 90; www.visitkarlskrona.se; Stortorget 2; ⊙9am-7pm Jun-Aug, shorter hours rest of year) In-ternet access, tour bookings and super-helpful staff who get lots of practice communicating face-to-face with curious visitors. Great range of interesting, inexpensive and well-timed tour options.

❶ Getting There & Away

Karlskrona is 56km east of Karlshamn and 135km south of Kalmar, the gateway to Öland.
Blekingetrafiken (☑0455-56 00; www.blekingetrafiken.se) operates public transport in the local area while SJ Rail offers frequent direct train services to Karlshamn (99kr, one hour) and Kristianstad (172kr, 1½ hours), Lund (241kr, 2½ hours) and Malmö (241kr, 2¾ hours).
Svenska Buss (☑0771-67 67 67; www.svenska buss.se) runs daily services to/from Stockholm (420kr, nine hours).

Stena Line (☑ 031-85 80 00; www.stenaline. com) ferries to Gdynia, Poland, start at 389kr. The journey takes about 9½ hours and boats depart from Verkö, 10km east of Karlskrona. Fares vary dramatically; check prices and book online for the best deals.

The free **Äspoleden** (www.trafikverket.se/as-poleden) car ferry shuttles between Karlskrona and the island of Äspo between 6am and midnight, at least hourly.

All buses depart from the bays adjacent to Karlskrona Centralstation.

Ronneby (☑ 010-109 54 00; www.swedavia. com) airport is 33km west of Karlskrona and has limited regular domestic connections.

For local taxis, call **Zon Taxi** (☑ 0455-230 50; www.zontaxi.se) or book online through the website.

GOTLAND

Gotland is the largest island in the Baltic Sea (2994 sq km in diameter), situated off Sweden's southeastern coast. Archaeological finds have revealed that the history of human life on the island predates the Christian tradition, stretching back some 8000 years. Sparsely populated and barely developed, considering its long history of occupation, the charm of the island is its tranquil, almost haunting, beauty.

Gotland's capital Visby, with its intact city walls, is a medieval marvel, magnificent in its authenticity. From the hilltop behind its striking cathedral, overlooking the Baltic, you could easily believe you were somewhere in the Mediterranean, or if you've an active imagination, that you've slipped way back in the annals of time. Come for Medieval Week, when everyone dresses the part, and it's even easier to believe.

Outside Visby, wheels are essential for exploring the island's diverse landscapes – sandy shores, grassy meadows, secluded coves and historical hamlets.

A God-pleasing 92 medieval churches can be found in the surrounding villages, of which more than 70 still have original frescoes. A few also contain extremely rare medieval stained glass.

❶ Getting There & Away

AIR

Gotlands Flyg (☑ 0771-44 00 10; www. gotlandsflyg.se) offers daily flights between Visby and Stockholm Bromma year-round, and between Visby and Malmö from June to Septem-

ber. Prices start at 392kr one way; book early for discounts, and enquire about standby fares.

NextJet (☑ 0771-90 00 90; www.nextjet.se) operates daily flights from Stockholm Arlanda to Visby (June to September). Prices start at 495kr one way.

BOAT

Destination Gotland (☑ 0771-22 33 00; www. destinationgotland.se; Korsgatan 2, Visby) operates year-round car ferries between Visby and both Nynäshamn (three hours, one to six times daily) and Oskarshamn (three to four hours, one or two daily). Seating is reserved and private cabins with two plank sofas, a writing desk, TV and bathroom with shower and toilet are available for the roughly three-hour journey. Cabins accept four passengers, so if you want one for yourself, you have to pay the fee for four people. Pets are allowed on board so to avoid a dog-smelly ride, request an allergy-friendly cabin.

Gotlandsbåten (www.gotlandsbaten.se; Färjeleden 2, Visby) runs ferries from Västervik to Visby (three hours, one or two daily) from June to August. Regular one-way adult tickets for the ferry start at 295kr, but from mid-June to mid-August there is a far more complicated fare system; some overnight, evening and early-morning sailings in the middle of the week have cheaper fares.

With each carrier, transporting a bicycle costs around 60kr; a car usually starts at 375kr, although tiered pricing operates in summer. Advance reservations are *strongly* recommended.

❶ Getting Around

There are more than 1200km of roads in Gotland, typically running from village to village through picture-perfect landscapes. Cycling on these is heavenly, and bikes can be hired from a number of places in Visby. The forested belt south and east of Visby is useful if you bring a tent and want to take advantage of the liberal camping laws.

Many travel agents and bike-hire places on the island also rent out camping equipment. In Visby, hire bikes from **Gotlands Cykeluthyrning** (☑ 0498-21 41 33; www.gotlandscykeluthyrning. com; Skeppsbron 2; bikes adult/child per day from 120/80kr, per week from 600/400kr; ⏰9am-6pm Jun-Aug, shorter hours rest of year) at the harbour. It also rents tents (100/500kr per day/week), or you can hire the 'camping package': two bikes, a tent, a camping stove and two sleeping mats (per day/week 370/1850kr), which is a brilliant way to see the island, and great value.

Kollektiv Trafiken (☑ 0498-21 41 12; www.got-land.se/kollektivtrafiken; single ride 80kr) runs buses to all corners of the island. The most useful routes, which run up to seven times daily, operate between Visby and Klintehamn (on the southwest coast), Burgsvik (in the far south) and Fårösund (in the north, with bus connections to Fårö). A one-way ticket will not cost more than 80kr (to bring a bike on-board add 40kr), but enthusiasts will find a monthly ticket good value at 760kr.

For car hire, try **Avis** (🖉 0770-82 00 82; www.avis.com) or **Europcar** (🖉 08-462 4848; www.europcar.com/location/sweden) for longer term rentals from the airport or snag a cheap deal by the marina with island operator **Visby Harbour Car Rental** (Visby Gästhamn Holmen 1; ⊘ Aug & Sep).

Visby

🖉 0498 / POP 23,576

Gotland's picturesque, medieval capital, Visby, is a delight in every way. Even if you saw nothing else of the wealth of fascination the island has to offer, a stroll among Visby's tangle of cobbled lanes, lined with painted cottages sprouting colourful wildflowers from cracks in their pavement, will not be forgotten quickly.

You'll have your finger on the shutter at almost every turn, snapping scenes that could come straight from a storybook – hauntingly beautiful ruined Gothic churches, the astounding, mostly intact 12th-century ramparts surrounding the Old Town, and the truly magnificent Saint Maria Cathedral

Visby swarms with summer holiday-makers. For many, Medieval Week means the chance to don all manner of fancy garb and parade around as knights, queens, peasants and strumpets, dining, drinking and dancing against a Unesco World Heritage backdrop – surprisingly convincing and fun! Others will prefer to visit during quieter times to ponder Visby's charms, undistracted.

⊙ Sights

★ Gotlands Museum   MUSEUM
(🖉 0498-29 27 00; www.gotlandsmuseum.se; Strandgatan 14; incl Konstmuseet adult/child 120kr/free; ⊘ 11am-4pm Tue-Sun; 🖼️) Gotlands Museum is one of the mightiest regional museums in Sweden. While highlights include amazing 8th-century, pre-Viking picture stones, human skeletons from chambered tombs and medieval wooden sculptures, the star turn is the legendary Spillings treasure horde. At 70kg it's the world's largest booty of preserved silver treasure.

★ Visby Sankta
Maria domkyrka   CATHEDRAL
(Visby Saint Maria Cathedral; www.visbydf.se; Norra Kyrkogatan 2; ⊘ 9am-9pm Jul & Aug, to 5pm rest of year) Visby's church ruins contrast with the stoic and utterly awe-inspiring Sankta Maria *kyrka*. Built in the late 12th and early 13th centuries and heavily touched up over the years, its whimsical towers are topped by baroque cupolas. Soak up the beautiful stained-glass windows, carved floor slabs and ornate carved reredos. The cathedral is used for intimate music concerts in summer. The best place to view the cathedral is from behind – climb all those stairs up the hillside for astounding views.

St Karins Kyrka   RUINS
(Stora Torget) One of the most stunning of Visby's medieval churches, it's often used for performances. In winter, local children skate on an artificial ice rink within the stone walls. Can you imagine?

Norderport   LANDMARK
The northern gate of Visby's city wall is a good entry point if you're short on time. Follow the wall in a southwesterly direction until you find the tallest rampart, (Langa Lisa – six storeys high), and then continue on past the Maiden tower and the Love gate (holding someone special's hand?) until you reach the gunpowder store called Kruttornet – that's the oldest section of the ramparts, built around 1150.

⚔ Festivals & Events

Medeltidsveckan   CULTURAL
(Medieval Week; www.medeltidsveckan.se; ⊘ Aug) Weeklong medieval festival held in early August throughout the streets of Visby, with axe throwing, archery, live music and feasting.

🛏 Sleeping

Fängelse Vandrarhem   HOSTEL €
(🖉 0498-20 60 50; www.visbyfangelse.se; Skeppsbron 1; dm/s/d 300/450/750kr; 🛜) This hostel offers beds year-round in the small converted cells of an old prison. It's in a handy location, between the ferry dock and the harbour restaurants, and there's an inviting terrace bar in summer. Reception is open from 9am to 2pm, so call ahead if you are arriving outside these times.

Hotel St Clemens   HOTEL €€
(🖉 0498-21 90 00; www.clemenshotell.se; Smedjegatan 3; r/ste from 1295/2195kr; 🅿️🛜🐾) Located

Visby

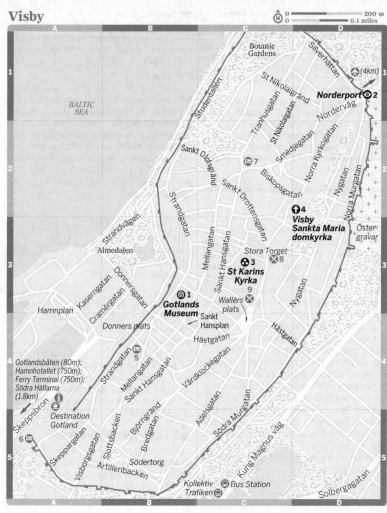

Visby

at the southeastern corner of the botanical garden, this family-run hotel is just a stone's throw away from the vine-covered ruins of the ghostly St Clemens *kyrka*. It takes up five historical buildings and has two gardens and a summery floral theme in the rooms.

★ **Clarion Hotel Wisby**　　HISTORIC HOTEL **€€€**
(☎ 0498-25 75 00; www.clarionwisby.com; Strandgatan 6; s/d from 1880/2190kr; 🅿 @ 🛜 🏊) Top of the heap in Visby is the luxurious, landmark Wisby. Medieval vaulted ceilings and sparkling candelabras contrast with eye-catching contemporary furnishings. The gorgeous

pool (complete with medieval pillar) occupies a converted merchant warehouse. Don't miss the 11th-century chapel, just inside the entrance. The Kitchen & Table restaurant receives rave reviews from readers.

✖ Eating

★ Lilla Bjers Farm Pub
GASTROPUB €€
(☎ 0498-65 24 40; www.lillabjers.se; Lilla Bjers 410; ⊗ noon-3pm & 5pm-midnight) About 7km southwest of Visby, Lilla Bjers is an award-winning farm eatery with a great outdoorsy feel, locavore food (as local as homegrown can be!), chilled beer and cider, and wholesome good vibes.

Surfers
ASIAN €€
(☎ 0498-21 18 00; www.surfersvisby.se; Södra Kyrkogatan 1; small plates 90-120kr; ⊗ 5pm-2am) Not your normal Chinese restaurant abroad, the speciality here is Szechuan finger food designed to share and ranging from Chinese dumplings to traditional twice-cooked pork. There's plenty of heat in the dishes, which are complemented by the other Surfers' speciality: zingy cocktails (from 100kr) made with fresh fruit juice – they're good for you. Honest.

Bolaget
FRENCH €€
(☎ 0498-21 50 80; www.bolaget.fr; Stora Torget 16; mains 190-260kr; ⊗ 5-10pm Mon & Tue, 11.30am-2pm & 5-10pm Wed-Fri, 1-10pm Sat; ☎) Take a defunct Systembolaget shop, chip the 'System' off the signage, and reinvent the space as a buzzing, French bistro-inspired hot spot (fried frog legs, anyone?). Staff members are amiable and the summertime square-side bar seating is perfect for a cool break.

ⓘ Information

Gotlands Turistbyrå (☎ 0498-20 17 00; www.gotland.info; Donners Plats 1; ⊗ 8am-7pm daily summer, 9am-5pm Mon-Fri & 10am-4pm Sat rest of year) The tourist office is conveniently located at Donners Plats and can help with accommodation and advise on what is going on during your stay. It also organises free tours during the summer months.

ⓘ Getting There & Away

The **airport** (Visby Flygplats 8; ☎ 010-109 52 00; www.swedavia.com/visby; Visby Flygplats 8) is 4km northeast of Visby, with regular year-round flights (p444) to Stockholm. In the summer months there are also flights to other destinations, including Malmö and Gothenburg. Catch a taxi into town (around 200kr); there is an airport bus during summer.

Car ferries (p444) operate in the summer between Visby and destinations including Nynäshamn (three hours, one to six times daily), Oskarshamn (three to four hours, one or two daily) and Västervik (three hours, one or two daily). Prices start at 275kr.

Buses depart from the **bus station** (www.gotland.se/busstationsflytt; Kung Magnus Väg; ⊗ 7am-10pm Mon-Fri, to 8pm Sat, 8am-4pm Sun) on Kung Magnus Väg; destinations include Klintehamn, Burgsvik and Fårösund. A one-way ticket costs a maximum of 80kr (plus 40kr to bring a bike on board).

NORRLAND

In Norrland, the northern half of Sweden, the population is sparse – reindeer outnumber cars, and much of the landscape consists of deep-green forest. It's a paradise for nature lovers who enjoy hiking, skiing and other outdoor activities; in winter in particular, the landscape is transformed by snowmobiles, dog-sleds and the eerie aurora borealis. The north is home to the Sami people, and it's possible to take part in traditional Sami pastimes, such as reindeer herding.

Gävle

☎ 026 / POP 71,033
Infamous among certain naughty youngsters because its name sounds a lot like a Swedish swear word, Gävle (Yerv-luh) is a lively university town that's been a prosperous industrial centre since the late 19th century, when it exported local timber and iron. Founded in 1446, Gävle is officially Norrland's oldest town, but not much of its original incarnation remains due to a devastating fire in 1869. A vibrant culinary scene and a host of oddball attractions in and around town appeal to a motley crew of beachgoers, would-be arsonists, whisky connoisseurs and trainspotters, and make Gävle linger-worthy for a day or three.

Coffee-lovers may be surprised to hear that Gevalia Coffee, nowadays a subsidiary of Kraft Foods, was started by Victor Theodore Engwall in Gävle in 1853.

⊙ Sights

★ Mackmyra Whisky
DISTILLERY
(☎ 026-54 18 80; www.mackmyra.se; Kolonnvägen 2; ⊗ restaurant 11am-9pm Sat) Mackmyra Svensk Whisky, established in 1999 as the first Scandinavian malt-whisky distillery,

offers tasting sessions that must be booked in advance via the website. You'll find the distillery, warehouse, and visitor center with restaurant just outside Gävle.

Gamla Gefle
HISTORIC SITE

(www.facebook.com/gamlagefle) A fire in 1869 wiped out most of the old wooden buildings that formed the town's core. Today the little cluster that survived the fire is preserved in the rickety area that is Gamla Gefle, just south of the river. There are lovely cobble-stoned streets, colourful houses adorned with bright flower boxes in summer, and a feeling of community pride on display.

Heliga Trefaldighets kyrka
CHURCH

(www.svenskakyrkan.se/gavle; Kaplansgatan; ⊙11am-4pm Mon-Sat, 10am-2pm Sun) The oldest church in Gävle has an 11th-century rune stone inside, as well as incredible woodcrafted decoration – the work of German artisan Ewardt Friis. The tower, completed in 1781, leans by about half a metre. The church is one of only a few buildings north of the Gävle river that escaped the devastating 1869 fire.

Sleeping & Eating

★ Gefle Vandrarhem
HOSTEL €

(Gävle Youth Hostel; ☑026-62 17 45; www.gefle-vandrarhem.se; Södra Rådmansgatan 1; dm/s/d 220/395/480kr; ⊙mid-Jan–early Dec; ℗ 🛜) Set in one of Gamla Gefle's old-style wooden buildings around a flowering courtyard, this quiet hostel with good guest kitchen is popular with travellers of all ages. Breakfast buffet costs 75kr. It's about a 10-minute walk from the station, has free wi-fi and there are laundry facilities available.

Elite Grand Hotel Gävle
HOTEL €€

(☑026-400 73 00; www.elite.se; Kyrkogatan 28; s/d from 750/950kr; ℗ 🛜) This beautifully restored art-deco hotel, in a massive building that originally opened as a hotel in 1901, has a lot going for it, not least its super-central location and bright, contemporary decor. The restaurant and bar are superb, overlooking the Gävle river.

★ Matildas
FUSION €€

(☑026-62 53 49; www.matildas.nu; Timmermansgatan 23; mains from 170kr; ⊙5pm-late Tue-Sat) The menu at this small, stylish bistro is short, sweet and seasonal, with a real depth of flavour to the dishes, wonderful attention to presentation and a relaxed ambience.

Feast on lobster tacos, oysters paired with champagne, crispy pork belly and home-made black pudding with lingonberry. The home-brewed beer, served by the delightful owners, goes down very smoothly.

ⓘ Information

Tourist Office (☑026-17 71 17; www.visit-gavle.se; Drottninggatan 22; ⊙8am-5pm Mon-Fri, 10am-2pm Sat) This very efficient office has brochures aplenty on the city and surrounding area.

ⓘ Getting There & Away

BUS

Long-distance bus services leave from behind the train station. For Ybuss departures, take a 'Busstaxi' from the train station to Gävlebro. **Ybuss** (www.ybuss.se) runs daily to Sundsvall (250kr, 2¾ to 3¼ hours, three to six daily) and Umeå (415kr, 6½ to 7½ hours, three daily). **SGS Bussen** (https://sgsbussen.se) serves Stockholm (160kr, two hours, five to seven daily).

TRAIN

There are numerous daily services to Stockholm (from 165kr, 1½ to 2¼ hours) via Uppsala (from 109kr, 45 minutes to 1¼ hours) and Sundsvall (from 106kr, 2¼ hours). One or two trains run to Kiruna (from 745kr, 14¼ hours), via Luleå (from 755kr, 10 hours), and three to Östersund (from 285kr, 3½ hours).

Sundsvall

☑060 / POP 51,350

Your first views of central Sundsvall may be one of the most pleasant (or mind-boggling) surprises of your visit to the Bothnian coast. The city was a well-off timber town exporting to the world when it was burned to the ground in 1888, after a spark from a steamboat set the town brewery alight. The central city was levelled in half a day. Civic leaders, finding that the town's timber barons were actually over-insured, then decided that their city should be rebuilt in stone and brick, buildings separated by wide avenues. This new start produced a construction boom and incredibly ornate stone buildings, all built within a decade of the fire, that stand to this day.

Sundsvall's main appeal lies less in any one specific sight than in the Bothnian Coast's most cosmopolitan city as a whole, complete with highly strollable boulevards and a clutch of great restaurants.

⦿ Sights & Activities

★ **Stenstan Visitor Centre** MUSEUM
(☑ 060-658 58 00; http://stenstanvisitorcenter.se; Storatorget; ☉ 10am-6pm Mon-Fri, 10am-4pm Sat, noon-4pm Sun) FREE This incredibly high-tech multimedia museum shares space with the tourist office at the Stadhus on the central square of Storatorget. Besides showing films of the 1888 fire and its aftermath, it features touch-screen tables and picture frames that allow you to follow the reconstruction of central Sundsvall through old photos, and information on each rebuilt building such as the background of the architect and original drawings. The centre's technology is now being exported to museums around the world.

Kulturmagasinet MUSEUM
(www.sunsvall.se/kulturmagasinet; Sjögatan; ☉ 10am-7pm Mon-Thu, to 6pm Fri, 11am-4pm Sat & Sun) FREE Down near the harbour, Kulturmagasinet is a magnificent restoration of some old warehouses and now contains the town library and Sundsvall Museum, which has engaging exhibits on the history of Sundsvall, natural history and geology. There's a permanent art exhibition upstairs featuring 20th-century Swedish artists and superb temporary exhibitions.

Alnö Gamla Kyrka CHURCH
(☉ noon-6pm mid-Jun–mid-Aug) This magnificent church, a mixture of 12th- and 15th-century styles, sits 2km north of the bridge (at Vi) on Alnö island, just east of Sundsvall. The upper wall and ceiling paintings, likely done by one of Albertus Pictor's pupils, have survived intact. Even better is the late-11th-century carved wooden font across the road; the upper part combines Christian and Viking symbolism, while the lower part shows beasts that embody evil. Catch bus 1 to Vi, then walk 1km north.

🛌 Sleeping

★ **Lilla Hotellet** HOTEL €
(☑ 060-61 35 87; www.lilla-hotellet.se; Rådhusgatan 15; s/d 750/900kr; 🛜) In a stone building designated a historical monument (since it was built the year after the great fire), this small family-run hotel has a great location and a friendly vibe. The eight spacious rooms with high ceilings have interesting architectural details, such as ceramic tile stoves. Throw in a good breakfast and this is a really good budget option.

Best Western Hotel Baltic HOTEL €€
(☑ 060-14 04 40; www.baltichotell.com; Sjögatan 5; s/d from 690/1090kr; P 🛜) This centrally located place has bright, modern rooms inside a stone building erected after the 1888 fire. Now part of the Best Western chain, it's near the port and the Kulturmagasinet.

Elite Hotel Knaust HOTEL €€
(☑ 060-608 00 00; www.elite.se; Storgatan 13; s/d from 830/1100kr; P 🛜) In a striking 19th-century building on Sundsvall's main pedestrian drag, this opulent hotel is full of old-world charm. Besides the grand, lobby-dominating (and much photographed) marble staircase, the rooms are decorated in classic Scandinavian style and have high ceilings. The breakfast buffet is excellent.

✗ Eating & Drinking

★ **Tant Anci & Fröcken Sara** CAFE €
(☑ 060-785 57 00; http://tantanci.se; Bankgatan 15; mains from 79kr; ☉ 10am-10pm Mon-Thu, to 8pm Fri, 11am-5pm Sat; ☑) ⦿ Humongous bowls of soup or salad are the speciality at this frilly organic cafe, where you can also get hearty sandwiches, giant bowls of pasta and pastries.

Udda Tapas Bar TAPAS €
(☑ 073-098 66 07; www.uddasundsvall.se; Esplanaden 17; tapas 40-85kr; ☉ 5-11pm Mon-Thu, to 2am Fri & Sat) Head for the roof terrace of this congenial bar on summer evenings to savour the likes of clams with lemongrass, smoked reindeer with Dijon mustard, lamb tacos and yellow beets with honey and feta, along with a glass of wine or a local brew. DJs kick it up a notch on weekends.

★ **Oscar Matsal & Bar** BAR
(☑ 060-12 98 11; www.oscarmatsal.se; Bankgatan 11; ☉ 11am-2pm Mon-Fri & 5-10pm Mon-Thu, to 3am Fri & Sat) The hottest watering hole in town with retro decor triples as a sophisticated bistro and a nightclub where you can knock back Tom Collinses while checking out the latest live band.

ℹ️ Information

Tourist Office (☑ 060-658 58 00; www.visitsundsvall.se; Storatorget; ☉ 10am-6pm Mon-Fri, 10am-4pm Sat, noon-4pm Sun) Inside the Stadhus, the tourist office shares its space with the Stenstan Visitor Centre.

❶ Getting There & Away

AIR

Sundsvall-Timrå Airport (Midlanda Airport; ☑ 070-522 03 12; www.sdlairport.se) is 21km north of Sundsvall; flights serve Gothenburg, Stockholm and Visby (summer only). Charter flights head out to places including Crete, Mallorca and Gran Canaria.

BUS

Buses depart from the Sundsvall bus station, near Kulturmagasinet. **Ybuss** (p475) runs to Gävle (from 257kr, 2¾ to 3¾ hours) and Stockholm (320kr, 4½ to six hours). Länstrafiken Västerbotten buses 10 and 100 run to Umeå (320kr, 5¼ hours) via other coastal towns.

TRAIN

Trains run west to Östersund (from 279kr, 2½ hours) and south to Gävle (from 106kr, 2¼ hours) and Stockholm (from 325kr, 3½ to five hours). The station is just east of the town centre on Landsvagsalen, which is a continuation of Köpmangatan.

Höga Kusten

Cross the Höga Kustenbron, the spectacular suspension bridge over the Ångerman river – Norrland's answer to the Golden Gate Bridge and one of the longest in the world (1867m) – and you find yourself amid some of the most dramatic scenery on the Swedish coastline. The secret to the Höga Kusten's (High Coast's) spectacular beauty is elevation; nowhere else on the coast do you find such a mountainous landscape, with sheer cliffs plunging straight down to the sea, as well as lakes, fjords and dozens of tranquil islands, covered in spruce and pine forest. The region is recognised as a geographically unique area and was listed as a Unesco World Heritage Site in 2000.

Höga Kusten stretches from north of Härnösand to Örnsköldsvik, and it's a wonderful area for scenic drives along narrow, twisty roads, though you can't really say that you know the Höga Kusten without visiting its tranquil islands.

The Islands

ULVÖN
☑ 0660

The largest island in the Höga Kusten archipelago, Ulvön is famous for its regatta (mid-July) and for the production of *surströmming* (fermented herring). It's possible to purchase the noxious (or delightful, depending on your outlook) stuff in the shops at Ulvöhamn, the island's one-street village and main port. A cycle path leads through the picturesque fishing settlement with traditional red-and-white wooden houses drowning in colourful flower blossoms in summer, past the tiny 17th-century chapel decorated with colourful murals, and onwards to the preserved 17th-century fishing village of Sandviken in the northern part of the island.

🍴 Sleeping & Eating

★ **Ulvö Hotell**   HOTEL €€
(☑ 0660-22 40 09; www.ulvohotell.se; Ulvö Hamngata 105; r from 1075kr; 🛜 🏊) Ulvö Hotell, with its superb restaurant, bar and pool area, makes a great place to stay on the island. The rooms feature a cream-and-charcoal colour scheme and quality furnishings. Located at the eastern end of the village, its restaurant is popular with day trippers and has a seasonal menu featuring local ingredients.

UlvöByn Café & Bistro   SWEDISH €€
(☑ 070-309 28 84; http://ulvobyn.se; Ulvö Hamngata 142; mains from 155kr; ☉ 10am-10pm Jun-Aug, plus weekends & holidays) Ulvöhamn's top cafe is about halfway along the street and caters for everybody with plates such as *Stekt strömming på spisbröd* (fried herring on crispbread; 75kr) through to full main courses. It's a very convivial atmosphere with both outdoor and indoor seating, plus friendly service.

❶ Information

A good website is www.ulvon.info though it is only in Swedish.

❶ Getting There & Away

MF Ulvön & MF Minerva (☑ 070-651 92 65; http://en.mfulvon.se; return adult/6-19yr 150/90kr) Between mid-June and mid-August, ferries leave Köpmanholmen for Ulvöhamn (adult/six to 19 years 150/90kr return, 1½ hours, six daily), three of them stopping at Trysunda on the way. From late May to mid-June and mid-August to mid-September, reduced services call at Ulvöhamn twice daily and at Trysunda once or twice daily. Both destinations are served daily the rest of the year.

M/S Kusttrafik (☑ 0613-105 50; www.hkship. se; one way/return 150/225kr) Ferry to Ulvön leaves Ullånger for Ulvöhamn via Docksta daily at 9.30am, returning from Ulvöhamn at 3pm, between June and August.

TRYSUNDA

A small island with a namesake village consisting of cute fisher's houses clustered around a little U-shaped bay, Trysunda has an attractive wooden chapel, dating back to 1655 – the oldest along the Bothnian Coast. There are also some great secluded spots for bathing, reachable by the walking paths that run through the woods; just pick your own flat rock by the water or else head to the cove at Björnviken, on the eastern side of the island. You can walk around the whole of Trysunda in an hour or two.

🛏 Sleeping

Trysunda Gästhamn GUESTHOUSE €

(☑ 0660-430 38; http://trysundavandrarhem.se; s/d 300/600kr; ☺ May-Sep; 🛜) Overnight stays are available at Trysunda Gästhamn, an easy-to-spot from the ferry, red waterfront guesthouse that usually has boats tied up out front. The rooms are pretty compact, but there's use of a guest kitchen. If you don't feel like cooking up a storm, there is a cafe on-site. The six-bed cottage goes for 3000kr per night.

ℹ Getting There & Away

MF Ulvön & MF Minerva (p450) Between mid-June and mid-August, ferries leave Köpmanholmen for Ulvöhamn, three of them stopping at Trysunda (adult/six to 19 years 120/80kr, 30 minutes) on the way. From late May to mid-June and mid-August to mid-September, reduced services call at Trysunda once or twice daily. Both destinations are served daily the rest of the year.

Östersund

☑ 063 / POP 49,806

This pleasant town by Lake Storsjon, in whose chilly waters is said to lurk a rarely sighted monster, is a relaxed and scenic gateway town for further explorations of Norrland. It's remote enough that if you are approaching by car, you can expect to see almost as many reindeer as cars. The town dates from 1786 and was a lucrative trading centre.

Today, its appeal lies in its air of relaxation: in summer, people flock to the terrace bars and cafes of this Unesco-designated 'city of gastronomy', or wander the pedestrianised shopping streets in the stroll-friendly centre. One of the best ways to appreciate Östersund is to take the footbridge across to the adjacent island of Frösön and gaze back at the city in profile, ideally around sunset. Seen in that light, this fun-loving university town is hard to resist.

👁 Sights

⭐ Mus-Olles Museum MUSEUM

(☑ 0640-220 60; www.musolles.com; Sjövik 453, Ytterån; adult/child 100kr/free; ☺ 8am-4pm late Jun-late Aug; 🅿) If you're into collections of stuff, this is the place to come, about 34km northwest of Östersund and 1 km north of the E14. Per-Olov Nilson was a charismatic collector extraordinaire who first opened his museum in 1906. He hoarded more than 150,000 objects, including 25,000 related to packaging, then formed a trust, which now operates the museum, to run things once he died (in 1955). This fascinating museum, including a cafe and various buildings, is on Per-Olov's old property.

⭐ Jamtli MUSEUM

(www.jamtli.com; Museiplan; adult/child 70kr/free, entry late June–late Aug free; ☺ 11am-5pm daily late Jun-late Aug, Tue-Sun rest of year; 🅿♿) Jamtli, 1km north of the centre, consists of two parts: the open-air museum, comprising painstakingly reconstructed wooden buildings, complete with enthusiastic guides wearing 19th-century period costume; and the indoor museum, home to the **Överhogdal Tapestries**, the oldest of their kind in Europe – Christian Viking relics from AD 1100 that feature animals, people, ships and dwellings. Another fascinating display is devoted to Storsjöodjuret (the lake monster), including taped interviews with those who've seen it, monster-catching gear and a pickled monster embryo.

Moose Garden ANIMAL SANCTUARY

(☑ 070-363 60 61; www.moosegarden.com; Orrviken 215, Orrviken; adult/child 140/90kr; ☺ tours 11am & 1pm late Jun–mid-Aug; 🅿) Head to Moose Garden, 16km southwest of Östersund, to get up close and personal with the King of the Forest – or at least, some tame ones. You get to learn all about the moose, pat one and get as many photos as you like. There is also accommodation here in the form of Moose Lodges (from 690kr).

Badhusparken BEACH

(www.vinterparken.se) The waterfront park is the town's most popular stop for sunbathing and a brisk swim. In winter the lake turns into Sweden's largest ice-skating rink (rent your skates here; 160kr per day) and you can also swim in the specially cut hole in the ice further south along the waterfront before making a spirited dash to the nearby mobile sauna and spa (140kr).

🛏 Sleeping & Eating

STF Ledkrysset Hostel   HOSTEL €
(📋 063-10 33 10; http://ostersundledkrysset.se; Biblioteksgatan 25; dm/s/d 180/350/520kr; 🛜) This well-run, central hostel is in a converted old fire station and is your best shoestring bet.

⭐ Hotel Emma   HOTEL €€
(📋 063-51 78 40; www.hotelemma.com; Prästgatan 31; s/d from 720/895kr; 🅿🛜) The individually styled rooms at super-central Emma nestle in crooked hallways on two floors, with homey touches such as squishy armchairs and imposing ceramic stoves; some rooms have French doors facing the courtyard. The breakfast spread is a delight. Reception hours are limited, so call ahead if arriving late or early.

Wedemarks Konditori & Bageri   CAFE €
(📋 063-51 03 83; http://wedemarks.se; Prästgatan 27; snacks 60-80kr; ⊙8am-10pm Mon-Fri, 10am-5pm Sat, 11am-4pm Sun; 🛜) This glorious cafe has been sweet-toothing its customers since 1924; this is the place to try a slice of typical Swedish delights such as the traditional Princess layer cake with its topping of bright green marzipan. If you are in a savoury mood, go for a succulent vegie or beef sandwich or shrimp-filled baked potato.

⭐ Innefickan
Restaurang & Bar   FUSION €€€
(📋 063-12 90 99; www.innefickan.se; Postgränd 11; mains from 210kr; ⊙5pm-late Tue-Sun) With a cosy cellar ambience – all exposed brick and contemporary art pieces – Innefickan packs a great deal of creativity into its succinct menu. Try the carpaccio with wasabi and coriander; the veal with chanterelles and pumpkin purée is expertly seared, and rhubarb is transformed into something far greater than the raw material in this place's capable hands.

ℹ Information

Tourist Office (📋 063-701 17 00; www.visitostersund.se; Rådhusgatan 44; ⊙9am-5pm Mon-Fri, 10am-3pm Sat & Sun) Efficient office opposite the town hall.

ℹ Getting There & Away

AIR
The **airport** (📋 063-19 30 00; www.swedavia.se/ostersund; Frösön) serving both Östersund and Åre is on Frösön island, 11km west of the town centre. The airport bus leaves regularly from the bus terminal (adult/child 90/45kr).

SAS flies to Stockholm. During the ski season, the airport receives charter flights from London Heathrow, Manchester, Amsterdam and Copenhagen.

BUS
Daily bus 45 runs north at 7.15am from Östersund to Gällivare (532kr, 11¼ hours) via Arvidsjaur (460kr, seven hours) and Jokkmokk (574kr, 9½ hours) and south to Mora (284kr, 5¼ hours, two daily) from the **bus station** (📋 0771-10 01 10; http://ltr.se; Gustav III Torg; ⊙6am-10.30pm Mon-Fri, 6.30am-7.30pm Sat, noon-10pm Sun).

TRAIN
In summer, the daily 7.05am **Inlandsbanan** (p476) train heads north to Gällivare (1378kr, 14½ hours) and one heads south to Mora (596kr, six hours). SJ departures include two trains daily to Stockholm (701kr, five hours) via Uppsala, and up to six daily trains heading west to Åre (146kr, 1¼ hours).

Åre

📋 0647 / POP 1417

Beautifully situated in a mountain valley by the shores of Åresjön lake, Åre is Sweden's most popular skiing resort and visitors invade the village during the December-to-May skiing season. Things don't drop off much for summer though, as this small village is taking on the mantle of the adventure capital of Sweden. In July, Åre hosts the Åre Bike Festival and the hard-core Åre Extreme Challenge that has its competitors running, paddling and cycling for glory. Besides traditional sports, winter and summer bring a bewildering array of mountain-related activities that you can try your hand at, such as dog-sledding, snowmobile safaris, paragliding, white-water rafting and hill-carting. There's even a chocolate factory to help with après-adventure recovery.

⊙ Sights & Activities

⭐ Kabinbanan   CABLE CAR, VIEWPOINT
(adult/child 150/110kr; ⊙10am-4pm daily late Jun-late Sep) Bringing you almost to the top of Mt Åreskutan, this gondola is worth taking for the awesome views alone. The seven-minute ride departs from behind Åre's main square and whisks you up to a viewing platform (1274m) complete with Åre's most expensive cafe. Hike up to the peak from there.

Åre Bergbana   FUNICULAR
(adult/child 60kr/free) This lovely old mountain railway was completed in 1910 along with the first ski lifts in Åre. These days, the funicular is run by SkiStar during winter

and Hotel Fjällgården keeps it operating in the evenings and at other times to get guests to the hotel. The trip takes seven minutes and is included for hotel guests.

Åre Chokladfabrik FACTORY
(Åre Chocolate Factory; ✉ 0647-155 80; https://arechokladfabrik.se; Björnänge 801; ⊙ 10am-5pm) It's hard to drive past this place at the eastern end of town on the E14. These guys have been producing handmade chocolates, truffles and caramels since 1991, and if you want to see why they've been so successful, drop by and try some of the chocolate up for tasting. It's seriously good stuff!

★ JoPe Fors & Fjäll RAFTING, ADVENTURE SPORTS
(✉ 0647-314 65; http://en.jope.se; Hosbacken 7, Undersåker) Challenging white-water rafting and mountain tours in summer; ice climbing and heliskiing in winter with a Nature's Best accredited operator.

★ Åre Bike Park MOUNTAIN BIKING
(http://bikingare.com) In summer the slopes of Mt Åreskutan become an enormous playground dedicated to downhill biking. More than 30 trails span 40km of track, ranging from beginner to extreme (the trails are graded using the same system as ski slopes). The Kabinbanan cable car, Bergbanan funicular, VM6 and Hummelliften chairlifts are fitted with bike racks.

🛏 Sleeping & Eating

STF Åre Torg HOSTEL €
(✉ 0647-515 90; www.svenskaturistforeningen.se/aretorg; Kabinbanevägen 22b; dm/s/d 295/540/690kr; ❄ 🛜) This large, renovated hostel sits virtually right on the main square. All rooms are identical windowless cubes with four glossy dark-wood bunks, ventilated from the inside. All open onto an enormous common space, with an indoor 'patio' with tables in front of each room and a cafe serving light bites during the day. Spotless guest kitchen and bathrooms.

Hotell Fjällgården HOTEL €€
(✉ 0647-145 00; www.fjallgarden.se; s/d from 745/1390kr; P 🛜) Among the trees and with great views at the top of Åre's funicular since 1910, this is as much an activity centre as hotel. On top of all the outdoor activities, there's a top restaurant and après-ski bar, often including live music. Rooms run from simple skier rooms to suites – and the hotel keeps the funicular running to get you here.

★ Copperhill Mountain Lodge LODGE €€€
(✉ 0647-143 00; https://copperhill.se; Åre Björnen; r from 1440kr; P 🛜) Beautifully constructed of wood and stone with copper accents, this lodge looks down on Åre from its lofty mountain perch. Its stylish, contemporary rooms are grouped according to precious metals; Gold Suites at the top, Brass, Zinc, Copper, Silver...you get the idea. The spa, Niesti Restaurant, and library and Fireside Lounge & Bar just add to the ambience.

★ Havvi i Glen SAMI €€€
(✉ 070-600 64 76; www.havviiglen.se; Glen 530, Åsarna; mains 195-265kr, tasting menu 1395kr) A proud standard-bearer for the Slow Food Sápmi movement, Havvi i Glen initiates you into the richness of mountain Sami cuisine, with game, mushrooms and berries featuring prominently on its seasonal menu. Expect the likes of thinly sliced reindeer steak with blueberry chutney, smoked Arctic char with sea buckthorn, and cloudberry sorbet. The website provides directions and opening hours.

★ Fäviken Magasinet SWEDISH €€€
(✉ 0647-401 77; http://favikenmagasinet.se; per person 3000kr) This intimate 16-seat, five-table mountain restaurant has one of Sweden's finest culinary reputations, drawing strictly on seasonal Jämtland produce and traditions such as drying, pickling and salting. There are also divine double rooms here for 2500kr, including breakfast. It's at Fäviken – turn north at Järpen, 15km east of Åre. Book well ahead for both the restaurant and accommodation.

ℹ Information

Tourist Office (✉ 0647-163 21; www.visitare.com; St Olafsväg 33; ⊙ 10am-6pm Mon-Fri, to 3pm Sat & Sun; 🛜) Inside the public library in the train station building. Plenty of info on the area, including maps of hiking trails and brochures on outdoor activities.

ℹ Getting There & Away

BUS
Bus 155 runs east to Östersund (185kr, two hours, one or two daily). Bus 157 runs west to Duved (30kr, 10 minutes, up to 10 daily) and bus 571 connects Duved to Storlien (110kr, 30 minutes, daily).

TRAIN
Åre has east-bound trains for Östersund (155kr, 1¼ hours, six daily) and to Stockholm (from 822kr, from seven hours, five daily). To get to Trondheim, Norway (296kr, 2½ hours, two daily), change at Storlien (98kr, 45 minutes, two daily).

Umeå

📍 090 / POP 121,030

Umeå has claims to fame on several counts: it was the European Capital of Culture in 2014; it has the second-largest art gallery in Sweden; it's home to Europe's greatest museum collection of vintage guitars; and it is the former residence of Stieg Larsson, author of *The Girl with the Dragon Tattoo*. Its location, a mere 400km below the Arctic Circle, means it is also popular with Northern Lights seekers.

A youthful college town, Umeå has a long and fascinating history. The town was founded in 1622, and was home to the indigenous Sami people whom visitors can learn about at a couple of excellent museums. Aside from its grand slam of cultural sights, Umeå has a superb choice of restaurants and bars, plenty of green spaces, and great shopping. It makes an excellent stopover on your way further north, as well as a destination in its own right.

◉ Sights

★ **Guitars – The Museum**　　　MUSEUM
(📞 090-580 90; www.guitarsthemuseum.com; Vasagatan 18-20; adult/student 150/100kr; ⊗ noon-6pm Mon-Sat) If you're into the six-string, then this result of two brothers' lifelong hobby, a huge collection of vintage guitars, is for you. Want to see a 1959 Les Paul Standard, identical to the one on which Keith Richards played the 'It's All Over Now' riff? They've got it. Or perhaps a 1958 Gibson Flying V, made famous by ZZ Top?

Västerbottens Museum　　　MUSEUM
(📞 090-16 39 00; www.vbm.se; Helena Elizabeths väg, Gammliavägen; ⊗ 10am-5pm, to 9pm Wed; 🅿️ 🚼) FREE The star of the Gammlia museum complex, the engrossing Västerbottens Museum traces the history of the province from prehistoric times to today. Exhibitions include an enormous ski-through-the ages collection starring the world's oldest ski (5400 years old), and an exploration of Sami rock art and shaman symbols. There are excellent temporary exhibitions as well as regular workshops and activities for children. There is also a superb cafe specialising in organic fare. Take bus 2 or 7 or walk 1km from the station.

Älgens Hus　　　ANIMAL SANCTUARY
(📞 0932-500 00; www.algenshus.se; Västernyliden 23, Bjurholm; adult/child 130/65kr; ⊗ noon-6pm Tue-Sun mid-Jun–mid-Aug; 🚼) This moose park, 70km west of Umeå along Rte 92, near Bjurholm, is your chance to meet the (tame) King of the Forest face to face. In Swedish, these are elk, but English-speakers know these giants as moose. There's a museum, video explanations of a year in the life of a moose, and even a small dairy where the ultra-rare moose cheese is produced; at 6000kr per kilogram, this is the most expensive cheese you'll ever taste.

🍴 Sleeping & Eating

★ **Stora Hotellet Umeå**　　　BOUTIQUE HOTEL €€
(📞 090-77 88 70; www.storahotelletumea.se; Storgatan 46; s/d/ste from 1000/1150/6000kr; 🅿️ 🛜) First opened as a hotel in 1895, Stora Hotellet had major renovations to coincide with the city being named European Capital of Culture in 2014. The six categories of rooms have names such as Superstition, Adventure and Mystique, and if you're after a bit of historical ambience, this is a top place to stay. The hotel's restaurant, Gotthards Krog, is superb.

U&Me Hotel　　　HOTEL €€
(📞 090-206 64 60; http://umehotel.se; Storgatan 46; r from 800kr; 🛜) This new-concept hotel in central Umeå is super cool. You'll spot the massive white building from miles away, and the hotel is on floors six to 13. Below is the city's continental indoor square and cultural hub known as Väven. This is where you'll check in on tablets, have breakfast at the bakery and cafe, and even issue your own room key.

Två Fiskare　　　SEAFOOD €€
(📞 090-765 70 20; www.tvafiskare.se; Storgatan 44; mains from 95kr; ⊗ 10am-6pm Mon-Fri, to 4pm Sat) This place takes fish very seriously indeed. Not only does it sell it fresh, it also prepares a handful of exquisite seafood and fish dishes daily for those in the know. Crabcakes, fish soup, smoked salmon…the dishes will depend on what is flapping fresh that day. Undecided? Then opt for the classic fish and chips, served in newspaper, the traditional way.

★ **Koksbaren**　　　SWEDISH €€€
(📞 090-13 56 60; www.koksbaren.com; Rådhusesplanaden 17; mains from 255kr; ⊗ 5-11pm Mon-Sat; 🛜) Expect stunning culinary combinations at this sophisticated restaurant on the corner near the train station. Virtually everything is made here, including the ketchup and the 'smoked' mayonnaise. The speciality is dry cured steaks with a choice of rib eye, sirloin or filet mignon. The bright yet classy dining area adds to the agreeable eating experience.

Reservations recommended.

ℹ️ Information

Tourist Office (☎ 090-16 16 16; www.visitumea.se; Rådhusesplanaden 6a; ⏰10am-6pm Mon-Fri, 10am-4pm Sat, 11am-3pm Sun) Centrally located with helpful staff who can advise on places to stay and what's going on.

ℹ️ Getting There & Away

AIR

Umeå Airport (☎ 01-109 50 00; www.swedavia. com/umea; Flygplatsvägen) is 5km south of the city centre. SAS and Norwegian fly daily to Stockholm's Arlanda and Bromma, Braathens Regional Aviation (formerly Malmö Aviation) to Gothenburg and Stockholm, and Direktflyg to Östersund and Luleå.

Airport buses run to the city centre (45kr, 20 minutes).

BOAT

Wasaline (☎ 090-18 52 14; www.wasaline.com; Blå Vagen 4, Holmsund) operates ferries between Umeå and Vaasa (Finland) once or twice daily (360kr one-way, four hours, Sunday to Friday) from Holmsund, 20km south of Umeå. A bus to the port leaves from near the tourist office an hour before RG Line's departures.

BUS

The **long-distance bus station** (☎ 090-70 65 00; Järnvägsallén 2; ⏰ ticket office 7am-6pm Mon-Fri, 9am-3pm Sat, 11am-6pm Sun) is directly opposite the train station. Ybuss runs services south to Gävle (395kr, 6½ to 7½ hours) and Stockholm (450kr, 9¼ to 10 hours), stopping at all the coastal towns.

Buses 20 and 100 head up the coast to Haparanda (368kr, 6½ to 7¾ hours) via Luleå (340kr, four to five hours) and Skellefteå (197kr, two to 2½ hours).

Local buses leave from Vasaplan on Skolgatan.

TRAIN

Departures include three daily trains to Stockholm (from 550kr, 6½ hours), while the northbound trains to Luleå (315kr, 5½ hours) stop in Boden, from where there are connections to Kiruna (685kr, 7½ to 8½ hours) and Narvik (in Norway; 452kr, 11 hours).

Luleå

☎ 0920 / POP 74,800

Luleå is the capital of Norrbotten, chartered in 1621, though it didn't become a boom town until the late 19th century when the Malmbanan railway was built to transport iron ore from the Bothnian coast to Narvik (Norway). The town centre moved to its present location from Gammelstad, 9km to the northwest, in 1649 because of the falling sea level (8mm per year), due to postglacial uplift of the land.

A laid-back university town and an important high-tech centre, Luleå claims more than its fair share of top-notch restaurants for a town its size, as well as an enticing archipelago of islands off its coast and a sparkling bay with a marina.

💿 Sights

★ Gammelstad   HISTORIC SITE

(☎0920-45 70 10; www.lulea.se/gammelstad) **FREE** The Unesco World Heritage–listed Gammelstad, Sweden's largest church town, was the medieval centre of northern Sweden. The 1492-built stone **Nederluleå church** has a reredos worthy of a cathedral and a wonderfully opulent pulpit. It has 420 wooden houses (where the pioneers stayed during weekend pilgrimages) and six church stables remaining.

Guided tours (80kr) leave from the Gammelstad tourist office at 11am, 1pm and 3pm (mid-June to mid-August). Bus 9 runs hourly from Luleå; disembark at the Kyrkbyn stop.

Luleå Archipelago   ISLAND

(www.lulea.se/skargard) This extensive offshore archipelago contains over 1700 large and small islands, most of them uninhabited and therefore perfect for skinny-dipping, berry picking, and camping. The larger islands, decorated with classic red-and-white Swedish summer cottages, are accessible by boat from Luleå. Facilities are limited, so most visitors come as picnicking daytrippers.

Teknikens Hus   MUSEUM

(www.teknikenshus.se; University Campus; adult/under 4yr 70kr/free; ⏰10am-4pm mid-Jun–Aug; 👶; 🚌4, 5) Curious minds of all ages will love the gigantic educational playground that is Teknikens Hus, within the university campus 4km north of town. The museum has hands-on exhibitions about everything from hot-air balloons and rocket launching to the aurora borealis. Take bus 4 or 5 to Universitetsentrén.

🛏️ Sleeping & Eating

★ Clarion Sense   HOTEL €€

(☎0920-45 04 50; www.clarionsense.se; Skeppsbrogatan 34; s/d/ste from 1095/1295/3595kr; 🛜🛗) Top dog in Luleå's sleeping scene is the super-central, ultra-modern Clarion Sense. Popular with the business set (and anyone who's not averse to a bit of pampering), it offers generously proportioned rooms, all classic charcoals and creams with contemporary bold splashes of colour. The fitness centre and sauna seal the deal.

★ **Treehotel** BOUTIQUE HOTEL €€€
(070-572 77 52, 0928-104 03; www.treehotel. se; Edeforsväg 2 A, Harads; r 4700-7200kr; P) A spaceship suspended in the trees. A mirror cube reflecting sunlight and surrounding spruces. A giant bird's nest...The seven tree rooms that make up Sweden's most mind-boggling, award-winning lodgings sit just off Rte 97, about halfway between Luleå and Jokkmokk, in the midst of pristine forest. There are saunas and spas to relax stiff muscles after hiking, kayaking or dogsledding.

★ **Bastard Burgers** BURGERS €€
(http://bastardburgers.se; Stationsgatan 29; burgers from 109kr; 11am-8pm Mon-Thu, to 9pm Fri & Sat, noon-5pm Sun) Bastard Burgers is a big hit with locals in Luleå. While the signature burger is known as The Bastard, it goes international with the New York Original Streetburger, the Berlin Cheesedog (65kr) and the Chicago Beefdog (65kr). This is where it's at, with some top beers on offer, too.

★ **Hemmagastronomi** FUSION €€
(0920-22 00 02; www.hemmagastronomi.se; Norra Strandgatan 1; tapas from 75kr; 10am-10pm Mon-Sat) Is it a bakery? Is it a deli? Is it a bar? Is it a bistro? Hemmagastronomi wears many hats and we love them all. Come for a leisurely lunch, or for a bit of romance in the evening under dimmed lights over softshell-crab tapas and seafood platters, complemented by the wide-spanning wine list.

ℹ Information

Tourist Office (0920-45 70 00; www.lulea. nu; Skeppsbrogatan 17; 10am-6pm Mon-Fri, to 4pm Sat & Sun) Inside Kulturens Hus, a block down from Storgatan.

ℹ Getting There & Away

AIR

Luleå Airport (010-109 48 00; www.swedavia.se/lulea) is 10km southwest of the town centre. There are daily flights to Stockholm and Gothenburg. Bus 4 connects it to the city centre.

BUS

Buses 20 and 100 run north to Haparanda (190kr, 2½ hours) and south to Umeå (320kr, four to five hours), stopping at all the coastal towns. Bus 44 connects Luleå with Gällivare

(325kr, 3½ to 4½ hours) and Jokkmokk (245kr, three hours) up to five times daily.

TRAIN

There are overnight trains to Stockholm (840kr, 14 to 15 hours) via Gävle (same price, 11¾ to 12½ hours) and Uppsala (same price, 14 hours). Two daily trains connect Luleå with Narvik (Norway), 485kr, 7¼ to 8¼ hours) via Kiruna (295kr, 3¾ to 4¼ hours) and Abisko (472kr, 5½ to 6½ hours).

Arvidsjaur

0960 / POP 6529
If you've come from another town along the E45, Arvidsjaur, with its busy, bustling main street, will seem like a virtual metropolis. Established several centuries ago as a Sami marketplace and meeting spot, Arvidsjaur is home to a number of Sami families who still make a living from reindeer herding.

Between December and April dozens of test drivers from different car companies descend on the town to stage their own version of *Top Gear* – putting fast machines through their paces on the frozen lakes. This is also hiking, hunting and fishing country; outdoor enthusiasts use Arvidsjaur as a base for all sorts of activities.

◉ Sights & Activities

★ **Lappstaden** HISTORIC BUILDING
(Lappstadsgatan; tours 50kr; tours 6pm mid-Jun–mid-Aug) FREE The first church was built in Arvidsjaur in 1607, and church-attendance laws (urged by zealous priests and enforced by the monarchy) imposed a certain amount of pew time upon the nomadic Sami. To make their church visits manageable, they built small, square cottages with pyramid-shaped roofs (*gåhties*) for overnighting. Eighty *gåhties* are preserved here, just across Storgatan from the modern church.

★ **Sports Cars on Ice** SNOW SPORTS
(0960-137 20; www.laplandlodge.se; Östra Kyrkogatan 18; 3 hr ice driving 5900kr) These guys, based at Lapland Lodge, organise ice driving (three to six hours) in an Audi TT Quattro so you can be just like all those other test drivers in town who are working.

Nymånen Dogsledding SNOW SPORTS
(070-625 40 32; www.nymanen.com; per person from 1250kr) Go dog-sledding with one of the largest Siberian-husky kennels in Lapland, certified ecofriendly by Nature's Best.

🛏 Sleeping & Eating

★ Lapland Lodge
HOTEL €€

(☑0960-137 20; www.laplandlodge.se; Östra Kyrkogatan 18; B&B s/d/f 690/850/950kr, hotel s/d 1490/1890kr; P🐾) Next to the church, this friendly place offers a range of room configurations in a top location near the main street. Contemporary comforts sit amid antique style accented with old wooden skis, antlers and snowshoes. An outdoor hot tub and sauna are available, and snowmobile, ice-driving and husky-sledding tours run in winter.

Rent Your Own Island
CABIN €€

(☑070-573 37 36; http://natursafari.se; Pitevägen 41, Abborrträsk; per day/week 1600/9800kr) There are not too many opportunities to rent your own island with a log cabin, sauna, outdoor hot tub, boat transportation and fishing licence in Lapland. The cabin has two double and three single beds and is the perfect spot to get away from it all. The hot tub costs extra. It's available year-round, but email for up-to-date details.

★ Hans På Hörnet
CAFE €

(http://hanspahornet.blogspot.se; Storgatan 21; mains from 59kr; ⏰8.30am-5.30pm Mon-Fri, 10am-3pm Sat) This very local spot has a popular buffet lunch (90kr), and also serves up inexpensive salads, sandwiches and pies. This is the place to try *palt*, a Swedish meat-filled dumpling.

🛍 Shopping

★ Arctic Glass
GLASS

(☑0960-121 05; http://arcticglas.se; Renvallen 104; ⏰10am-6pm) Located 4km west of town on E45, this little place has refined glass products with Sami-inspired designs. There's some nice stuff on display and for sale, including candle holders, wine glasses, goblets, bowls and vases, mostly handmade on-site. About 200m down a side-road, look for signs so you won't miss it.

ℹ Information

Tourist Office (☑0960-175 00; www.arvidsjaur. se; Storgata 14b; ⏰10am-6pm Mon-Fri, 10am-4.30pm Sat & Sun Jun-Aug) On Storgatan, the town's main road. The staff are helpful here.

ℹ Getting There & Away

AIR

Arvidsjaur Airport (☑0960-173 80; www.ajr. nu), 11km east of the centre, has daily connections to Gällivare and Stockholm-Arlanda with Nextjet (www.nextjet.se). It also has direct winter connections with Stuttgart, Frankfurt-Hahn, Munich and Hanover with FlyCar (www.fly-car.de).

BUS

The bus station is at Västlundavägen, in the town centre. Useful bus routes include:

Bus 45 South to Östersund (440kr, 7¼ hours); north to Gällivare (311kr, 3¾ hours) via Jokkmokk (215kr, 2¼ hours)

Bus 104 To Arjeplog (130kr, one hour).

TRAIN

Arvidsjaur is connected by daily **Inlandsbanan** (p459) trains in summer to Östersund (728kr, 8¼ hours), Gällivare (420kr, 5¾ hours) and Jokkmokk (265kr, 3½ hours).

Jokkmokk

☑0971 / POP 2790

The capital of Sami culture, and the biggest handicraft centre in Lapland, Jokkmokk (meaning 'river bend' in Sami) not only has the definitive Sami museum but is also the site of a huge annual winter market gathering. Just north of the Arctic Circle, it's a tranquil place and the only town in Sweden that has a further-education college that teaches reindeer husbandry, craft making and ecology using the Sami language. Jokkmokk is a jumping-off point for visiting the four national parks that are part of the Laponia World Heritage Area and makes a great base for all manner of outdoor adventures year-round.

◉ Sights

★ Ájtte Museum
MUSEUM

(☑0971-170 70; www.ajtte.com; Kyrkogatan 3; adult/child 80/40kr; ⏰9am-6pm) This illuminating museum is Sweden's most thorough introduction to Sami culture. Follow the 'spokes' radiating from the central chamber, each dealing with a different theme – from traditional costume, silverware, creatures from Sami folk tales and 400-year-old painted shamans' drums, to replicas of sacrificial sites and a diagram explaining the uses and significance of various reindeer entrails. The beautifully showcased collection of traditional silver jewellery features heavy collars, now making a comeback among Sami women after a long absence.

★ Sameslöjdstiftelsen Sami Duodji
GALLERY

(☑0971-128 94; www.sameslojdstiftelsen.com; Porjusvägen 4; ⏰1-5.30pm) FREE This centrally located Sami gallery and crafts centre is your one-stop shop for diverse, authentic Sami handicrafts of the highest quality: from leatherwork, clothing in Sami colours and silver jewellery to bone-inlaid wood carvings and Sami knives in reindeer-antler sheaths. Most items are available for purchase.

Gamla Kyrkan　　　　　　CHURCH
(Old Church; Storgatan; ⊙10am-6pm) This octagonal red wooden church was built in 1976 to replace and replicate its 1753 predecessor that was destroyed by fire. The colour scheme is inspired by Sami clothing and the design reflects the Sami building style; in winter, the space between the timbers used to hold coffins awaiting the spring thaw, which allowed for graves to be dug.

🛏 Sleeping & Eating

STF Jokkmokk Vandrarhem　　HOSTEL €
(☑070-366 46 45; www.svenskaturistforeningen. se; Åsgatan 20; dm/s/d from 250/480/700kr; P@🕾) This family-run STF hostel has a lovely setting among green lawns and trees, right behind the tourist office. It's a creaky, cheerful old wooden house originally built for forestry workers nearly 100 years ago, with numerous bunk beds, compact private rooms, guest kitchen, TV lounge and basement sauna. Breakfast costs 90kr.

★**Hotell Akerlund**　　　　HOTEL €€
(☑0971-100 12; http://hotelakerlund.se; Herrevägen 1; s/d from1195/1395kr; P🕾) This pleasant central hotel rises above a slightly shabby outward appearance – it's coming up to 100 years as an inn – by having a very sharp lobby and rooms. After changing ownership and its name (formerly Hotel Gästis) in 2015, it underwent extensive renovations and is a top place to stay. The attached restaurant is shaped like a Sami *kåta* (hut).

★**Ájtte Museum Restaurant**　　SWEDISH €€
(www.ajtte.com/besoka/restaurang-ajtte; Kyrkogatan 3; lunch buffet 90kr, mains from 95kr; ⊙9am-6pm) This Sami restaurant makes it possible to enhance what you've learned about the local wildlife by sampling some of it – from *suovas* (smoked and salted reindeer meat) to reindeer steak and grouse with local berries. The weekday lunchtime buffet is very popular and serves home-style Swedish dishes.

❶ Information

Tourist Office (☑0971-222 50; www.destinationjokkmokk.se; Stortorget 4; ⊙9.30am-6.30pm Mon-Fri, 10am-5pm Sat & Sun) Very helpful staff. Stocks numerous brochures on activities and tours in the area.

❶ Getting There & Away

BUS

Buses arrive and leave from the bus station on Klockarvägen.

Bus 45 Connects Jokkmokk with Östersund (507kr, 9¾ hours) via Arvidsjaur (215kr, 2¼ hours). It also heads north to Gällivare (142kr, 1½ hours)

Bus 44 Runs to Luleå (237kr, 2¾ hours) via Gällivare (142kr, 1½ hours)

TRAIN

In the summer only, daily **Inlandsbanan trains** (p459) head south to Östersund (993kr, 12 hours) via Arvidsjaur (129kr, 3¾ hours) at 9.14am, and north to Gällivare (154kr, 2¼ hours) at 6.18pm.

Gällivare

☑0970 / POP 18,425

Gällivare (Váhtjer in Sami) and its northern twin, Malmberget, are surrounded by forest and dwarfed by the bald Dundret hill. After

---

JOKKMOKK WINTER MARKET

Winter travellers shouldn't miss the annual Sami **Jokkmokk Winter Market** (www. jokkmokksmarknad.se), held the first Thursday through Saturday in February. The oldest and biggest of its kind, it attracts some 30,000 people annually; it's like a yearly party for Sami traders to make contacts and see old friends, while visitors can splurge on the widest array of Sami *duodji* (handicrafts) in the country.

The event has been going strong since 1605, when King Karl IX decreed that markets should be set up all over in Lapland to increase taxes, spread Christianity and exert greater control over the nomadic Sami. The Winter Market is preceded by the opening of the smaller Historical Market and several days of folk music, plays, parades, local cinematography, photography exhibitions, food-tasting sessions and talks on different aspects of Sami life – all of which segues into the Winter Market itself. It's the most exciting (and coldest!) time to be in Jokkmokk, with temperatures as low as -40°C, so wrap up warm!

Kiruna, Malmberget (Ore Mountain) is the second-largest iron-ore mine in Sweden. And as with Kiruna, the area's sustaining industry is simultaneously threatening the town with collapse into a great big pit, so buildings are gradually being shifted to sturdier ground. Gällivare's biggest attractions are ore-oriented, and even if you don't descend into the subterranean gloom, a visit to Malmberget casts a melancholy spell – many of its houses have been abandoned in anticipation of their imminent destruction.

The strong Sami presence in Gällivare is reflected in its monuments. The bronze statue opposite the church, by local sculptor Berto Marklund, is called *Tre seitar* (*seite* being a Sami god of nature) and symbolises the pre-Christian Sami religion. The nearby granite sculpture *Same*, by Allan Wallberg, depicts a sitting Sami in North Kaitum costume.

◎ Sights & Activities

Laponia Visitor
Centre Gällivare   CULTURAL CENTRE
(📞0970-166 60; https://laponia.nu; ⊘9am-5pm Mon-Fri) FREE Upstairs in the train station and looked after by the tourist office, this lovely exhibition about Sami culture, specifically life in autumn, is well worth visiting. The displays and videos are insightful and the place has been beautifully set up. If the door isn't open, the helpful staff in the tourist office will unlock it for you.

Gällivare & Dundret Tour   TOURS
(adult/child 350/170kr) Dundret (823m) is a nature reserve with excellent views of the town, Malmberget and the Aitik copper mine, and a favourite spot for viewing the midnight sun. The tourist office organises three-hour tours (from 10pm early June through to the end of July) from the train station that take you through the past, present and future of Gällivare, and include refreshments.

🛏 Sleeping & Eating

★ Bed & Breakfast Gällivare   B&B €
(📞0970-156 56; www.bbgellivare.se; Laestadiusvägen 18; s/d/tr/q 585/685/980/1100kr; 🅿🛜) Marita's is a lovely spot atop a small hill, about an 800m (15-minute) walk north of the station. This two-storey B&B is her pride and joy and Marita loves chatting with her guests. Bathroom facilities are shared, but there's a generous buffet included in the reasonable rates, good wi-fi and free parking outside.

Quality Hotel
Grand Hotel Lapland   HOTEL €€€
(📞0970-77 22 90; www.nordicchoicehotels.com; Lasarettsgatan 1; s/d from 1540/1650kr; 🅿🛜🏊🎳) This modern, business set-oriented hotel opposite the train station is in a great location with gym, pool, bowling alley and steakhouse to complement its airy, comfortable rooms. The ground-level **Vassara Steakhouse** (mains from 245kr) is popular with locals and serves local specialities such as reindeer, Arctic char and cloudberry tiramisu.

Sofias Kök   SWEDISH €
(📞0970-554 50; www.sofiaskok.se; Storgatan 19; lunch buffet 95kr, mains from 80kr; ⊘10am-9pm Mon-Thu, 9.30am-3am Fri, noon-3am Sat, 1-9pm Sun) A very local spot for a good-value lunch buffet and Swedish standards such as chunky pea soup. In the evening you can nurse a pint with the local barflies.

❶ Information

Tourist Office (📞0970-166 60; www.gellivarelapland.se; Central Plan 4; ⊘7.30am-9pm daily late Jun-Aug, 9am-5pm Mon-Fri Sep-May) Inside the train station. Organises mine and midnight-sun tours and looks after the Laponia Visitor Centre Gällivare upstairs. Baggage storage available.

❶ Getting There & Away

AIR
Gällivare Lapland Airport is 7km east of the city and has flights to/from Stockholm-Arlanda.

BUS
Regional buses depart from the train station.
Bus 10 To Malmberget; departs from directly opposite the Gällivare church
Bus 45 Runs to Östersund (483kr, 11 hours) via Jokkmokk (also covered by bus 44, 142kr, 1½ hours) and Arvidsjaur (311kr, 3¾ hours)
Bus 44 Runs via Jokkmokk to Luleå (310kr, 3½ to 4¾ hours)
Bus 52 To Kiruna (180kr, 1¾ to two hours)

TRAIN
The **Inlandsbanan** (Inland Railway; www.inlandsbanan.se; ⊘mid-Jun–mid-Aug) train runs south to Östersund (507kr, 11¼ hours, one daily at 7.50am) via Jokkmokk (154kr, 1½ hours) and Arvidsjaur (420kr, 4½ hours).

Other departures include the westbound train to Narvik (360kr, 4¾ to 5¼ hours) via Kiruna (147kr, one to 1¼ hours) and Abisko (175kr, three hours), and the eastbound train to Luleå (258kr, 2½ to three hours).

SLEEP IN THE ICE AT JUKKASJÄRVI

The tiny village of Jukkasjärvi is 20km east of Kiruna, 200km north of the Arctic Circle, and is surrounded by lakes, fir trees and reindeer. It is also home to one of Sweden's most famous attractions: the extraordinary Icehotel. Aside from this blockbuster of a sight, though, this tiny village is well worth a stroll. The only road, Marknadsvägen, passes by some simple rustic homes that are still owned by local families (some of whom are somewhat bemused by the village's Icehotel fame). The street eventually peters out when it reaches the historic wooden church. It is remarkable that this village has remained charmingly unchanged, despite its fame as one of the most extraordinary holiday destinations in the world.

Every winter, from December onwards, the **Icehotel** (☑ 0980-668 00; www.icehotel. com; Marknadsvägen 63; s/d/ste from 2400/3300/5400kr, cabins from 2000kr; ☉ Dec-Apr; P 🤶) seems to grow organically from ice blocks taken from the Torne river, while international artists flock from all over to carve the ice sculptures that make its frozen rooms masterpieces. Snuggle up between reindeer furs on a bed of snow and ice in the igloo-like 'cold rooms'; thankfully, the bathrooms are heated...

From a humble start in 1989 as a small igloo, originally built by Yngve Bergqvist to house an art gallery, the Icehotel has grown into a building comprising an entrance hall and a main walkway lined with ice sculptures and lit with electric lights, with smaller corridors branching off towards the 67 suites. The beds are made of compact snow and covered with reindeer skins, and you are provided with sleeping bags used by the Swedish army for Arctic survival training, guaranteed to keep you warm despite the -5°C temperature inside the rooms (and in winter that's nothing – outside the hotel it can be as low as -30°C).

There are heated bathrooms near the reception, and you leave most of your possessions in lockers so that they don't freeze. Stuff your clothes into the bottom of your sleeping bag, otherwise they'll soon resemble a washboard. Come morning, guests are revived with a hot drink and a spell in the sauna. Guests spend just one night in the Icehotel itself (it's not a comfortable night's sleep for most), so the hotel provides 30 satellite Aurora Houses – bungalows decorated in contemporary Scandinavian style, with skylights for viewing the northern lights.

This custom-built 'igloo' also has an **Ice Church**, popular for weddings (giving new meaning to the expression 'cold feet')! Outside the winter season, the hotel offers tours (295kr) that initiate visitors into the process of building this unique hotel and include a visit to see the rooms in Icehotel 365. Opened in 2016 as a year-round 'ice experience', **Icehotel 365** (☑ 0980-668 00; www.icehotel.com; Jukkasjärvi; ste from 5500kr; P 🤶) is insulated, allowing the frigid rooms to house ice sculptures and an ice bar, even in summer.

Winter adventures on offer include snowmobile safaris, skiing, ice-fishing, dog-sledding (you can even arrange a dog-sled pick-up from the airport!), Sami culture tours and northern-lights safaris, while summer activities comprise hiking, rafting, paddleboarding, canoeing, fishing and all-terrain-buggy tours.

Kiruna

☑ 0980 / POP 22,900

Scarred by mine works, the 'current' Kiruna may not be the most aesthetically appealing city, but it's a friendly place with the highest concentration of lodgings and restaurants in the northwestern corner of Sweden. Its proximity to great stretches of hikeable wilderness and the proliferation of winter activities make it an excellent base.

The citizens of Kiruna (Giron in Sami) have for many years had to live with the news that their city is on the verge of collapsing into an enormous iron mine. Fortunately a solution is under way: the building of a new city 3km to the east, largely funded by the mining company. Although just about the entire existing central city will be demolished, both the historic church and clock tower will be moved. To see what the new city will look like in 2033, check out the excellent model, plans and pics at the tourist office.

🏃 Activities

Active Lapland　　　　　　　SNOW SPORTS
(☑ 076-104 55 08; www.activelapland.com; Solbacksvägen 22; tours from 1250kr) This experienced operator offers 2½-hour dog-sled rides (1250kr), rides under the northern

lights (highly recommended), and airport pick-ups by dog sleigh (5400kr). They'll even let you drive your own dog-sled (3200kr).

A City on the Move
GUIDED TOUR

(☑070-578 04 98; www.kirunastorytelling.se; adult/youth 450/250kr; ☺10am & 2pm Mon-Fri) This 2½-hour guided tour by minibus takes visitors through 'the move', visiting the oldest parts of town that are due to disappear and the new centre of Kiruna, 3km to the east. The starting point is Kiruna tourist office; you'll need to pre-book.

Kiruna Guidetur
OUTDOORS

(☑0980-811 10; www.kirunaguidetur.com; Vänortsgatan 8) These popular all-rounders organise anything from overnighting in a self-made igloo, snowmobile safaris and cross-country skiing outings in winter, to overnight mountain-bike tours, rafting and quad-biking in summer. Book via the website, or visit the shop on the main square.

⭐ Festivals & Events

Kiruna Festival
MUSIC

(http://kirunafestivalen.nu; ☺late Jun-early Jul) The big one of the Kiruna party scene, this four-day music festival features top acts in late June or early July.

Snöfestivalen
ART, CULTURAL

(Kiruna Snow Festival; www.snofestivalen.com) In the last week of January, this festival is focused on snow sculpting. The tradition began in 1985 as a space-themed snow-sculpture contest to celebrate the launching of a rocket from nearby space base, Esrange. It now draws artists from all over to create ever more elaborate and beautiful shapes. The festival also features Sami reindeer-sled racing and other activities.

🛏 Sleeping & Eating

⭐ SPiS Hotel & Hostel
HOSTEL €

(☑0980-170 00; www.spiskiruna.se; Bergmästaregatan 7; dm/d from 305/535kr, hotel s/d 995/1195kr; P 🛜) This catch-all hotel-and-hostel combo features modern hotel rooms and cosy dorms in central Kiruna. There's a deli, bakery and top-quality restaurant as part of the complex, plus a handy communal guest kitchen and an even handier supermarket just a few minutes' stroll away. Look for the orange building.

⭐ Hotel Arctic Eden
BOUTIQUE HOTEL €€

(☑0980-611 86; www.hotelarcticeden.se; Föregatan 18; s/d 1000/1300kr; P 🛜 🏊) At Kiru-

na's fanciest lodgings the rooms are a chic blend of Sami decor and modern technology; there's a plush spa and indoor pool, and the friendly staff can book all manner of outdoor adventures. A Sami-inspired, family-owned place, it has a fine restaurant and an excellent handicraft store. Part of the complex, the Arctic Thai & Grill is flooded with customers.

⭐SPiS
SWEDISH €€

(☑0980-170 00; www.spiskiruna.se; Bergmästaregatan 7; mains from 185kr) With a top deli and bakery, breakfast and lunch buffets, and a quality dinner menu, SPiS is considered the best place to eat in Kiruna. The restaurant has won numerous awards and its four-/five-course menus (565/755kr) with wine pairings are the way to go. The Meat Locker has amazing options including the 500g entrecôte (495kr).

⭐ Camp Ripan Restaurang
SWEDISH €€

(☑0980-630 00; www.ripan.se; Campingvägen 5; lunch buffet weekday/weekend 100/125kr, dinner mains from 175kr; ☺11am-2pm & 6-9.30pm Mon-Fri, noon-2pm & 6-9.30pm Sat & Sun; P 🛜 🍴) The lunch buffet is good value, but the real draw is the Sami-inspired à la carte menu featuring local, seasonal produce. The restaurant, located at the local campground, hosts regular culinary events, like a four-course meal with drinks accompanied by a spellbinding northern lights slide show, as well as cookery demonstrations.

ℹ Information

Tourist Office (☑0980-188 80; www.kirunalapland.se; Lars Janssonsgatan 17; ☺8.30am-6pm Mon-Fri, to 4pm Sat & Sun) Inside the Folkets Hus visitor centre; has internet access and can book various tours.

ℹ Getting There & Away

AIR

Kiruna Airport (☑010-109 46 00; www.swedavia.com/kiruna), 7km east of the town, has flights to Stockholm (two to three daily), as well as several weekly flights to Luleå and Umeå. The **airport bus** (one way 110kr) is timed to meet Stockholm flights and runs between the tourist office and the airport during peak season.

BUS

Buses depart from the centrally located **bus station** (☑980-124 00; www.ltnbd.se/kiruna; Hjalmar Lundbohmsvägen 45; ☺7am-4pm Mon-Fri).

Bus 91 Runs to Narvik (Norway; 320kr, 2¾ hours) via Abisko (210kr, 1¼ hours) and Riksgränsen (240kr, two hours)

Bus 50 To Jukkasjärvi (48kr, 30 minutes)
Bus 10 & 52 To Gällivare (195kr, 1¾ hours)

TRAIN

Kiruna station has been closed and torn down. The 'Temporary Station' is a make-do affair a couple of kilometres to the north of the old station. There is a daily overnight train to Stockholm (from 696kr, 17½ hours) that departs at 4pm. Other destinations include Narvik (Norway; 227kr, 3½ to 3¾ hours) via Abisko (199kr, 1½ to two hours), Luleå (385kr, 4¼ hours) and Gällivare (139kr, 1¼ hours).

Abisko

📞 0980 / POP 85

Easy access to spectacular scenery makes Abisko (Ábeskovvu in Sami) one of the highlights of any trip to Lapland. The 75-sq-km Abisko National Park spreads out from the southern shore of scenic lake Torneträsk. It's framed by the striking profile of Lapporten, a 'gate' formed by neighbouring hills that serves as the legendary gate to Lapland. This is also the driest part of Sweden and consequently has a relatively long hiking season. In winter, people come to see the northern lights; in summer they come to hike and to see the midnight sun.

⊙ Sights & Activities

Hiking is the big draw here – trails are varied in both distance and terrain, and while most people come here to tackle part (or all) of the 450km-long Kungsleden, there are plenty of shorter rambles.

Excellent day hikes include the 8km hike to the Kårsa rapids, over the Ábeskoeatnu river and then along the left fork of the signposted Kårsavagge (Gorsavággi in Sami) trail through birch and pine forest, and the great 14km, four-hour return hike along the Paddus nature trail, past an STF reconstruction of a traditional Sami camp. It leads to Báddosdievvá, a former Sami sacrificial site with awesome views of Lapporten and lake Törnetrask.

Longer hikes include the trip to the Gorsajökeln glacier, staying overnight at the STF hut at the heart of the Kårsavagge valley, west of Abisko (15km each way), and the 39km-long Rallarvägen (Navvy Rd) to Riksgränsen, running parallel to the railway line and used by railway construction workers in the early 20th century. A good side venture from Rallarvägen is the 10km return trip to the enormous boulders and impressive rock formations of Kärkevagge (Gearggevággi)

valley from Låktatjåkka (short train/bus ride from Abisko). Trollsjön (Rissájáurre), the 'Sulphur Lake', is at the end of the valley, its clear blue waters named after the colour of burning sulphur.

For hikes in this area, employ maps *Fjällkartan BD6* or *Calazo Kungsleden* (120kr), both available at the STF lodge and Naturum.

★**Aurora Sky Station**   VIEWPOINT
(www.auroraskystation.se; ⊙9pm-1am Dec-Mar, 9.30am-4pm Jun-Sep & 10pm-1am Tue, Thu & Sat mid-Jun–mid-Jul) Across the highway from the STF Turiststation, a chairlift takes you up Mt Nuolja (1164m), where you can enjoy epic views from the deck of the Panorama Café. In summer this is a prime spot from which to see the midnight sun – the lift is open 10pm to 1am three days per week in June and July. In winter, come to view the northern lights.

Lights Over Lapland   TOURS
(📞0760-754 300; www.lightsoverlapland.com; 3hr photography tours 1195kr, 4-day expeditions 18,500kr) If you've always dreamed of chasing the northern lights with a camera in hand, here's your opportunity to learn from a professional photographer. Tours range from nightly photo excursions departing from STF Abisko to four-day expeditions that comprise dog-sledding, gourmet meals, Icehotel visits and accommodation at STF Abisko.

🛏 Sleeping & Eating

★**STF Abisko Turiststation
& Abisko Mountain Station**   HOSTEL €
(📞0980-402 00; www.abisko.nu; hostel dm/tw 295/885kr, hotel d 1540kr; ⊙year-round; 🅿🛜🐾) This 350-bed place overlooking Torneträsk lake is a massive hiker destination. There's huge demand for the excellent facilities: guest kitchens, a basement sauna, a supply shop and an excellent restaurant. There are single and twin rooms in the main building, two- and four-bed rooms in the Youth Hostel Keron (shared shower and toilet) and cabins with private facilities for self-caterers.

Abisko.net   HOSTEL €
(📞0980-401 03; www.abisko.net; Lapportsv 34A; dm/d from 250/600kr; 🅿🛜) This friendly backpackers' delight is spread over two buildings, with comfortable doubles and dorms with wide bunks, sharing guest kitchens and a wonderful sauna. Brothers Tomas and Andreas keep a large team of sled dogs;

dog-sledding, snowmobiling, ice-fishing, snowshoe tours and northern lights tours are all available here. Cross under the railway tracks 150m east of Abisko Östra station.

❶ Information

Naturum (📞 0980-788 60; www.national-parksofsweden.se; ⊙ 9am-6pm Tue-Sat early Jul-Sep & Feb-Apr) Effectively the national park visitors centre, the Naturum has detailed exhibitions, a reference library, maps and booklets for sale and extensive information on the Kungsleden. Helpful staff are happy to answer questions and make suggestions based on the amount of time you have.

❶ Getting There & Away

BUS

Buses stop at Abisko Östra (main village) and Abisko Turiststation – the start of the Kungsleden – five minutes apart. Bus 91 runs southeast to Kiruna (175kr, 1¼ hours) and west to Narvik (Norway; 185kr, 1½ hours).

CAR

It's a 94km drive from Kiruna to Abisko, taking about an hour in summer driving conditions.

TRAIN

Abisko has two train stops: Östra station puts you in the centre of tiny Abisko village, 2km to the east and outside of the national park, while Abisko Turiststation is across the highway from the Naturum, inside the national park.

Trains run to Kiruna (125kr, 1¼ hours) and to Narvik (120kr, 1¾ hours).

Kungsleden

Kungsleden (King's Trail) is Sweden's most important hiking and skiing route. It runs for around 450km from Abisko in the north to Hemavan in the south, through Sami herding lands consisting of spectacular mountainous wilderness that includes Sweden's highest mountain, Kebnekaise (2111m), fringed with forests, speckled with lakes and ribboned with rivers.

The route is split into five mostly easy or moderate sections, with Svenska Turistföreningen (STF: Swedish Tourist Association) mountain huts (www.swedishtouristas-sociation.com; dm from 360kr, sites 100kr; ⊙ late Feb-early May & late Jun–mid-Sep), each staffed by a custodian, spaced out along the route. They are 10km to 20km from one another (first come, first served), and there are four STF mountain lodges and two hostels en

route. Many of the mountain huts sell provisions (check which ones on the website), and kitchen facilities are provided, but you'll need your own sleeping bag and there's no electricity. The section between Kvikkjokk and Ammarnäs is not covered by the STF, so you'll need to be prepared to camp.

Insect repellent is a must in summer to avoid becoming a walking mosquito buffet, and you have to be prepared for changeable weather.

Abisko to Kebnekaise

From Abisko it's 86km to Kebnekaise Fjällstation (around five days of hiking), and 105km to Nikkaluokta if you're leaving the trail at Kebnekaise (around seven days).

This, the most popular section of the Kungsleden, runs through the dense vegetation of Abisko National Park, mostly following the valley, with wooden boardwalks over the boggy sections and bridges over streams. The highest point along the trail is the Tjäkta Pass (1150m), with great views over the Tjäktavagge valley.

There are five STF huts along the trail: Abiskojaure (in a lovely lakeside setting), Alesjaure (with a sauna and a great view from the mountain ridge), Tjäkta (before Tjäkta Pass), Sälka and Singi. The STF has mountain lodges at Abisko (p462) and **Kebnekaise** (📞 0980-550 00; www.svenskaturistforeningen.se/kebnekaise; dm/d/q 420/1550/2100kr; ⊙ mid-Feb–early May & mid-Jun–mid-Sep; 🛜).

Kebnekaise to Saltoluokta

This section is 52km (four to six days) from Kebnekaise Fjällstation and 38km from Singi to Saltoluokta.

South of Singi, 14km from Kebnekaise, this quieter section of the trail runs through peaceful valleys and beech forest. Row yourself 1km across Teusajaure lake and then cross the bare plateau before descending to Vakkotavare through beech forest.

A bus runs from Vakkotavare to the quay at Kebnats, where there's an STF ferry across Langas lake to Saltoluokta Fjällstation. STF has a mountain lodge at **Saltoluokta** (📞 0973-410 10; www.swedishtour-istassociation.com/facilities/stf-saltoluokta-moun-tain-station; dm/s/d from 345/545/760kr; ⊙ Mar-Apr & mid-Jun–mid-Sep; 🛜), and four huts en route, at Singi, Kaitumjaure, Teusajaure and Vakkotavare.

Saltoluokta to Kvikkjokk

This section is 73km, or four to six days of hiking. From Saltoluokta, it's a long and relatively steep climb to Sitojaure (18km, six hours), where you cross a lake using the boat service run by the hut's caretaker, followed by a boggy stretch with wooden walkways. At Aktse (an excellent base for side trips into Sarek National Park), on the shores of Laitaure lake, you are rewarded with expansive views of the bare mountainous terrain, before you cross the lake using the row boats provided and pass through pine forest to reach Kvikkjokk.

STF has a lodge at **Kvikkjokk** (☑0971-210 22; http://kvikkjokkfjallstation.se; dm/s/d from 365/695/960kr; ☺mid-Feb–May & mid-Jun–Oct; **P 🕏**), and huts at Sitojaure, Aktse and Pårte.

Kvikkjokk to Ammarnäs

This is the wildest and most difficult section of the park, recommended for experienced hikers only. It stretches for 157km, or seven to 10 days of hiking. Bring your own tent, as accommodation is very spread out.

Take the boat across Saggat lake from Kvikkjokk before walking to Tsielejåkk, from where it's 55km to the next hut at Vuonatjviken. Then cross Riebnesjaure lake and another one from Hornavan to the village of Jäkkvikk, from where the trail runs through Pieljekaise National Park. From Jäkkvikk it's only 8km until the next hut, followed by another stop at the village of Adolfström. Cross Iraft lake before making for the cabins at Sjnjultje. Here the trail forks: either take the direct 34km route to Ammarnäs or take a 24km detour to Rävfallet, followed by an additional 20km to Ammarnäs.

Ammarnäs to Hemavan

This section is 78km, or four to six days' hiking. Much of the southern section of the Kungsleden runs through Vindelfjällen Nature Reserve. This trail is the easiest of the five sections, mostly consisting of a gentle ramble through beech forest and wetlands, and over low hills. There's a long, steep climb (8km) through beech forest between Ammarnäs and Aigert, but at the top you are rewarded with an impressive waterfall.

To reach Syter, cross the wetlands using the network of bridges, stopping at the hut by Tärnasjö lake for a spell in the sauna. The hike up to Syter peak (1768m) from Syter hut is greatly recommended and the view on the way down to Hemavan, taking in Norway's Okstindarnas glaciers, is particularly spectacular.

STF has a hostel at **Hemavan** (☑0954-300 02; www.svenskaturistforeningen.se/hemavan; r from 460kr; **P @ 🗷 🕏**), and five huts en route at Aigert, Serve, Tärnasjö, Syter and Viterskalet.

🛈 Getting There & Away

The Kungsleden is reasonably straightforward to access from its most popular entry points, but if you're aiming for a remoter part of the trail, you may have to contend with limited (or, outside peak season, practically nonexistent) bus services.

Frequent trains stop at Abisko en route from Kiruna to Narvik (Norway). **Inlandsbanan** (p459) trains stop at Storuman (for Hemavan), Sorsele, Arvidsjaur (for Arjeplog), Jokkmokk and Gällivare in summer.

There are bus routes to other starting points along the Kungsleden:

Kiruna–Nikkaluokta Bus 92 (110kr, 70 minutes, two daily)

Gällivare–Ritsem via Kebnats and Vakkotavare Bus 93 (200kr, 3¼ hours, daily)

Jokkmokk–Kvikkjokk Buses 47 and 94 (178kr, 2¼ hours, daily)

Arjeplog–Jäkkvik Bus 104 (105kr, 1¼ hours, daily on weekdays)

Sorsele–Ammarnäs Bus 341 (119kr, 1¼ hours, one to three daily)

Umeå–Hemavan via Tärnaby Bus 31 (275kr, 5¼ hours, one to three daily)

Kallax Flyg helicopters (☑0980-810 00; www.kallaxflyg.se; adult/2-11yr 850/500kr) transport hikers twice daily between Nikkaluokta and Kebnekaise from late June to late August and daily until late September, while **Fiskflyg** (www.fiskflyg.se; Strömgatan 43, Porjus; adult/child under 7yr 1250/625kr) has helicopter flights from Kvikkjokk. If you wish to be dropped off in a wilderness location of your choice, that can also be arranged.

UNDERSTAND SWEDEN

History

Sweden's history can be seen as a play in three acts.

Act I Fur-clad hunter-gatherers – the predecessors of the Sami – are followed by the Vikings' raiding and plundering, only to be subdued by the Christians.

Act II The action is split between the court and the battlefield. Royal dynasties follow one another in rapid succession: there's fratricide by poisoned pea soup; an androgynous girl-king; a king is assassinated at a masked ball and another during battle. Sweden's territory expands and then rapidly contracts.

Act III Sweden is largely untouched by the turmoil of the world wars and focuses on improving the lives of its own citizens before turning its sights to the rest of the world. Sweden welcomes scores of refugees and the homogenous-looking cast quickly becomes a diverse one.

From First Settlement to Christianity

Around 9000 BC, hunter-gatherers followed the retreating ice into Sweden.

By 600 AD, the Svea people of the Mälaren valley (just west of Stockholm) had gained supremacy, and their kingdom, Svea Rike, gave the country of Sweden its name: Sverige.

The Viking Age was under way by the 9th century, and initial hit-and-run raids along the European coast were followed by major military expeditions, settlement and trade.

Stubbornly pagan for many centuries, Sweden turned to Christianity in the 10th century and by 1160, King Erik Jedvarsson (Sweden's patron saint, St Erik) had virtually wiped out paganism.

Intrigue & Empire-Building

In 1319 Sweden and Norway were united as one kingdom. But after the Black Death in 1350 created a shortage of candidates for the throne, Denmark intervened and, together with Norway, joined Sweden in the Union of Kalmar in 1397, resulting in Danish monarchs on the Swedish throne.

A century of Swedish nationalist grumblings erupted in rebellion under the young nobleman Gustav Vasa. Crowned Gustav I in 1523, he introduced the Reformation and a powerful, centralised nation state. The resulting period of expansion gave Sweden control over much of Finland and the Baltic countries. Gustav Vasa's sons did not get on – to the point that Johan dispatched his brother, King Erik, to the afterlife via some poisoned soup.

The last of the Vasa dynasty – Kristina – was a tomboy and a willful, controversial character who eventually abdicated the throne in 1654 and fled to Rome, dressed as a man.

King Karl XII's adventures in the early 18th century cost Sweden its Baltic territories. The next 50 years saw greater parliamentary power, but Gustav III led a coup that brought most of the power back to the crown. An aristocratic revolt in 1809 fixed that (and lost Finland to Russia). The constitution produced in that year divided legislative powers between king and *riksdag* (parliament).

During a gap in royal succession, Swedish agents chose Napoleon's marshal Jean-Baptiste Bernadotte (renamed Karl Johan) as regent. He became king of Norway and Sweden in 1818, and the Bernadotte dynasty still holds the Swedish monarchy.

World Wars & Beyond

In spite of rapid industrialisation, around one million Swedes fled poverty for a brighter future in America in the late 19th and early 20th centuries. Sweden declared herself neutral in 1912, and remained so throughout the bloodshed of WWI. Swedish neutrality during WWII was ambiguous: letting German troops march through to occupy Norway and selling iron ore to both warring sides tarnished Sweden's image, leading to a crisis of conscience at home and international criticism.

At the same time, Sweden was a haven for refugees from Finland, Norway, Denmark and the Baltic states; for downed allied aircrew who escaped the Gestapo; and for many thousands of Jews who escaped persecution and death.

Throughout the 1950s and 1960s the Social Democrats continued with the creation of folkhemmet (the welfare state), with the introduction of unemployment benefits, childcare and paid holidays. The standard of living for ordinary Swedes rose rapidly.

NOBEL ACHIEVEMENTS

In his will, Alfred Nobel (1833–96), the inventor of dynamite, used his vast fortune to establish the Nobel Institute and the international prizes in 1901. This idea was reportedly sparked by an erroneous report in a French newspaper, a premature obituary in which the writer condemned Nobel for his explosive invention ('the merchant of death is dead,' it declared). Prizes are awarded annually for physics, chemistry, medicine and literature, as well as the Peace Prize. An awards ceremony is held in Stockholm on 10 December, while the Peace Prize is awarded in Oslo in the presence of the King of Norway.

Recent Years

World recession of the early 1990s forced a massive devaluation of the Swedish krona, and with both their economy and national confidence shaken, Swedes voted narrowly in favour of joining the European Union (EU) in 1995. Since then, Sweden's economy has improved considerably, with falling unemployment and inflation. A 2003 referendum on whether Sweden should adopt the euro resulted in a 'no' vote.

The global economic crisis again affected Sweden towards the end of 2008. As ever, economic tensions fed social anxieties. An annual survey about ethnic diversity, conducted by Uppsala University researchers, indicated twice as many Swedes had an 'extremely negative' attitude towards racial diversity in 2008 than in 2005.

Sweden has been embroiled in the extradition scandal involving Wikileaks founder Julian Assange. Wanted in Sweden on sexual assault charges, Assange has opted to take refuge in the Ecuador embassy in London, as the Swedish courts cannot guarantee that he would then not be turned over to the Americans afterwards.

People

With 9.6 million people spread over the third-largest area in Western Europe, Sweden has one of the lowest population densities on the continent. Most Swedes live in the large cities of Stockholm, Göteborg, Malmö and Uppsala. Conversely, the interior of Norrland is sparsely populated.

The majority of Sweden's population is considered to be of Nordic stock, and about 30,000 Finnish speakers form a substantial minority in the northeast, near Torneälven (the Torne river). More than 180,000 citizens of other Nordic countries live in Sweden.

Around 20% of Sweden's population are either foreign born or have at least one non-Swedish parent. The 10 largest immigrant groups are from Finland, former Yugoslavia, Iraq, Poland, Iran, Germany, Denmark, Norway, Turkey and Somalia, and there are around 45,000 Roma.

Swedish music stars José González and Salem Al Fakir and film director Josef Fares are testament to Sweden's increasingly multicultural make-up. Some 200 languages are now spoken in Sweden.

Sweden first opened its borders to mass immigration during WWII. At the time it was a closed society, and new arrivals were initially expected to assimilate and 'become Swedish'. In 1975 parliament adopted a new set of policies that emphasised the freedom to preserve and celebrate traditional native cultures.

Not everyone in Sweden is keen on this idea, with random hate crimes – including the burning down of a Malmö mosque in 2004 – blemishing the country's reputation for tolerance. As hip-hop artist Timbuktu (himself the Swedish-born son of a mixedrace American couple) told the *Washington Post*, 'Sweden still has a very clear picture of what a Swede is. That no longer exists – the blond, blue-eyed physical traits. That's changing. But it still exists in the minds of some people.'

Gender equality has made great inroads in Swedish society, with plenty of childcare leave allocated to both parents, and legislation in place to prevent sexual discrimination.

Arts

Design

Sweden is a living gallery of inspired design, from Jonas Bohlin 'Tutu lamps' to Tom Hedquist milk cartons. While simplicity still defines the Nordic aesthetic, new designers are challenging Scandi functionalism with bold, witty work. A claw-legged 'Bird Table' by Broberg Ridderstråle and a table made entirely of ping-pong balls by Don't Feed the Swedes are two examples of playful creations from design collectives such as Folkform, DessertDesign and Defyra.

Aesthetic prowess also fuels Sweden's thriving fashion scene. Since the late 1990s and continuing today, local designers have aroused global admiration: Madonna dons Patrik Söderstam trousers, and Acne Jeans sell like hot cakes at LA's hip Fred Segal. In fact, these days Sweden is exporting more fashion than pop.

Pop Music

Any survey of Swedish music must at least mention ABBA, the iconic, dubiously outfitted winners of the 1974 Eurovision Song Contest (with 'Waterloo'). More current Swedish successes are pop icon Robyn, indie melody-makers Peter Björn & John, and the exquisitely mellow José González, whose cover of the Knife's track 'Heartbeats' catapulted the Gothenburg native to international stardom. Other Swedish exports include Roxette, The Hives, Mando Diao, The Cardigans, Kent, Lisa Ekdahl, The Hellacopters, Nicolai Dunger and Ace of Base, while Swedish songwriters and producers have been sought after by the likes of JLo and Madonna.

Environment

Sweden occupies the eastern side of the Scandinavian peninsula, sharing borders with Norway, Finland and Denmark (the latter a mere 4km to the southwest of Sweden and joined to it by a spectacular bridge and tunnel).

Sweden's surface area (450,000 sq km) is stretched long and thin. Around one-sixth of the country lies within the Arctic Circle, yet Sweden is surprisingly warm thanks to the Gulf Stream: minimum northern temperatures are around –20°C (compared with –45°C in Alaska).

The country has a 7000km-long coastline, with myriad islands – the Stockholm archipelago alone has up to 24,000. The largest and most notable islands are Gotland and

THE SAMI IN SWEDEN

Europe's only indigenous people, the ancestors of the Sami migrated to the north of present-day Scandinavia, following the path of the retreating ice, and lived by hunting reindeer in the area spanning from Norway's Atlantic coast to the Kola Peninsula in Russia, collectively known as Sápmi. By the 17th century, the depletion of reindeer herds had transformed the hunting economy into a nomadic herding economy. Until the 1700s, the Sami lived in siida – village units or communities, migrating for their livelihoods, but only within their own defined areas. Those areas were recognised and respected by the Swedish government until colonisation of Lapland began in earnest and the Sami found their traditional rights and livelihoods threatened both by the settlers and by the establishment of borders between Sweden, Norway, Finland and Russia.

Sweden's Sami population numbers around 15,000 to 20,000, and there are 10 Sami languages spoken across Sápmi, which belong to the Finno-Ugrian language group and are not related to any Scandinavian language. Sami education is now available in government-run Sami schools or regular municipal schools. Of the 6000 or so Sami who still speak their mother tongue, 5000 speak the North Sami dialect.

Sami beliefs and mythology have traditionally revolved around nature, with the noaidi (shamans) bridging the gap between the physical and the spiritual worlds. From 1685, the Sami were forcibly converted to Christianity and Sweden's policies regarding the Sami were tinted with social Darwinism, deeming them to be an inferior race fit only for reindeer herding, up until after WWII, when the Sami began to actively participate in the struggle for their rights, forming numerous associations and pressure groups.

The Sami in Sweden are represented by the Samediggi (Sami parliament), which oversees community matters and acts in an advisory capacity to the Swedish government, though it does not have the power to make decisions regarding land use. The Swedish state is yet to ratify the International Labour Organisation's Convention 169, which would recognise the Sami as an aboriginal people with property rights, as opposed to just an ethnic minority.

From the 1970s onwards, there has been a revival of traditional Sami handicraft, such as leatherwork, textiles, knife-making, woodwork and silverwork. Since then, high-quality Sami handwork that uses traditional designs and materials has borne the Sami Duodji trademark and can be found all over Lapland.

The booklet *The Saami – People of the Sun & Wind*, published by Ájtte, the Swedish Mountain and Saami Museum in Jokkmokk, is a fantastic introduction to the Sami and is available at tourist shops around the area. Visit Sápmi (p462) is an excellent resource for all things Sami. Also, look for the 'Naturens Bäst' logo, which indicates that an excursion or organisation has been approved by Svenska Ekoturismföreningen (www.ekoturism. org), the country's first ecotourism regulating body.

Öland on the southeast coast, and the best sandy beaches are down the west coast, south of Gothenburg.

Forests take up nearly 60% of Sweden's landscape and the land is dotted with around 100,000 lakes. Vänern is the largest lake in Western Europe, at 5585 sq km. Kebnekaise (2111m), part of the glaciated Kjölen Mountains along the Norwegian border, is the highest mountain in Sweden. The southern part of the country is mostly farmland.

Wildlife

Thanks to Sweden's geographical diversity, it has a great variety of European animals, birds and plants. The big carnivores – bear, wolf, wolverine, lynx and golden eagle – are all protected species. The elk (moose in North America), a gentle, knobby-kneed creature that grows up to 2m tall, is the symbol of Sweden. Elk are a serious traffic hazard, particularly at night: they can dart out in front of your car at up to 50km/h. Around 260,000 domesticated reindeer, also no fun to run into on a highway, roam the northern areas under the watchful eyes of Sami herders. The musk ox is another large herbivore. Forests, lakes and rivers support beaver, otter, mink, badger and pine marten, and hundreds of bird species (including numerous sea birds) populate the country.

National Parks

Sweden had the distinction of being the first country in Europe to establish a national park (1909). There are now 29, along with around 2600 smaller nature reserves; together they cover about 9% of the country. The organisation Naturvårdsverket (www.swedishepa.se) oversees and produces pamphlets about the parks in Swedish and English, along with the excellent book *National-parkerna i Sverige* (National Parks in Sweden). Four of Sweden's large rivers (Kalixälven, Piteälven, Vindelälven and Torneälven) have been declared National Heritage Rivers in order to protect them from hydroelectric development.

Environmental Issues

Ecological consciousness in Sweden is very high and reflected in concern for native animals, clean water and renewable resources.

Swedes are fervent believers in sorting and recycling household waste – you'll be expected to do the same in hotels, hostels and camping grounds. Most plastic bottles and cans can be recycled in supermarkets with around Skr1 returned per item.

Two organisations that set standards for labelling products as ecologically sound are the food-focused KRAV (www.krav.se), a member of the International Federation of Organic Agriculture Movements, and Swan (www.svanen.se), which has a wider scope and certifies entire hotels and hostels.

Linked to the environmental concerns is the challenge of protecting the cultural heritage of the Sami people. The harnessing of rivers can have massive (negative) impact on what has historically been Sami territory, whether by flooding reindeer feeding grounds or by diverting water and drying up river valleys. In general, the mining, forestry and space industries have wreaked havoc on Sami homelands.

Food & Drink

Epicureans around the world are smitten with Sweden's new-generation chefs and their inventive creations. Current luminaries include Bocuse d'Or recipient Mathias Dahlgren, TV chef Niklas Ekstedt and New York–based Marcus Samuelsson.

Staples & Specialities

While new-school Swedish cuisine thrives on experimentation, it retains firm roots in Sweden's culinary heritage. Even the most avant-garde chefs admire simple, old-school *husmanskost* (plain cuisine) such as *toast skagen* (toast with bleak roe, *crème fraiche* and chopped red onion) and *köttbullar och potatis* (meatballs and potatoes, usually served with lingonberry jam, or *lingonsylt*). Seafood staples include caviar, gravlax (cured salmon) and the ubiquitous *sill* (herring), eaten smoked, fried or pickled and often accompanied by capers, mustard and onion. The most contentious traditional food is the pungent *surström-ming* (fermented Baltic herring), traditionally eaten in August and September in a slice of *tunnbröd* (thin, unleavened bread) with boiled potato and onions and ample amounts of *snaps*.

In the north of Sweden, the bounty of the wilderness enhances the menu, from reindeer and elk steak and Arctic char (fish) to mushrooms and berries (including cloudberry-based desserts).

Where to Eat & Drink

Most hotels and some hostels provide breakfast buffets laden with cereals and yoghurt plus bread, fruit, cold cuts, cheese and the like. Sweden is the inventor of the smörgåsbord – a vast buffet of Swedish specialities and served as brunch in many establishments. Many cafes and restaurants offer a daily lunch special called *dagens rätt* or *dagens* lunch (main course, salad, bread, cold drink and coffee) at a fixed price between 11.30am and 2pm, which makes it considerably cheaper to eat out in the middle of the day than in the evenings.

To counter the mid-afternoon slump, Swedes enjoy *fika*, an almost mandatory coffee break. *Konditori* are old-fashioned bakery-cafes where you can get a pastry or a *smörgås* (sandwich), but there are also many stylish, modern cafes where you can enjoy people-watching over pricier Italian coffees, gourmet salads, bagels and muffins.

Pure vegetarian restaurants (especially buffets) are increasingly common, and there will usually be at least one vegetarian main-course option on the menu at ordinary restaurants.

Drinking

Lättöl (light beer, less than 2.25% alcohol) and *folköl* (folk beer, 2.25% to 3.5% alcohol) can be bought in *mataffär* (supermarkets) everywhere. *Mellanöl* (medium-strength beer, 3.6% to 4.5% alcohol), *starköl* (strong beer, over 4.5% alcohol) and wines and spirits can be bought only at outlets of the state-owned alcohol store – Systembolaget – which is open until about 6pm on weekdays and slightly shorter hours on Saturday.

Sweden's trademark spirit, *brännvin*, also called aquavit and drunk as *snaps*, is a fiery and strongly flavoured drink that's usually distilled from potatoes and spiced with herbs.

The legal drinking age in Sweden is 18 years, although you have to be 20 years old to buy alcohol at a Systembolaget.

SURVIVAL GUIDE

ℹ Directory A–Z

ACCOMMODATION
Cabins & Chalets

Camping cabins and chalets *(stugor)* are common at campgrounds and scattered through the countryside. Most contain four beds, with two- and six-person cabins sometimes available. They're good value for small groups and families, costing between 350kr and 950kr per night. In peak summer season, many are rented out by the week (generally for 1000kr to 5000kr).

The cheapest cabins are simple, with bunk beds and little else (bathroom and kitchen facilities are shared with campers or other cabin users). Chalets are generally fully equipped with their own kitchen, bathroom and even living room with TV. Bring your own linen and clean up yourself to save cleaning fees of around 500kr.

Pick up the catalogue *Campsites & Cottages in Sweden* from any tourist office, or check out www.camping.se.

Camping

Camping is wildly popular in Sweden, and there are hundreds of campgrounds all over the country. Most open between May and September. The majority are busy family-holiday spots with fantastic facilities, such as shops, restaurants, pools, playgrounds, beaches, walking trails, canoe or bike rentals, minigolf, kitchens and laundry facilities. Campgrounds are usually a combination of tent and/or RV sites, primitive camping huts (duvet provided; bring your own sheets) and sometimes more luxurious suites.

Camping prices vary (according to season and facilities) from around 250kr for a small site at a basic ground to 350kr for a large site at a more luxurious campground. Slightly cheaper rates may be available if you're a solo hiker or cyclist.

You must have a Camping Key Europe card to stay at most Swedish campgrounds. Buy one online at www.camping.se or pick it up at your

> **ℹ SLEEPING PRICE RANGES**
>
> The below room prices are for a double room in the summer season (mid-June through August); standard weekday prices during the rest of the year might be twice as high. Breakfast is normally included in hotel room prices, but usually costs extra in hostels.
>
> € less than 800kr
>
> €€ 800–1600kr
>
> €€€ more than 1600kr

ℹ️ EATING PRICE RANGES

The following price categories for listings refer to the average price of a main dish, not including drinks.

€ less than 100kr

€€ 100–200kr

€€€ more than 200kr

first campground. One card (150kr per year) covers the whole family.

Hostels

Sweden has more than 450 hostels (vandrarhem), usually with excellent facilities – they're often more like budget hotels. Most hostels aren't backpacker hang-outs but are used as holiday accommodation by Swedish families, couples or retired people. Another quirk is the scarcity of dormitories; hostels are more likely to have singles and doubles of almost hotel quality, often with en-suite bathrooms. About half are open year-round; many others open from May to September, some only from mid-June to mid-August in more remote locations.

Be warned: some Swedish hostels keep very short reception opening times, generally from 5pm to 7pm, and 8am to 10am. The secret is to prebook by telephone – reservations are recommended in any case, as good hostels fill up fast. If you're stuck arriving when the front desk is closed, you'll usually see a number posted where you can phone for instructions. (Hostel phone numbers are also listed online with STF and SVIF.)

Sleeping bags are usually allowed if you have a sheet and pillowcase; bring your own, or hire them (50kr to 65kr). Breakfast is usually available (70kr to 95kr). Before leaving, you must clean up after yourself; cleaning materials are provided. Most hostels are affiliated with Swedish Tourist Association (STF; www.swedishtouristassociation.com) or Sveriges Vandrarhem i Förening (SVIF; www.srif.se/en), but there are other unaffiliated hostels also with high standards of accommodation.

Hotels

Sweden is unusual in that hotel prices tend to fall at weekends and in summer (except in touristy coastal towns), sometimes by as much as 50%. We list the standard summer rates, as that's when most people will be visiting, but be aware that prices may be nearly double at other times of year. Many hotel chains are now also offering a variety of low rates for online booking. Hotel prices include a breakfast buffet unless noted in individual reviews.

There are a number of common midrange and top-end chains. Radisson and Elite are the most luxurious. Scandic is known for being environmentally friendly, and usually has great breakfast buffets. The top-end Countryside chain has the most characterful rooms, in castles, mansions, monasteries and spas.

Best Western (www.bestwestern.se)

Countryside (www.countrysidehotels.se)

Elite (www.elite.se)

First (www.firsthotels.com)

Nordic Choice (www.nordicchoicehotels.se)

Radisson (www.radisson.com)

Scandic (www.scandichotels.com)

Sweden Hotels (www.swedenhotels.se)

Your Hotel Worldwide (www.yourhotelsworldwide.net)

ACTIVITIES

Sweden is a canoeing and kayaking paradise (canoes are more common). The national canoeing body is Kanotförbundet (Kayak & Canoe Federation; www.kanot.com). It provides general advice and lists approved canoe centres that hire out canoes.

There are thousands of kilometres of hiking trails in Sweden, particularly in the north. The best hiking time is between late June and mid-September, when trails are mostly snow-free. Large ski resorts cater to downhill skiing and snowboarding.

SkiStar (www.skistar.com) manages the largest resorts and has good information on its website. Winter activities in the north include dogsledding, snowmobiling, and cross-country skiing.

CHILDREN

Sweden is a very easy, friendly place to travel with children. Museums almost always have dedicated playrooms with hands-on learning tools. Restaurants offer highchairs and kids' menus. There are safety features for children in hire/rental cars. Hostels generally have family rooms, and campgrounds are often equipped with swimming pools and playgrounds.

DISCOUNT CARDS

Gothenburg, Malmö, Stockholm and Uppsala offer tourist cards that provide discounts on major attractions, transport and more (see individual city sections for details).

The **International Student Identity Card** (ISIC; www.isic.org; fee $25) offers discounts on admission to museums, sights, public transport and more. **Hostelling International** (HI) cards get you discounts on accommodation.

Seniors get discounts on entry to museums, sights, cinema and theatre tickets, air tickets and other transport. No special card is required. Show your passport as proof of age (the minimum qualifying age is 60 or 65).

GAY & LESBIAN TRAVELLERS

Sweden is a famously liberal country; it was a leader in establishing gay and lesbian registered partnerships, and since 2009 its gender-neutral marriage law has given same-sex married couples the same rights and obligations as heterosexual married couples. The national organisation for gay and lesbian rights is **Riksförbundet för Sexuellt Likaberättigande** (RFSL; Map p386; ☑ 08-50 16 29 00; www.rfsl.se; Sveavägen 59; ☻10am-3pm or 4pm Mon-Fri, closed most of Jul & Aug; ☖Rådmansgatan).

There are gay bars and nightclubs in the big cities, but ask local RFSL societies or your home organisation for up-to-date information. The *Spartacus International Gay Guide* (www.spartacusworld.com), published by Bruno Gmünder Verlag (Berlin), is an excellent international directory of gay entertainment venues, but it's best used in conjunction with more up-to-date listings in local papers; as elsewhere, gay venues in the region can change with the speed of summer.

Another good source of local information is the free monthly magazine *QX*. You can pick it up at many clubs, shops and restaurants in Stockholm, Gothenburg, Malmö and Copenhagen (Denmark). The magazine's website (www.qx.se) has excellent information and recommendations in English.

One of the capital's biggest parties is the annual **Stockholm Pride** (p395), a five-day festival celebrating gay culture. The extensive program covers art, debate, health, literature, music, spirituality and sport.

INTERNET ACCESS

Most hotels have free wi-fi, and some have computers and printers in the lobby or business centre. Nearly all public libraries offer free internet access, but often the half-hour or hour slots are fully booked in advance by locals, and certain website categories may be blocked. Many tourist offices offer a computer terminal for visitor use (usually free or for a minimal fee).

Internet cafes are rarely found in Sweden as the vast majority of Swedes have internet access at home.

Wireless internet access at coffee shops is nearly universal and usually free; ask for the password when you order. At bus and train stations and airports, you often have to sign up for an account (usually free) to access the wi-fi.

MONEY
ATMs

The simplest and usually cheapest way to get money in Sweden is by accessing your account using an ATM card from your home bank. Bankomat ATMs are found adjacent to many banks and around busy public places such as shopping centres. They accept major credit cards as well as Plus and Cirrus cards.

Credit Cards

Visa and MasterCard are widely accepted, American Express, Discover and Diners Club less so. Credit cards can be used to buy train tickets and on domestic ferries. Electronic debit or credit cards can be used in most shops; in fact, the trend is towards card-only transactions, and many places no longer accept cash.

If your card is lost or stolen in Sweden, report it to your credit-card agency.

American Express (☑ 336-393 11 11)
Diners Club (☑ 08-14 68 78)
MasterCard (☑ 020-79 13 24)
Visa (☑ 020-79 56 75)

Moneychangers

Forex (☑ 0771-22 22 21; www.forex.se) is the biggest foreign money exchange company in Sweden, with good rates and branches in major airports, ferry terminals and town and city centres.

Tipping

➡ **When to Tip** Tipping is rare and usually reserved for great service.

➡ **Restaurants & Bars** Not expected except with dinner – service is figured into the bill, but a small gratuity (10% to 15%) for good service is customary. Tipping bartenders is increasingly common.

➡ **Taxis** Tipping is optional, but most people add an extra 10-20kr.

➡ **Hotels** Service is figured into the bill, but a small tip (around 10kr a day) for housekeeping is appreciated.

OPENING HOURS

Except where indicated, we list hours for high season (mid-June to August). Expect more limited hours the rest of the year.

Banks 9.30am to 3pm Monday to Friday; some city branches open to 5pm or 6pm.

Bars & Pubs 11am or noon to 1am or 2am.

Government Offices 9am to 5pm Monday to Friday.

Restaurants 11am to 2pm and 5pm to 10pm, often closed on Sunday and/or Monday; high-end restaurants often closed for a week or two in July or August.

Shops 9am to 6pm Monday to Friday, to 1pm Saturday.

PUBLIC HOLIDAYS

Midsummer brings life almost to a halt for three days: transport and other services are reduced, and most shops and smaller tourist offices close, as do some attractions. Some hotels close between Christmas and New Year. Upscale restaurants in larger cities often close for a few weeks in late July and early August.

School holidays vary, but in general the kids will be at large for Sweden's one-week sports holiday (February/March), the one-week Easter break, Christmas, and from June to August.

Many businesses close early the day before and all day after official public holidays.

Nyårsdag (New Year's Day) 1 January
Trettondedag Jul (Epiphany) 6 January
Långfredag, Påsk, Annandag Påsk (Good Friday, Easter Sunday and Monday) March/April
Första Maj (Labour Day) 1 May
Kristi Himmelsfärdsdag (Ascension Day) May/June
Pingst, Annandag Pingst (Whit Sunday and Monday) Late May or early June
Midsommardag (Midsummer's Day) Saturday between 19 and 25 June
Alla Helgons dag (All Saints Day) Saturday, late October or early November
Juldag (Christmas Day) 25 December
Annandag Jul (Boxing Day) 26 December

Note also that Midsommarafton (Midsummer's Eve), Julafton (Christmas Eve; 24 December) and Nyårsafton (New Year's Eve; 31 December) are not official holidays but are generally nonworking days for most of the population.

TELEPHONE

Swedish phone numbers have area codes followed by a varying number of digits. Look for business numbers in the Yellow Pages (www.gulasidorna.se).

Public telephones are increasingly rare, although you may find them at transport hubs, including train and bus stations. They accept phonecards or credit cards. Telia phonecards (telefonkort) cost 50kr and 120kr (for 50 and 120 units, respectively) and can be bought from Telia phone shops and newsagents.

Mobile Phones

Local SIM cards are readily available (around 100kr) from providers such as Tre, Telia, Comviq and Telenor; you then load them with at least 110kr worth of credit. You can buy SIM cards from Pressbyrå locations, including at Arlanda Airport, and purchase top-ups at many stores, including petrol stations.

Phone Codes

For international calls dial 00, followed by the country code and then the local area code. Calls to Sweden from abroad require the country code (46) followed by the area code and telephone number (omitting the first zero in the area code).

Mobile-phone codes start with 010, 070, 076, 073 and 0730. Toll-free codes include 020 and 0200 (but toll-free numbers can't be called from public telephones or abroad).

Directory assistance (☏118 119) International.
Directory assistance (☏118 118) Within Sweden.
Emergency services (☏112) Toll free.

TIME

Sweden is one hour ahead of GMT/UTC and is in the same time zone as Norway and Denmark as well as most of Western Europe. When it's noon in Sweden, it's 11am in London, 1pm in Helsinki, 6am in New York and Toronto, 3am in Los Angeles, 9pm in Sydney and 11pm in Auckland. Sweden also has daylight saving time: the clocks go forward an hour on the last Sunday in March and back an hour on the last Sunday in October.

Timetables and business hours are quoted using the 24-hour clock, and dates are often given by week number (1 to 52).

TOILETS

Public toilets in parks, shopping malls, libraries, and bus or train stations are rarely free in Sweden, though some churches and most museums and tourist offices have free toilets. Pay toilets cost 5kr to 10kr, usually payable by coin or text message, except at larger train stations and department stores (where there's an attendant).

TOURIST INFORMATION

Most towns in Sweden have centrally located tourist offices (turistbyrå) that provide free street plans and information on accommodation, attractions, activities and transport. Brochures for other areas in Sweden are often available. Ask for the handy booklet that lists addresses and phone numbers for most tourist offices in the country.

Most tourist offices are open long hours daily in summer; from mid-August to mid-June a few close down, while others have shorter opening hours – they may close by 4pm, and not open at all at weekends. Public libraries, hostels and large hotels are good alternative sources of information.

TRAVELLERS WITH DISABILITIES

Sweden is one of the easiest countries in which to travel around in a wheelchair. People with disabilities will find transport services, ranging from trains to taxis, with adapted facilities – contact the operator in advance for the best service.

Public toilets and some hotel rooms have facilities for those with disabilities. Some street crossings have ramps for wheelchairs and audio signals for visually impaired people, and some grocery stores are wheelchair-accessible.

For further information about Sweden, contact **De Handikappades Riksförbund** (☏08-685

80 00; www.dhr.se), the national association for the disabled.

Also, contact the travel officer at your national support organisation; they may be able to put you in touch with tour companies that specialise in travelling with disabilities.

Download Lonely Planet's free Accessible Travel guide from http://lptravel.to/AccessibleTravel.

VISAS

Citizens of EU countries can enter Sweden with a passport or a national identification card (passports are recommended) and stay indefinitely. *Uppehållstillstånd* (residence permits) are no longer required for EU citizens to visit, study, live or work in Sweden.

Non-EU passport holders from Australia, New Zealand, Canada and the US can enter and stay in Sweden without a visa for up to 90 days. Australian and New Zealand passport holders aged between 18 and 30 can qualify for a one-year working-holiday visa. For longer stays, you'll need to apply for a visitor's permit instead of an entry visa. These must be applied for before entering Sweden. An interview with consular officials at your nearest Swedish embassy is required – allow up to eight months for this process. Foreign students are granted residence permits if they can prove acceptance by a Swedish educational institution and are able to guarantee that they can support themselves financially.

Citizens of South Africa and many other African, Asian and some eastern European countries require tourist visas for entry to Sweden (and any other Schengen country). These are only available in advance from Swedish embassies (allow two months); there's a non-refundable application fee of €60 for most applicants. Visas are good for any 90 days within a six-month period; extensions aren't easily obtainable.

Migrationsverket (www.migrationsverket.se) is the Swedish migration board and handles all applications for visas and work or residency permits.

🛈 Getting There & Away

AIR

Stockholm Arlanda (p401) links Sweden with major European and North American cities. **Göteborg Landvetter** (p431) is Sweden's second-biggest international airport. **Stockholm Skavsta** (p401) is located 100km south of Stockholm, near Nyköping, and is mainly used by Ryanair flights. **Sturup Airport** (p418) in Malmö serves the south of the country and is also a major international hub.

LAND & SEA

Direct access to Sweden by land is possible from Norway, Finland and Denmark (via the Öresund toll bridge).

Nettbuss Express (☑ 0771-15 15 15; www. nettbuss.se) Long-distance buses within Sweden and to Oslo (Norway) and Copenhagen.
Sveriges Järnväg (SJ; ☑ 0771-75 75 99; www. sj.se) Train lines with services to Copenhagen and Oslo.
Swebus Express (p475) Long-distance buses within Sweden and to Oslo and Copenhagen.

Denmark

Bus Swebus Express runs between Gothenburg and Copenhagen (229kr, 4½ hours, daily). Nettbuss Express runs regular buses on the same route. Both offer student, youth (under 26) and senior discounts.

Train Öresund trains operated by Skånetrafiken (www.skanetrafiken.se) run every 20 minutes from 6am to midnight (and once an hour thereafter) between Copenhagen and Malmö (one-way from 99kr, 45 minutes) via the bridge. The trains usually stop at Copenhagen airport. From Copenhagen, change in Malmö for Stockholm trains. Frequent services operate between Copenhagen and Gothenburg (407kr, four hours) and between Copenhagen, Kristianstad and Karlskrona.

Car & Motorcycle You can drive from Copenhagen to Malmö across the Öresund bridge on the E20 motorway. Tolls are paid at Lernacken, on the Swedish side, in either Danish or Swedish currency (single crossing per car/motorcycle 520/265kr), or by credit or debit card.

Sea Stena Line (☑ 031-704 00 00; www. stenaline.se; passenger from 179kr) Three-hour crossing from Gothenburg to Fredrikshavn. Up to six ferries daily.

Helsingør–Helsingborg is the quickest route and has frequent ferries (crossing time around 20 minutes).

HH-Ferries (☑ 042-19 80 00; www.hhferries. se) A 24-hour service. Pedestrian/car and up to nine passengers 52/525kr. Pedestrians can bring bicycles along at no extra charge.

BornholmsTrafikken (☑ 0411-55 87 00; www. faergen.dk/ruter/bornholmerfaergen.aspx) Conventional and fast services (1½ hours, 80 minutes, two to nine times daily). Car with five passengers from 1030kr.

Germany

Bus Flixbus runs direct daily services from Gothenburg to Berlin (766kr, 12 hours, daily), as well as through Jönköping (622kr, 19 hours).

Train Hamburg is the central European gateway to Scandinavia, with direct trains daily to Copenhagen and a few on to Stockholm. Direct overnight trains and Swebus Express buses run daily between Berlin and Malmö via the Trelleborg–Sassnitz ferry (www.berlin-night-express. com; from 450kr, nine hours).

Sea TT-Line (www.ttline.com) Car and up to five passengers Trelleborg–Rostock 500kr (12 services daily, 5.5 hours), Trelleborg–Trave-münde 800kr (eight services daily, seven hours). Berths are compulsory on night cross-ings.

Finland

Helsinki is called Helsingfors in Swedish, and Turku is Åbo.

Stockholm–Helsinki and Stockholm–Turku ferries run daily throughout the year via the Åland islands. These ferries have minimum-age limits; check before you travel.

Bus Frequent bus services run from Haparanda (Sweden) to Tornio (Finland; 20kr, 10 minutes). Tapanis Buss (www.tapanis.se) runs express coaches from Stockholm to Tornio via Haparanda twice a week (735kr, 15 hours). **Länstrafiken i Norrbotten** (☏ 0771-10 01 10; www.ltnbd.se) operates buses as far as Karesuando, from where it's only a few minutes' walk across the bridge to Kaaresuvanto (Finland).

There are also regular regional services from Haparanda to Övertorneå (some continue to Pello, Pajala and Kiruna) – you can walk across the border at Övertorneå or Pello and pick up a Finnish bus to Muonio, with onward connec-tions from there to Kaaresuvanto and Tromsø (Norway).

Car & Motorcycle The main routes between Sweden and Finland are the E4 from Umeå to Kemi and Rd 45 from Gällivare to Kaaresu-vanto; five other minor roads also cross the border.

Sea Viking Line ships go to Åland from Stock-holm and Kapellskär two or three times daily.

Eckerö Linjen (☏ 0175-258 00; www.ecker-olinjen.fi; passenger/car 30/130kr) Runs to the Åland islands from Grisslehamn.

Tallink & Silja Line (☏ 08-666 60 01; www.tallink.ee; Cityterminalen) Runs from Stock-holm to Talinn (around 15 hours). Ticket and cabin berth from about 1195kr.

Viking Line (☏ 08-452 40 00; www.vikingline.fi) Ticket and cabin berth from about 1000kr.

Silja Line (☏ 08-22 21 40; www.silja.com) Eleven hours. Deck place 138kr, cabins from 478kr; prices are higher for evening trips. From September to early May, ferries also depart from Kapellskär (90km northeast of Stock-holm); connecting buses operated by Silja Line are included in the full-price fare.

Viking Line (p474) Operates routes to Turku from Stockholm and, in high season, also from Kapellskär.

Norway

Bus Nettbuss runs from Stockholm to Oslo (from 379kr, 7½ hours, three daily) and from Gothenburg to Oslo (from 219kr, four hours,

several daily). Swebus Express has the same routes with similar prices. In the north, buses run once daily from Umeå to Mo i Rana (eight hours) and from Skellefteå to Bodø (nine hours, daily except Saturday); for details, contact **Länstrafiken i Västerbotten** (p378) and **Länstrafiken i Norrbotten** (p378).

Train SJ trains run twice daily between Stockholm and Oslo (450kr to 1000kr, five hours), and at night to Narvik (800kr, about 20 hours). You can also travel from Helsing-borg to Oslo (856kr, seven hours, twice daily), via Gothenburg.

Car & Motorcycle The main roads between Sweden and Norway are the E6 from Gothen-burg to Oslo, the E18 from Stockholm to Oslo, the E14 from Sundsvall to Trondheim, the E12 from Umeå to Mo i Rana, and the E10 from Kiruna to Bjerkvik.

Sea There's a daily overnight **DFDS Seaways** (☏ 031-65 06 80; www.dfdsseaways.com) ferry between Copenhagen and Oslo (from €94 per passenger plus €85 per vehicle), via Helsingborg. Passenger fares between Helsingborg and Oslo (14 hours) cost from 1100kr, and cars 475kr, but the journey can't be booked online; you'll need to call. A **Color Line** (☏ 0526-620 00; www.colorline.se) ferry between Strömstad and Sandefjord (Norway) sails two to six times daily (2½ hours) year-round. Tickets cost from €22; rail pass hold-ers get a 50% discount.

❶ Getting Around

AIR

Despite the large number of smaller airports, domestic airlines in Sweden tend to use **Stock-holm Arlanda** (p401) as a hub. Flying domestic is expensive on full-price tickets, but discounts are available on internet bookings, student and youth fares, off-peak travel, return tickets booked in advance and low-price tickets for accompanying family members and seniors.

Airlines catering to domestic air travel include the following:

Braathens Regional Aviation (☏ 010 722 10 00; www.flygbra.se) Ängelholm, Gothenburg, Halmstad, Kalmar, Malmö, Östersund, Ron-neby, Stockholm, Sundsvall, Umeå, Visby and Växjö.

SAS (☏ 0770-72 77 27; www.flysas.com) Ängelholm-Helsingborg, Arvidsjaur, Borlänge, Gällivare, Gothenburg, Halmstad, Hemavan, Hultsfred, Jönköping, Kalmar, Karlstad, Kiruna, Kramfors, Kristianstad, Linköping, Luleå, Lycksele, Malmö, Mora, Norrköping, Örebro, Örnsköldsvik, Oskarshamn, Oskersund, Skel-lefteå, Stockholm, Storuman, Sundsvall, Sveg, Torsby, Trollhättan, Umeå, Vilhelmina, Visby and Västerås.

Air Passes

Visitors who fly SAS to Sweden from the UK can add on a Visit Scandinavia/Nordic Airpass, allowing one-way travel on direct flights between any two Scandinavian cities serviced by SAS and its partner airlines. For the latest, call SAS at 800-221-2350 or check www.flysas.com.

BOAT
Canal Boat

Canals provide cross-country routes linking Sweden's main lakes. The longest cruises, on the Göta Canal from Söderköping (south of Stockholm) to Gothenburg, run from mid-May to mid-September, take at least four days and include the lakes between.

Rederiaktiebolaget Göta Kanal (☑ 031-80 63 15; www.gotacanal.se) operates three ships over the whole distance at fares from 12,295kr to 17,125kr per person for a four-day cruise, including full board and guided excursions.

Ferry

An extensive boat network and the five-day Båtluffarkortet (Boat Hiking Pass; 445kr, plus 20kr for card) open up the attractive Stockholm archipelago. Gotland is served by regular ferries from Nynäshamn and Oskarshamn, and the quaint fishing villages off the west coast can normally be reached by boat with a regional transport pass – enquire at the Gothenburg tourist offices.

BUS

There is a comprehensive network of buses throughout Sweden and you can travel on any of the 24 good-value and extensive *länstrafik* networks as well as on national long-distance routes. In general, travelling by bus is cheaper than by train.

Express Buses

Swebus Express (☑ 0771-21 82 18; www. swebus.se) has the largest network of express buses; in the north it operates as Ybuss. Generally, tickets for travel between Monday and Thursday, and tickets purchased over the internet or more than 24 hours before departure are cheaper; if you're a student or senior, ask about fare discounts.

Svenska Buss (☑ 0771-67 67 67; www. svenskabuss.se) and **Nettbuss** (p473) also connect many southern towns and cities with Stockholm; prices are often slightly cheaper than Swebus Express prices, but services are less frequent.

North of Gävle, regular connections with Stockholm are provided by several smaller operators, including **Ybuss** (☑ 060-17 19 60; www.ybuss.se), which has services to Sundsvall, Östersund and Umeå.

Bus Passes

Good-value daily or weekly passes are usually available from local and regional transport offices, and many regions have 30-day passes for longer stays or summer travel. These can be bought online, from most newsagents, and from tourist information offices.

CAR & MOTORCYCLE

Sweden has good roads, and the excellent E-class motorways rarely have traffic jams.

Bringing Your Own Vehicle

If you're bringing your own car, you'll need vehicle registration documents, unlimited third-party liability insurance and a valid driving licence. A right-hand-drive vehicle brought from the UK or Ireland should have deflectors fitted to the headlights to avoid dazzling oncoming traffic. You must carry a reflective warning breakdown triangle.

Driving Licence

An international driving permit isn't necessary; your domestic licence will do.

Hire

To hire a car you have to be at least 20 (sometimes 25) years of age, with a recognised licence and a credit card.

International rental chains have desks at Stockholm Arlanda and Göteborg Landvetter airports and bus stations, and offices in most major cities.

Avis (☑ 0770-82 00 82; www.avisworld.com)
Europcar (☑ 020-78 11 80; www.europcar.com)
Hertz (☑ 0771 21 12 12; www.hertz-europe.com)
Mabi Hyrbilar (☑ 08-612 60 90; www.mabi. se/english) National company with competitive rates.

Road Hazards

In the north, elk (moose, to Americans) and reindeer are serious road hazards; around 40 people die in collisions every year. Look out for the signs saying *viltstängsel upphör*, which mean that elk may cross the road, and for black plastic bags tied to roadside trees or poles, which mean Sami have reindeer herds grazing in the area. Report all incidents to police – failure to do so is an offence.

In Gothenburg and Norrköping, be aware of trams, which have priority; overtake on the right.

Road Rules

Drive on and give way to the right. Headlights (at least dipped) must be on at all times when driving. Seatbelts are compulsory, and children under seven years old should be in the appropriate harness or child seat.

The blood-alcohol limit in Sweden is 0.02% – having just one drink will put you over. Random checks are not unheard of. The maximum speed on motorways (signposted in green and called E1, E4, etc) is 120km/h, highways 90km/h, narrow rural roads 70km/h and built-up areas 50km/h. The speed limit for cars towing caravans is 80km/h. Police using hand-held radar speed detectors have the power to impose on-the-spot fines of up to 1200kr.

TRAIN

Sweden has an extensive and reliable railway network, and trains are almost always faster than buses, although not necessarily cheaper. (Exceptions include local commuter trains in large urban and suburban areas, which make frequent stops.)

Inlandsbanan (☑ 0771-53 53 53; www.inlands-banan.se; Storsjöstråkket 19, Östersund) One of the great rail journeys in Scandinavia is this slow and scenic 1300km route from Kristine-hamn to Gällivare. Several southern sections have to be travelled by bus, but the all-train route starts at Mora. It takes seven hours from Mora to Östersund (596kr) and 15 hours from Östersund to Gällivare (1378kr). A pass allows two weeks' unlimited travel for 1995kr.

Sveriges Järnväg (p473) National network covering most main lines, especially in the southern part of the country.

Tågkompaniet (☑ 0771-44 41 11; www.tagkom-paniet.se) Operates excellent overnight trains from Gothenburg and Stockholm north to Boden, Kiruna, Luleå and Narvik, and the lines north of Härnösand.

Costs

Ticket prices vary depending on the type of train, class, time of day, and how far in advance you buy the ticket. Full-price 2nd-class tickets for longer journeys cost about twice as much as equivalent bus trips, but there are various discounts available for advance or last-minute bookings. Students, pensioners and people aged under 26 get a discount. When buying in ad-vance, you pay more for the flexibility to change your ticket.

All SJ ticket prices drop from late June to mid-August. Most SJ trains don't allow bicycles to be taken onto trains (they have to be sent as freight), but some in southern Sweden do; check when you book your ticket.

Train Passes

The Sweden Rail Pass, Eurodomino tickets and international passes, such as Interrail and Eurail, are accepted on SJ services and most regional trains.

The Eurail Scandinavia Pass (www.eurail.com) entitles you to unlimited rail travel in Denmark, Finland, Norway and Sweden; it is valid in 2nd class only and is available for four, five, six, eight or 10 days of travel within a two-month period (prices start at US$303 for five days). The X2000 trains require all rail-pass holders to pay a supplement of 75kr. The pass also provides free travel on Scandlines' Helsingør to Helsing-borg route, and 20% to 50% discounts on the following ship routes.

Route	Operator
Frederikshavn–Gothenburg	Stena Line
Grenå–Varberg	Stena Line
Helsinki–Åland–Stockholm	Silja Line
Stockholm–Riga	Silja Line
Stockholm–Tallinn	Silja Line
Turku–Åland–Stockholm/ Kappelskär	Silja Line
Turku/Helsinki–Stockholm	Viking Line

Some of the main rail routes across the country:
➸ Stockholm north to Uppsala–Gävle–Sunds-vall–Östersund
➸ Stockholm west to Örebro–Karlstad–Oslo
➸ Stockholm west to Örebro–Gothenburg
➸ Stockholm south to Norrköping–Malmö–Copenhagen

Survival Guide

Directory A-Z

Accommodation

Scandinavia has a wide range of accommodation, from hostels to boutique hotels and self-catering cottages. Booking ahead in summer is a good idea and is essential year-round in Iceland, where the tourist boom has squeezed accommodation availability.

Camping grounds Camping is very popular. Most camping grounds have good-value cabins.

Hotels Generally bland, chain options. Outside of major cities there are often discount rates in summer and on weekends.

Hostels There is a great network in Sweden and good options in other countries.

Self-catering From urban apartments to wilderness cottages, self-catering is an excellent option across the region.

B&Bs, Guesthouses & Hotels

➡ B&Bs, where you get a room and breakfast in a private home, can often be real bargains. Pensions and guesthouses are similar but usually slightly more upmarket.

➡ Most Scandinavian hotels are geared towards business travellers and have prices to match. But excellent hotel discounts are often available at certain times (eg at weekends and in summer in Finland, Norway and Sweden) and for longer stays. Breakfast in hotels is usually included in the price of the room.

➡ If you think a hotel is too expensive, ask if it has a cheaper room. In non-chain places it can be easy to negotiate a discount in quiet periods.

Camping

➡ Camping is immensely popular throughout the region. The Camping Key Europe card (www.campingkey.com) offers good benefits and discounts.

➡ Camping grounds tend to charge per site, with a small extra charge per person. Tent sites are often cheaper than van sites.

➡ National tourist offices have booklets or brochures listing camping grounds all over their country.

➡ In most larger towns and cities, camping grounds are some distance from the centre. If you've got no transport, the money you save by camping can quickly be outweighed by the money spent commuting in and out of town.

➡ Nearly all mainland Scandinavian camping grounds rent simple cabins – a great budget option if you're not carrying a tent. Many also have more upmarket cottages with bedrooms, bathrooms and proper kitchens, perfect for families who want to self-cater.

➡ Camping other than in designated camping grounds is not always straightforward but in many countries there's a right of common access that applies. Tourist offices usually stock official publications in English explaining your rights and responsibilities.

Hostels

Hostels generally offer the cheapest roof over your head. In Scandinavia hostels are geared towards budget travellers of all ages, including families, and most have dorms and private rooms.

Most hostels are part of national Youth Hostel Associations (YHA), known collectively throughout the world as Hostelling International (www.hihostels.com).

BOOK YOUR STAY ONLINE

For more accommodation reviews by Lonely Planet authors, check out http://lonelyplanet.com/scandinavia/hotels/. You'll find independent reviews, as well as recommendations on the best places to stay. Best of all, you can book online.

You'll have to be a YHA or HI member to use some affiliated hostels (indicated by a blue triangle symbol) but most are open to anyone. Members get substantial discounts; it's worth joining, which you can do at any hostel, via your local hostelling organisation or online. There's a particularly huge network of HI hostels in Denmark and Sweden.

Comfort levels and facilities vary markedly. Some hostels charge extra if you don't want to sweep your room out when you leave.

Bookings Some hostels accept reservations by phone; they'll often book the next hostel you're headed to for a small fee. The HI website has a booking form you can use to reserve a bed in advance – but not all hostels are on the network. Popular hostels in capital cities can be heavily booked in summer and there may be limits placed on how many nights you can stay.

Breakfast Many hostels (exceptions include most hostels in Iceland) serve breakfast, and almost all have communal kitchens where you can prepare meals.

Linen You must use a sleep-sheet (ie a cotton or silk sleeping bag) or linen in hostels in most Scandinavian countries; regular sleeping bags are not permitted. It's worth carrying your own sleep-sheet or linen, as hiring these at hostels is comparatively expensive.

Travellers with disabilities Specially adapted rooms for visitors with disabilities are common, but check with the hostel first.

Self-Catering

There's a huge network (especially in Norway, Sweden, Denmark and Finland) of rental cottages that make excellent, peaceful places to stay and offer a chance to experience traditional Scandinavian life.

Many Scandinavians traditionally spend their summers in such places. Renting a cottage for a few days as part of a visit to the region is highly recommended.

University Accommodation

➡ Some universities and colleges rent out students' rooms (sometimes called 'summer hotels') to tourists from June to mid-August.

➡ These are usually single or twin rooms with a kitchenette (but often no utensils). Enquire directly at the college or university, student information services or local tourist offices.

Children

Most of Scandinavia is very child friendly, with domestic tourism largely dictated by children's needs.

Bigger camping grounds and spa hotels are particularly kid-conscious, with heaps of facilities and activities designed with children in mind.

In Denmark, Finland, Norway and Sweden you'll find excellent theme parks, waterparks and holiday activities. Many museums have a dedicated children's section with toys, games and dressing-up clothes.

Iceland is something of an exception: children are liked and have lots of freedom, but they're treated as mini-adults, and there aren't many attractions tailored specifically for kids.

For more information, pick up a copy of Lonely Planet's *Travel with Children*.

Practicalities

➡ Cots (cribs) are standard in many hotels but numbers may be limited.

➡ Baby food, infant formula, soy and cows' milk, disposable nappies (diapers) etc are widely available in Scandinavian supermarkets.

➡ Car-rental firms hire out children's safety seats at a nominal cost, but advance bookings are essential.

➡ High chairs are standard in many restaurants but numbers may be limited.

➡ Restaurants will often have children's menu options, and there are lots of chain eateries aimed specifically at families.

➡ Breastfeeding in public is common and often officially encouraged.

➡ Many public toilets have baby-changing facilities.

Customs Regulations

From non-EU to EU countries For EU countries (ie Denmark, Sweden, Finland and Estonia), travellers arriving from outside the EU can bring duty-free goods up to the value of €430 without declaration. You can also bring in up to 16L of beer, 4L of wine, 2L of liquors not exceeding 22% vol, or 1L of spirits, 200 cigarettes or 250g of tobacco.

Within the EU If you're coming from another EU country, there is no restriction on the value of purchases for your own use.

Åland islands Arriving on or from the Åland islands (although technically part of the EU),

---

PRACTICALITIES

Smoking Widely forbidden, but some countries have dedicated smoking rooms in hotels and smoking areas in bars. Vaping laws depend on the country.

Tap Water Safe to drink throughout.

Weights & Measures The metric system is used across the region, though old local miles are still referred to sometimes.

carries the same import restrictions as arriving from a non-EU country.

Other Nordic countries Norway, Iceland and the Faroe Islands have lower limits.

Discount Cards

Seniors cards Discounts for retirees, pensioners and those over 60 (sometimes slightly younger for women; over 65 in Sweden) at museums and other sights, at public swimming pools, spas and with transport companies. Make sure you carry proof of age around with you.

Student cards If you are studying in Scandinavia, a local student card will get you mega-discounts on transport and more.

Camping Key Europe (www.campingkeyeurope.com) Discounts at many camping grounds and attractions, with built-in third-party insurance. In Denmark and at some Swedish camping grounds, it's obligatory to have this or a similar card. It covers up to a whole family with children under 18. Order through regional camping websites, or buy from camping grounds throughout the region (this is sometimes cheaper). It costs around €16 depending on where you get it.

Camping Card International (www.campingcardinternational.com) Widely accepted in the region, this camping card can be obtained from your local camping association or club.

European Youth Card (www.eyca.org) If you're under 30, you can pick up this card in almost any European country (some specify a maximum age of 26 though). It offers significant discounts on a wide range of things throughout the region. It's available to anyone for a small charge, not just European residents, through student unions, hostelling organisations or youth-oriented travel agencies.

Hostelling International (www.hihostels.com) The HI membership card gives significant discounts on

accommodation, as well as some transport and attractions.

International Student Identity Card (www.isic.org) Discounts on many forms of transport, reduced or free admission to museums and sights, and numerous other offers – a worthwhile way of cutting costs. Check the website for a list of discounts by country. Because of the proliferation of fakes, carry your home student ID as back up. Some places won't give student discounts without it. The same organisation also issues an International Youth Travel Card for under-30s, as well as the International Teacher Identity Card.

Electricity

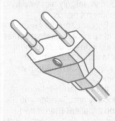

Type C
220V/50Hz

Etiquette

Greetings Shake hands with men, women and children when meeting them for the first time.

Shoes Take them off when entering someone's home.

Saunas Naked is normally the way to go.

Gifts Bring flowers, pastries, wine or chocolate when invited to someone's house.

Food

Scandinavian cooking, once viewed as meatballs, herring and little else, has wowed the world in recent years with New Nordic cuisine, a culinary revolution that centred on Copenhagen. While the crest of that wave has now passed, the 'foraging' ethos it championed has made a permanent mark here and worldwide. Its focus is on showcasing local produce prepared using traditional techniques and contemporary experimentation, and focused on clean, natural flavours.

In the wake of Noma, which became known as the world's best eatery, numerous upmarket restaurants have opened and flourished across the region's capitals, which are all now a foodie's delight. Traditional eateries still abound, however; they focused on old-school staples like herring, salmon, pork and beef, accompanied by root vegetables, berries and mushrooms. The pleasures of wandering a Scandinavian food market are memorable, particularly in summer when the short but intense season festoons the land with nature's bounty.

LGBT Travellers

Denmark, Finland, Iceland, Norway and Sweden are very tolerant nations, although public displays of affection are less common in rural areas, particularly Lapland.

See individual countries for specific information.

Health

Travel in Scandinavia presents very few health problems. The level of hygiene is high and there are no endemic diseases.

The extreme winter climate poses a risk; you must be aware of hypothermia and frostbite. In summer, biting insects such as mosquitoes, are more of an annoyance than a real health risk.

Health Insurance

Citizens of the European Economic Area (EEA) are covered for emergency medical treatment in other EEA countries (including Denmark, Finland, Iceland, Norway and Sweden) on presentation of a European Health Insurance Card (EHIC). However they may be liable to pay a daily or per-appointment fee as a local would. Enquire about EHICs at your health centre, travel agency or (in some countries) post office well in advance of travel.

Citizens from countries outside the EEA should find out if there is a reciprocal arrangement for free medical care between their country and the country visited. If not, travel health insurance is recommended.

Availability & Cost of Health Care

The standard of health care is extremely high and English is widely spoken by doctors and medical-clinic staff. Even if you are covered for health care here, you may be required to pay a per-visit fee as a local would. This is likely to be around €30 to €100 for a doctor or hospital visit.

Internet Access

➡ Wireless (wi-fi) hot spots are rife. Numerous cafes and bars, and nearly all hostels and hotels offer the service for free. A number of towns and cities in the region have free public wi-fi across the centre.

➡ Data is cheap. Buy a local SIM card, pop it in an unlocked phone, laptop or USB modem, and away you go. Deals may mean you pay as little as €15 to €20 for a month's unlimited access.

➡ Internet cafes are increasingly uncommon, but libraries provide free or very cheap internet service.

Legal Matters

Scandinavia is a law-abiding sort of place with professional, competent law enforcement. See individual countries for details.

Money

ATMs Widespread, even in small places. This is the best way to access cash in Scandinavia. Find out what your home bank will charge you per withdrawal before you go, as you may be better off taking out larger sums.

Cash cards These are much like debit or credit cards but are loaded with a set amount of money. They also have the advantage of lower withdrawal fees than your bank might otherwise charge you.

Changing money All Scandinavian currencies are fully convertible.

Charge cards These include cards like American Express and Diners Club. Less widely accepted than credit cards because they charge merchants high commissions.

Debit and credit cards Scandinavians love using plastic, even for small transactions, and you'll find that debit and credit cards are the way to go here.

Foreign currencies Easily exchanged, with rates usually slightly better at exchange offices rather than banks. Avoid exchanging at airports if possible; you'll get better rates downtown. Always ask about the rate and commission before handing over your cash.

Tax A value-added tax (VAT) applies to most goods and services throughout Scandinavia. International visitors from outside the European Economic Area can claim back the VAT above a set minimum amount on purchases that are being taken out of the

country. The procedure for making the claim is usually pretty straightforward.

Tipping Isn't required in Scandinavia. But if you round up the bill or leave a little something in recognition of good service, it won't be refused.

Travellers cheques Rapidly disappearing but still accepted in big hotels and exchange offices.

Taxes & Refunds

A value-added tax (VAT) is added on most goods and services across the region. Visitors from outside the European Economic Area (EEA) are eligible for a refund of this tax on large purchases. See individual countries for details.

Opening Hours

Except where indicated, we list hours for high season (mid-June to August). Expect more limited hours the rest of the year.

Banks 9.30am to 3pm Monday to Friday; some city branches open to 5pm or 6pm.

Bars & Pubs 11am or noon to 1am or 2am.

Government Offices 9am to 5pm Monday to Friday.

Restaurants 11am to 2pm and 5pm to 10pm, often closed on Sunday and/or Monday; high-end restaurants often closed for a week or two in July or August.

Shops 9am to 6pm Monday to Friday, to 1pm Saturday.

Post

Scandinavian postal services are uniformly reliable, though not cheap. See national postal websites for postage rates and post office locations:

Denmark (www.postnord.dk)

Finland (www.posti.fi)

Iceland (www.postur.is)

Norway (www.posten.no)

Sweden (www.postnord.se)

Public Holidays

Major Christian holidays are generally taken across the region, with additional public holidays specific to each country. See individual countries for details.

Safe Travel

Scandinavia is a very safe place to travel, with very low crime rates. Extreme winter temperatures must be taken seriously: wear proper protective clothing when outdoors.

Telephone

To call abroad dial 00 (the IAC, or international access code from Scandinavia), the country code (CC) for the country you are calling, the local area code (usually dropping the leading zero if there is one) and then the number.

Emergencies The emergency number is the same throughout Scandinavia: 112.

Internet Calling via the internet is a practical and cheap solution for making international calls, whether from a laptop, tablet or smartphone.

Mobile phones Bring a mobile that's not tied to a specific network (unlocked) and buy local SIM cards.

Phone boxes Almost nonexistent in most of Scandinavia.

Phonecards Easily bought for cheaper international calls.

Reverse-charge (collect) calls Usually possible, and communicating with the local operator in English should not be much of a problem.

Roaming Roaming charges for EU phones within the EU have been abolished and are low for other European Economic Area (EEA) countries.

Mobile Phones

➡ Local SIM cards are cheap and widely available. They need to be used with an unlocked phone.

➡ Data packages are cheap and easy.

➡ There is a normal tariff for EU SIM cards in EU countries; otherwise, expect to pay roaming rates.

Telephone Codes

Country	Country Code (CC)
Denmark	☑45
Finland	☑358
Iceland	☑354
Norway	☑47
Sweden	☑46
Estonia (Tallinn)	☑372

Use the country code to call into that country. Use the international access code (IAC) ☑00 to call abroad from that country.

Toilets

Public toilets are usually good, but often expensive; they can cost €1 or €2 or equivalent to enter.

Tourist Information

Facilities Generally excellent, with piles of regional and national brochures, helpful free maps and friendly employees. Staff are often multilingual, speaking English and other major European languages.

Locations Tourist information offices at train stations are often in the town hall or central square of most towns.

Opening hours Office hours are longer over summer, with reduced hours over winter; smaller offices may open only during peak summer months.

Services Offices will book hotel and transport reservations and tours; a small charge may apply.

Websites Most towns have a tourist information portal, with good information about sights, accommodation options and more.

Travellers with Disabilities

➡ Scandinavia leads the world as the best-equipped region for travellers with disabilities. By law, most institutions must provide ramps, lifts and special toilets for people with disabilities; all new hotels and restaurants must install disabled facilities. Most trains and city buses are also accessible by wheelchair.

➡ Some national parks offer accessible nature trails, and cities have ongoing projects in place designed to maximise disabled access in all aspects of urban life.

➡ Iceland is a little further behind the rest of the region – check access issues before you travel. Scandinavian tourist office websites generally contain good information on disabled access.

➡ Before leaving home, get in touch with your national support organisation – preferably the 'travel officer' if there is one. They often have complete libraries devoted to travel and can put you in touch with agencies that specialise in tours for the disabled. One such agency in the UK is Can Be Done (www.canbedone.co.uk).

➡ Download Lonely Planet's free Accessible Travel guide from http://lptravel.to/AccessibleTravel.

Visas

➡ Denmark, Estonia, Finland, Iceland, Norway and Sweden are all part of the Schengen area. A valid passport or EU identity card is required to enter the region.

TIME

Scandinavia sprawls across several time zones. The 24-hour clock is widely used. Note that Europe and the US move clocks forwards and back at slightly different times. The following table is a seasonal guide only.

CITY	TIME IN WINTER	TIME IN SUMMER
New York	11am (UTC -5)	noon (UTC -4)
Reykjavík	4pm (UTC)	4pm (UTC; no summer time)
London	4pm (UTC)	5pm (UTC +1)
Oslo, Copenhagen, Stockholm	5pm (UTC +1)	6pm (UTC +2)
Helsinki, Tallinn	6pm (UTC +2)	7pm (UTC +3)

➡ Most Western nationals don't need a tourist visa for stays of less than three months. Nationals of many other countries, including South Africa, China and India, will require a Schengen visa.

➡ A Schengen visa can be obtained by applying to an embassy or consulate of any country in the Schengen area.

Volunteering

There's not a great deal of scope for volunteers who don't speak local languages in Scandinavia. Volunteering on farms in exchange for bed and board is relatively common. See individual countries for details.

Work

➡ English teaching and working as an au pair are popular choices for travellers looking for work in Scandinavia.

➡ If you're aged between 18 and 30, Scandinavian and looking for short-term work in another Nordic nation, www.nordjobb.org is a useful website.

➡ See individual countries for useful national websites.

Transport

GETTING THERE & AWAY

Scandinavia is easily accessed from the rest of Europe and beyond. There are direct flights from numerous destinations into Sweden, Norway, Denmark and Finland. There is less choice to Iceland.

Denmark, Sweden and Norway can be accessed by train from Western Europe, while Baltic and North Sea ferries are another good option for accessing these Nordic countries.

Flights, cars and tours can be booked online at lonelyplanet.com/bookings.

Entering the Country/Region

Entering and leaving Scandinavia is very easy and usually achieved with minimal waiting time.

Air

As well as the many national carriers that fly directly into Scandinavia's airports, there are several budget options. These routes change frequently and are best investigated online.

Airports & Airlines

The following are major hubs in Scandinavia:

Stockholm Arlanda Airport (www.swedavia.com/arlanda) Sweden

Helsinki Vantaa Airport (www.helsinki-vantaa.fi) Finland

Copenhagen Kastrup Airport (www.cph.dk) Denmark

Reykjavík Keflavík Airport (www.kefairport.is) Iceland

Oslo Gardermoen Airport (www.osl.no) Norway

SAS (www.flysas.com) is the national carrier for Sweden, Norway and Denmark, Finnair (www.finnair.com) for Finland and Ice-landair (www.icelandair.com) for Iceland. Other important regional airlines include Norwegian (www.norwegian.com).

Departure tax is included in the price of a ticket.

Land

Bus

Without a rail pass, the cheapest overland transport from Europe to Scandinavia is the bus, though a cheap flight deal will often beat it on price. Eurolines (www.eurolines.com), a conglomeration of coach companies, is the biggest and best-established express-bus network, and connects Scandinavia with the rest of Europe. Advance ticket purchases are usually necessary and sometimes cheaper.

Car & Motorcycle

Driving to Scandinavia means driving into Denmark from Germany (and on to Sweden

---

CLIMATE CHANGE & TRAVEL

Every form of transport that relies on carbon-based fuel generates CO_2, the main cause of human-induced climate change. Modern travel is dependent on aeroplanes, which might use less fuel per kilometre per person than most cars but travel much greater distances. The altitude at which aircraft emit gases (including CO_2) and particles also contributes to their climate change impact. Many websites offer 'carbon calculators' that allow people to estimate the carbon emissions generated by their journey and, for those who wish to do so, to offset the impact of the greenhouse gases emitted with contributions to portfolios of climate-friendly initiatives throughout the world. Lonely Planet offsets the carbon footprint of all staff and author travel.

via the bridge-tunnel), going through Russia or taking a car ferry.

Train

→ Apart from trains into Finland from Russia, the rail route into Scandinavia goes from Denmark, then on to Sweden and then Norway via the Copenhagen–Malmö bridge-tunnel connection. Hamburg and Cologne are the main gateways in Germany for this route.

→ See the exceptional Man in Seat 61 website (www.seat61.com) for details of all train routes.

→ Contact Deutsche Bahn (www.bahn.com) for details of frequent special offers, reservations and tickets.

→ For more information on international rail travel (including Eurostar services), check out www.voyages-sncf.com.

Sea

Services are year-round between major cities: book ahead in summer, at weekends and if travelling with a vehicle. Many boats are amazingly cheap if you travel deck class (without a cabin). Many ferry lines offer 50% discounts for holders of Eurail, Scanrail and InterRail passes. Some offer discounts for seniors, and for ISIC and youth-card holders; enquire when purchasing your ticket. There are usually discounts for families and small groups travelling together. Ferry companies have detailed timetables and fares on their websites. Fares vary according to season.

Baltic Countries

There are numerous sailings between Tallinn, Estonia and Helsinki, Finland, operated by Eckerö Line, Linda Line (fast boats), Tallink/Silja Line and Viking Line. Tallink/Silja also sails from Tallinn to Stockholm via Mariehamn, and DFDS Seaways runs from Paldiski (Estonia) to Kappel-skär (Sweden).

Stena Line runs from Nynäshamn, Sweden to Ventspils, Latvia. Tallink/Silja does a Stockholm to Riga run.

DFDS operates between Karlshamn (Sweden) and Klaipėda (Lithuania).

Germany

Denmark BornholmerFærgen runs between the island of Bornholm and Sassnitz, in eastern Germany. Scandlines runs from Rødby to Puttgar-ten, and between Gedser and Rostock. There's also a service from Havneby, at the southern tip of the Danish island of Rømø, to List on the German island of Sylt; this is run by Syltfähre.

Finland Finnlines runs from Helsinki to Travemünde.

Norway Color Line runs daily from Oslo to Kiel.

Sweden Stena Line runs Trelleborg to Rostock, Trelleborg to Sassnitz and Gothenburg to Kiel. TT-Line runs Trelleborg to Travemünde and Trelleborg to Rostock. Finnlines runs Malmö to Travemünde.

Poland

Denmark TT Line runs between the island of Bornholm and Świnoujście.

Sweden Polferries runs Ystad to Świnoujście, as does Unity Line, while TT-Line runs Trelleborg to Świnoujście. Polferries also links Nynäshamn with Gdańsk. Stena Line runs between Karlskrona and Gdynia.

Russia

St Peter Line runs from St Petersburg, Russia to Helsinki, Finland; Tallinn, Estonia; and Stockholm, Sweden.

GETTING AROUND

Air

→ Flights are safe and reliable. They can be expensive, but often cheaper than land-based alternatives for longer journeys, and can save days of travelling time.

→ There are reduced rates for internet bookings on internal airline routes. The main budget operators in the region are Ryanair and Norwegian.

→ There are good bus and train networks between airports and city centres.

Bicycle

Scandinavia is exceptionally bike friendly, with loads of cycle paths, courteous motorists, easy public transport options and lots of flattish, picturesque terrain.

Bike shops Widespread in towns and cities.

Hire Bike hire is often from train station bike-rental counters, tourist offices, camping grounds. In some cases it's possible to return hire bikes to another outlet so you don't have to double back. Several cities have bike-sharing schemes accessible for a small fee.

No-nos Cycling across the Øresund bridge between Denmark and Sweden is prohibited. A new summer-only bike ferry opened in 2017 as an alternative.

On public transport Bikes can be transported as luggage, either free or for a small fee, on slower trains and local buses in Scandinavia.

Theft Not uncommon in big cities; take a decent lock and use it when you leave your bike unattended.

Boat

Ferries are a major part of Scandinavian travel, connecting islands and countries on both the Baltic and North Sea sides.

Ferry

You can't really get around Scandinavia without using ferries extensively. The shortest routes from Denmark (Jutland) to Norway and from southern Sweden to Finland are ferry routes. Denmark is now well connected to mainland Europe and Sweden by bridges.

Ferry tickets are cheap on competitive routes, although transporting cars can be

Train & Ferry Routes

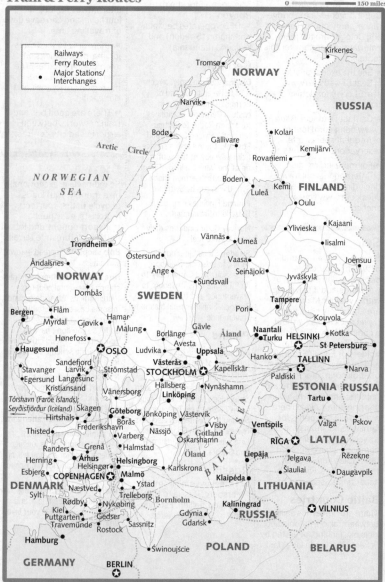

FERRY COMPANIES

The following is a list of the main ferry companies operating to and around Scandinavia, with their websites and major routes. See websites for contact telephone numbers, times, durations and sample fares.

BornholmerFærgen (www.faergen.com) Denmark (Bornholm)–Sweden, Denmark (Bornholm)–Germany.

Color Line (www.colorline.com) Norway–Denmark, Norway–Germany, Norway–Sweden.

DFDS Seaways (www.dfdsseaways.com) Denmark–Norway, Sweden–Lithuania, Sweden–Estonia.

Eckerö Line (www.eckeroline.fi for Finland–Estonia; www.eckerolinjen.se for Finland–Sweden) Finland (Åland)–Sweden, Finland–Estonia.

Finnlines (www.finnlines.com) Germany–Sweden, Sweden–Finland, Germany–Finland.

Fjord Line (www.fjordline.com) Denmark–Norway, Norway–Sweden.

Linda Line (www.lindaline.fi) Finland–Estonia.

Polferries (www.polferries.pl) Sweden–Poland.

St Peter Line (www.stpeterline.com) Sweden–Russia, Finland–Russia, Estonia–Russia.

Scandlines (www.scandlines.com) Denmark–Germany.

Smyril Line (www.smyrilline.com) Denmark–Faroe Islands–Iceland.

Stena Line (www.stenaline.com) Denmark–Norway, Denmark–Sweden, Sweden–Germany, Sweden–Poland, Sweden–Latvia.

Syltfähre (www.syltfaehre.de) Denmark–Germany (Sylt).

Tallink/Silja Line (www.tallinksilja.com) Finland–Sweden, Finland–Estonia, Sweden–Estonia, Sweden–Latvia.

TT-Line (www.ttline.com) Sweden–Germany, Sweden–Poland, Denmark (Bornholm)–Poland.

Unity Line (www.unityline.eu) Sweden–Poland.

Viking Line (www.vikingline.com) Sweden–Finland, Finland–Estonia.

Wasaline (www.wasaline.com) Finland–Sweden.

costly. Bicycles are usually carried free. On some routes, train-pass holders are entitled to free or discounted travel.

Weekend ferries, especially on Friday night, are significantly more expensive. Teenagers are banned from travelling on some Friday-night ferries due to problems with drunkenness.

Denmark–Faroe Islands–Iceland Smyril Line runs the popular *Nörrona* ferry from Hirtshals, Denmark to Seyðisfjörður, Iceland via Tórshavn on the Faroe Islands.

Denmark–Norway There are several connections. From Hirtshals, Fjord Line sails to Bergen, Kristiansand, Langesund and Stavanger. Color Line goes to Kristiansand and Larvik. From Frederikshavn, Stena Line goes to Oslo. From Copenhagen, DFDS Seaways goes to Oslo.

Denmark–Sweden Stena Line runs the connections Grenå to Varberg and Frederikshavn to Gothenburg. The short Helsingør to Helsingborg crossing is covered by Scandlines, while BornholmerFærgen goes from Rønne on Bornholm to Ystad.

Norway–Sweden Fjord Line and Color Line connect Strömstad, Sweden, with Sandefjord, Norway.

Sweden–Finland Connections from Stockholm to Helsinki or Turku via Åland are operated by Tallink/Silja and Viking Line. Eckerö Line runs from Grisslehamn to Eckerö on Åland, Finnlines runs Kapellskär to Naantali, while further north, Wasaline connects Umeå with Vaasa.

Steamer

➡ Scandinavia's main lakes and rivers are served by boats during summer, including some historic steamers. Treat these as relaxing, scenic cruises; if you view them merely as a way to get from A to B, they can seem quite expensive.

➡ Sweden has numerous routes. Most leave from Stockholm and sail east to the Stockholm archipelago and west to historic Lake Mälaren. You can also cruise the Göta Canal, the longest water route in Sweden.

➡ The legendary *Hurtigruten* ferry provides a link between Norway's coastal fishing villages.

➜ In Finland, steamships ply the eastern lakes, connecting the towns on their shores.

Bus

Buses provide a viable alternative to the rail network in Scandinavian countries, and are the only option in Iceland and parts of northern Sweden, Finland and Norway.

Cost Compared to trains, they're usually cheaper and slightly slower. Connections with train services (where they exist) are good.

Advance reservation It's rarely necessary to book ahead. But you do need to prepurchase your ticket before you board many city buses, and then validate your ticket on board.

International routes There are regular bus services between Denmark and Sweden, and Sweden and Norway. Services between Finland and Norway run in Lapland, and you can change between Swedish and Finnish buses at the shared bus station of the border towns of Tornio/Haparanda.

Car & Motorcycle

Travelling with a vehicle is the best way to get to remote places and gives you independence and flexibility.

Scandinavia is excellent for motorcycle touring, with good-quality winding roads, stunning scenery and an active motorcycling scene – just make sure your wet-weather gear is up to scratch. The best time for touring is May to September. On ferries, motorcyclists rarely have to book ahead as they can generally be squeezed in.

Bringing Your Own Vehicle

Documentation Proof of ownership of a private vehicle should always be carried (this is the Vehicle Registration Document for British-registered cars). You'll also need an insurance document valid in the countries you are planning to visit. Contact your local automobile association for further information.

Border crossings Vehicles crossing an international border should display a sticker showing their country of registration. The exception is cars with Euro-plates.

Safety It's compulsory to carry a warning triangle in most places, to be used in the event of a breakdown, and several countries require a reflective jacket. You must also use headlamp beam reflectors/converters on right-hand-drive cars.

Driving Licences

An EU driving licence is acceptable for driving throughout Scandinavia, as are North American and Australian licences, for example. If you have any other type of licence, you should check to see if you need to obtain an International Driving Permit (IDP) from your motoring organisation before you leave home.

If you're thinking of going snowmobiling, you'll need to bring your driving licence with you.

Fuel

Fuel is heavily taxed and very expensive in Scandinavia. Most types of petrol, including unleaded 95 and 98 octane, are widely available; leaded petrol is no longer sold. Diesel is significantly cheaper than petrol in most countries. Usually pumps with green markings deliver unleaded fuel, and black pumps supply diesel.

Car Hire

Cost Renting a car is more expensive in Scandinavia than in other European countries. Be sure you understand what's included in the price (unlimited or paid kilometres, injury insurance, tax, collision damage waiver etc) and what your liabilities are. Norway is the most expensive so it may pay to rent a car in neighbouring Sweden and take it across.

Insurance Decide whether to take the collision damage waiver. You may be covered for this and injury insurance if you have a travel-insurance policy: check.

Companies The big international firms – Hertz, Avis, Budget and Europcar – are all present. Sixt often has the most competitive prices. Using local firms can mean a better deal. Big firms give you the option of returning the car to a different outlet when you've finished with it, but this is often heavily charged.

Booking Prebooking always works out cheaper. Online brokers often offer substantially cheaper rates than the company websites themselves.

Fly/drive combination SAS and Icelandair often offer cheaper car rentals to their international passengers. Check their websites for deals.

Border crossings Ask in advance if you can drive a rented car across borders. In Scandinavia it's usually no problem.

Age The minimum rental age is usually 21, sometimes even 23, and you'll need a credit card for the deposit.

Motorcycle and moped rental Not particularly common in Scandinavian countries, but possible in major cities.

Insurance

Third-party motor insurance This is a minimum requirement in most of Europe. Most UK car-insurance policies automatically provide third-party cover for EU and some other countries. Ask your insurer for a Green Card – an internationally recognised proof of insurance (there may be a charge) – and check that it lists all the countries you intend to visit.

Breakdown assistance Check whether your insurance policy offers breakdown assistance overseas. If it doesn't, a European breakdown-assistance policy, such as those provided by the AA or the RAC, is a good investment. Your motoring organisation may also offer reciprocal coverage with affiliated motoring organisations.

Road Conditions & Hazards

Conditions and types of roads vary widely across Scandinavia, but it's possible to make some generalisations.

Iceland Specific challenges include unsealed gravel roads, long, claustrophobic single-lane tunnels, frequent mist and the wild, lonely, 4WD-only F-roads. See the videos at www.drive.is for more info.

Main roads Primary routes, with the exception of some roads in Iceland, are universally in good condition. There are comparatively few motorways.

Minor roads Road surfaces on minor routes are not so reliable, although normally adequate.

Norway There are some particularly hair-raising roads in Norway. Serpentine examples climb from sea level to 1000m in what seems no distance at all on a map. These roller coasters will use plenty of petrol and strain the car's engine and brakes, not to mention your nerves! Driving a campervan on this kind of route is not recommended.

Tolls In Norway there are tolls for some tunnels, bridges, roads and entry into larger towns, and for practically all ferries crossing fjords. Roads, tunnels, bridges and car ferries in Finland and Sweden are usually free, although there's a hefty toll of €56 per car on the Øresund bridge (www.oresundsbron.com) between Denmark and Sweden.

Winter Snow tyres are compulsory in winter, except in Denmark. Chains are allowed in most countries but almost never used.

Livestock on roads Suicidal animals, including sheep, elk, horses and reindeer, are a potential hazard. If you are involved in an animal incident, by law you must report it to the police.

Road Rules

➡ Drive on the right-hand side of the road in all Scandinavian countries.

➡ Seatbelts are compulsory for the driver and all passengers.

➡ Headlights must be switched on at all times.

➡ In the absence of give-way or stop signs, priority is given to traffic approaching from the right.

➡ It's compulsory for motorcyclists and their passengers to wear helmets.

➡ Take care with speed limits, which vary from country to country.

➡ Many driving infringements are subject to on-the-spot fines in Scandinavian countries. In Norway these are stratospheric. Drink-driving regulations are strict.

Hitching

➡ It's neither popular nor particularly rewarding to hitch in most of the region. In fact, it's some of the slowest in the world. Your plans need to be flexible.

➡ Hitching is better in Denmark and Sweden than Norway and Finland.

➡ It's sometimes possible to arrange a lift privately: scan student notice boards in colleges.

➡ After hitching, the cheapest way to get around is as a paying passenger in a private car. Various carsharing websites are good places to start. Try www.blablacar.com or www.ridefinder.eu.

➡ Hitching is never entirely safe, and we don't recommend it. Travellers who hitch should understand that they are taking a small but potentially serious risk.

Train

Trains in Scandinavia are comfortable, frequent and punctual. As with most things in the region, prices are relatively expensive, although train passes can make travel affordable. There are no trains in Iceland nor in far-north Finland and Norway.

Costs Full-price tickets can be expensive; book ahead for discounts. Rail passes are worth buying if you plan to do a reasonable amount of travelling. Seniors and travellers under 26 years of age are eligible for discounted tickets in some countries, which can cut fares by between 15% and 40%.

Reservations It's a good idea (sometimes obligatory) to make reservations at peak times and on certain train lines, especially long-distance trains. In some countries it can be a lot cheaper to book in advance and online.

Express trains There are various names for fast trains throughout Scandinavia. Supplements usually apply on fast trains and it's wise (sometimes obligatory) to make reservations at peak times and on certain lines.

Overnight Trains

These trains usually offer couchettes or sleepers. Reservations are advisable, particularly as sleeping options are generally allocated on a first-come, first-served basis.

Couchettes Basic bunk beds numbering four (1st class) or six (2nd class) per compartment are comfortable enough, if lacking a little privacy. In Scandinavia, a bunk costs around €25 to €50 (on top of the train fare) for most trains, irrespective of the length of the journey.

Sleepers This is the most comfortable option, offering beds for one or two passengers in 1st class and two or three passengers in 2nd class.

Food Most long-distance trains have a dining car or snack trolley – bring your own nibbles to keep costs down.

Car Some long-distance trains have car-carrying facilities.

Train Passes

There is a variety of passes available for rail travel within Scandinavia, or in various European countries including Scandinavia. There are cheaper passes for students, people under 26 and seniors. Supplements (eg for high-speed services) and reservation costs are not covered by passes, and terms and conditions change – check carefully before buying. Pass-holders must always carry their passport on the train for identification purposes.

EURAIL PASSES

Eurail (www.eurail.com) Offers a good selection of different passes available to residents of non-European countries; passes should be purchased before arriving in Europe.

Eurail Scandinavia Pass This pass gives a number of days' travel in a two-month period, and is valid for travel in Denmark, Sweden, Norway and Finland. It costs €215 for three days in 2nd class, up to €353 for eight days. There are also single-country passes.

Eurail Global Pass This pass offers travel in 28 European countries – five or seven days in a month, 10 or 15 days in a two-month period or unlimited travel from 15 days up to three months. It's much better value for under-28s, as those older have to buy a 1st-class pass.

Select Pass Provides a number of days' travel in a two-month period; you can choose up to four adjoining countries.

Discounts Most passes offer discounts of around 25% for under-28, or 15% for two people travelling together. On most Eurail passes, children aged between four and 11 get a 50% discount on the full adult fare. Eurail passes give a 30% to 50% discount on several ferry lines in the region; check the website for details.

INTERRAIL PASSES

If you've lived in Europe for more than six months, you're eligible for an InterRail (www.interrail.eu) pass. InterRail offers two passes valid for train travel in Scandinavia.

InterRail One Country Pass Offers travel in one country of your choice for three/four/six/eight days in a one-month period, costing €119/150/201/241 in 2nd class for Denmark or Finland, and €175/199/259/300 for Sweden or Norway.

Global Pass You can travel in 30 European countries with this pass and it costs from €267 for five days' travel in any 15, to €632 for a month's unlimited train travel.

Discounts On both the above passes, there's a discount of around 20% for under 28s. Inter-Rail passes give a 30% to 50% discount on several ferry lines in the region; check the website for details.

Language

This chapter offers basic vocabulary to help you get around Scandinavia. If you read our coloured pronunciation guides as if they were English, you'll be understood. Note that the stressed syllables are indicated with italics.

Some phrases in this chapter have both polite and informal forms (indicated by the abbreviations 'pol' and 'inf' respectively). The abbreviations 'm' and 'f' indicate masculine and feminine gender respectively.

DANISH

Danish has official status in Denmark and the Faroe Islands.

All vowels in Danish can be long or short. Note that aw is pronounced as in 'saw', eu as the 'u' in 'nurse', ew as 'ee' with rounded lips, oh as the 'o' in 'note', ow as in 'how', and dh as the 'th' in 'that'.

Basics

Hello.	Goddag.	go·da
Goodbye.	Farvel.	faar·vel
Excuse me.	Undskyld mig.	awn·skewl mai
Sorry.	Undskyld.	awn·skewl
Please.	Vær så venlig.	ver saw ven·lee
Thank you.	Tak.	taak
You're welcome.	Selv tak.	sel taak
Yes.	Ja.	ya
No.	Nej.	nai

How are you?
Hvordan går det?   vor·*dan* gawr dey

Good, thanks.
Godt, tak.   got taak

What's your name?
Hvad hedder   va *hey*·dha
De/du? (pol/inf)   dee/doo

My name is ...
Mit navn er ...   mit nown ir ...

Do you speak English?
Taler De/du   *ta*·la dee/doo
engelsk? (pol/inf)   eng·elsk

I don't understand.
Jeg forstår ikke.   yai for·*stawr i*·ke

Accommodation

campsite	campingplads	kaam·ping·plas
guesthouse	gæstehus	ges·te·hoos
hotel	hotel	hoh·tel
youth hostel	ungdomsherberg	awng·doms· heyr·beyrg

Do you have a ... room?	Har I et ... værelse?	haar ee it ... verl·se
single	enkelt	eng·kelt
double	dobbelt	do·belt

How much is it per ...?	Hvor meget koster det per ...?	vor maa·yet kos·ta dey peyr ...
night	nat	nat
person	person	per·sohn

WANT MORE?

For in-depth language information and handy phrases, check out Lonely Planet's *Western Europe Phrasebook*. You'll find it at **shop.lonelyplanet.com**.

Signs – Danish

Indgang	Entrance
Udgang	Exit
Åben	Open
Lukket	Closed
Forbudt	Prohibited
Toilet	Toilets

Eating & Drinking

Can you recommend a ...?	Kan De/du anbefale en ...? (pol/inf)	kan dee/doo an·bey·fa·le in ...
bar	bar	baar
cafe	café	ka·fey
restaurant	restaurant	res·toh·rang

What would you recommend?
Hvad kan De/du anbefale? (pol/inf) — va kan dee/doo an·bey·fa·le

Do you have vegetarian food?
Har I vegetarmad? — haar ee vey·ge·taar·madh

I'll have ...
..., tak. — ... taak

Cheers!
Skål! — skawl

I'd like the ..., please.	Jeg vil gerne have ..., tak.	yai vil gir·ne ha ... taak
bill	regningen	rai·ning·en
menu	menuen	me·new·en

breakfast	morgenmad	morn·madh
lunch	frokost	froh·kost
dinner	middag	mi·da
beer	øl	eul
coffee	kaffe	ka·fe
tea	te	tey
water	vand	van
wine	vin	veen

Emergencies

Help!	Hjælp!	yelp
Go away!	Gå væk!	gaw vek

Call ...!	Ring efter ...!	ring ef·ta ...
a doctor	en læge	in le·ye
the police	politiet	poh·lee·tee·et

I'm lost.
Jeg er faret vild. — yai ir faa·ret veel

I'm ill.
Jeg er syg. — yai ir sew

I have to use the telephone.
Jeg skal bruge en telefon. — yai skal broo·e en tey·ley·fohn

Where's the toilet?
Hvor er toilettet? — vor ir toy·le·tet

Shopping & Services

I'm looking for ...
Jeg leder efter ... — yai li·dha ef·ta ...

How much is it?
Hvor meget koster det? — vor maa·yet kos·ta dey

That's too expensive.
Det er for dyrt. — dey ir for dewrt

Where's ...?	Hvor er der ...?	vor ir deyr ...
an ATM	en hæve-automat	in he·ve·ow·toh·mat
a foreign exchange	et veksel-kontor	it veks·le·kon·tohr

market	marked	maar·kedh
post office	postkontor	post·kon·tohr
tourist office	turist-kontoret	too·reest·kon·toh·ret

Transport & Directions

Where's ...?
Hvor er ...? — vor ir ...

What's the address?
Hvad er adressen? — va ir a·draa·sen

Numbers – Danish

1	en	in
2	to	toh
3	tre	trey
4	fire	feer
5	fem	fem
6	seks	seks
7	syv	sew
8	otte	aw·te
9	ni	nee
10	ti	tee

493

Can you show me (on the map)?
Kan De/du vise mig — kan dee/doo vee·se mai
det (på kortet)? (pol/inf) — dey (paw kor·tet)

Where can I buy a ticket?
Hvor kan jeg købe — vor ka yai keu·be
en billet? — in bi·let

What time's the ... bus?	*Hvad tid er den ... bus?*	va teedh ir den ... boos
first	*første*	feurs·te
last	*sidste*	sees·te

One ... ticket (to Odense), please.	*En ... billet (til Odense), tak.*	in ... bee·let (til oh·dhen·se) taak
one-way	*enkelt*	eng·kelt
return	*retur*	rey·toor
boat	*båden*	w·dhen
bus	*bussen*	boo·sen
plane	*flyet*	flew·et
train	*toget*	taw·et

ESTONIAN

Double vowels in written Estonian indicate they are pronounced as long sounds.

Note that air is pronounced as in 'hair', aw as in 'law', ea as in 'ear', eu as in 'nurse', ew as ee with rounded lips, oh as in the 'o' in 'note', ow as in 'how', uh as the 'a' in 'ago', kh as in the Scottish *loch,* and zh as the 's' in 'pleasure'.

Basics

Hello.	*Tere.*	te·re
Goodbye.	*Nägemist.*	nair·ge·mist
Excuse me.	*Vabandage.* (pol)	va·ban·da·ge
	Vabanda. (inf)	va·ban·da
Sorry.	*Vabandust.*	va·ban·dust
Please.	*Palun.*	pa·lun
Thank you.	*Tänan.*	tair·nan
You're welcome.	*Palun.*	pa·lun
Yes.	*Jaa.*	yaa
No.	*Ei.*	ay

How are you?
Kuidas läheb? — ku·i·das lair·hep
Fine. And you?
Hästi. Ja teil? — hairs·ti ya tayl
What's your name?
Mis on teie nimi? — mis on tay·e ni·mi
My name is ...
Minu nimi on ... — mi·nu ni·mi on ...

Signs – Estonian

Sissepääs	Entrance
Väljapääs	Exit
Avatud/Lahti	Open
Suletud/Kinni	Closed
WC	Toilets

Do you speak English?
Kas te räägite — kas te rair·git·te
inglise keelt? — ing·kli·se keylt
I don't understand.
Ma ei saa aru. — ma ay saa a·ru

Eating & Drinking

What would you recommend?
Mida te soovitate? — mi·da te saw·vit·tat·te
Do you have vegetarian food?
Kas teil on taimetoitu? — kas tayl on tai·met·toyt·tu
I'll have a ...
Ma tahaksin ... — ma ta·hak·sin ...
Cheers!
Terviseks! — tair·vi·seks

I'd like the ..., please.	*Ma sooviksin ..., palun.*	ma saw·vik·sin ... pa·lun
bill	*arvet*	ar·vet
menu	*menüüd*	me·newt
breakfast	*hommikusöök*	hom·mi·ku·seuk
dinner	*õhtusöök*	uhkh·tu·seuk
lunch	*lõuna*	luh·u·na
beer	*õlu*	uh·lu
coffee	*kohv*	kokv
tea	*tee*	tey
water	*vesi*	ve·si
wine	*vein*	vayn

Emergencies

Help!	*Appi!*	ap·pi
Go away!	*Minge ära!*	ming·ke air·ra
Call ...!	*Kutsuge ...!*	ku·tsu·ge ...
a doctor	*arst*	arst
the police	*politsei*	po·li·tsay

I'm lost.
Ma olen ära eksinud. — ma o·len air·ra ek·si·nud
Where are the toilets?
Kus on WC? — kus on ve·se

Numbers – Estonian

1	üks	ewks
2	kaks	kaks
3	kolm	kolm
4	neli	ne·li
5	viis	vees
6	kuus	koos
7	seitse	say·tse
8	kaheksa	ka·hek·sa
9	üheksa	ew·hek·sa
10	kümme	kewm·me

Shopping & Services

I'm looking for ...
Ma otsin ...   ma o·tsin

How much is it?
Kui palju see maksab?   ku·i pal·yu sey mak·sab

That's too expensive.
See on liiga kallis.   sey on lee·ga kal·lis

bank	pank	pank
market	turg	turg
post office	postkontor	post·kont·tor

Transport & Directions

Where's the ...?
Kus on ...?   kus on ...

Can you show me (on the map)?
Kas te näitaksite   kas te nair·i·tak·sit·te
mulle (kaardil)?   mul·le (kaar·dil)

Where can I buy a ticket?
Kust saab osta pileti?   kust saab os·ta pi·let·ti

What time's the ... bus?	Mis kell väljub ... buss?	mis kel vairl·yub ... bus
first	esimene	e·si·me·ne
last	viimane	vee·ma·ne

One ... ticket (to Pärnu), please.	Üks ... pilet (Pärnusse), palun.	ewks ... pi·let (pair·nus·se) pa·lun
one-way	ühe otsa	ew·he o·tsa
return	edasi-tagasi	e·da·si·ta·ga·si

boat	laev	laiv
bus	buss	bus
plane	lennuk	len·nuk
train	rong	rongk

FINNISH

Double consonants are held longer than their single equivalents. Note that eu is pronounced as the 'u' in 'nurse', ew as 'ee' with rounded lips, oh as the 'o' in 'note', ow as in 'how', and uh as the 'u' in 'run'.

Basics

Hello.	Hei.	hay
Goodbye.	Näkemiin.	na·ke·meen
Excuse me.	Anteeksi.	uhn·tayk·si
Sorry.	Anteeksi.	uhn·tayk·si
Please.	Ole hyvä.	o·le hew·va
Thank you.	Kiitos.	kee·tos
You're welcome.	Ole hyvä.	o·le hew·va
Yes.	Kyllä.	kewl·la
No.	Ei.	ay

How are you?
Mitä kuuluu?   mi·ta koo·loo

Fine. And you?
Hyvää. Entä itsellesi?   hew·va en·ta it·sel·le·si

What's your name?
Mikä sinun nimesi on?   mi·ka si·nun ni·me·si on

My name is ...
Minun nimeni on ...   mi·nun ni·me·ni on ...

Do you speak English?
Puhutko englantia?   pu·hut·ko en·gluhn·ti·uh

I don't understand.
En ymmärrä.   en ewm·mar·ra

Eating & Drinking

What would you recommend?
Mitä voit suositella?   mi·ta voyt su·o·si·tel·luh

Do you have vegetarian food?
Onko teillä   on·ko teyl·la
kasvisruokia?   kuhs·vis·ru·o·ki·uh

I'll have a ...
Tilaan ...   ti·laan ...

Cheers!
Kippis!   kip·pis

Signs – Finnish	
Sisään	Entrance
Ulos	Exit
Avoinna	Open
Suljettu	Closed
Kielletty	Prohibited
Opastus	Information

I'd like the ..., please.	Saisinko ...	sai·sin·ko ...
bill	laskun	luhs·kun
menu	ruoka-listan	ru·o·kuh·lis·tuhn
breakfast	aamiaisen	aa·mi·ai·sen
lunch	lounaan	loh·naan
dinner	illallisen	il·luhl·li·sen
bottle of (beer)	pullon (olutta)	pul·lon (o·lut·tuh)
(cup of) coffee/tea	(kupin) kahvia/teetä	(ku·pin) kuh·vi·uh/tay·ta
glass of (wine)	lasillisen (viiniä)	luh·sil·li·sen (vee·ni·a)
water	vettä	vet·ta

Emergencies

Help!	Apua!	uh·pu·uh
Go away!	Mene pois!	me·ne poys
Call ...!	Soittakaa paikalle ...!	soyt·tuh·kaa pai·kuhl·le ...
a doctor	lääkäri	la·ka·ri
the police	poliisi	po·lee·si

I'm lost.
Olen eksynyt. — o·len ek·sew·newt

Where are the toilets?
Missä on vessa? — mis·sa on ves·suh

Shopping & Services

I'm looking for ...
Etsin ... — et·sin ...

How much is it?
Mitä se maksaa? — mi·ta se muhk·saa

That's too expensive.
Se on liian kallis. — se on lee·uhn kuhl·lis

Where's the ...?	Missä on ...?	mis·sa on ...
bank	pankki	puhnk·ki
market	kauppatori	kowp·pa·to·ri
post office	posti-toimisto	pos·ti·toy·mis·to

Transport & Directions

Where's ...?
Missä on ...? — mis·sa on ...

Numbers – Finnish

1	yksi	ewk·si
2	kaksi	kuhk·si
3	kolme	kol·me
4	neljä	nel·ya
5	viisi	vee·si
6	kuusi	koo·si
7	seitsemän	sayt·se·man
8	kahdeksan	kuhk·dek·suhn
9	yhdeksän	ewh·dek·san
10	kymmenen	kewm·me·nen

Can you show me (on the map)?
Voitko näyttää sen minulle (kartalta)? — voyt·ko na·ewt·ta sen mi·nul·le (kar·tuhl·tuh)

Where can I buy a ticket?
Mistä voin ostaa lipun? — mis·ta voyn os·taa li·pun

What time's the ... bus?	Mihin aikaan lähtee ... bussi?	mi·hin ai·kaan lah·tay ... bus·si
first	ensimmäinen	en·sim·mai·nen
last	viimeinen	vee·may·nen

One ... ticket, please.	Saisinko yhden ... lipun.	sai·sin·ko ewh·den ... li·pun
one-way	yksisuun-taisen	ewk·si·soon·tai·sen
return	meno-paluu	me·no·pa·loo

Where does this ... go?	Minne tämä ... menee?	min·ne ta·ma ... me·nay
boat	laiva	lai·vuh
bus	bussi	bus·si
plane	lentokone	len·to·ko·ne
train	juna	yu·nuh

ICELANDIC

Double consonants are given a long pronunciation. Note that eu is pronounced as the 'u' in 'nurse', oh as the 'o' in 'note', ow as in 'how', öy as the '-er y-' in 'her year' (without the 'r'), dh as the 'th' in 'that', and kh as the throaty 'ch' in the Scottish loch.

Basics

Hello.	Halló.	ha·loh
Goodbye.	Bless.	bles
Please.	Takk.	tak
Thank you.	Takk fyrir.	tak fi·rir

Signs – Icelandic

Inngangur	Entrance
Útgangur	Exit
Opið	Open
Lokað	Closed
Bannað	Prohibited
Snyrting	Toilets

You're welcome.	*Það var ekkert.*	thadh var e·kert
Excuse me.	*Afsakið.*	af·sa·kidh
Sorry.	*Fyrirgefðu.*	fi·rir·gev·dhu
Yes.	*Já.*	yow
No.	*Nei.*	nay

How are you?
Hvað segir þú gott? kvadh se·yir thoo got

Fine. And you?
Allt fínt. En þú? alt feent en thoo

What's your name?
Hvað heitir þú? kvadh hay·tir thoo

My name is ...
Ég heiti ... yekh hay·ti ...

Do you speak English?
Talar þú ensku? ta·lar thoo ens·ku

I don't understand.
Ég skil ekki. yekh skil e·ki

Eating & Drinking

What would you recommend?
Hverju mælir þú með? kver·yu mai·lir thoo medh

Do you have vegetarian food?
Hafið þið ha·vidh thidh
grænmetisrétti? grain·me·tis·rye·ti

I'll have a ...
Ég ætla að fá ... yekh ait·la adh fow ...

Cheers!
Skál! skowl

I'd like the ...,	*Get ég*	get yekh
please.	*fengið ... takk.*	fen·gidh ... tak
bill	*reikninginn*	rayk·nin·gin
menu	*matseðillinn*	mat·se·dhit·lin

breakfast	*morgunmat*	mor·gun·mat
lunch	*hádegismat*	how·de·yis·mat
dinner	*kvöldmat*	kveuld·mat

bottle of (beer)	*(bjór)flösku*	(byohr)·fleus·ku
(cup of)	*kaffi/te*	ka·fi/te
coffee/tea	*(bolla)*	(bot·la)

glass of (wine)	*(vín)glas*	(veen)·glas
water	*vatn*	vat

Emergencies

Help!	*Hjálp!*	hyowlp
Go away!	*Farðu!*	far·dhu

Call ...!	*Hringdu á ...!*	hring·du ow ...
a doctor	*lækni*	laik·ni
the police	*lögregluna*	leu·rekh·lu·na

I'm lost.
Ég er villtur/villt. (m/f) yekh er vil·tur/vilt

Where are the toilets?
Hvar er snyrtingin? kvar er snir·tin·gin

Shopping & Services

I'm looking for ...
Ég leita að ... yekh lay·ta adh ...

How much is it?
Hvað kostar þetta? kvadh kos·tar the·ta

That's too expensive.
Þetta er of dýrt. the·ta er of deert

Where's the ...?	*Hvar er ...?*	kvar er ...
bank	*bankinn*	bown·kin
market	*markaðurinn*	mar·ka·dhu·rin
post office	*pósthúsið*	pohst·hoo·sidh

Transport & Directions

Where's ...?
Hvar er ...? kvar er ...

Can you show me (on the map)?
Geturðu sýnt mér ge·tur·dhu seent myer
(á kortinu)? (ow kor·ti·nu)

Numbers – Icelandic

1	*einn*	aydn
2	*tveir*	tvayr
3	*þrír*	threer
4	*fjórir*	fyoh·rir
5	*fimm*	fim
6	*sex*	seks
7	*sjö*	syeu
8	*átta*	ow·ta
9	*níu*	nee·u
10	*tíu*	tee·u

Where can I buy a ticket?		
Hvar kaupi ég miða?		kvar *köy*·pi yekh *mi*·dha

What time's the ... bus?	*Hvenær fer ... strætisvagninn?*	*kve*·nair fer ... *strai*·tis·vag·nin
first	*fyrsti*	*firs*·ti
last	*síðasti*	see·dhas·ti

One ... ticket (to Reykjavík), please.	*Einn miða ... (til, Reykjavíkur) takk.*	aitn *mi*·dha ... (til *rayk*·ya·vee·kur) tak
one-way	*aðra leiðina*	*adh*·ra *lay*·dhi·na
return	*fram og til baka*	fram okh til *ba*·ka

Is this the ... to (Akureyri)?	*Er þetta ... til (Akureyrar)?*	er *the*·ta ... til (a·ku·ray·rar)
boat	*ferjan*	*fer*·yan
bus	*rútan*	*roo*·tan
plane	*flugvélin*	*flukh*·vye·lin

NORWEGIAN

There are two official written forms of Norwegian, *Bokmål* and *Nynorsk*. They are actually quite similar and understood by all speakers. It's estimated that around 85% of Norwegian speakers use *Bokmål* and about 15% use *Nynorsk*. In this section we've used *Bokmål* only.

Each vowel can be either long or short. Generally, they're long when followed by one consonant and short when followed by two or more consonants. Note that aw is pronounced as in 'law', eu as the 'u' in 'nurse', ew as 'ee' with pursed lips, and ow as in 'how'.

Basics

Hello.	*God dag.*	go·*daag*
Goodbye.	*Ha det.*	*haa*·de
Please.	*Vær så snill.*	veyr saw snil
Thank you.	*Takk.*	tak
You're welcome.	*Ingen årsak.*	*ing*·en *awr*·saak
Excuse me.	*Unnskyld.*	*ewn*·shewl
Sorry.	*Beklager.*	bey·*klaa*·geyr
Yes.	*Ja.*	yaa
No.	*Nei.*	ney

How are you?		
Hvordan har du det?		*vor*·dan haar doo de

Fine, thanks. And you?		
Bra, takk. Og du?		braa tak aw doo

What's your name?		
Hva heter du?		vaa *hey*·ter doo

My name is ...		
Jeg heter ...		yai *hay*·ter ...

Do you speak English?		
Snakker du engelsk?		*sna*·ker doo *eyng*·elsk

I don't understand.		
Jeg forstår ikke.		yai fawr·*stawr* *i*·key

Accommodation

campsite	*campingplass*	*keym*·ping·plas
guesthouse	*gjestgiveri*	*yest*·gi·ve·ree
hotel	*hotell*	hoo·*tel*
youth hostel	*ungdoms-herberge*	*ong*·dawms·heyr·beyrg

Do you have a single/double room?		
Finnes det et enkeltrom/dobbeltrom?		*fi*·nes de et *eyn*·kelt·rom/*daw*·belt·rom

How much is it per night/person?		
Hvor mye koster det pr dag/person?		vor *mew*·e *kaws*·ter de peyr daag/*peyr*·son

Eating & Drinking

Can you recommend a ...?	*Kan du anbefale en ...?*	kan doo *an*·be·fa·le en ...
bar	*bar*	baar
cafe	*kafé*	ka·*fe*
restaurant	*restaurant*	res·tu·*rang*

I'd like the menu.		
Kan jeg få menyen, takk.		kan yai faw me·*new*·en tak

What would you recommend?		
Hva vil du anbefale?		va vil doo *an*·be·fa·le

Do you have vegetarian food?		
Har du vegetariansk mat her?		har doo ve·ge·ta·ree·*ansk* maat heyr

I'll have ...		
Jeg vil ha ...		yai vil haa ...

Signs – Norwegian	
Inngang	Entrance
Utgang	Exit
Åpen	Open
Stengt	Closed
Forbudt	Prohibited
Toaletter	Toilets

Numbers – Norwegian

1	*en*	en
2	*to*	taw
3	*tre*	trey
4	*fire*	*fee*·re
5	*fem*	fem
6	*seks*	seks
7	*sju*	shoo
8	*åtte*	*aw*·te
9	*ni*	nee
10	*ti*	tee

Cheers!
Skål! skawl

I'd like the bill.
Kan jeg få kan yai faw
regningen, takk. *rai*·ning·en tak

breakfast	*frokost*	*fro*·kost
lunch	*lunsj*	loonsh
dinner	*middag*	*mi*·da
beer	*øl*	eul
coffee	*kaffe*	*kaa*·fe
tea	*te*	te
water	*vann*	van
wine	*vin*	veen

Emergencies

Help!	*Hjelp!*	yelp
Go away!	*Forsvinn!*	fawr·*svin*

Call a doctor/the police!
Ring en lege/politiet! ring en *le*·ge/po·lee·*tee*·ay

I'm lost.
Jeg har gått meg vill. yai har gawt mai vil

I'm ill.
Jeg er syk. yai er sewk

I have to use the telephone.
Jeg må låne yai maw *law*·ne
telefonen. te·le·*fo*·nen

Where are the toilets?
Hvor er toalettene? vor eyr to·aa·*le*·te·ne

Shopping & Services

I'm looking for ...
Jeg leter etter ... yai *ley*·ter e·*ter* ...

How much is it?
Hvor mye koster det? vor *mew*·e *kaws*·ter de

That's too expensive.
Det er for dyrt. de eyr fawr dewrt

Where's ...?	*Er det ...?*	eyr de ...
an ATM	*en minibank*	en *mi*·nee·bank
a foreign exchange	*valuta veksling*	va·*lu*·ta· *vek*·sling
market	*marked*	*mar*·ked
post office	*postkontor*	*pawst*·kawn·tawr
tourist office	*turist- informasjon*	tu·*reest*· in·fawr·ma·*shawn*

Transport & Directions

Where is ...?
Hvor er ...? vor ayr ...

What is the address?
Hva er adressen? va ayr aa·*dre*·seyn

Can you show me (on the map)?
Kan du vise meg kan du vee·se ma
(på kartet)? (paw *kar*·te)

Where can I buy a ticket?
Hvor kan jeg kjøpe vor kan yai *sheu*·pe
billett? bee·*let*

One one-way/return ticket (to Bergen), please.
Jeg vil gjerne ha yai vil *yer*·ne haa
enveisbillett/ en·veys·bee·*let*/
returbillett re·*toor*·bi·*let*
(til Bergen), takk. (til *ber*·gen) tak

What time's the ... bus?	*Når går ... buss?*	nawr gawr ... bus
first	*første*	*feur*·ste
last	*siste*	*si*·ste

boat	*båt*	bawt
bus	*buss*	bus
plane	*fly*	flew
train	*tåg*	tawg

SWEDISH

Swedish is the national language of Sweden and it also has official status in neighbouring Finland.

Vowel sounds can be short or long – generally the stressed vowels are long, except when followed by double consonants. Note that aw is pronounced as in 'saw', air as in 'hair', eu as the 'u' in 'nurse', ew as 'ee' with rounded lips, oh as the 'o' in 'note', and fh is a breathy sound pronounced with rounded lips, like saying 'f' and 'w' at the same time.

Basics

Hello.	*Hej.*	hey
Goodbye.	*Hej då.*	hey daw

Please.	*Tack.*	tak
Thank you.	*Tack.*	tak
You're welcome.	*Varsågod.*	var·sha·*gohd*
Excuse me.	*Ursäkta mig.*	oor·*shek*·ta mey
Sorry.	*Förlåt.*	feur·*lawt*
Yes.	*Ja.*	yaa
No.	*Nej.*	ney

How are you?
Hur mår du? hoor mawr doo

Fine, thanks. And you?
Bra, tack. Och dig? braa tak o dey

What's your name?
Vad heter du? vaad *hey*·ter doo

My name is ...
Jag heter ... yaa *hey*·ter ...

Do you speak English?
Talar du engelska? taa·lar doo *eng*·el·ska

I don't understand.
Jag förstår inte. yaa feur·*shtawr in*·te

Accommodation

campsite	*campingplats*	*kam*·ping·*plats*
guesthouse	*gästhus*	*yest*·hoos
hotel	*hotell*	hoh·*tel*
youth hostel	*vandrarhem*	*van*·drar·hem

Do you have a single/double room?
Har ni ett enkelrum/dubbelrum? har nee et *en*·kel·rum/*du*·bel·rum

How much is it per night/person?
Hur mycket kostar det per natt/person? hoor *mew*·ket *kos*·tar de peyr nat/*peyr*·shohn

Eating & Drinking

Can you recommend	*Kan du rekommendera*	kan doo re·ko·men·*dey*·ra
a bar?	*en bar?*	eyn bar
a cafe?	*ett kafé?*	et ka·*fey*
a restaurant?	*en restaurang?*	en res·taw·*rang*

I'd like the menu.
Jag skulle vilja ha menyn. yaa *sku*·le *vil*·ya haa me·*newn*

What would you recommend?
Vad skulle ni rekommendera? vaad *sku*·le nee re·ko·men·*dey*·ra

Do you have vegetarian food?
Har ni vegetarisk mat? har nee ve·ge·*taa*·risk maat

I'll have ...
Jag vill ha ... yaa vil haa ...

Cheers!
Skål! skawl

I'd like the bill.
Jag skulle vilja ha räkningen. yaa *sku*·le *vil*·ya haa *reyk*·ning·en

breakfast	*frukost*	*froo*·kost
lunch	*lunch*	lunsh
dinner	*middag*	*mi*·daa
beer	*öl*	eul
coffee	*kaffe*	*ka*·fe
tea	*te*	tey
water	*vatten*	*va*·ten
wine	*vin*	veen

Emergencies

| Help! | *Hjälp!* | yelp |
| Go away! | *Försvinn!* | feur·*shvin* |

Call a doctor!
Ring efter en doktor! ring *ef*·ter en *dok*·tor

Call the police!
Ring efter polisen! ring *ef*·ter poh·*lee*·sen

I'm lost.
Jag har gått vilse. yaa har got *vil*·se

I'm ill.
Jag är sjuk. yaa air fhook

I have to use the telephone.
Jag måste använda telefonen. yaa *maws*·te an·*ven*·da te·le·*foh*·nen

Where are the toilets?
Var är toaletten? var air toh·aa·*le*·ten

Shopping & Services

I'm looking for ...
Jag letar efter ... yaa *ley*·tar *ef*·ter ...

How much is it?
Hur mycket kostar det? hoor *mew*·ke *kos*·tar de

Numbers – Swedish

1	*ett*	et
2	*två*	tvaw
3	*tre*	trey
4	*fyra*	*few*·ra
5	*fem*	fem
6	*sex*	seks
7	*sju*	fhoo
8	*åtta*	*o*·ta
9	*nio*	*nee*·oh
10	*tio*	*tee*·oh

That's too expensive.
Det är för dyrt.   de air feur *dewrt*

Where's ...?	*Var finns det ...?*	var fins de ...
an ATM	*en bankomat*	eyn ban·koh·*maat*
a foreign exchange	*ett växlings-kontor*	et *veyk*·slings·kon·tohr
market	*torghandel*	*tory*·han·del
post office	*posten*	*pos*·ten
tourist office	*turistbyrå*	too·rist·bew·raw

Transport & Directions

Where's ...?
Var finns det ...?   var finns de ...

What's the address?
Vilken adress är det?   *vil*·ken a·*dres* air de

Can you show me (on the map)?
Kan du visa mig (på kartan)?   kan doo *vee*·sa mey (paw *kar*·tan)

Where can I buy a ticket?
Var kan jag köpa en biljett?   var kan yaa *sheu*·pa eyn bil·*yet*

A one-way/return ticket (to Stockholm), please.
Jag skulle vilja ha en enkelbiljett/returbiljett (till Stockholm).   yaa *sku*·le *vil*·ya haa eyn en·kel·bil·*yet*/re·*toor*·bil·*yet* (til *stok*·holm)

What time's the ... bus?	*När går ... bussen?*	nair gawr ... *bu*·sen
first	*första*	*feursh*·ta
last	*sista*	*sis*·ta
boat	*båt*	bawt
bus	*buss*	bus
plane	*flygplan*	*flewg*·plaan
train	*tåg*	tawg

Behind the Scenes

SEND US YOUR FEEDBACK

We love to hear from travellers – your comments keep us on our toes and help make our books better. Our well-travelled team reads every word on what you loved or loathed about this book. Although we cannot reply individually to your submissions, we always guarantee that your feedback goes straight to the appropriate authors, in time for the next edition. Each person who sends us information is thanked in the next edition – the most useful submissions are rewarded with a selection of digital PDF chapters.

Visit **lonelyplanet.com/contact** to submit your updates and suggestions or to ask for help. Our award-winning website also features inspirational travel stories, news and discussions.

Note: We may edit, reproduce and incorporate your comments in Lonely Planet products such as guidebooks, websites and digital products, so let us know if you don't want your comments reproduced or your name acknowledged. For a copy of our privacy policy visit lonelyplanet.com/privacy.

OUR READERS

Many thanks to the travellers who used the last edition and wrote to us with helpful hints, useful advice and interesting anecdotes: Gaëlle Le Provost, Joyce Lee, Danielle Wolbers

WRITER THANKS

Anthony Ham

Special thanks to Gemma Graham for sending me to the most beautiful country on earth. At Lonely Planet, I'm grateful to the following for their patience and wisdom: Genna Patterson, Joel Cotterell, Sandi Kestell, Elizabeth Jones, Kellie Langdon and Andrea Dobbin. Countless Norwegians were unfailingly helpful, and Miles Roddies deserves special thanks for the shared memories. And to my family – os quiero.

Carolyn Bain

It's always a joy to return to Denmark and spend time with my Danish family, the Østergaards. Tusind tak, as ever, for welcoming me back. Warm thanks to my cowriters on this project, Cristian Bonetto and Mark Elliott, and to regional tourism pros Heidi Lindberg and Helle Mogensen for kind assistance. This trip was special for the friendships forged: mange tak to Sif Orellana, Catrine Engelgreen, Trine Nissen and especially Mia Sinding Jespersen for hygge and heart.

Oliver Berry

As always thanks to all the people who helped out on this adventure, including Magnus Svendsen, Kristina Johansen, Karl Larsen, Nina Hedstrom, Jenny Eriksen and Jon Nordlie. A hearty thank you to my fellow authors Anthony Ham and Donna Wheeler, and to Gemma Graham for steering the ship home to port. And thanks to Rosabella for all the long-distance calls, words of encouragement and keeping my spirits up during the long days (and nights) of write-up.

Cristian Bonetto

For their priceless insight, generosity and friendship, tusind tak to Martin Kalhøj, Mette Cecilie Smedegaard, Christian Struckmann Irgens, Mads Lind, Mia Hjorth Lunde and Jens Lunde, Mary-Ann Gardner and Lambros Hajisava, Sophie Lind and Kasper Monrad, Anne Marie Nielsen, Sanna Klein Hedegaard Hansen and Carolyn Bain. In-house, many thanks to Gemma Graham.

Mark Elliott

A very special thank you to the wonderful Sally Cobham for love, company and great insight. En-route, thanks also to Elisabeth and Jens, Uve Horst, Mikayl, Annette, Morgens Grønning, Jens and the beer club in Helsingør, Peter Andreas, Klaus, Stine, Ole Rasmussen at NaturparkÅmosen, Henning Vingborg, Kevin, Eddie, Jesper, David, Michael, Bent and Marianne at Kiss the Frog, Katerin at Søbygaard, Helle and Jacob, Urt and Ties at Insp!

Catherine Le Nevez

Kiitos paljon/ tack så mycket first and foremost to Julian, and to all the locals, tourism professionals and fellow travellers who provided insights, inspiration and good times. Huge thanks too, to Destination Editor Gemma Graham, my Finland and Scandinavia co-authors, and all at Lonely Planet. As ever, *merci encore* to my parents, brother, *belle-sœur* and *neveu*.

Virginia Maxwell

Greatest thanks to my travelling companion and navigator, Max Handsaker. Thanks also to Peter Handsaker for holding the fort at home, and to the extremely helpful staff at the tourist offices in both the Finnish regions that I researched.

Craig McLachlan

Hej hej! A hearty thanks to everyone who helped out during my research trip around Sweden, but especially to my exceptionally beautiful wife, Yuriko, who kept me on track, focussed and constantly smiling. Jämtland and the Bothnian Coast and Swedish Lapland were a joy to explore, and a big part of that joy comes from meeting and talking to happy Swedes! – thanks to you all.

Hugh McNaughtan

Thanks to Gemma for the chance to research this glorious little city, and to Toomas and the other kind Estonians who showed me so much. And to Tas, Maise and Willa, always.

Becky Ohlsen

Thanks to my mom, Christina, for rounding up a bunch of extra info from her friends; Paul Smith for inspiring the pinball quest; James Borup for the brewery intel; the Auld Dub in general; and all the various editors in-house at Lonely Planet for helping whip the resulting content into shape.

Andy Symington

Gratitude is due to my fellow authors for their helpful contributions and recommendations, as well as the whole Lonely Planet team. Particular thanks go to Carolyn Bain, Gemma Graham and Michelle Bennett.

Mara Vorhees

Kiitos a million times over to my Finnish family, Outi and Kauko Ojala, for their in-depth knowledge of Finland, and for their hospitality and the laughs over the course of 30 years. *Kiitos* another million times to my American family – my parents, my kiddos, and my favourite travel companion of all time.

Benedict Walker

My thanks to Gemma Graham for taking me on for this project, to Michal Greenberg for helping me to find a home in Germany, to Ida Sarah Lina Burguete Kirkman and MacGyver, the Lindqvists in Älmhult, and to Mum, Trish Walker, who never gives up on me. Special thanks to Vicki Kirkman, for not giving up either, and to Lauren Kirkman, my travel agent.

Donna Wheeler

I'm ever grateful to the city of Oslo, possibly the kindest place on Earth. I am deeply indebted to Arvild Bruun and to Barry Kavanagh for the inspiring leads and delightful company. Thanks also to Daniel Nettheim, Claudia Van Tunen, Chris Wareing, Mark Steiner and Hugo Race. And as ever, thanks to Joe Guario in Melbourne for your love through the wires.

ACKNOWLEDGEMENTS

Climate map data adapted from Peel MC, Finlayson BL & McMahon TA (2007) 'Updated World Map of the Köppen-Geiger Climate Classification', Hydrology and Earth System Sciences, 11, 163344.
Cover photograph: Grass roof in Norway, Shaun Egan/AWL©

THIS BOOK

This 13th edition of Lonely Planet's *Scandinavia* guidebook was curated by Anthony Ham and researched and written by Anthony Ham, Alexis Averbuck, Carolyn Bain, Oliver Berry, Cristian Bonetto, Belinda Dixon, Mark Elliott, Catherine Le Nevez, Virginia Maxwell, Craig McLachlan, Hugh McNaughtan, Becky Ohlsen, Andy Symington, Mara Vorhees, Benedict Walker, and Donna Wheeler.

This guidebook was produced by the following:

Destination Editors Gemma Graham, James Smart, Clifton Wilkinson

Product Editors Heather Champion, Sandie Kestell

Senior Cartographer Valentina Kremenchutskaya

Book Designer Gwen Cotter

Assisting Editors Sarah Bailey, Andrew Bain, Imogen Bannister, Michelle Bennett, Nigel Chin, Lucy Cowie, Michelle Coxall, Pete Cruttenden, Melanie Dankel, Andrea Dobbin, Bruce Evans, Carly Hall, Jennifer Hattam, Gabrielle Innes, Helen Koehne, Alex Knights, Kellie Langdon, Jodie Martire, Anne Mulvaney, Kristin Odijk, Charlotte Orr, Susan Paterson, Chris Pitts, Sarah Reid, Gabrielle Stefanos, Sarah Stewart, Ross Taylor, Fionnuala Twomey, Sam Wheeler, Simon Williamson

Assisting Cartographers Mark Griffiths, Gabriel Lindquist

Cover Researcher Naomi Parker

Thanks to Egill Bjarnason, Kate Kiely, Jessica Ryan

Index

Map Legend

Sights

- Beach
- Bird Sanctuary
- Buddhist
- Castle/Palace
- Christian
- Confucian
- Hindu
- Islamic
- Jain
- Jewish
- Monument
- Museum/Gallery/Historic Building
- Ruin
- Shinto
- Sikh
- Taoist
- Winery/Vineyard
- Zoo/Wildlife Sanctuary
- Other Sight

Activities, Courses & Tours

- Bodysurfing
- Diving
- Canoeing/Kayaking
- Course/Tour
- Sento Hot Baths/Onsen
- Skiing
- Snorkelling
- Surfing
- Swimming/Pool
- Walking
- Windsurfing
- Other Activity

Sleeping

- Sleeping
- Camping
- Hut/Shelter

Eating

- Eating

Drinking & Nightlife

- Drinking & Nightlife
- Cafe

Entertainment

- Entertainment

Shopping

- Shopping

Information

- Bank
- Embassy/Consulate
- Hospital/Medical
- Internet
- Police
- Post Office
- Telephone
- Toilet
- Tourist Information
- Other Information

Geographic

- Beach
- Gate
- Hut/Shelter
- Lighthouse
- Lookout
- Mountain/Volcano
- Oasis
- Park
- Pass
- Picnic Area
- Waterfall

Population

- Capital (National)
- Capital (State/Province)
- City/Large Town
- Town/Village

Transport

- Airport
- Border crossing
- Bus
- Cable car/Funicular
- Cycling
- Ferry
- Metro station
- Monorail
- Parking
- Petrol station
- S-Bahn/Subway station
- Taxi
- T-bane/Tunnelbana station
- Train station/Railway
- Tram
- Tube station
- U-Bahn/Underground station
- Other Transport

Routes

- Tollway
- Freeway
- Primary
- Secondary
- Tertiary
- Lane
- Unsealed road
- Road under construction
- Plaza/Mall
- Steps
- Tunnel
- Pedestrian overpass
- Walking Tour
- Walking Tour detour
- Path/Walking Trail

Boundaries

- International
- State/Province
- Disputed
- Regional/Suburb
- Marine Park
- Cliff
- Wall

Hydrography

- River, Creek
- Intermittent River
- Canal
- Water
- Dry/Salt/Intermittent Lake
- Reef

Areas

- Airport/Runway
- Beach/Desert
- Cemetery (Christian)
- Cemetery (Other)
- Glacier
- Mudflat
- Park/Forest
- Sight (Building)
- Sportsground
- Swamp/Mangrove

Note: Not all symbols displayed above appear on the maps in this book

Mara Vorhees

Finland Mara writes about food, travel and family fun around the world. Her work has been published by BBC Travel, Boston *Globe*, Delta Sky, Vancouver *Sun* and more. For Lonely Planet, she regularly writes about destinations in Central America and Eastern Europe, as well as New England, where she lives. She often travels with her twin boys in tow, earning her an expertise in family travel. Follow their adventures and misadventures at www.havetwinswilltravel.com.

Benedict Walker

Sweden An Australian BA (Communications) graduate and travel agent by trade, Ben whittled away his twenties gallivanting around the globe before landing his first Lonely Planet gig, *Japan*. Aside from writing guidebooks, he's also written and directed a play, toured Australia managing the travel logistics for top-billing music festivals and is currently exploring his original major of photography and film-making. Join his journeys on Instagram: @wordsandjourneys.

Donna Wheeler

Norway Donna became a travel writer after various careers as a commissioning editor, creative director, digital producer and content strategist. She has written guidebooks for Lonely Planet for more than ten years, including the *Italy*, *Norway*, *Belgium*, *France*, *Austria* and *Australia* titles. Donna's work on contemporary art, architecture and design, food, wine, wilderness and cultural history also can be found in a variety of other publications. She loves cities, mountains and the sea.

Belinda Dixon

Iceland Only happy when her feet are sandy, Belinda has been (gleefully) travelling, researching and writing for Lonely Planet since 2006. A trained radio journalist, her innate nosiness means few likely-looking sleep spots go unexplored. Belinda is also an adventure writer – see her VideoBlog posts at https://belinda dixon.com

Mark Elliott

Denmark Mark Elliott had already lived and worked on five continents when he co-wrote *Asia Overland*, one of the first guides to help backpackers cross the then-new states of the former USSR. He has since authored (or co-authored) around 60 books including dozens for Lonely Planet. He also acts as a travel consultant, occasional tour leader, video presenter, speaker, interviewer and blues harmonicist.

Catherine Le Nevez

Finland Catherine has travelled to around 60 countries, completing postgraduate qualifications in Creative Arts in Writing, Professional Writing, and Editing and Publishing along the way. Over the past dozen-plus years she's written scores of Lonely Planet guides and articles, as well as work for online and print publications. Her top travel tip is to go without any expectations.

Virginia Maxwell

Finland Based in Australia, Virginia spends at least half of her year updating Lonely Planet destination coverage in Europe and the Middle East. Though the Mediterranean is her major area of interest, Virginia also writes LP guides to Finland, Armenia, Iran and Australia. Follow her @maxwellvirginia on Instagram and Twitter.

Craig McLachlan

Sweden Craig has covered destinations all over the globe for Lonely Planet for two decades. Based in Queenstown, New Zealand for half the year, he runs an outdoor activities company and a sake brewery, then moonlights overseas for the other half. Craig is also a Japanese interpreter, pilot, photographer, hiking guide, tour leader, karate instructor and budding novelist. Check out www.craigmclachlan.com.

Hugh McNaughtan

Tallinn A former English lecturer, Hugh swapped grant applications for visa applications, and turned his love of travel intro a full-time thing. Having done a bit of restaurant-reviewing in his home town (Melbourne) he's now eaten his way across four continents. He's never happier than when on the road with his two daughters. Except perhaps on the cricket field...

Becky Ohlsen

Sweden Becky is a freelance writer, editor and critic based in Portland, Oregon. Though raised in the mountains of Colorado, Becky has been exploring Sweden since childhood, while visiting her grandparents and other relatives in Stockholm and parts north. When she's not covering ground for Lonely Planet, Becky is working on a book about motorcycles and the paradoxical appeal of risk.

Andy Symington

Andy has worked on over a hundred books and updates for Lonely Planet (specialising in Europe and Latin America), and has published articles on numerous subjects for a variety of newspapers, magazines and websites. He part-owns and operates a rock bar and has written a novel. When he's not travelling the world, he can be found in his adopted home in northern Spain. Andy wrote the Plan and Survival Guide sections of this book.

OUR STORY

A beat-up old car, a few dollars in the pocket and a sense of adventure. In 1972 that's all Tony and Maureen Wheeler needed for the trip of a lifetime – across Europe and Asia overland to Australia. It took several months, and at the end – broke but inspired – they sat at their kitchen table writing and stapling together their first travel guide, *Across Asia on the Cheap*. Within a week they'd sold 1500 copies. Lonely Planet was born.

Today, Lonely Planet has offices in Franklin, London, Melbourne, Oakland, Dublin, Beijing and Delhi, with more than 600 staff and writers. We share Tony's belief that 'a great guidebook should do three things: inform, educate and amuse'.

OUR WRITERS

Anthony Ham

Norway Anthony is a freelance writer and photographer who specialises in Spain, East and Southern Africa, the Arctic and the Middle East, working for Lonely Planet and other publications in the US, UK and Australia. An Australian, Anthony found his spiritual home in Madrid: arriving on a one-way ticket in 2001, he finally left ten years later, speaking Spanish with a Madrid accent and married to a local. Now back in Australia, Anthony continues to travel the world in search of stories.

Alexis Averbuck

Iceland Alexis has travelled and lived all over the world, from Sri Lanka to Ecuador, Zanzibar and Antarctica. For Lonely Planet, Alexis specializes in Iceland, France, Greece and Antarctica. She also writes for the BBC, international magazines and newspapers and online platforms, presents travel TV programs and exhibits her oil paintings and watercolors.

Carolyn Bain

Denmark A travel writer and editor for more than 20 years, Carolyn has lived, worked and studied in various corners of the globe, including Denmark, London, St Petersburg and Nantucket. She has authored more than 50 Lonely Planet titles, with her all-time favourite research destination being Iceland. Her love of the country recently led her to relocate from Melbourne, Australia to Reykjavík.

Oliver Berry

Norway Oliver has been a writer and photographer for Lonely Planet for more than a decade, working on more than thirty guidebooks. His writing for Lonely Planet and other newspapers and magazines has won several awards, including The Guardian Young Travel Writer of the Year and the TNT Magazine Peoples Choice Award. Read more at www.oliverberry.com.

Cristian Bonetto

Denmark Cristian has contributed to over 30 Lonely Planet guides, including *Denmark*, *Pocket Copenhagen* and *Sweden*. His musings on travel, food, culture and design appear in numerous publications around the world, including the *Telegraph* (UK) and *Corriere del Mezzogiorno* (Italy). When not on the road, you'll find the reformed playwright in his hometown, Melbourne. Instagram: @rexcat75.

OVER PAGE | MORE WRITERS

Published by Lonely Planet Global Limited
CRN 554153
13th edition – June 2013
ISBN 978 1 78657 564 7
© Lonely Planet 2018   Photographs © as indicated 2018
10 9 8 7 6 5 4 3 2 1
Printed in China